Birds of Kenya and Northern Tanzania

Field Guide Edition

Dale A. Zimmerman, Donald A. Turner, and David J. Pearson

Illustrated by Dale A. Zimmerman, Ian Willis, and H. Douglas Pratt

Princeton University Press

Princeton, New Jersey

Princeton Field Guides

Rooted in field experience and scientific study, Princeton's guides to animals and plants are the authority for professional scientists and amateur naturalists alike. **Princeton Field Guides** present this information in a compact format carefully designed for easy use in the field. The guides illustrate every species in color and provide detailed information on identification, distribution, and biology.

Birds of Europe with North Africa and the Middle East, by Lars Jonsson
Coral Reef Fishes, by Ewald Lieske and Robert Myers
Birds of Kenya and Northern Tanzania: Field Guide Edition, by Dale A. Zimmerman, Donald A. Turner, and David J. Pearson

Copyright © 1999 Text and maps: Dale A. Zimmerman, Donald A. Turner, and David J. Pearson
Copyright © 1999 Illustrations: Dale A. Zimmerman, Ian Willis, and H. Douglas Pratt

Published in the United States, Canada, and the Philippine Islands by Princeton University Press, 41 William Street, Princeton, New Jersey 08540

In the United Kingdom, published by Christopher Helm (Publishers) Ltd, a subsidiary of A & C Black Publishers Ltd, 38 Soho Square, London W1D 3HB

Library of Congress Catalog Card Number 99-60206

ISBN-13: 978-0-691-01022-9 (pbk.)
ISBN-13: 978-0-691-01021-2 (cloth)

http://pup.princeton.edu

Printed in Singapore by Imago

10 9 8 7 6 5 4 3 2

CONTENTS

PREFACE

This field guide is an abridged edition of the authors' *Birds of Kenya and Northern Tanzania* published in 1996. It treats all species known from the region, including a few vagrants added to the avifauna subsequent to the appearance of that publication. Although the vast majority of persons who have provided us with comments on the earlier book decidedly favoured its format and its detailed treatment, a significant number expressed the desire for something smaller that could be conveniently carried on foot-excursions away from their tents or safari vehicles. They still wanted all benefits of the 'big book' available in the field, plus something less weighty and nearer 'pocket-sized' to have with them at all times.

Some serious birders dismember large regional books, separating the text from the fascicle of plates which they keep available for instant reference in a shoulder bag or rucksack, but most eschew such drastic measures. Although *Birds of Kenya and Northen Tanzania* was not designed for hand-carrying, we have seen several excised sets of plates bound with hard protective covers to withstand rough, prolonged use on treks in the bush. After lengthy deliberation, we decided to condense as much information as possible into a smaller and more portable format to meet the obvious demand, but we stress that this new guide is not intended as a substitute for the original book to which we refer our present readers for many details and the extensive supplementary material.

Of necessity, the new species accounts are greatly abbreviated, and all have been re-written, but most of the present material has been taken directly from the original book. We have updated our treatment with occasional modifications, a few additions and corrections. Extensive deletion was required throughout, the accounts being reduced by about half from those of the larger book. Many comments on taxonomy, the separate sections on behaviour and ecology, descriptions of some less common vocalizations, pointers for identification of certain birds in the the hand, and other useful features have been eliminated or drastically reduced. We have also condensed our treatment of subspecies. Literature references have been sacrificed, and users will have to consult the larger book for these. The glossary is much smaller. The lengthy discussions of climate and habitats, appendices, gazetteer and bibliography have been eliminated. For these the reader must refer to the earlier volume. Range statements have been severely reduced, the space instead devoted to retention of distribution maps for most species. (Despite lessened utility of ranges depicted on a reduced scale, a small map is vastly better than none; and presenting maps within the text is, we believe, preferable to having them isolated in a separate section of the book. Maps have been omitted for vagrants, a few truly rare species, and those of extremely restricted distribution.) Abridgement notwithstanding, our aim has been to present more identification-related information than is found in most modern field-books of this size.

At the species level we have made three taxonomic deviations from our original treatment, one in the Musophagidae, one in the Laniidae and one in the Malaconotidae. *Nicator* is now treated as a bush-shrike (as it was years ago) rather than with the bulbuls.

The text again is the product of all three authors. The colour plates are those of the original book. These were designed by Zimmerman who painted 79 of them (including all of the passerines). Ian Willis and H. Douglas Pratt produced 25 and 20 plates respectively. Turner and Pearson executed the distribution maps. Zimmerman prepared the introductory material, plate-caption pages and all line drawings (several of which are new in this book).

ACKNOWLEDGEMENTS

Space limitations preclude listing here the many individuals and institutions who contributed so significantly to the earlier book. However, we wish to thank each of them once again, and also express our appreciation to the numerous reviewers of that volume in the scientific and popular press. Specifically providing assistance and/or responding to queries relating directly to this field guide have been Thomas Brooks, Adrian Craig, Kimball Garrett (Los Angeles County Museum), Mary LeCroy (American Museum of Natural History), Jeremy Lindsell, and David Willard (Field Museum of Natural History). Dustin Huntington again has rendered invaluable assistance with computer-disk conversion of the manuscript. Marian Zimmerman has contributed significantly by reading and correcting the hundreds of text pages in various drafts, and she has offered much valued advice. Once again, it has been a pleasure to work with Robert Kirk, of A & C Black, who has been the driving force behind this enterprise.

INTRODUCTION

This volume describes and illustrates the 1089 bird species definitely recorded from the Republic of Kenya, and coverage extends south through ecologically similar territory to 5° 30′ south latitude in Tanzania, embracing an additional 34 bird species not found in Kenyan territory. These northern Tanzanian birds are shown on three separate colour plates (122–124), although the text treats them in taxonomic sequence alongside their Kenyan relatives.

Excluded are the birds of extreme northwestern Tanzania, and those found only west of a line southward from Mwanza on the southern shore of Lake Victoria. These western species are more typical of the Ugandan/central African fauna and are beyond the scope of this book. Our arbitrary southern boundary has been dictated by practical considerations. It was clearly desirable to include all species in the popular tourist destinations of Serengeti and other northern Tanzanian national parks, plus the intriguing Usambara Mountains so close to the Kenyan border. In more southern areas, however, access problems limit or preclude easy visitation to many choice sites, and the many different montane endemics and miombo woodland birds alone would have expanded our species list to unwieldy proportions. Nevertheless, many of the book's included species are widespread in eastern Africa, so that our coverage effectively embraces some 90 per cent of the 1046 birds known from Tanzania, 85 per cent of Uganda's 1008 species, and a majority of those in southern Ethiopia, Somalia and Sudan as well.

THE SPECIES ACCOUNTS

Species are treated following a brief family summary. Introductory paragraphs are also provided for a few large subfamilies or genera. These contain information relating to the group as a whole, not repeated under the various species headings. Each species account begins with the bird's English name (see below) followed by its scientific name—trinomial if only one subspecies of a polytypic species is present in the region, binomial if (a) no subspecies are recognized or (b) if two or more are present here (in which case they are named beyond). Following the name and colour-plate number is an approximation of the bird's length in inches.

An asterisk (*) preceding the name indicates a lack of either specimen or suitable photographic evidence of the species in our region. One of those so marked (Green Crombec) is supported by tape recordings.

Initial remarks under the species' name concern important recognition features, typically relating to the bird's appearance, but at times reflecting some behavioural trait, important habitat or diagnostic distributional point as well. Plumage descriptions are not necessarily complete. They are designed to supplement the figures on the colour plates, sometimes ignoring features that are obvious from the illustration. Where most or all species in a group share a common broad feature such as brown upperparts or white underparts, these may receive no mention unless the context so demands. *Adult plumage, and similar or identical sexes, should be assumed unless otherwise indicated.* Amount of descriptive detail varies with the complexity of the group or variation within the species. Birds that are difficult to identify are treated more fully than those that are well-marked or unmistakable. Noteworthy features or unique combinations important to identification are printed in italics. Where necessary, male and female are mentioned separately, as, if applicable, are breeding and non-breeding adult plumages and different colour morphs. The term *juvenile* refers to the bird's first real plumage following the natal down. Immature is used for any subsequent stage preceding adult plumage, although it is often appropriate to specifically mention a first-winter dress. We also use *subadult* for certain plumages in species requiring several years to reach 'full' adult status. Significant subspecific differences are indicated. For some polytypic species, ranges of the various races receive only brief mention, and subspecies characterized by only minor differences are not described (although virtually all that are recognized by us are at least named). Similar species likely to be sources of confusion are also referred to where necessary. Terms used in species descriptions are identified on the bird topography drawings and/or are defined in the glossary.

Relative numerical status is expressed in the terms *abundant, common, fairly common, uncommon, scarce,* or *rare,* designations intended only as a rough guide. (A bird may be abundant one season, rare or absent the next, and numbers may vary greatly between areas. The same term also differs in meaning between groups; a 'common' weaver or dove is far more numerous than a 'common' buzzard or eagle.) A *casual* species is one recorded only 5–10 times in the region, but, considering its normal range, is one that can be expected to turn up again. *Occasional* species appear every few years, but not regularly. *Accidental* or *vagrant* birds have been found once or twice but are not likely to be seen again. (Some pelagic species, currently so considered, may prove to be casual or regular with increased offshore observation.)

Resident species are those present in the region year-round, and *such status is assumed unless otherwise stated*. *Palearctic migrants* visit East Africa during the northern autumn and winter following breeding in Eurasia. Some remain here for a few months as *winter residents*, but others move through as *passage migrants* to 'winter' quarters in southern Africa. *Intra-African migrants* regularly move into or through our region, e.g. Plain Nightjars disperse southward into Kenya following nesting in northeast Africa, and the southern race of African Golden Oriole spends April to August with us after breeding in the southern tropics. A few *Malagasy migrants* such as Madagascar Lesser Cuckoo and Madagascar Pratincole breed on Indian Ocean islands before spending a significant portion of their year in Africa.

Descriptions of vocalizations, usually given under call or song, are based wherever possible on our own tape recordings and field notes, supplemented by those of our colleagues. A few descriptions are based on reports in the literature, references to which are found in *Birds of Kenya and Northern Tanzania*.

Geographic distribution within our region is briefly outlined in the text, under **Range** for all resident species, under **Range/status** for palearctic, afrotropical and other migrants. (For vagrants, only **status** is considered.) Distributions are elucidated in terms of cities, major towns, districts (and/or 'regions' in Tanzania), important topographic features, national parks and game reserves. Many of those mentioned are located on the two maps on the front covers. A few features require definition: the *eastern Kenyan plateau* encompasses the generally dry regions north, east, and south of the highlands. In the *Rift Valley*, that great trough intersecting Kenya from the north and continuing south to Malawi, lie the important *Rift Valley lakes* of Turkana, Baringo, Bogoria, Nakuru, Elmenteita, Naivasha and Magadi in Kenya, Natron and Manyara in northern Tanzania. The *western Kenyan highlands* are those west of the Rift, the *central highlands* are to the east. *Rift Valley highlands* may be used for elevated areas in or immediately adjacent to the Rift. The *Masai Steppe* is an extensive shelf of dry country extending from Tanzania's Rift wall east to the Pangani River valley below the Pare Mts.

Elevation limits (in metres) are often provided, but are omitted for most altitudinally widespread species. Highlands are considered to be those areas above 1500 m (5000 ft), lowlands below 500 m (1640 ft). Habitat terminology is discussed below.

Seasonal status and habitat are usually dealt with in the captions facing the colour plates, but where convenient, occasional comments are included with range statements or elsewhere in the species account. A **Taxonomic Note** terminates certain accounts where our treatment differs from that of other recent authors, or where we wish to direct attention to a particular point of classification.

THE ILLUSTRATIONS

Experienced observers know that positive species identification often involves more than matching an unfamiliar bird with a book illustration, but in most cases a person will first consult the colour plates. Similar species are grouped together among the plates wherever practical, but there may be additional birds to consider before deciding on a species name. This is particularly true in challenging groups such as larks, cisticolas and greenbuls that include numerous confusingly similar species. Sometimes, too, quite unrelated birds resemble one another. It is always wise to consult the text.

The family sequence of the plates does not parallel that of the text. Among the non-passerines, 'waterbirds' precede 'landbirds.' Otherwise we have kept related groups together when practical, but there are exceptions. Plates 1 and 2, for example, depict pelagic species regardless of their taxonomic affinities. Optimal space utilization, an overriding consideration in plate design, has resulted in unconventional placement of some small families. Ostriches thus appear with other large ground birds, far from their traditional lead position. Sequence of passerine families is also at variance with the text.

Some superficially similar but rather distantly related groups are placed near one another for easier visual comparisons; pipits are near the larks, and penduline tits, white-eyes and Little Yellow Flycatcher are with the warblers. The pitta and broadbill follow the motacillids, as near the beginning of the Passeriformes as available space permitted. The 34 species restricted (in our region) to northern Tanzania are depicted on the three final plates. Plates and text are conspicuously cross-referenced to avoid location problems.

We have endeavoured to illustrate birds in typical postures for the species, yet still show essential field marks. Where space has permitted, we have included additional figures of flying birds or spread tails if these aid identification. Important subspecific differences have also been illustrated. Ideally, these are full-size (as with the races of Yellow Wagtail), but at times small inset figures must suffice (e.g. White-headed Barbet). Most figures of flying birds are also to a smaller scale. A dividing line across a plate indicates two different size scales, and usually family separation. We offer no apology for crowded plates; purely aesthetic considerations have sometimes been sacrificed in favour of illustrating additional plumages or subspecies. For a few species, we have shown both worn and freshly plumaged birds as feather abrasion and fading can profoundly alter basic appearance. All passerines and most non-passerines have been painted from specific museum specimens, often supplemented by photographs of living birds. For polytypic species the bird figured usually represents a particular race and is so identified in the captions. Ten species, all vagrants, are illustrated only in black and white, either in the text or on an appropriate plate-caption page.

PLATE CAPTION NOTES

Captions opposite each colour plate provide key information in skeletal form, typically including relative abundance, migratory status, indication of habitat, and sometimes a brief reference to geographic range within our region. Captions for a few crowded plates are necessarily brief, but with those exceptions we have tried to provide identification 'essentials' opposite the plates to avoid the need for constant page-flipping to the text.

DISTRIBUTION MAPS

Maps are provided for most species, and show at a glance broad aspects of the bird's *recent* range (from *c.* 1960 to 1996). Solid black portions of the maps indicate the distribution of breeding and presumed breeding residents; open hatching (with diagonal lines) shows the non-breeding range of both East African residents and species breeding elsewhere but migrating through or into our region. It is understood that the map reflects distribution *only in areas of suitable habitat* within the broadly designated range. Black dots indicate either isolated breeding records or breeding colonies. Open dots show sites of isolated non-breeding records, both early (to 1950) and recent (through 1996). For a few species (e.g. Black Heron) open dots may indicate former breeding sites. Not reflected in the maps is former distribution of species which have suffered a major reduction in range in recent decades. Open dots are also used for records of rare or little known migrants. International boundaries are represented by dashed lines. For simplicity, the only physical features depicted are Lake Turkana, the eastern edge of Lake Victoria, and the Tana and Athi–Galana–Sabaki rivers.

Readers may note discrepancies between certain of our distribution maps and those for the same species that have appeared in other publications. As we know some available maps to have been based in part on questionable or erroneous sight records, we have interpreted them with great caution. Other maps have been based partially on earlier published range statements, some of which were in error or based on unverifiable information. We have disregarded these in preparing our own maps, relying instead on carefully considered data and many thousands of specimens in European, American and African museums.

HABITAT TERMINOLOGY

(For an expanded discussion of vegetation and bird habitats see *The Birds of Kenya and Northern Tanzania*.) The following terms are used throughout. *Desert* and *semi-desert* occupy extensive areas of low precipitation (especially in the north), grading into *grassland* as rainfall increases. *Bush* refers to a broad range of shrub or low tree growth, mainly under 5 m in height. It grades into *bushed grassland* with widely spaced thickets of shrubby growth, or into *savanna*—extensive grassy areas with scattered trees. *Scrub* is applied to varied assemblages of low shrubs or coarse perennial herbs 2–3 m in height. Bush and scrub may be deciduous or evergreen, thorny or unarmed.

In higher-rainfall areas, bush and savanna merge into denser *woodland* (in semi-desert areas usually confined to riparian strips), differing from savanna in its more nearly continuous tree canopy (over 20% coverage). Woodland grades into *forest* with its closed upper tree canopy of interlaced crowns. Forest is categorized as *riparian* (along watercourses), *lowland* (below 1000 m) and *highland* or *montane* (above 1500 m). Some anomalous major tracts, such as the western Kakamega and Nandi forests, are 'highland' in terms of elevation yet support many 'lowland' bird species. Although certain coastal Kenyan forests, and that in the Shimba Hills, have been treated as *lowland rainforest*, our region supports almost no stands that can be so considered. Except for small remnant coastal patches, most of it is in narrow riparian strips or other sites where the trees are maintained by ground water, not rainfall (e.g. the Lake Manyara Forest). Locally at higher elevations is a high-rainfall, temperate or *intermediate rainforest*, e.g. near Kakamega, at 1520–1820 m (5000–6000 ft), and the quite different Amani Forest as low as 900 m (*c.* 3000 ft) in the Usambara Mts. Structurally and floristically distinct from these are other montane forests such as those on Mt Elgon, Mt Kenya, the Aberdares and Kilimanjaro, also in high-rainfall areas. Less well-developed, but species-rich, 'dry' *evergreen forests* (precipitation *c.* 750 mm or 30 inches), exist on the Taita and Chyulu hills.

More localized habitats are *moorland*, above 3000 m (c. 10,000 ft), and thickets of montane *bamboo*, sometimes with intermediate belts of scrubby *Hagenia/Hypericum* woodland and *giant heath* (*Erica, Philippa*), forming a dwarf subalpine forest or shrub association. The moorlands themselves are characterized by coarse tussock grasses and impressive giant species of *Lobelia* and *Senecio*. In the alpine zone above the moors, vegetation is reduced to scattered low plants in sheltered sites, and there are few birds.

In swamps or along rivers, palms of several kinds form belts of specialised habitat. Picturesque doum palms (*Hyphaene*) are characteristic of watercourses in northern and eastern Kenya. *Papyrus swamps*, consisting of nearly pure stands of the giant sedge *Cyperus papyrus*, are prominent around Lake Victoria and scattered elsewhere. *Mangrove swamps* form an important coastal environment. Throughout the region, increasingly large areas of human-modified or -created habitats are superimposed on the original vegetational pattern. Locally attractive to birds are well-wooded *gardens* associated with rural or suburban residences. Croplands, pastures and cultivated fields, some in various stages of abandonment and regrowth, we lump together under the term *cultivation*. In the highlands are extensive *plantations* of introduced *Eucalyptus* or exotic conifers (with little to offer, for most birds).

The large *alkaline* ('soda') *lakes* (e.g. Nakuru, Magadi and Natron) support a different biota from *freshwater lakes* such as Naivasha. (Lakes Turkana and Baringo, though alkaline, are fresh enough to support rich fish populations.) Smaller freshwater *ponds*, artificial impoundments behind dams, and sewage treatment ponds provide important resting and feeding areas for many species. Extensive irrigated fields, as in the Mwea and Ahero rice schemes, are also important for waterbirds and waders. Temporarily flooded land, inundated after heavy rains, may persist for months as marsh, swamp or open water, providing breeding and feeding areas. Coastal habitats include sand and coral-rock *beaches*, and the tidal *estuaries* and *mudflats* so essential to palearctic-breeding shorebirds on passage and during their winter sojourn in East Africa.

TAXONOMY AND SCIENTIFIC NOMENCLATURE

Sources for our decisions on family sequence are cited in *The Birds of Kenya and Northern Tanzania*. In general, our taxonomic treatment parallels that of the recent volumes of *The Birds of Africa* (Academic Press, 1992, 1997), with a few important exceptions at both generic and specific levels. Users of East African bird books published prior to the 1990s will notice numerous unfamiliar names, plus a few changes at the family level. Authorities differ in their treatment of certain allopatric forms, and standard zoological nomenclature provides no convenient intermediate category to designate populations believed to be evolutionarily between mere subspecific standing and 'full' species status. In East Africa, a few such birds have, in our opinion, diverged sufficiently from their near relatives to be very strong candidates for species status, yet are not universally recognized as such. We treat each under a separate English name, and indicate in brackets after the generic name, the species to which it seems most closely related (and/or under which it is treated by other authors) e.g. Somali Ostrich, *Struthio (camelus) molybdophanes*. Where applicable, trinomial designations are used throughout, as we treat subspecies in greater detail than do many field guides. Although many of these geographic races differ only in minor ways from one another, others are readily recognizable under field conditions. Still others may be elevated to specific status in the future.

ENGLISH NAMES

English names are those of *The Birds of Kenya and Northern Tanzania* (one exception: 'Blue-eared Starling' of that work is modified to Greater Blue-eared Starling). In the few cases where our preferred names differ from those used in *The Birds of Africa*, we provide alternative names from that work. Where space permits, we include current names that differ in southern Africa for certain widespread species shared by both regions, but we have not attempted to provide alternatives for all of these.

NEW SPECIES ADDED TO THE KENYA LIST

The following species have been added to the Kenya list since this book was originally published in 1999:

Eurasian Griffon Vulture *Gyps fulvus* 1, Amboseli NP; 20 January 2000 (see *Bull ABC* 8[1], 59-60).
Cassin's Hawk Eagle *Spizaetus africanus* Re-identification of bird collected on Mt Elgon in April 1926, originally identified as Booted Eagle *Hieraaetus pennatus* (see *Bull ABC* 8[2], 138-139).
Common Crane *Grus Grus* First–year bird near Eldoret; 4–5 October 1999 (accepted on basis of photograph submitted).
Spotted Sandpiper *Actitis macularia* 1, Mt Lodge, Mt Kenya region; 4–5 September 1999 (see *Bull ABC* 8[1]; 48-49).
Rufous-tailed Weaver *Histurgops ruficaudus* 4, Mara GR; 4 July 2000 (short range extension, but first confirmed record for Kenya, 10kms sw. of Keekorok Lodge).

UNCONFIRMED
River Prinia *Prinia fluviatilis* A new population of this West African species, representing a considerable range extension eastwards, was found near Lokichokio in NW Kenya in July 2001. Identification was verified by comparing vocalizations with published recordings. This record is subject to confirmation by the Records Committee of Nature Kenya (formerly EANHS).

ABBREVIATIONS USED IN THE TEXT AND PLATE CAPTIONS

Measurements		
cm	centimetres	
mm	millimetres	
m	metre(s)	
mi	mile(s)	
km	kilometre(s)	
ft	foot; feet	
in. or "	inch(es)	

Geographical or directional	
n.	north(ern)
s.	south(ern)
e.	east(ern)
w. or west.	west(ern)
cent.	central
L.	lake
mt(s)	mountain(s), mount(s)
NP(s)	national park(s)

NR	national reserve
GR(s)	game reserve(s)
R.	river

Other	
ad.	adult
br.	breeding
imm.	immature
incl.	including
juv.	juvenile
non-br.	non-breeding
opp.	opposite
sec.	second
sp.	species (singular)
spp.	species (plural)
sq.	square

TERMS RELATING TO BIRD IDENTIFICATION

The following glossary covers morphological terms used in the text excepting many of those for parts labelled on the accompanying drawings (unless elaboration is necessary). Also included are certain other definitions relating to behaviour, distribution and taxonomy.

Air sacs: components of the bird's respiratory system; extensions from the lungs to several areas of the body cavity, into certain large bones and under the skin.

Allopatric: relating to two or more congeneric forms whose breeding ranges do not overlap.

Axillaries (axillars): long inner wing-lining feathers, lying between underside of wing and body.

Booted: referring to an undivided tarsal sheath, i.e. one not consisting of separate scales or scutes.

Brood parasite: a bird which lays its eggs in the nest of another species (the **host** species) and plays no parental role in raising the young, e.g. Old-World cuckoos and the New-World cowbirds.

Carpal: pertaining to the wrist area at the bend of the wing.

Cere: in hawks, owls and parrots, the soft basal covering on the maxilla. The nostrils open in, or at the edge of this structure which may be swollen and/or distinctively coloured.

Cheek: technically the side of the jaw (i.e. the malar region), but loosely considered to be the general auricular region.

Commissure: the line of closure of the two mandibles.

Congeneric: belonging to the same genus.

Conspecific: belonging to the same species.

Crepuscular: active at twilight.

Crissum: the under tail-coverts together with the feathers in the vent region; sometimes contrastingly coloured as in d'Arnaud's Barbet.

Cryptic: aiding in concealment.

Culmen: the dorsal ridge of the maxilla.

Decurved: curved downward, as the bill of a curlew.

Dimorphic: having two distinct morphs or colour phases. See **Polymorphic**.

Distal: farthest from the body; pertaining to the tip of an appendage.

Diurnal: active by day.

DNA: standard abbreviation for deoxyribose nucleic acid.

Dorsal: pertaining to the upper surface; opposite of ventral.

Eclipse plumage: a dull plumage worn by males of certain brightly coloured birds (e.g. some sunbirds and male ducks) following breeding.

Emarginate: pertaining to a primary feather that is notched or abruptly narrowed along the edge, usually near the tip. Also refers to a slightly forked or notched tail.

Endemic: confined to a particular region. Turacos and mousebirds are *endemic* to Africa.

Family: a taxonomic category immediately above the genus in rank, composed of a genus or several genera. Family names of birds and other animals invariably end in -*idae*.

Feather tract (pteryla): a tract or area of skin to which contour feathers are restricted.

Filoplume: an inconspicuous, specialized, hairlike feather, usually most noticeable on the hindneck.

Flight feathers: as used here, the long wing feathers or remiges (primaries and secondaries); strictly, the remiges and rectrices taken collectively.

Foot: the tarsus and toes, collectively.

Forked: referring to a tail with the outer feathers distinctly longer than the innermost, as in terns.

Form: as used here, a deliberately non-committal term applied to species and/or subspecies when a more specific taxonomic designation is not desirable or practical in a particular context.

Gape: the mouth opening; sometimes used to refer to the rictus (*q.v.*)

Gape flange: expanded soft tissue of the rictus as in young birds and adults of some cuckoo-shrikes; in raptors, may be extended far back to below the eye.

Genus (pl. **genera**): a taxonomic category between family and species; a group of close-ly related species.

Gonys: the lower median ridge of the mandible; usually smoothly curved but forms a dis-tinct **gonydeal angle** in gulls and some other birds.

Graduated: referring to a tail in which the innermost rectrices are longest, the others becoming progressively shorter toward the sides.

Greater coverts: see **Secondary coverts.**

Gular: pertaining to the throat.

Hackles: long slender feathers on the neck, as in a Vulturine Guineafowl.

Holarctic region: the palearctic and nearctic regions, collectively.

Host: the individual, or species, which incubates the eggs and raises the young of avian **brood parasites,** *q.v.*

Humerus: the upper arm bone.

Immature: in this book, used to refer to the plumage(s) replacing juvenile feathering and preceding adult plumage.

Indigenous: native to a particular country or region. (See endemic.)

Invertebrate: an animal lacking a spinal column or 'backbone'; insects, molluscs, worms *et al.*

Iridescence: a type of shiny or 'metallic' structural coloration, essentially independent of feather pigments; well developed in sunbirds and glossy starlings.

Iris (pl. **irides**): the coloured contractile diaphragm of the eye, surrounding the pupil.

Lamellate: possessing numerous thin plates or lamellae, as along the sides of a duck's bill.

Lappet: a wattle, especially at the corner of the mouth.

Lesser Coverts: see **Secondary coverts.**

Lore (pl. **lores**; adj. **loral**): the space between bill and eyelid; may be bare or feathered.

Malar region: the side of the jaw, posterior to the bill. At times marked by a **malar stripe** bordering the upper edge of the throat.

Mandible: the lower part of the bill (often called 'lower mandible'); the plural is used with reference to both upper and lower portions.

Mandibular ramus (pl. **rami**): the projection of the mandible extending posteriorly on each side of the jaw.

Maxilla: the upper half of the bill; often termed 'upper mandible.'

Median coverts: see **Secondary coverts.**

Monotypic: containing only one type or representative. A monotypic species includes no recognized subspecies.

Morph: a plumage 'colour phase' of a polymorphic or dimorphic species.

Morphological: pertaining to form or structure.

Moult (molt): the periodic process of shedding old feathers and replacing these with new ones.

Nearctic region: the biogeographical region comprising North America south to the trop-ics.

Neotropical region: the New World tropics; one of the world's six major biogeographi-cal regions.

Nidicolous: refers to bird species in which young remain in the nest for some time fol-lowing hatching.

Nidifugous: refers to species whose young leave the nest soon after hatching.

Nocturnal: active at night.

Nominate subspecies (race): the first population of a polytypic species to be described. Designated by repetition of the specific epithet, e.g. *Amadina fasciata fasciata.*

Nuchal: pertaining to the nape.

Orbital ring: a circle of bare skin surrounding the eye, as opposed to the feathered eye-ring.

Palearctic region: one of the world's six major biogeographical regions, comprising Eurasia south to the Himalayas and North Africa.

Panel: an elongated wing patch formed by more or less contrasting feather edges, as in the primaries of various cisticolas. See wing edgings.

Passerine: pertaining to the Order Passeriformes, the 'perching birds.'

Patagium (adj. patagial): the fold of skin between the carpal area of the wing and the body.

Pectinate: comb-like, i.e. bearing numerous tooth-like projections.

Pectoral patch: a clearly defined dark area of plumage on either side of the breast.

Pelagic: pertaining to the open sea.

Plumage: a bird's feathers, collectively. Also used more specifically for a particular feather coat or feather generation between moults. Each species has a characteristic plumage sequence.

Polymorphic: having two (then often called dimorphic) or more distinct, genetically determined colour morphs within a species, independent of age, sexual, seasonal or subspecific variation.

Polytypic: having two or more taxonomic divisions within the category referred to. Usually applied to those species divisible into subspecies.

Posthumerals (posthumeral quills): in some birds, the large, often long, inner wing feathers, usually lacking the rigidity of remiges, lying along or near the trailing edge of the humerus. Sometimes confusingly called tertiaries or tertials (q.v.), but not a feather series comparable with secondaries or primaries, and distinct from the true tertiaries which arise from the humerus in certain very large birds.

Postocular stripe: a (usually dark) line behind the eye; the posterior part of an **eye-line**.

Powder-down feathers: highly modified body feathers, short, silky and disintegrating at the tips into a very fine powder that produces a characteristic bloom on the bird's plumage, best developed in herons (among East African birds).

Primary extension: the length of that portion of the primaries visible beyond the ends of the secondaries in a folded wing.

Primaries: the outermost flight feathers of the wing, those attached to the bird's hand bones and digits.

Proximal: refers to the part of an appendage near the body; opposite of distal.

Race: see **subspecies**.

Raptor: a bird with strong claws and sharp talons for tearing prey. Usually used with reference to the diurnal Falconiformes (hawks and relatives) but applies also to owls. (adj. **raptorial**).

Rectrix: a tail feather.

Recurved: curved upward, as an avocet's bill.

Remex: a flight feather of the wing, either a primary or secondary.

Scute(s): the horny plates or scales, as in a scutellate tarsus.

Secondaries: the series of flight feathers (remiges) arising from, and attached to the ulna. The more or less differentiated inner secondaries are sometimes called **tertials** (q.v.)

Secondary coverts: partially overlapping feathers covering the bases of the secondaries. (Includes **greater, median** and **lesser coverts**; usually refers to the upper wing surface, but a comparable series exists on the underside (cf. **wing-lining**).

Serrate: saw-toothed.

Shaft streak: a narrow longitudinal mark along the central axis of a feather.

Sibling Species: two or more very closely related species, nearly identical morphologically but each usually distinct vocally or behaviourally.

Species (sg. & pl.): in the vernacular, a 'kind' of bird (or other organism). As defined by Ernst Mayr, a group of "actually or potentially interbreeding populations which are reproductively isolated from other such groups."

Speculum: A bright, sharply contrasting patch near the rear edge of a wing, especially the iridescent areas on the secondaries of waterfowl; conspicuous in flight.

Spur: a sharp projection (corneous modified skin over a bony core) as on the tarsus of a spurfowl or from near the carpal joint on the wing (as in Spur-winged Plover).

Streamer: exceptionally long slender outermost or innermost rectrices as in a tern or tropicbird.

Subadult: applies to the later (older) stages of immature birds (*i.e.* those two or three years old) in those species which require more than one year to reach full maturity.

Rachis: the shaft of a feather.

Subspecies (sg. & pl.): a geographic *race* of a species; a population (or group of populations) morphologically and geographically defined. The subspecies of a species interbreed freely where (and if) their ranges overlap, thereby producing intermediate populations sharing characteristics of each form but readily assignable to neither. Designated trinomially in scientific nomenclature. See **species**.

Supercilium: that part of the head immediately above the eye; in many birds marked by a **superciliary stripe** (or 'superciliary')

Supra-: a prefix meaning 'above.' Supraloral lines are above the lores.

Sympatric: applied to two congeneric species whose breeding ranges overlap; the opposite of allopatric.

Tarsus (pl. **tarsi**): technically, the **tarsometatarsus**, together with the tibia, loosely termed 'leg' (although the tarsus and toes anatomically constitute a bird's *foot*). Typically featherless, and covered with smooth scales, but feathered in sandgrouse, most owls and some other birds.

Taxon: any taxonomic unit—order, family, genus, species, etc.

Taxonomy (adj. **Taxonomic**): the science of classification of plants and animals according to their natural relationships.

Tertials: a term now generally avoided by ornithologists but perpetuated by birders to apply to a few differently coloured or patterned inner secondaries, or to strongly differentiated proximal secondaries or adjacent specialized posthumeral feathers (usually elongated and pointed) in shorebirds, larks *et al.* True tertiaries or tertials, originating on the humerus, are found only in certain large, long-winged birds such as albatrosses.

Tibia (pl. **tibiae**): the **tibiotarsus** ('drumstick') of the leg; partly bare in numerous birds such as herons, but largely feathered in most small birds (entire tibia featherless in Golden Pipit). Often casually designated as the 'thigh,' (especially if the feathering contrastingly coloured), but the true thighs are seldom visible in a living bird.

Tomia (sg. **tomium**): the hard cutting edges of the bill. There are maxillary tomia (one on each side) and comparable mandibular tomia, mutually apposed in the closed bill.

Trinomial: designation of a bird's scientific name by a generic name and both specific and subspecific epithets, e.g. *Anthreptes collaris elachior*; in other words, the name of a subspecies.

Ulna: the posterior and heavier forearm bone to which a bird's secondaries are attached.

Underparts: the feathers from chin to under tail-coverts, usually not including underside of the tail.

Upperparts: the feathered dorsal surface from forehead to upper tail-coverts, usually including the scapulars and wing-coverts, sometimes also the upper surface of the tail.

Vane: the flattened part of a feather, attached to the shaft (rachis); divided into outer and inner **webs**.

Vent: the opening of the cloaca to the surface of the body; the feathers of this region, between lower belly and under tail-coverts.

Ventral: pertaining to the underside of the body; opposite of dorsal.

Vertebrate: any 'backboned' animal (Subphylum Vertebrata) supporting a vertebral column—bony fish, amphibian, reptile, bird or mammal.

Wattle: a fleshy, largely unfeathered appendage of the head or neck, usually more or less wrinkled and often brightly coloured, as the **eye-wattles** of paradise flycatchers or wattle-eyes.

Web: of feather, see **vane**. Of toes, a thin flexible membrane attached to the sides of (and often connecting) the toes of various waterbirds.

Wing edgings: contrastingly coloured edges of the flight feathers, becoming less conspicuous as the outer web of the feather wears away.

Wing-lining: the under wing-coverts considered collectively.

Zygodactyl: two toes (nos. 2 and 3) in front and two (1st and 4th) directed backward, as in woodpeckers, cuckoos *et al.*

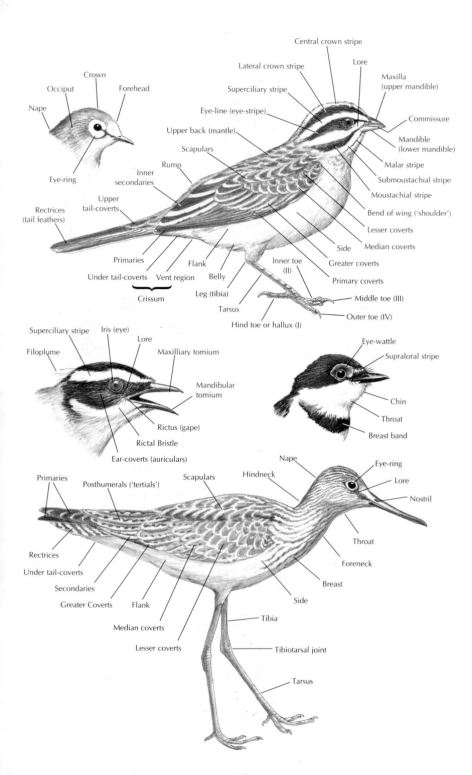

Central crown stripe

Lateral crown stripe

Lore

Maxilla
(upper mandible)

Superciliary stripe

Crown

Occiput

Forehead

Nape

Eye-line (eye-stripe)

Commissure

Upper back (mantle)

Mandible
(lower mandible)

Scapulars

Malar stripe

Eye-ring

Rump

Inner
secondaries

Submoustachial stripe

Moustachial stripe

Rectrices
(tail feathers)

Upper
tail-coverts

Bend of wing ('shoulder')

Lesser coverts

Side

Median coverts

Primaries

Flank

Inner toe
(II)

Greater coverts

Under tail-coverts   Vent region

Belly

Primary coverts

Crissum

Leg (tibia)

Middle toe (III)

Tarsus

Outer toe (IV)

Hind toe or hallux (I)

Superciliary stripe

Iris (eye)

Lore

Eye-wattle

Filoplume

Maxilliary tomium

Supraloral stripe

Mandibular
tomium

Chin

Throat

Rictus (gape)

Breast band

Rictal Bristle

Ear-coverts (auriculars)

Nape

Eye-ring

Posthumerals ('tertials')

Scapulars

Hindneck

Lore

Primaries

Nostril

Rectrices

Throat

Under tail-coverts

Foreneck

Secondaries

Breast

Greater Coverts

Flank

Side

Median coverts

Tibia

Lesser coverts

Tibiotarsal joint

Tarsus

Cere

Operculum

Facial
wattles
incl.
lappets

Crest

Cere

Ear-tuft

Gape flange

Facial disc

Nail

Lamellae

Orbital ring

Casque

Nasal tuft

Gonydeal
angle

Lappet

Frontal shield

Casque

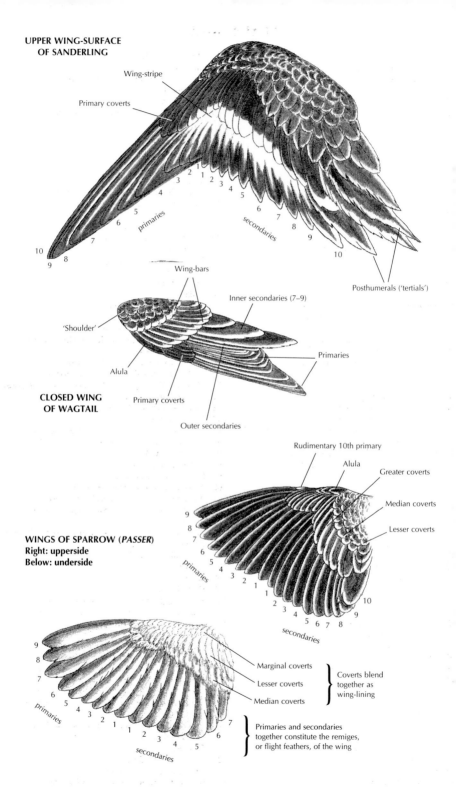

UPPER WING-SURFACE OF SANDERLING

Wing-stripe

Primary coverts

primaries

secondaries

Posthumerals ('tertials')

Wing-bars

Inner secondaries (7–9)

'Shoulder'

Alula

Primary coverts

Primaries

Outer secondaries

CLOSED WING OF WAGTAIL

Rudimentary 10th primary

Alula

Greater coverts

Median coverts

Lesser coverts

WINGS OF SPARROW (*PASSER*)
Right: upperside
Below: underside

primaries

secondaries

Marginal coverts

Lesser coverts

Median coverts

} Coverts blend together as wing-lining

primaries

secondaries

} Primaries and secondaries together constitute the remiges, or flight feathers, of the wing

PLATES 1–124

PLATE 1: PELAGIC BIRDS (FRIGATEBIRDS, TUBENOSES AND BOOBIES)

1 GREATER FRIGATEBIRD *Fregata minor* **Page 277**
Usually far from shore. Long, pointed wings and long, forked (when spread) tail. The most likely frigatebird in our area. **1a. Adult female**. Grey chin and throat merge with white breast (throat black in vagrant Lesser Frigatebird (see p. 277) **1b. Immature**. White or pale chestnut head. **1c. Adult male**. Entirely black underparts. (Lesser shows small white flank/wing-lining patches.)

2 BLACK-BROWED ALBATROSS *Diomedea melanophris* **Page 270**
Rare north to latitude of Mombasa. Underside of wings with white centre, black borders. **2a. Adult**. Upperside. **2b. Adult**. Underside.

3 SHY ALBATROSS *Diomedea cauta* **Page 270**
Wanderer to Pemba Channel, possibly regular Aug.–Sept. Black mark at junction of underside of wing and body, and black notch near carpal joint.

4 WEDGE-TAILED SHEARWATER *Puffinus pacificus* **Page 271**
Scarce; recorded between Shimoni and Lamu. Wings held forward, slightly bowed and angled. Long wedge-shaped tail with even sides. Smaller Jouanin's Petrel (p. 272). shows different tail outline. **4a. Adult**. Upperside. **4b. Adult**. Underside.

5 AUDUBON'S SHEARWATER *Puffinus lherminieri* **Page 271**
Uncommon but regular offshore, mainly north of Kilifi. Fluttering flight. Dark brown cap extends below eyes; under tail-coverts dark. (Flanks and sides also brown in *P. l. persicus*. See text. Mascarene Shearwater, *P. atrodorsalis*, is black, not dark brown, above and has white under tail-coverts. (See figure below.)

6 BROWN BOOBY *Sula leucogaster* **Page 275**
Vagrant. Smaller and longer-tailed than Masked Booby. White confined to lower breast, belly and under tail-coverts and central part of underwing. Female illustrated.

7 MASKED BOOBY *Sula dactylatra melanops* **Page 275**
Uncommon but regular in Pemba Channel. **7a. Immature**. Whitish collar more or less conspicuous; white area on underside of wing encloses dark stripe parallel to leading edge. (Similar to rare Brown Booby; see text.) **7b. Adult**. Black tail and yellow bill distinguish this species from similar Red-footed Booby. (Extralimital Cape Gannet, possible in Tanzanian waters, has pale blue-grey bill and yellow wash on head.)

8 RED-FOOTED BOOBY *Sula sula rubripes* **Page 275**
Casual, Aug.–March. Plumage variable. Feet red. **8a. Brown morph**. **8b. White morph**. White tail distinctive.

Mascarene Shearwaters

HDP

PLATE 2: PELAGIC BIRDS (STORM-PETRELS, TROPICBIRD AND MARINE TERNS)

1 BLACK-BELLIED STORM-PETREL *Fregetta tropica*   **Page 274**
Vagrant. Black mid-ventral line on white belly.

2 WILSON'S STORM-PETREL *Oceanites oceanicus*   **Page 273**
Uncommon, but probably annual, April–Dec. Small and dark. Flight fluttery, usually just above water, the feet often pattering on the surface. Feet project beyond tail in flight.

3 LEACH'S STORM-PETREL *Oceanodroma leucorhoa*   **Page 273**
Vagrant. Feet do not project beyond forked tail in flight.

4 BROWN NODDY *Anous stolidus pileatus*   **Page 356**
Uncommon offshore throughout the year. Numerous near breeding islands, June–Sept. Wedge-shaped tail. **4a. Adult**. Tail darker than the back. Whitish cap contrasts sharply with dark loral area. **4b. Immature**. White restricted to forehead. Feathers of upperparts and wings pale-tipped.

5 LESSER NODDY *Anous t. tenuirostris*   **Page 356**
Rare, but perhaps regular off s. Kenya and in Pemba Channel. Tail of adult appears greyish, paler than the back. Whitish cap often extends below eyes, not contrasting with loral area; bill longer and thinner than in Brown Noddy.

6 WHITE-TAILED TROPICBIRD *Phaethon l. lepturus*   **Page 274**
Uncommon but regular in Pemba Channel, Aug.–March. Occasional farther north at other times. (Immature has different pattern and lacks tail streamers; see text.)

7 WHITE-CHEEKED TERN *Sterna repressa*   **Page 354**
Locally common, sometimes in large flocks north of Mombasa, uncommon farther south. Occasionally seen from shore. **7a. Non-breeding plumage**. Darker, and narrower-winged than similar Common Tern. **7b. Breeding plumage**. Grey above, including rump; black cap separated from dark grey underparts by broad white facial streak.

8 SOOTY TERN *Sterna fuscata nubilosa*   **Page 355**
Regular and sometimes common at sea; rarely seen from shore. Breeds erratically in Lamu area. Feeds by daintily dipping or hovering near surface. **8a. Juvenile**. Pale lower belly/crissum and forked tail separate it from noddies. **8b. Adult**. White on forehead and underparts.

9 BRIDLED TERN *Sterna anaethetus antarctica*   **Page 355**
Fairly common at sea; rare inshore. Associates with Brown Noddy and Sooty Tern. **9a. Juvenile**. Paler than young Sooty Tern; whitish collar on hindneck. **9b. Adult**. Back brownish grey, usually separated from black cap by whitish collar. White of forehead extends back above eyes.

Red-tailed Tropicbird, Phaethon rubricauda. *Probable in Kenyan waters, but no substantiated records. See text.*

PLATE 3: SMALLER TERNS IN FLIGHT (See also Plates 2 and 5)

1 BLACK TERN *Chlidonias n. niger*   **Page 356**
Rare inland migrant. **1a. Spring adult** (rare in East Africa). **1b. Winter adult.** Rump and
tail grey. Dark grey patches on sides of breast.

2 WHITE-WINGED TERN *Chlidonias leucopterus*   **Page 356**
Common migrant on large inland lakes. Scarce at coast. Some present all year. **2a.
Winter adult. 2b. Juvenile.** Dark back patch, pale wings. **2c. Spring adult.**

3 GULL-BILLED TERN *Sterna n. nilotica*   **Page 352**
Locally common migrant, Aug.–April, on large inland lakes. Smaller numbers along
coast. Stocky, thick-billed. **3a and 3d. Spring adults.** Pale grey above. **3b. Juvenile. 3c.
Winter adult.**

4 WHISKERED TERN *Chlidonias hybridus delalandii*   **Page 355**
Widespread inland. Breeds in small colonies on freshwater lakes. Suggests short-tailed
Sterna. **4a. Non-breeding adult.** Back and tail uniformly grey. **4b. Juvenile.** Brown back
with buff feather edges. **4c. Breeding adult.** White facial stripe separates black cap from
dark underparts; bill dark red.

5 ROSEATE TERN *Sterna dougallii bangsi*   **Page 354**
Coastal. Present all year; locally abundant, May–Oct. More slender and appears whiter
than other terns. Bill long and narrow. **5a. Juvenile.** Narrow whitish forehead band, mot-
tled back, white collar and pale grey rump, dark carpal bar. Bill black. **5b and 5d.
Breeding adults.** All-red bill and feet, very long outer rectrices. **5c. Non-breeding adult.**
Narrow black bill may show some dull red at base; white forehead.

6 COMMON TERN *Sterna h. hirundo*   **Page 354**
Common/abundant along coast, Aug.–Dec. and in April. Scarce on Rift Valley lakes.
Shorter, greyer than Roseate Tern. **6a. First-winter bird** (some juvenile feathers). Dark-
edged outer rectrices; base of bill orange. **6b and 6d. Spring adults.** Dark trailing primary edge; outer rectrices darker-edged and shorter than in Roseate Tern. Bill usually black
(becomes largely red after birds leave East Africa). **6c. Non-breeding adult.** White forehead and forecrown.

7 LITTLE TERN *Sterna a. albifrons*   **Page 355**
Status uncertain (April specimens from coast and Lake Naivasha). **7a. Juvenile.** First-winter birds may retain many juvenile feathers. **7b and 7d. Spring adults.** Black only on outer
2 or 3 primaries (outer 3 or 4 in Saunders's); tail white (not pale grey). **7c. Non-breeding
adult.** Usually inseparable from Saunders's Tern. See text.

8 SAUNDERS'S TERN *Sterna (albifrons) saundersi*   **Page 355**
Abundant coastal migrant, most numerous Oct.–April. Status at Lake Turkana uncertain
(one Oct. specimen record). **Breeding adult.** White forehead patch less elongate than in
Little Tern.

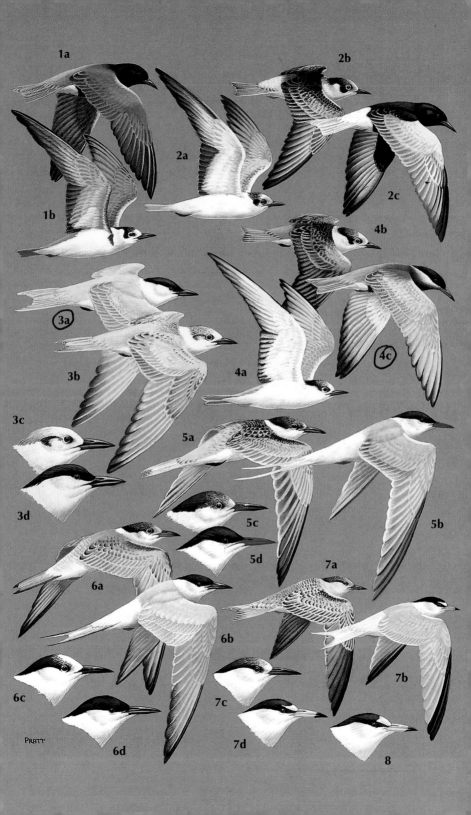

PRATT

PLATE 4: LARGER TERNS AND SKIMMER IN FLIGHT (See also Plate 5)

1 CASPIAN TERN *Sterna caspia*   **Page 353**
Annual winter migrant to Lake Turkana and the coast north of Mombasa. Size may suggest gull, but tern-like bill and habits distinctive. **1a. Juvenile acquiring first-winter plumage. 1b. Winter adult. 1c. Spring adult.**

2 SANDWICH TERN *Sterna s. sandvicensis*   **Page 353**
Uncommon migrant to n. Kenyan coast. Vagrant to Rift Valley lakes. **2a. Juvenile. 2b. Winter adult. 2c. Spring adult.**

3 LESSER CRESTED TERN *Sterna b. bengalensis*   **Page 353**
Present along coast throughout the year. Vagrant to Rift Valley lakes. **3a. Breeding adult. 3b. Non-breeding adult. 3c. First-year bird.**

4 GREATER CRESTED TERN *Sterna bergii*   **Page 353**
Coastal. Less common than Lesser Crested Tern. Two races: *S. b. velox*, with darker grey upperparts, on n. Kenyan coast; paler *S. b. thalassina* along south coast and in Pemba Channel. **4a. *S. b. velox*, breeding adult. 4b. *S. b. velox*, juvenile. 4c. *S. b. velox*, non-breeding adult. 4d. *S. b. thalassina*, breeding adult. 4e. *S. b. thalassina*, non-breeding adult.**

5 AFRICAN SKIMMER *Rynchops flavirostris*   **Page 357**
Resident at Lake Turkana; uncommon and irregular elsewhere. **5a. Newly fledged juvenile. 5b. Non-breeding adult. 5c and 5d. Breeding adults.**

African Skimmer flock

PLATE 5: SMALL GULLS, TERNS AND SKIMMER (See also Plates 3, 4, 7 and 8)

1 GREY-HEADED GULL *Larus cirrocephalus poiocephalus* **Page 351**
Common on inland lakes; rare at coast. Larger, stouter, longer tarsi and thicker bill than Nos. 2 and 3. **1a. Non-breeding adult.** Suggestion of breeding pattern; sometimes faint ear spot. **1b. Juvenile.** Broad white collar. **1c. Breeding adult.** Dove-grey hood, pale eyes. **1d. First-year.** Fainter head markings and tail band than 3c; primaries dark.

2 SLENDER-BILLED GULL *Larus genei* **Page 352**
Scarce palearctic migrant to lakes Turkana and Nakuru; rare elsewhere. Long-billed; shallow sweeping forehead. **2a. Spring adult. 2b. Winter adult. 2c. First-winter.** From 2b by two-toned bill, dark band across wing, dark tail tip.

3 BLACK-HEADED GULL *Larus ridibundus* **Page 351**
Uncommon palearctic migrant, inland and coastal. Slender bill of medium length. **3a. Spring adult. 3b. Winter adult. 3c. First-winter.** Two-toned bill.

4 WHITE-CHEEKED TERN *Sterna repressa* **Page 354**
Coastal, mainly beyond the reef; present all year. **4a. Breeding adult.** White facial streak; grey underparts. **4b. Non-breeding adult.** Suggests Common Tern, but darker grey and bill and legs shorter.

5 ROSEATE TERN *Sterna dougallii bangsi* **Page 354**
Coastal; present all year. Elegant pearl-white appearance. **5a. Breeding-plumaged adult.** Long outer tail feathers; pink bloom on underparts; bill becomes red when breeding (See Plate 3). **5b. Non-breeding adult.** White forehead and crown, shorter outer tail feathers, narrow black carpal bar.

6 LESSER CRESTED TERN *Sterna b. bengalensis* **Page 353**
Common all year along coast; regular on lower Tana River; vagrant to Rift Valley lakes. Crested, with slender orange or orange-yellow bill. **6a. Breeding adult.** Entire top of head black. **6b. Non-breeding adult.** Extensive white on crown.

7 COMMON TERN *Sterna h. hirundo* **Page 354**
Common palearctic migrant along coast; large offshore flocks. Many immatures over-summer. Scarce on Rift Valley lakes. **7a. Late-spring adult.** (Bill usually black in our region, becoming red after leaving East African waters.) **7b. Winter adult.** Broader black carpal bar than in non-breeding Roseate Tern.

8 GREATER CRESTED TERN *Sterna bergii* **Page 353**
Coastal. Large, with heavy, pale yellow or greenish-yellow bill drooping at tip. **8a. S. b. velox, breeding adult.** Visitor north of Malindi. **8b. S. b. velox, non-breeding adult. 8c. S. b. thalassina, non-breeding adult.** South of Mombasa and in Pemba Channel.

9 SAUNDERS'S TERN *Sterna (albifrons) saundersi* **Page 355**
Common migrant along coast, Oct.–April; also on lower Tana River and Lake Turkana. Small size, rapid wingbeats. See text and Plate 3. **9a. Non-breeding adult.** Differs from 5b and 7b in size and wing action. See text. **9b. Breeding adult.** Black-tipped yellow bill. 'Square' white forehead patch does not extend behind eyes as in Little Tern.

10 CASPIAN TERN *Sterna caspia* **Page 353**
Uncommon migrant along coast and at Lake Turkana. Large and crested, with heavy red bill. **10a. Winter adult. 10b. Spring adult.**

11 SANDWICH TERN *Sterna s. sandvicensis* **Page 353**
Uncommon palearctic migrant on n. Kenyan coast; accidental inland. Pale and crested. Yellow bill tip inconspicuous at distance. **11a. Winter adult. 11b. Spring adult.**

12 AFRICAN SKIMMER *Rynchops flavirostris* **Page 357**
Locally common at Lake Turkana; sporadic elsewhere; rare along coast. Appears less elongate than shown.

13 GULL-BILLED TERN *Sterna n. nilotica* **Page 352**
Migrant, Aug.–April, locally common on large inland lakes; less numerous along coast. Stockier, greyer above than Sandwich Tern, with heavier bill. **13a. Winter adult. 13b. Spring adult.**

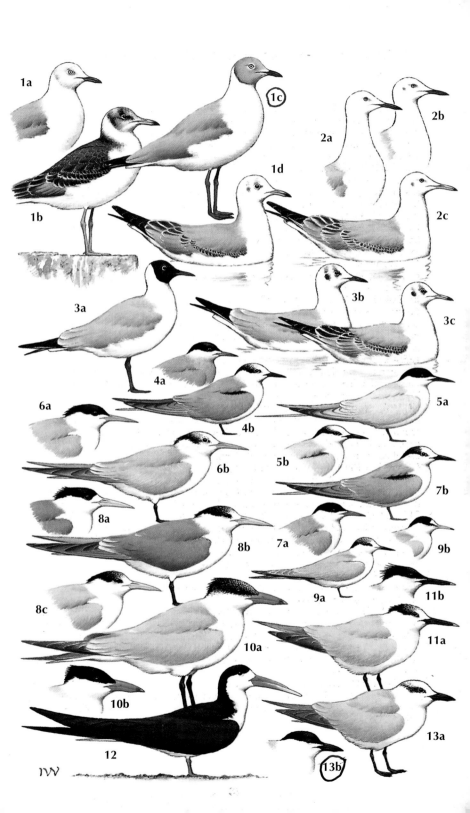

PLATE 6: LARGE GULLS (See also Plates 7 and 8)

1 SOOTY GULL *Larus hemprichii* **Page 350**
Coastal resident, at times common; some breed north of Lamu. Long-winged and long-billed. **1a. Juvenile acquiring first-year plumage**. Pale head and dorsal feather edgings. **1b. Non-breeding adult**. Head/neck pattern less well defined than in breeding plumage. **1c. Breeding adult**. White neck patch separates dark hood from grey-brown breast. Bill pale, with black band and red tip.

2 LESSER BLACK-BACKED GULL *Larus fuscus* **Page 351**
Palearctic migrant, common Oct.–April along coast and on larger inland lakes; some oversummer. Somewhat smaller and lighter in build than Heuglin's Gull. **2a. *L. f. fuscus*, second-winter**. Bill largely pale yellowish. **2b. *L. f. fuscus*, first-winter**. Bill blackish. **2c. *L. f. fuscus*, winter adult**. Black of back same shade as primaries. **2d. *L. f. graellsii*, second-winter**. Dense streaking on back and neck; medium grey on back. **2e. *L. f. graellsii*, winter adult**. Medium grey.

3 HEUGLIN'S GULL *Larus heuglini* **Page 350**
Regular along n. Kenyan coast, Nov.–March; sometimes fairly common (but no Kenyan specimens). Flocks with Lesser Black-backed Gulls. See text. **3a. (Presumed) *L. h. taimyrensis*, pale adult**. (Illustration from bird photographed at Malindi, Dec. 1992.) **3b. (Presumed) *L. h. taimyrensis*, darker adult**. (From bird photographed at Malindi, Jan. 1983.) **3c. *L. h. heuglini*, second-winter**. Bill blackish. **3d. *L. h. heuglini*, winter adult**. Bill yellow with red or black-and-red spot. Black primaries slightly darker than back. Bill somewhat larger than in *L. f. fuscus*; head and neck usually with some dark streaking.

4 KELP GULL *Larus dominicanus vetula* **Page 351**
Vagrant from s. Africa. **4a. Juvenile/first-winter**. Bill blackish. **4b. Non-breeding adult**.

5 GREAT BLACK-HEADED GULL *Larus ichthyaetus* **Page 352**
Uncommon palearctic migrant, Dec.–March, mainly along coast and at Lake Turkana. Large, with long sloping forehead and thick bill drooping at tip. **5a. Late-spring adult**. **5b. First-winter**. Dusky eye patch extends over hindcrown. Nape and often side of breast densely dark-streaked or spotted; pale greyish patch on wing; broad blackish tail tip. **5c. Winter adult**.

Adult White-eyed Gull, Larus leucophthalmus *(No substantiated record from our region.)*
See text.

1a

1b

1c

2a

2b

2d

3a

3b

2e

3c

4a

2c

3d

4b

5a

5b

5c

DALE A. ZIMMERMAN
1995

PLATE 7: SUBADULT GULLS IN FLIGHT (See also Plates 5, 6 and 8)

1 HEUGLIN'S GULL *Larus heuglini taimyrensis* **Page 350**
Birds apparently representing this form regular along Kenyan coast, from Tana River delta south to Malindi, Nov.–March. See text. **1a. First-winter. 1b. Second-winter.**

2 LESSER BLACK-BACKED GULL *Larus f. fuscus* **Page 351**
Common migrant along coast, Oct.–April, less numerous on inland lakes. A few over-summer. Slightly smaller and lighter in build than Heuglin's Gull. **2a. First-winter. 2b. Second-winter.**

3 SOOTY GULL *Larus hemprichii* **Page 350**
Present along coast throughout year, some breeding in the north. Long-winged and long-billed. **3a. First-year. 3b. Second-year.**

4 BLACK-HEADED GULL *Larus ridibundus* **Page 351**
Locally common palearctic migrant. Shorter-billed and shorter-tailed than Slender-billed Gull. **4a. First-winter.** More sharply marked than Slender-billed Gull. **4b. Winter adult.**

5 SLENDER-BILLED GULL *Larus genei* **Page 352**
Scarce to uncommon palearctic migrant. **First-winter** bird is longer-tailed and has less distinct postocular spot than more numerous Black-headed Gull.

6 GREY-HEADED GULL *Larus cirrocephalus poiocephalus* **Page 351**
Common on inland lakes; rare at coast. Heavier and thicker-billed than Black-headed and Slender-billed Gulls. **Juvenile/first-year** bird also darker on head and with less white in primaries.

7 GREAT BLACK-HEADED GULL, *Larus ichthyaetus* **Page 352**
Uncommon migrant, Dec.–March, mainly along coast and at Lake Turkana. Appears longer and more 'front-heavy' than other large gulls, owing to long bill and long sloping forehead. **7a. First-winter. 7b. Second-winter.**

First-winter Kelp Gull, Larus dominicanus. *Vagrant in our region. See text.*

PLATE 8: SKUAS AND ADULT GULLS (See Plates 5, 6 and 7 for other gull plumages)

1 POMARINE SKUA *Stercorarius pomarinus*   Page 348
Scarce, Oct.–March, on coast and Rift Valley lakes. Size of large gull, thick-necked, deep-chested. Bill long, deep, with prominent gonydeal angle. **1a. Spring adult, light morph**. Rounded and twisted central tail feathers; black cap. **1b. Adult, dark morph**. Uncommon. Identify by size, build, shape of central tail feathers. **1c. Immature** (and similar non-breeding adult). Barred upper tail-coverts/rump; heavy build.

2 LONG-TAILED SKUA *Stercorarius longicaudus*   Page 349
Vagrant. Less massive than larger species, flight more buoyant and tern-like; wings long and narrow, with less white in primaries (only two shafts white). **Immature** variable, wing-lining more barred than in non-breeding adult. (Adult figured below.)

3 ARCTIC SKUA or PARASITIC JAEGER *Stercorarius parasiticus*   Page 349
Rare migrant on coast and on Rift Valley lakes. Smaller, less massive than Pomarine, more falcon-like in flight. **3a. Immature**. Upper tail-covert barring buff and brown, less black and white than in young Pomarine. **3b. Adult, pale morph**. Central tail feathers straight and pointed. Any dark breast band evenly grey, not mottled or barred.

4 GREY-HEADED GULL *Larus cirrocephalus poiocephalus*   Page 351
The common gull of inland lakes; rare on coast. **Breeding bird** has pale grey hood, more dark in primaries than Nos. 7 and 8. Eyes yellowish white.

5 SOOTY GULL *Larus hemprichii*   Page 350
Common along coast (less numerous in south, June–Sept.). Long wings, long bill. **Breeding adult**.

6 LESSER BLACK-BACKED GULL *Larus f. fuscus*   Page 351
Sometimes common on coast and Lake Turkana, Oct.–April. See text.

7 BLACK-HEADED GULL *Larus ridibundus*   Page 351
Regular migrant mainly on Rift Valley lakes. **Spring adult** has dark brown hood.

8 SLENDER-BILLED GULL *Larus genei*   Page 352
Scarce migrant on lakes Turkana and Nakuru; rare elsewhere. More elongate than No. 7, with longer bill and slimmer neck. Bill dark red to orange.

9 GREAT BLACK-HEADED GULL *Larus ichthyaetus*   Page 352
Uncommon Dec.–March. Local but regular on coast, irregular on Lake Turkana; rare elsewhere. **Spring adult** has black hood and bold white eye crescents.

Adult Long-tailed Skua

PLATE 9: STORKS AND CRANES

1 WHITE STORK *Ciconia c. ciconia*   **Page 283**
Common palearctic migrant in grasslands and grain fields, Nov.–April; a few oversummer in Kenyan highlands. In high flight, white tail is diagnostic. **1a and 1b. Adults.**

2 YELLOW-BILLED STORK *Mycteria ibis*   **Page 284**
Common and widespread along shallow rivers and lakeshores. Breeding adult has pink wing-coverts. In flight shows black tail, unlike White Stork. **2a and 2b. Breeding adults.**

3 WOOLLY-NECKED STORK *Ciconia episcopus microscelis*   **Page 283**
Fairly common on coastal lagoons; local and uncommon elsewhere. Dark back and wings contrast with white posterior underparts. **3a and 3b. Adults.**

4 ABDIM'S STORK *Ciconia abdimii*   **Page 283**
Intra-African migrant, Oct.–April, often in large flocks with White Storks. White belly and (in flight) white back; bill, legs and feet dull greenish grey. **4a and 4b. Adults.**

5 SADDLE-BILLED STORK *Ephippiorhynchus senegalensis*   **Page 283**
Local and uncommon in swamps, marshes and flooded grassland. **5a and 5c. Adult females.** Eyes yellow. **5b. Juvenile.** Dark bill; dark plumage areas grey-brown. **5d. Adult male.** Eyes dark brown.

6 AFRICAN OPEN-BILLED STORK *Anastomus l. lamelligerus*   **Page 284**
Locally common in Lake Victoria basin, se. Kenya and ne. Tanzania. Glossy plumage; unique bill. **Adult.** (Juv. duller and browner; bill shorter, with narrow tomial gap.)

7 BLACK STORK *Ciconia nigra*   **Page 283**
Regular palearctic migrant, Oct.–April; uncommon in and near wetlands. **7a and 7b. Adults.** White belly, red bill and legs; back and rump dark. (Juvenile has dull olive-green bill and legs.)

8 MARABOU STORK *Leptoptilus crumeniferus*   **Page 284**
Widespread; locally common on town and village outskirts. Joins vultures at carcasses. **8a and 8b. Breeding adults. 8c. Non-breeding adult.**

9 DEMOISELLE CRANE *Anthropoides virgo*   **Page 325**
Palearctic vagrant. Grey, with black foreneck and long breast feathers. Elongated secondaries droop over tail. **Adult.**

10 GREY CROWNED CRANE *Balearica regulorum gibbericeps* **Page 326**
Fairly common and widespread in wetlands above 1300 m. Rare at Lake Turkana and in coastal lowlands. **10a and 10b. Adults.** Largely grey neck; white cheek patch scarlet at top. (Juvenile more rufous, with smaller crest.)

11 BLACK CROWNED CRANE *Balearica pavonina ceciliae*   **Page 326**
Rare at n. Lake Turkana. Neck blackish; cheek patch white above, pink below; short pinkish throat-wattle. **Adult.**

PLATE 10: IBISES, SPOONBILLS AND FLAMINGOS

1 GLOSSY IBIS *Plegadis f. falcinellus*   **Page 285**
Widespread in permanent wetlands. Appears all black at a distance. Feet project beyond tail in flight. **1a and 1c. Adults. 1b. Juvenile.**

2 AFRICAN GREEN or OLIVE IBIS *Bostrychia olivacea akeleyorum*   **Page 285**
Scarce in montane forests. Feeds on forest floor and in clearings. Rarely seen, except when flying to and from roosts at dusk and dawn. Little or no overlap of range with Hadada. **Adult.**

3 HADADA IBIS *Bostrychia hagedash brevirostris*   **Page 285**
Common and widespread in wet areas, along forest borders, in cultivation, Nairobi city parks and suburbs. Feet do not project beyond tail in flight. **3a and 3b. Adults.** (Juvenile similar but duller.)

4 AFRICAN SPOONBILL *Platalea alba*   **Page 286**
Widespread on inland waters; local in coastal lowlands. Forehead unfeathered. **4a. Immature.** Dull yellowish bill and facial skin. **4b. Adult. 4c. Subadult.**

5 SACRED IBIS *Threskiornis a. aethiopicus*   **Page 284**
Widespread in wetlands, including coastal estuaries. **5a. Juvenile. 5b. Breeding adult. 5c. Non-breeding adult.**

6 EURASIAN SPOONBILL *Platalea leucorodia*   **Page 285**
Fairly regular at Lake Turkana, scarce elsewhere. Forehead entirely feathered; bill largely black. **6a. First-winter.** No yellow on bill tip; facial skin dark. **6b. Spring male acquiring breeding plumage.** (Non-breeding adult has no crest or yellow on lower neck.)

7 GREATER FLAMINGO *Phoenicopterus (ruber) roseus*   **Page 286**
Largely confined to brackish and soda lakes in Rift Valley, where locally common. Uncommon at coast. **7a, 7c and 7d. Adults.** Bill pink with black tip. **7b. Immature.** Greyer plumage; black-tipped grey bill.

8 LESSER FLAMINGO *Phoeniconaias minor*   **Page 286**
Abundant on Rift Valley soda lakes. **8a. Immature. 8b. Juvenile. 8c, 8d and 8e. Adults.**

Lesser Flamingo

PLATE 11: LARGE HERONS AND HAMERKOP (See also Plates 12 and 13)

1 PURPLE HERON *Ardea p. purpurea*　　　　　　　　**Page 282**
Widespread and locally common in wetlands with extensive reedbeds. Colourful, slender. Less chestnut on wings than much larger Goliath Heron. Bill long and slim. **1a. Juvenile. 1b and 1c. Adults.**

2 BLACK-HEADED HERON *Ardea melanocephala*　　　**Page 282**
Commonest heron; widespread in open grassland, cultivation. Often on dry ground. **2a and 2b. Adults.** Black crown, nape and hindneck; underside of wings strongly two-toned (unlike Grey Heron). **2c. Juvenile.** Appears largely grey above, whitish to pale grey below.

3 GOLIATH HERON *Ardea goliath*　　　　　　　　　**Page 282**
Uncommon and local, mainly around larger lakes and swamps. Very large with massive bill. **3a, 3b and 3c. Adults. 3d. Juvenile.**

4 GREY HERON *Ardea c. cinerea*　　　　　　　　　　**Page 281**
Widespread and uncommon in wetlands. **4a, 4b and 4c. Adults.** Blackish flight feathers contrast with grey wing-coverts above; wings more uniformly grey below. **4d. Juvenile.**

5 HAMERKOP *Scopus u. umbretta*　　　　　　　　　　**Page 282**
Widespread and fairly common at swamp edges, lakesides and along rivers. **5a, 5b and 5c. Adults.** (Juvenile similar.)

Nest of Hamerkop

1a
1c
1b
2a
2c
2b
3c
4b
4c
3a
3b
4d
3d
4a
5c
5a
5b

HDP

PLATE 12: SMALL HERONS (See also Plates 11 and 13)

1 DWARF BITTERN *Ixobrychus sturmii*   **Page 278**
Widespread but uncommon in reedbeds and seasonal swamps. Secretive. **1a. Juvenile. 1b. Adult.**

2 LITTLE BITTERN *Ixobrychus minutus*   **Page 278**
Widespread in permanent marshes. Skulks in reeds. Nominate race present Oct.–May.
2a. *I. m. minutus*, first-winter. 2b. *I. m. minutus*, adult male. 2c. *I. m. payesii*, adult female. 2d. *I. m. payesii*, juvenile. 2e and 2f. *I. m. payesii*, adult males.

3 SQUACCO HERON *Ardeola ralloides*   **Page 280**
Widespread in wetlands. White wings may be largely concealed by body feathers. **Non-breeding adult.** (See Plate 13 for breeding plumage.)

4 MADAGASCAR SQUACCO or MALAGASY POND HERON *Ardeola idae*
Page 280
Uncommon non-breeding migrant, May–October, inland to Mwea NR and Ngorongoro Crater. **Non-breeding adult.** (See Plate 13 for breeding plumage.)

5 RUFOUS-BELLIED HERON *Ardea rufiventris*   **Page 280**
Uncommon and local; regular in nw. Mara GR and Tarangire NP. **5a and 5c. Adult males. 5b. Adult female.**

6 GREEN-BACKED or STRIATED HERON *Butorides striatus atricapillus*
Page 281
Fairly common along coastal creeks, well-vegetated lakes and rivers. **6a and 6c. Adults. 6b. Juvenile.**

7 BLACK-CROWNED NIGHT-HERON *Nycticorax n. nycticorax*   **Page 278**
Locally common in permanent wetlands. Nocturnal. **7a. Juvenile. 7b. Subadult. 7c and 7d. Adults.**

8 WHITE-BACKED NIGHT-HERON *Gorsachius leuconotus*   **Page 278**
Scarce along shaded river banks and in mangroves. Nocturnal. **8a. Juvenile. 8b and 8c. Adults.**

Black Herons feeding

PLATE 13: HERONS and EGRETS (See also Plates 11 and 12)

1 GREAT EGRET *Casmerodius albus melanorhynchos* **Page 281**
Widespread in wetlands. Large size; dark line from base of bill extends behind eyes; bill colour variable. Legs and feet black. **1a. Non-breeding adult. 1b. Courting adult.** (Amount of yellow at base of bill varies. Eyes may be briefly red.) **1c. Immature.**

2 YELLOW-BILLED or INTERMEDIATE EGRET *Mesophoyx intermedia brachyrhyncha* **Page 281**
Less common than Great Egret; smaller, with shorter neck and bill; black gape line from bill does not extend past eye; legs and feet black. **2a. Non-breeding adult. 2b. Immature. 2c. Breeding adult.**

3 CATTLE EGRET *Bubulcus i. ibis* **Page 279**
Common and widespread; not restricted to wet places. Small, stocky, heavy-jowled. **3a. Breeding adult. 3b. Juvenile.** (Tarsus colour varies; see text.) **3c. Non-breeding adult.**

4 MADAGASCAR SQUACCO or MALAGASY POND HERON *Ardeola idae* **Page 280**
Breeding-plumaged adult rare in East Africa. (Non-breeding plumage on Plate 12.)

5 SQUACCO HERON *Ardeola ralloides* **Page 280**
Fairly common and widespread in wetlands. **5a and 5b. Breeding adult.** White wings obscured in perched bird.

6 WESTERN REEF HERON *Egretta gularis schistacea* **Page 279**
Uncommon along coast (Mida Creek) and at Lake Turkana; rare at other Rift Valley lakes. Bill longer, heavier and deeper than in Little or Dimorphic Egrets, never black. (Caution: Little Egrets feeding in some Rift Valley lakes may show pale, soda-encrusted bills.) Legs and feet largely greenish olive, the toes, and often front of tarsi, yellow. **6a. White morph. 6b and 6c. Dark morph.** (Amount of white in wing varies individually.)

7 LITTLE EGRET *Egretta g. garzetta* **Page 279**
Common and widespread except along open coastal areas, where scarce. Toes greenish yellow (partly black in rare dark morph). Largely black bill (basal half of gonys pale). **7a. White morph, non-breeding.** Lores usually grey. **7b. Dark morph, breeding. 7c. White morph, breeding.** Lores yellow, or dull peach colour at onset of breeding season (orange during peak courtship activity).

8 DIMORPHIC EGRET *Egretta (garzetta) dimorpha* **Page 279**
Strictly marine. Strongly dimorphic; dark birds common, as are pied intermediates. May show yellow spot on mandible. Tibiae always dark (unless whitewashed with excrement); tarsi black, often with yellowish or greenish 'anklets' extending up front of tarsi. **8a. White morph, non-breeding.** Facial skin grey; toes or parts of tarsi yellow or greenish. **8b. White morph, courting.** Toes, lores and base of bill bright rose-pink. **8c and 8d. Dark morph, breeding.** Toes bright yellow or orange-yellow; base of bill bright yellow; lores and facial skin yellow-green. White in wing variable in extent or lacking. (Bare parts of non-breeders as in 8a.) **8e. Dark morph, courting.** Facial skin and bill base bright rose-pink. **8f. Juvenile/immature.** Largely grey, greyish blue or nearly lavender; some pale brown and white on wings and neck. *E. (g.) dimorpha* not known inland; similar grey birds seen on Rift Valley lakes may be young of dark-morph *E. g. garzetta*. (Grey immature of *E. gularis schistacea* has larger, paler bill.)

9 BLACK HERON *Egretta ardesiaca* **Page 280**
Local, mainly at coast, Lake Jipe and Rift Valley lakes. **Adult** shaggy-crested. Eyes dark; toes orange or orange-yellow. (Juv. duller, greyer, lacks long plumes; toes yellow.)

PLATE 14: PELICANS, CORMORANTS AND DARTER

1 GREAT WHITE PELICAN *Pelecanus onocrotalus*   **Page 274**
Common on alkaline lakes in Rift Valley. Secondaries largely black. **1a. Breeding adult.**
Pinkish-orange face (briefly shows swollen orange-red knob at base of culmen at peak of
courtship activity). **1b, 1c and 1d. Non-breeding adults. 1e. Immature.** Mottled plumage
replaces uniform dark brown of juvenile.

2 PINK-BACKED PELICAN *Pelecanus rufescens*   **Page 275**
Widespread on lakes, rivers and coastal saltpans. Secondaries brownish grey. **2a and 2b.
Adults.** Greyish white. Pinkish back and rump visible only in flight. Develops shaggy
crest, and pouch becomes deep yellow, when breeding. **2c. Juvenile.**

3 LONG-TAILED CORMORANT *Phalacrocorax a. africanus*   **Page 276**
Widespread on freshwater lakes, ponds and swamps with ample fringing vegetation.
Long-tailed, with small bill. Adults red-eyed. **3a. Immature.** (Juvenile similar but brown-
eyed, and may be paler below.) **3b. Post-breeding adult. 3c. Breeding adult.** (Non-breeding adult may have white underparts, but eyes are red.

4 GREAT CORMORANT *Phalacrocorax carbo lucidus*   **Page 276**
Locally common, often in large flocks on Rift Valley lakes. Wanders to coastal estuaries.
Heavy-billed and short-tailed. **4a. Immature.** Brownish, with whitish underparts, darken-
ing with age. **4b and 4c. Breeding adults.** White flank/thigh patch.

5 AFRICAN DARTER *Anhinga rufa*   **Page 276**
Formerly fairly common in freshwater areas with fringing trees. Now scarce in Kenyan
highlands. Long, broad tail, sinuous neck, sharp-pointed bill. **5a. Female. 5b. and 5c.
Adult males.**

Shoebill. Vagrant in Kenya. See text.

HDP

PLATE 15: GREBES, GEESE AND DUCKS (See also Plate 16)

1 WHITE-FACED WHISTLING DUCK *Dendrocygna viduata* **Page 287**
Common and widespread in wetlands below 1500 m. White face, long black neck, black belly and tail. **1a and 1b. Adults.**

2 FULVOUS WHISTLING DUCK *Dendrocygna bicolor* **Page 287**
Widespread visitor (rarely breeds) below 1500 m, often in large flocks. Broad black line on back, whitish U-shaped patch on upper tail-coverts. **2a and 2b. Adults.**

3 GREAT CRESTED GREBE *Podiceps cristatus infuscatus* **Page 269**
Increasingly scarce resident on lakes of cent. Rift Valley, Arusha NP and Ngorongoro Crater. **3a. Breeding adult. 3b. Juvenile.**

4 LITTLE GREBE *Tachybaptus ruficollis capensis* **Page 270**
Widespread. Most numerous on larger Rift Valley lakes and in Arusha NP. **4a. Breeding adult. 4b. Non-breeding adult.**

5 BLACK-NECKED or EARED GREBE *Podiceps nigricollis gurneyi* **Page 270**
Local on Rift Valley lakes, sometimes common July–Nov. Wanders elsewhere; sporadic in n. Tanzania. **5a. Breeding adult. 5b. Worn, post-breeding adult.** (No black-and-white non-breeding plumage in East African birds.)

6 EGYPTIAN GOOSE *Alopochen aegyptiacus* **Page 287**
Common on freshwater lakes, ponds, river banks (sometimes fields) up to 3000 m. **6a. Juvenile.** Forewing patch grey. **6b, 6c and 6d. Adults.** Variable; forewing patch white. **6e. Gosling.**

7 WHITE-BACKED DUCK *Thalassornis l. leuconotus* **Page 287**
Locally common on lakes and ponds with emergent vegetation. Avoids open water. **7a and 7b. Adults.**

8 AFRICAN PYGMY GOOSE *Nettapus auritus* **Page 288**
Local on secluded, well-vegetated lakes and swampy pools near coast. **8a and 8c. Males. 8b. Female.**

9 SPUR-WINGED GOOSE *Plectropterus g. gambensis* **Page 287**
Locally common in freshwater wetlands up to 3000 m. **9a. Female.** No forehead caruncles. **9b. Male. 9c. Juvenile.**

10 KNOB-BILLED or COMB DUCK *Sarkidiornis m. melanotos* **Page 288**
Widespread on freshwater lakes, ponds, flooded grassland up to 3000 m. **10a. Breeding male. 10b. Non-breeding male. 10c. Juvenile. 10d. Female.** Grey rump/lower back.

Southern Pochards, male (left) and female (right)

PLATE 16: DUCKS (See also Plate 15)

1 MACCOA DUCK Oxyura maccoa   **Page 292**
Only East African stiff-tail. Uncommon in Kenyan highlands; more numerous in n. Tanzania. Squat, thickset, large head and bill; swims low in water. **1a. Male. 1b. Female.**

2 HOTTENTOT TEAL Anas hottentota   **Page 290**
Widespread on alkaline and freshwater lakes. Often common inland; rare on coast. Dark crown and blue-grey bill diagnostic. **2a. Female.** Exposed secondaries-brown. **2b. Male.** Secondaries green.

3 RED-BILLED TEAL Anas erythrorhyncha   **Page 290**
Common and widespread inland; local on coast.

4 COMMON TEAL Anas c. crecca   **Page 289**
Regular, Nov.–March, in highlands and Rift Valley. Small, compact. **4a. Female.** Sometimes has paler loral area than shown, never as pale as 6b. **4b. Male.** Head looks dark at distance; yellowish buff patch on sides of black under tail-coverts.

5 CAPE TEAL Anas capensis   **Page 289**
Largely confined to alkaline Rift Valley lakes where common.

6 GARGANEY Anas querquedula   **Page 289**
Widespread, Oct.–April. Common in Kenya, less so in n. Tanzania. **6a. Male. 6b. Female.** Sharper head pattern than 4a; pale loral spot.

7 YELLOW-BILLED DUCK Anas u. undulata   **Page 290**
Common in Kenyan highlands, much less so in n. Tanzania. Green speculum (blue in northern A. u. rueppelli) conspicuous in flight.

8 AFRICAN BLACK DUCK Anas sparsa leucostigma   **Page 288**
Uncommon on mountain streams, mainly above 1850 m. Shy and wary. White-bordered blue or purple speculum conspicuous in flight.

9 EURASIAN WIGEON Anas penelope   **Page 289**
Uncommon on fresh water, Nov.–March, typically above 1800 m. No recent Tanzanian records. **9a. Female, rufous morph.** Some birds are much greyer. **9b. Male.**

10 MALLARD Anas p. platyrhynchos   **Page 288**
Vagrant. No definite recent records of wild birds. **10a. Male. 10b. Female.** Bill orange with dusky markings; no white patch in secondaries. See text.

11 GADWALL Anas s. strepera   **Page 289**
Rare on freshwater Kenyan lakes. Small white patch in secondaries distinctive in flight, sometimes visible on water. **11a. Female.** Grey-brown; orange-sided bill. **11b. Male.** Grey with black rear end.

12 NORTHERN SHOVELER Anas clypeata   **Page 291**
Locally common, Oct.–early April. Long spatulate bill. **12a. Female. 12b. Sub-eclipse male** (autumn, early winter). **12c. Male** (breeding plumage, late Dec.–April).

13 NORTHERN PINTAIL Anas a. acuta   **Page 290**
Fairly common and widespread, Nov.–early April. **13a. Male. 13b. Female.** Slender; plain head on long neck.

14 FERRUGINOUS DUCK Aythya nyroca   **Page 292**
Scarce and local, Oct.–March. Usually with Southern Pochards. **14a. Female.** Duller than male; brown-eyed. **14b. Male.** White-eyed. Appears black at distance, with white rear end.

15 COMMON POCHARD Aythya ferina   **Page 291**
Rare on open water (six records, Dec.–March). Long bill, peaked forehead. **15a. Female.** Hoary face patches, sooty rear. **15b. Male.**

16 SOUTHERN POCHARD Netta erythrophthalma brunnea   **Page 291**
Locally common on highland waters, mainly Nov.–Feb. **16a. Female.** Pied face, white rear end. **16b. Male.** Dark, with long pale grey bill.

17 TUFTED DUCK Aythya fuligula   **Page 292**
Scarce on highland waters and Lake Turkana, Nov.–March. Short crest on hindcrown usually evident. **17a. Male. 17b. Female.** White loral patch often lacking; can show white under tail-coverts.

PLATE 17: COURSERS, PRATINCOLES AND THICK-KNEES

1 MADAGASCAR PRATINCOLE *Glareola ocularis* **Page 335**
Malagasy migrant to East African coast, April–Sept.; locally abundant north of Kilifi (especially Sabaki River estuary Aug.–Sept.). **1a and 1b. Non-breeding plumage.** Shorter tail with shallower fork than in Collared Pratincole; dark brown throat and breast; rufous belly patch; white subocular streak.

2 ROCK PRATINCOLE *Glareola n. nuchalis* **Page 335**
Local on rocks in Nzoia River, w. Kenya. White postocular stripe joins hindneck collar. Short white stripe on underside of wing; feet red. **2a and 2c. Adults. 2b. Juvenile.**

3 COLLARED PRATINCOLE *Glareola pratincola fuelleborni* **Page 334**
Locally common along Rift Valley lakes and coastal estuaries. Long pointed wings, deeply forked tail. **3a and 3d. Breeding adults.** Creamy buff throat with black border; belly white. **3b. Immature.** Throat border blurred, breast mottled. **3c. Juvenile.** Buff feather edges, short tail.

4 BLACK-WINGED PRATINCOLE *Glareola nordmanni* **Page 334**
Rare palearctic passage migrant; associates with Collared Pratincole. Underside of wing entirely black; no white trailing edge.

5 VIOLET-TIPPED COURSER *Rhinoptilus chalcopterus* **Page 333**
Local in se. Kenya/n. Tanzania. May–Nov. Uncommon in open bush and woodland. Nocturnal. Shape and head pattern suggest Crowned Plover.

6 TWO-BANDED COURSER *Rhinoptilus africanus gracilis* **Page 333**
Uncommon on short-grass plains and alkaline flats in s. Kenya/n. Tanzania. Two black breast bands; pale buff superciliary stripe. (Larger-eyed and often paler than shown.)

7 HEUGLIN'S COURSER *Rhinoptilus cinctus* **Page 333**
Uncommon in dry bush and semi-desert scrub. Largely nocturnal. Cryptic pattern, chestnut neck and breast bands.

8 CREAM-COLOURED COURSER *Cursorius cursor* **Page 334**
Vagrant to Lake Turkana. Sandier-coloured than smaller Somali Courser, with different tail and under wing pattern, relatively shorter bill and tarsi. **8a and 8b. Adults.**

9 TEMMINCK'S COURSER *Cursorius temminckii* **Page 334**
The commonest courser; widespread on short-grass plains mainly south of the Equator. Dark brown above; rufous belly with black central patch.

10 SOMALI COURSER *Cursorius somalensis littoralis* **Page 334**
Locally common on short-grass plains and semi-desert in n. and e. Kenya. Pale, with distinctive head pattern, whitish legs and feet. **10a and 10b. Adults.**

11 SPOTTED THICK-KNEE *Burhinus capensis* **Page 332**
Locally common in dry bush. Largely nocturnal. Boldly spotted upperparts; relatively unpatterned closed wing. **11a and 11b. Adults.**

12 EURASIAN THICK-KNEE or STONE-CURLEW *Burhinus o. oedicnemus* **Page 331**
Scarce palearctic migrant, Oct.–March, regular in n. Kenya; scarce elsewhere. Narrow white wing-bar bordered above and below by black. **12a and 12b. Adults.**

13 SENEGAL THICK-KNEE *Burhinus senegalensis inornatus* **Page 332**
Local near rivers and lakeshores in n. and nw. Kenya (e.g. lakes Turkana and Baringo). Nocturnal. Finely streaked; no white bar on closed wing. Bill large, yellow at base; legs and feet yellowish. **13a and 13b. Adults.**

14 WATER THICK-KNEE *Burhinus v. vermiculatus* **Page 332**
Widespread along river banks and lakeshores. Broad grey wing panel, narrowly streaked with black. Base of bill greenish; legs and feet olive. **14a and 14b. Adults.**

15 EGYPTIAN-PLOVER *Pluvianus aegyptius* **Page 333**
Vagrant to northern shores of Lake Turkana. **15a and 15b. Adults.**

PLATE 18: LARGE PLOVERS

1 BROWN-CHESTED PLOVER *Vanellus superciliosus* **Page 337**
Vagrant, mainly in Lake Victoria basin and w. Serengeti NP. **1a and 1b. Adults**. Broad chestnut breast band, black crown. **1c. Juvenile**. Brownish crown, yellow on face.

2 BLACK-WINGED PLOVER *Vanellus melanopterus minor* **Page 337**
Locally common above 1500 m on short-grass plains, cultivated fields. Broader breast band and larger, more diffuse white forehead patch than smaller Senegal Plover; legs and feet dull red; orbital ring purplish red. Broad diagonal white wing-stripe in flight. **2a and 2b. Adults.**

3 SENEGAL PLOVER *Vanellus lugubris* **Page 336**
Local and nomadic, mainly below 1500 m, on open or bushed grassland in the Lake Victoria basin, Mara GR, Tsavo, Arusha NP and the coastal lowlands. Small. Sharply defined white forehead, white trailing wing edge; legs and feet dark slate-grey; faint orbital ring dull yellow. **3a and 3b. Adults.**

4 BLACKSMITH PLOVER *Vanellus armatus* **Page 336**
Common in highlands and on Rift Valley wetlands north to Lake Baringo. White cap and hindneck patch; black flight feathers. **4a and 4b. Adults.**

5 BLACK-HEADED PLOVER *Vanellus tectus* **Page 336**
Locally common in dry thorn-bush. Long crest; wing pattern as in Crowned Plover. **5a and 5b. V. t. latifrons.** Ne. Kenya, Meru and Tsavo NPs. Large white forehead patch. **5c. V. t. tectus.** Nw. Kenya south to Lake Bogoria. Small forehead patch.

6 CROWNED PLOVER *Vanellus c. coronatus* **Page 337**
Widespread. Fairly common on dry plains and cultivated land. Ringed crown; broad diagonal white wing stripe includes primary coverts. Highly vocal. **6a, 6b and 6c. Adults. 6d. Juvenile**

7 AFRICAN WATTLED PLOVER *Vanellus senegallus lateralis* **Page 337**
Western. Local on moist short-grass plains. **7a and 7b. Adults.**

8 SPUR-WINGED PLOVER *Vanellus spinosus* **Page 336**
Common on n. river banks and lakeshores; uncommon at coast; rare on s. Rift Valley lakes, where replaced by Blacksmith Plover. **8a and 8b. Adults.**

9 LONG-TOED PLOVER *Vanellus c. crassirostris* **Page 335**
Local in marshes and swamps. Forewing (incl. primary coverts) white. **9a and 9b. Adults.**

10 PACIFIC GOLDEN PLOVER *Pluvialis fulva* **Page 338**
Uncommon coastal migrant, scarce inland. **10a. Adult in nearly full breeding plumage. 10b. Immature.** (Winter adult similar, but less yellowish.)

11 GREY PLOVER *Pluvialis squatarola* **Page 338**
Common coastal migrant, occasional inland. Black axillaries (grey in Pacific Golden Plover). **11a and 11b. Adults in non-breeding plumage. 11c. Adult in nearly full breeding plumage.**

Northern Lapwing, Vanellus vanellus. *Vagrant in Kenya. See text.*

1a
1c
1b
2a
2b
3a
3b
6a
4a
4b
5a
5b
5c
6b
6c
6d
7a
7b
8a
8b
9a
9b
11b
10a
10b
11a
11c

DALE A. ZIMMERMAN
1994

PLATE 19: SMALL PLOVERS

1 KITTLITZ'S PLOVER *Charadrius pecuarius*   **Page 339**
Common around Rift Valley lakes. **1a. Adult**. Rich buff underparts. **1b. Juvenile**. Buff superciliary stripe and collar.

2 WHITE-FRONTED PLOVER *Charadrius marginatus tenellus*   **Page 339**
Locally common on sandy n. Kenyan coast and on sandbars in Galana/Athi Rivers. Sporadic at Lake Turkana. Thin black eye-line; white of forehead extends behind eye. **2a. Adult. 2b. Juvenile**.

3 LITTLE RINGED PLOVER *Charadrius dubius curonicus*   **Page 338**
Uncommon but regular, Oct.–April, along rivers, lakeshores and saltpans. Yellow orbital ring; no orange on bill; legs and feet pinkish or yellowish. **3a. Spring adult. 3b. Winter adult**.

4 CHESTNUT-BANDED PLOVER *Charadrius pallidus venustus*   **Page 339**
Locally common on Rift Valley soda lakes. Small, with narrow chestnut breast band, long-legged appearance. **4a. Adult male**. Black frontal bar and eye-line. **4b. Juvenile**. Narrow, broken greyish breast band. **4c. Adult female**. Broader breast band than male; no black on head.

5 KENTISH PLOVER *Charadrius a. alexandrinus*   **Page 339**
Migrant in small numbers, regular at Lake Turkana, Oct.–April; rare elsewhere. Small, slim. Pale, with dark bill, dark patch or bar at side of breast. **5a. Spring male**. Rufous nape. **5b. Spring female**.

6 RINGED PLOVER *Charadrius hiaticula tundrae*   **Page 338**
Common and widespread along coast and inland waters, Sept.–early May; some over-summer. Portly, with stubby bill, orange legs. No prominent orbital ring (unlike Little Ringed Plover). **6a. Spring adult**. Dense black facial area and breast band; base of bill orange. **6b. Juvenile**. Paler, incomplete breast band. **6c. Winter adult**. Bill largely dark.

7 THREE-BANDED PLOVER *Charadrius t. tricollaris*   **Page 339**
Widespread on inland waterways. Pale-eyed, with red orbital ring and bill base; double breast band. **7a. Juvenile**. Greyish forehead. **7b. Adult**. White forehead.

8 GREATER SANDPLOVER *Charadrius leschenaultii crassirostris*   **Page 340**
Common along coast, Aug.–early May; many first-year birds oversummer. Scarce inland. Bill larger and tarsi longer than in Lesser Sandplover. **8a. Spring male**. Chestnut breast band, black ear-coverts. **8b. Winter adult**. Grey-brown breast band and ear-coverts. **8c. Spring female**. Trace of rufous breast band, grey-brown ear-coverts.

9 CASPIAN PLOVER *Charadrius asiaticus*   **Page 340**
Regular, Aug.–April, on short-grass plains in Mara GR/Serengeti NP, where large numbers winter; mainly passage migrant elsewhere (often common on muddy shores at Lake Turkana, and on short grass in Tsavo East NP). Slim, with small head, slender bill. **9a. Spring male**. (Female usually has grey-brown breast band.) **9b. Winter adult**.

10 LESSER or MONGOLIAN SANDPLOVER *Charadrius mongolus pamirensis*   **Page 340**
Common along coast, Aug.–early May; many first-year birds oversummer. Scarce but regular inland, especially along Rift Valley Lakes. A smaller, shorter-legged and smaller-billed version of Greater Sandplover. **10a. Spring female**. Sooty-brown mask, trace of rufous on nape and breast. **10b. Winter adult**. Same pattern as 8b, but with different proportions. **10c. Spring male**.

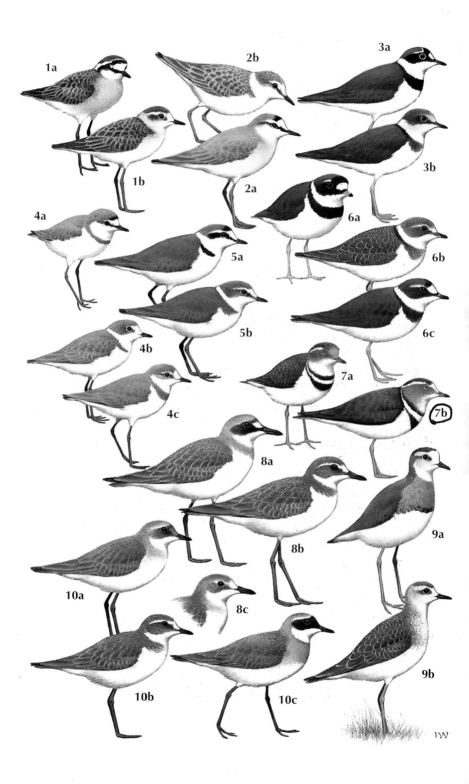

עשר

PLATE 20: SMALL SANDPIPERS (See also Plate 21)

1 TEMMINCK'S STINT *Calidris temminckii*   **Page 341**
Local and uncommon in freshwater wetlands, Oct.–April. Rare along coast; accidental in
n. Tanzania. Legs and feet yellowish or olive; tail tip projects beyond primary tips.
1a. Spring adult. 1b. Winter adult.

2 RED-NECKED STINT *Calidris ruficollis*   **Page 341**
Vagrant. **2a. Pale spring adult.** Wing-coverts grey (rufous-edged in spring Little Stint).
2b. Bright spring adult. 2c. Pale winter adult. From 3c by paler feather centres above.
See text.

3 LITTLE STINT *Calidris minuta*   **Page 341**
Common and widespread, Aug.–May. Bill, legs and feet black. See text. **3a. Spring adult.**
3b. Juvenile. 3c. Winter adult.

4 LONG-TOED STINT *Calidris subminuta*   **Page 342**
Rare migrant on coast and inland lakeshores. Smaller-headed, longer-necked than Little
Stint. Oversized toes often obscured by mud; legs and feet yellow or greenish; bill fine,
slightly decurved. **4a. Spring adult.** Often shows obscure whitish V on back (as do some
Little Stints). **4b. Winter adult.**

5 BROAD-BILLED SANDPIPER *Limicola falcinellus*   **Page 343**
Annual at Sabaki estuary, Aug.–April; rare elsewhere; usually on mudflats. Long, dark bill
decurved at tip; double (forked) superciliary stripe. **5a. Spring adult. 5b. Winter adult.**
Greyer above than in spring; dark patch may be visible at bend of wing.

6 SANDERLING *Calidris alba*   **Page 343**
Widespread along coast, Aug.–April; some oversummer. Scarce on inland lakes. Feeds at
water's edge, running ahead of breaking waves. Compact, with short, stout black bill.
6a. Winter adult. Pale, with black 'shoulder' mark. **6b. Juvenile. 6c. Spring adult.**

7 CURLEW SANDPIPER *Calidris ferruginea*   **Page 342**
Common and widespread, Aug.–May; some young birds oversummer. Evenly decurved
bill, long-legged appearance. **7a. Juvenile. 7b. Winter adult. 7c. Spring adult.**

8 DUNLIN *Calidris alpina*   **Page 342**
Vagrant. Similar to Curlew Sandpiper but more compact, with shorter neck, shorter tarsi,
bill decurved only at tip. **8a. Winter adult. 8b. Spring adult.**

9 RUFF *Philomachus pugnax*   **Page 344**
Common inland, Aug.–May; some oversummer. **Spring female** ('Reeve') shown. Portly,
small-headed, short-billed; plumage strongly 'scaled'; legs and feet pinkish red or orange;
slow, deliberate movements. (See also Plate 23.)

10 PECTORAL SANDPIPER, *Calidris melanotos*   **Page 342**
Vagrant. Streaked breast sharply demarcated; short bill. **10a. Juvenile female. 10b.**
Winter adult.

11 BUFF-BREASTED SANDPIPER *Tryngites subruficollis*   **Page 343**
Vagrant. Plump, plover-like, short-billed; yellow legs and feet. (Some birds more whitish,
less buff, than adult illustrated.)

PLATE 21: FLYING SANDPIPERS AND PLOVERS (Winter adults, except as indicated)

1 BUFF-BREASTED SANDPIPER *Tryngites subruficollis*   **Page 343**
Vagrant. See text. **1a. Below. 1b. Above.**

2 PECTORAL SANDPIPER *Calidris melanotos*   **Page 342**
Vagrant; most likely on fields, muddy shores, wet grasslands. Dark wings.

3 CURLEW SANDPIPER *Calidris ferruginea*   **Page 342**
Common on coast, Aug.–early May; some all year. Local inland. White upper tail-coverts; long, evenly decurved bill. **3a. Juvenile. 3b. Adult.**

4 BROAD-BILLED SANDPIPER *Limicola falcinellus*   **Page 343**
Uncommon on mudflats, Aug–Apr. Bill decurved near tip, striped head, black leading wing edge. **4a. Juv.** Pale-striped back; centre of rump black. **4b. Adult.** Grey rump.

5 DUNLIN *Calidris alpina*   **Page 342**
Vagrant. Resembles No. 3, but black line down centre of rump/upper tail-coverts.

⑥SANDERLING *Calidris alba*   **Page 343**
Common/abundant on coast, late Aug.–Apr.; some all year. Occasional inland. Pale grey, with brilliant white wing-stripe; short, stout bill.

7 LITTLE STINT *Calidris minuta*   **Page 341**
Common and widespread, Aug.–May, especially on Rift Valley lakeshores; less numerous on coastal mudflats. Narrow white wing-stripe, grey tail sides. **7a. Juv. 7b. Adult.**

8 LONG-TOED STINT *Calidris subminuta*   **Page 342**
Rare, Nov–May. See text. **8a. Juvenile. 8b. Adult.**

9 WHITE-FRONTED PLOVER *Charadrius marginatus tenellus*   **Page 339**
North Kenyan coast, Athi/Galana rivers. Toes do not extend beyond tail.

10 KITTLITZ'S PLOVER *Charadrius pecuarius*   **Page 339**
Local inland, especially Rift Valley. Toes extend beyond tail.

11 CHESTNUT-BANDED PLOVER *Charadrius pallidus venustus*   **Page 339**
Rift Valley soda lakes in s. Kenya and n. Tanzania. Small; toes project beyond tail.

12 TEMMINCK'S STINT *Calidris temminckii*   **Page 341**
Oct.–Apr., on muddy shores; uncommon in Rift Valley; rare on coast. Plain above; white tail sides.

13 CASPIAN PLOVER *Charadrius asiaticus*   **Page 340**
Winters on Mara/Serengeti Plains. Locally common migrant on L. Turkana shores and grass-lands in Tsavo East NP; uncommon elsewhere. Tips of toes project beyond largely dark tail.

14 KENTISH PLOVER *Charadrius a. alexandrinus*   **Page 339**
Small numbers regular at L. Turkana, Oct.–Apr.; occasional elsewhere, incl. coast. Paler and greyer than Ringed and Little Ringed Plovers, with broad white tail sides.

15 LITTLE RINGED PLOVER *Charadrius dubius curonicus*   **Page 338**
Uncommon, Oct.–early Apr., mainly along Rift Valley lakes and larger rivers. Local on coast. No noticeable wing-stripe, obscure head pattern (more striking in spring).

16 RINGED PLOVER *Charadrius hiaticula tundrae*   **Page 338**
Common and widespread, Sept.–early May; some on coast all year. Plump, large-head-ed; bright wing-stripe broader on primaries.

17 GREY PLOVER *Pluvialis squatarola*   **Page 338**
Common along coast, Aug.–Apr.; occasional on inland lakeshores. Large, stocky, with white upper tail-coverts. (See also Plate 18.)

18 PACIFIC GOLDEN PLOVER *Pluvialis fulva*   **Page 338**
Uncommon/regular on coast; scarce/irregular inland. No noticeable wing-stripe. (From below, wing-linings uniformly grey. See also Plate 18.)

19 GREATER SANDPLOVER *Charadrius leschenaultii crassirostris*   **Page 340**
Common/abundant on coast, Aug.–May; some all year. Uncommon at Lake Turkana. Large bill; toes project well beyond tail tip.

⑳THREE-BANDED PLOVER *Charadrius t. tricollaris*   **Page 339**
Widespread on inland waterways, local on coast. Dark, long-tailed, white head stripes; white on secondaries, but none on primaries.

21 LESSER or MONGOLIAN SANDPLOVER *Charadrius mongolus*   **Page 340**
Common on coast, late Aug.–May; some all year. Scarce on Rift Valley lakes. Wing-stripe less distinct than in No. 19, bill smaller, toes hidden by tail.

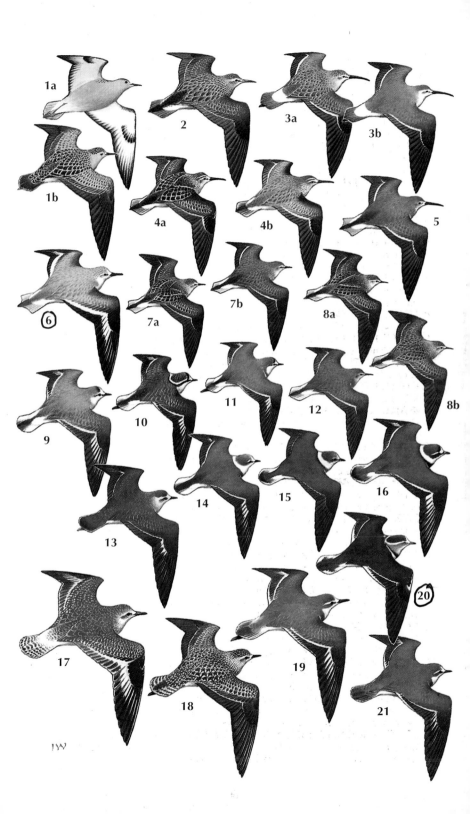

PLATE 22: SANDPIPERS, SHANKS AND PHALAROPES (Adults)

1 TEREK SANDPIPER *Xenus cinereus*   **Page 347**
Common coastal migrant, Aug.–April; scarce inland. Long upcurved bill and bright yellow-orange legs and feet. **1a and 1b. Winter.**

2 COMMON SANDPIPER *Actitis hypoleucos*   **Page 347**
Common and widespread, Aug.–April. **2a and 2b. Winter.** Tail extends well beyond primary tips. Bobbing motion on land. In stiff-winged low flight, wings remain below the
horizontal.

3 COMMON GREENSHANK *Tringa nebularia*   **Page 346**
Common and widespread, Sept.–April. **3a and 3b. Winter.** Bill slightly upturned. Hoary
head/neck; in flight, long white wedge on back, but wing pattern different from that of
No. 4.

4 COMMON REDSHANK *Tringa totanus ussuriensis*   **Page 346**
Uncommon; largely coastal. **4a and 4b. Winter.** Shorter, bulkier than Spotted Redshank;
forehead dark. In flight, large white wing patches, unlike Common Greenshank and
Marsh Sandpiper.

5 SPOTTED REDSHANK *Tringa erythropus*   **Page 346**
Widespread on inland waters, Nov.–May. More slender than Common Redshank, with
longer tarsi and longer, thinner bill. **5a and 5c. Winter.** Forehead white. In flight, lacks
strong contrast; pale wing patches marbled. **5b. Spring.** Plumage mostly blackish. Legs
and feet dark red.

6 MARSH SANDPIPER *Tringa stagnatilis*   **Page 346**
Common and widespread on wetlands, Sept–April. Some oversummer. Suggests diminutive Common Greenshank with straight, needle-thin bill. Legs and feet pale greenish or
yellow-green. **6a and 6c. Winter.** In flight, toes project well beyond tail. **6b. Spring.**

7 WOOD SANDPIPER *Tringa glareola*   **Page 347**
Common and widespread on freshwater wetlands, Aug.–early May. Bold white superci-
iary stripe. Slim and long-necked compared with more compact Green Sandpiper. **7a and
7b. Winter.** Prominently spangled above. Tail finely barred.

8 GREEN SANDPIPER *Tringa ochropus*   **Page 347**
Common along rivers, streams and roadside pools, Aug.–early April. Stockier than Wood
Sandpiper, with narrow superciliary stripe, dark olive legs and feet. **8a and 8b. Winter.**
Dark olive-brown, with faint pale speckling. In flight, shows bold tail bars and strong con-
trast between white rump and dark wings/back.

9 GREY PHALAROPE *Phalaropus fulicarius*   **Page 348**
Vagrant. Bill shorter and thicker than in Red-necked Phalarope. **9a and 9c. Winter.** Paler
grey above than Red-necked Phalarope. **9b. Spring female.**

10 RED-NECKED PHALAROPE *Phalaropus lobatus*   **Page 348**
Regular offshore, Oct.–April, at times in large flocks. Scarce inland on Rift Valley lakes.
Needle-like bill. **10a. Spring female. 10b. Spring male. 10c and 10d. Winter.**

11 RED KNOT *Calidris c. canutus*   **Page 343**
Vagrant. Stocky, with short neck and bill; tarsi short and greenish. **11a and 11c. Winter.**
May show traces of red spring plumage. **11b. Spring.**

PLATE 23: GODWITS, CURLEWS, RUFF AND TURNSTONE

1 RUDDY TURNSTONE *Arenaria i. interpres*   **Page 348**
Common on coast, Sept.–April; rare inland. **1a and 1b. Spring Adults. 1c. Winter Adult.**

2 RUFF *Philomachus pugnax*   **Page 344**
Common and widespread inland, Aug.–May; rare at coast. Legs and feet pink, pinkish
red or orange in adults. Movements sluggish, deliberate. See Plate 20 for spring female.
2a. Spring male. Flight pattern same for both sexes at all ages; conspicuous white oval
patches straddling upper tail-coverts. **2b. Winter female. 2c. Winter male**. White-
necked individual **2d. Juvenile female. 2e. Juvenile male**. Buff face and underparts,
scaly upperparts; legs and feet greenish or olive-brown.

3 WHIMBREL *Numenius p. phaeopus*   **Page 345**
Common along coast, especially Aug.–April; rare inland. Bill kinked downward near
tip, crown boldly striped. **3a and 3b. Winter.** Adults in flight appear compact and dark,
with white rump narrowing to point. (Immature similar.)

4 EURASIAN CURLEW *Numenius arquata orientalis*   **Page 345**
Uncommon but regular on coast, mainly Aug.–April; a few in summer. Occasional
inland. Larger, slightly paler than Whimbrel, with longer bill evenly decurved throughout its length. **4a and 4b. Winter adults**. Paler flight feathers than Whimbrel; no head
stripes. (Immature similar.)

5 BAR-TAILED GODWIT *Limosa l. lapponica*   **Page 345**
Uncommon on coast, mainly Aug.–Oct.; rare inland. Prefers shallow water. Lacks white
in wing; tail finely barred; legs much shorter than in Black-tailed Godwit.
5a. Spring female. Bright individual. **5b and 5c. Winter adults**. Upperparts noticeably
streaked; white extends up back; toes barely project beyond tail. **5d. Spring male**. Russet
extends to under tail-coverts.

6 BLACK-TAILED GODWIT *Limosa l. limosa*   **Page 345**
Common to fairly common inland, mainly Oct.–April, in wetlands. Scarce on coast.
Gregarious; often in deep water. Broad black tail band and large white wing-stripe.
6a and 6b. Winter adults. Feet project well beyond tail in flight. **6c. Spring adult**. Barred
flanks, white posterior underparts.

*Winter male Ruff. Largely white individual, with bill yellow, orange or pink at base,
orange or reddish legs and feet*

PLATE 24: LARGE PIED WADERS, SNIPE AND PAINTED-SNIPE

1 CRAB-PLOVER *Dromas ardeola*   **Page 330**
Present on coast all months, most numerous Aug.–April. **1a and 1b. Adults**.

2 EURASIAN OYSTERCATCHER *Haematopus ostralegus longipes*   **Page 330**
Uncommon on coast. Sporadic at lakes Turkana, Baringo and Nakuru. **2a. Winter**. White on lower throat. **2b. Spring**. All-black head and neck.

3 BLACK-WINGED STILT *Himantopus h. himantopus*   **Page 331**
Widespread in wetlands, including coastal creeks and saltpans. Dusky head markings variable. **3a and 3b. Adults**.

4 PIED AVOCET *Recurvirostra avosetta*   **Page 331**
Fairly common on alkaline Rift Valley lakes; scarce elsewhere. **4a and 4b. Adults**.

5 GREATER PAINTED-SNIPE *Rostratula b. benghalensis*   **Page 330**
Uncommon. Widespread in marshy areas and recently inundated grassland. **5a. Adult female. 5b and 5c. Adult males**.

6 PINTAIL SNIPE *Gallinago stenura*   **Page 345**
Vagrant from Asia (3 Kenyan records, Oct.–Jan.). Similar to Common Snipe. Bill averages shorter; less contrasting pale back lines, plainer breast, paler and faded-looking wing-coverts especially noticeable in flight, along with virtual lack of pale rear edge to secondaries. **6a. Adult and first-winter. 6b. Tail** shape unique, with ultra-narrow outer tail feathers (unlikely to be seen in the field).

7 AFRICAN SNIPE *Gallinago nigripennis aequatorialis*   **Page 344**
Local resident of *high-elevation* marshes and bogs (w. and cent. Kenyan highlands; common on moorlands of Mt Elgon, Mt Kenya; also Kilimanjaro and Crater Highlands in Tanzania.) Longer-billed, darker-breasted than Common Snipe. **7a. and 7c. Adult and first-year. 7b. Tail** with much white.

8 JACK SNIPE *Lymnocryptes minimus*   **Page 344**
Scarce and sporadic palearctic migrant, mainly Nov.–Feb. Small size, short bill. On ground, shows all-dark crown, double buff facial stripes, no flank bars. **8a. Adult and first-winter. 8b. Tail** dark, with no white or chestnut.

9 GREAT SNIPE *Gallinago media*   **Page 344**
Uncommon to scarce palearctic migrant, Oct.–Dec. and April–May. Lake edges, flooded grasslands, dry fields. Flight mode and shape distinct. Barred belly, white wing-bars. **9a. Adult and first-winter. 9b. Tail** with broad white sides.

10 COMMON SNIPE *Gallinago g. gallinago*   **Page 344**
Palearctic migrant, Oct.–March, when the commonest snipe below 2000 m in marshes, along lake edges and in wet fields. **10a. Adult and first-winter. 10b. Tail** mostly rufous, with little white.

PLATE 25: GALLINULES, RAILS, JACANAS AND FINFOOT (See also Plate 26)

1 AFRICAN WATER RAIL *Rallus caerulescens*   **Page 323**
Widespread in cent. Kenyan highlands south to Mara GR, Amboseli area and Arusha NP; scarce elsewhere. **1a. Adult. 1b. Juvenile.**

2 BLACK CRAKE *Amaurornis flavirostris*   **Page 324**
Common and widespread. **2a. Juvenile.** White on throat variable. **2b. Adult.**

3 AFRICAN JACANA *Actophilornis africanus*   **Page 329**
Common and widespread on waters with floating vegetation. **3a. Juvenile. 3b and 3c. Adults.**

4 LESSER MOORHEN *Gallinula angulata*   **Page 325**
Local and uncommon intra-African migrant, mainly April–August. Largely yellow bill; no red on legs. **4a. Adult. 4b. Immature. 4c. Juvenile.**

5 LESSER JACANA *Microparra capensis*   **Page 329**
Scarce. In flight, white trailing edge on secondaries and pale wing-coverts distinctive. **5a and 5b. Adults.**

6 COMMON MOORHEN *Gallinula chloropus meridionalis*   **Page 324**
Common and widespread above 1400 m. Scarce in coastal lowlands. Largely red bill/frontal shield and red tibial 'garters'. **6a. Juvenile. 6b and 6c. Adults. 6d. Downy young.**

7 ALLEN'S GALLINULE *Porphyrio alleni*   **Page 324**
Local and uncommon on cent. Rift Valley lakes (mainly Naivasha and Baringo), June–Sept. Rare in n. Tanzania. **7a. Juvenile.** Rail-like, with streaked upperparts. **7b. Adult.** Bluish frontal shield.

8 PURPLE SWAMPHEN *Porphyrio porphyrio madagascariensis*   **Page 324**
Local and uncommon. **8a. Adult.** Large; all-red bill and frontal shield **8b. Subadult.** Underparts pale purplish grey, shading to buffy white on belly.

9 RED-KNOBBED COOT *Fulica cristata*   **Page 325**
Locally abundant (especially on Lake Naivasha and some n. Tanzanian lakes). **9a. Non-breeding adult.** Inconspicuous knobs at base of frontal shield. **9b. Breeding adult. 9c. Downy young.**

10 AFRICAN FINFOOT *Podica senegalensis somereni*   **Page 326**
Scarce and local on well-shaded streams and rivers with overhanging vegetation. Shy and elusive. **10a. Female. 10b. Male.**

PLATE 26: CRAKES AND FLUFFTAILS (See also Plate 25)

1 WHITE-SPOTTED FLUFFTAIL *Sarothrura pulchra centralis*   **Page 321**
Locally common along wooded streams in w. Kenya. **1a. Female**. Rear body tiger-striped between rufous foreparts and tail. **1b and 1c. Males**. Scattered large white body spots.

2 STRIPED FLUFFTAIL *Sarothrura affinis antonii*   **Page 322**
Confined to tussock grass at high elevations. Few recent records. **2a. Female**. Rich buff; heavily spotted breast/belly, barred back and flanks. **2b and 2c. Males**. White-striped back; scaly/streaky pattern below.

3 STREAKY-BREASTED FLUFFTAIL *Sarothrura boehmi*   **Page 322**
Rare intra-African migrant, April–May, in flooded grasslands. Very short black tail. **3a. Female**. Dusky breast, barred flanks and under tail-coverts. **3b and 3c. Males**. White-striped back, narrowly streaked lower breast and sides.

4 RED-CHESTED FLUFFTAIL *Sarothrura rufa*   **Page 322**
Common in w. Kenyan marshes and swamps, less so elsewhere. Rarely seen on dry ground. **4a. Female**. Barred flanks, pale breast. **4b and 4c. Males**. Body and wings black with fine white markings.

5 BUFF-SPOTTED FLUFFTAIL *Sarothrura e. elegans*   **Page 321**
Uncommon in w. Kenyan forests. Occasional elsewhere during rains. **5a. Female**. Large dark eyes on pale face. Buff spots above, spot-barring below. **5b and 5c. Males**. Buff-spangled above, white-spotted below.

6 BAILLON'S CRAKE *Porzana pusilla obscura*   **Page 323**
Uncommon and local in wetlands. Irregular black and white marks on brown upper-parts. **6a. Juvenile**. Buff face and breast; barring on flanks, sides and breast. **6b. Adult male**. Blue-grey face and breast, strongly barred flanks, all-green bill, red eyes.

7 SPOTTED CRAKE *Porzana porzana*   **Page 323**
Scarce palearctic migrant in wet places, Nov.–April. **7a and 7b. Males**. Stocky; yellow chicken-like bill, reddish at base; spotted white foreparts, buff under tail-coverts. (Female browner on neck/breast.)

8 STRIPED CRAKE *Aenigmatolimnas marginalis*   **Page 323**
Scarce intra-African migrant, May–Nov., in wetlands. Bill heavy. **8a. Juvenile**. Plain light brown back, buffy-brown foreparts, dull white belly and crissum. **8b. Male** Rufous-brown head, neck and flanks, tawny or buff crissum. **8c. Female**. Grey foreparts, tawny or buff crissum.

9 CORNCRAKE *Crex crex*   **Page 323**
Scarce palearctic migrant in savanna/grassland; regular mid-April in Mara GR. **9a and 9b. Adults**. Buffy brown, with barred flanks and pale flesh-brown bill, grey superciliary stripe and foreneck. (Female may show little or no grey.) In flight, has large orange-rufous wing patches.

10 AFRICAN CRAKE *Crex egregia*   **Page 322**
Uncommon in wet grassy places; regular intra-African migrant, April–Sept. **10a. Juvenile**. Brownish-buff foreparts, obscure brown flank barring. **10b and 10c. Adults**. Grey foreparts, narrow white superciliary stripes.

PLATE 27: TURNICIDS, QUAIL, STONE PARTRIDGE AND FRANCOLINS (See also Plate 28)

1 BLUE QUAIL *Coturnix adansonii*   **Page 314**
Rare intra-African 'rains migrant' in wet grassland; may breed on Pemba Island. **1a and 1b. Males. 1c. Female.** Heavily barred underparts.

2 HARLEQUIN QUAIL *Coturnix d. delegorguei*   **Page 315**
Common and widespread in grassland and savanna. Concentrations coincide with periods of heavy rain. **2a and 2b. Females.** Sides of breast spotted; primaries plain brown. **2c and 2d. Males.** Bold face pattern; underparts appear dark in flight.

3 COMMON QUAIL *Coturnix coturnix erlangeri*   **Page 314**
Fairly common local resident of highland grain fields and grassland. Inconspicuous, but trisyllabic call frequently heard. **3a and 3b. Females.** Streaked sides, spots across breast, buff bars on primaries. **3c. Male.** Chestnut face, striped crown. (Some birds have chestnut underparts. Paler migrant *C. c. coturnix* has whitish cheeks in both sexes.)

4 QUAIL-PLOVER *Ortyxelos meiffrenii*   **Page 320**
Local and uncommon in dry grassland. Somewhat nocturnal; solitary. Suggests small courser. On bare ground, employs slow, chameleon-like locomotion. Wing pattern unique; flight lark-like. **4a. Female. 4b and 4c. Males.**

5 COMMON BUTTON-QUAIL *Turnix sylvatica lepurana*   **Page 320**
Locally common in grassland, savanna, abandoned cultivation. Solitary (or in small loose groups during rainy season). Pale buff wing-coverts contrast with dark flight feathers. **5a. Adult male. 5b. Adult female. 5c. Immature male.**

6 BLACK-RUMPED BUTTON-QUAIL *Turnix hottentotta nana* **Page 321**
Rare in moist grassland and marsh edges. Secretive. **6a and 6b. Adult females.** Black rump and tail; long buff streak on scapulars. Wings lack contrast of Common Button-quail. (Male has black or pale rufous crown, speckled malar area, whitish or buff throat.)

7 RING-NECKED FRANCOLIN *Francolinus streptophorus*   **Page 315**
Rare and local on grassy escarpments in w. Kenya (Mt Elgon, Samia Hills and the Maragoli Escarpment). **Male** illustrated. (Female similar.)

8 CRESTED FRANCOLIN *Francolinus sephaena*   **Page 317**
Locally common in lowland bush, dry scrub, open riverine woodland, dense thickets. Small; runs with tail erect; frequently in small groups. **8a and 8c. F. s. grantii.** Widespread, except in coastal lowlands and extreme ne. Kenya. **8b. F. s. rovuma.** Coastal. Short brown streaks on underparts.

9 HILDEBRANDT'S FRANCOLIN *Francolinus hildebrandti* **Page 317**
Locally common in scrub and thickets near wooded areas, especially in cent. Rift Valley. Sexes distinct. **9a. F. h. altumi,** male. **9b. F. h. altumi,** female. **9c. F. h. hildebrandti,** female.

10 STONE PARTRIDGE *Ptilopachus p. petrosus*   **Page 315**
Local on rocky slopes and in gorges in n. and nw. Kenya. Shy and elusive. Runs and hops among boulders, tail erect. May perch in trees. Vocal at dawn and dusk.

11 COQUI FRANCOLIN *Francolinus coqui*   **Page 315**
Widespread in savanna, grassy bush and thicket borders. *F. c. coqui* uncommon in coastal lowlands; *F. c. hubbardi* locally common in cent. Rift Valley, w. Kenyan highlands, Mara GR south to Serengeti NP. (*F. c. maharao*, not shown, uncommon and local east of Rift Valley.) **11a. F. c. hubbardi,** female. **11b. F. c. hubbardi,** male. **11c. F. c. coqui,** female. **11d. F. c. coqui,** male.

PLATE 28: FRANCOLINS AND GUINEAFOWL (Adults, except as indicated. See also Plate 27)

1 ORANGE RIVER FRANCOLIN *Francolinus levaillantoides archeri* **Page 316**
Local and rare in n. Kenya (Mt Kulal and Huri Hills). Underparts with short fine streaks.

2 MOORLAND FRANCOLIN *Francolinus psilolaemus elgonensis* **Page 316**
Local; high elevations on Mt Elgon and (similar *F. p. psilolaemus*) on Mt Kenya and the Aberdares.

3 SHELLEY'S FRANCOLIN *Francolinus shelleyi uluensis* **Page 316**
Locally common in grassland/open savanna in cent. and s. Kenya; uncommon in n. Tanzania. (Similar *F. s. macarthuri* uncommon in Chyulu Hills.) Belly heavily barred with black; wings show much rufous in flight. **3a and 3b. Adults.**

4 CHESTNUT-NAPED FRANCOLIN *Francolinus castaneicollis atrifrons*
Page 318
Vagrant (?) along edge of s. Ethiopian highlands near Moyale, in forest edge and juniper woods. Underparts nearly plain creamy buff (unlike well-marked Ethiopian races).

5 RED-WINGED FRANCOLIN *Francolinus levaillantii kikuyuensis* **Page 316**
Scarce in remnant grasslands in w. and sw. Kenyan highlands. Ochre/orange band between throat and black-and-white neck ring. Wings extensively rufous. **5a and 5b. Adults.**

6 SCALY FRANCOLIN *Francolinus squamatus maranensis* **Page 317**
Locally fairly common in forest, bamboo and dense forest-edge bush. Bill entirely red or vermilion (brown above and orange below in presumed immatures). (*F. s. schuetti*, west of Rift Valley, similar but paler.)

7 JACKSON'S FRANCOLIN *Francolinus jacksoni* **Page 318**
Common along montane-forest edges on Mt Kenya and in the Aberdares; rare on Mt Elgon.

8 RED-NECKED SPURFOWL *Francolinus afer* **Page 318**
8a *F. a. cranchii*. Locally common in Lake Victoria basin, Mara GR and Serengeti NP. **8b.** *F. a. cranchii*, **juv. 8c.** *F. a. leucoparaeus*. Local in Kenyan coastal lowlands. (E.Tanzanian birds may be the similar *F. a. melanogaster*; species also present in Tarangire NP.)

9 YELLOW-NECKED SPURFOWL *Francolinus leucoscepus* **Page 318**
Locally common in open light bush and savanna, in most national parks and game reserves. Pale buff wing patch conspicuous in flight. In n. Tanzania, hybridizes with Grey-breasted Spurfowl (see Plate 122). **9a and 9b. Adults.**

10 HELMETED GUINEAFOWL *Numida meleagris* **Page 319**
Widespread in bush, woodland, savanna and shrubby grassland: *N. m. reichenowi* common south of the Equator; *N. m. meleagris* uncommon in n. Kenya; *N. m. somaliensis* in northeast south to Wajir. (*N. m. mitrata* in coastal lowlands.) **10a.** *N. m. reichenowi*, **adult. 10b.** *N. m. reichenowi*, **imm. 10c.** *N. m. reichenowi*, **juv. 10d.** *N. m. reichenowi*, **downy young. 10e and 10f.** *N. m. meleagris*, **adults. 10g.** *N. m. somaliensis*, **adult.**

11 CRESTED GUINEAFOWL *Guttera pucherani* **Page 319**
Local in forest and dense woodland: *G. p. pucherani* coastal, inland to eastern edge of Kenyan highlands and to Lake Manyara; *G. p. verreauxi* in w. Kenyan highlands (incl. Mau, Nandi and Kakamega Forests) east to southern Aberdares; also in Mara GR and Serengeti NP. **11a.** *G. p. verreauxi*, **adult.** Unspotted purplish black collar; dark brown eyes; no red on face. **11b.** *G. p. verreauxi*, **downy young. 11c.** *G. p. pucherani*, **adult.** Bluish dots extend up to throat skin; red eyes and much red on face.

12 VULTURINE GUINEAFOWL *Acryllium vulturinum* **Page 319**
Locally common in dry bush and savanna from n. and e. Kenya south to Mkomazi GR and the Masai Steppe. **12a. Adult. 12b. Downy young.**

PLATE 29: BUSTARDS (See also Plate 30)

1 WHITE-BELLIED BUSTARD *Eupodotis senegalensis canicollis* **Page 328**
Widespread in shrubby grassland. **1a. Male. 1b. Female. 1c. Subadult male**.

2 CRESTED BUSTARD *Eupodotis ruficrista gindiana* **Page 327**
Widespread in northern and eastern areas, in dry bush and scrub below 1250 m.
2a. Female. 2b. Male.

3 BLACK-BELLIED BUSTARD *Eupodotis m. melanogaster* **Page 328**
Local in moist grassland. Slightly smaller, slimmer, longer-legged and with slightly thinner bill than Hartlaub's Bustard. **3a, 3b and 3c. Adult males**. Head pattern less bold and
with less white in wing than Hartlaub's; hindneck buffy brown, lower back to tail
brown. In display, shows black bands on brown tail. **3d. Adult female**. Neck pale buffy
brown or tan and finely vermiculated; appears plain. Lower back to tail brownish.
3e. Juvenile male. Neck brownish.

4 HARTLAUB'S BUSTARD *Eupodotis hartlaubii* **Page 328**
Locally common, mostly below 1500 m. Prefers drier habitat than Black-bellied, but the
two sympatric in places (e.g. Nairobi and Meru NPs). **4a, 4b and 4c. Adult males**.
Sharper face pattern than Black-bellied; broader black postocular line and dark line
from eye to throat bordering bright white ear-coverts. Neck greyish, not buffy brown.
Much white in wings; rump and tail appear black. **4d. Immature male**. Neck grey.
4e. Female. Neck finely streaked or speckled, not vermiculated, with cream central line
down front. Upper breast with blackish marks. Lower back and tail grey.

5 HEUGLIN'S BUSTARD *Neotis heuglinii* **Page 327**
Northern Kenya. Uncommon in lava desert, bush and shrubby grassland. Blue-grey
neck, chestnut band on lower breast. **5a and 5b. Adult males**. Black crown and face.
(Some males, and many females, show white line on centre of crown.) Some primaries
white along most of their length. **5c. Juvenile male**.

6 DENHAM'S BUSTARD *Neotis denhami jacksoni* **Page 326**
Local and uncommon in grassland above 1500 m. **6a and 6b. Females**. Rufous on hindneck; white patch at base of primaries. (Male similar but larger; see Plate 30.)

Male White-bellied Bustard

PLATE 30: LARGE GROUND BIRDS (See also Plate 29)

1 ABYSSINIAN GROUND HORNBILL *Bucorvus abyssinicus* **Page 397**
Scarce and local in nw. Kenya, mainly in short-grass areas below 1000 m. **1a and 1c. Males.** Blue facial skin; lower neck red. **1b. Female.** Gular skin entirely blue.

2 SOUTHERN GROUND HORNBILL *Bucorvus leadbeateri* **Page 397**
Uncommon and local in grassland and savanna. In pairs or small groups. **2a. Female.** Chin/upper throat with small violet-blue patch. **2b and 2c. Males.** Chin and throat red. **2d. Juvenile.** Brownish yellow facial skin.

3 SECRETARY BIRD *Sagittarius serpentarius* **Page 292**
Uncommon but widespread in grassland, open savanna and cultivation. Usually in pairs. **3a and 3b. Adults.**

4 KORI BUSTARD *Ardeotis kori struthiunculus* **Page 327**
Widespread. Uncommon in grassland, savanna and semi-desert. **4a and 4b. Adults. 4c. Male in display.**

5 ARABIAN BUSTARD *Ardeotis arabs* **Page 327**
Rare in n. Kenyan border areas. Few recent records. Smaller than Kori Bustard; no black on wing-coverts or lower neck.

6 DENHAM'S BUSTARD *Neotis denhami jacksoni* **Page 326**
Scarce and local in grassland above 1500 m, mainly on Laikipia Plateau and near Maralal. **Male in courtship display.** (See also Plate 29.)

7 SOMALI OSTRICH *Struthio (camelus) molybdophanes* **Page 269**
Uncommon in e. and ne. Kenya. Usually in pairs or solitary in savanna, bush or scrub, less often on plains. **7a. Breeding male. 7b. Non-breeding female. 7c. Juvenile.**

8 COMMON OSTRICH *Struthio camelus massaicus* **Page 269**
Widespread. Locally fairly common. Solitary or gregarious. **8a. Breeding male. 8b. Downy young. 8c. Non-breeding female. 8d. Non-breeding male. 8e. Breeding female.**

Displaying Common Ostrich

PLATE 31: VULTURES AND PALM-NUT VULTURE

1 LAMMERGEIER *Gypaetus barbatus meridionalis* **Page 295**
Scarce around mountains and inselbergs, mainly alpine areas of mts Elgon, Kenya, Meru and Kilimanjaro. **1a. Adult**. Rusty-tinged head and underparts, black mask and beard. **1b. Juvenile**. Pale face, hooded appearance; black secondaries. Head whitens with age.

2 PALM-NUT VULTURE *Gypohierax angolensis* **Page 305**
Local in coastal lowlands; also Lake Jipe and Tana River; usually near water. Heavy bill. **2a. Adult**. White plumage areas often earth-stained; bare face pinkish or pale orange. **2b. Juvenile**. Dark brown, with pale face; feathered head and neck.

3 HOODED VULTURE *Necrosyrtes monachus pileatus* **Page 295**
Widespread, but now urban only in w. Kenya; largely confined to national parks and game reserves. Compact, short-tailed, slender-billed. **3a. Juvenile**. Greyish-white face; sepia down on head. **3b. Adult**. Pink or red face; 'woolly' head.

4 EGYPTIAN VULTURE *Neophron p. percnopterus* **Page 295**
Widespread but uncommon. Nests on cliffs, forages in open country. Solitary or in pairs. **4a. Adult**. Shaggy neck, yellow face. **4b. Juvenile**. Pale face and foreneck. Dark hood blends into rest of plumage. Bases of secondaries grey (black in juvenile Lammergeier).

5 RÜPPELL'S GRIFFON VULTURE *Gyps r. rueppellii* **Page 296**
Locally common in dry open country; roosts and nests on cliffs. Most numerous large vulture in n. Kenya. Long-necked; slightly larger and heavier-billed than White-backed Vulture. **5a. Juvenile**. From adult White-backed by darker neck/head down and slightly paler bill. **5b. Adult**. Scaly pattern and yellowish-horn bill unique.

6 AFRICAN WHITE-BACKED VULTURE *Gyps africanus* **Page 296**
Commonest vulture in most national parks and game reserves. Nests in trees. Bill blackish at all ages. **6a. Juvenile**. Head/neck with pale down; underparts buff-streaked. No white on back. **6b and 6c. Adults**. Bill, head and neck blackish; white back patch visible when wings spread.

7 WHITE-HEADED VULTURE *Trigonoceps occipitalis* **Page 296**
Uncommon in open/semi-open country. Pink bill with blue cere at all ages. **7a. Juvenile**. Bill colour and angular head distinctive. **7b. Adult female**. (Male has grey secondaries; see figure below.)

8 LAPPET-FACED VULTURE *Torgos t. tracheliotus* **Page 296**
Uncommon to fairly common and widespread in national parks and game reserves. Huge size and massive bill. Often solitary. **8a and 8c. Adults**. **8b. Juvenile**.

Male White-headed Vulture

PLATE 32: VULTURES AND EAGLES OVERHEAD (See plates of perched birds for status and habitat notations)

(1) LAPPET-FACED VULTURE *Torgos t. tracheliotus*   **Page 296**
1a. Juvenile. Long, broad wings with pinched-in inner primaries. No contrast on wings, or forewing slightly paler with some obscure pale lines. **1b. Adult**. Whitish leg feathers and forewing line.

(2) RÜPPELL'S GRIFFON VULTURE *Gyps r. rueppellii*   **Page 296**
2a. Adult. Pale-mottled body, lines of crescent-shaped marks on wing-linings. **2b. Juv.** Ochre-brown, buff-streaked body and wing-linings contrast with blackish flight feathers. Single white forewing line in youngest birds makes separation from young African White-backed Vulture difficult or impossible. See text.

(3) AFRICAN WHITE-BACKED VULTURE *Gyps africanus*   **Page 296**
3a. Adult. Pale wing-linings and body. **3b. Juv.** Plumage identical to 2b, but wing tips often more tapering. See text.

(4) HOODED VULTURE *Necrosyrtes monachus pileatus*   **Page 295**
4a. Adult. Whitish down showing through the tibial feathers (not depicted on plate) may suggest miniature Lappet-faced Vulture, but no white line on wing-linings. **4b. Juv.** Dark, except for paler feet and head.

(5) WHITE-HEADED VULTURE *Trigonoceps occipitalis*   **Page 296**
5a. Adult female. Inner secondaries all white (greyish, and separated from dark forewing by white line, in male). **5b. Juv.** White line on wing; from adult male by all-brown body.

(6) LAMMERGEIER *Gypaetus barbatus meridionalis*   **Page 295**
Narrow pointed wing tips and long, wedge-shaped tail. **6a) Adult. 6b. Juv.**

(7) EGYPTIAN VULTURE *Neophron p. percnopterus*   **Page 295**
7a. Adult. Wedge-shaped white tail. **7b. Juv.** Dark, with paler tail; body and wings lighten with each moult.

(8) VERREAUX'S EAGLE *Aquila verreauxii*   **Page 307**
Adult. Pinched-in wing base, white primary patch.

(9) BATELEUR *Terathopius ecaudatus*   **Page 298**
Juvenile. Protruding head, short tail (longer than in adult), narrow wing tips.

(10) LONG-CRESTED EAGLE *Lophaetus occipitalis*   **Page 308**
Adult. Blunt, broad wings; long, two-banded tail; white primary patches.

(11) LESSER SPOTTED EAGLE *Aquila p. pomarina*   **Page 305**
This species and No. 14 slightly shorter-winged and shorter-tailed than larger *Aquila* spp. **11a. Adult**. Wing-coverts paler than remiges; pale carpal crescents. **11b. Juv.** Greater coverts and flight feathers pale-tipped in fresh plumage.

(12) STEPPE EAGLE *Aquila nipalensis orientalis*   **Page 306**
12a. Juv. White central wing band, trailing wing edges and tail tip; pale inner primaries, barred flight feathers. **12b. Pale subadult**. Body darker than wing-coverts; pale throat. **12c. Adult**. Body and wing-coverts darker than flight feathers.

(13) TAWNY EAGLE *Aquila r. rapax*   **Page 306**
Shape as in Steppe Eagle; plumage variable as in that species. **13a. Adult**. (Typical mottled bird.) Faint barring on flight feathers. **13b. Juv.** Cinnamon-brown (fading to yellowish tawny, then blond); pale inner primaries; obscure pale grey mid-wing line. As warm tones wear and fade, difficult to separate from imm. Steppe Eagle, but Tawny lacks pale tips to under primary coverts.

14 GREATER SPOTTED EAGLE *Aquila clanga*   **Page 305**
Shape differs slightly from that of Lesser Spotted Eagle, the wings broader and tail shorter. **14a. Adult**. Coverts and body darker than flight feathers and tail; pale carpal crescents as in Lesser Spotted. **14b. Juv.** Buff spotting on belly; streaks on breast (evident at close range); pale tips on remiges and tail feathers.

15 IMPERIAL EAGLE *Aquila heliaca*   **Page 306**
Longest wings of any East African *Aquila*. **15a. Juv.** Buff-streaked body and wing-coverts, dark secondaries, pale inner primaries; greater coverts all grey. **15b. Adult**. Coverts and body darker than remiges, tail broadly black-banded.

82

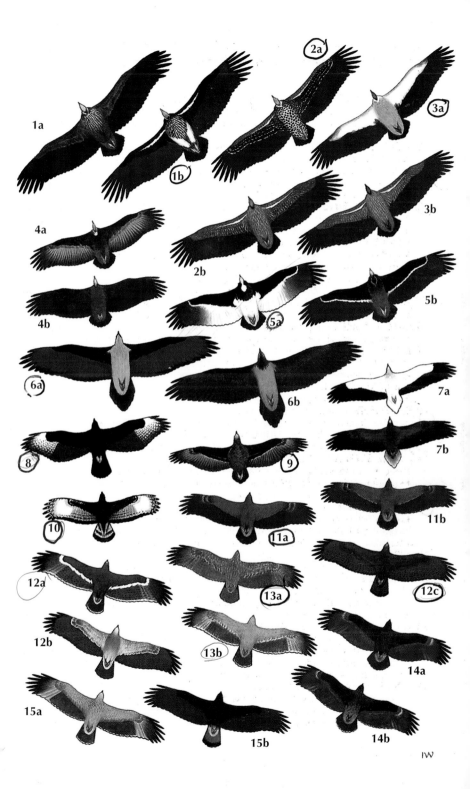

PLATE 33: BUZZARDS, ACCIPITERS AND CHANTING GOSHAWKS OVERHEAD (See plates of perched birds for status and habitat notations)

1 AUGUR BUZZARD *Buteo a. augur*   **Page 304**
Very broad wings, short tail; black carpal marks shared by pale adult and juvenile. **1a. Pale adult.** Black band at rear wing edge, rufous tail. **1b. Dark adult.** Blackish body and wing-coverts, rufous tail. **1c. Juv.** Pale buff body and wing-coverts; dull brown tail with darker subterminal band; rear edge of wing grey.

2 MOUNTAIN BUZZARD *Buteo oreophilus*   **Page 304**
Suggests Common Buzzard, but body and wing-linings densely spotted; no rufous, except for tibial barring.

3 COMMON (STEPPE) BUZZARD *Buteo buteo vulpinus*   **Page 303**
Variable. (Common brown morph resembles Mountain Buzzard, but lacks spots. Dark morph identical to 4b.) Usually a pale breast patch on all morphs. **3a. Juv., rufous morph.** Rear edge of wing obscurely grey, barred tail, streaked body (not barred as in adult). **3b. Adult, rufous morph.** Like 4a, but has dark hood; black band on rear edge of wing. Some have uniformly rufous or chestnut body/wing-coverts (barred at close range).

4 LONG-LEGGED BUZZARD *Buteo r. rufinus*   **Page 304**
More aquiline proportions than Common Buzzard. **4a. Typical adult.** Warm brown wing-linings and body, whitish head, black belly patches; pale rufous to almost whitish tail with no discernible barring. **4b. Dark adult.** Black-banded grey tail. Identical to dark morph of Common Buzzard. **4c. Juv.** Paler, buffier than adult, barred tail, suffused grey band on wings.

5 EURASIAN HONEY BUZZARD *Pernis apivorus*   **Page 294**
Differs from *Buteo* spp. in flat-winged soaring, slimmer and more protruding head; adult has bands across primaries and unique tail pattern of two dark basal bands, one at tip. (Juvenile on Plate 39.) **5a. Typical adult. 5b. Dark adult. 5c. Light adult.**

6 GRASSHOPPER BUZZARD *Butastur rufipennis*   **Page 303**
Slim silhouette suggests harrier. Whitish underwing, rufous body.

7 EASTERN PALE CHANTING GOSHAWK *Melierax poliopterus*   **Page 300**
Outer wings of both *Melierax* fuller than in sparrowhawks, and tail tip strongly rounded. Grey hood and black wing tips common to **adults** of both chanting goshawks, the two impossible to separate with view of underparts only.

8 GREAT SPARROWHAWK *Accipiter m. melanoleucus*   **Page 303**
Large; pinched-in outer wing and long tail typical of all sparrowhawks. **8a. Rufous-breasted juv. 8b. White-breasted juv.**

9 DARK CHANTING GOSHAWK *Melierax m. metabates*   **Page 300**
Juvenile. (No criteria for separating young of two *Melierax* species in ventral view.)

10 RUFOUS-BREASTED SPARROWHAWK *Accipiter r. rufiventris*   **Page 302**
Plain rufous wing-linings and body; throat and under tail-coverts whitish. (Juv. on Plate 42.)

11 LIZARD BUZZARD *Kaupifalco m. monogrammicus*   **Page 303**
Stocky proportions, black throat streak, single white tail band. (From above, shows white upper tail-coverts.)

12 LEVANT SPARROWHAWK *Accipiter brevipes*   **Page 301**
Pointed wings (less so when primaries spread in soaring). **12a. Juv.** Black-spotted on white; more banded on wing-linings. **12b. Adult female.** Black-tipped pale wing, chestnut barring. (Male has more contrasting black wing tips, paler body barring.)

13 SHIKRA *Accipiter badius sphenurus*   **Page 301**
Small and compact, with blunt wings. **13a. Juv.** Brown-spotted buff body/wing-linings; faint flight-feather barring. **13b. Adult.** Dusky-tipped pale wings; body/wing-linings faintly barred pinkish brown.

14 EURASIAN SPARROWHAWK *Accipiter n. nisus*   **Page 302**
Pale superciliary stripe in female and juvenile. **14a. Juv.** Ragged barring on body. **14b. Adult female.** Neat grey body barring (smaller male has chestnut barring).

15 GABAR GOSHAWK *Micronisus gabar aequatorius*   **Page 300**
15a. Dark morph. Grey barring on flight feathers and tail; red cere, legs and feet distinguish it from dark Ovambo Sparrowhawk. **15b. Pale morph.**

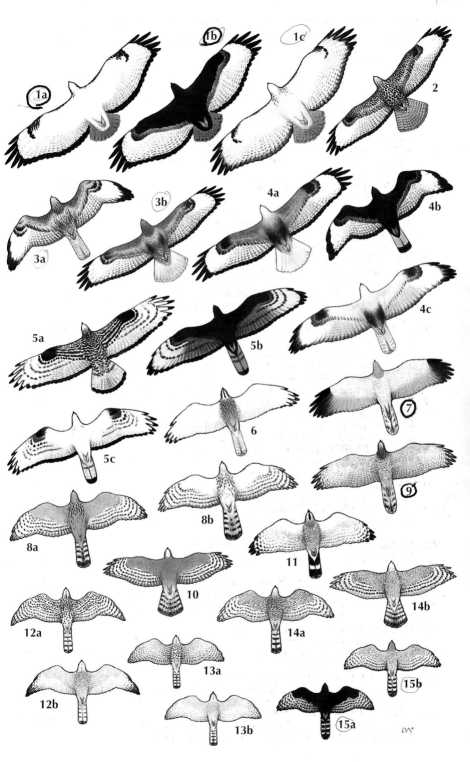

PLATE 34: MISCELLANEOUS LARGE RAPTORS OVERHEAD

1 AFRICAN HARRIER-HAWK *Polyboroides t. typus*   **Page 298**
Broad oblong wings and long tail; small protruding head. **1a. Adult. 1b. Dark juvenile.**
Chocolate head and body contrast with ginger-brown coverts; greater coverts dark-tipped; light patch at base of primaries.

2 PALM-NUT VULTURE *Gypohierax angolensis*   **Page 305**
Broad wings, short tail, protruding head/neck. Faster wingbeats than true vultures.
2a. Adult. Black secondaries, white-tipped tail. **2b. Juv.** Plain brown; distinctive shape.

3 OSPREY *Pandion h. haliaetus*   **Page 293**
Distinctive wing shape, black carpal patches and mid-wing band.

4 BATELEUR *Terathopius ecaudatus*   **Page 298**
Adult male. Very short tail, white wing-linings, broad black band on secondaries.
(Female's wings largely white, with narrow black band; see figure facing Plate 40.)

5 BOOTED EAGLE *Hieraaetus pennatus*   **Page 308**
Faint pale wedge on inner primaries. **5a. Dark morph.** Dark brown wing-linings, paler unbarred tail. **5b. Light morph.** Pale tail darker at tip.

6 BLACK KITE *Milvus migrans parasitus*   **Page 295**
Shallowly forked tail (unforked when fully spread); angular wings are evenly narrow, with pale primary panel (see Plates 43 and 44).

7 SHORT-TOED SNAKE EAGLE *Circaetus gallicus beaudouini*   **Page 297**
Whitish body with dark foreparts; barring evident at close range.

8 WAHLBERG'S EAGLE *Aquila wahlbergi*   **Page 307**
Straight, parallel-edged wings and narrow tail. **8a. Light morph.** Pale body and wing-linings, dark flight feathers and tail. **8b. Dark morph.** Body/wing-linings darker than flight feathers; primary bases pale.

9 BROWN SNAKE EAGLE *Circaetus cinereus*   **Page 297**
9a. Juvenile. 9b. Adult. Spread tail shows narrow white bands.

10 SOUTHERN BANDED SNAKE EAGLE *Circaetus fasciolatus*   **Page 297**
Barred body and wing-linings; plain brown head/breast; tail multi-banded.

11 BANDED SNAKE EAGLE *Circaetus cinerascens*   **Page 298**
Compact, with large head. White wing-linings; single broad white central tail band.

12 BLACK-CHESTED SNAKE EAGLE *Circaetus pectoralis*   **Page 297**
12a. Juvenile. White-mottled cinnamon body and wing-coverts (become paler with age).
12b. Adult. White, with black head and upper breast, black bands on rear edge of wing.

13 AFRICAN HAWK-EAGLE *Hieraaetus spilogaster*   **Page 307**
Long wings 'pinched in' at base. **13a. Juv.** Body and wing-linings usually darker and rustier than in 14a; primaries mostly unbarred. **13b. Adult.** White forewing and body with dark streaks; broad black terminal tail band, black tips to white flight feathers.

14 AYRES'S HAWK-EAGLE *Hieraaetus ayresii*   **Page 308**
Broad rounded wings and long tail with dark subterminal band at all ages. **14a. Juv.** Rich buff body and wing-linings, barred primaries. **14b. Adult.** Body with dark blotches, not streaks; wing-linings dark; tail and secondaries broadly barred.

15 VERREAUX'S EAGLE *Aquila verreauxii*   **Page 307**
Severely 'cut-away' inner secondaries; long broad wings; long tail. **Juv.** Pale primary panel and forewing; black breast and carpal patches.

16 AFRICAN FISH EAGLE *Haliaeetus vocifer*   **Page 304**
Very broad wings (well curved on rear edge); short tail, long head/neck. **16a. Juv.** White on primaries and upper breast; black-banded tail. **16b. Adult.**

17 AFRICAN CROWNED EAGLE *Stephanoaetus coronatus*   **Page 308**
Relatively short, broad wings and long tail, both boldly banded. **17a. Juv.** Whitish body, buff or pale rufous-buff wing-linings. **17b. Adult female.** Chestnut forewing; mid-wing band of black blotches; breast barred buff and black. (Male often barred white and black on breast.)

18 MARTIAL EAGLE *Polemaetus bellicosus*   **Page 309**
Long, broad wings and short tail. **18a. Adult.** Dark wings (unlike Black-chested Snake Eagle). **18b. Juv.** (Body gradually darkens with age.)

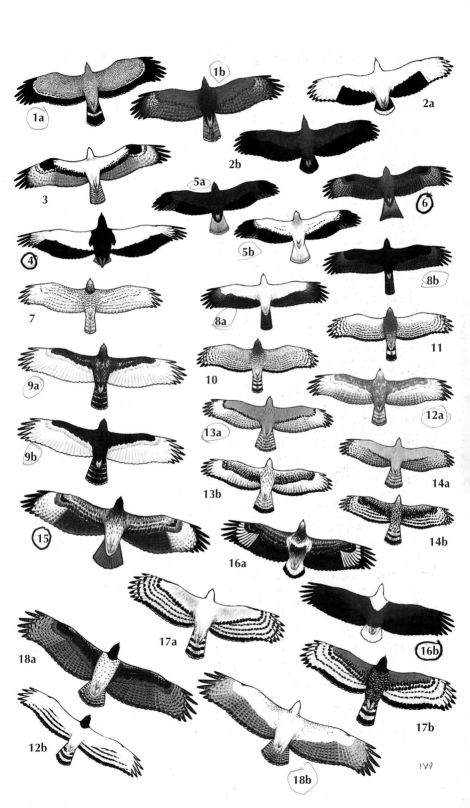

PLATE 35: EAGLES, BUZZARDS, AND OTHER RAPTORS IN FLIGHT
(See plates of perched birds for status and habitat notations)

1 VERREAUX'S EAGLE *Aquila verreauxii*   **Page 307**
Wings very narrow basally. **1a. Adult.** Black, with white rump and primary patches and white lines on back. **1b. Juvenile.** Pale upper tail-coverts and primary patches; rufous nape, cream crown.

2 GREATER SPOTTED EAGLE *Aquila clanga*   **Page 305**
2a. Pale juv. (rare). Whitish mid-wing line, pale primary panel and rump/tail-coverts; fulvous-buff forewing and body. **2b. Adult.** Very dark, with pale area on primary bases and upper tail-coverts. **2c. Dark juv.** White upper tail-coverts; pale spots on wing-coverts and back.

3 STEPPE EAGLE *Aquila nipalensis orientalis*   **Page 306**
3a. Juvenile. From 6a by dull earth-brown body and wing-coverts, wider, brighter rear edges to secondaries and tail in fresh plumage, and brighter white primary patch; rump dark. **3b. Adult.** Pale back mark, tawny nape (usually), whitish primary patch; flight feathers and tail sometimes barred.

4 LESSER SPOTTED EAGLE *Aquila p. pomarina*   **Page 305**
Slimmer wings and longer tail than Greater Spotted Eagle. **4a. Adult.** Dull brown, palest on smaller wing-coverts, with white inner primary flash and U on tail-coverts. **4b. Juv.** Warm brown wing-coverts and body; outer median coverts tipped with white; white patches on back, tail-coverts and primaries.

5 IMPERIAL EAGLE *Aquila heliaca*   **Page 306**
Proportions as in Steppe and Tawny Eagles. **5a. Adult.** Large cream nape patch, grey tail with black tip, white lines on back. **5b. Juv.** Probably inseparable from 2a at distance except for proportions, although buff rather than fulvous-buff hue on body and wing-coverts.

6 TAWNY EAGLE *Aquila r. rapax*   **Page 306**
Proportioned like Steppe Eagle. **6a. Juv.** Pale fulvous-brown body and wing-coverts in fresh plumage. **6b. Tawny adult.** Highly variable, depending on degree of wear and fading. Roughly streaked and mottled tawny and blackish brown. **6c. Imm.** Pale, worn and bleached individual.

7 COMMON (STEPPE) BUZZARD *Buteo buteo vulpinus*   **Page 303**
Wings and tail less attenuated than in Long-legged Buzzard. **7a. Brown juv.** Brown head/wing-coverts, pale greater-covert tips in fresh plumage, and finely barred grey-brown tail. **7b. Rufous adult.** Red-brown wing-coverts and head; orange-rufous tail may have terminal barring.

8 LONG-LEGGED BUZZARD *Buteo r. rufinus*   **Page 304**
More aquiline proportions than other *Buteo* spp. **8a. Pale adult.** Creamy brown wing-coverts merge with white of head and neck; pale rufous-orange tail almost white at base. **8b. Juv.** Dark barring on pale grey-brown tail. **8c. Dark adult.** Sooty head, body and wing-coverts, grey tail with broad black band at tip. Indistinguishable from dark morph of Common Buzzard.

9 AFRICAN FISH EAGLE *Haliaeetus vocifer*   **Page 304**
Adult. All-white tail, head and neck.

10 PALM-NUT VULTURE *Gypohierax angolensis*   **Page 305**
Adult. Distinctive wing and tail patterns, but sometimes confused with African Fish Eagle.

11 GRASSHOPPER BUZZARD *Butastur rufipennis*   **Page 303**
Slender; prominent rufous wing patches.

12 AFRICAN CUCKOO-HAWK *Aviceda cuculoides verreauxii*   **Page 293**
Cuckoo-like shape, grey head, boldly banded tail.

13 AFRICAN HARRIER-HAWK *Polyboroides t. typus*   **Page 298**
Broad black rear band and tips to wings; whitish band on mid-tail.

14 LONG-CRESTED EAGLE *Lophaetus occipitalis*   **Page 308**
Broad-tipped wings with striking white primary patches; bold tail bands.

15 BOOTED EAGLE *Hieraaetus pennatus*   **Page 308**
Buteo-like shape; flight feathers and tail wholly dark. **15a and 15b. Pale adults.** Cream middle wing-coverts and scapular patches and U on tail-coverts; small white 'headlights' at forewing bases (in all plumages.)

16 LIZARD BUZZARD *Kaupifalco m. monogrammicus*   **Page 303**
Stout and compact; white rear edge to secondaries, white tail-coverts and tail band.

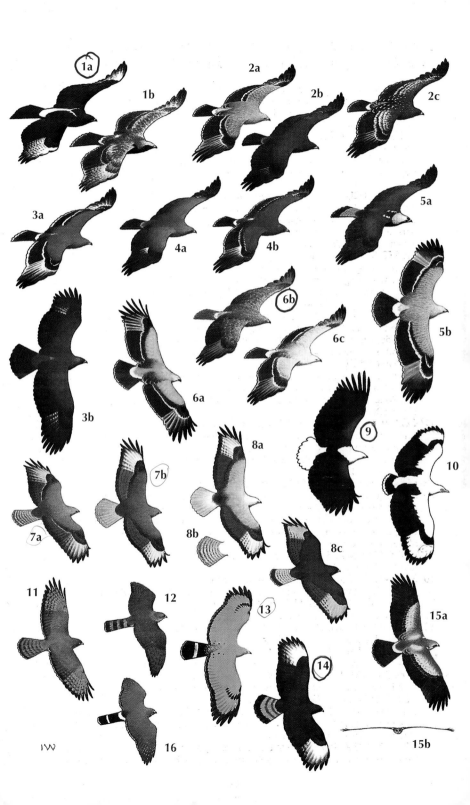

PLATE 36: FLYING SPARROWHAWKS, CHANTING GOSHAWKS, PYGMY FALCON AND HARRIERS (See plates of perched birds for status and habitat notations)

1 GREAT SPARROWHAWK *Accipiter m. melanoleucus*   **Page 303**
Typical adult white below, with blackish flank patches. (See Plate 44 for dark morph.)

2 AFRICAN GOSHAWK *Accipiter tachiro sparsimfasciatus*   **Page 300**
Heavily barred underparts. See text. **2a and 2b. Female**. (Male, Plate 42, blackish slate above.)

3 OVAMBO SPARROWHAWK *Accipiter ovampensis*   **Page 302**
Three white central spots in tail. See text.

4 SHIKRA *Accipiter badius sphenurus*   **Page 301**
Grey, with dark primary tips and plain-looking tail.

5 DARK CHANTING GOSHAWK *Melierax m. metabates*   **Page 300**
5a. Adult. Medium-dark grey, with barred upper tail-coverts. **5b. Juvenile**. Dull brown, with broadly barred upper tail-coverts.

6 LITTLE SPARROWHAWK *Accipiter m. minullus*   **Page 301**
Small; narrow white band on upper tail-coverts and two white tail spots.

7 PYGMY FALCON *Polihierax semitorquatus castanonotus*   **Page 309**
Female. Small. Rapid undulating flight; white wing spots, banded tail. (Male, Plate 46, has grey back.)

8 EASTERN PALE CHANTING GOSHAWK *Melierax poliopterus*   **Page 300**
8a. Adult. Pale grey, with unbarred white upper tail-coverts. **8b. Juvenile**. Brownish, with white-looking upper tail-coverts. (Varying degrees of dark barring do not cover the entire white patch as in 5b; see text.)

9 GABAR GOSHAWK *Micronisus gabar aequatorius*   **Page 300**
Small size; shape and actions sparrowhawk-like; white upper tail-coverts.

10 EURASIAN MARSH HARRIER *Circus a. aeruginosus*   **Page 299**
10a. Typical male. Three-toned wing pattern. **10b. Dark morph** (very rare). Black, except for grey tail and white areas under wings. **10c. Juvenile**. Cream crown and throat, pale bases of flight feathers below.

11 MONTAGU'S HARRIER *Circus pygargus*   **Page 299**
11a. Juvenile. Slim, with graceful, wavering flight. White upper tail-coverts; buff wing-covert patches; pale rufous-brown underparts (13a very similar). **11b. Adult male**. All outer primaries black; narrow blackish wing-bar.

12 AFRICAN MARSH HARRIER *Circus ranivorus*   **Page 299**
12a. Adult male. General brown tone relieved by barred flight and tail feathers, whitish on forewing. **12b. Juvenile**. Barred flight feathers and tail; cream breast band.

13 PALLID HARRIER *Circus macrourus*   **Page 299**
13a. Juvenile. Virtually identical to juv. Montagu's Harrier (11a). Close view reveals pale collar, often buffier underparts. **13b. Adult male**. Pale grey, with narrow black wedge at wing tips.

PLATE 37: FALCONS and KITES OVERHEAD (Adults except as indicated)

1 LANNER FALCON *Falco b. biarmicus*   **Page 309**
Large, with long wings and tail. **1a. Adult.** Pale, lightly spotted body and wing-linings. **1b. Juv.** Heavily blotch-streaked body; wing-linings dark.

2 PEREGRINE FALCON *Falco peregrinus minor*   **Page 310**
More compact than Lanner. (For migrant *F. p. calidus*, see text.) **2a. Adult.** Broad black 'moustache'; finely barred body and wing-linings not contrasting with flight feathers. **2b. Juv.** Resembles adult, except for bold streaks on rustier body.

3 TAITA FALCON *Falco fasciinucha*   **Page 310**
Small, compact, short-tailed. Stiff shallow, 'parrot-like' wingbeats. White throat/cheeks shade into rufous body; wing-linings also rufous.

4 EURASIAN HOBBY *Falco s. subbuteo*   **Page 311**
Slim, elegant shape; dashing flight. Boldly streaked underparts, chestnut crissum (lacking in juv.).

5 BAT HAWK *Macheiramphus alcinus anderssoni*   **Page 294**
Crepuscular. Suggests dark, broad-winged falcon. Variable amount of white on throat, small white eye marks. (See plate 44 for juv.)

6 SOOTY FALCON *Falco concolor*   **Page 312**
Grey, with sooty wing tips and pale throat; no barring; tail tip wedge-shaped.

7 GREY KESTREL *Falco ardosiacus*   **Page 313**
Grey body and wing-linings as in Sooty Falcon, but flight feathers and tail finely barred.

8 DICKINSON'S KESTREL *Falco dickinsoni*   **Page 312**
Greyish-white head and upper tail-coverts, ladder-like tail pattern.

9 AFRICAN HOBBY *Falco cuvieri*   **Page 311**
Shape and flight style of Eurasian Hobby, but faintly streaked underparts and wing-linings deep rufous.

10 ELEONORA'S FALCON *Falco eleonorae*   **Page 312**
Rakish, with very elongated wings and tail. Dark wing-linings contrast with pale flight-feather bases and heavily streaked rufous body.

11 AMUR FALCON *Falco amurensis*   **Page 311**
Somewhat more compact than kestrels; usually gregarious. **11a. Male.** White wing-linings; otherwise like Red-footed Falcon. **11b. Female.** Pale body heavily blotched with black; white wing-linings finely spotted away from edge; crissum pale tawny buff.

12 RED-FOOTED FALCON *Falco vespertinus*   **Page 312**
Shape and flight action as in Amur Falcon. **12a. Male.** Blackish wing-linings show minimal contrast with dark grey flight feathers, tail and body; crissum chestnut. **12b. Female.** Rich buff wing-linings and body; flight feathers and tail barred.

13 RED-NECKED FALCON *Falco chiquera ruficollis*   **Page 311**
Finely barred body, wings and tail appear grey at a distance; throat white; tail tip broadly black-banded; rusty cap/nape. (For juv., see Plate 45.)

14 LESSER KESTREL *Falco naumanni*   **Page 313**
Lighter in build than Common Kestrel; tail tip often strongly wedge-shaped. **14a. Male.** White wings, lightly speckled pale buff body, dark primary tips; no moustachial marks. **14b. Female.** Virtually identical to Common Kestrel. See text.

15 COMMON KESTREL *Falco t. tinnunculus*   **Page 313**
Regularly hovers. (Resident race on Plate 46.) **15a. Male.** Black band at tip of pale tail; dark-streaked buff body and pale buff wing-linings; crown and cheeks grey, lightly streaked with brown. **15b. Female.** Tail wholly barred; body and wing-linings boldly streaked.

16 BLACK-SHOULDERED KITE *Elanus c. caeruleus*   **Page 294**
Habitually hovers. White underparts, with black primary tips and upper leading wing edges.

17 AFRICAN SWALLOW-TAILED KITE *Chelictinia riocourii*   **Page 294**
Tern-like, with black carpal patches. (Juv. has much shallower tail fork.)

18 FOX KESTREL *Falco alopex*   **Page 313**
Tawny-buff wing-linings and whitish flight feathers; finely barred tail.

19 GREATER KESTREL *Falco rupicoloides arthuri*   **Page 313**
Black-edged whitish under wing-surface, tawny body, bold tail barring.

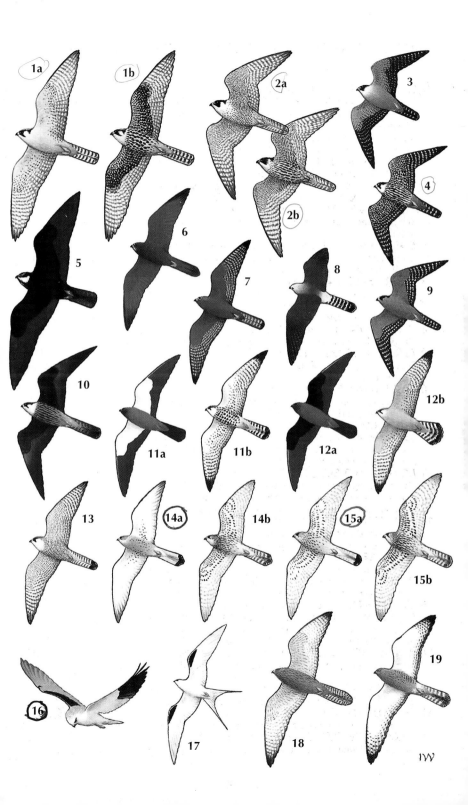

PLATE 38: *AQUILA* EAGLES (For flight figures, see Plates 32 and 35)

1 VERREAUX'S EAGLE *A. verreauxii* **Page 307**
Uncommon/scarce around rocky hills, gorges, mountains. **1a. Adult**. Coal-black plumage relieved by white lines on back. **1b. Juv.** Black from face to belly; rufous-buff on upperparts.

2 GREATER SPOTTED EAGLE *A. clanga* **Page 305**
Rare palearctic migrant, mainly near Rift Valley soda lakes. Like commoner Lesser Spotted Eagle, lacks 'baggy' leg feathering typical of larger *Aquila* spp. **2a. Typical adult**. Dusky brown, with pale under tail-coverts. **2b. Typical juv.** Blackish brown; whitish spots most evident on wing-coverts; buff-streaked breast. **2c. Pale juv.** (rare). Similar to Tawny Eagle, but with white rear edges on greater wing-coverts and secondaries. See text.

3 IMPERIAL EAGLE *A. heliaca* **Page 306**
Scarce palearctic migrant, Nov.–March. **3a. Adult**. Pale 'mane', white 'braces', black-tipped grey tail. **3b. Juv.** Buff-streaked body, plain buff head and leg feathering.

4 LESSER SPOTTED EAGLE *A. p. pomarina* **Page 305**
Regular palearctic migrant, Nov.–early Dec.; a few remain to March in Rift Valley and nearby highlands, mainly in savanna, open woods and farmland. At close range nostrils seen as circular, not oval as in Tawny and Steppe Eagles; yellow gape skin extends to below middle of eye. **4a. Juv.** Warm brown, with white spots on greater (and sometimes median) wing-coverts; buff nape patch, faint streaks on body and leg feathers. **4b. Adult**. Dull brown; feathered tarsi narrow.

5 TAWNY EAGLE *A. r. rapax* **Page 306**
Common and widespread in open country. Solitary or in pairs. Yellow of gape extends to below middle of eye. Plumage variable; darker birds often scruffy. **5a. Dark adult**. Tawny-brown, varying from very dark to lighter ginger-brown; mixture of dark or dark-centred feathers typical. **5b. Juv.** (fresh plumage). Pale tawny, with narrow white wing bands. **5c. Pale adult**. Pale buff to whitish blond. Whitish upper tail-coverts but no white on wings. (Bleached and worn juveniles and subadults similar.)

6 STEPPE EAGLE *A. nipalensis orientalis* **Page 306**
Common palearctic migrant in interior highlands and open plateau country, often in small to large groups. Yellow skin of gape extends to below rear edge of eye (unique among *Aquila*). **6a. Adult**. Dark brown; barred secondaries evident only at close range. **6b. Juv.** Medium brown; greater wing-coverts and secondaries edged with broad white bands.

7 WAHLBERG'S EAGLE *A. wahlbergi* **Page 307**
Most numerous Aug.–April. Widespread in dry wooded, bushed or cultivated country. Little larger than Black Kite, from which distinguished by short crest (often difficult to see) and long feathered tarsi. **7a. Paler adult**. Medium-brown body contrasts with black flight feathers and tail. (See Plate 34 for rare pale extreme.) **7b. Typical dark adult**. Uniform dark brown.

PLATE 39: BUZZARDS, HONEY BUZZARD, OSPREY AND EAGLES

1 COMMON (STEPPE) BUZZARD *Buteo buteo vulpinus*   **Page 303**
Fairly common palearctic migrant, Oct.–Nov. and March; some winter, mainly in lightly
wooded country. Variable. (See also Plates 33, 35 and 44.) **1a. Rufous adult**. White breast
band barred; pale pinkish-rufous tail plain or barred, with broader subterminal band.
1b. Rufous juvenile. Streaked breast; all tail bars narrow; pale-edged greater coverts.

2 MOUNTAIN BUZZARD *Buteo oreophilus*   **Page 304**
Resident of montane forest, adjacent moorlands and fields. Little plumage variation.
Highly vocal, unlike Common Buzzard. **2a. Adult**. Heavily blotched/spotted underparts;
wide subterminal tail band. **2b. Juv**. Buffier below, with fewer spots than adult; finer tibial barring; tail bars equal.

3 AUGUR BUZZARD *Buteo a. augur*   **Page 304**
Common and widespread in highlands. Bulky, with very short tail, especially adult. (For
dark morph, see Plate 44.) **3a. Light adult**. Black above, pure white below, with rufous
tail (often a narrow black subterminal band); secondaries barred. **3b. Light juv**. Brown
above, with pale-edged feathers; dull brown or red-brown tail longer than in adult,
barred and with wider subterminal band.

4 LONG-LEGGED BUZZARD *Buteo r. rufinus*   **Page 304**
Rare palearctic migrant in open country. Aquiline size and proportions. **4a. Adult**. Pale
head, dusky belly and leg feathers; plain tail very pale rufous to whitish orange. **4b. Juv**.
Streaked below, with dull, barred tail; head, body and wing-coverts paler than on young
Common Buzzard.

5 OSPREY *Pandion h. haliaetus*   **Page 293**
Palearctic migrant along large lakes, estuaries, coastal creeks. Perches in open, plunges
for fish. Black facial mask on white head; bushy crest.

6 EURASIAN HONEY BUZZARD *Pernis apivorus*   **Page 294**
Uncommon palearctic migrant in wooded areas, Oct.–April. Sluggish, soars on flat, not
upward-angled wings; small head. Adult yellow-eyed; 3 bands on tail. **6a. Typical adult**.
Heavily barred below. **6b. Rufous/cinnamon adult**. Pale-barred below. **6c. Pale juv**.
Black eye patch on white head; dark-eyed; dark-streaked underparts, 4 tail bands.

7 AFRICAN CROWNED EAGLE *Stephanoaetus coronatus*   **Page 308**
Uncommon in montane forest and woodland. Large, with short erectile crest. **7a. Adult**.
Banded/mottled underparts, pale yellow eyes, bright yellow cere and toes. **7b. Juv**. Pale
buff or whitish head and underparts, banded tail, black-spotted leg and tarsal feathers;
grey eyes, light yellow toes.

8 MARTIAL EAGLE *Polemaetus bellicosus*   **Page 309**
Widespread in open country. Impressive, crested, large-footed. **8a. Adult**. Dark grey-
brown hood, spotted underparts; blue-grey cere and toes. **8b. Juv**. White face, underparts
and tarsi; brown eye, whitish or grey cere and toes.

PLATE 40: SNAKE EAGLES, FISH EAGLE AND BATELEUR (For flight figures see Plates 32, 34 and 35)

1 SHORT-TOED SNAKE EAGLE *Circaetus gallicus*   **Page 297**
Bulky head, owl-like yellow eyes. *C. g. gallicus* a vagrant; western *C. g. beaudouini* of uncertain status. **1a. *C. g. gallicus*, typical adult**. Breast streaked grey-brown; short crescentic bars on white belly. **1b. *C. g. gallicus*, adult (dark-hooded form)**. Heavily marked below; dark head and breast. **1c. *C. g. beaudouini*, imm.** Buffy white head and underparts; separation from post-juvenile Black-chested Snake Eagle difficult (see text). **1d. *C. g. beaudouini*, adult**. Darker than 1a, with narrow barring below.

2 BROWN SNAKE EAGLE *Circaetus cinereus*   **Page 297**
Fairly common in bush, savanna, open country with baobab trees. Upright posture, owl-like head, bright yellow eyes. **2a. Adult**. Sooty brown, with banded tail, yellow eyes and bare whitish tarsi. **2b. Juv.** Usually shows whitish markings on underparts and face.

3 BLACK-CHESTED SNAKE EAGLE *Circaetus pectoralis*   **Page 297**
Thinly distributed in open or lightly wooded country. **3a. Adult**. Sharp separation between dark and light areas below. **3b. Juv.** Mottled rufous and white underparts (and possibly rufous on face), scaly-patterned wing-coverts, plain grey tail.

4 BANDED SNAKE EAGLE *Circaetus cinerascens*   **Page 298**
Scarce and local in riverine or moist woodland. Stocky; similar to No. 5, but tail shorter and differently patterned. Brown extends from throat to lower breast, barring restricted to lower belly; single white tail band. (Juv. resembles 5b, but tail as adult.)

5 SOUTHERN BANDED SNAKE EAGLE *Circaetus fasciolatus*   **Page 297**
Coastal and near-coastal forests; uncommon. **5a. Adult.** White barring up to chest; banded grey and dark brown tail shows two or three white bands below. **5b. Juv.** Pale-mottled head and breast (some almost whitish-headed); belly white; tail as adult.

6 AFRICAN FISH EAGLE *Haliaeetus vocifer*   **Page 304**
Widespread along coastal and fresh waters. Wing tips project well beyond short tail. **6a. Adult.** White head, back, bib and tail. **6b. Juv.** Whitish-mottled head and leg feathers; black eye-line.

7 BATELEUR *Terathopius ecaudatus*   **Page 298**
Widespread in dry bush and grassland. Extremely short tail. **7a. Juv.** Grey face, buff head contrasting with blackish-brown body; tail longer than adult's. **7b. Adult female (cream-backed morph)**. Partly grey secondaries and pale grey forewing; feet project beyond chestnut tail. See flight figure below. **7c. Adult male (rufous-backed morph)**. All-black secondaries (grey-centred in female), red face and feet, pale grey forewing.

Female Bateleurs

PLATE 41: CHANTING GOSHAWKS, *HIERAAETUS* AND GREAT SPARROWHAWK (See also Plates 33, 36 and 42)

1 DARK CHANTING GOSHAWK *Melierax m. metabates*   **Page 300**
Northwestern Kenya and Mara/Serengeti; fairly common.**1a. Juv.** Wholly dark-barred upper tail-coverts only safe way to separate from 2a, but these usually concealed in perched bird. Breast sometimes slightly mottled or plain grey-brown, but see comments under 2a.; no white greater-covert tips. **1b. Adult.** Red or coral-pink cere instantly separates from 2b. Tarsi usually pinkish red; grey wing-coverts and back washed with brownish; upper and under tail-coverts barred.

2 EASTERN PALE CHANTING GOSHAWK *Melierax poliopterus*   **Page 300**
Common in dry country north, east and south of the Kenyan highlands, in and (mainly) east of the Rift Valley; west of Rift only on Loita Plains. Nowhere alongside Dark Chanting Goshawk. Tarsi longer than in that species. **2a. Juv.** Plumage often identical to 1a, except for less barred (and white appearing) upper tail-coverts, (always?) white-tipped greater coverts in fresh plumage, and finer, fainter, more widely spaced dark under- tail-covert barring. Breast streaking and mottling equally variable in young birds of both species. **2b. Adult.** Readily distinguished from 1b by yellow cere and longer, typically orange-red tarsi; upper tail-coverts white or occasionally partly barred; under tail-coverts plain white; darker 'saddle' on back contrasts with pure grey wing-coverts; greater coverts white-tipped (unless worn).

3 BOOTED EAGLE *Hieraaetus pennatus*   **Page 308**
Uncommon palearctic migrant, Oct.–April, mainly in dry woodland and bush. Buzzard-sized, with striking pale wing-coverts and scapular patches and smoky mask. **3a. Rufous adult.** Dull cinnamon/rufous head and underparts. **3b. Light adult.** White or off-white underparts, variably dark-streaked. (For dark morph, see Plate 44.)

4 AYRES'S HAWK-EAGLE *Hieraaetus ayresii*   **Page 308**
Scarce and local in moister, more wooded habitats than African Hawk-Eagle. Stocky and long-legged. **4a and 4b. Adults.** (Males may be more white-faced than shown, and females entirely black-headed except for white throat.) All-dark wings, densely black-blotched underparts and leg feathers. Tail pattern as in 5b. **4c. Juv.** Buff or pale rufous underparts (may be very narrowly dark-streaked) and face; pale scaly upperparts.

5 AFRICAN HAWK-EAGLE *Hieraaetus spilogaster*   **Page 307**
Uncommon and local in open woodland and scrub, usually in drier areas. More attenuated, lankier appearance than Ayres's Hawk-Eagle. **5a. Juv.** Rich rufous with dark streaks below; wings and back plain dark brown, as cheeks; lacks pale eyebrow of juv. Ayres's. **5b and 5c. Adults.** Silvery grey secondary bases; plain white underparts (including leg feathers), not splotched as in Ayres's. In flight, whitish primary panel and broad black rear border to pale grey (dark-barred) secondaries.

6 GREAT SPARROWHAWK *Accipiter m. melanoleucus*   **Page 303**
Widespread in forest, woodland, wooded suburbs. Largest accipiter. **6a. Typical adult.** (For dark morph, see Plate 44.) **6b. Rufous-breasted juv.** Cinnamon-rufous underparts dark-streaked down to belly, streaks heaviest across breast. Similar to juv. Ayres's Hawk-Eagle in same habitat, except for dense streaking. **6c. White-breasted juv.** White ground-colour only difference from 6b.

PLATE 42: ACCIPITERS (See also Plates 33, 36, 41 and 44)

1 LITTLE SPARROWHAWK *Accipiter m. minullus*   **Page 301**
Local and uncommon in woodland. Very small and compact, especially male. **1a. Adult female**. Dark grey above, with two white central tail spots and white upper tail-coverts. **1b. Juv. female**. Narrow white band on upper tail-coverts; 2–3 white spots on central tail; heavy dark spotting and barring below.

2 SHIKRA *A. badius sphenurus*   **Page 301**
Uncommon but widespread in dry country. **2a. Adult male**. Faintly barred with pinkish rufous below, except for unmarked white leg feathering; closed tail plain grey; eyes red. **2b. Juv.** Breast heavily spotted, rest of underparts barred with brown; dark central throat stripe. **2c. Adult female**. Darker subterminal tail band than in male; eyes orange.

3 OVAMBO SPARROWHAWK *A. ovampensis*   **Page 302**
Rare in woodland; few confirmed records. Long, slender and small-headed. In very close view, long, slender middle toe diagnostic. **3a. Typical adult**. Grey barring extends onto throat and chin. (Other adult accipiters are white-throated.) White shaft marks between dark bands on upper tail-surface. (For dark morph, see Plate 44.) **3b. Rufous-breasted juv.** Broad white superciliary stripe, finely streaked breast. **3c. Light-breasted juv.**

4 RUFOUS-BREASTED SPARROWHAWK *A. r. rufiventris*   **Page 302**
Widespread in montane forest and plantations; shy, unobtrusive. **4a. Adult**. Bright rusty underparts and cheeks; white throat; slaty-black upperparts, with dark-capped appearance. **4b. Juv.** Well marked with dull rufous below; leg feathers plain.

5 GABAR GOSHAWK *Micronisus gabar aequatorius*   **Page 300**
Widespread in woodland and bush. White upper tail-coverts (all ages). **5a. Juv.** Streaked breast, rest of underparts barred; no pale superciliary stripe; white rear border on secondaries. **5b. Adult**. Red cere, tarsi and toes; grey hood. (Dark morph on Plate 44.)

6 LEVANT SPARROWHAWK *A. brevipes*   **Page 301**
Rare palearctic migrant in bush or open savanna. **6a. Adult male**. Pure dove-grey above, including cheeks (cf. 7b); resembles large Shikra, with similar red eyes and rufous-pink barring, but leg feathers also barred and often rufous wash on breast. **6b. Adult female**. Larger and browner than male, with stronger barring; narrow dark central throat stripe. **6c. Juv.** Rows of large blackish-brown spots and black central throat stripe.

7 EURASIAN SPARROWHAWK *A. n. nisus*   **Page 302**
Scarce palearctic migrant in wooded or bushed country. Conspicuous white superciliary stripe in female and juv. Adults yellow-eyed (unlike Levant Sparrowhawk). **7a. Adult female**. Dark grey or grey-brown above, including cheeks; white throat; dark brown barring below. **7b. Adult male**. Dark slate-grey above, chestnut barring on cheeks and underparts. **7c. Juv. female**. Browner than adult female, with narrower, more jagged barring on underparts (including leg feathers).

8 AFRICAN GOSHAWK *A. tachiro sparsimfasciatus*   **Page 300**
Widespread in wooded areas, including Nairobi suburbs. **8a. Juv. female** (male smaller). White superciliary stripes; blackish lines of spots on underparts, except for barred leg feathering. **8b. Adult male**. Slaty black above, including cheeks, which contrast with white throat; chestnut barring below. (Female is larger, sometimes greatly so; browner above and with coarser brown barring below.)

9 GREAT SPARROWHAWK *A. m. melanoleucus*   **Page 303**
Large size. **Typical adult** shown. (For other plumages, see Plates 41 and 44.)

PLATE 43: CUCKOO-HAWK, KITES, HARRIERS, AND GRASS-HOPPER AND LIZARD BUZZARDS (For flight figures, see Plates 33–37)

1 AFRICAN CUCKOO-HAWK *Aviceda cuculoides verreauxii* **Page 293**
Uncommon in wooded areas. Shy, retiring. Crested; long wings (tips reach end of tail); adult suggests large Eurasian Cuckoo. **1a. Juv.** Short whitish superciliary stripe; sometimes sparsely spotted/blotched underparts. **1b. Adult male.** Grey breast sharply demarcated from boldly rufous-barred belly and flanks. (Female larger, browner, with broader paler barring.)

2 AFRICAN SWALLOW-TAILED KITE *Chelictinia riocourii* **Page 294**
Local and uncommon; mainly northern; a few near Longonot in cent. Rift Valley. **Adult** figured. (Juv. has much shorter tail and rufous-edged feathers on back and wings.)

3 GRASSHOPPER BUZZARD *Butastur rufipennis* **Page 303**
Intra-African migrant in eastern bush country, Nov.–March. Shape suggests both *Buteo* and harrier. Rufous wing patches distinctive. **3a. Adult.** Dark-streaked pale tawny underparts, dark throat stripe, yellow eyes. **3b. Juv.** Faint throat stripe, dark moustache on tawny-buff head; pale rufous feather edging above, tail plain apart from dark terminal band; brown eyes.

4 AFRICAN MARSH HARRIER *Circus ranivorus* **Page 299**
Local and uncommon, mainly in wet highland areas. See No. 7. **4a. Adult.** Cream/buff 'frosting' on face, breast, leading wing edge; no grey in wings, and barred brown tail. **4b. Juv.** Buff patch on nape and throat, ragged band across breast and wing edge; buff speckling on coverts and back.

5 BLACK-SHOULDERED KITE *Elanus c. caeruleus* **Page 294**
Widespread in open areas. Short-tailed, large-headed. **5a. Juv.** Cinnamon wash on breast; white-edged feathers above. **5b. Adult.** Pale grey above; black epaulettes.

6 LIZARD BUZZARD *Kaupifalco m. monogrammicus* **Page 303**
Fairly common in coastal lowlands, where conspicuous on roadside poles, wires; scarce elsewhere. Stocky; black central throat stripe, red cere and tarsi. (Juv. similar.)

7 EURASIAN MARSH HARRIER *Circus a. aeruginosus* **Page 299**
Fairly common, Oct.–April, in wetlands, moist grassland. Long-legged and long-tailed. **7a. Adult male.** Plain grey tail and wing patch; more buff on head and breast than African Marsh Harrier. **7b. Juv.** Creamy white crown and throat, sometimes all-dark head. (Female similar, but usually with cream-edged forewing and yellowish buff breast patch.)

8 BLACK KITE *Milvus m. migrans* **Page 295**
Adult nominate *migrans*, present Oct.–March. Black bill contrasts with yellow cere; black-streaked head and neck greyer than in resident *parasitus* or migrant *aegyptius*, both yellow-billed. (*M. m. parasitus* on Plate 44.)

9 AFRICAN HARRIER-HAWK *Polyboroides t. typus* **Page 298**
Uncommon but widespread in wooded areas, including Nairobi suburbs. Bare face, small head, shaggy 'mane,' long legs and long tail. **9a. Dark juv.** Chocolate-brown, with pale face; paler feather edges form large patch on wing-coverts. **9b. Pale juv.** Large pale wing patch; mottled/streaked head and underparts. **9c. Non-breeding adult.** Yellow face; black spots above, white band across tail. **9d. Breeding adult.** Bare face flushes red or pink with excitement.

10 PALLID HARRIER *Circus macrourus* **Page 299**
Locally fairly common, Oct.–early April, especially in se. Kenya, n. Tanzania. **10a. Adult female.** Darker face than 11a, giving a masked appearance; darker cap and eye-line, paler, broader collar. Usually inseparable from 11a. **10b. Juv.** Darker, more extensive dark facial areas, pale collar; underparts often paler and buffier than 11b.

11 MONTAGU'S HARRIER *Circus pygargus* **Page 299**
Locally common, Oct.–early April, in open high plateau areas, including agricultural lands. Brown 'ring-tailed' birds as shown here require care and close views to separate from 10a. (For males of both species, see Plate 36.) **11a. Adult female.** Black rear border of ear-coverts and whitish face; vague collar. **11b. Juv.** Face and collar similar to female; pale rufous-brown underparts with faint dark streaking.

PLATE 44: DARK-PLUMAGED RAPTORS (Adults, except as noted)

1 LONG-CRESTED EAGLE *Lophaetus occipitalis* **Page 308**
Widespread in wooded and cultivated country.

2 AUGUR BUZZARD *Buteo a. augur* **Page 304**
Dark morph. Locally common in highlands. Short, reddish tail, pale-barred secondaries.

3 BROWN SNAKE EAGLE *Circaetus cinereus* **Page 297**
Fairly common resident in bush, woodland. Large owl-like head, yellow eyes. (See Plate 40.)

4 BOOTED EAGLE *Hieraaetus pennatus* **Page 308**
Dark morph. Duller above than light morph (Plate 41); under tail-coverts may be darkly mottled or all dark.

5 AYRES'S HAWK-EAGLE *Hieraaetus ayresii* **Page 308**
Dark morph. This plumage not recorded in East Africa. Tail pattern as in light morph (Plates 34 and 41); may show some white breast markings.

6 WAHLBERG'S EAGLE *Aquila wahlbergi* **Page 307**
Dark extreme. (For lighter plumage, see Plate 34.)

7 BLACK KITE *Milvus migrans parasitus* **Page 295**
Common, especially near water and human settlements. Forked tail. *M. m. aegyptius* also yellow-billed. (See Plate 43 for migrant nominate race.)

8 BAT HAWK *Macheiramphus alcinus anderssoni* **Page 294**
Uncommon and local in woodland, forest edge, villages. Crepuscular; roosts by day in leafy tree. Suggests bulky, broad-winged falcon in flight. **8a. Adult**. White throat and eye marks; short crest. **8b. Juvenile**. White or whitish on belly.

9 COMMON (STEPPE) BUZZARD *Buteo buteo vulpinus* **Page 303**
Dark morph. Mainly grey tail with broad black subterminal band.

10 AFRICAN GOSHAWK *Accipiter tachiro sparsimfasciatus* **Page 300**
Dark morph. Fairly common in wooded areas. Indistinct pale spots on tail; eyes yellow.

11 GABAR GOSHAWK *Micronisus gabar aequatorius* **Page 300**
Dark morph. Locally common in woodland and bush. Red bill base, legs and feet.

12 OVAMBO SPARROWHAWK *Accipiter ovampensis* **Page 302**
Dark morph. Rare and local in woodland and riparian trees. White arrowheads in centre of tail; red eyes.

13 GREAT SPARROWHAWK *Accipiter m. melanoleucus* **Page 303**
Dark morph. Rare in wooded areas. *Accipiter* shape, plain tail, white throat.

14 EURASIAN MARSH HARRIER *Circus a. aeruginosus* **Page 299**
Dark morph. Very rare. Typical harrier shape; pale grey tail.

15 EURASIAN HONEY BUZZARD *Pernis apivorus* **Page 294**
Dark morph. Uncommon in woodland, forest edge, Oct.–April. Black terminal and two narrower basal tail bands.

16 RED-FOOTED FALCON *Falco vespertinus* **Page 312**
Male. Palearctic vagrant. Orange-red bare parts.

17 ELEONORA'S FALCON *Falco eleonorae* **Page 312**
Male, dark morph. Scarce palearctic migrant. Larger, with more attenuated shape than Red-footed Falcon, and yellow bare parts.

PLATE 45: FALCONS (See also Plates 37 and 44)

1 LANNER FALCON *Falco biarmicus* **Page 309**
Commonest large falcon; widespread. Longer-tailed than Peregrine. **1a. F. b. abyssinicus,** **adult**. N. Kenya. Underparts streaked and barred. **1b. F. b. biarmicus, adult**. Cent./se. Kenya, n. Tanzania. Rufous crown/nape with black forecrown; pale buff below with sparse spotting; tail evenly barred. **1c. F. b. biarmicus, juv.** Tawny crown/nape, heavily streaked below; plain tail.

2 BARBARY FALCON *Falco p. pelegrinoides* **Page 310**
Rare in rough arid country. **2a. Adult**. Fine barring below; dusky-tipped tail with indistinct barring. **2b. Juv.** Sandy crown, nape and underparts, finely streaked below; tail barred.

3 SAKER FALCON *Falco c. cherrug* **Page 310**
Rare palearctic migrant, mainly in Rift Valley, Oct.–March. Heavily built; often pale-headed, with white superciliary stripe. See text. **3a. Adult. 3b. Juv.** Densely streaked head and body, tail almost plain above.

4 PEREGRINE FALCON *Falco peregrinus minor* **Page 310**
Scarce resident of open country with cliffs and crags; also in Nairobi city centre. Pale migrant race *calidus* present Oct.–March. **4a. Adult**. Blackish crown/nape and broad moustachial marks; densely barred body. **4b. Juv.** Rusty-washed body heavily streaked; tail evenly buff-barred.

5 EURASIAN HOBBY *Falco s. subbuteo* **Page 311**
Palearctic migrant in open country, Oct.–Dec., March–May; some winter in highlands. **5a. Adult**. Black cap, narrow moustachial marks; rufous leg feathers and crissum. **5b. Juv.** Buff scaling on brown upperparts and crown; heavily streaked underparts, the leg feathers and crissum buffy white.

6 AFRICAN HOBBY *Falco cuvieri* **Page 311**
Uncommon in Lake Victoria basin and w. Kenyan highlands. Small, slender and dark. **6a. Adult**. Underparts deep rufous; upperparts darker than in Eurasian Hobby. **6b. Juv.** More heavily marked below than adult; upperparts browner.

7 TAITA FALCON *Falco fasciinucha* **Page 310**
Rare near cliffs and gorges, typically in dry areas. Chunky, rather short-tailed. **7a. Juv.** Pale feather edges above; more heavily streaked below than adult. **7b. Adult**. Rufous nape patches diagnostic; head pattern otherwise suggests Peregrine; upperparts plain slate-grey, rufous below with contrasting white throat.

8 RED-NECKED FALCON *Falco chiquera ruficollis* **Page 311**
Uncommon in coastal lowlands south of Mombasa; elsewhere, scarce in open country with palms. Kestrel-sized, finely barred above and with broad black tail band. **8a. Adult**. Bright rufous crown and nape; broad black-and-white barring below. **8b. Juv.** Head pattern blackish brown; dull rufous underparts barred with black.

9 ELEONORA'S FALCON *Falco eleonorae* **Page 312**
Palearctic migrant, scarce in autumn, rarer in spring, in woodland, bush and grassland, mainly in cent. Kenyan highlands; rare in n. Tanzania. Long primaries reach tip of long tail. **9a. Light adult**. Streaked rufous underparts contrast with white throat/cheeks. **9b. Juv.** Pale-edged feathers above, pale buff below with heavy streaking.

PLATE 46: SMALLER FALCONS (See also Plates 37 and 45)

1 FOX KESTREL *Falco alopex* **Page 313**
Northern Kenya; uncommon near cliffs in dry areas. Rich chestnut, streaked above and below; indistinctly marked tail.

2 GREATER KESTREL *Falco rupicoloides arthuri* **Page 313**
Cent. and s. Kenya, n. Tanzania; fairly common in savanna, grassland. Stocky, with large head; pale rufous throat; barred above, finely streaked pale cinnamon underparts. **2a. Juv.** Entirely streaked below, cinnamon tail bands, dark eyes. **2b. Adult.** Barred flanks, grey tail bands, pale eyes.

3 COMMON KESTREL *Falco tinnunculus* **Page 313**
F. t. tinnunculus a widespread palearctic migrant in open country and farmland. Rustier *rufescens* a resident of rocky hills in and near Rift Valley. **3a. F. t. tinnunculus, female.** Spotted/barred above; buff with dark streaks below. **3b. F. t. tinnunculus, male.** Grey head and banded tail; spotted back. **3c. F. t. rufescens, female.** Dark, heavily marked throughout. **3d. F. t. rufescens, male.** Darker than 3b, back heavily spotted, tail finely barred.

4 DICKINSON'S KESTREL *Falco dickinsoni* **Page 312**
Vagrant in Kenya; rare in n. Tanzania except on Pemba Island, where common in open wooded areas and palm groves. Small and stocky. **4a. Adult.** Slate-grey, large greyish white head, barred tail. Figure should show broad, bright yellow orbital ring. **4b. Juv.** Narrower, duskier tail barring, barred on flanks.

5 GREY KESTREL *Falco ardosiacus* **Page 313**
Local in Serengeti and w. Kenya, in savanna and bushed grassland. Wing tips fall short of tail tip. All grey, with yellow bill base, orbital skin and feet. Usually appears more robust than in illustration.

6 LESSER KESTREL *Falco naumanni* **Page 313**
Locally common palearctic migrant in open or wooded country, Oct.–May. **6a. Female.** Slighter build than Common Kestrel, with finer breast streaks, longer central tail feathers. **6b. Male.** Grey wing patch, no moustachial marks; lightly spotted underparts.

7 PYGMY FALCON *Polihierax semitorquatus castanonotus* **Page 309**
Fairly common in dry thorn-bush. Very small; white face, red feet. **7a. Juv. male.** Rusty-buff streaks below, scaly rufous edges above. (Juv. female is chestnut on back.) **7b. Adult female.** Chestnut back. **7c. Adult male.** All grey above.

8 RED-FOOTED FALCON *Falco vespertinus* **Page 312**
Palearctic vagrant in open country. **8a. Male.** Slate-grey, with chestnut crissum; red on bill and feet. **8b. Female.** Unmarked rusty buff crown and underparts. **8c. Juv.** Rufous crown, white collar, streaked underparts, barred black-and-cream tail.

9 SOOTY FALCON *Falco concolor* **Page 312**
Uncommon migrant in bush and grassland, late Oct.–Nov., sporadic March–early May. **9a. Adult.** Wings reach or extend slightly beyond tail tip (much shorter in Grey Kestrel); dark moustachial streaks contrast with pale chin. **9b. Juv.** Buffy yellow below with slate-grey streaks, these darkest (often dense) on breast; buff cheeks and throat, with dark moustachial streaks; blue-green orbital ring and cere.

10 AMUR FALCON *Falco amurensis* **Page 311**
Palearctic passage migrant in open country, Nov.–Dec., late March–early May. **10a. Male.** White wing-linings; somewhat paler than Red-footed Falcon. **10b. Female.** Heavily marked white underparts with barred leg feathers, warm buff crissum. **10c. Juv.** Dark grey crown, heavily streaked buff underparts; grey tail narrowly barred with black.

PLATE 47: PARROTS AND SANDGROUSE

1 GREY PARROT *Psittacus e. erithacus*   **Page 363**
Kakamega Forest. Virtually extirpated from Kenya.

2 AFRICAN ORANGE-BELLIED PARROT *Poicephalus r. rufiventris*   **Page 363**
Eastern. Widespread in dry bush and scrub below 1200 m, often near baobab trees.
2a. Male. 2b. Female.

3 FISCHER'S LOVEBIRD *Agapornis fischeri*   **Page 364**
Tanzania (locally common in Serengeti NP). Introduced or escaped birds at various sites
in Kenya. Feral coastal populations north to Mombasa.

4 HYBRID LOVEBIRD *Agapornis fischeri* X *A. personatus*   **Page 364**
Birds exhibiting various combinations of characters common in cent. Rift Valley and elsewhere.

5 YELLOW-COLLARED LOVEBIRD *Agapornis personatus*   **Page 364**
Mainly Tanzanian. Introduced/escaped birds at several Kenyan localities. Feral population around Mombasa.

6 RED-HEADED LOVEBIRD *Agapornis pullarius ugandae*   **Page 364**
Western Kenya, mainly near Ugandan border. Local and shy. Often in sorghum fields.

7 BROWN-HEADED PARROT *Poicephalus cryptoxanthus*   **Page 363**
Coastal. Locally common in coconut palms.

8 BROWN PARROT *Poicephalus meyeri saturatus*   **Page 363**
Mainly western. Locally common in savanna and open woodland. (Similar *P. m. matschiei* in Tanzania north to Tarangire NP and Lake Manyara.)

9 RED-FRONTED PARROT *Poicephalus gulielmi massaicus*   **Page 363**
Locally fairly common in highland juniper and *Podocarpus* forests.

10 LICHTENSTEIN'S SANDGROUSE *Pterocles lichtensteinii sukensis* **Page 358**
N. Kenya. Uncommon in open dry bush, especially stony areas with scattered acacias.
Crepuscular drinker, in pairs or small groups. **10a. Female. 10b. Male.**

11 FOUR-BANDED SANDGROUSE *Pterocles quadricinctus*   **Page 358**
Locally common in nw. Kenya, south to n. Kerio Valley and Laikipia Plateau, generally
in less arid country than Lichtenstein's. Mainly nocturnal; crepuscular drinker, in flocks.
In pairs or small groups during the day. **11a. Male 11b. Female**

12 BLACK-FACED SANDGROUSE *Pterocles decoratus*   **Page 357**
Locally common in dry bush and shrubby grassland below 1600 m. Flocks drink after
sunrise and before dusk, sometimes with No. 14. Usually in pairs during the day.
12a. Female. 12b. Male.

13 YELLOW-THROATED SANDGROUSE *Pterocles gutturalis saturatior* **Page 358**
Locally common on grassland in s. and sw. Kenya, south in Tanzania west of the Masai
Steppe. Diurnal drinker, in flocks. **13a. Female. 13b. Male.**

14 CHESTNUT-BELLIED SANDGROUSE *Pterocles exustus olivascens* **Page 357**
Widespread in dry bush and open country below 1500 m. Vocal, high-flying flocks go to
water after sunrise and before sunset. Often in pairs during the day. **14a. Female.
14b. Male.**

PLATE 48: *STREPTOPELIA* DOVES

1 LAUGHING DOVE *S. s. senegalensis*   **Page 362**
Common and widespread below 1800 m. Greyish blue wing-coverts; white confined to
tail corners (Juv. lacks band of spots on chest, entire breast is paler than in adult; head
more rufous.) **1a and 1b. Adults.**

2 EUROPEAN TURTLE DOVE *Streptopelia turtur*   **Page 362**
Casual in our region. Note black-and-white patch on side of neck, broad rufous margins
on wing-coverts. **2a and 2b. Adults.**

3 AFRICAN WHITE-WINGED DOVE *Streptopelia reichenowi*   **Page 362**
Restricted to Daua River in extreme ne. Kenya. **3a and 3b. Adults.**

4 DUSKY TURTLE DOVE *Streptopelia l. lugens*   **Page 362**
Locally common in highlands. Large black patch on side of neck. (Juv. paler and browner, with more extensive rufous feather edging.) **4a and 4b. Adults.**

5 RING-NECKED DOVE *Streptopelia capicola somalica*   **Page 362**
Common and widespread from sea level to 2000 m. Eyes almost black. This eastern race,
ranging west to Samburu GR, Lake Baringo, Kibwezi, Namanga and Arusha, is paler and
greyer than browner western *tropica*. (Juv. has much buff feather edging above.) **5a, 5b
and 5c. Adults.**

6 AFRICAN MOURNING DOVE *Streptopelia d. perspicillata*   **Page 361**
Common below 1400 m. Eyes yellow (may be pale creamy orange); bare orbital ring
orange-red. (*S. d. elegans* of ne. Kenya south to Malindi is paler, with white lower belly
and breast. Juveniles of both races brownish on crown and breast; eyes pale brown.)
6a, 6b and 6c. Adults.

7 RED-EYED DOVE *Streptopelia semitorquata*   **Page 361**
Widespread from sea level up to 3000 m. Eyes dark red, appearing black at a distance.
Tail tip pale grey, not white. (Juv. brown-eyed, with pale rufous feather edges above, and
obscure blackish band on nape.) **7a, 7b and 7c. Adults.**

African Mourning Dove

NDP

PLATE 49: PIGEONS AND DOVES (See also Plate 48)

1 BRUCE'S GREEN PIGEON *Treron waalia*   **Page 359**
Northern Kenyan border areas only. In village fig trees and savanna watercourses.
Greyish head, neck and breast, yellow belly, and yellowish feet.

2 AFRICAN GREEN PIGEON *Treron calva gibberifrons*   **Page 359**
Widespread in wooded areas. Favours fruiting fig trees. (Tail green in coastal *T. c. wakefieldi*, grey in other races. Pemba Green Pigeon on Plate 124.) Yellow-green head and
underparts; feet scarlet. **2a and 2b. Adults.**

3 FERAL PIGEON or ROCK DOVE *Columba livia*   **Page 361**
Common in towns and cities. Plumage variable. Blackish birds numerous in Nairobi and
Mombasa.

4 OLIVE PIGEON *Columba arquatrix*   **Page 360**
Widespread in highland forests above 1600 m. High-flying flocks make extensive daily
movements. **4a and 4b. Adults.**

5 SPECKLED PIGEON *Columba g. guinea*   **Page 361**
Locally common around cliffs and buildings (urban and rural). **5a and 5b. Adults.**

6 EASTERN BRONZE-NAPED PIGEON *Columba delagorguei sharpei* **Page 360**
Locally common in highland forests. Shy. Pairs or small flocks feed in forest canopy and
on ground. **6a. Female. 6b and 6c. Males.**

7 NAMAQUA DOVE *Oena c. capensis*   **Page 360**
Locally common in dry bush, scrub and cultivation, mainly below 1600 m. Solitary, or
in small groups at waterholes. **7a. Juvenile. 7b. Adult female. 7c and 7d. Adult males.**

8 EMERALD-SPOTTED WOOD DOVE *Turtur chalcospilos*   **Page 359**
Common and widespread in low, dry areas, including bush and coastal forest. **8a and 8b.
Adults.** Bill black in northern birds, dull red with black tip in those south of the Equator.

9 TAMBOURINE DOVE *Turtur tympanistria*   **Page 359**
Widespread. Locally fairly common in wooded habitats in high-rainfall areas. Solitary;
usually on ground, often in forest clearings or on footpaths. **9a. Female. 9b and 9c.
Males.**

10 LEMON DOVE *Aplopelia l. larvata*   **Page 361**
Uncommon in highland forests. Terrestrial; shy. **10a and 10b. Adults.**

11 BLUE-SPOTTED WOOD DOVE *Turtur afer*   **Page 360**
Western. Common in moist bush, woodland and forest edge. Favours more humid habitats than Emerald-spotted Wood-Dove. Darker than that species, and bill yellowish-
tipped.

PLATE 50: TURACOS

1 EASTERN GREY PLANTAIN-EATER *Crinifer zonurus*   **Page 366**
Western. Locally common in savanna and edges of cultivation. Large rounded head with shaggy nuchal crest; brown face. In flight, white band near tip of wing; long tail grey basally.
1a and 1b. All plumages.

2 WHITE-BELLIED GO-AWAY-BIRD *Criniferoides leucogaster*   **Page 366**
Fairly common and widespread in savanna, bush and woodland below 1500 m. Pointed crest; much white in wings and tail. In flight, white on primary bases, not near wing tip. Bill of **female (2a)** pea-green, that of **male (2b)** black.

3 BARE-FACED GO-AWAY-BIRD *Corythaixoides personata leopoldi* **Page 366**
Locally common in bushed and wooded grassland in Mara GR, Serengeti and Tarangire NPs. (*C. p. personata*, with more extensive green breast patch, a vagrant in extreme northern Kenya.) Black face contrasts with otherwise white neck, bushy crest arising from forehead. In flight, wings and tail plain greyish. **3a and 3b. Adults.**

4 GREAT BLUE TURACO *Corythaeola cristata*   **Page 364**
Scarce and local in a few w. Kenyan forests. Large size, black-tipped tail (basally yellowish below); no red in wings. **4a, 4b and 4c. Adults.**

5 ROSS'S TURACO *Musophaga rossae*   **Page 364**
Uncommon in western riverine forests and forest edge. Violet-blue with red crest and yellow bill; much red in wings. **5a and 5b. Adults.**

6 HARTLAUB'S TURACO *Tauraco hartlaubi*   **Page 365**
Common and widespread in highland forests. Dark bushy crest and white facial markings; much red in wings. **6a, 6b and 6c. Adults.**

7 PURPLE-CRESTED TURACO *Tauraco porphyreolophus chlorochlamys*
                                                                                Page 365
Rare and local in Thika and Machakos Districts in Kenya and Lake Manyara NP. Dark crest like Hartlaub's, but no white on face. Bill black; much red in wings. **7a and 7b. Adults.**

8 WHITE-CRESTED TURACO *Tauraco leucolophus*   **Page 366**
Uncommon and local in w. and nw. Kenya. Head largely white, bill yellowish; much red in wings.

9 SCHALOW'S TURACO *Tauraco schalowi*   **Page 365**
Uncommon to fairly common in riparian woodland in and near Mara GR and Serengeti NP, also in Tanzania's Crater and Mbulu highlands. Long pointed crest, dark red bill; much red in wings.

10 BLACK-BILLED TURACO *Tauraco schuetti emini*   **Page 365**
Scarce and local in w. Kenyan forests. Short green crest, small black bill; much red in wings.

11 FISCHER'S TURACO *Tauraco f. fischeri*   **Page 365**
Locally fairly common in coastal forests and dense woodland inland along the Tana River and in Usambara Mts. White-tipped reddish crest, bright red bill; much red in wings.

Dale A. Zimmerman
1986

PLATE 51: CUCKOOS (See also Plate 52)

1 KLAAS'S CUCKOO *Chrysococcyx klaas* **Page 370**
Common and widespread in woodland and forest edge. White outer tail feathers obvious in flight. **1a. Juvenile. 1b. Adult female. 1c. Adult male.**

2 DIEDERIK CUCKOO *Chrysococcyx caprius* **Page 370**
Common and widespread in dry woodland, savanna and bush. White spots on wings and on sides of tail. **2a. 'Rufous' juvenile. 2b. 'Green' juvenile.** (Some birds are intermediate between 2a and 2b.) **2c. Adult female. 2d. Adult male.**

3 AFRICAN EMERALD CUCKOO *Chrysococcyx c. cupreus* **Page 369**
Local in highland-forest canopy. Vocal, but seldom seen. **3a. Adult female.** Wings rufous-barred; white underparts barred with iridescent green. **3b. Juvenile.** Crown and nape barred. **3c. Adult male.** Brilliant green above, bright yellow lower breast and belly. **3d. Immature male.** Barred with white and iridescent green below.

4 MADAGASCAR LESSER CUCKOO *Cuculus rochii* **Page 369**
Present April–Sept. Nearly identical to No. 5. Under tail-coverts may be nearly plain, as shown, but often barred in centre and at tip, occasionally throughout. Flying bird, as in 5b, shows blackish upper tail-coverts contrasting with grey back (unlike Eurasian and African Cuckoos).

5 ASIAN LESSER CUCKOO *Cuculus poliocephalus* **Page 369**
Asian migrant, present Nov.–Dec. and March–April in coastal areas, some inland to Tsavo NP late Nov.–Dec. Winter records from West Usambara Mts. Buff under tail-coverts usually boldly barred with black. **5a and 5b. Adults.**

6 EURASIAN or COMMON CUCKOO *Cuculus c. canorus* **Page 368**
Widespread palearctic migrant, uncommon in autumn, numerous March–April. Bill blackish with yellow or greenish-yellow base. **6a. Female, rufous morph. 6b. Juvenile.** Usually plain grey rump/upper tail-coverts; crown incompletely barred. **6c. Adult male.** Limited yellow on bill base; outer rectrices incompletely barred. **6d. Adult female, grey morph.** Some rufous-brown on breast (may extend to hindneck and crown).

⑦ AFRICAN CUCKOO *Cuculus gularis* **Page 368**
Intra-African 'rains migrant.' Uncommon in savanna, bush and acacia woodlands. Bill mainly yellow, with black tip. **7a. Juvenile.** Barred rump/upper tail-coverts; crown barred throughout. **7b. Adult male.** Much bright yellow or orange-yellow on bill; tail bars complete. (Female shows rufous-brown on sides of breast, as in female Eurasian Cuckoo.) **7c. Adult female.** Grey upper tail-coverts as in Eurasian Cuckoo (not blackish as in No. 4 and No. 5).

8 BLACK CUCKOO *Cuculus clamosus* **Page 368**
Widespread and fairly common in woodland, savanna and forest edge. **8a. C. c. clamosus, juvenile.** Dull sooty brown throughout. **8b. C. c. clamosus, adult.** Glossy blue-black; may show faint buff bars on underparts. **8c. C. c. clamosus/gabonensis intergrade** ('jacksoni'). Western Kenyan forests.

⑨ RED-CHESTED CUCKOO *Cuculus s. solitarius* **Page 367**
Common and widespread in wooded areas and suburban gardens. Highly vocal before and during rains. **9a. Juvenile. 9b. Adult male.** Throat grey. Upper breast variable: russet with dark bars, as shown, or brighter rufous and unbarred. Many males similar to female (9c), but with grey throat. **9c. Adult female.** Throat whitish to pale buff. Upper breast never barred, usually pale in centre.

1a 1b 1c 2a 2b 2c 2d 3a 3b 3c 3d 4 5a 5b 6a 6b 6c 6d 7a 7b 7c 8a 8b 8c 9a 9b 9c

PRATT

PLATE 52: CUCKOOS AND COUCALS

1 BLACK AND WHITE or JACOBIN CUCKOO *Oxylophus jacobinus*   **Page 367**
Widespread 'rains migrant' in dry bush and thickets, mostly below 1500 m. **1a. O. j. serratus, dark morph**. Rare; migrant from s. Africa. (Light morph, uncommon in rainy season, April–Sept., similar to that of *O. j. pica*.) **1b. O. j. pica, light morph**. Fairly common migrant. Breeds in Rift Valley and in west (March–Aug.) and in se. Kenya (Nov.–Dec.).

2 LEVAILLANT'S CUCKOO *Oxylophus levaillantii*   **Page 367**
Uncommon intra-African migrant; few breeding records. Most numerous west of Rift Valley, May–Sept. Disjunct coastal population. **2a. Dark morph**. Large size; shows white in tail. Mainly coastal. **2b. Light morph**. Some individuals more heavily streaked than shown.

③ GREAT SPOTTED CUCKOO *Clamator glandarius*   **Page 367**
Uncommon in open wooded areas, savannas and cultivation. Most numerous Oct.–March. **3a. Adult**. (First-year birds have some black in crown and rufous in primaries.) **3b. Juvenile**. Rufous primaries evident in flight.

4 YELLOWBILL *Ceuthmochares a. aereus*   **Page 370**
Uncommon in forest thickets and tangles. Shy and secretive. Western race shown here is dark, with blue tail iridescence. Eastern *C. a. australis* is paler below, with green-glossed tail.

5 BARRED LONG-TAILED CUCKOO *Cercococcyx montanus patulus*   **Page 369**
Local in montane forests on e. Mt Kenya and s. Aberdares; common in Usambara Mts. Shy; seldom seen, but highly vocal Oct.–March. Vagrant to coastal forests.

6 THICK-BILLED CUCKOO *Pachycoccyx audeberti validus*   **Page 367**
Uncommon in coastal woods (especially *Brachystegia*). Perches in tall treetops; displays in flight above forest canopy. Hawk-like in flight. **6a. Adult. 6b. Juvenile**.

7 SENEGAL COUCAL *Centropus s. senegalensis*   **Page 371**
Locally common in thickets and sugarcane in w. Kenya, mainly near Ugandan border. Smaller than Blue-headed Coucal of wetter areas. **7a. Juvenile**. Dark-crowned, primaries plain except at tips. Tail blackish. **7b. Adult**. Black on head lacks blue gloss.

8 BLACK COUCAL *Centropus grillii*   **Page 371**
Widespread in moist and wet habitats. Smaller than other coucals. Seasonally dimorphic. **8a. Breeding adult. 8b. Non-breeding adult**. No superciliary stripe, strongly barred tail. (Grey-eyed juvenile similar.)

9 BLUE-HEADED COUCAL *Centropus monachus fischeri*   **Page 371**
Local in papyrus swamps, wet thickets and tea plantations. **9a. Adult**. Large. Resembles Senegal Coucal, but head glossed with blue. **9b. Juvenile**. Primaries barred throughout. Tail dark brown.

⑩ WHITE-BROWED COUCAL *Centropus s. superciliosus*   **Page 371**
The common coucal. Widespread in bush and moist thickets, often near water. Superciliary stripes in all plumages. **10a. Juvenile. 10b. Adult**. Crown dark brown in fresh plumage (black in darker race *loandae* of n. Tanzania and sw. Kenya).

1a

1b

2b

3a

3b

2a

4

5

7a

6a

8a

9a

6b

8b

7b

10a

9b

10b

DALE A. ZIMMERMAN
1995

PLATE 53: NIGHTJARS (See also Plate 54)

1 DONALDSON-SMITH'S NIGHTJAR *Caprimulgus donaldsoni*   **Page 377**
Common in dry e. and se. Kenya, west to Horr Valley and Lake Baringo; also Mkomazi GR and Masai steppe in n. Tanzania. Small size, small white tail corners; yellowish-edged scapulars. Short whistling song. **1a. Brown female. 1b and 1d. Grey-brown female. 1c and 1e. Rufous male.**

2 NUBIAN NIGHTJAR *Caprimulgus nubicus torridus*   **Page 378**
Fairly common in e. and se. Kenya, mainly Nov.–March. Most birds silvery grey and rufous. Not vocal in our region. **2a. Dark-tailed male. 2b. Grey-tailed male. 2c. Grey-tailed female.**

3 GABON NIGHTJAR, *Caprimulgus fossii welwitschii*   **Page 380**
Resident on Pemba Island; local non-breeding visitor in se. and coastal Kenya, also Serengeti/Mara region. Pale trailing secondary edges; central rectrices not extending beyond others. Churring song. **3a and 3c. Males.** Dark, with contrasting whitish wing bands and trailing edge, much like male Slender-tailed Nightjar, except for tail tip. **3b and 3d. Females.** Wings paler, less contrasting than in male, pale areas buff or cinnamon-buff (including patch on primaries).

4 SLENDER-TAILED NIGHTJAR *Caprimulgus clarus apatelius*   **Page 380**
Common and widespread in dry areas below 2000 m. Similar to Gabon Nightjar, but central rectrices extend slightly beyond the others, and tail often paler and greyer. Churring song. **4a and 4b. Males. 4c and 4d. Females.**

5 MONTANE NIGHTJAR *Caprimulgus p. poliocephalus*   **Page 377**
Common in highlands (including Nairobi suburbs). Generally dark, with prominent nuchal collar. Shrill whistling song. **5a, 5b and 5c. Males.** Broad white tail sides (usually concealed at rest). **5d. Female.** Somewhat browner, less dusky; reduced white in tail. (See Plate 123 for Tanzanian *C. p. guttifer.*)

6 AFRICAN WHITE-TAILED NIGHTJAR *Caprimulgus n. natalensis*   **Page 379**
Western Kenya. Uncommon in wet grassy swamp and forest edges. Buff, with dark sides of face. Stocky, rather short-tailed. Monotonous 'tocking' song. **6a and 6c. Males.** Tail sides broadly white (as in much darker Montane Nightjar). **6b and 6d. Females.** Tail narrowly buff-edged. Lacks wing-covert bands of darker Gabon Nightjar.

7 FIERY-NECKED NIGHTJAR *Caprimulgus pectoralis*   **Page 377**
7a and 7b. *C. p. nigriscapularis,* males. Local and uncommon in w. Kenyan forest remnants, moist thickets and riparian woods. Shrill whistling song. (Female has buff-tinged wing and tail spots.) **7c, 7d and 7e. *C. p. fervidus,* females.** Fairly common in wooded areas of coastal lowlands, inland along lower Tana River and in Shimba Hills. Richly coloured. (Male has brighter white wing patches, no buff in white tail corners.)

8 DUSKY NIGHTJAR *Caprimulgus fraenatus*   **Page 379**
Common and widespread in dry country (between 650 and 2000 m). Generally dark, with black and creamy-buff scapulars. Churring song. **8a and 8b. Females.** Greyer than male; tail corners dingy buffy grey. **8c and 8d. Males.** Blacker than female; lacks warm tones of Fiery-necked Nightjar. White tail spots larger than in Donaldson-Smith's Nightjar.

PLATE 54: NIGHTJARS (See also Plate 53)

1 PLAIN NIGHTJAR *Caprimulgus inornatus*   **Page 379**
Widespread in dry bush, mainly Oct.–April. Possibly breeds in nw. Kenya. Rather plain above; no white throat patch. Pale wing-bar; very large white tail corners in male. Silent in most of our region. **1a and 1b. Brown males. 1c and 1d. Rufous males. 1e. Brown female.**

2 EURASIAN NIGHTJAR *Caprimulgus europaeus*   **Page 380**
Widespread migrant in wooded and cultivated areas, Oct.–Nov. and March–April. Blackish 'shoulder', pale wing-bar; dark ear-coverts; no nuchal collar. Typically rests on tree branches. Silent in East Africa. **2a. *C. e. unwini*, female. 2b. *C. e. unwini*, male. 2c. *C. e. europaeus*, female.**

3 STAR-SPOTTED NIGHTJAR *Caprimulgus stellatus simplex*   **Page 378**
Locally common on lava-rock deserts in n. Kenya (south to Lake Baringo). Plain; much white on throat. Clear yelping *hweu* or *pew* call. **3a and 3b. Brown males. 3c. Rufous female. 3d. Rufous-and-grey female.**

4 FRECKLED NIGHTJAR *Caprimulgus t. tristigma*   **Page 378**
Local on rocky outcrops and escarpments. Dark plumage, finely marked above; no nuchal collar. Barking or yelping *ow-wow* call. **4a and 4b. Males. 4c and 4d. Females.**

5 STANDARD-WINGED NIGHTJAR *Macrodipteryx longipennis*   **Page 381**
Rare migrant in nw. Kenya, vagrant south to Lake Baringo. Possibly breeds in nw. border areas. Rarely vocal in our region. **5a. Breeding male. 5b, 5c and 5d. Females.** Darker and shorter-tailed than female Pennant-winged Nightjar.

6 PENNANT-WINGED NIGHTJAR *Macrodipteryx vexillarius*   **Page 381**
Locally common migrant in western areas, July–early Sept. and Jan.–Feb.; casual east to Nairobi. Flies immediately after sunset. Largely silent in our region. No white in tail in either sex. **6a and 6b. Breeding males. 6c, 6d and 6e. Females.** Long tail; wings long and pointed.

7 LONG-TAILED NIGHTJAR *Caprimulgus climacurus sclateri*   **Page 381**
Northwestern Kenya. Scarce and local in savanna and bush south to the Turkwell River. Birds moulting central rectrices resemble Slender-tailed Nightjars. Song a low rapid churring or purring. **7a and 7b. Brown females. 7c. Rufous male.** (Some individuals are more chestnut.)

PLATE 55: LARGER OWLS

1 BARN OWL *Tyto alba affinis* **Page 372**
Uncommon in and near towns, buildings, cliffs, kopjes. Pale, with white, heart-shaped face.

2 AFRICAN GRASS OWL *Tyto capensis* **Page 372**
Terrestrial. Scarce in highland marshes, grassland, moorlands. Dark-backed. Smaller buff wing patches than Marsh Owl, and no white trailing edge; white sides of tail show in flight; dark brown, unbarred central rectrices. **2a and 2b. Adults**. (Juvenile has darker facial disc.)

3 SHORT-EARED OWL *Asio f. flammeus* **Page 376**
Palearctic vagrant. Typically in open grassy marshes. Pale and heavily streaked; eyes yellow. **3a and 3b. Adults**.

4 MARSH OWL *Asio c. capensis* **Page 376**
Locally common in highland grassland. Large buff patch in primaries, pale trailing edge to secondaries; eyes dark. **4a and 4b. Adults**.

5 AFRICAN LONG-EARED OWL *Asio abyssinicus graueri* **Page 376**
Mt Kenya: rare in *Hagenia* forest and adjacent giant-heath zone. Slender; tawny face; 'ear-tufts' near centre of forehead.

6 AFRICAN WOOD OWL *Strix woodfordii nigricantior* **Page 376**
Widespread and fairly common in forest and woodland. Round-headed; dark eyes; barred underparts.

7 CAPE EAGLE-OWL *Bubo capensis mackinderi* **Page 374**
Uncommon to scarce and local near highland cliffs and ravines, on alpine peaks and moorlands (but sometimes nests in trees). Richly coloured with bold blotching on breast; yellow-orange eyes.

8 SPOTTED EAGLE-OWL *Bubo africanus* **Page 374**
Fairly common; widespread in varied habitats. Dull grey or brownish, with dark blotching on breast. **8a. *B. a. africanus***: w. and s. Kenya to n. Tanzania. Smaller, less richly coloured than Cape Eagle-Owl; eyes yellow. **8b. *B. a. cinerascens***: n. Kenya south to Kerio Valley, Baringo and Meru Districts. Eyes brown; smaller, more boldly marked than Verreaux's Eagle-Owl.

9 VERREAUX'S EAGLE-OWL *Bubo lacteus* **Page 374**
Common and widespread in wooded areas. Uniformly pale, except for black facial-disc margins. Dark eyes and pink eyelids conspicuous by day. 'Ear-tufts' often inconspicuous at night.

10 PEL'S FISHING OWL *Scotopelia peli* **Page 375**
Tana and Mara Rivers, rare and local in dense riparian trees. **Male**. Round head may appear smaller in resting bird. Markings variable. (Female and young are paler.)

DALE A. ZIMMERMAN
1994

PLATE 56: SMALLER OWLS

When active at night, the four scops owls usually compress their 'ear-tufts' and appear quite round-headed; they are shorter-tailed than the *Glaucidium species*.

1 SOKOKE SCOPS OWL *Otus ireneae*   **Page 373**
Locally common in Arabuko–Sokoke Forest and East Usambara foothills. Nocturnal.
1a. Rufous morph (some individuals much paler than shown). **1b. Brown morph.**
1c. Grey morph.

2 AFRICAN SCOPS OWL *Otus s. senegalensis*   **Page 373**
Common in savanna, bush, acacia scrub. Nocturnal. Similar to Eurasian Scops Owl, but slightly smaller and highly vocal. See text. **2a. Grey morph. 2b. Grey-brown morph.**

3 WHITE-FACED SCOPS OWL *Otus l. leucotis*   **Page 373**
Uncommon in dry-country acacia bush and woodland. **3a. Juvenile. 3b. Adult.**

4 EURASIAN SCOPS OWL *Otus s. scops*   **Page 373**
Scarce palearctic migrant. Silent in East Africa. See text. **4a. Rufous-brown morph.**
4b. Brownish grey morph.

5 AFRICAN BARRED OWLET *Glaucidium capense scheffleri*   **Page 375**
Uncommon in Kenyan coastal forest and woodland; scarce inland to Kibwezi and Iltalal; rare in n. Tanzania. Partly diurnal.

6 RED-CHESTED OWLET *Glaucidium tephronotum elgonense*   **Page 375**
Western Kenya. Uncommon in highland forest. Mainly nocturnal. Individuals vary in density of ventral spotting and in wing colour.

7 PEARL-SPOTTED OWLET *Glaucidium perlatum licua*   **Page 375**
Common in dry woodland, savanna, riparian trees, except in Lake Victoria basin and coastal lowlands. Often wags tail or pumps it up and down. Shows large 'eye spots' on back of head (see figure below). Partly diurnal; especially vocal at dusk.

Pearl-spotted Owlet (back view)

1a

2a

1b

2b

1c

3b

3a

4a

4b

5

6

7

DALE A. ZIMMERMAN
1993

PLATE 57: SWIFTS

1 LITTLE SWIFT *Apus a. affinis*   **Page 385**
Widespread. Common in towns and around buildings, bridges. Square-tipped tail; white rump patch extends to sides. **1a, 1b and 1c. Adults.**

2 MOTTLED SPINETAIL *Telacanthura ussheri stictilaema*   **Page 382**
Uncommon in eastern areas, especially in bush with baobab trees; local around se. Mt Kenya. Resembles Little Swift, but flight more fluttery and shows narrow white band across lower belly. **2a and 2b. Adults.**

3 HORUS SWIFT *Apus h. horus*   **Page 384**
Locally common, March–Sept., mainly in cent. Rift Valley and Arusha District. Absent Oct.–February. Shallow tail fork; outer rectrices not elongated as in White-rumped Swift. **3a and 3b. Adults.**

4 WHITE-RUMPED SWIFT *Apus caffer*   **Page 384**
Widespread (except n. and ne. Kenya), but uncommon. More slender, with narrower white rump band than Horus Swift; deeply forked tail often appears pointed. **4a and 4b. Adults.**

5 SCARCE SWIFT *Schoutedenapus m. myoptilus*   **Page 382**
Local, typically over highland forest, but also over adjacent plains. Slender, with pointed or long-forked tail; throat slightly paler than body. **5a and 5b. Adults.**

6 BÖHM'S SPINETAIL *Neafrapus boehmi sheppardi*   **Page 382**
Uncommon; eastern and coastal; often around baobab trees. Tiny; wings narrower near body; looks tailless; flight fluttery and bat-like. Sympatric in places with Mottled Spinetail. **6a and 6b. Adults.**

7 SABINE'S SPINETAIL *Rhaphidura sabini*   **Page 382**
Rare over and near Kakamega Forest and Mt Elgon, w. Kenya. Few recent records.

8 AFRICAN PALM SWIFT *Cypsiurus parvus laemostigma*   **Page 383**
Low-flying; common below 1400 m, typically around palm trees. Pale grey with grey throat; slender. **8a and 8b. Adults.**

9 FORBES-WATSON'S SWIFT *Apus berliozi bensoni*   **Page 384**
Coastal; scarce migrant, Oct.–Feb. In flocks. Large white throat patch and often whitish forehead. Resembles imm. Eurasian Swift. See text.

10 AFRICAN BLACK SWIFT *Apus barbatus roehli*   **Page 383**
Locally common in highland-forest areas, and ranges far over plains and bush. Resembles Eurasian Swift, but from above body darker than inner wing feathers. Breeds and roosts in trees, sometimes in cliffs. See text. **10a and 10b. Adults.**

11 ALPINE SWIFT *Apus melba africanus*   **Page 385**
High-flying; typically near major mountains, but also over distant open areas and the coast.

(12) MOTTLED SWIFT *Apus a. aequatorialis*   **Page 384**
Widespread, often with other swifts. Breeds in cliffs (e.g. in Hell's Gate NP), but ranges widely over open country. Large size, pale body, mottled underparts.

13 NYANZA SWIFT *Apus niansae*   **Page 383**
13a and 13b. A. n. niansae. Common to abundant in Rift Valley highlands. Breeds in cliffs (e.g. in Hell's Gate NP) and quarries. Browner than other swifts; body/inner-wing contrast as in darker African Black Swift. **13c. A. n. somalicus.** Collected once near Mt Kenya. Status uncertain. See text.

14 EURASIAN or COMMON SWIFT *Apus a. apus*   **Page 383**
Common in large flocks, autumn and spring; less numerous in winter. Lacks strong body/inner-wing contrast of Nos. 10 and 13. (Immature shows much whitish about the face, resembling Forbes-Watson's Swift. *A. a. pekinensis*, common near coast Nov.–Dec., is browner, less blackish; more like Nyanza Swift, but pale-faced.)

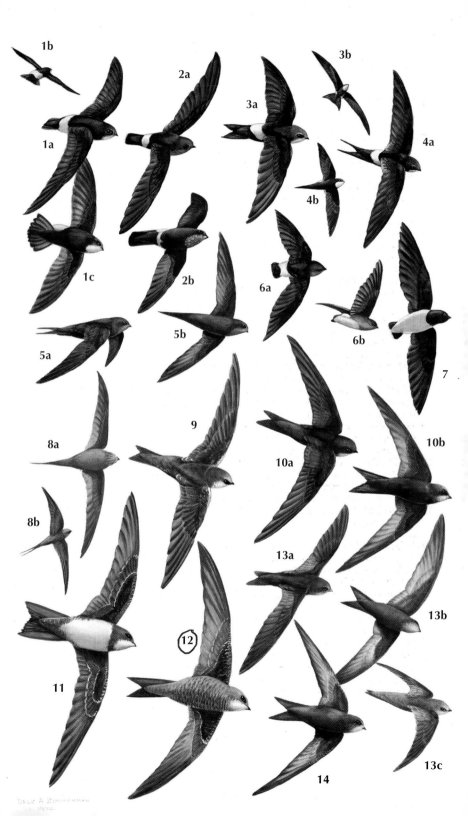

PLATE 58: MOUSEBIRDS AND TROGONS

1 BLUE-NAPED MOUSEBIRD *Urocolius macrourus pulcher*   **Page 386**
This and two similar races common and widespread in dry bush and thorn-scrub, usually in small groups. (Juvenile lacks blue nape, has pink facial skin and greenish bill.)

2 SPECKLED MOUSEBIRD *Colius striatus kikuyuensis*   **Page 385**
Common and widespread in various moist habitats, including towns and gardens, from
sea level to over 2500 m. Avoids arid regions. Eye colour variable. (Similar coastal race
mombassicus slightly paler and brown-eyed.)

3 WHITE-HEADED MOUSEBIRD *Colius leucocephalus turneri*   **Page 385**
Local in dry bush below 1400 m from Samburu and Shaba GRs northward. (Paler south-
ern nominate race uncommon in and near Amboseli and Tsavo West NPs and other
Kenyan/Tanzanian border areas.)

4 NARINA TROGON *Apaloderma n. narina*   **Page 386**
Uncommon in forest and rich woodland, mainly at lower elevations, but also on isolated mountains in n. Kenya. **4a and 4d. Males. 4b. Female. 4c. Immature.**

5 BAR-TAILED TROGON *Apaloderma vittatum*   **Page 386**
Uncommon in highland forest, mainly above 1600 m; overlaps with Narina Trogon in
Kakamega Forest and Arusha NP. **5a and 5c. Males. 5b. Female.**

Blue-naped Mousebirds

1

2

3

4a

4b

4c

5a

5b

5c

4d

DALE A. ZIMMERMAN
1994

PLATE 59: KINGFISHERS (Most juveniles have dusky or blackish bills and duller plumage)

1 SHINING-BLUE KINGFISHER *Alcedo quadribrachys guentheri*   **Page 388**
Vagrant, w. Kenya. Lustrous blue above, chestnut below; black bill.

2 HALF-COLLARED KINGFISHER *Alcedo semitorquata tephria*   **Page 388**
Wooded Tanzanian streams; casual in se. Kenya. Turquoise above, tawny below. Bill blackish.

3 AFRICAN PYGMY KINGFISHER *Ispidina p. picta*   **Page 389**
Widespread in forest, thickets, dense bush, often far from water. **3a. Adult**. Lilac on orange-rufous face. Bill red. **3b. Juv.** Black bill; hint of lilac ear-coverts.

4 MALACHITE KINGFISHER *Alcedo cristata galerita*   **Page 388**
Widespread. Fairly common near water. **4a. Adult**. Paler blue than Pygmy K. Floppy crest; no lilac. **4b. Juv.** Black-billed, face duller than in juv. Pygmy.

5 WOODLAND KINGFISHER *Halcyon s. senegalensis*   **Page 387**
Fairly common in western wooded areas. Black-and-red bill. (Migrant race *cyanoleuca* has black postocular mark and blue wash on crown.)

6 STRIPED KINGFISHER *Halcyon c. chelicuti*   **Page 388**
Fairly common in savanna, open woodland. Rump/tail flash blue in flight.

7 GREY-HEADED KINGFISHER *Halcyon l. leucocephala*   **Page 387**
Fairly common in wooded areas, often near water. (See text for other races.) **7a. Male**. Chestnut belly and crissum, red bill. **7b. Juv.** Chestnut lacking or reduced to wash on flanks. Bill blackish, sometimes dull reddish below.

8 MANGROVE KINGFISHER *Halcyon senegaloides*   **Page 388**
Coastal. Fairly common. Bill all red; back greyish blue; no buff on underparts; feet blackish.

9 BROWN-HOODED KINGFISHER *Halcyon albiventris orientalis*   **Page 387**
Common in woodland, savanna, forest edge, sometimes near water. This race mainly coastal. (*H. a. prentissgrayi*, interior e. Kenya and Tanzania, has darker, often unstreaked crown.) Bill red, dark brown at tip; feet reddish. (Female has sooty brown back.)

10 GIANT KINGFISHER *Megaceryle m. maxima*   **Page 389**
Uncommon on wooded rivers, streams and lakes. **10a. Male**. Breast chestnut; throat and wing-linings largely white. **10b. Female**. Upper breast slaty and white; rest of underparts and wing-linings chestnut.

11 PIED KINGFISHER *Ceryle r. rudis*   **Page 389**
Common on lakes, rivers, coastal estuaries. Often hovers. **11a. Male**. Two black breast bands. **11b and 11c. Females**. One breast band, often incomplete.

Blue-breasted Kingfisher Halcyon malimbica. *Vagrant in far-western Kenya.*
Large. Black-and-red bill; blue breast.

Dale A. Zimmerman
1987

PLATE 60: BEE-EATERS

1 BLUE-BREASTED BEE-EATER *Merops variegatus loringi*   **Page 392**
Uncommon and local in moist grassland, marshes, papyrus swamps near Lake Victoria.
Whitish cheeks below black mask; throat patch dark purplish blue. (Juvenile much like
juv. Little Bee-eater, but slightly larger.)

2 LITTLE BEE-EATER *Merops pusillus cyanostictus*   **Page 391**
Common and widespread. Black throat patch bordered with bright blue; no white on side
of face. **2a. Adult. 2b. Juvenile.**

3 CINNAMON-CHESTED BEE-EATER *Merops oreobates*   **Page 392**
Locally common in wooded highlands. Larger and darker than Nos. 1 and 2. **3a. Juvenile.**
Greener below than Little Bee-eater. **3b. Adult.** Underparts cinnamon-chestnut.

4 SOMALI BEE-EATER *Merops revoilii*   **Page 392**
Local in arid/semi-arid parts of n. and e. Kenya. Pale; lower back, rump and tail-coverts
bright cobalt-blue.

5 CARMINE BEE-EATER *Merops nubicus*   **Page 391**
5a. *M. n. nubicus*. Migrant from northern tropics, Sept.–March, common along coast and
locally inland in se. Kenya, scarce in Rift Valley. Some breed in far north. **5b. *M. n. nubicoides*.** Rare vagrant.

6 MADAGASCAR BEE-EATER *Merops s. superciliosus*   **Page 390**
Fairly common non-breeding migrant, May–Sept. Also breeds locally in coastal lowlands
(especially Lamu and Pemba Islands). Distinguished from No. 7 by duller green upperparts, dark olive-brown crown, white forehead, chin and cheek stripe. Superciliaries
white, yellow or blue; underside of wings ochreous. (Juv. short-tailed, with greenish
crown, cinnamon-buff throat, pale blue-tinged breast.)

7 BLUE-CHEEKED BEE-EATER *Merops p. persicus*   **Page 390**
Locally common palearctic migrant, late Oct.–early April, often along lake edges. Bright
green above. Whitish forehead merges with pale blue above eyes; cheeks usually pale
blue, but may be greenish or white; chin (and sometimes upper throat) yellow; underside
of wings cinnamon or coppery rufous. **7a and 7b. Adults.**

8 BLUE-HEADED BEE-EATER *Merops m. muelleri*   **Page 391**
Kakamega and South Nandi forests, w. Kenya; uncommon. (Juv. has little or no red on
chin.)

9 WHITE-THROATED BEE-EATER *Merops albicollis*   **Page 391**
Non-breeding migrant from northern tropics, Sept.–April. A few breed in extreme north
and near Lake Magadi in the south, April–May. **9a and 9b. Adults.** (Juv. has pale yellowish throat.)

10 EURASIAN BEE-EATER *Merops apiaster*   **Page 389**
Common and widespread palearctic migrant in autumn and March–April. Some winter.
10a and 10c. Spring males. (Female paler below, with greener scapulars.) **10b. Autumn
male** (Aug.–Oct.). Crown variably green-tinged.

11 WHITE-FRONTED BEE-EATER *Merops b. bullockoides*   **Page 391**
Locally common in cent. Kenyan Rift Valley, on lower slopes of Kilimanjaro and Mt
Meru. Local in Kerio Valley and n. Mara GR. **11a. Male.** (Female similar; juv. paler, bluer
above, little or no red on throat.) **11b. Yellow-throated variant.** Rare.

PLATE 61: ROLLERS AND HOOPOE

1 **BROAD-BILLED ROLLER** *Eurystomus glaucurus suahelicus*   **Page 394**
Uncommon in wooded areas with tall trees. Perches high. Dark plumage, short yellow bill. **1a. Juvenile. 1b and 1c. Adults.**

2 **ABYSSINIAN ROLLER** *Coracias abyssinica*   **Page 393**
Locally common in dry country west of Lake Turkana; occasional south to Laikipia Plateau and Mara GR. Irregular in ne. Kenya. **2a and 2b. Adults.** Bright azure underparts; long tail.

3 **EURASIAN ROLLER** *Coracias g. garrulus*   **Page 393**
Common, Oct.–April, in open woodland and bush in eastern areas. Uncommon autumn migrant in and west of Rift Valley. Short, stocky; flight feathers black. **3a. First-winter. 3b and 3c. Spring adults.**

4 **LILAC-BREASTED ROLLER** *Coracias caudata*   **Page 393**
Widespread. Fairly common in open bush, woodland and cultivation up to 2000 m. **4a and 4d. *C. c. caudata*, adults.** Resident north to Pokot and Maralal, east to the Tana River. **4b. *C. c. caudata*, juvenile. 4c. *C. c. lorti*, adult.** Migrant from Somalia; west to Marsabit, south to Meru NP, occasionally to Tsavo area.

5 **RUFOUS-CROWNED or PURPLE ROLLER** *Coracias n. naevia*   **Page 394**
Widespread but uncommon in dry bush and woodland, up to 2000 m. Scarce in n. Tanzania. **5a. Juvenile. 5b and 5c. Adults.**

6 **HOOPOE** *Upupa epops*   **Page 394**
U. e. africana a fairly common and widespread resident in savanna, bush and other open habitats; in all plumages primaries entirely black. Migrant *U. e. epops*, regular Oct.–March in same habitats, has white band across primaries (as do races *waibeli* and *senegalensis*). **6a and 6d. *U. e. africana*, males.** Secondaries largely white basally. **6b. *U. e. africana*, female.** Secondaries similar to those of *U. e. epops*. **6c. *U. e. epops*, male.**

Hoopoe (U. e. africana)

PLATE 62: WOOD-HOOPOES AND SCIMITARBILLS

1 GREEN WOOD-HOOPOE *Phoeniculus purpureus*   **Page 395**
The common wood-hoopoe, widespread in acacia woodland and savanna. **1a.** *P. p.*
marwitzi, **juvenile. 1b.** *P. p. niloticus*, **adult.** (Nw. Kenya.) **1c.** *P. p. marwitzi*, **adult male.**
1d and 1e. *P. p. marwitzi*, **adult female.**

2 BLACK-BILLED WOOD-HOOPOE *Phoeniculus s. somaliensis*   **Page 396**
Fairly common in ne. Kenya (where it replaces Green Wood-hoopoe). **2a. Female.**
2b. Male.

3 VIOLET WOOD-HOOPOE *Phoeniculus damarensis granti*   **Page 396**
Local in riverine woodland east of the Rift Valley, typically associated with doum palms,
mainly below 1000 m. Violet-blue on body, green on lower throat.

4 FOREST WOOD-HOOPOE *Phoeniculus castaneiceps brunneiceps*   **Page 395**
Formerly along Ugandan border in w. Kenya. Probably extirpated. **4a, 4b, 4c and 4d.**
Male, variations. 4e. Female.

5 WHITE-HEADED WOOD-HOOPOE *Phoeniculus bollei jacksoni*   **Page 395**
Fairly common in highland forests of w. and cent. Kenya. **5a. Immature. 5b. Adult.**

6 COMMON SCIMITARBILL *Rhinopomastus cyanomelas schalowi*   **Page 396**
Fairly common in open woodland, savanna and bush, except in arid areas. **6a. Female.**
6b and 6c. Males.

7 ABYSSINIAN SCIMITARBILL *Rhinopomastus minor cabanisi*   **Page 397**
Uncommon in dry bush. No white in wings or tail. **7a and 7c. Adults. 7b. Juvenile.**

Black Scimitarbill Rhinopomastus aterrimus. *Not known in Kenya,*
but may extend into our region near Ethiopian border. See text.

PLATE 63: HORNBILLS (*Tockus* and *Bycanistes*) (All adults except as noted. See Plate 30 for ground hornbills)

1 JACKSON'S HORNBILL *Tockus jacksoni* **Page 398**
Locally common in nw. Kenya. White spots on wing-coverts. **1a. Male.** Bill sharply bicoloured. **1b. Female.**

2 VON DER DECKEN'S HORNBILL *Tockus deckeni* **Page 398**
Common and widespread in n. and e. Kenya and n. Tanzania. Wings unspotted in adults. **2a. Male.** Bill orange-red and ivory, with black tip. **2b. Female.**

3 RED-BILLED HORNBILL *Tockus e. erythrorhynchus* **Page 397**
Common and widespread below 1400 m. Bill largely red. **3a. Juvenile.** Bill dull red. **3b. Male. 3c. Female.**

4 EASTERN YELLOW-BILLED HORNBILL *Tockus flavirostris* **Page 398**
Uncommon and local in n. and e. Kenya, mainly below 1200 m. **4a. Male. 4b. Female.**

5 AFRICAN GREY HORNBILL *Tockus nasutus* **Page 399**
Widespread but uncommon in savanna and acacia woodland. **5a. *T. n. nasutus*, male. 5b. *T. n. nasutus*, female. 5c. *T. n. epirhinus*, male.**

6 HEMPRICH'S HORNBILL *Tockus hemprichii* **Page 398**
Uncommon in n. and nw. Kenya. Local around cliffs, gorges and ravines between 900 and 1200 m. Dull red bill, much white in tail. **6a. Male. 6b. Female.**

7 CROWNED HORNBILL *Tockus alboterminatus geloensis* **Page 399**
This race and paler *T. a. suahelicus* widespread in forest and riverine woods. **7a. Male. 7b. Female.**

8 TRUMPETER HORNBILL *Bycanistes bucinator* **Page 399**
Fairly common but local in cent. Kenya and coastal lowlands, also in the East Usambaras and North Pare Mts in ne. Tanzania. White on wings mainly confined to tips of secondaries and inner primaries. **8a. Male. 8b. Female.**

9 BLACK-AND-WHITE-CASQUED HORNBILL *Bycanistes subcylindricus subquadratus* **Page 400**
Locally common in western forests. Much white in wings and tail. **9a. Male. 9b. Female.**

10 SILVERY-CHEEKED HORNBILL *Bycanistes brevis* **Page 399**
Locally common in cent. and e. Kenya and n. Tanzania. Wings entirely dark above. **10a. Male. 10b. Female.**

PLATE 64: BARBETS

1 WHITE-HEADED BARBET *Lybius leucocephalus* **Page 403**
Local in open wooded areas. **1a. L. l. leucocephalus, adult**. W. Kenya. Black tail and upper back; dark-streaked belly; white varies on breast and wings. **1b. L. l. albicauda, juvenile**. S. Kenya/n. Tanzania. Lower breast and abdomen brownish in both adults and young. **1c. L. l. senex, adult**. Cent. Kenya south to Chyulu Hills. Largely white, with blackish wings and upper back.

2 GREEN BARBET *Stactolaema o. olivacea* **Page 401**
Common in coastal forests and in the East Usambaras. Dull greenish olive, with dark brown head, large black bill.

3 GREY-THROATED BARBET *Gymnobucco bonapartei cinereiceps* **Page 400**
Fairly common in western forests. Small groups perch in tall dead trees. Drab brown, with greyer head, pale yellowish eyes; erectile straw-coloured tufts at bill base.

4 WHITE-EARED BARBET *Stactolaema leucotis kilimensis* **Page 400**
Local in se. Kenya and ne. Tanzania. White belly, rump and flaring postocular streak. **4a and 4b. Adults**.

5 RED-FRONTED BARBET *Tricholaema diademata* **Page 403**
Uncommon but widespread in dry woodland. **5a. Juvenile..** Forehead black. **5b. Adult**. Scarlet forehead; yellow superciliary stripes. Pattern similar to that of smaller Red-fronted Tinkerbird (Plate 65).

6 BLACK-THROATED BARBET *Tricholaema melanocephala stigmatothorax*
Page 403
Fairly common and widespread in dry thorn-bush and scrub below 1500 m. Largely immaculate sides; dark line from brown throat to lower breast or belly.

7 SPOT-FLANKED BARBET *Tricholaema lachrymosa radcliffei* **Page 403**
Locally common in moist acacia woods and tall riverine forest. Adults have spotted sides; black of throat reaches only to upper breast. **7a. Female**. Brown eyes. **7b. Male**. Yellow eyes; rounded spots. (Eastern and northern nominate race has teardrop-shaped spots.)

8 HAIRY-BREASTED BARBET *Tricholaema hirsuta ansorgii* **Page 402**
Kakamega Forest. Rare. Black polka-dots on yellowish underparts, white superciliary and whisker marks, yellowish speckling above. (Female has yellow speckling on crown, is brighter yellow below.)

9 BROWN-BREASTED BARBET *Lybius melanopterus* **Page 404**
Uncommon in eastern riverine woodland and coastal forest. Red head, brownish breast band, white belly.

10 BLACK-COLLARED BARBET *Lybius torquatus irroratus* **Page 404**
Local in coastal woodland. **10a. Adult male**. Black band separates yellow belly and red throat. **10b. Juvenile**. Largely dark head and breast.

11 BLACK-BILLED BARBET *Lybius guifsobalito* **Page 404**
Local in Lake Victoria basin and western border areas. Black belly and bill.

12 DOUBLE-TOOTHED BARBET *Lybius bidentatus aequatorialis* **Page 404**
Fairly common in western forests, woodlands, cultivation. White flank patch; ivory bill.

13 YELLOW-SPOTTED BARBET *Buccanodon d. duchaillui* **Page 402**
Local in w. Kenyan forests. Yellow superciliary stripes; no whisker marks.

14 YELLOW-BILLED BARBET *Trachylaemus purpuratus elgonensis* **Page 404**
Fairly common in w. Kenyan forests where the only barbet with bright yellow bill.

15 RED-AND-YELLOW BARBET *Trachyphonus erythrocephalus* **Page 405**
Widespread in open woodland, savanna, thorn-bush and scrub. **15a. T. e. versicolor, male**. Blackish crown, limited red on face. **15b. T. e. versicolor, female**. Largely yellow crown, red-and-white ear-coverts. **15c. T. e. erythrocephalus, male**. Black crown, throat patch; much red on sides of face. **15d. T. e. erythrocephalus, female**. Crown and face mostly red.

16 D'ARNAUD'S BARBET *Trachyphonus darnaudii* **Page 405**
Common and widespread in dry habitats. Smaller than No. 15. May show some orange on head. **16a. T. d. usambiro, male**. (Mara GR to Serengeti NP). Large. Bill blackish. **16b. T. d. darnaudii, male**. Blackish brown above; crown orange-red, yellow and black. **16c. T. d. boehmi, male**. Blackish brown above; forehead and crown black. **16d. T. d. darnaudii, female**. Pale brownish above; crown orange and black.

PLATE 65: TINKERBIRDS, SMALL WOODPECKERS AND WRY-NECKS

1 **EASTERN GREEN TINKERBIRD** *Pogoniulus simplex*   **Page 401**
Local and uncommon in coastal forest, inland to foothills of East Usambara Mts. Lemon-yellow rump. **1a. Adult. 1b. Immature**.

2 **MOUSTACHED GREEN TINKERBIRD** *Pogoniulus leucomystax*   **Page 401**
Uncommon in highland forests (as low as 900 m in East Usambaras). White moustachial stripes, golden-yellow rump.

3 **SPECKLED TINKERBIRD** *Pogoniulus scolopaceus flavisquamatus*   **Page 401**
Extirpated. Formerly rare in w. Kenyan forests. Large bill, pale eye.

4 **YELLOW-RUMPED TINKERBIRD** *Pogoniulus bilineatus*   **Page 402**
Common in forest canopy, riparian woods, tall suburban trees. Double white stripes on face; blackish back. **4a. *P. b. jacksoni*, adult** (highlands). **4b. *P. b. fischeri*, juvenile** (coastal woods).

5 **YELLOW-FRONTED TINKERBIRD** *Pogoniulus c. chrysoconus*   **Page 402**
Fairly common in moist areas of w. Kenya below 1500 m, in savanna, riparian thickets and suburban trees. Yellow forehead (black in juvenile).

6 **RED-FRONTED TINKERBIRD** *Pogoniulus pusillus affinis*   **Page 402**
Common in dry country below 2000 m. Vocally similar to No. 5, but no range overlap. **6a. Adult**. Red forehead. **6b. Juvenile**. Black forehead.

7 **CARDINAL WOODPECKER** *Dendropicos fuscescens*   **Page 410**
Common and widespread. Streaked on breast. Races *hartlaubii* and *hemprichii* in savanna and bush, *lepidus* in forest. **7a. *D. f. hartlaubii*, female**. Pale; heavily barred above. **7b. *D. f. hartlaubii*, male. 7c. *D. f. hemprichii*, male**. Darker, heavily barred. **7d. *D. f. lepidus*, male**. Golden olive above, obscurely barred. **7e. *D. f. lepidus*, female**.

8 **SPECKLE-BREASTED or UGANDA SPOTTED WOODPECKER** *Dendropicos poecilolaemus*   **Page 410**
Uncommon and local in w. Kenya. Usually low-foraging in riverine woods and thickets. **8a. Male**. Breast and neck finely spotted. **8b. Female**. Fine speckling on breast.

9 **EURASIAN WRYNECK** *Jynx t. torquilla*   **Page 408**
Scarce palearctic migrant in Kenya. Typically perches vertically, the bill angled upward. Feeds regularly on the ground.

10 **RED-THROATED WRYNECK** *Jynx r. ruficollis*   **Page 408**
Uncommon in cent. and w. Kenya above 1500 m. Regular in Lake Nakuru NP. Often on dead trees, fenceposts, usually in open woods or clearings.

PLATE 66: WOODPECKERS

1 GREY WOODPECKER *Dendropicos goertae rhodeogaster* **Page 411**
Widespread. Fairly common in open wooded areas. **1a. Male.** Red on belly centre, crown, rump and upper tail-coverts. Some western birds show little or no red below. **1b. Female.**

2 BROWN-BACKED WOODPECKER *Picoides obsoletus ingens* **Page 412**
Uncommon in woodland, forest edge, wooded suburbs. Brown above, with whitish wing and tail spots; variably streaked below. **2a. Female.** No red on hindcrown. **2b. Male.** Large red hindcrown patch. Eyes grey, dark red or red-brown.

3 FINE-BANDED or TULLBERG'S WOODPECKER *Campethera tullbergi taeniolaema* **Page 410**
Fairly common in Kenyan highland forests. Heavily barred below. Face appears plain grey at distance. **3a. Male. 3b. Female.**

4 BUFF-SPOTTED WOODPECKER *Campethera nivosa herberti* **Page 410**
Small. Forages low in w. Kenyan forest undergrowth where uncommon. Face and throat streaked. **4a. Male. 4b. Female.**

5 BROWN-EARED WOODPECKER *Campethera c. caroli* **Page 410**
Uncommon in western Kenyan forests. Underparts spotted, dark patch on side of head. **Female.** (Male has crimson on hindcrown and nape.)

6 BEARDED WOODPECKER *Dendropicos namaquus schoensis* **Page 411**
Widespread but uncommon in open wooded areas. Large, rather variable, but pattern diagnostic. (For other races, see text.) **6a. Male. 6b. Female.**

7 YELLOW-CRESTED WOODPECKER *Dendropicos xantholophus* **Page 411**
Scarce to uncommon in western Kenyan forests. Large; golden yellow on head often indistinct in male, lacking in female. Facial pattern suggests Bearded Woodpecker, but back dull brownish olive and habitats differ.

8 GREEN-BACKED or LITTLE SPOTTED WOODPECKER *Campethera c. cailliautii* **Page 409**
Local and uncommon in eastern woods. (Greener western race *nyansae* from South Nyanza and Mara GR south to Serengeti NP.) **8a. Male.** Greenish above with yellowish white spots; no prominent malar stripes; throat and breast spotted. **8b. Female.** Crown black with pale spots.

9 NUBIAN WOODPECKER *Campethera nubica* **Page 408**
Common and widespread in acacia woodland, bush and savanna. **9a. C. n. nubica, male.** Red malar stripe. **9b. C. n. pallida, female.** Blackish malar stripe.

10 GOLDEN-TAILED WOODPECKER *Campethera abingoni kavirondensis* **Page 409**
Local in riverine woodland in Mara GR and Serengeti NP (*C. a. suahelica* in n. Tanzania). **Male.** Dense black streaking from chin to upper breast.

11 MOMBASA WOODPECKER *Campethera mombassica* **Page 409**
Locally common in coastal and Tana River forests and the Usambaras. **Female.** Heavily streaked below. (Male similar, but with red-spotted and red-edged forehead/crown.)

Dale A. Zimmerman
1986

PLATE 67: HONEYGUIDES AND HONEYBIRDS

1 WAHLBERG'S HONEYBIRD *Prodotiscus r. regulus*   **Page 407**
Uncommon in acacia woodland, bush, and forest edge. Brown back; small, sharp-pointed bill. **1a. Juvenile**. Three lateral pairs of rectrices all white. **1b. Adult**. Dark T-pattern on tail.

2 CASSIN'S HONEYBIRD *Prodotiscus i. insignis*   **Page 408**
A scarce bird of forest edges and clearings in w. Kenya. Bright golden olive above; underparts dingy olive-grey; side of face greyish olive.

3 PALLID HONEYGUIDE *Indicator meliphilus*   **Page 407**
Uncommon in acacia woodland and forest edge. Stubby bill, no dark malar stripes, nearly plain golden olive back. **3a. Juvenile**. Olive extreme. **3b. Adult**. Greyer individual.

4 EASTERN HONEYBIRD *Prodotiscus zambesiae ellenbecki*   **Page 408**
Uncommon in open woodland, forest edge and suburban gardens east of Rift Valley. **4a and 4b. Adults.** Face grey, with narrow white eye-ring. Underparts pale grey and whitish (buffier in juvenile), outer rectrices sometimes with small dusky tips.

5 LEAST HONEYGUIDE *Indicator exilis pachyrhynchus*   **Page 407**
Uncommon in forests in w. Kenya. Small and dark. **5a. Juvenile**. Facial marks less prominent, underparts darker than adult. Smaller and stubbier-billed than Thick-billed Honeyguide; lores olive. **5b. Adult**. Small white loral spot, pale mandible base, dark malar stripes.

6 LESSER HONEYGUIDE *Indicator minor teitensis*   **Page 406**
Locally common in forest edge, savanna and acacia woodland. Paler, less well marked than Least Honeyguide; dark malar stripes sometimes faint. **6a and 6b. Adults**.

7 THICK-BILLED HONEYGUIDE *Indicator c. conirostris*   **Page 407**
Uncommon in western Kenyan forests. Dark olive-grey below, with no obvious facial markings.

8 SCALY-THROATED HONEYGUIDE *Indicator variegatus*   **Page 406**
Uncommon in forest edge, savanna, riverine woodland. Large, with scaly breast and streaked throat.

9 GREATER or BLACK-THROATED HONEYGUIDE *Indicator indicator* **Page 406**
Uncommon but widespread in woodland, savanna and forest edge. **9a. Juvenile**. Brownish olive above, yellow throat and breast, whitish rump patch. **9b and 9d. Adult males**. Black throat, white cheeks; bill usually pinkish, but may be dull brown; golden yellow on wing often concealed. **9c. Adult female**. Drab; streaked upper tail-coverts and yellow near bend of wing usually concealed; indistinct barring on chin and upper throat, pale wing-covert edges.

DALE A. ZIMMERMAN
1986

PLATE 68: GOLDEN PIPIT, LONGCLAWS, PITTA AND BROADBILL

1 GOLDEN PIPIT *Tmetothylacus tenellus*   **Page 422**
Widespread in dry country below 1000 m; locally common after rains. **1a and 1b. Adult males**. Large yellow wing patches. **1c. Subadult male**. Duller, less yellow on face. **1d. Adult female**. Slim, brownish buff, some yellow on belly, wings and tail.

2 ROSY-BREASTED LONGCLAW *Macronyx ameliae wintoni*   **Page 423**
Local and uncommon in wet grasslands. **2a. Adult male**. Red throat. **2b. Adult female**. **2c. Juvenile**. Brownish, with necklace of dark streaks. Hint of pink on belly.

3 YELLOW-THROATED LONGCLAW *Macronyx c. croceus*   **Page 423**
Widespread and locally common in grassland and cultivation. **3a and 3b. Adult males**. **3c. Adult female**. Resembles male; black may be less extensive than shown; sides of upper breast streaked. **3d. Juvenile**. Rich buffy brown, yellow confined to lower breast and belly; short breast streaks.

4 SHARPE'S LONGCLAW *Macronyx sharpei*   **Page 423**
Uncommon to scarce and local at high elevations. **Male** bright yellow below with necklace of streaks in all plumages. (Female similar.)

5 PANGANI LONGCLAW *Macronyx aurantiigula*   **Page 423**
Common in e. and se. Kenyan grassland. In n. Tanzania west to Lake Manyara and Tarangire NPs. **5a. Male. 5b. Female**.

6 AFRICAN PITTA *Pitta angolensis longipennis*   **Page 412**
Rare southern migrant, mainly April–Oct.; primarily coastal. **6a, 6b and 6c. Adults**.

7 AFRICAN BROADBILL *Smithornis capensis meinertzhageni*   **Page 412**
Scarce in w. Kenyan forests. Similar races elsewhere, all declining. **7a, 7b and 7c. Adults**. White back patch visible in display flight.

African Broadbill nest

PLATE 69: WAGTAILS

(1) YELLOW WAGTAIL *Motacilla flava*   **Page 420**
Common and widespread palearctic migrant, Sept.–April, mainly in moist areas (including pastures, lawns, roadsides and shorelines) below 2000 m. Gregarious. Forms large roosts in swamps, tall grass, trees. Variable; males greenish-backed; females and young birds often brownish above. Most birds yellow below. Autumn/winter adult males much duller than in spring, but, unlike females, have yellow throats. Some races have bold superciliary stripes.
1a. *M. f. beema*, male, spring. Crown pale grey.
1b. *M. f. beema*, male, winter.
1c. *M. f. thunbergi*, male, spring. Dark grey crown, blackish face, reduced superciliary stripe or none.
1d. *M. f. thunbergi*, female, spring.
1e. *M. f. lutea*, male, winter. Yellow superciliary.
1f. *M. f. leucocephala*, male, spring. Head largely whitish.
1g. *M. f. feldegg*, female, spring.
1h. *M. f. feldegg*, male, spring. Top and sides of head black.
1i. *M. f. feldegg*, male, winter.
1j. *M. f. lutea*, yellow-headed male, spring.
1k. *M. f. lutea*, first-winter female.
1l. *M. f. flava*, male, spring. (Some individuals paler than shown.) Blue-grey crown, dark face.
1m. *M. f. flava*, adult male, winter.
1n. *M. f. flava*, first-winter female.

(2) GREY WAGTAIL *Motacilla c. cinerea*   **Page 419**
Widespread palearctic migrant, Oct.–March, especially along highland-forest streams. Very long tail; yellowish-green rump; white superciliary stripe; wing-stripe obvious in flight. Usually solitary. **2a. Adult male, spring. 2b. Adult female, winter. 2c. Adult male, winter. 2d. First-winter male**. (Spring female similar.)

3 WHITE WAGTAIL *Motacilla a. alba*   **Page 419**
Uncommon palearctic migrant, Nov.–March (common at Lake Turkana). Regular at sewage works, oxidation ponds. Sides of head white. **3a. Adult male, winter. 3b. First-winter male. 3c. Adult male, spring**.

4 MOUNTAIN WAGTAIL *Motacilla clara torrentium*   **Page 420**
Local along highland streams up to 3000 m (below 700 m in E. Usambara Mts). **Adult male** slender; light bluish grey; narrow breast band.

(5) AFRICAN PIED WAGTAIL *Motacilla aguimp vidua*   **Page 419**
Common and widespread, often around towns and villages, lake edges and riversides. **(5a) Adult male**. Black and white above; white superciliary stripe. **5b. Juvenile**. Brownish grey above; flanks washed with brown. Much white on wings.

6 CAPE WAGTAIL *Motacilla capensis wellsi*   **Page 420**
Uncommon around lakes and swamps, in other moist areas and cultivation, mostly above 2000 m. **Adult male** olive-grey or olive-brown above; narrow breast band on buff-tinged underparts. Wing-coverts largely brown.

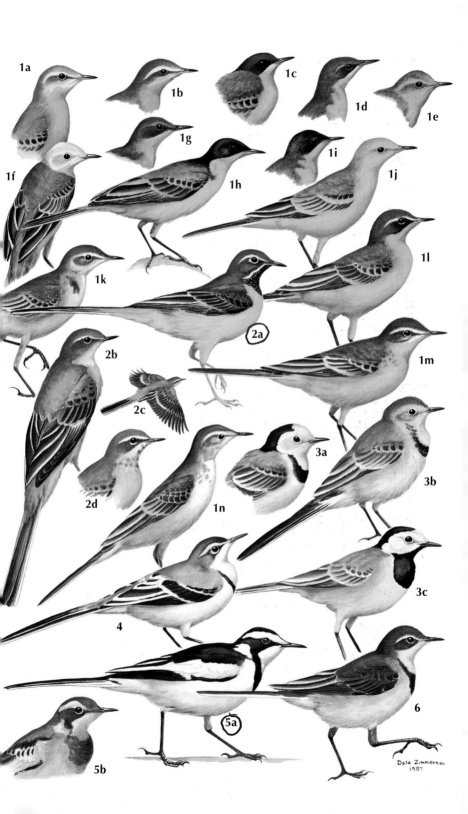

PLATE 70: PIPITS

1 RED-THROATED PIPIT *Anthus cervinus* Page 422
Palearctic migrant, late Oct.–April. Heavily streaked (including rump), buff and blackish above; fine bill, boldly streaked underparts. Usually in groups on wet ground. **1a. Male, winter.** Some pink on face/throat. **1b. Male, spring.** Bright tawny-pink from face to breast. **1c. First-winter.** (Oct.–Dec.) **1d. Adult male, autumn.** Buff throat.

2 BUSH PIPIT *Anthus caffer blayneyi* Page 422
Scarce and partly nomadic in bushed grassland. Small; no malar stripe. **2a. Adult, worn plumage.** Breast streaks narrow and sharp. **2b. Adult, fresh plumage.** Rich rufous-buff wing edgings.

3 SOKOKE PIPIT *Anthus sokokensis* Page 422
Scarce and local in coastal forests. Small; heavy black breast streaks. Solitary and shy.

4 TREE PIPIT *Anthus trivialis* Page 421
Palearctic migrant, Oct.–April, above 1500 m. Heavily streaked; olive-tinged upperparts; dark malar stripes. Bill heavier than in Red-throated Pipit.

5 GRASSLAND PIPIT *Anthus cinnamomeus lacuum* Page 420
The common East African pipit. Widespread in open habitats. **5a. 'Jackson's Pipit'**, *A. (c.) latistriatus.* Possibly a form of Grassland Pipit. Status unclear; see text. **5b. Juvenile.** Dark; flanks streaked; mandible pinkish. **5c. Adult, fresh plumage.** Flanks unstreaked; bright buff feather edges above; mandible yellowish, tarsi pinkish. **5d. Adult, worn plumage.**

6 MALINDI PIPIT *Anthus melindae* Page 421
North Kenyan coast and lower Tana River Valley, on short-grass flats subject to flooding. Dull, not contrastingly streaked above; mandible and feet orange-yellow. **6a. Immature(?).** Narrowly streaked individual. **6b. Breeding adult.** Heavily streaked individual.

7 PLAIN-BACKED PIPIT *Anthus leucophrys* Page 421
Locally common on short-grass plains. Slim; unstreaked back, limited breast streaking, buff outer tail feathers. **7a. Adult A. l. goodsoni.** Laikipia Plateau/ cent. Rift Valley. Pale; indistinct breast streaks. **7b. Immature A. l. goodsoni.** Sharper breast streaks. **7c. Adult A. l. zenkeri.** Western: Mt Elgon south to w. Serengeti NP.

8 TAWNY PIPIT *Anthus c. campestris* Page 420
Rare palearctic migrant. **Adult** slender, pale and faintly marked. Wagtail-like, with horizontal carriage. Walks and runs rapidly, pumping tail.

9 LONG-BILLED PIPIT *Anthus similis hararensis* Page 421
Rift Valley scarps and Arusha NP. Locally common on rough stony ground. Large; long-billed and long-tailed. Lightly streaked below. Does not pump tail. **9a. Juvenile.** Streaks extend onto flanks; wing edgings tawny-buff or light rufous; long tail edged with rich buff. **9b. Adult, fresh plumage.** (Some birds greyer, more diffusely streaked than shown; worn individuals darker and more uniform above.)

10 STRIPED PIPIT *Anthus lineiventris* Page 422
Rocky, grassy slopes in se. Kenya (rare) and ne. Tanzania. Large and well streaked; greenish yellow wing edgings. Wary and unobtrusive.

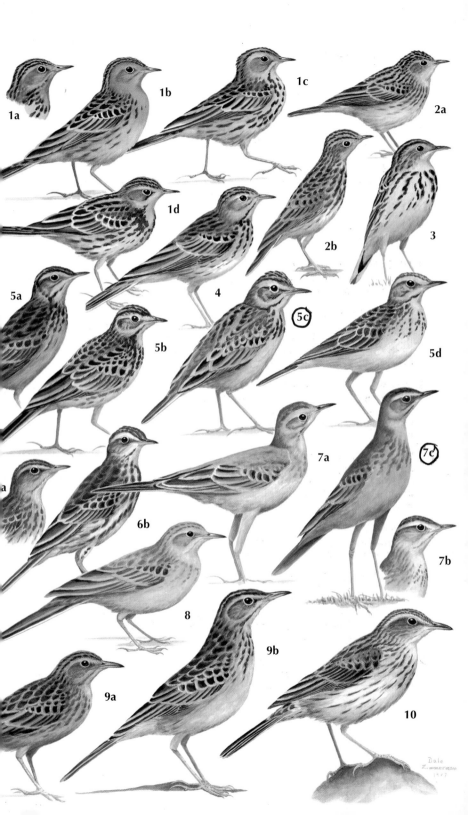

PLATE 71: LARKS (See also Plate 72)

1 FISCHER'S SPARROW-LARK *Eremopterix leucopareia* **Page 418**
Common, widespread; often in flocks on dry short-grass plains. **1a. Imm. male.** Resembles adult male, but cheeks duller. **1b. Adult male.** Black mid-ventral line; whitish cheeks. **1c. Juv. female.** Scaly or speckled above; mottled on breast. **1d. Adult female.** Rufous face, buff throat and upper breast.

2 CHESTNUT-HEADED SPARROW-LARK *Eremopterix signata* **Page 418**
Locally common on dry plains in n. and se. Kenya; some wander to coast. **2a. Juv. female.** Tawny about eyes. **2b. Juv. male.** Buffy brown; diffusely streaked below. **2c and 2d. Adult males.** White crown and cheek patch; black or chestnut on face and throat. **2e. Imm. male.** Reddish face with large whitish cheek patch. **2f. Adult female.** Crown darker than in immature male; face and throat buff.

3 CHESTNUT-BACKED SPARROW-LARK *Eremopterix leucotis madaraszi*
Page 418
Scarce and local wanderer, favouring black 'cotton' soils. **3a. Imm. female.** Chestnut wing-coverts, black belly. **3b. Adult male.** Chestnut back, white cheeks and nape band. **3c. Adult female.** Darkly streaked; chestnut wing-coverts.

4 SINGING BUSH LARK *Mirafra cantillans* **Page 413**
Widespread in grassland, with some bush. Well patterned in fresh plumage, with dark spot on sides of lower neck; rufous primary edgings often conspicuous in flight; outer rectrices white. See text. **4a. Presumed *M. c. chadensis*** (Kenyan–Sudanese border), **adult in fresh plumage**. **4b. *M. c. marginata*, adult male in fresh plumage.** Dark inner secondaries ('tertials') with broad cream edges; **4c. *M. c. marginata*, adult male in worn breeding plumage.** Duller; dark foreneck patches reduced or absent. **4d. *M. c. marginata*, juv.** Scaly-looking above; suggestion of dark submarginal lines on secondaries; bill mainly pinkish.

5 SOMALI SHORT-TOED LARK *Calandrella somalica* **Page 417**
Locally fairly common on dry plains. Prominent facial pattern; dark area at sides of lower neck; white tail edges obvious in flight. **5a. *C. s. athensis*.** S. Kenya, n. Tanzania. Whitish orbital/postocular areas contrast with dark ear-coverts. **5b. *C. s. megaensis*.** N. Kenya. Buffier than *athensis*.

6 GREATER SHORT-TOED LARK *Calandrella brachydactyla longipennis*
Page 416
Palearctic vagrant. Pale, with small yellowish bill.

7 MASKED LARK *Spizocorys personata* **Page 417**
Locally common in northern Kenyan deserts. **7a. *S. p. yavelloensis*.** South to Dida Galgalu Desert. **7b. *S. p. intensa*.** Northeast of Isiolo.

8 FRIEDMANN'S LARK *Mirafra pulpa* **Page 414**
Scarce and irregular in dry grassland with scattered shrubs. Sporadic in Tsavo area. See text.

9 SHORT-TAILED LARK *Pseudalaemon fremantlii delamerei* **Page 417**
Local on short-grass plains and in dry open bush.

10 RED-CAPPED LARK *Calandrella cinerea* **Page 416**
Widespread in highlands, south to n. Tanzania. Common on short-grass plains. **10a. *C. c. williamsi*** (Kenyan highlands), **juv.** Dark crown with fine speckling, scaly back pattern; large blotches at sides of mottled breast. **10b. *C. c. williamsi*, adult male** (with crest erected). Darker and more heavily streaked than *saturatior*. **10c. *C. c. saturatior*, adult male** (sw. Kenya, n. Tanzania).

11 CRESTED LARK *Galerida cristata somaliensis* **Page 417**
Common in sandy deserts of n. Kenya. **11a. Juv. female. 11b. Adult female.** (Male similar.)

12 THEKLA LARK *Galerida theklae huriensis* **Page 418**
Local on rocky substrate in n. Kenyan deserts. Darker, less sandy-coloured, than Crested Lark.

PLATE 72: LARKS (*Mirafra*) (See also Plate 71)

1 RED-WINGED LARK *Mirafra h. hypermetra* **Page 415**
Locally common in bushed grassland below 1300 m east of Rift Valley. Large, with rufous primaries; black neck patches conspicuous in adult (lacking in Rufous-naped Lark). **1a. Rufous adult. 1b. Pale adult in worn plumage. 1c. Pale juvenile. 1d. Rufous juvenile. 1e. Pale adult in fresh plumage.**

2 RUFOUS-NAPED LARK *M. africana* **Page 414**
Widespread and common in grassland above 1300 m east to Emali Plains and Arusha District. Stocky, short tailed, with rufous primaries. No black neck patches. **2a. *M. a. harterti*, adult.** Emali Plains. **2b. *M. a. tropicalis*, adult.** Crater and Mbulu Highlands of n. Tanzania north to Mt Elgon. **2c. *M. a. athi*, adult.** Cent. Kenyan highlands south to Kilimanjaro. **2d. *M. a. athi*, juvenile.** Darker, duskier than juv. Red-winged Lark.

3 FLAPPET LARK *M. rufocinnamomea* **Page 415**
Widespread. Uncommon in shrubby grassland, savanna and bush clearings. Outer rectrices tawny, buff or rufous. More slender, bill smaller, tail longer, back more scaly or spotted than in Rufous-naped Lark. **3a. *M. r. torrida*, adult.** Central; Huri Hills south to interior n. Tanzania. **3b. *M. r. fischeri*, juvenile.** Coastal; juveniles of other races similar. Darker, more uniform than young of other *Mirafra* species. **3c. *M. r. kawirondensis*, adult.** Western. Buff outer rectrices. **3d. *M. r. fischeri*, adult.** Coastal.

4 FAWN-COLOURED LARK *M. africanoides intercedens* **Page 415**
Fairly common in dry open bush and shrubby grassland. Slender-billed; blackish lores and distinct white superciliary stripes. **4a. Rufous adult. 4b. Brown adult. 4c. Juvenile.**

5 GILLETT'S LARK *M. gilletti* **Page 416**
Rare in open thorn-scrub in extreme northeastern Kenya. Resembles Fawn-coloured Lark, but rump and upper tail-coverts grey; breast streaks brownish rufous.

6 PINK-BREASTED LARK *M. poecilosterna* **Page 416**
Widespread; locally common in dry open *Acacia* and *Commiphora* bush below 1500 m. Perches in trees. Pipit-like; no white in tail. **6a. Light extreme. 6b. Dark extreme. 6c. Juvenile.** Paler than Rufous-naped and Flappet Larks; no dark loral area.

7 WILLIAMS'S LARK *M. williamsi* **Page 414**
Locally common in northern lava deserts, often with Masked Lark. Obscurely streaked to nearly plain above; heavy-billed. Variable. (Cf. Friedmann's Lark and Singing Bush Lark on Plate 71.) **7a. Worn adult female. 7b. Freshly plumaged adult female, dark morph.** More uniform above and with darker ear-coverts than White-tailed Lark. **7c. Freshly plumaged adult male, rufous morph.** Upperparts red- or orange-brown with sparse pale streaking; wing-coverts broadly edged with pale rufous; whitish semi-collar behind ear-coverts.

8 WHITE-TAILED LARK *M. albicauda* **Page 413**
Uncommon in open grassland on black 'cotton' soils. **Freshly-plumaged adult** blackish above.

9 COLLARED LARK *M. collaris* **Page 415**
Uncommon/scarce on red desert soils in n. and ne. Kenya.

1a

1b

1c

1d

1e

2a

2b

2c

2d

3a

3b

3c

3d

4a

4b

4c

5

6a

6b

6c

7a

7b

7c

8

9

DALE A ZIMMERMAN
1992

PLATE 73: SWALLOWS (See Plate 74 for flying birds)

1 ROCK MARTIN *Hirundo fuligula fusciventris* **Page 427**
Common around rocky sites and near tall buildings. Cinnamon throat/upper breast.
White tail spots usually concealed in perched bird.

2 BANDED MARTIN *Riparia cincta suahelica* **Page 424**
Locally common in open grassland. Large size; broad breast band; white supraloral lines.

3 MASCARENE MARTIN *Phedina borbonica madagascariensis* **Page 427**
Vagrant to coastal areas. Possibly more regular at Lake Jipe in June.

4 PLAIN MARTIN or AFRICAN SAND MARTIN *Riparia paludicola ducis*
Page 424
Common in open country in highlands. Dull brownish throat and breast.

5 BLUE SWALLOW *Hirundo atrocaerulea* **Page 425**
Scarce intra-African migrant in w. Kenyan grasslands, April–Sept. White at sides usually
concealed.

6 SAND MARTIN or BANK SWALLOW *Riparia r. riparia* **Page 424**
Common palearctic migrant, Sept.–May, mainly in the west. Small size, large breast
band; no white above lores.

7 RED-RUMPED SWALLOW *Hirundo daurica emini* **Page 426**
Fairly common in the highlands. Blue-black under tail-coverts.

8 MOSQUE SWALLOW *Hirundo senegalensis saturatior* **Page 426**
Uncommon but widespread; most numerous in west. Large size, pale cheeks.

9 RUFOUS-CHESTED SWALLOW *Hirundo semirufa gordoni* **Page 426**
Uncommon in Lake Victoria basin and Mara GR, especially near wet areas. Dark blue of
crown extends below eyes; under tail-coverts and rump rufous.

10 LESSER STRIPED SWALLOW *Hirundo abyssinica unitatis* **Page 427**
Locally common. Widespread, often around buildings. Largely rufous head and rump;
striped underparts.

11 GREY-RUMPED SWALLOW *Pseudhirundo g. griseopyga* **Page 424**
Uncommon in w. and cent. Kenya, mainly in grassland and cultivation. Rump grey or
brownish grey. **11a. *P. g. griseopyga*, adult. 11b. *P. g. 'andrewi'*.**

12 WIRE-TAILED SWALLOW *Hirundo s. smithii* **Page 425**
Widespread and fairly common, especially near water. **12a. Adult.** Chestnut cap; pure
white underparts. **12b. Juvenile.** Dull brown cap; buff-tinged underparts.

13 BARN SWALLOW *Hirundo r. rustica* **Page 425**
Widespread palearctic migrant. Common to abundant, Aug.–early May; some present all
year. **13a. Adult.** Chestnut throat and blue breast band. **13b. Juvenile.** Dull blue upperparts; brownish breast band.

14 COMMON HOUSE MARTIN *Delichon u. urbica* **Page 427**
Common palearctic passage migrant. Winters locally in highlands. White rump and
underparts may be buff-tinged in winter.

15 BLACK SAW-WING or ROUGH-WING *Psalidoprocne holomelas massaicus*
Page 427
Common and widespread near forests, high-elevation grasslands. (Smaller nominate race
uncommon in coastal forests.)

16 WHITE-HEADED SAW-WING or ROUGH-WING *Psalidoprocne a. albiceps*
Page 428
Locally common in the west; scarce elsewhere. **16a. Juvenile.** Stockier and browner than Black
Saw-wing, tail fork less deep. **16b. Adult male.** Head largely white. **16c. Adult female.** Throat
white; may show some white on crown.

17 ANGOLA SWALLOW *Hirundo angolensis* **Page 426**
Widespread in w. Kenya. Locally fairly common east to Nyahururu and Nanyuki.
Underparts dingy grey-brown; breast band incomplete.

18 ETHIOPIAN SWALLOW *Hirundo aethiopica* **Page 426**
Common in coastal areas and n. Kenya. Resembles small Barn Swallow, but breast band
narrow and incomplete, tail less forked. **18a. *H. a. aethiopica*, adult. 18b. *H. a. aethiopica*, juvenile. 18c. *H. a. amadoni*, adult.**

DALE A. ZIMMERMAN
1993

PLATE 74: SWALLOWS IN FLIGHT (Adults unless otherwise stated)

1 MASCARENE MARTIN *Phedina borbonica madagascariensis*   **Page 427**
Vagrant to coastal lowlands, inland to Lake Jipe. Dark wing-linings, streaked underparts, square tail.

2 ROCK MARTIN *Hirundo fuligula fusciventris*   **Page 427**
Widespread near gorges, cliffs, kopjes, tall buildings. Brown-backed; white spots evident in spread tail.

3 SAND MARTIN or BANK SWALLOW *Riparia r. riparia*   **Page 424**
Common and widespread migrant, Sept.–May, mainly western. Small size, brown wing-linings. Flight rather slow, with few long glides.

4 BANDED MARTIN *Riparia cincta suahelica*   **Page 424**
Locally common in grassland. Flight leisurely, often low. Brown upperparts, white wing-linings.

5 PLAIN or AFRICAN SAND MARTIN *Riparia paludicola ducis*   **Page 424**
Widespread and common, especially in the highlands. No breast band; dingy grey-brown throat, breast and sides.

6 BLACK SAW-WING or ROUGH-WING *Psalidoprocne h. massaicus* **Page 427**
Common in wooded areas and grassland in highlands; often flies just above ground. (Uncommon coastal race, *P. h. holomelas,* is smaller and shorter-tailed.)

7 BLUE SWALLOW *Hirundo atrocaerulea*   **Page 425**
Scarce in shrubby grassland in w. Kenya, April.–Sept. Appears all black at distance.

8 WHITE-HEADED SAW-WING *Psalidoprocne a. albiceps*   **Page 428**
Locally common in shrubby grassland and forest edge in w. Kenya. **Adult male** has large-ly white head. (Female differs from No. 6 in having shallow tail fork.)

9 RED-RUMPED SWALLOW *Hirundo daurica emini*   **Page 426**
Fairly common in the highlands, often near buildings. Rufous rump, blue-black under tail-coverts; no white in tail. Flight relatively slow and leisurely.

10 RUFOUS-CHESTED SWALLOW *Hirundo semirufa gordoni*   **Page 426**
Western. Uncommon in open areas below 1700 m. Rufous rump, under tail-coverts and wing-linings; dark blue of head extends below eyes; white tail spots.

11 MOSQUE SWALLOW *Hirundo senegalensis saturatior*   **Page 426**
Uncommon but widespread in open woodland, cultivation, clearings, below 2600 m. Large, with white wing-linings, pale cheeks, rufous rump and under tail-coverts; no white tail spots in this race, but present in eastern *H. s. monteiri.*

12 LESSER STRIPED SWALLOW *Hirundo abyssinica unitatis*   **Page 427**
Widespread below 2000 m, usually near buildings. Streaked underparts; rufous on rump and head.

13 BARN SWALLOW *Hirundo r. rustica*   **Page 425**
Common and widespread migrant, late Aug.–May; scarce other months. **13a. Adult male**. Glossy blue-black upperparts and breast band; white tail spots. (Female has shorter outer rectrices.) **13b. Juvenile.** Duller above with faint gloss; dusky brown breast band.

14 WIRE-TAILED SWALLOW *Hirundo s. smithii*   **Page 425**
Widespread and common, often near water. Shining blue above with chestnut cap; white below. Wire-like outer rectrices often broken or missing (or difficult to discern). (Juvenile on Plate 73.)

15 COMMON HOUSE MARTIN *Delichon u. urbica*   **Page 427**
Palearctic migrant, mainly in highlands. Small, high-flying; fluttery flight; white rump.

16 ANGOLA SWALLOW *Hirundo angolensis*   **Page 426**
Widespread in w. Kenya. Dull underparts and wing-linings.

17 ETHIOPIAN SWALLOW *Hirundo a. aethiopica*   **Page 426**
Common along coast; widespread in n. Kenya. Steel-blue above, with chestnut forehead.

18 GREY-RUMPED SWALLOW *Pseudhirundo g. griseopyga*   **Page 424**
Uncommon in grassland, open cultivation. Flight fluttery, slow, usually low; nests in holes in flat ground or in termitaria. Grey rump.

PLATE 75: BULBUL, BRISTLEBILL, LEAF-LOVE, LARGER GREEN-BULS AND NICATOR

AKA - YELLOW VENTED

1 COMMON BULBUL *Pycnonotus barbatus*　　　　**Page 434**
1a *P. b. tricolor*. Widespread, except in n. and e. Kenya. **1b.** *P. b. dodsoni*. Common in dry country of n. and e. Kenya. White ear patch, mottled breast.

2 HONEYGUIDE GREENBUL *Baeopogon i. indicator*　　**Page 433**
Uncommon in canopy of w. Kenyan forests. Dark, with much white in tail; eyes white in male (greyish in female).

3 EASTERN NICATOR *Nicator gularis*　　　　**Page 503**
Secretive. Fairly common in eastern forest undergrowth (especially near coast). **Male** large; pale yellow or white spots; stout hooked bill. (Female smaller, with spot in front of eye white, not yellow.)

4 SHELLEY'S GREENBUL *Andropadus masukuensis kakamegae*　**Page 430**
Fairly common in some w. Kenyan forests. Forages at all levels; clings to tree trunks. Grey head, pale eyelids; small bill. (See Plate 123 for ne. Tanzanian race.)

5 RED-TAILED BRISTLEBILL *Bleda syndactyla woosnami*　**Page 434**
Fairly common near ground in western forests. **5a. Adult male.** Yellowish below; pale blue orbital skin; eyes red (brown in female). **5b. Juvenile.** Rufous wash on flanks; orbital skin yellow or yellowish green.

6 MOUNTAIN GREENBUL *Andropadus nigriceps*　　**Page 430**
Widespread and conspicuous in highland forest and forest edge. **6a. A. n. nigriceps.** Nguruman Hills and n. Tanzania. Greyish head and breast, blackish crown; grey eyelids. **6b. A. n. kikuyuensis.** W. and cent. Kenyan highlands. Grey head, white eyelids; yellow belly. (For *A. n. usambarae* of ne. Tanzania, see Plate 123.)

7 ZANZIBAR SOMBRE GREENBUL *Andropadus importunus*　**Page 431**
Common and conspicuous in coastal scrub and thickets. **7a. A. i. insularis, adult.** Eastern lowlands. Plain; eyes pale. **7b. A. i. insularis, juvenile.** Yellow eyelids and gape; eyes brown. **7c. A. i. fricki.** Local in cent. Kenyan highlands. Slightly darker, heavier-billed than 7a; juvenile also has yellowish eyelids.

8 STRIPE-CHEEKED GREENBUL *Andropadus milanjensis striifacies*　**Page 430**
Locally common in Taita and Chyulu Hills forests south into n. Tanzania. Robust; striped cheeks; eyes pale grey.

9 JOYFUL GREENBUL *Chlorocichla laetissima*　　**Page 434**
Uncommon in canopy of w. Kenyan forests, typically in small groups. Vocal, conspicuous. Large size, bright yellow underparts.

10 YELLOW-BELLIED GREENBUL *Chlorocichla flaviventris centralis*　**Page 433**
Eastern. Common in coastal forest, dense bush; less numerous inland; scarce in cent. Kenyan highlands. Large; dull yellowish below; white on eyelids.

11 YELLOW-THROATED LEAF-LOVE *Chlorocichla flavicollis pallidigula*
Page 434
Locally common in w. Kenya. Retiring, but highly vocal. Large; pale throat feathers often raised. Eyes dull yellow to pale brown.

PLATE 76: GREENBULS AND BROWNBULS

1 **ANSORGE'S GREENBUL** *Andropadus ansorgei kavirondensis*   **Page 429**
Common in subcanopy of Kakamega Forest. Small; olive-grey below; narrow light eye-ring.

2 **LITTLE GREY GREENBUL** *Andropadus gracilis ugandae*   **Page 428**
Scarce. Subcanopy of Kakamega Forest. Yellowish belly; bright tawny flanks and sides.

3 **YELLOW-WHISKERED GREENBUL** *Andropadus l. latirostris*   **Page 429**
Commonest highland greenbul in forest and riparian undergrowth. **3a and 3b. Adults.**
Yellow throat feathers. **3c. Juvenile.** Blackish malar stripes; mottled orange-and-black bill.

4 **SLENDER-BILLED GREENBUL** *Andropadus gracilirostris*   **Page 429**
Fairly common and conspicuous in highland-forest treetops. Olive-green above, plain grey below; slender black bill.

5 **CAMEROON SOMBRE GREENBUL** *Andropadus c. curvirostris*   **Page 428**
W. Kenyan forests; uncommon in tall shrubbery and creepers. Dark olive-grey throat contrasts with darker breast; small dark bill; greyish white eyelids.

6 **LITTLE GREENBUL** *Andropadus v. virens*   **Page 429**
Fairly common in w. Kenyan forest undergrowth. Small, dark, short billed; throat, breast and flanks uniformly olive; feet orange to yellowish brown. (Similar race *zombensis* common in Shimba Hills and ne. Tanzania.)

7 **TORO OLIVE GREENBUL** *Phyllastrephus hypochloris*   **Page 431**
Dense undergrowth in Kakamega Forest. Uncommon and shy. Slender-billed; mainly plain olive, paler than Little Greenbul; suggestion of yellow-and-grey streaking below; tail dark rufous. Feet bluish or olive.

8 **CABANIS'S GREENBUL** *Phyllastrephus cabanisi*   **Page 431**
Widespread and common in forest undergrowth, usually in small noisy groups; flicks wings. **8a. *P. c. placidus*.** East of Rift Valley. Olive-brown with rufous tail; whitish or cream throat; eyes usually grey. **8b. *P. c. sucosus*.** West of Rift Valley. Yellower below than *placidus*; eyes usually greyish tan. (Immature has still brighter yellow underparts.)

9 **NORTHERN BROWNBUL** *Phyllastrephus strepitans*   **Page 432**
Widespread, fairly common in forest undergrowth and thickets, often in noisy family groups. Rump and upper tail-coverts bright rufous-brown; narrow whitish eye-ring; eyes red-brown.

10 **TERRESTRIAL BROWNBUL** *Phyllastrephus terrestris suahelicus*   **Page 432**
Uncommon in coastal forest undergrowth, often on ground; shy and secretive. Duller, slightly more olive-brown than Northern Brownbul, intermediate in colour between that species and Fischer's Greenbul; rump and tail-coverts not rufous; white throat contrasts rather sharply with breast. Eyes dark red-brown.

11 **FISCHER'S GREENBUL** *Phyllastrephus fischeri*   **Page 432**
Common in coastal forest undergrowth; secretive. Olive-brown above with whitish throat, rufous-tinged tail; eyes cream. Bill long and slender in **male**, much shorter in female, resembling bill of Cabanis's Greenbul.

12 **GREY-OLIVE GREENBUL** *Phyllastrephus cerviniventris*   **Page 431**
Kiambu, Thika, Taveta, Arusha and Moshi Districts. Local in forest undergrowth and riverine thickets. Pale eye-ring; feet pale straw colour or pinkish white.

13 **YELLOW-STREAKED GREENBUL** *Phyllastrephus flavostriatus tenuirostris*
    Page 433
Two Kenyan records. More numerous in Usambara and South Pare forests in ne. Tanzania. Crown grey; yellow streaks on greyish white underparts; long, slim, dark brown bill; eyes grey.

14 **TINY GREENBUL** *Phyllastrephus debilis rabai*   **Page 433**
Uncommon in coastal forest undergrowth. Small size; grey crown and face; eyes pale yellow; underparts yellow-streaked. (*P. d. albigula* of Tanzania's Usambara Mts has olive crown.)

DALE A. ZIMMERMAN
1987

PLATE 77: GLOSSY STARLINGS (as seen in strong sunlight)

Highly iridescent, the colours appearing markedly different with changing light conditions: brilliant in strong sunlight, darker and often largely black in shade or when viewed against the light.

1 RÜPPELL'S LONG-TAILED STARLING *Lamprotornis purpuropterus* **Page 513**
Common in lightly wooded and open country. Long purple or bronze-purple tail.

2 HILDEBRANDT'S STARLING *Lamprotornis hildebrandti* **Page 513**
Locally common in bush and woodland. Often on ground with Superb Starlings. **2a. Juv.** Brown or blackish-brown head; faint spotting on underparts. **2b. Adult.** Eyes red; breast paler than belly.

3 SHELLEY'S STARLING *Lamprotornis shelleyi* **Page 513**
Local and uncommon. Mostly a non-breeding visitor in dry e. and se. Kenya (south once to n. Tanzania); possibly resident in far north. Typically in *Commiphora* bush. Underparts uniformly dark chestnut; eyes orange.

4 SUPERB STARLING *Lamprotornis superbus* **Page 514**
Common and widespread below 2200 m. Feeds on ground. **4a. Adult.** White band separating dark breast and rufous-orange belly; eyes cream. **4b. Juv.** White breast band faint or lacking; eyes brown, soon turning greyish.

5 GOLDEN-BREASTED STARLING *Cosmopsarus regius* **Page 514**
Locally common in dry n. and e. Kenya and ne. Tanzania. Yellow underparts; long narrow tail. **5a. Adult.** Upperparts mostly iridescent blue; wings often show purple; head green. **5b. Juv.** Brownish head and breast; much duller and shorter-tailed than adult.

6 SPLENDID GLOSSY STARLING *Lamprotornis s. splendidus* **Page 512**
Scarce in Mt Elgon forests. Mostly arboreal. Large and broad-tailed; coppery patch on side of neck; velvety-black wing band; wings noisy in flight. **6a. Female.** Underparts more blue, less purple, with less coppery iridescence. **6b. Male.** Throat and breast violet, with band of brassy or coppery iridescence.

7 PURPLE STARLING *Lamprotornis purpureus amethystinus* **Page 512**
Scarce in w. Kenya. On ground or in trees, at times with other starlings. Large, bright yellow eyes; relatively short-tailed and long-billed; purplish head and underparts.

8 BRONZE-TAILED STARLING *Lamprotornis chalcurus emini* **Page 513**
Nw. Kenya. Local and uncommon in trees or on ground, often with Greater Blue-eared Starling; wings noisy in flight. **8a and 8b. Adults.** Purple-and-blue tail may appear bronze as bird flies against the light.

9 GREATER BLUE-EARED STARLING *Lamprotornis chalybaeus* **Page 512**
9a. L. c. cyaniventris, adult. Common in the highlands; also east and west of Lake Turkana. Larger and bluer than *L. c. sycobius*. **9b. L. c. cyaniventris, juv.** Sooty brown, washed with green or blue, belly dull black; eyes grey-brown. **9c. L. c. sycobius, adult.** Uncommon in n. Tanzania, also seasonally on Kenyan coast, inland to Tsavo and Kibwezi. Smaller, greener than *L. c. cyaniventris*, with magenta-violet flanks and belly. Closely resembles Lesser Blue-eared Starling.

10 BLACK-BELLIED STARLING *Lamprotornis corruscus mandanus* **Page 511**
Common in coastal forests and woods, inland along Tana River to Kora NR. (Larger race *jombeni* scarce/uncommon in Meru Forest and Nyambeni Hills.) **Male.** No black spots on wing-coverts; belly and crissum black (dark sooty in female).

11 LESSER BLUE-EARED STARLING *Lamprotornis c. chloropterus* **Page 512**
Western Kenya. Locally common in bush and woodland. **11a. Juv.** Dark brownish head, dull brown or brownish-grey underparts; dark eyes. (Juv. *L. c. elisabeth* of ne. Tanzania has rufous-brown underparts.) **11b. Adult.** Smaller, greener than No. 9, with narrower dark ear-covert patch, shorter tail.

PLATE 78: STARLINGS AND OXPECKERS

1 SHARPE'S STARLING *Cinnyricinclus sharpii*   **Page 515**
Uncommon in highland forests. Small-billed; upperparts blue-black. **1a. Juv**. Arrowhead-shaped spots on underparts; duller above than adult; orange-brown eyes. **1b. Adult male**. Pale tawny-buff belly and flanks; yellow eyes. Female slightly duller.

2 ABBOTT'S STARLING *Cinnyricinclus femoralis*   **Page 514**
Uncommon in montane-forest canopy. Dark above and on breast; eyes yellow. **2a. Male**. Blue-black of breast extends to point on upper belly. **2b. Female**. Upperparts and breast brown, heavily streaked below.

3 VIOLET-BACKED STARLING *Cinnyricinclus leucogaster verreauxi*   **Page 514**
Flocks seasonally common and widespread in forested areas, riverine woods, fruiting trees. **3a. Female**. Rufous-tawny feather edges in fresh plumage; shows rufous primary patch in flight. **3b. Male**. Magenta-violet to blue iridescence above, white below.

4 MAGPIE-STARLING *Speculipastor bicolor*   **Page 515**
Flocks in northern semi-deserts, scrub, dry woodland; nomadic. White patch at base of primaries in all plumages; eyes red in adults. **4a. Female**. Less glossy than male; black band across breast. **4b. Male**. Head and upperparts glossy blue-black. **4c. Juv**. Dark brown above, on throat and on breast; eyes brown.

5 FISCHER'S STARLING *Spreo fischeri*   **Page 515**
Locally common in dry bush country below 1400 m. Greyish or brownish grey above; crown much paler; lores blackish. **5a. Juv**. Brownish on back and breast; eyes dark brown; bill largely yellow. **5b. Adult**. Greyer; eyes white; bill black.

6 WATTLED STARLING *Creatophora cinerea*   **Page 516**
Widespread. Commonly in large flocks, often with ungulates. Plumage and bare parts variable, but rump whitish in all plumages. **6a. Non-breeding male**. No wattles; head largely feathered. **6b. Male in full breeding plumage**. Bare yellow facial skin; long black wattles. **6c. Male acquiring breeding plumage**. Head well feathered; greenish-and-yellow skin near eyes; wattles variable. **6d. Juv**. Brownish, with darker wings; yellow or greenish skin along sides of throat and behind eyes. **6e. Adult female** (and some non-breeding males). Dark malar streak; bare postocular skin.

7 WHITE-CROWNED STARLING *Spreo albicapillus horrensis*   **Page 515**
Uncommon in flocks in arid n. Kenya. White or whitish crown, wing patches, wing-linings and belly; underparts variably streaked. Feeds on ground or in fruiting *Salvadora* shrubs. **7a, 7b and 7c. Adults**. Upperparts shining olive-green, showing much gloss in strong light; wings and tail bluer. Eyes white. **7d. Juv**. Browner, less glossy; pale tawny-white crown. Eyes brown, becoming paler with age. Bill mostly yellow.

8 RED-BILLED OXPECKER *Buphagus erythrorhynchus*   **Page 516**
Common near large wild mammals, locally with livestock. No rump/back contrast. **8a. Adult**. Yellow eye-wattles; all-red bill. **8b. Immature**. Darker than adult; bill, eyes and orbital skin dark. **8c. Juv**. Similar to 8b, but bill yellow.

9 YELLOW-BILLED OXPECKER *Buphagus a. africanus*   **Page 516**
Locally common, but less widespread than Red-billed Oxpecker. Often with buffalo and rhino. Larger than Red-billed, with pale creamy buff rump; no eye-wattles. **9a. Adult**. Expanded base of bill yellow, tip red. **9b. Juv**. Bill dark; plumage duskier than adult's.

DALE A. ZIMMERMAN
1992

PLATE 79: 'RED-WINGED' STARLINGS (As seen in strong sunlight)

1 RED-WINGED STARLING *Onychognathus morio* **Page 511**
Widespread around cliffs, city buildings, mainly 1000–2400 m. In pairs or small flocks.
Long pointed tail less extreme than in No, 3. Bill heavy. **1a and 1c. Males. 1b. Female.**
Head and neck grey with dark streaks.

2 BRISTLE-CROWNED STARLING *Onychognathus salvadorii* **Page 511**
Local in n. Kenya near cliffs, rocky gorges. Velvety 'cushion' on head; very long, pointed tail. Much rufous in primaries. **Male** illustrated. Female smaller with greyer head,
smaller 'cushion'.

3 SLENDER-BILLED STARLING *Onychognathus tenuirostris theresae* **Page 511**
Locally common in cent. Kenyan highlands, at higher elevations than No. 1, and often
around waterfalls. Rufous primaries obvious in flight. Bill slender. **3a. Female.** Glossy
blue-black, some grey-tipped feathers. **3b. Male.**

4 WALLER'S STARLING *Onychognathus w. walleri* **Page 510**
Locally common in highland forests. Short-tailed. Forms large noisy post-breeding flocks.
Primaries largely rufous. **4a and 4c. Males. 4b. Female.** (Western race *elgonensis* shows
less grey on head.)

5 STUHLMANN'S STARLING *Poeoptera stuhlmanni* **Page 510**
Fairly common in w. Kenyan forest treetops. Iris brown, yellow peripherally. **5a and 5b.
Males.** All black at distance, glossed blue in strong light; no rufous in wings. **5c and 5d.
Females.** Dark grey with bluish gloss; rufous primaries show in flight.

6 KENRICK'S STARLING *Poeoptera kenricki bensoni* **Page 510**
Local in montane forests on Mt Kenya and Nyambeni Hills. Species' eye colour grey or
yellow, the latter perhaps more common in smaller Tanzanian race *kenricki*; *bensoni*
usually grey-eyed. **6a. Male.** Black with faint bronzy gloss; no rufous in wings. **6b.
Female.** Grey; primaries largely rufous as in female Stuhlmann's.

Bristle-crowned Starlings

PLATE 80: ORIOLES AND CORVIDS

1 EURASIAN GOLDEN ORIOLE *Oriolus o. oriolus* **Page 507**
Regular palearctic migrant, Oct.-Dec. and March–April, common in spring in coastal lowlands. Scarce, Jan.–early March. **1a. Older adult female.** Yellow underparts with faint olive streaks. **1b. Adult male.** Black on lores, none behind eyes; wings largely black. **1c. First-winter male** (first-winter female similar). Bend of wing darker than side of neck; no grey postocular stripe; wing feathers not obviousy yellow-edged. Some immatures of both sexes more heavily streaked. Bill brown, becoming pinkish.

2 AFRICAN GOLDEN ORIOLE *Oriolus auratus notatus* **Page 507**
Regular intra-African migrant, April–August, in wooded habitats, especially coastal forest; less common inland. **2a. Adult male.** Much yellow wing edging; black stripe through eye. **2b. Adult female.** Grey eye-line. **2c. Immature male.** Resembles 1c, but bend of wing little darker than back and neck; grey eye-line extends behind eye; bold yellow wing edging. Bill black.

3 GREEN-HEADED ORIOLE *Oriolus chlorocephalus amani* **Page 507**
Local and uncommon in southern Kenyan coastal forest; more numerous in Usambara Mts. Greenish head, yellow collar.

4 BLACK-HEADED ORIOLE *Oriolus larvatus rolleti* **Page 506**
Common below 2300 m in open woods, acacia savanna, forest edge; locally in mangroves. **4a. Adult.** Central tail feathers olive; inner secondaries ('tertials') edged with pale yellow, outer secondaries with whitish; greater coverts mainly grey. **4b. Juvenile.** Throat and breast densely streaked.

5 WESTERN BLACK-HEADED ORIOLE *Oriolus brachyrhynchus laetior*
  Page 507
Fairly common in Kakamega Forest, w. Kenya. **5a. Adult.** Outer secondaries edged with slate-grey, not whitish; inner secondaries ('tertials') edged with olive, not yellow. Central rectrices yellow-olive. **5b. Juvenile.** Head dusky olive; breast faintly streaked.

6 MONTANE ORIOLE *Oriolus percivali* **Page 506**
Locally common in Kenyan highland forests. Some hybridization with No. 4 (see text). **6a. Adult.** Central tail feathers black; wings with more black than in Nos. 4 and 5. **6b. Juvenile.** Faintly streaked below the dark throat.

7 PIAPIAC *Ptilostomus afer* **Page 508**
Scarce in w. Kenya near Ugandan border; often with large mammals. **7a, 7b and 7c. Adults.** Eyes purple or red-violet; bill black. **7d. Juvenile.** Eyes brown; bill largely pink.

8 CAPE ROOK *Corvus capensis* **Page 509**
Local in grassland, semi-desert and cultivation. Slender bill; plumage browner when worn. **8a and 8b. Adults.**

9 FAN-TAILED RAVEN *Corvus rhipidurus* **Page 509**
Locally common near cliffs, rocky hills in n. Kenya. Very short tail exceeded by wing tips in perched bird. **9a and 9b. Adults.**

10 DWARF or BROWN-NECKED RAVEN *Corvus (ruficollis) edithae* **Page 508**
Common in arid n. Kenya. Ruffled feathers of nape, neck and breast show white bases. Plumage browner when worn. **10a, 10b and 10c. Adults.**

11 HOUSE CROW *Corvus s. splendens* **Page 508**
Common along coast north to Malindi. Grey neck, sooty grey underparts. Tail extends well beyond wing tips in perched bird. **11a and 11b. Adults.**

12 PIED CROW *Corvus albus* **Page 509**
Widespread up to 3000 m, including all urban areas. **12a and 12b. Adults.**

13 WHITE-NAPED RAVEN *Corvus albicollis* **Page 509**
Locally common around mountains, escarpments and rocky hills. Wing tips extend beyond tail tip. In flight, appears short-tailed, broad-winged. **13a and 13b. Adults.** (Juv. duller and browner; some black streaks on nape.)

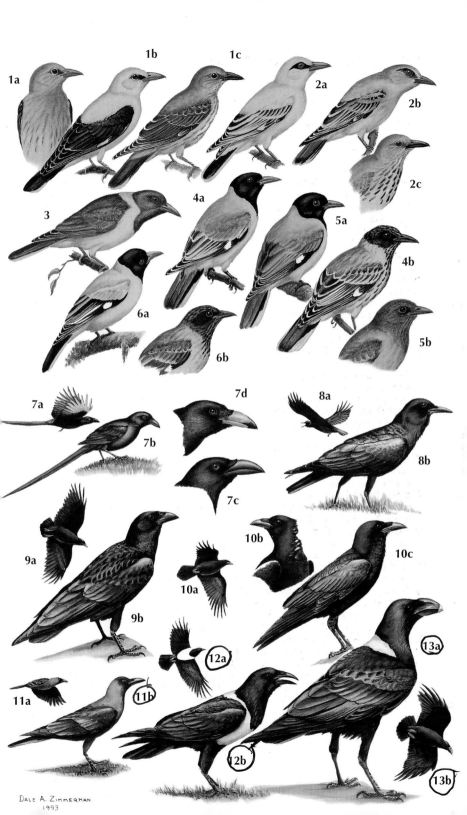

PLATE 81: CUCKOO-SHRIKES AND DRONGOS

1 RED-SHOULDERED CUCKOO-SHRIKE *Campephaga phoenicea*   **Page 504**
Scarce and local in riverine thickets and open wooded habitats near Ugandan border in w. Kenya. **1a. Male. 1b. Female**. Upperparts greyish or grey-brown with no olive tinge.

2 BLACK CUCKOO-SHRIKE *Campephaga flava*   **Page 504**
Largely an intra-African migrant, May–Oct., when common and widespread in bush, woodland and forest edge. **2a. Female**. Upperparts greyish olive; underside of tail largely yellow. **2b. Male, all-black morph. 2c. Male, yellow-shouldered morph**.

3 PURPLE-THROATED CUCKOO-SHRIKE *Campephaga quiscalina martini*
Page 504
Uncommon in forest and forest edge in the highlands. **3a and 3b. Males**. Throat/breast glossed with purple. Mouth red or orange-red. **3c. Female**. Upperparts plain olive; head mostly grey.

4 PETIT'S CUCKOO-SHRIKE *Campephaga petiti*   **Page 504**
Fairly common in Kakamega and Nandi Forests, w. Kenya. **4a and 4b. Males**. Prominent rictal skin and mouth-lining bright orange-yellow. **4c. Female**. Upperparts barred with black; underparts plain except for bars on sides of lower throat and upper breast. **4d. Immature male**. Plain above, barred below (sometimes more heavily than shown). (Juv. heavily black-spotted below.)

5 WHITE-BREASTED CUCKOO-SHRIKE *Coracina pectoralis*   **Page 505**
Rare in savanna and open woodland in w. Kenya and n. Tanzania. **5a. Female. 5b. Male**.

6 GREY CUCKOO-SHRIKE *Coracina caesia pura*   **Page 505**
Local in highland forests. Quiet and inconspicuous; perches motionless for long periods. **6a. Female. 6b. Juvenile male. 6c. Adult male**. Blackish lores and chin.

7 SQUARE-TAILED DRONGO *Dicrurus ludwigii sharpei*   **Page 506**
Local in w. Kenyan forests and (similar nominate race) in Tana River, coastal forests, and Usambara Mts. Tail slightly notched, not splayed. Highly vocal. **7a. Adult**. Eyes red. **7b. Juvenile**. Eyes brown.

8 VELVET-MANTLED DRONGO *Dicrurus modestus coracinus*   **Page 506**
Scarce in Kakamega Forest, w. Kenya. Less glossy than Common Drongo; back and rump velvety black; no pale wing flash in flight.

9 COMMON DRONGO *Dicrurus a. adsimilis*   **Page 505**
Widespread and common in varied habitats, including forest edge. Shows pale silvery wing flash in flight. **9a. Adult**. Eyes red. **9b. Immature**. Eyes brown; skin at corners of mouth pale; less 'fork-tailed' than adult. **9c. Juvenile**. Eye colour variable from amber or grey-brown to yellowish grey; underparts mottled grey-brown, with varying amounts of buff on feather tips.

DALE A. ZIMMERMAN
1993

PLATE 82: BUSH-SHRIKES (See also Plate 83)

1 MARSH TCHAGRA *Tchagra m. minuta* **Page 498**
Uncommon and local in wet grasslands, marsh edges. Solid black crown. Black V on back (obsolete in rare coastal/Usambara race *T. m. reichenowi*). **1a. Male. 1b. Female. 1c. Juvenile.**

2 BRUBRU *Nilaus afer minor* **Page 497**
Widespread in savanna, open woodland and bush. **Male** illustrated. (Female has black replaced by brown or blackish brown. Western *N. a. massaicus* has dark brownish-chestnut sides and flanks.)

3 BROWN-CROWNED TCHAGRA *Tchagra australis emini* **Page 498**
Widespread. Common in moist bush, woodland, bushed grassland, on or near ground in dense shrubbery. Skulking; sings from bushtops and in flight. **3a and 3b. Adults.** (Coastal birds are smaller, paler and greyer below.)

4 BLACK-CROWNED TCHAGRA *Tchagra s. senegala* **Page 497**
Locally common in shrubbery of wooded and bushed habitats. Skulking; conspicuous only in song-flight. Sympatric with No. 3 in many areas. **Male** illustrated (female similar).

5 THREE-STREAKED TCHAGRA *Tchagra j. jamesi* **Page 498**
Local and uncommon in dry bush below 1000 m. Sings on the wing like No. 4. Skulking. Some birds have narrow, incomplete central crown stripe. (Eastern *T. j. mandana* more sandy buff, less grey, than *jamesi*.)

6 BOCAGE'S or GREY-GREEN BUSH-SHRIKE *Malaconotus bocagei jacksoni* **Page 498**
Western Kenya, in Nandi and Kakamega forests only. Arboreal, usually in canopy. **Male** illustrated (female similar).

7 PINK-FOOTED PUFFBACK *Dryoscopus angolensis* **Page 503**
Uncommon in w. Kenyan forest canopy (Nandi, Kakamega). **7a. Male. 7b. Female.**

8 PRINGLE'S PUFFBACK *Dryoscopus pringlii* **Page 503**
Local and uncommon in dry northern and eastern *Acacia* and *Commiphora* bush, often with mixed-species flocks in low trees, shrubbery. Eyes crimson; basal half of mandible pale. **8a. Male.** Tail edged and tipped with dull white in fresh plumage. **8b. Female.** Dull, with narrow white eye-ring and white loral area.

9 NORTHERN PUFFBACK *Dryoscopus gambensis malzacii* **Page 502**
North of the Equator in lightly wooded areas. Arboreal. **9a. Male.** Rump grey (as in female Black-backed Puffback); scapulars grey or dull whitish, underparts dull white. **9b. Female.** Tawny buff underparts, buff wing edgings, orange eyes.

10 BLACK-BACKED PUFFBACK *Dryoscopus cubla* **Page 503**
Male clean-cut, bright white below, with white rump. Female has grey rump, white supraloral stripes. Coastal race *affinis* has all-black wings. **10a. D. c. affinis, immature female. 10b. D. c. affinis, male. 10c. D. c. hamatus, male. 10d. D. c. hamatus, female.**

11 SLATE-COLOURED BOUBOU *Laniarius funebris* **Page 502**
Common and widespread in scrub, bush and thickets below 2000 m. Dark bluish slate. **11a. Adult male. 11b. Juvenile.**

12 TROPICAL BOUBOU *Laniarius aethiopicus* **Page 501**
12a. L. f. major. West of Rift Valley. **12b. L. f. ambiguus.** Highlands east of Rift Valley. **12c. L. f. sublacteus, normal morph.** Coastal, inland to Garissa, Taita Hills, Lake Jipe, East Usambara and North Pare mts. **12d. L. f. sublacteus, black morph.** Coastal only; glossy black, not dull slate as in No. 11.

13 SOOTY BOUBOU *Laniarius leucorhynchus* **Page 502**
Accidental in our region. Wholly sooty black or brownish black. Bill heavy, black in adults, ivory in young birds. **Adult female** illustrated. (Male slightly glossier.)

PLATE 83: BUSH-SHRIKES (See also Plate 82)

1 LÜHDER'S BUSH-SHRIKE *Laniarius l. luehderi*　　　**Page 501**
Western Kenyan forest undergrowth, forest-edge tangles. Shy and skulking. **1a. juv.** Buffy
yellow on breast and sides; olive above, with rufous upper tail-coverts (barred with black)
and tail. **1b. Adult.**

2 RED-NAPED BUSH-SHRIKE, *Laniarius ruficeps rufinuchalis*　　　**Page 501**
Eastern. Locally common in thickets in dry bush country; long white wing-stripe, white-
sided tail. Shy and skulking. **2a. Juv.** Olive-grey above, with suggestion of black mask.
2b. Adult. Forecrown black (orange-red in *L. r. kismayensis* around Kiunga).

3 PAPYRUS GONOLEK *Laniarius mufumbiri*　　　**Page 501**
Papyrus swamps around Lake Victoria. Locally common. **3a. Immature.** Yellowish buff
throat; pinkish or brick-red breast; crown greyish olive mixed with black. **3b. Adult.**
Golden-yellow crown; white in wing and on under tail-coverts.

4 BLACK-HEADED GONOLEK *Laniarius erythrogaster*　　　**Page 500**
Western Kenya. Fairly common in dense shrubbery, brushy cultivation and thickets.
4a. Adult. Entirely black above; lower belly and crissum yellowish buff. **4b. Juv.** Barred
yellowish buff and black below; flecked with red when moulting into adult plumage.

5 FOUR-COLOURED BUSH-SHRIKE *Malaconotus quadricolor nigricauda*
　　　Page 499
Uncommon in eastern lowland-forest undergrowth and thickets. Skulking. Supraloral
region orange or yellow; some red below black breast band. Tail black (olive-green in
female).

6 DOHERTY'S BUSH-SHRIKE *Malaconotus dohertyi*　　　**Page 499**
Uncommon in Kenyan highland-forest undergrowth, dense thickets with bamboo above
2200 m. Shy and skulking. **6a. Adult.** Red forehead and under tail-coverts; no red below
the black breast band. **6b. Adult, yellow morph.** Rare. No red pigment.

7 SULPHUR-BREASTED BUSH-SHRIKE *Malaconotus sulfureopectus similis*
　　　Page 499
Widespread in dry woodland, acacia savanna, forest edge; arboreal. Small bill.
7a. Immature. Grey head, upper back; suggestion of white superciliary stripe. **7b. Adult.**
Bright yellow superciliary stripe; black facial mask; broad orange breast band.

8 GREY-HEADED BUSH-SHRIKE *Malaconotus blanchoti approximans* **Page 500**
Widespread but uncommon in bush and woodland; arboreal. Large, with heavy bill, grey
head, white tips to wing feathers; yellow eyes. Chestnut on breast; may extend to flanks,
but lacking in northwestern race *catharoxanthus*.

9 ROSY-PATCHED BUSH-SHRIKE *Rhodophoneus cruentus*　　　**Page 500**
Locally common. Near or on ground in dry bush and semi-desert. Long, white-cornered
tail and rosy red rump patch conspicuous in flight. **9a and 9d. R. c. hilgerti,** male. North
of Equator. Red throat/breast patch with no black border. (Female has black-bordered
white throat similar to 9c.) **9b. R. c. cathemagmenus,** male. South of Equator. Black border to red throat/breast patch. **9c. R. c. cathemagmenus,** female. White throat, with black
border expanded to form patch on upper breast.

10 BLACK-FRONTED BUSH-SHRIKE *Malaconotus nigrifrons*　　　**Page 499**
Fairly common in highland forest; arboreal. Black forehead and mask. Underparts variable. **10a. Golden-breasted morph.** Widespread. **10b. Red-breasted morph.** Western and
cent. Kenyan highlands and Mt Kilimanjaro. Some individuals duller red below.
10c. Buff-breasted morph. Mt Kenya, Taita Hills, Usambara Mts.

DALE A. ZIMMERMAN
1987

PLATE 84: SHRIKES (See also Plate 85)

1 YELLOW-BILLED SHRIKE *Corvinella corvina affinis* **Page 494**
Uncommon and local in w. and nw. Kenya, now mainly on and near ne. Mt Elgon. **Adult**.
Brown, long tail, yellow bill. Wings show much rufous in flight.

2 MAGPIE SHRIKE *Urolestes melanoleucus aequatorialis* **Page 494**
Local in acacia savanna/bush in e. Mara GR and n. Tanzania. **Adult**. Large and long-
tailed; tail length and amount of white in wings variable. Only shrike with black underparts.

3 LONG-TAILED FISCAL *Lanius cabanisi* **Page 496**
Common in dry open savanna/bush mainly east of the Rift Valley; also in coastal lowlands. Larger than Common Fiscal, with longer, broader tail. **3a. Adult male**. Back dark
grey; no white on scapulars. **3b. Juv.** Large; closely barred above.

4 GREY-BACKED FISCAL *Lanius e. excubitoroides* **Page 495**
Common in moist bush and cultivation, mainly in the west, and cent. Rift Valley.
Adult male. Pale grey on back, much white at tail base. (Female has rufous on flanks.)

5 COMMON FISCAL *Lanius collaris humeralis* **Page 496**
Widespread in highlands above 1500 m; often common in open country, cultivation,
towns and gardens. Slender, with long narrow tail. **5a. Juv.** Heavily barred. **5b. Adult
male**. Back black, scapulars pure white. (Female shows trace of chestnut on flanks.)

6 MACKINNON'S FISCAL *Lanius mackinnoni* **Page 495**
Uncommon at forest edge and in cultivation in w. Kenyan highlands. **Adult female**. Grey
above, with white scapulars, black facial mask. (Male lacks chestnut flank patch.)

7 LESSER GREY SHRIKE *Lanius minor* **Page 495**
Widespread palearctic migrant, common late March–early May in open country.
Occasional in autumn. **7a. Spring adult**. Grey above, with black forehead; in fresh
plumage, shows pink tinge on breast and sides. **7b. Autumn adult** (Oct.–Nov.). Some
dark barring on forehead. **7c. First-winter**. Upperparts tinged brownish; no black on forehead; bill pale at base.

8 SOMALI FISCAL *Lanius somalicus* **Page 496**
Uncommon and local in semi-desert areas of n. Kenya. Short-tailed. **Adult male**. Crown,
nape and hindneck black; centre of back pale grey; white on scapulars and secondary
tips. (Female lacks chestnut flanks.)

9 TAITA FISCAL *Lanius dorsalis* **Page 496**
Common in dry bush and savanna below 1500 m. **Adult male**. Lacks white secondary
tips of Somali Fiscal. (Female usually has trace of chestnut on flanks.)

10 MASKED SHRIKE *Lanius nubicus* **Page 497**
Scarce palearctic migrant; most records from Lake Baringo. Favours acacias near water.
Dainty, with slender bill. **10a. First-autumn female**. Brownish grey above; extent of barring variable. Resembles adult by Dec. **10b. Adult male**. (Female similar but duller: back
and nape feathers tipped with brownish, lower back greyer, all white areas buffier.)

11 WOODCHAT SHRIKE *Lanius senator niloticus* **Page 496**
Uncommon palearctic migrant in w. and nw. Kenya, Nov.–March. **11a. First-autumn
bird** with remnant juvenile plumage. More rufous than young Masked Shrike. Similar to
Juv. Red-tailed and Red-backed Shrikes (Plate 85), but scapulars and 'shoulders' paler,
and head markings less contrasting. **11b. Adult male**. Rufous on head; white scapulars
and upper tail-coverts. **11c. Adult female**. Duller and often much smaller than male.
11d. First-winter female. Still duller; face pattern more obscure.

PLATE 85: SHRIKES AND HELMET-SHRIKES (See also Plate 84)

1 RED-BACKED SHRIKE *Lanius collurio* **Page 494**
Palearctic migrant (Nov.–Dec. and April) in open habitats. Some winter in se. Kenya, ne. Tanzania. **1a. *L. c. kobylini*, ad. male. 1b. *L. c. collurio*, ad. male. 1c. *L. c. pallidifrons*, ad. female. 1d and 1e. *L. c. collurio*, first-winter.** Variable barring; underside of tail grey.

2 RED-TAILED or ISABELLINE SHRIKE *Lanius isabellinus* **Page 494**
Common migrant and winter resident Nov.–April. in open habitats, mainly east of Rift Valley. **2a. *L. i. phoenicuroides*, ad. female.** Brown above; tail rufous beneath. **2b. *L. i. phoenicuroides*, typical ad. male.** Brown above, crown more rufous. **2c. *L. i. phoenicuroides*, first-winter.** Barring fainter than on young of No. 1; tail rufous beneath. **2d. *L. i. phoenicuroides*, pale ad. male.** Pale greyish above with paler crown; white below. **2e. *L. i. isabellinus* (= *speculigerus*), ad. male.** Sandy grey above, tail pale rufous. White primary patch; cinnamon wash below.

3 Hybrid RED-BACKED X RED-TAILED SHRIKE *L. collurio* X *L. isabellinus*
3a. Male. Grey upperparts, black-and-white tail. **3b. Male.** Back rufous; tail rufous or rufous-edged, no white.

4 GREY-CRESTED HELMET-SHRIKE *Prionops poliolophus* **Page 493**
Uncommon from Serengeti NP and Mara GR north to Lake Nakuru. Dark grey crest; no eye-wattle. Flight pattern similar to that of *P. plumatus*.

5 WHITE-CRESTED HELMET-SHRIKE *Prionops plumatus* **Page 492**
Uncommon in woodland and bush. Restless, nomadic, noisy and gregarious. Yellow eye-wattle; crest whitish to pale grey. **5a. *P. p. cristatus*.** Nw. Kenya. Large; curly-crested; closed wings largely black. **5b. *P. p. vinaceigularis*.** Eastern. Moderate crest; little or no white in closed wing. **5c and 5d. *P. p. poliocephalus*.** Southern. Small; short-crested; long white wing-stripe.

6 CHESTNUT-FRONTED HELMET-SHRIKE *Prionops scopifrons kirki* **Page 493**
Locally common in coastal Kenyan woods, often in flocks with No. 7. (Similar to *P. s. scopifrons* in E. Usambaras. Interior Kenyan *keniensis* lacks whitish on crown.)

7 RETZ'S HELMET-SHRIKE *Prionops retzii graculina* **Page 493**
Fairly common in coastal woods; uncommon inland to Kibwezi, Mkomazi GR and Arusha NP. Gregarious. **7a and 7b. Adults. 7c. Juv./imm.**

8 NORTHERN WHITE-CROWNED SHRIKE *Eurocephalus rueppelli* **Page 493**
Common in dry bush and open woodland below 1600 m. Conspicuous; sometimes in small groups. **8a and 8b. Adults. 8c. Juvenile.**

Southern Grey Shrike, Lanius meridionalis pallidirostris. *Vagrant. See text.*

PLATE 86: WATTLE-EYES AND BATISES

1 **YELLOW-BELLIED WATTLE-EYE** *Dyaphorophyia concreta graueri* **Page 491**
Kakamega and Nandi Forests; scarce in tall undergrowth. Yellow belly, apple-green eye-wattles. **1a. Male**. Yellow throat. **1b. Female**. Chestnut throat.

2 **JAMESON'S WATTLE-EYE** *Dyaphorophyia jamesoni* **Page 491**
Kakamega and Nandi Forests; fairly common in low undergrowth. White belly, blue eye-wattles. **2a. Adult male**. Glossy greenish black above and on throat. **2b. Juvenile**. Pale rufous throat.

3 **CHESTNUT WATTLE-EYE** *Dyaphorophyia c. castanea* **Page 491**
Kakamega and South Nandi Forests; fairly common in high undergrowth, low trees. Plum-coloured eye-wattles. **3a. Female**. Chestnut above and on breast. **3b. Male**. White collar and back, broad black breast band.

4 **COMMON WATTLE-EYE** *Platysteira cyanea nyansae* **Page 490**
Western. Widespread in woodland, forest edge, riparian trees. Scarlet eye-wattles, long white wing-stripe. **4a. Immature female**. Pale rufous wing stripe; rufous-tinged white throat; suggestion of adult's pattern. **4b. Adult female**. Maroon-chestnut throat. **4c. Adult male**. White throat bordered by broad black breast band.

5 **BLACK-THROATED WATTLE-EYE** *Platysteira p. peltata* **Page 490**
Local and uncommon in forest and riparian trees, this race east of Rift Valley to the coast. (West of the Rift, *P. p. mentalis* has greener gloss.) **5a. Male**. Narrow breast band across white underparts; eyes dark brown. **5b. Female**. Throat/upper breast glossy black.

6 **PYGMY BATIS** *Batis perkeo* **Page 490**
Northern and eastern; fairly common in dry areas, mostly in low *Acacia* scrub-savanna. Small, short-tailed and with white supraloral stripe not extending behind eye. **6a. Female**. Pale line from bill to above front of eye only; orange-tawny breast band; throat usually washed with buff. **6b. Male**. Pattern suggests Chin-spot, but white supraloral line does not extend as superciliary stripe, breast band narrower, tail shorter.

7 **GREY-HEADED BATIS** *Batis o. orientalis* **Page 490**
Rare in far-northern dry country; known with certainty only from Ethiopian border. Complete superciliary stripe typically extends behind eye in both sexes (shorter in worn birds). See text. **7a. Male**. **7b. Female**. Breast band broad, deep chestnut, not cinnamon or tawny; in hand, shows trace of rufous on white nuchal spot.

8 **BLACK-HEADED BATIS** *Batis minor* **Page 489**
Uncommon to fairly common in savanna and open wooded habitats in the west (*B. m. erlangeri*) and southeast (*B. m. minor*). See text. **8a. *B. m. erlangeri*, female**. Like female Chin-spot Batis, but lacks throat spot and crown usually darker (often as black as side of face). **8b. *B. m. erlangeri*, male**. Typically blackish-crowned, but some can be greyer. (Worn Chin-spot similar.) **8c. *B. m. minor*, male**. Crown medium grey to blackish; breast-band width variable (typically narrower than in Chin-spot). **8d. *B. m. minor*, female**. Crown grey to blackish; breast band often narrow, but quite broad at sides. Commonly mistaken for No. 7, and some individuals seem intermediate with that species. See text.

9 **CHIN-SPOT BATIS** *Batis molitor* **Page 488**
Commonest batis; widespread in various wooded habitats except in arid regions, Lake Victoria basin and on coast. With wear, grey crown becomes darker and white superciliary stripes narrower. **9a. Male**. Breast band broad (especially in centre). **9b. Female**. Chestnut throat spot and breast band. (*Cf.* female Pale Batis.)

10 **FOREST BATIS** *Batis mixta ultima* **Page 489**
Coastal forest and evergreen thickets; fairly common in undergrowth. (Nominate Tanzanian race, on Plate 124, may be in montane forest canopy). Short-tailed; eyes red or orange. **10a. Female**. Tawny wing patch; frosty light cinnamon throat and breast. **10b. Male**. Eye colour distinctive.

11 **PALE or EAST COAST BATIS** *Batis soror* **Page 489**
Coastal. In Kenya, primarily in *Brachystegia;* in the Usambara Mts, below1000 m in other open woodland. Paler and shorter-tailed than Chin-spot **11a. Male**. Yellow eyes, narrow breast band. **11b. Female**. Pale tawny or cinnamon (not chestnut) throat spot and breast band; superciliary stripe faintly rufous-tinged.

DALE A. ZIMMERMAN
1986

PLATE 87: FLYCATCHERS AND SHRIKE-FLYCATCHER

1 SILVERBIRD *Empidornis semipartitus*   **Page 455**
Western acacia savanna and other open habitats, mainly below 1600 m. **1a. Juvenile. 1b. Adult.**

2 PALE FLYCATCHER *Bradornis pallidus murinus*   **Page 455**
Widespread; typically in moister habitats than African Grey Flycatcher. **2a. Juvenile.** Dorsal pale areas buff or tawny; throat streaked. **2b. Adult.** Pale grey-brown above, with plain unstreaked crown. (Coastal race *B. p. subalaris* paler, with almost no trace of breast band.)

3 AFRICAN GREY FLYCATCHER *Bradornis m. microrhynchus*   **Page 455**
Common and widespread, except in coastal lowlands and Lake Victoria basin. **3a. Adult.** Greyer than Pale Flycatcher, with streaked forecrown and smaller bill. **3b. Juvenile.** Paler than juv. Pale Flycatcher; throat unstreaked.

4 ASHY FLYCATCHER *Muscicapa caerulescens cinereola*   **Page 454**
Local; forest borders and acacia woodland. Ashy blue-grey, with white supraloral streak and eye-ring; tail grey. (Western *M. c. brevicaudata* more bluish-tinged above.)

5 LEAD-COLOURED FLYCATCHER *Myioparus plumbeus orientalis*   **Page 455**
Uncommon in riverine and acacia woods. Darker than Ashy Flycatcher, with white-edged black tail, this often raised and actively flirted.

6 AFRICAN DUSKY FLYCATCHER *Muscicapa adusta interposita*   **Page 453**
Common and widespread in highlands. Small; plain except for lighter wing-feather edges and tips, which wear away to leave more uniformly brown plumage.

7 SWAMP FLYCATCHER *Muscicapa aquatica infulata*   **Page 453**
Mainly in Lake Victoria basin. Fairly common in papyrus swamps.

8 WHITE-EYED SLATY FLYCATCHER *Melaenornis f. fischeri*   **Page 454**
Common and widespread in highlands. (See Plate 124 for Tanzanian *M. f. nyikensis*.) **8a. Adult. 8b. Juvenile.**

9 CHAPIN'S FLYCATCHER *Muscicapa lendu*   **Page 453**
Only in Kakamega and North Nandi Forests, where scarce. Short, dark bill with yellow gape; narrow greyish supraloral line. Sluggish; perches in foliage 10–20 m above ground.

10 SPOTTED FLYCATCHER *Muscicapa striata neumanni*   **Page 453**
Widespread palearctic migrant, often common Oct.–April. Variable streaks on crown, throat and breast, faint in some birds. Bill entirely black.

11 GAMBAGA FLYCATCHER *Muscicapa gambagae*   **Page 453**
Local and uncommon in n. and e. Kenyan thorn-scrub and savanna. Shorter-winged than Spotted Flycatcher; head rounder; bill shorter, with buff or yellowish mandible.

12 AFRICAN SHRIKE-FLYCATCHER *Bias flammulatus aequatorialis*   **Page 491**
Uncommon in west Kenyan forest canopy. Sideways wagging of tail diagnostic. **12a. Female.** Rufous rump, crissum and wing-feather edgings. **12b. Male.** Rump and under-parts white.

13 SEMI-COLLARED FLYCATCHER *Ficedula semitorquata*   **Page 456**
Uncommon palearctic migrant in w. Kenya. See text for similar Pied Flycatcher. **13a. Spring male.** Suggestion of partial white collar. Often shows white bar on median coverts. **13b. Adult male, autumn/winter.** Brownish, with bold black-and-white wing pattern. **13c. Female.** Duller than autumn male.

14 COLLARED FLYCATCHER *Ficedula albicollis*   **Page 456**
Palearctic vagrant. See text. **14a. Male, spring.** Complete white collar. **14b. Female.** Somewhat darker and browner than female Semi-collared. May show vague pale nuchal collar or suggestion of dark breast band.

PLATE 88: MONARCH FLYCATCHERS, BLACK-AND-WHITE FLY-CATCHER AND BLACK FLYCATCHERS

1 RED-BELLIED PARADISE FLYCATCHER *Terpsiphone rufiventer emini*
Page 488
Western Kenya, only in Kakamega Forest interior; scarce. Interbreeds with No. 3. **Adult male**. Black head sharply defined from body; solid rufous underparts. (Female greyer on throat.)

2 HYBRID RED-BELLIED X AFRICAN PARADISE FLYCATCHER **Page 488**
T. r. emini X *T. viridis ferreti*. Kakamega Forest. Now more numerous than typical *T. rufiventer*. **2a. Female, rufous-breasted type**. Paler on belly than 'pure' *rufiventer*; black or grey of throat extends onto breast. **2b. Male, grey-and-rufous type**.

3 AFRICAN PARADISE FLYCATCHER *Terpsiphone viridis* **Page 487**
Common and widespread in wooded areas and gardens. **3a. T. v. ferreti, male, white morph. 3b. T. v. plumbeiceps, male**. Coastal, no white in wing. **3c. T. v. ferreti, male, rufous morph**. Rufous above, grey below, glossy black head with blue eye-wattle; central rectrices sometimes short. **3d. T. v. ferreti, female, rufous morph**.

4 BLACK-AND-WHITE FLYCATCHER *Bias musicus* **Page 492**
Rare in Meru, Ngaia (and formerly coastal) forests; also in Usambara Mts. Stocky, long crest, yellow eye. Highly vocal. **4a. Female. 4b. Male**.

5 BLUE-MANTLED CRESTED FLYCATCHER *Trochocercus cyanomelas bivittatus*
Page 487
Uncommon in forest undergrowth throughout coastal lowlands, inland to the Chyulu Hills and Kitovu Forest (Taveta Dist.), North Pare Mts, Arusha and Moshi districts. **5a. Male**. White wing patch. **5b. Female**. Grey above, with white eye-ring and wing-bars.

6 NORTHERN BLACK FLYCATCHER *Melaenornis edolioides* **Page 454**
Locally common west of the Rift Valley near wooded areas and in cultivation. Dull black. **Adult** figured. (Juv. like 7b, but dull black.)

7 SOUTHERN BLACK FLYCATCHER *Melaenornis pammelaina* **Page 454**
Locally common in dry woodland east of the Rift Valley. No overlap with No. 6. **7a. Adult**. Glossy blue-black. **7b. Juvenile**. Duller, with tawny buff spots.

8 DUSKY CRESTED FLYCATCHER *Trochocercus nigromitratus* **Page 487**
W. Kenya: uncommon in Kakamega and Chemoni forest undergrowth. Dull bluish slate, with black face and crest.

9 AFRICAN BLUE FLYCATCHER *Elminia longicauda teresita* **Page 487**
W. Kenya: locally common in woodland, forest edge and gardens. Pale blue; active and confiding.

10 WHITE-TAILED CRESTED FLYCATCHER *Trochocercus albonotatus* **Page 487**
Fairly common in montane forests of the w. and cent. Kenyan highlands and Usambara Mts. Much white in frequently fanned tail.

DALE A. ZIMMERMAN
1986

PLATE 89: BABBLERS AND CHATTERERS (*Turdoides*)

1 SCALY CHATTERER *T. aylmeri kenianus*   **Page 437**
Uncommon in dry *Commiphora* scrub. Brown, not rufous; scaly throat and breast. Pale bluish grey or whitish skin surrounding pale eyes.

2 RUFOUS CHATTERER *T. r. rubiginosus*   **Page 436**
Widespread in dense bush and thickets below 1500 m. Pale bill; eyes usually pale.

3 SCALY BABBLER *T. s. squamulatus*   **Page 436**
Uncommon in coastal forest and thickets, along Tana River and in extreme ne. Kenya. Dark face and ear-coverts, orange-yellow eyes, scaly breast, whitish chin.

4 ARROW-MARKED BABBLER *T. jardineii emini*   **Page 435**
Locally common north to Lake Nakuru NP, in thickets, forest edge and shrubby woodland. Orange-yellow eyes, sharp-pointed white feather tips, dark lores.

5 BLACK-LORED BABBLER *T. sharpei*   **Page 435**
Locally common in forest edge, thickets and dense bush. White eyes, black lores. **5a. *T. s. vepres*.** White throat patch, but ventral plumage variable. (See text.) Nanyuki and Timau Districts. **5b. *T. s. sharpei*.** Underparts mottled throughout. Common around lakes Naivasha and Elmenteita.

6 BROWN BABBLER *T. plebejus cinereus*   **Page 436**
Uncommon in nw. Kenya, south to the Equator. Yellow eyes, pale lores and chin; white feather tips on breast.

7 NORTHERN PIED BABBLER *T. h. hypoleucus*   **Page 436**
Cent. Kenya and n. Tanzania. Common in some Nairobi suburbs. White eyes, dark flanks and patch on sides of breast.

8 HINDE'S BABBLER *T. hindei*   **Page 436**
Local in cent. Kenyan highlands. Variable. White feather edgings, tawny-cinnamon rump/upper tail-coverts. Red or orange-red eyes. **8a. Light variation. 8b. Dark variation.**

Black-lored Babblers

DALE A. ZIMMERMAN
1989

PLATE 90: ILLADOPSES, HILL BABBLER AND THRUSHES (Part)

1 MOUNTAIN ILLADOPSIS *Illadopsis p. pyrrhoptera*   **Page 438**
On or near ground in montane Kenyan forests. Grey below, with brownish flanks and crissum; throat whitish.

2 AFRICAN HILL BABBLER *Pseudoalcippe a. abyssinica*   **Page 437**
Arboreal in highland forest. Grey head sharply defined from tawny-rufous back; throat and breast grey.

3 BROWN ILLADOPSIS *Illadopsis fulvescens ugandae*   **Page 438**
Western Kenyan forests (notably Kakamega). On ground and in undergrowth. Tawny below, with white throat; may show faint malar streaks; tail fairly long.

4 SCALY-BREASTED ILLADOPSIS *Illadopsis albipectus barakae*   **Page 439**
Terrestrial in Kakamega and Nandi forests. Dull olive-brown above, mottled below. Tarsi long and pale (usually whitish grey to greyish pink). **4a. Typical adult**. Prominent scaly breast markings. **4b. Juvenile**. Some orange-rufous on face; bill largely dark. **4c. Less scaly adult**. Faint to very faint breast markings.

5 PALE-BREASTED ILLADOPSIS *Illadopsis r. rufipennis*   **Page 438**
Terrestrial in w. Kenyan forests only. (See Plate 124 for Tanzanian *I. r. distans*.) **5a. Adult**. Plain below, throat and belly whitish. Tarsi blue-grey or brownish grey. **5b. Juvenile**. Base of mandible bright yellow to orange.

6 GREY-CHESTED ILLADOPSIS *Kakamega poliothorax*   **Page 438**
Uncommon on ground in Kakamega and Nandi Forests, w. Kenya. Rufous-brown upperparts, grey breast and flanks.

7 BROWN-TAILED ROCK CHAT *Cercomela scotocerca turkana*   **Page 449**
Uncommon in dry, rocky bush country south to Baringo District. Plain; narrow eye-ring.

8 RED-TAILED or FAMILIAR CHAT *Cercomela familiaris falkensteini*   **Page 449**
Rocky hillsides and escarpments. Rufous rump and sides of tail; lateral rectrices darker at tips.

9 COMMON REDSTART *Phoenicurus p. phoenicurus*   **Page 446**
Palearctic migrant in w. and nw. Kenya. **Female**. Lateral rectrices entirely rufous. (Male on Plate 93.)

10 BROWN-CHESTED ALETHE *Alethe poliocephalus carruthersi*   **Page 443**
Forests in w. and cent. Kenya; terrestrial. **10a. Adult**. Brownish breast band, white superciliary stripes. **10b. Juvenile**. Densely rufous-spotted; tail dark. (Young robin-chats show rufous in tail.)

11 ALPINE CHAT *Cercomela sordida ernesti*   **Page 449**
High montane grassland and moorland. Upright posture.

⑫ SOOTY CHAT *Myrmecocichla nigra*   **Page 450**
Western grasslands (Mara/n. Serengeti Plains). **12a. Female**. Plain dark brown. **12b. Male**. Black, with white 'shoulders'.

⑬ NORTHERN ANTEATER CHAT *Myrmecocichla aethiops cryptoleuca*
                                                          Page 450
Widespread in eroded dry grassland. Both sexes brownish black, with large white patches in primaries (usually concealed at rest). **13a and 13b. Adults**.

DALE A. ZIMMERMAN
1988

PLATE 91: THRUSHES (*Turdus, Monticola, Zoothera, Neocossyphus*)

1 LITTLE ROCK THRUSH *Monticola r. rufocinereus* **Page 450**
Local and uncommon in highlands, mainly on cliffs, rocky slopes and in forested ravines. Rufous rump and much of tail; grey throat and breast. Crepuscular. **1a. Male. 1b. Female.**

2 COMMON ROCK THRUSH *Monticola saxatilis* **Page 450**
Fairly common palearctic migrant, Oct.–April, in largely open country. **2a and 2b. Spring males.** Greyish blue head, largely rufous underparts, white on back. **2c. Autumn male.** Restricted rufous; much light feather edging. (Intermediates between b and c relate to degree of feather wear plus a gradual body moult, Dec.–Feb.) **2d. Female.**

3 RED-TAILED ANT THRUSH *Neocossyphus r. rufus* **Page 444**
On and near ground in coastal forests, Shimba Hills and East Usambara Mts. Shy; attends ant swarms; flicks tail. Plain brown and rufous, tail brighter.

4 WHITE-TAILED ANT THRUSH *Neocossyphus poensis praepectoralis* **Page 444**
Uncommon in Kakamega and Nandi forests. Usually near ground; follows ant columns; flicks tail. White tail corners conspicuous in flight.

5 SPOTTED GROUND THRUSH *Zoothera guttata fischeri* **Page 451**
Migrant from southern tropics. Scarce in coastal forests, April–Oct. Shy; forages in leaf litter.

6 ORANGE GROUND THRUSH *Zoothera gurneyi chuka* **Page 451**
Uncommon in highland forests. Shy and skulking. Feeds on ground, sings from canopy trees or undergrowth. Eye-ring broken (unlike adult of No. 7); pale band across ear-coverts, large bill. See text for racial differences.

7 ABYSSINIAN GROUND THRUSH *Zoothera piaggiae kilimensis* **Page 451**
At higher elevations than Orange Ground Thrush, the two largely allopatric. Shy. **7a. Juvenile.** Eye-ring small and broken; ear-coverts and crown mostly rufous-brown, latter spotted with buff. (Juv. Orange Ground Thrush has dark crown and light band across ear-coverts, as in adult.) **7b. Adult.** Eye-ring large and complete; ear-coverts plain, head rufous-tinged.

8 TAITA THRUSH *Turdus (olivaceus) helleri* **Page 452**
Taita Hills forests (se. Kenya); very rare and shy. See text.

9 BARE-EYED THRUSH *Turdus tephronotus* **Page 452**
Uncommon in eastern *Commiphora* bush and scrub. Forages on ground inside thickets; shy. Extensive bare orbital skin; throat heavily streaked; bill orange-yellow.

10 OLIVE THRUSH *Turdus olivaceus abyssinicus* **Page 451**
Common in wooded highlands (including city suburbs and gardens, where it forages on lawns). **10a. Juvenile.** Heavily spotted below; orange or yellow-orange eye-ring and bill. **10b. Adult.** Breast dark; orange eye-ring and bill. (See Plate 124 for n. Tanzanian races.)

11 AFRICAN THRUSH *Turdus pelios centralis* **Page 452**
Western Kenya, east locally to Lake Nakuru NP and Laikipia Plateau. Fairly common in woodland, cultivation, forest edge. Resembles pale Olive Thrush; bill yellow.

PLATE 92: THRUSHES (robin-chats, scrub robins, chats)

1 WHITE-BROWED SCRUB ROBIN *Cercotrichas leucophrys* **Page 445**
Common and widespread in bush and scrub. Lower back and tail rufous, tail tipped black and white. Prominent superciliary stripes; variable white in wing. **1a. C. l. zambesiana.** West and south of Kenyan highlands to Mara GR and Serengeti NP; also coastal. Broad white wing-bars, reddish back. **1b. C. l. brunneiceps.** S. Kenya, Rift Valley highlands, Crater Highlands and Mt Meru. White in wing extends to inner secondaries. Back darker and browner than 1a. **1c. C. l. vulpina.** Dry interior se. Kenya. Lightly streaked below; much white in wing; head grey-brown, contrasting with back. (Other races include the greyer-headed *C. l. leucoptera*, Turkana to Magadi, and paler northeastern *C. l. eluta* ranging south to the Tana River.)

2 RUFOUS BUSH CHAT *Cercotrichas galactotes familiaris* **Page 446**
Fairly common palearctic migrant in dry bush and scrub, Nov.–early April. Pumps tail like scrub robin. Pale grey-brown, with largely rufous rump and tail, latter white-tipped with black subterminal band.

3 BROWN-BACKED SCRUB ROBIN *Cercotrichas hartlaubi* **Page 446**
Western and cent. Kenyan highlands, uncommon in wooded areas, thickets, gardens. Terminal half of tail black with white tips; narrow white wing-bars.

4 CAPE ROBIN-CHAT *Cossypha caffra iolaema* **Page 443**
Widespread in highland towns, cultivation and wooded habitats. **4a. Juvenile.** Mottled and spotted, tail as adult's but duller. (See text for distinctions from other juvenile robin-chats.) **4b. Adult.** Lower breast and sides grey.

5 EASTERN BEARDED SCRUB ROBIN *Cercotrichas q. quadrivirgata* **Page 446**
Common in dense moist thickets and wooded areas in coastal lowlands, inland to Mt Endau, Kibwezi, Taveta and North Pare Mts. Chestnut on tail-coverts, but none on tail.

6 RED-CAPPED ROBIN-CHAT *Cossypha natalensis intensa* **Page 441**
Common in coastal forests, April–Nov. (Similar *C. n. hylophona* breeds in thickets and riverine forest at Taveta and in sw Kenya.) Shy. No head stripes, wings bluish.

7 BLUE-SHOULDERED ROBIN-CHAT *Cossypha cyanocampter bartteloti*
Page 442
Local in Kakamega, Kaimosi and Nandi Forests. Skulks in undergrowth; very shy. Pale blue 'shoulders' sometimes concealed. Rump buffy olive; underparts mostly rich tawny-buff; outer rectrices narrowly black-edged.

8 SNOWY-HEADED ROBIN-CHAT *Cossypha niveicapilla melanota* **Page 443**
Local in remnant forest, riverine thickets and forest edge in w. Kenya. Black back, white crown, no superciliary stripes.

9 SPOTTED MORNING THRUSH *Cichladusa g. guttata* **Page 444**
Common in dry thickets and dense bush below 1600 m, especially along watercourses. Chestnut tail with no dark central feathers; heavily spotted below.

10 COLLARED PALM THRUSH *Cichladusa arquata* **Page 444**
Uncommon and local in coastal lowlands, usually near palms. Forages low, in or near thickets. Chestnut tail; narrow black band around throat/breast.

11 RÜPPELL'S ROBIN-CHAT *Cossypha semirufa intercedens* **Page 442**
Common in Kenyan highland forest east of the Rift Valley, south to n. Tanzanian mountains. Blackish central rectrices, prominent superciliary stripes. Orange nuchal collar somewhat less distinct than in No. 12.

12 WHITE-BROWED ROBIN-CHAT *Cossypha h. heuglini* **Page 442**
Common in woodland, forest edge and gardens. Avoids arid country and most highland areas occupied by Rüppell's Robin-Chat. Central rectrices brown. Slightly larger than Rüppell's, with broader superciliary stripes. (Some birds more olive above.)

13 CLIFF CHAT *Thamnolaea cinnamomeiventris subrufipennis* **Page 450**
Uncommon and local on Rift Valley scarps, cliffs and in rocky gorges. **13a. Male.** Glossy black above, with white wing patches. **13b. Female.** Dark grey, with chestnut belly.

PLATE 93: THRUSHES (akalats, Irania, chats *et al.*)

1 COMMON STONECHAT *Saxicola torquata axillaris* **Page 447**
Fairly common and widespread in open country above 1800 m. **1a. Female**. Indistinct superciliary stripes; white stripe in wing. **1b. Male**. White wing-stripes and collar; chestnut bib.

2 WHINCHAT *Saxicola rubetra* **Page 447**
Fairly common palearctic migrant in cent. Rift Valley, western grasslands and cultivation, Oct.–March. Buffy white superciliary stripes, dark cheeks. **2a. Male**. **2b. Female**.

3 WHITE-STARRED ROBIN *Pogonocichla stellata intensa* **Page 439**
Widespread in highland forests. Black-and-yellow tail pattern diagnostic (except in Mt Elgon race). **3a. Juvenile**. Strongly patterned below; base of bill yellow. **3b. Adult**. Bluegrey head and wings; white spot above eye. (See Plate 124 for immature plumage of *P. s. orientalis*.)

4 EQUATORIAL AKALAT *Sheppardia a. aequatorialis* **Page 441**
Fairly common in w. Kenyan forest undergrowth. Robin-like; orange below. **4a. Adult**. Russet on rump and upper tail-coverts; tail brown; face greyish. **4b. Juvenile**. Duller; mottled and spotted.

5 FOREST ROBIN *Stiphrornis erythrothorax* **Page 440**
Vagrant in w. Kenya. Yellow-orange throat and breast; white supraloral spot.

6 COMMON REDSTART *Phoenicurus p. phoenicurus* **Page 446**
Uncommon palearctic migrant, Oct.–March. Local in w. and nw. Kenya. **Male** has tail largely bright rufous; throat black, heavily veiled with white in early winter; breast rufous, veiled with white. (For female, see Plate 90.)

7 GREY-WINGED ROBIN *Sheppardia p. polioptera* **Page 441**
Local in w. Kenyan forests. Rufous tail, rufous-orange underparts; blue-grey on wing-coverts. **7a. Immature**. Variable white supraloral spot. **7b. Adult**. Robin-chat-like pattern; crown dark slate-grey.

8 EAST COAST AKALAT *Sheppardia gunningi sokokensis* **Page 441**
Tana River and coastal forests, East Usambara lowland forest. **8a. Adult male**. Underparts yellow-orange and white. (Female similar.) **8b. Adult male in display** (showing erectile white loral feathers).

9 NIGHTINGALE *Luscinia megarhynchos hafizi* **Page 444**
Skulking palearctic migrant, mainly in cent. and e. Kenya, Nov.–March. Brown above, with rufous tail; breast plain greyish white.

10 SPROSSER or THRUSH-NIGHTINGALE *Luscinia luscinia* **Page 445**
Skulking palearctic migrant, east of Rift Valley, Nov.–early April. Abundant in Tsavo region Nov.–Dec. Slightly darker than Nightingale, with mottled breast.

11 IRANIA or WHITE-THROATED ROBIN *Irania gutturalis* **Page 446**
Locally common palearctic migrant, Nov.–March, in dry thickets along watercourses. Long black tail in both sexes. Shy and secretive. **11a. Adult male, autumn**. **11b. Spring male**. **11c. Female**. Traces of orange on sides and flanks; ear-coverts often tawny.

PLATE 94: THRUSHES (Wheatears)

1 ISABELLINE WHEATEAR *Oenanthe isabellina*   **Page 448**
Common and widespread migrant, Oct.–March. Paler, more uniform in colour, larger-billed than Northern Wheatear; superciliary stripe broader. Wings contrast little with body; wing-linings white. (Lores black in spring male, greyer in female and autumn birds.)

2 NORTHERN WHEATEAR *Oenanthe o. oenanthe*   **Page 447**
Common and widespread migrant, late Sept.–March. Smaller-billed than Isabelline Wheatear; wing-linings dusky. **2a. Winter female**. Wings noticeably darker than body. (Unworn autumn birds have broader, pale buff feather edges, resembling Isabelline.) **2b. Adult male, autumn**. Dark face patch, pale buff throat/breast, grey or brownish-grey back.

3 DESERT WHEATEAR *Oenanthe deserti*   **Page 448**
Palearctic vagrant. Black tail, white only at extreme base. **3a. Spring male**. Black of face and throat connected to black wings. **3b. Female**. Pale sandy or greyish-buff head and breast.

4 PIED WHEATEAR *Oenanthe p. pleschanka*   **Page 447**
Fairly common and widespread migrant in dry bushed grassland, Oct.–March. Small-billed; black band at tail tip narrow (may be incomplete); white of rump extends to lower back; wing-linings black. **4a. Female**. Darker than Northern or Isabelline Wheatears; throat and breast often dusky. **4b. First-winter male**. Brown crown and back; throat feathers pale-tipped. **4c. Adult winter male**. Crown and nape feathers grey-tipped; black body feathers brownish-tipped. **4d. Spring male**. Clean-cut black-and-white pattern.

5 HEUGLIN'S WHEATEAR *Oenanthe (bottae) heuglini*   **Page 448**
Extreme nw. Kenya. Brick-red below, black facial stripe, narrow white superciliary stripe; broad black tail band. **5a. Male**. **5b. Female**. Breast feathers white-tipped in fresh plumage.

6 BLACK-EARED WHEATEAR *Oenanthe hispanica melanoleuca*   **Page 448**
Palearctic vagrant. Facial mask (sometimes throat also) blackish, separated from black wings by pale body plumage. Black tail band incomplete (occasionally so in Pied Wheatear). Variable sandy-buff wash above and below; some very pale. **6a. Spring male, black-throated form**. Largely white or creamy white above and below. **6b. Spring male, white-throated form**. Much paler than Northern Wheatear. **6c. Female**. Variable; ear patch typically darker than in female Pied Wheatear.

7 ABYSSINIAN BLACK or SCHALOW'S WHEATEAR *Oenanthe lugubris schalowi*
Page 448
Locally common near eroded gullies in cent. Rift Valley, around Mt Meru and in Crater Highlands. Orange-buff or rufous rump, crissum and tail base. **7a. Juvenile**. Dark dusky brown, variably speckled with pale buff; belly paler; rump and tail as in adult; no superciliary stripes. **7b. Adult female**. Dusky brown above; streaked from chin to breast. **7c. Adult male**. Streaked, pale brown crown; white belly.

8 CAPPED WHEATEAR *Oenanthe pileata livingstonii*   **Page 449**
Locally common on open grassland above 1400 m. Upright posture. Sexes alike, with broad black breast band connected to facial mask. **8a. Adult**. **8b. Juvenile**. Brown, heavily spotted with pale buff; pale superciliary stripes.

PLATE 95: WARBLERS (*Acrocephalus, Bradypterus et al.*)

1 LESSER SWAMP WARBLER *Acrocephalus gracilirostris*   **Page 459**
Common wetland resident. **1a. Adult *A. g. parvus*.** Blackish tarsi, orange gape. (Rump more rufous in eastern *leptorhynchus*.) **1b. Juvenile *A. g. jacksoni*.** Rufescent on breast and flanks.

2 BASRA REED WARBLER *Acrocephalus griseldis*   **Page 458**
Palearctic migrant, Nov.–April, in moist thickets, rank grass and wet places. Common in winter in lower Tana River valley. Regular autumn migrant through the Tsavo region. Large, long-billed, olive-brown, with no rufescent or bright buff tones.

3 GREAT REED WARBLER *Acrocephalus a. arundinaceus*   **Page 457**
Palearctic migrant, Nov.–April, in tall grass, green thickets and reedbeds, often near lakes and rivers. Large, heavy-billed, buff sides. Usually has faint streaks on throat.

4 AFRICAN REED WARBLER *Acrocephalus baeticatus cinnamomeus*   **Page 458**
Local wetland resident in Lake Victoria basin, cent. Rift Valley; occasional farther east. Small; bright buff below, rufous above; legs and feet brown or grey. (*A. b. suahelicus* is a common resident on Pemba Island.)

5 EURASIAN REED WARBLER *Acrocephalus scirpaceus fuscus*   **Page 458**
Palearctic migrant, Oct.–May, in scrub and cultivation, as well as moist thickets and reedbeds. Common in Lake Victoria basin. Slight rufous tinge to rump, broken eye-ring. Tarsi variable. See text.

6 GREATER SWAMP WARBLER *Acrocephalus rufescens ansorgei*   **Page 459**
Locally common resident of papyrus swamps around Lake Victoria. Large, long-billed; drab brown above, brownish grey below; feet large.

7 BROAD-TAILED WARBLER *Schoenicola brevirostris alexinae*   **Page 465**
Uncommon in wet grassland, moist meadows. Skulking. Tail large and graduated.

8 MARSH WARBLER *Acrocephalus palustris*   **Page 458**
Palearctic migrant, common Nov.–Jan. in bush and scrub. Less numerous April–May. Some winter. Rare west of Rift Valley. More olive-brown than Eurasian Reed Warbler, seldom with rufescent tones. Pale throat may contrast with buffier breast. Feet often pinkish brown, usually paler than in No. 5.

9 CINNAMON BRACKEN WARBLER *Bradypterus cinnamomeus*   **Page 464**
Locally common in undergrowth of highland-forest clearings, brushy edges, bracken and bamboo. Rufous-brown above, on flanks and on breast. Superciliary stripes prominent.

10 AFRICAN MOUSTACHED WARBLER *Melocichla m. mentalis*   **Page 465**
Uncommon in rank streamside vegetation. Skulking except when singing. Shy. Pale eyes, black malar marks, heavy bill.

11 LITTLE RUSH WARBLER *Bradypterus baboecala*   **Page 463**
Fairly common in reedbeds, swamps and along streams. Variable streaks on throat and upper breast; tail broad. Two populations, with different songs (see text). **11a. Adult *B. b. elgonensis*.** Whitish below, streaks few, restricted. (Adult *B. b. moreaui* darker, duller brown, less rufous, above.) **11b. Juvenile *B. b. moreaui*.** Yellowish wash below, streaking heavier.

12 EVERGREEN FOREST WARBLER *Bradypterus lopezi mariae*   **Page 464**
Skulking resident of montane-forest undergrowth. (Somewhat brighter race *usambarae* in Taita Hills, the Pare and Usambara mts.) Creeps through low vegetation with tail elevated. Difficult to see, but quite vocal. Dark breast/throat streaking often obsolete. Tail generally worn, the feathers pointed.

13 WHITE-WINGED WARBLER *Bradypterus carpalis*   **Page 464**
Locally common in interior of papyrus swamps around Lake Victoria. Forages low.

DALE A. ZIMMERMAN
1986

PLATE 96: WARBLERS (palearctic migrants except Nos. 1–3)

1 BROWN WOODLAND WARBLER *Phylloscopus umbrovirons mackenzianus*
    Page 463
Fairly common in montane wooded areas. Yellow-olive wing and tail edgings.

2 UGANDA WOODLAND WARBLER *Phylloscopus budongoensis*   **Page 463**
Fairly common in Kakamega and Nandi Forests, w. Kenya. Arboreal. Striped face.

3 GREEN HYLIA *Hylia p. prasina*   **Page 482**
Uncommon in Kakamega and Nandi forests, w. Kenya. Heavier and darker than No. 2.

4 WILLOW WARBLER *Phylloscopus trochilus*   **Page 463**
Common Sept.–early May (esp. Mar.–Apr.) in wooded areas. Tarsus colour usually pale yellowish brown. **4a. *P. t. yakutensis*; 4b. *P. t. acredula,* spring** (some are greener); **4c. *P. t. acredula*, first-winter.**

5 CHIFFCHAFF *Phylloscopus collybita abietinus*   **Page 462**
Uncommon Nov.–Mar. in montane forest. Browner than No. 4. Tarsi usually dark.

6 WOOD WARBLER *Phylloscopus sibilatrix*   **Page 462**
Scarce, Nov.–Apr., in wooded areas at mid-elevations. Yellow breast sharply separated from white belly. Wings longer, tail shorter than in No. 4.

7 ICTERINE WARBLER *Hippolais icterina*   **Page 460**
Uncommon, Oct.–Apr., in open woods, bush etc., in and west of Rift Valley. Light wing panel in fresh plumage. **7a. Spring. 7b. First-winter.**

8 UPCHER'S WARBLER *Hippolais languida*   **Page 460**
Fairly common, Nov.–Apr., mainly in dry bush east of the highlands. Larger, paler and greyer than Olivaceous Warbler, with heavier blackish tail; prominent wing panel in fresh plumage. Tarsi pinkish grey.

9 OLIVACEOUS WARBLER *Hippolais pallida elaeica*   **Page 459**
Common, late Oct.–Apr., in bush, woodland, riparian trees. Long bill, pinkish or pale orange below. **9a. Spring. 9b. First-winter** (Oct.–Dec.).

10 OLIVE-TREE WARBLER *Hippolais olivetorum*   **Page 460**
Uncommon, mainly Oct.–early Dec., and Mar.–Apr., in dry open wooded areas. Large; long bill with bright orange or yellow below. Superciliary shorter than Nos. 8 and 9.

11 GARDEN WARBLER *Sylvia borin woodwardi*   **Page 461**
Fairly common, late Sept.–Apr., in moist bush, woodland and forest edge. Plain brownish, with stubby bill, faint superciliary stripe and narrow pale eye-ring.

12 COMMON WHITETHROAT *Sylvia communis icterops*   **Page 461**
Locally common, Oct.–Apr., in dry woods and bush. White throat and eye-ring. **12a. Female.** Sandy wing edgings, white eye-ring; tail white-edged. **12b. Male.** Crown greyer; iris usually yellowish.

13 BARRED WARBLER *Sylvia n. nisoria*   **Page 461**
Common, Oct.–Apr., in dry country. Large. **13a. Male.** Variably barred; iris yellow. Some birds paler than shown. **13b. Female.** Barring distinct or lacking (similar first-winter. may be brown-eyed).

14 BLACKCAP *Sylvia atricapilla dammholzi*   **Page 462**
Common, late Oct.–early April, in woodland, forest edge and cultivation. **14a. Male.** Grey or olive-grey, with solid black cap. **14b. Female.** Olive-brown above, with rufous-brown cap, white lower eyelid.

15 GRASSHOPPER WARBLER *Locustella naevia*   **Page 457**
Vagrant. Streaky brown skulker with broad tail, slim pointed bill; very long, narrowly streaked under tail-coverts.

16 RIVER WARBLER *Locustella fluviatilis*   **Page 457**
Fairly common in se. Kenya, Nov.–Jan. and late Mar.–Apr., in green bush and thickets. Skulking. Plain brown above, with broad rounded tail; long dark under tail-coverts pale tipped; throat streaked.

17 SAVI'S WARBLER *Locustella luscinioides fusca*   **Page 457**
Vagrant. Warmer brown than River Warbler. Plain throat often bordered by necklace of faint spots; superciliary stripe indistinct.

18 SEDGE WARBLER *Acrocephalus schoenobaenus*   **Page 457**
Common, Nov.–May, in low growth along lake edges or (esp. spring) in drier areas. Streaked above; bold creamy superciliary stripes.

Dale A. Zimmerman
1988

PLATE 97: UNSTREAKED CISTICOLAS

1 SINGING CISTICOLA *Cisticola cantans pictipennis*   **Page 466**
Common in leafy vegetation, gardens and hedges in the highlands. Rufous wing panel
and crown contrast with greyish back; loral spot dark.

2 RED-PATE CISTICOLA *Cisticola ruficeps mongalla*   **Page 468**
Nw. Kenya. Local in grassy bush near Lokichokio. Larger and longer-tailed than Tiny
Cisticola, with relatively larger bill. **Breeding plumage** figured. (See also Plate 98).

3 TINY CISTICOLA *Cisticola nanus*   **Page 468**
Uncommon in dry bush country in and east of Rift Valley. Very small and short-tailed.
3a. Adult male. Rufous cap, white loral line; back streaks fainter with wear. **3b. Juvenile**.
Rufous-tinted throughout; bill ochre.

4 LONG-TAILED or TABORA CISTICOLA *Cisticola angusticaudus*   **Page 469**
Sw. Kenya and n. Serengeti NP. Uncommon and local in open *Acacia* woodland. Prinia-
like, with long slender tail, rufous cap.

5 RED-FACED CISTICOLA *Cisticola erythrops sylvia*   **Page 467**
Widespread; locally common in rank undergrowth in moist hollows and near water.
5a. Adult male. Face reddish, no rufous wing panel. **5b. Ad. female, rufous** bird. Rufous
below, throat whitish. **5c. Juv.** Ochre on bill; tail spots distinct from below.

6 RATTLING CISTICOLA *Cisticola chiniana heterophrys*   **Page 470**
Common along coast and inland to East Usambara Mts, in varied habitats. (See Plate 98
for heavily streaked inland races.) Nearly plain above, the back with narrow dark shaft
streaks; wing edgings and crown more rufous than back.

7 HUNTER'S CISTICOLA *Cisticola hunteri*   **Page 468**
Common above 2400 m in brushy places, bracken, forest edge. Dark and drab, with
obscurely streaked back, often very grey below; dark-lored. Indulges in animated duet or
group singing. **7a. Adult.** Loral spot dark grey, not black; crown dull. **7b. Juv.** Duller and
rustier above, paler below than adult; bill yellow-ochre; tail spots well defined.

8 CHUBB'S CISTICOLA *Cisticola c. chubbi*   **Page 468**
Locally common in w. Kenya, in shrubbery and thickets near forest edge. **8a. Adult.**
Reddish brown cap, black loral spot, plain back, long tail. **8b. Juv.** More uniformly
coloured above; bill yellowish; tail spots dull.

9 TRILLING CISTICOLA *Cisticola w. woosnami*   **Page 467**
Sw. Kenya, south in Tanzania to Lake Manyara, Arusha and Moshi areas. Locally common in grassy bush and savanna. Stocky and dull. **9a. Adult female**. Tail spots conspicuous in flight; crown dull chestnut-brown. Bill heavy, well curved, greyish pink below.
9b. Adult male. Bill large, greyish below; little contrast between back and dull chestnut
crown and wing edgings. **9c. Juv.** Rufous, with grey eyes, yellow-ochre bill (smaller than
in juv. Whistling Cisticola); crown can be rufous.

10 SIFFLING CISTICOLA *Cisticola b. brachypterus*   **Page 472**
Fairly common and widespread in bush, savanna, woodland clearings. **Breeding adult**
small, drab, a few obscure back streaks, sometimes nearly plain. (See also Plate 99.)

11 FOXY CISTICOLA *Cisticola troglodytes*   **Page 468**
Northwestern Kenya; rare and local. Small and rufous, similar to larger juvenile Whistling
Cisticola, including grey eye, but bill brownish pink.

12 WHISTLING CISTICOLA *Cisticola lateralis antinorii*   **Page 467**
W. Kenya. Scarce and local in forest edge, woodland and bush. **12a. Adult male**. Large,
bulky, plain. Like Trilling Cisticola, but darker, duller, dusky-crowned, larger-billed; clear
whistling song. **12b. Adult female**. Plain, smaller than male; bill pinkish with brown culmen. **12c. Juv. female** (male similar but much larger). Rufous, with grey eyes.

13 ROCK CISTICOLA *Cisticola aberrans*   **Page 467**
Very local on rock outcrops, boulder-strewn hillsides in se. and sw. Kenya, n. Tanzania.
Runs mouse-like over bare rock surfaces, around boulders; tail often elevated or in
motion. **13a. *C. a. teitensis*, presumed non-breeding plumage**. Se. Kenya, ne. Tanzania.
Upperparts rufous-tinted, underparts rich buff. **13b. *C. a. emini*, fresh breeding plumage**
(presumably this race; no Kenyan specimen; illustration from photographs). Bill and loral
spot blackish; noticeable eye-ring; rufous crown and nape contrast with brown back;
underparts white or buff, greyish on sides.

PLATE 98: LARGER STREAKED CISTICOLAS

1 RATTLING CISTICOLA *Cisticola chiniana* **Page 470**
Common and widespread in dry shrubby habitats. Sexes similar in plumage, but males larger than females. Heavily streaked above, usually including crown (but see *C. c. heterophrys* on Plate 97); bill strong. **1a. *C. c. ukamba*, male**. Kenyan highlands and Rift Valley north of Nairobi. **1b. *C. c. humilis*, female**. Southern Kenyan/n.Tanzanian highlands; duller, but boldly marked. **1c. *C. c. victoria*, female**. W. Kenya to Serengeti NP. Less patterned; crown nearly plain. **1d. *C. c. victoria*, male**. **1e. *C. c. humilis*, juv.** Yellowish below. Bill smaller than that of Croaking Cisticola. Back less boldly streaked than in young Winding and Levaillant's Cisticolas.

2 WINDING CISTICOLA *Cisticola galactotes* **Page 469**
Common and widespread. Slimmer, smaller billed than Rattling Cisticola; boldly streaked. **2a. *C. g. haematocephalus*, female**. Coastal race; in varied habitats; pale lores, rufous wing panel, dull crown. **2b. *C. g. amphilectus*, breeding adult**. Inland, typically near water or in low damp areas. Black-streaked grey back, plain rufous crown and wing patch; tail greyish centrally. **2c. *C. g. amphilectus*, non-breeding adult**. As 2b, but buff-and-black streaks, streaked crown, rufous-and-black tail. **2d. *C. g. amphilectus*, juv.** Similar to 2c, but faintly yellow below; tail colour intermediate between 2b and 2c.

3 CARRUTHERS'S CISTICOLA *Cisticola carruthersi* **Page 470**
Lake Victoria papyrus swamps. Like Winding Cisticola (*C. g. amphilectus*), but tail blackish, bill smaller, and wing edgings brown, not rufous.

4 LYNES'S or WAILING CISTICOLA *Cisticola (lais) distinctus* **Page 471**
Locally common on rocky brushy hillsides and in ravines from Laikipia Plateau and cent. Rift Valley to e. Serengeti. Underparts and face rufous-tinted.

5 BORAN CISTICOLA *Cisticola b. bodessa* **Page 471**
Locally common in n. Kenya in scrub and on rocky, grassy hillsides and slopes. Duller than Rattling Cisticola and crown essentially unstreaked.

6 LEVAILLANT'S CISTICOLA *Cisticola tinniens oreophilus* **Page 469**
Local in highland tussock-grass meadows and marshes. Slim; bright rufous-and-black upperparts. **6a. Adult**. Head unstreaked; back heavily streaked (sometimes nearly solid black). **6b. Juv.** Yellowish below; crown and nape streaked.

7 STOUT CISTICOLA *Cisticola robustus* **Page 470**
Common in tall grassland with moist hollows, 1200–2500 m. Stocky build, boldly streaked back, unstreaked rufous nape; pronounced sexual size difference. **7a. Adult male**. Heavy-bodied; rather short tail. **7b. Juv.** Yellow below, upperparts decidedly rufous. **7c. Adult female**. Much smaller than male.

8 ABERDARE CISTICOLA *Cisticola aberdare* **Page 470**
Locally common in moist highland grassland (above 2300 m) near Molo, Mau Narok and Aberdare Mts. Like Stout Cisticola, but somewhat darker, with streaked nape. **Adult male** figured. (Female similar but much smaller, rufous of nape may not extend onto back.)

9 RED-PATE CISTICOLA *Cisticola ruficeps mongalla* **Page 468**
Local in grassy bush near Lokichokio in nw. Kenya. **Non-breeding female** figured. (Male similar.) Top of head and nape rufous; distinct white superciliary stripe; bill relatively long. (For breeding adult, see Plate 97.)

10 CROAKING CISTICOLA *Cisticola natalensis* **Page 470**
Uncommon and local in open wooded habitats and tall grass with shrubs. Heavy bill. Some birds have plumages intermediate between those figured. **10a. *C. n. kapitensis*, adult male, perennial plumage**. Tail relatively short; suggestion of rufous on nape. **10b. *C. n. kapitensis*, imm. female**. Buff-and-black streaks; long tail; bill and feet yellowish. (Non-breeding adult similar but paler, with pinkish bill and feet.) **10c. *C. n. strangei*, adult male, perennial plumage**. Dull; lores grey or dusky; short-tailed. Some individuals paler and greyer on sides of crown, neck and back.

DALE A. ZIMMERMAN
1987

PLATE 99: SMALLER STREAKED CISTICOLAS

1 SIFFLING CISTICOLA *Cisticola brachypterus* **Page 472**
Fairly common in shrubby grassland savanna and bush. Dull, often indistinctly streaked.
1a. *C. b. brachypterus*, non-breeding. W. Kenya. Heavily streaked back; crown mottled; nape not streaked. (Breeding plumage on Plate 97.) **1b. *C. b. katonae*.** Widespread in highlands. Nape not streaked. (*C. b. kericho* is similar but less heavily streaked.) **1c. *C. b. reichenowi*.** Coastal. Plainer, slightly reddish, unstreaked crown; back faintly streaked. **1d. *C. b. katonae*, juvenile.** Similar to adult, but washed yellowish below and grey-eyed; bill more yellowish; tail longer than in adults.

2 TANA RIVER CISTICOLA *Cisticola restrictus* **Page 471**
Rare; lower Tana River only. Suggests Lynes's and Ashy Cisticolas. Sides grey; tail-feather tips red-brown or buff (not white); crown more reddish brown. See text.

3 ASHY CISTICOLA *Cisticola cinereolus* **Page 472**
Locally common in low scrub and bush in dry areas, mainly east of Rift Valley. Less numerous in Tanzania. **3a. Juvenile.** Faintly yellow on face and breast; grey-eyed; ochre-billed. **3b. Adult.** Pale, generally greyish, uniformly streaked above.

4 ZITTING CISTICOLA *Cisticola juncidis uropygialis* **Page 472**
Local in low grassy areas, especially near lakes. Bright rump, pale collar contrasts with back and crown. **4a. Female.** Less contrast above, more whitish below than male. **4b. Non-breeding adult.** Plumage acquired by some southern birds. Longer-tailed, brighter above than usual perennial dress. **4c. Juvenile.** Rufous-tinged above, yellowish below.

5 BLACK-BACKED CISTICOLA *Cisticola e. eximius* **Page 473**
Formerly in low grasslands in w. Kenya. Now very rare or extirpated. **5a. Juvenile.** Yellowish below; similar to juv. *ayresii* but paler, with dark subloral spot. **5b. Breeding male.** Stub-tailed, bright rufous on rump and flanks; back boldly streaked; crown plain, lores dark. **5c. Non-breeding adult.** Streaked crown, pale loral area.

6 PECTORAL-PATCH CISTICOLA *Cisticola brunnescens* **Page 473**
Widespread and locally common in grasslands from 1400 to 2000 m in Kenya, up to 2500 m in n. Tanzania. Heavily streaked above; white-tipped short tail obvious in flight. **6a. *C. b. hindei*, non-breeding male. 6b. *C. b. nakuruensis*, breeding male.** Plain rufous crown centre, black subloral spots; often a dark smudge on sides of breast. **6c. *C. b. nakuruensis*, non-breeding male.** Uniformly streaked above (may show faint collar); pectoral patch often lacking; no subloral spot. (For juvenile, see text.)

7 DESERT CISTICOLA *Cisticola aridulus tanganyika* **Page 473**
Widespread, often common on dry, short-grass plains. **7a. Juvenile.** White below, unlike Pectoral-patch and Wing-snapping Cisticolas. **7b and 7c. Adults.** Similar to non-breeding Pectoral-patch Cisticola, but tail longer, rump plain rusty buff.

8 WING-SNAPPING CISTICOLA *Cisticola ayresii mauensis* **Page 474**
Locally common in Kenyan grasslands above 2150 m. Replaces Pectoral-patch at high elevations. Much darker and brighter above; rump rustier than back. **8a. Juvenile.** **8b. Breeding male.** Often black-crowned. **8c. Non-breeding male.** More uniformly streaked; resembles Pectoral-patch, but rump rust-red. **8d. Adult female.** Generally darker above than male.

DALE ZIMMERMAN
1987

PLATE 100: AFRICAN WARBLERS (*Apalis* and relatives)

1 GREY APALIS *Apalis c. cinerea*   **Page 477**
Widespread and common in forest and forest-edge trees. **1a. Adult**. Back grey, outer rectrices white, tail appears all white from below. **1b. Juvenile**. Olive-brown above; dull yellow below, darker on throat.

2 BUFF-THROATED APALIS *Apalis rufogularis nigrescens*   **Page 476**
Locally common in w. Kenyan forests. In canopy, often in mixed-species flocks. **2a. Female**. Buff or pale tawny on throat, upper breast; tail all white from below. **2b. Male**. Blackish brown above, creamy white below; underside of tail white.

3 BAR-THROATED APALIS *Apalis thoracica*   **Page 478**
Local in forest trees and undergrowth. **3a. A. t. fuscigularis**. Taita Hills. Dark throat, grey back. **3b. A. t. griseiceps**. Chyulu Hills and n. Tanzania. White throat, narrow breast band, yellow-green back.

4 CHESTNUT-THROATED APALIS *Apalis p. porphyrolaema*   **Page 476**
Fairly common in forest trees at high elevations. Chestnut throat, underside of tail largely dark.

5 BLACK-HEADED APALIS *Apalis melanocephala*   **Page 477**
Common in forest trees in e. and cent. Kenya and n. Tanzania. Dark above; tail long, most feathers white-tipped. **5a. Male A. m. nigrodorsalis**. Uncommon in cent. Kenyan highlands. **5b. Female A. m. melanocephala**. Common in coastal forest and along lower Tana River. (Paler *A. m. moschi* common in n. Tanzanian forests.)

6 BROWN-HEADED APALIS *Apalis alticola*   **Page 477**
Fairly common in forest edges of the Nguruman Hills in se. Kenya, also at Loliondo, Crater and Mbulu Highlands of n. Tanzania. Resembles Grey Apalis, but underside of tail grey with white feather tips.

7 WHITE-WINGED APALIS *Apalis c. chariessa*   **Page 478**
Very rare in riparian trees along lower Tana River. **7a. Male**. Glossy blue-black, with white wing panel; throat white. **7b. Female**. Olive-backed, with white wing panel; throat grey.

8 BLACK-THROATED APALIS *Apalis j. jacksoni*   **Page 477**
Fairly common in Kenyan highlands, mostly in forest-edge trees. **8a. Male**. Black face and throat, with bold white stripes from bill. **8b. Female**. Largely grey head with white facial stripes.

9 BLACK-COLLARED APALIS *Apalis p. pulchra*   **Page 478**
Fairly common in Kenyan highland-forest undergrowth and at edges. Wags tail constantly.

10 YELLOW-BREASTED APALIS *Apalis flavida*   **Page 476**
Common and widespread in open wooded habitats. **10a. Male A. f. golzi**. Distinct black breast spot (lacking or faint in female). **10b. Female A. f. pugnax**. Longer-tailed than *golzi*; breast spot indistinct or lacking in female (but pronounced in male); broad yellow tail-feather tips. **10c. Juvenile A. f. flavocincta**. N. Kenya. Upperside of tail brown, not olive-green as in southern races; no black on breast; head may be brownish. (For other races, see text.)

11 BUFF-BELLIED WARBLER *Phyllolais pulchella*   **Page 481**
Fairly common in savanna and open woodland; partial to acacia trees. Pale buff underparts; white outer tail feathers; bill yellowish below.

12 RED-FRONTED WARBLER *Spiloptila rufifrons*   **Page 479**
Near ground in dry bush country. *Apalis*-like; wags long, often erect tail. **12a. S. r. rufidorsalis**. Tsavo East NP. Rufous wash on back. **12b. S. r. rufifrons**: N. Kenya to n. Tanzania, except in range of 12a. Rufous crown contrasts with dull grey-brown back. **12c. Male S. r. rufidorsalis**. Blackish breast band in some. (See text.)

13 GREY WREN-WARBLER *Calamonastes simplex*   **Page 475**
Widespread in low-elevation bush and dry woods, except in sw. Kenya and adjacent Tanzania. Constantly flirts tail. Feet dark grey or blackish. Barring on underparts indistinct.

14 PALE WREN-WARBLER *Calamonastes undosus*   **Page 475**
Local in north-cent. Tanzania and north to Serengeti NP, Loliondo and Mara GR. Feet pinkish orange; ventral barring conspicuous; limited tail action.

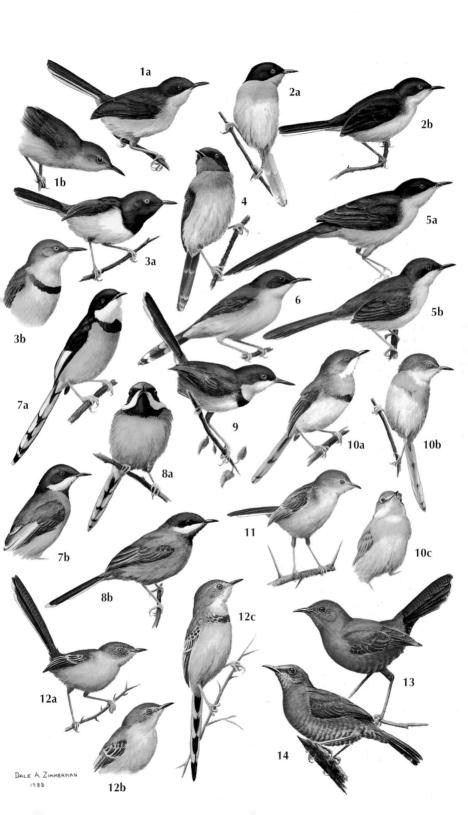

DALE A. ZIMMERMAN
1988

PLATE 101: AFRICAN WARBLERS (*Prinia, Parisoma et al.*)

1 BROWN PARISOMA *Parisoma lugens jacksoni*   **Page 482**
Uncommon in Kenyan highlands and Crater Highlands of n. Tanzania. Favours acacia
trees. Narrow white tail-feather edges and tips.

2 BANDED PARISOMA *Parisoma boehmi*   **Page 482**
Fairly common in acacia trees. **2a. *P. b. boehmi*, adult male**. Black breast band, white
wing-stripe; throat spots variable; eyes yellowish. **2b. *P. b. boehmi*, juvenile**. No breast
band. Buff on sides, wing-bars; white-edged tail, dark eyes. **2c. *P. b. marsabit*, adult
female**. Breast band incomplete. Paler than southern birds, very little buff below.

3 WHITE-CHINNED PRINIA *Prinia leucopogon reichenowi*   **Page 474**
Common in undergrowth in w. Kenyan woodland and forest edge. Long-tailed; creamy
white throat contrasts with dark face.

4 TAWNY-FLANKED PRINIA *Prinia subflava melanorhyncha*   **Page 474**
Common, usually in small noisy groups, in scrub, woodland and brushy habitats. Tawny
brown, with long slim tail; white superciliary stripe, dark loral spots. **4a. Breeding male**.
Bill black. (Non-breeding birds have horn-coloured bill, longer tail, are darker above.)
4b. Juvenile. Like non-br. adult, but faintly yellowish below, more rufescent above.

5 PALE PRINIA *Prinia somalica*   **Page 474**
Fairly common in dry open bush in n. Kenya; rare south to Tsavo West NP. Pale brown-
ish grey upperparts. Often feeds on ground. **5a. Adult**. Creamy white below. **5b. Juvenile**.
Pale buff on breast, more sandy brown above.

6 BANDED PRINIA *Prinia bairdii melanops*   **Page 474**
Locally common in w. Kenyan forest undergrowth. Shy; skulks in rank herbage.
6a. Adult. Barred below, long tail, yellowish eyes; white wing spots. **6b. Juvenile**.
Browner, less blackish than adult, buff wing spots; only suggestion of bars below.

7 RED-WINGED WARBLER *Heliolais erythroptera rhodoptera*   **Page 475**
Scarce and local in w. Kenya, fairly common in e. Tanzania; feeds in undergrowth, sings
from trees in bushed grassland, open woods, old cultivation. Prinia-like, with large bill,
maroon-rufous wings. **7a. Breeding adult**. Greyish to grey-brown above; bill black.
7b. Non-breeding adult. More rufous above; bill pale, tail longer.

8 BLACK-FACED RUFOUS WARBLER *Bathmocercus rufus vulpinus*   **Page 465**
Common in forest undergrowth in w. Kenya. Skulking, but highly vocal. **8a. Adult
female**. Olive-grey back, black face and throat. **8b. Adult male**. Largely rufous, with
black face and mid-ventral line. **8c. Juvenile male. 8d. Juvenile female**.

9 YELLOW-BELLIED HYLIOTA *Hyliota f. flavigaster*   **Page 482**
Western: Mt Elgon/Kongelai Escarpment; Fort Ternan to Mara GR. Uncommon in savanna, woodland and tall bush. Arboreal. **9a. Male**. Glossy blue-black above, yellowish
tawny below. **9b. Female**. Dark grey above, with faint bluish gloss on back and tail.

10 SOUTHERN HYLIOTA *Hyliota australis slatini*   **Page 482**
Uncommon in Kakamega and Nandi Forests, w. Kenya. Arboreal. **10a. Male**. Dull black
above; belly white. **10b. Female**. Brownish above. (Darker *H. a. usambarae* rare in
Usambara Mts.)

11 KRETSCHMER'S LONGBILL *Macrosphenus k. kretschmeri*   **Page 479**
Formerly in Kitovu Forest near Taveta, se. Kenya. Now apparently restricted to mountains
in ne. Tanzania. Greenbul-like. Long slender bill; eyes pale.

12 GREY-CAPPED WARBLER *Eminia lepida*   **Page 479**
Fairly common in dense tangled vegetation on river banks, in moist ravines, forest edges
and cultivation. **Adult** bright olive-yellow above, with grey head, black eye-line and
chestnut throat. Chestnut on bend of wing often concealed.

PLATE 102: AFRICAN WARBLERS, LITTLE YELLOW FLYCATCHER AND WHITE-EYES

1 YELLOW-BELLIED EREMOMELA *Eremomela icteropygialis abdominalis*
Page 480
Uncommon in open woodland and bush. Avoids drier habitats. Yellow extends from middle underparts to vent. (Western *E. i. griseoflava* yellow only on lower belly.)

2 YELLOW-VENTED EREMOMELA *Eremomela flavicrissalis* **Page 480**
Uncommon in arid scrub and semi-desert in n. and e. Kenya, in more extreme habitats than Yellow-bellied Eremomela. **2a. Adult.** Yellow (often pale) confined to extreme lower belly and vent region. No olive on lower back as in *E. i. griseoflava*. **2b. Juvenile.** Buff wing edgings. Yellow faint and restricted.

3 GREEN-BACKED EREMOMELA *Eremomela pusilla canescens* **Page 481**
Western Kenya. Uncommon and local in savanna, open woodland and on shrubby slopes. Bright yellow belly, grey crown, narrow blackish mask.

4 GREEN-CAPPED EREMOMELA *Eremomela scotops kikuyuensis* **Page 481**
Uncommon and local in wooded habitats, often with mixed-species flocks. Arboreal. Greenish-olive forecrown, yellow throat and breast. (Entire underside pale yellow in coastal race *occipitalis*. *E. s. citriniceps* of sw. Kenya to Serengeti NP is brighter, but has greyish white belly.)

5 TURNER'S EREMOMELA *Eremomela turneri* **Page 481**
Uncommon in canopy of Kakamega Forest, w. Kenya. **5a. Adult.** Black breast band, rufous forecrown. **5b. Juvenile.** Hint of breast band or none, pale yellow below, olive above, sometimes with rufous forehead. Feet pink.

6 YELLOW-THROATED WOODLAND WARBLER *Phylloscopus ruficapillus minullus* **Page 463**
Common in forest remnants on Taita Hills and in ne. Tanzanian mountains. Tawny-brown crown, yellow face and under tail-coverts.

7 DARK-CAPPED YELLOW WARBLER *Chloropeta natalensis massaica*
Page 465
Uncommon in low leafy vegetation in moist places from 1100 to 2300 m. Suggests flycatcher, with broad bill and rictal bristles, often upright posture. **7a. Adult.** Blackish crown, yellow underparts. **7b. Juvenile.** Blackish brown crown; tawny buff throughout.

8 MOUNTAIN YELLOW WARBLER *Chloropeta similis* **Page 466**
Largely replaces No. 7 at higher elevations (1850–3000+ m) mainly in forest-edge vegetation. Less flycatcher-like and lacks dark crown of preceding species.

9 PAPYRUS YELLOW WARBLER *Chloropeta gracilirostris* **Page 465**
Scarce in papyrus swamps around Lake Victoria. Flanks russet brown, rump tinged rufous; toes and claws large and dark.

10 LITTLE YELLOW FLYCATCHER *Erythrocercus holochlorus* **Page 486**
Common in Kenyan coastal forests, Shimba Hills and East Usambara Mts. Arboreal. Tiny, warbler-like; bright yellow underparts, narrow yellowish eye-ring.

11 MONTANE WHITE-EYE *Zosterops poliogaster* **Page 483**
Common in highland forest. Eye-ring broad in all races. **11a. Z. p. silvanus.** Taita Hills and Mt Kasigau. Much grey below (female paler). **11b. Z. p. kulalensis, male.** Mt Kulal, n. Kenya. Yellow mid-ventral streak. **11c. Z. p. mbuluensis.** Mostly Tanzanian. (In Kenya, on Chyulu Hills and Ol Doinyo Orok.) Yellow forehead blends with yellow green crown. **11d and 11e. Z. p. kikuyuensis.** Cent. Kenyan highlands. Yellow forehead contrasts with crown. (For Tanzanian *Z. p. eurycricotus*, see Plate 124.)

12 YELLOW WHITE-EYE *Zosterops senegalensis* **Page 483**
Common in wooded habitats above 1500 m (to 3400 m on Mt Elgon, in moorland). Narrow eye-ring and restricted yellow forehead band. Darker than Abyssinian White-eye, and greenish on sides and flanks. **12a. Z. s. jacksoni.** Widespread in Kenyan highlands. **12b. Z. s. jacksoni/stuhlmanni intergrade.** Kakamega Forest, w. Kenya. Plumage variable. (*Z. s. stierlingi* of Usambara Mts is darker on flanks, deeper yellow on belly.)

13 ABYSSINIAN WHITE-EYE *Zosterops abyssinicus flavilateralis* **Page 483**
Locally common in bush, savanna, forest edge and gardens. Widespread in and east of Rift Valley (common in Nairobi suburbs). Small and pale; eye-ring narrow; no obvious black loral area, no greenish wash on sides. (Far-northern *Z. a. jubaensis* is greyer above.)

DALE A. ZIMMERMAN

PLATE 103: AFRICAN WARBLERS (crombecs, camaropteras), TITS AND CREEPER

1 SOMALI LONG-BILLED CROMBEC *Sylvietta isabellina*   **Page 480**
Uncommon in dry scrub and bush in n. and e. Kenya. Pale coloration; long bill.

2 RED-FACED CROMBEC *Sylvietta whytii jacksoni*   **Page 479**
Fairly common in open woodland, bush and savanna, in moister areas than No. 3. No facial stripes; face/underparts uniform buffy rufous. (Other races more olive-brown.)

3 NORTHERN CROMBEC *Sylvietta brachyura leucopsis*   **Page 479**
Fairly common in dry open woodland and bush, less so in the highlands. Facial stripes; throat and much of face whitish. (Superciliary stripes pale tawny in western *S. b. carnapi*.)

4 WHITE-BROWED CROMBEC *Sylvietta l. leucophrys*   **Page 480**
Local and uncommon in Kenyan highland forest and bamboo. Greenish wings, brown cap, bold white superciliaries. **4a. Adult.** Throat/breast whitish to pale grey. **4b. Juvenile.** Throat, breast and sides olive-brown; belly yellow; superciliaries yellow.

5 GREEN CROMBEC *Sylvietta virens baraka*   **Page 480**
Locally in dense bush and second-growth riparian woods near Ugandan border. Dull greyish olive back, olive wings, grey-brown breast band and narrow whitish superciliaries.

6 GREY-BACKED CAMAROPTERA *Camaroptera brachyura*   **Page 475**
Common in forest, dense bush, garden shrubbery. Yellow-green wings; back usually grey or brownish, sometimes olive; underparts vary. **6a. Adult, C. b. tincta.** W. Kenya. Throat, breast and back grey. (Some birds paler grey on throat and breast.) **6b. Juv., C. b. erlangeri.** Coastal Kenya and interior ne. Tanzania. Upperparts olive, breast pale yellowish. **6c. Juv., C. b. abessinica.** N. Kenya. Brownish above and on breast; flanks faintly barred. (Adult greyer, lacks barring.)

7 OLIVE-GREEN CAMAROPTERA *Camaroptera chloronota toroensis*   **Page 476**
Common in forest undergrowth and vines in Kakamega and Nandi Forests, w. Kenya. **7a. Juvenile.** Dark-chested extreme figured; some birds paler, more yellowish. **7b. Adult.** Pale tawny on face and breast; throat white.

8 AFRICAN PENDULINE TIT *Anthoscopus caroli*   **Page 485**
Uncommon in open woodland, savanna and forest edge in moister areas than No. 9. Tiny; bill sharp and conical; tail short. Darker than No. 9, forehead paler than crown. Variable. **8a. A. c. sylviella.** Interior e. Kenya to Longido and Kibaya in n. Tanzania. Grey above, buff or rusty below; forehead usually buff, sometimes whitish. (*A. c. sharpei* near Lake Victoria similar, but darker below, with whitish forehead.) **8b. A. c. robertsi.** Se. Kenya and ne. Tanzania. Greyish olive above, pale yellowish to pale ochre-buff on belly and crissum. **8c. A. c. roccattii.** W. Kenya. Olive above, with yellow forehead, dull yellow below.

9 MOUSE-COLOURED PENDULINE TIT *Anthoscopus musculus*   **Page 485**
Uncommon in bush, savanna and open woodland in dry areas. Bill conical, sharp. Bright extreme shown; some birds nearly white below.

10 WHITE-BELLIED TIT *Parus albiventris*   **Page 485**
Fairly common in wooded habitats, including suburban gardens. Black, with white belly and wing markings. **10a. Juvenile.** Dull greyish black. **10b. Adult.** Glossy black.

11 NORTHERN GREY TIT *Parus thruppi barakae*   **Page 484**
Fairly common in dry n. and e. savanna and scrub. Whitish cheeks.

12 RED-THROATED TIT *Parus fringillinus*   **Page 485**
Locally common in acacias in s. Kenya/n. Tanzania. Rufous-buff face and throat; much white in wing.

13 NORTHERN BLACK TIT *Parus leucomelas guineensis*   **Page 484**
Rare and sporadic in moist wooded areas of w. Kenya. Black, with white wing patch, yellow eyes.

14 DUSKY TIT *Parus funereus*   **Page 484**
Fairly common in Kakamega and Nandi forests, w. Kenya. Arboreal. Usually with mixed-species flocks. Dull blackish throughout; eyes red.

15 SPOTTED CREEPER *Salpornis spilonota salvadori*   **Page 486**
Rare and local in acacias near Kapenguria, nw. Kenya. Creeps on tree trunks.

PLATE 104: LONG-TAILED SUNBIRDS (mostly males; for females, see Plate 107) (Pectoral tufts often wholly or partly concealed)

1 MALACHITE SUNBIRD *Nectarinia famosa cupreonitens* **Page 525**
Locally common in highland-forest edge, open areas; mostly above 1800 m. **1a. Non-breeding male.** (Birds in moult may show dark mid-ventral line, scattered shiny feathers.) **1b. Breeding male.** Yellow pectoral tufts.

2 SCARLET-TUFTED MALACHITE SUNBIRD *Nectarinia j. johnstoni* **Page 525**
Mainly on moorlands (above 3000 m), lower in cool wet seasons. Darker, bluer green than Malachite Sunbird, with scarlet pectoral tufts; very long central rectrices. **2a. Breeding male. 2b. Immature male.** Variable; mostly greyish brown with limited green iridescence. Tail short.

3 BRONZE SUNBIRD *Nectarinia k. kilimensis* **Page 524**
Common above 1200 m in gardens, cultivation, forest edge. **Adult male** with iridescent green head and breast, bronzy or brassy gloss.

4 GOLDEN-WINGED SUNBIRD *Nectarinia r. reichenowi* **Page 525**
Highland forest edge, cultivation; mostly above 1800 m, lower in wet season. Yellow wing and tail patches in all plumages. **4a. Breeding male.** Velvety black with bronzy and coppery iridescence (lacking in non-breeding plumage). **4b. Adult female.** Yellowish below, blackish mask, short tail.

5 TACAZZE SUNBIRD *Nectarinia tacazze jacksoni* **Page 524**
Highland forest, giant heath and gardens above 1800 m. **5a. Breeding male.** Green to brassy-green head; ruby-violet iridescence on body. **5b. Non-breeding male.** Mostly greyish, with black belly, dark face; shoulders, rump and upper tail-coverts metallic red-purple. Iridescence increases on head and body as moult progresses.

6 BEAUTIFUL SUNBIRD *Nectarinia pulchella* **Page 526**
Common in dry acacia woodland and savanna. **6a. Juvenile male, *N. p. pulchella*.** Nw. Kenya **6b. Non-breeding male, *N. p. pulchella*. 6c. Breeding male, *N. p. pulchella*.** Green belly, yellow sides to breast. **6d. Breeding male, *N. p. melanogastra*.** E. and s. Kenya, n. Tanzania. Black belly, yellow on breast.

⑦ RED-CHESTED SUNBIRD *Nectarinia erythrocerca* **Page 525**
Lake Victoria basin. Fairly common near lakeshore. **7a. Adult male.** Breast band darker, deeper red than in male Beautiful or Black-bellied Sunbirds; also larger, heavier. **7b. Juvenile male.** Extent of black throat patch variable. Older immatures may show red or green feathers.

8 BLACK-BELLIED SUNBIRD *Nectarinia nectarinioides* **Page 526**
Locally common in dry eastern areas south to ne. Tanzania. Favours riverine acacias. **8a. Adult male, *N. n. nectarinioides*.** Southern. Orange-red breast band. (Beautiful Sunbird shows much more yellow.) Intergrades with 8b along Northern Uaso Nyiro River. **8b. Adult male, *N. n. erlangeri*.** N. Kenya. Lacks yellow pectoral tufts; breast band pure red.

PLATE 105: SUNBIRDS (See also Plates 104, 106 and 107)

1 PYGMY SUNBIRD *Anthreptes p. platurus*   **Page 518**
Northwestern Kenya. Irregular in arid and semi-arid bush country. **Male.** (Female on Plate 107.)

2 COLLARED SUNBIRD *Anthreptes collaris garguensis*   **Page 518**
Common in forest and forest edges. **2a. Male. 2b. Female.**

3 VARIABLE SUNBIRD *Nectarinia venusta*   **Page 520**
Widespread in bush, forest edge, cultivation and gardens. **3a.** *N. v. falkensteini,* **breeding male.** Common except in ne. Kenya; intensity of yellow varies. **3b.** *N. v. albiventris,* **breeding male.** Common in arid ne. Kenya. **3c.** *N. v. falkensteini,* **imm. male.** (Juvenile male also black-throated but lacks iridescence.)

4 ORANGE-TUFTED SUNBIRD *Nectarinia bouvieri*   **Page 523**
Scarce at forest edge and in moist scrub in w. Kenya. **4a. Adult male.** Orange pectoral tufts (not always visible), violet forehead, blue chin. **4b. Imm. male.** Long bill, coppery/green wing- and upper tail-coverts.

5 MARICO SUNBIRD *Nectarinia mariquensis suahelica*   **Page 522**
Common and widespread in bush, savanna, open woodland. **5a. Adult male.** Broad maroon breast band; larger bill than Purple-banded Sunbird. **5b. Juv. male.** Yellow primary edges; mottled breast and sides.

6 PURPLE-BANDED SUNBIRD *Nectarinia bifasciata*   **Page 522**
N. b. tsavoensis. Common in dry se. bush, but not on coast. **6a. Imm. male. 6b. Adult male.** Much narrower maroon breast band than in *N. b. microrhyncha.* Smaller and smaller-billed than Violet-breasted Sunbird. **6c. Female.** (Some lack black throat; see Plate 107.) *N. b. microrhyncha.* Common along coast north to Malindi; scarce in west (Lake Victoria basin south to w. Serengeti NP). **6d. Breeding male.** Bill smaller than in Marico Sunbird. **6e. Non-breeding male.** Like black-throated female, but with green wing-coverts and dark wings. May show green throat feathers.

7 VIOLET-BREASTED SUNBIRD *Nectarinia chalcomelas*   **Page 523**
Uncommon on n. Kenyan coast; scarce (seasonal?) inland to lower Tana River. **Male** larger, heavier, longer-billed than Purple-banded Sunbird; large violet breast patch with no maroon along lower edge.

8 GREEN-HEADED SUNBIRD *Nectarinia verticalis viridisplendens*   **Page 519**
Fairly common in w. and cent. Kenyan highlands in forest, riparian woods and gardens. Long curved bill; iridescent head often appears blue. **8a. Adult male. 8b. Adult female. 8c. Juv. male.** Blackish forehead, face and throat.

9 HUNTER'S SUNBIRD *Nectarinia hunteri*   **Page 520**
Common in drier country than Scarlet-chested Sunbird. **9a. Imm. male.** Throat and chin black (some green at sides). **9b. Adult male.** Vivid scarlet breast with little blue iridescence; throat and chin black (shining green at sides); violet iridescence on 'shoulders' and rump. **9c. Juv. female.** Yellowish below, with dark barring; pale throat, short eyebrow.

10 AMETHYST SUNBIRD *Nectarinia amethystina kalckreuthi*   **Page 519**
Fairly common in wooded habitats and gardens. **10a. Juv. male.** Streaked yellowish underparts; black throat; long superciliaries. **10b. Adult male.** Throat and 'shoulder' iridescent ruby, rose-violet or amethyst; forecrown green or turquoise. (Inland *N. a. kirkii* lacks purple on upper tail-coverts.)

11 SCARLET-CHESTED SUNBIRD *Nectarinia senegalensis lamperti*   **Page 520**
Common in gardens and open wooded habitats in moister areas than Hunter's Sunbird. **11a. Adult male.** Green chin and throat; red patch suffused with shining blue (visible at close range). **11b. Juv. male.** Variable; usually whitish below and heavily barred; throat blackish; no superciliary stripes. **11c. Imm. male.** Glittering green chin and throat; red patch shows more blue than in Hunter's Sunbird.

12 GREEN-THROATED SUNBIRD *Nectarinia rubescens kakamegae*   **Page 519**
Kakamega and Nandi forests only; in canopy, often with mixed-species flocks. **Male** has narrow violet band below green gorget often not visible. (Female on Plate 107.)

DALE A ZIMMERMAN
1992

PLATE 106: SUNBIRDS (adults, except as indicated) (See also Plates 104, 105 and 107)

1 **AMANI SUNBIRD** *Anthreptes pallidigaster*   **Page 518**
Local in coastal *Brachystegia* woodland and East Usambara Mts. **1a. Female**. Plain, with blue-black tail. **1b. Male**. (Orange pectoral tufts not always visible.)

2 **PLAIN-BACKED SUNBIRD** *Anthreptes reichenowi yokanae*   **Page 517**
Uncommon in coastal forest, Shimba Hills NP and East Usambara Mts. **2a. Male**. Black forehead and throat show blue gloss in bright light. **2b. Female**. Faint pale superciliary stripes; white eyelid feathering.

3 **SUPERB SUNBIRD** *Nectarinia superba buvuma*   **Page 523**
Rare near Mumias and Busia along Kenya-Ugandan border. **3a. Female**. Large bill; long yellow superciliary stripes; belly and under tail-coverts yellow or yellow-orange. **3b. Male**. Blue crown, violet-blue and maroon underparts.

4 **MOUSE-COLOURED SUNBIRD** *Nectarinia veroxii fischeri*   **Page 519**
Uncommon in coastal bush, thickets, mangroves and gardens. **Female**. Sexes similar. (Scarlet pectoral tufts may be concealed).

5 **OLIVE SUNBIRD** *Nectarinia olivacea changamwensis*   **Page 519**
Fairly common in forest, other wooded habitats. Yellow pectoral tufts in both sexes (lacking in females of inland race). **5a. Female. 5b. Male**.

6 **GREEN SUNBIRD** *Anthreptes rectirostris tephrolaemus*   **Page 518**
Uncommon in w. Kenya. (Kakamega, Nandi and Kericho forest canopy.) **Male**. (Female on Plate 107.)

7 **COPPER SUNBIRD** *Nectarinia cuprea*   **Page 523**
Common resident in bush, cultivation and forest edge in and near Lake Victoria basin. **Male**. (Female on Plate 107.)

8 **SHINING SUNBIRD** *Nectarinia habessinica turkanae*   **Page 526**
Uncommon in dry northern Kenya; partial to acacias and flowering aloes. **Male**. Only far-northern sunbird with bright scarlet breast band. (Female on Plate 107.)

9 **OLIVE-BELLIED SUNBIRD** *Nectarinia chloropygia orphogaster*   **Page 521**
Uncommon in w. Kenya below 1550 m, in bush, forest edge and cultivation. **Male**. Belly dark olive-brown; yellow tufts not always evident. (Female on Plate 107.)

10 **EASTERN DOUBLE-COLLARED SUNBIRD** *Nectarinia mediocris*   **Page 521**
Fairly common in highland forest, gardens, bamboo and giant heath, 1850–3700 m. **Male**. Narrow scarlet breast band; longer tail, longer bill and slightly more golden-green than No. 11; upper tail-coverts blue. (Female on Plate 107.)

11 **NORTHERN DOUBLE-COLLARED SUNBIRD** *Nectarinia preussi kikuyuensis*
Page 521
Common, 1700–2800 m. Overlaps preceding species above 1800 m. **Male**. Broad scarlet breast band; tail and bill shorter than in No. 10; bluer green above; upper tail-coverts violet. (Female on Plate 107.)

12 **EASTERN VIOLET-BACKED SUNBIRD** *Anthreptes orientalis*   **Page 517**
Widespread in dry bush and savanna below 1300 m. **12a. Male**. Rump blue-green; underparts white. **12b. Female**. Underparts entirely white; tail dark blue with white feather tips.

13 **ULUGURU VIOLET-BACKED SUNBIRD** *Anthreptes neglectus*   **Page 517**
Rare in coastal and Tana riverine forest, also in Shimba Hills. Fairly common in East Usambara Mts. **13a. Male**. Grey below; dull brown sides of face and collar. **13b. Female**. Iridescent violet crown and back; grey throat/breast, olive-yellow belly.

14 **WESTERN VIOLET-BACKED SUNBIRD** *Anthreptes l. longuemarei*   **Page 517**
Scarce and local in w. Kenyan gardens, cultivation and forest edge in high-rainfall areas. **14a. Juvenile**. Underparts entirely pale yellow. **14b. Female**. Yellow belly; violet tail and upper tail-coverts. **14c. Male**. Upperparts uniformly violet.

PLATE 107: DULL-PLUMAGED SUNBIRDS (Adult females except as indicated) See text for field marks

1 OLIVE-BELLIED SUNBIRD *Nectarinia chloropygia orphogaster* **Page 521**
Western Kenya. Local below 1550 m in bush and forest edge.

2 VARIABLE SUNBIRD *Nectarinia venusta falkensteini* **Page 520**
Common, widespread below 3000 m in gardens, bush and cultivation.

3 NORTHERN DOUBLE-COLLARED SUNBIRD *Nectarinia preussi kikuyuensis*
Page 521
Common in Kenyan highlands, 1700–2800 m, in forest edge and gardens.

4 EASTERN DOUBLE-COLLARED SUNBIRD *Nectarinia m. mediocris* **Page 521**
Fairly common between 1850 and 3700 m in forest, subalpine vegetation, gardens.

5 SHINING SUNBIRD *Nectarinia habessinica turkanae* **Page 526**
Uncommon in arid n. Kenya. **5a. Female. 5b. Juvenile male.**

6 PYGMY SUNBIRD *Anthreptes p. platurus* **Page 518**
Irregular in dry bush in nw. Kenya.

7 ORANGE-TUFTED SUNBIRD *Nectarinia bouvieri* **Page 523**
Western Kenya. Scarce and local in forest edge in Busia/Kakamega areas.

8 GREEN SUNBIRD *Anthreptes rectirostris tephrolaemus* **Page 518**
Western Kenya. Mainly forest treetops.

9 VIOLET-BREASTED SUNBIRD *Nectarinia chalcomelas* **Page 523**
Mainly in coastal shrub-savanna and thickets, inland to lower Tana River.

10 BEAUTIFUL SUNBIRD *Nectarinia p. pulchella* **Page 526**
Common in dry country.

11 BLACK-BELLIED SUNBIRD *Nectarinia nectarinioides* **Page 526**
Locally common in riverine acacias in dry country. **11a. Juvenile male. 11b. Female.**

12 PURPLE-BANDED SUNBIRD *Nectarinia bifasciata* **Page 522**
Common in bush, scrub and gardens. **12a. *N. b. tsavoensis*.** Southeastern (but not coastal).
12b. *N. b. microrhyncha*. Common along coast; scarce in Lake Victoria basin.

13 RED-CHESTED SUNBIRD *Nectarinia erythrocerca* **Page 525**
Lake Victoria shores and islands, east to Ruma NP, Ahero and Migori.

14 GREEN-THROATED SUNBIRD *Nectarinia rubescens kakamegae* **Page 519**
W. Kenya in Kakamega and Nandi forest canopy.

15 COPPER SUNBIRD *Nectarinia cuprea* **Page 523**
Fairly common in bush and cultivation in and near Lake Victoria basin.

16 MARICO SUNBIRD *Nectarinia mariquensis osiris* **Page 522**
Widespread in open bush and savanna.

17 AMETHYST SUNBIRD *Nectarinia amethystina* **Page 519**
Widespread, fairly common in wooded habitats. **17a. *N. a. kirkii*.** Highlands. **17b. *N. a. kalckreuthi*.** Coastal.

18 HUNTER'S SUNBIRD *Nectarinia hunteri* **Page 520**
Common in dry areas of n. and e. Kenya, ne. Tanzania.

19 SCARLET-CHESTED SUNBIRD *Nectarinia senegalensis lamperti* **Page 520**
Fairly common and widespread, except in dry areas; avoids forest.

20 OLIVE SUNBIRD *Nectarinia olivacea vincenti* **Page 519**
Fairly common in forest west of Rift Valley. (This race lacks yellow pectoral tufts.)

21 SCARLET-TUFTED MALACHITE SUNBIRD *Nectarinia j. johnstoni* **Page 525**
Alpine moorlands above 3000 m.

22 TACAZZE SUNBIRD *Nectarinia tacazze jacksoni* **Page 524**
Fairly common in wooded highlands above 1800 m.

23 BRONZE SUNBIRD *Nectarinia k. kilimensis* **Page 524**
Common and widespread in highland gardens, cultivation and forest edge. **23a. Adult female. 23b. Juvenile male.**

24 MALACHITE SUNBIRD *Nectarinia famosa cupreonitens* **Page 525**
Local in open areas above 1800 m. **24a. Female. 24b. Juvenile.**

PLATE 108: SPARROWS, PETRONIA, SPECKLE-FRONTED WEAVER

1 CHESTNUT SPARROW *Passer eminibey*   **Page 528**
Locally common in bush and open wooded habitats. Gregarious. **1a. Male** acquiring
adult plumage. Largely chestnut. (Adult on Plate 115.) **1b. Female**. Trace of chestnut
above eye and on throat.

2 SOMALI SPARROW *Passer castanopterus fulgens*   **Page 528**
Locally common in villages and along watercourses in n. Kenya. Gregarious when not
breeding. **2a. Female juvenile**. Resembles female House Sparrow, but brighter above,
darker below. **2b. Non-breeding male**. Bright rufous on scapulars and wings, pale yellowish below; bill horn-colour. **2c. Breeding male**. Bright rufous crown and nape, yellow
cheeks and underparts; bill black.

3 HOUSE SPARROW *Passer domesticus indicus*   **Page 528**
Local and uncommon; spreading inland from coastal towns along highways and railroads
in se. Kenya/ne. Tanzania. **3a. Female**. Buff superciliary stripes and wing-bars. **3b. Male**.
Black face and throat, white cheeks and sides of neck.

4 RUFOUS SPARROW *Passer r. rufocinctus*   **Page 527**
Common in pairs in cultivation and open habitats in and near Rift Valley highlands. Pale
eyes. **4a. Female**. Dusky throat. **4b. Male**. Black throat patch, grey-and-rufous head.

5 GREY-HEADED SPARROW *Passer griseus*   **Page 527**
Common and widespread in varied habitats. Polytypic, with noticeable intergradation
between at least some forms. Bill black in breeding season, otherwise dull grey or brown
above, dull yellowish below. **5a. *P. g. ungandae*, adult**. West of Rift Valley. Grey head,
dull rufous or rufous-brown back, white throat. **5b. *P. g. ungandae*, juvenile**. Browner,
short dark streaks on back. **5c. *P. g. gongonensis*, breeding male**. 'Parrot-billed Sparrow'.
In and east of Rift Valley from Lake Turkana, south to ne. Tanzania. Larger than *ungandae*;
underparts evenly grey; bill stout. **5d. *P. g. gongonensis*, non-breeding female**. **5e. *P. g.
swainsoni***. 'Swainson's Sparrow'. Ethiopian border areas. Back dull brown; dark grey
below, with white belly, whitish throat. **5f. *P. g. suahelicus***. 'Swahili Sparrow'. Sw.
Kenya, n. Tanzania. Back and head uniformly coloured.

6 YELLOW-SPOTTED PETRONIA *Petronia pyrgita*   **Page 528**
Widespread, but uncommon and inconspicuous in bush, savanna and dry woodland
below 1500 m. **6a. Juvenile**. Brownish. Recalls House Sparrow, but with prominent eye-
ring; bill pale. **6b. Adult**. Greyish or brownish above, with white eye-ring. Small yellow
throat spot sometimes visible.

7 SPECKLE-FRONTED WEAVER *Sporopipes frontalis emini*   **Page 533**
Uncommon in dry bush and open savanna. Black forehead and crown with white speckling; tawny-rufous nape, bold moustachial stripe. Feeds on ground, Gregarious when not
breeding.

1a
1b
2a
2b
2c
3a
3b
4a
4b
5a
5b
5c
5d
5e
5f
6a
6b
7

DALE A. ZIMMERMAN
1990

PLATE 109: SPARROW-WEAVERS, BUFFALO-WEAVERS, SOCIAL WEAVERS *et al.*

1 GROSBEAK-WEAVER *Amblyospiza albifrons melanota*   **Page 533**
Locally common near marshes, swamps; also visits woodland, suburban gardens, forest.
1a. Female. Heavy bill; bold streaking. **1b. Male**. Heavy bill; dark, with white forehead (variable), white wing patches. (Eastern races are black-headed.)

2 BLACK-CAPPED SOCIAL WEAVER *Pseudonigrita cabanisi*   **Page 532**
Locally common in dry open savanna and bush. Gregarious . Feeds on ground. **2a. Adult**. Black cap; large pale bill. **2b. Juvenile**. Brown head, dull horn-coloured bill.

3 GREY-CAPPED SOCIAL WEAVER *Pseudonigrita arnaudi*   **Page 532**
Locally common in bush and open woodland. Short tail with pale tip. Gregarious.
3a. Juvenile. Brownish grey cap, dark cheeks, blackish lores. **3b. *P. a. dorsalis*, adult**, Sw. Kenya, Serengeti NP. Pale cap; centre of back grey. **3c. *P. a. arnaudi*, adult**, Mainly in and east of Rift Valley. Grey-brown back.

4 DONALDSON-SMITH'S SPARROW-WEAVER *Plocepasser donaldsoni*
    Page 529
Locally common in n. Kenya. Conspicuous in Isiolo District game reserves. Scaly, mottled plumage, buff cheeks, black whisker mark; white rump.

5 CHESTNUT-CROWNED SPARROW-WEAVER *Plocepasser superciliosus*
    Page 532
Local and uncommon on thinly wooded hillsides and in thorn-bush in nw. Kenya. Chestnut cap; bold head pattern.

6 WHITE-BROWED SPARROW-WEAVER *Plocepasser mahali melanorhynchus*
    Page 529
Common in *Acacia* bush, savanna and dry woodland below 1400 m. White superciliary stripe, much white in wings, white rump and upper tail-coverts. Often in small flocks. Feeds on the ground. **6a and 6b. Adults**.

7 RED-HEADED WEAVER *Anaplectes rubriceps*   **Page 544**
Uncommon in lightly wooded areas. Quiet and unobtrusive. **7a. Male *A. r. leuconotus***. Red and white, with black face, red bill. **7b. Female**. Orange-red bill, wing and tail edgings (rarely yellow). (Juvenile on Plate 114.) **7c. Male *A. r. jubaensis***. All red.

8 WHITE-HEADED BUFFALO-WEAVER *Dinemellia dinemelli boehmi*   **Page 529**
Common in dry bush and savanna below 1400 m. Orange-red on rump, tail-coverts and bend of wing; white head and wing patches. Noisy. Feeds on ground with starlings. **8a and 8b. Adults**.

9 WHITE-BILLED BUFFALO-WEAVER *Bubalornis albirostris*   **Page 529**
Locally common in nw. Kenya, south to lakes Baringo and Bogoria. Noisy in nesting colonies. **9a. Adult male**. Mostly black, bill ivory-white (blackish in female and non-breeding male). **9b. Juvenile.** White mottling below; bill black.

10 RED-BILLED BUFFALO-WEAVER *Bubalornis niger intermedius*   **Page 529**
Noisy and gregarious. Feeds on ground with starlings and weavers. Common and widespread in bush and savanna.**10a. Adult female**. Dark brown above, spotted and streaked below; bill brown or horn colour, pinkish at base. **10b. Juvenile**. Generally tan above, cheeks grey; bill largely yellowish orange or yellowish pink; throat and breast barred. **10c. Adult male**. Mostly black, with reddish bill.

DALE A. ZIMMERMAN
1990

PLATE 110: WHYDAHS, INDIGOBIRDS AND QUELEAS

1 PARADISE WHYDAH *Vidua paradisaea*   **Page 558**
Fairly common in dry country. **1a. Breeding male.** Buff nape; unusual tail, with two long tapering feathers. **1b. Breeding female.** Larger than female indigobirds; dark marks on side of head; large dark bill; breast plain or with necklace of fine streaks. **1c. Juvenile.** Plain; bill larger than in juv. Pin-tailed Whydah.

2 BROAD-TAILED PARADISE WHYDAH *Vidua obtusa*   **Page 559**
Rare. (Possibly extirpated from Kenya.) **2a. Breeding male.** Similar to *V. paradisaea,* but long tail feathers much wider, equally broad almost to tips. **2b. Female.** Paler bill than female of No. 1; less distinct face pattern. (See text.)

3 STRAW-TAILED WHYDAH *Vidua fischeri*   **Page 558**
Uncommon/fairly common in dry areas below 2000 m. **3a. Breeding male.** Buff and black, with 4 long straw-like central tail feathers; bill red. **3b. Female and non-breeding male.** Crown rufous-tinged; bill and feet red. **3c. Juvenile.** Dull rusty brown.

4 STEEL-BLUE WHYDAH *Vidua hypocherina*   **Page 558**
Uncommon and local in dry areas. **4a. Breeding male.** Dark shiny blue, with 4 long, slender tail feathers; white tufts beside rump often concealed. **4b. Female and non-breeding male.** In fresh plumage, brightly patterned; wing feathers edged buffy rufous, upper tail-coverts and black tail feathers white-edged and -tipped (but much duller when worn). Tiny bill pale grey.

5 PIN-TAILED WHYDAH *Vidua macroura*   **Page 558**
Common and widespread, mainly in moist areas, including cultivation. **5a. Breeding male.** Black and white, with long, slender floppy tail; red bill. **5b. Non-breeding male.** Black-and-white head stripes; red bill. Tail variable. **5c. Adult female.** Buff-and-brown head stripes; bill dusky or blackish above, reddish below (becoming all red after breeding). Much white on inner webs of rectrices. **5d. Juvenile.** Plain, with suggestion of superciliary stripe; blackish bill (becoming red in a few weeks).

6 VILLAGE or COMMON INDIGOBIRD *Vidua chalybeata*   **Page 557**
Widespread, especially in moist areas, often around dwellings. **6a. *V. c. centralis,* breeding male.** Dark blue-black, wings browner; bill whitish; feet orange, red or salmon-pink. **6b. *V. c. amauropteryx,* breeding male.** Bill and feet red or orange; plumage slightly more blue-green than in 6a. **6c. *V. c. centralis,* juvenile.** Suggests small female House Sparrow; no central crown stripe; bill pale. **6d. *V. c. centralis,* adult female.** Patterned like female Pin-tailed and Paradise Whydahs, but breast plain, usually dingy greyish buff; bill greyish pink, paler below.

7 PURPLE INDIGOBIRD *Vidua purpurascens*   **Page 557**
Uncommon and local in bush and shrubby woodland. **Breeding male** black with dull purple sheen; bill and feet white. Plumage identical to that of male Variable Indigobird. (See text.)

8 RED-BILLED QUELEA *Quelea quelea aethiopica*   **Page 544**
Common in dry savanna, bushed grassland and cultivation. **8a. Non-breeding female.** Heavy red bill; yellow wing edgings. **8b. Breeding male.** Red bill; black face and throat.

9 CARDINAL QUELEA *Quelea cardinalis rhodesiae*   **Page 544**
Locally common in tall moist grassland. **Breeding male** with brownish hindcrown and nape, rest of head to upper breast red. (Female on Plate 112.)

10 RED-HEADED QUELEA *Quelea erythrops*   **Page 544**
Sporadic in Lake Victoria basin and coastal lowlands. **Breeding male** has entire head red; barred blackish on throat; bill large, grey. (Female on Plate 112.)

DALE A ZIMMERMAN
1990

PLATE 111: BREEDING MALE BISHOPS AND WIDOWBIRDS (*Euplectes*)

1 RED-COLLARED WIDOWBIRD *Euplectes ardens* **Page 547**
Locally common in grassland, cultivation, moist brushy habitats. **1a. E. a. suahelica.** Highlands of Kenya and n. Tanzania. Crown and nape red. **1b. E. a. tropicus.** E. Tanzania north to Taita Hills and lower Tana River. Crown and nape black.

2 WHITE-WINGED WIDOWBIRD *E. albonotatus eques* **Page 547**
Common in bushed grassland and cultivation. White wing patch.

3 LONG-TAILED WIDOWBIRD *E. progne delamerei* **Page 548**
Locally fairly common in Kenyan highland grasslands, above 1800 m. **3a. At rest,** scarlet and buff wing-coverts may be partially concealed. **3b. Courtship flight** slow and erratic, with bustle-like dangling tail.

4 JACKSON'S WIDOWBIRD *E. jacksoni* **Page 549**
Locally common in grasslands of Kenyan and n. Tanzanian highlands. Long curved tail, tawny 'shoulders.'

5 YELLOW-MANTLED WIDOWBIRD *E. macrourus* **Page 547**
Locally common in moist grasslands of w. Kenya and adjacent areas of n. Tanzania. **5a. E. m. macrourus, yellow-backed form**. High grasslands, Mara GR to n. Serengeti NP. **5b. E. m. macrocercus, yellow-shouldered form**. Widespread at lower elevations in w. Kenya.

6 HARTLAUB'S MARSH WIDOWBIRD *E. hartlaubi humeralis* **Page 548**
Uncommon and local in w. Kenyan marshes and moist grassland, often alongside No. 7. Buffy-orange 'shoulder' patch; long tail.

7 FAN-TAILED WIDOWBIRD *E. axillaris phoeniceus* **Page 547**
Common in w. Kenyan marshes, local in n. Tanzanian and cent. Kenyan highlands. Short tail often fanned. (Coastal race *E. a. zanzibaricus* is larger-billed and wing-coverts may be black-tipped.)

8 NORTHERN RED BISHOP *E. f. franciscanus* **Page 546**
Local in Rift Valley around lakes Baringo and Bogoria, in marshes and tall wet grassland. Head extensively black; tail-coverts largely conceal tail.

9 ZANZIBAR RED BISHOP *E. nigroventris* **Page 546**
Southeastern; most numerous in coastal lowlands. Top of head entirely red; throat to belly black.

10 BLACK-WINGED RED BISHOP *E. h. hordeaceus* **Page 546**
Species widespread; this race locally common in moist grassland and cultivation in coastal lowlands. Wings black, not brown. (Western *E. h. craspedopterus* has white under tail-coverts.)

11 SOUTHERN RED BISHOP *E. orix nigrifrons* **Page 546**
Local in western marshes, rice fields and tall grass. Forehead and belly black, breast scarlet; tail-coverts do not conceal tail.

12 YELLOW BISHOP *E. capensis crassirostris* **Page 546**
Fairly common, mainly above 1400 m, in cultivation, moist scrub, forest edge and roadsides. Lower back and 'shoulders' largely yellow.

13 YELLOW-CROWNED BISHOP *E. afer ladoensis* **Page 545**
Local and uncommon in marshes, rice fields and moist grassland, mainly in w. and cent. Kenyan highlands and Arusha District. Top of head and most of back yellow.

14 FIRE-FRONTED BISHOP *E. diadematus* **Page 545**
Seasonally abundant in east and southeast following heavy rains. Scarlet or orange forehead patch.

15 BLACK BISHOP *E. gierowii ansorgei* **Page 545**
Western Kenya. Uncommon in moist grassland, sugarcane and scrub. Scarlet hindcrown, neck and breast band; yellowish upper back. (Mainly Tanzanian *E. g. friederichseni* is smaller, with broader breast band.)

PLATE 112: DULL-PLUMAGED BISHOPS, WIDOWBIRDS, QUE-LEAS, AND PARASITIC WEAVER (See text for field marks)

1 PARASITIC WEAVER *Anomalospiza imberbis*　　　**Page 549**
Local and uncommon in moist grassland. **1a. Breeding female** (somewhat worn). **1b. Juvenile male. 1c. Non-breeding female** (fresh).

2 RED-HEADED QUELEA *Quelea erythrops*　　　**Page 544**
Scarce, sporadic, mainly Lake Victoria basin and coastal lowlands. **Female.**

3 CARDINAL QUELEA *Quelea cardinalis*　　　**Page 544**
Common in open moist places, especially tall grassland. **Female.**

4 RED-BILLED QUELEA *Quelea quelea aethiopica*　　　**Page 544**
Common in dry savanna, bushed grassland and cultivation. **Juvenile male.**

5 ZANZIBAR RED BISHOP *Euplectes nigroventris*　　　**Page 546**
Southeastern, mostly near coast. **Female.**

6 NORTHERN RED BISHOP *Euplectes franciscanus*　　　**Page 546**
(Southern Red Bishop *E. orix*, nearly identical.) **Female.**Uncommon at lakes Baringo and Bogoria; in marshes and wet grassland.

7 FIRE-FRONTED BISHOP *Euplectes diadematus*　　　**Page 545**
Local in *Acacia* and *Commiphora* bush north to Meru NP. **Female.**

8 BLACK-WINGED RED BISHOP *Euplectes hordeaceus craspedopterus*
　　　Page 546
Western. In wet grassland and cultivation north to Mt Elgon. **Female.**

9 YELLOW-CROWNED BISHOP *Euplectes afer ladoensis*　　　**Page 545**
Local in marshes in w. and cent. Kenyan highlands and Arusha District. **Female.**

10 RED-COLLARED WIDOWBIRD *Euplectes ardens suahelica*　　　**Page 547**
Locally common in highland grasslands. **10a. Female. 10b. Non-breeding male.**

11 YELLOW-MANTLED WIDOWBIRD *Euplectes m. macrourus*　　　**Page 547**
Moist grasslands in Mara/Serengeti. (Nearly identical *E. m. macrocercus* local in w. Kenyan scrub and grassy bush.) **Female.**

12 WHITE-WINGED WIDOWBIRD *Euplectes albonotatus eques*　　　**Page 547**
Locally common in tall grass, bush, brushy habitats.
12a. Non-breeding male. 12b. Female.

13 YELLOW BISHOP *Euplectes capensis crassirostris*　　　**Page 546**
Widespread in moist bush and cultivation in highlands.
13a. Non-breeding male. 13b. Adult female.

14 BLACK BISHOP *Euplectes gierowii ansorgei*　　　**Page 545**
Western. Uncommon in moist scrub, shrubby tall grass, sugarcane. **14a. Female. 14b. Non-breeding male.**

15 FAN-TAILED WIDOWBIRD *Euplectes axillaris phoeniceus*　　　**Page 547**
Western. In marshes, low wet places. (Similar *E. a. zanzibaricus* local in coastal lowlands.) **Female/juvenile.**

16 LONG-TAILED WIDOWBIRD *Euplectes progne delamerei*　　　**Page 548**
Local in Kenyan highland grasslands. **16a. Non-breeding male. 16b. Female.**

17 HARTLAUB'S MARSH WIDOWBIRD *Euplectes hartlaubi humeralis* **Page 548**
Western. Local, uncommon in marshes and wet grasslands. **Female/juvenile.**

18 JACKSON'S WIDOWBIRD *Euplectes jacksoni*　　　**Page 549**
Locally common in highland grasslands. **Female.** (Non-breeding male larger, darker and browner, breast streaks mostly at sides; wings with broad tawny feather edges.)

PLATE 113: *PLOCEUS* WEAVERS (part) AND PARASITIC WEAVER

1 PARASITIC WEAVER *Anomalospiza imberbis*   **Page 549**
Local and uncommon in moist grassland. Canary-like; short-tailed, heavy-billed.
1a. Breeding male. Underparts bright yellow, unstreaked; bill black. **1b. Immature male.**
Variably streaked on sides and crown; paler bill. (Females and juvenile on Plate 112.)

2 SLENDER-BILLED WEAVER *Ploceus pelzelni*   **Page 534**
Lake Victoria basin in marshes and swamps. Small size, slim bill. **2a. Juvenile.** Pale bill.
2b. Adult female. Black bill. (Male on Plate 115.)

3 AFRICAN GOLDEN WEAVER *P. subaureus aureoflavus*   **Page 535**
Eastern, usually near water. Common at coast, local inland. **3a. Breeding male.** Eyes
orange or pink; bill black; rufous-orange on face. **3b. Non-breeding female.** Eyes pink;
bill pale buffy brown; underparts yellow and white. **3c. Juvenile female.** Eyes brown;
underparts largely white. **3d. Breeding female.** Eyes orange or pink; bill black; underparts
yellow.

4 GOLDEN PALM WEAVER *P. bojeri*   **Page 538**
Fairly common at Kenyan coast, inland to Kibwezi, Meru NP and Samburu GR.
4a. Breeding male. Brilliant orange-yellow head; orange-rufous on upper breast; eyes
dark brown, bill black. **4b. Immature male.** Duller yellow; bill light below. **4c. Adult
female.** Lightly streaked back, underparts yellow; two-toned bill.

5 TAVETA GOLDEN WEAVER *P. castaneiceps*   **Page 538**
Locally common in Amboseli–Taveta region, Arusha and Moshi Districts and Lake Jipe.
5a. Adult male. Rufous on hindcrown and upper breast; eyes dark brown. **5b. Adult
female.** Heavily streaked back, yellow underparts; two-toned bill; eyes dark brown. (Juv.
on Plate 116.)

6 NORTHERN BROWN-THROATED WEAVER *P. castanops*   **Page 539**
Uncommon around Lake Victoria in papyrus and lakeside trees. **Subadult male.** Rufous-
brown throat, pale eyes. (Adult male on Plate 115; female and juv. on Plate 116.)

7 ORANGE WEAVER *P. aurantius rex*   **Page 538**
Rare along Lake Victoria shore and islands. **Male.** Bright orange-yellow; eyes pale grey;
bill pale, slender. (Female on Plate 116.)

8 JACKSON'S GOLDEN-BACKED WEAVER *P. jacksoni*   **Page 539**
Locally common near water. **Adult female.** Heavily streaked back, bright yellow superciliary stripe; breast and sides orange-buff. (Male on Plate 115.)

9 BAGLAFECHT WEAVER *P. baglafecht*   **Page 533**
Race *reichenowi* (**Reichenow's Weaver**) common in highland towns, forest edge, cultivation. **9a. P. b. reichenowi, juvenile.** Olive head, buff-and-brown-streaked back, buffy
yellow below. **9b. P. b. reichenowi/stuhlmanni intergrade, juvenile female.** Head blackish (more extensively black in male). W. Kenya (Bungoma–Siaya area). (Other plumages
on Plates 114 and 116.)

10 HOLUB'S GOLDEN WEAVER *P. xanthops*   **Page 535**
Fairly common in gardens, cultivation, wet areas and edges of woodland in the highlands. Large, with heavy black bill; eyes pale yellow. **10a. Adult male.** Orange wash on
throat and upper breast. **10b. Adult female.** Duller, more olive above; no orange on
throat.

DALE A. ZIMMERMAN
1989

PLATE 114: *PLOCEUS* WEAVERS (part) AND MALIMBE (Adults, except as indicated)

1 RED-HEADED WEAVER *Anaplectes rubriceps leuconotus* **Page 544**
Uncommon in savanna and other open habitats. **Juvenile**. (Other plumages on Plate 109.)

2 CLARKE'S WEAVER *Ploceus golandi* **Page 542**
Kenyan coastal-forest endemic. **2a. Female**. Bright yellow on wings, yellow streaks on belly. **2b. Male**. Black head and upperparts; yellow on wings.

3 DARK-BACKED WEAVER *P. bicolor* **Page 542**
Forest species; fairly common. **3a. *P. b. kersteni***. Black back. (East of Rift Valley; mainly coastal and in Usambara Mts.) **3b. *P. b. mentalis***. Grey back. (W. Kenyan forests.)

4 BROWN-CAPPED WEAVER *P. insignis* **Page 535**
Highland forest. Forages nuthatch-like on trunks and large branches. **4a. Male**. Chestnut crown. **4b. Female**. Black crown.

5 BAGLAFECHT WEAVER *P. baglafecht* **Page 533**
Widespread. Race *reichenowi* common in various highland habitats, including towns. **5a. *P. b. emini*, non-breeding female**. Black-streaked grey back, white lower breast and belly. **5b. *P. b. reichenowi* (Reichenow's Weaver), adult male**. Black face patch, pale eyes. **5c. *P. b. reichenowi*, adult female**. Black head, pale eyes. (Other plumages on Plates 113 and 116.)

6 COMPACT WEAVER *P. superciliosus* **Page 533**
Western Kenya. Uncommon in moist grassy areas, woodland edge. Solitary nester. Heavy, deep-based bill; black face and throat. **6a. Breeding female**. Dark crown. **6b. Breeding male**. Yellow crown, grading to chestnut on forehead. (Non-breeding male on Plate 116.)

7 YELLOW-MANTLED WEAVER *P. tricolor interscapularis* **Page 542**
Rare. Solitary canopy species of w. Kenyan forests (possibly extirpated). **7a. Female**. Black, with yellow band on upper back. **7b. Juvenile**. Rufous-brown crown and upper back. **7c. Male**. Yellow band on upper back; chestnut underparts.

8 RED-HEADED MALIMBE *Malimbus r. rubricollis* **Page 543**
Kakamega Forest treetops. Nuthatch-like in habits; in pairs. **8a. Female**. Black forehead and forecrown. **8b. Male**. Scarlet from forehead to nape.

9 VIEILLOT'S BLACK WEAVER *Ploceus nigerrimus* **Page 542**
Western Kenyan forests and forest edge. Gregarious. **9a. Male**. All black, with yellow eyes. **9b. Female**. Dark olive, with heavily streaked back; pale eyes.

10 BLACK-NECKED WEAVER *P. nigricollis melanoxanthus* **Page 535**
Widespread but uncommon. In pairs in dry bush and open woodland. **10a. Female**. Yellow superciliary stripe, black bill. **10b. Male**. Rich golden-yellow head, black bib. **10c. Juvenile male**. Resembles female, but with pale bill.

11 BLACK-BILLED WEAVER *P. melanogaster stephanophorus* **Page 535**
Western Kenyan forests. Solitary or in pairs, usually low in undergrowth or vine tangles. Black, with yellow face, narrow black mask. **11a. Female**. Yellow throat. **11b. Male**. Black throat.

DALE A. ZIMMERMAN
1989

PLATE 115: *PLOCEUS* WEAVERS (part) AND CHESTNUT SPARROW (Breeding males except as indicated)

1 JACKSON'S GOLDEN-BACKED WEAVER *Ploceus jacksoni*　　**Page 539**
Locally common in acacia woodland and scrub near water, cultivation, tall sedges. Back golden yellow, underparts rich chestnut. (Female on Plate 113.)

2 YELLOW-BACKED WEAVER *P. melanocephalus fischeri*　　**Page 539**
Confined to swamps and reedbeds in Lake Victoria basin where locally common. Yellow collar separates black head from yellow-olive back. (Female on Plate 116.)

3 JUBA WEAVER *P. dichrocephalus*　　**Page 539**
Locally common in riverine bush in Daua River Valley near Mandera in ne. Kenya.
3a. Chestnut-headed individual. 3b. Black-headed individual. (Female on Plate 116.)

4 NORTHERN BROWN-THROATED WEAVER *P. castanops*　　**Page 539**
Uncommon in papyrus and lakeside trees around Lake Victoria. Chestnut throat; white eyes. (Subadult male on Plate 113, female and juv. on Plate 116.)

5 RÜPPELL'S WEAVER *P. galbula*　　**Page 539**
Vagrant (?) along ne. Kenyan border. Chestnut face and throat; orange or orange-red eyes. (Female on Plate 116.)

6 LITTLE WEAVER *P. l. luteolus*　　**Page 534**
Fairly common in bush and woodland in nw. Kenya south to Lake Baringo. Small bill; black face, forecrown, throat. (Female on Plate 116.) (Similar *P. l. kavirondensis* scarce and local in sw. Kenya.)

7 SLENDER-BILLED WEAVER *P. pelzelni*　　**Page 534**
Fairly common in swamps, marshes, waterside trees around Lake Victoria. Small size, slender bill. (Female and juv. on Plate 113.)

✓⑧ BLACK-HEADED or VILLAGE WEAVER *P. cucullatus*　　**Page 541**
Locally common. Highly gregarious when breeding. **8a. *P. c. bohndorffi*.** Western. Large bill, black scapulars. **8b. *P. c. paroptus*.** N. and e. Kenya, ne. Tanzania. Black-and-yellow back; large bill; red eyes. (Females and juv. on Plate 116.)

9 SPEKE'S WEAVER *P. spekei*　　**Page 541**
Widespread. Common in savanna, bush, cultivation, towns and villages, 1400–2200 m. Black-and-yellow back, no black on crown; creamy eyes. (Female on Plate 116.)

✓⑩ LESSER MASKED WEAVER *P. i. intermedius*　　**Page 540**
Local in savanna, bush and cultivation, in both dry and humid areas below 1500 m. Pale eyes, grey feet, black crown. (Female and juv. on Plate 116.)

11 NORTHERN MASKED WEAVER *P. t. taeniopterus*　　**Page 541**
Local in Lake Baringo area and n. Lake Turkana, near water. Dark brown eyes, pinkish feet; crown deep chestnut; black of throat extends to upper breast. (Female and juv. on Plate 116.)

✓⑫ VITELLINE MASKED WEAVER *P. velatus uluensis*　　**Page 540**
Widespread in dry savanna and thorn-bush. Black confined to throat, face; eyes red. (Female on Plate 116.)

13 HEUGLIN'S MASKED WEAVER *P. heuglini*　　**Page 540**
Scarce and local in nw. Kenya, south to Kitale and Bungoma areas. Black face and throat extending to point on breast; back nearly plain; pale eyes. (Female on Plate 116.)

✓⑭ SPECTACLED WEAVER *P. ocularis suahelicus*　　**Page 534**
Widespread. Uncommon in tangled vegetation along forest and swamp edges. **14a. Female.** No black on throat. (Western *P. o. crocatus* has less rufous on face.) **14b. Male.** Black throat patch.

15 CHESTNUT WEAVER *P. r. rubiginosus*　　**Page 542**
Seasonally abundant, mainly in dry areas. Highly gregarious when breeding. **15a. Non-breeding male.** Rufous-buff and black back stripes, chestnut breast; eyes red, bill heavy. **15b. Breeding male.** Mostly rufous-chestnut, with black head; eyes red. **15c. Adult female.** Rufous wash on sides of breast, whitish wing edging; heavy bill; eyes brown. **15d. Immature male.** Eyes red; bill dusky above, paler below.

16 CHESTNUT SPARROW *Passer eminibey* (for comparison)　　**Page 528**
Locally common in dry country. Much smaller than Chestnut Weaver. Small bill, brown eyes, no black on head. **Adult male.** (Female on Plate 108.)

PLATE 116: *PLOCEUS* WEAVERS (mostly females and juveniles)

1 LITTLE WEAVER *Ploceus l. luteolus*   **Page 534**
Fairly common in acacia bush and woodland in nw. Kenya south to Baringo. **Female**.
Small size, small bill. (Male on Plate 115.)

2 ORANGE WEAVER *P. aurantius rex*   **Page 538**
Female. Rare along L. Victoria shores and islands. Pale slender bill; eyes pale. (Male on
Plate 113.)

3 NORTHERN BROWN-THROATED WEAVER *P. castanops*   **Page 539**
Uncommon in papyrus and lakeside trees around L. Victoria. Usually near water.
3a. Female. Slender black bill; short black eye-line; pale eyes. **3b. Juvenile male.** Slender
bicoloured bill; brown-and-buff-streaked back, brown eyes. (Subadult and adult males on
Plates 113 and 115.)

4 COMPACT WEAVER *P. superciliosus*   **Page 533**
W. Kenya. Local in moist bush, cultivation and wet grassland. **Non-breeding adult**.
Largely brown, with blackish brown crown and eye-line.

5 RÜPPELL'S WEAVER *P. galbula*   **Page 539**
Vagrant (?) in ne. Kenyan border areas. **Female**. Bright yellow wing edgings, usually trace
of chestnut on face; bill short and thick; eyes chestnut. (Male on Plate 115.)

6 YELLOW-BACKED WEAVER *P. melanocephalus fischeri*   **Page 539**
Confined to swamps and reedbeds in the L. Victoria basin. **Female**. Tawny-buff breast,
yellow superciliary stripe, brown-and-black streaked back. (Male on Plate 115.)

7 TAVETA GOLDEN WEAVER *P. castaneiceps*   **Page 538**
Locally common in Amboseli–Taveta region, Lake Jipe, Arusha and Moshi Districts.
Juvenile. Bicoloured bill (as in Golden Palm Weaver), dark eye-line and yellow super-
ciliary stripe, strongly streaked back. (Adults on Plate 113.)

(8) LESSER MASKED WEAVER *P. i. intermedius*   **Page 540**
Local in savanna, bush and cultivation, in dry and humid areas below 1500 m. Blue-grey
feet, rather slender bill. (Male on Plate 115.) **8a. Juvenile male.** Pale bill; eyes brown.
8b. Breeding female. Grey bill; eyes pale tan or cream.

9 JUBA WEAVER *P. dichrocephalus*   **Page 539**
Locally common in riverine bush in Daua River Valley near Mandera, ne. Kenya. **Female**.
Small bicoloured bill. (Males on Plate 115.)

10 NORTHERN MASKED WEAVER *P. t. taeniopterus*   **Page 541**
Local in Lake Baringo area and northern L. Turkana; near water. **10a. Juvenile**. Tan or buff;
yellow superciliary stripe; white eyes; bill mostly blue-grey; feet pinkish. **10b. Adult female**.
Similar, but brown-eyed; breast, head and wing-linings more yellowish. (Male on Plate 115.)

11 VITELLINE MASKED WEAVER *P. velatus uluensis*   **Page 540**
Widespread in dry savanna and thorn-bush. Similar to No. 9, but adults orange- or red-
eyed; feet pinkish flesh; bill smaller; superciliary stripe duller. **11a. Non-breeding female**.
Sides pinkish buff, back tan or buff with black streaks; eyes dull red. (Young similar, but
eyes brown.) **11b. Breeding female.** Side and back more olive, breast more yellow; eyes
bright orange-red. (Male on Plate 115.)

12 SPEKE'S WEAVER *P. spekei*   **Page 541**
Common in savanna, bush, cultivation, towns and villages. Large; bill heavy and long;
superciliary stripe indistinct or lacking; back well streaked. **12a. Adult female**. Dull olive
and yellow; eyes pale; bill dark or partly dark. **12b. Juvenile**. Paler olive-yellow; eyes
brown; bill pale; whiter below (Male on Plate 115.)

13 HEUGLIN'S MASKED WEAVER *P. heuglini*   **Page 540**
Scarce and local in nw. Kenya, south to Kitale and Bungoma areas. **Adult female**. Bill
short, dark; back faintly streaked; eyes pale (Male on Plate 115.)

14 BAGLAFECHT (EMIN'S) WEAVER *P. baglafecht emini*   **Page 533**
Mt Loima and Kongelai Escarpment. **Juvenile male**. Head blackish; back streaked grey
and black. (Other plumages and races on Plates 113 and 114.)

15 BLACK-HEADED (VILLAGE) WEAVER *P. cucullatus*   **Page 541**
Locally common. Highly gregarious when breeding. Large and large-billed. **15a. *P. c.
bohndorffi*, breeding female**. Western. Bill black; eyes red. **15b. *P. c. paroptus*, non-
breeding female**. N. and e. Kenya, ne. Tanzania. Grey-backed, yellow and white below,
yellow eyebrow; eyes red. **15c. *P. c. paroptus*, early immature male**. Similar to female,
but brown-eyed and sides more pinkish buff, less grey. (Adult males on Plate 115.)

DALE A. ZIMMERMAN
1990

PLATE 117: WAXBILLS AND RELATIVES

1 QUAIL-FINCH *Ortygospiza atricollis muelleri*   **Page 555**
On ground in open grassland. Tiny, short-tailed, heavily barred. **1a. Male.** Black throat band; contrasting face pattern. **1b. Female.** Duller; lacks black on face and throat.

2 LOCUST-FINCH *Ortygospiza locustella uelensis*   **Page 555**
Rare in w. Kenya. Red-orange in wings and on upper tail-coverts. **2a. Male. 2b. Female.** Whitish underparts, barred flanks.

3 CUT-THROAT FINCH *Amadina fasciata alexanderi*   **Page 556**
Fairly common in dry areas; on ground or in trees around water holes. Heavily barred; large pinkish grey bill, chestnut belly patch. **3a. Female.** Sides of face strongly barred. **3b. Male.** Red band across throat.

4 ZEBRA WAXBILL *Amandava subflava*   **Page 555**
Uncommon in moist grassland, rice fields. Yellow or orange underparts, orange or red upper tail-coverts, strongly barred sides. **4a. *A. s. subflava*, male.** Western. Orange below; red superciliary stripe. **4b. *A. s. clarkei*, male.** Eastern. Yellow below; orange confined to breast and crissum. **4c. *A. s. clarkei*, female.** Pale yellowish below; orange tail-coverts.

5 COMMON WAXBILL *Estrilda astrild*   **Page 554**
Common and widespread in grassy and shrubby places, near ground. Gregarious. Brown rump and tail, red eye-line. **5a. *E. a. massaica*, male.** Southern and central areas east of Rift Valley. Pinkish below, including throat. **5b. *E. a. minor* male.** Coastal. Browner, less pink, below; throat whitish. **5c. *E. a. massaica*, juvenile.** Bill grey, eye-line orange, faint barring below.

6 BLACK-CROWNED WAXBILL *Estrilda n. nonnula*   **Page 554**
W. Kenya, at lower elevations than No. 7. Fairly common near ground in cultivation, grassy forest edge, brush. Under tail-coverts white, head black only on crown; bill blackish. **6a. Juvenile.** Whitish to pale buffy brown below, no red on flanks; bill blackish. **6b. Male.** Underparts whitish; flanks tinged with pink. (Female paler grey above.)

7 BLACK-HEADED WAXBILL *Estrilda atricapilla graueri*   **Page 554**
W. and cent. Kenya. Fairly common along edges of montane forest. Lower belly and crissum black; duller than No. 6, and black of head more extensive. **7a. Male.** Flanks red, some pink on bill. **7b. Juvenile.** Dusky below, no red on flanks, bill all black.

8 CRIMSON-RUMPED WAXBILL *Estrilda rhodopyga centralis*   **Page 553**
Widespread; fairly common in bush, grassy areas, cultivation, often in dry areas. Upper tail-coverts red. **8a. Juvenile.** Face plain or with faint eye-line. **8b. Adult.** Red line through eye, as in Nos. 5 and 9.

9 BLACK-RUMPED WAXBILL *Estrilda troglodytes*   **Page 554**
W. Kenya only. Uncommon in scrub, thickets, rice fields. Pale, with black upper tail-coverts and tail. (Juv. lacks red eye-line, has black bill.) Often in flocks with other waxbills.

10 YELLOW-BELLIED WAXBILL *Estrilda quartinia kilimensis*   **Page 553**
Fairly common in gardens, grassy clearings, forest edge in highlands. Olive back. **10a. Adult.** Bicoloured bill. **10b. Juvenile.** All-black bill.

11 FAWN-BREASTED WAXBILL *Estrilda p. paludicola*   **Page 553**
Uncommon, local in moist grassland in w. Kenya. Tawny brown back, red bill. (Juvenile has black bill.)

12 BLACK-FACED WAXBILL *Estrilda erythronotus delamerei*   **Page 554**
Lake Victoria basin; Thika and Nairobi areas south to Tanzania. Local in *Acacia* woods and bushed grassland; in undergrowth or trees. **12a. Male.** Black of face extends to chin and upper throat; belly and crissum black. **12b. Female.** Chin black; belly/crissum pinkish grey.

13 BLACK-CHEEKED WAXBILL *Estrilda charmosyna*   **Page 555**
Locally common in dry n. and e. Kenya, south to Tsavo East NP. Wanders to eastern edge of highlands during droughts. **Male.** Chin whitish, crissum pale pink.

14 AFRICAN SILVERBILL *Lonchura cantans orientalis*   **Page 555**
Small flocks in dry bush and scrub, on ground or in trees. **Adult.** Blue-grey bill, black rump and tail.

15 GREY-HEADED SILVERBILL *Lonchura griseicapilla*   **Page 556**
Widespread, typically in less arid country than No. 14. Usually on or near ground. White rump, black tail. **15a. Adult.** Blue-grey head with black-and-white-speckled face. **15b. Juvenile.** Duller; no speckling on face.

DALE A ZIMMERMAN
1990

PLATE 118: ESTRILDIDS (cordon-bleus, pytilias and firefinches)

1 RED-CHEEKED CORDON-BLEU *Uraeginthus b. bengalus*　　**Page 552**
Widespread. Common in wooded areas, bush and gardens. Feeds on ground. Confiding.
1a. Male. Red facial patch. **1b. Female.** Like male, but no red. **1c. Juvenile.** Brownish head, dusky bill. (Some birds may have blue cheeks.)

2 BLUE-CAPPED CORDON-BLEU *Uraeginthus cyanocephalus*　　**Page 552**
Fairly common in arid and semi-arid country. Feeds on ground. More wary than No. 1. Paler and brighter blue than Red-cheeked, with longer tail. **2a. Male. 2b. Immature female. 2c. Adult female.**

3 PURPLE GRENADIER *Uraeginthus ianthinogaster*　　**Page 553**
Fairly common in bush and thickets, on or near ground. Widespread except in north and east. Blue or purplish blue rump, black tail; adults red-billed. **3a. Juvenile.** Mostly tawny. **3b. Female.** Silvery blue around eyes. **3c. Male.** Largely violet-blue below (extent of rufous variable); blue on face.

4 ORANGE-WINGED PYTILIA *Pytilia afra*　　**Page 550**
Rare and local in dense bush; skulking. Formerly more widespread. See text. Orange in wings separates it from Green-winged Pytilia. **4a. Male. 4b. Female.**

5 GREEN-WINGED PYTILIA *Pytilia melba soudanensis*　　**Page 549**
Common on or near ground in dense bush, thickets and scrub. Golden olive wings, red bill. **5a. Female. 5b. Male.**

6 BLACK-BELLIED FIREFINCH *Lagonosticta r. rara*　　**Page 552**
Western. Uncommon, local in tall grass, overgrown cultivation. Black belly and crissum, pink patch on bill. **6a. Male.** Body plumage deep wine-red. **6b. Female.** Red loral spot, rosy-pink breast, grey throat.

7 AFRICAN FIREFINCH *Lagonosticta rubricata hildebrandti*　　**Page 552**
Widespread but uncommon and shy. On or near ground in dense cover at forest edge or in thickets. Bill grey or bluish; belly and crissum black. Shy; avoids human habitation. **7a. Female.** Brown, with pale throat. **7b. Male.** Bright rose-red on head and underparts; back dark brown. **7c. Juvenile.** Pale, with black crissum.

8 JAMESON'S FIREFINCH *Lagonosticta rhodopareia taruensis*　　**Page 552**
Uncommon and local in dry bush country; avoids towns. On and near ground. **8a. Male.** Largely pink, including back; bill and feet bluish. **8b. Female.** Red loral spot; more rose-pink than 7a. Under tail-coverts barred.

9 RED-BILLED FIREFINCH *Lagonosticta senegala ruberrima*　　**Page 551**
Common ground feeder in towns, villages, cultivation, bush. Confiding. **9a. Female.** Dusky brown; loral spot and mandible red; under tail-coverts barred/spotted. **9b. Male.** Wine-red, with dusky brown belly and crissum; bill largely red; eye-ring yellow. **9c. Juvenile.** Brown, with pale belly; red loral spot small or lacking; bill brown above, pink below.

10 BAR-BREASTED FIREFINCH *Lagonosticta rufopicta*　　**Page 551**
Western. Local on ground in cultivation, grassy thicket borders. Sexes alike. Large red bill, blue-grey eye-ring, faint white bars on sides and breast.

DALE A ZIMMERMAN
1990

PLATE 119: ESTRILDIDS (mannikins, twinspots *et al.*)

1 BLACK-AND-WHITE MANNIKIN *Lonchura bicolor*   **Page 556**
Local in forest clearings, forest edge, moist bush and cultivation. **1a.** *L. b. nigriceps*.
'Rufous-backed Mannikin'. Kenyan highlands and coastal lowlands, inland to Usambara
and Pare mts, Arusha and Moshi areas. **1b.** *L. b. poensis*, **adult**. Widespread below 2000
m. west of Rift Valley. **1c.** *L. b. poensis*, **juvenile**.

2 BRONZE MANNIKIN *Lonchura cucullata scutata*   **Page 556**
Common, widespread. Feeds on ground in open habitats, cultivation and gardens.
2a. Adult. 2b. Juvenile.

3 MAGPIE-MANNIKIN *Lonchura fringilloides*   **Page 556**
Rare in se. Kenya and Usambara Mts in moist thickets, forest edge, bush. One record
from Alupe on Kenya-Ugandan border.

4 WHITE-BREASTED NEGROFINCH *Nigrita f. fusconota*   **Page 549**
Uncommon in Kakamega Forest canopy.

5 GREY-HEADED NEGROFINCH *Nigrita canicapilla schistacea*   **Page 549**
Fairly common in highland forests, in canopy and undergrowth. **5a. Adult**. White-edged
grey crown and nape; white wing dots. **5b. Juvenile**. Dull grey-brown, with suggestion of
grey stripe on head and neck.

6 BLACK-BELLIED SEED-CRACKER *Pyrenestes o. ostrinus*   **Page 551**
Rare in Busia District, w. Kenya, in moist grassy bush, forest edge. **6a. Female**. Brown,
with much red in tail. **6b. Male**. Red tail, no red on bill.

7 RED-HEADED BLUEBILL *Spermophaga r. ruficapilla*   **Page 551**
Common in w. Kenyan forest undergrowth; scarce in cent. Kenyan highlands. (Paler-
backed *S. r. cana* uncommon in East Usambara Mts.) No red on tail. Adults with bright
red-and-blue bill. **7a. Juvenile**. Brown, with only trace of red on bill. **7b. Male**.
7c. Female.

8 ABYSSINIAN CRIMSONWING *Cryptospiza salvadorii kilimensis*   **Page 550**
Highland forest clearings and edges; terrestrial, shy. (In n. Tanzania, see Red-faced
Crimsonwing on Plate 124.) Variably red on wings, upper tail-coverts. **8a. Juvenile male**.
8b. Adult male (Female similar, with less red, none on eyelids.)

9 PETERS'S TWINSPOT *Hypargos niveoguttatus macrospilotus*   **Page 550**
Eastern, especially coastal lowlands. On or near ground in damp bush, thickets.
9a. Juvenile. Tawny brown, with grey bill; trace of white spotting. **9b. Male. 9c. Female**.

10 GREEN-BACKED TWINSPOT *Mandingoa nitidula chubbi*   **Page 550**
Uncommon in coastal lowlands, Usambara and Pare mts; scarce in cent. and se. Kenyan
highlands, in damp forest undergrowth and moist thickets. **10a. Juvenile male**. Tawny
buff face, olive on wings. **10b. Adult male**. Red face (pale orange-tawny in female).

11 BROWN TWINSPOT *Clytospiza monteiri*   **Page 551**
Scarce in w. Kenya, on or near ground in moist savanna, bushed grassland and thickets.
Furtive and shy. **11a Juvenile**. Grey head, red upper tail-coverts; no white spots below.
11b Male. Small red throat patch. **11c Female**. Whitish throat.

DALE A. ZIMMERMAN
1991

PLATE 120: CANARIES (*Serinus*)

1 AFRICAN CITRIL *Serinus citrinelloides* **Page 560**
Widespread in highlands along forest borders, roadsides, in gardens. **1a. *S. c. kikuyuensis*, male** (Kenyan highlands west to Kakamega). Black face. **1b. *S. c. kikuyuensis*, female.** Streaked below; bold superciliary stripes. **1c. *S. c. brittoni*, adult** (w. Kenya). Both sexes like female *kikuyuensis,* but face greyer; slightly more yellow-green below. **1d. *S. c. brittoni*, juvenile.** Browner and buffier than adult. **1e. *S. c. hypostictus*, female** (s. and sw. Kenya and Tanzania). Face greyer than in other races, superciliaries less bold. **1f. *S. c. hypostictus*, male.** Less heavily streaked than female.

2 PAPYRUS CANARY *S. koliensis* **Page 561**
Fairly common in Lake Victoria basin, in and near papyrus. Resembles streaked plumages of African Citril, but bill shorter, stubbier, with more curved culmen. **2a. Female.** Mask greyish, extends onto forehead; heavy ventral streaking. **2b. Male.** Brighter yellow; less streaked; mask dusky, not reaching forehead.

3 YELLOW-FRONTED CANARY *S. mozambicus* **Page 561**
Fairly common at coast and below 2200 m in the west, in second growth, scrub and bush. Mainly in moist habitats. Bold facial pattern. Forehead and underparts entirely yellow. In Mara GR ofen with No. 4 in mixed flocks. **3a. Juvenile.** Pale, spotted breast. **3b. *S. m. barbatus*, male** (western). Bright olive-green above. **3c. *S. m. mozambicus*, female** (coastal; East Usambara foothills). Brownish olive above.

4 WHITE-BELLIED CANARY *S. dorsostriatus* **Page 561**
Widespread and locally common in dry bush and savanna below 1600 m. White belly; streaked on sides and flanks. **4a. *S. d. maculicollis*, female.** White extends from belly to under tail-coverts. **4b. *S. d. dorsostriatus*, male** (southern). Less white; crissum yellowish. **4c. *S. d. dorsostriatus*, female.** Duller than male, short breast streaks.

5 YELLOW-CROWNED CANARY *S. canicollis flavivertex* **Page 560**
Common along forest borders, in pastures and gardens in highlands. Often sings from tall trees. **5a. Male.** Yellow crown, much yellow in wings and tail. **5b. Female.** Variably streaked below, yellow wing edgings, white belly.

6 BRIMSTONE CANARY *S. sulphuratus sharpii* **Page 561**
Widespread in bush, cultivation in w. and cent. Kenyan highlands. Large; heavy-billed; olive 'whiskers'. **6a. Female.** Often dull; faintly streaked below. **6b. Male.** Plain bright yellow below. **6c. Both sexes in flight.** Little contrast between rump and back.

7 NORTHERN GROSBEAK-CANARY *S. donaldsoni* **Page 562**
Scarce in dry bush and semi-desert north of Equator. **7a and 7b. Males.** Large, with very large (often pinkish) bill; underparts bright yellow, with some white on belly. Yellow rump contrasts with back. (Female on Plate 121.)

8 SOUTHERN GROSBEAK-CANARY *S. buchanani* **Page 562**
Uncommon in dry bush south of Equator. Large and pink-billed; dull; rump slightly more yellow than back. Often in mixed-species flocks. **8a. Female. 8b. Male.**

PLATE 121: SEEDEATERS, BUNTINGS AND ORIOLE-FINCH

1 YELLOW-RUMPED SEEDEATER *Serinus reichenowi* **Page 560**
Widespread in open bushed habitats. Small flocks common in roadside weeds, scrub, cultivation. Siskin-sized; yellow rump evident in flight. **1a and 1b. Adults**.

2 BLACK-THROATED SEEDEATER *Serinus atrogularis somereni* **Page 560**
Kakamega–Ukwala area of w. Kenya. Status uncertain. Throat heavily mottled with black; superciliary stripes less distinct than in Yellow-rumped Seedeater.

3 STREAKY SEEDEATER *Serinus s. striolatus* **Page 559**
Common in gardens, scrub, woodland openings and cultivation in the highlands. Feeds on ground. Boldly and sharply streaked below; broad facial streaks.

4 THICK-BILLED SEEDEATER *Serinus burtoni* **Page 560**
Fairly common in highland-forest undergrowth, low trees. Large, dull, heavy-billed; olive wing and tail edgings. **4a. *S. b. albifrons*** (east of Rift Valley). White forehead. **4b. *S. b. tanganjicae*** (west of Rift Valley). Dark forehead.

5 NORTHERN GROSBEAK-CANARY *Serinus donaldsoni* **Page 562**
Scarce in open bush, semi-desert, north of Equator. **Female**. Brown and streaky, large pale bill, yellow rump. (Male on Plate 120.)

6 STRIPE-BREASTED SEEDEATER *Serinus (reichardi) striatipectus* **Page 559**
Local and uncommon on shrub-covered slopes with scattered trees. Dark cheeks contrast with white superciliary stripes; crown finely streaked black and white; broad diffuse streaking below.

7 STREAKY-HEADED SEEDEATER *Serinus (gularis) elgonensis* **Page 559**
Rare on scrub-covered slopes, Mt Elgon (one specimen). Black-and-white crown streaks; largely plain underparts, with white throat.

8 HOUSE BUNTING *Emberiza striolata saturatior* **Page 563**
Local in rocky deserts of n. Kenya, often in flocks around wells. **8a. Male**. Rufous/tawny, with dusky throat streaks. **8b. Female**. Pale sandy rufous; throat faintly streaked.

9 CINNAMON-BREASTED ROCK BUNTING *Emberiza t. tahapisi* **Page 563**
Locally common in rocky places and on stony ground. **9a. Female**. Head streaked brown and buff. **9b. Male**. Head streaked with black and white.

10 GOLDEN-BREASTED BUNTING *Emberiza flaviventris kalaharica* **Page 563**
Common in highland gardens, open woods, forest edge. Feeds on ground; sings from high trees. **10a. Adult male**. Golden yellow below, with white flanks and belly; back may appear solid rufous as grey feather edges wear; rump grey. **10b. Juvenile**. Pale yellow below; brown-and-buff head stripes.

11 SOMALI GOLDEN-BREASTED BUNTING *Emberiza poliopleura* **Page 563**
Common in dry bush and scrub in e. and n. Kenya. Shy. **11a. Juvenile**. Less yellow than young Golden-breasted, and usually with fewer breast streaks. **11b. Adult male**. Brighter above than Golden-breasted, with white-edged feathers; rump pale grey; flanks and tail sides with more white.

12 BROWN-RUMPED BUNTING *Emberiza affinis forbesi* **Page 563**
Rare and local in nw. Kenya. On or near ground in bush, on brushy slopes or escarpments. Yellow extends to flanks and belly; rump brown.

13 ORTOLAN BUNTING *Emberiza hortulana* **Page 562**
Palearctic vagrant. On ground in open areas. **13a. Adult female, winter**. Pale yellow throat/upper breast; whitish eye-ring; white outer tail feathers. **13b and 13c. First-winter**. Bold white eye-ring; white in tail.

14 ORIOLE-FINCH *Linurgus olivaceus elgonensis* **Page 562**
Uncommon in highland forest undergrowth. **14a. Adult male**. Short yellow-orange bill. **14b. Immature (?) female**. Short, dull orange bill; wing edgings yellow and white. Some individuals obscurely streaked below.

1a

2

1b

3

4a

4b

5

6

7

8a

8b

10a

9a

9b

11a

10b

11b

12

13a

13b

14a

14b

13c

DALE A. ZIMMERMAN
'89

PLATE 122: NORTHERN TANZANIAN BIRDS (See also Plates 123 and 124)

1 WHITE-THROATED SWALLOW *Hirundo albigularis*　　　　**Page 425**
Widespread in southern Africa; vagrant to Lake Jipe. Breast band narrow in centre (not of equal width throughout as in Barn Swallow); throat white. **1a and 1b. Adults.** (Immature has brown breast band, lacks chestnut on forehead.)

2 SOUTHERN CORDON-BLEU or BLUE WAXBILL *Uraeginthus angolensis*
　　　　Page 553
Vagrant from south of our region. (Normally north to Handeni and Naberera.) Both sexes pale brown from forehead to lower back; bill slate-grey or pinkish, with black cutting edges. (Female Red-cheeked Cordon-bleu has less blue on sides of head and neck. Female Blue-capped Cordon-bleu is paler; male is blue from forehead to nape; juvenile has tan breast.)

3 SPIKE-HEELED LARK *Chersomanes albofasciata beesleyi*　　　　**Page 416**
Confined to treeless short-grass plains 30–50 km north of Arusha. Upright posture; short, white-tipped tail.

4 SWALLOW-TAILED BEE-EATER *Merops h. hirundineus*　　　　**Page 392**
Ranges north to Tanga, possibly wanders farther. (Similar northern race *heuglini* approaches Kenyan border in Uganda and Sudan.) Deeply forked bluish tail in adults and young.

5 ASHY STARLING *Cosmopsarus unicolor*　　　　**Page 514**
Locally common in dry bush, savanna and acacia woodland. Feeds on ground. Common in Tarangire NP.

6 OLIVE-FLANKED ROBIN-CHAT *Cossypha anomala mbuluensis*　　　　**Page 441**
Only in Nou Forest, Mbulu Highlands. Forages in forest undergrowth and on ground. Flicks wings; slowly raises and lowers tail. Other robin-chats have rufous on breast.

7 BENNETT'S WOODPECKER *Campethera bennettii scriptoricauda*　　　　**Page 409**
Reportedly uncommon in Kilimanjaro area, North Pare Mts, and from Handeni southward. (Formerly on Kenyan coast.) Throat speckled in centre (unlike Nubian Woodpecker) and bill extensively yellow below. **7a. Male. 7b. Female**.

8 RUFOUS-TAILED WEAVER *Histurgops ruficaudus*　　　　**Page 532**
Locally common and conspicuous in acacia savanna in Ngorongoro Crater and se. Serengeti NP. Gregarious; feeds on ground; nests colonially in trees.

9 GREY-BREASTED SPURFOWL *Francolinus rufopictus*　　　　**Page 319**
Locally common in Serengeti NP. Tarsi and toes dark brown (red in Red-necked Spurfowl); sides of breast grey. Some hybridization with Yellow-necked Spurfowl in area of overlap in se. Serengeti.

10 DUSKY LARK *Pinarocorys n. nigricans*　　　　**Page 416**
Flicks wings constantly. A miombo-woodland bird of w. Tanzania, accidental in our region. Favours recently burnt ground.

11 CRESTED BARBET *Trachyphonus vaillantii suahelicus*　　　　**Page 405**
Scarce and irregular at Lake Manyara and Tarangire NPs, and around the West Usambara Mts. Forages on ground in dry areas, especially in vicinity of termitaria.

PLATE 123: NORTHERN TANZANIAN BIRDS (Usambara Mts) (See also Plate 124)

1 BANDED GREEN SUNBIRD *Anthreptes rubritorques*   **Page 518**
Fairly common in forest canopy of both Usambara ranges. Short-tailed. **1a. Female.** Olive-green above, pale greyish yellow below, with faint yellowish streaks. **1b. Male.**

2 RED-CAPPED FOREST WARBLER *Orthotomus m. metopias*   **Page 478**
Common in West Usambaras, rare in East Usambaras (formerly at Amani). Skulks in forest undergrowth.

3 LONG-BILLED APALIS *Apalis m. moreaui*   **Page 478**
Rare and local in East Usambaras only. Forages in dense vine tangles at forest edge.

4 FÜLLEBORN'S BLACK BOUBOU *Laniarius fuelleborni*   **Page 502**
Common in undergrowth and low trees in West Usambara forests. **Female** figured; male deeper black, especially on head.

5 SHELLEY'S GREENBUL *Andropadus masukuensis roehli*   **Page 430**
Fairly common in Usambara and South Pare mountain forests. (Kenyan *A. m. kakamegae* on Plate 75.)

6 CABANIS'S BUNTING *Emberiza cabanisi orientalis*   **Page 563**
Fairly common in open areas of East Usambaras and around Ambangulu in Western range. No white subocular streak, unlike other yellow-breasted buntings. **6a. Male. 6b. Female.**

7 USAMBARA WEAVER *Ploceus n. nicolli*   **Page 543**
Rare; apparently now restricted to forest and forest edge in West Usambaras. **7a. Male.** Forehead dull yellow; brownish yellow wash on nape. **7b. Female.** Head brownish black.

8 MOUNTAIN GREENBUL *Andropadus nigriceps usambarae*   **Page 430**
Common in forests of West Usambaras and South Pare Mts; scarce or rare north to Taita Hills in se. Kenya. Black superciliary stripe diagnostic. (Black-crowned *A. n. nigriceps*, also in n. Tanzania, on Plate 75.)

9 WHITE-CHESTED ALETHE *Alethe fuelleborni*   **Page 443**
Common in Usambara forest undergrowth. Accidental or casual in South Pare Mts.

10 DAPPLED MOUNTAIN ROBIN *Modulatrix orostruthus amani*   **Page 437**
Rare in East Usambara montane forest. Forages low, often in streamside undergrowth.

11 USAMBARA GROUND ROBIN *Sheppardia montana*   **Page 440**
Fairly common in West Usambara forests above 1650 m.

12 SPOT-THROAT *Modulatrix s. stictigula*   **Page 437**
Rare in montane-forest undergrowth in both Usambara ranges; most numerous above 1500 m. Forages on ground; shy.

13 SHARPE'S AKALAT *Sheppardia sharpei usambarae*   **Page 440**
Fairly common in both Usambara ranges. Forages on or near ground.

14 SWYNNERTON'S ROBIN *Swynnertonia swynnertoni rodgersi*   **Page 440**
Rare in East Usambara lowland-forest undergrowth; feeds on ground. (Female duller, head more olive.)

15 USAMBARA EAGLE-OWL *Bubo vosseleri*   **Page 374**
Rare in forest and wooded borders of tea plantations in both Usambara ranges.

16 MONTANE NIGHTJAR *Caprimulgus poliocephalus guttifer*   **Page 377**
Local and uncommon at forest edge and grassland between 1075 and 1700 m.

PLATE 124: NORTHERN TANZANIAN BIRDS (including Pemba Island specialities)

1 **PEMBA WHITE-EYE** *Zosterops vaughani*   **Page 484**
Only white-eye on Pemba Island.

2 **FOREST BATIS** *Batis m. mixta*   **Page 489**
Locally common above 900 m on Tanzanian mountains. **Female** is brown-eyed, darker, less hoary and with shorter superciliary stripes than female *B. m. ultima* of coastal forests (see Plate 86). Male resembles male *ultima*.

3 **PEMBA SUNBIRD** *Nectarinia pembae*   **Page 523**
Common on Pemba Island. **3a. Female. 3b. Adult male. 3c. Immature male.**

4 **MONTANE WHITE-EYE** *Zosterops poliogaster eurycricotus*   **Page 483**
Common in montane areas of Arusha NP, Kilimanjaro, Mt Meru, Essimingor, Lossogonoi Plateau and Lolkissale. No yellow on forehead, little on underparts. (*Z. p. mbuluensis*, of other Tanzanian mountains, on Plate 102.)

5 **WHITE-TAILED BLUE FLYCATCHER** *Elminia albicauda*   **Page 487**
Locally common in forest edge and riverine forest in the Mbulu and Crater Highlands. Active; twists, droops wings and fans tail.

6 **ZITTING CISTICOLA** *Cisticola juncidis uropygialis*   **Page 472**
Rufous form (restricted to Pemba Island).

7 **PALE-BREASTED ILLADOPSIS** *Illadopsis rufipennis distans*   **Page 438**
Common in East Usambaras, less so at Ambangulu in West Usambaras. Shy. Forages on and near ground in dense forest undergrowth. (Kenyan *I. r. rufipennis* on Plate 90.)

8 **OLIVE WOODPECKER** *Dendropicos griseocephalus kilimensis*   **Page 411**
Local in montane forests. Dark olive on breast; unbarred blackish tail. **8a. Male. 8b. Female.**

9 **WHITE-STARRED ROBIN** *Pogonocichla stellata orientalis*   **Page 439**
This subspecies only in Usambara Mts. Other races elsewhere in n. Tanzania. **Immature** shown. (See Plate 93 for adult and juvenile of this species.)

10 **RED-FACED CRIMSONWING** *Cryptospiza reichenovi australis*   **Page 551**
Fairly common in highland-forest undergrowth and along forest borders. As low as 300 m in East Usambara foothills. **10a. Male.** Broad red orbital/loral area (unlike Abyssinian Crimsonwing). **10b. Female.** Diffuse pale orbital area.

11 **SOUTHERN GREY-HEADED SPARROW** *Passer diffusus mosambicus*
                                          Page 527
Only *Passer* on Pemba Island. Replaced on adjacent mainland by *P. griseus*.

12 **JAVA SPARROW** *Padda oryzivora*   **Page 557**
Uncommon and local on Pemba Island. **12a. Adult male. 12b. Juvenile.**

13 **WHITE-EYED SLATY FLYCATCHER** *Melaenornis fischeri nyikensis*   **Page 454**
Mbulu and Crater highlands. Eye-ring narrower and body plumage duller than more widespread *M. f. fischeri* (on Plate 87).

14 **PEMBA GREEN PIGEON** *Treron pembaensis*   **Page 359**
Only green pigeon on Pemba Island; grey head and underparts.

15 **KURRICHANE THRUSH** *Turdus libonyanus*   **Page 452**
Coastal lowlands and formerly East Usambara foothills. Present status uncertain. White throat bordered by dark streaks.

16 **PEMBA SCOPS OWL** *Otus pembaensis*   **Page 373**
Only small owl on Pemba Island. **16a. Orange-rufous morph. 16b. Pale rufous morph.**

17 **OLIVE THRUSH** *Turdus olivaceus*   **Page 451**
Common in wooded highlands. **17a. *T. o. deckeni*, male.** Mt Kilimanjaro, Monduli, Kitumbeine, Longido and in extreme s. Kenya at Ol Doinyo Orok. (Still darker and duller *T. o. oldeani* of the Crater and Mbulu Highlands not illustrated.) **17b. *T. o. roehli*, male.** North Pare and Usambara mts. (See Plate 91 for *T. o. abyssinicus*.)

DALE A.
ZIMMERMAN
1995

OSTRICHES, FAMILY STRUTHIONIDAE

Flightless ratite birds, the largest of living species. They are powerful runners, with long sturdy legs and only 2 toes on each foot. The thick thighs lack feathers. The small head and long neck are also largely unfeathered except for fine bristles. The bill is short, flat and blunt-tipped; eyes are large with long lashes.

COMMON OSTRICH *Struthio camelus*   Plate 30 ✔

Height 7–8 ft. **Male** brownish black with white wings, tail and lower neck ring. In *S. c. massaicus*, parts of head and neck are thickly covered with woolly white down. *Pinkish skin of neck, sides of body and legs* becomes brighter in breeding season when dark-tipped greyish pink bill is also bright pink and front tarsal scutes turn red; eyes dark brown. Male of *S. c. camelus* has bald crown ringed with short stiff brown feathers; bill yellowish above, pink to red below. Head, most of neck, bare sides of body and legs pinkish. **Female** *massaicus* is grey-brown with pale feather edges; neck and legs pale pinkish to creamy grey-brown. Brownish bill becomes reddish or black with pink base when breeding; eyes brown. **Immature** similar. Female *camelus* has darker brown body feathers with pale edges; bill as in *massaicus*; neck and legs grey-brown, turning pink; tarsal scutes red in breeding season. **Downy young** striped buff and black on head and neck; body dappled black, buff and whitish above. **Juvenile** darker than adult female, with grey neck and legs. Males acquire whitish wing and tail feathers in their second year. (Some Kenyan populations may include in their ancestry domesticated birds representing extralimital subspecies and freed following collapse of early ostrich farming operations.) **Call** of male a deep booming *ooom, ooom, booo-ooooo*, descending, at times with an extra terminal *ooom*. **Range**: *S. c. massaicus* from Serengeti Plains east to Ngorongoro Crater and Arusha Dist., north to Kilgoris, Nairobi and Tsavo West NP; also around Naro Moru, Timau and on Laikipia Plateau, west to Baringo Dist. and Maralal. *S. c. camelus* only near Lokichokio on the Lotikipi Plains (now largely extirpated).

SOMALI OSTRICH *Struthio* (*camelus*) *molybdophanes*   Plate 30 ✔

Height 7–8 ft. This northern ostrich is more of a browser than *massaicus*, often in bush and scrub; usually solitary or in pairs. **Male** differs from other forms in its deeper black plumage, *blue-grey neck and legs, and black scutes on lower tarsi and toes, those on upper tarsi deep pink*, turning bright red when breeding (when thighs and neck become bluer). Bill pink above, whitish below, with horn-yellow or brownish tip, bright pink when breeding. *Eyes pale brownish grey.* In both sexes, the bare crown has a raised, dull yellow-brown horny hump surrounded by dense hair-like feathers; sparse down elsewhere on the head and neck. Plumage of **adult female** and **immature** browner than in *massaicus*; female's eyes pale blue-grey. **Call** as in other ostriches. **Range**: From e. side of Lake Turkana to Wajir, and south to Samburu and Shaba GRs, Meru and Tsavo East NPs. **Taxonomic Note**: Mitochondrial DNA studies show considerable divergence of Somali Ostrich from other forms. Morphological and ecological differences and reported interbreeding difficulties also suggest that *molybdophanes* is specifically distinct.

GREBES, FAMILY PODICIPEDIDAE

Aquatic diving birds with short wings, long necks, pointed bills and rudimentary tails. The legs are set far back on the body, the tarsi laterally flattened, the toes lobed. Flight is fast and direct with rapid wingbeats, the bird pattering across the water surface on take-off, and landing on its belly (not feet-first like ducks). Gregarious for much of year, but separating into pairs for breeding. Sexes are alike.

GREAT CRESTED GREBE *Podiceps cristatus infuscatus*   Plate 15

Length 18–22". Large, with a long thin erect neck and long greyish bill. Dark above, white below; face and sides of neck white; crown and eye-lines black. In flight, shows long white patches on front and rear edges of inner part of wings. **Adult** has conspicuous black-and-rufous ruff on face and black ear-tufts; eyes red. Apparently no distinct non-breeding plumage in East African birds. **Juvenile** paler, with striped head and neck and no ruff. Usually silent; harsh barking and honking **calls** when breeding. **Range**: Local (and now scarce) on freshwater and alkaline lakes in cent. Rift Valley, Laikipia Plateau, Arusha NP and Ngorongoro Crater.

BLACK-NECKED or EARED GREBE *Podiceps nigricollis gurneyi*   Plate 15

Length 11–13". A small grebe with *short, slender, slightly upturned* bill. Blackish above and on head and neck, with *golden tufts behind the bright red eyes*; sides and flanks chestnut; belly white. Shows small white patch on rear of wing in flight. No separate black-and-white non-breeding plumage (unlike northern races), but post-breeding birds become worn, faded and dull. (Little Grebe is more compact, shorter-necked, has differently shaped head and bill, and chestnut foreneck.) **Call** a soft *preeip*. **Range**: Local, breeding erratically on Rift Valley lakes, mainly Bogoria and Elmenteita; wanders to Lake Turkana, Marsabit, Nairobi and Tsavo regions, Lake Lygarja in Serengeti NP, Crater Highlands and Arusha NP.

LITTLE GREBE or DABCHICK *Tachybaptus ruficollis capensis*   Plate 15

Length 9-11.5". Small and dark, with rounded head, short neck and stubby bill. **Breeding plumage** dark brown above and dusky below with *chestnut throat and foreneck*. Eyes brown; bill dark with *pale yellow spot near rictus*. **Non-breeding plumage** grey-brown above, merging to whitish below; throat and neck grey. Usual **call** a whinnying trill; alarm note *whit, whit*. **Range**: Widespread. Most numerous on larger lakes of Rift Valley highlands and in Arusha NP.

ALBATROSSES, FAMILY DIOMEDEIDAE

Large web-toed seabirds, superficially somewhat gull-like, but considerably larger and with proportionately much longer wings. The strong hooked bill is covered by horny plates and with laterally positioned tubular nostrils. Most species nest on islands in southern oceans. They feed on squid taken from the surface of the sea, and soar on stiff wings for extended periods, rarely coming near land in our region. Underwing patterns, and colours of head, bill and upperparts are important in identification.

*BLACK-BROWED ALBATROSS *Diomedea melanophris* subsp.   Plate 1

Length 32–37"; wingspan *c.* 8'. Soars in sweeping glides with bowed wings. Follows ships; usually rests on sea when winds light or calm. **Adult** suggests a *very long-winged*, black-backed gull with a white rump. White head shows *narrow black eye-lines and dusky lores*; underparts white. *Wings black above, typically white along centre below, with broad blackish tip and border* (white centre strip broadest in older birds); tail grey. Bill bright yellow or orange-yellow, red at tip, narrowly black at base; eyes brown in nominate *melanophris*, yellow in *D. m. impavida*; feet bluish white. **Juvenile** has grey or dusky bill, largely white head with dark eye-marks, grey nape and collar; underside of wings much darker than in adult, the pale central area smaller. **Immature** has white head and *black-tipped, dull yellowish bill*; pale areas beneath wings greyer than in adult. See Shy Albatross. **Status**: Rare visitor from southern oceans. Several sightings in Kenyan waters north to Mombasa,1955-1990.

SHY ALBATROSS *Diomedea cauta*   Plate 1

Length 35–39"; wingspan 7-8'. Differs from Black-browed Albatross in greyer back and somewhat paler wings, longer and thicker bill, and from beneath, by *black spot near body at base of leading edge of black-bordered, black-tipped wings*. **Adult** grey-brown on upper back, shading to darker brown adjacent to the contrasting white rump. Blackish around eyes. Head colour varies racially: white with grey cheeks in nominate *cauta* (only race recorded to date in our waters), grey-brown with white forehead and forecrown in *salvini*, darker and all grey in *eremita* which has yellow bill with black spot at tip of

270

mandible (yellowish grey with yellow tip in other races; no black spot in *cauta*). Feet pinkish, bluish at joints. **Immature** grey-billed (or with black mandible tip in *D. c. cauta*; entire bill black-tipped in *salvini*). Nape grey, or whitish in *cauta*, and partial collar similar to young Black-browed. **Status:** Visitor from southern oceans, possibly regular Aug./Sept. in Pemba Channel (14 sightings, photos, 1989-90). Specimen from Mombasa (Oct.).

PETRELS AND SHEARWATERS, FAMILY PROCELLARIIDAE

Web-toed, 'tube-nosed' birds rarely seen from shore, and little known in East African waters. The hooked bill is covered with horny plates. The nostrils are separated by a partition but lie in a common tube at base of culmen. Larger species fly with bursts of quick wingbeats alternating with banking and gliding on long, narrow, rigid wings. The smaller prions have a more erratic flight, typically just above the waves. Most species are highly migratory. General build and flight characteristics are important in identification.

*PINTADO or CAPE PETREL *Daption capense*   Figure on p. 272
Length 14–16"; wingspan *c.* 3'. *Pied upperparts* and white tail with broad black terminal band render this vagrant unmistakable. Commonly follows ships, often alighting nearby; feeds on water surface. **Call** a high *chichichichi*. **Status:** One sight record off Mombasa (Sept. 1974).

WHITE-CHINNED PETREL *Procellaria aequinoctialis*   Figure on p. 272
Length 20–23"; wingspan 4-5'. A large, *dark brown* petrel with a *greenish white or ivory bill* (culmen and mandibular groove blackish). *Small white chin patch* difficult to see, and not always present. Feet black. Sometimes soars high. Follows ships. **Status:** Vagrant (apparently *P. a. aequinoctialis*) from southern waters; photographed off Shimoni, Sept.1990.

*WEDGE-TAILED SHEARWATER *Puffinus pacificus*   Plate 1
Length 16–18"; wingspan 3'. Large and dark, with a long wedge-shaped tail and slender dark grey bill. *Holds wings forward, slightly bowed and angled.* **Dark morph** wholly blackish brown with darker primaries and tail; may show paler bands across upper wing-coverts. Rare **pale morph** not reported off East Africa. Does not follow ships. (Smaller Jouanin's Petrel has shorter thicker bill, sides of tail uneven owing to shorter outer feathers; flies rapidly. Flesh-footed Shearwater, *P. carneipes*, not yet recorded here, has pale bill, pale bases to underside of primaries, and holds wings straighter in flight. See White-chinned Petrel.) **Status:** Scarce. Several sight records, Shimoni to Lamu; maximum of 12 birds seen off Mtwapa, Dec.1991. Breeds in western Indian Ocean.

AUDUBON'S SHEARWATER *Puffinus lherminieri*   Plate 1
Length 12"; wingspan 27". A small, stocky shearwater with distinctive fluttering flight. *Upperparts dark brown, including cap which extends to below eyes;* underparts white except for *brown under tail-coverts.* In Persian Gulf race *persicus*, brown extends to axillaries, sides of breast and flanks; wings dark beneath, with a restricted pale central area. Bill narrow and blackish; *feet flesh-pink*, the tarsi dusky on outer sides. Solitary or in small flocks. Flight involves *rapid wing-flapping interspersed with short glides.* May rest on the water with wings partly raised. (Little and Mascarene Shearwaters, *P. assimilis* and *P. atrodorsalis* [not yet recorded in our region, but which must be considered], are *black*, not brown, above and have *white* under tail-coverts. Little is short-tailed, almost stubby billed. Mascarene's long wings and tail and slender bill are reminiscent of Manx Shearwater, *P. puffinus*; it has wedge of black extending down from rump, between white flanks and crissum; except for narrow dark margin on front edge, wing-linings pure white; remiges mostly dusky grey to blackish below; feet *blue-grey and black.* Probable Mascarenes have been seen far east of Mombasa in May and June. See figure facing Plate 1.) **Range/status:** Uncommon most months, mainly north of Kilifi. One found dead inland at Limuru (Oct. 1963) was *P. l. bailloni* which breeds on Mascarene islands, but *persicus* and *nicolae* could reach East African waters.

Vagrant procellariiform birds: 1. White-chinned Petrel; 2. Jouanin's Petrel; 3. Pintado or Cape Petrel; 4. Matsudaira's Storm-petrel; 5. Antarctic Prion; 6. Slender-billed Prion

ANTARCTIC or DOVE PRION *Pachyptila desolata* **Figure on p. 272**
Length 10.5"; wingspan 24". The most likely prion in East African waters. *Blue-grey above*, darker on crown, with white superciliary stripes, blackish eye-lines, and *bold, dark, open M-shaped band across wings and back*; tail wedge-shaped with black tip. *Dark smudge or patch on each side of lower neck and breast* contrasts with white cheeks and throat (this mark present to a lesser degree in other prions which might also reach East Africa). Wings whitish beneath with dusky tips and rear margins; bill 12-15 mm wide and, like feet, pale blue. Flight rapid and twisting, close to waves. Higher flight erratic, almost bat-like, as bird flutters up and over ship. **Status**: Southern ocean vagrant. Two heads found on beach at Watamu in Aug. 1988, are the only regional specimens. Prions seen near Malindi in Sept. 1983, and one photographed off Shimoni, Sept. 1990, appeared to be *desolata*, (as were four collected in se. Somalia, Aug. 1979).

SLENDER-BILLED PRION *Pachyptila belcheri* **Figure on p. 272**
Length 10"; wingspan 22". A vagrant similar to the preceding species, but dark *patches on sides of lower neck/breast smaller, shorter and less conspicuous*; upperparts paler blue-grey, the *M-mark much less bold*; underparts paler; *black of tail tip more restricted; outer tail feathers noticeably pale above*. Typically narrower bill (10–14.5 mm wide) sometimes diagnostic if bird in hand, but note overlap with Antarctic Prion. **Status**: One found dead at Watamu, Aug. 1984.

JOUANIN'S PETREL *Bulweria fallax* **Figure on p. 272**
Length 12–13"; wingspan 30–33". A rare blackish brown petrel with rather heavy head and bill, long slender wings and *long wedge-shaped tail*. Close view reveals grey tips to feathers of chin and forehead; often shows pale brown diagonal band or series of pale spots on upper wing-coverts, doubtless varying with moult. Bill black, or with the plates pale horn, held slightly downward; feet pinkish. Flies rapidly in *swooping zig-zagging arcs, with bowed wings held slightly forward*, and 'towers' 15–20 m above water like *Pterodroma* petrels. Seldom follows ships, but flies alongside. (Similar but larger Wedge-tailed Shearwater has slower wingbeats and slender, dark grey bill held more horizontally. Flesh-footed Shearwater, *Puffinus carneipes*, is larger with slender pale bill. Mascarene Petrel, *Pterodroma aterrima*, is slightly larger with shorter, more square-tipped tail. Bulwer's Petrel, *B. bulwerii*, is smaller, slimmer, with proportionately smaller head and bill. Of these four species, only Wedge-tailed S. is known in East African waters, but all are possible and require consideration.) **Status**: Vagrant (?) from nw. Indian Ocean; 3 December specimens from Malindi and off Mtwapa.

STORM-PETRELS, FAMILY HYDROBATIDAE
Small dark pelagic birds with erratic and often fluttering flight low over the water. The slender short bill has a terminal hook, and the nostrils are united in a tube on the culmen. Often in flocks, feeding daintily from the sea surface. Nesting is in holes and burrows on distant oceanic islands. Some are highly migratory. Identification relies in part on feeding action and flight characteristics.

*WILSON'S STORM-PETREL *Oceanites oceanicus* **Plate 2**
Length 6–7.5"; wingspan 15–17". A small *sooty black* pelagic bird with *white rump, square or slightly rounded tail tip*, and a *pale band across the upper wing-coverts*. Sides of tail white beneath; wings rather short and rounded. Legs long and slender; the black toes, *often projecting beyond the tail* in flight, are joined by inconspicuous *yellow webs*. When feeding, skips across water with wings raised, feet pattering on the surface. Gregarious; often follows ships. (Leach's Storm-petrel is larger with forked tail, shorter tarsi and different habits.) **Range/status**: Uncommon visitor from subantarctic breeding areas to offshore waters between Shimoni and Kiunga, April–Dec.

LEACH'S STORM-PETREL *Oceanodroma leucorhoa* **Plate 2**
Length 7.5–9"; wingspan 18–19". A vagrant storm-petrel, more slender and longer-winged than Wilson's, with *forked tail* and *white rump divided by greyish centre* (difficult to see in the field), pale bar across upper wing-coverts, and *dark feet not projecting beyond tail*. Flight erratic and buoyant, the deep wingbeats alternating with swooping

glides. Often solitary. Does not follow ships. **Status**: Vagrant. A beached specimen, pre-sumably of nominate race, found dead south of Mombasa (Feb. 1967), and 3 sight records, April, Oct., Dec., from Kilifi, Watamu, and Mtwapa.

*MATSUDAIRA'S STORM-PETREL *Oceanodroma matsudairae* **Figure on p. 272**
Length 9–10"; wingspan 22". A vagrant *dark-rumped* storm-petrel, larger than Leach's and dark brown except for *paler diagonal bar on upper wing-coverts and small white patch formed by bases of outer primary shafts*; tail forked. Normal flight heavier and more lethargic than that of Leach's. **Status**: Two sight records off Mombasa, July and Aug. 1981. Regularly migrates to western Indian Ocean from breeding areas south of Japan.

BLACK-BELLIED STORM-PETREL *Fregetta tropica* **Plate 2**
Length 8"; wingspan 18". A vagrant *white-rumped* storm-petrel, larger than Wilson's; black above, and with a *dark central line on the white belly; wing-linings also white*. Flies low and foot-patters like other storm-petrels. Seldom follows ships, but often flies beside or ahead of them. (White-bellied Storm-petrel, *F. grallaria*, not recorded here but known in s. African waters, is paler with all-white belly and crissum. **Status**: Single birds found dead in June at Watamu (1988) and Malindi (1994).

TROPICBIRDS, FAMILY PHAETHONTIDAE
Medium-sized aerial pelagic birds with stout pointed bills, very short tarsi, long tern-like wings, and wedge-shaped tails with greatly elongated narrow central feathers. Adult plumage is white with black markings. They fly high, the fluttering wingbeats alternating with soaring glides; birds hover and plunge for fish or squid. Nesting is colonial on oceanic islands.

WHITE-TAILED TROPICBIRD *Phaethon l. lepturus* **Plate 2**
Length 32" ; wingspan 3'. Black diagonal bar on wing-coverts and black primary bases form bold patches on wings; long white tail feathers have black shafts, and black cres-cent-shaped eye-marks are evident; bill and feet yellow. **Juvenile** has black wing tips and heavy black barring on upperparts; lacks large black bar on wings and has no tail stream-ers; yellow bill is dark tipped. **Range/status**: Regular in Pemba Channel off Shimoni, Aug.–March; occasional between Malindi and Kiunga, Sept.–Nov. **Note**: Deep-sea fish-ermen have at times reported tropicbirds with orange or reddish tail streamers from n. Kenyan waters. (*P. rubricauda* lacks the black bar and patch on the wing and has red streamers; juvenile has black bill, no black on wing tips. *P. aethereus*, like *lepturus*, has white tail streamers, but has heavily barred back, much black on wing tips, and overhead it shows distinct barring on inner secondaries; juv. has yellow/orange bill, black nuchal collar and much black on primaries.)

PELICANS, FAMILY PELECANIDAE
Very large swimming birds with short tarsi and fully webbed toes. The hook-tipped bill is long and straight, and between its tip and the throat is a large extensible gular pouch (for holding fish) suspended from the mandible. Wings are long and broad, tail short. Flocks soar effortlessly; flight ponderous with the long neck retracted. Breeding is colonial.

GREAT WHITE PELICAN *Pelecanus onocrotalus* **Plate 14**

Length 55–70"; wingspan 8–10'. **Adult** mainly white; *in flight, tip and rear half of wing black*. Pouch usually yellow; *feet yellowish or orange*; bill greyish and pink, becoming bright yellow and bluish with red nail in breeding season, when both sexes develop swollen orange-red knob at base of culmen (turns pink and shrinks after eggs are laid). When breed-ing, plumage tinged pinkish, and small occipital crest develops. **Juvenile** dark brown with blackish flight-feathers and pouch. **Immature** (8–10 weeks) greyer with pale-edged brown wing-coverts, short crest and dark grey bill. By fly-ing age (10–12 weeks) plumage paler grey except for black flight feathers; pouch black but later mottled with ochre-yellow; feet grey. Silent except in breeding colonies where mooing, deep grunting and a continuous humming are evident. Loafs on lakeshores in

dense flocks. Feeds in tightly packed, co-ordinated flotillas, all birds submerging heads and necks in unison. Flies in V-formations and commonly soars. (Smaller Pink-backed Pelican is greyer with pinkish or grey bill, pouch and feet; in flight, trailing edge of wings is grey, not black.) **Range**: Thousands inhabit alkaline Rift Valley lakes; breeds on Elmenteita, less often on Natron and Manyara. Wanders to other lakes, rivers and estuaries.

PINK-BACKED PELICAN *Pelecanus rufescens*   **Plate 14**

Length 53–60"; wingspan 7–8'. Smaller and duller than Great White Pelican. **Adult** *greyish white*, with small black loral spot; *head tufted*, with a dark shaggy crest when breeding. Wing tips dark above and below, but *secondaries brownish grey* (not black as in Great White). *Pinkish back and rump may show in flight*; belly also washed with pink. Bill and pouch greyish; *feet grey or pinkish*; when breeding, pouch is deep yellow with fine dusky vertical lines; orbital skin is pink, orange and yellow; feet deep pink. **Juvenile** brownish grey on back and wings, browner on head and neck, white on rump, back and belly; bill pale dull yellow with grey pouch; feet greyish pink. Almost silent; guttural notes in breeding colonies. Usually in small groups, but forages singly. Colonies often small, usually in tall trees. **Range**: Widespread inland and on coastal estuaries and saltpans.

BOOBIES, FAMILY SULIDAE

Large, short-legged, web-toed seabirds that catch fish and squid by plunging with partly folded wings, sometimes from considerable heights. The long, stout, conical bill, pointed wing tips and wedge-shaped tail contribute to a streamlined appearance. Sexes are alike or similar. Breeding is colonial, on islands or cliffs, the nests built on the ground or in trees.

MASKED BOOBY *Sula dactylatra melanops*   **Plate 1**

Length 32–36". **Adult** *white* with *black flight feathers and tail* and *yellowish bill*; bare facial and gular skin blackish; feet grey. (Extralimital Cape Gannet, *Morus capensis*, has pale blue-grey bill and yellow wash on crown and nape, but would be difficult to distinguish from Masked Booby at a distance.) **Juvenile** dark grey-brown above, with dark brown head, dull olive bill, and sometimes a narrow white hindneck collar; *underside of wing shows dark stripe parallel to leading edge, plus broad dark trailing edge and tip*. **Immature** still dark, but white collar becomes wider, and bill turns pale greenish yellow. Upperparts finally whiten from rump forward. (Brown Booby differs from young Masked in having dark brown of neck extending to upper breast and continuous with upperparts; never has hindneck collar; underwing pattern also differs.) **Call** a high double honk sometimes heard at sea. Solitary except on nesting islands. Flies quite high, and its plunge-dives are impressive. **Range**: Regular in Pemba Channel Aug.–Feb., presumably from breeding colony on Latham Is., Tanzania.

*BROWN BOOBY *Sula leucogaster*   **Plate 1**

Length 25–29". Smaller, more lightly built, and longer-tailed than Masked Booby, its quicker wing action reminiscent of a large cormorant. **Adult** brown with white lower breast, belly and under tail-coverts; wings white beneath with dark tips and borders; bill yellow or sometimes greenish grey, slim and tapering. Bare facial and gular skin yellow or whitish; legs and feet yellow. **Immature** resembles adult, but has grey bill and facial skin, and *underside of wings sullied with brown* as is belly. See young Masked Booby. Usually flies close to water, diving at an angle, but may plunge vertically from a greater height. Pursues flying-fish in the air. **Call** a high *schweee*, and a honking *aar*. **Range/status**: Seen in Pemba Channel, Aug.–Sept., and from Kilifi northward mainly Jan.–Feb.

RED-FOOTED BOOBY *Sula sula rubripes*   **Plate 1**

Length 26–30". A scarce polymorphic booby, usually with *red feet and white tail*, blue-grey bill and face. **Adult** plumage variable: (1) white with black flight feathers and *black patch on underside of carpal area*; (2) white with dark brown back and upperside of wings; (3) brown with white rump, belly and tail; (4) wholly brownish. **Juvenile/imma-**

ture brown with yellowish grey feet and dark bill. Readily approaches ships and fishing boats, often perching on rigging. **Status**: 7 records, Aug.–March, including specimens from Kilifi, Mombasa and Watamu. Brown morph reported off Shimoni and at Latham Is., Tanzania.

CORMORANTS, FAMILY PHALACROCORACIDAE

Large, upright-perching, short-legged aquatic birds with fully webbed toes; the strong hooked bill has a small bare gular pouch at its base; tail stiff and rounded. The long neck is outstretched in flight. Plumage is not fully waterproof, and the short wings are often held outstretched to dry (and for thermo-regulation) when at rest. They swim low in the water, bill tilted upward, and dive from the surface, pursuing prey underwater, using feet but not the wings in swimming. Nests of sticks are built on the ground or in trees.

√ **GREAT CORMORANT** *Phalacrocorax carbo lucidus* **Plate 14**

Length 31.5–40". A large gregarious cormorant with a *short tail*, our race black with *white cheeks, foreneck and upper breast*. **Breeding adult** has white thigh patches, and black plumage glossed with green; lores orange (male) or scarlet (female). Bill grey; *eyes green*; gular pouch dark olive; feet black. Rare all-black individuals are known. **Non-breeding** birds are duller, with no white thigh patches, and bill is white at base; gular pouch and skin below eyes is yellow or olive. **Juvenile/immature** brownish above and entirely dull white below, darkening with successive moults; bill greyish above, dull yellow below; gular pouch yellow. Infrequent **call** a guttural *korrrrk*, but usually silent away from breeding colonies (typically on large lakes with rocky or open shores). **Range**: Widespread. Numerous at lakes Victoria, Naivasha, Nakuru, and Turkana. Wanders to smaller lakes and estuaries. Scarce in n. Tanzania.

√ **LONG-TAILED or REED CORMORANT** *Phalacrocorax a. africanus* **Plate 14**

Length 20–22". Much smaller than Great Cormorant with *relatively long tail and small bill*. **Breeding adult** black with faint greenish gloss; feathers of back to upper tail-coverts whitish-margined; wing-coverts and scapulars bronzy grey with black tips. Short bristly frontal-crest feathers white basally; ephemeral tufts of white filoplumes behind eyes. Bill yellow with brown culmen; bare facial skin yellow-orange to red; *eyes red*. Seasonal variation poorly known. Some non-breeding birds, red-eyed and probably adult, are white below, and some have dark feathers on breast. **Juvenile** whitish or buff below, and brown-eyed. Typically solitary or in small groups on reedy lakeshores and swampy pools. **Call** a bleating *kakakakakoh* at roost; soft croaking, hissing, and cackling at nest. **Range**: Widespread. Reaches the coast, but more numerous inland.

DARTERS, FAMILY ANHINGIDAE

Large, slender and cormorant-like, but with a serrated dagger-like bill and a markedly long stiff tail (distinctive outer rectrices are laterally grooved or fluted, as are the longest scapulars). When swimming, often only the small head and part of the long neck are above water.

AFRICAN DARTER *Anhinga rufa* **Plate 14**

Length 28–31". Somewhat larger and much longer-tailed than Long-tailed Cormorant, with small head, *pointed bill* and *long snaky neck*. **Male** largely black, with oil-green gloss, but neck chestnut with long white lateral stripes. Bill yellow, ivory, brownish or dark grey; bare gular skin cream-coloured; *eyes orange-red*. **Female** has entirely brownish neck, with faint or no white stripes; bill dark grey above, often pinkish below; eyes as in male. **Juvenile** *much paler* than adult, brownish above with buff feather edges, later developing *long buff streaks on scapulars and inner secondaries*; whitish on throat and foreneck, buff from breast to belly. Solitary. Perches upright, often with wings outstretched. Flies strongly, with characteristically kinked neck. Usually silent. **Range**: Formerly widespread, but now regular only along lower Tana River.

FRIGATEBIRDS, FAMILY FREGATIDAE

Large aerial seabirds with exceptionally long pointed wings, long, deeply forked tail and slender hooked bill. The legs are short, feet small and weak, toes partially webbed. Skilful fliers, soaring for long periods with only occasional deep wingbeats, they neither walk nor swim, but snatch food on the wing from sea surface or beach, and harass and steal from other seabirds. Male's balloon-like scarlet throat sac is inflated when breeding on distant islands.

GREATER FRIGATEBIRD *Fregata minor* (*aldabrensis?*)   **Plate 1**
Length 34–40"; wingspan 6–7'. Most of the unidentified frigatebirds seen almost annual-ly at sea off the Kenyan coast during August probably are this species. **Male** black with scarlet throat patch (seldom visible) and pale brownish bar on upperside of wing. **Female** has grey chin and throat merging into white upper breast. **Juvenile** blackish brown above with paler wing-bar; white or pale chestnut head and throat separated from white belly patch by rufous band; other underparts and underside of wings dark. **Immature** largely white below after breast band is lost through moult; upperparts paler brown than adult and the wing-bar paler. **Subadult female** is white from chin to upper breast, and with sep-arate white belly patch. See Lesser Frigatebird. **Status**: Few acceptable records including a specimen from the Tana River mouth and a skull from Kiunga (both Aug.); sight records of adult males from Watamu and Lamu in Aug. and Sept.

*LESSER FRIGATEBIRD *Fregata ariel*   **(Not illustrated)**
Length 28–32"; wingspan 5.5–6'. Only slightly smaller than Greater Frigatebird, but **adult male** easily identified by *small white patches on upper flanks extending onto wing-lin-ings*; *no pale bar on upperside of wing*. **Female** has *black chin and throat* (as well as black cap), and *white of breast extends as a spur onto the wing-linings*. **Juvenile and immature** have similar white breast and wing pattern, but belly is dark. There are numer-ous transitional stages to full adult plumage. **Status**: Vagrant; accepted sight records of adult males at Watamu (Jan. 1980) and Malindi (Dec. 1994). Unidentified frigatebirds seen in Kenyan waters Dec.-Jan. are probably this species. (No evidence supports a pub-lished report of Christmas Island Frigatebird, *F. andrewsi*, in Kenyan waters.)

SHOEBILL, FAMILY BALAENICIPITIDAE

A unique bird which shares several characteristics with storks and herons, but skeletal evidence and DNA-DNA hybridization data indicate a closer relationsip to pelecaniform birds.

SHOEBILL or WHALE-HEADED STORK *Balaeniceps rex*   **Fig. facing Plate 14**
Length 48"; stands *c*. 1 m tall. A huge, *all-grey* wetland bird with a *massive bill*. Pale bluish grey with slate-grey flight-feathers and greyish white belly and crissum. A *short pointed occipital crest* is always erect or nearly so. *Clog-shaped, hook-tipped bill* mot-tled green and brown, yellowish horn or pinkish, with irregular blotches and streaks, but often appears grey; eyes greyish to pale yellow; legs and feet dark slate. **Juvenile/Imm-ature** darker, brown-tinged above. Normally silent away from nest except for resonant bill-clattering. Preys on fish, particularly lungfish. Sluggish, standing stiff-legged and motionless for long periods in papyrus or flooded grassland. Pace slow and deliberate, its long toes enabling it to move on floating vegetation. Soars on thermals with head and neck retracted. **Status**: Vagrant. Early unverified reports from ne. Lake Victoria area. One photographed in nw. Mara GR (Sept.–Nov. 1994) and (same bird) Amboseli NP (Dec. 1994 to late 1996).

HERONS, EGRETS AND BITTERNS, FAMILY ARDEIDAE

Long-legged wading birds with spear-like bills for taking aquatic prey, insects and rodents. The toes are long, with the middle nail pectinate. Wings are long and broad, flapped deeply and steadily in sustained flight when the long neck is prominently kinked and retracted (unlike storks, ibises, spoonbills, and cranes). The neck is also retracted at rest, but stretched with activity. Plumage is lax, with long feathers on neck, breast and back; well-developed powder-down patches are hidden on breast and sides of rump.

Some species develop long filamentous head plumes when breeding, at which time bare parts may become brightly coloured. Several species crepuscular or nocturnal. All typically feed in wet places, although some hunt on dry ground. They usually nest colonially in trees or reeds, but bitterns are more solitary.

LITTLE BITTERN *Ixobrychus minutus*   Plate 12

Length 11–15″. A small secretive heron; climbs about in papyrus and tall marsh vegetation. When disturbed, it may 'freeze' motionless, with outstretched neck and bill pointing upward. *Pale forewing patches conspicuous in flight.* **Male** *I. m. minutus* largely greenish black above with pale buff face, neck, underparts, and wing patches. Eyes yellow; bill greenish yellow; legs and feet yellowish to green. **Female** browner above, *streaked below*, and with smaller wing patches. Breeding *I. m. payesii* slightly smaller, with chestnut neck and sides of face. **Juvenile** like female but mottled above and more heavily streaked below. Flight fairly fast, often with dangling feet. See Dwarf Bittern. Flight **calls** *kwer*, *quar* or *kerack*; when breeding has a rapid *gak-gak-gak-gak* and a gurgling *ghrrrrr*. **Range/status**: Resident *I. m. payesii* breeds at lakes Naivasha and Baringo, and near Nairobi. Elsewhere recorded mainly after heavy rains, and some birds perhaps intra-African migrants. Palearctic *I. m. minutus* present in small numbers Oct.–early May.

DWARF BITTERN *Ixobrychus sturmii*   Plate 12

Length 10–12″. *Smaller than a Little Bittern* and equally secretive. Hides in reed beds and marshes. Flies with slow steady wingbeats, the neck sometimes outstretched. **Adult** wholly *dark slate grey above, buff below with heavy dark grey streaking* from throat to belly, and *black line down centre of foreneck.* Bill dark greenish with black tip; legs and feet yellowish green (bright orange during courtship); eyes red-brown; loral and orbital skin bluish. **Juvenile** has pale buff feather edges above and underparts more rufous. (Young Green-backed Heron is heavily streaked below, but is larger, paler, has whitish wing-covert tips and is less secretive.) **Call**, when breeding, a deep *hoo-hoo-hoo*. When flushed, utters a loud croak. **Range**: Widespread in suitable wetlands during periods of high rainfall.

WHITE-BACKED NIGHT-HERON *Gorsachius leuconotus*   Plate 12

Length 20–22″. A retiring and seldom-seen bird of shaded streams and mangroves; crepuscular and nocturnal. Head largely black with short dark plumes, *broad white eye-ring and yellowish loral skin*; neck and breast brownish rufous, contrasting with dark brown wings and back, the latter with *elongate white patch showing in flight*. Eyes large and yellow (darker when breeding); bill black with some yellow along base of mandible; legs and feet greenish or orange-yellow, the tarsi rather short. **Juvenile** light, spotted and streaked with white, the white back patch obscure; underparts buff with pale tawny streaking. Flight **call** a sharp *kraak*, more raspy than call of Black-crowned Night Heron. **Range**: Mara, upper Tana, Grumeti and Moshi rivers. Recent records from Mida Creek and near Shimoni (Ramisi River). Formerly on Pemba Island.

✓ BLACK-CROWNED NIGHT-HERON *Nycticorax n. nycticorax*   Plate 12

Length 22–24″. A stocky nocturnal heron, roosting by day in reed beds or swamps. **Adult** has *black crown and back* with 2 long white occipital plumes; *wings, rump, and tail grey*; face, neck and underparts white. Eyes large and red; bill black; legs and feet pale yellow (briefly red during courtship). **Subadult** less clean-cut, dark grey on crown and back, dirty white below, with brown eyes. **Juvenile/immature** dark brown above with whitish spots which disappear after a year or so; greyish underparts streaked with dark brown; bill yellowish; eyes orange-yellow, later brown; legs and feet yellow-green. **Call** a short *quok*, sometimes heard overhead at night. **Range**: Local near permanent water. Breeds regularly at Garsen, sporadically elsewhere.

CATTLE EGRET *Bubulcus i. ibis*   Plate 13 ✓

Length 19–21". A common gregarious heron of dry or wet open areas, often with large herbivores. Stocky, short-legged and 'heavy jowled', hunched when resting, but neck extended when active. Flocks fly to roost in long lines and Vs. **Non-breeding adult** and **juvenile** white; tarsi greenish yellow or blue-grey; eyes and loral skin pale yellow; bill yellow. **Breeding adult** has deep buff crown, nape, back and breast plumes. Bare parts bright yellow, orange-red when breeding. (Yellow-billed Egret is larger, longer necked, and has black tarsi at all ages.) **Call** a harsh croaking *kark-kark, krok* at breeding colonies; otherwise silent. **Range**: Widespread. Breeds regularly at Kisumu and Garsen, sporadically at other localities including North Kinangop and Emali.

LITTLE EGRET *Egretta g. garzetta*   Plate 13 ✓

Length 22–25.5". A common slender white heron with long, largely *black bill*, black or mostly black tarsi, and *yellow toes* (features shared with coastal Dimorphic Egret). **Breeding adult** has 2 long firm occipital plumes, filmy 'aigrette' plumes arising from back and scapulars and reaching to tail tip, and long lanceolate feathers on breast. Mainly black bill typically *pale horn or dull flesh on basal half of mandible, particularly along gonys*; eyes pale yellow. The normally *grey or bluish grey loral/orbital skin* becomes pale yellow, greenish yellow or dull peach colour at onset of breeding season, and lores turn bright orange during courtship. Rare **dark morph** is *slate-grey, bluish grey or black*, usually white on chin and throat. Normal **juvenile** is white with no elongate plumes. **Immature** has somewhat longer breast feathers and short dorsal plumes. **Call** a soft to harsh *gwaa* or a short guttural *kow*. Feeds alone or in groups. Dashes about in shallow water, actively pursuing fish, but rests with slouched posture for long periods. Foot-stirs to flush prey. **Range**: Widespread on fresh and alkaline waters, and along coastal creeks and estuaries (rarely on open seashore). Breeds at Garsen, Kisumu, Lake Jipe, and on rocky islets in Lake Turkana where mixed pairs of dark and white morphs have been photographed.

DIMORPHIC EGRET *Egretta (garzetta) dimorpha*   Plate 13

Length 22–25.5". Perhaps not specifically distinct from Little Egret, but an *entirely marine* bird in East Africa. **White morph** subtly longer-necked than Little Egret, and may show small amounts of black streaking on body and wings. Colours of bare parts slightly different: yellow or yellowish olive of toes extends upward as 'anklets' (and sometimes covering nearly entire front of tarsus); *these yellow areas bright pink or orange-red as breeding season begins*. Lores and prominent narrow 'saddle' across base of maxilla sometimes grey *(in non-breeding birds)*, but more often bright yellow as is orbital ring; all turn *bright deep pink during courtship*; eyes pale yellow. *More common* **dark morph** is blackish with white chin and upper throat, sometimes with a narrow white line down foreneck, and/or some white on the primary coverts (as in *E. gularis*), this showing as a *small but conspicuous white patch in flight*. Intermediates between dark and white morphs common. Bare facial parts as in white morph, with bill all black or showing yellow patch on sides of mandible (but unlike Madagascar birds never largely yellow); tarsi olive or black and olive; toes olive-yellow to orange. **Juvenile** and **immature** slate-grey or pale blue-grey to almost lavender-grey. Bare parts as in non-breeding adults, but lores dark grey with narrow yellow line from mandible base to below eye. (Non-breeding Little Egret is grey-lored. [Breeding Littles unlikely on marine shores or islands]. Rare dark Little probably indistinguishable. Western Reef Heron always differs in bill colour. Black Heron is smaller, with shaggy crest.) **Call** a low *gar* similar to call of Little Egret. Active, scurrying around in search of prey and stirring tidepools with feet; frequently wades belly-deep. Breeds colonially. **Range**: Common on open shores, reefs and creeks south of Shimoni. Breeds regularly on Kisite and Pemba islands and small coral islets. Occasional north to Kilifi and Mida Creek. **Taxonomic Note**: *E. garzetta, E. dimorpha* and E. *gularis* are considered conspecific by some authorities.

WESTERN REEF HERON *Egretta gularis schistacea*   Plate 13

Length 22–26 ". Resembles Little Egret, but with a *longer, heavier and deeper bill* that is *yellowish, pinkish brown, horn-brown or brownish olive*, and often appears to *droop slightly at the tip*; legs and feet dark brown or brownish olive. Often stands with slouched

279

posture or rests on tarsi. Waits for prey or stealthily stalks in crouched position prior to lightning-quick thrusts. Unlike Little and Dimorphic egrets, seldom runs in active pursuit of prey. **White morph** has two long occipital plumes, elongate scapular 'aigrettes' extending beyond the tail, and lanceolate upper breast feathers. Legs and feet olive-green or dark olive (apparently never black). **Dark morph** blackish with well-defined white chin and throat, and variable amounts of white on primary coverts (evident in flight); bare-part colours as in white morph. **Immature dark morph** light grey or slate-grey with yellow or orange-yellow toes; pale yellow eyes ringed by greenish yellow skin, and yellow lores in both morphs. **Call** a guttural *kawww*. **Range/status**: Uncommon non-breeding visitor from ne. Africa, mainly on coast south to Kilifi, but frequent at Lake Turkana; occasional on lakes Nakuru and Magadi.

BLACK HERON or BLACK EGRET *Egretta ardesiaca*   Plate 13

Length 19–20". A *shaggy-crested, slaty black* heron, *dark-eyed* and with conspicuous *orange or orange-yellow toes* (briefly red when courting); feet otherwise black as are legs and bill. *Eyes deep brown* with narrow powder-blue orbital ring. **Juvenile** duller, slightly paler, without head plumes. **Call** a low *cluck*, but generally silent. Feeds along marshy lake margins. Forms canopy over lowered head by spreading wings up and forward down to the water surface. This pose is maintained while mud is stirred with foot to flush prey; flocks may canopy in unison. Flies with steady quick wingbeats. (Dark morphs of preceding 3 species lack the shaggy crest and show some white on the throat.) **Range**: Local on lower Tana River and Lake Jipe. Currently breeds only near Garsen (formerly at Kisumu).

√ SQUACCO HERON *Ardeola ralloides*   Plates 12, 13

Length 17–18". Small and short-necked, mainly buffy or brownish and well camouflaged when standing in marsh grass or reeds, but *in flight shows conspicuous white wings, lower back, rump and tail*. **Non-breeding adult** brown on back, head and neck; breast pale buff with dark brown streaks; belly white. Bill greenish yellow with dusky tip; lores, legs and feet yellow-green, eyes yellow. **Breeding plumage** paler and buffier, the streaking largely confined to head which supports black-edged white plumes; also long cinnamon-buff plumes on upperparts, neck and breast. Bill azure-blue with distinct black tip; lores bluish, and legs and feet bright red as nesting begins. **Juvenile** like non-breeding adult, but wings and tail tip tinged brown and breast more heaviy streaked. See Madagascar Squacco Heron. **Call** a harsh grating *krruk*. **Range**: Widespread. Breeds regularly near Garsen, sporadically elsewhere.

MADAGASCAR SQUACCO or MALAGASY POND HERON *Ardeola idae*
Plates 12, 13

Length 17.5–19". *Stockier and heavier-billed* than Squacco Heron. Less secretive than that species, often feeding in open areas. **Non-breeding plumage** dark brown above, without buffy appearance of Squacco, and *head/neck streaking blacker and bolder, ending more abruptly against white lower breast and belly*. Bill olive-horn with blackish tip; lores, orbital skin and eyes yellow; legs and feet dull olive-yellow. **Breeding plumage** (rare in Africa) white with pale buff wash on upperparts (becomes snow-white in Madagascar); long white plumes on nape, back, foreneck and breast. Bill cerulean blue with black tip; lores greenish; eyes yellow; tarsi and toes rose-pink. **Call** a grating *krruk*, louder than Squacco's. **Range/status**: Non-breeding migrant from Madagascar, May–Oct., regular in coastal areas and inland to Nairobi, Nakuru and Arusha NPs and Ngorongoro Crater.

RUFOUS-BELLIED HERON *Ardeola rufiventris*   Plate 12

Length 15.5". Small, compact and dark. **Male** dark slate-grey with *chestnut 'shoulders', belly, rump and tail*. **Female** sooty grey-brown, with *buffy white streak on throat and fore-neck*; chestnut parts as in male. Adults show chestnut wing-linings and much chestnut on upperside of wing in flight. Bill brown with yellowish mandible turning rufous brown when breeding; eyes, lores and tarsi yellow, all turning red in breeding males. **Juvenile** resembles female but neck and breast streaked with buffy brown. **Call** a crow-like *kar*, and a croaking *kraak*. **Range**: Local in permanent swamps in Tarangire NP and nw. Mara GR. Occasional wanderers elsewhere.

GREEN-BACKED or STRIATED HERON *Butorides striatus atricapillus* Plate 12 ✔

Length 16″. A small, short-legged heron with hunched posture, typical of mangrove creeks and shaded river or lake edges with overhanging vegetation where it creeps among low waterside branches and roots. **Adult** dark greyish green above with erectile greenish black crown feathers; grey below with white throat and a broad buff line down foreneck. Legs and feet yellow (orange or red-orange when breeding); bill blackish with greenish yellow base (wholly black at onset of breeding); eyes yellow (deep orange when breeding). **Juvenile** streaked buff and brown, with whitish wing-feather tips. Shy and solitary. Mainly diurnal but also feeds at night. (Dwarf Bittern is smaller, heavily black-streaked on underparts, with dark line down centre of throat.) **Call** a sharp *kyah* when disturbed. **Range**: Widespread except in n. Kenya (where now scarce at Lake Turkana owing to falling water levels).

YELLOW-BILLED or INTERMEDIATE EGRET *Mesophoyx intermedia brachyrhyncha* Plate 13 √

Length 24–27″. Suggests a small, short-necked Great Egret, but the *bill is smaller* and the *dark 'gape line' extends back only to below the eye.* Acquires long plumes on back and breast when breeding. Bill yellow, often blackish at tip, becoming orange-red with yellow tip when breeding. Tarsi and toes blackish brown; tibiae paler brown, briefly pinkish red during courtship, but soon turning yellow for remainder of breeding season when yellow line also extends down sides of tarsi. Lores yellow, turning bright green when breeding; yellow eyes briefly turn bright red when courting. **Juvenile** resembles non-breeding adult. Often solitary except when breeding. See Cattle Egret. **Call** a low *kwark*, but usually silent except in nesting colony. **Range**: Widespread in suitable wetlands, but scarce along coast. Breeds regularly at Kisumu and Garsen, occasionally in Rift Valley.

GREAT EGRET *Casmerodius albus melanorhynchos* Plate 13 √

Length 33–36″. A fairly common tall white heron with long curved neck and a *black gape line extending from bill to behind the eye.* **Non-breeding adult** has *long yellow bill, black legs and feet, including toes*; lores dull yellowish green. **Breeding adult** develops long white back plumes; *bill becomes all or partly black,* the lores turn bright green, and the normally yellow eyes are briefly red. **Juvenile** and **immature** have black-tipped yellow bill. See Yellow-billed Egret. **Call** a deep raucous croak, *krrrawk, krrrawk*. **Range**: Widespread in wet inland and coastal habitats. Breeds regularly near Kisumu and Garsen, sporadically elsewhere.

GREY HERON *Ardea c. cinerea* Plate 11 ✔

Length 35–39″. A large grey-backed heron. **Adult** has *whitish head*, neck and underparts, and broad *black eye-lines extending into a black occipital plume*; also has narrow black streaks down front of neck and *black 'shoulders'.* In flight, from above, *blackish flight feathers contrast with grey wing-coverts, back and tail; wings uniformly grey beneath.* Bill and eyes yellowish; tarsi yellow-brown, all becoming orange or vermilion during courtship. (Adult Black-headed Heron has black crown and nape, black legs, and white wing-linings.) **Juvenile/immature** more uniformly grey (sometimes washed with brown) including crown and most of underparts, with white only on face and neck and no black epaulettes; bill dark, turning yellow in second year. Solitary except when breeding. Feeds day and night in water or on dry land; also scavenges along coast. **Call** a harsh *hraaank* in flight; at nest, a deep grunting *ur-ur-ur-ur*. **Range**: Widespread in wetlands, inland and coastal; breeding sites scattered.

PURPLE HERON *Ardea p. purpurea*   **Plate 11**

Length 31–33". A richly coloured, *slender* heron with sinuous neck and long slim bill. **Adult** has grey back and wings, black cap, a black-streaked, rufous-and-white neck, and black belly. Develops elongate chestnut scapular and back plumes when breeding, and yellow bill is then more orange. Tarsi black in front, as are tops of toes; feet and legs otherwise yellowish. (Goliath Heron is much larger, heavier, lacks black cap and and has dark bill; in flight, its wings show much more chestnut below.) **Juvenile** and **immature** much browner than young Grey Heron, and have some black stripes on brownish foreneck; otherwise dull white below. Typically feeds in tall marsh vegetation where difficult to see, but not shy. **Call** a harsh *kraak* or *kreek*. **Range**: Widespread and locally common in wetlands. Breeds near Garsen, in some years at Lake Jipe and in Rift Valley.

✓**GOLIATH HERON** *Ardea goliath*   **Plate 11**

Length 47–60". *Huge* size, *grey-and-chestnut plumage*, and *large grey-ish black bill* distinctive. **Adult** grey above with *rufous-chestnut head and neck, deep chestnut 'shoulders' and belly*; white foreneck and breast streaked with black; legs and feet black. In flight, *wings appear uniform-ly grey above and* have *chestnut coverts beneath*. **Juvenile** browner with rufous-buff feather edges above; breast and belly buffy white streaked with dark brown. **Immature** brownish grey above, the chestnut areas paler than in adult; neck pattern obscure, and no chestnut epaulettes; bill pale below. Solitary. Flies with slow ponderous wingbeats, feet usually hanging below horizontal. **Call** a deep raucous *koworrh-koworrh-worrh-worrh*. **Range**: Local on larger lakes, rivers and permanent swamps. Breeds sporadically at lakes Baringo and Naivasha and along Mara River, occasionally elsewhere.

✓**BLACK-HEADED HERON** *Ardea melanocephala*   **Plate 11**

Length 33–36". The commonest East African heron, often on open grass-land or cultivated ground as well as in aquatic habitats. **Adult** has *most of head and hindneck black*, contrasting with *white throat and foreneck*. Upperparts darker than Grey Heron, and in flight shows strongly *two-toned underwing pattern, the whitish linings contrasting with black flight feathers* (uniformly grey in Grey Heron). Legs and upper half of bill black (yellowish in Grey Heron); yellow eyes turn red early in breeding sea-son. **Juvenile/immature** grey on head and hindneck. **Call** a raucous croaking *kaaaak* in flight. At nest, a loud *kowk* and other calls. **Range**: Widespread, although absent from much of arid n. and e. Kenya. Breeds at Usa River, Njoro, and near Kisumu; smaller colonies elsewhere.

HAMERKOP, FAMILY SCOPIDAE

This unique bird shares with herons the pectinate middle toenail and rather long legs, but protein studies suggest a closer relationship with storks.

✓**HAMERKOP** *Scopus u. umbretta*   **Plate 11**

Length 19–22". A heavy billed brown waterbird with large 'hammer-shaped' crested head and short neck; bill, legs and feet black. Feeds in shallow water. Flaps and glides on broad wings with neck extended. Solitary or in pairs. Builds massive nest of sticks and mud, with side entrance hole, in tree crotch. **Call** a loud strident yelping, *yik-purrrr,yik-yik-yik-purr-purr-yik-yik*. **Range**: Widespread along swamp edges, lake-sides, sluggish rivers and streams.

STORKS, FAMILY CICONIIDAE

Large, long-legged and long-necked birds with long, heavy bills and basally webbed toes. The head may be partly bare. They fly with neck and legs extended; some soar on long, broad wings. Most are voiceless, but engage in bill-clattering when nesting. They feed on open ground and in shallow water, and frequently loaf near feeding areas, often resting on their tarsi. Legs and upper tarsi often 'whitewashed' with the bird's excrement (for thermoregulation), concealing true colours. Some species are long-distance migrants. Our residents nest in trees, either colonially or as isolated pairs. The sexes are much alike.

WHITE STORK *Ciconia c. ciconia*   Plate 9 ✔

Length 40–48″. A large stork with *white body and tail*, contrasting black flight feathers, and red bill, legs and feet. (Yellow-billed Stork, similar in high flight, distinguished by black tail.) **Immature** duller, with dark brown flight feathers. Usually in loose flocks, mainly on grassland or cultivated ground; soars on thermals; assembles at large insect concentrations or grass fires. **Range/status**: Palearctic migrant, mainly Nov.–April, but some remain all year. Often numerous on e. Serengeti Plains and in Ngorongoro Crater. Marked migrations in Kericho/Mara area.

BLACK STORK *Ciconia nigra*   Plate 9 ✔

Length 38–40″. A tall dark stork, white from lower breast to under tail-coverts, and with dull *red bill and legs*. Upperparts mainly black with purple and green gloss; black wings show small white triangle next to body on underside. **Immature** brownish above, with dull olive-green bill, legs and feet. (Abdim's Stork is smaller with shorter greenish grey bill, blue facial skin, and white lower back.) **Range/status**: Palearctic migrant, regular but uncommon in Kenya, Oct.–April, especially along the Athi-Galana rivers. Occasional in w. Kenya. Scarce in n. Tanzania.

ABDIM'S STORK *Ciconia abdimii*   Plate 9 ✔

Length 30-32″. A small black-and-white stork of grassland and cultivated areas. Largely black with purplish gloss, but *white from lower breast to under tail-coverts and on rump/lower back*. Bill dull grey-green with reddish tip; legs and feet greenish grey, tinged red on toes and tibiotarsal joints. Facial skin bluish with red around eyes. **Juvenile** has adult pattern but is duller and browner. Gregarious, sometimes in flocks of hundreds or thousands, often with White Storks. Soars on thermals when migrating. **Range/status**: Mainly a non-breeding migrant from the northern tropics, late Oct.–mid-April. Has bred in n. and w. Kenya.

WOOLLY-NECKED STORK *Ciconia episcopus microscelis*   Plate 9

Length 33–34″. A solitary stork of coastal lagoons and inland riversides. *Black, glossed bluish and purple, with woolly white neck, white belly and long stiff white under tail-coverts projecting beyond the deeply forked black tail*. Blackish bill is red along culmen and at tip; dark red eyes are ringed with bare blackish skin; tarsi and toes dusky red. **Juvenile** and **immature** are much duller and browner with reduced gloss, the crown dark at first, whitening with age. **Range**: Coastal lowlands (where fairly common) and along inland streams and rivers, especially in se. Kenya. An uncommon wanderer elsewhere, although it has bred in Mara GR.

SADDLE-BILLED STORK *Ephippiorhynchus senegalensis*   Plate 9 ✔

Length 57″. An uncommon, tall, spectacular stork of wet places. **Adult** *black and white* with a *yellow saddle-shaped frontal shield* and small yellow wattles at base of the *enormous black-and-red bill*. *Pinkish red tibiotarsal joints and toes* mark the otherwise dark legs and feet. Eyes dark brown in male, bright yellow in female. **Juvenile** largely grey-brown, including bill (which lacks saddle). **Immature** duller than adult with greyish flight feathers; bill black and red but without saddle; legs and feet greenish. **Range**: Local and uncommon in large wetlands. Regular on coast north of Malindi, May–Sept. Scattered breeding records from lower Tana River west to Lake Victoria and Mara GR, south to Serengeti and Arusha NPs.

√ **MARABOU STORK** *Leptoptilus crumeniferus* **Plate 9**

Length 60″. Huge and unmistakable with massive grey or pinkish horn bill, naked pinkish head with white ruff, and a bare pendent inflatable throat pouch; may also show inflatable bright orange-red swelling just above ruff at base of hindneck. **Non-breeding adult** slate-grey above, with greenish gloss on wing-coverts; underparts white. Legs and feet black but often whitened with the bird's excrement. **Breeding plumage** paler blue-grey with broadly white-edged secondary coverts and larger, fluffier white under tail-coverts; bare skin brighter than in non-breeding bird, with the throat pouch and most of head red, pale blue nape, black forehead and lores, and lines of black warts from ear region to occiput. **Juvenile** and **immature** duller, with more hair-like feathers on head; wings brownish (becoming blackish and slightly glossed in 2nd or 3rd year); coverts pale-edged; bare skin often yellow-tinged. Usually silent apart from bill clattering and loud wheezy whine of air across flight feathers in low flight, but moans, moos and squeals at nest; **call** of courting bird a repeated hoarse whinnying, *wu-wuwuwuwuwuwuwuwa-ekk*. A gregarious scavenger at offal and rubbish dumps; consorts with vultures at carcasses, and also captures live vertebrate prey. Soars and cruises at great height with neck retracted. Inactive for long periods, standing motionless or squatting on tarsi. **Range**: Widespread, but only small numbers breed in a few widely scattered traditional tree colonies (e.g. at Kitale, Wajir, Garissa, Kibwezi, Hunter's Lodge and Lake Manyara).

√ **AFRICAN OPEN-BILLED STORK** *Anastomus l. lamelligerus* **Plate 9**

Length 32–37″. A rather small blackish stork of shallow water where small groups feed on molluscs. Unique feathers of underparts extended as stiff, lustrous, curly filaments (visible at close range as is purplish and green plumage gloss). Large brownish bill is pale basally, and shows prominent *tomial gap* (larger in male). Legs and feet black. **Juvenile/immature** duller and browner with whitish feather tips, the bill at first shorter and straighter with only a narrow gap. Perches and roosts in trees; nests colonially. Large flocks at times circle high in the air. **Call** a loud raucous croaking or honking, *horrrnkh-horrrnkh*. **Range**: Mainly below 1500 m on inland waters and brackish coastal lagoons. Nests regularly near Garsen and (a few) at Kisumu.

✔ **YELLOW-BILLED STORK** *Mycteria ibis* **Plate 9**

Length 38–42″. A pinkish white waterside stork with *black tail* and flight feathers, *long yellow, slightly decurved bill, bare red face,* and bright pink legs and feet. **Juvenile** grey-brown with dull greyish yellow bill, dusky orange face and brown legs. **Immature** resembles adult but lacks pinkish tinge to white body plumage, and bare parts are much duller. Small groups feed in shallow water, walking slowly with bills immersed, stirring with feet to disturb prey. Flocks spend much time resting on grassy banks or in trees. **Range**: Widespread along lake edges, rivers, coastal estuaries, and other wet places. Breeds regularly near Kisumu, sporadically elsewhere.

IBISES AND SPOONBILLS, FAMILY THRESKIORNITHIDAE

Large, long-necked wading birds which typically fly with flapping and intermittent gliding, the neck fully extended. Mostly gregarious, feeding in shallow water, wet grassland, or forest clearings. Ibises have long decurved bills and relatively short tarsi; spoonbills have straight spatulate bills and long tarsi. Toes are webbed at the base. The sexes are alike. Some species are solitary nesters; others breed colonially, often over water with herons.

√ **SACRED IBIS** *Threskiornis a. aethiopicus* **Plate 10**

Length 25–32″. Mainly white with wrinkled *bare black head and neck* and *strongly decurved blackish bill.* Tail concealed by iridescent blue-black plume-like scapulars and long inner secondaries; remiges tipped with glossy greenish black. Flanks tinged golden or brownish yellow when breeding. Eyes brown, with dark red orbital ring when breeding; legs and feet black (tarsi tinged red). In flight, *white wings with narrow black trailing edges* distinctive. Adult shows bare red skin beneath wings near body. **Juvenile** has mottled black-and-white feathering on head and neck, lacks plumes, and has broader black wing margins. **Immature** may have partially feathered head, some plume-like inner secondaries and scapulars. Feeds in shallow water, fields and on mudflats. Flies in V-formations between roosts and feeding sites. Nests in large colonies. **Call** a harsh croak in flight, but mostly silent away from nesting sites. **Range**: Widespread in and near water, including coastal lagoons and estuaries. Breeds annually near Kisumu, Garsen and Lake Turkana, irregularly elsewhere.

HADADA or HADEDA IBIS *Bostrychia hagedash brevirostris*   Plate 10

Length 30–35". A *stocky, dark short-legged* ibis, brownish grey with bronze gloss above, *iridescent green and purplish wing-coverts*, and whitish stripe below cheeks. Black bill has red culmen; legs and feet dark grey, toes sometimes crimson above. **Juvenile** duller. **Call** a loud raucous *HAAA* or a longer *HA-HAA-DE-DAH* or *HAA-HAA-HAA*. Highly vocal, especially at dawn and dusk when flying to and from feeding grounds. Flight slow, rather jerky, bill angled downward. Roosts communally in trees but pairs nest singly. (Scarce African Green Ibis is crested, restricted to montane forests, and differs vocally.) **Range**: Widespread in high-rainfall areas, along streams, forest edges, lakeshores and in cultivation. Has become common in Nairobi suburbs in recent years.

AFRICAN GREEN or OLIVE IBIS *Bostrychia olivacea akeleyorum*   Plate 10
Length 29". A scarce *highland forest* ibis resembling Hadada, but with a *loose mane-like crest* and more general greenish wash on head, neck and underparts; upperparts and wing-coverts iridescent green and bronze. Bill dull dark red; bare skin on lores and above eyes dusky blue; area below eyes to ear-coverts pale brown; legs and feet dull orange-brown with greenish tinge, pinkish brown or (when breeding?) dull dark red. **Juvenile/immature** duller and with shorter crest. **Call** a single *GARR*, and a resonant *GARRA-GARRA* or *AKA-A* uttered by flying groups at dawn and dusk. Pairs or small groups feed in glades within dense forest, and perch in trees. Flight strong and direct. Rarely observed except when calling in crepuscular flight to and from roosts. A solitary breeder. **Range**: In Kenya, now confined to areas from 2000 to 3700 m on the Aberdares and Mt Kenya; in n. Tanzania known from s. Kilimanjaro and locally near 1000 m in East Usambaras.

GLOSSY IBIS *Plegadis f. falcinellus*   Plate 10

Length 22–25.5". A dark ibis with slender decurved bill and long legs. Appears black at a distance, but at close range **breeding adult** is mainly chestnut with purple gloss, the back and wings iridescent green. Bill, legs and feet dull brown; bare pale blue or purplish lores bordered by narrow white lines. **Non-breeding adult** brownish black, flecked with white on head and neck. **Juvenile** and **immature** sooty brown with some greenish gloss, head and neck brownish grey with white spots. Flocks may contain hundreds of birds, flying in compact lines, with fluid wingbeats and long glides; may feed singly. **Call** a croaking *gra-gra-gra*. **Range**: Widespread in wetlands. Now breeds only near Garsen.

*EURASIAN SPOONBILL *Platalea leucorodia*   Plate 10
Length 34–35". Differs from common African Spoonbill in having *feathered area between eyes, black spatulate bill with yellow tip, and black legs*. Bare yellow skin at bill base and on chin and throat; some dark skin on lores; eyes red. In spring, develops partially yellow crest at rear of crown, and yellowish neck patch. **First-year bird** has black primary tips, and gradually assumes adult coloration, the pinkish bill darkening from base, the pinkish legs turning olive-grey, then blackish; facial skin dark. (Black-legged young African Spoonbill has unfeathered face.) **Range/status**: Scarce migrant, occasional at Lake Turkana, less often at lakes Nakuru and Naivasha. (Kenyan birds may represent the nominate palearctic race, but *archeri* of the Red Sea coast is also possible here.)

AFRICAN SPOONBILL *Platalea alba*   **Plate 10**

Length 36″. A large white wading bird with a long spatulate bill. **Adult** has *bare red face*, grey bill with pink edges, and long pinkish red legs; eyes pale blue-grey. **Juvenile** and **immature** have *dull yellow bill and facial skin, blackish legs and feet*, and *black primary tips*. Feeds in shallow water, bill immersed and sweeping from side to side. Flight graceful with shallow wingbeats and long glides, often in lines and Vs. Infrequent **call** a barking *ark-ark*. **Range**: Widespread on inland waters. Breeds regularly near Kisumu and Garsen, and sporadically in or near Rift Valley. Local along coast.

FLAMINGOS, FAMILY PHOENICOPTERIDAE

Tall slender wading birds of shallow saline or alkaline waters, characterized by long sinuous neck, lamellate bill bent sharply downward at the midpoint, pink and white plumage, extremely long legs and short webbed toes. Flocks fly in long skeins and Vs with neck and legs fully extended, pointed wings beating steadily. Both species feed with bill immersed, head upside-down. Mud and water are taken in, then expelled past the filtering lamellae, the thick tongue acting like a piston. Highly gregarious and nomadic. Breeding sporadic, in large colonies, the nest a mound of mud with a shallow depression at the top.

✓ GREATER FLAMINGO *Phoenicopterus* (*ruber*) *roseus*   **Plate 10**

Length 50–55″. Very tall. White **adult** plumage washed with pink, the wing-coverts and axillaries bright coral-red; flight-feathers black. *Bill pink with black tip*; legs and feet bright coral-pink. **Juvenile** brownish grey, with no red on wings; bill pale grey with black tip; eyes yellow; legs grey. **Immature** white, tinged pink, with greyish head and neck, bill and legs gradually becoming pink. **Calls** include a loud goose-like double honk, *ka-hanh*, a conversational *kuk-kuk, kuk-kuk. . .*, and a nasal *knyaaa*. Feeding flocks maintain a continuous 'kucking.' **Range**: Mainly brackish and soda lakes of the Rift Valley, breeding sites at Elmenteita and Natron. Small numbers regular on coast

✓ LESSER FLAMINGO *Phoeniconaias minor*   **Plate 10**

Length 32–35″. Much smaller than Greater Flamingo and more richly coloured. **Adult** mainly deep pink with *dark red, black-tipped bill*, bright red legs and feet, and largely red wings with black flight feathers; eyes yellow. **Juvenile** greyish with grey bill and legs. **Immature** whitish with no red in wings. Usual **calls** a low *murr-err, murr-err* at rest, and a high-pitched *kwirrik* in flight. Flocks produce a continuous humming or murmuring. Gathers in immense numbers on Rift Valley soda lakes where often in tightly packed flocks. **Range**: Largely confined to Rift Valley soda lakes from Manyara north to Turkana. Hundreds of thousands breed regularly on Natron, occasionally Magadi and Logipi. Concentrations of feeding birds can exceed one million at lakes Nakuru and Bogoria. Seldom seen far from the Rift Valley.

DUCKS AND GEESE, FAMILY ANATIDAE

Strong-winged, heavy-bodied waterbirds, whose broad flattened bill has a nail-like tip. Tarsi are short and thick and the front toes webbed. Sexes differ in palearctic species, but are similar in most residents. Adults' post-breeding moult is complete and rapid, leaving birds flightless for a few weeks. During this period, males of palearctic species (and a few southern breeders) acquire their dull non-breeding or 'eclipse' dress, retained for a month or two, then replaced by the bright breeding plumage in autumn or early winter. Some northern birds retain partial eclipse plumage until arrival in East Africa. Northern Shoveler and Garganey moult into a supplementary 'sub-eclipse' plumage retained for several months before moulting into breeding dress. Females of palearctic species have moults corresponding to those of males, but there is little seasonal difference between female plumages.

The subfamilies in East Africa are Dendrocygninae (whistling ducks), Thalassorninae (White-backed Duck), Plectropterinae (Spur-winged Goose), Tadorninae (the duck-like geese *Sarkidiornis* and *Alopochen*) and Anatinae, represented by the tribes Anatini (dabbling ducks), Aythyini (diving ducks) and Oxyurini (stiff-tails).

FULVOUS WHISTLING DUCK *Dendrocygna bicolor* **Plate 15**

Length 18–21". Long-necked and long-legged. This and the following species stand more upright than most ducks. *Rich rufous-brown* or fulvous below and on head, dark brown above with a broad *blackish line down back of neck*, and a *broad pale line along the flanks*. In flight appears long-necked and broad-winged, and feet project well beyond the tail; a *whitish U-shaped patch on upper tail-coverts* separates brown back and wings from black tail. Duller **juvenile** has a less showy white tail-covert patch. **Call** a low whistled *tsu-ee*. Large flocks produce a persistent whistling day and night. **Range**: Widespread on wetlands below 1500 m, but breeding confirmed only near Arusha.

WHITE-FACED WHISTLING DUCK *Dendrocygna viduata* **Plate 15**

Length 17–19". A dark duck. *White face contrasts with long blackish neck* and chestnut breast; sides barred buffy white and dark brown; *belly and tail blackish without white U of preceding species.* Duller **juvenile** has light brown face patch. Often flocks with Fulvous Whistling Duck. Usual **call** a sibilant 3-note whistle, *swee-swee-sweeu*. **Range**: Widespread below 1500 m, mostly in freshwater wetlands.

WHITE-BACKED DUCK *Thalassornis l. leuconotus* **Plate 15**

Length 15–16". A thickset, *large-headed* duck with *white patch at base of the heavy bill*. Face and crown dark, merging into tawny buff on neck; dark *body coarsely barred brown and tawny buff*; white lower back patch normally visible only in flight, when bird looks tail-less and large-footed. Usually in pairs or small groups among floating vegetation. Flies reluctantly, pattering across surface to take wing; usually dives to escape danger. See Maccoa Duck. **Call** a clear whistled *tu-wheet* or *si-weet-weet*. **Range**: Cent. and w. Kenyan highlands and north-cent. Tanzania (common in Arusha NP); also along coast, in Lake Victoria basin, and on Lake Paradise, Mt Marsabit.

SPUR-WINGED GOOSE *Plectropterus g. gambensis* **Plate 15**

Length 30–39". The largest African waterfowl: a *long-necked and long-legged* black-and-white goose. Glossy black with green and bronze reflections; cheeks/chin and belly white. *Bill, bare loral and orbital skin, legs and feet dark pink*. In flight, shows conspicuous white forewing patch. Male substantially larger than female and with caruncles forming a low comb on base of bill. **Juvenile** browner with lower face white-feathered. Wary. Pairs or flocks fly to feeding areas at dawn, dusk or at night. Flight **call** a soft rolling or bubbling whistle, *cherrut* or *cherwit*. **Range**: Local in wetlands below 3000 m. Wanders widely.

 EGYPTIAN GOOSE *Alopochen aegyptiacus* **Plate 15**

Length 25–29". A common buffy brown goose (some birds noticeably greyer) with a *chestnut-brown eye patch* continuing around base of bill, similar small patch on lower breast, and narrow chestnut collar around lower neck. In flight, *white forewing* conspicuous against black primaries; secondaries edged with iridescent green. From below, white wing-linings contrast with dark flight feathers. Eyes orange; bill, legs and feet bright pink. Duller **juvenile** lacks face and breast patches, and forewing panel grey, not white; bill, legs and feet yellowish grey. A bird of lakes, ponds and river banks; grazes in fields. Swims with rear end held high. Usually in pairs. Female's display **call** a strident nasal *hur-hur-hur-hur-hur. . .* accelerating and becoming staccato; male has throaty wheezing or hissing; both sexes give a honking *ha-ha-ha-ha-*

ha before taking flight. **Range**: Almost ubiquitous below 3000 m on permanent lakes, ponds and sandy river banks.

KNOB-BILLED DUCK *Sarkidiornis m. melanotos* Plate 15

Length 22–30". A large black-and-white dabbling duck. *Head, neck and underparts white,* the head and upper neck finely speckled with black. Back and wings glossy black with green and bronze reflections. **Male** has large, fleshy, black comb at base of bill. **Female** smaller and with grey rump/lower back. Eyes dark brown; bill black, legs and feet dark grey. In overhead flight, dark wings contrast with white body. **Juvenile** more brownish on head and upperparts, mottled below, with trace of glossy green on wings. Typically in small flocks, feeding in shallow water and on land; often perches in trees. **Call** a low croak when flushed; otherwise silent. **Range**: Widespread from coast to 3000 m, in freshwater wetlands. Has bred in se. Kenya and in Serengeti NP.

AFRICAN PYGMY GOOSE *Nettapus auritus* Plate 15

Length 12–13". A compact colourful duck about the size of a Hottentot Teal. Dark *green above with white face and neck; bright tawny cinnamon on chest and flanks.* **Breeding male** has light green patches at sides of foreneck, and bright yellow bill. In flight, looks small and dark with white belly, the dark wings with a large white patch on secondaries. (Paler Hottentot Teal shows only narrow line of white.) **Eclipse male, female**, and **juvenile** lack neck patches and have dull greyish olive bills. Pairs or small groups inhabit heavily vegetated secluded waters. **Call** of male a soft whistled *choo-choo-pee-pee.* **Range**: Local on coastal freshwater lakes and swamps, including Pemba Island. Scarce inland.

*MALLARD *Anas p. platyrhynchos* Plate 16

Length 20–25". A rare vagrant in East Africa. **Male** unmistakable with *dark glossy green head and neck, narrow white collar and purplish brown breast.* Sides of body pale grey, back darker, the scapulars black and buff; rump and upper tail-coverts black, and 2 black tail feathers curl up and forward; outer rectrices mainly white. In flight, wings show *white-bordered blue or purple speculum,* white belly and wing-linings. Bill olive-green or yellowish; feet orange. **Female** is generally buffy brown with dark brown streaking and mottling; crown, nape and eye-lines dark brown, contrasting with buffy brown superciliary stripes; face and foreneck; wings as in male. *Bill usually dull orange with blackish markings,* but may be dull brownish, olive or yellowish brown. (Female Gadwall is slimmer, has white patch on secondaries, her smaller grey bill is yellow-orange at sides, and feet yellower than in Mallard.) **Call** of female a repetitive *quack*; male has a soft *kreep*. **Status**: Undoubted wild birds shot near Marsabit, 1928–29, but no specimens preserved. Reports from Lake Naivasha (Dec. 1938) perhaps based on feral birds. No satisfactory recent records.

AFRICAN BLACK DUCK *Anas sparsa leucostigma* Plate 16

Length 19–22". A large sooty black *river* duck with *bold white scalloping on upperparts* (forming bands on some individuals). *Blue or purplish-blue speculum bordered by white and black bands,* evident in flight and often on water. Bill pinkish or pinkish grey with black 'saddle'; feet yellowish. In overhead flight, white inner wing-linings contrast with generally dark wings. (In flight, similar Yellow-billed Duck shows less prominent speculum borders and more white on underside of wings.) **Juvenile** browner with sparse buff spotting above, dusky and white barring on belly; speculum dull; bill blue-grey. Pairs haunt fast-flowing highland streams with wooded banks. Feeds by head-dipping or up-ending to take prey from beneath stones in strong current. **Call** a mallard-like *quack* (female) and a soft wheezy *peeshp* (male). **Range**: Local above 1850 m in highlands of w. and cent. Kenya and n. Tanzania, especially on Mt Kenya, Aberdares, Mt Meru, Kilimanjaro, and between 1200 and 2200 m in the West Usambaras.

CAPE TEAL   *Anas capensis*   **Plate 16**

Length 17–19". A *pale* dabbling duck with a distinctive *rose-pink bill*. Plumage mottled brownish grey, the head ash-grey with fine speckling. Eyes yellowish to orange-brown; feet dull yellowish brown. In flight shows green speculum broadly bordered with white. Typically forms small flocks on soda lakes. See Red-billed Duck. **Call** a soft nasal whistle or a low nasal quack. **Range**: In Kenya, on alkaline Rift Valley lakes but wanders to fresh water. In n. Tanzania, common in Arusha NP, less so at Lake Manyara, Ngorongoro Crater and Lake Lygarja (Serengeti NP).

EURASIAN WIGEON   *Anas penelope*   **Plate 16**

Length 18–20". Medium-sized with a *steep forehead, short blue-grey bill* and rather pointed tail. **Male in breeding plumage** has *chestnut head with yellowish buff forehead and crown*, grey body, white line along sides and black under tail-coverts. In flight shows white forewing and greenish speculum. **Female/first-winter male** greyish or rufous-brown, finely mottled; head paler, but blackish around eyes. Speculum blackish; forewing grey-brown; belly white. Eclipse male like female but retains white forewing; sides more rufous. See female Northern Pintail. Gregarious, often with other waterfowl on freshwater lakes and ponds. Swims with pointed tail angled upward. **Call** of male a loud whistled *wheeeoo*; female utters a low *grrr*. **Range/status**: Uncommon palearctic migrant, Nov.–March, mainly in Rift Valley and above 1800 m in w. and cent. Kenyan highlands. Scarce in n. Tanzania.

GADWALL   *Anas s. strepera*   **Plate 16**

Length 18–22". A rare, subtly patterned dabbling duck. **Breeding-plumaged male** mainly *grey* with browner head and *black rear end*, some chestnut in upper wing-coverts; belly white. *Bill blackish; legs and feet orange-yellow.* **Female** and **first-autumn** birds mottled brown with dark eye-lines, duller and greyer than female Mallard which also has more pointed flank markings, darker crown and eye-lines, and less sloping forehead. *Bill greyish with orange sides* (usually orange near tip and base, not sides, in Mallard). In flight (and sometimes on water) both sexes show *small square white patch on secondaries*. **Call** of male a low whistle and a throaty *bek* or *nheck*; female gives a descending Mallard-like *kak-ak-ak-ak-ak*. **Range/status**: Palearctic migrant, the 10 Kenyan records mostly of single birds on freshwater lakes in the west, northwest and Rift Valley.

COMMON or GREEN-WINGED TEAL   *Anas c. crecca*   **Plate 16**

Length 13–15". A small dabbling duck, little larger than a Hottentot Teal, with rather steep forehead and short bill. **Male** has *chestnut head with buff-bordered shining green band from lores to nape*; grey body with white line along sides, and creamy patch on under tail-coverts. Bill, legs and feet slate-grey. **Female** mottled brown with dark eye-lines, shorter-necked and shorter-billed than female Garganey, and head pattern less bold, forewing browner, belly less white; also distinguished by *flesh-pink at base of maxilla*, and pale line along under tail-coverts near each side of tail. In flight, both sexes show *bright green speculum* with white borders. Small groups or singles associate with other migrant ducks. Typically feeds near waterside vegetation. Rises abruptly and flies rapidly, usually low. **Call** of male a high ringing *crreek-crreek*; female a short high-pitched *quack*. **Range/status**: Regular palearctic migrant Nov.-March, mainly above 1400 m on ponds in and west of Rift Valley; occasional in Amboseli and Tsavo West NPs. Rare in n. Tanzania.

GARGANEY   *Anas querquedula*   **Plate 16**

Length 15–16". Small, with relatively long neck and large dark grey bill. **Breeding-plumaged male** (late Jan. onwards) has bold *white stripe from eye to nape*, chestnut-brown head, neck and breast, and *pale grey sides*. In flight shows *pale blue-grey forewing* and *dark green speculum broadly bordered with white in front and behind*; overhead, the mainly white wing-linings contrast with broad black leading edge. **Female** and **first-winter male** pale mottled brown with *bolder head pattern* than female

Common Teal; dark crown and eye-lines contrast with pale buff stripes above and below eyes and *short dark subloral lines* near base of bill; speculum brownish (greyer in young birds); throat and belly bright white. **Sub-eclipse male** like female but wing as in breeding male, brighter white throat, and broader streaking on head and neck. May gather in tightly packed flocks of hundreds or thousands. Prefers sheltered shallow pools with emergent vegetation. See female Northern Pintail. **Call** of male a dry *krik-krik* and, in spring, a crackling *rrar-rrar-rrar;* female has a harsh *gack.* **Range/status:** Palearctic migrant, mainly late Oct.–April. Widespread in Kenya, most numerous on Rift Valley lakes and in w. and cent. highlands; also on lower Tana River and in the southeast. In n. Tanzania, regular in Ngorongoro Crater; also in Lake Manyara and Arusha NPs.

YELLOW-BILLED DUCK *Anas u. undulata*   Plate 16

Length 20–23″. A mottled brownish grey duck with broad pale feather edges and a long, *largely bright yellow bill.* In flight, shows white winglinings and green speculum (in nominate *undulata*) with white borders. Legs and feet red-brown to dark grey. **Female** duller with paler bill. **Juvenile** has broader and buffier feather edges. Slightly darker northern race *rueppelli* has deeper yellow bill and a blue speculum. Pairs or small flocks forage in marshy freshwater ponds and lakes. (African Black Duck, occasionally on ponds, is darker and has pinkish or greyish bill.) **Call** of female a hoarse descending Mallard-like *quack-quack-quack;* male gives a soft low whistle. **Range:** Widespread *A. u. undulata* is common in cent. and w. Kenyan highlands and Rift Valley lakes; regular in Ngorongoro Crater but scarce in most of n. Tanzania. Old Marsabit records and some Ol Bolossat sightings may refer to *rueppelli.*

NORTHERN PINTAIL *Anas a. acuta*   Plate 16

Length 20–26″. Slender and long-necked. **Breeding-plumaged male** (Dec.–April) has *dark brown head, white throat and neck stripe* and long *pointed central tail feathers.* Body grey with buffy white patch at rear of flanks and black under tail-coverts. Eyes yellow to brownish yellow; bill pale blue-grey with black culmen, tip and edges. Legs and feet dark grey. White-bordered bronzy green speculum, long neck, pointed tail and dark head obvious in flight. **Female** and **first-winter** bird mottled brown, sometimes with warm tawny tinge; face rather plain; slim-necked and with short pointed tail. Bill and feet grey. In flight, appears brownish with paler belly and *conspicuous white trailing edge on brown speculum;* wings largely grey beneath. Young male shows partly green speculum. See females of Garganey, Gadwall and Eurasian Wigeon. Flocks in shallow water, often with Garganey or Shoveler. **Call** of male a weak mellow *prrip-prrip;* female quacks. **Range/status:** Palearctic migrant, mainly Nov.–early April, especially in cent. and w. Kenyan highlands and Rift Valley. Occasional in se. Kenya, including coastal estuaries. Regular in Ngorongoro Crater, Lake Manyara and Arusha NPs.

✔ RED-BILLED TEAL *Anas erythrorhyncha*   Plate 16

Length 17–19″. A medium-sized dabbling duck with a *red bill, buffy white cheeks and dark brown crown and nape.* Pale feather edges produce a scalloped or spotted effect on the dark brown body. Legs and feet dark grey. In flight shows unique pattern of *whitish secondaries contrasting with otherwise dark wings.* **Juvenile** streaked rather than spotted below; bill dull pink. (Cape Teal has pink bill, finely speckled pale grey head, green speculum and dull yellowish feet.) **Call** of male a soft whistling *whizzzt,* female a guttural *krraak.* **Range:** Widespread from s.-cent. Kenya through n. Tanzania, but rare in most coastal areas except Tana and Sabaki estuaries.

✔ HOTTENTOT TEAL *Anas hottentota*   Plate 16

Length 12–14″. A common small duck with *dark crown and dark smudge on sides of neck* contrasting with *pale buff face* and foreneck. Mottled dark brown above; buff with dark spotting and barring below. Pattern recalls Red-billed Teal, except for neck patches and *greyish blue bill* with black culmen and edges; legs and feet dark blue-grey. In flight shows large green speculum with broad white rear margin. Female duller than male with browner crown and less well defined neck patch. Dabbles in reedy shallows, and spends much time loafing on shores, often hidden in vegetation. Flies low across water with head and neck elevated. **Calls** include a harsh *tsetzetze* and a higher *ke-ke-ke*. **Range**: Local on freshwater and alkaline lakeshores and ponds. Scarce near coast.

NORTHERN SHOVELER *Anas clypeata*   Plate 16

Length 17–20″. Identified in all plumages by the *oversized, semi-spatulate bill*. **Male in breeding plumage** (after late Dec.) has *dark glossy green head* and *large chestnut patch on sides and belly* contrasting with white breast; under tail-coverts black. Bill black in breeding plumage, otherwise brown; *legs and feet bright orange*; eyes yellow to orange. In flight shows *pale blue forewing*, large green speculum with narrow white bar in front and white wing-linings; appears 'front-heavy' with long bill, long neck and short tail. **Female** and **first-winter** bird mottled light buffy brown, head paler but hindneck and eye-stripe dark; tail pale-edged; bill grey-brown with orange sides and base; legs and feet orange; eyes brown. Blue forewing as in male. **Partial eclipse male** female-like but rufous on flanks and belly, darker brown on head and with darker feather edges on breast and sides. **Sub-eclipse male** intermediate between eclipse and breeding plumages with a *whitish facial crescent* (often mottled) on dark head. Gregarious, sometimes in large flocks. Swims with rear end raised and head down, bill tip almost touching the water. **Call** of male a gruff *took-took*; female quacks. **Range/status**: Palearctic migrant, late Oct.–early April, locally common on lakes in Rift Valley and adjacent highlands. Uncommon elsewhere.

SOUTHERN POCHARD *Netta erythrophthalma brunnea*
Plate 16 and fig. opp. Plate 15

Length 19–20″. A large *dark* diving duck with a steep forehead. **Male** blackish below with chestnut flanks, blackish brown above, dark maroon-brown on face and neck. In flight looks black and long-necked, with *broad white band along entire length of the flight feathers*. Bill long, *bluish grey* with black nail; legs and feet dark grey; eyes bright red. **Female** dark brown with unique head pattern: *whitish patch near base of bill and white crescent from behind eye to sides of neck*; under tail-coverts also white. Flight pattern, bill and feet as in male; eyes red-brown. **Juvenile** light brown, darker on back, pale buff on bill base and throat; under tail-coverts whitish. Young male much darker than female on neck and underparts. Often in compact flocks on open water. Dives frequently, but also feeds like dabbling duck. Patters across water when taking wing. See female Maccoa and Ferruginous Ducks. **Call** a low nasal *prerr-prerr* from male in flight; female has a descending nasal *krrrrow*. **Range**: Rift Valley and w. Kenyan highlands up to 3000 m; generally scarce elsewhere and although some breed in cent. Kenya and n. Tanzania, mainly a non-breeding visitor with peak numbers Nov.–Feb.

COMMON POCHARD *Aythya ferina*   Plate 16

Length 17–19″. A stocky, open-water diving duck with steep forehead and relatively long bill. **Male** distinctive with *very pale grey body* (almost white in bright sunlight), *rich chestnut head* and neck, and *black breast and rear end*. Bill with wide pale grey band between black tip and darker grey base; eyes orange-yellow or red; legs and feet grey. In flight shows broad *pale grey stripe along the flight feathers*, darker grey forewing and whitish wing-linings. **Female** brown on head, neck and breast with diffuse pale greyish buff or whitish areas at base of bill and on sides of head, and a pale postocular line; back dark grey-brown, sides and flanks paler and greyer. Bill has narrow pale grey subterminal band behind broad black tip; eyes brown. Young birds in early winter may show remnants of brown juvenile plumage. **Call** of female a growling *krrr*; male usually silent. **Range/status:** Rare palearctic migrant, Dec.–March; 6 Kenyan records (Kisumu, Ol Bolossat, Lake Turkana), 1 in Arusha NP.

FERRUGINOUS DUCK or WHITE-EYED POCHARD *Aythya nyroca* **Plate 16**
Length 15–16″. A *dark* diving duck, smaller than Southern Pochard with which it may associate. Rests higher in water than that species, tail angled upward. **Male in breeding plumage** dark chestnut with blackish brown back, at distance appearing black except for *white under tail-coverts, white eyes* and black-tipped grey bill with obscure pale grey band. Head more rounded than in Southern Pochard, with steeper forehead and shorter bill. **Female** duller and browner, with *brown eyes.* **First-winter** bird resembles female but white under tail-coverts barred with brown; eyes grey in young male. In flight, both sexes show broad whitish stripe along flight feathers and white belly. (Dark female Tufted Duck also shows white under tail-coverts, but has shorter bill, different head shape, and *usually* yellow eyes.) **Call** of female a harsh *gaaa.* **Range/status:** Scarce palearctic migrant, Oct.–March. Kenyan records at lakes Naivasha and Nakuru, Ol Bolossat, Endebess, Marsabit, Thika and Nairobi.

TUFTED DUCK *Aythya fuligula* **Plate 16**

Length 16–18″. A diving duck with steep rounded forehead and tuft or bulge at rear of crown. **Male in breeding plumage** *black with white sides, flanks and belly, and long drooping crest at back of head.* Bill blue-grey with narrow whitish subterminal band; eyes yellow; legs and feet grey. In flight, contrasting black-and-white pattern includes broad white stripe on secondaries shading to grey on primaries; much white on underside of wings. **Female** dull dark brown with *short crest or tuft on hindcrown.* Some birds show whitish areas on lores and/or white under tail-coverts (cf. Ferruginous Duck). Wing pattern as in male. Eyes yellow, occasionally brown. **First-winter male** browner on back, greyer on sides than adult, with shorter crest. Full adult plumage usually not acquired prior to spring departure; eyes brown at first, becoming yellowish. Solitary or in small groups on open water. See Ferruginous Duck. **Call** of female a short low growl when flushed. Usually silent. **Range/status:** Scarce palearctic migrant, Nov.–March, on Turkana and other lakes at medium to high elevations in cent. and w. Kenyan highlands. Rare wanderer south to Arusha NP and Ngorongoro Crater.

MACCOA DUCK *Oxyura maccoa* **Plate 16**

Length 19–20″. Squat and thick-necked, with a broad bill. Swims low in water, often with the stiff tail angled upward. **Breeding male** rich chestnut with *black head* and bright *cobalt-blue bill*; centre of belly and under tail-coverts whitish. Wings uniformly dark above. **Eclipse male**, **adult female** and **juvenile** dark brown with broad whitish line below eyes; lower face and throat also whitish; bill dull grey. Male's head more blackish. Usually in pairs or small groups on alkaline or freshwater lakes. When alarmed the body largely submerges. Dives frequently. Reluctant to take wing, but flies rapidly and low after pattering across water. **Calls** of male include guttural croaks and whistles, and a vibrating *prrr* when displaying. Female makes grunting notes. **Range:** Local in Kenyan Rift Valley and cent. and w. highlands. In n. Tanzania regular in Arusha NP and in the Crater Highlands (where common at times).

SECRETARY BIRD, SAGITTARIIDAE
One species, confined to Africa, distantly related to other Falconiformes. Long-legged, and adapted to a pedestrian mode of life; bill raptorial for dispatching living prey, but the toes are weak, with short and rather blunt claws.

SECRETARY BIRD *Sagittarius serpentarius* **Plate 30**

Length 49–59 ″. A large bird, usually in pairs, hunting on foot with measured gait in open grassland. *Long-projecting central tail feathers and drooping head plumes* conspicuous, as are the long legs. Plumage mainly grey, with *crest, belly, leg and flight feathers and two broad tail bands* black. Bare orbital skin orange. **Juvenile** similar but duller. When soaring overhead the black remiges, projecting long tarsi and tail are diagnostic. **Call** a croaking *korr-orr-orr* in display, and mewing notes at roost.
Range: Widespread in s. Kenya and n. Tanzania, mainly in areas of moderate rainfall.

VULTURES, EAGLES, HAWKS, KITES, AND ALLIES, ACCIPITRIDAE

Strong-flying, mainly diurnal, birds of prey, typically with broad, rounded wings, short strong tarsi, and raptorial bill and toes. Females are larger than males, and may differ in appearance. Excepting a few unique forms (e.g. Osprey, Cuckoo-Hawk, Honey Buzzard, Bateleur and Bat Hawk), the majority can be grouped as follows. **VULTURES**: Mostly large, open-country carrion feeders that soar for extended periods on long wings, most taking flight as late morning thermals develop. Feathering is usually reduced or absent on face and neck, the tarsi unfeathered and the toes adapted to walking. Useful identification criteria are head, neck and bill colours, and, in flight, overall shape and ventral pattern. *AQUILA* **EAGLES**: Large dark open-country birds with long broad wings, rather short tails, powerful bills and feathered tarsi. Adults quite uniform in colour; immatures paler with patterned rump and wings. Identification relies heavily on flight silhouette and wing pattern. **SNAKE EAGLES**: Medium-sized to large raptors, large-headed and thick-necked, with long loose feathering on occiput or nape, prominent yellow eyes (in adults) and long bare tarsi. They feed mainly on snakes. **HAWK-EAGLES and ALLIES**: Powerful raptors of wooded country, preying largely on mammals and birds. Tarsi feathered and adults pale-eyed, with strongly patterned underparts and barred tail; immatures may be markedly different. **BUZZARDS (*Buteo*)**: Sluggish, rodent-eating raptors of wooded or open country, thickset with short square or rounded tail, bare yellow tarsi, and brown eyes. They soar with wings held in a shallow V, and the tail fanned. Pattern of tail, underparts, and underside of wings are important in identification. **SPARROWHAWKS, GOSHAWKS, CHANTING GOSHAWKS**: Slender, bird-eating hawks with short, rounded wings, rather long tail, small sharp bill, and long bare tarsi. Chanting goshawks (*Melierax*) are longer-winged than accipiters, less dashing in pursuit of prey, flying with rather languid wingbeats. Gabar Goshawk (*Micronisus*) resembles *Accipiter* in proportions, habits and hunting behaviour, but is like *Melierax* in colour, voice and habitat preference. Identification depends partly on plumage pattern and coloration. **HARRIERS**: Slim-bodied and long-winged, with long tail and long bare tarsi; the small head has an owl-like facial disc. They fly low over open country, tilting lightly from side to side, wings typically held in a shallow V, seeking rodents and birds. Identification based on coloration and on rump, tail and dorsal wing patterns. **KITES**: A diverse group of graceful, buoyant fliers; relatively weak-footed, small-billed, and with moderately to strongly forked tail. They feed on insects, small vertebrates and carrion.

OSPREY *Pandion h. haliaetus*   Plates 34, 39

Length 22–23″. A large long-winged raptor associated with water. Dark brown above and white below with a narrow breast band of dusky streaks; *head white with broad dark line through* eyes; tail barred; feet grey. Flight outline distinctive, *well-angled, often bowed wings that are white below with large black carpal patches, black primary tips* and narrowly barred flight feathers. Wingbeats slow and loose. At a distance may suggest a large gull. Hovers, and catches fish by plunging feet-first. **Call** an occasional melodious *chewk-chewk-chewk*. **Range/status**: Uncommon palearctic migrant on lakes, rivers and along coast, mainly Oct.–March; a few remain year-round.

AFRICAN CUCKOO-HAWK *Aviceda cuculoides verreauxii*   Plates 35, 43

Length 16″. An uncommon woodland or forest raptor with *short tarsi* and *short occipital crest*. Retiring, often in dense cover. Shape and colour pattern suggest a large cuckoo. Slim; *long wings extend nearly to tip of the long tail*. **Male** dark brownish grey above, *greyer on throat and upper breast; lower breast, belly and sides white with chestnut barring*; blackish tail has 3 broad grey bands. In flight shows dense chestnut-barred wing-linings. Cere greenish yellow; eyes dark brown; tarsi yellow. **Female** browner above, buffier below, with broader, paler barring, and *yellow eyes*. **Juvenile** dark brown above with short white superciliary stripes; underparts and wing-linings white with dark spots; eyes grey or brown. Flight graceful, somewhat kite-like; soars in display. Feeds on insects and lizards, mostly caught on the ground. **Calls** include a single explosive *tohew*; near nest, a whistled *choo-titti-too* from perch. Soaring birds utter a mewing *peeoo*. **Range**: Has bred in Kenyan highlands (twice) and the southeast. Known mainly in cent. and s. Kenya including coastal lowlands (most records May–Nov.) Scarce in n. Tanzania (Usambara Mts, Arusha and Serengeti NPs).

EURASIAN HONEY BUZZARD *Pernis apivorus*   Plates 33, 39, 44

Length 20–24″. Body slimmer, *head smaller* than in buteonine buzzards, and *lores feathered. Soars with the long wings held flat and straight, head protruding noticeably, ample tail well fanned; glides with distal half of wing somewhat depressed. **Adult** *heavily barred below with streaked throat.* Underside of wings whitish with *bold barring and prominent black carpal patches;* tail pattern diagnostic: *2 dark bars near base, a broader one at tip.* Typically grey-brown above; some birds uniform dark brown on body and wing-linings, others rufous or much paler and lightly marked below. Cere dark grey; large *eyes bright yellow or orange* (brown in *Buteo* spp.); bare tarsi yellow. Dark-eyed **juvenile** variable, but *small head* distinctive. Usually dark brown above, but some birds have light-mottled wing-coverts. Underparts blackish or dull rufous, or white with dark streaks and a *black eye patch on all-white head.* Tail pattern less distinct than adult's, with 4 evenly spaced bars and underside of flight feathers darker, the barring less prominent; shows *pale primary patch and often white upper tail-coverts.* Secretive and sluggish; perches in or below canopy. Feeds on ground on insects. Plaintive whistling *kee-er* **call** rarely heard in Africa. **Range/status**: Uncommon palearctic migrant, Oct.–April, mainly in Kenyan highlands e. of Rift Valley and on coast.

BAT HAWK *Macheiramphus alcinus anderssoni*   Plates 37, 44

Length 18″. An uncommon dark *crepuscular* hawk with *long pointed wings, rather long tail, crested head and small bill.* Cruises with glides and slow wingbeats, suggesting a dark broad-winged falcon. Blackish brown, with indistinctly barred tail, white eyelids (especially upper); throat dark or whitish with dark central streak; eyes yellow; tarsi whitish. **Juvenile** has white or whitish belly. Rests by day in tree, emerging at dusk to hunt small bats and birds. **Call** a high-pitched falcon-like *keerik-keerik-keerik.* **Range**: Local in higher-rainfall areas below 2000 m. Regular at Lake Baringo, Kakamega, Taveta and several coastal sites from Shimoni north to Malindi. Rare in n. Tanzania.

✓ **BLACK-SHOULDERED KITE** *Elanus c. caeruleus*   Plates 37, 43

Length 12–14″. A small, pale grey-and-white hawk with relatively large head and short tail; wings broad-based but long and pointed, with *large black 'shoulder' patches.* **Adult** grey above with white face and underparts; some black around the rather large orange or red eyes; outer primaries contrastingly black beneath. Cere and feet yellow. **Juvenile** *tinged tawny on neck and breast;* scapulars and wing-coverts browner, with white edging; the black 'shoulders' white-spotted. Usually seen on wires or trees in open grassy or cultivated country. *Glides on raised angled wings; hovers persistently.* **Call** a weak shrill whistle, *eet-eet-eet-eet. . .,* and short chipping notes. **Range**: Widespread in areas of moderate rainfall. Breeds regularly in and around Nairobi NP.

AFRICAN SWALLOW-TAILED or SCISSOR-TAILED KITE *Chelictinia riocourii*
Plates 37, 43

Length 12″. *Graceful and tern-like,* with a *deeply forked tail.* Plain pure pale grey above and white below, the wings with a narrow black bar along edge of carpal area below. When perched, tail feathers project well beyond wing tips. Tarsi short and yellow; cere grey; eyes red. **Juvenile** shorter tailed; back and wing feathers edged with rufous. Gregarious, roosting and breeding colonially; sometimes flying alone. Soars, hovers and hangs montionless against the wind. **Calls** include a rasping chatter and a thin mewing on breeding grounds. **Range/status**: Mainly a non-breeding visitor from n. tropics, Nov.–March. Regularly reaches cent. and sometimes se. Kenya; occasional influxes. Breeds locally near Lake Turkana; a few pairs also resident in Longonot/Suswa area of cent. Rift Valley.

BLACK KITE *Milvus migrans* Plates 34, 43, 44 V

Length 20–24". An often common brown raptor whose *shallowly forked tail is frequently spread and twisted in slow buoyant flight.* Long narrow wings usually held flat and angled at wrist. **Adult** of *M. m. parasitus* warm brown with *yellow bill* and *dark brown eyes*; underside of flight feathers and tail faintly barred. **Juvenile** buffier, paler and distinctly streaked below; *bill black.* **Adult** *M. m. migrans* has greyer, black-streaked head/neck and a more prominent buff bar on upper wing-coverts; *black bill* contrasts with yellow cere; eyes brown, grey, pale yellow or ivory. Paler **juvenile** streaked white on head and underparts; pale area at base of primaries shows in flight. Some apparent immature *migrans* are pale-headed, whitish-faced, with black streak or patch through eyes; bill and eyes as in adult. *M. m. aegyptius* like *migrans* but browner on head and neck, more rufous below and on the distinctly barred tail; adult *yellow-billed.* Opportunistic feeder, often around human habitation. (Common Buzzard has broader wings and lacks tail fork; Grasshopper Buzzard shows large rufous wing patches in flight. African Marsh Harrier has longer, square-tipped tail.) Flight **call** a quavering, loud, slow whistle, *kiiiiiiiiiii-errrrrrrr,* second part lower. From perch, a plaintive, descending *wheeeeeeeeuu;* when excited, *keeeeee-kik-kik-kik-kik.* **Range:** Widespread. *M. m. parasitus* present all months, breeds Sept.–March; palearctic *M. m. migrans,* mainly in cent. Kenya, Oct.–March; Red Sea race *aegyptius,* present at same time, said to be more coastal.

LAMMERGEIER *Gypaetus barbatus meridionalis* Plates 31, 32 V

Length 43". A very large, scarce vulture of mountains and high cliffs. Soars over slopes with *wings held slightly below horizontal.* Distinctive, with *long, pointed, dark wings, long wedge-shaped tail,* conspicuous *white head with black mask with bristly 'beard.'* Underparts whitish or pale buff, often rusty on head and neck. **Juvenile** blackish on head and neck, pale brown below. **Immature** has whitish head, rufous-brown underparts. (Dark young Egyptian Vulture is much smaller, shorter-tailed, and soars on flat, straight wings.) **Call,** at nest, a shrill *cheek-a-cheek-a-cheek;* in aerial display, a whistling *fweeee.* **Range:** Local on Mt Elgon, Cheranganis, Loldaiga Hills, Mt Kenya, Kilimanjaro and Mt Meru; occasional near Gol Mts (Serengeti) and Ngorongoro Crater. Formerly at Hell's Gate.

EGYPTIAN VULTURE *Neophron p. percnopterus* Plates 31, 32

Length 23–28". Small and *slender-billed* with rather narrow wings and a *wedge-shaped tail.* Slim and graceful in flight, soaring with wings straight and flat. **Adult** *white or pale buff with black flight feathers and bare orange-yellow face.* **Juvenile** dark brown with grey facial skin. Body of **immature** becomes paler with each moult; face orange-yellow by second year. Usually silent. **Range:** Widespread below 2000 m in open country with rocky crags, especially in Kenyan Rift Valley south of Naivasha, and in n. Tanzania from Arusha District west to the Serengeti Plains.

HOODED VULTURE *Necrosyrtes monachus pileatus* Plates 31, 32 V

Length 26–30". A *small dark brown* vulture with *slender bill* and a *short tail.* **Adult** has *largely bare pink head and neck, the hindcrown covered with buffy white down.* White tibial feathers noticeable in flight, suggesting miniature Lappet-faced Vulture, but shows no discrete white stripe near leading edge of wing (although remex bases broadly pale below) and body all dark; feet pale blue. **Juvenile** has bare whitish face and throat (can flush red with excitement), brown down on hindcrown, brown tarsi, and dark tibial feathers; underside of wings dark. Gregarious where common. (Overhead, Lappet-faced Vulture shows white stripe near leading edge of wing and has larger white tibial patches.) Essentially silent. **Range:** Widespread but declining. Still present in most national parks and game reserves. Now around towns and villages only in w. Kenya and lower Tana River area.

295

✔ **AFRICAN WHITE-BACKED VULTURE** *Gyps africanus* **Plates 31, 32**

Length 35–39″. The common large vulture of most southern national parks and game reserves. *White lower back and rump* of adult conspicuous as bird takes wing. Body brown, becoming paler and buffier with age; old birds almost white. Underparts light brown with faint pale shaft-streaks; unfeathered head and neck blackish with whitish ruff. *Bill heavy and blackish, cere grey; eyes dark brown;* feet dark grey. In flight shows *wholly pale wing-linings and black flight feathers.* **Juvenile** darker, the body (including back), wing-coverts and ruff slate-grey with white streaks; head and neck felted with white down; skin of face and neck greenish. **Immature** becomes plainer and paler with age, and back whitens after about fourth year. Flying young birds appear largely dark brown beneath, the wing-linings with *narrow white line near leading edge.* Gregarious at carrion and at roosts in tall trees. **Call**, chatters and squeals at carcasses and roosts. (Slightly larger Rüppell's Griffon has longer neck, no white on back, and wings are dark beneath with narrow white lines near leading edge. Older birds have 'scaly' plumage, pale eyes and bill.) **Range**: Widespread in open or lightly wooded areas with large mammals, mainly below 2300 m. Absent from Lake Victoria basin and coast south of Malindi.

✔ **RÜPPELL'S GRIFFON VULTURE** *Gyps r. rueppellii* **Plates 31, 32**

Length 38–42″. Proportioned much like the preceding species, but **adult** has *long, heavy, yellowish horn bill, 'scaly' whitish edges on body feathers and upper wing-coverts, yellow or amber eyes,* and no white on back. Underparts whitish, somewhat mottled; head and long blackish neck bare except for sparse whitish down. Cere, facial skin and feet grey. In flight, shows *narrow white stripe near front edge of wing-linings, and more diffuse pale lines just behind.* **Juvenile** and **early immature** plumages tawny fulvous, plain above and broadly pale-streaked below; bill dark grey; eyes brown; *down on head and neck also brown* (whitish in young White-backed). In flight, younger birds with a single white stripe on wing-linings not safely distinguishable from White-backed. Full adult plumage reportedly takes 6–7 years to acquire. **Call** a querulous shriek when feeding, plus hisses and grunts. **Range**: Widespread in dry open country within flight range of nesting/roosting cliffs. The most numerous large vulture in n. Kenya, and present in all parks and reserves. Breeds at Mt Nyiru, Marsabit, Ololokwe, Hell's Gate, near Magadi, and Gol Mts. (e. Serengeti).

✔ **LAPPET-FACED or NUBIAN VULTURE** *Torgos t. tracheliotos* **Plates 31, 32**

Length 39–45″. Similar in soaring outline to Rüppell's Griffon, but with *more wedge-shaped tail.* **Adult** blackish brown with *white-streaked underparts.* Head and back of neck bare and pink (red when excited), and with *fleshy lappets on sides of face.* Large bill ivory or pale horn; cere greyish; eyes dark brown; feet blue-grey. In flight shows *prominent white leg feathering,* and wings are dark beneath *with narrow white stripe near leading edge.* **Juvenile** blackish, without white tibial patches; bare head and neck dull pink. Early **immature** has brownish bill, and may show some white on back and upper wing-coverts, this gradually disappearing; tibial feathers take 5–6 years to become wholly white. Usually silent. Roosts and nests in trees on open plains. See Hooded Vulture (which can appear similar in flight if size not evident). **Range**: Widespread on open plains with large herbivore populations. In all game parks, but most numerous in Mara GR and Serengeti NP.

✔ **WHITE-HEADED VULTURE** *Trigonoceps occipitalis* **Plates 31, 32**

Length 31–33″. A uniquely patterned vulture with *colourful face and bill,* a peaked, somewhat triangular white head, white crop patch, belly and tibial feathers, and, in female, largely white inner secondaries (these dark grey or blackish in male); black ruff on hindneck. Bare face pink, turning red in excitement; *bill bright pink with blackish tip;* cere and mandible base pale blue; eyes dark yellow; feet pale pink. **Juvenile** has brown crown and lacks white on secondaries and belly; distinguished in flight by white line separating wing-linings and flight feathers; bill pale pink. **Immature**

intermediate between juv. and adult. Normally silent. Begins foraging early in day, and often arrives first at carcasses. Kills small mammals and young birds. Roosts and nests in trees. **Range**: Widespread (but uncommon) in open and lightly wooded country with large mammals. Present in most game parks; most frequent in Mara GR, Tsavo and Serengeti NPs.

SHORT-TOED SNAKE EAGLE   *Circaetus gallicus*   Plates 34, 40

Length 24–27″. A *pale* vagrant eagle with *large rounded head and prominent yellow eyes*. Tarsi bare. **Adult** *C. g. gallicus* usually *grey-brown above, head and breast mottled with paler brown and rest of underparts white with sparse brown or chestnut spots and mottling*. Some birds darker above and on breast; others have whitish head and underparts, ventral spotting nearly obsolete. Wings mainly white below with narrow dark rear edges and tips, and usually barred remiges; tail grey with 3 dark bars. **Juvenile** resembles adult. Darker *C. g. beaudouini* has 3–4 indistinct tail bars, grey-brown upper breast, white *lower breast and belly narrowly barred with brown*. **Juvenile** streaked whitish on head but otherwise largely rufous-brown, the flanks, crissum and tail barred. **Immature** (second year) has blotched underparts, later largely whitish. (Imm./subad. Black-chested Snake Eagle distinguished by absence of dark markings on wing-linings, always present in Short-toed.) Silent in Africa. Frequently hovers. **Status**: Palearctic *C. g. gallicus* collected once at Lake Turkana (Oct. 1988). Kenyan reports of *beaudouini* unsubstantiated.

BLACK-CHESTED SNAKE EAGLE   *Circaetus pectoralis*   Plates 34, 40

Length 25–27″. An uncommon open-country eagle with long broad wings and a large rounded head. **Adult** *blackish brown on upperparts, head and breast; white below. Eyes large, bright yellow; bare tarsi whitish.* In overhead flight appears white with black head and breast, barred remiges, and 3 broad black bands on tail. (Martial Eagle has same general pattern but is larger, broader-winged, with dark wing-linings, darker remiges, dark-spotted underparts; also has feathered tarsi and short crest.) **Juvenile** paler, brown above, *rufous on face and underparts*; underside of wing and tail plainer than in adult; *eyes yellow*. **Immature** may have whitish face and throat, dark breast band, and dark blotching on white belly similar to *C. gallicus*, but no dark markings on wing-linings. Display **calls** a musical *weeu-weeu* and a ringing *kwo-kwo-kwo* recalling Fish Eagle. Frequently hovers with slowly beating wings. Preys largely on snakes. **Range**: Widespread on lightly wooded plains and in more open country at all elevations.

BROWN SNAKE EAGLE   *Circaetus cinereus*   Plates 34, 40, 44

Length 26–28″. Plain brown with a rounded, *owl-like head, yellow eyes and long bare whitish tarsi*. Perches upright on treetops. In flight, *silvery flight feathers contrast below with dark brown wing-linings*; entire wing dark brown above; tail shows 3 often inconspicuous narrow bands. **Juvenile** paler, often with white mottling on nape and belly and/or white streaks on crown. Flies with slow deep wingbeats; rarely hovers; soars on long flat wings, mainly in display when it gives loud **call**, *kok-kok-kok-kaaw*. (Other all-brown eagles have feathered tarsi, darker flight feathers, unbarred tail and dark eyes; none has owl-like head. Juv. Bateleur is short-tailed and brown-eyed. Juv. Black-chested Snake Eagle is rufous below.) **Range**: Widespread at low to medium elevations with scattered tall trees, favouring areas with baobabs.

SOUTHERN BANDED SNAKE EAGLE   *Circaetus fasciolatus*   Plates 34, 40

Length 22–24″. A stocky *eastern forest eagle, brownish on head and breast; rest of underparts narrowly barred brown and white. Narrowly white-tipped tail has 4 broad black bands alternating with 3 equal greyish bands above*; and in flight from below shows 2–3 white bands, plus the white tip. Wings whitish beneath, with dark barring throughout. Eyes, cere and feet yellow. **Juvenile** paler, buffy white below, dark-streaked on throat; crown and nape brown with white streaks; flanks and tibial feathers tawny-barred; dark tail bands (except subterminal one) narrower than in

adult. Some **immatures** almost whitish on the head, and show suggestion of adult pattern below. Perches quietly in leafy cover, or at times exposed on large branch. Flies with quick, shallow wingbeats; occasionally soars. **Call**, from perch, a high-pitched rapid *ko-ko-ko-ko-kaah* or *k-k-k-k-kaw-aw*, and a sonorous *kowaa*. **Range**: Coastal Kenya, inland along lower Tana River; once near Voi. Locally common in East Usambara Mts.

BANDED SNAKE EAGLE   *Circaetus cinerascens*   Plates 34, 40

Length 22–24″. A scarce bird of riverine woods and small forest patch-es, mainly western. **Adult** differs from preceding species in its *shorter tail with a single broad white band*, and *brown of the breast extends to flanks and belly*; white barring only on lower belly and underside of tail. Wings whitish below, the flight feathers prominently barred but coverts plain. Cere and bill base orange-yellow; eyes pale creamy yellow; feet yellow. **Juvenile** pale brown above with buff feather edges; crown whitish with dark streaks; *underparts greyish white or buffy white, darker buff on breast and with some brown on belly and leg feathers*. Tail as in adult. Bill and eyes brown; *cere yellow; feet whitish*. **Immature** paler eyed and streaked below; later brown with barred flanks and belly. Inconspicuous; typically perches in large tree near river or swamp. **Call**, in circling aerial display, a loud staccato *kok-kok-kok-kok-ko-ko*, dropping in pitch. From perch gives a repeated mournful *ko-aaagh*. **Range**: Local in w. Kenya and on rivers at e. edge of cent. highlands south to Kibwezi. Rare in n. Tanzania. No East African breeding record.

✔ BATELEUR   *Terathopius ecaudatus*   Plates 32, 34, 40

Length 22–28″. *Glides continuously over open country, its wings raised in marked 'V,' canting from side to side.* Unique flight silhouette unmis-takable: *extremely short tail* and *long, broad-based wings with curved rear edge narrowing to pointed tip.* Cowled head large and owl-like with erectile feathers apparent on perched bird. Head and much of body black, usually with *chestnut tail and back, and pale grey upper wing-coverts* ; female also has grey secondaries, her wings white below but black confined to tips and narrow trailing edges; male's black remiges contrast below with white wing-linings. *Cere, bare facial skin, and feet bright red.* In **light morph**, usu-ally in more arid regions, back and tail vary from cream to pale brown. **Juvenile** brown, streaked with darker brown below; *tail blackish brown, longer than adult's.* Cere and facial skin greenish blue-grey; eyes dark brown; feet grey. **Immature** blackish with white mottling on underside of wings. Facial skin yellowish; feet pinkish. **Call**, from perch, a soft, *ko-ko-ko-ko-koaaagh*, recalling Banded Snake Eagle; other calls near nest. **Range**: Widespread in dry bush and grassland.

AFRICAN HARRIER HAWK or GYMNOGENE   *Polyboroides t. typus*
Plates 34, 35, 43

Length 24–26″. An unusual large grey woodland or forest hawk with a *small head* (but *long nape feathers*), *long black tail with a single broad white band*, and long wide wings broadly tipped black; underparts fine-ly barred black and white. Eyes dark brown; *cere and bare face yellow*, the latter flushing pink or red-orange in excitement. *Yellow tarsi excep-tionally long.* In flight, wings appear grey with broad black tips and trail-ing edges. **Juvenile** uniformly dark brown above and below; primaries tinged whitish at base, more or less barred; tail with 4 narrow darker brown bands. Face dark grey; cere and bill greenish yellow, tipped black; eyes yellowish brown. **Immatures** vary from bright gingery or tawny brown to chocolate or blackish above, pale buff or whitish on forehead/forecrown, and streaked with pale buff below. Pale tawny flanks, leg feathers and crissum may be brown-barred; tail as in juv. Some have few dark markings; all underparts pale tawny buff. Best identified by overall proportions and small head. **Call**, from perch, a tremulous whistled *su-ee-oo* or *su-eeeeeee*. In flight a thin *peeeeeeeee*, and a plaintive *ur-eet ur-eet . . .* Often soars. Probes tree cavities with bill and feet for insects and bird nests, clinging to trunk with wings. Often robs weaver nests. **Range**: Widespread (but uncommon) in higher-rainfall areas and along wooded water-courses in drier country.

PALLID HARRIER *Circus macrourus*   Plates 36, 43 ✓

Length 16–19″. Slim, narrow-winged and long-tailed. **Male** *pale grey above* with *small black wedge at wing tips,* the pattern quite gull-like. **Female** brown above, with *white bar across upper tail-coverts* and *strongly barred tail*; underparts streaked buffy brown; flight feathers and tail pale grey below with dark barring. At close range dark cheek contrasts sharply with obvious pale collar. Very similar to female Montagu's, but wing pattern distinctive, with the *secondaries unbarred above, and largely dark below*. **Juvenile** resembles female but unstreaked pale rufous-buff below; underside of secondaries dark grey. Generally silent. Falcon-like when soaring. Hunts on grassy plains, perching on ground or low posts. (Female and young Montagu's harriers similar to Pallid, but have reduced pale collar and more whitish face, are darker rufous and more streaked below.) **Range/status**: Palearctic migrant, mainly Oct.–early April. Outnumbered in highlands by Montagu's Harrier, but often the more numerous species in se. Kenya and on the Masai Steppe.

MONTAGU'S HARRIER *Circus pygargus*   Plates 36 43

Length 17–18.5″. Another migrant harrier of grassland and farming country, similar to Pallid Harrier but **male** has *narrow black bar across secondaries and much more black in wing tips*. Head to upper breast dark grey; whitish elsewhere below with rufous streaks on flanks. Wings pale beneath except for black primaries and 2 black bands on secondaries. **Female** like Pallid, but has only indistinct pale collar behind black facial mark, and distinguished in flight by *broad black bands on undersides of secondaries plus distinct black trailing edge*. Rare **dark morph** charcoal-grey or sooty black in male, with or without silvery areas at base of primaries and tail, chocolate-brown in female with greyish white primary bases (plain, barred or mottled); tail boldly banded in female, almost plain in male. **Juvenile** like Pallid, but deep rufous or chestnut below, and lacks pale collar. **First-year male** has greyish head and upperparts and white belly combined with wing/tail pattern of adult female. Silent. Solitary or in loose groups; roosts communally, sometimes with Pallid Harrier. **Range/status**: Palearctic migrant, mainly Oct.–early April. Locally common in grassland and farmland, especially in higher plateau country at 1500 to 2500 m, in Uasin Gishu and Laikipia districts, Rift Valley highlands, Mara GR, Serengeti/Ngorongoro and Arusha area.

AFRICAN MARSH HARRIER *Circus ranivorus*   Plates 36, 43 ✓

Length 18–20″. An uncommon *brown* hawk, usually near highland marshes or other wetlands. Smaller and more lightly built than Eurasian Marsh Harrier. Both sexes have *whitish leading wing edges. Pale brown with dark streaking below, more rufous on belly and rump; tail narrowly grey-banded above and below; primaries darker than coverts above,* and undersides of flight feathers prominently barred. Rare **dark morph** uniform deep brown, lacks pale markings, shows some rufous on breast and wing-coverts, and tail bands are narrower (absent in dark-morph Eur. Marsh Harrier). **Juvenile** plainer and darker above than adult; dark brown below with *variable pale breast band*; nape and chin usually whitish, but crown dark. **Call** a high-pitched *fee-uu* in display. Alarm call *kek-kek-kek-kek*. **Range**: Local and uncommon, mainly in cent. Kenyan highlands. Has bred on w. Kilimanjaro.

EURASIAN MARSH HARRIER *Circus a. aeruginosus*   Plates 36, 43, 44

Length 19–22″. *More heavily built and broader-winged than other harriers.* Typical **male** has dark brown back and wing-coverts, black outer primaries that contrast sharply with *pale grey inner flight feathers and tail; forewing often cream*; head and underparts rufous-buff with dark streaks; black-tipped flight feathers pale grey beneath. Rare **dark morph** *blackish above with silvery grey tail; wings show broad white band on bases of remiges* below. Normal **female** *dark brown with plain brown tail; crown, throat and front edge of wings usually cream; variable yellowish breast patch*; wings all dark beneath, the primary bases somewhat paler. **Dark-morph** female *brown with pale cream nape patch* and some white or tawny at base of primaries below.

Juvenile resembles normal female but darker, with pale buff cap and throat. Generally silent. Hunting flight less buoyant and often higher than that of other harriers. **Range /status**: Palearctic migrant, Oct.–April. Mainly in w. and cent. Kenya and n. Tanzania in moist grassland and cultivation below 2500 m.

GABAR GOSHAWK *Micronisus gabar aequatorius*   Plates 33, 36, 42, 44

Length 11–14″. A *small* accipitrine hawk, usually in rather dry woodland and thorn-bush. Typical grey **adult** shows *broad white band on upper tail-coverts*; *underparts barred grey and white below the grey breast*; tail broadly banded with blackish above, grey below. *Cere and tarsi red*; eyes dark red-brown. **Dark morph** *black except for grey banding on tail and flight feathers.* **Juvenile** browner above than any *Accipiter*, with *white upper tail-coverts*; underparts white with *brown-streaked throat and breast and brown barring on belly and flanks. Wings appear scaly with pale-edged upper coverts.* (Juv. E. Pale Chanting Goshawk is much larger, the breast less boldly streaked than in young Gabar, and only the greater and median coverts are pale-edged; usually shows whitish superciliaries lacking in Gabar. Ovambo and Little Sparrowhawks have white spots on upper tail surface. Rare dark-morph Ovambo has orange-yellow, not red, cere and tarsi. Shikra lacks white on upper tail-coverts.) **Call** differs from that of any small *Accipiter*: a reedy piping *kwew-he, kwew-he. . .*, or *kik-kik-kik-kik-kik*. **Range**: Widespread below 2000 m in low-rainfall areas.

DARK CHANTING GOSHAWK *Melierax m. metabates*   Plates 33, 36, 41

Length 17–22″. A large, grey, upright-perching hawk of western bush and savanna. Note the *pinkish red or coral-pink cere and similar long slender tarsi*. (Cere yellow in more eastern *M. poliopterus*.) **Adult** grey above and from head to breast, wing-coverts washed with brownish as is back; underparts and *upper and under tail-coverts narrowly barred grey and white*; primaries black; wings otherwise grey above and white below. Long tail has blackish central feathers, the others broadly grey-barred and white-tipped. **Juvenile** dull brown above with whitish superciliary stripes and *fully barred upper tail-coverts*; white-tipped brown tail broadly barred with darker brown. Underparts variable, sometimes much like young Eastern Pale Chanting Goshawk, or the whitish throat brown-streaked and sharply defined from plain or lightly mottled pale grey-brown breast band; most underparts and underside of flight feathers barred. Cere grey; eyes pale yellow; tarsi and toes yellowish olive. **Call** a melodious piping *whee-pee-pee-pee*, and a long high-pitched *kleee-yeu*. **Range**: Nw. Kenya from Lokichokio south to Kongelai, Kerio Valley and lakes Baringo and Bogoria; also Serengeti NP to s. and w. Mara GR, Aitong and Lemek.

EASTERN PALE CHANTING GOSHAWK *Melierax poliopterus*
Plates 33, 36, 41

Length 18–25″. A common dry-bush species, differing from Dark Chanting Goshawk in several features: *yellow cere, longer orange-red tarsi, less fully barred or plain white upper tail-coverts* and generally *paler grey* plumage, pure grey wing-coverts, less prominent tail barring, and *plain white under tail-coverts*. **Juvenile** resembles Dark Chanting, but tarsi longer, and some birds heavily dark-streaked on breast. Upper tail-covert barring can be fairly dark and heavy, but the bars always short and not reaching the feather edges, thus much more white visible than on Dark Chanting's completely barred coverts. Under tail-coverts have finer, fainter, more widely spaced barring than in Dark Chanting. Fresh greater wing-coverts (always?) white-tipped as in adult. **Calls** similar to those of Dark Chanting, but slightly lower-pitched. **Range**: North, east and south of the Kenyan highlands, mainly east of Rift Valley, but in the Rift around lakes Turkana, Magadi and Natron, and west of Rift only on dry e. Loita plains. Nowhere resident alongside Dark Chanting Goshawk.

AFRICAN GOSHAWK *Accipiter tachiro*   Plates 36, 42, 44
Length 15–18″. The commonest accipiter of more humid areas; in wooded habitats from forests to city suburbs. Unobtrusive except in frequent soaring display (not limited to

breeding season). Somewhat crepuscular. **Male** *dark slate, almost black, above; whitish below with fine rufous or chestnut barring,* grey face and white throat; tail has indistinct grey bars above, is narrowly white-tipped, and may show small white spots on central feathers; beneath, tail is grey-ish with brown bands which may be lacking on outer two feathers. Wings pale below, narrowly barred. *Bare parts yellow.* **Female** *much larger, browner above, more coarsely brown-barred below.* **Adult dark morph** *brownish black with grey tail bands.* **Juvenile** dark brown above (feathers at first rufous-edged) with white superciliary stripes; may show white spot on nape. *Buffy white below with dark central throat stripe and large dark brown drop-shaped spots; flanks broadly barred; tibial feathers closely barred or with chestnut spots.* Eyes brown; cere greenish grey or olive. (Juv. Cuckoo Hawk resembles young African Goshawk, but has long wings, shorter tarsi, and short occipital crest. See Ovambo Sparrowhawk.) **Call** a repeated sharp *krit* or *kwik* from perch or in circling flight. **Range:** *A. t. sparsimfasciatus* widespread from coast up to 3000 m. Smaller *A. t. pembaensis* only on Pemba Island.

SHIKRA or LITTLE BANDED GOSHAWK *Accipiter badius sphenurus*
Plates 33, 36, 42

Length 11–12″. An uncommon *pale* little hawk of bush and woodland. *Grey above and on sides of face; underparts finely barred with pale rufous or pinkish chestnut;* throat white; folded tail usually plain above, but shows 5 dark bands beneath. (Some females have dark terminal band on upper surface.) Wings whitish beneath, with faint barring and darker tips. Cere and tarsi yellow; eyes red (male) or orange (female). **Juvenile** brown above with buff-tipped wing-coverts; *dark line down centre of throat, breast heavily blotched and rest of underparts barred with russet-brown.* Dark tail bands narrower than adult's. **Immature** darker, with narrower, less blotchy ventral streaks. (Little Sparrowhawk and Gabar Goshawk have white upper tail-coverts; Gabar has red tarsi. See also scarce Ovambo, Eurasian, and Levant Sparrowhawks.) **Call** a rapid, high-pitched *kee-wick, kee-wick* (male), and *kee-uh* or a descending *keew-keew-keew* (female), plus an aggressive *kee-kee-kee-kee-kee.* Flight typically accipitrine; often soars. **Range:** Widespread at low to medium elevations.

LEVANT SPARROWHAWK *Accipiter brevipes*   Plates 33, 42
Length 13–15″. A rare migrant in dry open bush. Suggests a large Shikra, but *wings longer,* somewhat falcon-like, and flight less dashing than that of most accipiters; commonly soars and glides. Plain grey above with *darker cheeks than Shikra.* Closed tail plain above, but shows 5-6 narrow dark bars beneath. Eyes *dark red,* cere greenish yellow, tarsi yellow. **Male** dark blue-grey above with darker wing tips, white below with narrow chestnut barring heaviest on breast; *wings white beneath with sharply defined black tips.* **Female** grey-brown above, *heavily brown-barred below, and with prominent short streaks on throat;* wings lightly barred beneath. **Juvenile** brown, with white spot on hindneck, heavily spotted underparts, *black central throat stripe;* wings strongly barred beneath. **Call** like that of Shikra. **Status:** 6 records from Tsavo West and Meru NPs (Nov.-Dec.).

LITTLE SPARROWHAWK *Accipiter minullus*   Plates 36, 42

Length 9–11″. An uncommon, *small and rather short-tailed* hawk of wooded areas, including city suburbs. Flies fast with much twisting and turning; glides briefly above trees but seldom soars. **Adult** dark slate grey above with *white upper tail-coverts and 2 large white spots on upperside of closed tail* (appearing as broken white bars when feathers spread). Underparts white, finely barred with brown and washed with rufous on sides. In flight from below, shows narrowly barred remiges and pale tail with 3 broad dark bands. *Dark sides of head contrast with white throat.* Eyes yellow-orange; cere, tarsi and toes yellow. (Gabar Goshawk has red cere and tarsi. Other small sparrowhawks have dark upper tail-coverts.) **Juvenile** dark brown above with blackish crown, *usually a narrow band of white on upper tail-coverts.* Underparts with short, dark brown streaks composed of large circular or drop-shaped spots. *Buff-tipped, dark brown tail has 2 or 3 white spots* and 3 or 4 dark bands on upper surface (outer rectrices have

numerous narrow bars underneath). Eyes pale grey or brown, later turning yellow; cere greenish. **Call** a rapid reedy high-pitched *kek-kek-kek-kek-kek* (female) or a softer *kew-kew-kew-kew*. . . (male). **Range**: *A. m. minullus* in w. and cent. Kenya and parts of n. Tanzania; paler *tropicalis* in the coastal lowlands.

OVAMBO SPARROWHAWK *Accipiter ovampensis* Plates 36, 42, 44
Length 12–16″. A rare hawk with a *rather small head*; typically in dry woods or riparian groves. **Adult** of **light morph** plain slate-grey above and on face, chin and sides of throat, *finely barred with grey or brownish grey below*. Tail grey above, with *long-triangular white marks along the feather shafts*, between the broad blackish bands, showing as 3 or 4 white streaks below the often white coverts and white tip. (Similar species all lack these white shaft marks; Shikra is smaller, with *pinkish rufous* barring below; Gabar Goshawk has grey head/breast and *red* tarsi; Little Sparrowhawk has *yellow* cere and tarsi, unbanded tail with 2 *broad oval* white spots; African Goshawk has *whitish* throat, *brown* barring below, yellow eyes, and white *patches or bars* on central rectrices.) The exceptionally long, slim middle toe (35–45 mm) is a sure distinction from other accipiters if it can be seen. **Dark morph** *dull black except for white shaft marks on the dark grey tail*, and often some white on upper tail-coverts; dark barring on greyish underside of tail and remiges; wing-linings black. (Black Gabar Goshawk has boldly banded tail; larger black Great Sparrowhawk has no tail bands.) Eyes of both morphs orange-yellow to dark red; *cere, base of bill, tarsi and toes bright orange-yellow or yellowish orange.* **Juvenile** dark brown above; *broad white superciliary stripes and dark patch behind eyes; head and underparts whitish or dull rufous with narrow dark breast streaks and barred flanks*; cere and feet yellow. (Montane Rufous-breasted Sparrowhawk differs from rufous-morph juv. Ovambo in dark grey or brown head with no superciliaries.) **Call** a repeated high-pitched *wheet-wheet-wheet*. . .; also a shorter whistled *kee-kee, kee-kee,* and a slurred *QUEE-u*. **Range**: Mt Elgon and Trans-Nzoia south to Nakuru, Nairobi and Tsavo River (12 specimens). Reliably recorded in recent years only in nw. Mara GR and near Namanga. One n. Tanzanian record (North Pare Mts).

EURASIAN SPARROWHAWK *Accipiter n. nisus* Plates 33, 42
Length 11–15″. A scarce winter visitor in open country or woodland. Both sexes *plain* above, barred below and under wings; tail rather long with 4–5 dark bands. **Male** *slate grey above, with rufous cheeks/ear-coverts, and underparts barred rufous-brown*; eyes orange-yellow to orange-red; tarsi yellow or orange-yellow. **Female** *dark grey-brown above, with whitish throat and large pale superciliary stripes* separating dark crown from dark ear-coverts; nape often white; *barring of underparts dark brown*; eyes yellow or orange. **Juvenile** browner than adult female above, throat/upper breast streaked, rest of underparts with narrow ragged barring. (Rufous-breasted Sparrowhawk is plainer and brighter below, darker above. Shikra is smaller, paler grey, with pinkish ventral barring, grey cheeks, unbarred central rectrices, and red eyes. African Goshawk is similar in size to female *A. nisus*, but *slaty* above with dark cheeks. Levant Sparrowhawk has blue-grey cheeks, dark red eyes—thus different facial expression; its central rectrices plain above; male's wings white below with sharp black tips.) **Call** a chattering *kek-kek-kek-kek-kek*. **Range/status**: Palearctic migrant, Nov.–Feb., recorded from Lake Turkana and cent. Kenyan highlands to Tsavo West NP.

RUFOUS-BREASTED SPARROWHAWK *Accipiter r. rufiventris* Plates 33, 42

Length 13–16″. An unobtrusive hawk of *montane forest and woodland*. Slaty or blackish above, *cheeks and underparts largely rufous with little barring*; throat paler, under tail-coverts white; underside of tail and flight feathers boldly barred. Eyes, cere, and feet yellow. **Juvenile** dark brown above with rufous feather edges; *dark-streaked on breast* and *barred with pale rufous on belly and flanks*; tibial feathers plain dull rufous. Some brown-backed **immatures** nearly plain rufous below. **Call** a staccato *kek-kek-kek*, or *chek-chek-chek*, and a long mewing *weeeeeeuu*. **Range**: Local up to 3000 m in w. and cent. Kenyan highlands, Arusha NP, on Kilimanjaro, and in W. Usambaras.

GREAT or BLACK SPARROWHAWK *Accipiter m. melanoleucus*
Plates 33, 36, 41, 42, 44

Length 18–23″. A *large*, long-tailed hawk of wooded areas, including city suburbs. **Adult** black above and white below, *with mottled black patches on sides and flanks; dark sides of head contrast sharply with white throat;* tail broadly barred above, whitish below with several narrow bars and broader dark tip; wings white below with narrow dark barring on remiges. Except for black side patches, appears white in overhead flight. Eyes dark red to amber; cere and feet yellow. Rare **dark morph** all black (including unbarred tail) except for white throat. **Juveniles** variable. One morph dark brown above, *rufous or chestnut-buff below with short dark streaks on neck and breast;* pale morph white below with dark streaks (not drop-shaped spots as in juv. African Goshawk). Eyes dark at first, later greyish. **Call** a sharp *kyip,* and a loud ringing *ku-ku-ku-ku-ku.* Usually silent away from nest. **Range**: Along coast and in w. and cent. Kenyan highlands, up to 3000 m. Scarce in interior n. Tanzania.

GRASSHOPPER BUZZARD *Butastur rufipennis*   Plates 33, 35, 43

Length 16–17″. A slim insectivorous hawk of open bush country where it perches conspicuously on low trees; Shows *large rufous wing patches* in flight. **Adult** brown above, darker on head; *throat white with dark central streak;* underparts pale tawny with black shaft streaks; tail barred above and below; underside of wings whitish. Bare parts yellow except dark bill tip. **Juvenile** rufous-tinged above, tawny-buff on head and underparts with dark moustache marks; tail unmarked apart from dark terminal band; little yellow on bill; eyes brown. Solitary or in small loose parties. Attracted to fires. Takes insect prey on the ground. **Range/status**: Migrant from n. tropics, mainly Nov.–March. Regular in e. Kenya including places in coastal lowlands where some appear to winter. Scarce in n. Tanzania.

LIZARD BUZZARD *Kaupifalco m. monogrammicus*   Plates 33, 35, 43

Length 14–15″. *A small, thickset grey hawk with reddish cere, short red tarsi, dark central throat stripe, and white upper tail-coverts.* Head, back and breast plain grey; lower underparts *finely barred grey and white;* eyes dark red-brown with narrow red orbital ring. In flight, short blackish tail shows white tip and 1 or 2 broad white bands; wings white beneath with narrow grey barring. Browner **juvenile** has pale buff feather edges above, indistinct throat stripe, brown eyes and orange-yellow cere and tarsi. Perches prominently on branch, pole or wire, scanning the ground below. Flight low and undulating, series of quick wingbeats are followed by glides on partly closed wings; rapidly swoops up to perch; soars above trees during display. **Call**, when breeding, a clear somewhat gull-like whistle, *klioo-klu-klu-klu-klu,* repeated at intervals from perch; also a prolonged, high-pitched mewing *peeeeeoooooo,* and a low *kraa-kraa.* **Range**: Coastal lowlands (where fairly common). Local inland, mainly in high-rainfall areas below 1500 m. Scarce in n. Tanzania.

COMMON or STEPPE BUZZARD *Buteo buteo vulpinus*
Plate 33, 35, 39, 44

Length 18–20″. A migrant buzzard of woodland and open country. Variable; usually warm brown above, *more mottled from head to breast and with a broad pale band across lower breast; rest of underparts barred brown and white.* Eyes dark brown, cere and tarsi yellow. In flight, wing shows *large pale patch in primaries,* bordered beneath by the black tip, rear margin and carpal mark. **Rufous morph** has rusty wing-linings, sometimes a paler line on median coverts connecting to broad pale breast band (or the breast and wing-linings uniform fox-red); tail whitish or pinkish orange, plain, narrowly barred throughout, or with broad blackish subterminal band. (Long-legged Buzzard easily confused with rufous morph but is longer-winged, usually with more whitish head and breast, darker belly, and tail often unbarred—rarely true of Common.) **Brown morph** has tones more subdued; tail pale brown, barred, and broad band near tip. Rare **dark morph** (identical in plumage to dark Long-legged B.) has black-

303

ish brown body and wing-linings, and barred greyish tail with broad black band near tip. (Mountain Buzzard is darker above, whitish below with heavy streaking and blotching; usually at higher altitudes than Common.) **Juvenile** resembles adult of same morph but more streaked below, lacks clear-cut dark rear wing edges and tail band. Commonly soars with wings slightly raised. Solitary or in migrant flocks. Silent in Africa. **Range/status**: Widespread palearctic passage migrant, mainly Oct.–Nov. and March. Some winter.

MOUNTAIN or FOREST BUZZARD *Buteo oreophilus*   Plates 33, 39

Length 18". A fairly common *montane* buzzard with *heavy brown splotching on breast, belly, flanks and wing-linings*; tibial feathers and crissum rufous-barred. Flight feathers whitish beneath, the secondaries barred; wing tips and trailing edges blackish. Tail brown above, pale grey below with faint narrow barring and broader subterminal band. Flight silhouette identical to that of Common Buzzard. Eyes grey-brown; cere and tarsi yellow. **Juvenile** paler than young Common; buffier below and more lightly marked than adult, and underside of flight feathers less sharply barred; tail bars of equal width. Eyes pale yellowish brown. Soars in pairs above montane forest and adjacent farms or moorland. Quite vocal; **call** a loud mewing *peeeoo-peeeoo*. **Range**: Widespread above 2000 m. **Taxonomic Note**: Listed as *B. tachardus* by some authors.

LONG-LEGGED BUZZARD *Buteo r. rufinus*   Plates 33, 35, 39

Length 22–26". *Larger and longer-winged* than other buzzards; *somewhat aquiline.* Wingbeats slower and deeper than those of Common Buzzard; wings held flatter when gliding, but slightly raised and held forward when soaring; *commonly hovers.* Plumage variable. Typical **adult** warm brown above with *cream-coloured head and neck*, rufous or buff below, usually *chestnut-brown on belly and tibial feathers.* (Some individuals evenly buff below.) Eyes brown; cere and tarsi yellow. In flight shows *large white patch at base of primaries*, and flight feathers are darker above than wing-coverts; from below, white wing panels contrast (more strongly than in Common Buzzard) with dark tips, rear margins and large carpal patches; *tail pale orange-rufous to whitish, with no visible barring* (unlike Common Buzzard); wing-linings rufous. **Rufous morph** has chestnut breast and wing-linings. **Dark morph** differs from dark Common Buzzard only in proportions. **Juvenile** paler than juv. Common, with more oval or circular carpal marks, buff, with light head, dark belly streaks and barred brownish-grey tail. Silent in Africa. **Range/status**: Rare palearctic migrant, Oct.–April; 12 Kenyan records (Lake Turkana and Marsabit, south to Nairobi, Narok and the Tsavo area).

✔ AUGUR BUZZARD *Buteo a. augur*   Plates 33, 39, 44

Length 22–24". The commonest highland buzzard, very broad-winged, and with diagnostic *short rufous tail* in adults. **Light morph** black above, white below, with chin and throat black in female, white in male; secondaries barred pale grey. Wings white beneath, black at tips and on rear margins. Tail may show narrow black subterminal band. **Dark morph** blackish below and on wing-linings. **Juvenile** *longer tailed than adult*, usually brown above, pale buff below, boldly streaked on throat, sides of breast and flanks; tail brown or red-brown with narrow dark bars and black subterminal band; wings patterned beneath as in adult, but barring of remiges fainter. **Dark juvenile** brownish black below and on wing-linings, heavily barred on remiges and tail. **Immatures** show mixture of white and brown-streaked underparts. Soars on markedly raised wings; frequently hovers or hangs motionless in the wind. **Call** a loud crowing *erawk-erahk-erahk*, and a longer, higher *ah-waaaa, ah-waaaa. . . .* **Range**: Widespread between 1500 and 3000 m in cent. and w. Kenya and n. Tanzania. Resident above 4000 m on Mt Elgon, Mt Kenya and Kilimanjaro.

✔ AFRICAN FISH EAGLE *Haliaeetus vocifer*   Plates 34, 35, 40

Length 25–29". A large white-tailed waterside eagle. **Adult** has entire *head, back, breast and tail white* contrasting with black wings and *chestnut belly*; large bill black with yellow base; cere, facial skin and feet also yellow; eyes brown. In flight, head projects well forward, and tail appears very short; linings of broad wings chestnut, underside of flight feathers black. **Juvenile** unkempt looking, streaky brown with *whitish breast patch; tail whitish with broad dark tip; dark wings show white patch on primaries beneath; cere and tarsi grey.* **Immature** *largely white below and on tail, with black superciliary region, wings and belly.* **Call** a loud ringing or yelping *wee-ah, kyo-kyo-kyo-kyo,* somewhat gull-like, uttered with head thrown back, often in duet. **Range**: Widespread on coastal creeks, inland lakes and rivers (but may stray far from water). Most numerous on Rift Valley lakes and Lake Victoria.

PALM-NUT VULTURE   *Gypohierax angolensis*   Plates 31, 34, 35

Length 24". A large vulturine eagle with broad rounded wings and short rounded tail. **Adult** *white* with *black lower back, scapulars, secondaries, greater coverts and tail base. Overhead, black secondaries and primary tips contrast with otherwise white wings.* Bare orbital skin pink, red or orange; bill and eyes yellow; cere pale blue-grey; feet flesh-pink or yellowish. **Juvenile** brown, darker on secondaries and tail, with *dull yellow face patch* and black bill; eyes brown; feet dull whitish. **Immature** mottled brown, black, and white. Perches in trees and walks on ground, scavenging along shorelines and floodplains. Soars well. Feeds on oil-palm fruits where available. **Call** a low-pitched *pruk-kurr,* or *kwuk-kwuk-kwuk.* **Range**: The coast, mainly south of Mombasa, including Pemba Island; Tana River to Meru NP; Lake Jipe-Taveta area and Tsavo River. Wanders to N. Uaso Nyiro and upper Tana rivers and Thika. Inland in Tanzania to East Usambaras, Moshi and Lake Manyara NP.

LESSER SPOTTED EAGLE   *Aquila p. pomarina*   Plates 32, 35, 38

Length 24–26". A large migrant eagle of open woodland, bush and farmland. Bill smaller than in Steppe Eagle, and yellow gape margin extends back only to below middle of eye; nostrils circular, not oval; *tarsal feathering less bulky* than in other *Aquila* species. In flight, *head projects less than in Tawny and Steppe eagles,* and rear edge of wings is typically straighter. Soars with *wings held flat or slightly drooped, the short rounded tail fanned*; from above, often shows *whitish U on upper tail-coverts, small pale area in primaries, and white spot on lower back*; from below, *remiges and tail usually appear darker than body and wing-linings.* **Adult** dull brown with head, neck and forewings somewhat buffier. **Juvenile** (through first winter) dark brown, often with small pale nape patch, pale streaks on underparts and white spots on wing-coverts (which soon wear away). Wing-linings may appear uniform with flight feathers. White upper tail-coverts and primary patches more conspicuous than in adults. Solitary or in groups. Frequently soars and hangs motionless in updraughts. Insectivorous. Perches in trees, but primarily a ground feeder. See Tawny, Steppe and Greater Spotted Eagles. **Call** a barking *kow-kow-kow.* **Range/status**: Palearctic migrant, mainly Oct.–early Dec. A few remain to March near Rift Valley lakes and in adjacent highlands.

GREATER SPOTTED EAGLE   *Aquila clanga*   Plates 32, 35, 38

Length 26–30". A rare dark eagle closely resembling Lesser Spotted (and some birds probably not distinguishable). Soars and glides with flat or drooping wings like that species, but differs slightly in outline with *broader wings and shorter tail.* In flight from above, both species show pale patch at base of primaries; in Greater Spotted this is less distinct at a distance. **Adult** typically *darker* and duller than Lesser Spotted, rather uniform *sooty* brown (purplish-glossed in fresh plumage) and *wing-linings appear darker than flight feathers.* (Dark adult Steppe Eagle has longer tail, more protruding head, gape extending to back of eye.) **Juvenile** *blackish or sooty brown,* some birds nearly as unmarked as Lesser Spotted, but in fresh plumage may show rows of large white spots on wing-coverts almost obscuring the brown areas; however, those coverts otherwise contrast little with remiges. In flight, shows white U on upper tail-coverts and white patch on primaries; wing-linings dark as in adult. **Pale morph** (juv. only?) has blackish flight feathers contrasting with rufous-buff coverts and body. (Compare buffy brown juv. Tawny and Imperial Eagles.) **Call** a yapping *kyak-kyak-kyak.* **Range/status**: Palearctic migrant; 12 records, Oct.–Feb., mainly from around Kenyan Rift Valley lakes.

✓ TAWNY EAGLE *Aquila rapax*   Plates 32, 35, 38

Length 26–29". The common resident brown eagle of bush and savanna. Often appears ragged, less elegant than other *Aquila* species. At rest, shows bulky tarsal feathering and heavy bill like Steppe Eagle, but distinguished by the yellow *gape flange extending back only to below middle of eye*. **Adults** vary from dark tawny brown to pale buff and occasionally almost white; flight feathers and tail always dark brown. Northern *A. r. belisarius* is darker, less rufous, more streaky than widespread *A. r. rapax*. Flapping flight rather heavy and clumsy; wings held flat when gliding or soaring; tail broad and rounded with buff upper coverts. **Juvenile** much paler cinnamon or tawny, with pale bars along upper wing-coverts and along rear wing edges; underside marked by obscure pale mid-wing line and pale inner-primary panel. (Juv. Steppe Eagle has bold *white* line along middle of wing below, and broad white band on upper tail-coverts. Lesser Spotted Eagle is typically darker below, with pale patch at base of primaries above, white spot on back and whitish U on upper tail-coverts.) **Immatures** vary. Year-old birds may be pale cream, light buff or nearly white, with contrasting dark flight feathers. Other birds dark (to almost blackish), often well streaked or blotched, and some show dark head and/or breast contrasting with pale body and wing-coverts. Adult plumage acquired in 3–4 yrs. Prey ranges in size from termites to dik-dik; feeds at carcasses with vultures, and robs other raptors of food. **Call** a barking *kiok* or *kowk*, plus other sounds at nest. Somewhat more vocal than wintering palearctic eagles. **Range**: Widespread. Most birds are *A. r. rapax*, but *belisarius* collected at Lake Turkana.

✓ STEPPE EAGLE *Aquila nipalensis orientalis*   Plates 32, 35, 38

Length 30". A common winter eagle of bush and grassland. Darker and more regal-looking than similar Tawny Eagle. Tarsi heavily feathered; bill long and powerful, the *wide yellow gape extending back to a point below rear edge of eye* (thus longer, more prominent than in Tawny). **Adult** dark brown with buff patch on nape, indistinctly barred tail and flight feathers and bulky tarsal feathering. Flight outline like Tawny Eagle's, with wings held flat, primary tips often slightly raised, and shorter *inner primaries creating slightly pinched-in look*. (Lesser Spotted Eagle soars with straighter edged and slightly drooping wings, has shorter tail and less protruding head; lacks broad white stripe on underside of wing, has narrower, more U-shaped white band on upper tail-coverts.) **Juvenile** buffy or greyish brown, often with pale nape and hindcrown. In flight, *blackish tail and remiges contrast with grey-brown wing-coverts above*, the pattern striking, with *white primary patches, stripe along coverts, rear wing edges and tail-covert band. Below, wing-linings broadly outlined in white*. (Juv. Tawny lacks this white line, the bands on upper tail-coverts and wings are buff, not white, and remiges lack heavy barring.) **Immatures** variable. During 6-year transition to adult, white underwing line is replaced by darker feathers, often producing a ragged effect, and *wing-linings become pale, always in contrast with darker body*. Remiges barred; pale bands on upper wing-coverts gradually lost through wear and moult. May be in small flocks on migration. Feeds on the ground, and consorts with vultures at carrion. Usually silent. **Range/status**: Palearctic migrant, late Oct.–March, mainly in n. and e. Kenya, Rift Valley highlands, Mara GR and n. Tanzania.

*IMPERIAL EAGLE *Aquila h. heliaca*   Plates 32, 35, 38

Length 28–33". A large grassland eagle that soars with its long broad wings held flat, *square-tipped tail* slightly spread, and head markedly protruding. **Adult** blackish brown with distinctive *pale golden crown and nape, pale greyish tail base and narrow white scapular stripes*. **Juvenile** brownish buff with dark streaking, especially on breast. In flight, pale upperwing-coverts obvious; also shows narrow white bar along edge of coverts, white patch in primaries, and broad white rump patch; below, shows pale inner-primary panel (as in juv. Tawny Eagle). **Immature** still paler with little streaking below, becoming mottled or blotchy as adult feathers appear; may show adult head pattern and greyish tail base while retaining pale underparts. Adult plumage may take 6–7 yrs. to acquire. Flies high over open country (usually with other *Aquila* eagles). Silent. (Steppe Eagle is smaller, stockier, with shorter, more wedge-shaped tail. Adult is darker below, lacks white on scapulars and grey tail base, and head is not as pale. Juv. Steppe has bold white line on wings beneath; otherwise resembles juv. Imperial with buff body and pale under-sides of inner primaries, but is smaller-billed, and both tail and flight feathers are brown-er. Greater Spotted Eagle has shorter tail.) **Range/status**: Scarce palearctic migrant, Nov.–March, in Rift Valley, Mara GR, Meru and Tsavo NPs. One Tanzanian record (Olduvai).

WAHLBERG'S EAGLE *Aquila wahlbergi*   Plates 34, 38, 44

Length 22–24″. Smallest of the brown eagles, *little larger than a Black Kite*. Short occipital crest diagnostic but not always conspicuous. Soars with its *long, parallel-edged wings held flat*, the *long narrow square-tipped tail* usually folded, and head projecting far forward. Usual **dark morph** nearly *uniform dark brown*, sometimes golden-buff on crown and scapulars. In flight, *dark wing-linings and body contrast slightly with paler remiges, especially the primary bases*; tail faintly barred below. Cere and feet bright yellow. Uncommon **pale morph** buffy white or cream, with dark remiges and tail; underparts lightly marked with dark shaft streaks or spots. **Juvenile** resembles adult of dark morph but slightly paler below. Typically hangs against breeze with narrowed tail depressed. Perches inconspicuously. (Other *Aquila* eagles are larger, bulkier, with broader wings and tail; none is crested. Dark Booted Eagle has narrower wing tips, frequently spread paler tail, light band on upper wing-coverts, and narrow whitish U on upper tail-coverts. Brown Snake Eagle has bare tarsi, large head, bright yel-low eyes, silvery underwing surfaces, and barred tail. Black Kite has forked tail, differ-ently shaped wings.) **Call** a clear shrill *kleeeee-ay* in display. No other brown eagle has similar whistled call. **Range**: Widespread in dry country, mainly Aug.–April when it breeds; many presumably spend remaining months north of Kenya.

VERREAUX'S or BLACK EAGLE *Aquila verreauxii*   Plates 32, 34, 35, 38 ✔

Length 32–38″. An uncommon, large black eagle of rocky hills and gorges, distinctive in soaring flight with its *long distally broad wings greatly narrowed at base*, raised in shallow V and the primary tips upturned. Tail quite long; large bill and head project well forward. **Adult** *has large white patches on primaries and white of rump/lower back extends as lines along sides of upper back*. **Juvenile** rich tawny brown on back, *buff from forehead to hindneck*, wing-coverts edged with pale buff, *and pale back heavily streaked with brown*; face, foreneck and breast blackish, blending into buff belly. In flight, *wing-linings and primary patches pale buff*; remiges and tail barred below. Adult plumage acquired after 3–4 years. Usually nests on cliffs. Feeds primarily on hyraxes. Pairs perform spectacular swooping and somersaulting dis-plays. **Call** a staccato *cluck*, a harsh barking *chyaw* and a ringing *whaee-whaee-whaee*; also a mewing *weeeeooo* in display. **Range**: Rather widespread in suitable habitat above 1000 m, mainly in dry areas.

AFRICAN HAWK-EAGLE *Hieraaetus spilogaster*   Plates 34, 41

Length 24–26″. An uncommon *black-and-white* (adult) or *rufous* (young) hawk-like eagle of open woodland and scrubby hillsides. Soars on long, flat, *rounded wings distinctly narrowed* at the base; tail rather long. **Adult** blackish above and *white below including tarsal feathering*, with short dark streaks on throat and breast. In flight, *whitish 'window' at base of primaries* conspicuous from above; *wings white beneath, with narrow black trailing edges and broad mottled black band across the greater coverts*; remiges unbarred. *Narrowly barred tail has broad black tip*. Cere and feet green-ish yellow; eyes yellow. (Smaller Ayres's Hawk-Eagle lacks clear windows in wings, has heavily barred remiges, and adult has boldly banded tail.) **Juvenile** dark brown above, *rufous with narrow black shaft streaks below and on wing-linings*; remiges white, faintly barred below; barred tail greyish; eyes brown. (Rufous juv. Great Sparrowhawk has long bare yellow tarsi.) Dark-backed **immature** has whitish underparts with broad dark streaks; eyes brownish yellow. Adult plumage acquired in 3–4 years. Soars frequently. Powerful and dashing, taking prey to size of guineafowl and hare. **Call** a musical *klu-klu-klu-klu-klu-klu*, or *kweee-u, kweee-u*. **Range**: Widespread in drier country, at low to medium elevations, in cent. and s. Kenya and n. Tanzania.

BOOTED EAGLE *Hieraaetus pennatus*   Plates 34, 35, 41, 44

Length 19–20". *Buzzard-sized*, with rather narrow wings and long tail. **Pale morph** warm brown above, head and neck more tawny with darker streaks; underparts white with fine brown streaking on breast. In flight from below, *dark flight feathers contrast with white wing-linings and body*; tail greyish and *unbarred*, slightly rounded when soaring; above, shows *broad buff band across wing-coverts*, and *narrow whitish U on upper tail-coverts* accentuated by dark remiges and tail. **Dark morph** uniform dark brown on head, underparts and wing-linings; appears dark below except for *paler tail and small pale wedge in inner primaries*. **Rufous morph** has dull chestnut or tawny brown head and underparts. Flying toward observer, *small white 'landing lights' at junction of wings and body* a diagnostic feature of all morphs. Some birds intermediate between dark and light extremes. **Juvenile** resembles adult of same morph, but pale birds have chestnut wash below. Soars and glides with wings flat, but relaxed looking with primary tips slightly drooping, *tail usually slightly spread and flexed from side to side* as in Black Kite. See Wahlberg's Eagle and Ayres's Hawk-Eagle. Generally silent in East Africa. **Range/status**: Uncommon but regular palearctic migrant, mainly late Oct.–early April, at low to medium elevations, including the coast.

AYRES'S HAWK-EAGLE *Hieraaetus ayresii*   Plates 34, 41, 44

Length 18–22". A scarce, rather stocky raptor of forest and woodland, smaller than African Hawk-eagle. In flight, broad rounded wings held stiff and flat, long tail slightly spread. Perched, **adult** appears blackish above with *small white forehead spot*, short whitish line above eyes, white underparts with *heavy black spotting* extending to tibial feathers, and *boldly banded tail*; short occipital crest inconspicuous. Primary shafts black (white in African Hawk-Eagle). Eyes yellow or orange, cere and feet greenish-yellow. Rare dark morph unrecorded in East Africa. Flying adult darker than African Hawk-Eagle below, with *boldly barred remiges and no white primary patch*. May show *white 'landing lights' at base of each wing* as in Booted Eagle. **Juvenile** grey-brown above, rufous from crown to upper back, scaly looking with white edges to wing-coverts and scapulars. *Pale rufous superciliary stripes* usually present; *underparts almost plain rich buff or pale rufous* (some narrow black streaks on breast); eyes pale grey-brown. In flight shows pale tawny rufous body and wing-linings, heavily barred remiges and tail. (Juv. Booted is paler, less rufous than young Ayres's and less heavily barred on wings and tail. Juv. African Hawk-Eagle is similarly rufous or buff below, but lacks pale feather edges on upperparts.) Soars briefly above canopy, and hunts over adjacent open country. Takes medium-sized birds, stooping from a height, and pursues prey at speed through canopy. **Call** a high whistling *wheep-hip-hip-hip-wheeeep* in aerial display, a piping *kip-kip-kip* when perched. **Range**: Local up to 3000 m in w. and cent. Kenyan highlands, Shimba and Chyulu hills, lower Tana River and Arabuko-Sokoke forests, Arusha NP and Usambara Mts.

✓ LONG-CRESTED EAGLE *Lophaetus occipitalis*   Plates 32, 35, 44

Length 21–23". *Blackish brown* with a *long floppy crest, broad grey tail bars and whitish tarsal feathering*; cere, eyes and toes yellow. *Large white primary patches* prominent in flight. Flies with shallow flaps and glides; when soaring, short rounded wings held flat. **Juvenile** browner with some white mottling and a shorter crest. Usual **call** a repeated screaming *keeeeeeah* or *keerr-wee*, sometimes with a sharp high-pitched *kek-kek-kek-kek* (which may be given separately). Frequents woodland, forest edge and partly cultivated country. Perches conspicuously on tree or pole, peering downward for rodents or lizards. **Range**: Widespread at medium elevations, but ranging up to 3000 m.

AFRICAN CROWNED EAGLE *Stephanoaetus coronatus*   Plates 34, 39

Length 32–36". An impressive *crested* forest eagle, *large* and *long-tailed*; perches bolt-upright, usually half-hidden in or under canopy. **Adult** blackish brown above; head and *throat rich brown, rest of underparts heavily barred and mottled tawny buff and black*. Eyes, cere and *toes yellow*. Overhead flight pattern diagnostic, the broad rounded wings with wide black rear margins and *rufous wing-linings broadly bordered by black*; tail whitish with *3–4 broad black bands.* **Juvenile** *pale grey* above, head and underparts largely white with *black spots on legs;* wings and tail banded as in adult but *wing-linings pale rufous-buff; remiges and tail with 3–4 heavy black bands.* Eyes and cere grey; toes light yellow. Adult plumage acquired after 3–4 years. (Juv. Martial Eagle, an open-country bird, has *white* wing-linings, closely barred *dark* remiges, a short tail with numerous narrow dark bars, and plain white tarsi.) Soars to great height over forest and vocal male indulges in distinctive swooping display flight, flapping rapidly at top of each undulation. **Call** a melodious, far-carrying *kewee, kewee, kewee*; female gives a deeper *koowi, koowi. . .*, each note repeated 15–30 times. Flight remarkably silent and owl-like; partly crepuscular. Preys on large birds and mammals to size of duiker or young impala, and favours colobus monkeys. **Range**: Local from coast up to 3000 m in Kenyan highlands, Usambaras, Kilimanjaro and Arusha NP.

MARTIAL EAGLE *Polemaetus bellicosus*   Plates 34, 39

Length 31–33". A *noticeably short-tailed* crested eagle of *plains and open bush.* **Adult** *dark grey-brown on head, upperparts and breast; rest of underparts white with small dark spots; underside of wings dark*, the remiges closely barred as is tail. Eyes yellow; cere and *toes blue-grey*. (Black-chested Snake Eagle is smaller with white under wing-surface, more prominently barred flight feathers and tail and bare tarsi.) **Juvenile** and **immature** have *white face, underparts, tarsi and wing-linings*, the latter lightly mottled. Eyes brown; *cere and toes whitish or grey*. (This pattern maintained through several moults for 4–5 years). (Juv./imm. Crowned Eagle has black-spotted legs like *adult* Martial). **Subadult** plumage, worn briefly, has throat and breast more spotted, wing-linings mottled with dark brown. Soars high; rarely hovers. Perches prominently on dead trees. Takes large birds and medium-sized mammals in long shallow dives from air or from high perch. **Call** a musical ringing *koweeo-koweeo-koweeo. . .*, and a loud clear *klee-klee-klee, klooee, klooee, klooee. . .* in display; a liquid *kluweeo* when perched. **Range**: Widespread, mainly in drier open country at low to medium elevations.

FALCONS, FAMILY FALCONIDAE

Distinct from other diurnal raptors, with fairly short tarsi, large strong toes, and short, well-hooked, 'toothed' bill. Typically swift and dashing in flight, pursuing birds and small mammals by stooping or hovering, and some catch aerial insects. Most species are solitary, but some are gregarious on migration and at roosts. Adults usually show black 'moustaches'; young are browner, more streaked below. Species identification, often difficult, is based on structure, plumage and flight characteristics.

PYGMY FALCON *Polihierax semitorquatus castanonotus*   Plates

Length 8". A diminutive, somewhat shrike-like falcon of dry bush. Mainly grey above with white face, nuchal collar and underparts; female has *chestnut patch on back*. In flight shows *white rump, white-spotted wings and black-and-white-barred tail*. Cere, orbital ring and feet red, eyes pale brown. **Juvenile** washed with rufous on back, with buff on finely streaked breast. Perches on exposed branches or treetops; flight owl-like, low and undulating. **Call** a high-pitched *kikiKIK*, repeated. **Range** coincides with that of White-headed Buffalo-Weaver whose unoccupied nests it uses.

LANNER FALCON *Falco biarmicus*   Plates 37, 45

Length 15–18". The commonest large falcon, usually near cliffs or rock outcrops in dry country. Distinguished from Peregrine by *rufous crown and nape*, in flight by *pale buff wing-linings*, blunter, longer wings and longer tail. **Adult** *F. b. biarmicus* is slaty or grey-brown above, *paler on rump, pale buff below with sparse brown spotting*. Black band through eyes, and narrow blackish moustachial marks, contrast with pale buff cheeks. Cere, orbital ring and feet yellow. Northern *abyssinicus* is more heavily streaked and barred below, and crown is dark chestnut. **Juvenile** (both races) dark

slaty brown above with pale rufous or creamy buff crown, *heavily streaked underparts, whitish throat, and dark wing-linings contrasting with pale flight feathers.* Cere and orbital ring blue-grey; feet pale yellow. See Saker and Barbary Falcons. **Calls** a harsh *kak-kak-kak . . .*, and a shrill *kiree-kiree.* **Range**: *F. b. abyssinicus* from Lake Baringo northward, *F. b. biarmicus* in the south.

SAKER FALCON *Falco c. cherrug* Plate 45

Length 17–22". A rare falcon, larger than Lanner, with broader-based wings and *paler head* (often appears whitish at distance), faint moustachial marks, darker postocular streaks, and *whitish superciliary stripes* (lacking in Lanner). Back feathers rusty-edged in fresh plumage. *Brown tail shows pale yellowish spots at sides,* and *incomplete bars on central feathers* (all rectrices completely barred in adult Lanner.) Underparts often more heavily spotted than adult Lanner. In flight, brown wing bases and back noticeably paler than blackish primaries; remiges appear silvery below; wing-linings variably marked. Cere, orbital ring and feet pale yellowish. **Juvenile** darker above than adult; heavily streaked below. Difficult to separate from juv. Lanner, but crown and nape usually more whitish. (Juv. Peregrine is darker above with heavier moustachial marks and wings barred beneath.) Cere and feet grey. In flight, juv. Saker's dark wing-linings contrast with almost translucent primaries (unlike Peregrine). Flies with slow, 'loose' wingbeats until prey is sighted, then quickly accelerates, making capture in air or less often on the ground after powerful stoop. Soars on flat or slightly lowered wings. **Range/status**: A few records, mainly in Kenyan Rift Valley, Oct.–March; single records near Kilimanjaro (Feb.) and Ngorongoro Crater (Jan.).

PEREGRINE FALCON *Falco peregrinus* Plates 37, 45

Length 13–19". Compact and heavy; generally dark with white throat/upper breast; *wings broad-based* but pointed at tips; narrowly barred tail relatively shorter than in Lanner. Crown blackish in **adult.** Wings well barred beneath, appearing grey at distance. *F. p. minor dark blue-grey above with broad blackish moustachial marks* (bolder than in Lanner) and white cheeks; creamy buff below, the dark spotting and barring dense along sides and flanks. Eyes large, dark brown; cere, orbital ring and feet bright yellow. Larger migrant race *calidus* paler above, white below with reduced spotting and barring, and has narrower, more pointed moustachial marks. **Juvenile** dark brown above, heavily streaked below, with broader moustachial marks and darker crown than juv. Lanner, yellowish (not blue-grey) cere, and pale-barred upper tail surface. Wing-linings darker than in adult. Juv. *calidus* resembles juv. Barbary Falcon, quite different from resident *minor* with its buff crown and narrowly streaked underparts. **Immature** may show mixed streaking and barring below. **Call** a shrill *kek-kek-kek. . ..* **Range/status**: *F. p. minor* an uncommon resident of cliffs in open country (has nested in downtown Nairobi); palearctic *calidus*, present Oct.–March, accounts for most birds in atypical habitats.

BARBARY FALCON *Falco pelegrinoides* Plate 45

Length 13–16". A rare dry-country falcon, easily confused with Lanner. **Adult** *pale* bluish grey above, paler on rump, with rufous on sides of crown and nape, blackish moustachial marks and white cheek patches. Differs from Lanner in more slender build, more diffuse black eye-lines, dark crown centre, reduced and *less distinct barring on pale pinkish buff underparts,* and (always?) less clearly defined tail barring above. Resembles Peregrine in silhouette and flight habits. **Juvenile** warm *dark brown above with narrow yellowish or buff collar on nape,* sandy buff below with narrower, lighter brown streaking than in juv. Peregrine or Lanner; tail barred (unlike young Lanner); feet blue-grey. **Status** unclear. Collected at Loyangalani (Nov. 1958); injured bird examined at Timau (Feb. 1981); reported seen near Isiolo and in Tsavo West NP.

TAITA FALCON *Falco fasciinucha* Plates 37, 45

Length 11–12". A rare chunky falcon of cliffs and gorges, *shaped like a miniature short-tailed Peregrine. Wingbeats stiff, shallow, somewhat parrot-like.* **Adult** dark slate-grey above with paler rump, distinctive *rufous nape patches, black crown and bold dark moustachial marks; chin and throat whitish or pale buff*; rest of underparts and wing-linings rufous, darker on flanks, with narrow dark shaft streaks; tail faintly barred above and below, with buff tip; bill dark; cere, eye-ring, and feet yellow. (African Hobby has narrower wings, deep rufous or chestnut cheeks and underparts; tail unbarred above.) **Juvenile** browner with buff feather edges above; more streaked below and with barred wing-linings. **Calls** a squealing *kree-kree*, and a loud *kek-kek-kek-kek*. **Range:** Specimens from near Voi and Nanyuki. Sight records from Lewa Downs, Samburu GR, Ololokwe, Baringo, near Lokitaung, Gol Mts (Serengeti NP) and Olosirwa (Crater Highlands), some poorly documented.

EURASIAN HOBBY *Falco s. subbuteo*　　　　　Plates 37, 45

Length 12–14″. An agile, often gregarious dark-backed falcon of savanna, bush and farmland. **Adult** *slate-grey above including unbarred tail*; underparts cream or buff with heavy black streaks, the *tibial feathers and crissum rich chestnut*; tail unbarred; broad black moustachial marks and black cap contrast with white cheeks and throat; *wing-linings buff with dense dark spots*. Bill steel-blue; cere, orbital ring and feet yellow or yellow-orange. In flight appears more slender than Peregrine. **Juvenile** browner above with pale buff feather edges; more heavily streaked below; tibial feathers and crissum buff; cere, orbital ring and feet pale greenish yellow. (Heavier Peregrine is barred above, including tail. Female and juv. Amur Falcon are more lightly built, paler below, tail barred above, have orange or red feet. Eleonora's Falcon is darker chestnut below, has contrasting dark wing-linings and paler remiges. Juv. Sooty Falcon paler above than young Hobby, more diffusely streaked below, with slightly projecting central rectrices.) **Call** a repeated *kew-kew-kew-kew-kew*. . .. Partly crepuscular. **Range/status:** Palearctic passage migrant, Oct.–early Dec. and March–early May, up to 2500 m; scarce near the coast. Occasionally winters in the highlands.

AFRICAN HOBBY *Falco cuvieri*　　　　　　　Plates 37, 45

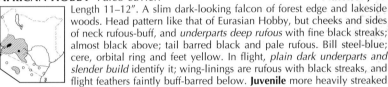

Length 11–12″. A slim dark-looking falcon of forest edge and lakeside woods. Head pattern like that of Eurasian Hobby, but cheeks and sides of neck rufous-buff, and *underparts deep rufous* with fine black streaks; almost black above; tail barred black and pale rufous. Bill steel-blue; cere, orbital ring and feet yellow. In flight, *plain dark underparts and slender build* identify it; wing-linings are rufous with black streaks, and flight feathers faintly buff-barred below. **Juvenile** more heavily streaked below, and browner above than adult; back feathers rufous-tipped and tail more boldly barred; cere greenish white. (Paler Eurasian Hobby has more contrasting black streaks, no rufous under wings. Taita Falcon is stockier, peregrine-like, with rufous nape patches and white throat.) **Call** a high *kiki-keeee*, and a harsher *kik-kik-kik-kik*. . .. Partly crepuscular. **Range:** Lake Victoria basin and w. Kenyan highlands up to 2200 m. Often seen along lakeshore near Kisumu. Scarce in n. Tanzania.

RED-NECKED FALCON *Falco chiquera ruficollis*　　　Plates 37, 45

Length 12–14″. An uncommon kestrel-sized falcon typically *associated with Borassus palms* in low hot country. **Adult** pale *blue-grey above* (with fine black barring), forecrown to hindneck rufous, as is narrow band across breast; barred black and white on lower underparts; short black moustachial marks accent white face and throat; narrowly barred tail has *broad black subterminal band* conspicuous in flight. When perched, wing tips do not reach tip of tail. **Juvenile** darker above, dark brown instead of rufous on head; *underparts dull rufous or buff, boldly barred with black below the whitish throat;* may suggest Eleonora's Falcon or juv. Amur Falcon but they are streaked, not barred below. Perches inconspicuously, often hidden by foliage. Partly crepuscular. **Call** a shrill *keep-keep-keep*. . .. **Range:** Coastal lowlands, mainly south of Mombasa, lower Galana River, and along the Tana upstream to Meru NP; also around Lokichokio, Lake Turkana and along N. Uaso Nyiro River. Rare inland in n. Tanzania.

AMUR FALCON *Falco amurensis*　　　　　　　Plates 37, 46

Length 12″. A dark, *usually gregarious* falcon, often seen gliding on scythe-like wings in open country. **Adult male** slate-grey with chestnut tibial feathers, lower belly and crissum.

In flight, *white wing-linings and silvery grey flight feathers* contrast with dark tail, body, and wing bases. *Cere, orbital ring, and feet red.* (Vagrant Red-footed Falcon has dark wing-linings.) **Female** has slate-grey upperparts and tail with faint blackish barring, blackish crown and short moustachial marks on white cheeks. Pale buff *underparts boldly blotched and barred with black*; legs and crissum more rufous; tail strongly barred. (Similar Eurasian Hobby is unbarred above, including tail.) **Juvenile** resembles female but is browner with paler crown, and more streaked below. (Juv. Red-footed Falcon has white nuchal collar and barred black-and-cream tail.) Usually silent except for infrequent *kew-kew-kew* call at communal roosts. **Range/status**: Palearctic passage migrant, Nov.–Dec. and late March–early May in cent. and se. Kenya. Common in Tsavo region in autumn. Recorded on coast in April. Few n. Tanzanian records except near Lake Jipe and in Mkomazi GR.

*RED-FOOTED FALCON *Falco vespertinus*   Plates 37, 44, 46
Length 12″. Vagrant in open country. **Male** differs from similar Amur Falcon in *dark grey wing-linings.* **Female** *almost plain rufous-buff below and from crown to hindneck*; pale face has black moustachial marks and dark area around eyes. In flight, rich buff wing-linings contrast with barred flight feathers. **Juvenile** has rusty crown, whitish nuchal collar and black-streaked buff underparts. **Call** similar to Amur Falcon's. **Status**: 4 Kenyan records, Oct., April, May.

DICKINSON'S KESTREL *Falco dickinsoni*   Plates 37, 46
Length 11–12″. A small stocky kestrel, both sexes slate grey above with contrasting whitish head and rump; face marked by *broad, bright yellow orbital ring*; cere and tarsi also yellow; *tail strongly barred* black and pale grey. **Juvenile** browner with *barred flanks and blue-green cere.* (Larger Grey Kestrel has less strongly barred tail, dark grey head and rump with less pronounced orbital ring.) **Call** a high *keee-keee*, but usually silent. **Range**: In Kenya, a rare visitor north to Nairobi and Meru NPs, June–August. Rare in n. Tanzania excepting Pemba Island where common.

ELEONORA'S FALCON *Falco eleonorae*   Plates 37, 44, 45

Length 14–16″. *Sleek and streamlined, with long narrow wings* (reaching tail tip), and *hobby-like head pattern.* Adult of usual **pale morph** *slaty black above with unbarred tail, rufous-buff underparts with black streaks, blackish wing-linings, and dark trailing wing edges.* Rare **dark morph** appears all blackish at distance, but paler grey flight-feather bases and tail evident at close range. Cere and orbital ring pale blue in males, pale yellow in females; feet yellow in both sexes. **Juvenile** shows buff feather edges above; underparts buff with heavy black streaks; spotted wing-linings appear brown. Partly crepuscular; often associated with rain-storms. Feeds on birds and insects taken in the air. (Eur. Hobby is smaller, shorter-tailed, paler below and underwing surface lacks contrasting pattern. Juv. Sooty Falcon is shorter tailed, and dull yellowish, not pale buff below.) **Call** a high sharp *ki-ki-kik-ki-ki. . .* **Range/status**: Uncommon palearctic passage migrant, late Oct.–Nov., and March–early May, in varied habitats, mainly in cent. Kenyan highlands. Rare in n. Tanzania.

SOOTY FALCON *Falco concolor*   Plates 37, 46

Length 13–14″. A narrow-winged falcon with *tail somewhat wedge-shaped owing to slight projection of central feathers.* Adult slate-grey with head and wing tips darker than rest of plumage. Cere and orbital ring yellow; feet orange-yellow (reddish in some males). **Juvenile** *dull buffy yellow below* with slate-grey streaking, *often solidly blotched on breast.* Head pattern recalls that of Eurasian Hobby or Eleonora's Falcon. Cere blue-green; feet pale yellowish green. Mainly crepuscular, in bush and grassland. (Eleonora's Falcon is larger, longer-tailed, with contrasting underwing pattern; dark-morph adult more blackish than typical Sooty Falcon. Grey Kestrel is stockier, shorter winged, has barred under tail, more uniformly grey face, different habits and slower flight. Eur. Hobby has *darker streaks* and bolder face pattern than young Sooty. Juv. Hobby and Eleonora's Falcon not as yellowish below, and less densely streaked on

breast.) **Call** a shrill *kikikik.* **Range /status**: Passage migrant from North Africa/Arabia, regular in small numbers in cent. and e. Kenya, late Oct.–Dec., less often Feb.–early May, at low to medium elevations. Few n. Tanzanian records.

GREATER KESTREL *Falco rupicoloides*   Plates 37, 46

Length 14″. The *white eyes* distinguish adults of this grassland falcon. Stockier and larger-headed than Common Kestrel, and with broader wings, it is rufous above, with bold black barring on back and wings; paler cinnamon below with dark-streaked breast and belly; *rump and tail barred grey and black* in adult. Head streaked, but *no moustachial marks* (unlike female Common and Lesser Kestrels). Wings whitish below. **Juvenile** is brown-eyed, has streaked flanks, and tail is rufous with black barring. Rather sluggish; occasionally hovers. **Call** a double *kweek-kweek*; also sharp *chik* or *kwit* notes. **Range**: *F. r. arthuri* from Serengeti Plains north to Nairobi, Naro Moru and Nanyuki. Birds in n. and nw. Kenya may represent the paler Ethiopian race *fieldi* (no Kenyan specimens).

FOX KESTREL *Falco alopex*   Plates 37, 46

Length 14–15″. A large *chestnut* kestrel of northern dry rocky country, where it soars and glides along cliff faces. *Long graduated tail* has incomplete dark bars, the *chestnut plumage otherwise relieved only by black streaking above and below*; *no moustachial marks*; eyes pale brownish yellow. In flight, wings whitish beneath with tawny-buff linings. **Juvenile** more heavily streaked than adult, tail more clearly barred. (Female and juv. of local dark race of Common Kestrel are duller, more spotted and barred above, with dark moustachial marks, barred under wing surface, and shorter rounded tail with dark terminal band.) **Call** a high-pitched *kee-kee-kee-kee.* **Range**: Near Lake Turkana and around Lokichokio and Kamathia. Has wandered south to Kongelai Escarpment, Lake Baringo and Ngong Hills.

GREY KESTREL *Falco ardosiacus*   Plates 37, 46

Length 12–13″. An uncommon, *rather stocky* falcon of bushed grassland and savanna, *grey with a conspicuous broad yellow orbital ring. Wing tips do not reach tail tip in perched bird.* Shows dark shaft streaks at close range; tail almost plain above. (Dickinson's Kestrel has whitish head and rump, strongly barred tail. Sooty Falcon is slimmer, with much longer wings.) **Juvenile** more brownish grey than adult. Sluggish; sometimes hovers. Utilises old nests of other birds (especially Hamerkop). **Call** *keek-keek-keek,* and a harsh twittering. **Range**: W. Serengeti Plains, Mara GR and Nyanza north to Mt Elgon, occasionally east to Lake Baringo, Nakuru and Kedong Valley.

LESSER KESTREL *Falco naumanni*   Plates 37, 46 ✓

Length 11–13″. A small falcon, *usually in loose flocks* over plains or farmland. *Slightly wedge-shaped tail* has black band near narrow white tip. Perched, at close range, the diagnostic *white claws* are evident. **Male** pale *chestnut on back with crown, nape, rump and most of tail bluegrey;* creamy buff or pinkish buff below with sparse fine spots. In flight, shows *blue-grey band across greater coverts*, rufous-chestnut forewing and blackish primaries; wings whitish below. **Female** and **juvenile** *chestnut, spotted and barred with black above*, with indistinct dark moustachial marks; underparts with finer streaks than female Common Kestrel, and central rectrices longer. **Call** a high-pitched *kikikikikiki.* Communal roosts, in trees, may hold thousands of birds. Commonly pursues aerial insects; glides frequently, but hovers less persistently than Common Kestrel. **Range/status**: Palearctic migrant, locally common Oct.–May, mainly in upland areas of s. Kenya and n. Tanzania.

COMMON or ROCK KESTREL *Falco tinnunculus*   Plates 37, 46 ✓

Length 12–13″. A small falcon that habitually hovers with tail fanned and depressed. **Male** of nominate race has rufous *back spotted with black*, blue-grey crown and nape, and a grey tail with *broad black subterminal band* and narrow white tip; underparts pale buff streaked with black. In flight, blackish primaries contrast with rufous coverts above, the wings pale beneath with faint markings. **Female** and **juvenile** *rufous-brown, heavily spotted and barred above,* and with brownish moustachial streaks; narrowly barred chestnut tail has broad dark tip; more heavily marked below and under wings than male. Adults of local breeding race *rufescens are* darker and more rufous below than nominate birds, the male more slaty on head and on the noticeably barred tail. Coastal *archeri* is smaller than similar *tinnunculus* and more heavily barred above. Solitary. Resident birds usually near rock outcrops and cliffs but may nest in trees and buildings. **Call** a shrill *kee-kee-kee-kee-kee-kee* or *kik-kik-kik-kik*-kik . . .. **Range/status**: *F. t. tinnunculus* a widespread palearctic migrant, Oct.–March, at medium to higher elevations; *rufescens* an uncommon resident, mainly in Rift Valley and adjacent highlands. Somali race *archeri* at least formerly in Lamu area.

QUAIL AND FRANCOLINS, FAMILY PHASIANIDAE

Terrestrial, cryptically patterned birds, short-tailed, with thickset bodies and short rounded wings. Sedentary residents, excepting the quail, and usually in pairs or small coveys. They prefer to run when approached, but flight is fast and direct with rapid wingbeats, for short distances. Quail are small, sexually dimorphic birds, seldom seen unless flushed. Francolins and the bare-throated spurfowl are larger, with heavier bills. The tarsi are sturdy, and prominently spurred in males of some species. Except in Coqui and Hildebrandt's Francolins, the sexes are similar.

COMMON QUAIL *Coturnix coturnix*   **Plate 27**

Length 7–8″. Although fairly common locally, less frequently encountered than Harlequin Quail; usually seen only when flushed from grassland or crops. Paler plumage and *broad pale side stripes* separate it from Harlequin. **Male** of resident *C. c. erlangeri* is chestnut-faced with long whitish head stripes, and chestnut or buff throat encloses a dark central patch. Sandy brown above with various dark markings and short white streaks; buff underparts *streaked with white and brown on sides and flanks.* **Female** is paler, lacks dark face and throat patch, but has dark spots across breast. *Buff bars on primaries* separate female from female Harlequin Quail in the hand, but are seen only rarely in the field. Feet yellowish or pinkish brown. **Rufous morph** chestnut on throat, rufous on sides and flanks. **Juvenile** like female, but flanks heavily barred. *C. c. coturnix* is paler above and on face than resident birds, both sexes have whitish cheeks, and male shows bolder throat mark bordered by white below. See female Blue Quail and Common Button-quail. **Call** of male a ventriloquial trisyllabic *wheet, wit-it,* repeated several times, or with different rhythm, *whik-wik, whik.* In flight, a higher *tree-tree.* Most vocal at dawn and dusk. **Range**: *C. c. erlangeri* in w. and cent. Kenya highlands, Crater Highlands, Arusha area and West Usambara Mts. Palearctic *C. c. coturnix* recorded in n. Kenya (Lake Turkana, Huri Hills, Maralal); early specimens south to Kisumu, Nairobi, Loita Hills and Tsavo.

BLUE QUAIL *Coturnix adansonii*   **Plate 27**

Length 5″. A rare *small dark* quail of wet or lush grassland. **Male** *slaty blue* with *chestnut on inner wings, wing- and upper tail-coverts. Bold black-and-white face/throat pattern includes no white above eyes.* **Female** distinguished from other quail by *heavily black-barred sides and flanks.* Tarsi and toes yellowish in both sexes. (Common Button-quail is buffier and greater coverts are usually pale-edged.) **Call** described as a descending trisyllabic piping whistle the first note loud and shrill. **Range/status**: Intra-African migrant in Kenya. (Formerly bred from Kitale south to Ngong Escarpment.) Scattered rainy-season records in w. and s. Kenya and n. Tanzania; may still breed on Pemba Island. **Taxonomic Note**: Often considered conspecifc with Asian *C. chinensis.*

HARLEQUIN QUAIL *Coturnix d. delegorguei* Plate 27 ✔

Length 5.5–6". The common grassland quail. **Male** blackish brown above, streaked with buffy white. Black-and-white face pattern includes *long white superciliary stripes continuing down sides of neck*; white throat contrasts with *black central underparts and black-streaked rufous sides and flanks*. In flight, appears dark with short pale back streaks. Feet dusky white or brownish pink. **Female** difficult to distinguish from Common Quail in flight, but darker above, and with variable *dark spotting* on sides of breast. In the hand, note *plain brown primaries without buff barring*, and *rich rufous-buff under tail-coverts*. Highly gregarious with locally large concentrations. Flushes readily but runs and hides after dropping again to ground. Shy but quite vocal. **Call** of male a loud rapid *whit-whit* or *whit-whit-whit,* when close sounding more like *tswic-tswic-tswic*; no pause after first note as in Common Quail. Female may answer with soft *quick-ik*. When flushed, a squeaky rolled *skreeee*. **Range**: Widespread except in the north. Strongly nomadic, its movements coinciding with onset of the rains.

STONE PARTRIDGE *Ptilopachus p. petrosus* Plate 27

Length 9.5–11.5". A small, bantam-like bird, running and hopping over boulders on *rocky hillsides and gorges*, its *long broad cocked tail* distinctive. At a distance appears dark and uniform above; fine barring, strongest on sides and flanks, is evident at close range. Head 'scaly'; throat and neck dark-speckled; breast buff in male, paler and more whitish in female. Bare facial skin dull red; bill dark reddish brown, yellowish at tip; tarsi and toes dark red. **Juvenile** more distinctly barred throughout. (Crested Francolin often runs with cocked tail, but shows whitish superciliaries and pale streaks on back; it favours flat ground.) **Call**, at dawn and dusk, a far-carrying whistled *oueek-oueek-oueek* or *weet-weet. . .*, sometimes more rolling, *rrr-weet, rrr-weet. . .*, often in duet or chorus. **Range**: Nw. Kenya, from Turkwell River gorge south to Kongelai Escarpment; more local from Laikipia and Lewa Downs north to N. Uaso Nyiro River, Baragoi, the Ndotos and South Horr.

COQUI FRANCOLIN *Francolinus coqui* Plate 27 ✔

Length 8.5–10.5". A *small* francolin of *grassy areas*, including forest edges. **Male** of coastal *F. c. coqui* has *ochre face and neck; underparts barred with black-and-white* except for plain pale throat; crown and spot on ear-coverts rufous; streaked brown, buff and black above, and with rufous and buff cross-bars. Brown flight feathers may show traces of rufous on inner webs, but *no large rufous patch*; tarsi and toes yellow. **Female** has buffier face with *2 black streaks on each side of head, the lower pair joining around the pale throat; upper breast vinaceous pink or pinkish brown;* other underparts buffy white, heavily barred with black. Western *F. c. hubbardi* has dark brown (not rufous) crown and an unbarred buff belly (both sexes); female has grey upper breast. Eastern and northern *maharao* is more narrowly barred below, and usually shows some rufous on primaries. **Juvenile** similar to female but paler and more mottled rufous-buff above, buff below. Noisy near dusk. Often walks slowly with outstretched neck almost horizontal. **Call** of male *hubbardi* a shrill, squeaky *KO-ki, KO-ki, KO-ki. . .* or *KWI-ki, KWI-ki. . .*. Another call, *chur-INK-CHINK-CHERRA-cherra-cherra-cherra-cherra* from coastal birds. Alarm call a harsh *churr-churr* and gives shrill squeaks when flushed. **Range**: *F. c. coqui* in coastal lowlands north to Arabuko-Sokoke Forest, inland to near Mt Kasigau; *hubbardi* local from cent. Rift Valley to w. Kenyan highlands, Mara GR and Serengeti NP; *maharao* local east of Rift Valley from Tarangire NP and Arusha Dist. north to Selengai and Machakos; also in the Huri Hills.

RING-NECKED FRANCOLIN *Francolinus streptophorus* Plate 27

Length 12–13". A rare western species of grass-covered rocky escarpments. Shows *rufous face and neck*, white throat and superciliaries; *hindneck and breast are barred black and white*, forming a broad contrasting band. Brown above with narrow whitish streaks; underparts rufous-buff *blotched with dark brown*; bill black; tarsi pale yellow. **Female** has darker brown crown, cinnamon-barred underparts with buffy white streaks, and back, rump and upper tail-coverts are buff-barred. **Call** of 2 ventriloquial dove-like coos, the first lower, followed by a soft piping trill. **Range**: Formerly on s. Mt Elgon, Samia Hills near Busia, Maragoli Escarpment, and near Fort Ternan; bred on ne. Elgon in August 1993.

RED-WINGED FRANCOLIN *Francolinus levaillantii kikuyuensis* **Plate 28**
Length 14–15″. A large, warmly coloured francolin of high grassland; now scarce. *Much orange-buff on face and neck*, enclosing dark and light lines connected with the black-and-white-barred collar; breast buff with broad rufous streaks and dark brown spots; belly buff, vermiculated and broadly barred with black. In flight, shows orangey hindneck and *more rufous in wings than Shelley's Francolin, the colour extending to primary coverts and outer secondaries*. Tarsi yellow or yellowish brown. (Other 'red-winged' francolins lack the narrow rufous-ochre or orangey ring separating white throat from adjacent black-and-white feathering. Moorland F. is much larger and shows more rufous in the wings.) **Juvenile** duller; black-and-white pattern less distinct. Secretive. Shrill chattering squeal accompanies whirr of wings when flushed (as with other red-winged species). Advertising **call** a loud chanting *ki-al-de-werk* or *tee-til-eet*. **Range**: Once extensive distribution in w. and sw. Kenyan highlands now severely fragmented. Recent records from Soy-Webuye-Kitale area (where rare), Lumbwa, Koru, Lolgorien and nw. Mara GR. Early specimens from n. Serengeti NP.

MOORLAND FRANCOLIN *Francolinus psilolaemus* **Plate 28**
Length 16–18″. A large, richly coloured species of *alpine moorlands*. Has *extensively rufous primaries* and otherwise resembles Shelley's Francolin, but ground-colour of underparts buff or rufous-buff, not whitish, and *no heavy black bars on belly*. Orange-buff of face extends from eyes down sides of neck, bordered by lines of black-and-white speckling; the lower lines encircle the pale buff throat, separating it from the black-spotted rufous lower neck/upper breast; hindneck mottled black and rufous, but otherwise buffy brown above with cream shaft streaks and dark barring. Underparts mostly buff, heavily blotched with chestnut and finely barred with black. Tarsi pale brownish yellow. Birds on Mt Elgon, often separated as *F. p. elgonensis*, are more rufous (especially on breast). Male's **call** said to be almost identical with that of Shelley's Francolin. **Range**: Local on higher parts of Mau Escarpment, the Aberdares, and ranging down to 2300 m on n. Mt Kenya where wheat fields now extend to the moorlands. Fairly common above 3000 m on Mt Elgon.

SHELLEY'S FRANCOLIN *Francolinus shelleyi* **Plate 28**

Length 11–12″. Four francolins (Red-winged, Moorland, Orange River and Shelley's) show prominent rufous remiges in flight. Adults of these have black bills and yellow feet, as do Ring-necked and Coqui (which lack large rufous wing patches). Shelley's, locally common in acacia-grassland, is the most frequently encountered. Sides of head are tawny buff with *black-flecked white postocular lines broadening on neck*; similar *black-and-white band extends down sides of neck, enclosing the white throat* (a buff band may encircle throat, *outside* the black-and-white area). Upperparts blotched and barred with brown, and with buff shaft streaks; underparts basically *whitish*, not buff or cream; breast and sides heavily streaked with chestnut; *lower breast and belly extensively black-barred*. *F. s. macarthuri* is slightly darker. Tarsi and toes dull yellow. Usually shy and secretive (except in Nairobi NP). Vocal at dusk. **Call** a repeated 4-note *ski-UK skiki-eu* or *ker-kIRRrr, ker-kek*; a shrill squeal when flushed. **Range**: *F. s. uluensis* in Kenyan highlands from Laikipia and Mt Kenya south to Naivasha, Ngong, Nairobi, Athi Plains and Machakos, also from Bura and Taveta to Tsavo West NP, Mkomazi GR, North Pare Mts, Arusha NP and Crater Highlands; *macarthuri* is restricted to the Chyulu Hills.

ORANGE RIVER FRANCOLIN *Francolinus levaillantoides archeri* **Plate 28**
Length 11.5–12″. A rare northern bird similar to Shelley's Francolin, but *creamy buff below with short black streaks throughout*, sparse broader chestnut streaks on breast and flanks, and *faint dusky bars on lower belly and crissum*. **Call**: *Ki-KEET, ki-KIT*, the repeated phrase faster, more strident and higher-pitched than similar call of *F. shelleyi uluen-*

sis. **Range**: Huri Hills (1100–1350 m) and Mt Kulal (collected, Oct. 1973) but status unclear. **Taxonomic Note**: This race merged with Somali *lorti* by some authors.

CRESTED FRANCOLIN *Francolinus sephaena*   Plate 27 ✓

Length 9.5–11.5". Small and bantam-like, often seen running in dry scrub with *tail cocked* and *crown feathers raised. Largely black tail conspicuous in flight.* Racially variable. **Male** of widespread *F. s. grantii* rich brown above with *short white streaks, bold white superciliary stripes and black moustachial stripes* that merge with chestnut or brown spots around the plain white throat. Upper breast has band of triangular dark spots; underparts otherwise whitish or buff with coarse vermiculations, often heavy on white-streaked breast and flanks; bill black, tarsi dull red. **Female** and **juvenile** more densely barred. Coastal *rovuma* lacks dark moustachial stripes and has numerous short brown streaks on underparts. Northern *spilogaster* is larger with narrower ventral streaking. In pairs or small coveys, often on bare ground, dirt roads and tracks. Vocal on moonlit nights and at intervals throughout the day. **Call** a high, strident, squealing cackle, given rapidly and often in duet or chorus, *kerra-kreek, kerra-kreek. . .* and an antiphonal *kee, kek-kerra. . .* repeated frequently, the first note uttered by one bird, second and third by another. **Range**: *F. s. grantii* widespread below 1500 m, but now largely absent from Lake Victoria Basin, *rovuma* in coastal lowlands, *spilogaster* near Moyale.

SCALY FRANCOLIN *Francolinus squamatus*   Plate 28

Length 12–13". A dark, *red-billed* and *red-legged* francolin of *highland evergreen forest and forest edge.* Dark brown above with black-and-buff feather edgings; lower back, rump and upper tail-coverts with dusky vermiculations; underparts appear scaly with pale feather edges (markings less coarse and belly paler in western birds); spurred tarsi orange-red. **Juvenile** more rufous-brown above with black arrowhead markings, barred with black and white below. Forages in clearings and glades, but retreats to safety of forest when disturbed. Noisy at dawn and dusk, sometimes at night. **Call** a loud grating *ke-RAAK, ke-RAAK*, or *kerrAK-KAK-KAK*, repeated and increasing in volume; often in chorus from roosts. **Range**: Widespread from Mt Elgon, the Cheranganis and Mt Nyiru south to Mara GR, n. Nairobi suburbs (now scarce), Chyulu Hills, the Ngurumans, Arusha NP and Kilimanjaro. In places adapts to dense bush as forest disappears. *F. s. schuetti* mostly west of Rift Valley, *maranensis* to the east; *usambarae* formerly in the Usambara Mts but no recent records.

HILDEBRANDT'S FRANCOLIN *Francolinus hildebrandti*   Plate 27 ✓

Length 12.5–16". A sturdy, *sexually dimorphic* francolin of dense bush, forest edge and thickets, often on rocky hillsides. **Male** *F. h. hildebrandti* whitish below, *heavily spotted with black*; neck with fine black-and-white streaks grading into whitish U-shaped marks on dark back. Upperparts mostly brown, faintly vermiculated; grey head finely white-speckled, the crown and ear-coverts brown, *forehead and lores black.* Bill brown above, orange-yellow to red at base, and mandible usually red; tarsi typically coral-red, sometimes orange-yellow; toes dusky black. *F. h. altumi* has upper breast heavily spotted and mottled, but flanks sparsely so. (Males of n. Kenyan birds, once separated as *helleri*, more reddish brown above and more extensively white below; females more olive-brown, less grey.) **Female** smaller, *rich tawny or rufous-buff below* with some whitish feather edges; *underparts almost uniform buff in F. h. hildebrandti.* Bill brown above, usually red or orange below and at gape; tarsi red. **Juvenile** resembles female, but buffy brown underparts spotted and streaked (rather than blotched) with black; upperparts as in female but more distinctly barred. Vocal at dawn and dusk. **Call** a raucous *kek-kerek-kek-kek* with variations, often in chorus. **Range**: *F. h. altumi* in Kenyan Rift Valley north to Nakuru, in w. highlands from Elgeyu to Nguruman Hills, e. Mara GR. and Ugandan border; *hildebrandti* from Marsabit and the Ndotos to Maralal and Ololokwe, and from Chyulu Hills and Voi south to the North Pare Mts., Arusha, Longido, Tarangire and Lake Manyara NPs and Crater Highlands.

JACKSON'S FRANCOLIN *Francolinus jacksoni* Plate 28

Length 15–19". A large *montane* francolin of forest edge, bamboo and giant heath, *boldly streaked chestnut and white below*, with white throat and *red bill and tarsi*. Rufousbrown above; lores chestnut. Female noticeably smaller than male. **Juvenile** duller, with some barring on belly. Forages in thick shrubby growth and adjacent openings. Often on dirt roads and tracks in wet weather. **Call** a high-pitched loud cackling reminiscent of Scaly Francolin. **Range**: Above 2500 m on Mt Kenya and the Aberdares (fairly common); fewer in high parts of the Mau Forest and Cherangani Hills; 2 records from Mt Elgon (one from the Ugandan side where generally replaced by Moorland Francolin).

*CHESTNUT-NAPED FRANCOLIN *Francolinus castaneicollis atrifrons*
Plate 28

Length 16–18". A large, *red-billed and red-legged* Ethiopian francolin *with black forehead and superciliary stripes*. This race quite plain, lacking the rich chestnut dorsal coloration and heavy ventral streaking of some others; only a faint rufous tinge to sides of head. Crown dull brown; neck and back feathers broadly bordered with dull white, those on upper back with buffy white U- or V-shaped markings; lower back to upper tail-coverts olive-brown. *Underparts pale creamy buff*; foreneck feathers, below the plain throat, have V-shaped brown marks; sides and flanks with dusky shaft streaks and faint sparse barring; tibial feathers dull brown. Tarsi coral-red, double-spurred in male. In Ethiopia, inhabits broad-leaved forest edge and juniper woods; small groups are vocal and feed in the open. **Call** (subspecies?) said to be a raucous *kek-kek-kek-kerak*. **Status** unclear; known in Kenya from a single sight record south of Moyale (June 1975).

✓RED-NECKED SPURFOWL *Francolinus afer* Plate28

Length 14–16". A bird of dense bush (in moister habitats than those occupied by Yellow-necked Spurfowl). Plumage variable, but adults of all races have *bare red throat, orbital skin, bill, tarsi and toes*. **Adult** of black-bellied *F. a. leucoparaeus* has brown crown and black forehead; upperparts otherwise dark brown with blackish mottling; sides of face grey-streaked. Upper breast greyish with narrow black streaks, and *some white streaking* on the black belly patch (which is smaller in female). In flight, pale brown outer primary webs evident, but no prominent buff patch as in Yellow-necked Spurfowl. Tarsi spurred in male. Smaller *F. a. cranchii* is more uniform brownish grey, the vermiculated greyish white underparts sparsely streaked with rufous. **Juvenile** duller and browner, black-streaked on back, brown-barred below; feathered throat speckled with brown; tarsi greyish red, bill blackish. (Grey-breasted Spurfowl of n. Tanzania has dark brown tarsi and orange or pinkish red skin on face and throat.) **Call** a repeated squealing cackle, *ku-WAAARK* or *ko-RAAAK*, higher-pitched than Yellowneck's similar call. **Range**: *F. a. leucoparaeus* in coastal Kenya north to Shimba Hills, and from Lamu northwards; *cranchii* local in Lake Victoria basin (especially Ruma NP), and south to Mara GR and n. Serengeti NP. Also (race?) in Tarangire NP. Coastal birds south of Tanga, and inland to Korogwe, may represent the southern *melanogaster*.

✓YELLOW-NECKED SPURFOWL *Francolinus leucoscepus* Plate28

Length 14–17". A fairly common francolin of light bush and savanna. *Bare yellow throat* and orange or vermilion facial skin diagnostic. Dark brown above with buffy white barring and shaft streaks; underparts streaked dark brown and buffy white. Bill blackish, orange-red at base below; tarsi blackish. In flight, wings show *conspicuous pale buff patch in primaries*. Female lacks spurs. **Juvenile** has grey and blackish vermiculations above, and a paler yellow throat. In n. Tanzania see Grey-breasted Spurfowl. Usual **call** a series of loud, raucous, grating notes, *ko-WAAARK, ko-WAAARK*, lower pitched than call of Red-necked Spurfowl; also a longer *ka-WEEEERRRk, ka-WEEEERRRK, KREEEK*-kraak-kraak-kraak-kraak.. **Range**: In Kenya, widespread below 2300 m (now numerous only in protected areas); absent from Lake Victoria basin and most of the highlands. Confined in northwest to Ilemi Triangle and Ugandan border areas. Reaches coast between Sabaki and Tana rivers. In n. Tanzania from Mkomazi GR west to e. Serengeti NP where it meets and hybridises with Grey-breasted Spurfowl.

GREY-BREASTED SPURFOWL *Francolinus rufopictus* Plate 122 ✔
Length 13–16″. Restricted to n. Tanzania. Similar to Yellow-necked Spurfowl (including buff patch in primaries conspicuous in flying bird), but with *pinkish red or orange bill and throat, white moustachial streaks and red-orange facial skin.* Tarsi dark brown, not red as in Red-necked Spurfowl. Grey-brown above with chestnut streaks on upper back; *sides of neck and breast grey* with sepia streaks; dull whitish belly streaked with chestnut and sepia. **Juvenile** has blackish vermiculations on upperparts, black-and-white barring below. Pairs or small groups inhabit open acacia woodland and dense riparian thickets. **Call** similar to that of Yellow-necked Spurfowl. **Range**: Seronera River valley in cent. Serengeti NP, southeast to Lake Lygarja where it interbreeds with Yellow-necked Spurfowl.

GUINEAFOWL, FAMILY NUMIDIDAE

Large terrestrial game birds with characteristic pale-dotted and vermiculated dark plumage. Small, largely bare head has bony casque or feathered crest, and often small facial wattles and tufts of nasal bristles. The sexes are alike. Highly vocal, with distinctive strident rattling calls. Often treated as a subfamily of Phasianidae.

CRESTED GUINEAFOWL *Guttera pucherani* Plate 28

Length 18–20″. A *forest* bird with *shaggy crest* of curly feathers covering top of head. Black plumage spotted with small round *bluish dots.* These extend to the naked *cobalt-blue neck* in eastern *G. p. pucherani* ('Kenya Crested Guineafowl') which also has *red throat, face and eyes.* Western *verreauxi* has shaggier crest, *unspotted broad blackish collar* around lower neck, *dark brown eyes*, vermilion throat and foreneck but *no red on sides of face.* Both forms show pale brown wing patches in flight.
Juvenile *verreauxi* lacks blue spots, is dusky below with buff and rufous feather edges, rusty brown and buff-spotted above, with black-and-rufous barring on wing-coverts; bare face and throat are grey. Shy and retiring, but on paths or dirt roads at dawn or after heavy rains. Cocks tail when alarmed. May fly with loud cackling into tree canopy if disturbed, and feeds partly on arboreal fruits. Usual alarm **call** a fast rattling *chuk-chuk-chukkkkkrrrrr*, lower and less strident than calls of Helmeted Guineafowl. **Range**: *G. p. pucherani* along coast, inland to Lake Manyara NP, and e. edge of cent. Kenyan highlands, meeting (but apparently not intergrading with) *verreauxi* in s. Aberdares. Latter race also from Mt Elgon and the Cheranganis south to Kakamega and Mau forests, Lolgorien, Mara GR and n. Serengeti NP.

VULTURINE GUINEAFOWL *Acryllium vulturinum* Plate 28

Length 24–28″. A bizarre, tall, *long-tailed* guineafowl of dry bush. *Black, white and brilliant blue*, with *striped lanceolate feathers* on neck, back and breast; lower breast and belly bright blue on sides, black centrally; wings and rear half of body black with white dots; secondaries lilac-edged. Bare head and neck grey, with *band of short dense chestnut feathers on occiput.* Eyes red; bill pale yellowish green; tarsi black.
Juvenile grey-brown, mottled and barred rufous-brown, buff and black; blue of underparts and long neck and breast feathers dull. Large flocks forage in the open near cover. Usual **call** a strident metallic rattle or trill, *chink-chink-chink-cheenk-cheek-krrrrrrrrr* higher than call of Helmeted Guineafowl; lower *chink* contact notes among foraging birds. **Range**: N. and e. Kenya, west to Lake Turkana, Rumuruti and Isiolo; local in and near the Tsavo parks including Lake Jipe, Mkomazi GR and the Masai Steppe; also local on coast from Karawa north to Kiunga.

✔ **HELMETED GUINEAFOWL** *Numida meleagris* Plate 28 ✔

Length 23–25″. The common guineafowl of bush and savanna, with bony casque on the crown, bare blue skin on head and neck, and small gape wattles. Dark plumage fine-dotted and vermiculated with white. Bill pale, with dense tuft of bristles on cere; tarsi blackish. Northern *N. m. meleagris* has finely white-barred collar below black hindneck, short or elongate brownish casque; facial skin and *flat rounded gape wattles pale blue.* Southern *reichenowi* has throat and entire hindneck black,

blue facial skin with *pointed red gape wattles*, its casque long and dark. *N. m. soma-liensis* resembles *meleagris* but has small stumpy casque, much longer bristles at base of bill, a row of black filoplumes on mid-line of hind neck, and blue wattles that are some-what pointed and red-tipped. *N. m. mitrata* has similar wattles but otherwise is more like *reichenowi* except for smaller casque. **Juvenile** grey brown with small buff spots, rufous-brown barring above, and fine black speckling. **Immature** plumage as in adult, but neck well-feathered and casque smaller. In large flocks much of year. Common **call** a raucous strident *kik-kik-kik-kik-kaaaaaa*; contact call of soft metallic *chink* notes. **Range**: Widespread, but uncommon in the north. *N. m. meleagris* south to edge of Kenyan high-lands; *somaliensis* in ne. Kenya south to Wajir; *mitrata* in coastal lowlands; *reichenowi* elsewhere south of the Equator.

BUTTON-QUAIL AND QUAIL-PLOVER, FAMILY TURNICIDAE

Small terrestrial grassland and bush birds resembling true quail (Phasianidae), but differ-ing behaviourally and anatomically. They run swiftly in cover, but in the open at least some may employ peculiar chameleon-like, forward-backward rocking movement, pro-gressing extremely slowly. They are plump-bodied birds with short tail, short broad wings (longer in *Ortyxelos*) and cryptic plumage; bill is short, slender and arched; hind toe absent. The female is slightly larger and more brightly coloured than male; she does the courting and primary vocalizing. Male does most of the incubating, and he cares for the young.

QUAIL-PLOVER *Ortyxelos meiffrenii*   Plate 27

Length 4.5–5″. A tiny, uncommon grassland bird, *suggesting a miniature courser* or plover. Usually seen first in lark-like flight when flushed from grass and showing *rounded wings strikingly patterned with rufous, black and white*. **Male** *rufous-brown above with broad cream-coloured or pale buff superciliary stripes and similar streaks and U-shaped marks on back* and scapulars; wing-coverts cream or white with rufous markings. Some birds show rufous-brown postocular lines extending to sides of neck, others entirely pale around eyes except for rufous smudge on ear-coverts. Underparts whitish with buff breast, sometimes with rufous-bordered cream spots; sides may show rufous wash. Bill greenish brown to pale green; eyes light brown; tarsi and toes whitish flesh or creamy yellow (said to be dark pink in some birds). **Female** similar but breast dark rufous brown. **Juvenile** paler, less rufous than adult, more vermiculated above. Solitary. Runs rapidly and stands erect, but if disturbed may crouch and freeze; slow rocking loco-motion (see above) used on bare ground or in sparse cover. Flushes silently, almost underfoot, and flies in slightly undulating, erratic flight, further spreading wings and ele-vating tail before dropping into the grass. Somewhat nocturnal, at times active in rainy weather, and said to be vocal on moonlit nights. **Call** a soft low whistle likened to the sound of wind blowing through a pipe. **Range**: Local in dry n. and e. Kenya, recorded at Turkwell River, Lake Baringo, Samburu and Shaba GRs, Kora NR, Meru, both Tsavo and Tarangire NPs; to be expected in Mkomazi GR.

COMMON BUTTON-QUAIL *Turnix sylvatica lepurana*   Plate 27

Length 5.5–6″. A *tiny, very short-tailed, quail-like* bird, usually seen in flight when *dark brown flight feathers contrast with paler buff wing-coverts*, post-humerals and some scapulars. *Flight slower, more fluttery, less whirring than quail's*; feet may dangle, rail-like, at take-off; body appears more slender than in true quail which also have longer, nar-rower, uniformly dark wings. Appears more quail-like when hunched in grass; *upperparts dull rufous-brown with indistinct scaly pattern and nar-row black bars. Long pale patch* formed by buff edges of some wing feathers and scapu-lars noticeable in fresh plumage, this patch spotted with rufous/dark brown, and con-trasting with brown outer remiges. Rufous crown has pale buff median stripe; face pale buff and black-speckled as are sides of throat; *breast bright orange-rufous* with *bold black U-shaped spots on sides/upper flanks*. Female brighter than male. *Bill pale grey, eyes whitish*; feet pale flesh-pink. **Juvenile/Immature** have duller crown and a *band of dark spots across breast*. When flushed, flies low and not far, raises wings very briefly on

alighting; runs after landing and reluctant to flush again. Vocal day and night, mostly at dawn and dusk. **Call** of courting female a deep resonant droning *hoom, hoom, hoom. . . that* may develop into a soft 'drumming,' slower and deeper than call of Red-chested Flufftail. Also gives 2 long penetrating notes, the first high-pitched and longer, the second lower and shorter. Male said to give a sharp *tuc-tuc,* and a high kestrel-like *kee-kee-kee-kee.* **Range**: Local in major grasslands of Serengeti NP, Mara GR, cent. Rift Valley, the Tsavo parks, and Arusha Dist.

BLACK-RUMPED BUTTON-QUAIL *Turnix hottentotta nana*   **Plate 27**
Length 5.5". A scarce and secretive bird of wet grasslands and marsh edges. *Diagnostic black rump and tail* evident in flight. On ground, appears rich buff or orange-rufous from face to breast, and barred sides and flanks separate it from *T. sylvatica.* Scapulars also broadly edged golden-buff or orange-rufous. Belly white (not dark as in Harlequin Quail, which also shows dark rump). **Male** has speckled malar area, usually black forehead and crown, and whitish or golden buff throat; these orange-rufous in **female**. Wing-coverts are paler than remiges, but show less contrast than in Common Button-quail which appears more uniformly rufous-brown above (although rump/upper tail-coverts somewhat darker). Eyes pale creamy tan or whitish, sometimes pale blue-grey; feet light pink or whitish. **Call** a *Sarothrura*-like *ooooop-oooooop,* and a series of shorter resonant *hoo* notes. **Range**: Trans-Nzoia area of nw. Kenya where once apparently regular; few records since 1950.

RAILS AND RELATIVES, FAMILY RALLIDAE

A diverse family including the small, partly terrestrial flufftails and large, heavy-set, aquatic coots and gallinules. Plumage tends to be cryptic, with marked sexual dimorphism exhibited only by the flufftails. All rallids have fairly short rounded wings, short tails, long tarsi and long slender toes. Flight appears weak and laboured, but several perform long-distance movements. Most are birds of marshes and swamps, but the *Crex* species inhabit grassland and some flufftails live in forest. Some, notably the flufftails, are highly vocal.

WHITE-SPOTTED FLUFFTAIL *Sarothrura pulchra centralis*   **Plate 26**

Length 6–7". Fairly common but shy and skulking in swampy forest and thick riverine bush. **Male** *rufous-chestnut from head to breast, on upper back and tail*; rest of plumage *black with white spots.* **Female** rufous-chestnut as in male, but rest of plumage *coarsely barred brown and rufous,* and rufous tail is black-barred. **Juvenile** browner than female, more barred on breast. See Buff-spotted Flufftail. Vocal all day. **Call** a short whistled note rapidly repeated 6–14 times, *yew-yew-yew-yew-yew. . .,* likened to tinkerbird's song, but louder, more mellow; also a faster, high pitched *wuwuwuwu. . ..* **Range**: Nandi and Kakamega forests to Busia Dist. and along Ugandan border south of Mt Elgon.

BUFF-SPOTTED FLUFFTAIL *Sarothrura e. elegans*   **Plate 26**

Length 6-7". An uncommon crake of rank *forest undergrowth,* usually not associated with water. **Male** bright rufous-chestnut from head to upper breast; otherwise *black below, densely spotted with whitish and buff*; upperparts dark brown with *much buff spotting; tail barred rufous and black.* **Female** brown above with paler, partly black-rimmed, buffy brown spots; *underparts heavily barred* except for whitish throat; belly with broader dark brown bars; tail banded rufous-brown, buff and black.
Juvenile uniform sepia-brown, paler below, white on mid-belly. Vocal in evening, at night and early morning in cloudy, misty weather. **Call** a far-carrying, hollow wail, with the resonance of a tuning fork; starts low, rises in pitch toward end, and lasts up to 4 sec.
Range: Nandi and Kakamega forests and Kitale area in w. Kenya. Isolated records from Lake Turkana and Maralal to cent. Kenya, Mara GR, Kilimanjaro, Usambaras and Pemba Island suggest a broader range.

RED-CHESTED FLUFFTAIL *Sarothrura rufa*   Plate 26

Length 6–7". A common but elusive bird of *swamps and marshes.* **Adult male** *bright rufous from head to breast and upper back; rest of plumage black with short white streaks,* changing to spots on the *largely black tail.* When flushed, front third of bird appears rufous, the rest black. Western *elizabethae* has longer white streaks and no spots. **Female** dark brown above with buff speckling and feather edging, appearing scaly or barred in *elizabethae*, more spotted in *S. r. rufa.* Tail almost plain blackish brown; throat white, other underparts buffy white with dark mottling and barring. (Female Striped Flufftail resembles *rufa*, but has broadly banded tail and is confined to higher elevations.) **Juvenile** dusky black above, somewhat greyer below, the throat and mid-belly whitish. **Call** a series of upslurred whistles, about one per sec. and in long series, *huer-huer-huer-huer. . .*, or *tui-tui-tui . . .*, often followed by a high-pitched *ki-ki-ki-ki-ki-ki.* **Range**: Local up to 2700 m, *elizabethae* in w. Kenya, east to Timboroa and Molo; nominate *rufa* in cent. Kenya (incl. Nairobi and Thika areas), Arusha area, South Pare and Usambara mts (formerly on Pemba Island).

STREAKY-BREASTED FLUFFTAIL *Sarothrura boehmi*   Plate 26

Length 6–7". A secretive bird of *flooded grasslands.* **Male** *black above with thin white streaks,* has bright rufous head and neck with contrasting white throat. *Breast and belly whitish with extensive dark streaking. Black tail very short.* (Red-chested Flufftail is similar above, but rufous on throat, breast and upper back.) **Female** *blackish* (not brown) above, with fine white streaks and feather edges; much paler below than female Red-chested, *almost plain white on throat* and belly. **Juvenile** sooty black, whitish on throat and mid-belly. **Call** a hollow hoot repeated at 2 sec. intervals, *hooh. . . hooh. . . hooh . . .*, like someone blowing across an open bottle; also a higher-pitched, faster *gaWOO, gaWOO, gaWOO. . .* or *koo-AH, koo-AH. . .*, accelerating, and sometimes ending with *blip-blip-blip-blip.* **Range/status**: Scarce intra-African migrant following heavy April/May rains. Early records from Kitale, Kisumu and Machakos; recently at Thika, Nairobi NP and Mumias. Juv. at The Ark (Aberdare Mts) July 1990.

STRIPED FLUFFTAIL *Sarothrura affinis antonii*   Plate 26

Length 5.5–6". Scarce, and restricted to *montane grasslands and moors.* **Male** plain rufous at both ends, black in the middle, streaked with buff above, with white below. (White-spotted Flufftail has body and wings spotted, not streaked.) **Female** dusky brown above with bright scaly buff feather edges; *tail broadly banded rufous and black or* (on birds from Mt Kenya and Aberdares) *sooty with slight traces of rufous.* **Call** a rather slow, repetitive hoot, *huuw-huuw-huuw-huuw. . .* each note starting softly, increasing in volume, then fading slowly away. Also gives a series of grunts, and a rapid *ti-ti-ti-tititi* that fades to a slower *tee-tee-teee-teee.* **Range**: Above 3000 m on the Aberdares, Mt Kenya and Mt Elgon; one caught and ringed June 1977 in the Nguruman Hills (near site of early collection in Jan. 1909).

AFRICAN CRAKE *Crex egregia*   Plate 26

Length 7.5–9". A *short-billed*, brown-and-grey crake of wet grassland and marshes. Shows *narrow white superciliary stripes,* and *heavy black-and-white barring on flanks, belly and crissum.* **Adult** dark olive-brown above, with white throat; grey from sides of head to breast. *Bill grey with pink or reddish base;* eyes red or orange; orbital skin pink; legs and feet olive. **Juvenile** has grey of face and breast replaced by dull brownish buff, more obscure *brown* flank barring, faint superciliaries, and brown bill; eyes grey-green or brown. (Spotted Crake has white-spotted neck, breast and wing-coverts, olive-green tarsi and red-brown eyes.) **Call** a short hard *kik* or *kak*, and a series of 8–9 rapid, high-pitched, whistling notes, somewhat trilled: *kik-kik-kik-kik-ik-ik-ikiki-ikikikikik*; also has a harsh, Corncrake-like *churrr.* **Range/status**: Local and uncommon intra-African migrant, mainly April–Sept. Has bred in w. and cent. Kenya, and near Lake Manyara, but most records from Lake Victoria basin, Lake Baringo and s. Kenyan coast (probably non-breeding birds from southern tropics).

CORNCRAKE Crex crex   Plate 26

Length 10.5″. A large *grassland* crake, buff-and-brown, with *tawny-rufous wing-coverts diagnostic in flight*. Olive-buff above with black streaks; head buff with *broad grey superciliaries*; foreneck and breast greyish tawny; underparts mainly buffy white with *broad brown barring on sides and flanks*. Bill *pale pinkish-brown or flesh-pink*; legs and feet *pale flesh-pink*. Shy and secretive. When flushed, flies only a short distance, with dangling feet. **Range/status**: Uncommon palearctic passage migrant, Oct.–Dec. and March–April). Less frequent than formerly; recent records mainly from cent. Kenya, Mara GR (April) and Tsavo West NP (Nov.–Dec.).

AFRICAN WATER RAIL Rallus caerulescens   Plate 25

Length 11–12″. A large rail of swamps and freshwater marshes, with *long red bill* and *red legs, barred flanks* and red eyes. Blackish on crown, otherwise dark brown above, mostly dark slate-grey below, whitish on throat; *flanks barred black and white; under tail-coverts white*. **Juvenile** sooty brown above, with heavy brown barring on flanks, blackish or dull red bill, legs and feet. Secretive. Constantly flicks tail when walking in the open at dawn or dusk. Runs rapidly with long strides and swims well. Flies low with dangling feet. **Call** a high-pitched *pree* followed by a rapid loud pumping *pi-pi-pi-pip-pip* . . ., also a loud *kew-kew-kew*. . ., the 10–20 notes gradually slowing and dropping in pitch. **Range**: Widespread but uncommon. Most numerous from cent. Kenyan highlands and Rift Valley south to Mara GR, Amboseli NP, Lake Jipe and Arusha NP.

BAILLON'S CRAKE Porzana pusilla obscura   Plate 26

Length 6–7″. A *small, short-billed* marsh crake, rich brown above and grey below. **Male** *flecked with black and white on upper back and wing-coverts*. Face, neck and underparts largely slaty blue-grey, *flanks and crissum barred black and white* (but less boldly than in African Crake, which has different bill colour and lacks white markings on upperparts). Bill, legs and feet greenish or greenish grey; eyes red. **Female** similar but whitish on throat and upper breast. **Juvenile** pale buff below, mottled on breast, barred on sides and flanks and more heavily on crissum. (Little Crake, *Porzana parva*, unsubstantiated in our region, resembles Baillon's, but is slightly larger and paler above, with *whitish scapular stripes,* unpatterned wing-coverts, and longer, thinner bill.) Forages on mud or floating vegetation at marsh edges. **Call** a dry rattling trill, *ti-ti-ti-ti-ti-ti-ti-tirrrrr*, lasting 2–3 sec. and repeated, mainly at night. **Range**: W. Kenya east to Thika and Mombasa, south to near Arusha. No East African breeding records. (Palearctic *P. p. intermedia* possibly also present Nov.–April.)

SPOTTED CRAKE Porzana porzana   Plate 26

Length 8–9.5″. A *brownish, bar-flanked* marsh crake, *extensively white-speckled* and with narrow white streaking on upperparts. **Male** has slate-grey face and throat, brown-tinged neck and breast, all dotted with white; lower underparts buffy white with *brown-barred sides and flanks*. Eyes red-brown, *bill yellowish green or greenish yellow with red base*; tarsi and toes olive-green to greenish yellow. Similar **female** has less grey on foreparts, and sides of head and neck more heavily spotted. (African Crake is not white-spotted; adult's neck and breast are plain grey. Adult Striped Crake has bright cinnamon crissum, no red at base of bill.) Less skulking than most crakes. *Constantly flicks tail, showing buff under tail-coverts.* **Call** a short *kreck* or *krrick* when alarmed; generally silent in Africa. **Range/status**: Uncommon palearctic migrant, Oct.–April. Recorded at Lake Turkana and in w., cent. and se. Kenya, mainly on spring passage.

STRIPED CRAKE Aenigmatolimnas marginalis   Plate 26

Length 8–9″. A large-toed, heavy-billed crake of marshes and swamps. **Male** *rich tawny to orange-buff on head, neck and breast*, and with *white-streaked brown upperparts*. Upper tail-coverts are brighter, more orange-brown, and *cinnamon under tail-coverts* flash as bird habitually flicks tail; tawny cinnamon lower flanks also contrast with whitish belly; sides/upper flanks olive-brown with white feather edges. Bill orange-brown; eyes golden brown with *orange or yellow orbital ring*; tarsi and very long toes jade-green. **Female** similar but dark grey on head, paler *blue-grey on neck and breast*, the feathers white-edged; flanks and crissum as in male. Orbital skin, tarsi and toes yellowish green. **Juvenile** *plain unstreaked* brown above with tawny buff foreparts, dull white on belly and crissum; bill yellow-brown, feet blue-grey. Secretive, but stands in the open to dry plumage after rain. **Call** a sharp repetitive *tak-tak-tak-tak* at night or on dark cloudy days. **Range/status**: Scarce intra-African migrant, presumably from southern tropics, mainly May–Nov. Scattered Kenyan records from w., cent., and s. areas and the coast.

BLACK CRAKE *Amaurornis flavirostris* Plate 25

Length 7–8″. The most frequently seen rail. Unmistakable with *plain dull black plumage, short greenish yellow bill, and red legs, feet and eyes*. **Immature** *olive-brown above and grey below* (sometimes with variable amounts of white on cheeks and throat). Bill dull greenish yellow, brightening with age; tarsi and toes pinkish flesh, later bright orange; eyes pale brown at first. **Juvenile** *dark chocolate-brown*; feet blackish slate; bill slaty with pink base, becoming greenish yellow. Not shy. Active all day, often in the open. **Calls** include a throaty *coo-crr-chrooo*, and a rippling *weet, eet, eet, eet*, and a series of loud wheezing sounds from dense cover. **Range**: Widespread in w. and cent. Kenya, much of n. Tanzania, and on coast.

ALLEN'S GALLINULE *Porphyrio alleni* Plate 25

Length 10–12″. A uncommon dark gallinule with *greenish blue frontal shield, dark red bill*, and *dark red tarsi and toes*. **Adult** has *blackish head*, dark green upperparts and bright purplish blue underparts except for white under tail-coverts. (Moorhens have olive or grey-green tarsi and toes.) **Juvenile** dark brown above, pale buff below with white throat and belly, rich buff under tail-coverts; bill brown with red base, frontal shield olive-brown; legs and feet pale pink. Shy. Favours sites with floating vegetation. Swims and dives well. Flicks tail when walking; runs rapidly with lowered head, and often climbs in vegetation. **Calls** include a sharp *kik*, a metallic *kleerk* and a dry nasal *kekk*, singly or rapidly repeated; also a series of sharp, frog-like sounds ending with a chur:*kik-kik-kik-kik-ki-kier-kier-kierr-kierr-kiurrrrrrrr*; in flight, a sharp *kli-kli-kli*. **Range**: Local. Present all year at Lake Baringo (most numerous June–Sept.) Mostly scattered records elsewhere.

PURPLE SWAMPHEN *Porphyrio porphyrio madagascariensis* Plate 25

Length 15–18″. A *large* gallinule of papyrus swamps and reedbeds, especially those with water-lilies. *Size and massive red bill* distinctive. **Adult** mainly *blue and dull purple* with bronzy green back, white under tail-coverts and pinkish red tarsi and toes. **Subadult** bluish and olive-brown above, generally pale grey on head, neck and underparts; bill, legs and feet duller than in adult. **Juvenile** dull brown below but readily identified by heavy reddish bill. Vocal day and night. **Calls** include wide variety of shrieks, whistles, neighing, and especially grunting and cackling sounds, sometimes in excited chorus. Contact call a clucking *aak aak aak . . .* or *cuk-cuk-cuk-cuk*. Alarm note a loud *kree-ik*. **Range**: Local (and now uncommon) in Kenyan Rift Valley, near Nairobi, Thika, Amboseli, Lake Jipe, Mombasa, and from Arusha NP west to Ngorongoro Crater and the Mbulu Highlands.

COMMON MOORHEN *Gallinula chloropus meridionalis* Plate 25

Length 12–14″. A perky slate-grey swimmer with *yellow-tipped red bill and red frontal shield rounded posteriorly*. Blackish on head, tinged olive-brown on the back, and a conspicuous *line of broad white streaks along sides*; under tail-coverts white with black central patch. Legs and feet yellowish green with *orange-red 'garters' around tibiae*. (Lesser Moorhen is smaller, the bill red only on culmen, and no red bands on legs; juvenile paler and buffier; frontal shield pointed at base.) **Immature** dark brown above, buffy slate below with some white on throat and buff-tinged flank stripes. Bill greenish brown, yellow at tip. **Juvenile** brown, with buffy white throat, whitish in centre of breast and belly, olive-brown bill/frontal shield, and olive legs with yellow tibial bands. Swims in open water or among floating vegetation; dives readily; walks with high-stepping gait, often jerking tail. Climbs among reeds and waterside branches. **Calls** a single loud *quaarrk* or *kraak,* and a double or triple *kik-kik* or *kek-kek-kek.* **Range:** Widespread in w. and cent. Kenya, and in much of n. Tanzania. Local along coast and at Lake Turkana.

LESSER MOORHEN *Gallinula angulata*   Plate 25

Length 9–10.5″. A *small* moorhen with *largely yellow bill, red only along culmen,* and *red frontal shield pointed (not rounded) on forehead;* legs and feet yellowish green with no red tibial bands. Body dark grey with line of white streaks on sides; head blackish; back olive-brown. White under tail-coverts have black mid-line, visible when tail flicked upward as bird swims or walks. **Immature** paler and browner than adult, but *grey on face and throat;* some black around base of bill; pale brownish grey below, more buffy brown on breast; bill yellowish, frontal shield orange. **Juvenile** olive-brown above, *whitish below with some buff on sides of breast;* bill dull yellow; legs and feet grey-green. Shy; remains in or near cover. **Call** a soft *pyup,* and a sharp high *kik* or *tik.* **Range/status:** Intra-African migrant, April–Aug., during and after the long rains. Has bred in Nairobi/Thika area and near Arusha, but mainly a visitor to Lake Victoria basin, cent. Kenyan highlands and coastal lowlands.

RED-KNOBBED or CRESTED COOT *Fulica cristata*   Plate 25

Length 16–18″. A common *slate-grey* swimming bird with a *white bill and frontal shield.* During breeding season develops 2 dark red knobs at top of frontal shield, these dull and much smaller after nesting. Eyes red when breeding, otherwise dull red-brown; tarsi and broadly lobed toes olive or greenish when breeding, slate-grey most of year. **Juvenile** dull brown above, flecked with white on head and neck, whitish around base of bill and on throat; mostly pale grey below; bill, legs and feet grey. Swims with pumping motion of head; patters across water before taking wing. Dives frequently. Highly gregarious. Usual **calls** a low *hoo-hoo,* a harsh, somewhat metallic *kik-kik* or *kerrk,* and a disyllabic *co-up.* **Range:** Widespread on permanent Kenyan waters, most numerous in highlands and on freshwater Rift Valley lakes. Small numbers on most freshwater n. Tanzanian lakes, particularly in the Crater and Mbulu highlands.

CRANES, FAMILY GRUIDAE

Stately, long-necked, long-legged birds of marshes, grassland, and cultivation. Plumage mainly grey, the same in both sexes. Some species have ornamental plumes or crests, and the large secondaries hang down over the short tail. Many individuals pair for life, holding large territories when breeding, and performing elaborate dancing displays. Gregarious outside breeding season, sometimes forming large flocks. Flight is strong and often sustained, with head and neck held below the horizontal, imparting a distinctive hunchbacked appearance.

DEMOISELLE CRANE *Anthropoides virgo*   Plate 9

Length 38″. Pale blue-grey with black foreparts. White postocular stripes continue as a tuft of long drooping feathers along hindneck; flight feathers black; long inner secondaries extend and droop well beyond the dark grey tail. Bill olive-grey with reddish tip; legs and feet black. **Immature** duller and more ash-grey, the breast feathers and postocular tuft short and grey. Feeds in open grassland, savanna and marshland. **Call** a soft purring when feeding; in the air, a low raspy sound. **Status:** Palearctic vagrant; 8 adults and an immature photographed near Malindi Jan. 1986, seen again near Mt Kenya in March.

✓**GREY CROWNED CRANE** *Balearica regulorum gibbericeps* **Plate 9**

Length 43–44″. A tall wetland crane, slate-grey with *white, black and chestnut wings, velvety black forehead/forecrown,* and *crest of bristly straw-coloured feathers; large bare white cheek patch bordered with red above; pendulous red wattle* hangs from black throat. Bill, legs and feet black, eyes pale blue. (Rare Black Crowned Crane is darker, particularly on neck; cheek patch is largely pink with smaller area of white.) **Juvenile** has rufous feather edges above, rufous head and neck, short tawny crest, whitish cheeks and brown eyes. Gregarious except when breeding. **Call** a loud honking from perch or in flight, members of a pair often calling in unison, *ku-waank, oo-waank. . .,* or *ka-oo-ga-lunk. . .* A low booming sequence, often by several displaying birds calling together, may continue for several minutes; also a low purring while feeding. **Range**: Widespread above 1300 m in w. and cent. Kenya and much of n. Tanzania. Has wandered to the coast and to Lake Turkana.

BLACK CROWNED CRANE *Balearica pavonina ceciliae* **Plate 9**
Length 36–38″. A rare northern crane resembling the preceding species but *black,* not slate-grey, and the bare *face patch largely pink, white only on upper quarter;* short throat wattle rose-pink. **Juvenile** also dark, with rufous feather edges. **Calls** like those of preceding species, and often a single *wonk* or *ka-wonk.* **Status**: A few sight records on n. shores of Lake Turkana.

FINFOOT, FAMILY HELIORNITHIDAE

A shy, somewhat grebe-like waterbird with a long body, thin neck, and small head with a fairly long tapered bill. The short tarsi are set far back and the long toes are lobed, with well developed claws. When alarmed, swimming bird submerges, often leaving only the head above water. On shore it waddles duck-like. It frequently rests on emergent rocks or logs, and climbs in branches overhanging the water.

AFRICAN FINFOOT *Podica senegalensis somereni* **Plate 25**

Length of male, 21–26″; female 18–20″. A scarce long-bodied bird of shaded riverbanks. *Swims with pumping neck motion,* the ample black tail spread out flat on the water surface. **Male** has black crown and neck washed with iridescent green, a narrow *whitish line from eyes down sides of the dark slaty blue neck;* back dark brown, glossed greenish, and rather heavily *white-spotted* as are brown sides and flanks. *Bill coral red;* eyes red-brown; *feet mainly bright orange-red.* **Female** duller, browner above, with buffy white throat and foreneck, and more *distinct white neck line;* bill dusky above, red below. **Juvenile** resembles female but is brown above, and tawny buff breast and flanks are faintly spotted. Infrequent **call** a sharp *skwack* or a duck-like *kwack, kwak-wak-wak-wak.* **Range**: In Kenya, on the Tana and Galana rivers and tributaries, and the Naro Moru, Mbagathi, Migori, Mara and Ramisi rivers. In n. Tanzania, in Moshi Dist. and the East Usambaras.

BUSTARDS, FAMILY OTIDIDAE

Large to very large terrestrial birds of grassland, bush and semi-desert scrub. All have rather short bills, long slender necks, stout bodies, short tails and fairly long legs with only 3 toes on each foot. They walk purposefully, head moving back and forth, pausing briefly to feed. Flight is strong, heavy, with slow deliberate wingbeats, the neck extended crane-like. Males are brighter and generally larger than females. Plumage of most species is cryptically vermiculated above, white, buff or black below. The smaller *Eupodotis* species can be quite vocal, whereas *Neotis* and *Ardeotis* are almost silent except during the male's elaborate courtship displays.

DENHAM'S or JACKSON'S BUSTARD *Neotis denhami* **Plates 29, 30**
Length 33–46″. A large grassland bustard with *bright orange-rufous hindneck,* less extensive in female. **Male** dark brown above with much black and white mottling on wing-coverts; foreneck and breast light grey; belly white; black crown has white central stripe

and is bordered below by white superciliaries and black eye-lines. **Female** has centre of crown brown, foreneck buff with dark brown vermiculations. Bill dull yellowish white with dark culmen and tip in both sexes; tarsi yellowish white; eyes brown. **Juvenile** resembles adult but shows some variation in neck and throat colour and extent of crown stripe. Usually solitary. Breeding male struts and displays with enormously inflated neck and breast, tail either raised or lowered, with body almost vertical. **Call** an infrequent barking *kaa-kaa*, and during courtship a resonant booming. **Range**: *N. d. jacksoni* very local in cent. Serengeti NP, n. Masai Mara GR, east to Narok and lower sw. slopes of Mau Escarpment; main stronghold now the Laikipia Plateau and high grasslands northwest of Maralal. Birds near Lokichokio may be *N. d. denhami*.

HEUGLIN'S BUSTARD *Neotis heuglinii*   Plate 29

Length 26–35". A large bustard of northern thorn-bush and lava fields. Black cap, blue-grey neck and white belly may suggest smaller Whitebellied Bustard, but *breast is rich chestnut bordered below by a narrow black band, and bill is black above, yellowish below*. Upperparts mostly light brown with dark brown and buff barring. Black crown (especially in female) may have a white central stripe; face and chin black in male, mainly grey in female. *In flight, mostly white outer primaries contrast with otherwise dark wings*. Legs pale yellow; eyes dark. **Immature male** resembles female but has large white nape patch and blackish streak below and around eyes. Shy, wary and nomadic. Voice unrecorded. **Range**: East side of Lake Turkana, south to Marsabit and Turbi, Rhamu/El Wak area and Shaba GR (regular?), occasionally to Bura, n. Tsavo East NP and Galana Ranch.

KORI BUSTARD *Ardeotis kori struthiunculus*   Plate 30 ✔

Length 41–50"; A *very large, thick-necked and distinctly crested* bustard of open grassland. Greyish brown above with the grey vermiculated neck and breast feathers filamentous and erectile. Black sides of crown . and postocular stripes extend back to straggling crest. *Chequered blackand-white pattern near bend of wing and black patches at sides of lower neck* are diagnostic. In flight, shows pale diagonal band across upper wing-coverts, white-barred inner primaries, and black-and-white-banded tail. Legs and feet pale yellowish or creamy white; eyes yellowish. In far northern Kenya see Arabian Bustard. Solitary or in pairs, although 15–20 birds may congregate at grass fires or on recently harvested wheat fields. Courting male erects lax neck feathers, and raises spread tail vertically to show fluffy white under coverts. **Call** of displaying male a deep resonant *voomp. . .voomp. . .voomp*. **Range**: Widespread below 2000 m. Most numerous from the Rift Valley highlands south to Mara GR, Loita Plains, Amboseli NP and inland n. Tanzania. Local from Tana River south to the Tsavo parks and Shimba Hills.

ARABIAN BUSTARD *Ardeotis arabs*   Plate 30

Length 33–36". A rare, large-crested bustard of dry n. Kenya. Smaller and slimmer than the similar (and partly sympatric) Kori, paler and more tawny above, *without black on wing-coverts and sides of lower neck*. Shows several *rows of creamy or buffy white spots on wing-coverts* (less distinct in juvenile). Eyes yellow-orange. Flight pattern similar to Kori's. Display **call** said to be a rasping or croaking *pah pah*. **Range**: Northern border areas (Collected in Turkana, Jan. 1932; photographed near Ileret, Jan. 1989.)

CRESTED BUSTARD *Eupodotis ruficrista gindiana*   Plate 29 ✔

Length 18–21". A small, black-bellied and pale-eyed bustard of *thornscrub or dry bush*. **Male** has *almost plain rufous-buff head with drooping crest; a narrow black stripe extends down foreneck to the belly*, and much white on adjacent wing edges. Upperparts tawny brown with large pointed brown spots; most of neck buffy grey; breast grey with white patches at sides. In flight, dark wings show long white diagonal central band and vermiculated black-and-white tail appears grey with a broad black tip. Eyes, legs and feet cream-coloured. **Female** and **juvenile** more buff-flecked on

327

crown and nape, rufous-buff around eyes, densely flecked and barred with brown on neck. (See Black-bellied and Hartlaub's Bustards.) Secretive; alone or in pairs. **Calls** of displaying male include short series of melancholy whistles, *kweu, kweu, kweu . . .*, and some harsh strident calls and whistles continuing up the scale and ending on a sustained high note; also has a descending high piping, *kee-keea, k'keea, k'keea . . .*, suggesting Crested Francolin's call. After impressive aerial display, male gives a low *tuck-tuck-tuck, chuk chuk chuk chuk . . .* as he follows female. A loud whistled *KWEEEE-kwer. . . KWEEEE-kwer-kwer . . .* is repeated frequently on moonlit nights. **Range**: Widespread in dry n. and e. Kenya, mainly below 1300 m; south of the highlands it ranges west to Olorgesailie and Lake Natron, south through Tarangire NP and the Masai Steppe. **Taxonomic Note**: Some authors consider *gindiana* specifically distinct from *ruficrista*.

WHITE-BELLIED BUSTARD *Eupodotis senegalensis canicollis*   **Plate 29**

Length 19–24″. The only small East African bustard with a *bluish grey neck and white belly* in both sexes. **Male** tawny brown above and on breast, *black on forehead/forecrown; sides of head are white with black lines along lower crown border, below eyes and from chin to cheeks.* Bill deep bright pink, almost red when breeding, tip and culmen dusky; legs and feet pale creamy yellow. **Female** resembles male but has tan cheeks, blue-grey forehead and crown, and brown-and-buff subocular line; throat patch reduced to black-and-white speckling; lower throat and front of neck and breast sandy buff with fine dusky vermiculations. **Sub-adult male** has brownish face, white superciliaries, grey neck with white throat, and suggestion of blackish head pattern; bill dull yellowish with dusky tip. **Juvenile** has grey crown, largely whitish face with no black, and the mainly tawny buff neck is whitish in front. Pairs or family groups forage in bushy grassland and savanna. (Young remain with adults for long periods, unlike other bustards.) Birds frequently call to each other in early morning and evening. **Call** a very loud guttural *k'wuka WHUKa, k'wuka WHUKa . . .*, or *ka-warrak, ka-warrak . . .*, sometimes preceded by some low, frog-like *gaa* notes. **Range**: Widespread in cent., s. and se. Kenya, and in n. Tanzania where most numerous in Serengeti NP. Local (and scarce) in n. Kenya.

 BLACK-BELLIED BUSTARD *Eupodotis m. melanogaster*   **Plate 29**

Length 23–25″. A thin-necked bustard of *open grassland*, more typical of higher-rainfall areas than the similar Hartlaub's Bustard. **Male** tawny buff with brown and black markings above, *including back and rump; tail brown and buff with 4–5 narrow dark brown bands.* (Hartlaub's has black lower back, dark brown rump and tail.) *Long neck almost uniformly buffy brown* (hindneck greyish in male Hartlaub's) with no obvious markings; top and sides of head buff with dark flecks; *lores and chin whitish*; throat dark with grey flecking. A thin black line down centre of foreneck, bordered narrowly with white, joins black underparts which contrast with white edge of closed wing. Whitish superciliary stripes border *thin black lines from eyes to black occipital feathers*, forming a short drooping crest. *Spread wing mostly white above, with broad brown central wedge extending from base to median coverts.* Outermost primary brownish black, most others with short black tips. Broad trailing edge of all but outermost secondaries black. Bill dull yellowish, brown on culmen; eyes light brown; legs/feet dull yellow. **Female** difficult to separate from Hartlaub's; differences discussed under that species. **Juvenile** duller, darker, with buff wing spots; crown dark grey. Solitary except when breeding. **Call** of displaying male a short rising wheezy whistle, *zhweeeeee*, as bird suddenly retracts his head onto the back; after a short pause, he emits a popping *quock* or *plop* followed by soft gurgling as head is slowly raised. **Range**: Local in w. and cent. Kenyan highlands north to Mt Marsabit and Huri Hills. In the south (after heavy rains) from Mara GR, Amboseli, Shimba Hills, and n. Tanzania from Mkomazi GR and Arusha NP west to the Lake Victoria basin.

HARTLAUB'S BUSTARD *Eupodotis hartlaubii*   **Plate 29**

Length 24–28″. Commonly mistaken for Black-bellied Bustard but slightly stockier and more contrastingly marked; bill appears slightly heavier. **Male** has similar white-bordered black foreneck stripe connecting with black belly, but *hindneck greyish*, not brown, and *side of face more sharply patterned*: large white spot on and below ear-coverts contrasts with heavy black postocular line above and with another from eye to throat. Crown is brownish black with buffy white speckling. *Shows more white on the closed wing than does Black-bellied Bustard*, has *darker crown, chin and throat* (the latter all black in some birds, a 'pepper-and-salt' pattern in others). In flight, shows *black from lower back to the dark brown, faintly banded tail; wings have more white than in Black-bellied,* with smaller and narrower dark wedge extending from body to coverts. **Female** darker than that species, with *cream-coloured line down foreneck; rest of neck streaked or somewhat spotted, not finely vermiculated; upper breast with discrete blackish markings, not vermiculations; lower back to tail basically grey,* not brownish. **Immature male** shows dull adult pattern, no solid black on throat; eyes dark yellow. Generally prefers drier sites than Black-bellied Bustard, but following heavy rains, both species may appear together in several localities. Displaying male struts with raised tail, inflated throat/upper neck, and gives a 3-part **call**: a soft *click* followed by *pop!*, then (as head is lowered onto the breast) a deep prolonged *oooooooohm*. **Range**: In Kenya, local in dry grasslands from Nairobi NP southeast through Amboseli NP to the Tsavo parks (where fairly common). Regular after rains in Meru NP and Marsabit. In n. Tanzania scattered records from Mkomazi GR, Arusha Dist., Tarangire NP and seasonally in e. Serengeti NP.

JACANAS, FAMILY JACANIDAE

Sometimes called 'lily-trotters,' jacanas are long-legged, rail-like birds of swampy pools and marshy lake edges. Their exceedingly long toes and claws enable them to walk easily on floating vegetation where they feed and nest.

AFRICAN JACANA *Actophilornis africanus*   **Plate 25**

Length 12". Unmistakable, with *chestnut wings and body, white face and foreneck, and bright blue bill and frontal shield*. Legs and feet slate-grey or blue-grey, the long claws dark brown. *White underparts of* **juvenile** glossy golden-yellow at sides of breast, rufous on flanks; also has *small grey or blue-grey frontal shield*, broad whitish buff superciliary stripes and generally brown upperparts. Half-grown young distinguished from Lesser Jacana by small frontal shield, *uniform black cap and hind-neck, chestnut secondaries and wing-linings.* Various strident **calls** include a harsh rattle, a guttural *kyowrrr*, a grating *kreep-kreep-kreep* and a loud, high-pitched *weep-weep-weep-weeep*, recalling a flufftail (*Sarothrura*) **Range**: Widespread below 3000 m on fresh water with floating or emergent vegetation.

LESSER JACANA *Microparra capensis*   **Plate 25**

Length 6–6.5". Suggests a juvenile African Jacana but much smaller. *Blackish brown above and white below, with golden rufous forehead, prominent white superciliary stripes, and cinnamon crown and nape.* Crown shiny black in some, presumably older, individuals. White face and sides of head marked by *narrow rufous line from bill through eyes to nape.* White underparts with yellowish buff patch on sides of neck and breast. Rump and tail cinnamon-rufous. In flight shows *pale brown panel across wing,* and *black flight feathers with prominent white trailing edge.* Forages on floating vegetation, but shy and easily overlooked. Flight swift and strong; *raises wings on alighting, revealing black wing-linings.* **Juvenile** has buff feather edges above, and *rump and upper tail-coverts are black.* **Call** a soft *kruk* or *koop* repeated several times; also a higher complaining *shrrree shree shree*, and a soft *tchrr-tchrr-tchrr*. **Range**: Local and uncommon in cent., w. and s. Kenya; vagrant(?) in Arusha and Tarangire NPs.

PAINTED-SNIPES, FAMILY ROSTRATULIDAE

Shape suggests true snipe (Scolopacidae), but behaviour more rail-like. The eyes are large and set well forward, and the long slender bill is hard-tipped and bent downward apically. The usual sex roles are reversed: the female is more brightly coloured, and the male builds the nest, incubates the eggs, and cares for the downy young.

GREATER PAINTED-SNIPE *Rostratula b. benghalensis* **Plate 24**

Length 9–10". An uncommon, long-billed marsh-dweller, plump and short-tailed, with a striking head pattern: *buff crown stripe, white or yellowish eye-ring and postocular stripes; also a bold white stripe on sides of breast* and rows of *large black-bordered golden-buff spots on flight feathers.* **Female** is chestnut on neck and from face to upper breast, black on back. Bill orange or pinkish, greenish at base and paler at tip, or dull olive with reddish tip; eyes dark brown; tarsi greyish green. **Male** paler and duller, the face and upper neck grey-brown and streaked; breast and back barred; bill greenish brown. **Juvenile** resembles male but is paler, without a distinct breast stripe. Skulking, nocturnal and crepuscular; also active on dull days. Usually flushes silently, flying on barred, *rounded* wings, feet dangling, and showing a conspicuous golden V on back. Upon alighting, or when feeding, the rear end bobs up and down. **Call** of breeding female a repeated hollow hooting, *koh-koh-koh. . .,* and a loud mellow *booo.* **Range:** Widespread, but highly erratic and seasonal. Largely absent from arid n. and e. Kenya.

CRAB-PLOVER, FAMILY DROMADIDAE

The single species differs from other shorebirds not only in structure but in its tunnel-nesting habits, single white egg and nidicolous young. It is endemic to the Red Sea region and winters southward along the East African coast.

CRAB-PLOVER *Dromas ardeola* **Plate 24**

Length 15–16". A large pied coastal wader with *heavy pointed black bill.* **Adult** white with black back, inner scapulars, wing tips and outer webs of primaries; mainly white tail is grey in centre. Crown and nape greyer in non-breeding plumage; legs and feet blue-grey. **Juvenile** dark grey on back, streaked grey on crown and hindneck; inner wing feathers pale grey, not white. Solitary or gregarious, foraging plover-like. Head often carried low, but long neck is stretched up and forward when alarmed. Flight often low over the water, direct and unhurried, neck extended and feet trailing, but at times flies higher in flocks, lines or V's, the neck then retracted. **Call** a low *kerrk,* and a sharper *chee-rruk* in flight. Flocks produce a continuous harsh chatter. **Range/status**: Migrant from ne. African and Arabian coasts, present all months, mainly Aug.–April. Most numerous in Lamu Archipelago, Mida Creek, and on s. Kenyan coast.

OYSTERCATCHERS, FAMILY HAEMATOPODIDAE

Large, heavily built waders with a distinctive long laterally compressed and colourful bill, sturdy pink legs, and each foot with three partly webbed toes. They typically inhabit rocky beaches, exposed reefs and offshore islands.

EURASIAN OYSTERCATCHER *Haematopus ostralegus longipes* **Plate 24**

Length 16–17". A heavy, black-and-white coastal bird with a *bright orange-red bill, robust pinkish legs and feet,* red eyes and eyelids. Brownish black above and from head to breast; white of underparts extends up beside bend of wing. In flight shows *broad white stripe on wings, and the white back, rump, and tail base contrast with otherwise blackish upperparts and tail tip.* **Immmature** and **non-breeding adults** have whitish collar across throat, lacking in breeding plumage. First-year bird is browner above than adult, with duskier and usually more pointed bill, and *greyish legs and feet.* Usually solitary. **Call** a plaintive far-carrying *kleep* in flight, and a sharp repeated *kip!* or *pic!* **Range/status**: Uncommon but regular palearctic migrant along the coast. A few inland records from lakes Turkana, Baringo and Nakuru.

STILTS AND AVOCETS, FAMILY RECURVIROSTRIDAE

Slender graceful waders with thin bills and exceptionally long thin legs. The three toes are more or less webbed. Plumage is largely black and white.

PIED AVOCET *Recurvirostra avosetta* **Plate 24** ✔

Length 17". Unmistakable with *strongly recurved bill, long slender blue-grey legs* and distinctive pied plumage. The black feathers become brownish with wear and fading. Eyes red (unlike European birds). In flight, appears *largely white with black on wing tips, wing-coverts, scapulars and crown*; feet project well beyond the tail. (Wings of flying Crab-plover show more black, and heavy bill usually visible.) **Juvenile** has the dark plumage areas brown rather than black, and all white feathers are buff-tinged. **Call** a clear melodious *kluit* or *kleep*. Gregarious. Feeds in shallows, sweeping bill from side to side; also swims. Flight strong on stiff wings. **Range:** Widespread inland, but numerous only on alkaline Rift Valley lakes. Some breed at Lake Magadi and on most alkaline lakes in n. Tanzania.

BLACK-WINGED STILT *Himantopus h. himantopus* **Plate 24** ✔

Length 15". A slender *black-and-white* wader with *thin straight black bill* and *extremely long pinkish or red legs*. **Breeding male** glossy black above with mainly white head and neck; hindcrown and nape occasionally dark grey. In flight, wings appear entirely black, both above and below; middle back also black with pointed wedge of white extending from upper tail-coverts and rump; feet extend far beyond the whitish tail. **Breeding female** duller, less glossy above than male and head and neck white or merely with dark-tipped feathers. **Non-breeding adult** has white tips obscuring the greyish crown and nape, and appears mostly white-necked and white-headed. **Juvenile** sepia-brown from above with extensive buff feather tipping; legs and feet duller, more greyish pink. In flight shows pale trailing wing edges. Usually in groups. Wades in deep water, picking insects from surface. **Call** a persistent *pip-pip-pip. . ..* **Range**: Widespread inland and on coastal creeks and saltpans. Most numerous Aug.–April, but some breed in the Rift Valley May–July.

THICK-KNEES, FAMILY BURHINIDAE

Large-headed, somewhat plover-like birds (known as dikkops in southern Africa) which inhabit stony or sandy dry habitats and shorelines. Characterized by stout bill, large glaring yellow eyes, long yellowish legs with swollen tibiotarsal joints, and cryptically-coloured plumage. Largely crepuscular and nocturnal, they rest in the shade during the day, often squatting on their tarsi. Standing posture is typically hunched, but they feed actively with walking or trotting gait interrupted by frequent stops. They also run rapidly, with head and neck extended forward. Flight is fast, fluid and silent, the rather long tail obvious and white wing patches conspicuous. Their loud semi-melodious calls, heard after sundown, are sometimes mistaken for those of nightjars.

EURASIAN THICK-KNEE or STONE CURLEW *Burhinus o. oedicnemus*
Plate 17

Length 16–17". Resembles resident Senegal and Water Thick-knees, with heavily streaked upperparts, neck and breast, but distinguished from them by a *narrow white bar on the lesser coverts bordered both above and below by black*. Legs and feet dull yellow. Bill smaller than in other thick-knees, black-tipped with basal half or more yellow. In flight, shows black wing tips and trailing edge, with 2 white patches at base of primaries. Wings longer and more pointed than in other African thick-knees, and the wingbeats less fluttery. Feet do not project beyond tail. **Juvenile** paler, less heavily marked, wings at first lacking the well-defined contrasting black-and-white bands of adult. (Water Thick-knee is riparian, lacks lower black border to white wing-bar, and shows broad grey panel on the closed wing. Senegal Thick-knee is more finely marked, has much less yellow on its larger bill, and closed wing has no narrow white bar.) Solitary or in small groups in open sandy country or short grassland. **Call** a melodious *cur-LEEE*. Largely silent in East Africa. **Range/status**: Scarce palearctic migrant, Oct.–March, mainly in n. Kenya but recorded south to Nairobi, Amboseli, Mara GR, and (once) Serengeti NP.

SENEGAL THICK-KNEE *Burhinus senegalensis inornatus*   **Plate 17**

Length 12.5–15″. *Finely-streaked* and with *no narrow white bar on the closed wing*; instead, a *wide, pale grey panel bordered above by black. Bill proportionately large, black* with yellow at base of maxilla; legs and feet yellowish. White primary patches prominent in flight. (Water Thick-knee has narrow white bar on wing-coverts separated from pale grey panel by series of narrow black streaks; base of bill dull greenish, not yellow; legs more olive or greenish. Adult Eurasian is larger, more coarsely marked, its white wing-bar bordered above and below by black; immature has more uniformly brown wings.) Prefers sandy country near water. Solitary, in pairs or small flocks. Rests in shade by day. Often forages along shorelines, at times near Water Thick-knees. Vocal at dusk. **Call** a double whistled note, shriller than that of Eurasian and Water thick-knees. Song, *pi-pi-pi-pi-pi-PII-PII-PII-PII-PII-pii-pii-pii-pii*, louder in middle of series then tapering off; thinner and higher-pitched than similar call of Spotted Thick-knee. **Range**: Local in n. and nw. Kenya. Regular at Lake Turkana, occasional south to Lake Baringo.

WATER THICK-KNEE *Burhinus v. vermiculatus*   **Plate 17**

Length 15–16″. More restricted to water's edge than other thick-knees. Closed wing shows a *broad grey panel narrowly streaked with black*, bordered above by narrow white and black bands, and by a black one below. Further differs from its relatives in having fine crossbars and ver-miculations on the body feathers, visible at close range, and a *dull greenish (not yellow) bill base.* Legs and feet olive or greenish. **Juvenile** somewhat more finely marked with buff wing-covert edges. In pairs or small groups on open river banks or lake edges by day, especially when overcast. Somewhat more diurnal than other thick-knees, but most active and vocal at night (when ranging at least one km from water). **Call** a rapid series of piping whistles, rising in pitch and volume, then subsiding with long melancholy notes, *wi-wi-wi-wi-wee-wee-WEE-WEE-WEE-WEE-WEE-WEEI-weeu-weeeu-weeeu-weeeu.* Alarm call a triple *kwa-lee-vee*; also gives a single harsh *whee*. **Range**: Local throughout n. Tanzania and Kenya except at Lake Turkana (where replaced by Senegal Thick-knee). Most numerous at lakes Victoria and Jipe, on coastal creeks and Pemba Island.

✓ **SPOTTED THICK-KNEE** *Burhinus capensis*   **Plate 17**

Length 17″. Boldly *spotted* upperparts and lack of pronounced pattern on closed wing distinguish this *dry-country* species. The face also browner and less patterned than in other thick-knees, and tail strongly barred. Bill black with basal third yellow; legs and feet yellow. In flight shows double white primary patches. Northern *B. c. maculosus* is brighter, more tawny, than the southern nominate race. Usually crouch-es or walks away when disturbed. If flushed, flies low and silently, with rapid wingbeats; briefly holds wings spread upon alighting. Often encountered on roads and tracks at night. **Call**, mainly at night, a musical piping whinny, rising in pitch and volume then subsiding: *pi-pi-peo-PEO-PEO-PEO-PI-pi-pee-pee-pee.* Also has a rapid *qui-qui-qui-qui . . .*, and a descending *wuk-i-kik, wuk-i-kik, quee-quee-quee-quee-quee . . .*. **Range**: Widespread north, east and south of the Kenyan highlands, from the coast up to 2000 m; *B. c. maculosus* south to Lake Bogoria, Samburu GR and Meru NP; *B. c. capensis* elsewhere.

COURSERS AND PRATINCOLES, FAMILY GLAREOLIDAE

Somewhat plover-like birds of deserts, plains and shorelines. Two distinct subfamilies: **CURSORIINAE**, including the rare waterside Egyptian-plover (*Pluvianus*), and the com-moner *Rhinoptilus* and *Cursorius*, long-legged ground birds that run rapidly and fly strongly. Some are crepuscular or nocturnal and difficult to observe. **GLAREOLINAE**, the pratincoles (*Glareola*), are medium-sized aerial feeders with long tern-like wings, short bills, short tarsi, and usually a forked tail. The sexes are alike in both groups.

*EGYPTIAN-PLOVER *Pluvianus aegyptius*   **Plate 17**
Length 7.5–8″. A unique northern lakeside bird with strikingly patterned plumage: blue-grey above, *orange-buff below*, with *black cap, sides of head, upper back and breast band* contrasting with white superciliaries and throat. Short-legged and not especially plover-like. In flight, the *broadly triangular wings are mainly white with broad black diagonal band*, black patch on forewing and narrow black trailing edge; short grey tail has white tip. **Juvenile** duller with some rusty brown on head and wings. Forages along water, sometimes scratching (with both feet, following a forward jump), or running after prey, often with spread wings. Flight fast and flickering, low over water. Runs with spread wings upon landing. **Call** a high-pitched *cherk-cherk-cherk*, usually in alarm. **Status**: One Kenyan record (near Todenyang, nw. Lake Turkana, August 1971).

TWO-BANDED COURSER *Rhinoptilus africanus gracilis*   **Plate 17** ✔

Length 8–9.5″. A slender, thin-necked courser of sandy or alkaline flats and short-grass plains, identified by the *2 black breast bands. Buff face* is marked by *large dark eyes under bold, pale buff superciliary stripes.* Scaly buffy brown above, buff to whitish below; legs and feet yellowish white. In flight shows a *broad rufous band along rear of wing, and white upper tail-coverts* form a narrow strip at base of the black tail; toes project well beyond tail tip. **Juvenile** sandier above, more finely marked; upper breast band faint in younger birds; outer primaries tipped with buffy white. Nocturnal and diurnal. Confiding; seldom flies far when flushed. (More intricately patterned Heuglin's Courser is stockier, has chestnut stripe on neck and no rufous in wings.) **Call** a thin, plover-like *peeuee*, rising at end, and a sharper repeated *kik, kik, kik . . .* when disturbed. Whistling alarm call, *wheeu wheeu pip-pip-pip-pip-pip.* **Range**: Interior n. Tanzania north to Loita Plains, Olorgesaillie, Kajiado, and Amboseli and Tsavo West NPs.

HEUGLIN'S or THREE-BANDED COURSER *Rhinoptilus cinctus*   **Plate 17** ✔

Length 10–11″. A fairly robust, cryptically patterned courser of dry bush and scrub, often seen resting in shade of shrub by day, or on sandy roads at night. Scaly brown above like Two-banded Courser, but *chestnut stripes, one on each side of the neck, converge in a point above a broad mottled brown breast band that is bordered below by narrower black, white and chestnut bands*; belly white. Long pale superciliary stripes contrast with scaly brown crown and rich buff face patch. Bill black with yellow base; eyes brown; legs and feet yellowish. In flight, shows *white upper tail-coverts and outer rectrices* and rather *uniformly dark wings*. The 2 races are similar. Largely nocturnal. Solitary or in small groups. **Call** a loud whistled *pieu*; after dark, a repetitive *whik-er, whik-er, whik-er.* **Range**: Widespread (but uncommon). *R. c. cinctus* north, east and south of the Kenyan highlands, and into n. Tanzania east of Rift Valley; *emini* from Nyanza and Mara GR south through Serengeti NP to Tabora District.

VIOLET-TIPPED or BRONZE-WINGED COURSER *Rhinoptilus chalcopterus*
                                                          Plate 17

Length 10–11″. An uncommon nocturnal courser of open bush and woodland. Distinctive, with long *dark red legs*, plain brown neck and upperparts, a *single black band across lower border of brownish breast*, and bold head pattern with *white forehead, superciliaries and sides of throat*, and contrasting dark face patch. Eyes large, *dark brown*, with narrow purplish red orbital ring; bill black with dull red mandible base. Flight pattern suggests a *Vanellus* plover, with white rump, greyish diagonal wing-covert band, black flight feathers and white wing-linings. Iridescent violet primary tips seldom obvious unless spread wings seen at close range. (Crowned Plover, sometimes active at night, is stockier, has yellowish eyes, *bright* pinkish red legs and black forehead.) **Call** a penetrating trisyllabic *gee-leew-eee* much like piping of Spotted Thick-knee, and a ringing *ki-kooi*; also a harsh flight call. **Range/status**: Mainly a non-breeding migrant from the s. tropics, May–Nov. Local in ne. Tanzania and se. Kenya north to Malindi and Meru NP.

SOMALI COURSER *Cursorius somalensis littoralis* Plate 17

Length 8–8.5". A *pale,* long-legged diurnal courser of semi-arid plains in n. Kenya. Mainly creamy brown with *white belly and under tail-coverts,* and long white superciliary stripes bordered below by *black postocular lines which meet in a V on the nape* as do the superciliaries; hindcrown grey. Largely black bill thin and decurved; *legs and feet pale yellowish cream.* In flight, black primaries contrast with pale brownish upper wing-coverts and grey secondaries as in Cream-coloured Courser, but unlike that species, *wing-linings are mainly pale greyish,* and *from below, inner part of wing contrasts with blackish outer half;* feet project well beyond white-edged tail, which has dusky subterminal spot on central feathers and broader blackish tips on the others. **Juvenile** blotched and barred with dark brown above; basal half of bill yellowish brown; distal half of tail is barred. See Cream-coloured and Temminck's Coursers. Runs rapidly, stopping at brief intervals to feed or look around; bobs head. May crouch and stretch neck forward. Flight noticeably jerky. **Call** a sharp *whit-whit* on ground and in flight. **Range**: N. Kenya, south through Buffalo Springs and Shaba GRs and Meru NP to Tsavo East NP at Aruba and adjacent Galana Ranch.

*CREAM-COLOURED COURSER *Cursorius cursor* Plate 17

Length 8.25–9.5". A palearctic vagrant, sandier in tone than Somali Courser, with *underside of wings entirely dark,* and both bill and tarsi relatively shorter. **Adult** has slightly different tail pattern (central feathers plain sandy buff, the others with narrow subterminal blackish bars). **Juvenile** tail pattern like that of adult, distinct from that of young Somali Courser in which distal half of rectrices barred. Dorsal body plumage more finely barred than in that species. **Call** said to be a sharp piping whistle. **Status**: Sight records along the east shore of Lake Turkana, Jan.–Feb. 1987.

✓ TEMMINCK'S COURSER *Cursorius temminckii* Plate 17

Length 7.5–8". The commonest and most widespread courser, patterned on head like northern Somali Courser, with black-and-white postocular stripes, but *darker brown,* the *belly rufous with a blackish central patch*; also rufous on crown, nape and cheeks. In flight, black flight feathers contrast with generally pale brown upperparts; underside of wing entirely dark. Legs and feet whitish. **Juvenile** has duller head pattern and is somewhat barred above. Diurnal; in pairs or small nomadic flocks, often on recently burnt grassland. **Call** a piercing metallic *enrr-enrr-enrr* or *keer-keer* recalling a squeaking hinge. **Range**: N. Tanzania and s. Kenya, overlapping range of Somali Courser in Tsavo East NP, Buffalo Springs and Shaba GRs. Wanders up to 2800 m; seasonal at lower elevations. Most numerous in Serengeti NP, Mara GR, Nairobi NP and around Naro Moru.

✓ COLLARED PRATINCOLE *Glareola pratincola fuelleborni* Plate 17

Length 9.5–10". On the ground, suggests a squatty, long-winged plover. In *graceful tern-like flight, shows white patch on lower rump/upper tail-coverts, deeply forked black tail* with much white on outer feathers, and *long wings with narrow white rear edges and chestnut linings.* **Breeding plumage** plain brown with *creamy buff throat bordered by thin black line;* belly whitish; bill black, red basally; short tarsi black. **Non-breeding adult** has less distinct throat border, and breast is more mottled. **Juvenile** has feathers of upperparts tipped with buff, and pale throat lacks dark border; tail shorter than in adult. See Black-winged and Madagascar Pratincoles. Noisy flocks assemble on lakeshores or riverine flats. Hawks insects in the air and runs after them on the ground. Nests colonially or in isolated pairs. **Call** a chattering *kik, kik, kirrik.* **Range**: Local along lakes and rivers below 1800 m, mainly seasonal. Breeds April–Sept. in low-rainfall areas including lakes Turkana, Magadi and Manyara and Amboseli NP.

*BLACK-WINGED PRATINCOLE *Glareola nordmanni* Plate 17

Length 9–10". At rest, appears darker brown, less sandy or buffy above, than Collared Pratincole. Distinguished in flight by *entirely black underwing surface* (but Collared Pratincole can appear black-winged in poor light) and *lack of white on trailing edge of wing*. Also has more black on lores, and less red on base of bill (not extending to nostril). **Juvenile** dark brown with buff-edged feathers above; wing-linings as in adult. **Call** similar to that of Collared Pratincole but lower-pitched and more strident. **Range/status**: Rare palearctic passage migrant, Oct.–Nov. and March–April. The few Kenyan records are from north of Marsabit, lakes Baringo anad Naivasha, Ahero (near Kisumu), Lessos and Mara GR.

MADAGASCAR PRATINCOLE *Glareola ocularis*   Plate 17
Length 9–10″. Distinguished from Collared Pratincole by *shorter, shallowly forked tail, mostly brown throat/foreneck, white subocular streaks and rufous belly patch* contrasting with the white lower belly. On flying bird note short, shallowly forked tail and absence of white on trailing edge of wings; upper tail-coverts white as in Collared; wing-linings partly chestnut. Bill black with red base. Highly gregarious. Rests on dunes and adjacent sand or mudflats. Flocks hawk insects, especially in evening, often high in the air over open habitats and at times over coastal forest. **Call** a repeated sharp *wick-wick-wick*. **Range/status**: Malagasy migrant, April–Sept. on East African coast. Hundreds regular at Sabaki River mouth.

ROCK PRATINCOLE *Glareola n. nuchalis*   Plate 17
Length 7–7.5″. A *small, short-tailed* pratincole associated with *emergent rocks in rivers*. Mainly dark brownish grey with white lower belly and crissum; narrow *white postocular stripes meet to form collar across hindneck* below the black cap. The only East African pratincole with dull *orange to coral-red tarsi*; bill red basally. In flight white upper tail-coverts and tail base contrast with largely black, slightly forked tail; wings all dark above, but below shows distinctive *white stripe along base of secondaries*. **Juvenile** lacks white stripes on head, is finely spotted with buff on upperparts and breast; tarsi dull orange-red. Pairs or small groups perch on exposed riverine rocks, less often on tree limbs overhanging water. Hawks insects in the air, especially in early morning or late evening. **Call** a faint *kip-kip*, and a harsh *kek-kek-kek*. In display gives a purring trill. **Range**: Breeds along the Nzoia River in w. Kenya, from Mumias south to Ukwala. Seen once on lower Tana near Garsen (Feb. 1985).

PLOVERS, FAMILY CHARADRIIDAE
A widespread family of 'shorebirds' characteristic of grasslands, fields, mudflats and beaches. Compact and large-headed with short straight bills and relatively long legs. Sexes similar, usually plain above; many species have white wing stripes or patches that are conspicuous in flight. Three genera in our region: *Vanellus*, large residents or short-distance migrants (and one vagrant) with broad, rounded wings, most with bold black-and-white wing markings and white-based black tail, quite vocal, some both day and night; *Pluvialis*, large palearctic migrants with long pointed wings, mottled upperparts, and black underparts in breeding plumage; *Charadrius*, both residents and palearctic migrants, small, short-necked, often with dark breast bands.

NORTHERN LAPWING *Vanellus vanellus*   Illus. opp. Plate 18
Length 11.5″. A highly distinctive plover, dark with green gloss above (more brownish, less gloss in female) and white below, with a long black crest. The broad black or brownish black breast band, black or brown crown and dark marks around eyes and on cheeks contrast with otherwise buffy white face and (in non-breeding plumage) the whitish throat; some magenta gloss on scapulars, and some violet on wing-coverts; under tail-coverts orangey cinnamon. Rather short tarsi dull red. In deep-flapping flight, broad rounded wings dark above and with white linings, and a few of the outer primaries with pale grey-brown tips; sides of back and rump white, and white upper tail-coverts and tail base contrast with broad black tip. **Call** a plaintive *wee-ip*. **Status**: Palearctic vagrant; one at Sabaki Estuary, Feb. 1995-Aug. 1996.

LONG-TOED PLOVER *Vanellus c. crassirostris*   Plate 18
Length 12″. A long-necked marsh plover with upright stance, *white face and foreneck*, black hindneck and breast; upperparts grey-brown; belly white. *Bill pink with dark tip; legs and feet pinkish red*; eyes red. In flight, *white forewing* and rump band contrast with

black flight feathers and tail. **Juvenile** has buff feather-edging above, all black areas tinged brown. Forages on floating vegetation or in shallow water. **Call** a metallic *kik-k-k-k-k*. . .. **Range**: Fairly common in Lake Victoria Basin, occasional in Uasin Gishu and Trans-Nzoia districts; also at lakes Baringo and Naivasha, Thika, Amboseli NP, Lake Jipe, lower Tana River and in Ngorongoro Crater; sporadic at Lake Manyara and in Tarangire NP.

✓BLACKSMITH PLOVER *Vanellus armatus*   Plate 18

Length 11–12". A distinctive black, grey and white plover of inland shores and wetlands. *Face, neck and breast black, with contrasting white cap* and white patch on hindneck; back black; folded wings mainly grey. In flight, *black flight feathers contrast with grey upper wing-coverts*; wing-linings, rump and tail white, the latter with broad black tip. Bill, legs and feet black; eyes dark red. **Juvenile** has white crown feathers tipped with brown, chin and throat whitish, and all black feathers buff-tipped. (Spur-winged Plover has black cap, white cheeks and brownish back.) Usual **call** a repeated *klink klink klink* (likened to a blacksmith hammering on an anvil). **Range**: Common resident in n. Tanzania, north along Kenyan Rift Valley lakes to Baringo, and to Maralal, and east to Lake Jipe; wanders to middle and lower Tana River and Tsavo East NP. Scarce in w. Kenya. Overlaps Spur-winged Plover at Lake Baringo and in Amboseli NP.

✓SPUR-WINGED PLOVER *Vanellus spinosus*   Plate 18

Length 10.5". A bird of inland waterways, grey-brown on back, with *white cheeks and sides of neck, black breast and upper belly joined to chin by a black mid-ventral line*; crown and hindneck also black. In flight, a white diagonal bar separates brown forewing from black flight feathers; broad black tail tip contrasts with white base and upper tail-coverts; under tail-coverts and wing-linings also white. Bill, legs and feet black, eyes dark red. **Juvenile** shows brown and white speckling. (Crowned, Black-winged, and Wattled Plovers show similar flight pattern from above, but lack extensive black underparts. Flying Blacksmith Plover similar from underneath but has black back and no white wing stripe.) **Calls** include a repeated metallic *pitt, pitt, pitt* . . ., and a loud *ti-ti-terr-er*. **Range**: Common south to Kisumu, Lake Bogoria, Galana and Sabaki rivers, Tsavo East and Amboseli NPs. A few on coast south to Garsen, although rarely on open shore. Replaced by Blacksmith Plover on Rift Valley lakes south of Bogoria. Frequent at Lake Manyara NP; rare elsewhere in n. Tanzania.

✓ BLACK-HEADED PLOVER *Vanellus tectus*   Plate 18

Length 10". A *red-legged dry-country* plover with a *long thin black crest*. *White chin and white nape patch are sandwiched between black of crown and neck;* back brown; underparts white. Eyes yellow; *base of bill and small loral wattles red*. White forehead patch more extensive in eastern *latifrons*. In flight, a long white diagonal wing-stripe contrasts with black tip and trailing edge; tail white with broad black terminal band. **Juvenile** has shorter crest, and buff-tinged upperparts. **Call** a short whistled *kir-kir-kir* of alarm, and a loud, shrill *kwairrr*. **Range**: In Kenya, locally common in dry bush: *V. t. latifrons* south to Meru NP, Kora NR, Tsavo East NP, lower Tana River, the Tsavo parks and once to n. Tanzania (Arusha); northwestern *V. t. tectus* south to Kerio Valley and lakes Baringo and Bogoria.

SENEGAL PLOVER *Vanellus lugubris*   Plate 18

Length 9–10". A brown-backed *grassland* plover of *low elevations*. Dark grey of head/upper breast separated from white belly by a *narrow black band*; *small white forehead patch sharply defined from grey crown*. *Legs and feet dark slate grey or blackish*; inconspicuous *orbital ring dull yellowish*; *eyes yellow* (narrowly red peripherally). In flight, *white secondaries* contrast with otherwise dark wings, and white tail has broad sub-terminal black band. **Juvenile** has forehead patch and breast demarca-

tion line partly obscured by pale feather tips, and wing-coverts tipped with buff. (Larger Black-winged Plover, typically at higher elevations, has shorter dark red tarsi, head and neck paler grey and forehead patch usually larger and more diffuse; wings show bold diagonal white stripe and black trailing edge in flight.) Often noticeable on burnt or heavily grazed grassland. **Calls** include a melodious *kitti-kooee,* a piping *klu-WIT,* repeated, and a wailing alarm call. **Range**: Local north to Lake Baringo and Meru NP. Nowhere resident. Regular April–Aug. near coast, June–Aug. in Tsavo area, Nov.–May from Lake Victoria basin to Mara GR and adjacent n. Tanzania, Jan.–April in Arusha NP.

✔BLACK-WINGED PLOVER *Vanellus melanopterus minor*   Plate 18 **V**

Length 10.5″. A *highland* species of grassland and ploughed fields. Resembles Senegal Plover but slightly larger and heavier, and with *much broader black band on lower breast*; white forehead patch also larger, not as sharply defined, and often with short pale superciliary extensions. Bill black; *legs and feet dull red; orbital ring purplish red; eyes orange-yellow.* More white on wings than in Senegal Plover; in flight, *broad white diagonal band* separates brown forewing and black flight feathers. **Juvenile** pale brown from head to breast; much buff feather-edging above. **Call,** *che-che-chereek,* higher and more strident than call of Senegal Plover. When disturbed, a loud, rapid metallic *kay-kay-kay-kay. . . .* **Range**: Locally common on high grassland and cultivation between 1500 and 3000 m. Breeds at higher elevations March–July, then moves lower. In Kenya, widespread in w. and cent. highlands, and (after breeding) Mara GR. Resident in Crater Highlands and Arusha District.

CROWNED PLOVER *Vanellus c. coronatus*   Plate 18 **V**

Length 12″. A noisy conspicuous plover of dry grassy plains, with brown back, brown chest and white belly. Easily identified by *white ring on black crown, red bill base and long legs red*; eyes yellow. In flight shows *broad white diagonal wing-stripe,* white tail with broad black band. **Juvenile** has more obscure head pattern, duller bare parts and much buff feather-edging. **Call** a strident *erEEK,* an excited *kree-kree-kreeip-kreeip,* or *WEEK-EEEK-EEEK*; a chattering *tri-tri-tri-tri* in display. **Range**: Widespread, at times as high as 3000 m. Absent from coastal areas south of Malindi; scarce in Lake Victoria basin.

AFRICAN WATTLED PLOVER *Vanellus senegallus lateralis*   Plate 18

Length 13.5″. A large plover of short grass near wet areas. Unique with *long yellow facial wattles* and smaller red ones on forehead. Generally greyish brown, with white forecrown, *black chin and throat, and streaked neck. Bare parts yellow, the bill black-tipped.* In flight, shows diagonal white wing-stripe, white upper-tail coverts and tail, the latter with a broad dusky subterminal band. **Juvenile** has small wattles, lacks black chin, and white of forehead obscure. Solitary. Raises wings vertically upon alighting. (Black-winged and Crowned Plovers have similar flight patterns, but are red-legged and show much more white below.) **Call** a shrill high-pitched *kip, kip, kip;* alarm call *ke-WEEP, ke-WEEP.* **Range**: Fairly common but local in Mara GR and Serengeti NP, less numerous in Lake Victoria Basin and w. Kenyan highlands. Wanders to Rift Valley lakes, including Turkana, and rarely Tsavo West NP.

BROWN-CHESTED PLOVER *Vanellus superciliosus*   Plate 18

Length 9″. A small black-legged plover, accidental in our region. May associate with Senegal Plover on grasslands. *Broad chestnut band separates grey neck/upper breast from white belly; face grey with short yellow loral wattles at base of black bill; crown and nape black, forehead pale chestnut*; eyes yellow. In flight, shows short white diagonal wing-stripe, white upper tail-coverts and white tail with partial black subterminal band. **Juvenile** has brownish grey face and neck shading to dull brown on breast, dark brown on hindcrown, dull rufous on forecrown/forehead; wattles and orbital skin yellow, legs and feet olive. **Call** a harsh penetrating flight call, likened to squeak of a rusty hinge. **Range/status**: Vagrant from West Africa, July–Oct. Recorded at Kisumu, Ruiru near Nairobi and Serengeti NP.

(COMMON IN HAWAII)

PACIFIC GOLDEN PLOVER Pluvialis fulva   **Plates 18, 21**

Length 9–10". *Smaller, slimmer and browner than Grey Plover, with grey axillaries and wing-linings and different call.* In flight, toes project beyond tail tip (unlike extralimital American Golden Plover, *P. dominica*, known as a vagrant in s. Africa.) Favours grassy plains as well as shorelines. **Non-breeding plumage** greyish brown above *spangled with pale golden-yellow; prominent buffy yellow superciliary stripes extend well behind eyes.* Underparts lightly mottled greyish or brownish buff, with white belly and crissum. In flight shows only a faint wing-stripe. Legs and feet dark grey. In **breeding plumage**, *yellow-spangled upperparts separated from black face and underparts by broad white area at sides of breast continuing as a narrow white line along sides and flanks.* (*P. dominica* shows more white at sides of breast than *fulva*, but usually no continuous white flank line; belly grey, not white, in non-breeding plumage, and primary extension longer, with 4 visible feather tips.) **Juvenile** resembles non-breeding adult but superciliaries and breast more yellowish; flanks and belly lightly barred with dark brown. **Calls** a clear whistled *tu-ee*, a plaintive *klee* and a dry *chuwit*. **Range/status**: Scarce palearctic migrant almost annual on coast (Tana River delta to Malindi); irregular on Rift Valley lakes and at Aruba Dam in Tsavo East NP.

GREY or BLACK-BELLIED PLOVER *Pluvialis squatarola*   **Plates 18, 21**

Length 11–12". A *large, stocky, shoreline plover with a stout black bill* and dark grey legs and feet. Posture characteristically hunched; feeding behaviour lethargic. **Breeding plumage** (Aug.–Sept. and March–May) black from face to belly, and sides of neck and breast bordered by broad white line; under tail-coverts white. **Non-breeding plumage** mottled brownish grey above, white below with dusky mottling on breast; sides of face marked by diffuse dark eye-line and smudge on ear-coverts accentuating the pale superciliary stripe. In flight shows *white upper tail-coverts and white streak on upperside of wings,* and from below *black axillaries contrast with whitish wing-linings and belly.* **Juvenile** browner than non-breeding adult, and finely spotted with yellowish buff. **Call** a far-carrying trisyllabic whistle, *tlee-oo-ee.* **Range/status**: Palearctic migrant, Aug.–April, common on coastal flats, occasional inland, mainly in Rift Valley. A few young birds oversummer.

RINGED PLOVER *Charadrius hiaticula tundrae*   **Plates 19, 21**

Length 7–8". Small and compact, with a single *dark breast band, narrow white collar and stubby bill. Legs and feet orange,* the tarsi rather short. Crown and back dark brown, underparts white. In **breeding plumage** (Sept. and April–May), bill orange with black tip, white forehead broadly bordered by black, and narrow white superciliaries contrast with black mask. In **non-breeding plumage**, black replaced by dusky brown, the superciliaries usually continuous with the pale forehead, and bill may be all black. **Juvenile** resembles non-breeding adult but breast band paler, reduced and sometimes broken in centre; tarsi dull orange-yellow. In flight shows strong white wing-stripe; sides of rump, lateral tail-coverts and tip of tail also white. **Call** a distinctive melodious whistle with rising inflection, *too-li*; a sharper *too-i* or *wip* when alarmed. **Range/status**: Palearctic migrant, common Sept.–early May on coastal flats and beaches, and on inland lakeshores and river edges. A few oversummer on coast.

LITTLE RINGED PLOVER *Charadrius dubius curonicus*   **Plates 19, 21**

Length 6–6.5". Separated from the common Ringed Plover by *diagnostic call,* smaller, *slimmer build,* and *lack of obvious wing-stripes.* **Adult** also distinguished by *yellow orbital ring,* dull pinkish or yellowish legs, and lack of orange on the bill (only a trace of yellow at base, below). In **breeding plumage**, a narrow white crown band behind the black frontal bar. **Non-breeding** bird has black replaced by brown, forehead buff-tinged, and (*contra* Ringed Plover) the superciliary stripes barely extend behind eyes. **Juvenile** has smaller eye-ring and obscurely patterned brownish head; breast band usually broken. **Call** a far-carrying, descending *pee-o.* **Range/status**:

Palearctic migrant, Oct.–April, mainly on Kenyan Rift Valley lakes and larger rivers. Local on coastal flats; rare in n. Tanzania.

KITTLITZ'S PLOVER *Charadrius pecuarius* Plate 19, 21

Length 5.5–6". Forages on dry flats near inland lakes and ponds, as well as on shorelines. Small, *rich buff below*, with *distinctive black-and-white head pattern*: white superciliary stripes and black eye-lines which meet around hindneck, and white forehead bordered behind by black bar. Legs and feet dark greenish grey. In flight, shows dark leading wing edge, white wing-stripe, white tail sides; toes project beyond tail (unlike White-fronted and Kentish Plovers). **Juvenile** lacks black frontal bar and bold face pattern, but buff forehead is continuous with pale superciliaries and nape band; breast pale buff with brownish patches at sides. **Call**, in flight, *trip* or *pip;* also a trilling *tri-rit-rit-rit.* Alarm call a rough *chrrrt.* **Range**: Inland lakes, mainly in Rift Valley; local on coastal salt flats and on lower Tana River.

THREE-BANDED PLOVER *Charadrius t. tricollaris* Plate 19, 21 ✔

Length 7". A solitary plover of riverbanks and lakesides. Unique, with *2 black breast bands, red orbital ring and paler red bill base*; greyish face marked by broad white superciliary stripes which meet around hindneck; *eyes pale brown*; legs and feet red-orange. Tail rather long. In flight shows narrow white wing stripe and white tail edges. **Juvenile** has less distinct head pattern, and pale feather edges above. **Call** a high-pitched *pi-peep* or *peeep.* **Range**: Inland waters and coastal lagoons and creeks north to Malindi.

KENTISH PLOVER *Charadrius a. alexandrinus* Plates 19, 21

Length 6". A small *pale* plover of sandy beaches and saltpans, grey-brown above and white below, with *fine dark bill, dark grey or brown legs and feet, white hindneck collar and dark patches at sides of breast.* **Breeding-plumaged male** has black frontal bar, black line through eyes, white forehead continuous with short superciliary stripes; *cap usually tinged chestnut.* In **female** and **non-breeding male**, black is replaced by brown. In flight, shows narrow white wing-stripe, and white-sided upper tail-coverts/tail. (White-fronted Plover usually washed tawny below, lacks dark breast patches and sharp white nuchal collar; it has a large white forehead patch. Lesser Sandplover is larger, lacks nuchal collar and has more diffuse smudges at sides of breast.) **Call** a soft *kittip* or *teu-it*, sometimes a simple *pit* or *pit-wit-wit*; alarm note a hard *prrrr.* **Range/status**: Palearctic migrant, regular at Lake Turkana, Oct.-April. Occasional on Rift Valley lakes south to Magadi and on Kenyan coast.

WHITE-FRONTED PLOVER *Charadrius marginatus tenellus* Plates 19, 21

Length 6". An active plover of beaches and sandbars, brown or rufous-brown above; white underparts often with *tawny wash and pale rufous patches at sides of breast. Broad white forehead band extends back to short superciliary stripes.* Adult shows black frontal bar and eye-lines, and often a pale buff or rufous (not white) collar. Bill black; legs and feet greenish or yellowish grey. Wing tips do not reach tail tip on standing bird. In flight, shows distinct white wing-stripe and white at sides of rump and tail. **Juvenile** lacks black forecrown, is less tawny below. (Juv. Kittlitz's Plover has pale superciliaries extending to hindneck, and toes project beyond tail in flight.) **Calls** a low *wit,* and a dry trilling *trrrr* of alarm. **Range**: Common on n. Kenyan coast, less so on Galana and Athi river sandbars. Wanders to Lake Turkana.

CHESTNUT-BANDED PLOVER *Charadrius pallidus venustus* Plates 19, 21

Length 5". A *small*, relatively long-legged plover of alkaline lakes; wings short, their tips not reaching tip of the short tail in standing bird. Adult the *only small plover with a narrow chestnut breast band* on white underparts. Both sexes have white forehead and chestnut forecrown; male has black frontal band connecting to black eye-lines (lacking in female). Bill *slender* and black; legs and feet dark grey. **Juvenile** has incomplete greyish breast band and no black or chestnut. In flight, white wing-stripe and white sides of tail obvious. **Call** a soft *chup* or a dry *drreet* or *d'weeu*; also a plaintive *hweet* of alarm. **Range**: Common at lakes Magadi and Natron. Also known in Suguta Valley south of Lake Turkana, at Amboseli NP, and many small n. Tanzanian lakes from Serengeti NP east to Lake Manyara.

LESSER or MONGOLIAN SANDPLOVER *Charadrius mongolus pamirensis*
Plates 19, 21

Length 7.5–8". Mainly coastal. Ringed Plover-sized, with dark grey or blackish legs and feet (sometimes green-tinged); no pale band on hind-neck. Compared to Greater Sandplover (with which it associates), Lesser has *more rounded head, shorter bill and shorter and darker tarsi; toes do not project beyond tail tip in flight*. **Non-breeding plumage** grey-brown above with whitish forehead and superciliary stripes. Underparts white with broad brownish grey pectoral patches. Narrow white stripe on wings and white edges of tail and upper tail-coverts evident in flight. **Breeding plumage** (April–May) distinctive with *broad chestnut breast band and hindneck, black mask and forehead*. **Juvenile** buffier than non-breeding adult, with warm buff wash across breast, buff feather edges on back and wing-coverts. **Call** a short hard *chitik* or *trrrrk* (distinct from usual soft call of Greater Sandplover). **Range/status**: Palearctic migrant, common late Aug.–early May. Some young oversummer. Frequent at Lake Turkana, otherwise rare inland.

GREATER SANDPLOVER *Charadrius leschenaultii crassirostris*   **Plates 19, 21**

Length 8.5–10". A *heavy-billed* plover of beaches and sandflats, larger than a Curlew Sandpiper, with *greenish grey tarsi*. Compared to Lesser Sandplover, *bill is longer and thicker, head more angular with more sloping forehead, tarsi paler and longer*, and *toes project well beyond the tail in flight*. **Non-breeding plumage** as in Lesser Sandplover but separated by above characters. In **breeding plumage** has chestnut band across upper breast and chestnut hindneck; male shows *striking face pattern* with black mask and frontal band enclosing a white forehead bisected by a black median line (female may lack mask). **Juvenile** resembles non-breeding adult but buffier. **Calls** a soft trilled *trrrrri* and a short dry *trrip*. **Range/status**: Palearctic migrant, common on coast and offshore islands, Aug.–early May; some young remain all year. Frequent at Lake Turkana, otherwise rare inland.

CASPIAN PLOVER *Charadrius asiaticus*   **Plates 19, 21**

Length 7–8". A *grassland* or lakeshore bird, suggesting a small Golden Plover. Shows *distinct pale superciliary stripes* and *white forehead*, a small dark postocular line (usually extending through eye), a *broad brown breast band*, and yellowish (sometimes greenish or grey) legs. Folded wings extend beyond tail tip, as do tips of toes in flying bird. In **non-breeding plumage**, upperparts, crown and postocular patches are brown, the breast band mottled. In **breeding plumage** (Jan.–April), **male** has more contrasting head pattern; breast band chestnut with blackish lower border; **female** resembles non-breeding adult but may show some chestnut on breast. **Juvenile** has bright buff feather edges above, and a mottled buff-and-grey breast band. Sometimes in large flocks; often tame. (Both sandplovers have thicker bills, shorter wings, lateral breast patches and different head patterns; neither is likely on inland plains.) **Call** a loud sharp high-pitched *tjeep* or *tchup*; also a soft *kik-kik-kik. . .*, and a shrill *quit*. **Range/status**: Locally common palearctic migrant, Aug.–April. Large flocks winter in Serengeti NP, Mara GR and at Lake Turkana. Also in Tsavo East NP during Feb.

SANDPIPERS AND RELATIVES, FAMILY SCOLOPACIDAE
A diverse group of shorebirds, typically long-necked, long-legged and slender-billed. Excepting one local breeder and 3 Siberian/nearctic vagrants, ours are palearctic migrants,

arriving in Africa after breeding at high latitudes. Breeding plumage (seen here July–Sept. and March–May) is usually brighter than basic non-breeding dress. Juveniles may be boldly patterned above, but moult by Nov. into first-winter body plumage, and then resemble non-breeding adults. Flight patterns are important in identification, and calls are diagnostic. Major groups are: **(1) STINTS & OTHER SMALL SANDPIPERS** (e.g. *Calidris, Limicola*), relatively short-legged, with bold wing-stripes, often brightly patterned upperparts in breeding plumage; **(2) SNIPES** (*Gallinago, Lymnocryptes*), superbly cryptic, long-billed marshbirds, including 1 breeding species; **(3) CURLEWS** (*Numenius*) **and GODWITS** (*Limosa*), large with curved, straight or slightly upturned long bills; **(4) GREENSHANK & allies** (*Tringa*), slender, long-legged, small to medium-sized, with white rump and barred tail, wings almost unpatterned, loud ringing calls; **(5) PHALAROPES** (*Phalaropus*), dainty, lobe-toed, aquatic or pelagic swimmers; sometimes seen on shores; breeding-plumaged females brighter than males.

LITTLE STINT *Calidris minuta* Plates 20, 21

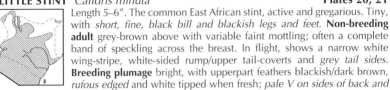

Length 5–6". The common East African stint, active and gregarious. Tiny, with *short, fine, black bill and blackish legs and feet.* **Non-breeding adult** grey-brown above with variable faint mottling; often a complete band of speckling across the breast. In flight, shows a narrow white wing-stripe, white-sided rump/upper tail-coverts and *grey tail sides.* **Breeding plumage** bright, with upperpart feathers blackish/dark brown, *rufous edged* and white tipped when fresh; *pale V on sides of back and another, greyer V formed by pale scapular tips; face and neck rufous* with dusky streaking; dim superciliary stripes and throat whitish. **Juvenile** (Sept.–Oct.) has *whitish forehead, face and underparts* contrasting with dark-streaked crown and dark buff- or rufous-edged dorsal feathers, buff breast band (usually sharply streaked dusky brown at sides), and *prominent whitish V on back.* See Red-necked Stint. **Calls** a sharp high *chit* or *tit*, and *chi-chi-chit* or a trilled *tilililili.* **Range/status**: Widespread migrant, Aug.-May, abundant on alkaline Rift Valley lakes, common on coastal saltpans and mudflats.

RED-NECKED STINT *Calidris ruficollis* Plate 20

Length 5–6.5". A rare dark-legged sandpiper easily mistaken for Little Stint except in full **breeding plumage** when *brick-red head, neck and breast* are obvious. **Non-breeding adult** differs subtly from Little in appearing *more elongate* and squatty (owing to longer wings and shorter tarsi); *upperparts greyer, less spangled, the dark feather centres reduced to fine shaft streaks*; shows *clear white wedge between grey breast sides and edges of wings; darker lores* contrast more with whitish forehead; never a complete speckled breast band. In **partial breeding plumage** usually shows slightly rufescent throat (white in Little), *unmarked* rufous areas on face and neck (these streaked or spotted in Little); *grey* posthumerals ('tertials') and inner wing-coverts with dark shaft streaks (brown with broad rufous/buff edges in Little); light V on back less prominent and only in fresh plumage (V usually obvious even in worn Little Stints). **Juvenile** greyer, less buff, without pale dorsal V; *wing-coverts and posthumerals dull grey with buff edges (not dark-centred and rufous-edged as in Little),* contrasting with more brightly patterned back and scapulars; sides of breast grey or buffy grey. **Call** a rolling *chirrk*, and a dry coarse *chit* or *prip*, similar to calls of Little Stint; also a sharp squeaky *week* and, when flushed, a short trilled *tirrwi-chit-chit.* **Status**: Vagrant; 3 Kenyan records (at coast, Lake Magadi) May, July and August.

TEMMINCK'S STINT *Calidris temminckii* Plates 20, 21

Length 5–6". An inconspicuous *yellowish- or olive-legged* stint of freshwater marshes, typically feeding in shallow water among sedges or grasses. Comparatively *plain,* with *narrow pale eye-ring* and diagnostic *white tail sides,* evident when bird is flushed. *Appears elongate, with relatively long tail projecting beyond primary tips.* **Non-breeding plumage** uniformly brownish grey above and across faintly streaked upper breast which is darker at sides; appears somewhat hooded; throat white. **Breeding plumage** browner, more mottled, breast more streaked; no pale dorsal V-marks or strong rufous tones; usually shows some grey winter feathers in E. Africa. **Juvenile** grey-brown or greyish above, *distinctly scaly with pale buff feather edges,* and *narrow*

blackish subterminal bar on some back feathers, scapulars and wing-coverts. (These scaly feathers unique among stints, recalling juv. Red Knot.) Some scapulars appear black-spot-ted; greyish or *brownish wash on sides of breast*; note the *pale eye-ring on plain grey face.* **Calls** include a repeated trilling or ringing *tiriri* or *treee*, and a longer rising *titititi-titititi.* **Range/status**: Local but regular migrant in Kenya, Oct.–April, mainly in Rift Valley; rare on coast and in n. Tanzania.

LONG-TOED STINT *Calidris subminuta*   Plates 20, 21

Length 5–6″. *Longer-necked* than Little Stint. *Legs and feet pale yellowish or greenish, not black; toes noticeably long and spindly, appearing oversized, and projecting beyond tail in flying bird* (unlike other African stints). **Non-breeding plumage** mottled brown above with light streaking on neck and breast; *top of head and eye-lines dark, contrast-ing with prominent whitish superciliary stripes.* In flight shows *greyish outer tail feathers*, and short white wing-stripe. Fine black bill dull yellow at base below. **Breeding plumage** tawny brown above, the feathers broadly edged rufous and whitish; may show indistinct whitish V on back. Crown and ear-coverts streaked dark brown and rufous; nape and faint superciliary stripes paler. Neck and sides of breast heavily streaked, but greyish buff breast centre usually plain. **Juvenile** brightly patterned like breeding adult; *dark rufous-streaked crown* contrasts with greyish hindneck and long white superciliaries; whitish Vs on scapulars and back; feather edges orange-buff to chestnut; breast finely streaked, often in centre. Feeds like Little Stint. Crouches low when disturbed; stands upright with stretched neck if alarmed. Often 'towers' when flushed. (Temminck's Stint is plainer, with longer wings, *white* outer rectrices and narrow eye-ring. Little and Red-necked Stints are dark-legged.) **Call** a soft rolling *cherrp* or *chulip.* **Range/status**: Rare migrant at Kenyan Rift Valley lakes, Malindi and Sabaki Estuary.

PECTORAL SANDPIPER *Calidris melanotos*   Plates 20, 21

Length 8–9″. A rare medium-sized brownish sandpiper of marshy pools. Size and colour variable. Head rather small, bill short, and *brown-streaked breast sharply demarcated* from white belly. In **non-breeding plumage** upperparts streaked/mottled black and buff or light brown; pale superciliary stripes evident but not prominent; neck and breast buffy brown to whitish, finely and closely streaked with brown. *Bill, legs and feet dull yellow-ish olive.* In flight dark wings show suggestion of pale stripe; rump dark in centre, whitish on sides. **Juvenile** has rufous crown-feather and scapular edges, whitish superciliaries and dark loral lines; breast buffier, streaks finer than in adult, and pale buff back and scapular lines more prominent. (Female Ruff may suggest Pectoral, but is more scalloped, not well-striped above and with unstreaked breast.) Usual **call** a distinctive reedy *krrik-krrik.* **Status**: Nearctic/Siberian vagrant; 2 Kenyan records, Lake Naivasha (May) and Mombasa (Sept.).

DUNLIN *Calidris alpina*   Plates 20, 21

Length 6–8.5″. In **non-breeding plumage** resembles Curlew Sandpiper but slightly small-er, more portly, with *shorter tarsi, less conspicuous superciliary stripes and darker grey breast.* Long black *bill decurved only near tip*, not evenly curved throughout its length as in Curlew Sandpiper. Flight pattern as in Little Stint, with white wing-stripe, dark rump centre and greyish tail sides. Bright **breeding plumage** is mottled *rufous above*, heavily streaked on neck and breast and with a *black patch on belly.* **Juvenile** buffy brown with rufous-buff scaling above; breast streaks expand into dark blotches on flanks. **Call** a high nasal *treer* or *treerp.* **Range/status:** Rare migrant; 4 inland Kenyan sight records.

CURLEW SANDPIPER *Calidris ferruginea*   Plates 20, 21

Length 7–9″. A common wader, with black legs and feet, and a relative-ly long, *decurved black bill.* Our only small sandpiper with combination of *all-white upper tail-coverts and long white wing-stripe.* **Non-breeding plumage** grey-brown above and white below, with whitish superciliary stripes and faint streaking on neck and breast; rump white at sides, dark-barred centrally. **Partial breeding plumage** (Aug. and April–May) *mot-tled chestnut and white below*, mainly white on belly and under tail-coverts; blackish bars on flanks and belly; chestnut and whitish feather edges above. **Juvenile** (Sept.–Oct.) similar to non-breeding adult, with buff feather edging, cinnamon

wash on breast. **Call** a soft *churrup.* **Range/status**: Widespread migrant, Aug.–late May; more local inland, mainly on passage. A few first-year birds oversummer.

SANDERLING *Calidris alba*   **Plates 20, 21** ✔

Length 8″. Primarily coastal. Forages restlessly at water's edge, following a wave, then retreating hastily before the next breaker. Runs with body horizontal and head held low. **Non-breeding plumage** *whitish* looking, with *stout black bill and short black legs*; grey smudges on sides of breast, and *black at bend of wing.* Long white wing-stripe and white-sided dark rump/upper tail-coverts obvious in flight. Traces of black-speckled rufous **breeding plumage** often present on head, breast and upperparts in August and late April. (Acquires full spring plumage after leaving East Africa.) **Juvenile** (Sept.–Nov.) blackish above with pale buff spots and feather edges, brown crown, dark loral marks and darker ear-coverts. **Call** a distinctive sharp *twick* or *kick-kick*; sometimes a short trilling note. **Range/status:** Common migrant on coastal beaches and coral flats, late Aug.–April; some young remain through summer. Occasional on inland lakes Aug.–Nov. A few winter at Lake Turkana.

RED KNOT *Calidris c. canutus*   **Plate 22**

Length 9–10″. A *stocky,* medium-sized coastal wader with *short neck and bill. Legs and feet dull greenish, the tarsi short.* **Non-breeding plumage** *pale grey and 'scaly' above* (fine black shaft streaks visible at close range), whitish superciliary stripes obvious; underparts white, faintly streaked on neck and breast, and finely scalloped along sides. Some birds have pale rufous wash on breast. In flight shows short, narrow white wing-stripe and whitish rump. **Breeding plumage** mottled chestnut and black above, bright *rufous-chestnut below* with variable blackish speckling on white lower belly and crissum. **Juvenile** browner than non-breeding adult, with buff feather edges and buff-tinged breast. **Call** a whistling *twit-wit* in flight, and a low *utt.* **Range/status**: Rare migrant; 5 coastal records (Apr., Sept., Nov.).

BROAD-BILLED SANDPIPER *Limicola falcinellus*   **Plates 20, 21**

Length 6.5″. Suggests a miniature snipe or a very long-billed stint. Slightly larger than Little Stint, with a *long dark bill kinked downward at tip.* Forages slowly with persistent vertical probing. **Non-breeding plumage** pale grey above, including central rump and tail-coverts. Pale *superciliary stripe forks in front of the eye*, but upper branch, below crown, often narrow and inconspicuous. Dark patagial/carpal patch often shows on closed wing. Underparts white with indistinct grey streaks from sides of breast to flanks. Black bill at times olive or yellowish at base, and the *short, dark brown tarsi* may be olive-tinged. In flight, appears *pale grey with broad blackish leading wing edges and dark flight feathers,* inconspicuous wing-stripe and white on sides of rump/tail-coverts. Breeding-plumaged *L. f. sibirica* much more reddish than European *L. f. falcinellus,* boldly patterned with rufous, black and white above. **Juvenile** has bolder, more *snipe-like pattern* than adult, with broad white superciliaries and narrower buff crown stripes; dark brown above with rufous-and-buff feather edges, and pale double V on back; dark carpal area as in adult; sharply defined dark breast streaks do not reach flanks. In flight shows *conspicuously black rump, central rectrices and upper tail-coverts* (retained in first-winter bird); wing-stripe conspicuous. **Call** a rough *chrreek* when flushed, and a quick *chitter-chitter* in flight. **Range/status**: Uncommon migrant, Aug.–April, regular at Sabaki estuary north of Malindi; occasional elsewhere on coast and Rift Valley lakes.

*BUFF-BREASTED SANDPIPER *Tringytes subruficollis*   **Plates 20, 21**

Length 7.5″. Small, plump and plover-like, typically with *evenly buff underparts* (some autumn/winter birds pale whitish buff on belly) with dark flecking at sides of breast. Upperparts mottled buffy brown. *Pale buff face accentuates the dark eye;* no obvious superciliary stripe. Bill short and dark, *legs and feet yellow.* In flight appears plain brown above, wings white underneath with dark carpal 'comma' and trailing edge; sides of rump buff. Stretches neck when alarmed. See juv. Ruff. Prefers dry short-grass plains, dried mudflats. Infrequent **calls** include a soft *churrp* or sharp *tik* when flushed and a low trill. **Status**: Nearctic vagrant; 1 sight record from Lake Turkana (Dec. 1973).

RUFF *Philomachus pugnax*   **Plates 20, 23**

Length, male, 11–12"; female, 9". Stocky, small-headed and long-necked, with a rather short dark bill; *legs and feet of adults bright orange or pink-ish*. Often forages while running. In flight shows a *distinctive light oval patch on either side of dark rump and upper tail-coverts* (sometimes a single U-shaped light patch) and a narrow white wing-stripe. **Non-breeding plumage** (Sept.–Feb.) brown-mottled or barred above and on sides of breast and flanks, with brownish buff head and neck, or breast may be plain grey-brown. Female **breeding plumage** and **spring male** (March–May) brighter and browner, more distinctly patterned above, heavily mottled on neck, breast and flanks. Male usually has pinkish or orange bill base; some have white neck, others an entirely white head, upper back, scapulars and underparts. (Breeding plumage, with elaborate ruff, acquired after departure.) **Juvenile** scaled buff above, buffier below than adult; legs and feet greenish, yellowish or brownish olive. **Call** an infrequent *tooi*. **Range/status:** Regular migrant, mainly Aug.–May. Common on Rift Valley lakes, and on irrigated fields and flooded grassland in the highlands; scarce at coast. A few young oversummer.

JACK SNIPE *Lymnocryptes minimus*   **Plate 24**

Length 7.5". A *small, relatively short-billed Snipe* with *double pale superciliary stripes bordering the dark crown*; neck and breast well streaked. In flight buff stripes on back obvious, but *tail dark and wedge-shaped, showing no white or chestnut*. Rises more slowly than Common Snipe, flies directly and alights within 50 m. Infrequent weak low calls when taking wing. **Range/status:** Scarce migrant, Nov.-Feb., on lakes and swamps, in Rift Valley, Mara GR and cent. Kenyan highlands; 2 n. Tanzanian records: Serengeti NP and Tabora.

COMMON SNIPE *Gallinago g. gallinago*   **Plate 24**

Length 10-10.5". Widespread in winter on marshes and wet fields. *Long-billed*, with pale central crown stripe and *bold black stripes above, through and below eyes*. Back patterned rich brown and blackish with *vivid golden-buff stripes along edges of scapulars*. Streaked and barred with brown from head to breast; rest of underparts white, with some dark barring on flanks. In flight shows whitish trailing edge to secondaries, and a *rufous-tipped tail with little white at the sides*. Tail of 12–18 feathers (usually 14); wings narrow and pointed (unlike African Snipe). Rises explosively giving harsh rasping *scaaap* **call***;* climbs quickly with rapid zig-zagging, and usually flies far before landing. **Range/status:** Common migrant Oct.–March, when *the most numerous snipe below 2000 m.*

AFRICAN SNIPE *Gallinago nigripennis aequatorialis*   **Plate 24**

Length 12". The resident *highland* snipe. On the ground, similar to Common Snipe, equally long-billed, but *more blackish above*, and the *more boldly streaked neck and breast contrast strongly with white belly*. In flight shows white trailing edge to secondaries and conspicuous pale body stripes like Common Snipe, but has *broader, more rounded wings and prominent white tail sides* evident as bird alights; *flight slower and more fluttery than that of Common Snipe; flies lower with less zig-zagging*. Circular breeding display flight (day or night) involves repeated stooping to near ground with low humming *whur-whur-whur-whur*. . . produced by spread vibrating outer tail feathers. **Call** a harsh *scaap* or *scaip* similar to that of Common Snipe. **Range/status:** Local in marshes and bogs, mainly 1900–4000 m, but recorded as low as 1500 m. Widespread in w. and cent. Kenyan highlands and south to the Crater Highlands and Kilimanjaro.

GREAT SNIPE *Gallinago media*   **Plate 24**

Length 11". *Bulkier and darker than Common Snipe, and more barred on flanks and belly; bill somewhat shorter*. Further separated by *broad white tail sides, bold whitish wing-covert tips* and spotted (not streaked) neck and breast. Rectrices number 14–18 (usually 16). Rises rather slowly in silent, direct (not twisting) flight. A bird of wet fields, lake edges or dry short grassland. **Call** an occasional short croak when disturbed; *hoo-hoo* sound reportedly heard from Kenyan birds on ground in May. **Range/status**: Uncommon to scarce migrant, mainly on passage Oct.–Dec. and April– May.

PINTAIL SNIPE *Gallinago stenura*   Plate 24

Length 10″. A rare visitor, similar in size, build and pattern to Common and African Snipes. With practice, distinguishable at close range by paler, less richly coloured upperparts, less prominent back stripes, and in flight by *paler, more fawn-coloured wings without white trailing edges and toes projecting well beyond the end of the short tail*. In the hand shows *26–28 tail feathers* (more than other snipes), the *outer 8 pairs narrow and pin-like*. Rises more slowly and directly than Common Snipe, and the reedy *krreek* or *squik* **call** weaker and lower pitched. **Status**: Vagrant; 3 Kenyan records, Oct.–Jan., from Lake Naivasha and Mombasa.

BLACK-TAILED GODWIT *Limosa l. limosa*   Plate 23

Length 16″. A large, graceful, long-legged wader with a long straight bill; forages on marshy shores and irrigated fields, often in deep water. In flight shows *broad white wing-stripe* and black trailing wing edge, plus *broad black tail band contrasting with white rump*. **Non-breeding plumage** dull brown above, light brownish on head, neck and breast, white on belly; narrow whitish superciliary stripes bordered below by dark eye-lines. Bill blackish with basal third pinkish; legs and feet grey or blue-grey. In **breeding plumage** (March–April), head and breast are chestnut, the flanks, sides and belly white barred with black; base of bill orange-pink. **Calls**, *kik* or *keuk*, and in flight a loud excited *wicker-wicker-wicker*. **Range/status**: Common migrant, Oct.–early April, at lakes Turkana and Naivasha, also regular at Lake Nakuru, lower Tana River and Ahero. Scarce elsewhere, including n. Tanzania. Some oversummer.

BAR-TAILED GODWIT *Limosa l. lapponica*   Plate 23

Length 15″. Mainly coastal. Large, with a long, *slightly upturned bill*; blackish tarsi shorter than in Black-tailed Godwit, the toes barely projecting beyond the tail in flight. **Non-breeding plumage** pale mottled brownish grey above, whitish below, greyer and lightly streaked on head, neck and breast; pale superciliary stripes. In flight shows *whitish rump patch narrowing to a point on the back, finely barred tail and almost uniformly dark wings*. Bill blackish with basal half pink or pinkish yellow. **Breeding plumage** (Aug.–Sept.) mottled blackish and rich brown above, male reddish chestnut on head and underparts; female dull rufous or buff on neck and breast, whitish on belly. Feeds in shallows on open shores. Usual **call** a low *kirruk-kirrruk*. Rather quiet. **Range/status**: Uncommon coastal migrant, mainly Aug.–Oct.; a few winter in Sabaki-Mida Creek area near Malindi; rare on Rift Valley lakes.

WHIMBREL *Numenius p. phaeopus*   Plate 23

Length 16″. A large dusky brown coastal wader with *long bill decurved toward the tip*, and *boldly striped head pattern*. Neck and breast heavily streaked, flanks and underside of wings barred. Bill blackish brown, paler brown or pinkish at base; legs and feet blue-grey. In flight appears mainly brown above with narrowly barred tail and *white rump patch narrowing to a point on the lower back*. **Call** a rippling *pipipipipipipipi* or *whiwhiwhiwhiwhi*. **Range/status**: Common coastal migrant, mainly Aug.–April, but present in all months. Occasional at lakes Victoria and Turkana; rare elsewhere.

EURASIAN CURLEW *Numenius arquata orientalis*   Plate 23

Length 21-23″. Larger than Whimbrel and with a *longer and heavier bill decurved throughout its length*; *lacks Whimbrel's strong head pattern* and is lighter, more buffy brown. On the wing recalls Whimbrel, but *flight feathers paler* and wingbeats slower, somewhat gull-like. Bill dark brown, pinkish at base; legs and feet blue-grey. **Calls** include *quoi-quoi,* a longer more ringing *coor-lew,* and a rapid Whimbrel-like *tuyuyuyuyu* of alarm. Occasional loud song a long melodious bubbling trill, accelerating and rising in pitch. **Range/status:** Uncommon coastal migrant, mainly Aug.–April; a few present all year. Occasional inland, mainly on Rift Valley lakes.

SPOTTED REDSHANK *Tringa erythropus*   Plate 22

Length 12″. Slender with long neck, *long red legs* and *long straight red-based bill.* **Non-breeding plumage** grey above with conspicuous white spotting on wings; white below, the neck and breast faintly streaked; *whitish superciliary stripes contrast with dark eye-lines.* In flight, greyer above than Greenshank, white rump and back appearing as a more discrete patch, and white-spotted secondaries give paler-looking rear wing edge; tail narrowly barred. **Breeding plumage** (April–May) *sooty black* with whitish spots above; white wedge on back and white wing-linings obvious in flight. Mandible base dull dark red; legs and feet dark red or red-brown. Active; often wades in deep water, probing with head submerged; swims readily and up-ends to feed. Flight **call** a sharp rising whistle, *chu-it;* also a short *kip* of alarm, and a scolding *chick-chick-chick.* **Range/status:** Regular migrant inland, Nov.–May, rather uncommon.

COMMON REDSHANK *Tringa totanus ussuriensis*   Plate 22

Length 11″. Fairly large and long-necked; *base of bill, legs and feet orange-red.* **Non-breeding plumage** dull grey-brown above, white below with light streaking on neck and breast; often shows white eye-ring; pale superciliary stripes indistinct. In flight the *white inner primaries and secondaries contrast with dark outer primaries,* and *white rump patch extends in a wedge onto the back.* **Breeding plumage** warmer brown, heavily streaked below. **Juvenile** buffier, well-patterned above, with yellow-orange legs. (Spotted Redshank is more slender, longer-legged, greyer above and lacks white wing patches). **Call** a ringing *tew-hew-hew,* first note highest, and a yelping *tuuu* or *twek* of alarm. **Range/status:** Uncommon migrant, coastal and inland; winters regularly at Mida Creek and in Tana River delta. Rare in n. Tanzania.

MARSH SANDPIPER *Tringa stagnatilis*   Plate 22

Length 9″. An active wader, feeding at surface of shallow water. Slender, thin-necked, with a *very fine straight bill.* Suggests a diminutive Greenshank. **Non-breeding plumage** pale brownish grey above, white below with light streaking on sides of neck and breast. Pale superciliary stripes usually inconspicuous on light face. In flight, *plain dark wings* contrast with *white rump extending to a point on the back,* and toes project well beyond the narrowly barred tail. Bill black, greenish toward base; legs vary from greyish green to yellow. **Breeding plumage** (Feb.–April) darker on upperparts, the head and neck more heavily streaked, and breast boldly black-spotted. Legs often yellow to orange-yellow. **Juvenile** (Aug.–Sept.) is much browner above, with cream feather edges. (Larger Common Greenshank, similarly patterned, has a longer, stouter, slightly upturned bill, proportionately shorter tarsi, and different call.) **Call** a single rather dry *cheeo* when flushed; alarm call a sharp *chip,* often repeated. **Range/ status:** Migrant, mainly late Aug–April. Common inland on muddy and marshy shores, especially on Rift Valley lakes. Scarce on coast. Some first-year birds oversummer.

COMMON GREENSHANK *Tringa nebularia*   Plate 22

Length 12″. Large and long-necked, with a long, *slightly upturned, thick-based bill, and greenish legs and feet.* **Non-breeding plumage** brownish grey above, white below with light streaking on sides of neck and breast. In flight from above, *plain dark wings separated by white rump and wedge of white on back;* white tail narrowly barred with black. Bill blackish with basal half greenish grey or blue-grey Browner **breeding plumage** (Feb.–April) is streaked and barred above, most heavily on face, neck and breast. **Juvenile** (Aug.–Sept.) is dark brown above with buffy feather edges, lightly speckled and barred on sides of breast. Picks food from water surface and also scythes from side to side with bill held flat. **Call** a far-carrying, fluty *tew-tew-tew*, usually given in flight; also a complaining *tyip*. **Range/status**: Common migrant, coastal and inland, late Aug.–April; many first-year birds oversummer.

GREEN SANDPIPER *Tringa ochropus*   Plate 22

Length 9″. A robust *dark-backed* solitary wader with fairly short *olive-green legs; underside of wings entirely dark*, contrasting with white belly in flight, when it also shows white rump, upper tail-coverts and tail, the latter with 2–3 black bars toward tip; *toes barely extend beyond tail tip*. Often along rivers and streams. Bobs up and down. Takes off erratically, quite snipe-like, calling repeatedly. 'Towers' and descends in rapidly executed loops. **Non-breeding plumage** *olive-brown above* with fine whitish speckling; white below, olive at sides of breast; white supraloral streak and narrow white eye-ring contrast with blackish eye-line; faint streaking on face, neck and breast (bolder in **breeding plumage**, Feb.–April). **Juvenile** sparsely spotted with dull buff above. **Call** a loud ringing *clewit-lewit* or *clewit-weet-weet*. **Range/status**: Migrant, Aug.–early April, mainly inland, but on creeks and lagoons at coast.

WOOD SANDPIPER *Tringa glareola*   Plate 22 ✓

Length 8″. A *slender* inland wader with *white superciliary stripes*, straight bill and *long yellowish green or pale olive legs*. In flight, appears dark above with *white rump and upper tail-coverts* like Green Sandpiper, but tail barring narrower, *toes project well beyond tail tip*, and *pale wing-linings* merge with white belly; white shaft of outer primary noticeable at close range. In **non-breeding** and **juvenile** plumages, *upperparts paler and browner than in Green Sandpiper*, with pale buff speckling. **Breeding plumage** (March–May) more boldly spotted above, flanks boldly barred. **Call** a loud *chiff-iff, chiff-iff-iff*, and a persistent sharp *chip-chip-chip. . .* of alarm. **Range/status**: Common migrant inland, late July–early May.

COMMON SANDPIPER *Actitis hypoleucos*   Plate 22

Length 7.5″. A solitary, short-legged sandpiper of ditches, pools and shores. *Incessant teetering motion* is characteristic, as is *low, stiff-winged flight* in which shallow wing strokes alternate with short glides. Olive-brown above with whitish superciliary stripes, white below, and *brownish patches on sides of breast* separated from bend of wing by white wedge. In flight, centre of rump and tail uniform with back, *white wing-stripe and barred white sides of the long rounded tail* conspicuous. Bill olive-grey or dark brown, ochre or pinkish at base; legs and feet dull greenish grey or rarely yellowish olive. **Breeding plumage** (March–April) noticeably streaked above and on neck and breast. Often perches on rocks and tree roots. **Call** a high-pitched *twee-wee-wee*, and a long-drawn *tweeee* of alarm. **Range/status**: Common migrant, inland and on coast, mid-July–April, marked passage in Aug.–Sept.

TEREK SANDPIPER *Xenus cinereus*   Plate 22

Length 9–10″. An orange-legged coastal wader with a *long, upturned black bill, orange to dull red at the base*. An active feeder at water's edge; probes with bill held nearly flat; also scythes in Avocet fashion. Bobbing suggests Common Sandpiper. **Non-breeding plumage** grey-brown above with blackish 'shoulders' sometimes conspicuous. Underparts white, the neck and sides of breast grey-tinged and faintly streaked. In flight appears plain above except for *white rear edge to secondaries*. **Breeding plumage** more streaked above and below, broadly so on scapulars which may form a blackish V. **Calls** include a fluty *tuu-hu* or *tew-tew-tew*, and a sharper *twit-wit-wit-wit*. **Range/status**: Common migrant, late Aug.–April in various coastal habitats including coral reefs. A few remain all year. Occasional on Rift Valley lakes.

347

RUDDY TURNSTONE *Arenaria i. interpres* **Plate 23**

Length 8–10″. A plump coastal shorebird with *distinctively patterned plumage*, a *short, slightly uptilted, blackish bill and short orange legs.* Forages among shoreline debris, turning over small stones and seaweed. **Non-breeding plumage** mottled dusky brown and black above; dark brown sides of face and bold blackish breast patch contrast with white chin and belly. Bold flight pattern involves broad white wing-stripe, white back/upper tail-coverts, black bar on rump and broad black tail tip. **Breeding plumage** rufous and black above, with *intricate black-and-white head/neck pattern.* **Juvenile** duller brown above and on breast than non-breeding adults, with pale patches on head; legs and feet dull yellowish-brown at first, soon turning orange. **Calls** a hard *kitititit* or *tuk-a-tuk*, and a sharp *keeoo.* **Range/status**: Common coastal migrant, mainly late Aug.–April. Occasional inland, Sept.–Nov.

RED-NECKED PHALAROPE *Phalaropus lobatus* **Plate 22**

Length 7″. Mainly pelagic; usually seen swimming. A dainty open-water bird with slender neck and *black, needle-like bill.* **Non-breeding plumage** grey above with white sides of neck and underparts, and a bold *black eye patch*; white wing-stripe and dark centre of rump and tail prominent in flight. In **breeding plumage**, buff lines on grey back and rufous upper breast and sides of neck diagnostic; throat white; male duller and more brownish above than female. **Call** a Sanderling-like *twick* or *kwick.* **Range/status**: Regular offshore migrant, Oct.–April, often in flocks. Scarce inland, mainly on Lake Turkana and other Rift Valley lakes. Rare in n. Tanzania (records from Tabora, Serengeti NP, Arusha NP).

GREY or RED PHALAROPE *Phalaropus fulicarius* **Plate 22**
Length 8″. Slightly larger and stockier than Red-necked Phalarope, and with *shorter and thicker bill*, often yellowish at the base. In **non-breeding plumage**, paler and more uniformly grey than Red-necked. **Breeding plumage** bright rufous below with *black cap and white cheeks.* **Call** a sharp, high-pitched *wit*, shriller than call of Red-necked. **Range/status**: Rare migrant, most likely at sea. Five Kenyan records, including one photographed in Nairobi NP, Sept. 1979.

SKUAS OR JAEGERS, FAMILY STERCORARIIDAE

Hook-billed piratical seabirds now often included in Laridae, and quite gull-like in general appearance, especially when swimming or standing on the shore. More often they are seen in flight, pursuing gulls or terns and forcing them to disgorge their food. They are typically marine (although a few appear on Rift Valley lakes), migrants from Arctic breeding areas. (Unidentified *Catharacta* skuas, rarely reported off the coast, are probably vagrants from southern oceans.) Adult *Stercorarius* in breeding plumage, most likely here in August or in spring, have projecting central tail feathers with diagnostic shapes. Adult plumage apparently takes up to 4 years to acquire. The highly variable immatures have central rectrices shaped like those of adults but much shorter. All 3 species are polymorphic, with either predominantly white or dark brown underparts, but intermediates exist. Sexes are alike. Barred winter adults begin to moult into breeding dress before spring migration. Most juveniles are brown (Long-tailed much greyer) and pale-barred above, dark-barred below; some are darker, more sooty brown with little pale feather-tipping. Identification of juveniles and non-breeding adults requires consideration of *shape, size, wingspread* and *flight style.* On young birds also note *general plumage colour, shape of central rectrices* (difficult to see, but diagnostic), *bill shape and colour* and *tail-covert markings.* Less important is extent of white on upperside of the primary bases (reflecting the number of ivory-white primary shafts visible—which depends on the degree to which the primaries are spread).

POMARINE SKUA *Stercorarius pomarinus* **Plate 8**
Length (adult) 25.5–31″. *Thick-necked, barrel-chested and broad-winged*, with steady, powerful, slow wingbeats, *suggesting a large gull.* (Deep regular strokes of normal flight quickly change in swift agile pursuit of gull or tern.) *Bill long, deep with strong hook and*

prominent gonydeal angle, often pale at base. **Spring adult** dark brown above with black cap; usual **pale morph** yellowish white below, darkly barred along sides and flanks, typically with a *mottled or barred dark breast band*; under tail-coverts dark brown. In flight, 5–6 white primary shafts show as prominent pale crescent at base of primaries above and below; *projecting central rectrices broad, twisted, and rounded at tips.* Uncommon **dark morph** wholly blackish brown below, *mottled* rather than evenly toned, with dull yellowish face. **Non-breeding adult** pale-barred on back, *dark-barred on upper tail-coverts*; cap margins blurry; chin and throat browner than in spring, and barring stronger on flanks and crissum; central tail-feathers shorter, more pointed. Some spring birds intermediate between breeding and non-breeding plumages. **Immature** resembles non-breeding adult, but wings more barred beneath and projecting rectrices short; pale legs and feet gradually become black. **Juvenile** usually has *pale bill base* (grey, brownish or dull yellow) contrasting with black tip and with *dark malar feathers. Head more uniformly dark than that of Arctic Skua, not paler on nape, faintly barred instead of streaked*; upper tail-coverts more conspicuously barred. Central rectrices broad, bluntly rounded, barely extending beyond others. Legs and feet pale blue; distal part of toes and webs black. **Status**: Scarce migrant, Oct.–March (10 coastal records, 4 from Rift Valley lakes).

*ARCTIC SKUA or PARASITIC JAEGER *Stercorarius parasiticus*   Plate 8
Length (adult)18–26.5". *Slimmer than Pomarine Skua, with narrower, more pointed wings.* Wingspan about that of a Grey-headed Gull. *Flight somewhat falcon-like.* **Adult** has *narrow, pointed central tail-feather projections 8–14 cm in length.* Bill black, tinged olive or slate at base; feet black. **Dark morph** *evenly dark smoky grey-brown, not mottled.* **Light morph** may lack dark breast band which, if present, is *evenly grey, not mottled or barred.* White primary shafts (3–5) usually provide less prominent 'flash' than in Pomarine. **Non-breeding adult** and **immature** resemble corresponding plumages of Pomarine; bill as in adult; blue-grey tarsal colour of juvenile gradually changes to black. **Juvenile** brighter warmer brown than young Pomarine or Long-tailed Skuas, with *rufous or tawny feather edgings producing scaly effect on back and wings*; underparts usually barred with uneven wavy lines except on flanks; *pale brown nape typically streaked like the face, malar area pale* (no dark area adjacent to bill as in Pomarine). *Upper tail-covert barring more brown and buff, less black and white, the bars wavy, not as straight and even as in Pomarine.* Bill dark blue-grey, blackish at tip. **Status**: Four acceptable Kenyan records of adults near Malindi (April), one from Lake Turkana (Oct.). Skuas thought to have been Arctics seen at lakes Nakuru and Turkana (Sept.–Nov.) and on coast (Mar.–Apr.).

LONG-TAILED SKUA *Stercorarius longicaudus*   Plate 8
Length (adult)19.5–23". Smaller, more *tern-like* than Arctic Skua, the wings appearing longer and narrower; flight more bouyant. Only 2 primaries with white shafts. **Spring adult (pale morph)** shows *neat, sharply defined black cap* separated by white collar from grey upperparts; *blackish secondaries contrast noticeably with greyish coverts.* (Arctic has more uniformly dark wings.) Underparts largely white, without breast band, but belly and crissum dark; *tail streamers straight, pointed, about* one-third *of bird's total length.* Tarsi greyish blue to wholly black. **Dark morph** very rare. **Non-breeding adult** generally buffy grey, dusky on face, collar, and breast; tail projections shorter. **Immature** variable; usually like non-breeding adult but with mostly barred under wing-coverts and axillaries. Tarsi as in adult. **Juvenile** greyish above, *finely barred with white, less scaly or scalloped* than the larger skuas; nape often pale, face usually finely streaked; breast typically uniform dark brownish grey; wing-linings, flanks, upper and under tail-coverts *strongly barred black and white.* Inch-long rectrix extensions blunt and rounded (tiny sharp points doubtless wear off before birds reach African waters). Lacks buff primary tips of young Arctic Skua. Bill grey-blue with black tip; tarsi greyish blue; toes and webs blackish and pale pink. **Status**: Adult in breeding plumage photographed at Lake Turkana, late Aug 1961; probable immature seen at Lake Nakuru late Aug. 1989.

GULLS, FAMILY LARIDAE, SUBFAMILY LARINAE
Mostly coastal scavengers, numerous at fishing centres; a few regular on inland waters. Generally larger than terns, and with broader, less pointed wings, heavier bills and square-tipped tails. They commonly settle on the water. Sexes are alike. The smaller species

appear adult in their second winter, medium-sized species in their third, and large gulls not until their fourth winter. Post-juvenile body moult occurs at 2–4 months of age, but juvenile wing and tail feathers are retained through the first year. A partial pre-nuptial moult replaces head and body feathers, some wing-coverts and inner wing feathers. A prolonged post-nuptial moult, resulting in basic 'winter' plumage, replaces all feathers and may take up to 5 months to complete. Intra-specific variation is therefore considerable. Important identification features include colour of bare parts, relative bill size, upper wing and tail patterns, and head markings.

SOOTY GULL *Larus hemprichii*   Plates 6, 7, 8

Length 17–18.5". A large dark *coastal* gull, long-billed and with long, broad rounded wings. Gregarious. **Adult** brownish grey above with *sooty brown head and greyish neck and breast; white collar on hindneck and small white marks above and below* eyes; wings blackish above with white trailing edge, dark below. *Bill yellowish with black subterminal band and red tip*; legs and feet greenish yellow; eyes dark brown. **First-year** bird paler and browner above with pale-edged wing-coverts, head to breast pale brown, dark brown around eyes and on nape. In flight, primaries and bar along secondaries blackish, forewing paler; *white rump/upper tail-coverts contrast with black tail*; bill blue-grey with black tip; feet dull grey or blue-grey; eyes brown. **Second-year** bird similar but plainer above, black of tail confined to tip. Adult plumage attained in third year. **Juvenile** resembles first-year bird, but body paler, upperparts browner with much buff feather-edging. Usual **call** a screaming *keeow*; also a more staccato *kek-kek-kek* at colonies. **Range**: On coast and offshore islands most months, although scarce south of Malindi June–Sept. Mainly a non-breeding visitor from ne. Africa and Arabia, although a few breed on islets off Kiunga (n. Kenya) July–Oct. (Similar extralimital **White-eyed Gull**, *Larus leucophthalmus,* regular on north coast of Somalia, is a possible vagrant. Paler and slimmer than Sooty Gull, it has narrower, more pointed wings. Non-breeding adult has white-flecked black head, bold white eye-crescents, a slender, black-tipped dark red bill, and yellowish feet. First-year bird is darker above than Sooty Gull, more uniformly brown. See figure opposite Plate 6.)

HEUGLIN'S GULL *Larus heuglini*   Plates 6, 7

Length 23–26". A coastal gull, *patterned like Lesser Black-backed* but slightly larger and bulkier with heavier bill. **Adult** medium grey to dark slate above; outer primaries grade to blackish distally, and have small white tips with a small white 'mirror' on outermost feather. Wings show white trailing edges. Bill usually yellow with red or black and red gonydeal spot; some Kenyan birds (third year?) show a large black mandibular spot, others a nearly complete subterminal blackish ring around the bill, fainter on maxilla. *Eyes pale yellow*, rim of the eyelids dark red. Apparent nominate *heuglini* dark slate above (almost as black as *L. f. fuscus*) show *greyish streaks on crown and neck* in non-breeding plumage; feet yellowish. Paler birds, presumably representing *taimyrensis-birulae* cline, are medium to dark grey above, with little head streaking, and yellowish or flesh-pink feet. (Note that some pale-backed birds may be *L. fuscus graellsii*, q.v.) **First-winter** *heuglini* resembles *L. f. fuscus*, but paler, with more barring and pale mottling above, more boldly marked on rump, and paler below; head whitish. Said to lack black bar on greater coverts, and to show grey panel near base of primaries (unlike Lesser Black-backed). Bill black or pink with black tip; feet pinkish. **Second-winter** bird greyer (pale in some *taimyrensis*, slaty in *L. h. heuglini*) with yellowish bill base; feet pink, yellow or almost whitish. **Calls** resemble those of Lesser Black-backed Gull. **Range/status**: Regular palearctic migrant, sometimes in substantial numbers, from Tana River delta to Malindi/Sabaki area, Nov.–March; occasional on south Kenya coast and at Lake Turkana. **Taxonomic Note**: Some authors consider *heuglini* and *taimyrensis* to be races of Herring Gull, *L. argentatus*; others merge them with *L. fuscus*. Yet another school of thought supports their separation as a third species owing to near-sympatry on their breeding grounds. *L. heuglini* may also include the forms *vegae, barabensis* and *armenicus* (any of which, like *cachinnans* or *michahellis*, might reach East African waters). Lack of specimen evidence precludes more meaningful analysis at present.

LESSER BLACK-BACKED GULL *Larus fuscus*   Plates 6, 7, 8

Length 20–24″. Large but rather slim, adult with *white head and tail* and (*L. f. fuscus*) *slaty black upperparts*. Wings show white trailing edges, small white outer primary tips and white 'mirror' on outermost feather; *underside whitish, dark near tip and along trailing edge*. Bill yellow with red gonydeal spot (variable dark markings in presumed third-year birds); eyes pale yellow, eyelids red; legs/feet usually yellow, but pinkish or greyish in some adult-plumaged birds. **First-winter plumage** mottled blackish brown above, paler on head, and neck heavily streaked; underparts and rump densely grey-marked; wings blackish; tail white, broadly tipped black. Bill blackish; eyes, legs and feet dull flesh-pink. **Second-winter** bird darker above, tail band as in first-winter; bill yellowish at base. Adult plumage attained in fourth year. Paler and greyer *L. f. graellsii* has especially dense head/neck streaking in first and second winters. (A second-winter Turkana specimen had largely black bill, extensively whitish at base, pale tan eyes and whitish flesh feet.) That race noticeably short-winged (400–447 mm) compared to similar *L. h. taimyrensis* (443–477 mm). **Range/status**: *L. f. fuscus* locally common palearctic migrant Oct.–April, on coast and larger inland lakes. A few immatures present all year in Kenya where Finnish- and Swedish-ringed birds have been recovered; *graellsii* collected once at Lake Turkana.

KELP GULL *Larus dominicanus* [*vetula*]   Plate 6

Length 23″. A vagrant black-backed gull with a *very heavy bill. Stockier and larger-headed than preceding two species.* **Adult** black above with white head, trailing wing edges, primary tips and 'mirror' on outermost primary. Wings of standing bird do not project as far beyond the tail as in Lesser Black-backed Gull. Bill yellow with red gonydeal spot; orbital ring orange-red; eyes usually dark brown; legs and feet blue-grey to olive-yellow (less pure yellow than in Heuglin's or Lesser Black-backed). **First-winter plumage** mottled greyish brown above; whitish head and underparts dark-streaked, ear-coverts and area around eyes dusky; rump white with coarse dark barring; tail blackish; all bare parts brown. In **second-winter**, head and underparts clearer white with brown streaking pronounced on breast, faint on head; back brown, primaries slate-grey, and tail white at base. Bill and feet grey-brown becoming olive-yellow in spring. **Calls** include a plaintive *meew*, a staccato *ko-ko-ko-ko* and a loud *keeyok*. **Status**: Southern vagrant. Adult photographed at Malindi, Jan. 1984.

GREY-HEADED GULL *Larus cirrocephalus poiocephalus*   Plates 5, 7,

Length 16–17″. The only common *inland* gull. Wings of adult grey above with *white wedge* from outer primary bases to bend; tip black with white mirrors; undersurface quite dark. In **breeding plumage** has *pale grey hood*, darker along rear margin, and often a pink 'bloom' on the white underparts; bare parts red except for *yellowish white* eyes. Hood less well-defined in non-breeders. **First-year plumage** differs in brownish diagonal bar across wing-coverts, dusky band along rear of secondaries, and dark tail band; the white head shows blackish smudges on crown and behind eyes. Juvenile wings and tail retained, faded and worn. Feet brownish red; bill pinkish with dark tip. **Juvenile** largely brown above including crown and sides of head; tail white with dark brown terminal band; no mirrors on primaries; *eyes dark*. Gregarious and noisy. **Call** a short harsh *garr* and a querulous *kwaar*. High-flying flocks especially vocal. **Range**: Breeds irregularly on several Rift Valley lakes. Rare at the coast.

BLACK-HEADED GULL *Larus ridibundus*   Plates 5, 7, 8

Length 13.5–14.5″. A medium-sized, *dark-eyed* gull with pale grey upperparts and a slender bill. Wings rather narrow and pointed, the upper surface with *long white leading edge from bend to tip*; only the primary tips black. Diagnostic *dark brown hood* of **breeding adult** replaced by white in **non-breeding plumage**, which shows *prominent blackish spot behind eye*. Bill, legs and feet red; eyes brown. **First-winter plumage** has leading edge of primaries white, rear edge of secondaries dark, and a dark diagonal bar across coverts; tail tipped blackish. Legs and feet dull orange; bill orange-red with blackish tip. (Grey-headed Gull has blackish wing tips at all ages, and under-

side of wings is dark; adult has pale eyes.) **Calls** similar to those of Grey-headed Gull. **Range/status:** Fairly common palearctic migrant on Rift Valley lakes, particularly Turkana and Nakuru. Uncommon elsewhere, including coast.

SLENDER-BILLED GULL *Larus genei*   Plates 5, 7, 8

Length 15–18" Similar in colour and wing pattern to Black-headed Gull, but *pale-eyed*, with *longer neck* and somewhat longer tail. Bill also longer, slightly drooping at tip and varying in colour from blackish red to bright orange; legs and feet usually scarlet. In flight, shows *flatter forehead and distinctive long-necked, hump-backed profile*. When swimming, neck less upright than in Black-headed, with *head held forward*. **Spring adult** has a pink 'bloom' on underparts (not evident at distance in bright light), and a pure white head. In **non-breeding plumage** shows a faint grey postocular mark. In **first-winter plumage** resembles Black-headed, but dark wing and postocular marks less distinct, and bill and feet typically brighter orange-yellow. **Range/status:** Fairly regular palearctic migrant on lakes Turkana and Nakuru. Rare elsewhere, including the coast. Occasional in summer.

GREAT BLACK-HEADED GULL *Larus ichthyaetus*   Plates 6, 7, 8

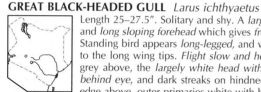

Length 25–27.5". Solitary and shy. A *large pale* gull with a *massive bill* and *long sloping forehead* which gives *front-heavy appearance* in flight. Standing bird appears *long-legged*, and with *attenuated rear end* owing to the long wing tips. *Flight slow and heavy.* **Non-breeding adult** pale grey above, the *largely white head with blackish shading around and behind eye*, and dark streaks on hindneck. Wing shows white leading edge above, outer primaries white with black markings near tip; underside pale. Bill yellow with black subterminal band; legs and feet greenish yellow. **Breeding plumage** has *black hood* marked by conspicuous small white crescents around eyes. **First-winter** bird resembles non-breeding adult but more black on wing tips, forewing mottled brown, blackish bar on secondaries, and broad black tail tip; pinkish bill tipped black; legs and feet grey. **Second-winter** bird has greyer wings, yellowish bill, legs and feet. **Call** a raven-like croaking *kuraak*. **Range/status:** Uncommon palearctic migrant, Dec.–March, mainly near Malindi/Sabaki delta and at Lake Turkana.

TERNS, FAMILY LARIDAE, SUBFAMILY STERNINAE

Mostly smaller and more slender than gulls, with forked tail and more pointed wings. Flight graceful and buoyant, the bill often angled downward. They rarely swim, and come to land for roosting. Nesting is colonial. Typical coastal terns (*Sterna*) show a black cap in breeding plumage, partially lost after nesting. They mature during their second or third years, and many young oversummer in non-breeding areas. Most dive to catch fish. Marsh terns (*Chlidonias*) are dark-bodied in breeding dress, but display marked seasonal plumage changes. The dark, white-capped noddies (*Anous*) are low-flying marine terns, which hover and swoop for food far out at sea.

✔ GULL-BILLED TERN *Sterna n. nilotica*   Plates 3, 5

Length 14–15". Large and stocky; *pale grey above (including rump)* and *white below*. Gull-like impression from *heavy black bill, strong black tarsi, rather broad wings and shallowly forked tail* is enhanced by heavier flight than that of most *Sterna* species. Hunts with slow shallow wing strokes over exposed flats, marshes or water, snatching prey from surface or hawking insects in the air. Black cap of **breeding adult** reduced to dark ear-coverts and streaks on nape in **non-breeding plumage**. In flight shows darker trailing edge on outer primaries. **First-winter** bird whiter than adult with distinct black facial patch; wing-coverts brown-tipped. **Calls** include a throaty *kirrr-uk, kay-ti-did* or *kay-rik*, and an almost metallic *kaaak*. **Range/status:** Locally common palearctic migrant, mainly late Aug.–early April, on large lakes, and on coast south to the Pemba Channel. Flocks regularly cross eastern Serengeti Plains in n. Tanzania, Jan.–March. A few present all year on Rift Valley lakes.

CASPIAN TERN *Sterna caspia* Plates 4, 5

Length 18.5–21″. A *very large* tern with *heavy red bill* (tipped dusky), and shaggy occipital crest. Size, rather broad wings, and shallow tail fork may suggest a gull, but bill and habits are tern-like. **Adult** pale grey above with slightly crested black cap, white-streaked in non-breeding plumage; underparts and rump white. Wings pale grey above, darker on primaries; whitish underside shows contrasting dark tips. Feet black. **First-winter** bird resembles non-breeding adult, but has brown-tipped wing-coverts, dusky secondaries and dark tail tip. Flies high and sometimes soars. Dives well. **Calls** include a hoarse *kaaa*, a shorter *kark* and a heron-like *kraah-aah*. **Range/status**: Presumed palearctic migrant, uncommon but regular on coast and at Lake Turkana; rare elsewhere. Winters in Malindi/Sabaki area and at Lake Turkana.

GREATER CRESTED TERN *Sterna bergii* Plates 4, 5

Length 18–19″. A *prominently crested* coastal tern, slightly smaller than Caspian. Appears elongate at rest, with long wings and *large pale yellow bill which droops at the tip*. Tail well forked. Flies with steady sweeping strokes. Sociable; usually in small groups within mixed larid flocks. **Breeding adult** has *black cap separated from bill by narrow white band*. In **non-breeding plumage**, black confined to back of head. Upperparts rather dark grey in *S. b. velox*, paler in *S. b. thalassina*; rump and tail pale grey in both races. Blackish outer primaries form a dark wedge at wing tip, noticeable above and below. In *velox*, silvery white inner primaries and secondaries contrast with dark grey forewing above. Feet black. Greyer **first-year** bird has much grey-brown on wing-coverts, and darker carpal and secondary bars. **Juvenile** darker grey above, barred and mottled black and white; crown blackish brown with white-edged feathers, crest browner and dusky mottling around eyes; wings and tail blackish; bill brown. (Lesser Crested Tern is smaller, more lightly built, paler above than *S. b. velox*, with smaller, brighter orange-yellow bill, all-black forehead in breeding plumage; entire crown of non-breeding bird is white.) **Calls** include a harsh *ki-ekk* or *kiii-rit*, a croaking *krrow*, and a high squealing *kreee-kreee*. **Range/status**: *S. b. velox* is a non-breeding visitor from Somalia and the Gulf of Aden, common south to Malindi, mainly Nov.–June. *S. b. thalassina* breeds in w. Indian Ocean to Latham Island off Dar es Salaam; sporadic along coast south of Mombasa and around Pemba Island.

LESSER CRESTED TERN *Sterna b. bengalensis* Plates 4, 5

Length 14–14.5″. A *crested* coastal tern with *long straight orange or orange-yellow bill* and pale ash-grey upperparts. Tail deeply forked; wings proportionately shorter than in Greater Crested Tern and flight more buoyant. In **breeding plumage**, entire cap *black from bill to nape*. **Non-breeding adult** has *white forehead, crown and part of occiput, black largely confined to nape and postocular areas;* flight feathers silvery edged; wing pale below with greyer primary tips. Feet black. **First-year** bird has dull yellow bill, blackish outer primaries and dusky secondaries. Gregarious, forming large flocks; associates with Greater Crested and Common Terns. **Calls** include a rough *kik-kerruk* or *kirrik* or *kreek-kreek*, and a high-pitched *krrr-eeep*. **Range/status**: Common non-breeding visitor from the Red Sea and coast of Somalia. Common in all months, especially Nov.–April. Extends inland along lower Tana River. Vagrants recorded on Rift Valley lakes including Naivasha, Nakuru and Turkana.

SANDWICH TERN *Sterna s. sandvicensis* Plates 4, 5

Length 14–16″. A crested coastal tern, similar in size and build to Lesser Crested. *Short white tail is not deeply forked.* Pale grey upperparts can appear white at a distance or in bright sunlight when *slender, yellow-tipped black bill* may seem all black. In **breeding plumage**, entire crown black. **Non-breeding adult** has white forehead and forecrown, less yellow on bill tip. Greyish white wings show only a narrow dusky trailing edge below near tip. Feet black. **First-year** bird has darker wing tips and brown flecking on coverts. **Calls** suggest Lesser Crested Tern: a grating *kirrick* or *keer-kwit*, and a lower *gwick* or *gwut*. **Range/status**: Uncommon palearctic migrant, mainly on n. Kenyan coast south to Malindi. Vagrant inland (once, Lake Baringo).

ROSEATE TERN *Sterna dougallii bangsi*   Plates 3, 5

Length 13–15″. A slender, exceptionally graceful coastal tern. *White appearance and long tail* of black-capped **breeding adult** distinctive. Upperparts very pale grey, outer primaries forming *darker grey wedge at wing tip; wings entirely white* below as are rump and underparts, the latter with a rosy 'bloom' when fresh; *long outer tail feathers greatly exceed wing tips in resting bird*. Long thin bill, *black or black with red base* in non-breeding season, turns *largely or wholly bright scarlet* at breeding time; feet bright red. **Non-breeding adult** and **first-year** bird have white forehead and crown, shorter outer tail feathers, narrow black carpal bar on wing, and brownish orange feet. (Common Tern is darker grey above, has blackish trailing edge on outer wing below, and has broader wings. White-cheeked Tern is more compact, greyer above, with shorter bill.) **Juvenile** Roseate has whitish forehead and scaly buffy grey back, white rump and hindneck, and black feet. **Calls** include a harsh *chirrik* or *chewik*, a higher-pitched *aaar* or *aaak*, and an insistent chatter at nesting colonies. **Range/status**: Breeds abundantly in Kiunga Islands, July–Sept., occasionally on Whale, Kisite and Pemba.

COMMON TERN *Sterna hirundo*   Plates 3, 5

Length 12–14″. A gregarious coastal tern; in **breeding plumage**, pale grey above with white rump and tail; black cap separated from pale greyish underparts by white sides of face; *underside of wing whitish with broad dusky trailing edge along primary tips*. In resting bird, *wing tips reach the ends of the moderately long outer tail feathers*. Bill usually all *black* (turning scarlet with black tip later in spring, after leaving East African waters); feet dull red or red-brown. **Non-breeding adult** has shorter outer tail feathers, white forehead and forecrown; lacks contrast between back and rump; blackish lesser coverts form a *broad carpal bar*, evident on closed wing. **First-year** bird resembles non-breeding adult but has dusky bar along secondaries; in August may show remnant brown juvenile feathers above, sooty-brown ear-coverts, orange bill base and orange feet. Large flocks roost on beaches and sandbanks; thousands feed offshore beyond the reef. (Breeding Roseate Tern is paler above, shows no contrast between back and rump, has longer bill and longer outer tail feathers, wings pure white below, wingbeats quicker and shallower. White-cheeked Tern is somewhat darker above with whitish primaries, in breeding plumage much darker below than Common and with grey rump; non-breeding adult has narrower carpal bar and less white on forehead than Common; White-cheeked is more compact with shorter tarsi, narrower wings.) **Call** a repeated *kik-kik-kik* and *KEE-agh* or *KEE-yarr*. **Range/status**: Abundant palearctic migrant on coast, mainly Aug.–Dec. and in April. Some winter in East African waters, and many first-year birds present April–Aug. Few records from Rift Valley lakes. Both nominate *hirundo* and *S. h. tibetana* appear to be represented in our region.

WHITE-CHEEKED TERN *Sterna repressa*   Plates 2, 5

Length 12–14″. A grey marine tern, distinctive in **breeding plumage** with *dark grey underparts and broad white facial streak* below black cap. Long outer feathers equal wing tips at rest. In flight, wings appear dark grey above, with *contrasting whitish primaries* and *narrow blackish trailing edges* both above and below. (Primaries of worn birds in late summer may be uniformly dark without obvious contrast.) Wing-linings largely grey. Bill red with dusky tip; legs and feet dark red. **Non-breeding adult** and **first-year** bird white below and on forehead, medium grey above, with *darker inner wing feathers than Common Tern; dark edge formed by black primary tips is longer than in that species and the black carpal bar narrower; wings narrower; rump and tail also greyer;* outer rectrices little elongated. Bill and tarsi blackish, both slightly shorter than in Common Tern. **Juvenile** has brownish back showing much white feather edging; largely grey wings with *conspicuously white primaries* and white-margined coverts; forehead, lores and much of forecrown white, lores largely black, tail tip brown. Basal half of mandible flesh-pink. Small groups assemble on beaches, larger flocks beyond the reef. Usual **call** a loud *kee-ERR* or *kee-EEEK* (*second syllable accented*, unlike Common Tern's call). **Range/status**: Breeds off n. Kenya in Kiunga Islands and on Tenewe Is. south of Lamu, July–Sept. Present along coast throughout the year.

BRIDLED TERN *Sterna anaethetus antarctica* Plate 2

Length 12–12.5″. A *pelagic* tern, usually well offshore. Dark above and white below, the *brownish grey back usually separated from black crown and nape by whitish hindneck; white of forehead extends over and behind eyes as narrow superciliary stripes;* sides of tail white. Bill and feet black. **First-year** bird has shorter tail with no white. **Juvenile** has pale-tipped dorsal feathers, less distinct head pattern, and wholly brownish tail. Solitary or gregarious. Perches on ships and floating debris but rarely settles on water. (Sooty Tern is larger, more blackish and uniform above with broader and shorter superciliary stripes.) **Call** a growling *kararrr* and softer notes from feeding birds. At colonies gives a barking *yup-yup*. **Range/status:** Breeds in Lamu and Kiunga archipelagos, erratically on Whale Is. off Watamu, July–Sept. Frequent all year at sea.

SOOTY TERN *Sterna fuscata nubilosa* Plate 2

Length 16–17″. A gregarious *pelagic* tern with *bounding, often soaring flight. Black above and white below with broad white forehead and superciliary stripes;* tail black and deeply forked, with white outer edges. Bill and feet black. **First-year** bird usually black from chin to breast. **Juvenile** sooty brown speckled with white; crissum and wing-linings pale whitish. Feeds mostly by dipping to sea surface. See Bridled Tern. Usual **call** a loud, nasal *ker-wacky-wack.* **Range:** Has nested on Tenewe and Kisite islands. Frequent at sea beyond the reef.

SAUNDERS'S TERN *Sterna (albifrons) saundersi* Plates 3, 5

Length 8.5–9.5″. A *small* gregarious coastal tern with narrow wings and rapid wingbeats. **Breeding plumage** pale grey above with black cap, and *white forehead area extending back only to anterior margin of eyes,* the patch appearing more 'square' in side view than in Little Tern; from the front, patch is triangular, not V-shaped as in Little. *Outer 3–4 primaries black, forming a dark wedge* on otherwise pale grey wings; shows more dark than Little Tern which has only outer 2 (sometimes 3) primaries black. All outer primary shafts black (outermost has a pale shaft in Little). Rump, upper tail-coverts and central tail feathers ash-grey (paler, almost white, in breeding Little). *Bill yellow with black tip;* legs and feet olive to red-brown, any yellow restricted to rear of tarsi and underside of toes. **Non-breeding adult** has blackish band through eyes, connecting around occiput; crown and lores mostly white. Loses distinctive wing pattern as primaries wear. Bill blackish; feet usually yellowish brown. **First-winter plumage** similar but has *dark tail tip and carpal bar.* (Non-breeding Common and Roseate terns are black-billed like non-breeding Saunders's, but are larger and vocally distinct.) Usual **call** *kidik,* or *kik-kik;* sometimes a long *keeeee.* **Range/status:** Migrant from southern Red Sea. Widespread, often abundant, Oct.–April. Inland on lower Tana River. Presumably this species sometimes present in numbers on Lake Turkana, where *saundersi* once collected in Oct.

LITTLE TERN *Sterna a. albifrons* Plate 3

Length 8.5–9.5″. Like common Saunders's Tern, but typical **breeding-plumaged adult** differs in having *white of forehead extending at least to rear margin of eyes,* in paler wing tip (*blackish only on the outer 2–3 primaries,* the outermost with a pale shaft), a white (not ash-grey) tail, and bright yellow to red-orange feet (duller in *saundersi*). However, these features are not always clear-cut and some birds appear intermediate. **Non-breeding adult** and **first-winter** bird not distinguishable in the field from Saunders's, as diagnostic head and wing patterns not evident, and both forms have largely grey rump and tail in these plumages. **Call** described as a rasping *kyik* or *cherk,* but not distinguishable from Saunders's. **Status** uncertain; 4 April specimens from coast and Lake Naivasha.

WHISKERED TERN *Chlidonias hybridus delalandii* Plate 3

Length 10″. Largest and most *Sterna*-like of the marsh terns. Often with White-winged Terns, hawking insects over water. Black cap of **breeding adult** separated from *dark grey underparts* by *white stripe on side of face;* under tail-coverts also white; upperparts grey;

bill and feet dark red. **Non-breeding adult** has white underparts, black streak through eyes to nape, and black-flecked crown; bill and feet dull red. In flight, silvery, black-tipped primaries obvious, but no contrasting white rump (unlike White-winged Tern). **First-year plumage** similar but with dusky bar across secondaries. **Juvenile** has rich brown back, pale grey wings and rump. **Call** a loud rasping *kerch* or *kreek*. Near nest, calls include a longer grating *kirrrik*. **Range**: Widespread inland on lakes and irrigated areas. A few breed in cent. Kenya (Lake Naivasha, Limuru) and n. Tanzania.

WHITE-WINGED TERN *Chlidonias leucopterus* Plate 3

Length 8–9". Commonest of the marsh terns, often in large flocks. **Breeding adult** unmistakable with *black body, head and wing-linings* contrasting with pale grey flight feathers and *white forewing, rump, tail and under tail-coverts*. Bill dark red; feet orange-red. Moulting adult has variably pied body plumage. **Non-breeding adult** mainly grey above with *whitish forehead/forecrown, collar, rump and tail*. White of underparts extends to wing-linings. Hindcrown and ear-coverts blackish as is a small preocular spot. Bill and feet dark red to black. **First-year** bird similar but with blackish carpal bar and dusky secondaries. Hawks insects far from water, and is attracted to grass fires or ploughing operations. **Call** a harsh *kreek-kreek*. **Range/status**: Palearctic migrant. Widespread inland; scarce at coast except near lower Tana River. Many first-year birds oversummer.

(*) BLACK TERN *Chlidonias n. niger* Plate 3

Length 8.5–9.5". A vagrant marsh tern (typically coastal or pelagic elsewhere in Africa). **Breeding-plumaged adult** *dark grey above, including wings*, sooty black on head and underparts except for white under tail-coverts; wing-linings pale; rump and tail dark grey. Bill blackish; feet dark red. **Non-breeding adult** and **first-winter** bird recall White-winged Tern, but *grey rump and tail uniform with back; dark grey patches on sides of breast* diagnostic. Bill slightly longer than in White-winged Tern; flies with slower, deeper strokes. See also non-breeding Whiskered Tern. Generally silent in Africa. Spring migrants may give a double *kik-kik*. **Status**: Rare palearctic migrant; 3 sight records (Sept., Oct., Feb.) from Lake Nakuru, Nairobi and Thika. Some doubt surrounds a late-April specimen from Kisumu.

BROWN NODDY *Anous stolidus pileatus* Plate 2

Length 14–17.5"; wingspan *c.* 32". A dark brown seabird, larger than Common Tern, with *wedge-shaped tail and greyish white cap sharply demarcated from dark lores and ear-coverts*; forehead white with narrow black band at base of bill, connecting the black lores. Wings and tail almost black; underside of wings pale with dark margins. Bill and feet black. **First-year** bird often much faded and worn, paler than adult. It and **juvenile** have white restricted to forehead, plus white-tipped feathers on upperparts and wings. Flight direct with heavy wingbeats and short glides, usually close to sea surface; hovers and swoops to snatch food. Nests colonially on rocky islands. (Smaller Lesser Noddy is more blackish, the wings more uniformly dark below; light cap extends to nape and merges evenly on lores and ear-coverts.) A variety of **calls**, some low and croaking, rather raven-like; others shrill. Mostly silent at sea. Highly vocal day and night at breeding colonies and roosts. **Range**: Breeds in Lamu Archipelago, June–Sept., on Latham Island off Dar es Salaam, Nov.–Feb. A few offshore in all months.

LESSER NODDY *Anous t. tenuirostris* Plate 2

Length 12–13.5"; wingspan *c.* 24". A marine tern, smaller than Brown Noddy, less brown, more greyish black, with relatively *longer and thinner bill and the light cap extending from bill to nape, often to below the eyes, and not sharply demarcated* from dark lores and ear-coverts. In flight, *tail appears paler than the back* (the reverse in Brown Noddy), narrower wings more uniformly dark below. Wing strokes more rapid, flight more erratic. Usually silent at sea. **Range/status**: Rarely recorded but perhaps regular beyond the reef. Flock of 200 or more near Mombasa, Aug.–Sept. 1976. Occasional Sept.–Dec. off Kipini and Shimoni.

SKIMMERS, FAMILY RYNCHOPIDAE

Peculiar fish-eating birds allied to terns and gulls, and sometimes included in Laridae. Feeding behaviour unique, involving the laterally compressed, knife-thin bill; the longer mandible slices the water at a 45-degree angle as bird flies rapidly back and forth, skimming surface; the shorter maxilla snaps down on any food item encountered. Breeds along freshwater shores, laying eggs in bare scrape in the sand.

AFRICAN SKIMMER *Rynchops flavirostris*   Plates 4, 5

Length 15–16". An uncommon long-winged blackish-and-white waterbird with tern-like flight. *Ultra-thin scissor-like bill bright vermilion and yellow.* **Breeding adult** blackish above except for white on secondary tips, upper tail-coverts and sides of forked tail; underparts white; feet red. **Non-breeding adult** has indistinct pale band on hindneck, and dull greybrown crown. Bill paler, more yellowish, feet more orange. **Juvenile** duller with buff feather edging above; bill of newly-flying young bird noticeably shorter than that of adult, brownish black, pale basally, becoming more yellow with age. Rests in groups on sandbanks and lakeshores. Flight slow, with quick upstroke. Nocturnal and diurnal. **Calls** include a sharp loud *kip* or *kik*, and a harsh *kreeee*. **Range:** Irregular at several widely scattered localities in Kenya. Breeds at Lake Turkana, with flocks at Allia Bay throughout year. Elsewhere, mainly on Rift Valley lakes, Sabaki estuary and lower Tana R. Rare in n. Tanzania.

SANDGROUSE, FAMILY PTEROCLIDAE

Stocky terrestrial birds, more pigeon-like than grouse-like. All species have long pointed wings for swift strong flight; the bill is small, and the short tarsi are feathered to the toes. The sexes differ, but both are rather cryptically patterned. Males usually have one or more breast bands and bold head patterns, whereas females are duller and often more extensively barred. Our species inhabit plains or dry bush. Noted for their morning and evening flights to waterholes, sandgrouse fly far from feeding and breeding areas, some species congregating in large flocks. They build no nest, laying their eggs on bare ground. The downy young are provided with water carried from remote sources on specialized belly feathers of the male.

CHESTNUT-BELLIED SANDGROUSE *Pterocles exustus olivascens*   Plate 47 ✓

Length 10.5–11". The only East African sandgrouse with *long, fine-pointed central tail feathers.* In flight shows *dark wing-linings continuous with dark belly.* **Male** has sandy or greyish buff neck and breast merging into *dark chestnut belly*, which is bordered by a narrow broken black breast band. Upperparts lightly scaled brownish or greyish buff, with large buff spots on scapulars, and a broad buff area on wings; orbital skin pale yellow-green. **Female** closely barred buff and brown above, the yellowish face surrounded by darker streaked crown, neck and upper breast, the latter separated from pale buff lower breast by narrow sepia line (sometimes double); belly dark, barred with buff at sides; wings have rows of buff spots. **Immature** olive-grey above with faint dark bars and pale feather edges; breast greyish pink with fine black vermiculations; no breast band; belly dark. **Juvenile** yellowish buff, tinged rufous, and finely vermiculated. (Larger female Yellow-throated Sandgrouse has dark belly and pointed tail, but central rectrices not elongated. Black-faced Sandgrouse is dark-bellied, but wing-linings are pale.) **Call** a repeated *gut-gurut, gut-gurut. . ..* Flock produces a low murmuring at waterhole. **Range**: Widespread south to Lake Baringo, Isiolo, Meru NP, Garissa and Bura. Also from Olorgesailie and Loita Plains south across the Serengeti to Lake Eyasi, east to Amboseli and Tsavo West NPs and the Masai Steppe.

BLACK-FACED SANDGROUSE *Pterocles decoratus*   Plate 47 ✓

Length 8–9". A small sandgrouse with pale wing-linings. Dark-bellied adults have contrasting *broad whitish area on lower breast.* **Male** barred above, *black from forehead to throat*, and with white superciliary stripes meeting on forecrown; white and buff areas of breast separated by a narrow black band. Bill pale orange or pinkish orange; bare orbital skin yellow. **Female** barred above; face/throat rather plain; *neck and breast streaked with* spots and short bars, sharply demarcated from broad white breast band. Paler *P. d. ellenbecki* is less heavily barred than *P. d. decoratus*; *loveridgei* also paler, greyer, less buff than other races. **Immature** male has no black breast band. **Juvenile** has rufous scapulars and finely barred wing-coverts. (Lichtenstein's and male Four-banded Sandgrouse black and white on head but neither has a black throat. Four-banded shows narrow white breast band; larger Lichtenstein's lacks white on breast and is strongly barred. Females of these lack white breast of female Black-faced.) **Call**, *see-u* when taking wing, followed by a whistled *whit-wi-wheeer*. Also *chucker-chucker-chuck-er* and a low *quick-quick-quick.* . .. **Range**: East and south of the Kenyan highlands. *P. d. ellenbecki* south to the Northern Uaso Nyiro and Tana rivers; *P. d. decoratus* in s. Kenya/n. Tanzania in and east of the Rift Valley; *loveridgei west of the Rift* from the Loita plains south to cent. Tanzania.

LICHTENSTEIN'S SANDGROUSE *Pterocles lichtensteinii sukensis*   Plate 47

Length 10–11". A bulky, heavily barred northern sandgrouse of dry stony bush country. Wing-linings pale in both sexes. **Male** has *black-and-white banded forecrown and forehead,* and *yellow orbital skin* bordered behind by short white bar; neck, upperparts and belly barred black and buff; wings have additional white bars. *Large buff breast patch is crossed by narrow black band and bordered below by a second broader band.* **Female** *narrowly barred black and buff almost throughout; ill-defined forehead patch and superciliary stripes whitish speckled with black;* bare orbital skin pale yellowish green. **Juvenile** resembles female but is duller and more closely barred. (Black-faced Sandgrouse has broad whitish breast patch; male has black throat and white superciliaries. Four-banded Sandgrouse is plain on throat and breast; male has narrow white breast band and one black forehead bar.) **Call** a high whistled *chitoo* or *quitoo-quitoo*, a low *quark-quark* and a soft *wheet. . . wheet. . .* in flight. **Range**: N. Kenya south to Kapenguria, Lake Bogoria, Northern Uaso Nyiro River and Lewa Downs.

FOUR-BANDED SANDGROUSE *Pterocles quadricinctus*   Plate 47

Length 10–11". Resembles Lichtenstein's Sandgrouse (including pale wing-linings) but *throat to upper breast plain.* **Male** has *black bar across the white forecrown,* a black mark above each eye, and *3 breast bands, the broad white central one bordered by chestnut above and black below;* hindcrown rufous-buff with black streaks; upperparts otherwise barred sandy buff and brown; belly finely barred black and white. **Female** *lacks breast bands and head markings; face, throat and upper breast rich buff;* lower breast barred buff and brown. **Juvenile** more rufous than adults, with finer barring; primaries broadly tipped rufous or buff. **Call**, in flight, a whistled *pir-rou-ee.* **Range**: Nw. Kenya, generally in less arid country than Lichtenstein's Sandgrouse; south to Kacheliba, n. Kerio Valley and on Laikipia Plateau near Mugie.

✔ YELLOW-THROATED SANDGROUSE *Pterocles gutturalis saturatior*   Plate 47

Length 10.5–12" *Large and stocky,* with *dark wing-linings* and a short graduated tail. **Male** has *pale yellowish buff throat and sides of face bordered by black;* black lores accent buff superciliary stripes. Breast dark buffy grey, browner on belly, nearly chestnut on crissum. Diffuse dark blotches on grey- to yellow-brown back and scapulars; large dull rufous patch on wing-coverts spotted with grey. **Female** boldly mottled and barred black and buff above, streakier on neck, with yellowish buff face and throat, blackish brown crown and black lores; lower neck/upper breast streaked yellowish buff and black; lower breast and belly chestnut barred with black. (Smaller female Chestnut-bellied Sandgrouse also has yellowish face and dark body/wing-linings, but lacks black lores, has broad pale area across lower breast, and the central tail feathers are very narrow.) **Call** a harsh *gluck-gluck-gluck* on take-off. In flight, *WHA-ha, WHA-ha. . .*, and *tweet-WEET, tweet-WEET.* . .. **Range**: S. Kenya from e. Mara GR, Loita Plains, Kajiado and Nairobi NP south into n. Tanzania west of the Masai Steppe.

PIGEONS AND DOVES, FAMILY COLUMBIDAE

Plump, small-headed birds with dense plumage, pointed wings, short tarsi and a short bill with a soft bare cere. With strong swift flight, many perform extensive daily or seasonal movements, and large numbers may assemble at food sources. Most species have characteristic calls, important in identification. The green pigeons (*Treron*) are arboreal fruit-eaters with distinctive plumage and sharp calls unlike the cooing of other columbids. Most *Columba* species are forest birds, often seen in fruiting trees, although a few are open-country ground-feeders. The turtle-doves (*Streptopelia*) are mainly ground-feeding birds of dry country. The small, short-tailed wood doves (*Turtur*) and the long-tailed Namaqua Dove (*Oena*) also feed on the ground.

AFRICAN GREEN PIGEON *Treron calva* Plate 49 ✔

Length 10–11″. A gregarious arboreal pigeon, *bright yellow-green on head and underparts*, grey to greyish olive above, with dull lilac at bend of wing; other wing feathers edged with pale yellow; crissum pale yellowish with dark grey feather centres, the longest coverts chestnut-tinged; bill cream-coloured with reddish base and cere; eyes pale blue; orbital ring brown; *feet scarlet*. Tail green in coastal *wakefieldi*, greyish in inland races. **Juvenile** duller, with no lilac on wings. **Call** an extended series of mellow trills followed by lower harsh creaking, barking, growling or whinnying, typically punctuated at the end with sharp *wick* or *tok* notes and often repeated. Also gives a separate *wik, ku-wik, k-ku-wik, ku-wik*. . .. **Range**: Sea level up to 2000 m. *T. c. gibberifrons* west of Rift Valley from Mt Elgon south to Serengeti NP; *brevicera* mainly east of the Rift, from Northern Uaso Nyiro and upper Tana rivers south to the Crater Highlands, Arusha and Moshi; *wakefieldi* on coast north to the Somali border, inland to Bura, Shimba Hills and the Usambara Mts.

PEMBA GREEN PIGEON *Treron pembaensis* Plate 124

Length 10″. The only green pigeon on Pemba Island, Tanzania, where fairly common in wooded areas. *Grey on head and breast*, with *contrasting yellow lower belly*, purple 'shoulder' patch and *chestnut, yellow and grey under tail-coverts*; feet bright yellow or yellowish orange. **Call** a soft *tiu*. . .*kiuriuu*, prolonged, but with little of the harsh grating quality typical of *T. calva*; also a soft *kiu-tiu-kiutiu, kiwrikek-wrikek* followed by a soft purring. **Range**: Pemba and adjacent coral islets.

BRUCE'S GREEN PIGEON *Treron waalia* Plate 49

Length 11–12″. This *northern* pigeon differs from African Green Pigeon in *greyish head, neck and breast, bright yellow belly* and *yellowish feet* and orbital ring; centre of under tail-coverts chestnut. *Bill whitish with dull lavender cere.* Favours riverine woods with fig trees. Long 'creaking' **call** extends into high sharp whistles, growls and yelping notes. **Range**: Lokichokio, Moyale and Ramu. Reports from Suam River and Marsabit unsubstantiated.

TAMBOURINE DOVE *Turtur tympanistria* Plate 49

Length 8–9″. A small dark-backed forest dove with *white forehead and superciliary stripes*, white or grey underparts, grey-tipped outer feathers on short dark tail, *rufous primaries* and two dark bars across back showing in flight; blue-black spots on wings; bill dark purple, tipped black. **Male** *pure white below*; **female** grey from chin to flanks, white only on mid-belly. **Juvenile** has dull head pattern like female, but is barred with tawny and dark brown above and has no wing spots; underparts mainly brownish. (In w. Kenya Blue-spotted Wood Dove has shining blue wing spots, pinkish breast, dark red bill with yellow tip, bolder bars on back, and all-dark tail tip.) **Call** a few hesitant coos leading into 18–20 faster, evenly pitched notes, *not decreasing in volume, and more prolonged than calls of wood doves* (and lower pitched than Emerald-spotted's call). **Range**: Local in high-rainfall areas, up to 2500 m, north to Marsabit and Mt Nyiru.

EMERALD-SPOTTED WOOD DOVE *Turtur chalcospilos* Plate 49 ✔

Length 6.5–8″. The common *dry-country* ground dove with bright *iridescent green wing spots*. In flight, shows *rufous primaries, two black bars across back*, and a *broad dark tail tip*; pale brown above, greyer on head; breast pinkish; bill all black in northern birds, dull red with black tip south of the Equator. **Juvenile** buff-barred above and with small dull wing spots. (In w. Kenya and Usambara Mts see Blue-spotted Wood Dove.) **Call** a long series of soft but penetrating notes, beginning slowly, with pauses, accelerating and descending in pitch: *cuwoo, cuwoo, co-oo-cuwoo coo cuwoo, cu-cu-cu-cu-cucucucucucu-cucucucucu. . .*, higher and more prolonged than Blue-spotted's call. **Range**: Widespread below 1600 m except in Lake Victoria basin where largely replaced by Blue-spotted Wood Dove.

BLUE-SPOTTED WOOD DOVE *Turtur afer*   Plate 49

Length 7–8″. A small ground dove, mainly western. Replaces Emerald-spotted Wood Dove in *more humid habitats*. Resembles that species, especially in flight, but darker brown above, deeper buff on belly, with iridescent *blue spots on wings* and has *yellow-tipped dark red bill*; head grey; chin to breast pinkish. **Juvenile** browner than adult, buff-barred above, with small dull wing spots and dull brown bill. Solitary, usually within cover. (Tambourine Dove is darker but white-faced, has fainter bands on back, grey-tipped outer tail feathers and dark bill. Extralimital Black-billed Wood Dove, *T. abyssinicus*, erroneously attributed to Kenya, has dark blue metallic wing spots and a black bill with dull carmine base.) **Call** a few soft, well-spaced coos followed by 6–8 faster, even notes, *coo, cooo, cuwoo, coo, cuwoo, cu-cu-cu-cu-cu-cu-cu-cu. . .*, slightly lower, less prolonged than call of Emerald-spotted. **Range**: Lake Victoria basin, north to Mt Elgon and Trans-Nzoia, east to Kakamega and Nandi districts, the Mau and Mara GR, at times to Rift Valley. Scarce on Pemba Island and in East Usambaras.

√ NAMAQUA DOVE *Oena c. capensis*   Plate 49

Length 8–9″. A small *long-tailed* dove of dry bush. The rufous primaries are conspicuous in flight as are two black bands, separated by pale buff across the grey-brown lower back; underparts and outer tail feathers mostly white. **Male** *black from forehead to upper breast*, head otherwise grey; *bill yellow-orange* with purplish base. **Female** has brown bill and whitish face, and is grey-brown from chin to breast. **Juvenile** has spotted throat and is barred on back and wing-coverts. **Call** a soft plaintive *hoo-ooooo*, rising slightly and repeated several times; also some rather sharp throaty notes. **Range**: Widespread, mainly below 1600 m; occasionally higher.

EASTERN BRONZE-NAPED PIGEON *Columba delegorguei sharpei*   Plate 49

Length 9.5–12″. A slaty-backed highland forest pigeon with grey or rufous-tinged underparts. **Male** dark-headed with *white collar across nape*, pinkish and green gloss on hindneck; tail black with a narrow dark grey tip. **Female** has *rufous crown and nape* glossed with coppery green as are neck and upper back; underparts dark buffy grey; bill blue-grey with pale tip. **Juvenile** dark grey-brown above, deep rufous below. Feeds on fruit in forest canopy, but also walks on ground, and is attracted to salty earth in clearings. **Call** a distinctive *hu-hu-COO-COO-COO-hu-hu-hu-hu-hu*, higher and more emphatic in middle, softer and lower at beginning and end. **Range**: Mathews Range and Mt Nyiru south through Kenyan highlands to Mt Hanang, Arusha NP, Kilimanjaro and Usambara Mts. Occasional on coast and Pemba Island.

OLIVE PIGEON *Columba arquatrix*   Plate 49

Length 15″. A *large dark* arboreal pigeon with *bright yellow bill, orbital ring and feet, white-speckled breast and wing-coverts*; pale grey hind-crown becomes dusky pink on upper back; rump and tail *blackish*; breast dark purple to slaty, dotted with white; belly to under tail-coverts slate-grey. **Juvenile** browner above, some blue-grey on wing-coverts and nape; rufous-brown underparts faintly white-spotted. **Call** a series of low notes, the first deep and rolling, *crrrooo, cw-w-w-oo, cw-w-w-oo, cw-w-oo*. **Range**: Typically above 1600 m, in and near forest, from the isolated northern mountains of Kulal, Nyiru and Marsabit south to the Nguruman and Chyulu hills, Crater and Mbulu highlands, east to Arusha NP, Kilimanjaro, Pare and Usambara mts.

SPECKLED PIGEON *Columba g. guinea* — Plate 49 ✔

Length 12–13.5″. A large open-country pigeon, often around cliffs or buildings. On flying bird note *pale grey rump* and grey tail with broad black tip and fainter dark band near mid-tail (lacking in Feral Pigeon). Unique are the *large red eye patches* and *vinous-chestnut/maroon upperparts*, boldly marked with *triangular white spots on wing-coverts*; grey from head to breast, the neck streaked with white and cinnamon. **Juvenile** much duller and browner. **Calls** include a series of deep rough coos, uttered rapidly and increasing in volume, *whu-whu-whu-whu-whu-whu-whu-whu-WHU. . .*, and *ooWOO ooWOO wu-wu-wu-wu-wu*; also a rough 'bowing call,' *hoo-uuu, hoo*, an owl-like *WHO-oo WHOO* or *whu-whooo* (first note slurred upward), and a deep harsh *kworr*. **Range**: Local in nw. Kenya, southeast to Tsavo area, Kilimanjaro and Moshi, west to Lake Victoria basin and Serengeti NP. Urban populations in Kisumu, Eldoret, Nakuru, Nairobi and Thika.

FERAL PIGEON or ROCK DOVE *Columba livia* — Plate 49 ✔

Length 12.5–13″. The common city pigeon. Wild-type birds mainly blue-grey, usually with *two black wing-bars, whitish or grey rump and black-tipped grey tail*. Plumage highly variable, from predominantly pale cinnamon-brown to white, grey, black or combinations of these. **Call** a guttural *ooorrh*, and a cooing *cu-roo-oo-oo* or *oo-roo-coo*. **Range**: Established in most towns and cities north to Kitale, Isiolo and Lamu.

LEMON or CINNAMON DOVE *Aplopelia l. larvata* — Plate 49

Length 9.5–10″. A shy dark forest-floor pigeon with a *whitish face* and *rich cinnamon underparts*. Brown above, with bronzy green, violet and pinkish iridescence from crown to back; tail brown, most feathers obscurely grey-tipped; orbital skin dark reddish. **Juvenile** dark brown on breast, the feathers rufous-edged as on upperparts. **Call** a deep, upslurred *whoo* or *cwoo*, repeated with short pauses between notes. **Range**: Isolated northern mountains of Kulal, Nyiru and Marsabit south to the Pare and Usambara mts, Kilimanjaro, Crater Highlands, Lake Manyara and Arusha NPs.

RED-EYED DOVE *Streptopelia semitorquata* — Plate 48 ✔

Length 12-13″. Largest and darkest of the black-collared doves, common at forest edges and in wooded gardens. *Brownish*, with grey crown and whitish forehead, and *wings entirely brown*; face to breast vinous pink, shading to grey on belly; *spread tail black at base with a broad grey terminal band*; dark red eyes appear black at a distance. **Juvenile** has pale rufous feather edges above, and black nuchal band is obscure. (African Mourning and Ring-necked Doves are smaller, paler with *white* tail tips, and Mourning is pale-eyed. Dusky Turtle Dove has rufous-edged wing feathers and black lateral neck spot instead of nuchal collar.) **Call** variable: (1) repeated syncopated call of 6 notes, the first 2 slower, last 4 faster, the accent varied, *coo COO, cu-cu-cu-cu* or *oo-woo, oo-WOO-oo-oo*; (2) *wu-wu-wu-wu WOO-cu*, also repeated in series; (3) a deep rough *whu-whu-whu, whu*, last note low and guttural; (4) a raspy bowing call, *WOOO-roo, WOOO-roo. . .* or *whrruu-whrruu. . .*; (5) a nasal alighting call, *uh-RHAao* or *u-WHA*. **Range**: Widespread up to 3000 m except in dry areas.

AFRICAN MOURNING DOVE *Streptopelia decipiens* — Plate 48 ✔

Length 11–12″. A common *pale* 'collared' dove of *dry country*, readily identified by the *pale yellow eyes ringed with orange-red*. Light grey-brown wings have *paler grey coverts along outer edges*. Grey crown and sides of head contrast with pale pinkish neck and breast; throat, belly and under tail-coverts white (breast also white in paler eastern *elegans*); *tail broadly white at corners* above; from beneath, terminal half is white. **Juvenile** brown on top of head, lighter brown on breast; eyes pale brown. (Ring-necked Dove has dark eyes without red orbital ring. Red-eyed Dove is darker with grey tail tip, pinkish face and dark eyes.) **Calls** (1) *WHOO-woooo*, followed by a rhythmical 3-note phrase accented on second syllable, *wu-WOO-oo, wu-WOO-oo. . .* and may end with *krrrrrrrrow* or *uh-krrrrrrrrrow*; (2) *hoo-WOO, hoo-WOO, hoo-WOO. .* ; (3)

a descending throaty purring *aaaooow* on alighting. **Range**: Typically below 1400 m, *S. d. perspicillata* from nw. Kenya south into n. Tanzania; *S. d. elegans* from ne. Kenya south to Kilifi District, reaching the coast north of Malindi.

✓RING-NECKED DOVE *Streptopelia capicola*   Plate 48

Length 10–10.5″. A *pale, almost black-eyed* 'collared' dove, often abundant in bush, savanna, woodland and cultivation. Grey-brown above, pale grey on outer wing-coverts and on head above the nuchal collar; underparts more pinkish grey to white on belly and crissum; tail brownish grey with narrow white edge and broad white corners, from beneath like that of African Mourning Dove. *S. c. somalica* paler and greyer than widespread browner *tropica*. **Juvenile** has much buff feather edging. (Red-eyed Dove is larger and darker, with grey lower belly and grey tail tip. African Mourning Dove has pale eyes.) **Calls** (1) a rhythmic *cuc-CURRRoo, cuc-CURRRoo. . .,* or *wuh-ROOoo, wuh-ROOoo . . .* repeated monotonously—a familiar sound of the East African bush; (2) *wuh-ka-RROOO, wuh-ka-RROOO. . .,* repeated; (3) bowing call a rolling *uk-carrroooo, uk-carrroooo. . .;* (4) alighting call a high raspy nasal *ka-waaaaaa.* **Range**: Widespread, mainly below 2000 m, but locally higher. *S. c. somalica* in e. and ne. Kenya, west to Lake Baringo, Samburu GR, Kibwezi, Namanga and Arusha, south on coast to Mombasa; *S. c. tropica* elsewhere.

AFRICAN WHITE-WINGED DOVE *Streptopelia reichenowi*   Plate 48

Length 10″. A pale 'collared' dove of extreme ne. Kenya, distinctive in flight with *large white crescent on wing-coverts* and white-tipped tail. At close range, note *white-feathered eye-ring* around *yellowish orange eye* . **Male** greyish on head and breast, with brownish black nuchal collar, white chin, throat and belly; **female** brownish on breast. **Juvenile** resembles female but feathers edged with buff. Typical of riparian woodland dominated by palms; also in adjacent shrubby grassland. **Call** a deep *kok-koorrr-kok-koorrr. . .,* repeated, and a low repeated *crooo-crooo. . ..* **Range**: In our region, only along the Daua River between Malka Mari and Mandera along the Ethiopian border.

EUROPEAN TURTLE DOVE *Streptopelia turtur*   Plate 48

Length 10–11″. A slim light brown dove with *black and white patch on sides of neck.* In flight shows *grey band on wings,* and *prominent white tail rim;* smaller *wing-coverts scaly with conspicuous rufous margins;* yellow eyes (the iris black peripherally) ringed by pinkish skin. **Juvenile** duller, without chequered neck patches; wing-coverts margined white and tawny; brownish breast has pale feather edges. **Call** a purring *rrrrrrr, rooooooorrrr.* **Range/ status**: Palearctic migarant, casual in our region (6 sight records, Lake Turkana to Amboseli NP, Oct.–Jan); subspecies uncertain.

DUSKY TURTLE DOVE *Streptopelia l. lugens*   Plate 48

Length 11–12″. A highland pigeon with large *black spot on sides of neck;* no nuchal collar; dark grey-brown above, dark grey on head and underparts; *prominent feather edging greyish on lesser wing-coverts, tawny on secondaries;* eyes orange, surrounded by red orbital ring. **Juvenile** paler and browner with extensive tawny feather edging. Often solitary, but numbers assemble at food sources (including Nairobi bird feeders). **Call** a deep slow *coo-or, coo-or, coo-or,* and a rough growling *oooh* repeated 2–4 times. **Range**: Between 1750 and 3200 m, from Maralal and Marsabit south to the Crater Highlands, Arusha NP and Kilimanjaro; also recorded at Moyale.

LAUGHING or PALM DOVE *Streptopelia s. senegalensis*   Plate 48

Length 9″. A small dry-country dove with *blue-grey wing-coverts,* a *black-speckled rufous band* across front and sides of neck, and white-cornered tail. Head pinkish grey, breast pinkish or vinous tawny; belly and crissum whitish; eyes brown or brownish red. Female paler than male and with fainter neck band. **Juvenile** lacks neck band, head is more rufous. Solitary or gregarious, often common in bush and dry cultivation. **Call** of 5–6 rather high short notes, rapid and dropping slightly in pitch at the end, *oo, cu-cu-oo-oo* or *oo-oo-kuWOOoo.* **Range**: Widespread, mainly below 1800 m.

PARROTS AND LOVEBIRDS, FAMILY PSITTACIDAE

Compact, colourful birds with powerful hooked bills, the nostrils opening in a fleshy cere. The legs are short, the tarsi stout and the first and fourth toes are directed backward. Most African species are short-tailed, with narrow pointed wings. With one exception the sexes are alike in our species. The distinctive flight is fast and direct, with rapid shallow wingbeats. Typically noisy, all species produce loud squawking or screeching sounds, especially in flight. Parrots nest in tree cavities. Lovebirds also use old nests of swifts, holes in buildings or termitaria and openings among palm-leaf bases.

GREY PARROT *Psittacus e. erithacus*   Plate 47

Length 11–12". A rare west Kenyan parrot, easily identified by its grey body plumage and *scarlet tail*; bare loral and orbital skin white, bill black. **Calls** include various high-pitched screeches and whistles. **Range**: Now only in Kakamega Forest where probably fewer than 10 birds survive.

RED-FRONTED PARROT *Poicephalus gulielmi massaicus*   Plate 47

Length 10–11". The green parrot of highland *Podocarpus* and *Juniperus* forests. *Red forehead, crown, and leading wing edges* evident in flight, as is yellow-green rump; orbital skin greyish yellow, bill ivory horn above, black below and at tip. **Juvenile** has buff crown and brown forewing edges. **Call** a shrill high-pitched screeching chatter in flight and when perched. Pairs or small groups feed in treetops; flocks undertake daily flights to and from feeding areas. **Range**: Local between 2000 and 3200 m from Mt Elgon, the Cheranganis and Maralal south to Kilimanjaro, Arusha NP and Crater Highlands.

BROWN PARROT *Poicephalus meyeri*   Plate 47

Length 8–9". A brown-and-green woodland/savanna parrot with *yellow crown band, 'shoulders,' forewing edges and wing-linings*. Head to upper back and breast dark brown; lower breast to tail-coverts green, as are lower back and rump; orbital skin dark grey, eyes dark red, bill blackish. **Juvenile** lacks yellow on crown and has less on wings. Usually in pairs; flies low and fast. (Female Orange-bellied Parrot shows no yellow and has dark brown wing-linings. Coastal Brown-headed P. lacks yellow on crown and upper wing surface and has pale eyes.) **Call** a shrill, high *cheek-cheek-cheek*, and a screeching *chweeee*. **Range**: *P. m. saturatus* widespread, between 600 and 2000 m, from Lokichokio and Lake Turkana south to Mara GR and Serengeti NP, east to Lewa Downs, Nanyuki and Naro Moru. *P. m. matschiei* of interior Tanzania extends north to Tarangire and Manyara NPs.

BROWN-HEADED PARROT *Poicephalus cryptoxanthus*   Plate 47

Length 9.5–10". Replaces Brown Parrot in *coastal lowlands*. Largely olive-green above, brighter green below and on rump; note the *grey-brown head* and *yellow wing-linings*; orbital skin blackish; eyes pale yellow; bill dark above, whitish below. **Juvenile** duller. Usually in small groups. Partial to baobab trees, but often roosts in coconut palms. **Call** a high screeching in flight, *chweer-eer chweer-eer chweek*; less piercing calls when perched. **Range**: Local in varied coastal habitats north to Lamu. Common near Kilifi, Shimoni and on Pemba Island; scarce elsewhere.

AFRICAN ORANGE-BELLIED PARROT *Poicephalus r. rufiventris*   Plate 47

Length 10". A *dry-country* parrot partial to *Commiphora* bush with baobab trees. Usually in pairs. **Male** *bright orange on belly and wing-linings*, green on rump, tail-coverts and leg feathers; rest of plumage pale grey-brown; eyes orange-red; bill, bare orbital skin and feet black. **Female** has *green belly and dark brown wing-linings*. (Brown Parrot is darker with yellow on crown and wings.) **Juvenile** resembles female, but male shows some orange. **Call** a repeated high screech. **Range**: Mainly below 1200 m in e. and ne. Kenya, west to the Ndotos, Samburu GR, Lewa Downs, Meru and the Tsavo NPs, south to Mkomazi GR, the Masai Steppe and west to Tarangire NP.

RED-HEADED LOVEBIRD *Agapornis pullarius ugandae*   **Plate 47**
Length 5". A scarce western lovebird, *green with red forehead, face and throat* (more orange in female) and pale blue rump. In flight shows *green-and-red tail with black sub-terminal band*, and *black wing-linings*; bill red. **Juvenile** resembles adult but has *yellow-ish face patch*. Pairs or small groups feed unobtrusively on millet, sorghum and other grasses, perching at times in low trees and shrubs. **Call** a squeaky twittering *si-si-si-si* in flight. When perched, a sharp thin *swee-seet* or *tswi-sitsit*, and a 3- or 4-note *skee-tee, tsyip-tsyip*. **Range**: Bushed grassland and cultivation along Kenya-Ugandan border from Malaba and Malikisi south to Alupe and Busia, east to Sio River near Mumias (formerly north to Kakamega and Mt Elgon).

✓**FISCHER'S LOVEBIRD** *Agapornis fischeri*   **Plate 47**

Length 6". A gregarious Tanzanian lovebird with *orange-red face, red bill and white orbital ring*; head mainly dull olive-brown, body bright green with yellow breast and collar, and pale blue wash on upper tail-coverts; green tail has black subterminal band. **Juvenile** duller. **Call** a shrill whistle; also utters a high-pitched twittering both in flight and when perched. **Range**: Local from southern Lake Victoria islands to the Wembere River, east to Serengeti NP and the Lake Eyasi depression; wanders east to Babati and Arusha District. Trapping for the overseas cagebird trade has seriously reduced numbers. Escaped birds frequent in Kenya. Feral populations along coast north to Mombasa. *A. fischeri X A. personatus* hybrids are locally common around Lake Naivasha, less numerous at Kisumu, Nakuru and Nairobi; they wander widely.

YELLOW-COLLARED LOVEBIRD *Agapornis personatus*   **Plate 47**

Length 5–6". A Tanzanian lovebird with a red bill, white cere, and bare white skin around eyes. Differs from Fischer's in its *dark brown head and broader yellow collar extending to the breast*. **Call** a shrill high-pitched screeching, from perch and in flight. **Range**: Interior Tanzania, north to Babati and Tarangire NP. In Kenya, feral birds breed around Mombasa, and a few near Naivasha appear to be nearly pure *personatus*, although most are hybrids (see under Fischer's Lovebird).

TURACOS, FAMILY MUSOPHAGIDAE

Good-sized arboreal birds with long broad tails and rounded wings. All are crested, and most have bare orbital or facial skin; their serrate bills are short and strong, sometimes brightly coloured, and expanded to form a frontal shield in *Musophaga*. The feet are strong, with semi-zygodactyl toes (the fourth reversible). They inhabit woodland, forest, savanna and bush, and are more or less sedentary. Mostly gregarious, their presence is invariably revealed by their loud raucous calls, often in chorus. Flight appears weak and laboured but they rapidly run, climb and bound with great agility along branches or through thick vegetation. Several species have brilliant red primaries prominent in flight, but go-away-birds and plantain-eaters lack bright colours. Sexes are alike or closely sim-ilar. They feed largely on fruits, flowers and buds, but also consume arthropods. Turacos are called louries in southern Africa. The family is endemic to this continent.

GREAT BLUE TURACO *Corythaeola cristata*   **Plate 50**
Length 30". The largest turaco, identified by size, overall greenish blue and yellow plumage, and *long wide tail with a broad black subterminal band*. Also distinctive are the bushy blue-black crest, yellow red-tipped bill, and *chestnut posterior underparts*. There is no red in the wings. Not shy; may feed and nest near dwellings and in wooded gardens. Glides from tree to tree on short broad wings. **Call** a loud guttural *cow-cow-cow-cow*, and a deep, resonant, rolling *kurru-kurru-kurru*. **Range**: Kaimosi, Kakamega and South Nandi forests in w. Kenya.

ROSS'S TURACO *Musophaga rossae*   **Plate 50**
Length 20–21". Another western turaco, striking *violet-blue* with *bright crimson crest, yellow bill and frontal shield*. In flight, brilliant red primaries contrast sharply with dark body and tail. Typical of riparian woodland; avoids heavy forest. **Call** a loud rolling *k-k-*

kkkow-kkow-kkow-kkow often repeated by others in the same or a near-by group; higher-pitched than calls of the green turacos. **Range**: Mt Elgon and Kapenguria south to Nandi and Tugen hills, West Mau, South Nyanza, Mara GR and Serengeti NP.

PURPLE-CRESTED TURACO *Tauraco porphyreolophus chlorochlamys*
Plate 50

Length 17–18″. A rare, dark green-and-blue turaco with *iridescent purple crown* and *shining green forehead and face; no white around eyes;* belly dull greenish grey; back mostly greyish blue, more violet-blue on wings and tail; primaries show bright red in flight. **Call** begins with a single loud high-pitched hoot, then continues as a raucous *kaw-kaw-kaw.* . .. **Range**: Now only near Thika, Ol Doinyo Sapuk NP, the Mua and Ulu hills and Kibwezi Forest in s.-cent. Kenya, and Lake Manyara NP. Formerly more widespread.

SCHALOW'S TURACO *Tauraco schalowi* **Plate 50**

Length 16″. The region's only turaco with a *long pointed crest* of white-tipped blue-green feathers, typically held erect. Green of head, neck and breast accented by red orbital skin, *dark red bill*, and black-and-white feathers from lores to behind eyes; head to breast mostly green, shading to dusky on belly; back and wings blue-green, more violet on rump and tail. Largely red primaries showy in flight. Solitary and shy. **Call** a slowly uttered series of 5–6 rough, cawing-barks, *haw, haw, haw.* . ., usually beginning with a shorter, higher pitched note. **Range**: One population in the Loita Hills and woods along the Talek and Mara rivers in sw. Kenya, west and north to Lolgorien, Rapogi and Kilgoris, south to n. Serengeti NP and Grumeti River; another ('*chalcolophus*') in forests of the Mbulu and Crater highlands. **Taxonomic Note:** Formerly considered conspecific with extralimital *T. livingstonii.*

BLACK-BILLED TURACO *Tauraco schuetti emini* **Plate 50**

Length 16″. A scarce *west Kenyan* turaco with *short rounded white-tipped crest* and *black bill* (dark red at base below); lower breast to under tail-coverts dusky; rump and tail violet-blue; primaries brilliant red; white line in front of and under the eye; orbital skin red. Solitary and shy. (Hartlaub's Turaco has rounded dark blue crest, that of Schalow's is long and pointed.) **Call** a repetitive husky *khaw, khaw, khaw.* . . often continuing for 10–15 seconds. **Range**: Kaimosi, Kakamega, and South Nandi forests of w. Kenya. Declining.

FISCHER'S TURACO *Tauraco f. fischeri* **Plate 50**

Length 16″. An *eastern* green-and-blue turaco with *white-tipped reddish crest*, blackish belly and largely red primaries; red orbital skin margined in front by a white line extending to the bill, and below by a small black patch, itself bordered by a white line to below the ear-coverts; *bill bright red.* Vocal but shy. **Call** a guttural cawing preceded by 2–3 higher notes. **Range**: Coastal forests south to Tanga, inland along Tana River to Garsen and Bura, Shimba Hills, Mrima Hill and up to 1500 m in the Usambara Mts.

HARTLAUB'S TURACO *Tauraco hartlaubi* **Plate 50**

Length 17″. The common *highland* turaco with *rounded bushy blue-black crest, white facial markings* and *bright red orbital patch;* throat, breast and upper back green; posterior parts glossy violet-blue; bright red primaries conspicuous in flight. Solitary or in small groups in wooded areas; less shy than many turacos. **Call** several rough, raucous *khaw* notes, harsher than those of other green turacos. **Range:** Between 1700 and 3000 m, from isolated montane forests on mts Kulal, Nyiru, Marsabit, the Ndotos and Mathews Range south to the Chyulu and Taita hills, Arusha NP, Mt Meru, Kilimanjaro, the Pare and West Usambara mts.

WHITE-CRESTED TURACO *Tauraco leucolophus*   Plate 50

Length 16″. A western green turaco with a *large white crest and yellow bill*. Forehead and area below crest blue-black, enclosing red orbital ring; rest of head white; upper back and breast green; posterior parts deep violet-blue above, violet-grey below; much red in primaries. Usually alone or in pairs in riverine forest and on wooded hillsides. **Call** a high-pitched hoot followed by a succession of low raucous barks, *whoo, khow-khow-khow-khow khow*. . .. **Range**: Suam River and Kongelai Escarpment to Marich Pass, and in Kerio Valley below Tambach, east occasionally to Tugen Hills and Baringo District. Small population along Sio River in Mumias District.

✔ BARE-FACED GO-AWAY-BIRD *Corythaixoides personatus*   Plate 50

Length 19″. A large dull-coloured turaco with *bare dark face, chin and upper throat*; bill also black. Forehead and crest ashy brown; *sides of face, neck, and chest white*; back, wings and tail grey-brown. Sage-green patch on breast merges into pinkish brown of belly. *C. p. leopoldi* has blackish face, small green breast patch, undersides of wings and tail pale grey. *C. p. personatus* has brown face, larger green breast patch, underside of wings and tail pale greenish. **Call** a loud, double *kow-kow*. **Range**: *C. p. leopoldi* is local in sw. Kenya, from Kisumu and Muhoroni south through Ruma NP and Mara GR to Serengeti NP, and locallly common in Tarangire NP. *C. p. personatus* reported once near the Ethiopian border west of Moyale.

✔ WHITE-BELLIED GO-AWAY-BIRD *Criniferoides leucogaster*   Plate 50

Length 20″. The crested grey-backed turaco of savanna, bush and open acacia woodland. *Pointed grey crest and long black tail with white median band* distinctive; white wing patch conspicuous in flight. Bill black in male, pea-green in female. Typical **calls** are a nasal *haa-haa-haa*, like bleating of sheep, and a single or repeated *gwa* (or *g'way*). Flies from tree to tree in loose straggling groups, calling loudly. **Range**: In Kenya, below 1500 m from northern borders south to Tsavo and Amboseli NPs, and along coast to near Malindi; absent from the sw. and cent. highlands. In n. Tanzania, from Mkomazi GR and Masai Steppe west to Tarangire NP, Lake Natron and lowlands north of Arusha.

EASTERN GREY PLANTAIN-EATER *Crinifer zonurus*   Plate 50

Length 20″. A large grey-brown turaco of open savannas in *western border areas*. Dark-headed with *shaggy white-tipped nape feathers* and a *long black-tipped tail*; white patch in wings and partly white outer tail feathers conspicuous in flight; bill dull yellow in adults, more greenish yellow in young birds. **Call**: *KWAH, kow-kow-kow-kow*. . . lasting 10–12 sec. Also a high-pitched squeal and a rapid yelping and cackling. **Range**: Suam River and Mt Elgon south to Lake Victoria basin, wandering to Mara River and Serengeti NP.

CUCKOOS AND COUCALS, FAMILY CUCULIDAE

Typical cuckoos (Subfamily Cuculinae) are long-tailed, long-winged arboreal birds, some small and superficially passerine in appearance, others larger and somewhat hawk-like. The tail is graduated, the bill often stout and slightly decurved, the feet strong with short tarsi and zygodactyl toes. Several species are polymorphic. Most are secretive, but breeding males have obtrusive and distinctive calls. Our species are brood parasitic, each specialising on a different host species or group of species. The non-parasitic coucals (subfamily Centropodinae, sometimes elevated to family status) are bulky, clumsy-looking birds with long broad tails, short wings and coarse plumage. They skulk in shrubbery, tall grass and rank herbage; flight is heavy, usually of short duration before the bird flops awkwardly into cover. The male constructs a globular grass and leaf nest with a side entrance; he alone incubates. Related to the Oriental malkohas is the unique Yellowbill (Subfamily Phaenicophaeinae). It builds a cup-shaped nest of twigs in dense vegetation.

BLACK-AND-WHITE or JACOBIN CUCKOO *Oxylophus jacobinus* Plate 52

Length 13″. A slender *crested* cuckoo, seasonally common in bush, dry woodland and thickets. *O. j. pica* is glossy bluish or greenish black above and white below; a small white patch at base of outer primaries is conspicuous in flight; tail white-tipped. *O. j. serratus is* greyish white below with fine streaks on throat and breast. It has a **dark morph**, *entirely black except for small white patch at base of primaries.* **Juvenile** brown above, buff-tinged below with buff tail-feather tips. (Larger Levaillant's Cuckoo is more robust, still longer-tailed, with boldly streaked throat/upper breast; its dark morph has white tail spots unlike black *jacobinus*.) **Calls** include a ringing *ker-wi-wi*, a sharp excited *kikikikiki*, and a yelping, somewhat hornbill-like *kyaOW-pi, kyaOW-pi, kyaOW-pi. . ..* **Range**: *O. j. pica* breeds in and west of Rift Valley, March–Aug. and in se. Kenya, Nov.–Dec.; also a 'rains migrant' throughout, but scarce Mar.–May. Large numbers move northwest across Serengeti, Feb.–Mar. Coastal migrants in April–May, presumably *pica*, may include birds from India. *O. j. serratus* is an uncommon non-breeding visitor from s. Africa north to w. and cent. Kenya, April–Sept. **Taxonomic Note**: The two *Oxylophus* species are placed in the genus *Clamator* by some authors.

LEVAILLANT'S CUCKOO *Oxylophus levaillantii* Plate 52

Length 15″. Suggests the more common Black-and-white Cuckoo, but larger, with *proportionately longer tail* and *heavily streaked throat*. **Light morph** glossy black above (faintly bluish or greenish); streaking may extend to sides; white on primaries and rectrix tips. **Dark morph** black except for white primary patch and *white spots on outer tail feathers* (absent in dark *jacobinus*). **Juvenile** brown above, rufous on wing-coverts and rectrix tips, with buff forehead, face and underparts; throat streaked. More skulking than *jacobinus*; hides in thick leafy cover. **Call** a low ringing *kuwu-weer, kuwu-weer. . .* and an excited *ku-wi-wi-wi*. **Range**: Intra-African migrant below 2000 m. Most frequent west of the Rift Valley May–Sept., less so in se. Kenya and on coast, March–Nov. Few breeding records. Rare in n. Tanzania.

GREAT SPOTTED CUCKOO *Clamator glandarius* Plate 52

Length 14–16″. A *large crested white-spotted* cuckoo with a long narrow tail and *long pointed wings*. Uncommon in savanna and open woodland where it often perches in tops of small trees. Grey-brown above, with *bold white spots and 3–4 white bars on wings*, more white spots on upper tail-coverts and tail; cream or yellow-buff throat and breast, whitish on belly; eyes brown or red. **Juvenile** has *entire top of head black*, throat/upper breast deep buff, and *rufous primaries* conspicuous in flight. First-year birds retain some rufous in wings plus a few black crown feathers. **Calls** include a mellow whistling *kweeu, kweeu, kweeu. . .*, an excited, harsh *kiu-ku-ku-ker* or *kiu, kirru-kirru*, and a trilled *kirrrrrrrrr* ending with loud cackling. **Range**: Mainly a migrant from the northern tropics, Oct.–March but present much of the year (and has bred) in parts of the Kenyan Rift Valley and adjacent highlands.

THICK-BILLED CUCKOO *Pachycoccyx audeberti validus* Plate 52

Length 14″. An uncommon *hawk-like* cuckoo of coastal Kenyan woods. Dark grey above and white below, with black-barred tail; not crested; wings long and pointed. **Juvenile** *dark brown above with bold white spots*, white on sides of face, wing-coverts and tail-feather tips. Cruising flight hawk-like and erratic with deliberate wingbeats. Performs buoyant, floppy display flight above the forest canopy. **Call** a repeated loud piping whistle, *REE-pipee, REE-pipee. . .* Displaying bird gives a loud *weer-wik*, a querulous *wheep-wheep-wheep*, and a sharp vibrating *titititititi*. **Range**: Local from Sokoke Forest north to Witu, and along lower Tana River to Garsen.

RED-CHESTED CUCKOO *Cuculus s. solitarius* Plate 51

Length 11–12″. A well-known but elusive canopy cuckoo with a highly distinctive call characteristic of various wooded habitats. Dark slate grey above, with *orange-rufous upper breast; throat pale buff in female, grey in male* (distinguishing it from w. Kenyan Black

Cuckoo); lower breast to under tail-coverts whitish with narrow black barring; tail sides spotted and barred with white; orbital ring yellow. **Juvenile**
black above and on throat and breast, with black-and-buff-barred underparts and white patch on nape (sometimes obscure); dark body feathers
'scaled' with narrow whitish tips. Male has loud three-note **call**, descending in pitch, *wip-wip-weeu,* repeated many times. (Barred Long-tailed
Cuckoo has similar call, but usually of 4–5 syllables.) Female gives an
excited *he-he-he-he-ha-he-ha-he* and an emphatic *quick-quick-quick. . ..* Vocal mainly just
before and during rains. **Range**: Widespread north to Mt Elgon and the Cheranganis, east to
Meru, Kitui and Tsavo, but only a rare or seasonal visitor to coastal lowlands. Movements
little understood, but generally a wet-season visitor to arid northern border areas.

BLACK CUCKOO *Cuculus clamosus* Plate 51

Length 11–12". Like Red-chested Cuckoo, more often heard than seen.
Fairly common in acacia woodland and savanna. Black, with small
white spots on tips of tail feathers, and, often, *faint buff bars on under
tail-coverts or breast.* **Juvenile** *dull sooty brown.* West Kenyan '*jacksoni*'
more like Ugandan *gabonensis,* with *chestnut throat, neck and breast
variably barred black,* as are the buff/whitish belly and flanks; tail plain
in adult, faintly barred in young. (Male Red-chested Cuckoo is easily
confused with these western birds, but its throat is grey. Juv. Red-chested is heavily
barred below and on tail.) Usual **call** a distinctive unhurried mournful whistle of 3 notes,
the last rising, *wur, wur, wurEE* or *hoo, hoo, hurEEE,* repeated many times. Also frequent
is a fast, excited-sounding *weurrri-weurrri-weurrri-WEURRRI,* or *cheudili-cheudili-
CHEUDILI. . .* rolling upward then fading and often ending with a subdued *chew-chew-
tew-tew-tew.* **Range**: *C. c. clamosus* from Turkwell River and the Ndotos south to Serengeti NP and Arusha, east to Tsavo West NP. Vocal mainly or only during the rains: in w.
Kenya/cent. Rift Valley, Feb.–Aug.; se.Kenya, Nov.–Feb.; Arusha area, Jan.–March.

EURASIAN or COMMON CUCKOO *Cuculus c. canorus* Plate 51

Length 12.5–13". A fairly large cuckoo with long pointed wings. **Male** grey
above, and from head to breast, otherwise barred black and white below;
tail blackish, the outer feathers with large white terminal spots, smaller
bar-like spots near shafts and on inner webs; from below appears mainly
black with narrow white markings. *Bill blackish with yellow base*; orbital
ring yellow; eyes orange-yellow. **Female** usually grey above, breast more
barred than male with rufous wash on sides; **rufous morph** barred rufous
and dark brown on upperparts, wings and tail; bare parts as in male. Variable **juvenile**
always has strongly barred wings and tail, and whitish nape patch. (African Cuckoo has
basal *half* of bill yellow, some complete white bars across outer tail feathers and distinctive
call. Both lesser cuckoos are much smaller, more compact and more heavily barred below.)
Call a chuckling *wuckel-wuckel-wuc-wuc-wuc-wuc. . ..* Well-known *cuc-koo* not heard
in East Africa. **Range/status**: Palearctic passage migrant, generally below 2000 m. Mainly
in se. Kenya/ne. Tanzania, Oct.–Dec., more numerous March–April (when sometimes
common at coast). Scarce in north and east.

AFRICAN CUCKOO *Cuculus gularis* Plate 51

Length 12–13". Distinguished from very similar Eurasian Cuckoo by
more *orange-yellow bill with distal half black,* by some *complete white
bars on outer tail feathers (thus tail not as black below),* by *brown eyes
in female,* and by *distinctive call.* **Male** grey above and from head to
breast; otherwise white with narrow black barring below; eyes orange;
eyelids bright yellow. **Female** somewhat more brownish grey above, and
barred breast often tinged with buff; eyelids yellow. No rufous morph.
Juvenile similar to young Eurasian, but rump, upper tail-coverts and crown more completely barred. **Call** a Hoopoe-like *oo-oo* or *hoo-hoop* (second syllable slightly higher),
repeated several times. **Range/status**: Calling in Serengeti NP, Jan.–Feb.; cent. Kenya,
Mar.–June; in Baringo District, Aug.–Sep.; in Tsavo Nov.– Dec. Few breeding records.
Movements not clear. Some birds may be intra-African migrants, others may merely follow the rains.

ASIAN LESSER CUCKOO *Cuculus poliocephalus*   Plate 51

Length 10–11″. Resembles a small Eurasian Cuckoo, but more compact and appearing *shorter-tailed*, and *dark tail and rump contrast with pale back* (unlike African and Eurasian Cuckoos). **Male** grey above, on throat and breast, boldly barred black and white on belly, sides and flanks. Buff crissum feathers usually heavily black-barred, but many birds have anterior and lateral under tail-coverts unbarred as is usual in *C. rochii*, and a few have entirely plain coverts; outer rectrices with large white spots. Some **females** similar to male, but tinged tawny and faintly barred on breast and sides of neck; others (common **rufous morph**) barred rufous on back, plain rufous on head and rump. **Juvenile** tawny from crown to nape and breast, the latter barred; tawny bars on flight feathers and tail. **Call** of male, 5–6 staccato notes, middle ones highest, *yok-yok chiki-chuchu*; rarely heard in Africa during northward passage. **Range/status**: Migrant from s. Asia, fairly common in March–April on coast north to Malindi (often moving with Eurasian Cuckoos). Some late Nov.–Dec. records from coastal forest (Arabuko-Sokoke) and Tsavo West NP. Recently found in winter in West Usambara Mts.

MADAGASCAR LESSER CUCKOO *Cuculus rochii*   Plate 51

Length 10–11″. Virtually identical to Asian Lesser Cuckoo (but no rufous morph females); unlikely in Nov.–Dec. when Asian Lesser is present in East Africa. Generally scarce in forest edge and woodland. Under tail-coverts *usually* plain creamy buff (longest central coverts barred, but not visible in side view of bird.) Some females may have *all* coverts heavily barred. Male longer-winged than male Asian Lesser (162–174 mm *vs.* 142–162 mm) but females same size. Madagascar Lesser present in Africa *Apr.–Sept.*, the Asian species, Nov.–April. In April, when there is some overlap, birds newly arrived from Madagascar are in *old worn plumage*, quite different from freshly moulted Asian birds about to depart. Four-note **call** distinctive, but apparently not heard here. **Range/status**: Most enter and leave Africa south of our region. Sight records, considered of this form, from w. Kenya (Saiwa NP, Kapenguria, Kitale, Eldoret, Kapsabet, Mumias and Ng'iya districts); also from East Usambara Mts, Sokoke and Lake Baringo (Aug.), and Nakuru (May). Old specimen records from Lamu and Mombasa. **Taxonomic Note**: Considered conspecific with *C. poliocephalus* by some.

BARRED LONG-TAILED CUCKOO *Cercococcyx montanus patulus*   Plate 52

Length 12.5–13″. A shy, secretive forest cuckoo. Small-bodied, with a *long broad tail* and *relatively short wings. Boldly barred with black and buffy white* below, with rufous and dark brown above; flight feathers and tail rufous-barred, the outer rectrices with white bars as well. From below, primaries lack white bars characteristic of other *Cuculus* species. Orbital ring yellow; bill blackish above, yellow below. **Juvenile** streaked below, and some scaly mottling on throat. **Call** a repetitive whining whistle, *wee-weoo, wee-weoo, wee-weoo*. . . rising in pitch and volume before stopping, the series then quickly followed by a ringing *wip-wip-weu-weu-wo*, much like Red-chested Cuckoo's call but usually of 4–5 notes. A variation begins with a raspy, nasal owlet-like *way-eu, way-eu* . . ., changing to a loud *PEE-tu, PEE-tu* . . ., repeated often before a final series of *whee-wee-whew-yer* phrases. Highly vocal in thick cover, mainly in evening and briefly at sunrise, or on moonlit nights. **Range**: Between 1700 and 2100 m on e. Mt Kenya and s. Aberdares, 900 to 1600 m in Usambaras (common). Probably resident, but overlooked except when vocal Oct.–March. Vagrants on the coast, Sept.–Nov., are perhaps wanderers from the Usambaras.

AFRICAN EMERALD CUCKOO *Chrysococcyx c. cupreus*   Plate 51

Length 8.5–9″. A brightly coloured cuckoo of highland forest canopy. **Male** *brilliant iridescent green with golden yellow lower breast and belly*; under tail-coverts barred black and white, sides of tail white; orbital ring and maxilla bright blue-green. **Female** shining green above with heavy tawny or rufous barring; *white underparts barred with irides-cent green* except sometimes on throat; *head mainly rufous-brown, flecked with white behind eyes* and sometimes from forehead to nape;

tail coppery-green, the white outer feathers barred with bronze-green near tip; orbital skin and feet blue. **Juvenile** female-like but crown and nape barred; lateral upper tail-coverts with only a very narrow pale edge, not a broad white stripe as in young Klaas's Cuckoo which further differs in buff-barred crown, absence of white flecks on head, and non-iridescent barring on underparts. **Call** of 4–5 clear whistled notes, *teeoo, tchew-tui* or *diu, dew-dui*. **Range**: Mathews Range, Ndotos and Mt Marsabit south through Kenyan highlands to Chyulu and Taita hills, Usambara Mts, Kilimanjaro, Arusha and Lake Manyara NPs and Mt Hanang; wanders beyond these areas during the rains.

KLAAS'S CUCKOO *Chrysococcyx klaas*　　　　　　　　　　**Plate 51**

Length 6–7". A small woodland cuckoo with *broad white tail sides* conspicuous in undulating flight. **Male** shining coppery green above with *small white postocular marks; underparts white with dark green patches on sides of breast*; orbital ring and bill pale green (brighter when breeding); eyes dark brown, feet olive. **Female** may resemble dull male except for brown-barred sides, but usually has plain bronzy brown head; upperparts mostly barred iridescent green and coppery brown; tail sides broadly white with dark spots near tip; *eyes brown or grey*. **Juvenile/immature** shining green above, lightly barred with *tawny buff*, including crown, and barred with brown or dark metallic green; buff wash on breast; pale edges of upper tail-coverts show as a *short white stripe on each side of tail base*. (Diederik Cuckoo is larger, white-spotted on wings; adult has red eyes, male heavily barred on flanks; young has white wing spots and largely red bill. Female and juv. Emerald resemble young Klaas's, but flecked or barred with *white* on head, and lack white streak at sides of upper tail-coverts.) **Call**, 3–5 high plaintive whistles, *swhee-hee, whee-hee, whee-hee-ki wee-ki*, or *weu-ki weu-ki weu-ki*, the series repeated 3–4 times per minute, often from treetop. **Range**: Widespread from sea level to 3000 m except in arid areas.

DIEDERIK CUCKOO *Chrysococcyx caprius*　　　　　　　**Plate 51**

Length 7–7.5". A fairly common small cuckoo of open country, distinguished from Klaas's by *white spots on wings* and along sides of tail. **Male** iridescent coppery green above, with the white superciliary stripe often broken above the red eye; underparts white with green barring on flanks. **Female** variable; browner above, often more barred below than male, with buff wash on throat and breast. Some show green streaks on throat; eyes rufous brown, often yellow peripherally. **Juvenile** has largely *coral-red bill*, is often *spotted* below as well as streaked on throat, barred on flanks and crissum; usually green with rufous barring above, broken white superciliaries, dark malar stripes, and much white spotting on wings and tail sides; some birds largely rufous above or intermediate with green form. **Call** a persistent plaintive whistle, *kew-kew-kew-kewk-iti* or *dee-dee-dee-DEEderik*, from exposed treetop perches and in rapid quivering flight with spread, sometimes raised, tail. **Range**: Widespread up to 2000 m. A wet-season visitor in most dry areas, and in n. and e. Kenya mainly confined to vicinity of permanent water.

YELLOWBILL *Ceuthmochares aereus*　　　　　　　　　　**Plate 52**

Length 13". A slender dark skulker with *conspicuous yellow bill*, bright blue skin behind the red eyes and greenish yellow lores. Western nominate race dark slaty blue above, grey below with paler throat. Eastern *C. a. australis* has glossy greenish grey upperparts, olive-grey head and underparts with buff throat. **Juvenile** more sooty above, pale brownish on throat and breast; wing-covert edges buff. **Call** of arresting high-pitched staccato notes accelerating into a harsh trill, *kik kik, kik, kik-ki-ki-kikikikikiki*; and a wailing *kweeu-eeep, kweeu-eeep;* also various scolds. **Range**: *C. a. aereus* from Kakamega and Nandi forests west to Uganda, south to Kericho, Lolgorien and Migori River. *C. a. australis* on Tanzanian coast (and islands) inland to the Usambara and North Pare mts, Arusha NP, Taveta area and Kilimanjaro; also along entire Kenyan coast (apparent migrants, mainly May–Nov.). Occasional near Nairobi, in Samburu GR and Tsavo area.

WHITE-BROWED COUCAL *Centropus superciliosus*   **Plate 52** ✔

Length 16″. The most widespread coucal, distinguished from its less common relatives by *whitish superciliary stripes* and dark ear-coverts; much whitish streaking on upper back and neck; wings light chestnut, long broad tail greenish black; eyes red. *C. s. loandae* is darker than *C. s. superciliosus*, with black (not brown) crown in fresh plumage. **Juvenile** has *buff* superciliaries, is streaked pale buff and brown from forehead to scapulars, black-barred on back and wing-coverts; tail bronzy greenish brown with faint buff/whitish bars. **Call** an accelerating hollow cooing, *hoo-hoo-hoo-hoo-huhuhuhuhuhuhu. . .*, and a series of gurgling notes likened to water being poured from a bottle. Pairs duet, and several birds may call together. Alarm note a sharp *TCHUK!*; also hisses. **Range**: *C. s. loandae* in n. Tanzania and sw. Kenya; supposedly nominate birds elsewhere, but precise limits of the two races unclear.

BLACK COUCAL *Centropus grillii*   **Plate 52**

Length 15″. Uncommon in marshes and wet grassland. Smaller and more compact than White-browed Coucal, with *shorter tail, shorter bill*, and *no superciliary stripes* in any plumage. *Eyes dark brown.* **Breeding adult** *black with orange-rufous wings.* **Non-breeding plumage** broadly barred rufous-buff and black on back and wings, *streaked tawny and black from forehead to scapulars*; pale shaft-streaks from head to breast and wing-coverts; *tail narrowly tawny-barred*; underparts buff with dusky feather edges on throat and breast, dusky barring on flanks. **Subadult breeder** has barring on remiges and tail, some retained for 2 years. **Juvenile** resembles non-breeding adult but barring extends onto face and forehead; pale shaft streaks as in adult; *rump and upper tail-coverts black with narrow dull buff or tawny bars*; flight feathers dull cinnamon with bold black bars; sides of breast brown-mottled with pale shaft streaks. (White-browed Coucal has pale superciliaries and unstreaked forehead/forecrown; young Senegal Coucal is longer tailed; both are red eyed.) **Call** a double *kutuk. . .kutuk. . .kutuk. . .* repeated at length; also a low hooting *hoo. . . hoo. . . hoo. . .*, and a 'water-bottle' call like that of White-browed Coucal but higher, faster and not rising at end. **Range**: Serengeti NP and Mkomazi GR (breeding Dec.–Feb.); otherwise scarce in n. Tanzania. In Kenya, local from Lake Victoria basin and Mara GR east to the Tana River delta. Seasonal in most areas; few breeding records.

SENEGAL COUCAL *Centropus s. senegalensis*   **Plate 52**

Length 15–16″. A *small, west Kenyan* coucal. Pattern that of the larger, more widespread Blue-headed Coucal, but *plain black, not blue-black, from forehead to nape*, and brighter rufous on back and wings; buffy white underparts with shiny feather shafts. **Juvenile** brown above, with creamy streaks and fine barring; wings barred brown, but *primaries plain except at tips* (juv. Blue-headed has barred primaries), rump and upper tail-coverts barred, underparts buff, and blackish tail has faint buff barring at tip; older **immature** is similar with all-black tail. (White-browed Coucal has pale superciliaries, lacking in juv. Senegal.) **Call** suggests that of White-browed but begins more slowly, descends and accelerates, *hoo-hoo-hoo-hu-hu-huhuhuhu. . . hoo. . .hoo huhu*, slowing before rising at end. 'Water-bottle' call like White-browed's. **Range**: Below 1300 m near Ugandan border in Bungoma, Busia and Mumias districts.

BLUE-HEADED COUCAL *Centropus monachus*   **Plate 52**

Length 18″. A *large*, heavy-looking coucal of papyrus swamps and moist thickets; also in tea planatations. **Adult** *shiny blue-black from crown to upper back*; lower back and wings chestnut-rufous; rump and tail black; underparts whitish or pale buff; eyes red. Western *C. m. fischeri* is darker, more olive-brown on wings. **Juvenile** has top of head dull black with fine buff shaft streaks, barred primaries, is dull rufous on breast and sides of neck, and the dark brown tail has only very narrow buff barring toward tip. (Along Ugandan border see Senegal Coucal.) **Call** slower and deeper than that of White-browed, *hoo, hoo, hoo, hoo-wu-wu-wu-wu-wu-wu hoo hoo, hu*, accelerating and dropping in pitch in the middle, then rising and slowing at end; also has a raucous cackle. **Range**: *C. m. monachus* in highlands from Kericho east to Nyeri and Meru, south to near Nairobi. *C. m. fischeri* from Lake Victoria basin north to Kakamega and Nandi districts, south to Ruma NP and Kilgoris. One old n. Tanzanian record (near Musoma).

BARN OWLS, FAMILY TYTONIDAE

Nocturnal raptors differing from typical owls (Strigidae) in their heart-shaped facial disc surrounding small dark eyes, but similar in being large-headed, with long rounded wings, short decurved bills, strongly curved sharp claws and soft plumage. The middle claw is pectinate (as in herons and some nightjars), the long slender tarsi are feathered, the toes covered with bristles. Sexes are alike or similar, although females are larger than males. They nest in burrows, buildings, tree or cliff cavities or (African Grass Owl) on the ground.

AFRICAN GRASS OWL *Tyto capensis*　　　　　　　　　　Plate 55

Length 14–16″. A scarce, dark-backed, ground-nesting owl with *whitish facial disc, dark brown lores, and white-edged tail*. Dark chocolate-brown above, finely speckled with white; tawny buff to creamy white below, with dense dark spotting on breast; tail whitish or dirty buff, *central feathers dark brown (not barred as in Marsh Owl); outer two pairs white*; eyes brown. Spread wing shows *tawny-buff area at base of outer primaries*, the patch much *less extensive than in Marsh Owl* in the same habitat; shows pale patagial area and *no white trailing edge*; wing-linings spotted and with a small dark carpal crescent. **Juvenile** has tawny-russet facial disc, white only toward throat, no white speckling on back, and golden brown underparts with small black spots. **Call** a soft, Barn Owl-like screech with a distinctive ending, *schreeeeeeow*, given during the day in response to disturbance. Contact call a series of steady clicks, rising and falling in intensity, suggesting distant frogs except for a regular pause between the clicks, series interspersed with squeaks and snores near nest. **Range:** Between 1600 and 3200 m, in the Crater Highlands and from the Mau, Aberdares and Mt Kenya to Laikipia and Uasin Gishu plateaus. Casual in Kakamega Forest glades, Sotik, Athi Plains and Arusha NP.

BARN OWL *Tyto alba affinis*　　　　　　　　　　Plate 55

Length 13–14″. A pale owl with *white heart-shaped face* enclosing *dark beady eyes*. Appears large-headed and short-tailed in flight, ghostly white in headlight beams at night. Often associated with human habitation; otherwise around cliffs and kopjes. A delicate mixture of golden-buff and pale grey above, with much black and white flecking; tail yellowish buff with grey-brown bars. Facial disc outlined by sepia or black, and a dark patch in front of each eye; underparts and entire underside of wings white, the former with small blackish dots. **Juvenile** darker above than adult, golden buff below. **Call** an eerie trilling screech, *schreeeeeeeeee*, or *eeeSHEEEEeeee*. Hisses loudly near nest. **Range**: Local from sea level to nearly 3000 m. Scarce in arid n. and ne. Kenya.

TYPICAL OWLS, FAMILY STRIGIDAE

Mostly nocturnal with large eyes (which see perfectly well in daylight) usually surrounded by a broad facial disc. Legs are shorter than in *Tyto*; both tarsi and toes may be well-feathered. Several species have well-developed 'ear-tufts' of erectile head feathers (which have nothing to do with the internal ears or with hearing). Exceptionally soft, nightjar-like plumage, apparently aided by the serrated leading outer primary edge, effectively muffles flight sounds, thus enabling them to approach prey silently. (Pel's Fishing Owl, adapted to underwater prey, does not have mechanisms for silent flight.) Cryptic feather patterns, plumage compression and ear-tuft erection render many owls inconspicuous when roosting during the day. The sexes are alike in colour, but females are usually larger than males. Some species exhibit different colour morphs. *Glaucidium* species moult all rectrices at once, the new tail requiring several weeks to reach full length. Owls occupy all land habitats, but most are woodland and forest-edge birds. All have distinctive calls, and are highly vocal during periods of full moon.

SOKOKE SCOPS OWL *Otus ireneae*   **Plate 56**

Length 6″. A small, polymorphic *coastal* species, most common in *Cynometra–Brachy-laena* forest on red soil in Kenya's Arabuko–Sokoke Forest. Roosts by day in dense thick-ets, ear-tufts erected and pale yellow eyes reduced to slits. *At night the small ear-tufts are barely visible.* Upperparts usually brownish grey with small black-and-white dots, and larger (but often inconspicuous) pale spots on scapulars; face buffy grey, outlined in black; densely vermiculated underparts pale grey, browner on breast, with fine speckling; wings have black-and-white markings on coverts, black and buffy white-barred pri-maries; tail grey-brown with incomplete dark bars. Some birds are rich vinous brown on head and breast, with white speckling and small black spots; others *largely rufous, pale or bright,* quite uniform except for short black crown streaks and white scapular spots (not always evident). **Call** a whistled *too-too-too. . . .*, reminiscent of a tinkerbird, uttered as a series of 8–10 notes repeated about 10 times per minute. **Range**: Between Kilifi and Malindi. Recently discovered between 200 and 400 m in East Usambara Mts.

PEMBA SCOPS OWL *Otus pembaensis*   **Plate 124**

Length 8″. The only small owl on Pemba Island where fairly common and widespread in forest and clove plantations. Varies from plain russet-brown and finely vermicu-lated pale rufous-buff below, to entirely rich russet-brown or orange-rufous with little or no streaking. Eyes yellow. **Call** a single monosyllabic *too* or *hoo* at irregular intervals. Male's call higher-pitched than female's; pairs duet. At dusk, 4–5 hoots in quick succes-sion, single notes for remainder of night. **Range**: Pemba Island, Tanzania.

EURASIAN SCOPS OWL *Otus scops*   **Plate 56**

Length 7″. Difficult to distinguish from resident African Scops which has broader black facial disc borders and heavier, more continuous black streaking below, but there is much variation. Inner part of Eurasian's ear-tufts and scapular edges pale buff or white. In the hand note that 10th (outermost) primary is longer than 5th (the reverse in African Scops). Eurasian Scops appears to be *silent in East Africa*, whereas *senegalensis* is quite vocal. (Call on breeding grounds a measured pure whistle, *peu .*
. . peu . . . peu. . ..) **Range/status**: Scarce palearctic migrant, Nov.–March, from Nandi, Eldama Ravine and Mt Kenya south to Nairobi, Tsavo West NP, and (once) North Pare Mts. Most are *O. s. scops* or the poorly differentiated *pulchellus*, but paler *turanicus* recorded in Tsavo West NP and at Bura.

AFRICAN SCOPS OWL *Otus senegalensis*   **Plate 56**

Length 6–6.5″. The common small 'eared' owl of savanna and bush country. Often vocal (unlike Eurasian Scops). Nocturnal, but may begin calling before dusk. Dimorphic, with some birds more rufous than oth-ers. Ear-tufts (inconspicuous as night) mainly dark, often with some white spots, but inner edges not, or usually not, broadly pale as in preceding species. Eyes yellow. Nominate race dark grey above, streaked and mot-tled with black, often with buff or tawny on neck and wing-coverts; scapulars boldly white-spotted; finely vermiculated underparts grey, with narrow dark shaft streaks, a few broad black marks and short white bars; centre of belly white. *O. s. nivosus* is smaller and paler grey below, with a few light brown marks on breast. Usual **call** a single short trill, *krruuup*, or *k-k-krruup*, repeated many times at intervals of 5–10 sec.—a common night sound in suitable habitat; varied to a soft purring *twrrr* or *terrrrup*. **Range**: *O. s. senegalensis* widespread in low-rainfall areas below 2000 m. *O. s. nivosus* is known from 3 specimens taken in se. Kenya.

WHITE-FACED SCOPS OWL *Otus leucotis*   **Plate 56**

Length 10″. A pale grey, dry-country owl with *black-bordered white face,* golden-yellow eyes, and *narrow black streaks on the underparts;* upperparts mostly vermiculated grey; white on scapulars and along edge of wing. *O. l. granti* is darker and greyer, often with heavier dark ventral streaks, but some nominate birds are almost as dark. **Juvenile's** facial disc grey. **Call** a mellow bisyllabic *co-croor* repeated at 5–6 sec. intervals. **Range**: *O. l. leucotis* below 1700 m in nw. Kenya, south to Turkwell and

Kerio rivers, Baringo, Samburu and Meru districts; *O. l. granti* scarce in South Nyanza, Amboseli and the Tsavo NPs, rare in much of n. Tanzania. Sight records from the Tana River are not racially assigned.

CAPE EAGLE-OWL *Bubo capensis mackinderi*   Plate 55

Length 20–24″. The *yellow-orange eyes* and *heavily blotched breast* identify this large 'eared' owl of the highlands. Mottled tawny and dark brown above; ear-tufts long and brown (shorter in juvenile). Roosts on rock ledges or in caves. Nests on ledges or in old nests of other raptors in trees. (Verreaux's Eagle-Owl is paler, more finely marked, and has dark eyes. Spotted Eagle-Owl lacks bright tawny buff coloration and is less heavily blotched on breast, ear-tufts are smaller, eyes yellow or brown.) **Call** a deep *hoooo* or *ho-hooo* or *ho-hooo-ho*. (Pairs apparently do not duet.) **Range**: High peaks and moorlands on Mt Kenya, Mt Elgon, Aberdares and Mau plateau; smaller isolated populations or pairs near cliffs and ravines in the Ngobit–Nakuru–Gilgil–Naivasha region, including Hell's Gate NP.

SPOTTED EAGLE-OWL *Bubo africanus*   Plate 55

Length 17–19″. An ecologically widespread, greyish or (more often) brownish 'eared' owl, finely barred below, with darker blotching on upper breast; mottled dark brown, buffy and white above, with some pale spots on back and wing-coverts. Northern *B. a. cinerascens* has pale brownish facial disc enclosing darker brown rings and *dark brown eyes*. Paler *B. a. tanae* has a light grey face with faint brown rings and *yellow eyes* like those of larger *B. a. africanus*. Young birds tend to be browner and less spotted than adults. Habitats vary from wooded ravines and rocky gorges to desert oases and suburban gardens. (Much larger Cape Eagle-Owl has more orange eyes and more boldly blotched ventral plumage. Larger and paler grey Verreaux's Eagle-Owl has whitish facial disc with broad black margins, dark brown eyes and bright pink upper eyelids.) **Call** of male a mellow *ho-hoo* (second note lower); female gives a tremulous *hoo, whoo-hoo* in duet with her mate or seconds after his call; both sexes also give single *hoo* notes. **Range**: Sea level to 2000 m. *B. a. cinerascens* south to Kerio valley, Baringo, Isiolo, Meru and Wajir districts; *B. a. tanae* along Tana River from Garissa to Garsen and inland to the Lali Hills; *B. a. africanus* in w., cent. and s. Kenya and n. Tanzania; along coast at Mombasa and Lamu.

VERREAUX'S EAGLE-OWL *Bubo lacteus*   Plate 55

Length 23–26″. The common large *dark-eyed* owl of acacia groves and riverine woodland. *Pale milky grey* or grey-brown below with fine dark vermiculations visible at close range; upperparts pale grey-brown with whitish vermiculations; *whitish facial disc broadly bordered laterally with black; deep brown eyes and bright pink bare upper eyelids* conspicuous; ear-tufts broad, rather short. **Juvenile** has narrower dark facial borders, shorter ear-tufts. Nocturnal, but frequently hunts during early evening; often on exposed perch in daytime. **Call** a deep husky *hoo-hoo*, singly or in series; female's voice deeper than that of male. Both sexes give an irregular grunting *wuh, wu-wuh-wuh*. **Range**: Common and widespread from sea level to near 3000 m, except in driest areas.

USAMBARA EAGLE-OWL *Bubo vosseleri*   Plate 123

Length 19″. A rare large owl of Tanzania's *Usambara Mountain forests*. Tawny brown above with darker brown barring; creamy underparts heavily blotched with tawny brown on breast, dark-barred on belly and crissum; face pale tawny, broadly black-bordered at sides; ear-tufts long and tawny brown; *eyes dull yellowish orange or pale orange-brown* (not dark brown) with bluish white eyelids; feet whitish. **Juvenile** has distinct line of white spots on scapulars until first moult; eyes probably brown. Strictly nocturnal; vocal only after dark (20.00 to 04.30 hours), not at dusk or dawn. Possibly restricted to forest canopy. **Call** a deep, far-carrying *ub-a-wb-a-wb-wb-a*, of several seconds duration, ventriloquial. **Range**: Between 200 and 1500 m in the Usambaras.

PEL'S FISHING OWL   *Scotopelia peli*   Plate 55

Length 24". A large, round-headed, *rufous* owl of *riverine trees*. Finely barred with dusky above, streaked and spotted with brown below; rufous-buff tail has narrow dark bars; *eyes dark brown.* **Juvenile** paler, at first *white with rufous wash* on head and underparts, the latter with faint dusky streaks; obscure dusky barring on back. **Call** an echoing hoot often followed by a deeper and softer grunt, *hoooommmmm-hut*, audible over great distance; also a repeated horn-like *hoom, hoom.* Pair may duet, male starting with a grunting *uh-uh-uhu*. . . leading to higher *hoommm*, answered by female's deeper hoot. Also gives a loud descending wail, *weeeeaaow.* **Range**: Local along major rivers from sea level to 1700 m. Known from the Tana upstream to Meru NP and Kiambere, and from secluded areas along the Mara. Formerly at Arusha Chini (south of Moshi) but no recent n. Tanzanian records.

PEARL-SPOTTED OWLET   *Glaucidium perlatum licua*   Plate 56

Length 7–7.5". A small, partly diurnal owl, common in woodland and savanna. Note the *prominent white 'eyebrows'* and *heavy chestnut streaks* on underparts; *long-tailed* (except in moult). Upperparts mainly warm brown with two *'eye-spots' on back of head*; crown and nape white-dotted; rows of larger white spots form bands on flight feathers and tail. If disturbed during the day it watches observer, not closing eyes like scops owl; when alarmed, pumps tail up and down and wags it sideways. Flight strong and undulating. (Barred Owlet is spotted on lower breast and belly, barred above and on breast; lacks occipital 'eye-spots.' Scops owls are differently patterned, have small ear-tufts and shorter tails.) **Call** variable. Most frequent is a prolonged series of loud penetrating whistles, *scheeu, scheeu, scheeu* . . ., rising in pitch and increasing in volume, at first accelerating, then notes gradually becoming more widely spaced and the pitch dropping slightly. Also gives a less harsh, higher-pitched *teeu* repeated a few times or in a long accelerating series, the notes beginning softly and becoming progressively louder. Pair members call to one another, sometimes duetting. Female's voice higher-pitched. Vocal day and night, especially at dusk. **Range**: Between 300 and 2000 m except in Lake Victoria basin, the driest parts of n. and e. Kenya and the coastal lowlands.

RED-CHESTED OWLET   *Glaucidium tephronotum elgonense*   Plate 56

Length 7.5–8". A uncommon small owl of *west Kenyan highland forests. Spotted below* with sepia or black; *rufous wash (sometimes faint) across breast and along sides* and flanks. Head grey with white eyebrows connecting along sides of bill and merging with white chin; may show vertical black band on each side of bill. Upperparts dark brown or rufous-brown; wings vary from strongly rufous-washed with tawny-banded flight feathers, to almost plain dark brown above; white beneath with dark tips and black bands. *Tail dark brown or black with 3–4 large white spots on inner webs of central feathers; also on inner webs of outer feathers where conspicuous from below.* **Call** a series of 4–20 hollow whistled notes, mechanical-sounding and uttered at 1-sec. intervals, *teu teu teu teu*. . ., or a more yelping *wook, wook, wook* . . ., also in series; at times a double note, *wu-wook, wu-wook* . . .. **Range**: Mt Elgon, North Nandi, Kakamega, Mau and Trans-Mara forests.

AFRICAN BARRED OWLET   *Glaucidium capense scheffleri*   Plate 56

Length 8–8.5". An uncommon, partly diurnal owl of eastern woods, larger and with more rounded head than Pearl-spotted Owlet, but with equally prominent white eyebrows. Heavily *spotted on lower breast and belly, barred buff and brown across upper breast* and on back; tawny-brown nuchal collar; many wing-coverts white tipped; face grey-brown. **Call** a series of 6-10 loud notes, increasing and decreasing in volume: kerr-kerr-kerr-kerr-KERR-KERR. . . or piu-piu-piu-piu-PIU-PIU-PIU-PIU-piu-piu-prr-prr. . ., often followed by a double trilled or purring whistle, the second note higher, chrr-chrrrr, chrr-chrrrr repeated and increasing in volume; also monotonously repeats a single note, weu-weu-weu-weu-weu . . .. **Range**: Coastal areas, and inland along the Tana River to Garissa. Scattered inland records from Kondoa, Mombo, Iltalal and Kibwezi.

AFRICAN WOOD OWL *Strix woodfordii nigricantior*   Plate 55

Length 13–14″. A medium-sized, *round-headed* woodland owl with *dark brown eyes* and broad white eyebrows. Pale facial disc darkens to brown around eyes. Underparts barred brown and whitish; crown and back dark brown with some white speckling; large whitish or buffy spots on scapulars. **Juvenile** has duller face. Pairs roost in dense foliage or creeper tangles. (Eagle-owls have ear-tufts, not always obvious; Verreaux's and northern race of Spotted dark-eyed, but their facial discs black-bordered and underparts not heavily barred.) **Call** easily confused with that of Spotted Eagle-owl. Individuals may give single hoots; pair duets with a loud, tremulous, fairly high-pitched *WHOOOO* or *WHEEOW* or *oo-WOW-oo* from female answered by male's single low *hooo*, a longer *whu, hu-hu-hu, hu-hu*, or *ooo-wow-wow-wow-oo-waau*. May call on dark cloudy days. **Range**: Coastal strip and inland to the Usambara and Pare mts, Kilimanjaro, Arusha and Tarangire NPs, Mt Hanang, Ngorongoro, Taita and Chyulu hills, cent. and w. Kenyan highlands north to the Cheranganis and Mt Ololokwe.

AFRICAN LONG-EARED OWL *Asio abyssinicus graueri*   Plate 55

Length 17″. A rare *montane forest* owl with *long, blackish brown ear-tufts near centre of forehead, rich tawny brown facial disc* and orange-yellow eyes. Upperparts dark brown with some paler tawny mottling. Underparts mottled tawny and dark brown on breast, irregularly barred tawny and whitish on belly; tail heavily barred brown and pale tawny brown. Strictly nocturnal. May feed over moorlands adjacent to forest. (Cape Eagle-Owl is much larger, with more laterally positioned 'ear-tufts,' belly and feet whitish.) **Call** believed to be a bisyllabic *OOOOO-oooomm*, prolonged and rising slightly in pitch. **Range**: Mt Kenya (one taken in *Hagenia* forest at 3350 m, Sept. 1961, and possible sight records from 2800 m in Aug. 1975, at 3500 m in July 1992.) **Taxonomic Note**: Often considered conspecific with the holarctic *A. otus*.

SHORT-EARED OWL *Asio f. flammeus*   Plate 55

Length 15″. A rare, y*ellow-eyed* ground owl of open marshy areas. *Pale tawny buff* with *broad dark streaks*, darker on breast; *face pale buff shading to dusky around eyes*; short ear-tufts in centre of forehead usually not noticeable. Dark carpal patch on pale underside of wings conspicuous in slow-flapping and gliding flight. Partly diurnal. Roosts on or near ground in tall grass or bushes. (Marsh Owl is much darker brown, has brown eyes. See African Grass Owl.) **Status**: Palearctic visitor; 5 Kenyan records including an early specimen from Mt Elgon. Some perhaps ship-assisted, as recorded at sea near Lamu and off Mida Creek. Two photographed Serengeti NP, Feb. 1996.

MARSH OWL *Asio c. capensis*   Plate 55

Length 12.5–15″. A *dark-eyed* brownish owl of *open grasslands. Dull brown* above, except for buff tail bars and *large pale buff patch in primaries conspicuous in flight. Secondaries darker with pale trailing edges.* Wings appear long; underside shows large dark patch at carpal joint; short ear-tufts on forehead seldom obvious; brown underparts barred and vermiculated with buff. **Juvenile** has darker, blackish-rimmed facial disc. Diurnal in cloudy weather. Roosts and nests on the ground. (African Grass Owl is larger with prominent white tail sides. Rare Short-eared Owl is paler and has yellow eyes.) **Call** a harsh croaking *zheeeow* or *creeow* ; also a repeated croaking, *crrk-crrk-crrk*. **Range**: Between 1300 and 2000 m north to cent. Rift Valley, Nairobi NP, Mt Kenya, Laikipia Plateau and Trans-Nzoia.

NIGHTJARS, FAMILY CAPRIMULGIDAE

Crepuscular or nocturnal birds with soft, intricately cryptic, owl-like plumage. They are big-headed, small-footed with large eyes, small weak bills and well-developed rictal bristles for funnelling insect prey, caught on the wing, into the huge gape. They spend their daylight hours well camouflaged on the ground or perched lengthwise on tree branches. Although solitary, numbers may be attracted to insect concentrations. The nocturnal calls are often distinctive, and most species are more readily identified by voice than by appearance. Some have long churring songs, others melodious whistles, and a few produce yelping or chucking sounds; however, the 4 non-breeding visitors are largely or entirely silent in East Africa. Several species exhibit grey, rufous or brown morphs, and plumage patterns of several are closely similar. Included in the following species accounts are some features such as wing length, useful for identification of birds in the hand, as nightjars are frequently found dead on roads, or are picked up alive at night when dazzled by bright light.

FIERY-NECKED NIGHTJAR   *Caprimulgus pectoralis*   Plate 53

Length 8.75–9.5″. A richly coloured nightjar of coastal woods (*C. p. fervidus*) and groves or thickets in far western Kenya (*C. p. nigriscapularis*). Hawks insects from trees, and its *whistling call* is also delivered from a tree branch. Plumage patterned as in Dusky Nightjar, but *general colour warm brown*, not grey-brown or dusky. *C. p. fervidus* shows broad black streaks on grey crown; black, cream and tawny scapulars; *broad rufous nuchal collar* and *rufous-brown ear-coverts*; breast dark rufous, finely barred with grey, black and buff. In flight, **male** shows *large white tail corners* (distal third of outer 2 pairs of feathers) and white spots near tips of outer 5 primaries; in **female**, all white areas buff-tinged. Wing much as in Dusky, but 10th (outermost) primary usually shorter than 7th; wing length 150–176 mm. Western *nigriscapularis* ('Black-shouldered Nightjar') typically has rufous-edged, black central crown streak and rufous nuchal collar marked with black. In the hand, note *deep rufous-and-buff underparts with sharp black barring on under tail-coverts*, and *blackish 'shoulders'*; outer two rectrices pale-tipped as in *fervidus*; wing 147–159 mm. **Call** of *fervidus* a quavering liquid whistle, trilled at end, *keeyou-wurr, qu-weerrrrrrr*; less often *whi-whi-whippi-eeeu* or *tuwurrr, turrr-r-r-r-r*; calls of *nigriscapularis* similar: *ki-yay-o kee-yairrrrrr* and *t'wip, tuwrr-r-r-r-r-r*. Both forms also give low chucking notes. (Montane Nightjar of the highlands has similar but shriller voice. Dusky N. has churring call.) **Range**: *C. p. fervidus* on coast, inland along lower Tana River and in Shimba Hills; *nigriscapularis* local in Siaya, Mumias, Busia and Bungoma districts. **Taxonomic Note**: The two forms are treated as separate species by some authors.

MONTANE NIGHTJAR   *Caprimulgus poliocephalus*   Plates 53, 123 ✔

Length 8.25–9″. A *dark* nightjar of the *highlands* with *shrill whistling call*. In flight, **male** flashes *broad white tail sides* and white bar near tip of outer 4 primaries. **Female** has buff wing spots, and different tail pattern (see plate). At rest, widespread nominate race resembles Dusky Nightjar with black-streaked crown, buff-spotted wing-coverts, and bold buff-and-black scapulars, but *head appears dark and rather plain, with contrasting buff or tawny nuchal collar*, and large white throat patches; white of tail usually concealed. Wing 146–160 mm. Male of smaller Tanzanian *C. p. guttifer* ('Usambara Nightjar') has dark rufous collar, larger white throat spots bordered posteriorly with black, less white on primaries and tail. (Male African White-tailed N. has similar tail pattern but is much buffier, has different call and prefers swampy grasslands. Dusky N. shows much less white in tail. Gabon and Slender-tailed Nightjars have whitish trailing secondary edges, narrow pale tail sides, and have churring calls. Vocally similar Fiery-necked Nightjar only in lowlands.) **Call** (from high perch) a shrill trilling whistle, *pee-yay-yo, pee-yairrrr or PEE-oo-wiirrrrr*, higher-pitched than call of Fiery-necked. *C. p. guttifer* gives a shorter, shriller *tur-eee-ur kurree*. **Range**: *C. p. poliocephalus* above 1500 m from Mt Elgon, the Cheranganis and Maralal, south to nw. Mara GR, Crater Highlands, Arusha NP and Kilimanjaro, east to Mt Kenya, Nyambeni and Chyulu hills. *C. p. guttifer* between 1100 and 1700 m in Usambara Mts. **Taxonomic Note**: Some authors treat the two forms as separate species.

DONALDSON-SMITH'S NIGHTJAR   *Caprimulgus donaldsoni*   Plate 53

Length 7–7.5″. The *smallest* African nightjar, locally *common in dry eastern thorn-scrub and open bush* where its *short whistling call* is a frequent sound on moonlit nights. Roosts under shrub during the day. In flight, both sexes show small white or whitish patch near wing tips and at tail corners. *Scapulars boldly edged with bright yellowish buff, wing-coverts and breast marked with pale spots*; crown black-streaked. Common rufous morph *largely cinnamon-rufous to deep russet* with buff spots on wings; tail rufous or grey.

Other birds grey or grey-brown overall, with tawny nuchal collar; central rectrices pale grey with 7–8 *faint* dark bars. Wing 119–147 mm. (Nubian Nightjar is larger and usually much paler, purer grey; scapulars have cinnamon tips instead of long yellow-buff edges. See Slender-tailed Nightjar.) **Call** (from ground) a whistled *pyew-yew-tew* or *tew-wi, piree*, repeated indefinitely. **Range**: Sea level to 1200 m, west to the Horr Valley, Lake Baringo and Loitokitok; in n. Tanzania only in Mkomazi GR and on the Masai Steppe west to Naberera.

NUBIAN NIGHTJAR *Caprimulgus nubicus torridus*   Plate 53

Length 8.25–9″. A beautiful pale nightjar of *dry bush and semi-desert. Crown silvery grey marked rufous and black in centre;* otherwise usually sandy or light silvery grey *with bright rufous-buff nuchal collar,* and *large sandy or rufous-buff spots on wing-coverts. Tail typically silvery grey centrally, with a few narrow blackish bands and vermiculations; sides rufous with dark bands* (but some pale-bodied birds have dark tails with almost no rufous). *Large rufous wing patch* (greater coverts and bases of many remiges) conspicuous when bird flushed during the day; in flight, appears pale buff or rufous with small white tail corners and whitish spots on primaries. Some birds tinged cinnamon-rufous overall, with rufous wing-covert spots. Pale-bodied birds may have dark tails with almost no rufous. A few are browner, almost dusky on throat and breast, but grey-crowned and with large rufous-buff spots above. Wing 140–164 mm. (Paler/greyer extremes of Donaldson-Smith's Nightjar have more *yellowish buff* scapular edges, but are best told by small size. Dusky N. is darker than darkest *nubicus*, and male has larger white tail corners.) **Call** a double *kwua-kwua*, steadily repeated, suggesting distant barking poodle. No Kenyan recordings known; perhaps silent here. **Range/Status**: Non-breeding visitor from Somalia, although a few June–Aug. records from Samburu GR and Ijara suggest some present all year. Ranges up to 1300 m, north and east of the highlands, south through Meru and Tsavo NPs to Lake Jipe, mainly Nov.–March. No Tanzanian records.

FRECKLED NIGHTJAR *Caprimulgus t. tristigma*   Plate 54

Length 9–10″. A *thickset, dark* nightjar of *rocky places,* with a distinctive yelping call; roosts on rocks by day, often exposed. *Almost uniformly blackish grey above with fine pale speckling;* few coarse markings and no contrasting nuchal collar; appears plain above except at close range. Head noticeably large; white throat patches prominent in **male**, which in flight shows small white tail corners and white spot on outer 3–4 primaries. **Female** lacks white tail spots. Wing 184–205 mm. (Plain Nightjar is smaller, paler, and has churring call. Star-spotted Nightjar also paler.) **Call** a 2–3-note *OW-wow* or *ow-WOW-WOW,* repeated; also an irregular *wuu-wu-wu-wuu,* and a triple *kluk-kluk-kluk* when disturbed. Calls from rock outcrops or from roofs of buildings. **Range**: Local below 2000 m along e. edge of cent. Kenyan highlands south to Tsavo and Taita hills; also common from Tugen Hills and adjacent Kerio Valley north to the Turkwell Gorge and Lokitaung. On kopjes in Serengeti NP, but scarce elsewhere in n. Tanzania.

STAR-SPOTTED NIGHTJAR *Caprimulgus stellatus simplex*   Plate 54

Length 8.75–9″. A *stocky, almost patternless* bird of *arid n. Kenya* where locally common in rock-strewn deserts with areas of bare sand. Plainer than Plain Nightjar, from which readily distinguished by *large white throat patch* and smaller white tail corners; head appears larger, tail shorter than in that species. Rufous, grey, buff or sandy brown, but always with *largely plain back* and *tiny, more or less stellate black spots on crown and scapulars.* (Rufous birds mistaken for Nubian Nightjar, even in the hand, but Nubian has larger spots on crown and conspicuous pale cinnamon spots on scapulars and wing-coverts. Freckled N. is much darker, almost blackish.) In flight, **male** shows small white tail corners, and white spots on outer 3–4 primaries. **Female** differs from female Plain N. in having white, not buff, spots on primaries and tail corners. Wing 151–162 mm; 7th primary about equal to outermost (10th). **Call** a repeat-

ed yelping *pweu, pweu, pweu. . .* (*c*.1.5 notes/sec.); also a guttural *churr-krrk*. **Range**: Northern borders south to Lodwar and Marsabit, casually to Kongelai Escarpment, Lake Baringo, n. Laikipia Plateau and Shaba GR. Some northern records possibly refer to *C. s. stellatus.*

PLAIN NIGHTJAR *Caprimulgus inornatus*   Plate 54

Length 9″. A northern and eastern nightjar of dry bush and shrubby grass-land. *Plain-looking, rather long-tailed and with no white throat patch.* Variable; pale cinnamon, rufous, or grey-brown above and on breast, but delicate pattern constant: fine black speckling (or less often, narrow sparse black streaks) on crown and scapulars; a few small streaks on back and nape; belly finely barred; pale bar on lesser coverts evident on perched bird. In flight, **male** shows very *large white tail corners*, and band of white spots on outer 4 primaries. In **female**, white of wings replaced by buff, and outer rectrices unbarred at tips but with no discrete pale patches. Wing 148–166 mm; outermost primary longer than 7th, the latter much shorter than 8th. (Star-spotted N. is plainer, with much white on throat, less on tail corners. Freckled N. is larger and black-ish. Eurasian N. shows pale wing-bar at rest, but is larger and boldly patterned.) Apparently silent here apart from a low *chuck* when disturbed, except perhaps in extreme nw. Kenya. **Call** on breeding grounds a prolonged rapid churring, recalling Eurasian Nightjar. **Range/status**: Intra-African migrant below 1800 m. Breeds from Sudan east to nw. Somalia, possibly in nw. Kenya. Moves south through n. and e. areas Oct.–Dec., returning Mar.–Apr., through Usambara Mts, coastal and Tsavo areas, west to Olorgesailie.

AFRICAN WHITE-TAILED or NATAL NIGHTJAR *Caprimulgus n. natalensis*
Plate 53

Length 8.5″. A *western* bird of tall wet grasslands, papyrus swamp edges and woodland borders. *Buffy and dark-cheeked,* with *large black spots on scapulars* and *large buff spots on dark brown breast; broad buff collar extends nearly from the whitish throat patch around hindneck; dark lores and auriculars contrast strongly with pale superciliary and moustachial stripes.* In flight, **male** shows broad *white tail sides* and white bar on outer 4–5 primaries. This bar partly buff/pale rufous in **female**, the outer rectrices buff-tipped. In the hand note *large breast spots and unmarked pale buff belly/crissum;* tarsi rather long; wing 145–167 mm. (Male Montane Nightjar of the high-lands, also has white-sided tail, but is a dark dusky bird with plainer head with more contrasting tawny-buff collar restricted to hindneck. Gabon and Slender-tailed Nightjars have much narrower pale tail edges. All differ vocally from *natalensis*.) **Call** (usually from ground), a *long-continued*, monotonous *tsuk-tsuk-tsuk-tsuk. . .* or *chook-chook-chook. .* .; at times a harder emphatic *kew-kew-kew. . .*, and in flight, a tremulous *wuwuwuwuwuwu*. **Range**: Mt Elgon and Trans-Nzoia south through Kakamega, Mumias and Busia districts to Yala Swamp and Lake Kanyaboli; reported once from Lake Baringo.

DUSKY NIGHTJAR *Caprimulgus fraenatus*   Plate 53

Length 8.25–9″. Common in open shrubby habitats (especially those with tall grass or dense herbage) where it roosts on ground. No truly distinctive features, but rather thickset, *dark* grey-brown with a few black streaks above, a *rufous-tawny nuchal collar, bold black and creamy buff markings on scapulars, cream-spotted wing-coverts* and *dark ear-coverts*; heavily *mottled* with black on crown and upper back; narrow white moustachial lines and a large white patch at each side of throat; dusky brown breast finely barred with buff; belly buff with dark barring. In flight, **male** shows white tail corners and white spots on outer 3–4 primaries; **female** paler above, often greyer; spots on primaries smaller, buff or pale tawny; tail corners dirty white. Wing 152–174 mm; outermost (10th) primary about equal to 7th. (Equally dark Montane Nightjar has white or buff tail sides. Eurasian N. is paler, greyer, longer-winged, longer-tailed and with *streaked* crown. Gabon N. has pale-edged tail, pale trailing wing edges and, in male, a white wing-covert bar. Slender-tailed N. shows slightly projecting central rectrices. Fiery-necked N. has rufous-brown cheeks.) **Call** a *steady* rapid churring, mechanical sounding and continuing for 50–60 sec., interrupted at times by a brief low

querk. The churring may begin with a soft *wowka-wowka* or end with *kyow-kyow-kyow.*
Flight note a liquid *quick.* **Range:** From below 650 m to 2000 m on Mt Elgon and Mt
Kenya. Mainly in dry country from Maralal and the Laikipia Plateau south through the
Rift Valley and adjacent highlands to Narok Dist., Amboseli NP and Arusha Dist. west to
Mbulumbulu, east to the Tsavo parks. Formerly at Marsabit, Wajir and Kisumu, but now
seems largely absent from n. and e. Kenya, Lake Victoria basin and coastal areas.

EURASIAN NIGHTJAR *Caprimulgus europaeus*   Plate 54

Length 9.25–10.5". Longer-winged and longer-tailed than most nightjars. Typically roosts in trees. *Dark ear-coverts, blackish 'shoulders' and
pale bar across lesser wing-coverts* often noticeable in perched birds;
crown and back streaked with black, and *no contrasting nuchal collar.*
In flight, male shows white tail corners, and white spots on outer 3–4 primaries; these absent in female. Nominate *europaeus* is brownish grey,
meridionalis more silvery grey, *unwini* distinctly paler, less extensively
black-streaked and with unbarred under tail-coverts, *plumipes* pale cinnamon-buff. In all
races, 7th primary much shorter than outer three (nos. 8–10); wing 178–202 mm. (Dusky
Nightjar has shorter tail, is darker with mottled crown, bold nuchal collar and more white
on primaries; female has buff primary spots.) **Call** a sharp *quoik* or nasal *kweep* in flight;
otherwise silent in Africa. **Range/status:** Palearctic migrant, late Oct.–Nov. and late
March–early April, when widespread to above 2000 m. Locally common in and east of
Rift Valley in autumn, regular near coast in spring.

GABON or MOZAMBIQUE NIGHTJAR *Caprimulgus fossii welwitschii*
Plate 53

Length 8.25–9". Resembles Dusky Nightjar in body colour and pattern,
but **male** has *white bar on lesser coverts* and *white trailing edge to secondaries* obvious in flight, as are the *narrow* white tail sides and corners.
Shares these features with Slender-tailed N. but *central tail feathers do
not extend beyond the others* as in that species; white spots on outer 5
primaries (on 6–7 in Slender-tailed). In **female**, pale areas of wings and
tail are cinnamon-buff. Resting bird appears *sooty brown with tawny
nuchal collar, densely mottled black crown,* broad black-and-buff scapular edging, dark
ear-coverts and white throat patch (sometimes divided). When flushed by day, male's
wings dark except for the whitish bands and rear edges; female shows more cinnamon
in flight feathers, and the pale primary band is half cinnamon (white only on inner webs
of outer 4 feathers). In the hand distinguished from Slender-tailed by *darker and shorter
central rectrices* (brownish grey or grey-brown with *mostly complete broad black bands*)
and at most a rudimentary white/buff spot on 6th primary; wing 149–170 mm, formula
as in Dusky Nightjar. **Call** a prolonged low churring, recalling Dusky Nightjar, but *alter-
nately accelerating and decelerating;* may end with a short hollow *whoop.* Flight call, *a-
whoop-whoop-whoop.* Although vocal in Tanzania, no definite Kenyan records of
singing birds. **Range:** Mainly below 1500 m, usually in areas of moderate rainfall, but
sometimes in places occupied by *C. clarus.* Resident on Pemba Island, and probably
breeds locally in cent. and n. Tanzania; non-breeding visitor to Tsavo area and the coast
north at least to Arabuko–Sokoke Forest and Mida Creek. Specimen records from
Serengeti NP and north to Mara GR, Kilgoris and Kericho. Reports from Olorgesailie,
Kiambu and farther north require confirmation.

✓ SLENDER-TAILED NIGHTJAR *Caprimulgus clarus*   Plate 53

Length 8.5–9.75". *Common* in dry bush, scrub and open country, often
seen hawking insects around safari lodge lights. Sings from ground or
low tree. Slim and long-tailed, the *central rectrices projecting 5–10 mm
beyond the others* in females, up to 25 mm in males, these feathers pale
grey or brownish grey and the *5–7 transverse blackish bands narrow,
incomplete, or obsolete on one web. Plumage otherwise as in Gabon
Nightjar, but paler and often greyer, top of head lighter, more streaked
than mottled.* Wing 133–155 mm, well-developed white or buff spots on 6–7 outer primaries (on 4–5 in Gabon). (Similar female Long-tailed Nightjar is often more rufous, less
dusky, usually longer tailed, its central rectrices with at least 9 bars.) **Call** a churring or

chattering, *continuing for several minutes: chk-chk-chk-chk-chk-chk-chk. . .* or *tu-tu-tu-tu. . ., each note evident* and the call steady except for slight acceleration toward end of series which ends with a soft *kyor-kyor*. Flight call, *wik-wik-wicku-wik-wicku*. **Range**: Widespread below 2000 m except along Ugandan border and in Lake Victoria basin (some early specimens from Kisumu). N. Kenyan birds are the longer-tailed *apatelius*, intergrading north of Equator with southern *C. c. clarus*.

LONG-TAILED NIGHTJAR *Caprimulgus climacurus sclateri*   Plate 54

Length 10.5–15.5″, including *8–10.5″ central rectrices*. Scarce and local in savanna and bushed grassland in nw. Kenya. Resembles Slender-tailed Nightjar except for long tail, although some birds strongly rufous-tinged. **Male** has narrow white tail edges and corners. In flight, long tail projects straight out behind; *white spots on outer 4 primaries only; white trailing edges and wing-bars formed by tips of secondaries and on lesser and middle wing-coverts* respectively. **Female** has shorter tail; pale areas of wing partly buff; wing length 138–160 mm. Birds with tail in moult easily confused with Slender-tailed N. Roosts on ground, but may perch on low tree branches at night. **Call** a steady, low-pitched, rapid churring or purring distinct from that of Slender-tailed and Gabon Nightjars; also a faint *tsip-tsip* and a twangy *chew-chew-chew*. **Range**: Probably resident near Lokichokio; undertakes regular seasonal movements as shown by records south to the Turkwell River and east to Lake Turkana.

PENNANT-WINGED NIGHTJAR *Macrodipteryx vexillarius*   Plate 54

Length 10–12″. Seasonal in bushed and open habitats in and west of the Rift Valley. Impressive **breeding-plumaged male** has *remarkably long inner primaries, the extremely elongated 2nd pair forming pale 'pennants' projecting over twice the bird's total length*; these and broad white wing-bars contrast with largely black flight feathers. **Non-breeding male** (Jan.–Feb.) has short pennants. Plumage generally rich brown above, with black mottling on crown, a tawny nuchal collar, and bold black-and-buff marks on scapulars; also a large white throat patch and distinctive *white belly*. **Female** has *long tail*, noticeably *small head*, no pennants, and *flight feathers are barred black and chestnut*; wings long and pointed. *Neither sex has white in the tail.* Outermost primary longer than adjacent one in male, usually so in female (unique among East African nightjars). Wing of female 177–195 mm. **Juvenile** plainer and more tan above, but with distinctive barred primaries as in adult female. Southbound migrating flocks often including breeding-plumaged males. Foraging begins immediately after sunset, the males flying high and swooping spectacularly. Rests on bare ground and on roads. **Call** a high-pitched bat-like or squeaking, *tseek-tseek-tseek . . .*, but mainly silent away from breeding grounds. (Smaller female Standard-winged Nightjar has wing under 185 mm, and relatively short tail; outermost primary always shorter than 9th.) **Range/Status**: Intra-African passage migrant to and from breeding grounds in the southern tropics. In our region July–early Sept., and Jan.–Feb. Ranges east to Nairobi and the cent. highlands. Scarce in n. Tanzania.

*STANDARD-WINGED NIGHTJAR *Macrodipteryx longipennis*   Plate 54

Length 7.25–8″. Rare in nw. Kenya (displaying males observed at Lokichokio in late March), usually in bushed grassland or savanna. Smaller, darker and shorter-tailed than female Pennant-winged; general colour greyer but pattern similar, with the *flight feathers barred blackish and rich tawny*, tawny nuchal collar, boldly marked scapulars and black-mottled crown; *no white in wings or tail*. **Breeding-plumaged male** has *shafts of 2nd primary extraordinarily elongated, each terminating in a broad flag-like racquet. In flight, these 'standards' appear as separate objects fluttering behind and above the bird.* **Non-breeding male** and **adult female** similar but without standards. **Juvenile** more sandy above, with fewer markings. Wing 158–184 mm, more rounded than in Pennant-winged N., with outermost primary shorter than 9th, 7th much shorter than 8th, and *lacking emargination*. Migrates in loose groups; sometimes singly. Does not fly as early in evening as Pennant-winged. Standards are moulted after arrival in non-breeding quarters. **Call** a high-pitched, strident, orthopteran-like trilling, *seeti-seeti-seeti-seeti. . .* or *tsi-tsi-tsi-tsi. . .*, but silent in non-breeding season. **Range/status**: Intra-African migrant breeding east to n. Uganda and s. Sudan, perhaps nw. Kenya, Jan.–May, moving north after breeding. Vagrant males (in full breeding dress) seen at Lake Baringo (Jan., Nov.) and in Mumias District (Dec.).

SWIFTS, FAMILY APODIDAE

Highly specialised aerial birds with long, slender wings and short square-tipped or forked tails. The head is flattened with large eyes, the bill tiny but the gape wide. All four toes are directed forward, their claws curved and sharp for clinging to vertical surfaces; the tarsi are very short. The plumage is mainly black, grey or brown, frequently offset by a white rump, tail-coverts, throat or belly; the sexes are alike. Juveniles are duller than adults, but of similar pattern. On the wing, swifts superficially resemble swallows, but their distinctive flight is typically fast with stiff wingbeats and much gliding. Most species are gregarious and flocks may produce screaming, rasping, or trilling calls. Swifts spend long periods aloft catching insects, their sole food. Colonial or solitary when breeding, most nest in cliff crevices, buildings, caves or hollow trees, one species on the undersides of palm leaves. Dark-rumped *Apus* swifts cannot always be positively identified in the field.

SABINE'S SPINETAIL *Rhaphidura sabini*   **Plate 57**
Length 3.5–4". A rare *white-bellied* swift associated with west Kenyan forests. *Long white upper tail-coverts cover centre of tail*; rest of upperparts, throat and breast glossy blue-black. Flight fluttery (but less bat-like than that of Böhm's Spinetail.) **Call** a weak, high-pitched twittering *tsu-sit-sit-sit sireeeeeeeeee sit-sit-sit*. **Range:** Kakamega Forest and on Mt Elgon. Few recent records.

MOTTLED SPINETAIL *Telacanthura ussheri stictilaema*   **Plate 57**

Length 5". Resembles Little Swift, but has an inconspicuous *narrow white band across lower belly* near the vent; *throat and breast mottled* dark brown and whitish, and tail square-tipped or slightly rounded (extended spine-like feather shafts not visible in the field). Flight appears more laboured than that of Little Swift, with longer wings but shorter inner secondaries. Uncommon; typically in deciduous bush or woodland with baobab trees, but seasonally higher. Nests in hollow tree or well shaft. **Call** a soft *tt-rrit, tt-rrit*, and *shree-shree-skiii-skirrrrrrrrreeeee* or *chiti-chiti-chiti skirrrrreeeeee*. **Range:** Usually below 1400 m, occasionally up to 2200 m, from coastal lowlands near Tanga inland to the Usambaras and Tarangire NP, along Upper Tana and Athi /Galana river systems to Kibwezi, Kitui, Meru NP and the Nyambenis. Regular near sw. corner of Mt Kenya at Kiganjo and Mountain Lodge, Sept.–Jan.

BÖHM'S SPINETAIL *Neafrapus boehmi sheppardi*   **Plate 57**

Length 3–3.25". A *tiny* white-bellied swift, *appearing tailless* in flight; *broad wings have pointed tips and pinched-in appearance near body*; upperparts black with broad white rump patch; throat, breast and sides brownish grey. *Flight bat-like, slow, fluttery and erratic.* Nests in hollow tree (especially baobab) or well shaft. **Call** a distinctive *sitsitsit-see-tsew* or *sitisitCHE-chew*; sometimes a high-pitched *srree-srree-seeep*. **Range:** Local. Most frequent in coastal lowlands north to the Tana River delta, inland to the Shimba Hills, Usambara Mts, disjunctly to near Kitui and Kibwezi in s. Kenya where alongside the more numerous Mottled Spinetail.

SCARCE SWIFT *Schoutedenapus m. myoptilus*   **Plate 57**

Length 6.5". A small *slim* swift, uniformly grey or brownish except for *slightly paler throat*. Wing length similar to that of Little Swift, but *tail long and deeply forked, pointed when closed, recalling African Palm Swift.* (Other dark-rumped swifts are heavier-bodied with less deeply forked tails, whitish throats.) Typically above highland forest but also over open grassland and bush as low as 1000 m. **Call** a distinctive metallic clicking, *tik, tik, tik . . .* preceding or following a short rapid trill or nasal chitter. **Range:** Common around Mt Kenya, often elsewhere in cent. and w. Kenyan highlands, Arusha NP, Kilimanjaro and West Usambaras. Recorded also in the Ngurumans,

Mara GR, Kakamega, Kapenguria, Laikipia Plateau, Mathews Range, Isiolo, Thika, Nairobi, Tsavo West NP and Mt Kasigau.

AFRICAN PALM SWIFT *Cypsiurus parvus* Plate 57

Length 5.5–6″. A *slender plain brownish grey* swift with a very *long pointed tail (deeply forked when spread)* and *narrow pointed wings*; throat not distinctly paler than body. Plumage has faint greenish gloss, slightly more intense in western *C. p. myochrous.* Forages low, often around palm trees. Nests on underside of palm or *Dracaena* leaf. Flight graceful and darting, with quick wingbeats and less gliding than most swifts. **Call** a thin high-pitched twittering scream, *skiiirrrrrrrrrr.* **Range:** Mainly below 1400 m, but breeds locally up to 1800 m. *C. p. laemostigma* common in coastal lowlands, inland to 36° E. *C. p. myochrous* in w. Kenya and adjacent n. Tanzania.

EURASIAN or COMMON SWIFT *Apus apus* Plate 57

Length 6.25–7″. Sooty black (*A. a. apus*) or paler sooty brown (*A. a. pekinensis*) with noticeable whitish throat, more prominent in *pekinensis. Wings almost uniform in colour with upper back,* the inner feathers *not* forming a contrasting paler patch. **Juvenile** has pale forehead and whitish lores, anterior to the black pre-orbital spot, merging with white throat to impart pale-faced appearance; body feathers more distinctly pale-margined than in adult. In the hand, distinguished from the following 3 swifts by 10th (outermost) primary being distinctly shorter than 9th instead of nearly equal. Largely or entirely silent in East Africa. (Similar African Black Swift has more blackish body contrasting above with paler secondaries/greater coverts. Nyanza S., also pale on innerwing area, is smaller, browner and has weaker flight. Mottled Swift is larger, browner, mottled below with less distinct pale throat. At coast see Forbes-Watson's Swift.) **Range/status:** Palearctic migrant, common in w. Kenya Sep.–Nov.; in Tsavo area and coastal lowlands, Nov.–Dec. (mostly *pekinensis*). Present Dec.–Feb. over Mara/Serengeti grasslands, and in wetter years from Tsavo and Kibwezi south to Moshi. Moves northward in March–April.

AFRICAN BLACK SWIFT *Apus barbatus roehli* Plate 57

Length 6.25–7″. *Blackish-bodied* with whitish throat as in Eurasian Swift. Resembles that species in size and build, but *dark body contrasts above with paler secondaries and greater coverts* when viewed under favourable conditions. Forehead always dark, without pale-fronted appearance of juvenile Eurasian Swift (from which distinguished in the hand by outer 2 primaries being of equal length.) Tail fork pronounced but more shallow than in Eurasian. (Nyanza Swift shows similar pale secondaries, but is somewhat smaller and sooty brown, not blackish; whitish throat less prominent.) Often in flocks of 100 or more around rock outcrops and over farmland or highland forest. Nests and roosts in cliff crevices and tree cavities. **Call** a shrill twittering scream from displaying flocks. **Range:** Local in w. Kenyan highlands, breeding mainly between 1600 and 2400 m, from Mt Elgon and the Cheranganis south to Trans-Mara area and Mara GR; also in Taita Hills, Arusha NP, North Pare and Usambara mts. Has been collected at Isiolo.

NYANZA SWIFT *Apus niansae* Plate 57

Length 5.5–6″. A distinctly *brown* swift with less contrasting *dull whitish chin and throat* than in slightly larger African Black Swift, but like that species *shows contrast between body and paler secondaries from above.* Smaller *A. n. somalicus* is paler and greyer brown, quite like extralimital Pallid Swift, *Apus pallidus,* which it further resembles in its large whitish throat patch. Breeds colonially in cliffs, rarely in buildings. Noisy at breeding sites. May flock with other swifts. (African Black and nominate Eurasian Swifts are darker with more prominent whitish throats. *A. apus pekinensis,* most likely in and near coastal lowlands, is paler brown. Mottled Swift is much larger, longer tailed and lacks dorsal body/innerwing contrast of Nyanza.) **Call** a descending twittering scream, reedy and strident, *zhiiiiiiiuuuuuuu* or *riiiiieeeeeee.* **Range:** *A. n. niansae* in w. and cent. Kenya; abundant in Rift Valley highlands and Arusha NP. Breeds in large

numbers (alongside Mottled Swift) in Hell's Gate NP near Naivasha. A specimen of ne. African *somalicus* has been collected near Mt Kenya, and periodic sight records of white-throated pale swifts from Mt Kenya, Meru and Embu districts may refer to this form and/or to *A. pallidus*; their identity remains questionable without specimens. (*A. p. brehmorum* has been taken at Moroto, Uganda, near the Kenyan border.)

FORBES-WATSON'S SWIFT *Apus berliozi bensoni*   Plate 57

Length 6.25–6.75″. A sooty brown *coastal* swift with well-forked tail. Often in silent flocks over or near coastal forest. *Large white throat patch* prominent, as is *whitish fore-head* of some birds. Others lack pale frontal feather tips and are grey-brown to the bill, although black pre-orbital spot always contrasts with pale sides of face and white throat. (Immature Eurasian Swift can appear equally pale-faced.) Generally paler than adult nominate Eurasian but nearly identical to *A. a. pekinensis* which is seasonally common along coast. **Call** a repeated metallic buzzy *dzhhh, dzhhh. . .*, given by birds *probably* of this species flying toward presumed roosts on offshore islands; (these calls distinct from known vocalizations of similar East African swifts). Also said to have a strident chittering scream, shorter and less shrill than that of Eurasian Swift. **Range/status**: Breeds in sea caves in se. Somalia. Scarce coastal migrant, Oct.–Feb. (specimens 6 Dec.–26 Jan.); recorded over Arabuko–Sokoke and Gedi forests, Kilifi, Diani, Gazi and Shimba Hills; probable at Mida Creek, Nov.–Dec.

√ MOTTLED SWIFT *Apus a. aequatorialis*   Plate 57

Length 8″. A fairly common, long-winged and long-tailed swift. *Mottling on underparts* visible at close range. At a distance appears grey-brown with an indistinct whitish throat patch; somewhat paler than smaller Nyanza and African Black Swifts with which it often associates, but upper wing surface uniform with back. Large size obvious when with other swifts, but can appear deceptively small if alone. Vocal around nesting/roosting sites on cliffs and rocky crags. Wanders widely over open country, frequently following rainstorms. **Calls** rather low-pitched, rapid and shrill, *tsirrrrrrrrrrrrrrr, tsit-tsit-tsit,* and *skwi-skwi-skwi-skwi skwirrrrrrrrrrrrrrrrr,* or *skiree-skiree chk-skirree-tsit.* **Range**: Widespread up to 3000 m or higher. Many breed in Hell's Gate NP alongside Nyanza Swift.

WHITE-RUMPED SWIFT *Apus caffer*   Plate 57

Length 5.5–6″. *Slim* and black, with contrasting *white throat* and *narrow U-shaped whitish rump* patch; *slender tail deeply forked* when feathers spread, but usually closed and *appearing pointed*; wings narrow and pointed, the secondaries with narrow whitish tips and edges. (Horus and Little Swifts are stockier and have broader white rump band; tail of Horus more shallowly forked, that of Little Swift short and square-tipped.) Typically uses old nests of Red-rumped and Striped Swallows under bridges or eaves, but may build its own in rock crevice or hollow tree. **Call** a short chatter, each note distinct, *chree-chree-chree-chree-chree*; near nest gives a longer trill beginning with several separated *tsip* notes. **Range**: Closely parallels that of Red-rumped Swallow. Widespread from the coast to over 2500 m, except in arid n. and ne. Kenya.

HORUS SWIFT *Apus h. horus*   Plate 57

Length 5–6″. A *stocky* black swift with broad *whitish band on rump* and *whitish throat patch* extending onto breast; tail distinctively shaped, the outer feathers somewhat bowed and not long-attenuated, the fork shallow. (White-rumped Swift is slimmer with deeply forked tail and narrow white rump band. Little Swift has square-tipped tail.) Nests and roosts in earth banks, using tunnels vacated by bee-eaters, kingfishers or martins. Forages over lakeshores and open country. **Call** a buzzy or reeling *rrrrreeeeeeeeee-ew*, lower-pitched than that of White-rumped Swift. **Range/status**: Breeding visitor (Mar.–Sept.) between 1600 and 2000 m in cent. Rift Valley and in Tanzanian border areas from Lake Natron to Kilimanjaro. Wanders north to Horr Valley, east to Tsavo and Taita Hills (Oct.–Dec.). Breeding range closely parallels that of White-fronted Bee-eater.

LITTLE SWIFT *Apus a. affinis*   Plate 57

Length 5–5.5". The common white-rumped swift of towns and villages. *Stocky,* with a *short, square-tipped tail,* pale forehead and narrow whitish line above black lores. Largely blackish except for *white throat* and *square white rump patch which extends down onto flanks.* Nests colonially under eaves of buildings or bridges and on cliff faces. (White-rumped and Horus Swifts have forked tails. Mottled Spinetail has darker mottled throat, white band on lower belly, is somewhat longer-winged but with shorter secondaries.) **Call** a shrill chittering trill, *tsitsitsitsitsitsitsi. . .,* or *si-si-tsiti-tsireeeeeeeeeeeeee.* **Range**: Widespread from sea level up to 3000 m except in arid areas.

ALPINE SWIFT *Apus melba africanus*   Plate 57

Length 8.5". A *large, high-flying* swift, dark brown above with white underparts crossed by a *broad brown breast band*; tail well forked. Nests in colonies on high crags. **Call** a strident rising and falling scream. **Range**: To above 4000 m on the higher mountains (Elgon, Kenya, Meru and Kilimanjaro), but wanders with Mottled and Scarce Swifts as far afield as Mt Marsabit, Mara GR, Serengeti, Tarangire, Amboseli, Tsavo area, Arabuko–Sokoke Forest and other coastal areas near Malindi.

MOUSEBIRDS, FAMILY COLIIDAE

Short-billed, crested birds with long, stiff graduated tails. The common name stems from their habit of scampering mouse-like along branches; they climb well, using bill and feet, and they frequently hang upside-down or assume other odd positions. The tarsi are short and thick, the sharp-clawed toes strong and the outer ones reversible. The birds roost communally, tightly bunched together, becoming torpid on cold nights. Flight is straight, with whirring beats of the short wings, alternating with long glides. Gregarious except when breeding.

SPECKLED MOUSEBIRD *Colius striatus*   Plate 58

Length 12–14". The familiar *brown* mousebird of gardens, cultivation and various open wooded habitats. The *brown crest* and contrasting whitish or silvery grey cheeks are distinctive. Fine barring on neck, throat and breast is more conspicuous in paler coastal birds. Bill black above with blue spot on culmen, pinkish below, sometimes black-tipped. Iris colour varies from brown in *mombassicus* to greenish yellow, white or pale brown in interior races. **Juvenile** has short crest, bare blackish nape and a narrow pale stripe down centre of back. (White-headed Mousebird has white median back stripe, but is greyish, not brown, above, has white on crown and a paler bill.) Usual contact **call** a soft *siu-siu;* also a *zik-zik* of alarm and a thin *seeeeeeeet, tseet chireeeeeet.* **Range**: Sea level to above 2500 m. Interior *C. s. kikuyuensis* in high-rainfall areas from Marsabit south to the Chyulu Hills and adjacent n. Tanzania; *mombassicus* in coastal Kenya, interior ne. Tanzania and Usambara Mts; *affinis* in coastal Tanzania; *cinerascens* in n. Tanzanian areas not occupied by other subspecies.

WHITE-HEADED MOUSEBIRD *Colius leucocephalus*   Plate 58

Length 12". A *broad-tailed, greyish* mousebird of dry bush country. Note the *white crown, crest and cheeks,* and bare dark orbital skin; *neck, back and breast narrowly barred black and white*; white streak on the grey back conspicuous when not concealed by the wings; underparts tawny buff, tinged vinaceous on breast and flanks; bill pale bluish grey or bluish white above, pale buff below. Northern *C. l. turneri* is darker and more heavily barred on hindneck. **Juvenile** has buff throat and breast. (Speckled Mousebird is browner and darker-billed, lacks white on crown.) **Call** a dry squeaky chatter, *tsik chiki-chiki,* a simpler *tsip-sip-sip. . .* or *tsik-tsik-tsik*; also a descending *tsip-tsip tseeeeeeeer.* **Range:** *C. l. leucocephalus* local below 1400 m from Mkomazi GR and Tsavo West NP at Maktau, east to Voi and Maungu, northwest to Kimana, Selengai and w. Amboseli NP; also on Tiva and Tana rivers north to Bura and possibly Garissa. *C. l. turneri* from the Horr Valley and Marsabit south to Samburu and Shaba GRs and Isiolo.

√ **BLUE-NAPED MOUSEBIRD** *Urocolius macrourus* **Plate 58**

Length 13–14″. A *slender-tailed, ash-grey* mousebird, common in dry country. *Crested head, turquoise-blue nape patch* and black-and-red bill characterize adults. *U. m. abyssinicus* has more white on throat and a darker breast than southern birds. **Juvenile** lacks blue on nape, has pink facial skin and greenish bill. Usually in small groups, and often far-flying (unlike Speckled Mousebird). **Call** a plaintive far-carrying whistle, *peeee, peeeeeeeeeee*; also shorter calls of same quality, *pyee, pyee, pyee. . .* or *pew t'lew*, repeated. **Range**: *U. m. pulcher* widespread up to 1900 m, including coastal areas north of Malindi; *massaicus* in ne. Tanzania, from lowlands around Arusha and Kilimanjaro and the Masai Steppe east to the coast near Tanga; *abyssinicus* along Kenya's northern border east to Moyale.

TROGONS, FAMILY TROGONIDAE

Colourful arboreal forest dwellers with lax plumage, large head, short neck, and long broad tail. The feet are weak with very short tarsi; two toes directed forward, two backward. At the base of the short curved bill are well-developed bristles. Their short rounded wings have strongly curved primaries. Trogons are stolid birds, typically perching upright with hunched posture. As they remain still for extended periods they are easily overlooked despite their bright colours (in males, bright red below, iridescent green above). Taking wing suddenly, they snatch insects from twigs and foliage or in the air. They nest in tree cavities.

NARINA TROGON *Apaloderma narina* **Plate 58**

Length 12″. A brilliant green-and-red forest bird with *underside of tail unmarked white*. **Male** shining green above and to upper breast, otherwise bright red below; wings largely grey; tail dark blue-green with 3 outer pairs of feathers white. Bill largely yellow; small bare patches of postocular, rictal and gular skin yellowish green and bright blue, that above eyes pale blue. Narrow orbital ring blue, greenish on coastal *A. n. littoralis*, which is also bronzier green above and pinkish red below. Long streak formed by white primary bases conspicuous on underside of wing in flight. **Female** brown on face and throat, greyish pink on breast, with red belly and crissum; bare facial skin blue or bronzy blue-green. **Juvenile** duller bronzy green above with large white spots on wings; underparts grey with fine buff barring, the breast more mottled with brown; orbital ring whitish. **Immature** resembles adult female, but has white spots on inner secondaries, and less pink on belly. **Call** somewhat ventriloquial, a soft double hoot, *hroo-HOO* or *oh-COO*, repeated several times, accented second note of each pair usually slightly higher; series begins softly and becomes louder. **Range**: *A. n. narina* in w. and cent. Kenyan highlands from mts Elgon, Kulal, Marsabit and Mathews Range south to Mara GR, the Ngurumans, Kibwezi and Taveta districts, Arusha and Lake Manyara NPs, and west to Serengeti NP (scarce). *A. n. littoralis* along coast, inland to East Usambara Mts, Shimba Hills and lower Tana River.

BAR-TAILED TROGON *Apaloderma vittatum* **Plate 58**

Length 11″. An uncommon highland forest bird. Resembles Narina Trogon, but *underside of tail barred with black*. **Male** also differs in bronzy blue-black head and throat, the patches of bare skin below eyes yellow or orange, one above eyes yellow or grey; sides of breast iridescent violet, blue and blue-green; tail mainly bluish or purplish black above. White streak on underside of primary bases conspicuous in flight. **Female** has brown head and light cinnamon breast. **Juvenile** white-bellied, with pale-tipped wing-coverts and inner secondaries. **Call** higher-pitched and more yelping than that of Narina, *yaow, yow, yow, yow. . .* or *wuk-wuk-wuk-wuk. . .* beginning softly and increasing in volume. Female utters a whining *chee-uu*. **Range**: Above 1600 m in the w. and cent. Kenyan highlands (formerly near Nairobi), and most n. Tanzanian mountains. Typically at higher elevations than Narina Trogon, but the two overlap in Kakamega Forest and Arusha NP.

KINGFISHERS, FAMILY ALCEDINIDAE

Small to medium-sized birds with large heads, long and often heavy pointed bills, short legs and small feet with strongly syndactyl toes. The mainly piscivorous *Alcedo*, *Megaceryle* and *Ceryle* inhabit aquatic environments, but *Ispidina* and *Halcyon* may seek terrestrial prey far from water. Most kingfishers are solitary, perching quietly and scanning the ground or water for long periods, darting down or plunging for prey. Some recent authors split the Alcedinidae into three families.

GREY-HEADED KINGFISHER *Halcyon leucocephala*   Plate 59 ✔

Length 8". A *dry-country* kingfisher with greyish or grey-brown head and *chestnut or pale tawny belly, bright cobalt-blue rump and tail* and *all-red bill*. *H. l. leucocephala* is black-backed, with blue-and-black wings. Blue of wings has strong violet cast in coastal *H. l. hyacinthina*. Migrant *pallidiventris* is pale grey on upper back, and pale tawny on belly. **Juvenile** duller, buff below with grey barring on neck and breast, and dusky red bill. (Brown-hooded Kingfisher has darker head, buffy white belly, pale cinnamon flanks, some streaking on sides.) **Calls** varied, a piping *tieu*, *WEEU-WEEU* chrrtili *weeu-ti-weeu*, a sharp *chirrrr-r-r-r-r*, falling in pitch, and a sharp *TSI-TSI-TSI-TSI*. . ., the notes given in long series, at times alternating with a high wavering twitter; also a clear *tew-uuuuuuuuuu*, and a clear descending *piuu piuu piuu*. . .. **Range**: Widespread resident *H. l. leucocephala* is joined by migrants from the northern tropics, Nov.–April. *H. l. hyacinthina* is an uncommon coastal resident, inland to Tsavo East NP and along the Tana River to Bura. *H. l. pallidiventris* visits from the southern tropics, Apr.–Sept., north to Kisumu, Nandi and Bungoma districts.

BROWN-HOODED KINGFISHER *Halcyon albiventris*   Plate 59 ✔

Length 7.5–8". A *red-billed* kingfisher of eastern woodland and forest edge. Differs from Grey-headed Kingfisher in *pale buffy white belly* and nuchal collar. Head greyish brown, lightly streaked on crown, and with faint whitish superciliary stripes; flanks buff or cinnamon, lightly and narrowly streaked in *H. a. prentissgrayi*; back black in male, sooty brown in female. (Mangrove Kingfisher has blue back.) Coastal *orientalis* paler, almost unstreaked on crown, nearly plain below with a few dark shaft streaks on buffy flanks. **Juvenile** browner above, more streaked below, with dusky scalloping on sides of breast; bill dusky red. **Calls**, a loud strident phrase of 4–5 notes, dropping in pitch, *KIEU*, *KI-ki-ki-ki*; a rapid descending trill, *PI-iiiiiiiirrrrr*, and a more even, drawn-out *pi-ee-ee*, *pi-ee-ee*. . .. **Range**: *H. a. orientalis* on coast, inland along Tana River to Garissa, in Shimba Hills and East Usambaras; *prentissgrayi* in interior e. Kenya and Tanzania south to Arusha, Tarangire and Lake Manyara NPs. Has wandered to Lake Baringo, Laikipia Plateau and Samburu GR.

WOODLAND KINGFISHER *Halcyon senegalensis*   Plate 59

Length 8–8.75". The *bicoloured bill, red above and black below*, separates adults of this woodland species from all other kingfishers in our region except the vagrant Blue-breasted. Azure-blue above, *including scapulars*, with much black on wings; pale grey and white below (breast may have faint greenish blue wash). *H. s. cyanoleuca* has the head pale blue, more like back than in grey-headed *H. s. senegalensis*, and black of eye-ring may extend in a point behind the eye. **Juvenile** has largely dusky bill and dark vermiculations on buffy grey neck and breast. Nests in tree cavities. **Call** a loud staccato note preceding a strident, slightly rising, then descending trill: *KEWK, kirrrr-r-r-r*; initial note may be omitted when birds duet. A short rapid call, *ski-ski-ski-ski*, at times has the notes doubled or tripled, *kiKEE-kiKEE-kikiKEE*, and may continue as an excited twitter. **Range**: *H. s. senegalensis* is west of the Rift Valley, mainly in the Lake Victoria Basin, Mara GR and Serengeti NP; at times alongside *cyanoleuca*, a migrant from the southern tropics, Apr.–Sept., from Lake Manyara and Tarangire NP north to Lake Baringo, Trans-Nzoia and Turkwell River valley.

BLUE-BREASTED KINGFISHER *Halcyon malimbica*   **Illus. opp. Plate 59**
Length 9–9.5″. A rare blue-and-black forest kingfisher much like the preceding species, but noticeably *larger, face and breast distinctly blue*, and *broad scapulars as well as wing-coverts are black* (looks black-backed in side view). The large bill is black below, with maxilla all red or extensively black at tip, at base and along lower edge. Usual **call** suggests Woodland's trill, but is much slower, *kew, kew, kew, ku-ku-ku-ku-ku-ku*. **Status**: Several sight records, 1994–1996, in riverine thickets in Mumias Dist. (habitat now largely destroyed). Kenyan birds doubtless represented the Ugandan race *prenticei*, not recognized by some authors.

MANGROVE KINGFISHER *Halcyon senegaloides*   **Plate 59**

Length 8.5–9″. A red-billed *coastal* kingfisher, resembling sympatric Brown-hooded, but with *stouter bill, grey head* and *pale greyish blue* back. **Juvenile** much duller, washed with yellowish buff from head to breast and sides, which are finely vermiculated and speckled with dusky; bill brownish. **Call** a series of sharp separated notes accelerating into a descending chatter, *KYI, KYI, KYI, ki-kik-ki-kikikikikiki*. **Range**: The coastal strip and offshore islands, north of Tanga, and inland along Tana River to Garsen and Baomo.

✓ **STRIPED KINGFISHER** *Halcyon c. chelicuti*   **Plate 59**

Length 6.5″. A *rather dull streaky* kingfisher of *dry bush and open savanna*. Mostly grey-brown above, but *in flight shows bright blue from lower back to tail*. Top of head buffy grey (male) or brownish (female), streaked with dark brown; black line from eyes around lower nape, bordering whitish sides of head and nuchal collar; underparts whitish, buffier on breast; *sides and flanks streaked with brown*; bill blackish above, orange-red below. **Juvenile** paler, with less blue in wings, crown darker and less streaked; breast feathers dusky-tipped; mandible dull red. **Call** distinctive and far-carrying, *KEW, kerrrrrrrrr*, the trill lower, descending and repeated. **Range**: From sea level to above 2000 m except in dry n. Kenya.

HALF-COLLARED KINGFISHER *Alcedo semitorquata tephria*   **Plate 59**
Length 7–7.5″. Scarce and local in ne. Tanzania, casual in se. Kenya. Bright *cobalt-blue above, rich tawny below*, with a *long black bill*, whitish throat, white patches on sides of neck and diagnostic *blue patch on each side of breast*. **Juvenile** duller below, scaled greyish on breast. (Black-billed juv. Malachite Kingfisher can be mistaken for Half-collared but is much smaller, with brownish cheeks and no blue breast patches.) **Call** a sibilant *tseeep* or *tsip-ip-ip-eep*. Song a very thin *tsip-tsip-tsiueep-tseep,tsiu-tseep-tseeueep-seep*. **Range**: Wooded streams flowing from Mt Kilimanjaro and in East Usambaras. Formerly in Kitovu Forest (Taveta Dist.). Recent records from Tsavo East and Shimba Hills NPs.

SHINING-BLUE KINGFISHER *Alcedo quadribrachys guentheri*   **Plate 59**
Length 6.5″. Vagrant along wooded streams in w. Kenya. Deep blue above, with *centre of back and rump glossy cobalt-blue*; underparts bright chestnut except for whitish throat; patch on side of neck buffy white; *bill black*. (Much smaller juvenile Malachite and African Pygmy Kingfishers also have blackish bills.) **Call** a sharp high *cheet*, given mainly in flight, and a high-pitched *seet-seet-seet-seet*. **Range**: Casual in Busia, Mumias, Nandi, Kakamega and Kapenguria districts (6 records, 1905–1993).

✓ **MALACHITE KINGFISHER** *Alcedo cristata galerita*   **Plate 59**

Length 4.5″. The familiar small waterside kingfisher with a *shaggy crest*. **Adult** blue above, with *bright red bill* and feet; *top of head (down to eyes) turquoise barred with black*; underparts and sides of head orange-rufous; throat and patch on side of neck white. (African Pygmy Kingfisher, usually found away from water, lacks crest, has chestnut between eye and the blue cap and on the hindneck.) **Juvenile** has *blackish bill*, is more greenish blue above and paler below than adult. **Call** a sharp high-pitched *seek*, usually in flight, and a squeaky chattering song, *tsiii-tsi-tswitswitswi tsewi-*

chui-chichi-chui. . ... **Range**: Widespread; from coastal creeks up to 3000 m. Regular at Lake Turkana but otherwise largely absent from n. and ne. Kenya.

AFRICAN PYGMY KINGFISHER *Ispidina picta* Plate 59

Length 4–4.5″. A diminutive, forest or woodland kingfisher resembling Malachite, but *without crest*, and *dark blue cap does not extend down to eyes*. **Adult** has *red bill*, dark blue upperparts; orange-rufous under-parts and face (lilac wash on ear-coverts in *I. p. picta*); throat white. *I. p. natalensis* is paler below, almost white on belly, and has a small blue patch on ear-coverts. **Juvenile** more greenish above and *black-billed*. **Call** a high-pitched *seet*. Song a long twittering, *chewtiCHIchew chewti-CHEEtew skitise-see tseu-tsieeu-chewtitseu* . ... **Range**: *I. p. picta* in w. Kenya north to Pokot District, se. Kenya (including coast), Arusha, Lake Manyara and Serengeti NPs. *I. p. natalensis* on Pemba Island and parts of coastal mainland; also present Apr.–Sept. as a non-breeding migrant from s. Africa on coast north to Malindi and inland to the East Usambaras.

GIANT KINGFISHER *Megaceryle m. maxima* Plate 59 ✓

Length 15–17″. An uncommon *crow-sized* kingfisher, dark-crested with white throat and a *large black bill*. Upperparts dark slate, finely spotted and barred with white. **Male** has *chestnut breast, white belly* and black-and-white-barred flanks. **Female** is *chestnut-bellied* with *densely black-and-white-speckled breast*. **Juvenile** male resembles adult, but has chest-nut on sides and flanks; juv. female has whitish band between breast and belly. *Hunts from perches along wooded rivers and lakes.* **Call** a sharp raucous *kyaahk* or *kahk*, repeated from perch; also *skyak-skyak-skyak-skirrrrrrrr* and a rattling *keriririririri* in flight. **Range**: The w. and cent. Kenyan highlands, Upper Tana and Athi rivers, Hunter's Lodge, Kitovu Forest, wooded streams flowing off Kilimanjaro and Mt Meru, and in the Usambaras. Wanders to the coast, once to Lake Turkana.

PIED KINGFISHER *Ceryle r. rudis* *L. VIC* Plate 59 ✓

Length 9–10″. A *black-and-white* crested kingfisher of lakes, streams and coastal waters. *Habitually hovers.* Crown bordered below by broad white superciliary stripes; ear-coverts black; cheeks and underparts white with 2 black breast bands in male, one partial band in female. **Juvenile** has brown-tinged breast. **Calls**, *tsiree-eee tsiktsiktsik.* . ., a repeated *tsee-ee TSEU*, and *kwik.* . . *kwik.* . .; on take-off, a sharp, *kikety-kick*. **Range**: Widespread below 2300 m. In n. Kenya confined to Lake Turkana and Daua River.

BEE-EATERS, FAMILY MEROPIDAE

Sleek attractive aerial feeders with long pointed wings, slightly decurved bills and small weak feet with syndactyl toes. Their tails are rather long, and in some species the two central rectrices extend well beyond the others. Body plumage is compact, often slightly lustrous, and shades of green predominate in a majority of species. Some are gregarious and highly social. Most larger species are colonial breeders, typically forming flocks and making long foraging flights to hawk insects high in the air. The smaller ones tend to nest in scattered pairs. They usually make only short foraging sallies before returning with prey to a perch. Nesting is in burrows excavated in earth banks or sometimes in almost flat ground.

EURASIAN BEE-EATER *Merops apiaster* Plate 60

Length 10.5–11″. A large greenish blue and rufous-brown bee-eater with a *yellow throat*. In overhead flight, wings appear translucent pale rufous with broad black rear borders. **Spring male** (after Jan.) has *golden-yellow scapulars that form a large V* along the rufous-brown back; rump yel-lowish; tail green, the *central feathers pointed and projecting an inch* beyond the others. In **non-breeding plumage** (Aug.–Oct.) back is green, scapulars greenish blue, and the yellow throat shows only a faint dark

border; central rectrices not greatly elongated. Many early-winter males are intermediate between the two above plumages. **Female** differs from spring male in her paler underparts, greener scapulars, and green feathers mixed in the rufous wing areas. **First-winter** bird generally greenish with rufous-brown crown, pale yellow throat, pale green or buff scapulars, and no projecting central rectrices. (Immature Madagascar Bee-eater without long central rectrices somewhat similar, but has cinnamon-buff throat and no rufous on crown.) High-flying migratory flocks are typically vocal. **Call** a far-carrying liquid *klroop-klroop*, or *chrreep-eep*. **Range/status**: Widespread palearctic passage migrant from sea level to over 2000 m. Common Sept.–Nov., more sporadic Mar.– April. Some winter in w. and cent. Kenya and n. Tanzania.

MADAGASCAR BEE-EATER *Merops s. superciliosus* Plate 60

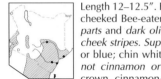

Length 12–12.5". Elegant, slim and long-tailed. Distinguished from Blue-cheeked Bee-eater by duller *olive-green* (not bright grass-green) *upperparts* and *dark olive-brown crown*, *white* (not pale blue) *forehead and cheek stripes. Superciliary stripes usually white* but may be pale yellow or blue; chin whitish, throat dull rufous. *Underside of wings ochreous, not cinnamon or rufous.* **Juvenile** lacks tail streamers, has greenish crown, cinnamon-buff throat and blue-tinged breast merging with pale green belly. Seasonally common in low bush and lightly wooded habitats, often beside water. **Call** a persistent *t'rreeo, t'rreeo* or *krreep, krreep*, sharper than call of Eurasian Bee-eater, but almost identical to that of Blue-cheeked. **Range/status**: Non-breeding migrant from farther south, May–Sept. Also breeds uncommonly and erratically in some coastal areas, e.g. Lamu and Pemba islands. Has bred along Tana River in Meru NP.

BLUE-CHEEKED BEE-EATER *Merops p. persicus* Plate 60

Length 12–12.5". A long-tailed, *bright green* bee-eater with black mask, mostly white forehead, *green crown*, and pale blue or whitish superciliary and cheek stripes *conspicuously brighter than the surrounding green plumage*; *yellow chin* merges with russet throat. Underside of wings *coppery rufous.* **First-winter** bird duller, more olive than adult, sometimes retaining pale-edged juvenile feathers; forehead green, narrowly yellowish at bill; chin pale yellowish buff grading into rufous-buff throat patch. Young resemble adults by mid-winter. (Madagascar Bee-eater has brown crown, white facial stripes and a larger dull rufous throat patch.) **Call** a rolling *prruuik* or *krreep-krreep* recalls Eurasian Bee-eater, but is softer, less melodious, more distinctly bisyllabic. **Range/status**: Regular palearctic migrant, late Oct.–early April, at lakes Victoria, Baringo, Jipe and Manyara, in mangroves on lower Tana River and coastal creeks south to Tanga.

Carmine Bee-eater

CARMINE BEE-EATER *Merops nubicus* Plate 60

Length 13–14". A large, highly gregarious *red-and-blue* bee-eater with long central tail feathers. Northern *M. n. nubicus* has *turquoise-blue head and throat*, the bright forehead and chin separated by a black mask; underparts and back largely pinkish red; rump and all tail-coverts bright pale blue. Vagrant *nubicoides* (considered specifically distinct by some authors) differs in having chin, *throat and cheeks bright pink.* **Juvenile** *nubicus* is brown on nape, more rufous on upper back; scapulars and inner secondaries olive-brown with pale blue edgings; tail dull carmine, tipped with brown; chin and throat blue; breast brown with pinkish feather edges; belly pale buff. **Call** a loud *gra-gra-grra* from perch. In flight, a repeated *cheeo-cheeo-cheeo, chrrip, chrrip,* or *kyee kyeeo*; also a shorter *chrk* or *tewp.* Feeding flocks produce a continuous chatter. **Range**: *M. n. nubicus* breeds erratically in northern border areas, more regularly (?) at Lake Turkana, Mar.–May; elsewhere mainly a non-breeding migrant from the northern tropics, Sept.–Mar., especially at coast where fairly common south to Tanga; occasional in se. Kenya and some cent. Rift Valley localities. *M. n. nubicoides* recorded at Lake Kanyaboli (June 1972) and in Kedong Valley (July 1977).

WHITE-THROATED BEE-EATER *Merops albicollis* Plate 60

Length 12–13". *Slender and long-tailed* with *bold black-and-white head pattern. Black crown, mask and rectangular patch on lower throat* contrast with white forehead, superciliaries and throat. Much of body pale green, almost white on belly; hindneck tawny; back olive-green becoming pale blue on rump and tail; closed wings appear mainly green with ochre-buff flight feathers. **Juvenile** more olive above, with many pale-tipped feathers; chin and throat light yellow; tail olive with short central feathers. Locally common in dry bush and woodland. **Call** a strident *tyrrr-tyrrr,* typically in ringing chorus from a flock (reminiscent of Madagascar Bee-eater); also a longer *pyeep-pyeep, pyueep-pyrrrrrrr.* **Range**: Widespread migrant from the northern tropics, Sept.–April, below 1400 m, including coastal lowlands south to Tanga. Small numbers breed in northernmost Kenya, April–May, and erratically around Lake Magadi and Olorgesailie in the south.

WHITE-FRONTED BEE-EATER *Merops b. bullockoides* Plate 60

Length 8.5–9.5". A colourful bee-eater with a square-tipped tail. Mainly green above; black mask offset by *whitish forehead, white chin and cheeks, and bright red* (very rarely yellow) *throat; all tail-coverts deep blue*; back of head, breast and belly pale cinnamon-buff. **Juvenile** much paler than adult, with little or no red on throat. Locally common in bush and woodland. **Call** a deep, somewhat nasal *gaaaa* or *gharrra,* and a sharp *kwaank* of alarm. **Range**: Local in Kenyan Rift Valley from Mt Suswa north to Menengai; also on lower slopes of Kilimanjaro and Mt Meru. Recorded in Kerio Valley and nw. Mara GR.

BLUE-HEADED BEE-EATER *Merops m. muelleri* Plate 60

Length 7.5". An uncommon, dark-plumaged solitary bee-eater of *west Kenyan forests.* Mainly *deep blue with russet back and scarlet chin* surrounded by black malar areas, sides of neck and lower throat; *forehead pale frosty blue,* darker on crown. **Juvenile** more ochre-brown on back, dusky turquoise below; cheeks to breast dusky; chin bluish with little or no red. **Song** a medley of well-spaced notes, some strident or piercing, others soft and nasal, *cherik, nyaa, sherik SKIEEK-skirk, chrrrr SKERIK.* Calls include a weak *tssip-tssip-tseeseeseesee* and a single thin *tseep* or *tseeup.* **Range**: Kakamega and South Nandi forests. Formerly at Nyarondo, Lerundo and Mt Elgon where no suitable habitat remains.

LITTLE BEE-EATER *Merops pusillus* Plate 60

Length 6". The smallest bee-eater; bright green above with long *black mask bordering the yellow throat.* Triangular *black patch on throat* is narrowly margined above with bright blue, and below by chestnut or cinnamon-brown on breast and belly. Flight feathers rufous with greenish edges; secondaries broadly tipped with black, producing striking flight pattern; *tail cinnamon-rufous with green central feathers and broad black terminal*

391

band. Blue superciliary stripes evident in *M. p. cyanostictus*, barely discernible in *meridionalis*. **Juvenile** *pale greenish below*, with no black throat patch. (See Blue-breasted Bee-eater. Larger Cinnamon-chested Bee-eater occupies different habitat, is darker below, has white cheeks, and a black-and-white-tipped green tail.) **Call** a soft sibilant *tseep* or *teesip*, and a sharper *tsip, tsip, tsip. . .*, alone or with additional notes to form a song: *tsip-tsip-tstip-teesip-siddip-seedle-tsip-tsip-tsee*. **Range:** *M. p. cyanostictus* widespread from sea level to above 2000 m in Kenya, intergrading with mainly Tanzanian *meridionalis* in the w. Kenyan highlands.

BLUE-BREASTED BEE-EATER *Merops variegatus loringi*   Plate 60
Length 6.5″. A small bee-eater of *moist grassland, lakeshores* and papyrus swamp margins in the Lake Victoria basin. Closely resembles the slightly smaller Little Bee-eater, but both adult and juvenile have narrow *whitish cheeks* below the black mask. Adult's *throat patch is dark purplish blue*, not black, and is bordered above with bright blue. **Call** lower-pitched, less sibilant than that of Little Bee-eater, *tseuk, tseuk, tseuk. . .* or a more song-like *tseuk-tseuk-cherrik-chewk*, with or without a terminal trilled *trrrip*. **Range:** Usengi, Yala Swamp and Lake Kanyaboli. Formerly east to Kisumu.

CINNAMON-CHESTED BEE-EATER *Merops oreobates*   Plate 60

Length 8–8.5″. A highland species of more wooded habitats than the smaller and paler Little Bee-eater. Locally common along forest paths, in riverine woods and wooded gardens. *Lacks blue superciliary stripes* present in Kenyan races of Little and Blue-breasted Bee-eaters. **Adult** has *chestnut breast, largely green tail with broad black subterminal band and white tip*; inner webs of most tail feathers faintly edged with dull cinnamon. White posterior cheek patch visible at close range. **Juvenile** bluish green above, with yellow throat and *greenish* breast which has infusion of pale cinnamon; belly and flanks buff, under tail-coverts pale green or greenish buff. **Call** a high *tsip* or *tseeip*, stronger and more persistently uttered than calls of Little Bee-eater. Song, *siddip-siddip, tsip-tse-tsee*. **Range:** Between 1600 and 2300 m or higher in the Kenyan highlands, north to Mt Nyiru and Mt Marsabit, east to Mt Kenya, south to Machakos and Nairobi, Mara GR, Crater Highlands, Lake Manyara and Arusha NPs, Kilimanjaro, Mt Meru, North Pare Mts and West Usambaras.

✓ SWALLOW-TAILED BEE-EATER *Merops h. hirundineus*   Plate 122
Length 8″. An extralimital, green bee-eater with a long, *deeply forked, bluish tail* in all plumages. **Adult** has bright green upperparts, black mask and yellow throat, and pale *green underparts* with narrow blue band on throat. Blackish trailing edge of rufous flight feathers conspicuous in flying bird. **Juvenile** duller, with no dark band on the greenish white throat. **Call** resembles that of Little Bee-eater, but drier and less sibilant. **Range:** Ranges north to Tanga in Tanzania. Old reports of specimens from Vanga and Shimba Hills cannot be verified. The northern race *heuglini* (recorded several times near Kenyan territory in Sudan and Uganda) can be expected as a vagrant in the extreme northwest of our region.

SOMALI BEE-EATER *Merops revoilii*   Plate 60

Length 6–6.5″. An uncommon, solitary *pale* bee-eater of *dry bush and semi-desert scrub*. *Lustrous cobalt-blue lower back, rump and upper tail-coverts* contrast in flight with dull green back; black mask bordered above by narrow blue superciliary stripes; *throat white; breast and belly pale cinnamon-buff*; under tail-coverts light cobalt-blue; flight-feather bases pale cinnamon, giving wings pale rufous appearance in flight. **Juvenile** duller than adult. **Call** an infrequent soft warbling, slightly descending and becoming fainter, *turee-turee-turee-turee-turee*. **Range:** Local in n. and e. Kenya from Lake Turkana and Mandera south to Isiolo area, Meru and the Tsavo NPs.

ROLLERS, FAMILY CORACIIDAE

Robust, upright-perching colourful birds with large heads, strong and rather corvine bills (the nostrils more or less concealed by frontal feathers) and short tarsi. The outer toe is basally united to the middle one and is reversible. Sexes are similar, with much blue, purple, rufous or cinnamon in the plumage. They are somewhat aggressive birds, perching prominently on vantage points in open country from which they either drop on their arthropod and vertebrate prey (*Coracias*) or pursue aerial insects (*Eurystomus*). In flight, rollers are exceptionally agile, and the name derives from their exuberant diving and rolling aerial displays which are accompanied by harsh croaking. They nest in cavities in trees or termitaria.

EURASIAN ROLLER *Coracias g. garrulus*   Plate 61 ✔

Length 12". Stocky, *greenish-blue* and *without long tail feathers*. **Spring adult** has *cinnamon-brown back*, whitish forehead/supraloral areas, bluish purple on bend of wing, lower back and rump; wings flash bright blue and black in flight, the black-tipped blue flight feathers contrasting with turquoise wing-linings below. **Autumn adult** duller with many feathers brown-tipped, the back more rufous. **First-winter** bird browner, pale greenish blue on head and wing-coverts, with little or no purplish on rump or wings, and no black spot on outer tail feathers. Infrequent **call** a croaking *ugrr-ugrr-ugrr . . .*, or a harsh noisy *kaarr* or *aaagh*. **Range/status**: Palearctic migrant, late Oct.–April, common in dry open woodland and bush below 1500 m in e. Kenya and ne. Tanzania where migrating flocks are frequent. Regular on autumn passage in and west of the Rift Valley, and in spring along the coast. The nominate race and the paler *semenowi* both occur.

ABYSSINIAN ROLLER *Coracias abyssinica*   Plate 61

Length 15.5–17" including *long outer tail feathers*. A streamlined roller of bushed grassland and acacia woodland in *dry northern Kenya*. *Bright azure-blue* with whitish face and rufous-brown back. In flight, *purplish blue rump and flight feathers contrast with azure-and-dark blue forewing*. Duller **juvenile** has crown, hindneck and breast tinged olive-brown, and no elongated outer rectrices. (Eurasian Roller can be mistaken for young Abyssinian, but is stockier, duller and has black flight feathers. Lilac-breasted Roller is lilac on lower throat and, usually, on breast.) **Call** a repeated raucous *aaaaarr, aaaaarr. . .* or *sckaaaa, sckaaaa . . .* from perch. In aerial display, a harsh *ga-ga-ga-ga-ga-ga-gaarrrr-GAARRRRRR*, building in volume. **Range**: Local west of Lake Turkana. Wanders Oct.–Mar. south to Kerio Valley, Baringo and Nakuru areas, occasionally to Nyanza, Laikipia Plateau, Samburu and Mara GRs. Sporadic visitor to the Moyale–Ramu–Mandera area of extreme ne. Kenya.

LILAC-BREASTED ROLLER *Coracias caudata*   Plate 61 ✔

Length 12.5–14" including long outer tail feathers. A fairly common, highly colourful roller with *bold white forehead/superciliary area, and white streaks from chin to azure breast*; blue-green on crown and nape, and with *largely lilac throat and breast* in *C. c. caudata*; lilac confined to throat and lower face in *C. c. lorti* which has greenish blue breast (sometimes with central lilac patch); bend of wing dark blue. *Flight feathers brilliant turquoise-azure basally, in flight forming large patch contrasting with dark wing tip*. **Juvenile** much duller, without elongated outer rectrices; crown and nape brownish, forehead/superciliaries buff; throat and breast rufous-tawny with buffy white streaks. **Call** loud and raucous: *keer, ka, kek-ke-ke-kek-keer-keer*, or a repeated guttural *errrack yecck yecck* , sometimes ending with a very loud *KRAAA-KRAAAACK*. **Range**: Widespread below 2000 m. *C. c. caudata* in n. Tanzania, and Kenya north to Pokot and Maralal areas, Northern Uaso Nyiro and Tana rivers; wanders to Lake Turkana. *C. c. lorti* mainly a non-breeding visitor from Somalia, west to Marsabit, south to Meru NP, Garissa, and Garsen, occasionally to the Tsavo parks (Jan.–March).

RUFOUS-CROWNED or PURPLE ROLLER *Coracias n. naevia*   **Plate 61**

Length 13". Robust and strong-billed, with a square-tipped tail; lacks extensively blue body plumage of the previous three species. *Face and underparts purplish brown streaked with white; rufous crown bordered by white superciliary stripes and white nape patch*; upper back olive, lower back lilac, more purple on rump; tail dark purplish blue with greenish central feathers; upperside of wings largely dark blue and purplish brown. **Juvenile** olive-green below with broad white streaks narrowing and more pinkish on throat. (Young Lilac-breasted Roller has rufous-tawny breast, often with some lilac, broader pale streaks on underparts, no white nape patch.) **Call** a repeated guttural *gah* in flight, and a deep nasal *wukhaa* or *ka-karaa*; also a throaty, somewhat bustard-like *guggiow* or *keeoh*, and a rough chuckling *chk-chk-chk-chk-chk.* . .. **Range**: Widespread up to 2000 m or higher. Seasonally numerous in parts of Kenya (Baringo District, Tsavo parks); scarce in much of n.Tanzania.

BROAD-BILLED ROLLER *Eurystomus glaucurus*   **Plate 61**

Length 9.5–10.5". A small dark and compact roller with a *short broad yellow bill*, uncommon and local in woodland, forest edge and open country with tall trees. *Rich cinnamon-brown above with blue rump and tail; underparts deep lilac*; flight feathers and outer wing-coverts mainly deep blue; crissum dark grey-blue in *E. g. glaucurus*, pure blue in other races; *suahelicus* has all upper tail-coverts deep blue; in *afer* the central coverts are brown, the others greenish blue. **Juvenile** dull rufous-brown above with blackish lores; head to breast dull brown, otherwise greenish blue or dull azure below; bill yellowish with brown culmen and tip. Crepuscular, pairs often wheeling around treetops in erratic noisy evening flights. **Call** a deep harsh *kaaar, kyaaar, kyaaaar*, and a chattering *kakakakaka-kaa-kaa-kakaka*. **Range**: *E. g. suahelicus* is a widespread resident from Mt Elgon, the Cheranganis, Samburu, and Tana River southward, but in interior n. Tanzania mainly a breeding migrant, Aug.–March. West African *afer* recorded in Lake Victoria basin; nominate Madagascan *glaucurus* known from Pemba Island, and flocks in w. Kenya July–Sept. may represent this form.

HOOPOE, FAMILY UPUPIDAE

A unique, smartly patterned, crested bird with a very slender long bill with which it probes for insects, mostly as it walks somewhat jerkily on the ground. Its tarsi are short but the toes are relatively long, the third and fourth fused basally. The cavity nest is in a tree, earth bank or wall. Southern races are more richly coloured than those in the north, and females may differ from males in wing pattern. Some authors have considered the African breeding forms as a species separate from *U. epops*, but there are no obvious differences in habits or vocalizations.

✓ HOOPOE *Upupa epops*   **Plate 61**

Length 10–11". Unmistakable, with pinkish rufous, tawny or cinnamon head, neck and underparts, and a *pointed black-tipped crest frequently raised in fan-like fashion*. *Black-and-white wings and tail striking in wavering, erratic, butterfly-like flight*. **Male** *U. e. africana* is more richly coloured than northern birds, and lacks the whitish subterminal band on crest feathers. **Female** is smaller, duller below with whitish abdomen and dusky-streaked flanks. **Juvenile** darker, more earth-brown. In all plumages *africana* has *all-black primaries*; *U. e. epops* is pale pinkish cinnamon, and shows a conspicuous white band across the primaries as do northern tropical *waibeli* and *senegalensis*. The latter has a *pale* tawny body whereas *waibeli* is *rich* tawny, almost as dark below as *africana*. **Call** a low penetrating *hoop-hoop* (suggesting African Cuckoo) or *oo-poo-poo*. **Range/status**: Widespread below 2000 m. *U. e. africana*, breeding north to about 2º N, and is fairly common throughout (numbers may fluctuate seasonally); *waibeli* is a non-breeding migrant (June–Aug.) from the northern tropics south to Nairobi; *senegalensis* is known in extreme ne. Kenya near Moyale and Mandera, and from Lodwar and the Horr Valley. *U. e. epops* is a palearctic migrant (Oct.–Mar.), mainly in dry n. Kenya, but reaching the cent. Rift Valley and rarely n. Tanzania (2 records).

WOOD-HOOPOES AND SCIMITARBILLS, FAMILY PHOENICULIDAE

Slim, small-bodied birds with long slender graduated tails, broad rounded wings, narrow decurved bills and short thick (sometimes partly feathered) tarsi. The plumage is largely iridescent black with green, violet or blue sheens, alike or similar in both sexes. Wood-hoopoes are agile arboreal birds, climbing and clinging to boughs and trunks, often hanging upside-down. The tail may be used as a brace, as in woodpeckers, but the unspecialized rectrices become badly worn as a consequence. All species feed mainly by extracting arthropods from bark crevices or decaying wood. They nest in tree cavities, and some breed cooperatively. The larger *Phoeniculus* species travel in small noisy groups, moving from tree to tree with floppy bounding flight, 'see-sawing' back and forth on alighting and calling excitedly. The smaller scimitarbills (*Rhinopomastus*) are quieter and less gregarious.

WHITE-HEADED WOOD-HOOPOE *Phoeniculus bollei jacksoni*   Plate 62

Length 12–14″. The only wood-hoopoe in Kenyan *highland forest* where fairly common. Iridescent green with an individually variable *whitish head* (buff on crown), blue-glossed wings, and long blue and purple tail; no white in wings or tail; bill and feet red. **Juvenile** lacks white on head, is duller overall, with *black bill*. (Juveniles of related species are also dark-billed but do not inhabit highland forest. Pale-headed morph of Forest Wood-hoopoe, probably extirpated from Kenya, has shorter straighter bill.) **Call** a prolonged, rippling chuckling chatter, higher-pitched than similar call of Green Wood-hoopoe, *shk-chk chickchickichichichichi-ch-ch-ch-ch*, often by several birds together; also a descending trilled *chirrrrrrrrrrrrrrrr*. Contact call a soft mellow *krrr*. **Range**: Mainly between 2000 and 3000 m, from Mt Elgon and Maralal south to the Kakamega and Mau forests, Ngong Hills (formerly), nw Mara GR and Nguruman Hills. In n. Tanzania only at Loliondo.

FOREST WOOD-HOOPOE *Phoeniculus castaneiceps brunneiceps*   Plate 62

Length 10″. A small, polymorphic central African species doubtless now extirpated from w. Kenya. Iridescent blue-green above with dark blue wings and violet tail; no white in wings or tail; bill grey, black at base, yellow along commissure. Head of **male** variable: *light chestnut-brown, buffy white, pale brown or greenish black;* **female** always brown-headed. **Juvenile** shorter-billed, duller, with dark brown head. **Call** a plaintive yelping *ueek ueek ueek. . .*, the quality recalling that of gull or African Fish Eagle. A rapid, high-pitched twittering chatter, given by one or more birds, suggests White-headed Wood-hoopoe. **Range**: Formerly along Sio River, Mumias District (and also known from Ugandan side of Mt Elgon). Extensive deforestation in w. Kenya precludes any likelihood of its return.

GREEN WOOD-HOOPOE *Phoeniculus purpureus*   Plate 62 ✓

Length 13–14.5″. The commonest wood-hoopoe, typical of acacia woodland. Despite not always appearing green (often blue and purple in the shade), *P. p. marwitzi* is *iridescent green on neck, back, throat and breast* (throat tinged blue or violet in some birds), blue/violet-blue on wings with some white on primary coverts and *broad white bar across primaries conspicuous in flight;* tail violet, several feathers with large white spot near tip; *bill and feet typically bright red,* but mandible and culmen may be black in shorter- and straighter-billed female. Easily mistaken for Violet Wood-hoopoe is *P. p. niloticus,* larger-billed, darker and more purplish overall than *marwitzi*, with crown, nape and back deeper violet-blue, tinged green; wings violet-blue, *inner secondaries purple* (not blue), *throat violet* and breast blue. **Juvenile** dull black with brownish chin and throat, *short black bill and black feet* becoming red in first year. (Violet Wood-hoopoe, not known west of the Rift Valley, distinguished *with care* by mostly violet-blue iridescence on head, back and breast with *only chin and throat green*. Black-billed Wood-hoopoe has largely black bill, often red near base below. All young wood-hoopoes have blackish bills, shorter and straighter than in adults.) **Call** a repeated chuckling, usually with one bird beginning with slow *wuk. . .wuk . .*, then several call together, the loud chattering chorus accelerating, and the pitch rising and falling: *whuh,*

wuk, wuk-ukuk, ukchuk-chuck-chukchukchukch-ch-ch-ch. Other notes a loud *kuk* of alarm, a braying *waaa* and a short *uk*. **Range**: *P. p. marwitzi* widespread below 2800 m, north to Mt Elgon, Laikipia Plateau, Mathews Range, Northern Uaso Nyiro and Tana rivers. Replaced by *P. p. niloticus* in nw. Kenya south to lakes Baringo and Bogoria, and by *P. somaliensis* in the northeast.

BLACK-BILLED WOOD-HOOPOE *Phoeniculus somaliensis*   Plate 62

Length 13–14". Known with certainty only in far ne. Kenya where fairly common in bush and riparian woodland. Resembles Green Wood-hoopoe in appearance and voice, but *bill black, sometimes red at base, more slender and more strongly decurved; iridescence more blue, less violet.* In *P. s. somaliensis,* crown and nape glossed with blue, back and breast dark violet-blue, wings green or blue-green, chin blue with turquoise gloss, tail violet with white subterminal spots on most feathers, and feet red. Ethiopian *P. s. neglectus* is slighty greener on head and upper back, with lower back brighter violet, also heavier billed than nominate race. **Juvenile** *neglectus* is dull black, with blue or greenish blue wash above, tawny buff feather edges on chin and throat, blue or violet wash on black lower throat and breast; wings and tail as in adult except for faint white primary tips; bill and feet blackish. (Green and Violet Wood-hoopoes usually have red or largely red bills but these can be black with red base in young Green. *P. p. marwitzi* mainly green-glossed on body, violet on tail; *P. p. niloticus* violet on inner wing feathers, throat and tail. Violet W. is more uniformly purplish or violet-blue.) **Range**: *P. s. somaliensis* in ne. Kenya west at least to Lodwar, but w. and s. limits not clearly defined. Reports that *P. p. niloticus* and *P. s. neglectus* are sympatric around Lake Turkana require substantiation.

VIOLET WOOD-HOOPOE *Phoeniculus damarensis granti*   Plate 62

Length 14–15". In and near dry *riverine woodlands east of the Rift Valley*; local and uncommon, often in association with doum palms. Closely resembles Green Wood-hoopoe (especially race *niloticus*) in size, appearance and habits, but *purplish or violet-blue on crown, nape, back, wings (often more coppery purple), breast and tail; lower throat green*; tail purplish blue; bill red, sometimes black at base; feet red. **Juvenile** duller, sooty black with buff-streaked chin and throat; bill blackish, almost straight, shorter than in adult, gradually becoming red and curved. (Race *marwitzi* of Green W. has green neck, back and breast; more violet northwestern *P. p. niloticus* often misidentified as *granti*. Black-billed W. has largely black bill; iridescence more blue and violet-blue. Note ranges.) **Call** resembles that of Green W. but somewhat louder and harsher. **Range**: Mainly below 1000 m. Specimens from Taveta, both Tsavo parks, Kibwezi, Kitui, Meru NP, the Tana, Athi–Galana–Tiva and Northern Uaso Nyiro rivers. Irregular in many localities. Northern limits unclear owing to frequent confusion with other species.

COMMON SCIMITARBILL *Rhinopomastus cyanomelas schalowi*   Plate 62

Length 11–12". A small wood-hoopoe with a *strongly decurved black bill* and *black feet.* Fairly common, usually alone or in pairs, in *moist savanna,* tall leafy bush and open woodland. Plumage blackish with violet-blue gloss; *white bar across primaries* and *white subterminal spots on outer tail* obvious in flight. **Female** duller below than male. **Juvenile** resembles adult but bill is shorter and straighter. (Juvenile Green W. is larger with more pointed tail, straighter bill and some buff on throat; bill and feet show some red except in very young birds.) Usual advertising **call** a mournful *woui* or *poui* given in groups of 2–7 notes for an extended period, the groups separated by intervals of a few seconds. Also gives a faster *woueek-week-week-weeek* and a descending *kui-kui-ker-ker-ker-ker-ker*. **Range**: Widespread from n. Tanzania north to Laikipia Plateau, the Cheranganis, Ndotos and Tana River; also in coastal woods north to the Somali border. (**Black Scimitarbill**, *R. aterrimus*, has been attributed to Kenya by some authors. There is no record from our region, although *R. a. notatus* could extend across the border from Ethiopia. It has a *shorter, less strongly curved dark bill, a short and only slightly graduated tail* with white spots on tips of the outer feathers, and a broad

white bar on the primaries. Its calls are a plaintive mournful *wuoi wuoi wuoi wuoi*, suggestive of *R. cyanomelas*, and *week-week-week* . . . recalling Forest Wood-hoopoe.)

ABYSSINIAN SCIMITARBILL *Rhinopomastus minor cabanisi*   **Plate 62**

Length 9–9.5″. A small *dry-country* scimitarbill with *bright orange, strongly decurved bill*, and *no white in wings or tail*. Black plumage is glossed dull violet above; tail bluer, somewhat rounded, shorter than in *R. cyanomelas*. **Juvenile** duller than adult, with dusky bill. **Call** a chattering *keree-keree-keree-keree-keree*. . ., each note rising then falling in pitch; also a loud yelping *kwee-u* or *peu*, repeated up to 15 times and varying slightly in pitch. **Range**: Widespread below 1400 m, except in higher-rainfall areas.

HORNBILLS, FAMILY BUCEROTIDAE

Medium-sized to large, mostly short-legged birds, noted for their large ridged or casqued bills, sometimes of remarkable shape. Plumage is basically black and white, but bill and bare skin on face and throat may be brightly coloured. Several species exhibit facial and gular wattles, and all have long eyelashes. The wings are rather short, the tail long. Flight is bouyant, with repeated flapping and gliding, undulating in the smaller *Tockus* species, and often distinctly audible, especially in the large *Bycanistes*. Most *Tockus* have simple monotonous clucking or piping calls; the braying or bleating of *Bycanistes* is exceptionally loud. Typically, after mating, the female seals herself into the nest cavity (in tree or cliff) with mud. The entrance hole is reduced to a small slit through which the male feeds his mate and their young for many weeks. The female emerges first, leaving the young to re-seal themselves in with excrement until ready to leave. The ground hornbills (*Bucorvus*), sometimes treated as a separate family, do not seal the nest-cavity entrance, and *B. leadbeateri* is a cooperative breeder; the bare throat is inflatable owing to its underlying air sac.

SOUTHERN GROUND HORNBILL *Bucorvus leadbeateri*   **Plate 30**

Length 38–40″. A massive-billed, *turkey-sized* terrestrial bird, *mainly black*, but *white primaries* conspicuous in flight; *bright red bare skin* around eyes and on neck where usually somewhat inflated; eyes pale yellow; bill black with small basal casque. Female smaller than male, with small violet-blue patch on chin and upper throat. **Juvenile** sooty brown, with smaller and greyer bill and brownish yellow facial skin. Pairs or small groups forage in open grassland and savanna. **Call** a deep resonant *ooom, ooom, ooo-ooom*, or *oomp-oomp-oomp*; sometimes a lion-like grunting, *uh-uh-uh*, or a single *ugh*. Often calls just before dawn, the sound far-carrying. **Range**: Local, from interior n. Tanzania north to Tsavo parks, Nairobi NP, cent. Rift Valley, Mt Elgon and Kapenguria. (Recent agricultural development in Kenyan highlands has severely reduced numbers.)

ABYSSINIAN GROUND HORNBILL *Bucorvus abyssinicus*   **Plate 30**

Length 40–43″. **Male** differs from the preceding species in having a yellow patch at the base of the maxilla, an *open-ended cylindrical casque*, and *blue* skin around eyes and on throat; skin on lower neck red. **Female** smaller, and all *bare skin dark blue*. **Juvenile** dark sooty brown with rudimentary casque and bluish grey skin. **Call** a series of deep booming grunts, *uuh, uh-uh-uh* and *who-OOru OO-ru*, slightly higher-pitched than call of Southern Ground Hornbill; suggests grunt of leopard. **Range**: Scarce local resident, mainly below 1000 m, in nw. Kenya south to the Kerio Valley and Baringo District and east to Lake Turkana. Generally in drier areas, with poorer grass cover, than those inhabited by Southern Ground Hornbill.

RED-BILLED HORNBILL *Tockus e. erythrorhynchus*   **Plate 63** ✓

Length 16–20″. A common, small 'black-and-white' hornbill with a *slender orange-red bill*. Blackish brown above with *white streak down centre of back*; crown dark grey, bordered by white superciliary stripes; *wing-coverts white-spotted*; central tail feathers black, outermost pair white, others black and white; bill black at base below in male, sometimes in female; orbital skin pale pink. Most birds are brown-eyed, but those in Turkana (and some in other northern areas) have yellow eyes. **Juvenile** has smaller duller bill and buffy white wing spots. **Call** a long series of similar notes, faint at first, becoming louder and more run together: *uk. . .uk. . .uk, wuck, wuck, wuck-wuck-wuck-WUCK-WUCK-WUCK-WUCK-WUCK, uhWUK, WUK-WUK-uhWUK-uhWUK. . .;* or *wuk-wuk-wuk-kaWUKwa-kaWUKa-wuka-wuka. . .,* higher-pitched than similar calls of related *Tockus* species. Pairs often duet. **Range**: Widespread in dry bush below 1400 m; absent from coastal lowlands and Lake Victoria basin.

EASTERN YELLOW-BILLED HORNBILL *Tockus flavirostris*   Plate 63

Length 20". Black-and-white with a *heavy yellow bill*, unique among East African hornbills. Pattern recalls Red-billed Hornbill, but tail has distinctive black subterminal band; bare throat patches pink in male, black in female. **Juvenile** has smaller, dull yellowish bill mottled with dusky, and upper breast streaked with dark grey; eyes dull grey, not yellow as in adults. Uncommon; most numerous among *Commiphora* and baobabs. **Call** deeper than that of Red-billed H., a long-continuing series of clucks, increasing in intensity toward end, *wuk-wuk-wuk-wuk-wuk-wuk-wuk-wuk-wuk-wuk-wuk-wuk-WUK-WUK-WUK-WUK-WUK. . ..* **Range**: N. Kenyan borders south to Lake Baringo in the west; in the east to Mkomazi GR and adjacent edge of the Masai Steppe; also north of Arusha and near Namanga and Longido.

VON DER DECKEN'S HORNBILL *Tockus deckeni*   Plate 63

Length 18.5". A small black-and-white hornbill with a *heavy bill (two-toned red and ivory with black tip in* **male**, *entirely black in* **female***)* and *no white spots on wing-coverts* (but has small white patch on central secondaries, conspicuous in flight). Bare orbital skin black, joining dusky-streaked ear-coverts; throat patches flesh-pink. (Adult Jackson's Hornbill has white spots on wing-coverts.) **Juvenile** resembles female with dark horn-coloured bill, but has small white spots on wing-coverts. Fairly common in thorn-bush and savanna. **Call** a continuous low even *cukcukcuk-cukcukcukcuk. . .,* or *whuh-whuh-whuh. . .* with little variation. **Range**: Widespread except in nw. Kenya (where replaced by Jackson's Hornbill), coastal lowlands south of Malindi, Lake Victoria basin and areas above 1600 m.

JACKSON'S HORNBILL *Tockus jacksoni*   Plate 63

Length 20". A *northwestern* hornbill, resembling Von der Decken's (the two considered conspecific by some), but differing in its *white-spotted wing-coverts*, and bill of **male** more *orange-red with creamy yellow tip.* **Juvenile** resembles adult but bill black, as in **female**, or mixed with dull orange-red. **Call** a monotonous series of notes on one pitch, suggesting Von der Decken's but higher, louder, more hollow and often slower, each note more distinct, *wek-wek-wek-wek-wek. . .,* or *wukk, wukk, wukk . . ..* **Range**: West of Lake Turkana, south to Nasolot NR, Kerio Valley and Baringo Dist. Status on e. side of Lake Turkana unclear; no known overlap with Von der Decken's, but specimens of both collected at the base of Mt Nyiru.

HEMPRICH'S HORNBILL *Tockus hemprichii*   Plate 63

Length 22–23". A rather large *northern* hornbill of dry rocky terrain. Dark brown with a *dull reddish bill* and *much white in the tail;* head washed with grey; wing-coverts and secondaries narrowly white-edged; bare orbital and gular skin black in male; *eyes brown;* female smaller with duller, dusky-based mandible, and pale greenish gular skin. (Crowned Hornbill has brighter red bill, white streaks behind *yellow* eyes and different tail pattern.) **Call** a series of high-pitched yelping whistles, *queeo, pipipipipipipipipi;* or *pwik, kwiwiwiwiwiwiwi;* also *pi-pi-pi-pi-pi-piew.* Call note a sharp *QUEEo* or *PEEo.* Breeds in cliff crevices. Non-breeders wander in small groups some distance from nesting areas. Flight slow and buoyant. **Range**: Between 900

and 1200 m on the Kongelai, Tambach and Kabarnet escarpments, and near Lake Baringo. Local movements to Laikipia Plateau and Menengai Crater; also on n. borders at Lokichokio, Kamathia, Huri Hills and Moyale.

CROWNED HORNBILL *Tockus alboterminatus*   Plate 63

Length 21.5". A fairly common, open-forest hornbill. Mostly blackish with *white belly, white tail corners and a red bill; white streaks from above eyes to nape*, and head *slightly crested*; bill orange-tinged at base, and with a low ridge-like casque; bare orbital and gular skin black; *eyes dull yellow*; female duller than male, with smaller bill and greenish yellow gular skin. Eastern *T. a. suahelicus* is much paler and browner above than the almost black-backed *geloensis*. **Juvenile** lacks ridge on bill, has brownish wing-covert edges. **Call** a shrill, piercing piping or whistling *squeek, pyi-pyi-pyi-pyi-pyi. . . or . . . pew-pew-pew-pew-pew*; in display, the repeated notes grouped together, rising and falling in pitch; contact note a single loud *KWEE* or *QUEW*. **Range**:*T. a. geloensis* up to 3000 m in the w. and cent. Kenyan highlands, south to Crater Highlands and Tarangire NP. *T. a. suahelicus* in coastal lowlands including Pemba Island, inland to Usambara and Pare mts, along Tana River, in Shimba Hills, Tsavo area, Mkomazi GR and north to Kibwezi and Kitui. Birds on Mt Kulal and the Ndotos not racially assigned.

AFRICAN GREY HORNBILL *Tockus nasutus*   Plate 63 ✔

Length 20". The *dull grey-brown* hornbill of acacia habitats. Has *long white stripe from eye to nape and another down centre of back*; sooty brown wing feathers edged white; bare gular skin dark grey; throat and breast pale grey-brown, belly white. *Bill of male black with cream patch at base of maxilla,* narrow pale lines/ridges across base of mandible; low ridge-like casque in nominate *nasutus*, this narrowly tubular and longer in *T. n. epirhinus*. **Female** similar, but *bill tip dark red* and *basal half of maxilla cream.* **Juvenile** dull brown with buffy white wing edgings and smaller, paler bill. Flight buoyant and deeply undulating. **Call** a penetrating rhythmic piping, *ki-ki-ki-ki-ki-ki, pi-KEW pi-KEW pi-KEW curee-curee-curee-curee*; a simpler *PEW-ku, PEW-ku, PEW-ku. . .*, and a more strident descending *PEW, PEW, pew, pew. . ..* **Range**: *T. n. epirhinus* is widespread in n. Tanzania, north uncommonly in coastal Kenya to Lamu. *T. n. nasutus* widespread below 1700 m in interior Kenya.

TRUMPETER HORNBILL *Bycanistes bucinator*   Plate 63

Length 23.5". A large pied hornbill, locally common in coastal and east-central riverine forests. Often in large noisy flocks. Largely black above, but white on upper tail-coverts and *rear half of wings* conspicuous in flight; throat and upper breast black, otherwise white below; casque large in male, smaller and extending only halfway along bill in female; *bare orbital and gular skin usually dark purple to purplish pink.* (All 3 *Bycanistes* show white tail corners in flight. Silvery-cheeked has *no* white in wings, more on lower back. Black-and-white-casqued has much white in wings but is only western.) **Call** a loud high nasal braying, *NHAAA NHAAA NHA-HA-HA-HA-HA-HA . . .*, often prolonged; a guttural croak when feeding. **Range**: Along coast north to lower Tana River. Inland populations in Taveta, Kibwezi, Thika and Maua districts and on upper Tana; local in East Usambara and North Pare mts. **Taxonomic Note**: Some authors sink *Bycanistes* in the genus *Ceratogymna.*

SILVERY-CHEEKED HORNBILL *Bycanistes brevis*   Plate 63

Length 27-28". A large black-and-white hornbill with *all-black wings* which in flight contrast with the *white lower back, rump and upper tail-coverts.* **Male** has silvery grey feather tips on cheeks and ear-coverts, an impressive *cream-coloured casque* projecting to or beyond the bill tip, and *grey or blue-grey orbital skin.* **Female** has smaller casque restricted to basal half of maxilla and tapered or abruptly truncated in front, and *pink orbital skin.* **Juvenile** shows brown-tipped feathers on head; casque as in female. (Trumpeter Hornbill has smaller darker bill, more white on underparts, and wings show much white in flight; white on upper tail-coverts but none on rump or back.) **Call** a loud raucous braying, *RAAAH RAAAH RAAAH . . .*; softer grunting and quacking calls when feeding. **Range:** Local in highlands *east* of the Rift Valley, south to Chyulu and Taita hills, and coastal lowlands north to Arabuko–Sokoke Forest. In ne. Tanzania, common in Usambara and Pare mts, on Kilimanjaro and Mt Meru, in Arusha and Lake Manyara NPs. Disjunct or seasonal populations in Nguruman and Loliondo forests astride Kenya-Tanzanian border. Regularly visits fruiting trees in Nairobi.

BLACK-AND-WHITE-CASQUED HORNBILL *Bycanistes subcylindricus subquadratus* **Plate 63**

Length 27–28". The large black-and-white forest hornbill of *western* areas, distinguished from Silvery-cheeked by *extensive white wing area* and more white in the tail; silvery grey facial feather tips less conspicuous than in that species. **Male** has *high wedge-shaped casque* (much shorter than that of Silvery-cheeked), *cream at base but apical half black* like rest of bill; bare orbital skin dull greyish pink. Casque of **female** reduced to low projection at base of bill; bare loral/orbital skin pale pink (red when breeding). **Juvenile** has brown facial feathering and no casque. Large numbers roost together, making long flights to and from tall trees in morning and evening. **Call** a very loud bleating or braying AAAR HAAARH, AAARH. . ., or AAAK AAAK AAAK AAAK-AAAK-AAK-AK, producing a remarkable din when many birds call together. Contact note a single querulous AARK; softer guttural notes when feeding. **Range:** Local above 1600 m west of Rift Valley from Mt Elgon, Cheranganis and Kakamega east to Molo, south to w. Mara GR and Serengeti NP.

BARBETS AND TINKERBIRDS, FAMILY CAPITONIDAE

Stocky, large-headed birds with stout pointed bills, often brightly coloured and strongly patterned, but some are clad in uniformly dull hues. Sexes are alike or similar. In the larger species, the bill is proportionately longer and heavier, with the maxillary tomia coarsely notched or 'toothed.' All have well-developed rictal and chin bristles, and *Gymnobucco* has bristly nasal tufts. Their wings are short and rounded, providing direct, strong but rather laboured (and typically audible) flight. With few exceptions the tail is quite short. The tarsi are short and strong, the toes zygodactyl. The terrestrial species hop rather awkwardly on the ground. The majority are associated with trees, nesting and roosting in cavities excavated in soft wood, but the *Trachyphonus* species breed in holes dug in termitaria or in the ground. Certain barbets are social; co-operative breeding is known in a few and suspected in others. Some authors place African barbets in a separate family, Lybiidae.

GREY-THROATED BARBET *Gymbobucco bonapartei cinereiceps* **Plate 64**

Length 6.5–7". A fairly common forest barbet with *pale eyes* and two prominent *erect tufts of bristly feathers at base of bill*. Mainly dark brown, greyer to almost black on face and forehead; elongate buff spots behind the brownish or straw-coloured nasal tufts; eyes cream or pale yellow. **Juvenile** uniform chocolate-brown, with shorter, darker tufts and dark eyes. Often in small vocal groups in dead treetops. **Call**, *chew* or *whew* notes repeated several times, and a sharper *yeek* in series; a nasal *nyaaa* and a buzzy *spzzz* when several birds are together. **Range:** Mt Elgon and Kapenguria south to Nandi, Kakamega and Mau forests, nw. Mara GR and nearby Olololoo Escarpment.

WHITE-EARED BARBET *Stactolaema leucotis kilimensis* **Plate 64**

Length 6.5–7". An eastern *pied* barbet of forest edge and riparian woods. *A broad white streak extends from near eye and flares on side of neck*; belly, *rump and tail-coverts white*, plumage otherwise black. **Juvenile** less glossy, and bill is pale at base. Perches for long periods on tall dead trees. **Call** a harsh rolling *chreeer* or *kyeeeee*, repeated 3–4 times, and a loud piercing *tseu tseu tseu tseu*. Several birds together produce various chattering and trilling notes. **Range:** Local on Nyambeni Hills, lower slopes of Mt Kenya,

Chyulu, Taita and Shimba hills, and in coastal Diani and Ganda forests. More common in Usambara and Pare mts, on Kilimanjaro, Mt Meru, and in Arusha NP.

GREEN BARBET *Stactolaema o. olivacea*   Plate 64

Length 6″. A stolid, *dull greenish olive* bird of *coastal Kenyan forests* and the Usambara Mts; more yellow-green on wings, paler on underparts; head and chin dark brown; eyes dull red or orange. **Juvenile** duller, with brown eyes. Common and frequently vocal, but difficult to locate high in forest trees. **Call** a loud repetitive *tyok tyok tyok. . .*, or *chock chock. . ..* Duets, and one calling bird often stimulates another. **Range**: Tana River delta south to Mrima Hill and Shimoni. Largely absent from Tan-zanian coast, but common in the East Usambaras.

SPECKLED TINKERBIRD *Pogoniulus scolopaceus flavisquamatus*   Plate 65

Length 4.5–5″. A central African bird, probably no longer in our region. *Dull* olive-brown above, blackish on crown, the yellowish-edged and -tipped feathers *appearing spotted or scaly*; underparts mottled, the faintly barred whitish chin and throat shading into olive-yellow breast and belly; sides of breast and *flanks streaked and spotted with dusky brown*; eyes pale or dark. **Juvenile** has more barred throat and yellowish-based bill. Unique long **call** starts with a single *cok*, repeated slowly, doubled to *cokok. . .*, later tripled, *cokok-kok . . .*, finally becoming 4–5 rapidly uttered syllables *cokok-kok-kok-kok*, etc.; middle portion of series closely resembles call of quail, *Coturnix coturnix*. Less frequent is a more typical tinkerbird-type *tok, tok, tok . . .*, and a faster trill recalling Moustached Green Tinkerbird. **Status**: Vagrant or extirpated. An old specimen (now untraceable) collected near Kitale in w. Kenya, and an unsubstantiated early sight record from Kakamega Forest.

EASTERN GREEN TINKERBIRD *Pogoniulus simplex*   Plate 65

Length 3.5″. An uncommon tiny bird of *coastal forest*, olive, with *lemon-yellow rump patch* and *yellow wing-bars*. (Moustached Green Tinkerbird is only in highlands. Green Barbet is much heavier, bigger-billed and lacks yellow rump. Yellow-rumped Tinkerbird is black and white with a striped face.) **Call** a rapid trill, at times preceded by a sin-gle *pop* or *tok*; differs from similar call of sympatric Yellow-rumped Tinkerbird in being higher-pitched, often faster and shorter. **Range**: Local from Arabuko–Sokoke Forest, Shimba Hills, Shimoni and Mrima Hill south to Tanga, and inland to the East Usambara foothills, meeting Moustached Green Tinkerbird around Amani.

MOUSTACHED GREEN TINKERBIRD *Pogoniulus leucomystax*   Plate 65

Length 3.5–4″. A *highland forest* bird, dark olive-green above with two *yellow wing-bars* (lower one often faint), *yellow rump* and *white mous-tachial stripes* widening toward the neck. Underparts greyish yellow-olive, darker on breast; belly yellowish; bill blackish with base of mandible yellow or whitish. **Juvenile** brighter yellow below. (Eastern Green Tinkerbird, at lower elevations, lacks prominent white mous-tachial streaks and differs vocally.) **Call** a dry rapid *chk-chk-chk-chk-chk* in groups of several syllables, separated by pause from next series, recalling that of Yellow-rumped Tinkerbird, but faster and of different quality. Variable trills, fast or slow, may change tempo within a series, or begin slowly and accelerate (6–20 notes/sec.) Has a sharp, woodpecker-like *pi-pik!* **Range**: Mt Elgon and Mt Nyiru south to the Mau, Mt Kenya, Aberdares and n. Nairobi suburbs, the Nguruman, Chyulu and Taita hills, Arusha NP, Kilimanjaro, Pare and Usambara mts.

YELLOW-RUMPED TINKERBIRD *Pogoniulus bilineatus* Plate 65

Length 4". The common *stripe-faced, black-backed* tinkerbird of the Kenyan highlands; also in coastal lowlands. Glossy black above with yellow wing-bars, yellow-edged flight feathers and a bright golden yellow rump; bill black. Coastal *P. b. fischeri* is whitish on throat, paler grey on breast, more yellow (less olive) on sides and differs vocally from highland *jacksoni*. **Juvenile** has yellowish olive feather tips on crown and back; bill yellowish brown. (Yellow-fronted and Red-fronted Tinkerbirds have bright forehead patches and white-striped backs, but are similar vocally and easily misidentified by voice alone.) **Call** not loud but far-carrying, *tonk-tonk-tonk-tonk*. . . or *tok, tok, tok*. . ., typically in groups of 3–7 notes, often for many minutes. A slower, more deliberate *whonk*. . . *whonk*. . . *whonk*. . . and a harsh *krreek, krreek*. . ., also in long series. Song of coastal race is a single *pup* quickly followed by a rapid dull trill (see Eastern Green Tinkerbird). **Range**: *P. b. jacksoni* up to 3000 m in w. and cent. Kenyan highlands south to nw. Mara GR. *P. b. fischeri* coastal (Tanga north to Arabuko–Sokoke Forest).

✓ RED-FRONTED TINKERBIRD *Pogoniulus pusillus affinis* Plate 65

Length 3.5–4.25". A fairly common *dry-country* tinkerbird with a black-and-white-*striped face* and, in **adult**, a *scarlet forehead*; streaked black and yellowish white from crown to back, yellow and white on wings; rump and tail-coverts yellow; mainly pale yellowish below. **Juvenile** lacks scarlet forehead patch. (Yellow-rumped Tinkerbird could be confused with juv. Red-fronted, but face patterns differ and Yellow-rumped has plain back.) **Calls** include a repeated trill (recalling those of the green tinkerbirds), a metallic *tonk, tonk, tonk, tonk*. . ., and a hollow *tok-tok-tok*. . ., both in series of *20 or more notes without pause*; and a faster trilled piping, at times with popping sounds; also some harsh croaks. **Range**: Below 2000 m, north to Kerio and Turkwell rivers, Mt Kulal, Marsabit and ne. border areas. Replaced by *P. chrysoconus* in n. Lake Victoria basin and along w. border. After breeding, may move from usual dry habitats to higher wetter sites.

YELLOW-FRONTED TINKERBIRD *Pogoniulus c. chrysoconus* Plate 65

Length 4–4.5". Larger and heavier-billed than Red-fronted Tinkerbird, and usually with *golden yellow forehead.* Inhabits moist savanna, riparian thickets and suburban shade trees. *Lacks superciliary stripes*, is *more lemon-yellow below*, and white cheeks are separated from throat by black moustachial stripes. Face pattern separates rare birds with orange-red forehead from *P. pusillus*. **Juvenile** lacks forehead patch. **Call** more uniform than that of Yellow-rumped T., with no periodic pauses within a series. The repetitive *tok tok tok*. . . is almost identical to one call of Red-fronted T. Often changes to *tu tu tu tu*. . . Also common are a bisyllabic *cok-ok, cok-ok, cok-ok*. . ., and an almost trilled *cok-k-k-k, cok-k-k-k* . . .. **Range**: Up to 1500 m in w. Kenya from Malaba and Busia border areas east to Bungoma, Mumias, Kisumu and Chemelil. Rare south of Ahero where replaced by Red-fronted Tinkerbird.

YELLOW-SPOTTED BARBET *Buccanodon d. duchaillui* Plate 64

Length 6–6.5". A black-and-yellow, crimson-crowned barbet of *west Kenyan forests.* Uncommon and usually high in the canopy. Velvety blue-black from hindcrown to back and on face, throat and breast, spotted with bright yellow above, and with a *broad yellow stripe from eyes to sides of neck*; yellow barring on black underparts and rump; bill black. **Juvenile** duller, with *black crown and forehead*, and *black-tipped orange or yellow bill*. **Call** a 2-sec. purring or snoring, *zhr-r-r-rrrrrrrrrrrr*; also a group chatter. **Range**: Nandi, Kakamega and West Mau forests.

HAIRY-BREASTED BARBET *Tricholaema hirsuta ansorgii* Plate 64

Length 6.5–7". A rare, canopy-feeding barbet of the Kakamega Forest, w. Kenya. Glossy black on forehead and face with white facial stripes; upperparts mostly brownish black, speckled with yellow, and most wing feathers yellow-edged; *throat streaked black and white*; breast yellow in male, orange-gold in female, with fine hair-like tips to some feathers; *lower breast, sides, flanks and under tail-coverts paler yellow or greenish yellow spotted with black*. **Juvenile** less spotted, more barred below. **Call** a deep short *hoop* or *oork* slowly repeated in short series, faster than similar call of Yellow-billed Barbet. **Status**: Few records, but some in late 1980s; a few may survive.

RED-FRONTED BARBET *Tricholaema diademata*   Plate 64

Length 5.75–6.5″. A thickset, dry-country barbet, with *red forehead patch and broad yellowish superciliary stripes* separating the black mask and crown. *Black back* and wings are streaked and spotted with yellow; yellow rump evident in flight. Underparts creamy white in *T. d. diademata*, with a few large blackish spots on lower flanks; in *T. d. massaica* spotted or streaked on flanks and belly. **Juvenile** duller; little or no red on forehead. (Red-fronted Tinkerbird is much smaller with black moustachial stripes.) **Call** a series of up to 15 hollow Hoopoe-like notes, *hoop-hoop-hoop. . .* often in duet; faster than call of Spot-flanked Barbet. **Range**: *T. d. diademata* in n. Kenya from Kongelai Escarpment, Kerio Valley and Mt Nyiru south to Baringo, Isiolo and Meru districts; *T. d. massaica* from Siaya, Kisumu, Nakuru and Kitui south into interior Tanzania.

SPOT-FLANKED BARBET *Tricholaema lacrymosa*   Plate 64 ✓

Length 5–5.5″. A small *black-bibbed* woodland barbet, *heavily spotted on sides and flanks*. Black above with bold white stripes on sides of head and scapulars; browner rump and upper tail-coverts heavily streaked with pale yellow as are flight-feather edges. Black side/flank spots drop-shaped in *T. l. lacrymosa*, smaller and more rounded in western *radcliffei*. Eyes yellow or yellow-orange in male, brown or red in female. **Juvenile** more greyish black above, with brown eyes. (Black-throated Barbet, typically in drier areas, has yellow-spotted upperparts, no black spots below.) **Call** a loud *hook. . . hook. . . hook. . .*, slower and higher-pitched than call of Red-fronted Barbet; also a croaking *grrrk, grrrk. . .*, a low *yek, yek, yek. . .* and a harsh nasal *nyaaa*. **Range**: *T. l. lacrymosa* from Kongelai Escarpment and Mt Nyiru south through e. Kenya to Moshi and Arusha districts. *T. l. radcliffei* in w. Kenya from Mt Elgon south to Crater highlands and Tarangire NP and w. edge of the Masai Steppe.

BLACK-THROATED BARBET *Tricholaema melanocephala stigmatothorax*
Plate 64

Length 5–5.5″. A dark brown-and-white barbet of *dry bush*. Head pattern suggests Spot-flanked Barbet, but may show yellow, orange, or red speckling on forehead; *elongated bright yellow spots on back*, yellow streaks on rump; *brown of throat and breast narrows to point* on the white belly. **Juvenile** darker, the yellow areas duller. **Call** of 4–6 grating notes, rapid and slightly descending, *skwi, tchee-tchew-tchew* or *ka-kaar-kaar-kaar-kaar*; also a nasal *nyaaa*. **Range**: Widespread below 1500 m from n. and e. Kenya south through Amboseli and Tsavo region to Mkomazi GR and west across the Masai Steppe to Tarangire NP, lakes Natron and Magadi.

WHITE-HEADED BARBET *Lybius leucocephalus*   Plate 64

Length 7–7.5″. A *white-headed, white-rumped* barbet of the highlands. Variable: *L. l. senex* is white except for wings and middle of back. *L. l. albicauda* is *white-tailed* like *senex*, but flanks, belly and wings are dusky brown spotted with white. *L. l. leucocephalus* has a *black tail, brown lower breast and belly with white streaks*, and *white-spotted scapulars and wings*. **Juvenile** blotched with brown on head and underparts, tail partly or wholly brown. Often in small groups in fruiting fig trees. Noisy displays involve elaborate posturing; the guttural churring or growling from a group is quite babbler-like. Other **calls** vary: those of *albicauda* build from a soft beginning, intensify, then fade, *chrrchrr-grr, grraak gwak, grrh, grrh, chrr-OW-chrrOW-chrrCHOW-chrrCHOW-chrr-tchao chrrak-akk-akk-akk.*; *senex* has harsher, loud wheezy chatter, *ch-ch-ch-ch-zhizh, zhizh-zhizh-zhizh-tchee-tchee-tchee . . .* and separate *skyrrrr*

notes; *L. l. leucocephalus* duets with repeated clear *pewp* notes, ending with short *it-it*. **Range**: *L. l. leucocephalus* from Ruma NP north to Mt Elgon and Kongelai Escarpment; *senex* in highlands mainly east of Rift Valley, south to the Chyulu Hills, intergrading with *albicauda* which ranges from Mara GR south into Tanzania, east to Taveta and Bura (Taita Hills Dist.).

BLACK-BILLED BARBET *Lybius guifsobalito* Plate 64

Length 6–6.5″. A solitary barbet of *western border areas. Blue-black*, and *red from forehead to breast*; brown *flight feathers broadly edged with pale yellow*, and *wing-coverts black with white streaks*. Red areas of **juvenile** more orange, forehead/crown dull black and throat brown with red feather tips. Usually seen on high exposed perch in savanna, bush or cultivation. Main **call** an antiphonal duet, with chatter preceding 10–20 *kik-ka-apoot* phrases (recalls Black-collared Barbet); also gives a single *wupp*. **Range**: Local along Kenya-Ugandan border from Mt Elgon south to Musoma.

BLACK-COLLARED BARBET *Lybius torquatus irroratus* Plate 64

Length 7–7.5″. A colourful barbet of *coastal woods. Red from forehead to upper breast*, a *broad black breast* band between the red and the pale yellow belly; crown to upper back black; lower back and rump brown with fine dark and yellowish vermiculations; dark brown wings have pale yellow feather edges. **Juvenile** blackish brown with white belly; scattered red feathers appear with age. (Brown-breasted Barbet has white belly, brown breast band and black leg feathers.) **Call** a sprightly antiphonal duet, *KEE, pup-up KEE, pup-up. . .* (*KEE* from one bird, *pup-up* from the second), repeated and often preceded or followed by a babbler-like *cheew-chewchewchew. . ..* Sometimes *pup, pup, pup. . .* given by single bird. **Range**: Coastal lowlands, inland to Shimba Hills and along lower Tana River.

BROWN-BREASTED BARBET *Lybius melanopterus* Plate 64

Length 7–7.5″. A *white-bellied, red-faced* eastern barbet with a *broad brown breast band; leg feathers and small flank patch black*. Red of forehead, face and throat grades into blackish crown with bright red feather tips in fresh plumage; bill pale. **Juvenile** shows little red, has largely brown throat and grey-brown breast. Uncommon in coastal woods or forest edge where small groups perch in dead treetops (sometimes fly-catching). **Call** a loud *whaak whaak whaak*. Does not duet. **Range**: Local from Tanga north to Lamu, inland along Tana River to Garissa, from Shimba Hills west to Mkomazi GR, North Pare Mts, lower slopes of Kilimanjaro and Mt Meru, Arusha and Moshi districts; also from Taveta and Rombo to Bura and Wundanyi in Taita Hills Dist. and along the Voi River in Tsavo East NP.

DOUBLE-TOOTHED BARBET *Lybius bidentatus aequatorialis* Plate 64

Length 8–8.5″. A black-and-red *highland* barbet with a *large ivory-coloured bill* and *yellow eye patch*. Mostly black above with small white patch on lower back and a narrow rosy wing-bar; largely *bright red below*; flanks, leg feathers and under tail-coverts black, and a *white fan-shaped patch* usually conspicuous on sides. Eye colour variable, but dark brown in most or all Kenyan birds; reportedly pale elsewhere. Female has blackish streaks on the red sides immediately above the white patches. **Juvenile** shows much less red below, has more greyish brown on throat and sides, and grey orbital skin. **Call** a harsh *kekk* or *krrek*, singly or repeated; also long purring *krrrrrrrrrrrrrrrr-ik*. **Range:** Between 1300 and 2300 m in w. Kenya, from Mt Elgon, Kapenguria and Saiwa NP south to w. Mau Forest, Mara GR and w. Serengeti NP.

YELLOW-BILLED BARBET *Trachylaemus purpuratus elgonensis* Plate 64
Length 9–10″. Solitary or in pairs in dense forest. Sluggish and long-tailed, with *vivid yellow bill and facial skin*. Blue-black above, with *deep maroon forehead, crown and face*, bright crimson along lower edge of dark throat/upper breast which are 'frosted' with short, silvery pink streaks; lower breast and belly yellow, grading into large yellow spots

on black sides and flanks; eyes red. **Juvenile** similar but with less red and no pink on throat/breast; more extensively yellow below. Usual **call** (a common forest sound) a low *whook* or *hoop*, frequently uttered for an extended period; varied to *wha-ook*. Displaying birds give a soft *wunk-wunk, oonk-oonk-oonk*; duetting birds utter a harsh *chaaa* preceding a rapid *wuk-wuk, wuk-wuk-wup* . . . . **Range**: Local in w. Kenya, between 1500 and 2800 m, from Mt Elgon south to Mau and Trans-Mara forests (formerly Molo). **Taxonomic Note**: Now often placed in *Trachyphonus*, but differs from those open-country social species in plumage, behaviour and voice.

CRESTED BARBET *Trachyphonus vaillantii suahelicus*   Plate 122

Length 9–9.5″. Tanzanian only. A large multicoloured barbet with *prominent black crest, red-speckled yellow face* and pale yellowish bill. Glossy black above with white spotting and scalloping; rump yellow, upper tail-coverts red; long black tail with white bars and tip; white-spotted black breast band; rest of underparts pale yellowish streaked with red. **Juvenile** browner above, paler yellow on face, with darker bill. **Call** a sustained purring (suggests ringing of a muffled alarm clock) lasting up to 20 seconds. Pairs often duet. Alarm call a loud sharp rattle recalling that of Red-and-Yellow Barbet. **Range**: In our region, only around edges of cultivation in the West Usambaras (scarce); periodically recorded at Lake Manyara and Tarangire NPs.

RED-AND-YELLOW BARBET *Trachyphonus erythrocephalus*   Plate 64

Length 8–9″. A gaudy, *boldly white-spotted* barbet with red-bordered *white ear-patches* and a reddish bill; throat and upper breast usually orange; black-and-white speckled band across yellow breast; red on under tail-coverts; tail boldly spotted with yellowish white. **Male** of *red-faced* nominate race with slightly crested, *glossy black crown* and a long median black throat patch. **Female** similar but browner, and *crown red with black spots*. *T. e. versicolor* is paler, more yellow, with less red on head. Northeastern *T. e. shelleyi* is smaller, much paler below, with little orange on throat and breast. **Juvenile** (all races) yellower than adult, with little orange; dorsal spots cream or yellowish, not white; throat greyish. Fairly common in open dry bush. Forages mainly on ground. (Smaller d'Arnaud's Barbet shows little or no orange-red coloration, has different face pattern, horn-coloured or blackish bill. In n. Tanzania see Crested Barbet.) **Call** a loud rollicking duet, *ko-quedeely-kwo, ko-tweedely-kwo*, repeated over and over. Alarm call a woodpecker-like *ki-ki-ki-ki*. **Range**: *T. e. versicolor* in n. and nw. Kenya south to the Kerio Valley, Lake Borgoria and Meru NP; intergrades with Ethiopian *T. e. shelleyi* in extreme northeast. *T. e. erythrocephalus* from s. Kenya (in and east of Rift Valley) south to Tarangire and Lake Manyara NPs, the Crater Highlands and Lake Natron.

D'ARNAUD'S BARBET *Trachyphonus darnaudii*   Plate 64 ✔

Length 6.5–7.5″. A common, *boldly spotted* bird of bush and scrub, smaller than Red-and-Yellow Barbet, with *no red on face*, and *under-parts black-speckled*, with *large black patch on lower throat* and a black-and-white-spotted breast band. *Forehead and crown yellow or orange and yellow, speckled with black* (*T. d. darnaudii* and *usambiro*), or *entirely black* (*boehmi*). Southwestern *usambiro* (considered specif-ically distinct by some authors) is larger and stockier, with a more dis-tinct breast band and *heavy barring on lower breast and belly*; plumage lacks orange tones, and bill is *blackish* (not pale grey or light greyish horn). **Juvenile** resembles adult, but crown of nominate *darnaudii* is dark brown with few or no light spots, and under-parts are paler yellow, brownish on throat. Typically excavates roosting and nesting holes in flat ground. Forages in low bushes and on ground. **Calls:** Rising and falling duet of *boehmi* and *darnaudii* recalls that of Red-and-Yellow Barbet, *tu-wa-tee-tootle, tu-wa-tee-tootle*. . . or *qu-wa-tew-chupup* . . . repeated numerous times. Duet of *usambiro* is a harsh grating, almost squealing, *cherk-a-SKRRRRRK* or *uk-ki-YERRRK*, repeated and not rising and falling in pitch; also a reedy repeated *kuWEEER* . **Range**: *T. d. darnaudii* in nw. Kenya south to Baringo Dist.; *boehmi* east of Rift Valley south through Tsavo area to ne.Tanzania, west to Tarangire and Lake Manyara NPs and Lake Natron; *usam-biro* in barren parts of Narok District, Mara GR and Serengeti NP east to Olduvai Gorge.

(Birds along Kenya-Tanzanian boundary at Muhoro Bay on Lake Victoria, with general appearance of *boehmi*, have calls of *usambiro* and may be intermediate between those forms.)

HONEYGUIDES, FAMILY INDICATORIDAE

Small arboreal birds, often unobtrusive, remaining still for long periods before abruptly flying with rapid and sometimes undulating flight, flashing their white outer tail feathers. Some are quite vocal, and certain species have traditional calling sites used for years. The dainty honeybirds are reminiscent of warblers in their movements. They and the small honeyguides sometimes feed by fluttering amid foliage, and they may pursue aerial insects. Except for the Greater Honeyguide, sexes are alike and young resemble adults. The well-known guiding behaviour, whereby a bird leads humans or ratels to bees' nests, seems to be restricted to the Greater, but all *Indicator* species feed on wax as well as insects, thus explaining their predilection for bees' nests. All studied members of the family are brood parasites, with the cavity-nesting barbets and woodpeckers serving as primary hosts of the *Indicator* species. The small, sharp-billed honeybirds (*Prodotiscus*) lay their eggs in open nests of passerine birds.

✓ **GREATER or BLACK-THROATED HONEYGUIDE** *Indicator indicator* **Plate 67**

Length 7–7.5". Most often seen in *undulating flight* through open woodland, the *white outer tail feathers* conspicuous. When perched, appears as *an upright compact bird*, the tail from below appearing white with dusky markings at sides and tip. **Adult male** greyish brown above, with obvious black throat patch and whitish cheeks. Golden 'shoulder' patch partly concealed; bill usually pink, but may be whitish or pale brown. **Female** plain brownish above with pale-edged wing feathers, light grey to white below; grey bill may show some pink. **Juvenile** normally yellow on throat, otherwise whitish below; upperparts olive-brown. **Immature** may retain some yellow on throat after the first moult. Usual **call** a loud, monotonous rolling *WHEET-Cher, WHEET-cher. . .* or *WHIT-purr, White-purr. . .*, repeated several times. Guiding call of both sexes a dry chattering rattle. Female gives loud *wit* or *weet* when interacting with barbets. Near favoured call sites produces a whirring, rustling or clapping sound with wings or tail. **Range**: Widespread from sea level to over 2500 m except in n. Kenya.

SCALY-THROATED HONEYGUIDE *Indicator variegatus* **Plate 67**

Length 7–7.5". An inconspicuous bird of canopy foliage in woodland or denser savanna. Compact and heavy-billed; olive-grey to yellow-olive above, greyer on head; *breast and sides olive-grey, heavily mottled or scaled*, contrasting with whitish belly and throat, the latter with narrow dark streaks. White outer rectrices obvious in flight. **Juvenile** greener above, more strongly marked below, and with narrow yellowish eye-ring. **Call** a rising purring trill, recalling an insect or frog, begins slowly and may last for several seconds. Also gives a loud vibrant trill, *trrrreeeeeee* or *treeeee-phew*, likened to a policeman's whistle. Has various other chattering and buzzing notes. **Range**: Widespread from sea level to over 2500 m, except in n. Kenya and dry interior n. Tanzania.

✓ **LESSER HONEYGUIDE** *Indicator minor teitensis* **Plate 67**

Length 5–5.5". A fairly common but unassertive stub-billed bird, olive-grey to yellow-olive above, greyer on crown and cheeks; underparts pale grey to dark ashy grey with olive tinge; chin and belly whitish, and flanks obscurely streaked. Whitish loral spots and poorly defined dusky malar streaks obvious in adults, lacking or obscure in **juvenile**, which is also greener than adult with somewhat streaked throat. A bird of woodland, savanna, tall bush and open forest. More active than larger honeyguides; often flycatches; flight even or undulating. **Call** a far-carrying *klee-eu* or *pew*, repeated indefinitely, each series followed by a brief pause before resumption. Less frequent is a clear *twee-wiweet. . .* with variations. Sometimes gives trill or rattle. **Range**: Widespread to above 2000 m, but local in n. Kenya.

THICK-BILLED HONEYGUIDE *Indicator c. conirostris*   Plate 67

Length 6". An increasingly scarce, dark honeyguide of heavy forest in w. Kenya. *Breast deep grey or olive-grey,* sometimes obscurely streaked, and a *stout blackish bill.* Upperparts yellowish olive, wings appearing almost golden yellow with bright flight-feather edgings; head and upper back dusky; face may show obscure streaks recalling Lesser Honeyguide, but usually appears plain and dark except for paler chin and posterior underparts. **Juvenile** darker and greener than adult, the chin and throat streaked with dusky. (Lesser Honeyguide is paler, less contrastingly streaked above. Where sympatric with Thick-billed in w. Kenya, Lesser confined to forest edge and more open habitats. In the east, where Thick-billed is absent, Lesser inhabits forest.) **Call** a husky *kiss-kiss-kiss-kiss* or lisping *tssp-tssp.* Louder calls in w. Africa (not reported from Kenyan birds) said to be indistinguishable from those of Lesser Honeyguide. **Range**: Mt Elgon, Cherangani, Kakamega and Nandi forests, and Saiwa NP. Gradually being replaced by Lesser Honeyguide as larger forest tracts disappear.

LEAST HONEYGUIDE *Indicator exilis pachyrhynchus*   Plate 67

Length 4.25–5". A *small,* dark *forest* honeyguide of *western* Kenya. (Similar but paler Pallid H. is a bird of open woodland.) *Facial marks and dark dorsal streaking more distinct than in larger Thick-billed Honeyguide* which often shares the same forest habitat. Usually evident is the *pale mandible base* (bill rarely all black), plus *black sub-moustachial or malar stripes* and *white loral spots.* Underparts olive-grey, heavily streaked on flanks, less so on sides. White outer rectrices conspicuous in flight. **Juvenile** less distinctly streaked above, and darker below than adult; facial marks often obscure or lacking. Usual **call** a short dry trill; less often a song-like *pew-pew-wheet-wheet* or *tew-tew-wheer wheer-wheer.* **Range**: Kakamega, Nandi, Sotik, Kericho and Mau forests.

PALLID HONEYGUIDE *Indicator meliphilus*   Plate 67

Length 4.25–5". A *paler, plainer eastern* counterpart of the Least Honeyguide, not found in heavy forest. Greyish *golden olive and nearly plain above,* greyer on face, more whitish with fine dusky streaks on chin and throat; rest of *underparts light grey; lacks dark malar stripes,* but *faint whitish loral spots* usually visible at close range, as is *pale pinkish mandible base.* White outer rectrices prominent in flight. Upperparts of some individuals noticeably greyer than in others. (Lesser Honeyguide, only slightly larger, may show only obscure malar stripes, but bill size and shape diagnostic.) **Juvenile** more yellowish green above, darker grey below than adult, with no loral spots. Repeated song-like **call** *pwee, pa-wee, pa-wee-wit,* or *pwee, wee-wee-wee-wee.* **Range**: Sigor and n. Kerio Valley southeast to Kibwezi, Taveta and se. Kenyan coast. Old records from Lake Manyara NP, North Pare and Usambara mts and the coast north of Tanga. **Taxonomic note**: Includes the former *narokensis* ('Kilimanjaro Honeyguide').

WAHLBERG'S HONEYBIRD *Prodotiscus r. regulus*   Plate 67

Length 4.75". Warbler-like in appearance and behaviour. Sharp-billed and brown-backed, with much white in the tail. Pale grey on breast, white or whitish elsewhere below. Silky white feathers flanking lower sides of rump normally concealed, but erected in display. **Juvenile** paler brown above and yellowish below, with outer 3 pairs of rectrices entirely white; gape flanges orange. A bird of acacias and riverine woods. (Other honeybirds are greenish above, and more typical of forest, but may visit wooded gardens and forest edge.) **Calls** include a short buzzy trill, a high *tseeu-tseeu,* a loud rasping *zeet-zeet* in flight, a single *zeep* and a soft chatter. **Range**: Kongelai Escarpment and Sigor south to Southern Uaso Nyiro River, Tsavo West NP, Shimba Hills and Kilifi District. Old records from Serengeti NP, Arusha and Moshi districts and the North Pare Mts.

CASSIN'S HONEYBIRD *Prodotiscus i. insignis*   **Plate 67**
Length 4.5". The *only west Kenyan honeybird*, scarce along forest edges and in clearings. Dull *olive-green* above; sides of face greyish olive, shading to dark olive-grey on underparts, paler in centre of belly; tail white with 4 dark central feathers. **Juvenile** greyer. **Call** an infrequent soft chatter. A weak *whi-hihi* reported in w. Africa. **Range**: Kakamega and Kaimosi areas.

EASTERN or GREEN-BACKED HONEYBIRD *Prodotiscus zambesiae ellenbecki*
Plate 67

Length 4.25". *The only olive-backed honeybird east of the Rift Valley.* Local and uncommon in open woodland, riparian strips and wooded gardens. Duller above, paler below than western Cassin's Honeybird, otherwise closely similar. **Juvenile** paler and greyer below, more yellowish olive above than adult. **Call** a harsh *skeee-aaa*, apparently from a courting bird; otherwise undescribed. **Range**: Cent. Kenyan highlands from Nairobi to Thika, Nyeri, Naro Moru and Meru districts, Arabuko–Sokoke Forest (in *Brachystegia* woodland), the Pare and Usambara mts, Arusha and Moshi districts, Lake Manyara NP and Oldeani.

WOODPECKERS AND WRYNECKS, FAMILY PICIDAE

The woodpeckers (Subfamily Picinae) are specialised bark-foragers, differing from the related barbets (Capitonidae) in their straight, chisel-tipped bills, long barbed tongues, and stiff pointed tail feathers which provide support on tree trunks. Their strong zygodactyl toes with sharp nails enable them to cling to smooth surfaces. Our species forage little on the ground. Present (although not common) in all forested and bushed habitats, they are resident birds, typically in pairs that maintain frequent vocal contact. They proclaim territory by rapidly 'drumming' on some resonant object such as a hollow branch. They roost and nest in cavities excavated in trees. All are sexually dimorphic in head colour or pattern. The two wrynecks (Jynginae) are superficially unlike woodpeckers with their soft rounded tails, cryptic nightjar-like plumage and lack of sexual dimorphism. Only occasionally do they cling to tree trunks, and they feed almost exclusively on ants and termites. Their flight is undulating as in woodpeckers.

EURASIAN WRYNECK *Jynx t. torquilla*   **Plate 65**

Length 7". An unusual bird, at a distance appearing mottled brownish grey with a *broad dark streak down the nape and back*, and narrow streaks on scapulars. At close range the vermiculated and barred dorsal plumage is evident, as are brown ear-coverts and a dark grey band from the eye down each side of the neck; underparts pale buff with *dark brown wavy bars on flanks and belly*, finer barring on throat and breast. Apparently silent in Kenya. **Range/status**: Scarce palearctic migrant; 15 widely scattered records south to the Chyulu Hills.

RED-THROATED WRYNECK *Jynx r. ruficollis*   **Plate 65**

Length 7–7.5". An uncommon bird of open wooded areas. Recalls Eurasian Wryneck, but is *bright rufous from chin to upper breast*; upperparts grey-brown, finely vermiculated and spotted, with a *broad dark streak from hindcrown to back*, and black-spotted scapulars; whitish lower breast and belly *streaked* with black; flanks and under tail-coverts dull rufous, the latter barred with black as is tail. **Juvenile** darker and more heavily barred. **Call** a loud squealing *yeea, yeea, yeea. . .* or *pyee, pyee, pyee, pyee, pyee.* **Range**: Cent. and w. Kenyan highlands, most numerous in Lake Nakuru NP. In Tanzania, scarce near Loliondo and near Mara/Serengeti border.

√ **NUBIAN WOODPECKER** *Campethera nubica*   **Plate 66**
Length 8". The familiar barred and spotted large woodpecker of acacia woods and savanna. *Combination of dark malar stripes (red in male, black with white speckles in female)* and *black-spotted underparts* distinguishes it from other similarly sized *Kenyan* woodpeckers; *dull yellow tail barred with olive-brown, the feather shafts bright yellow.* (Imm-

aculate throat and all-grey bill separate it from Bennett's W. in Tanzania. Mombasa and Golden-tailed Woodpeckers are *streaked* on breast, as is smaller Cardinal W. Golden-tailed W. is blackish on throat.) **Male** crimson from forehead to nape; **female** red only on nape; both have white superciliary stripes, pale spots above (wings more barred). *Coastal pallida* is paler, with smaller spots than nominate *nubica*. **Juvenile** darker, more heavily spotted below. **Call** a loud strident duet, *tyee, tyee, tyee, tyee-tyee-tyee-tyee-tyee, tee, tee*, accelerating, then often slowing at end; one bird begins, the second soon joins, more or less synchronously; series repeated several times. **Range:** *C. n. pallida* near coast from Kilifi north to Lamu. *C. n. nubica* from the Tsavo and Amboseli NPs northward, also south to lowlands around Kilimanjaro, Arusha, Tabora, Kilosa and Iringa; probably this race in Mkomazi GR.

BENNETT'S WOODPECKER *Campethera bennettii scriptoricauda*   Plate 122
Length 7–7.5″. A *Tanzanian* bird resembling Nubian Woodpecker, but *throat centrally speckled, not plain, and mandible pale yellow*. **Female** *lacks dark malar stripes*, is slightly *more yellowish above* and back is more narrowly barred. **Calls** include *wi-wi-wi-wi-wi* and a short *churr*. **Range**: Around Kilimanjaro (where apparently sympatric with Nubian W.) and North Pare Mts, and from Handeni southward. Formerly in Mombasa area.**Taxonomic Note:** Treated as a full species or as a race of *C. nubica* by some; said to intergrade freely with nominate *bennettii* in Malawi.

MOMBASA WOODPECKER *Campethera mombassica*   Plate 66

Length 8″. A large, streak-breasted woodpecker, fairly common in *coastal forest*. Golden-green above with *fine yellowish white spotting; underparts yellowish white, heavily streaked with black*; tail as in Nubian Woodpecker. **Male** has *red-tipped forehead/crown feathers and largely red nape*; malar stripes mixed red and black. **Female** and **juvenile** have olive-green forehead/crown speckled with buffy yellow; red only on nape. (Nubian, Bennett's and Green-backed Woodpeckers are spotted, not streaked, below.) Not known to drum. **Call** an accelerating nasal *keeoank-yaaaank-yaaaank-yaaank-yaank-yank-yank, yuk*; also a rough *ghrrrrrrrk*. **Range**: From Tanga north to Somali border, inland to Garissa, Shimba Hills and Usambara Mts. **Taxonomic Note**: Formerly considered a race of *C. abingoni*.

GOLDEN-TAILED WOODPECKER *Campethera abingoni*   Plate 66

Length 8″. An uncommon *western* counterpart of the preceding species, white without yellowish tint below and with *dense black streaking from chin to upper breast, sides and flanks*; spotted only on belly. Upperparts olive-green in *C. a. kavirondensis*, more yellowish green in *suahelica*, with cream-coloured spots merging into bars on rump; white ear-coverts streaked with black. **Male** has mostly crimson crown, nape and malar stripes. **Female** has blackish forehead and crown densely spotted with white, and black-and-white malar areas; nape red. (Smaller Green-backed Woodpecker has black-speckled throat and no malar stripes.) **Juvenile** more heavily streaked below, more barred on belly and sides than adult. Forages low, in and near riparian woods. **Call** a drawn-out, penetrating *skweeeeeeea*. **Range**: *C. a. kavirondensis* local in sw. Kenya, from Lolgorien and the Mara River south to w. Serengeti NP. *C. a. suahelica* in Arusha NP, Moshi District and North Pare Mts.

GREEN-BACKED or LITTLE SPOTTED WOODPECKER *Campethera cailliautii*
Plate 66
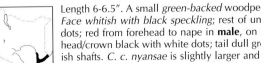
Length 6-6.5″. A small *green-backed* woodpecker with *no malar stripes*. *Face whitish with black speckling*; rest of underparts with round black dots; red from forehead to nape in **male**, on nape only in **female**; forehead/crown black with white dots; tail dull greenish yellow with brownish shafts. *C. c. nyansae* is slightly larger and brighter green above than eastern birds, with fine short yellowish *streaks* instead of spots, and heavier ventral spotting changes to barring on belly and sides. (Cardinal and Golden-tailed Woodpeckers are streaked below. Nubian and Mombasa Woodpeck-

ers show obvious malar stripes.) **Call** a fairly rapid *uweek uweek uweek uweek. . .*, the note repeated 20 times or more; also a shorter *kwee-kwee-kwee* or *kerree*. **Range**: *C. c. cailliautii* along coast north to the Somali border, inland along Tana River to Bura, Shimba Hills and East Usambaras. *C. c. nyansae* from Mwanza and w. Serengeti NP north to Mara GR, Lolgorien and South Nyanza.

FINE-BANDED or TULLBERG'S WOODPECKER *Campethera tullbergi taeniolaema* Plate 66

Length 7–7.5″. A *greenish* woodpecker of *montane forest canopy; finely barred body* appears plain at a distance. Olive-green above, browner on wings and tail and bright red on nape; blackish vermiculations on face, neck and throat merge into narrow bars on breast and belly; broader bars on flanks. Forehead and crown dull red in **male**, black with small white dots in **female**. **Juvenile** more greyish green, with darker barring below; head much as in adult female. **Call** a loud *kweek-kweek-kweek. . .*, often prolonged. **Range**: Local between 1750 and 3000 m from Mt Elgon and Cheranganis south to the Mau, Trans-Mara, Aberdare and Mt Kenya forests; also Nguruman Hills and nearby Loliondo District.

BUFF-SPOTTED WOODPECKER *Campethera nivosa herberti* Plate 66
Length 5.5–6″. An uncommon small woodpecker of *west Kenyan forest undergrowth.* Plain yellowish olive-green on back, with brown tail and white-spotted brown primaries; pale yellowish olive throat and face streaked with brown; *underparts olive (darker on breast), profusely spotted with dull yellow;* barred with dull yellowish white on flanks. **Male** has olive-brown forehead and crown and bright orange-red nape. **Female** lacks red, is brownish olive from forehead to nape. **Juvenile** resembles female but has greyish crown. **Call** a slightly descending rattle, *kee-kee-kee-kee-kee-kee-kee*, and a soft dry *chk chk chk-chk*. **Range**: Kakamega and South Nandi forests. Formerly on Mt Elgon.

BROWN-EARED WOODPECKER *Campethera c. caroli* Plate 66
Length 7–7.5″. A dark, *west Kenyan* forest woodpecker with buff-spotted face and throat and *large chestnut-brown patch on side of head*; top of head dark brown (some red on hindcrown and nape in male), back and wings golden olive; tail blackish; *olive underparts densely spotted with dull yellowish white*. **Juvenile** more olive-green above, with cinnamon ear patch and streaked chin, more barred on belly. **Calls** include a short *kwaa-kwaa-kwaa*, a single drawn-out *uwheeeeeu*, and a low trilled *trrrrrrrr*. **Range**: Kakamega Forest. Formerly on Mt Elgon.

SPECKLE-BREASTED or UGANDA SPOTTED WOODPECKER *Dendropicos poecilolaemus* Plate 65

Length 5.5″. An uncommon *west Kenyan* woodpecker of forest edge and riverine thickets. Often forages low. *Yellow-olive on back, faintly barred* from lower back to upper tail-coverts, the coverts and rump feathers red-tipped; face whitish with black streaks and spots; underparts pale olive-yellow or yellowish grey, *faintly speckled on upper breast*, and a few indistinct short streaks on belly; flanks faintly barred. **Male** *brown on forehead and forecrown*, red from hindcrown to nape. **Female** *black from crown to nape*. **Juvenile** greyish above and below, with little yellow; faintly dark-barred on back, and little or no red on rump/upper tail-coverts, but both sexes *red-crowned* (brighter and more extensive in male) and *black behind eyes and on nape*. **Call** a dry rattling *che-che-chi-chi-chichi*. **Range**: Mt Elgon and Kapenguria south to Busia, Mumias, Yala and Ukwala districts.

CARDINAL WOODPECKER *Dendropicos fuscescens* Plate 65
Length 5–5.5″. The common, *widespread small* woodpecker, conspicuously *streak-breasted* (other small woodpeckers have *spotted* underparts); has *orange or reddish rump/upper tail-coverts and yellow-shafted tail feathers*. **Male** plain brown on forehead and forecrown, red on hindcrown and nape. **Female** has brown forehead, black crown and nape. **Juvenile** duller than adult, both sexes with red crown. Variable; 3 of the 4 races contrastingly '*ladder-backed*' birds of savanna, tall bush or forest edge. The 4th, ***D. f.***

lepidus, of forest/dense woodland, is *almost plain golden olive above*, the faint dark barring inconspicuous. **D. f. massaicus** has yellowish wing-barring, is yellowish orange on rump/upper tail coverts; **hemprichii** is more sharply barred, has white barring on wings, and orange-red rump and tail-coverts; **hartlaubii** is more olive-brown above, more yellow-olive below with paler streaking. **Call** a soft, slow descending rattle, *kwee, kwee, kee-kee-kee-kikik*, repeated, or *chwi-chi-chi-chi-chi*, or a trilled *tri-tri-tri-trrrrrrr*. **Range**: *D. f. hemprichii* in e. and ne. Kenya south to the Northern Uaso Nyiro and Tana rivers, and along coast south to Kilifi; *massaicus* in n. and e. lowlands south of *hemprichii*, including Mombasa area; interbreeds with that race and with *hartlaubii* of se. Kenya/Tanzanian border areas from Chyulu Hills southward; *lepidus* in East Usambaras and Kenyan highlands up to 2600 m, interbreeding with *massaicus* in all contact zones.

BEARDED WOODPECKER *Dendropicos namaquus* Plate 66

Length 9″. A *large* dark woodland woodpecker, with two *broad black stripes* on a *whitish face*. Upperparts olive-brown with narrow pale barring, yellow-tinged on rump and upper tail-coverts; tail shafts yellow; chin/throat white, but other underparts olive-brown, closely pale-barred in nominate race, greyish with whitish *spots* in *schoensis*. **Male** has *white-speckled black forehead and forecrown*, red hindcrown/occiput and black nape. **Female** has entire top of head black, with white spots on forehead. **Juvenile** more olive above, less distinctly barred. **Call** a shrill *kwik-kwik-kwik*. . .; recalls Grey-headed Kingfisher. Drumming rather slow with last three or four taps separated. **Range**: *D. n. namaquus* from sea level to 2600 m, from interior n. Tanzania north to the Kenyan highlands, Meru and Tsavo NPs, and on coast from Kilifi to the Tana River. *D. n. schoensis* on n. Kenyan mountains and from Maralal, Karissia Hills and Laikipia Plateau south to Kerio Valley and Baringo Dist.

YELLOW-CRESTED WOODPECKER *Dendropicos xantholophus* Plate 66

Length 8–9″. A large dark woodpecker of *west Kenyan forests*. Head pattern resembles that of Bearded Woodpecker, but *forehead is brown*, and *hindcrown golden yellow* in male. Upperparts olive-brown washed with yellow on rump/upper tail-coverts; a few whitish bars on back; tail black; underparts, except for white throat, brown with white spots/bars on flanks, sometimes on belly. **Juvenile** has some yellow on hindcrown, is more olive above, greyer below, with more barring and less spotting than adult. **Call** a trilled, somewhat honeyguide-like *kerrreee, kerreee, kerrreee* followed by a descending *kwi-kwi-kwi-kwi*. . .. **Range**: Mt Elgon, North Nandi and Kakamega forests. Drumming accelerates at end (reverse of Bearded Woodpecker's).

GREY WOODPECKER *Dendropicos goertae* Plate 66

Length 7–7.5″. A *grey and golden-olive* woodpecker showing *bright red rump and upper tail-coverts* in flight. Fairly common in savanna and open woodland. Crown and nape of **male** red as, usually, is a patch on mid-belly/crissum (extensive in *D. g. rhodeogaster*, small and orange or yellow in western *centralis*); head mainly grey, entirely so in **female**; back and wings golden olive. **Juvenile** more greenish olive above, faintly barred below, with little red on belly. **Call** a weak *ch-ch-reeek-reeek-reeek*, a fast rattling *wik-wik-wik-wik-wik-wik*. . ., and a more emphatic *SKWI-SKWI-SKWI-skwi-skwi-skwi-skwi*. **Range**: *D. g. centralis* in w. and cent. Kenya north of Equator; *rhodeogaster* from Mt Kenya, Nyeri and Kisumu south to Serengeti NP, east to Arusha Dist. and w. slopes of Kilimanjaro.

OLIVE WOODPECKER *Dendropicos griseocephalus kilimensis* Plate 124

Length 6.5″. A red-rumped *Tanzanian forest* woodpecker, suggesting Grey Woodpecker, but *dark olive on breast* and with an *unbarred blackish tail*. **Male** dull golden olive-green on back, red from crown to nape, on rump and upper tail-coverts; head mainly grey (all grey in **female**). Underparts yellowish olive, more greyish on belly and crissum. **Juvenile** greyer, less yellowish below, darker above, paler red on rump. **Call** a laughing *yeh-yeh-*

yeh-yeh-yeh and week-week-week; a loud QUEEK of alarm. Does not have Grey Woodpecker's long rattle. **Range**: Local on Mt Meru, Kilimanjaro, Pare (scarce) and Usambara mts. Most numerous in West Usambaras between 1500 and 1850 m.

BROWN-BACKED WOODPECKER Picoides obsoletus   Plate 66

Length 5". A small brown-and-white woodpecker with boldly white-spotted wings. Back dull brown (blackish brown in P. o. crateri) barred with white from rump to tail. Bold brown ear patch and malar stripes bordered by white. Whitish underparts have fine faint brown streaks (darker and heavier in crateri). Top of head brown in **female**, with red occipital patch in **male**. **Juvenile** darker, with some barring below, red on crown in both sexes (more extensive in male). See Cardinal W. (D. f. lepidus). **Call** a loud, slightly descending SQUEE squee squee squee. . . and a chattering chew-chew-CHEW-CHEW-chew-chew-chew-chew. **Range**: P. o. ingens in cent. Kenyan highlands south to Thika and Nairobi NP; also Kongelai Escarpment and Saiwa NP, south to nw. Mara GR, Nguruman Hills and Loliondo. P. o. crateri ranges from the Crater Highlands south to Mbulu and Nou Forest. Shimba Hills and Arusha area birds not racially determined.

BROADBILLS, FAMILY EURYLAIMIDAE

Our single representative of this largely Asiatic family is a small thickset arboreal forest bird with large head and broad flat bill, short tarsi and strong syndactylous toes. The tail is short, the wings rounded.

AFRICAN BROADBILL Smithornis capensis   Plate 68

Length 5". Boldly streaked and somewhat flycatcher-like. Mainly olive-brown above; crown black in male, grey in female of eastern races, blackish in western meinertzhageni; white bases of lower back and rump feathers usually concealed at rest. The more narrowly streaked medianus is buffier below than the other races. In w. Kenyan forests see female Shrike-Flycatcher. **Call** a loud strident vibrating sound like that of an old-fashioned automobile horn: PR-R-R-R-R-R-RRRRRRUP, or KRRRRRRRROOOOO, produced during display flight or at rest. A soft plaintive tui-tui-tui or twee-o, twee-o . . . may alternate with the louder sound or be given separately. Both sexes perform remarkable display flight, describing a 1-m diameter circle around perch on rapidly vibrating wings, puffing out white on back and rump, and giving the 'klaxon horn' call. **Range**: S. c. meinertzhageni restricted to Kakamega and North Nandi forests; medianus formerly widespread in montane areas east of Rift Valley from Mt Kenya and Sagana Forest in Nyeri Dist. south to Nairobi suburbs and Chyulu Hills, but now rare and extirpated from most areas; also known from Usambara Mts, Kilimanjaro, Mt Meru, Arusha NP, Mbulumbulu and Marang forests; suahelicus in Shimba Hills and Arabuko–Sokoke Forest.

PITTAS, FAMILY PITTIDAE

Our species is a rare intra-African migrant from the southern tropics where it breeds; a secretive, brightly coloured, terrestrial forest bird, long-legged, short-tailed and with rounded wings.

AFRICAN PITTA Pitta angolensis longipennis   Plate 68

Length 7". A plump, somewhat thrush-like bird of the forest floor; scratches noisily for insects and molluscs in leaf litter; flirts tail as it walks. Cobalt-blue 'shoulders' and rump, and white patch at base of primaries prominent in flight; bright red under tail-coverts inconspicuous unless bird is perched on low tree branch. **Call** a querulous scolding skee-ow (Moreau) and a deep short trill followed by a sharp wing-clap. Usually silent.

Range/status: Formerly more or less regular Apr.–Oct. in coastal forests north to Gede, but few records after 1983. Widely scattered reports elsewhere, mainly of exhausted or dead vagrants in highland areas from Usambara Mts, Arusha Distr. and Ngorongoro Crater north to Nairobi, Timau and Kongelai.

LARKS, FAMILY ALAUDIDAE

Cryptically patterned, terrestrial birds of open areas, stouter-billed and generally bulkier than the superficially similar pipits (Motacillidae) of the same habitats. They walk, at times with a shuffling gait, and can run rapidly. Some are migratory or nomadic, abundant one year, rare or absent the next. Identification is complicated by subspecific variation, different colour morphs and by wear and fading of plumage. Larks have but one annual (postnuptial) moult, so worn birds are frequently encountered. Differences between these and freshly feathered individuals of the same species can be striking; abraded birds appear more uniform as light feather tips and edges wear away, leaving the dark central portions which become browner. Overall plumage coloration is often correlated with soil colour. The sexes are different only in sparrow-larks. Juveniles tend to be speckled or scalloped above.

SINGING BUSH LARK *Mirafra cantillans* · **Plate 71**

Length 5″. A fairly common lark of open or bushed grassland, quite nondescript when worn, except for whitish superciliaries and *white tail sides,* but in fresh plumage also shows *dark ear-coverts separated from dark pectoral patches by a partial whitish collar,* and a necklace of *spotted streaks across the breast.* Rufous-buff flight-feather edges (disappearing with wear) can make *wings appear largely rufous in flight. Breast patches absent in worn birds* (including some breeding adults). Rarely almost as dark as White-tailed Lark, but has brighter feather edges, fainter breast spots, less white in tail. (More coarsely streaked Somali Short-toed Lark has pale sandy buff, not rufous, primary edges, broad pale eye-ring and heavier bill. See Friedmann's Lark.) **Juvenile** buffier than adult, *scalloped with pale buff* on crown and back. **Song** a prolonged medley of tsips, trills, warbling and scratchy notes, fluctuating in pitch and intensity, some notes distinct, others run together, and often ending in a buzzy trill. Shorter songs include *chk chk tsitsitsiki-zreeeeeeeeeee* (from perch) and *tsit tsit tsit chreet chreet chreet tsikitswik-sik srisrisrisrisrisrisrisri* (in high circling or low hovering flight). **Range:** *M. c. marginata* from Turkana south to Arusha, Moshi, Mt Meru and Kilimanjaro lowlands. Widespread in drier parts of Rift Valley. Appears to move south with Nov./Dec. rains through Tsavo West NP. Replaced by White-tailed Lark in sw. Kenya. Birds near Sudan border may represent *M. c. chadensis* .

WHITE-TAILED LARK *Mirafra albicauda* **Plate 72**

Length 5″. *Prefers dense grass on black 'cotton' soils;* usually avoids overgrazed areas. Appears *blackish* compared to other grassland larks, and shows *much white in the spread tail* when flushed. (Faded birds are browner, resembling Singing Bush Lark.) Bases of secondaries and inner primaries show much cinnamon-rufous in flight, but *only outer two primaries edged rufous.* **Juvenile** scaly above. (Browner Singing Bush Lark has paler breast spots, frequently sings from bushes or while hovering. Blackish morph of Flappet Lark has deep buff tail sides and slimmer bill. Dark morph of Williams's Lark, only in lava desert, is heavily spotted on breast, thicker-billed and almost patternless on back. See Friedmann's Lark.) Distinctive **song** of separated sharp or throaty notes with an occasional whistle; lacks Singing Bush Lark's trills: *tsik trrr chi-chi tsik chrr tsik-tsik tsyuk. . ..* Male's circular song-flight takes place far above ground. **Range:** Mainly in the highlands from West Pokot, Siaya and Kitui districts to Athi–Kapiti Plains near Nairobi south to Serengeti NP and plains west of Arusha. Also on Lewa Downs near Timau.

WILLIAMS'S LARK *Mirafra williamsi* **Plate 72**

Length 5.5″. A *heavy-billed, almost plain-backed* lark of *northern deserts.* Secretive (unlike Masked Lark in same habitat); scuttles rodent-like among rocks and low shrubs. General coloration rufous to nearly black, matching the red soil and lava rocks of its habitat. Upperparts of worn birds show no pale streaks, and *dark streaking is more prominent on crown and nape than on back.* Outer tail feathers white. Bill largely ivory, more pinkish above. **Rufous morph** bright above, but back duller and browner than wings. Fresh wing-coverts, *inner flight feathers and central rectrices edged with pale reddish buff,* the primaries with rufous; lower throat and breast sparsely spotted with dark brown sometimes mixed with rufous; below this a streaky band of rufous flanked by red-brown pectoral patches; feet heavy, pale. **Dark morph** *deep vinous brown or blackish above;* sides of face with some chestnut; *breast mottled chestnut and dusky, with bold blackish pectoral patches; flanks heavily streaked;* small throat spots usually evident. Juvenile unknown. (Singing Bush Lark and Friedmann's Lark, in grassier habitats, are boldly streaked above, less well marked below, have bolder superciliaries and lack chestnut on breast.) **Song** of thin scratchy notes with louder sharper ones toward end: *tsit-tsitsit-sit-sureet-eet, tse-tseetsuleu-eet-sueet . . . chuck tseet tserk tsuk tsuk tser-SREET tsur-SREET tsri-tsri tsur-SREET tsri-tsri-tsri tsur-SREET . . ..* Sunrise display, within 3 m of ground, involves slow, jerky, laboured flight in which body and tail hang almost vertically, wingbeats accompanied by the sharp *tsur-SREET* phrase. Take-off call a short metallic *tseu.* **Range**: Rocky plains north of Marsabit (locally common in Dida Galgalu Desert); also east of Isiolo among low *Barleria* shrubs on rocky lava desert.

FRIEDMANN'S LARK *Mirafra pulpa* **Plate 71**

Length 5–5.5″. A rare bird resembling Singing Bush Lark but more richly coloured and more heavily streaked on nape and upper back, the streaking enhanced in fresh plumage by broad pale feather edges; superciliary stripes somewhat less prominent. Singing birds readily distinguished vocally and by *prominent white throat.* Further differs from Singing Bush Lark in its *red-brown* central rectrices, inner wing feathers and coverts each with a *fine dark submarginal line between feather centre and pale edge.* (Dark line also present on feathers of juv. *M. cantillans.*) Dark ear-coverts accentuated by white postauricular 'collar' extending partly around hindneck. Breast streaks aggregated into patch at sides of breast; sides and flanks with diffuse brown streaks. In fresh plumage, *head appears streaked* (more scalloped in *cantillans*); *scapulars and wings more reddish than back.* **Rufous morph** more reddish overall, less contrastingly patterned, the white areas washed with warm buff, and pale collar less distinct; may show some rufous at sides of breast with the brown streaks. **Juvenile** more rufous above than young Singing Bush Lark. Gregarious territorial birds share shrubby grassland with that species, Red-winged and Flappet Larks. Vocal at night and all day. **Song** a whistled *uREEu* or *ooEEoo,* accented in middle and nearly trisyllabic, from bush or tree and during laboured circular song-flight. **Range**: Irregular in both Tsavo parks (Nov.–Feb., Apr.–May and Aug.); and Mkomazi GR (Sept., Dec.–Jan.). Old records near Kibwezi and near Isiolo in n. Kenya.

RUFOUS-NAPED LARK *Mirafra africana* **Plate 72**

Length 6–7″. A *large stocky short-tailed* lark with conspicuous *rufous wings in flight.* Perches conspicuously on fences and rocks; rises from ground with jerky fluttering wing action, but sustained flight direct and somewhat undulating; walks and stands with upright stance. Highland race *athi* has *no distinct rufous nape;* western *tropicalis* more *reddish brown above with contrasting blackish streaks,* rufous on hindcrown, nape, and outer tail webs of se. Kenya still brighter rufous. **Juveniles** of all races dark-crowned, with bold dark spotting on breast and at sides of foreneck. (Similar Red-winged Lark is larger, longer-tailed, with prominent dark pectoral patches. Flappet Lark is smaller, slimmer, more scalloped or spotted above, relatively long tailed; rufous morph resembles *M. a. harterti* but is less heavily streaked above, with broader rufous tail edges and shorter bill.) Usual whistled **song** repeats a single phrase such as *weet-ureet* or *chi-witu-EEE* or *tew-tew-tewi-li.* A more complex *twee-tew-pewi-CHEE pewiCHEE* is similarly repeated, as is a prolonged complex series of sputtering, chirping and whistled notes. **Range**: *M. a. tropicalis* from Mt Elgon south to

414

Serengeti NP, Crater and Mbulu highlands and Mt Hanang; *athi* from Maralal, Laikipia Plateau and cent. Rift Valley south through cent. Kenyan highlands to plains around Kilimanjaro, Mt Meru and Arusha; *harterti* on Simba and Emali plains of se. Kenya.

RED-WINGED LARK *Mirafra h. hypermetra*　　　　Plate 72

Length 8.5-9". *Suggests Rufous-naped Lark*, and like that species shows *much rufous in the primaries* (especially in flight), but larger, longer-tailed, and with *dark patches on sides of chest* (less obvious in worn birds). Regularly sings and makes short vertical song-flights from shrubs; also sings while hovering. On ground, often assumes very upright stance with stretched neck. Dimorphic. (*M. africana harterti* can be confused with rufous morph of Red-winged, but is stockier and lacks the pectoral patches. Flappet Lark is much smaller, more barred or scalloped above, lacks pectoral patches and shows broad tawny or rufous tail sides.) **Song** of clear whistles—loud, melodious and variable, typically with variations on a single phrase: *tew-EE-tew, tew TEW-e-tew, WEE-tew, WEE-tew. . ., pee-tu-wee , teree-teree, cheet-twertiLEE . . ..* Also has a clear bubbling *tree, turquireedo-qureee-qureee* (last 2 notes higher), and complex songs uttered *continuously for several minutes, with imitations* of other larks, Ashy Cisticola *et al*. **Range**: N. and e. lowlands from Huri Hills and Marsabit south to Meru, the Tsavo NPs, Mkomazi GR and Masai Steppe, west to Tarangire NP. Prefers lower, drier country than Rufous-naped Lark, with no known range overlap. (Birds along Sudan border near Loki-chokio may represent the small race *kidepoensis*, not collected in Kenya.)

FLAPPET LARK *Mirafra rufocinnamomea*　　　　Plate 72

Length 5–5.5". Suggests a small, slender Rufous-naped Lark with *tawny or pale rufous outer tail-feathers* and *more spotted or barred upperparts*. Inconspicuous except for breeding male's loud rattle-like 'flappeting' from high above ground: *prrt. . . prrt. . . prrrrrrrt. . .*, presumably produced by wings, employed in undulating, circling courtship flight and when disturbed. Coastal *fischeri* usually dull earth-brown above, but a more heavily barred, cinnamon-brown morph is known; bright rufous or chestnut *torrida* is widespread inland; western *kawirondensis* is darker (with a rare blackish morph), less barred than eastern birds, the markings more streaky. More rufous-backed individuals may show only faint barring with some thin black shaft streaks; colour of underparts varies in all races. **Juvenile** more barred above than most adults. (More common Rufous-naped Lark is larger, heavier, shorter tailed, much larger billed, streaked rather than barred above. Fawn-coloured Lark is slimmer-billed, with whitish (not buffy) superciliaries, blackish loral lines and thin white tail edges; neither species flappets.) **Song** slow and melodious, the phrases well separated: *te-ew. . . eee eetieu. . . eet pee-ee. . . eet pee-ee. . . wee-it whur. . .weet we-EW. . . wee eetiEW. . ..* Call, *tuwee tuwee*. **Range**: *M. r. fischeri* on coast and inland to lower Tana River and Shimba Hills; *torrida* in n. and e. Kenya south to the Tsavo parks, Mkomazi GR, Arusha and Moshi districts and Mbulumbulu south through interior Tanzania; *kawirondensis* in Lake Victoria basin and Mara GR south to Serengeti NP and Maswa GR.

COLLARED LARK *Mirafra collaris*　　　　Plate 72

Length 5–6". A bright rufous-backed lark of sandy red soils in *northern Kenya. Black-and -white collar across the nape and sides of neck* unique; note also the *narrow black band across lower throat*. **Juvenile** has black spots on back and dusky spots on throat. Wary, elusive, and runs rapidly. Reportedly 'flappets'. **Song** described as a plaintive ascending whistling. **Range**: Mandera and Moyale areas south to Garissa (said to be common in areas supporting *Acacia turnbulliana*). In Somalia, inhabits tussock grass with low shrubs.

FAWN-COLOURED LARK *Mirafra africanoides intercedens*　　　　Plate 72

Length 5.5–6.5". A *trim, slender-billed*, often sharply patterned lark with *dark cheeks, bold white superciliaries and black lores*; tail edges white. **Brown and rufous morphs** illustrated. Rare dark **grey morph** (almost blackish above when worn) known from Loita Plains to Naivasha and Nakuru; birds in northern deserts are noticeably pale. **Juvenile** streaked brown and buff on back, with rufous flight feathers and dusky lores. (Juv. Pink-breasted Lark lacks rufous in the wings and has pale lores. In far ne. Kenya see Gillett's Lark.) **Song** a short thin *seet suweet sweet-sweet*, variable but the terminal double *sweet* typical. Also a colourless *tsee-tsee, tsi-tsi-tsi-tsitsi*. **Range**: Lodwar and Marsabit south through much of s. Kenya and across n. Tanzania from Serengeti and Tarangire NPs to foothills of North Pare Mts, Mkomazi GR and the Masai Steppe. Especially common in the Rift Valley.

GILLETT'S LARK *Mirafra gilletti (arorihensis ?)* Plate 72
Length 6–6.75". A rarely recorded bird of *extreme northeastern Kenya*. Resembles a rufous Fawn-coloured Lark, but slightly larger, less streaked above (especially on crown), with *grey rump and upper tail-coverts*, and light brownish rufous (instead of sepia) streaks on the breast. Juvenile unknown. In Somalia, prefers hard stony ground among sparse thorn bushes; not a grassland bird (Archer and Godman). **Call** undescribed. **Range**: Specimens taken near Mandera and El Wak along the Somali border in May 1901.

PINK-BREASTED LARK *Mirafra poecilosterna* Plate 72

Length 6–6.5". A slender *pipit-like* lark typical of dry *Acacia* and *Commiphora* bush; commonly *perches in trees. Face pinkish cinnamon with mottling of the same colour on breast and sides; no white in tail* and *wings and tail show no rufous*. **Juvenile** paler than young Rufous-naped and Flappet Larks; lacks dark lores of Fawn-coloured Lark. See Red-throated Pipit. Usual **call** a simple *tseet-tseet* or *pweet*. **Song** a series of up to seven rather squeaky high thin notes, often running into a short, descending, squeaky chatter, or a shorter *tseet-tseetsew-seet* or *tsit-tsit-tseu-tseet*, the last note higher. **Range**: North, east and south of the Kenyan highlands south to Mkomazi GR and eastern parts of the Masai Steppe.

DUSKY LARK *Pinarocorys n. nigricans* Plate 122
Length 7.5–8". A large *dark thrush-like* lark that favours recently burnt ground. Forages restlessly, stopping and flicking wings after each stop. Bold facial pattern distinctive; female paler and less well marked. Immature duller with much buffy brown feather edging on upperparts. **Call** a soft *wek-wek-wek*. **Starus**: Breeds in miombo zone of w. Tanzania. In our region known from a single specimen taken in Arusha NP, Oct. 1962.

SPIKE-HEELED LARK *Chersomanes albofasciata beesleyi* Plate 122
Length 4.5". A northern Tanzanian lark of barren treeless plains. Note *upright carriage* and the fairly *long decurved bill*, and distinctive *very short white-tipped tail*; flight undulating. **Juvenile** lacks rufous on nape and has less white feather tipping on upperparts than adult; breast diffusely speckled with brown, the feathers white-tipped; rest of underparts pale. **Flight call** a trilled *piree* or *tirrr* repeated several times. Alarm note, a harsh *skeee*. Southern African races sing *chip-kwip-kwip-kwip, ti-ti-ti-ti-ti, chirri-chirri-chirri* (Maclean). **Range**: Only near Kingerete, 30–50 km north of Arusha.

GREATER SHORT-TOED LARK *Calandrella brachydactyla longipennis* Plate 71
Length 5–5.5". A *pale* vagrant lark with a *short dull yellowish bill*, broad buffy white superciliaries bordered below by dark postocular lines, and broad white tail edges. Similar Somali Short-toed Lark is darker, with streaked breast and larger bill. **Call** a short chatter when flushed. **Status**: Palearctic. Normally winters from the Sahel to ne. Ethiopia. Known in Kenya from two specimen records (Athi River, Nov. 1899, and near Mombasa, Dec. 1964). **Taxonomic Note**: Included in *C. cinerea* by some authors.

√ RED-CAPPED LARK *Calandrella cinerea* Plate 71
Length 5.5–6". A gregarious highland lark of short grass and bare ground. *Rufous-chestnut crown* feathers often erected, particularly when it stands upright and alert. Shows whitish superciliaries and rufous patches on sides of breast; outer rectrices edged white (noticeable in flight). *C. c. saturatior* is brighter, more rufous above than the somewhat greyer *williamsi*. **Juvenile** lacks reddish tones, is scaly above with light feather edges; breast dark-spotted with dusky patch at each side. **Call** a hard *chip* or *chirrip* (sometimes

double) when flushed. Flocks in flight produce a soft twittering. A brief aerial song, infrequently heard, consists of a few thin harsh notes. **Range**: *C. c. williamsi* in the cent. Kenyan highlands, and south to Amboseli NP; *saturatior* from Mara GR south to Serengeti NP, east to Crater Highlands and Arusha.

SOMALI SHORT-TOED LARK *Calandrella somalica* Plate 71

Length 5–5.5 ". A gregarious lark of dry grassy plains, heavily streaked above, with a *large pale eye-ring or subocular semi-circle joining the creamy buff superciliary and postauricular areas. C. s. athensis* is dark brown and sandy buff, the pale wing edgings at first prominent, but wearing away prior to the annual moult. Edges of tail white; central rectrices almost black. Northern *megaensis* paler and sandier than *athensis*, but head and neck may show rich buff wash. (Singing Bush Lark lacks the distinctive facial pattern and usually shows prominent rufous primary edges. See also Williams's and Friedmann's Larks.) At very close range, *Calandrella* separated from all *Mirafra* species by concealed nostrils. **Call** a short trilling *trrrit* when flushed; flock produces a chittering sound. Prolonged trilling flight song of *athensis* recalls European Skylark: *trr-trr-treer, treer-treet-treer-trtrtrtr-tlee-tlee-treer. . ..* Song of presumed *megaensis* includes rapid medleys of scratchy and clear notes plus an occasional canary-like trill; suggests songs of Greater and Lesser Short-toed Larks, *C. brachydactyla* and *C. rufescens*, but with more distinct notes: *chlip-chlip-slureeet, chree-chree-chree, quree quree, tyee-tyee squiree. . . screet-weet, squirrrrrr.* **Range**: *C. s. athensis* from Nairobi NP south to Arusha. (Formerly north to Naivasha and plains below Mt Kenya.) Birds at Buffalo Springs GR (March) and Huri Hills (Nov.) probably *megaensis*, and hundreds south of Maralal (Nov.) almost certainly that race. **Taxonomic Note**: Often considered conspecific with palearctic *C. rufescens*.

MASKED LARK *Spizocorys personata* Plate 71

Length 5.5–6". A distinctive *northern desert* lark with white throat, *black face* and *heavy pink or yellowish horn bill*. Favours areas of lava rock on red soils. Head and neck grey-brown. Northern *yavelloensis* noticeably grey above, with grey breast; southern races browner. **Song** a rolling *chew-chi-chew, chew* or *tew-tew-tutew-tew*, and a thin metallic *tsik-tsik tseedleee*. Calls include a high-pitched *treeeeeee*, a single *chew*, a double *djew-djew*, and a repeated high *tee tee tee tee.* **Range**: *S. p. yavelloensis* from Ethiopian border south to Dida Galgalu Desert; *mcchesneyi* on Marsabit Plateau, *intensa* in e. Shaba GR and between Isiolo and Garba Tula.

SHORT-TAILED LARK *Pseudalaemon fremantlii* Plate 71

Length 5.5". Unique; *long-billed and short-tailed*, with a conspicuous *vertical black mark below the eye* and partly encircling ear-coverts. White superciliary stripes and dark patches on each side of foreneck add to the distinctive face pattern. Wanders in pairs or small groups, sometimes with *Calandrella* larks. Uncommon **rufous morph** rufous above instead of greyish and black. Northern *megaensis* noticeably paler than southern *delamerei*. **Juvenile** with whitish feather tips above and small brown spots on the breast. **Song** a slow deliberate whistle delivered from the ground: *seeu seeu. . . seeu seeu seeu. . . seeu seeu TEWleu*, slightly slurred. Take-off call a distinctive sharp *tewi*. **Range**: *P. f. delamerei* from Nairobi NP south to Amboseli NP and Arusha, west to Crater Highlands and Serengeti Plains; *megaensis* from the Ethiopian border south to Marsabit; sight records from near Maralal probably represent this race.

CRESTED LARK *Galerida cristata somaliensis* Plate

Length 6.75". A *sharply crested sand-coloured lark* of *sandy* deserts in northern Kenya. (Similar Thekla Lark of rocky deserts is darker above than Crested, has darker breast markings and differs vocally.) **Juvenile** has pale feather tips above and speckled crown. **Calls** include a thin *tee-tewit* and a slurred *seeureet* (higher at end), in flight or from the ground; when flushed, *cherrreet*. **Songs** loud, clear, and sweet, among them a slurred liquid *ti-TSI-oo, EEE-tsew-seeet*, a musical *tee-tee-tew TEW-e-tew*, a brief *sree-sree-reeu*, and a longer *weee-twee, tewee-tew, twee-too-ee-tooee*. A more complex warbling song of these phrases and a few scratchy notes, plus mimicry of other species, may last for 30 sec. or longer. **Range**: Lake Turkana basin south in the Rift Valley to Lokori and Kapedo, east to Turbi and Marsabit districts and the Kaisut Desert.

THEKLA LARK or SHORT-CRESTED LARK *Galerida theklae huriensis* Plate 71

Length 6.5″. A *conspicuously crested* lark of *rocky places* in arid n. Kenya. *Overall tone much darker and less sandy than Crested Lark*, the dorsal streaks and *breast spots heavier and blacker*; heavily marked extremes of Crested seldom if ever as boldly spotted as *G. t. huriensis* (but juvenile Thekla buffier than adult and with fainter breast streaks). Crest and *bill slightly shorter* than in Crested, and *light grey upper tail-coverts paler than grey-brown rump*. Unlike Crested Lark, seldom digs forcefully with bill. The two species may be together where habitats merge. Common **call** of Thekla a short buzzy *chureeeeet*, quite unlike thin clear whistles of Crested. Short songs from perched birds, *sweet seet sureet-tsew* and *tseet-tseet-chreet, chureet, tsur-reeeeeee*. In flight display, groups of scratchy notes and short trills precede a faster, longer and complex twittering. Mimics other species. **Range**: Huri Hills, Allia Bay, North Horr and Turbi south to Loyangalani and Marsabit districts. (Common in Dida Galgalu Desert.) **Taxonomic Note**: Considered a race of the Asian *G. malabarica* by some authors.

✓ FISCHER'S SPARROW-LARK *Eremopterix leucopareia* Plate 71

Length 4.5″. A common gregarious sparrow-like lark of short-grass plains; compact and short-tailed. **Male**'s *large white cheek patch plus dark throat and mid-ventral line* diagnostic. **Female** has *broad black line from belly to under tail-coverts* (not easily seen). **Juvenile** mottled above with pale buff nape patch, long tawny wing panel and small blackish belly patch. (Other sparrow-larks are thicker-billed and have whitish outer tail feathers; female Chestnut-headed paler and buffier than female Fischer's, with no dark mid-ventral line; female Chestnut-backed shows rufous or chestnut wing-coverts.) **Call** a low *chirrup* or *seet-eet*. Flocks utter a soft twitter. When breeding, a simple short song recalling a repeated *Passer* chirp given incessantly in rather high flight. **Range**: From Kongelai, Maralal, Meru NP and Tsavo West NP south beyond our limits.

CHESTNUT-BACKED SPARROW-LARK *Eremopterix leucotis madaraszi* Plate 71

Length 5″. A dark nomadic sparrow-lark with a predilection for black soils. Scarce and of erratic appearance; sometimes flocks with *E. signata*. **Male**'s *chestnut back and large white area on side of head and sides of breast* distinctive; also shows a *narrow whitish band on nape*. **Female** variable but always with *chestnut wing-coverts and black on face, fore-neck and centre of belly*; some are blackish-crowned and densely streaked on throat and breast. In flight, both sexes show *whitish grey upper tail-coverts and outer rectrices*. **Juvenile** resembles juv. Fischer's Sparrow-Lark but has *heavier bill*. See Chestnut-headed Sparrow-lark. **Song** a rather soft, variable *chitichu ch-ch-ch CHIwieu, ch-ch-ch CHIwieu. . ..* Call a sharp rattling *chirip-cheew*. **Range**: Erratic north, south and southeast of the Kenyan highlands, regular in parts of Meru and Tsavo East NPs; sporadic in Arusha, Tarangire and Serengeti NPs and on the Ardai Plains. Formerly (or rarely) on Kenyan coast.

CHESTNUT-HEADED SPARROW-LARK *Eremopterix signata* Plate 71

Length 4.5″. A pale sparrow-lark of dry plains in *northern Kenya*. **Male**'s *crown and nape auburn, chestnut or blackish*, with a *large circular white area on centre of crown*. **Female** sandy buff with *whitish patch on each side of head* and *pale rufous superciliaries*. Immature male resembles female but has *dull chestnut throat and upper breast and black-*

ish patch on lower breast and belly; suggests a lighter-coloured, larger-billed female Fisher's Sparrow-Lark. **Juvenile** pale brown and scalloped, with sandy buff face and nape; buff breast band mottled or streaked dusky. Freshly plumaged birds show pale buff wing-feather edgings; some individuals more uniformly tawny brown above and heavily streaked below. **Song** described as a short twittering. Call a sharp *chip-up*. **Range**: Dida Galgalu and Kaisut deserts near Marsabit south to Kapedo, Meru NP and Tsavo East NP. Wanders to Tsavo West NP, the lower Tana River and the coast north of Malindi. *E. s. signata* and more western *harrisoni* reportedly meet near Lake Turkana but limits of races uncertain. Little overlap with Fisher's Sparrow-Lark (both known from Buffalo Springs GR and Meru NP).

WAGTAILS, PIPITS, AND LONGCLAWS, FAMILY MOTACILLIDAE

Small ground birds with slender pointed bills. The moderate to long tail, with white or buff outer feathers, is habitually pumped up and down in wagtails and most pipits. Forward and backward head motion is also exaggerated, especially in wagtails, and all species walk rather than hop. Wagtails are slender and long-tailed with unstreaked plumage, mostly black and white, yellow and grey. Excepting adult *Tmetothylacus*, pipits are somewhat lark-like, brownish and cryptically marked above, and with similar elongated inner secondaries ('tertials'). Some are difficult to identify; the most useful field characters are colour of outer tail-feathers, degree of streaking, and vocalizations. Longclaws are grassland birds, more robust, shorter-tailed, and with more rounded wings than pipits. Their plumage is brown-streaked above, yellow or pink below, often with a black breast band. The feet are stout, the hind claw extremely long.

AFRICAN PIED WAGTAIL *Motacilla aguimp vidua*   Plate 69

Length 8". The common *black-and-white* wagtail of town and countryside, mostly black above, with black mask and breast band, large white wing patch and superciliary stripes. **Juvenile** brownish grey where adult is black, washed brownish on flanks; breast band may be brown. See White Wagtail. **Song** a sustained sequence of melodious whistling and piping notes, *weet-weet, wip-wip-wip, weet-wee-wee. . ..* Calls are a whistled *tuwhee* and *tseet-tseet-tseet. . .,* thin but loud. **Range**: Throughout, excepting arid n. and ne. Kenya.

WHITE WAGTAIL *Motacilla a. alba*   Plate 69

Length 7.5". A grey-and-white wagtail, characteristic of muddy shores. White sides of head contrast with dark crown/nape and *black crescent across upper breast.* In spring may have black chin and throat. Tail black with white sides. **Male** broadly white on forehead, black from crown to nape. **Female** and **first-winter male** may show little white on forehead and have grey nape and crown. (Cape Wagtail darker above, buff-tinged below.) **Call** a high-pitched double *tschizzic.* **Range/status**: Palearctic migrant, Nov.–Mar. Common at Lake Turkana, regular in cent. Kenyan highlands south to Nairobi; scarce elsewhere.

GREY WAGTAIL *Motacilla c. cinerea*   Plate 69 ✔

Length 7.5–8". A very *long-tailed* wagtail, *grey above with yellowish green rump.* Underparts mainly yellow, with buff flanks; throat white or (in spring male) black; superciliary stripes whitish. In flight shows white outer tail-feathers and *long white band across base of secondaries and inner primaries; tarsi pinkish brown or brownish flesh* (not black). Forages along highland forest streams. Pumps tail strongly during feeding pauses. (Shorter-tailed Yellow Wagtail is olive-green above without contrasting rump.) **Call** a sharp metallic *chitik!*; alarm note a shrill *si-heet.* **Range/status**: Palearctic migrant, late Sept.–Mar.; mainly in Kenyan highlands and Crater Highlands of n. Tanzania. At times lower, including coastal areas.

MOUNTAIN WAGTAIL *Motacilla clara torrentium* **Plate 69**

Length 6.75–7.5". Slender and especially *long-tailed*; characteristic of *highland forest streams*. *Light blue-grey on back*, with a *narrow black breast band*; tail broadly white-sided. **Juvenile** brownish above, buff-tinged below, with breast band reduced or absent. **Song** a sustained series of trilled musical phrases and short sibilant notes: *tsrrrrup, tsrrrrup . . . tsu-tse-seu, tsweu-tswii, trrrip . . ..* Call a loud *chizzik.* **Range**: Local in highlands of cent. and w. Kenya and n. Tanzania (recorded as low as 700 m at Taveta and lower in East Usambara Mts).

CAPE WAGTAIL *Motacilla capensis wellsi* **Plate 69**

Length 7.5–8". A dull *olive-brown*, relatively *short-tailed* wagtail of lake and swamp edges. Shows *narrow buffy white superciliary stripes* and dusky lores; whitish underparts (sometimes with faint salmon-pink wash) with narrow dark breast band; tail blackish with white outer feathers. **Juvenile** has buff wing edgings, yellowish underparts; recalls brownish juv. African Pied Wagtail but lacks the large white wing patch and has narrow superciliaries. (Female and young Yellow Wagtails lack black breast band. Young White Wagtail with narrow breast band resembles Cape, but is paler above, nearly pure white below.) **Song** a jumble of twittering notes, *tweep-tweep-tweep, witititi, cheep-tweep*, etc. Call a piping *tweep.* **Range**: Mau and Trans-Mara areas east to Naivasha, the Aberdares, Nyeri, Karatina and Limuru districts.

✔YELLOW WAGTAIL *Motacilla flava* **Plate 69**

Length 7". A gregarious wagtail of shorelines and short grassland, often accompanying large herbivores. Olive-green or brownish above, yellow or yellowish below; pale superciliary stripes usually prominent; tarsi black; *throat yellow in adult male, whitish or buff in female.* **Male's** head pattern varies racially (see plate). **Females** often racially indistinguishable; crown and face olive-brown or grey-brown, superciliaries buff or whitish. **First-winter** bird resembles female, but with sharper white wing-bars, and usually more whitish below; young males show adult head pattern by Dec. (Grey Wagtail has yellowish rump and longer tail.) **Call** *tseeip* or *tseer.* **Range/status**: Widespread, often abundant palearctic migrant, mid-Sep.–mid-Apr. Main races are *flava* (throughout), *lutea* (mainly eastern grasslands), *beema* (mainly eastern) and *thunbergi* (mainly western especially spring); *feldegg* local in wetlands, *leucocephala* scarce south to Arusha.

TAWNY PIPIT *Anthus c. campestris* **Plate 70**

Length 6.5". A slender *pale* pipit of short grassland. Almost uniform sandy brown above and with *only a few short dark brown streaks on buff breast*. Shows prominent creamy white superciliary stripes, brownish lores and ear-coverts, narrow dark brown malar stripes, and much pale wing edging; buffy white fringes of median coverts contrast strongly with blackish centres. Frequently pumps the *rather long, white-sided tail.* **First-winter** bird more streaked on breast, distinctly streaked above. (Grassland Pipit has similar tail pattern, but is less wagtail-like, has more upright carriage and differs vocally. Long-billed Pipit is darker and duller above, deeper buff below, with buffy white tail sides.) **Call** a loud *tseep* or *tseuc* on take-off and landing. **Range/status**: Rare palearctic migrant south to Lamu and Tsavo.

✔ GRASSLAND PIPIT *Anthus cinnamomeus* **Plate 70**

Length 6–6.5". The common East African pipit, streaked buffy brown above, and with *short dark streaks across buff upper breast*; face shows *pronounced pale superciliary and dark malar stripes*; sides of tail white. Broad, pale buff dorsal feather edges of fresh plumage largely lacking in worn adults. **Juvenile** duskier above, with heavy dark breast streaks extending to flanks; back blotched or spotted with black, the feathers narrowly buff-tipped. Coastal *A. c. annae* is paler, greyer and slightly smaller than inland *lacuum.* Dark 'Jackson's Pipit,' *A. (c.) latistriatus*, discussed below, is possibly not conspecific. (Long-billed Pipit is larger and darker with longer bill and tail,

less streaked above; has buffy white tail sides. Tree and Red-throated Pipits are smaller, extensively streaked below, with smaller bills and shorter legs. Larger Plain-backed Pipit almost unstreaked above and has buff tail edges. See Tawny Pipit.) **Song** *tree-tree-tree,* or *sreet-sreet-sreet,* sometimes continuing as *chew chew chee chew-chew-chew,* from low perch or in display flight. Take-off call a sharp *chip* or *trip.* **Range**: *A. c. lacuum* widespread to above 3000 m in cent. and s. Kenya, and n. Tanzania. *A. c. annae* is coastal. **Taxonomic Note**: Perhaps conspecific with Richard's Pipit, *A. (novaeseelandiae) richardi,* but most authors now treat the African birds as a separate species. The little-known *latistriatus,* described from w. Kenya in 1899, has not been positively recorded here again. It has been considered a race of Long-billed Pipit, a full species, or a dark morph or race of Grassland Pipit.

LONG-BILLED PIPIT *Anthus similis hararensis*   **Plate 70**

Length 7″. A rather *large, stocky* pipit with *relatively long bill* and a *long tail with buffy white sides, not pumped up and down* as in other pipits. Dusky brown above with diffuse streaking; warm buff below, with lightly streaked breast. Face marked with buff superciliaries and dark malar stripes. Often on thinly grassed *rocky hillsides or in dry gullies.* **Juvenile** darker with deep tawny edges to wing and outer tail feathers; breast spotting extends as streaks onto flanks. (Smaller Grassland Pipit is shorter billed, buffier, more distinctly streaked. Plain-backed Pipit is plainer, smaller billed, has darker buff sides to shorter tail.) **Song** a repeated series of disjointed notes, *chreep. . . shreep. . . chew-ee . . .* from the ground or in fluttering display flight. Call a metallic two-syllabled *che-vlee.* **Range**: Local to above 2500 m from Sudan border and Mt Kulal south to Arusha NP and Mt Hanang. Most numerous around cent. Rift Valley scarps.

PLAIN-BACKED PIPIT *Anthus leucophrys*   **Plate 70**

Length 6.5″. Distinctly *'plain-backed,'* and with noticeable upright stance; almost unstreaked above and with only *short faint breast streaks*; *broad-looking tail buff, not white,* at sides. Western *A. l. zenkeri* is rather *dark brown above* with contrasting *rufous-buff wing edgings* and *deep buff underparts,* and shows *narrow dark malar stripes.* Cent. Kenyan *goodsoni* paler and sandier above and below, the breast streaks pale and diffuse. **Juveniles** browner with pale buff wing edgings, and more distinct streaks on breast. (Long-billed Pipit is darker, has longer bill and longer tail with buffy white outer feathers, more prominent malar streaks and heavier body streaking.) **Song** (*goodsoni*) a monotonous sparrow-like *chwee, chweep, cheew,* or *tchwip-shee-cheree.* Alarm/flight call a thin soft *chissik;* on take-off, a sparrow-like *t-t-tit.* **Range**: *A. l. zenkeri* from Mt Elgon south to Mara GR and Serengeti NP; *goodsoni* in Rift Valley from Nakuru south through e. Mara GR to e. Serengeti Plains and Lake Eyasi; local east of the Rift (Laikipia, Ngobit, Naro Moru). Birds from Moyale, Mt Nyiru and Mt Hanang not racially assigned. Both forms collected at Nakuru and in Mara GR, and said to intergrade at Maralal and Kakamega. **Taxonomic Note**: *A. l. goodsoni* is much like the southern Buffy Pipit, *A. vaalensis,* and is sometimes considered conspecific.

MALINDI PIPIT *Anthus melindae*   **Plate 70**

Length 5.75–6.25″. A heavily streaked pipit of *seasonally flooded coastal grassland.* Similar in size and structure to Grassland Pipit but *bill bright yellow or orange-pink at base below.* Appears long-legged, the *tibiae partly bare; tarsi yellow to orange-flesh colour.* Streaking on *dark grey-brown upperparts* indistinct, but *underparts heavily and extensively streaked;* sides of tail white; pale superciliary stripes and dark malar stripes prominent. **Juvenile's** bare parts much duller. **Song** a repeated *creer* or *kwee* from low shrub. Flight call *tsweep* or *tirrip-tirrip-tirrip.* **Range**: N. Kenyan coast from Ngomeni to Karawa; less numerous in Tana River Delta north to Baomo.

TREE PIPIT *Anthus trivialis*   **Plate 70**

Length 6″. A slim pipit of *forest edges or other open wooded areas;* typically in small groups; flies to low tree branches when disturbed. Light *warm olive-brown* above, heavily streaked on back, but rump and *upper tail-coverts almost plain.* Underparts buffy white with *sharp blackish streaks across breast* (more obscure on flanks); malar stripes prominent, and narrow pale eye-ring evident at close range; sides of tail white. (Similar Red-throated Pipit in non-breeding plumage has more whitish underparts with heavier, more extensive streaking, browner upperparts and well-streaked rump; bill also finer. Grassland Pipit is larger, has longer bill and legs, more distinct superciliaries and different call.) **Call** a single *tseep*, usually as bird rises. **Range/status**: Palearctic migrant, Oct.–mid-April. Common in the highlands; local in lower drier parts of se. Kenya; sparse in the north and northeast, coastal lowlands and ne. Tanzania.

RED-THROATED PIPIT *Anthus cervinus* — Plate 70

Length 5.5–6". A small, heavily marked pipit of *open wet places.* Upperparts *brown or grey-brown, well-streaked from back to upper tail-coverts*, and with *bold streaking on the whitish breast and flanks*; sides of tail white. Many individuals show *pink on face* from Jan. onward; in full **breeding plumage** (Mar.–Apr.) face, throat and upper breast may be bright tawny-pink. **Non-breeding plumage** distinguished from Tree Pipit by *heavily streaked rump/upper tail-coverts* and *bolder streaking on sides and flanks*, less olive appearance, finer bill, and by **call**, usually a high-pitched thin *teeze* or *seeu* (at times a double *see-seeu*, longer and more piercing than call of Tree Pipit). **Range/status**: Palearctic migrant, late Oct.–mid-April, most numerous near Rift Valley lakes (especially Turkana and Baringo) and in adjacent highlands. Uncommon but regular south to the Crater Highlands, Arusha NP, and around Kilimanjaro.

STRIPED PIPIT *Anthus lineiventris* — Plate 70

Length 7". A *large, strong-billed* pipit of rocky hillsides in ne. Tanzania and se Kenya. *Long streaks extend from breast to belly and under tail-coverts.* No other large pipit is so extensively streaked below. *Greenish yellow edges to wing and tail feathers* diagnostic. **Song** a melodious whistling *whip-chew-chew whitty-pee-tee-tee, whip chew-chew . . ..* **Range**: In Kenya only between 1500 and 2000 m in the Taita Hills (rare). Also in Tanzania's Pare and Usambara mts, and on Mbulu escarpment above Lake Manyara.

BUSH PIPIT or LITTLE TAWNY PIPIT *Anthus caffer blayneyi* — Plate 70

Length 5–5.25". A *miniature* pipit of bushed grassland and open acacia groves. Sandy buff with bold dark brown streaks on back; rump and upper tail-coverts nearly plain. *Face rather plain, the buff superciliary stripes narrow.* Partially nomadic, its movements coinciding with the onset of rains. Favours heavily grazed areas with scattered shrubs. **Song** a repeated *zweep-tseer*; call a sibilant *tzee-eep*. **Range**: Cent. and n. Serengeti NP (common), north to Mara GR and Loita Hills. Sporadic from Tarangire NP and Monduli north to Kajiado, Simba and Ngong areas.

SOKOKE PIPIT *Anthus sokokensis* — Plate 70

Length 4.75". A small *coastal forest* pipit with *heavy black streaking both above and below*, that on the underparts broader on breast, sharper and narrower on sides and flanks; rump and upper tail-coverts rufous-tinged; wings with much pale feather edging and *two prominent wing-bars*. Contact **call** a high-pitched descending *sweer* or *tseeer* from ground or tree. Very high-pitched flight song, delivered above forest openings or canopy, consists of a repeated *eee-see* or *su-eeee-see* (middle note highest) separated from next phrase by a brief but distinct pause. **Range**: Sokoke–Arabuko Forest (dense *Afzelia*-dominated stands, but at least formerly in more open *Brachystegia* woodland); also in Mkongani Forest, Shimba Hills (Oct. 1992). Collected near Moa (north of Tanga) in 1931, but all recent Tanzanian records from well south of our area.

GOLDEN PIPIT *Tmetothylacus tenellus* — Plate 68

Length 5–6.25". A unique long-legged pipit of dry bush country. **Male** suggests a small longclaw with its yellow underparts and black breast band, but *in flight appears mostly yellow with black wing tips and a dark inverted 'T' on the yellow tail*; tibiotarsi unfeathered. **Female** only faintly yellowish below, but wing and tail feathers edged with bright yellow. Both sexes have yellow underwing surfaces. **Juvenile** *closely resembles Grassland Pipit but centre of belly faintly yellow-tinged,* and note the *suggestion of streaks on sides and flanks*; the *long bare dark tibiotarsi* distinguish it from Grassland Pipit; tarsi darker and browner than in that species. **Song** a series of sibilant whistles from perch or in display flight, *tsi-tsi-tsi-tsi, tsur-tsur, tsi-tsi-tsi-tsi* . . .. **Range:** Mainly below 1000 m from Marsabit, Samburu and Shaba GRs, Meru, Amboseli and the Tsavo NPs eastward, including the north coast. Occasional west to Lake Baringo and Nairobi NP. In n. Tanzania known from Longido, Arusha District and Mkomazi GR (Dec.–Feb.), and the Masai Steppe. Numbers fluctuate.

YELLOW-THROATED LONGCLAW *Macronyx croceus*   Plate 68

Length 8–8.75″. A stocky grassland bird, larger than any pipit, with streaked warm brown upperparts and *bright yellow underparts with a bold black V on breast. White tail sides and corners conspicuous in flight* (which consists of bursts of stiff wingbeats alternating with glides). Coastal *M. c. tertius* is smaller and brighter than nominate *croceus*. **Juvenile** buffy yellow with band of indistinct short streaks on breast, some birds rufous-tinged in fresh plumage. (Similar Pangani Longclaw has streaked, pale buff flanks and under tail-coverts, and more orange throat.) **Song** a far-carrying whistled *tirrEEoo, trip-tritri* or *twitilew-tree-eurr*; alarm call a loud piping *whip-pipipipi, tuwhip-pipipipi.* Usual call a repeated whistling *teuwhee* or *twee-eu.* **Range**: *M. c. croceus* from w. and cent. Kenya south to Serengeti NP. *M. c. tertius* along the coast.

PANGANI LONGCLAW *Macronyx aurantiigula*   Plate 68

Length 7.5–8″. Resembles Yellow-throated Longclaw but *flanks buffy white with dark streaks, throat orange-yellow* (more contrasting in male); *breast band narrower and sides more heavily streaked* than in Yellow-throated. Streaking of upperparts also paler, and yellow confined to centre of breast and belly. **Juvenile** buff below with incomplete band of streaks on yellow-washed breast. **Song** *syeet syeet syeet, churrie churrie, which which which-which, tee-er tee-er tee-er* . . ., each note repeated at least twice. One call is a very high-pitched *teeeeeeee.* **Range**: Below 1500 m from Meru NP and Kora NR south to Amboseli and Tsavo NPs, west to Athi Plains; reaches coast north of Malindi and in Tana delta area (where alongside Yellow-throated L.). In n. Tanzania from Mkomazi GR and the Masai Steppe west to Arusha, Tarangire and Lake Manyara NPs.

SHARPE'S LONGCLAW *Macronyx sharpei*   Plate 68

Length 6–6.75″. *Restricted to the Kenyan highlands.* Smaller than Yellow-throated Longclaw and lacking solid black V on breast; upperparts more boldly marked with rufous- or buff-edged black streaks. Underparts bright chrome-yellow with dark streaks across breast and along flanks. In flight, white shows at sides of tail, but less at corners than in Yellow-throated. Flight stiff-winged as in that species. **Song** a series of thin whistles rising in pitch: *tew tyo tew tee* or *tyo tyo tew-tee.* Calls include a sharp *tsit*, a long plaintive *tweeeee* and a thin rising *seeeu.* **Range**: Mt Elgon, the Uasin Gishu, Mau and Kinangop plateaus, s. Aberdares and n. Mt Kenya slopes. Always at higher elevations than *M. croceus*, with few areas of overlap. Populations declining.

ROSY-BREASTED LONGCLAW *Macronyx ameliae wintoni*   Plate 68

Length 7.5–8″. A slender, *red-throated* longclaw of open wet grassland. **Breeding male** has bright rosy red *chin and throat bordered by broad black band*; centre of breast and belly salmon-pink. **Female** much paler below with *pink wash on throat and belly.* Flying adult shows pale patch formed by buffy white edges of lesser coverts (unless plumage much worn). Tail appears longer than in other longclaws, the white conspicuous only at sides, not corners. **Juvenile** scalloped above, *buff below without breast band; belly pinkish* (sometimes in centre only). Flight less stiff-winged, more

pipit-like, than that of other longclaws. (Juv. Pangani Longclaw might be mistaken for this species but has no pink on belly.) **Song** a squeaky series of whistled notes, *pink-pink-pink-zheeenk* with a wheezing final syllable, often in hovering display flight. Call a plaintive *chuit-chuit*, and in alarm or excitement a sharper *chwit* or a metallic *tyang*. **Range:** Maralal, Laikipia Plateau, Naro Moru and Ngobit south to Nakuru and Nairobi NPs and the Athi Plains; locally in Mara GR, Serengeti NP and Ngorongoro Crater east to Ardai and Sanya Plains, Arusha Dist. Partially nomadic, with rainfall-related movements.

SWALLOWS AND MARTINS, FAMILY HIRUNDINIDAE

Graceful, long-winged fliers whose insect food is taken entirely on the wing. In most species the tail is long and forked with the outer feathers sometimes much elongated. The bill is short, flattened and with a wide gape; the feet are comparatively small. Although swallows superficially resemble swifts (Apodidae), their wings are broader and less scythe-like, their flight slower and more graceful. The sexes are similar in colour. Juveniles usually resemble adults except for duller, buff-edged body feathers and often shorter rectrices. Swallows tend to feed in groups, and some breed colonially. Nest type may be useful in identification. Most species build a nest of mud pellets—either a half-cup plastered to a wall, or retort-shaped with an entrance tube and affixed below an overhang, often in or on a building. A few nest in tree cavities or holes in the ground.

BANDED MARTIN *Riparia cincta* Plates 73, 74

Length 5.5–6". A *large brown-backed* grassland swallow with a broad brown breast band and white supraloral lines; sometimes shows a dark mid-ventral line from breast to belly, especially in *R. c. erlangeri; wing-linings white. Tail almost square-tipped.* **Juvenile** has buff-edged wing feathers. Flight slower, more leisurely and less fluttering than that of most swallows. Nests in sandbanks. (Migrant Sand Martin is smaller, with clearly forked tail and brown wing-linings; has no white supraloral lines.) **Song** a short *chirip-cherip-chee-chirup-tsri-ereee*, sometimes ending in a trill. Calls include a rapid *chrink-cherrunk, tsri-tserrunk* and a long nasal *schwaanh*. **Range:** *R. c. suahelica* in the Kenyan highlands south to Mara GR, Amboseli NP, Lake Jipe, and n. Tanzania. Ethiopian *erlangeri* has been collected at Naivasha, and sight records from n. Kenya probably are of this race.

PLAIN MARTIN or AFRICAN SAND MARTIN *Riparia paludicola ducis*
Plates 73, 74

Length 4.5". *Brown-backed*, with *grey-brown throat, breast, sides, and wing-linings;* tail slightly forked. **Juvenile** has buff feather edges on somewhat greyer upperparts. Nests colonially or in scattered pairs in earth banks. (Sand Martin has white throat and brown breast band. Rock Martin shows white tail spots, is pale cinnamon on throat and upper breast.) Often numerous in open high country near water. **Song,** *chee, wer-chi-cho wer-chi-cho.* Also a short descending trill, a low *chi-choo,* and a rough *chrrk* or *chickereek*. **Range:** W. and cent. Kenya south to Arusha NP and Crater Highlands. Records from Lake Turkana probably refer to *R. p. schoensis.*

✓ SAND MARTIN or BANK SWALLOW *Riparia r. riparia* Plates 73, 74

Length 5". *Brown-backed*, with a *dark brown breast band* across otherwise white underparts, but *wing-linings dark brown;* tail well forked. **Juvenile** shows buff or creamy feather edges on upperparts. See Banded Martin. **Call** a rough twittering, *ch-ch-ch-ch-chi-chi-chi-chi,* but usually silent when alone. Flocks produce a continuous deep churring. **Range/status:** Palearctic migrant, Sept.–May, mainly around lakes. Most numerous at Lake Victoria. Small numbers reach the coast, but generally scarce in e. Kenya and ne. Tanzania.

GREY-RUMPED SWALLOW *Pseudhirundo g. griseopyga* Plates 73, 74

Length 5–5.5". A small swallow of open (often recently burnt) grassland. *Grey-brown crown and grey rump are sharply demarcated from glossy blue-black back.* Early in breeding season, white of underparts briefly tinged with salmon pink. **Juvenile** duller above, often with larger superciliary stripes and darker smudges at sides of breast; rump browner, outer rectrices shorter. (Common House Martin is stockier with broader-based wings and less deeply forked tail; flight more lively, usually higher, with more gliding.) Nests in rodent holes in flat open ground. **Calls** a weak nasal *waanh* or *phew*, a harsh *chrree-chrr-chrr*, and a rough *chirrk, tsr-chrrrr*, the latter recalling Plain Martin. Infrequent song a weak sibilant twitter, *tsitsertsi-tsi-sisi*. **Range**: Mt Elgon and Laikipia Plateau south to Lake Victoria basin, cent. Rift Valley and Crater Highlands. Occasional on Serengeti and Ardai plains; vagrants north to Marsabit and Lake Turkana. Population around Naivasha and Kedong possibly augmented by winter migrants from southern tropics, June–Aug. **Taxonomic Notes**: Perhaps not generically distinct, as morphologically little different from *Hirundo*. The unique specimen from Lake Naivasha, originally described as *H. andrewi* and later accorded subspecific rank by some, may be merely an aberrant dark individual; no subsequent record.

BLUE SWALLOW *Hirundo atrocaerulea*   Plates 73, 74

Length 6.5–9". A slender *dark glossy blue* swallow of open or bushed grasslands in w. Kenya; appears black at a distance. Adult's *tail deeply forked with long, almost wire-like outer feathers*. Normally concealed long black-and-white feathers on sides and flanks sometimes show as conspicuous white patch on perched birds. **Juvenile/immature** sooty black with brownish throat, no long outer tail feathers. See Black Sawwing. **Calls** a harsh *tchur* and a soft *tchup-tchup*. A twittering *wi-wi-wi-wi-wi-wi* given by courting males prior to departure for breeding grounds. **Range/status**: Rare migrant from s. Africa, April–Sept., north to Ruma NP, Mumias, Busia and Bungoma districts, w. Kenya. Recorded only twice in n. Tanzania: Korogwe (Apr.) and Serengeti NP (Aug.).

WIRE-TAILED SWALLOW *Hirundo s. smithii*   Plates 73, 74

Length 4.5–7". A dainty swallow, dark metallic blue above, with *narrow blue-black patch on each side of upper breast*. No other white-breasted swallow has *wholly chestnut cap* and *long wire-like outer tail feathers* (sometimes missing or broken). Spread tail shows *white spots*. **Juvenile** has dull brownish crown, buff-tinged underparts and shorter outer tail feathers. (Ethiopian Swallow has incomplete breast band, is chestnut only on forehead.) **Song** a Barn Swallow-like twittering, *chirrrik erreeek*. Contact call a short *chwit* or *twit*. **Range**: Widespread except for arid areas of n. and ne. Kenya.

BARN SWALLOW *Hirundo r. rustica*   Plates 73, 74 ✓

Length 6–7.5". A seasonally common swallow with *shiny dark blue upperparts and breast band*; underparts vary from white to deep buff. *Rufous-chestnut forehead and throat become buff when faded. Deeply forked tail* has long narrow outer feathers (especially in male) *with prominent white spots.* Wing-linings buffy white. **Juvenile** (Sept.–Dec.) duller, faintly glossed above, with *pale buff forehead and throat* and dusky brown breast band; outer tail feathers less narrow and only slightly elongated. (Angola Swallow is greyer below, with broken breast band and lacks long outer tail feathers. Ethiopian Swallow has white or buff throat and incomplete breast band.) **Call**, *wit-wit*. Twittering song rarely heard in East Africa. **Range/status**: Palearctic migrant, widespread late Aug.–early May.

WHITE-THROATED SWALLOW *Hirundo albigularis*   Plate 122

Length 5.5–6.75". This vagrant from southern Africa suggests a Barn Swallow, but has *snow-white throat bordered by a blue-black breast band* (narrower in centre than at sides, not of even width as in *H. rustica*). Wings broader than Barn Swallow's, with white linings. **Juvenile** lacks chestnut on forehead and has brownish breast band. **Call** a high thin *sreek* or *seet-seet*, and a sharp twittering. **Status**: One collected at Lake Jipe, ne. Tanzania, July 1957, is the sole East African record.

ETHIOPIAN SWALLOW *Hirundo aethiopica*   Plates 73, 74

Length 5". Smaller than Barn Swallow, more steel-blue above, with *chestnut restricted to forehead*. Tail forked and white-spotted, but narrow outer feathers shorter than in adult Barn. Throat and upper breast buff in nominate birds, white in *amadoni*, and partly margined below by a *broken blue-black breast band*. **Juvenile** more dusky above, with buff forehead; outer tail feathers not elongated. (Angola Swallow is larger and grey-brown below. Wire-tailed Swallow has entire top of head rufous, and longer, narrower outer tail feathers.) Nest a mud cup. **Song** a prolonged squeaky twittering. Contact call a soft *cht*. **Range**: The common resident swallow of coastal lowlands. Also widespread from Ethiopian border south to the Kerio Valley and Laikipia Plateau. Most Kenyan birds represent the nominate race. *H. a. amadoni* of Somalia ranges south to Lamu and possibly Malindi.

ANGOLA SWALLOW *Hirundo angolensis*   Plates 73, 74

Length 5.5–6". Suggests a short-tailed, stocky Barn Swallow with *dingy grey-brown underparts* and *dusky wing-linings*. *Rufous of throat extends to breast, the dark pectoral band narrow and incomplete*; under tail-coverts dark-centred; tail well forked, with *large white spots*. **Juvenile** has buff throat and smaller tail spots. (Ethiopian Swallow is white below with unmarked under tail-coverts and pale wing-linings.) Builds mud nest like that of Ethiopian Swallow. **Song** a weak twitter. **Range**: Mt Elgon, Nakuru, Nyahururu and Nanyuki districts to nw. Mara GR. Status uncertain in Tanzania's Mara Region and w. Serengeti NP.

RED-RUMPED SWALLOW *Hirundo daurica emini*   Plates 73, 74

Length 7". A rufous-bellied grassland swallow with *blue-black under tail-coverts* and glossy blue back contrasting with *rufous of rump and sides of head*; underparts and *wing-linings rufous-chestnut*, paler on throat; tail plain, well-forked. **Juvenile** paler, shorter tailed and with some tawny wing-feather tips. (Larger Mosque Swallow has white wing-linings. Rufous-chested S. has no rufous on face, and blue extends down to below eyes. Both species have rufous under tail-coverts.) Nest of mud, flask-shaped. **Song** a few widely spaced metallic notes of 'squeaking hinge' quality: *yaannh . . . . . quer-yaannh skiaaaannh . . . . . cher-yaanng. . . . .* Flight calls include a soft *chmp*, a long *queesch* and *skeek-eek*. Alarm note a short *keer*. **Range**: Between 1200 and 2500 m from the northern Kenyan mountains south into n. Tanzania. Rare in lowland n. and e. Kenya and ne. Tanzania. Seasonal in some localities.

✦ MOSQUE SWALLOW *Hirundo senegalensis*   Plates 73, 74

Length 8". Distinguished from Red-rumped Swallow by *larger size, snow-white wing-linings, rufous under tail-coverts*, and *buff cheeks and throat*, paler than the rufous auriculars. Tail entirely dark in *H. s. saturatior*, with white spots on inner rectrix webs in eastern *monteiri*. (Rufous-chested Swallow is blue-black on sides of head and nape and has rufous wing-linings.) Slowly uttered, semi-musical **song** of creaking, whining and metallic notes, *muree rrrang crrik-crrik meeeu mreeeeeu rrrrreeeerang-rrrang*. Varied calls include a short nasal *haaarrnk*, a descending *tseeeu*, a cat-like *meeu* and various guttural notes. Builds covered mud nest in hollow baobab or other tree, occasionally on building. **Range**: Widespread (but uncommon) below 2600 m. Most numerous in Lake Victoria basin and coastal lowlands. *H. s. monteiri* in n. Tanzania and on coast north to the Somali border, inland to Kibwezi, intergrading with western *saturatior* near Nairobi.

RUFOUS-CHESTED SWALLOW *Hirundo semirufa gordoni*   Plates 73, 74

Length 7–7.5". A rather large swallow, uncommon in moist grassland. Glossy blue-black above, with *rufous rump*, underparts, and wing-linings. *Dark blue top of head extends below eyes across ear-coverts* giving a hooded appearance. Spread tail shows white spots; outer tail feathers much elongated in adult. **Juvenile** browner above, paler below, with buff-tipped secondaries and shorter outer tail feathers. Builds flask-shaped mud nest, sometimes in hollow tree. Unique **song** of growling notes and prolonged descending squeals, *chureek-cherrrrow-chiteeeerpereee squeeeeeeeee chrrierrow*. Call a plaintive *seeurr-seeurr* and a *weet-weet* of alarm. **Range**: Lake Victoria basin north to Kakamega, Nandi and Mumias districts, south to Mara GR and Mara region of n. Tanzania. Mainly a wet-season visitor.

LESSER STRIPED SWALLOW *Hirundo abyssinica unitatis*   **Plates 73, 74** 〜

Length 6–7". *Rump and most of head rufous,* and *entire underparts boldly streaked* black on white; back glossy blue-black; *tail has long narrow outer feathers and shows large white spots when spread*; wing-linings mostly white. **Juvenile** duller, with some blackish on head, shorter tail. Flask-shaped mud nest built under overhanging projection, usually on building. **Song** a pleasing tinny *rronh rrenh reenh rroonh reenh,* ascending or descending; usually introduced by some thin squeaky or buzzy notes. Flight call, *seent*. **Range**: Widespread below 2000 m, but largely absent from the highlands during cold June–Aug. period, returning with the rains to breed.

ROCK MARTIN *Hirundo fuligula fusciventris*   **Plates 73, 74**

Length 4.5". The only brown-backed swallow showing *white spots in the spread tail*, and with pale *cinnamon throat and upper breast*; wings quite broad at base, tail slightly forked. Flight appears leisurely with much gliding. **Juvenile** has feathers of upperparts tipped with buff. (Plain Martin dull brown on throat and breast, with no tail spots. Mascarene Martin is streaked below. Young Common House Martin shows pale grey rump.) Builds cup-shaped mud nest on cliff, rock outcrop or building. **Calls** include a low *wick* or *wik-wik*, a high-pitched *sree*, and some soft mellow twittering. Seldom vocal. **Range**: Widespread around cliffs, gorges and tall urban buildings in cent. and s. Kenya (more local in northwest) and n. Tanzania, typically between 1500 and 3000 m, but as low as 400 m in gorges near Lake Turkana. Rare in Lake Victoria basin.

COMMON HOUSE MARTIN *Delichon u. urbica*   **Plates 73, 74** 〜

Length 5–5.5". Small and rather thickset, glossy blue-black above with *white rump* and *white underparts,* these variably tinged buffy grey-brown in winter; tail black and well forked. Tarsi and toes uniquely white-feathered. **Juvenile** browner above, more dusky below and on rump. Typically forages high (lower in cloudy weather), often with swifts. See Grey-rumped Swallow. **Calls**, when perched, *bzreet, dzreet-dzreet cherrrang*; in flight, *dzurreet-dzeet chri-eet chree-eeet* and various higher notes. Contact call a harsh grating *chirrt* or *chirrup*; alarm note a shrill *tseep*. **Range/status**: Palearctic migrant, Sept.–April, in Kenyan highlands east to the Nyambenis, south to Mt Meru, Kilimanjaro and the Crater and Mbulu highlands.

MASCARENE MARTIN *Phedina borbonica madagascariensis*   **Plates 73, 74** Length 5–5.5". A stocky brown-backed swallow, the underparts *heavily streaked with dark brown from throat to belly*; sides and flanks washed with grey-brown. Almost square-tipped blackish tail shows no fork when spread; wing-linings dark. Flight sluggish with alternate fluttering and gliding, usually high. **Call** a wheezy *srree-zz*. **Range/status**: Casual visitor from Madagascar. Formerly recorded from Pemba Island. Four recent records: Lake Jipe, June 1978 and 1993; Watamu, June 1980; near Malindi, August 1989.

BLACK SAW-WING or ROUGH-WING *Psalidoprocne holomelas*
Plates 73, 74
Length 5.25–6". An all-black forest-edge swallow with a distinctively shaped tail. Male of highland *P. h. massaicus* has faint greenish gloss (duller in female) and grey-brown wing-linings; *tail longer than body, rather broad but very deeply forked* (less so in female). **Juvenile** has no gloss and shorter tail. Coastal *P. h. holomelas* is shorter-tailed and noticeably smaller. (Dark juv. White-headed Saw-wing usually shows slightly paler throat, is more sooty, tail is less forked and body appears stockier.) Excavates nest bur-

row in bank or road cut. Flight **calls** include *dzrrt-tsireeee* and a squealing *sqweeu*, a sharper *tseeeu-tseeu*, and a soft *chirp*. Perched birds give a nasal *chirranu-chirranu*, slightly drongo-like in quality; also *chirr-chirr-cheeru*. **Range:** *P. h. massaicus* above 1600 m in Kenyan highlands south to the Nguruman, Chyulu and Taita hills and all n.Tanzania highlands. Coastal *P. h. holomelas* in Shimba Hills, Arabuko–Sokoke and Marafu forests.

WHITE-HEADED SAW-WING or ROUGH-WING *Psalidoprocne a. albiceps*
Plates 73, 74

Length 5–6″. A *black* swallow with *white on the head*; stockier and with shallower tail fork than the preceding species. **Male** *white-headed* with black eye-lines. **Female** has *whitish throat*, and sooty feathering often intermixed with white on the crown. **Juvenile** *almost uniformly sooty brown*, somewhat paler on throat. Nests in holes in banks. See Black Saw-wing. **Call** an infrequent soft *brzt*. **Range:** Mt Elgon and the Cheranganis south to Nandi and Kakamega forests, Lake Victoria basin, Mara GR, Serengeti NP and the Crater and Mbulu highlands.; in Kenyan highlands east to Embu and Machakos districts (sporadic) and Taita Hills.

BULBULS, FAMILY PYCNONOTIDAE

Mostly retiring, secretive birds (Common Bulbul a notable exception), somewhat thrush-like but with shorter weaker feet. Plumage lax and soft, with hair-like filoplumes on nape. Crown or throat feathers often erected in excitement. Some species arboreal, but the majority inhabit undergrowth and tangles, and several are quite terrestrial. Brownbuls and certain others travel in small vocal groups, suggesting babblers. Songs often loud, lively and cheerful, with repeated notes or phrases, and many species indulge in spirited chattering, chuckling or churring; a few are remarkably quiet, their vocalizations poorly known. Sexes much alike in plumage but males larger and often longer-billed. Young resemble adults. Some forest greenbuls are difficult to identify, particularly those in the genus *Andropadus*. The *Phyllastrephus* species are longer-billed, often browner, and are more insectivorous, seen less often in fruiting trees. Important in greenbul identification are: foraging level and behaviour, tail colour (olive *vs.* rufous), throat and breast colour, colour of bare parts, bill size and shape, voice and range (some species strictly confined to either eastern or western forests; several highly localized). **Note**: The aberrant genus *Nicator*, once again considered a bush-shrike, is transferred to Malaconotidae.

CAMEROON SOMBRE or PLAIN GREENBUL *Andropadus c. curvirostris*
Plate 76

Length 6.5″. A dark brownish olive greenbul of *tall understorey shrubs and creeper tangles* in w. Kenyan forests. *Usually forages 3–10 m* above ground. Note the *whitish eyelids, short slender black bill, olive-grey throat and yellow-olive belly contrasting with darker olive breast*; dark tail is washed with rufous. Some (young?) birds are very dark-chested. Feet dark olive or greenish grey. **Juvenile** much brighter yellow on belly, greyer (less olive) on throat, breast, and flanks. (Sympatric Ansorge's and Little Grey Greenbuls are smaller, with brighter eye-rings. Little Greenbul, less easily seen, is more uniformly olive, has olive throat, broader bill, light yellowish brown feet.) Seldom-heard **song** of repeated slow, rather mournful, clear whistles, *wheetu-WEEu, wheetu WEEu . . ..* Call a short mellow trill, *chreeeeeee* or *pureeeeeee*, dropping slightly at the end. **Range:** Nandi and Kakamega forests of w. Kenya (fairly common); Migori River near Lolgorien. Formerly at Mumias and on Mt Elgon.

LITTLE GREY GREENBUL *Andropadus gracilis ugandae*
Plate 76

Length 6″. A *small* western greenbul, much like the commoner sympatric Ansorge's, including the narrow eye-ring, but *belly brighter, almost pure yellow centrally*, flanks bright tawny, and under tail-coverts pale brown; tail and upper coverts washed with rufous; feet greyish olive or blue-grey. **Juvenile** of *ugandae* undescribed (that of nominate West African *gracilis* brighter yellow below than adult, and has *yellowish eye-ring* and bill base). Forages on smaller tree branches at middle and lower levels. (Cameroon

Sombre Greenbul is larger, darker on breast, its eye-ring greyish; less likely than *gracilis* to forage on slender tree branches.) **Song** descriptions from West Africa unsatisfactorily differentiated from those of Ansorge's Greenbul; said to consist of five rapid jaunty notes *wheet-wu-wheet-wu-wheet*, rising at the end; in Uganda reportedly *HWEET-hwet-hwut*, second and third notes shorter and descending (the latter song, however, suspiciously like that of collected w. Kenyan *ansorgei*). **Range**: Kakamega Forest in w. Kenya (scarce).

ANSORGE'S GREENBUL *Andropadus ansorgei kavirondensis*   Plate 76

Length 5.75″. *Olive-grey belly and narrow white eye-ring* mark this *small*, short-tailed greenbul of the Kakamega Forest. Throat grey, breast and belly olive-grey, and *flanks warm rufous-olive.* **Juvenile** has still greyer head and breast. (Much rarer Little Grey Greenbul tends to forage higher, has yellowish belly; see Cameroon Sombre G.) **Song** an infrequent, thin whistle: *weet-wurt-eet*, last note highest; also a descending chatter or rattle. Songs in West Africa sometimes terminally accented like those of *A. gracilis*. **Range**: Kakamega Forest. Formerly Nyarondo Valley and s. slopes of Mt Elgon.

LITTLE GREENBUL *Andropadus virens*   Plate 76

Length 6″. A small forest greenbul, *short-tailed*, and with a *short broad bill.* Darker olive below than most other small greenbuls, the throat and breast *almost uniform*; belly yellow; some birds (immature?) deeper olive on breast. Tail and upper tail-coverts reddish brown; feet yellowish orange or yellowish brown. Coastal birds brighter than those in w. Kenya. **Juvenile** darker on crown, browner on wings and yellowish on throat but yellow of belly dull and restricted; crissum pale olive; *feet dull brown or yellowish brown.* (Juv. Yellow-whiskered G. has similar broad though longer bill, but bright orange feet, dusky malar streaks, dark dusky olive throat and breast and tawny under tail-coverts.) **Song** of *zombensis* a long hurried chatter starting with a low guttural *kwirk-kwirk-kwirk* or *chuk-chuk. . .*, accelerating into *chwukawuk-cherchickalee-chuck-chuck-chuck-tuwerrtlii-tuk-tuk*, all run together and often ending on a short high note. Song of western birds shorter (2–3 sec.), recalling Yellow-whiskered's, but faster and not progressively louder from a faint beginning: *chippity choppity chipity chop* or *chippity chop chippity cherp p'CHEEEEee*, thin and upslurred at end. Alarm call a rapid chatter. **Range**: *A. v. zombensis* on coast north to Mombasa (formerly Kilifi), inland to Shimba Hills, East Usambaras, Arusha and Moshi; *virens* in Kakamega and Nandi forests, riverine strips in Busia, Mumias and Rapogi districts, along Migori River near Lolgorien south to Tanzanian border.

YELLOW-WHISKERED GREENBUL *Andropadus l. latirostris*   Plate 76

Length 6.5–7″. The most numerous greenbul from 1500 to 3000 m, its protracted chattering a dominant feature of many wooded areas. Readily identified by the prominent *yellow streak on each side of the throat.* With 'whiskers' compressed may appear yellow-throated. Feet dark orange to yellowish brown. **Juvenile** *lacks yellow whiskers*, is browner above, less yellowish on belly, has *pale tawny under tail-coverts, bright orange or orange-yellow feet*, and *mottled yellow-orange and black bill.* Whiskers of moulting immature narrow and less prominent than adjacent dark malar areas. (Similar juv. Little Greenbul like young Yellow-whiskered but throat yellowish olive, under tail-coverts pale olive, and feet dull yellowish brown.) **Song**, 4–6 sec. long, delivered in short choppy bursts, at first very faint, becoming progressively louder before abrupt stop: *chuk, chik, chuk, chip, tsup chik-chik-chik tsuk chik-chik-tsuck*, repeated after 20–30 sec. Much slower than Little Greenbul's song, the individual notes more distinct. **Range**: Mt Elgon and the Cheranganis south to n. Tanzania at Loliondo; east of Rift Valley, from n. Kenyan mountains south to Nairobi and Ol Doinyo Orok.

SLENDER-BILLED GREENBUL *Andropadus gracilirostris*   Plate 76

Length 7″. A slim, slender-billed species of *forest canopy* (but ripening subcanopy berries lure it into lower branches). Longer-tailed than other *Andropadus* but with no obvious field marks; *from below appears plain grey* against the sky. Bright olive above, duller on crown; tail brownish olive above, much paler below; eyes brick-red or red-brown. **Juvenile** browner above, duller grey below than adult. (Ansorge's and Little Grey Greenbuls are smaller with darker underparts and rufous tinge to the short tail.) **Song** *twick-CHEWsee-tseu* or *chik-WEEo-chew*, is heard less often than a repeated short *cu-WEE-a* or *chew-WAYa*; also a scolding *chewi*. **Range**: Mt Elgon, Mathews Range and Mt Kenya south to Trans-Mara and Mau forests, the Aberdares and n. Nairobi suburbs. Two similar subspecies, *percivali* and *gracilirostris* intergrade in w. Kenya.

SHELLEY'S GREENBUL *Andropadus masukuensis*   Plates 75, 123

Length 6.5". A fairly common forest bird, the two distinct forms perhaps specifically distinct. **A. m. kakamegae** frequently seen *clinging to tree trunks*, has *grey head* contrasting with bright greenish olive upperparts (including tail) and yellowish olive underparts; narrow, *dull white eye-ring* noticeable. **Juvenile** paler headed but otherwise like adults. Tanzanian **A. m. roehli**, not reported as a tree-trunk forager, has mainly *olive-green head with only the face and throat greyish*, and underparts dull greyish olive. (Mountain Greenbul, *A. nigriceps kikuyuensis*, resembles *A. m. kakamegae*, but has much brighter underparts, more conspicuous eye-ring, is stockier, and tends to be at higher elevations.) **Call** of *kakamegae* unrecorded despite extensive observation; apparently nearly silent. *A. m. roehli* gives a loud simple *chew-ki, chew-ki, chew-ki* or *kew-kee, kew-kee . . .;* also a soft nasal *kwew, kwa, kwew* (Moreau). **Range**: *A.m. kakamegae* in Nandi and Kakamega forests, and (status?) Mau and Trans-Mara forests; formerly on Mt Elgon. Sight record from montane forest above Kericho. *A. m. roehli* in the Usambara and South Pare mts, as low as 500 m in East Usambara foothills.

MOUNTAIN GREENBUL *Andropadus nigriceps*   Plates 75, 123

Length 7". A *montane-forest* greenbul. Three distinct races: **kikuyuensis** of w. and cent. Kenya has *entire head slate-grey* contrasting with bright yellow-olive underparts (more yellow on belly) and greenish olive back, wings and tail; *broken greyish white eye-ring* readily visible at close range. Of the two southern races, **nigriceps** has *blackish forehead and crown* and dark grey hindneck, face and most of underparts grey, the flanks, sides and crissum yellowish olive; upperparts darker than in *kikuyuensis* and eye-ring greyer; **usambarae** is grey-headed like *kikuyuensis,* but with *black superciliary stripes extending from the lores.* **Juveniles** of all races darker than adults, and dull olive below. See Shelley's Greenbul. **Song** of Kenyan *kikuyuensis* a low nasal husky phrase of 1.5–2 sec, lacking the boisterous cheerful quality of extralimital *A. n. chlorigula*; in Rwanda, a bustling series of low nasal husky notes all on one pitch, and a more defined *jur-jitjur-dejur-jur-jerry*, upslurred at end. Voice of *usambarae* described as *hee-her-hee* (Moreau). N. Tanzanian races said to have "a conversational *kwew-ki-kwew-ki-kwew*, very like Shelley's Greenbul" (S. Keith). Call a short grating *churr*. **Range**: *A. n. kikuyuensis* locally common in high terrain from Mt Elgon to Mt Kenya, the Aberdares, Mau and Trans-Mara forests. Nominate *nigriceps* from Mt Hanang, the Crater and Mbulu highlands east to Kilimanjaro and Arusha NP, north to Loliondo and the Nguruman Hills. *A. n. usambarae* in West Usambara and South Pare mts occasionally north to Taita Hills. **Taxonomic Note**: Formerly considered conspecific with West African *A. tephrolaemus.*

STRIPE-CHEEKED GREENBUL *Andropadus milanjensis striifacies*   Plate 75

Length 7.5". Bright yellowish olive, almost *golden yellow on the belly,* with *dark face and contrasting pale eyes*; whitish streaking on auriculars visible only at close range. **Juvenile** is duller and greyer below with faintly streaked auriculars; eyes dark. Less shy than many greenbuls, often easily viewed at forest edge where several may gather to feed on small fruits. Forages in forest and forest edge from mid-level into the canopy where it hops or creeps along branches. (Mountain, Shelley's and Yellow-bellied Greenbuls are all dark-eyed.) Contact **call** *ookeri* or *u-ki-rii*. Taita Hills birds have two 'songs': a prolonged monotonous loud *piku-piku-piku-piku . . .* or *tchiku-tchiku-tchiku. . .*, and a more slowly uttered *qua quee-qua qua-quee-qua. . .* varied to *cha-CHWEE-kwa, cha-CHWEE-kwa-kwa*, etc., altered in excitement to *kwi-kwa-kwa-*

KWEEri and *chwi-chwa-choo-kwa-CHWEERi*. **Range**: Arusha NP, the Pare and Usambara mts and lower slopes of Kilimanjaro and Mt Meru, north to Taita and Chyulu hills, Mt Monduli and Ol Doinyo Orok (Namanga Hill).

ZANZIBAR SOMBRE GREENBUL *Andropadus importunus insularis* **Plate 75**

Length 6–7″. A *plain-looking, pale-eyed greenbul of thickets and scrub,* common in coastal lowlands. **Adult** has uniform brownish olive upper-parts, including sides of head; underparts pale yellowish olive, slightly browner on flanks. Central Kenyan birds described as *A. i. fricki* on basis of *prominent yellow eye-ring* in adult, but birds perhaps incompletely moulted immatures, as this feature characteristic of **juvenile** *insularis*. (Sympatric Yellow-bellied Greenbul is larger, darker olive-brown on upperparts, and with dark reddish eyes.) Persistent **song** typically a short, rapid, slurred *chweleee-tuweeueet-tuweeuleet,* higher-pitched at end; also *we-up-tchup-cheu-tew-WEEa* and *chuk, chreep churrreeep chweeeo* or variations. Usual call note a terminally accented *cheerurIP* or *wheerUP*. Also utters an emphatic, police-whistle-like *prrrreeep,* repeated indefinitely. Often sings in midday heat. **Range**: Coastal lowlands inland to Mkomazi GR, North Pare Mts. and Kilimanjaro; along Tana River to Garissa and Meru NP, and through Tsavo area to the Chyulu Hills, Kibwezi and Emali. Highland *'fricki'* in Thika, Embu and Meru districts; type specimen (but no subsequent records) from Ndoto Mts.

GREY-OLIVE GREENBUL *Phyllastrephus cerviniventris* **Plate 76**

Length 6″. 'Pale-footed Greenbul' would be a better name, as the *straw-coloured, whitish or pinkish tarsi and toes* are this drab bird's best field mark. Nondescript olive-brown except for *narrow whitish eye-ring* and *orange-yellow or golden brown eyes*; bill dark above, but mandible *largely pale horn or whitish*. Highly vocal groups display marked prefer-ence for dense streamside vegetation and groundwater forest, foraging low and constantly flicking wings and tail. Partly terrestrial. (The some-what similar brownbuls are brighter brown. Fischer's and Cabanis's Greenbuls are larg-er with prominent white or cream-coloured throats.) **Calls** varied: a somewhat raspy *yeckk yeckk yeckk . . .*, a repeated *cherkiyeck . . .*, a rapid *chirrrridichirr*, a descending trilling *tirrrrrrr*, and *weh-weh-weh-weh. . .* A mournful whistling *hee-heu, hee-heu, hee-heu* and *chewki-chiki-chew-chew-chew. . .*, with quality reminiscent of Yellow-bellied Greenbul's voice, may serve as songs. **Range**: Local in Kiambu and Thika districts of cent. Kenya, near Bura (Taita Dist.), Tanzanian border areas near Loitokitok and Taveta, Moshi and Arusha districts, Lake Manyara NP and East Usambara foothills at Mombo.

TORO OLIVE GREENBUL *Phyllastrephus hypochloris* **Plate 76**

Length 6–6.75″. An elusive and uncommon west Kenyan bird of forest undergrowth, its few distinctive markings not easily observed. *Fairly long blackish bill* separates it from confusing *Andropadus* species, but bill shorter and much broader at base than in Cabanis's Greenbul (which has pale tan or grey eyes, a light yellowish throat, is general-ly yellower below and browner on the back). Plumage *dull olive above except for dark rufous tail; underparts paler and obscurely streaked yellow and grey*. Feet dull greenish or bluish-grey; eyes brownish orange to russet-brown. **Juvenile** paler below, with pale rufous under tail-coverts and dark brown bill with yellow commissure and tip; recalls adult of sympatric Cabanis's, but is dark-eyed, duller above and below, more uniformly greyish olive on upper breast and belly, and the pale throat is duller and less contrasting. **Call** not known with certainty. A bird thought to be of this species uttered a loud song of three or four notes with quality of Little Greenbul's song, and consisting of a short phrase, *titiwah*, lower pitched at the end; or *titutawah* rapidly repeated two to four times. A shrill harsh chatter, *chrrrrrrrrrrtitiwah*, may precede the song. **Range:** Kakamega Forest; for-merly on Mt Elgon and at Lerundo.

CABANIS'S GREENBUL *Phyllastrephus cabanisi* **Plate 76**

Length 6.5–7.5″. A common, slender-billed, *highland forest* greenbul, with *bright rufous-brown tail* and *pale throat*. Travels in pairs or family groups in undergrowth, flicking wings and dipping the tail, its chuckling chatter a common forest sound. Eastern **P. c.**

placidus olive-brown above, with narrow whitish eye-ring and *creamy white chin and throat*; eyes typically pale brown or grey; *feet blue-grey or slaty blue.* **Juvenile** said to be dark rufous-brown above, and blotchy brown and creamy below with brown flanks. Immature more olive above than adult, darker (or with distinct broad olive-grey band) on breast. Adult **P. c. sucosus** brighter olive, less brown on back (thus greater contrast with reddish tail); eyelid feathers pale grey; *dark sides of breast accentuate the pale yellow throat; eyes pale greyish tan or pale grey*; feet as in *placidus.* **Juvenile** and immature bright olive above, pale yellow below (brighter than adult), more olive on sides and breast; eyelids yellowish; feet greenish grey. **Song**, *chrrrk, chrrrrrk, chrrrrrk-chrrrk, chwerrt-chwerrt*, often as a duet; or a less grating *prrip-prip-perrup-perrup. . .*, or *pru-ip, pru-ip, peerrip peerrip prrup prrup. . .* prolonged, the notes loud and explosive or soft with scolding quality. Song may contain various whistled notes. Contact call a low harsh churring. **Range**: *P. c. placidus* east of Rift Valley from northern mountains south through the highlands to Mt Kasigau, the Taita and Chyulu hills, Arusha NP, Kilimanjaro, Mt Meru and the Pare and Usambara mts. *P. c. sucosus* from the Crater and Mbulu highlands (some specimens intermediate with *placidus*) north to Mt Elgon and the Cheranganis.

FISCHER'S GREENBUL *Phyllastrephus fischeri*   Plate 76

Length 7". A *white-throated, pale-eyed, long-billed* bulbul of *coastal forest* usually in small chattering groups on or near the ground; indulges in much tail-flirting and wing-flicking. *Pale brownish olive above, dull rufous on tail.* White throat contrasts with brownish olive breast and flanks. Inconspicuous narrow whitish eye-ring around white, cream, or yellowish tan eyes. Male's bill much longer and more slender than that of female. **Juvenile** has *pale yellow belly* and grey eyes. (Similar Cabanis's Greenbul is allopatric. Brownbuls are dark-eyed.) **Call** *prurrit prurrit*, varied with protracted dry chattering and churring, plus a scolding *chiccck-chicccck-chiccck CHIKI-TIK. . .*, and a repeated rapid *chweeeeeeeeeeoh*, dropping at end. Chatter may accelerate into a distinctive descending *WREEE-ga-ga-ga-ga* , possibly a contact call (S. Keith). **Range**: From Somali border south along the coast, inland along lower Tana River, Shimba Hills and up to 600 m in East Usambaras.

NORTHERN BROWNBUL *Phyllastrephus strepitans*   Plate 76

Length 6–7". Travels babbler-like through dry undergrowth in noisy restless parties, repeatedly flicking wings. *Bright brown on back and tail, with strongly rufous-tinged wings, upper tail-coverts and rump* (unlike Terrestrial Brownbul). Inconspicuous, narrow whitish eye-ring and reddish brown eyes; bill black with pale tomial streak; feet blue-grey, darker than in Terrestrial B. **Juvenile** duller above; eyes dull brown. See Cabanis's and Fischer's Greenbuls. **Call** (often as duet or chorus) a rapid chattering reminiscent of *Turdoides* babblers; continues 5–10 sec. and is frequently repeated; higher pitched, faster than call of Terrestrial Brownbul, *skrrrk-skrrrrk-kk-kk-kk-kk-kk. . .*; or slower and softer at beginning and end: *chiak-chiak- chiak chchchch SKEY-OW skeyow chyow chyow chyow chyow.* **Range**: Coastal lowlands (where sympatric with Terrestrial B.), inland along Tana River to edge of the highlands, and through the Tsavo parks to Mkomazi GR and southern slopes of Kilimanjaro. In n. Kenya from Lake Baringo, Kerio Valley and Samburu GR north to Lokichokio and Ethiopian border areas.

TERRESTRIAL BROWNBUL *Phyllastrephus terrestris*   Plate 76

Length 6.75–7.5". Closely resembles the more common Northern Brownbul, but often in moister habitat and *mainly coastal* in distribution. *Less rufous above* than Northern B., particularly on wings and tail, and bill slightly larger. *Whitish throat contrasts with darker breast.* Scarce interior *bensoni* more olive-brown above than coastal *suahelicus*, and with more yellow streaking on underparts; whitish eyelids less prominent. **Juvenile** *suahelicus* paler and brighter than adult, more rufous on wings (*thus more like adult Northern Brownbul*). **Call** somewhat lower in pitch than that of Northern Brownbul: *chrrrrrk, chrrk-chrrk, chrrrrrk . . ..* Birds calling together

produce a churring sound. **Range**: *P. t. suahelicus* local in coastal lowlands north to Somali border, inland to Shimba Hills and forest patches on lower Tana River. *T. t. bensoni* known only from early records near Meru. (A specimen from Mt Endau, attributed to this species, is actually *P. strepitans*, casting doubt on subsequent sight record from near Murang'a).

YELLOW-STREAKED GREENBUL *Phyllastrephus flavostriatus tenuirostris*
Plate 76

Length 7–8". A pale, long-billed forest bulbul with a habit of *constantly raising or flicking one wing at a time*, revealing the yellow wing-linings. Faint light-yellow ventral streaks rarely visible in the field; crissum brownish yellow. Upperparts olive, with greyer head. (Terrestrial Brownbul also has faint yellow streaking, especially in the race *bensoni*, but is browner above.) **Song** of distinct loud downslurred notes followed by rapid notes on same pitch: *chwick chwerk chk chk chee qu-qu-qu chew chikichick*; or more distinctly two-parted, 3–4 nasal whistled notes followed by clear faster whistling, *yerk, chwip chweep cheweep whew-whew-whew-whew*, accelerating and slightly descending. Call a repeated *quee-chew* and various twittering notes that may lead into song. **Range**: Usambara and South Pare mts in ne. Tanzania. In Kenya known only from two early specimens (Murang'a, 1917, and Mt Kasigau, 1938).

TINY GREENBUL *Phyllastrephus debilis*
Plate 76

Length 5–5.5". A small *warbler-like* bird of eastern forest undergrowth (but sings from canopy in early morning). Coastal *P. d. rabai* has mainly olive-green upperparts with *sharply defined grey head* and greyish white *underparts streaked with yellow*; eyes usually white, cream or yellowish. *P. d. albigula* has a more olive crown, is greyer below with fewer yellow streaks; eyes yellow or yellow-orange. **Juvenile** *rabai* has greenish instead of grey lores and crown; eyes probably brown. **Song** of short *chit* notes variously combined with lower nasal sounds, *chitchitchit, chit-nya-nya-nya*. Call of *albigula* a gurgling *chrrrrrr*, of *rabai* a rasping rising *chicididididididi,* sometimes with other notes. **Range**: *P. d. rabai* in Arabuko–Sokoke Forest (scarce); apparently now absent from other Kenyan coastal sites, but extends up to 450 m in Shimba Hills; also in East Usambara foothills where replaced above 300 m by *albigula* which also ranges throughout West Usambaras.

HONEYGUIDE GREENBUL *Baeopogon i. indicator*
Plate 75

Length 7.5". A western forest canopy species; dark olive-grey with a *largely white tail* patterned somewhat like a honeyguide's, the resemblance heightened in flight. *Eyes white, cream or pale grey in male, grey or brown in female.* **Juvenile** (male) similar to adult but browner on crown and greyish white on belly; outer three pairs of rectrices entirely white; eyes dull greyish buff. Forages at all levels. Vocal throughout the day from concealed canopy perches. **Song** loud and distinctive, of several slurred, slightly squealing whistles with a prolonged, descending final note, the latter somewhat buzzy in quality and often fading away, *keerriup keeup kuileep turee TZEEeeeeewwww*; variable. Calls include a squealing catlike *teeueeep*, or *squeeeueee*, pitch dropping in the middle; sometimes interspersed with the song. **Range**: Kakamega and Nandi forests. Formerly Mt Elgon and along Yala River.

YELLOW-BELLIED GREENBUL *Chlorocichla flaviventris centralis*
Plate 75

Length 8–8.5". A large eastern greenbul of forest undergrowth, olive-brown above, *yellow below* (throat paler) and with prominent *white upper eyelid* (lower lid feathering less conspicuously whitish). Dark crown feathers frequently erected into a low bushy crest; eyes dark red or brown. **Juvenile** duller, head no darker than back; underparts paler than in adult; eyes grey-brown. **Song** a distinctive, querulous, somewhat nasal *qui quaaaa quer qua queree qwa*; or *quar-tooa, quar-tooa*, slowly delivered, the notes well spaced. Also *rreeek, rrreeek, rrreeek, yerrrk*, alternating with continued chatter. Prolonged *kerr quar, kerr quar. . .* perhaps a contact call. Two birds may call together asynchronously. **Range**: Coastal areas, inland along Tana River to Bura,

Shimba Hills, East Usambaras, base of Pare Mts, Lake Manyara and Mt Hanang. Local in and near Tsavo West NP west to Nairobi and Meru area, but now scarce in cent. Kenya where little suitable habitat remains. Formerly along Voi River and near Taveta.

JOYFUL GREENBUL *Chlorocichla laetissima* **Plate 75**

Length 8.25″. A large golden-yellow greenbul of w. Kenyan forests where a cheerful rollicking or bubbling chatter announces presence of a group moving through the trees. *Bright yellowish olive above*, with 'scaly' crown feathers, short yellowish superciliaries and yellow eyelids. **Juvenile** browner above, washed with greenish below. **Song** chuck-chuck-chweek-kweek-kuardl-chuker-erk-querk. In courtship, *chukliSKEEskeu*, repeated. **Range**: Mt Elgon south to Kericho and nw. Mara GR (Olololoo Escarpment). Conspicuous in Kakamega Forest.

YELLOW-THROATED LEAF-LOVE *Chlorocichla flavicollis pallidigula*
Plate 75

Length 8.5″. A *large noisy pale-throated* greenbul of *west Kenyan* riverine thickets and tangles where small, highly vocal family groups forage low in dense foliage, scolding all intruders. Appears large-headed with raised crown and throat feathers; flicks wings when disturbed. Dusky olive above, *crown greyer and somewhat dappled or scaly; tail olive-brown*. Chin and throat yellowish or cream; eyes dull yellow to light brown in male; whitish in female; appears long-legged. **Juvenile** browner, less olive than adult, and with whitish throat. (Cabanis's Greenbul, also with prominent pale throat, is smaller with reddish brown tail.) **Call** a loud twangy *skyow* or *chow* combined with various chattering, and squeaky notes to convey an impression of anger or irritation, *skyow-skyow-chyowk-chyowk, ch-ch-ch-ch-chchchchch. . .* with variations. Several birds may call together. **Range**: Local from Saiwa NP and Kitale south to Tanzanian border areas. Generally scarce east of 35° E.

✓ COMMON or DARK-CAPPED BULBUL *Pycnonotus barbatus* **Plate 75**

Length 6–7.5″. One of East Africa's best-known birds. Widespread *P. b. tricolor* almost black on head and throat; underparts otherwise white with *prominent yellow under tail-coverts*. Small eastern and northern *dodsoni* ('White-eared Bulbul') has whitish ear-coverts, mottled breast and more conspicuous whitish rectrix tips. Tanzanian *layardi* has black crown and face. Eyes of some birds in s. Kerio Valley prominently ringed by bare white orbital skin. **Juvenile** rufous-tinged above. **Songs** involve repetition of one note: *churtle-churtle-churtle-churtle*, or *wurtilee-wurtilee-wurtilee* given separately or intermingled. In excitement, variations explode in a jumble of frantic-sounding notes. Greeting vocalization *cheedle cheedle cheedlelit*, given with partly raised wings. Common calls of *tricolor*, *kwick kwerk kwee* or *kwee kwit kwert keert* and *kwee kerr-oh*; those of *dodsoni* higher and more shrill, *pwhic-pwer* or *chwiki-chwiki-chwiki*, etc. **Range**: Virtually ubiquitous except above 3000 m. and in dense forest. *P. b. tricolor* in w. and cent Kenya and Tanzania west of the Rift Valley; *layardi* in Tanzania east of the Rift, and in s. Kenya around Taveta and Loitokitok; *dodsoni* in n. and e. Kenya south to Mkomazi GR in ne. Tanzania; races freely interbreed in contact zones.

Aka: Yellow-vented Bulbul (margin note)

RED-TAILED BRISTLEBILL *Bleda syndactyla woosnami* **Plate 75**

Length 8–9″. A large stocky bulbul of the forest floor and low undergrowth in western Kenya. Conspicuous *pale blue or bluish white orbital skin, bright yellow underparts, plain rufous tail* and dark brownish olive back identify adults; eyes blood-red (male) or brown (female). **Juvenile** more or less *rufous above, on sides and flanks* and with *yellowish orbital skin*. **Call** a series of four or five quavering, minor-key, descending notes: *QUEEE, queee, queee, queee.* Much less frequent is a short monotonous *tung-tung-tung-tung-tung. . .* lasting for several seconds. West African birds give a distinctive, evenly pitched *querr-querr-querr-kiqurr, qurrrrrr-qurrrrrr. . . qurrrrrrrr. . .* with quality of Yellow-bellied Greenbul's notes. **Range**: North Nandi, Kakamega, and Iruru forests; on Mt Elgon and (once) in Saiwa NP.

BABBLERS, CHATTERERS AND ILLADOPSES, FAMILY TIMALIIDAE

Brownish birds, somewhat thrush-like, but stronger-footed and with shorter rounded wings. The long-tailed babblers and chatterers (*Turdoides*), named for their boisterous vocalizations, call in duet or chorus from thick cover or as they reassemble after flying weakly, one by one, across openings. Decidedly social, several birds roost together and rest side by side during the day, often preening one another. They are mostly ground foragers, but freely perch in shrubs and low trees in thickets, forest-edge undergrowth, dense bush and cultivation. Iris colour is important in identification of adult babblers. (All juveniles are brown-eyed.)

The illadopses (*Illadopsis* and *Kakamega*) are shy terrestrial birds of the leaf litter and lowest shrub stratum in deep forest. Master skulkers, all are similar in appearance, and their habits and habitat almost preclude good views. Vocal distinctions exist, but persistent confusion clouds identifications based on voice, as singing birds are not easily seen (and 3 or 4 species live together in certain forests). Brown Illadopsis is perhaps easiest to see and to identify, but Pale-breasted appears almost identical in a side view. Scaly-breasted is recognizable if its scaly underparts can be seen. Mountain Illadopsis is the only species in montane forest above 2200 m (but it ranges down to 1500 m, overlapping the other three). Only Pale-breasted inhabits n. Tanzania. Male illadopses are noticeably larger than females; plumage is the same in both sexes, as in *Turdoides*.

The African Hill Babbler (*Pseudoalcippe*) is a small arboreal bird of highland forest, distinct from other East African timaliids. Restricted in our region to ne. Tanzania are the *Modulatrix* species, both secretive forest-floor dwellers. Although frequently included in Turdidae, they reportedly have syringeal differences from thrushes, their juveniles are unspotted, and their behaviour is more suggestive of timaliids. We place them here following Jensen and Brogger-Jensen.

BLACK-LORED BABBLER *Turdoides sharpei*   Plate 89

Length 9". A typical gregarious babbler, grey-brown with *black lores* and *white eyes*. *T. s. sharpei* has somewhat mottled underparts with lighter feather edges and dark shaft streaks on chin and throat feathers (but without white-pointed tips or spots). Birds around Naivasha are paler-throated, have darker wings and tail, and may appear quite frosty-headed. The variable race *vepres* near Nanyuki has *chin and often the entire throat white*; rest of underparts dark brown with narrow pale scaly feather edges, more streaked on belly; those around Lewa Downs may suggest a streaky-breasted Northern Pied Babbler. (Arrow-marked and Brown Babblers have yellow or orange eyes and pointed white feather tips below.) **Call** of single birds a rough single or double note, *waaach* or *sqwaa-a,* repeated many times; also a muffled, *wher-ha* or *kurr-ack;*in duet or chorus, various harsh phrases, sometimes in long series, *ch-WAACKa WAACKa wAACKa. . . or wuk-wuk-wuk ye-ack, wee-ack wee-ak cherakkk-akk-akk. . .,* or *CHURRRi CHURRi CHURRi chchchchchch chichiwaka. . .,* often slower than many babbler vocalizations. Alarm note a cat-like *nyaaa.* **Range**: *T. s. sharpei* from Kongelai Escarpment and Mt Elgon south through the Lake Victoria basin and Lolgorien to w. Serengeti NP (southeast to Ndutu and Lake Masek) and in cent. Rift Valley from Solai south to Narok. *T. s. vepres* from the Laikipia Plateau south to Nanyuki, Timau and Lewa Downs. **Taxonomic Note**: Formerly considered conspecific with s. African *T. melanops.*

ARROW-MARKED BABBLER *Turdoides jardineii*   Plate 89

Length 8.5-9". A yellow- or orange-eyed, greyish brown babbler found *south of the Equator*. Note the conspicuous sharp white feather tips on throat and upper breast; crown and nape feathers have less prominent white tips and dark centres; lores, chin and auriculars brown. (Brown Babbler has whitish lores and chin, more scaly white feather edges on throat and breast, with the sharp white tips less pronounced.) **Call** a boisterous chuckling and chattering, *waaCHA, waaCHA. . .,* or *chyaa-chyaa-chyaa. . . chchchchch,* often slowing then accelerating. **Range**: *T. j. emini* west of Rift Valley, from Narok south to the Crater Highlands and Serengeti NP, and in cent. Rift at Naivasha (where sympatric with Black-lored Babbler) and Lake Nakuru NP. East of the Rift, *T. j. kirki* north to Tarangire and Lake Manyara NPs. Old records from Kilimanjaro, Taveta and East Usambaras.

435

BROWN BABBLER *Turdoides plebejus cinereus*   **Plate 89**

Length 8.5". The northern counterpart of Arrow-marked Babbler. Dull brown, *yellow-eyed* and *grey-faced,* with *whitish lores and chin*; crown and nape slightly mottled in fresh plumage (less so as pale margins wear); *throat and breast feathers with small white tips.* (Arrow-marked Babbler has dark lores and ear-coverts; chin not noticeably pale; white feather tips on breast larger and more sharply defined; belly and flanks more mottled or streaked.) **Call** a variable chattering and chuckling recalling Arrow-marked Babbler, and including a slow *tsuk-tsuk-tsuk.* . ., a harsh *skyrr, skyrr, skyrr, skyrr, chwrrr-chwrrr-chrrr-chrrchrrchr,* and a buzzier communal *chwerryer chwerryer chwerryer.* . .. Scold note a repeated buzzy *CHAY-o* given with partly spread and raised wings, and fanned tail. **Range:** Pokot and Maralal districts, and the Turkwell and Kerio valleys, south to Mogotio, Rumuruti and Nanyuki, south of equator only near Kisumu, Muhoroni and Fort Ternan. No overlap with Arrow-marked Babbler.

SCALY BABBLER *Turdoides s. squamulatus*   **Plate 89**

Length 9". A skulking, *scaly-looking coastal* babbler with largely *whitish chin* and *orange-yellow eyes.* Upperparts dark olive-brown, the crown, throat and neck feathers scaled with whitish edges; *auriculars and lores dark blackish brown.* **Call** a distinctive throaty *wuk-a-ha, wuk-a-ha . . .* and *ch'wuk ch'wuk . . .,* most reminiscent of Black-lored Babbler. Less vocal than other *Turdoides.* (Arrow-marked Babbler, in coastal thickets south of our area, has prominent white feather tips.) **Range:** Kilifi north to the Somali border, inland along Tana River to Garissa. Birds near Ramu along the Daua River (Ethiopian border) show much white on the head, more than in white-throated *jubaensis* from the nearby Juba River in s. Somalia; they reportedly resemble the more distant *T. s. carolinae.*

HINDE'S BABBLER *Turdoides hindei*   **Plate 89**

Length 8–9". Scarce Kenyan endemic, confined to fringes of cultivation and river valleys on e. and s. edges of the central highlands. A motley, *red-eyed* babbler that shows varying amounts of *broad white feather edging on head and back,* plus white wing-covert and secondary tips. Head and back can be almost blackish, wings and tail browner, *rump chestnut-brown, flanks and crissum tawny-cinnamon.* Some birds are much darker than others, and certain individuals suggest partial albinos. (Allopatric Brown and Arrow-marked Babblers have yellow or orange eyes, and *pointed* white markings on underparts; both are plainer brown above without the white scaling of Hinde's. Adult Black-lored and Northern Pied Babblers have white eyes.) **Call** a harsh chuckling and chattering, *cherak-chwak-chakchakchakchak . . .* or *kwerak-chk-chk-chk.* **Range:** Meru, Embu, Karatina, Murang'a, Thika and Machakos districts. Formerly at Athi River and in Kitui, Mwingi and Chuka districts. Reduction in range coincides with increased agricultural development.

NORTHERN PIED BABBLER *Turdoides hypoleucus*   **Plate 89**

Length 8–9". *White-eyed* and brown-backed, with *white underparts* bordered by *dark brown lateral breast patches and sides. T. h. rufuensis* is greyer above than nominate *hypoleucus,* with light scaly crown-feather margins. (Black-lored Babbler, also white-eyed, usually has dark underparts, but see *T. sharpei vepres.*) **Calls** much like those of Hinde's Babbler. **Range:** *T. h. hypoleucus* east of Rift Valley, from Meru and Nyeri districts south through the highlands to the Tanzanian border; occasional in Arusha NP and n. Kilimanjaro. *T. h. rufuensis* ranges north to Tarangire and Lake Manyara NPs.

RUFOUS CHATTERER *Turdoides rubiginosus*   **Plate 89**

Length 7.5–8". A generally rufous, *pale-billed* and *pale-eyed* babbler of dense bush and dry thickets. Browner above, mostly *cinnamon-rufous below.* Shows short silvery streaks on breast and forehead. Eastern *heuglini* is darker overall, rufous-tinged above (especially on head), with indistinct black shaft streaks on head and back. Western *emini* has greyer crown with extensions of the light forehead streaks. **Call** a shrill descending *tschyeerss,* repeated many times at intervals of 2–3 sec. Also chattering, growling and squealing sounds, a soft *queer,* and a long quavering whistle. **Range:** *T. r. rubiginosus* in n. and e. Kenya south to Mtito Andei, Amboseli NP, the Athi/Kapiti plains and Southern Uaso Nyiro River; *heuglini* on coast, inland to Voi, Taveta, Mkomazi GR and s. Kilimanjaro lowlands; Tanzanian *emini* west of the Rift Valley from lakes Eyasi and Masek and Maswa GR southward. Sight records from extreme ne. Kenya may refer to *T. r. sharpei.*

SCALY CHATTERER *Turdoides aylmeri*   Plate 89

Length 8.25–9″. Duller than Rufous Chatterer, with a *bare blue-grey patch around pale yellow eyes.* Pale cinnamon-brown below, the *broad buff feather edges of throat and breast producing a scaly effect*; lores ashy. Northern *boranensis* has darker centres to throat feathers, and Tanzanian *mentalis* is generally more greyish brown than eastern *kenianus.* **Call** an odd 'squeaking wood-screw' sound, varied by a thin high-pitched chatter and broken whistling. **Range:** North, east and south of the Kenyan highlands, typically in drier areas than Rufous Chatterer but the two often sympatric: northern *boranensis* from South Horr south to Barsaloi; *kenianus* from Meru NP and Garissa south to Mkomazi GR and North Pare foothills; *mentalis* in interior e. Tanzania from Lake Natron and the Masai Steppe south to Dodoma. Birds from Olorgesailie to Magadi may also be *mentalis.*

AFRICAN HILL BABBLER *Pseudoalcippe a. abyssinica*   Plate 90

Length 6″. An arboreal forest bird with a *small slim bill, grey head and nape sharply delineated* from bright rufous-brown back, grey underparts faintly mottled or streaked with white; belly whitish; *flanks and leg feathers washed with yellowish brown.* (Similar Mountain Illadopsis is a stockier terrestrial skulker, with grey of head more restricted and merging with olive-brown back and nape, dark slaty grey underparts and no white on belly.) **Song** usually clear and melodious, suggesting a thrush, composed of separated whistled phrases with frequent changes in pitch: *weu-tu-whu-yo-WUtu-CHeeu* or *CHEWi-WEUto-wuchiWEEtew.* Also a pure slurred whistling, *weu-TEEU-tu-WEU-weu-weu,* quite low-pitched. Some songs higher with more scratchy notes. **Range:** Northern Kenyan mountains south to Mau and Trans-Mara forests, Chyulu Hills, Crater and Mbulu highlands, Arusha NP, Kilimanjaro and Mt Meru, Pare Mts and West Usambaras.

SPOT-THROAT *Modulatrix s. stictigula*   Plate 123

Length 6.75″. A dark, chestnut-tailed forest bird of the Usambara Mts. Runs or flutters along forest floor when approached; hops with tail slightly elevated, probing in leaf litter and flicking leaves with bill. Noticeable *whitish or greyish eye-ring ,* and largely *rufous breast and sides,* and buffy white throat marked with small dark spots; upperparts brownish olive; flanks and crissum tawny rufous; belly whitish. **Juvenile**'s throat less speckled, and chin/throat patch less distinct. (Dappled Mountain-Robin and Pale-breasted Illadopsis have no chestnut on underparts.) **Song** recorded by Svendsen and Hansen in Udzungwa Mts consists of loud, shrill slurred whistles with some long-drawn higher notes, *skureet chierreet siureeee sreet seeu sheeu-tsi-chiu, seeeeeet, swee-ir-si-REEO,* the final note often loudest. Also gives a shorter *chiu chi-chi-CHEEO* and a shrill, descending *siuuuuu,* repeated. **Range:** Usambara Mts, both East (rare) and West (common between 900 and 2200 m, mainly above 1500 m).

DAPPLED MOUNTAIN-ROBIN *Modulatrix orostruthus amani*   Plate 123

Length 6.75″. A rare, streaky-breasted bird of the East Usambara Mts. Elusive, preferring dense undergrowth along streams. Brownish olive-green above with lores and sides of face dark olive; upper tail-coverts and tail russet-brown; underparts pale yellow, with *broad olive streaks on breast, upper belly and flanks*; lower belly and crissum washed with ochre, sometimes heavily. Bill brown or black, whitish at base below. Very rounded wings said to be obvious in flight. **Juvenile** olive below, darker and greener on breast.

Song (of *M. o. sanje* in Udzungwa Mts) rapid, clear and melodious, at times quite oriole-like: *qu qu-we wurdilee WEE-yew* or (*twee*) *turLEEa*; also a repetitious bulbul-like chatter: *chiquea chiquea chiquea*. Main call is a rising fluty whistle, *hoooo-reee*, much higher at end (Svendsen and Hansen). **Range**: East Usambaras (other races farther south in e. Tanzania). **Taxonomic Note**: Placed by some authors in a separate genus, *Arcanator*.

GREY-CHESTED ILLADOPSIS *Kakamega poliothorax*   Plate 90

Length 6.5″. A thrush-like bird of the forest floor and undergrowth in western Kenya. *Bright mahogany-rufous above*, more dusky on crown, wings and tail; throat and centre of belly whitish, shading to pure *grey on breast and sides*; eyes red-brown. Relatively small-billed and long-legged. Juvenile apparently undescribed. (Brown-chested Alethe appears bright brown above in dappled forest light but has light superciliary stripes and brownish breast band.) **Song** short, clear and loud, the rapidly uttered phrase somewhat oriole-like: *kew-ki-KEWI-eu* or *wi chi-yow kiWEEo*; sometimes more bulbul-like: *werk-kiyer-l'week* or *choik-kiyer-WEEK*. Calls incude *tseetseetseetsee* and a slightly churring *kwerriyer, kwerriyer* or *churriyer, churriyer*. **Range**: Kakamega and Nandi forests. Formerly at Lerundo and on Mt Elgon.

BROWN ILLADOPSIS *Illadopsis fulvescens ugandae*   Plate 90

Length 5.5–6″. Spends more time above ground in low shrubbery than other west Kenyan illadopses, often investigating vine tangles and clusters of dead leaves, thus more easily seen. *Longer-tailed* and *larger billed* than its relatives; *whitish throat* contrasts with *otherwise tawny-buff underparts*; lower edge of grey cheeks and ear-coverts dusky, forming *weak malar streaks*; no hint of scaly pattern on breast; flanks only slightly darker than belly; feet purplish grey or blue-grey. **Juvenile** almost rufous on back and wings; feet dull maroon. **Song** usually of a few short notes preceding longer minor-key whistles, the latter often with a pronounced 'twang': (1) *yik, youuuuuuuuuu,* (2) *yik chickik p'chyowww,* (3) *whik peeeeee, pyerrrrrr,* (4) *whik whik, CHIK-ti-fownnnnn,* the twangy end note given by one bird, the *chik* or *wick* notes by its presumed mate. Dawn song, which may end with twang of diurnal songs, is "a long-drawn husky whistle. . . often introduced by a couple of shorter, less musical attempts, and as the whistles are slowly repeated they vary . . . about half a tone, always low in the scale" (Chapin, Congo). Alarm call a nasal *tchaa* or *chwaa*. **Range**: Kakamega Forest and nearby Malaba Forest. Upper altitudinal limit probably *c.* 1600 m.

MOUNTAIN ILLADOPSIS *Illadopsis p. pyrrhoptera*   Plate 90

Length 4.75–5.25″. The common illadopsis of *montane* forest (ranges up to 2800 m). *Dark* and skulking. Rufescent olive-brown above, greyer and somewhat scaly on crown; upper tail-coverts dull rufous brown contrasting somewhat with the dark brown tail. *Dark grey face, breast and sides contrast with pale grey throat and brownish flanks and crissum*; belly grey, lighter than breast. **Juvenile** brighter russet-brown. See African Hill Babbler. **Song** of penetrating descending semitones, *TWEEK twe tyew tu-wer tu-wer*, mingled with much low chucking and chattering. Ugandan bird's songs attributed to this species (Keith and Gunn) confusingly like Brown Illadopsis, with short semi-staccato notes and longer descending minor-key semitones: *chick-waaaa-fiyownn* or *chikchi-fiyaaaa chiyaaaaa chiown*; sometimes more varied notes, e.g. *quili-waaa yew-yew-yeaow*. Also said to duet as does *I. fulvescens*. **Range**: West of Rift Valley from Mt Elgon and the Cheranganis south to North Nandi, Mau and Trans-Mara forests. Formerly rare in Kakamega Forest, perhaps wanderering from the Nandi.

PALE-BREASTED ILLADOPSIS *Illadopsis rufipennis*   Plates 90, 124

Length 5–5.5″. Easily confused with partly sympatric Scaly-breasted Illadopsis. *I. r. rufipennis* is paler below than that species, and virtually lacks dark edging on breast feathers. *Whitish throat and belly* accentuated by *olive-buff or pale brownish breast band, sides, flanks and crissum*; face greyish. Rictal skin and *mandible base bright yellow to orange*; feet blue-grey or purplish grey, usually darker than in Scaly-breasted, but sometimes pale yellowish white. In the hand, note that the rictal bristles are long (9-12 mm) and thin in *rufipennis*, short (4-6 mm) and thick in

438

albipectus. The feet of rufipennis are noticeably smaller than those of albipectus. Tanzanian distans, perhaps specifically distinct, has a large bill, the breast band is pale cold grey, not buff or brownish, and the flanks and crissum are olive-brown. **Juvenile** I. r. rufipennis has tawny lesser wing-covert tips, is brighter above than adult, and grey-faced, but lacks rufous or cinnamon of young Scaly-breasted. (Brown Illadopsis is more uniformly tawny-buff below, including belly, is larger and longer looking. Mountain Illadopsis resembles I. r. distans but is dark grey below.) **Song**: Kenyan birds' voices have not been adequately documented. In the Congo, Chapin attributed to rufipennis an ascending series of 3 or 4 short whistles introduced by 1 or 2 low chirps, but pursuing these songs he collected both this species and albipectus. In w. Uganda, the introductory chirps can resemble those which albipectus uses to introduce its own 2/3/4-note ascending whistles; they also resemble some notes of I. fulvescens. Ugandan rufipennis songs carefully studied by J. Lindsell recall I. fulvescens in form and tone, but following the introductory chirp or chirps is a SINGLE fulvescens-like whistle: chip PHEEEE or chirrip churrup PHEEEEE . Whistles in successive songs are all on the same pitch (unlike fulvescens) and the whistled notes are even, neither slurring upward or downward. The song of rufipennis has less volume than that of fulvescens; the initial chirp(s) often so faint that one hears only the whistled pheeee at a rate of about 1 every 5-8 sec. Call note a harsh chack. In the Usambaras, I. r. distans commonly utters two slow human-like whistles preceded by a softer short note: twik wureet weeee or chip wureet uweeee, often answered by second bird. Alarm note of distans said to be a grating ka-a-a-a followed by a throaty kwo-kwo. There is much 'conversational' churring between members of a group. **Range:** I. r. rufipennis in Kakamega and South Nandi forests; distans in the East Usambara Mts and around 1200 m in the West Usambaras. Birds in Ol Doinyo Orok (Namanga Hill) and Trans-Mara forests apparently show plumage characteristics of distans.

SCALY-BREASTED ILLADOPSIS Illadopsis albipectus barakae   Plate 90
Length 5–6". Very similar to the preceding species (with which partly sympatric) but breast feathers of west Kenyan birds usually appear scaly. Well-marked individuals are also scaly on the olive-brown sides and white belly, less so on back; long tarsi whitish grey to greyish pink or purplish pink, usually paler than in rufipennis. **Juvenile** brighter than adult, faintly yellowish on breast; head browner, less grey, with rufous feathering around the eyes, at times on forehead. (Some rufous feathers remain on immatures after other juvenile plumage moulted.) Feet whitish or pinkish grey. See Pale-breasted Illadopsis. **Song** of 2–4 ascending, semitone, minor-key notes often preceded by a softer introductory note inaudible at a distance: t'eee eee EEE, or t'wick yee HEEE, the louder notes penetrating and far-carrying. Seldom heard is a high-pitched warbler-like see-u, see-u, see-u preceded by a soft twittering titititititititi. More vocal (or with longer song season) than other illadopses. **Range**: Kakamega and Nandi forests, 1600 to 2100 m.

THRUSHES, CHATS AND RELATIVES, FAMILY TURDIDAE
Mostly small birds which occupy a broad range of habitats from deep forest to open plains. They are longer-legged than the related warblers and flycatchers (sometimes united with thrushes in the family Muscicapidae). The bill is rather slender, and the eyes tend to be large. Some species are undistinguished in appearance, but others have bold facial or tail patterns or bright colours. Several employ conspicuous wing or tail movements. The sexes are usually similar, but are different in some wheatears, chats and Irania. Juveniles are more or less spotted. Most East African breeders are solitary, but some migrants gather in small groups. Forest thrushes are shy and elusive, often feeding with other birds on invertebrates flushed by columns of army ants. Many stand quite upright when alert. Songs vary from unimpressive to powerful and melodious, and some species are among Africa's finest songsters. Twelve of our thrushes are long-distance migrants from the Palearctic.

WHITE-STARRED ROBIN Pogonocichla stellata   Plates 93, 124
Length 6". A small forest thrush that spreads and flirts its distinctively patterned tail. **Adult** has bright yellow underparts and a yellow tail with black central feathers and tip (yellow only at extreme tail base in Mt Elgon race). Back olive; dark grey head has small white

spot in front of each eye (another, usually concealed, on lower throat conspicuous in singing bird). Races differ in intensity of yellow and colour of wing edgings. **Juvenile** olive-green with pale spots above, dull yellow below where heavily marked with black chevrons; tail as adult; this plumage replaced by long-lasting **immature** dress, olive above, underparts varying racially: mottled yellow and olive in *intensa*; pale yellow with grey mottling in *helleri* and *orientalis*; olive narrowly streaked with yellow in *macarthuri*. **Song** a long series of squeaky phrases interspersed with low chattering: *ski-skurEE-skurEW, chrrg-chrr-chrr, ski-skurEE.* . . or *wi-wur-wihi, wi-wur-wihi, chrr-ch-chrr-chrr, wi-wur-wihi* . . .. Softer prolonged song, with creaking quality, alternates two notes, *treee-tur, treee-tur.* . .. In Tanzania, a clear song, *tuEET tuEET tuEET, eet eet tuEET.* . ., interspersed with ticking chatter. Calls include a soft *krrrrrrrr* and a harsh *pirrut-pirrut.* **Range**: *P. s. intensa* from Mbulu and Crater highlands north to Mathews Range, the Ndotos, Mt Nyiru and Mt Kulal; *orientalis* in the Usambaras; *guttifer* on Kilimanjaro and Mt Meru; *helleri* on Mt Lossogonoi, Pare Mts, Mt Kasigau and Taita Hills; *macarthuri* in Chyulu Hills; *elgonensis* on Mt Elgon.

SWYNNERTON'S ROBIN *Swynnertonia swynnertoni rodgersi* Plate 123
Length 4.5–5″. Suggests a White-starred Robin, but with *rich yellow flanks and breast,* and a *white crescent on the lower throat bordered below by black or dark grey.* Tail often carried at 45º angle. **Male** dark grey on head, wings and tail, bright olive-green on upper back, grey from lower rump to tail. **Female** duller, head more olive, throat pale buffy grey. **Juvenile** brown above with buffy yellow spots; breast pale yellow with brown feather tips; belly and crissum mottled grey and white. **Immature** browner above than adult female, paler below. **Song** a sweet, high, leisurely whistled series of 3–5 notes, slightly slurred, the first one or two higher. Birds south of our region usually sing 3 notes, *teeee ter tew,* penetrating and semi-mechanical, the quality recalling Black-faced Rufous Warbler or a *Batis.* **Range**: East Usambara mts (200–550 m).

FOREST ROBIN *Stiphrornis erythrothorax xanthogaster* Plate 93
Length 4.5″. Skulks in rainforest undergrowth. Only a vagrant east of Uganda. Olive-brown above, including tail; *throat and upper breast yellow-orange;* sides of breast and flanks grey, rest of underparts white. Shows *blackish cheeks* and *white spot in front of each eye.* **Juvenile** tawny-spotted above, with grey cheeks, whitish throat. (Equatorial Akalat is more uniform apricot below, the colour extending to sides of breast and belly; lacks supraloral spots.) **Song** a high-pitched squeaky and repetitive *ter-ter twee ter ter churrri.* Common call, a low hoarse *ch-chic.* **Range**: West and cent. Africa. Collected once (April 1966) near Kipkabus, w. Kenya.

USAMBARA GROUND ROBIN or USAMBARA AKALAT *Sheppardia montana*
Plate 123
Length 5.5″ A drab, long-legged robin of the *West Usambara forests* in ne. Tanzania. Frequently attends ant swarms with other thrushes. *Dull brownish olive* with *dark reddish brown upper tail-coverts,* whitish preorbital area, and a *usually concealed supraloral streak of orange-rufous* (visible during excitement). Throat and belly dull white; breast, sides and flanks olive-grey; crissum buffy white. **Juvenile** dark brown above, densely mottled with pale buff on back and wing-coverts; breast heavily mottled greyish white and dark brown. **Song** short and clear, *twi-tew LEEtiew* or *wi-TEW-TWI-i-chew.* Also said to give a series of extended high notes on the same pitch. Call a short guttural *querr* or *wurr,* and a repeated nasal *jaanh.* **Range**: West Usambara Mts at Mazumbai, Shagayu and Shume (locally common above 2000 m).

SHARPE'S AKALAT *Sheppardia sharpei usambarae* Plate 123
Length 5″. A robin-like bird of the Usambara Mts. Shy and skulking in open forest understorey. Forages on or near ground. Plain brownish olive above (browner on tail), with *short pale grey superciliary stripes; ear-coverts; sides of neck and underparts dull orange-buff.* **Juvenile** blackish above with buffy orange streaks and spots; underparts buff, more orange on breast, scalloped with black and dark brown. (Usambara Ground Robin behaves similarly, but is much duller and longer-legged.) **Song** tinkling and warbler-like, accelerating at end: *tee tu-wi tu-teetu-ti* or *tee, see see tuweee tuweeti.* Alarm call a more raspy

chatter mixed with clear staccato notes. **Range**: Between 900 and 1600 m in East and West Usambaras; as low as 600 m during cold periods in July/Aug.

EQUATORIAL AKALAT *Sheppardia a. aequatorialis*   Plate 93

Length 5″. An unobtrusive robin-like bird of *west Kenyan highland forest undergrowth. Grey on lores and around eyes*, olive-brown above, more *russet on rump, upper tail-coverts* and on edges of the brown tail feathers; *underparts dull apricot-orange, white in centre of breast and belly*; sides of breast brown. **Juvenile** dark brown mottled with tawny above and below, white on centre of belly. (Juv. Grey-winged Robin has tawny superciliaries, later becoming white, blue-grey 'shoulders' and plain tawny-orange tail. Sharpe's and East Coast Akalats are allopatric.) Easily overlooked **song** a low quavering *erriyerrk* or *yeeerrrr*, repeated at 1–2 sec. intervals, slightly reminiscent of African Scops Owl's call. Usual call a soft *whit*. Alarm call a low rattling *grrrrrrr* or *prrer*. **Range**: Kakamega and Nandi forests (1600–2200 m) south to the Sotik, Kericho, Mau and Trans-Mara forests. Formerly on Mt Elgon.

EAST COAST AKALAT or GUNNING'S ROBIN *Sheppardia gunningi sokoken-sis*   Plate 93

Length 4.5″. A *coastal forest* bird, in low dense undergrowth. Olive-brown above with *blue-grey lores, superciliary stripes and wing-coverts;* mostly *orange-yellow below* with white on belly; orange flanks faintly washed with olive. Erectile white supraloral feathers usually concealed but prominent during excitement. **Juvenile** dark brown above and below with tawny spotting; flanks pale yellowish. **Song** a clear rapid warbling, *uweela-uweela. . .*, or *tureea-tureea-tureea* with little change in pitch and lasting 2–3 sec.; oft-repeated in monotonous continuum for 1 min. or longer. A low *prrrt* accompanies flirting of wings and spreading of tail. **Range**: Arabuko–Sokoke, Shimba Hills and East Usambara lowland forests, and along lower Tana River from Garsen to Wenje; also known from Shimoni and Rabai.

GREY-WINGED ROBIN or ROBIN-CHAT *Sheppardia (Cossypha) p. polioptera*   Plate 93

Length 5.5–6″. This bird of western forests suggests both an akalat and a robin-chat. **Adult** has orange-rufous underparts, *dark slate-grey crown, broken white superciliary stripes* and plain rufous tail. **Juvenile** recalls adult Equatorial Akalat with its nearly plain *rufous-orange or orange-buff underparts, rufous superciliaries*, unpatterned tail and small erectile white supraloral feathers; crown dark with fine rufous streaks; *blue-grey wing-coverts*, at first rufous-tipped as are head feathers; ephemeral tawny or rufous spots above; rump and tail rufous. **Immature** has narrow or obscure whitish superciliaries and black lores. **Song** a soft, high-pitched *sureee-ta-twee-tuweee*, or a prolonged one with each note repeated: *tweet-tweet-tweet, turr-turr-turr, siweet-siyerrr, seet-seeet, titiur-titiur. . ..* Calls a soft *chut*, and *kwik-kwik-kwik*. **Range**: Mt Elgon, Kapenguria and Saiwa NP south to Kakamega (rare), Kaimosi, Nandi, Sotik and West Mau forests; also in gallery forest at Rapogi, Lolgorien and along the Migori River.

OLIVE-FLANKED ROBIN-CHAT *Cossypha anomala mbuluensis*   Plate 122

Length 5.5″. A Tanzanian robin-chat with white throat, *dark grey breast and sides,* and *long white superciliary stripes meeting across forehead*. Blackish above, with rufous-brown rump; orange-rufous upper tail-coverts and sides of tail contrast with blackish central rectrices and tail tip; *flanks washed with olive-rufous* and *crissum orange-rufous*. Flicks wings as it slowly raises and lowers tail. **Juvenile** (*C. a. grotei*, Ukaguru and Uluguru mts) mottled and speckled dark brown and buff above and on breast; centre of belly and crissum pale buff; upper tail-coverts buff or rufous. **Song** of two plaintive notes, *peee-FEUUUuR*, descending. **Range**: Nou Forest in Mbulu Highlands.

RED-CAPPED ROBIN-CHAT or NATAL ROBIN *Cossypha natalensis*   Plate 92

Length 6–7″. Highly vocal but shy and skulking. *Mostly bright orange-rufous including the head; slaty blue on back and wings*; crown rufous (brighter in coastal birds) or indistinctly streaked with black; central rectrices blackish; dark eyes conspicuous on the bright face. **Juvenile** mottled blackish and rufous above; underparts tawny with some dusky mottling. **Song** a melodious whistling often with mimicry of other birds: *twee tew, twee tew, chwe-witi-tew, tutututu, tee-tew. . .* and variations. Common call a slightly trilled, *prreep-prrup*, monotonously repeated. Alarm note, a guttural *gurr*. **Range/status**: *C. n. intensa* an intra-African migrant, late Apr.–Nov., from the southern tropics to Kenyan coast, scattered inland localities in ne. Tanzania, and gallery forest along the Tana River upstream to Garissa. *C. n. hylophona* breeds in several inland Kenyan localities including Mara GR.

RÜPPELL'S ROBIN-CHAT *Cossypha semirufa*   Plate 92

Length 7". A *highland forest* species closely resembling the more widespread White-browed Robin-Chat, but *central tail feathers blackish, not olive-brown*, and back and wings dark slate-grey; superciliaries slightly narrower than in White-browed. Northern nominate race is smaller, more olive and less slaty above than *intercedens*. **Juvenile** has faint superciliaries or none, plus much black scalloping above and below; crown marked with pale olive speckling and rufous streaks; wing-coverts rufous spotted. Variable but distinctive **song** of repeated loud whistles; mimics many bird species and other sounds; also persistently repeats a rolling three-note phrase, *rrrri-pru-ru, rrrri-pru-ru, rrrri-pru-ru. . ..* Alarm call a guttural *rack-k-k-k*. **Range**: *C. s. semirufa* on Mt Marsabit and near Moyale; *intercedens* from 1400 to 2300 m east of Rift Valley from cent. Kenya south to the Crater Highlands, Arusha NP, Mt Meru, Kilimanjaro and Pare Mts.

✓ WHITE-BROWED ROBIN-CHAT or HEUGLIN'S ROBIN *Cossypha heuglini*
Plate 92

Length 7.5–8". The most familiar East African robin-chat, common in a variety of moist wooded habitats. Strikingly coloured with black top and sides of head separated by *long white superciliary stripes*; back brownish olive, rump and upper tail-coverts rufous; underparts and tail orange-rufous except for *light or olive-brown central rectrices*. **Juvenile** mottled and scalloped tawny and black above, with rufous spots on crown and large tawny spots on wing-coverts; superciliaries indistinct; rufous underparts scalloped with black. **Song** an extended variable series of repeated rich whistled phrases *starting softly but markedly increasing in volume*, each repetition louder and more rapidly uttered than the last: *pwirri-pi-pirrr, Pwirri-Pi-Pirrr, PWIRRI-PI-PIRRR. . .,* or *oodle-teedle-teedle, OODLE-TEEDLE-TEEDLE, OODLE-TEEDLE-TEEDLE. . .* or *we-KEEa, WEKEEa, WEKEEA . . .,* mostly at dawn and dusk. Duets and sings antiphonally, the female giving a high-pitched *seeeeet;* sometimes pair chatters together *tickety-tickety-tickety* or *CHUCKitee CHUCKitee.* Less of a mimic than Rüppell's Robin-chat. Alarm call a harsh *tserk-tserk*. **Range**: *C. h. heuglini* in w. and cent. Kenya north to Mt Loima, Mt Marsabit and Mt Nyiru, and n. Tanzania east to Lake Manyara and Tarangire NP. *C. h.intermedia* on coast and inland along Tana River to Garissa, and the Usambara foothills. Avoids most highland areas occupied by Rüppell's Robin-chat.

BLUE-SHOULDERED ROBIN-CHAT *Cossypha cyanocampter bartteloti*
Plate 92

Length 6". Confined to *western Kenyan forests*. Very shy and skulking. Head pattern recalls White-browed Robin-chat; back and wings dark slate-grey with *bright blue 'shoulder' patches* (can be largely concealed); *rump buffy olive;* upper tail-coverts orange-rufous as are sides of tail; central rectrices and outer edge of outermost pair black. *Underparts rich tawny buff,* darker on flanks. **Juvenile** mottled tawny and blackish above, crown and wings rufous-spotted; underparts pale tawny with black markings on breast. Sustained **song** of low chuckling and clear whistles, each note or phrase repeated several times; may begin with slow rising whistles, followed by louder and softer phrases, *chreek chreek WUKERI-TEW-TEW-TEW, chick-chick-chuck-chuck chi-chew WHI-WHEW WEE-WHEW, WIKIYEW WIKIYEW tootoo-wee-wee, weetu weetu-weetu. . ..* Other songs entirely of melodious clear whistles, *wee-tee-tee-tee, tu-tee-tu, tooi-tooi-tooi. . .* Highly vocal at dusk and dawn. A *remarkable mimic* of other birds and human whistling. Common call a guttural dry croaking. **Range**: Kakamega, Kaimosi, and Nandi forests. Formerly on Mt Elgon.

SNOWY-HEADED or SNOWY-CROWNED ROBIN-CHAT   *Cossypha nivei-capilla melanota*   **Plate 92**

Length 8–8.75". The *solid white cap* distinguishes this *large black-backed* robin-chat of *western Kenya*. Forehead and sides of head black; white top of head separated from black back by an *orange-rufous collar* (more distinct than in other robin-chats); central rectrices black. **Juvenile** lacks white on head, its brownish crown densely speckled with rufous, and back mottled dark brown and rufous; rump and tail as in adult but central rectrices dark brown; underparts rufous, scalloped with dark brown. **Song** a loud, sustained, rapidly delivered mimicking of numerous bird species (and other sounds) interspersed with powerful whistles. Alarm note a low churrr. Contact call, a whistled wheeeeo-wheeeeo-wheeeeo. **Range**: Mt Elgon and Saiwa NP south to Lake Victoria basin, east to Kakamega, Nandi Hills, Kericho and Sotik, the Mau and Trans-Mara forests.

CAPE ROBIN-CHAT or CAPE ROBIN   *Cossypha caffra iolaema*   **Plate 92**

Length 6.5". A small *grey-bellied* robin-chat of highland gardens and forest edge. *Tawny-orange throat and breast* contrasts with *pale grey flanks and belly*; short white superciliary stripes separate dark grey crown from black sides of face; rump and tail rufous, the latter with brown central feathers. **Juvenile** brown above with tawny buff spots and streaks; underparts buff scalloped with black. **Song** a series of whistled phrases, repetitive and halting: t*eeu-cheeo. . . cheeo-tu-teeo. . . teeo-teeo-tu-weeoo. . . *. Mimics other species. Calls a low *turr-da-da*, and a plaintive descending *peeeeeuu*. **Range**: Above 1500 m from Mt Kulal, Mt Nyiru and Mt Elgon south through the Kenyan highlands to the Chyulu and Taita hills and all Tanzanian highland areas.

BROWN-CHESTED ALETHE   *Alethe poliocephala*   **Plate 90**

Length 6". A long-legged, short-tailed thrush of the forest floor. Dark chestnut-brown above, the dusky head marked by *whitish superciliary stripes*. Underparts dingy white with *grey-brown breast band and flanks and a white throat*; tail dark brown; long tarsi and toes pale whitish pink. Central highland birds duller and greyer about the face than western *carruthersi*. **Juvenile** blackish brown above heavily spotted with dull orange; breast buff and white with black scallops, otherwise greyish white below. Older young resemble adult, but duller and often with some orange spots on upperparts. **Song** of soft, widely separated minor-key single notes alternating with a double one: *pew. . . . . .pew-pee. . . . . pee. . . . . tew-tee. . . . . . pee. . . . . pew-pee. . ..* Less often gives 4–8 mournful minor-key whistles, descending and accelerating, *pee pee pee pee pee-pee. . ..* Utters a rough *chaggh* at swarms, and an ascending *schleeee*. Call a hollow repeated *keu*; also a repeated *tseeeep tyerrrr*, the first note higher and thinner, the second descending. **Range**: *A. p. carruthersi* west of Rift Valley, from Mt Elgon and Saiwa NP south to Kakamega, Nandi, West Mau and Trans-Mara forests; *akeleyae* in cent. Kenyan highlands from Meru and Embu districts south to Kieni, Gatamayu, Kiambu and n. Nairobi forests.

WHITE-CHESTED ALETHE   *Alethe fuelleborni*   **Plate 123**
Length 6.75". A dark-backed *white-bellied* terrestrial thrush of *Tanzanian mountain forests*. Stays near ground; flicks wings and tail when alarmed. *Face dark brown tinged grey above the eyes*; olive-brown to chestnut-brown back merges to dark rufous on rump/upper tail-coverts and chestnut on tail; central underparts white, but *dark grey from neck to flanks*; breast may appear somewhat scaly. **Juvenile** marked above with tawny orange spots, more streaky on head, and entire *underparts have blackish feather margins* and orange mottling; flanks greyish orange; crissum pale orange. **Call** a loud, somewhat buzzy, ascending *zhurreeee* or whistled upslurred *querrrrr-quiiiiiii*; sometimes a shorter faster *yerr-terwii*. Such phrases may initiate a whistled song. Also a penetrating whistled *wheeu*; alarm call, a rattling *skreeee*. **Range**: Between 500 and 2200 m in the Usambara

443

Mts. Disperses lower during the July–Aug. cold season. One record from South Pare Mts (Feb. 1960).

RED-TAILED ANT-THRUSH *Neocossyphus r. rufus* Plate 91

Length 8.5″. A plain thrush of coastal forests. Warm brown on head and back, otherwise rufous with central rectrices darker. **Juvenile** duller, more olive-brown above, more tawny-olive below. (Possibly confusing brownbuls have brown upperparts and a reddish tail, but are smaller, slimmer and not rufous below.) Commonly heard **call** a descending sibilant mournful *peeeyew* or *twit-teeeyew*, varying to *tsip-wi-wheeeer* or *seeyew-peeyew*, repeated. Song consists of these notes followed by a long descending trill, acccelerating and dropping in pitch. Gives a trilling *chrrrr-chrrrr* at ant swarms. **Range**: Coastal areas and inland along lower Tana River to Bura, in Shimba Hills and up to 950 m in the East Usambara Mts.

WHITE-TAILED ANT THRUSH *Neocossyphus poensis praepectoralis*
Plate 91

Length 8″. A dark, west Kenyan forest thrush with *large white tail corners* and a *broad rufous stripe across the primaries noticeable as the bird flies away*. Upperparts generally sooty brown, paler on throat and upper breast; rest of underparts dull rufous. Usually on or near ground, but sings from trees. Usual **call**, a 1-sec, shrill ascending whistle, *weeeeeeeeeeeet* or *wurrreeeeeeeet*, repeated. Alarm note, a sharp *sip-sip*, and also a low sharp *prrt-prrt* when flushed or in excitement. Seldom-heard song rich and *Turdus*-like, *wurreeet t'ree ueeeeeet. . ..* **Range**: Kakamega and Nandi forests.

✓ SPOTTED MORNING THRUSH or SPOTTED PALM THRUSH *Cichladusa guttata*
Plate 92

Length 6.5″. A spotted thrush of scrub and thicket; feeds on the ground with much flicking of wings and raising of *bright rufous tail*. Upperparts *rufous-brown*, underparts whitish or pale buff with *large black spots surrounding throat and extending down flanks*; shows small white superciliary stripes. Northern birds paler and duller, more whitish below, than richly coloured, heavily spotted *intercalans*; coastal *rufipennis* smaller, paler, with smaller spots. **Juvenile** resembles adult. See Collared Palm Thrush. Varied **song** of powerful clear whistled phrases, often with a chuckling introduction, and including mimicry of other species. Less complex song may begin with a penetratingly loud, descending whistle, *EEEEEEEEEu. . .*, or shorter *ee-eu*, repeated several times and leading into groups of simple notes: *ee-eu ee-eu ee-eu kewi-kewi-kewi. . ..* Regular low call, *PEE-u-priri-PEEeu*, at all times of day; alarm a harsh scolding *chaaaaa* or *skurrrr*. Prolonged, near-perfect imitations of Greater Honeyguide and other species frequent. **Range**: *C. g. guttata* from Lokichokio and Turkana Dist. (west of the lake) south to Lake Baringo; *intercalans* southeast of Lake Turkana and east of the highlands south to the Masai Steppe and Mkomazi GR; *rufipennis* on coast north of Malindi.

COLLARED PALM THRUSH *Cichladusa arquata* Plate 92

Length 7″. Typically asociated with coastal *palm groves*. Hops with the long tail elevated, and slowly pumps it up and down while flicking the wings. Sings from high perches. *Pale-eyed,* with diagnostic *narrow black band outlining pale buff throat and upper breast*. Warm rusty brown above, more rufous on *rump, tail and wings*. **Juvenile** *lacks black throat border*, is mottled with blackish above and with brown below, streaked on crown and nape; eyes brown. **Song** a medley of melodious whistled phrases and harsh scratchy notes, including mimicry. Call a piping *weet-weet*; alarm note a shrill *preee*; also chatters. **Range**: Coastal lowlands north to Lamu, inland to Shimba Hills and along lower Tana River to Wenje. Possibly a scarce resident in Lake Manyara NP.

NIGHTINGALE *Luscinia megarhynchos* Plate 93
Length 6.5″. A skulking, ground-feeding thrush of green bush and leafy thickets. Hops with drooped wings; cocks tail and flicks wings. *Rufous rump and tail* conspicuous; breast and flanks pale greyish brown (darker and distinctly mottled in similar Sprosser);

rest of underparts whitish. *L. m. africana* rich brown above with rufous-tinged head; larger *hafizi* is paler, the greyer brown back contrasting with rufous rump and tail, and darker eye-lines more distinct. **First-winter** bird shows buff greater covert tips. In the hand, larger 10th primary (longer than primary coverts) separates it from Sprosser; in the field, best distinguished by loud rich **song** (Dec.–March) of repeated phrases such as *cheoo-cheoo-cheoo. . .*, *jugg-jugg-jugg. . .* and *pichu-pichu-chipuchi*; often preceded by whistled crescendo, *whee-WHEE-WHEE*. Calls a plaintive *whet*, a hard *tucc,* and a grating *krrr.* **Range/status**: Palearctic migrant, Nov.–early April. Locally common below 1800 m from cent. and se. Kenya to ne. Tanzania; scarce west of Rift. Most inland birds *africana*, but *hafizi* predominates near coast. Occasional birds in and near Lake Victoria basin possibly nominate *megarhynchos*.

SPROSSER or THRUSH-NIGHTINGALE *Luscinia luscinia* Plate 93

Length 6.5". Another skulker of moist leafy thickets. Slightly darker than Nightingale, the *greyish brown breast with variable dark mottling*, and *whitish throat contrasting with dusky malar area.* The dark rufous-brown tail contrasts less with back than in nightingale. Often raises, spreads and moves tail from side to side. In the hand, note very short pointed 10th primary, shorter than primary coverts. **Calls** a high whistling *wheet*, a dry croaking *kh-krrrrrk*, and a soft *tuc*. Rich and powerful song includes whistles, harsh grating sounds, and a loud *chook-chook-chook*; less liquid, more guttural, than Nightingale's song, the phrases less well defined and without introductory crescendo. **Range/status**: Palearctic migrant, common east of Rift Valley, late Oct.–Dec., less so late March–April when sometimes on coast. Winters locally in se. Kenya and Mkomazi GR. Scarce in and west of Rift Valley where sporadic in autumn.

WHITE-BROWED SCRUB ROBIN *Cercotrichas leucophrys* Plate 92

Length 5.5–6.5". Common in bush and scrub. Raises and fans tail over back and droops wings; sings from near tops of shrubs or well concealed within. All races have *white superciliary stripes, rufous tail with black subterminal band and white corners*, and streaked breast. Two subspecies groups: (1) 'red-backed' *zambesiana, brunneiceps* and *sclateri* warm brown to brownish olive above, more rufous on rump, the distinct breast streaks blackish; *zambesiana* has white wing-bars, *brunneiceps* both wing-bars and white-edged secondaries; *sclateri* has more tawny brown back and paler streaks; (2) 'white-winged' *vulpina, leucoptera* and *eluta* rufous above with dark grey-brown head, less distinct greyish breast streaks, and large white wing patch. **Juvenile** mottled black and tawny; tail as in adult. (Brown-backed Scrub Robin has broader black tail band, narrow wing-bars; Rufous Bush Chat lacks white in wings.) **Songs** loud, variable and repetitious, shriller in white-winged races which sing one phrase indefinitely with no variation, e.g. the *sweet-sweet-sweet-siaweet-sweet* or *wureet see-titi-yew* of *C. l. leucoptera*. *C. l. vulpina* has similar short songs, e.g. *suree-sweet chew chew. . .*, but also more varied longer medleys of slurred whistles and shrill piping notes: *sieu pee-pee-pee-pee. . .*, and *tee-twee-tweeo, teet-wet-weo-twer, see-see-seeutwer, tchwee-tchweeo . . .; vulpina* also has chattering or rattling songs, *churee chi-chi-chichcichichichi* and *tsuree tsi-tsi-tsi-tsi-tsi. C. l. zambesiana* repeats clear slurred whistles interspersed with other notes: *siureeet-sreet-swureet-cheet. . .*, and has a rhythmic repetitive *see-surEET, see-surEET . . or t'weeoTWEET, t'weeoTWEET. . .; brunneiceps* sings *tee-tew t'pee . . .* or *werra-weeo, werra-weeo. . . werr-wi-weeo, werr-wi-weeo. . .*, changing after countless repetitions to series of new phrases; also has a slurred *slureet sreet turr chichichi*. Alarm note, a sharp *skirr* or *skee-ip*. **Range**: 'White-winged' races of drier country largely segregated ecologically from 'red-backed' (limited *brunneiceps/vulpina* intergradation around Simba): *leucoptera* in n. Kenya south to Embu, and at Magadi; *eluta* from extreme ne. Kenya south to the Tana River; *vulpina* from dry interior se. Kenya south to near Kilimanjaro; *zambesiana* west and south of Kenyan highlands to Serengeti NP, and on coast from Mombasa to Tana delta; *brunneiceps* at Naivasha, south in Rift Valley to the Crater Highlands and west of Kilimanjaro, east to Machakos and Simba; *sclateri* from Mbulu Highlands east to Tarangire NP.

BROWN-BACKED SCRUB ROBIN *Cercotrichas hartlaubi*   **Plate 92**

Length 6". The *broad blackish terminal tail band, narrow* white wing-bars and darker brown upperparts separate this *highland* scrub robin from White-browed. Breast faintly streaked. **Juvenile** mottled on crown and breast, and with buff superciliaries. **Song** loud, cheerful and protracted, including clear whistled notes, *pripri-weeoo-wee-oo-wi-wee-oo. . .*, or *weet wurdleyu EE-tsee. . .*, or simply *trrreee-EU.* Any of these phrases may be repeated many times with little variation. Some songs are of simpler phrases in which members of a pair duet. **Range**: Between 1500 and 2200 m in w. and cent. Kenyan highlands.

EASTERN BEARDED SCRUB ROBIN *Cercotrichas q. quadrivirgata*   **Plate 92**

Length 5.5–6.5". A shy *eastern* scrub robin with broad white superciliary and moustachial stripes; breast band and flanks tawny; *tail black, white-tipped except for central feathers*; small white patch on primary coverts and another at base of primaries. **Juvenile** mottled black and tawny above and on breast. **Song** sustained and varied, of whistled notes repeated to form musical phrases sometimes lasting many minutes and often preceded by three slow whistles, *whee, yeeu, weee*; may be delivered slowly with significant pauses between phrases, *wurk-wurk. . . oodle-ee-EE-oo. . . chur-rchurr. . . wurkilee-ee-ee. . .wurkelee-eeo-eeo. . ..* When faster, phrases run together and less melodious. Call a loud *chuk*; alarm call *chuk-churr* or *chak-chak-chizzzzz.* **Range**: Coastal lowlands and inland along the Tana River to Garissa, at Ngaia Forest (near Meru), Mt Endau, Kibwezi and Kitovu forests, and the North Pare Mts. Unconfirmed reports from Tarangire NP. Formerly along Voi and Galana rivers.

RUFOUS BUSH CHAT or RUFOUS SCRUB ROBIN *Cercotrichas galactotes*
                                                      Plate 92

Length 6". Differs from resident scrub robins in having *no white in the wings.* Upperparts mostly plain grey-brown or buffy brown, rufous on rump and upper tail-coverts, with *pale buff superciliary stripes*. Long graduated *rufous tail boldly tipped black and white*, frequently fanned and cocked over the back. **Call** a sibilant *sseeeep* and a squeaky double *si-sip.* (Song apparently not heard in East Africa). **Range/status**: Palearctic migrant, Nov.–early April, common below 1000 m in e. Kenya, more local in the north (south to Baringo and Samburu GR). Regular on passage (Nov.) in Tsavo West NP, but few records from ne. Tanzania. Most birds apparently *C. g. familiaris*, but darker *syriacus* also known in Kenya.

IRANIA or WHITE-THROATED ROBIN *Irania gutturalis*   **Plate 93**

Length 6–6.75". A skulking migratory thrush of dry bush and thickets. Grey upperparts and black tail distinctive. **Male** readily identified by *white throat and superciliary stripes* contrasting with *black cheeks.* Breast, flanks and wing-linings rufous-orange to pale cinnamon; belly and under tail-coverts white. Brown-tinged **female** has *orange-buff confined to flanks and wing-linings.* **First-winter** bird resembles female, but has whitish spots on greater coverts; adult body plumage acquired in Dec. **Call** a grating *krrrk.* Sings warbling subsong, and occasionally (Jan. onward), a long song of fluty whistles and scratchy, chattering or slurred notes, portions almost parrot-like in quality: *skwee-churrilee-cheek-cheek-cheek-chur-skweeilew-chur-chur, skwer skweeereri-tsik-tsik tsi-tsi-tsi. . ..* **Range/status**: Palearctic migrant, Nov.–early April; locally common from Isiolo and Meru districts south through Kitui, Tsavo and Taita–Taveta area to the Masai Steppe; a few west to Nairobi, Lake Manyara and Serengeti NP.

COMMON REDSTART *Phoenicurus p. phoenicurus*   **Plates 90, 93**

Length 5.5". A robin-like bird of dry woodland. *Regular quivering of dark-centred, bright rufous tail* attracts attention. **Adult male** grey above with *black face and throat* and rufous breast, all feathers pale-tipped when fresh; the broad white superciliary stripes also partly obscured by grey feather tips in fresh plumage. **Female** buffy brown below, uniformly brown on head and upperparts with *pale eye-ring.* (Similar Red-tailed Chat is greyer, has blackish band across tail tip, flicks wings frequently.) **First-winter male** has adult pattern largely obscured by buffy white feather tips. **Call** a high liquid *tic* or *quick* and a thin plaintive *hweet,* the two sometimes run together, *whit-tic-tic,* Song a short squeaky warbling ending in a mechanical trill rarely heard in East Africa. **Range/status:** Palearctic migrant, Oct.–early April. Mainly western, but occasional in cent. Rift Valley; rare in se. Kenya and n. Tanzania.

COMMON STONECHAT   *Saxicola torquata axillaris*   Plate 93

Length 5″. A small, plump, upright-perching chat of open country. *Pale rump* conspicuous in low flight. **Male** has *black head, throat and upperparts* with *white collar and rump* and *long white wing patch;* chestnut breast patch on white underparts. **Female** has rather plain brown head and streaked brown back; white wing panel smaller than in male; underparts tawny buff. See Whinchat. **Juvenile** mottled blackish brown above, mottled buffy brown below. **Song** a cheerful interrupted series of short notes and repeated phrases, these typically separated by 2-sec. intervals. Call a grating *hwee-trr-trr* or *terk-terk;* also a plaintive *weet.* **Range:** Cent. and w. Kenyan highlands, the Chyulu and Taita hills, south to the Crater and Mbulu Highlands, Arusha NP and ne. Tanzanian mountains.

WHINCHAT   *Saxicola rubetra*   Plate 93

Length 5″. Suggests Stonechat, perching prominently in open grassy areas, but posture less upright, head less rounded, and in all plumages shows *pale superciliary stripes* and *white sides to tail base.* Well-patterned **spring male** *mottled brown above including rump,* the *black cheeks and ear-coverts bordered by broad white stripes* above and below; underparts orange-buff. *White patches on wing-coverts* conspicuous in flight. **Female and winter male** have brown cheeks, buff superciliaries and smaller wing patches. **Call** a persistent *hu-tuc* or *hu-tuc-tuc.* Infrequent song a brief, clear warbling mixed with rattling notes, the phrases often in long series. **Range/status:** Palearctic migrant, late Sept.–early April. Mainly western, but regular in cent. Rift Valley. Rare in se. Kenya and n. Tanzania.

NORTHERN WHEATEAR   *Oenanthe oenanthe*   Plate 94

Length 5.5–6 ″. A terrestrial bird of open country (mainly in greener areas). Greyish or brown above, pale buff below; *white rump and white tail with black inverted T pattern show in low flight.* **Spring male** unmistakable, with pure grey back and blackish wings, and black *mask* below the white superciliaries. Pale brown-backed **female** has *dark brown wings contrasting with paler upperparts at rest and in flight;* superciliaries pale buff. Both sexes have *dusky wing-linings.* **Autumn/winter male** shows much brown above, the mask often brown. **First-winter** bird resembles adult female, but wing feathers broadly pale-edged. Male *O. o. libanotica* is paler grey than nominate *oenanthe* and buff only on throat and upper breast; black tail band narrower. (Plainer Isabelline Wheatear is slightly larger and paler, especially on wings; bill also heavier, tarsi thicker and longer, black tail band broader and wing linings white. Female Pied W. is darker brown with black wing linings.) **Call** a grating *chack-chack* or *eek-chack-chack.* Song of short phrases including whistles, trills, harsh *chack* notes and frequent mimicry. **Range/status:** Palearctic migrant, Sept.–March, common Oct.–early Nov. Winters mainly above 1300 m, but also on coast.

PIED WHEATEAR   *Oenanthe p. pleschanka*   Plate 94

Length 6″. Usually in dry bush country where it habitually perches on shrubs and low tree branches. In all plumages, shows rump/tail pattern as in Northern Wheatear, but *white extends farther up rump, and black band across tail tip is narrower* (occasionally broken); *wing-linings black.* **Spring male** black on face, throat/upper breast and back; forehead to nape white (sometimes white-throated, buff on breast, black only on face). In Oct.–Dec. pattern muted by grey and brown feather tips. **Female** ashy brown above, slightly mottled; dusky brown on throat and breast. (Isabelline and Northern Wheatears are larger-billed, longer-legged, paler above and on breast than female Pied, with more pronounced superciliaries and pale wing-linings.) **First-winter male** shows adult pattern, but strongly masked by buff and brown feather tips. **Call** a soft *perrt*, and a harsh *chack* or *zack*. Song (Feb.–Mar.) a short trilled *tri-tri-trreeee-tri*. **Range/status:** Palearctic migrant, Oct.–March. Widespread below 1500 m. but scarce in Lake Victoria basin and near coast.

BLACK-EARED WHEATEAR *Oenanthe hispanica melanoleuca.* **Plate 94**
Length 5.75". Resembles Pied Wheatear in plumage, form, and habits. **Male** differs in *cream or whitish back continuous with pale cap*; black of throat joins black cheeks and ear-coverts in some birds, others are white-throated. **Female** of this race perhaps inseparable in the field from female Pied, but slightly paler, less mottled above, paler on breast, ear patch usually darker, and without distinct superciliary stripes. **First-winter male** has heavy brown feather-tipping on crown and back, but is generally much paler above than Pied Wheatear. **Call** a rough *grrt*. **Status:** Palearctic vagrant (twice): Athi River, March–April 1984, and Lake Baringo, Dec. 1994.

*DESERT WHEATEAR *Oenanthe deserti* (*deserti?*) **Plate 94**
Length 5.75". The *almost wholly black tail* identifies this vagrant wheatear. **Spring male** has black throat and face, dark wings contrasting with buffy brown upperparts; often shows a paler line on scapulars; rump buffy white. *Black of wings continuous with throat patch* (unlike similar wheatears). **Female** variable, light sandy buff to greyish buff on head and breast. **Calls** a plaintive whistled *heeu* and a short soft chatter. **Status:** Palearctic vagrant (twice): Kiunga, Feb.1984 and Kerio Valley, Oct. 1996. (Specimens from Somalia are of nominate race.)

ISABELLINE WHEATEAR *Oenanthe isabellina* **Plate 94**

Length 6–6.75". A common pale wheatear of *open dry grassland and bare plains.* Both sexes resemble female Northern Wheatear, but are slightly *larger, more uniformly coloured* and with *white wing-linings;* dark terminal tail band broader than in Northern. In flight *lacks contrast between pale brown wings and sandy brown back* (but confusing first-winter Northern has fresh broad buffy wing edgings which reduce contrast). Isabelline has more robust bill, somewhat longer and heavier tarsi, and the slightly broader superciliary stripes are more diffuse in front of the eyes. Usual **call** *chack* or *chack-chack* like Northern Wheatear; also a high-pitched *wheet-whit* and a loud whistled wheew. Sings subdued subsong. **Range/status:** Palearctic migrant, Oct.–March. Widespread below 2000 m.

ABYSSINIAN BLACK or SCHALOW'S WHEATEAR *Oenanthe lugubris schalowi*
Plate 94

Length 6–6.75". The only wheatear with *rufous* instead of white in the tail. Resident on boulder-strewn slopes, hillsides and in eroded gullies. **Male** *largely black with white belly* and colourful rump/tail; pale crown more or less streaked with black. **Female** mostly sooty brown above, paler brown from chin to breast with darker streaking; rump/tail pattern as in male. **Juvenile** dusky brown, faintly speckled with pale buff; rump and tail as in adult. **Song** short and rapidly delivered, mainly of grating, somewhat buzzing notes, *skeerrreeet-siweek-chiureek*, repeated with short pauses; variable. **Range:** Cent. and s. Kenyan Rift Valley and associated highlands, from Nakuru south to Narok and Olorgesailie; disjunct Tanzanian populations in the Crater and Mbulu highlands, and around Mt Meru in Arusha District. Birds seen on Mt Kulal (Aug. 1985) possibly of the nominate Ethiopian race. **Taxonomic Note:** Merged with Mourning Wheatear (*O. lugens*) by some authors, but differs in behaviour, voice and plumage of both sexes.

HEUGLIN'S WHEATEAR *Oenanthe* (*bottae*) *heuglini* **Plate 94**
Length 5.5". A dark wheatear with a *dull brick-red breast* (veiled with whitish or buff in fresh plumage). Prefers short grass on black soil, and attracted to burnt ground. Almost

blackish above except for *buff rump*; upper tail-coverts and basal half of tail sides white. Blackish mask bordered above by white superciliary stripes; cheeks/throat whitish or rufous-buff shading into the darker breast; belly much paler, whitish in some birds; *wing-linings spotted with reddish-buff.* **Juvenile** dark brown above, with deep reddish buff spots; chin, throat and breast russet with dark brown feather tips. **Call** a harsh *chack.* Song, not recorded in our area, said to be extended and complex. (Extralimital Red-breasted Wheatear, *O. bottae,* of highland savanna, tussock grass and moorland in Ethiopia, is larger, chunkier, more upright-perching, with brighter rufous breast clearly separated from the white throat; narrow superciliaries and wing-linings cream-coloured.) **Range**: Nw. Kenya where (seasonally?) fairly common around Lokichokio and Todenyang. Recorded at Lake Turkana (June–July) and Lodwar (March). Vagrant at Kisumu (July).

CAPPED WHEATEAR *Oenanthe pileata livingstonii*   **Plate 94** ✔

Length 6.5 ". An upright-perching grassland wheatear. *Broad black breast band, forecrown and sides of head* contrast with white forehead, superciliaries and throat; back brown, more cinnamon on rump; upper tail-coverts and sides of tail white at base, rest of tail black. **Juvenile** brown, spotted with buff above; underparts pale buff with dark mottling on throat and breast. **Song** a short medley of trills, melodious whistles and some harsh notes; includes imitations of other birds. Calls include a thin *sueet* and varied ticking notes. **Range**: Cent. and se. Kenya, Mara GR and much of upland n. Tanzania. Largely resident above 1400 m; non-breeding visitor to lower areas, April–Sept.

RED-TAILED or FAMILIAR CHAT *Cercomela familiaris*   **Plate 90**

Length 6". Quiet and unobtrusive, this uncommon chat of rocky slopes frequently *flicks its wings and slowly raises and lowers its tail* (but no tail shivering as in similar female Common Redstart). Grey-brown above and mainly paler greyish below, with *rufous rump and tail, the latter with dark central feathers and tip.* Note the *narrow pale eye-ring.* **Juvenile** mottled dusky and buff, with adult tail pattern. **Song** a soft mixture of whistles, chattering and churring, *chur-chur-chur, sureet-sweet-sweet, her-chack-chack-chack. . ...* Call a shrill whistle; alarm call *chak-chak* or *whee-chak-chak.* **Range**: Suam and Kongelai escarpments and Kerio Valley, nw. Mara GR (Olololoo Escarpment), Serengeti and Lake Manyara NPs. N. Kenyan birds may be *C. f. omoensis* (no specimens); southern birds are *falkensteini*.

BROWN-TAILED ROCK CHAT *Cercomela scotocerca turkana*   **Plate 90**

Length 5.5". A *plain drab chat of rocky country in n. Kenya. Tail dark brown*; dull brown upperparts relieved by more rufous-brown ear-coverts and rump and a *narrow pale tan eye-ring* around the large dark eyes; wings faintly buff-edged in fresh plumage. See Red-tailed Chat. **Song** a thin but loud rapid phrase, *seeseesuweet* or *tcheesueet* repeated frequently. Call *chuke-chuke.* **Range**: Dry n. Kenya from Lokichokio east to Lake Turkana and Mt Marsabit, south to Lake Baringo and Shaba and Samburu GRs.

ALPINE CHAT or MOORLAND CHAT *Cercomela sordida*   **Plate 90**

Length 5.5–6". A tame brown chat which stands bolt-upright on rocks and boulders in *alpine* habitats. Tame. Flicks wings, and *often spreads the short, white-sided tail.* The two Tanzanian races are darker above and greyer below than Kenyan birds. **Juvenile** mottled with darker brown on breast. **Song**, a loud metallic piping. Call, a soft chirping *werp-werp.* **Range**: *C. s. ernesti* on Mt Elgon, the Cheranganis, Aberdares and Mt Kenya; *hypospodia* on Kilimanjaro (commonest bird above 3400 m); *olimotiensis* in the Crater Highlands above 2400 m. Small population on Mt Meru not racially determined.

449

✓ **NORTHERN ANTEATER CHAT** *Myrmecocichla aethiops cryptoleuca* **Plate 90**

Length 7". A *stocky, dark sooty brown* chat of open country, usually in small groups. Shows *large white wing patches in flight.* **Female** slightly browner than male, with faint buff feather edging on throat in fresh plumage. **Juvenile** sooty brown throughout. See female Sooty Chat. **Song** an attractive prolonged mixture of high thin whistles, rattling trills, and tsicking notes, often from several birds: *chwerchiwee tserk, chiwerchi-wee, tsick-tuweee tuwee, teeruweeeer tsick, tchu chiwer. . ..* Also has varied piping and whistling calls. **Range:** Cent. and w. Kenyan highlands. Largely replaced by Sooty Chat in Mara GR. In n. Tanzania at Loliondo, in Crater Highlands and on e. Serengeti Plains.

✓ **SOOTY CHAT** *Myrmecocichla nigra* **Plate 90**

Length 6–6.25". A stocky, rather short-tailed dark chat of the Mara/Serengeti grasslands. Raises and lowers tail, sometimes teetering slightly. **Male** *glossy black* with *white patch at bend of wing* (sometimes concealed in perched bird). **Female** and **juvenile** *plain sooty brown.* **Song** prolonged, sweet and musical, sometimes given in flight, *wee tewee tuweer, skwik-skueeeeer, cueee-eeeee-cuweeeer, eee-euwee-tee, tseuwee-tew-skeweeer-tsi-seet. . .* Mimics other species. **Range:** Mara GR south to n. Serengeti NP.

CLIFF CHAT *Thamnolaea cinnamomeiventris subrufipennis* **Plate 92**

Length 8". Look and listen for this colourful long-tailed chat around *rocky cliffs and ravines.* It slowly raises and lowers its tail, bringing it far above back, often fanned wide. **Male** glossy black with *large white 'shoulder' patch, rufous rump* and *upper tail-coverts* and *bright orange-rufous underparts*; narrow white band separates rufous belly from black breast. **Female** dull *slate-grey on head, breast and back*, with no white in wings. **Juvenile male** duller than adult with smaller wing patches. **Song** a loud continuous fluty warbling, replete with rapid-fire mimicry of other species; also a long series of well-spaced phrases, some sweet, others harsh: *tseeu tseeu, week-week-week, chir-chir-chir, tseuk tseuk tsuCHEEO, tsur WEEo tsik. . ..* **Range:** Lokichokio and n. Kenyan mountains south through cent. and s. Kenya (most numerous on Rift Valley scarps) to Serengeti, Lake Manyara and Tarangire NPs, Mkomazi GR and West Usambara Mts.

COMMON or MOUNTAIN ROCK THRUSH *Monticola saxatilis* **Plate 91**

Length 6.5–7.5". A *stocky*, ground-foraging thrush with *rather short rufous tail.* Favours open areas; perches upright on ground, rock or stump. **Spring male** *blue-grey on head, throat and back, dark rufous on underparts and wing-linings*, and with *whitish patch on lower back.* **Female** mottled brown above, buff with *dark crescentic markings below;* no white on back. **Autumn male** resembles female but shows some white on lower back, grey on crown and throat and (largely hidden) rufous feather bases on underparts. (Smaller Little Rock Thrush has relatively longer tail; in male, blue-grey of throat extends to breast, and rufous rump same shade as tail; female lacks strong mottling and barring.) **Call** a soft *chack-chack*, and a low throaty *kschirrrr.* **Range/status:** Palearctic migrant, late Oct.–early April. Widespread from coast to above 2000 m, except in arid areas.

LITTLE ROCK THRUSH *Monticola r. rufocinereus* **Plate 91**

Length 6". Crepuscular and unobtrusive. Inhabits cliffs, gorges and similar rocky places. **Male** smoky or brownish grey above, more bluish *grey from chin to breast; rest of underparts and rump rufous; tail darker rufous with black central feathers and tip.* **Female** duller above, ash-grey on throat and breast. **Juvenile** spotted with buff above and mottled buff and black below; rump and tail as in adult. (Red-tailed Chat and female Common Redstart are pale brown or buff below.) **Song** a short *tsurr-sureet, skeee, tsee-ee-tsurrrr* or *steeee skurrree skirrrrr*, the phrases fading terminally.

Range: Northern mountains and w. and cent. Kenyan highlands (most numerous on Rift and Kerio valley scarps). Rare in n. Tanzania (Longido, escarpment above Lake Natron, and in n. Serengeti NP).

SPOTTED GROUND THRUSH *Zoothera guttata fischeri* **Plate 91**

Length 7–8″. Restricted to coastal forests. *A large terrestrial thrush with bold black spots on the white underparts*; olive-brown above with 2 rows of *large white spots on wing-coverts*; *pale buff face has 2 heavy black vertical bars on cheeks and ear-coverts*; small white tail corners noticeable in flight. **Call** a sibilant *tsee-tseee*; otherwise silent here. **Range/status**: Non-breeding migrant from the southern tropics, April–Oct., recorded north to Lamu, but most records from Gedi and Arabuko–Sokoke forests.

ORANGE GROUND THRUSH *Zoothera gurneyi* **Plate 91**

Length 7–8″. More often heard than seen; a retiring ground bird of eastern forests. *Orange-rufous below*, whitish on belly, and with two bold white wing-bars. Note the *incomplete narrow white eye-ring* and *greyish ear-coverts crossed by an oblique pale band*. Bill especially long in *Z. g. chuka*; *tarsi yellowish*. Upperparts vary: olive-brown in *chuka*, grey in *otomitra*, grey-brown with greyish crown in *chyulu*. **Juvenile** mottled brown below. See Abyssinian Ground Thrush (mostly above 2000 m). Loud clear whistling **songs** short and simple without repetition of notes within a phrase (*tew turee keeu -turIP*, or *wuree tew-tew*) or the often slurred notes repeated several times before the same is done with a different phrase (*reee-eee tureee-tew, reee-eee tureee-tew. . . erreee tew-tew rriiiii. . .*); high, barely audible, 'whisper' notes often inserted between the loud whistles. Longer warbling phrases may be given with others in a complex extended performance. Some songs more quavering, *quee qui-urrrrr tur-turileee weet-weet*. Calls include *querk* and *cureek*. Often vocal until early afternoon, again in evening. **Range**: *Z. g. chuka* in s. Aberdares and e. Mt Kenya; *chyulu* in Chyulu Hills; *otomitra* in Taita Hills and n. Tanzania incl. Mt Meru (to 2400 m, in bamboo), Arusha NP, North Pare and Usambara mts. (900–1800 m; lower in cold seasons, e.g. to 260 m on Mrima Hill in se. Kenya, 450 m in East Usambaras).

ABYSSINIAN GROUND THRUSH *Zoothera piaggiae* **Plate 91**

Length 7.5″. Generally replaces similar Orange Ground Thrush above 2000 m in w. and cent. Kenya, and on the higher Tanzanian mountains; overlaps that species only on Mt Kenya (where it prefers dense bamboo) and in Aberdares. Best distinguished by *complete broad white eye-ring* and *no pale band on ear-coverts* which are rufous-olive; *forehead deep orange-rufous* as are throat, breast and sides; *tarsi whitish flesh-colour*. Kenyan races browner-backed (western *piaggiae* paler below, *kilimensis* orange-brown on breast); Tanzanian *rowei* paler below, more olive above than either northern race. **Juvenile** tawny above and on head, mottled brown below; wing-bars prominent. **Song** of classic thrush quality, of clear whistles with a few softer harsher notes, some phrases almost trilled. Some songs recall Orange Ground Thrush in that a phrase is repeated several times before switching to another. Others involve less repetition: *wurr teeu weeu. . . wur-weeu-tiWEE, (wichu-tsik) trrrrweeeu, seesurrWEE, tiuwee (chi-ku-chik) wurweeotuweee. . ..* **Range**: *Z. p. piaggiae* west of Rift Valley from Mt Elgon and the Cheranganis south to Trans-Mara forests; *kilimensis* on mountains east of the Rift (Nyiru, Kulal, Marsabit, Karissia Hills, Aberdares and Mt Kenya) and on Kilimanjaro; *rowei* in Loliondo and Magaidu forests of n. Tanzania and Nguruman Hills in s. Kenya.

OLIVE THRUSH *Turdus olivaceus* **Plates 91, 124**

Length 8–8.5″. The common large thrush of the highlands; a typical *Turdus*. *T. o. abyssinicus* is olive-brown above with *bright orange bill and bare orbital ring*; chin and throat buffy white with dusky streaks, becoming *greyish olive-brown on breast, dull tawny orange on flanks and most of belly*. Feet brownish orange. Tanzanian races are darker above: *deckeni* darker than *abyssinicus* on upperparts and breast, brownish tawny on sides and flanks; *oldeani* still darker, more sooty

grey, the flanks grey-brown without tawny hue; *roehli* nearer *abyssinicus*, but darker on upper breast and white from centre of breast to belly; bill more reddish. **Juveniles** dark above with tawny wing-covert tips, a band of dark spots across breast and onto the dull orange flanks; orbital ring yellowish. **Song** of rising and falling short phrases, often ending with higher soft trill: *wheeu - wheee - wheeu - wheee-wheeu-trrrrrrree*; at times more reeling: *rreeee-rreeeeetew-eeeeeee. . .*; dawn song a reedy *trrrip-trreeEET* or*weeu-HEE* or*tuwee-teelieu*; in midday a sweet, high *swee-turr-TEE-turr*, or similar repeated phrase. Calls include a soft *chk-chk-chk*, a guttural *gew* or *gew-gew*, and a scolding *tsrk, tsrk*. **Range**: *T. o. abyssinicus* from northern Kenyan mountains south to Chyulu and Nguruman hills. Replaced by Taita Thrush in Taita Hills. *T. o. oldeani* in Mbulu and Crater highlands, on Lolkissale, Hanang and Meru; *roehli* in North Pare and Usambara mts, *deckeni* on Kilimanjaro, Monduli, Kitumbeine, Longido and Ol Doinyo Orok.

TAITA THRUSH *Turdus (olivaceus) helleri*   **Plate 91**

Length 8.5". Confined to remnant *Taita Hills forests* where now very rare. Usually on the ground, and rarely perches more than 2 m above. Avoids secondary growth, scrub and cultivation. Differs from Kenyan race of Olive Thrush (not in the Taitas) in being *much darker above*, and *blackish from head to breast*; *orange-rufous restricted to flanks*; *belly and crissum white*; bill and feet bright orange; bare *orbital ring and postocular patches orange-yellow*. **Juvenile** duller and browner on upperparts; scapulars and. wing-coverts with orange tips and shaft streaks; breast heavily mottled. **Song** not known with certainty. A short *wee sewee slewp* and *wee tewer tuwee* (rising at end) may be attributable to Taita Thrush, but singing birds not observed. **Range**: Ngangao, Chawia and Mbololo forest patches (endangered; few pairs remain).

AFRICAN THRUSH *Turdus pelios centralis*   **Plate 91**

Length 8–8.5". Mainly *western. Resembles a faded Olive Thrush* with a *yellow bill*. Grey-brown above, paler below with light tawny flanks and dusky throat streaking; bare skin behind eye dusky brown; feet light grey, pale buff, or pale brownish green. Similar Olive Thrush is darker, more rufous below and has orange bill. **Juvenile** greyish below, mottled on breast and flanks. **Song** an extended caroling, mainly at dawn, of clear and slurred whistles, a few notes slightly quavering and throaty; most notes/phrases repeated 2–several times: *tureep tureep tureep weeu-weeu-weeu-cureep-churEEP. . .* or *trierieu trierieu ureetew-ureetew. . . slurreeep slurreeep swrp-swrp-swrp, weet-tweeyu tweeyu. . ..* **Range**: Mt Elgon and Kapenguria south to Lake Victoria basin and Lolgorien, east to Kabarnet, lakes Baringo and Elmenteita and Lake Nakuru NP (where sympatric with Olive Thrush); local on w. Laikipia Plateau. .

BARE-EYED THRUSH *Turdus tephronotus*   **Plate 91**

Length 8". The *large area of bare orange-yellow skin around the eyes* is unique among our large thrushes. A shy grey and tawny orange bird of dry eastern woodland and bush. Upperparts and breast grey; flanks tawny; throat white with black streaks. **Juvenile** pale greyish below with mottled breast. **Song** a short quavering trill with one or more higher-pitched notes: *quirrrrrrrrr turr chik*, or *squirrrrr-qyrrr tyip-tyip tew-tew-tew*, or *huu-huu-tsri-tsritsritsritsri*. Varied calls include *tsyik-tsyik-tsyik*, a rattling *chrrrrrr* and a soft mellow *tew-tew-tew* . **Range**: Below 1600 m from the Ndotos and ne. Kenyan border areas south to Mkomazi GR and the Masai Steppe, including coastal scrub north of Mombasa. Rare in coastal Tanzania where replaced by Kurrichane Thrush.

KURRICHANE THRUSH *Turdus libonyanus tropicalis*   **Plate 124**

Length 8.5". Southern counterpart of Bare-eyed Thrush. *Broken dark malar streaks border the whitish throat.* Breast buffy grey; flanks bright buffy orange; upperparts plain brownish grey; narrow orbital ring yellow; bill orange. **Juvenile** buff-spotted on wing-coverts, black-spotted on breast, sides and flanks; bill brownish. **Song** short and pleasing: *rrreeeee treeeeee qurileeeee*. Common call, a whistling *tsi-tseeoo*; also a higher sweet *tsurrreeeeee*. **Range**: Barely reaches our area around Tanga. Formerly recorded at Amani in East Usambaras.

FLYCATCHERS, FAMILY MUSCICAPIDAE

Small, mostly arboreal, insectivorous birds with somewhat flattened, broad-based triangular bills. Except in the migratory *Ficedula*, the sexes are alike, mostly grey or brown above and pale below. Juveniles are spotted. Most species feed by hawking insects in the air; many also take prey from the ground, and some glean from canopy foliage. Typically solitary or in pairs, they perch unobtrusively and most have unimpressive voices. Certain species formerly included in this family are now treated under Platysteiridae and Monarchidae.

SPOTTED FLYCATCHER *Muscicapa striata*   **Plate 87**

Length 5.5″. A *long-winged, streak-crowned* flycatcher of bush and light woodland, grey-brown above and whitish below with diffuse *dusky streaks on breast. Perches upright. Wing tips reach mid-tail.* Flicks wings when calling and on alighting. (Grey and Pale Flyctachers are more robust, lack breast streaks, have more rounded crowns and shorter wings. See Gambaga Flycatcher.) **Call** an insistent thin *tseet* or *see-tseet*, repeated several times; sometimes a longer *tsee, tsi-tsik*. **Range/status**: Palearctic migrant, Oct. April. Widespread on passage; winters in Rift Valley highlands, se. Kenya/ne. Tanzania, and on coast. Mostly *M. s. neumanni*, but nominate *striata* also occurs.

GAMBAGA FLYCATCHER *Muscicapa gambagae*   **Plate 87**

Length 4.5–5″. A bird of dry bush, streamside acacias and broad-leaf tree savanna. Smaller than Spotted Flyctacher and perches more horizontally. Flicks wings when calling. Gambaga has *shorter wings* (primary tips do not extend beyond upper tail-coverts), more rounded head *unstreaked on crown* (but feathers appear mottled at close range), and narrow whitish eye-ring broken in front by *dark loral spot, whitish supraloral line*; diffuse pale brownish *breast streaks less sharply defined* than in Spotted F.; sides and flanks brownish. **Juvenile**'s buff dorsal spotting subject to early wear as are adult's narrow white tail edges. See African Grey and African Dusky Flycatchers. **Call** a distinctive *chick*, or *zick-zick-zick*, or *zickzick-tzicktzick*, much sharper than any note of Spotted F. **Range**: (Scattered records) n. and e. Kenya south to the Kerio Valley, Garissa and the Tsavo parks.

AFRICAN DUSKY FLYCATCHER *Muscicapa adusta*   **Plate 87**

Length 4″. A small plain brown woodlland flycatcher with a short tail. At close range a *narrow pale tan eye-ring* noticeable. Quiet; occasionally flicks wings. The 3 subspecies differ slightly in colour (northern *marsabit* is richer rusty olive-brown above, more rufous-buff below than the others). **Juvenile** buff spotted on upperparts and breast; some yellow at base of bill. **Immature** retains buff greater covert tips, has pale secondary edges, is richer brown on breast, and buffier on belly than adult. See Gambaga and (in w. Kenya) Chapin's Flycatchers. **Call** a thin sibilant repetitive *ss-s-s-st* or *tseee*, and a sharp *trrt-trreet*. **Range**: *M. a. marsabit* at Marsabit and Moyale; *interposita* from the Ndotos, Mt Nyiru and Mt Loima south through the highlands to Mara GR and Serengeti NP; *murina* from Crater and Mbulu highlands east to the Pare and Usambara mts, Taita and Chyulu hills.

CHAPIN'S FLYCATCHER *Muscicapa lendu*   **Plate 87**

Length 5″. A scarce arboreal flycatcher of w. Kenyan forests; unobtrusive; perches upright on tree branch; makes long sallies for insects, sometimes low, but returns to high perch. Dark brown above, dingy below, darker on breast, with *short greyish supraloral stripes. Bill short*, black, grey at base below, yellow at gape. **Juvenile** has buff wing-feather tips, some yellow at base of bill. Smaller Dusky Flycatcher has no supraloral lines. **Call** a repeated short dry trill, *bzzzt-bzzzt-bzzzt-bzzzt*. **Range**: Kakamega and North Nandi forests.

SWAMP FLYCATCHER *Muscicapa aquatica infulata*   **Plate 87**

Length 5–5.5″. A *western lakeshore* bird, usually on grass or reed stems. Dark brown above with *broad brown breast band*, white throat and white belly. **Juvenile** *heavily* spotted above, mottled and streaked below. **Song** a soft squeaky *weesaseet-tsit-seetaseet*. Alarm note a short *pzitt*. **Range**: Lake Victoria basin, including Yala Swamp and Lake Kanyaboli; also at Saiwa NP. Occasionally wanders to Mara GR and Grumeti River in w. Serengeti NP.

✔ASHY FLYCATCHER *Muscicapa caerulescens* Plate 87

Length 5". A pale *grey or blue-grey* flycatcher of forest edge. *M. c. brevicaudata* blue-grey above, on breast and sides; *blackish loral line* and *short white supraloral streaks join narrow white eye-ring*. Eastern *cinereola* paler, more ashy grey, lacking bluish tone. **Juvenile** heavily spotted dark brown and buff above, speckled blackish on underparts. See Lead-coloured Flycatcher. Darts to catch aerial insects, flicks wings on return to mid-level perch. **Song** a rapid sibilant, slightly descending *tsip-tsip-tsetse-tseu*. **Range**: Western *M. c. brevicaudata* in Kakamega Forest and Kerio Valley (scarce), and (probably this race) Mara GR, Loita HIlls and Serengeti NP. *M. c. cinereola* on coast, inland to Bura, Shimba Hills, Kibwezi, Usambara and Pare foothills, also Tsavo East NP and north to Machakos (scarce). Formerly near Nairobi and Embu.

WHITE-EYED SLATY FLYCATCHER *Melaenornis fischeri* Plates 87, 124

Length 6–6.5". A grey highland flycatcher with a *broad white eye-ring* in widespread, blue-grey nominate race, the ring narrow in slate-grey *nyikensis* of Tanzania. **Juvenile** grey with whitish spots above and mottled black streaks below. Confiding and decidedly crepuscular. See Ashy Flycatcher. **Call** a barely audible, high-pitched *see* or *eeea*, sometimes extended to a chattering descending trill. Alarm note a loud *zit*. **Range**: *M. f. fischeri* in w. and cent. Kenyan highlands including most northern mountains (except Marsabit); south to Arusha NP, Kilimanjaro, Mt Meru and North Pare Mts. *M. f. nyikensis* in Crater Highlands, intergrading with *fischeri* from Mbulu Highlands northwards.

NORTHERN BLACK FLYCATCHER *Melaenornis edolioides* Plate 88

Length 7–7.5". A *dull blackish* flycatcher of *n. and w. Kenya*. Long tail almost *square-tipped; eyes dark brown*. (Paler northern race *schistacea* is dark grey rather than blackish.) **Juvenile** heavily spotted with tawny. Flies to ground for most prey, returning to same perch. Somewhat crepuscular. (Allopatric Southern Black Flycatcher has glossy blue-back plumage. Common Drongo has forked tail, red eyes and larger bill.) **Song** a soft sibilant *sweetchy* repeated at intervals. Calls harsh and scolding. **Range**: *M. e. lugubris* west of Rift Valley from Mt Elgon and Saiwa NP south to Mara GR and Serengeti NP, east to Kerio Valley, Kakamega and Kericho. *M. e. schistacea* in Ethiopian highlands south to Moyale.

✔SOUTHERN BLACK FLYCATCHER *Melaenornis pammelaina* Plate 88

Length 7". A somewhat drongo-like, *glossy blue-black* flycatcher of *dry country east and south* of the preceding species' range. **Juvenile** dull sooty black, with tawny buff spotting above, tawny scaling below. Perches quietly, usually on low bare branch. (Noisier Common Drongo has splayed forked tail, larger bill and red eyes. Male Black Cuckoo-shrike has yellow skin at gape and more rounded tail.) **Song** in midday a thin, high-pitched *tsee-tsee-sweeu, tsee-swooi, tsee-tsee. . ..* Longer dawn song also high and squeaky, *seet-skeet-sisi, skreee-tsew-tsreet seeet seeet*. Call, *tzeer*. **Range:** Mainly east of Rift Valley below 1800 m: in Kenya from Amboseli and Tsavo NPs north to Samburu and Shaba GRs, Mathews Range and the Ndotos; also along lower Tana River and on n. Kenyan coast (Boni Forest). Scarce in ne. Tanzania (Lake Manyara and Tarangire NPs, Arusha District and East Usambara Mts).

AFRICAN GREY FLYCATCHER *Bradornis microrhynchus* Plate 87

Length 5.5". The common round-headed *greyish* flycatcher of *dry country*. Has small *dusky streaks on crown*, but lacks streaking on breast; *wing edgings whitish; bill entirely black*. Northern *B. m. neumanni* brownish grey above, pale buff below with suggestion of dark breast band, whitish forehead and noticeable superciliary stripes. Eastern *burae* pale grey; southeastern *taruensis* smaller and markedly darker than *burae*; southern/southwestern *microrhynchus* larger and darker grey. **Juvenile** has pale streaks on head, buff spots elsewhere above, dark scaling and mottling on breast; paler than young Pale Flycatcher and *throat unstreaked*. Perches low; feeds mainly by dropping to ground. (Pale F. lacks crown streaks, is slightly browner with longer tail; longer bill pale at the base. Spotted Flycatcher has more pointed wings, streaked breast, less rounded head.) **Song** a soft squeaky *wit-wer-tsip, twititi . . ..* Call a thin squeaky *see*. **Range**: Widespread below 2000 m except on coast and near Lake Victoria. *B. m. neumanni* south to Kapenguria and Wajir; *burae* in e. Kenya west to Shaba GR, south to Lali Hills and lower Tana River; *taruensis* from Tsavo East NP south to Tanzanian border, intergrading near Simba with nominate *microrhynchus* of s. and sw. Kenya and n. Tanzania (intergrades with *neumanni* between Meru and the Athi River); *taruensis* and *burae* approach one another but do not intergrade. **Taxonomic Note**: *B. m. neumanni* (= *B. pumilus* of Mackworth-Praed and Grant) has been considered a separate species. *Bradornis* is merged with *Melaenornis* by some authors.

PALE FLYCATCHER *Bradornis pallidus* Plate 87 ✓

Length 6–6.75". A common light *brownish* flycatcher, typical of moister habitats than African Grey Flycatcher. Slimmer than that species, with longer tail, *longer bill* and *no streaks on crown*; usually has *pale tawny* (not white) wing edgings. *B. p. subalaris* is pale sandy brown above, with little trace of the dark breast band of darker southern races. Bill black, pale at base below. Perches upright; drops to ground to feed. **Juvenile** spotted with buff or tawny above and with dark streaks on underparts. *B. p. bafirawari*, pale grey-brown above and with similar breast band and flanks, is the only race in dry thorn-bush country, the usual habitat of Grey Flycatcher. (Spotted Flycatcher has streaks on crown and breast. See Gambaga Flycatcher.) **Song** a high twittering, *tree-tricky-trit-tricky-chee-witty. . .*, less squeaky than song of Grey F. Calls a soft *churr* and thin *see-see*. **Range**: *B. p. murinus* from nw. border areas and Mt Elgon south to Chyulu and Taita hills, Serengeti NP, east to the Mt Meru and Kilimanjaro foothills; *bafirawari* in ne. Kenya from Wajir south to Garba Tula and Garissa; *griseus* from Voi and Taveta south to Mkomazi GR and Tarangire NP; *subalaris* coastal, inland to East Usambaras, Shimba Hills and lower Tana River. **Taxonomic Note**: *B. p. subalaris* appears not to intergrade with neighbouring *griseus*, the two possibly not conspecific.

SILVERBIRD *Empidornis semipartitus* Plate 87 ✓

Length 7". A stunning flycatcher of open areas west of the Rift Valley, silvery grey above and tawny orange below. **Juvenile** with black-bordered tawny spots on upperparts, mottled buff and black on throat and breast. **Song** short, the phrases slightly thrush-like, sometimes with terminal note higher and thinner, *eee-sleeur-eeee* or *sweet siursur-eet-seet*; also a longer *eep-eep churEEerip, eeep-eep cherip chchch eee*, embellished with chattering and *seep* notes. **Range**: Kongelai Escarpment, and from Kerio Valley and Baringo Dist. south to Rongai; also in Lake Victoria basin and s. Mara GR south to Serengeti NP and Maswa GR. Has wandered to Lake Turkana, Lokochokio, Laikipia Plateau, Nairobi and Tarangire NP.

LEAD-COLOURED FLYCATCHER or GREY TIT-FLYCATCHER *Myioparus plumbeus* Plate 87

Length 5.5". Restless and *warbler-like*; frequently *raises, fans and wags tail*. Blue-grey above and whitish below, pale grey on throat and breast; under tail-coverts faintly tawny. Lores, short narrow superciliary stripes and eyelids whitish; *long blackish tail conspicuously white-sided*. Reminds Americans of a gnatcatcher (*Polioptila*). **Juvenile** browner above than adult, with buff spots on wing-coverts, and pale brown below; best identified

455

by size, behaviour, and white-edged tail. Ashy Flycatcher has no white in tail, bolder face pattern, is much less active. **Call** a plaintive repeated *peerri-peeeerr*. **Range**: *M. p. plumbeus* from Suam River, Kongelai Escarpment and Marich Pass to Kerio Valley and Lake Baringo; *oriental-is* on coast and inland to East Usambara foothills, Moshi, Arusha, Taveta and Kibwezi. Formerly in Tsavo East NP.

SEMI-COLLARED FLYCATCHER *Ficedula semitorquata*   Plate 87

Length 5″. A compact flycatcher of wooded areas, with long wings, rounded head and small bill. Black-and-white **spring male** (Feb.–March) has white forehead, *white band from throat to behind ear-coverts*, a large white panel on inner part of closed wing, smaller patch at base of primaries and often a short *narrow bar on median coverts*; also a white-sided black tail and a *grey rump patch*. **Female** and **first-winter male** grey-brown above with ashy wash on breast; pale wing areas buff, and smaller than in spring male, confined to edges of inner secondaries, bar on greater coverts, and small mark at base of primaries. Flight feathers and white-sided tail dark brown. **Adult winter male** has black-and-white wings, but body, head and tail as in female. See Collared and Pied Flycatchers. **Call** a repeated sharp *dzit*. **Range/status:** Uncommon palearctic migrant, Sept.–April, in w. Kenya (Mt Elgon, Kakamega Forest, Mara GR). Rare east to Nakuru and Nairobi.

COLLARED FLYCATCHER *Ficedula albicollis*   Plate 87

Length 5″. **Spring male** differs from Semi-collared F. in having a *complete white collar around hindneck* and a *white* rump patch; *lacks white bar on median coverts*. **Female and winter male** like Semi-collared, although some *may* show complete greyish collar. **Call** as in Semi-collared. **Status:** Palearctic vagrant. (Regular migrant west of our region.) One collected in Nyanza, Oct. 1972.

PIED FLYCATCHER *Ficedula hypoleucos*   Figure below

Length 5″. **Male** resembles Semi-collared F., but in spring lacks white partial collar, white bar on median coverts and pale rump patch, and has less white on forehead; *white patch on primary bases very small*. **Female** and **first-winter male** similar to Semi-collared, but typically browner, with narrower white wing-bar and inner secondary edges, and often *no white mark visible on primary bases*. In the hand, 9th primary shorter than 6th (usu-ally equal to or longer than 6th in other *Ficedula*). **Call** a repeated sharp *whit*. **Status:** Palearctic vagrant (winters mainly in West Africa); one specimen, Kakamega, Dec. 1965.

Pied Flycatchers

WARBLERS, FAMILY SYLVIIDAE

A diverse group of small, slender-billed insectivorous birds (only distantly related to the nine-primaried New World wood-warblers), sometimes merged with thrushes, babblers and flycatchers. The genera *Cisticola, Prinia, Spiloptila, Apalis, Heliolais, Camaroptera, Calamonastes* and *Eminia* are sometimes separated as the family Cisticolidae. The unique *Hylia* with its odd firm plumage, sunbird-like tongue and hyoid apparatus and apparent lack of any well-developed song, is probably not a warbler, but is so treated here following established tradition.

RIVER WARBLER *Locustella fluviatilis* Plate 96

Length 5.5″. A secretive bird of rank undergrowth. Dark olive-brown above, including the *broad rounded tail*; faint pale superciliary stripes; *whitish below with olive-brown sides; throat and upper breast with soft dark streaks; long, buffy brown under tail-coverts conspicuously pale-tipped.* Bill fine and pointed; tarsi flesh-pink. **First-winter** bird may be yellowish on face and throat. **Call** a repeated high-pitched *chik, chik* or *p'chick*. Song a metallic *zizizizizizizizi*. **Range/Status**: Palearctic passage migrant, frequent Nov.–Jan., occasional in April, mainly in e. Kenya from Samburu GR and Meru south to Kitui and Tsavo. A few winter. One n. Tanzanian record (Arusha NP, April).

GRASSHOPPER WARBLER *Locustella naevia* Plate 96

Length 4.5–5″. Skulking and unobtrusive. Upperparts warm olive-brown with soft black streaks on back, faint streaks on rufous-tinged rump. *Tail broad and rounded*, with *long, finely-streaked buff under coverts*. Underparts whitish, pale yellow or warm buff, with variable spotting on lower throat; sides brownish. **Call** a sharp *tuck, tchik* or *pitt* , repeated in alarm. Song a high-pitched continuous insect-like reeling or buzzing. **Status**: Palearctic vagrant; one caught and photographed in Nguruman Hills, June 1977 (subspecies uncertain).

SAVI'S WARBLER *Locustella luscinioides fusca* Plate 96

Length 5–5.5″. Like River Warbler but warmer brown above, sides rufous-tinged, less olive-brown; throat plain or bordered below with a necklace of *faint* diffuse spots; pale tips to under tail-coverts less pronounced. **Call** a sharp *chik* or *pitch*; in alarm a dry chatter. Song a far-carrying reel similar to that of Grasshopper Warbler but lower-pitched and more mechanical sounding. **Status**: Palearctic vagrant; recorded twice in Tsavo West NP (Dec.)

SEDGE WARBLER *Acrocephalus schoenobaenus* Plate 96

Length 5″. Distinguished from other small *Acrocephalus* by *bold cream superciliary stripes, heavily streaked back and plain rufous-tinged rump* which contrasts with the *dark blunt tail*. **First-winter** bird buffier than adult, with a necklace of faint spots across chest. Prefers lake edges and waterside vegetation. **Song** (less intense than on breeding grounds) a prolonged medley of harsh and sweet notes, faster, less rhythmic and more 'buzzing' than that of Eurasian Reed Warbler. Call a harsh *churr* and a sharp repeated *tuck*. **Range/status**: Palearctic migrant, Nov.–early May; winters in w. and cent. Kenya above 1800 m, locally in se Kenya (e.g. L. Jipe) and n. Tanzania. More numerous and widespread on April–early May passage.

GREAT REED WARBLER *Acrocephalus arundinaceus* Plate 95

Length 7–7.5″. Large, with *long, fairly thick bill, well-defined creamy buff superciliary stripes*, and ample tail. Olive-brown upperparts often tinged rufous on rump; *throat faintly streaked in adults*; bill horn brown, paler at base below; tarsi pale brown in adults, darker or greyer in young birds. Greyer *A. a. zarudnyi* lacks warm tones of *A. a. arundinaceus*. Faded and worn first-autumn birds lack throat streaks. (Smaller Basra Reed Warbler has more slender bill, is duller above, has no throat streaks. Greater Swamp Warbler is much greyer below.) **Song** loud and rhythmic, of harsh grating notes each repeated 2–3 times: *chirrk-chirrk kreek-kreek skyuk-skyuk*

syrrik-syrrik-syrrkk krruk-krruk . . .. Call a loud harsh *chack*. **Range/status**: Palearctic migrant, Nov.–April. Winters around Lake Victoria, in cent. Kenyan highlands and on lower Tana River. More widespread in spring in and east of Rift Valley. Few n. Tanzanian records; reportedly winters at Lake Eyasi.

BASRA REED WARBLER *Acrocephalus griseldis*   **Plate 95**

Length 5.5–6.25″. Smaller than Great Reed Warbler, with *long slender bill and dark greyish tarsi. Uniformly cold olive-brown above*; mostly whitish below with buff wash on sides of breast and flanks; throat never streaked. Narrow whitish superciliary stripes pronounced. Skulks in rank vegetation, often near water. Distinguished from dark-legged Lesser Swamp Warbler by cold plumage tones and long pointed wings. **Call** a harsh nasal *chaarr*. Song softer, less strident and rhythmic than Great Reed Warbler's; lacks grating quality; notes low and deliberate: *chwik-chwak-chook-charra, tchuk-tchuk-whee-er skweek skwak skuiir, swerwee cherak cherak. . .*; recalls song of Yellow-whiskered Greenbul. **Range/status**: Palearctic migrant, Nov.–mid-April, in e. lowlands. Frequent on southward passage in Tsavo West NP. Winters commonly in lower Tana River valley, sparingly elsewhere. Sparse on northward April passage along coast and inland to Tsavo.

EURASIAN REED WARBLER *Acrocephalus scirpaceus fuscus*   **Plate 95**

Length 5–5.5″. An olive-brown warbler with a rather long thin bill. Often *rufous-tinged above, especially on rump*; whitish below with buff wash on breast and sides; pale superciliary stripes. Tarsi pale brown to dark greenish brown (usually dark in young birds). Most Kenyan birds are of pale eastern race *fuscus;* warmer coloured birds may represent nominate race. Usually in dense green thickets. See African Reed, Basra Reed and Marsh Warblers. **Call** a soft or harsh *tchurr*. Song (heard Dec.–March) a rhythmic series of strident grating or squeaky notes, each repeated 2–3 times: *chup-chup-chic-chic-weet-weet-chip-churric-whit-whit-tsurric-tsurric. . ..* **Range/status**: Palearctic migrant, late Oct.–early May; common in Lake Victoria basin and cent. Kenya from Meru and Embu to Nairobi. A few along Tana and Athi/Galana rivers; scarce elsewhere. Marked spring passage through cent. Kenya.

AFRICAN REED WARBLER *Acrocephalus baeticatus*   **Plate 95**

Length 4.5–5″. A small brown warbler of rank grass and waterside shrubs. Similar to Eurasian Reed Warbler but more warmly coloured, smaller and shorter-winged. Inland *A. b. cinnamomeus* plain, *rather pale, reddish brown above* (brightest on rump) and *warm buff below* with throat and centre of belly whitish. Tarsi pale brown to greenish grey. **Juvenile** closely resembles adult. Pemba Island birds larger. (Eur. Reed and Marsh Warblers are larger, more olivaceous above, less buff below, with longer, more pointed wings. Marsh Warbler has whiter throat, usually pink tarsi and more rounded head. Fulvous juv. Lesser Swamp Warbler is larger and darker, with strong blackish tarsi and toes.) In the hand note that wing of *cinnamomeus* is below 58 mm (over 63 in Eurasian Reed) and with more rounded tip, the 9th primary shorter than 5th (usually longer than 6th in Eurasian Reed). **Call** as in Eurasian Reed Warbler. Song similar, a prolonged rhythmic *tshic-chic-churric-churric . . .*, thin, scratchy or squeaky. **Range**: *A. b. cinnamomeus* local in Lake Victoria basin and cent. Kenyan highlands; also Tarangire NP north and east to the Crater Highlands, Amboseli NP, Lake Jipe and Mkomazi GR. *A. b. suahelicus* on Pemba Island.

MARSH WARBLER *Acrocephalus palustris*   **Plate 95**

Length 5 ″. Resembles race *fuscus* of Eurasian Reed Warbler, from which distinguished with difficulty by slightly shorter and broader bill and more rounded crown (thus less attenuated, more *Sylvia*-like head shape), more uniform olive-brown upperparts (lacking rufescent tinge to rump except in some first-autumn birds), yellowish buff breast and pale cream throat; tarsi typically pinkish brown (but often dark greenish brown in young birds). In the hand, best distinction is position of 9th primary inner-web notch: at or above 3rd primary tip (below it in adult and *most* first-autumn Eur. Reed). Prefers herbaceous undergrowth. **Song** a prolonged rich, varied warbling with characteritic liquid trills, mimicking many bird species. Call a harsh dry *tchahh*, *kaahh* or *t-cherr* similar to Eur. Reed Warbler's note; also *cha-cha-cha*, a soft *tuc*, and a hard *Hippolais*-like *chek*. **Range/status**: Palearctic migrant, Nov.–early May. Abundant in autumn in cent./ inland se. Kenya and ne. Tanzania; less numerous in spring when also along coast. A few winter inland. Almost unknown west of Rift Valley.

GREATER SWAMP WARBLER *Acrocephalus rufescens ansorgei* Plate 95

Length 6.5–7″. A *large, dull-coloured, strong-footed* denizen of papyrus swamps in Lake Victoria basin. Actions recall Great Reed Warbler. Long slender bill obvious, and long dark (bluish grey or greenish grey) tarsi and *large toes* noticeable; dingy grey-brown above with *rufescent rump*; greyish underparts washed with brown or dull tawny on sides and flanks; throat and belly almost white, but *throat/breast contrast less than in Lesser Swamp Warbler*. Ill-defined superciliary stripes do not extend far behind eyes; *corners and interior of mouth dull yellow* (evident in singing bird). **Juvenile** tawny or yellowish brown above, washed with pale tawny on underparts. **Song** a mixture of gurgling and harsh churring phrases separated by short pauses, *churr, churr, chirrup, chuckle, cwiurok . . .*, or *krip-krr-krr-krr, kikweu-kikwer, kieru-kwee-kwee-kwee*. Call a single or double *chock*, and a low throaty *kweeok*. **Range**: Yala Swamp and Lake Kanyaboli east to Kisumu and Homa Bay.

LESSER SWAMP WARBLER *Acrocephalus gracilirostris* Plate 95

Length 5.5–6″. A common, highly vocal warbler of tall marsh vegetation and lakeshore shrubbery. *White throat contrasts with darker breast*; brown of upperparts brightest on rump. Dark brown bill salmon-pink, dull yellow, or grey at base below; *inside of mouth bright orange or scarlet*, and *corners of mouth bright yellow or orange*; tarsi dark grey or black. Highland *A. g. parvus* dark throughout above, the rump only slightly more rufescent; underparts (incl. crissum) grey-brown to brownish tawny; western *jacksoni* duller and paler brown, less warm-toned, belly and crissum almost white; *leptorhynchus* of eastern lowlands has brighter, more contrasting, rufescent rump/upper tail-coverts; underparts tinged with tawny buff. **Juvenile** (all races) more rufescent above than adults. (Greater Swamp Warbler differs vocally, usually has pale mandible, and gape and mouth lining dull yellow, not bright orange; *male* appears much larger and coarser. African Reed Warbler is smaller with paler tarsi and smaller bill than bright juv. Lesser Swamp.) Prolonged **song** a pleasing series of musical and harsh notes, clearer and higher-pitched than more guttural song of Greater Swamp W., e.g. *shkioo, cherk, tweeeoweeowew squeeo-squeeo squeeo squeeo, quewk weeoweeoweeo, chee-chee-chee . . .*; sometimes more rolling, *chrree-churree-churree, chrrrrr chak-chak, chirrweeoweeo-weeo-weeo, tsrrrk tsirrrr seeo-chick*. Calls include a harsh *chaa*, a hard *tchuck*, and a low *chierok*. **Range**: *A. g. jacksoni* on islands and shores of Lake Victoria; *parvus* in w. and cent. Kenyan highlands from Eldoret, Kapsabet and Nandi districts east to Lake Baringo, Naivasha and Nairobi, and Arusha NP, Mbulu Highlands, Lake Manyara and Serengeti NPs; *leptorhynchus* on coast north to lower Tana River, inland to Usambara Mts, Taveta, Amboseli NP and Kibwezi.

OLIVACEOUS WARBLER *Hippolais pallida elaeica* Plate 96

Length 5″. Smallest and commonest *Hippolais*. Plain grey-brown above and whitish below. Distinct whitish superciliary stripe barely extends behind eye; square-tipped tail whitish on corners when fresh. Worn autumn birds paler and greyer. Bill pale orange or pinkish below; tarsi pinkish grey or brownish grey. Forages *Phylloscopus*-like in shrubs or in the canopy of larger trees (especially river-bed acacias). Habitually calls and flicks tail. (Similar Upcher's Warbler is larger and paler grey with longer bill, bulkier tail and different song. See Olive-tree Warbler.) In the hand, 10th primary much longer than primary coverts (near coverts in Upcher's). **Song** a prolonged scratchy warble, with suggestion of an underlying Reed Warbler-like rhythm: *shweek-chirri seek-sik, siriskeei-chur-chweek chirr, seek-seek . . ..* Usual call a persistent hard, repeated *tac. . .tac* or *trrt . . .trrt*. Marsh Warbler (richer brown above, less white below, with darker lores) has similar hard call note. **Range/status**: Palearctic migrant, late Oct.–early April. Common in dry country below 1800 m, but scarce in arid e. and ne. Kenya.

UPCHER'S WARBLER *Hippolais languida*   Plate 96

Length 5.5". A bird of dry bush. Slightly larger than Olivaceous Warbler, with *longer slimmer bill, paler and greyer (less brownish) upperparts, and longer, bulkier tail.* Narrow whitish superciliary stripe readily discernible as is white on upper (and usually lower) eyelid. Newly moulted birds show *pale panel on closed wings (edges of secondaries)* and *blackish tail with narrow white outer edges.* Base of mandible pinkish; feet pinkish grey. Forages within low shrubs and tree canopy. *Pumps tail deliberately and moves it from side to side and in circular motion*, recalling a shrike. (Olivaceous Warbler has different tail action. Olive-tree Warbler is larger with heavier bill, longer tarsi, darker cheeks and less distinct superciliaries.) **Call** *tuc. . . tuc*, softer, less persistent than in Olivaceous. Song prolonged,with sweet warbling quality suggesting a *Sylvia*: *chuk-chuk-chuk swee-wee, skwiawer skiuirrri-ceek, chr-chr, tsi-tsi-tswee-swer.* **Range/status**: Palearctic migrant, Nov.–early April. Winters mainly below 1200 m. east of the highlands (locally common); widespread in arid north. Regular on southward migration in the Tsavo parks and extreme ne. Tanzania; rare at coast.

OLIVE-TREE WARBLER *Hippolais olivetorum*   Plate 96

Length 6". A slim *greyish* warbler of tall bush and dry woodland. Larger and slightly darker than Upcher's, with *larger bill* and *long slate-grey or blue-grey tarsi.* Brownish grey above and creamy white below; wings often appear browner than back; superciliary stripes shorter and narrower, and cheeks darker than in Upcher's and Olivaceous Warblers. In fresh plumage shows *prominent pale wing panel*, and the grey tail has narrow whitish edges and tips. *Bill flesh pink below, bright yellow or orange at base*; culmen dark. Constantly flicks tail, but without Upcher's vigour. In the hand, 10th primary much shorter than primary coverts, and 9th longer than 6th (shorter than 6th in Upcher's). **Song** harsh and grating, recalling Great Reed Warbler: *tchek-chek-kak-kak-kok, kek kek, chuk-chuck-chuk.* Call a loud harsh *chack* or *tcheck*; in alarm, a harsh nasal *chaaarr.* **Range/status**: Uncommon palearctic migrant, late Oct.–April, mainly on southward passage east of Rift Valley, from coast to above 1500 m; less frequent in spring. Few winter.

ICTERINE WARBLER *Hippolais icterina*   Plate 96

Length 5". A long-winged *Hippolais* of open woodland. Coloration may suggest a *Phylloscopus*, but lores are pale, there are no dark eye-lines, and movements more deliberate. Erects crown feathers in excitement. Greenish olive above, with *pale yellow superciliary stripes and underparts*, and in fresh plumage a *prominent wing panel* formed by yellowish edges of secondaries; bill dull white or pinkish below; feet blue-grey. (Apart from vagrant Melodious Warbler, other *Hippolais* lack olive and yellow tones.) However, autumn birds are often greyer, with little yellow below and inconspicuous wing panels. **Song** a loud sustained mixture of musical and discordant notes, including mimicry. Call a hard *tac*, a distinctive slurred *wipperueet*, and a less common *uwee.* **Range/status**: Palearctic migrant, Oct.–April, mainly west of Rift Valley. Some winter in acacia woodland in Mara GR and Serengeti NP.

MELODIOUS WARBLER *Hippolais polyglotta*   Figure opposite

Length 5". Very like Icterine Warbler, but with *shorter, more rounded wing* and slightly more rounded crown; more brownish olive above, often richer yellow below; lacks pale wing panel, even in fresh plumage. Tarsi usually brownish grey. Distinguished in hand by *shorter 9th primary* (shorter than 5th; longer than 5th in Icterine) and *relatively large 10th* (much longer than primary coverts). **Calls** distinctive and sparrow-like, a loud *chuck* and a churring *trr-trr.* **Status**: Palearctic vagrant; one trapped for ringing, Tsavo West NP, Nov. 1995.

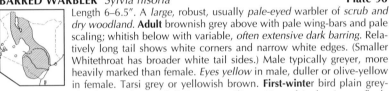

Melodious Warbler

BARRED WARBLER *Sylvia nisoria*   Plate 96

Length 6–6.5". A *large*, robust, usually *pale-eyed* warbler of *scrub and dry woodland*. **Adult** brownish grey above with pale wing-bars and pale scaling; whitish below with variable, *often extensive dark barring*. Relatively long tail shows white corners and narrow white edges. (Smaller Whitethroat has broader white tail sides.) Male typically greyer, more heavily marked than female. *Eyes yellow* in male, duller or olive-yellow in female. Tarsi grey or yellowish brown. **First-winte**r bird plain grey-brown above, with pale wing-bars and distinct superciliary stripes, *faint barring on flanks and under tail-coverts* only; eyes dark brown to yellowish brown or ochre. Shy and skulking. Erects crown and forehead feathers and pumps tail when excited. (Garden Warbler is dark-eyed, lacks pale wing-bars; Olive-tree Warbler is slimmer, with short superciliary stripes, dark eyes, long pointed bill orange-yellow at base below.) **Song** (Feb.–March) a low-pitched warbling, usually subdued, phrases often prolonged; includes rich musical notes and harsher sounds; recalls song of Garden Warbler, but softer, less throaty. Calls a harsh *chack-chack* or *ch-ch-check*, and a longer chatter. **Range/status**: Palearctic migrant, late Oct.–early April. Mainly below 1200 m north and east of highlands, from Lake Turkana area to Baringo, Isiolo and Meru NP, south to Kitui, lower Tana River, Tsavo and Amboseli NPs and inland ne. Tanzania.

COMMON WHITETHROAT *Sylvia communis*   Plate 96

Length 5.5". A rather long-tailed warbler of scrub and dry woodland. Brown or grey-brown above, with *pale rufous wing-feather edgings, and a white throat contrasting with pale buff underparts; tail prominently white-edged*. **Male** usually has grey crown and ear-coverts, and pinkish wash on breast; eyes pale yellowish to reddish brown; tarsi pale brown. **Female** has browner crown, little or no pink on breast, and pale brown eyes. **First-winter** bird resembles female but browner above and eyes usually dull grey-brown. See Garden Warbler and immature Barred Warbler. Our subspecies are *icterops, volgensis and rubicola*. **Call** a harsh *chaar* or low *chur* and a hard *tek*. Subdued song (Dec.–March) a rather scratchy prolonged warbling, higher-pitched, less rich than that of Garden Warbler. **Range/status**: Palearctic migrant, late Oct.–April. Mainly east of the highlands between 800 and 1200 m, from Isiolo and Meru NP south to Tsavo area and ne. Tanzania. Widespread on passage (Nov.–Dec. and April) when common in Mara GR, Tsavo West, Arusha and Tarangire NPs and Mkomazi GR.

GARDEN WARBLER *Sylvia borin*   Plate 96

Length 5.75". *A compact, stubby-billed* and *plain-looking* warbler of leafy bush and secondary growth. It has a noticeably *rounded head with subdued pattern* of short greyish or pale buff superciliary stripes, *narrow pale eye-ring accentuating the dark eye*, dusky

461

loral spot and short postocular line. *Uniformly dull grey-brown upper-parts* relieved only by narrow whitish primary tips in fresh plumage; may show a touch of white above primary coverts at edge of wing; underparts pale buff, darker on breast, sides and flanks. European nominate race is browner than widespread *S. b. woodwardi*. Tarsi grey or dark horn-brown. Unobtrusive; lacks 'nervous' wing and tail movements of some warblers. (Grey *Hippolais* species have flatter forehead and longer pointed bill. Young Barred Warbler is larger, longer-billed and longer-tailed, and has pale wing-bars.) **Call** a sharp *teck-teck*. Song rich and low-pitched, a sustained warbling with few pauses. **Range /status**: Palearctic migrant, late Sept.–April, mainly between 1000 and 1600 m. Common on southward passage in sw. Kenya and Serengeti NP, and from eastern highlands to Kibwezi and Tsavo area. Marked northward migration through cent. Kenya in April. Some winter from Serengeti NP east to Usambaras, and from the edge of the Kenyan highlands to Tsavo West NP. Most birds represent the Siberian race *woodwardi* but nominate race also known in Kenya.

✓ BLACKCAP *Sylvia atricapilla*   Plate 96

Length 5.75". A compact robust warbler of scrub and undergrowth, often in small parties. **Male** grey below, brownish olive-grey above with *black crown*; tail dusky black with outer feathers brown-edged. **Female** olive-brown above with *reddish brown cap*; underparts dull creamy or buffy tan, paler on throat; eyelids narrowly whitish. *S. a. dammholzi* generally paler and greyer above and whiter below than nominate *atricapilla*. **Call** a hard *tac tac*. Song (Jan.–March) a subdued varied warbling which may lead into a series of pure fluty notes; mimetic. **Range/status**: Palearctic migrant, late Oct.–early April, generally above 1500 m. Winters commonly from w. and cent. Kenyan highlands south to Serengeti and Arusha NPs and in all n. Tanzanian mountains. Most Kenyan wintering birds are *dammholzi*.

WOOD WARBLER *Phylloscopus sibilatrix*   Plate 96

Length 5". An active arboreal warbler mainly in broad-leaved trees at medium elevations. Frequently flycatches. Does not customarily flick wings or tail. Distinguished by *greenish upperparts, yellow superciliary stripes* and *yellow throat/upper breast sharply demarcated from the white belly*. Wings longer (extending beyond tail base) and tail shorter than in Willow Warbler. Bill brown above, yellowish below; tarsi yellowish brown. In hand, note long 9th primary, longer than 6th; (shorter than 6th in Willow.) **First-winter** bird may have somewhat greyer upperparts than adult, and is paler yellow on throat and breast. (Willow Warbler is less green above and lacks breast-belly contrast. Yellow-throated Woodland Warbler has brown crown, grey underparts and shorter wings.) **Call** a plaintive *püüü*. Song a high-pitched *sit-sit-sit-sit* . . . accelerating into a trill. **Range/status**: Scarce palearctic migrant, Nov.–early April, mainly in w. and s. Kenya. No valid Tanzanian records.

CHIFFCHAFF *Phylloscopus collybita abietinus*   Plate 96

Length 4.5". Closely resembles Willow Warbler but browner or buffier on breast and flanks, yellow-olive on wing edgings; tarsi typically *blackish or dark brown* (rarely light brown); superciliary stripes somewhat less pronounced; also has slightly more rounded head shape and smaller bill which, combined with shorter wings, produces a subtly more compact impression. Restless, forages with much rapid wing-flicking plus vertical pumping and lateral twitching of tail. In hand, distinguished from Willow Warbler by emarginate 5th primary. **Call**, *hweet*, typically more monosyllabic than that of Willow W. Distinctive song (usually from tall forest trees) an irregular repetition of two notes, one slightly higher pitched, *chif chaff chif chif chaff*. . ., given from Jan. onward. **Range/status**: Uncommon palearctic migrant Nov.–early March, in highland forest above 2000 m. Winters mainly on Mt Elgon, Mt Kenya and Aberdares. Occasional at lower elevations on passage. In n. Tanzania known from 3 early specimens taken on Kilimanjaro.

WILLOW WARBLER *Phylloscopus trochilus* Plate 96

Length 4.5″. Partial to acacia trees, but feeds at all levels from weedy herbs to tree canopy. Sometimes flicks wings and regularly pumps tail up and down. Olivaceous above and whitish below, with pale yellow superciliary stripes, dusky and yellowish streaking on throat and breast, and yellow at bend of wing. Tarsi typically pale yellowish brown, but can be blackish brown. Some *P. t. acredula* are greenish streaked above, yellow-streaked on breast, others much browner above, whiter below; *yakutensis* lacks olive and yellow tones, is grey-brown above, greyish white below, and has whitish superciliary stripes. Most **first-winter** *acredula* are extensively yellow below. See Wood Warbler and Chiffchaff. **Call** a bisyllabic *hooweet.* Song a melancholy liquid descending cadence, typically starting faintly, becoming louder, then fading away with distinctly phrased ending, . .*sweet sweet suEEtu.* **Range/status**: Common palearctic migrant, mid-Sept.–early May. Winters mainly in w. and cent. Kenya at 1000–2200 m. More widespread on passage, late March to April (mainly *P. t. acredula*, but some e. Siberian *yakutensis*).

UGANDA WOODLAND WARBLER *Phylloscopus budongoensis* Plate 96

Length 4″. A tiny arboreal warbler of w. Kenyan forests, easily overlooked except for its distinctive song. Olive-green above and on the sides; whitish superciliary stripes bordered below by black eye-lines. (Migrant *Phylloscopus* species wintering here are paler below and have less bold face patterns. Green Hylia is larger and much stockier with different voice.) **Juvenile** darker on crown and more olive on breast and flanks than adult. **Song** of 4 or 5 high notes, thin yet fairly loud: *see-su-su-eet* or *see-see-su-weet.* **Range**: Kakamega Forest and nearby North and South Nandi forests (where much less common); formerly at Nyarondo.

BROWN WOODLAND WARBLER *Phylloscopus umbrovirens mackenzianus*
Plate 96

Length 4–4.5″. A highland warbler, in forest, woodland and giant heath. Mostly *warm brown above with bright olive-green wing edgings* and *pale tawny superciliary stripes bordered below by dark eye-lines.* Usual **song** a clear descending series of musical notes, *tu-ti-teeo-teeo-teeo-teew,* or *titiri-titiri-cheeo-tu-tu;* also a long series of varied repeated phrases, *tseu-tsi-tsee-tsee chew, weechu weechu weechu, tsuchee tsuchee tsuchee, sweet sweet sweet sweet. . .,* typically with a brief pause after each group of similar notes and interspersed with occasional rapid trills. Alarm note, *tu-wiu.* **Range**: northern mountains and Mt Elgon south through all Kenyan and Tanzanian highlands except the South Pares and Usambaras.

YELLOW-THROATED WOODLAND WARBLER *Phylloscopus ruficapillus minullus* Plate 102

Length 4–4.5″. A colourful warbler of montane forest in se. Kenya and ne. Tanzania. Olive-green above with *lemon-yellow on face, throat and under tail-coverts; crown and nape tawny brown;* grey wash on breast. Duller **juvenile** has yellowish olive wash across breast. (Superficially similar Wood Warbler, present in winter, has white under tail-coverts and no brown on head.) **Song** sweet and variable, e.g. *tee-tuitee-tuitee,* or *see-see seesee seet* or *twee, tewi tewi tewi tewi,* the first note highest; other variations: *tee-pe-tee-pe-tee, pe-pe-tee,* and *turee-tsee-tsuiEEsee.* Call a high-pitched *seeu.* **Range**: South Pare and Usambara mts and Taita Hills where fairly common in the limited remaining habitat.

LITTLE RUSH WARBLER *Bradypterus baboecala* Plate 95

Length 5–5.75″. A skulking, dark brown warbler of *swamps and marshes*, conspicuous only in display when it flies low over the water or reeds with audible wing rattling, its ample tail well spread and held downward. *Short black streaks on lower throat* not always easy to see and racially variable (finer, sometimes almost lacking in *B. b. moreaui*). Dorsal colour also varies racially: rich rufous-brown in *elgonensis*, dark olive-brown in *centralis*, dark brown in *moreaui*. Buffy brown of cheeks extends across breast, separating whitish throat and belly; *tarsi brownish pink*. **Juvenile** richer brown above, yellowish below, the throat streaks narrow. **Song** of *B. b. elgonensis* and *centralis* a thin *seet* or sharper *zri* repeated 10–18 times, slowly at first then accelerating as they gradually fade away: *zri, zri, zri, zri - zri-zri-zri-zizizizizizizi*; reedy and somewhat insect-like. Southeastern *B. b. moreaui* has similar 'bouncing ball' pattern, but a much deeper, louder *turr - turr - turr-turr turr-turrturrturrturr* or *chwerk, chwerk . . . cherk-cherk-cherchercherCherk*, the notes all on same pitch, less measured, and acceleration less pronounced than in *elgonensis* (thus sounding like nominate southern African birds). Wing sounds, *prrt-prrt-prrt*, terminate each vocal display flight. Call note a single *chup*. (Broad-tailed Warbler in flight also produces audible wing whirring, but lacks throat streaks, has much larger tail and long, pale-tipped under tail-coverts.) **Range**: *B. b. elgonensis* in Kenyan highlands, Mara GR and Lake Victoria basin; *moreaui* along coast north to lower Tana River delta, inland to Lake Jipe, and Amboseli NP; *centralis* south of Lake Manyara and Tarangire NPs and in Mbulu Highlands.

WHITE-WINGED WARBLER *Bradypterus carpalis*   Plate 95
Length 6.5". A well-marked warbler of *papyrus swamps in the Lake Victoria Basin*. Note *the heavily streaked throat and breast, whitish patch on carpal area*, and *white-tipped wing-coverts*. **Juvenile** brown-backed like adult, but less clearly streaked below, dusky brown on sides, flanks and centre of belly; whitish on bend of wing, but not on wing-coverts. **Song** a succession of short loud notes with almost metallic resonance, starting slowly, accelerating, then fading away: *tsyik, tsyik, tsyik, tsyik-tsyik tyur-tyur-tyur-turtur-turtur*, often followed by 4–5 loud explosive whirring wingbeats, recalling Little Rush Warbler, but where the two species are sympatric, song of *baboecala* weaker and much higher-pitched. **Range**: Yala Swamp, Lake Kanyaboli and Usengi east to Kisumu and Kendu Bay.

EVERGREEN FOREST WARBLER *Bradypterus lopezi*   Plate 95

Length 5-5.75". A dark master skulker of dense low vegetation and debris in *highland forest*; hops and creeps with tail slightly elevated, flits quickly between adjacent perches but usually flies only a metre or two. *Short diffuse blackish streaks on lower throat and upper breast* diagnostic but inconspicuous; *tail feathers usually much frayed and pointed*. *B. l. mariae* deep olive brown above, dark grey below; *usambarae* warmer brown above, browner below than *mariae*. (Mountain Illadopsis is more robust, its tail rarely appearing threadbare. See Cinnamon Bracken Warbler.) **Song** varies in pitch and accenting, but usually of one note or short phrase repeated 8–20 times. Some begin softly and become louder: *p'chew-p'chew-p'chew-p'chew-p'chew. . .*, or *cher-TEE cher-TEE cher-TEE. . ..* Others of more even pitch: *chewi-chewi-chewi. . .*, or *wuchi-wuchi-wuchi. . .*, varied to a slower, softer *tewsi, tewsi . . ..* Call a hard emphatic *TCHEW!* or *chi-CHEW!*; *CHIR-U, CHIR-U* in *usambarae*, sometimes preceded by a high-pitched *see-see* (Moreau). Also a thin chatter of annoyance. Birds may duet. **Range**: *B. l. mariae* in Kenyan highlands incl. the Chyulu Hills, and in Tanzania in the Crater Highlands, Arusha NP, Mt Meru and Kilimanjaro; *usambarae* in the Usambara and Pare mts and Taita Hills.

CINNAMON BRACKEN WARBLER *Bradypterus c. cinnamomeus*   Plate 95

Length 5.5–6". A rich rufous-brown warbler of bracken and briars, often at forest edge. Shows prominent *pale superciliary stripes* and *whitish throat and belly*. Broad rectrices soon become worn and narrow. **Juvenile** darker dusky brown above, olive-brown and yellowish below. (Evergreen Forest Warbler in forest interior is darker olive-brown, not rufous-brown, with blackish streaks on throat.) **Song** highly variable, loud and ringing, with 1–several notes followed by a *slow* trill or repetition of a single note: *cheee, chur- tu-ur-ur-ur-ur-ur-rrrrrrr*, or *twee, twee, twee, chu-chu-chu-chu-chu. . ..* Call note a soft *tseep*; also a scolding *chrrrr*. **Range**: w. and cent. Kenyan highlands north to Mt Nyiru; n. Tanzanian mountains east to the West Usambaras.

BLACK-FACED RUFOUS WARBLER *Bathmocercus rufus vulpinus* **Plate 101**

Length 5". A shy, *black-faced* bird of w. Kenyan forest undergrowth. Often cocks tail forward over back. **Male** *bright rufous* with black from forehead to centre of breast and upper belly. Feet dark blue; normally concealed bright blue skin at sides of throat perhaps visible in singing males. **Female** has male's pattern but olive-grey replaces rufous. Dark olive or olive-grey **juvenile** lacks black, the male with rufous on wings and tail but female uniformly drab and best identified by shape and size. Young male later splotched black and rufous below. **Song** not bird-like, of loud, extremely penetrating, slowly uttered and prolonged notes often given antiphonally by a pair, but male also sings alone: EEEENH. . . EEEENH. . . EEEENH. . ., a characteristic sound of some western forests, ventriloquial and hard to trace; continues for long periods. *Quality similar to that of illadopsis voices.* Call a loud *chip*. **Range**: Sotik and Kericho north to the Kakamega and Nandi forests and southern slopes of Mt Elgon.

AFRICAN MOUSTACHED WARBLER *Melocichla mentalis* **Plate 95**

Length 7.5". A *large* skulking brown-backed warbler of rank herbage and dense grass along streams. *Long broad dark tail* shows buff feather tips; note the *black malar streaks at sides of white throat*, and rufous-tinged forehead; white shaft streaks on dark auriculars evident at close range; *eyes yellow or cream. M. m. orientalis* paler, more sandy brown on back than western birds. **Juvenile** has dark eyes, no rufous on forehead, and buff-tipped wing-coverts. **Song** loud, sprightly and rapidly delivered, of sharp notes and short warbling or bubbling phrases with numerous changes in pitch: *twip-twip-twip-twip chiWEE chipity-chip teu teu teu* , or *tsyk, tchuk TSYUK TSYUK TSYUK TSYUK chordilee-ideleee churdle-tweeee* and variations; bulbul-like quality well conveyed by Chapin's memory aid: "chirp-chirp-chirp-chirp, doesn't it tickle you?" Some songs have higher wispy notes added: *tsi-chireeee WIDDLEY WIDDLEY WEE, tsip-tsyip tsyip tsee* . . .. Calls a wheatear-like *tuck*, and a loud chatter. **Range:** Nominate race from Mt Elgon south to Ruma NP (Lambwe Valley), Mara GR and Serengeti NP (once); also from Meru NP, Embu and Nairobi south to the Taita and Chyulu hills, Kilimanjaro and Arusha. *M. m. orientalis* from East Usambaras (old records) southward. Formerly in Tsavo East NP.

BROAD-TAILED WARBLER *Schoenicola brevirostris alexinae* **Plate 95**

Length 6". A unique brown-backed warbler of wet grasslands, small bodied but with a *remarkably broad graduated tail, the wide black rectrices pale-tipped as are the very long dark under tail-coverts.* **Juvenile** similar but underparts yellowish-tinged. Creeps about in coarse grass. Usually seen when flushed from underfoot, flying a short distance with laboured flight, fanned tail bobbing; flushed again only with difficulty. Displaying male circles in a wide spiral, the wings producing a soft whirring. **Song** a weak metallic *cheep. . . cheep. . . cheep. . . cheep. . .*, or *simp . . . simp* . . ., from perch or in aerial display flight. Calls a harsh *chick* and a sharp *prit-prit*. **Range**: Mt Elgon south to Serengeti NP, east to Nakuru and Nairobi NPs, Chyulu Hills, Mt Meru and Arusha NP. Becoming scarce as grasslands disappear. **Taxonomic Note**: Often considered conspecific with the Indian *S. platyura.*

PAPYRUS YELLOW WARBLER *Chloropeta g. gracilirostris* **Plate 102**

Length 5.25". A scarce inhabitant of dense *papyrus swamps* fringing Lake Victoria. Resembles Mountain Yellow Warbler but with slimmer bill, larger tarsi, *much longer toes*, and *no yellow on lores*. **Song** sibilant or semi-whistling: a short series of notes described as *to-tslo-wee*, or *trslo-tschlee-wo*, or *tschlee-ow* (S. Keith). An erratic singer. **Range**: Yala Swamp, Lake Kanyaboli, Kisumu and Kendu Bay.

DARK-CAPPED or AFRICAN YELLOW WARBLER *Chloropeta natalensis massaica* **Plate 102**

Length 5.5". A yellow-breasted, *flycatcher-like* warbler of low rank vegetation, olive-brown above with a broad bill, well-developed rictal bristles, *long blackish tarsi and strong toes*; posture often upright; sidles up and down grass stems. This species of *moist* sites below 2300 m has *contrasting dark crown* lacking in Mountain Yellow Warbler. **Juvenile** tan or dull ochre-tawny with brown crown. **Song** a short musical warbling, *twiya twiya, wichuwichu wichu*, and a brief *chui chui, chuweya*. Alarm note a harsh *check*. **Range:** Mt Elgon and Saiwa NPs south to Kericho and Sotik, east to the Aberdares, Nairobi and Meru. Also in Chyulu and Taita hills, Arusha and Moshi districts, on lower slopes of Kilimanjaro and the Usambaras.

MOUNTAIN YELLOW WARBLER *Chloropeta similis* Plate 102

Length 4.75–5.5″. More warbler-like in habits and appearance than the preceding species which it largely replaces at higher elevations, usually along forest edges (although the two overlap around 1900 m on Kilimanjaro). *Uniformly olive-green above*, the crown coloured like the back; underparts bright yellow. **Juvenile** generally greenish olive, darker above. **Song** slow and melodious, with slurred whistles, canary-like warbling and trills, *turee tsk-tsk, sureeeee tur-tur-treeeeee chur, seewuree tchip-tchip-tchip-tchip*, or *reee-tew, purrreeee, skeeaskew, purreet-reeet*; variable, but with a wide range of pitch. **Range:** Mt Nyiru, Mt Elgon and the Cheranganis south and east to the Aberdares, Mt Kenya, the Crater and Mbulu highlands, Mt Hanang, Arusha NP, Mt Meru and Kilimanjaro.

CISTICOLAS are grass- or bush-warblers with subtle species distinctions complicated by racial, seasonal and individual variation. The following treatment applies only to populations in our area. (Differences may exist between local subspecies and those in other parts of a species' range; e.g. the nominate race of Singing Cisticola in Ethiopia has a stripe-backed non-breeding plumage, whereas Kenyan birds are always plain-backed.) Species identification may require knowledge of distribution, voice, behaviour, size and proportions as well as plumage. Colour and pattern are not especially varied and there is little sexual dimorphism. However, the *distinction between streaked and unstreaked species* is important. Obvious *contrast between head and back*, and *presence or absence of crown or nape streaking* can be diagnostic (streaks may be difficult to detect at a distance, in harsh light or on worn birds). *Colour of face and underparts* is noteworthy, as is that of the *tail-feather tips*. *Differences between abraded and fresh unworn plumage* must be borne in mind, as effects of feather wear combined with sun-fading can be considerable. Some silent birds in poor plumage cannot be safely named. Few East African cisticolas have distinct breeding and non-breeding plumages. Ours generally moult only once per year and wear a 'perennial' dress. Here, seasonal differences are exhibited only by Black-backed, Rock, Long-tailed, certain populations of Siffling, Croaking, and by some inland Winding Cisticolas. A few Zitting Cisticolas also moult twice per year. Juvenile plumage tends to be rufous-tinged and often yellow below. (No adult cisticola has yellowish underparts.) In most adults, feet are typically pale flesh-pink, and the eyes light brown; juveniles have more yellowish bills, and their eyes are grey or brownish grey.

√ SINGING CISTICOLA *Cisticola cantans* Plate 97

Length 5–5.75″. A plain-looking highland bird of dense, luxuriant herbaceous or shrub growth (not harsh thorn-bush). Largely avoids lower wetter sites occupied by similar Red-faced Cisticola. *Dull rufous crown and wing edgings contrast with unstreaked grey-brown back*; face buffy or whitish with a black subloral spot (more noticeable in males). (Red-faced is reddish on face, lacks contrast between rufous wing edgings and brown back, lacks dark subloral spot and is buffier below.) **Song** of loud, emphatic 2- or 3-syllabled phrases such as *wee-chew, tchew-whip, tchee-tchew-WHIP, o-ki-WEE*, etc., variously combined or a single phrase repeated. Pair members duet, one giving a repeated low *trr, trr*, the other singing short song phrases. Alarm call, *srrt-srrt-srrt.* **Range:** *C. c. belli* in w. Kenya (Mt Elgon, Siaya NP); *pictipennis* from Kakamega east to Mt Kenya, south to Nairobi and Machakos; also Taita Hills, Arusha NP and lower slopes of Mt Meru and Kilimanjaro.

RED-FACED CISTICOLA *Cisticola erythrops sylvius* Plate 97

Length 5–5.5″. A skulker of rank herbage and shrubbery in low wet places. Unlike the more confiding Singing Cisticola has *russet face*, its dim superciliaries more reddish than crown (which, like wings, does not contrast with the back). Olive-grey back becomes slaty with wear; *underparts tinged rufous-buff* (more whitish in Singing C.). **Songs** sometimes confusingly like those of *cantans*, but more emphatic, with many staccato notes, e. g. *pickup pickup pickup TWEE TWEE TWEE pickup pickup CHWEE CHWEE CHWEE. . .*, or *wuCHEE, wuCHEE, wuCHEE. . .;* at times a series of excited notes increases in volume: *chic-chic-chic-chic. . . CHEEP CHEEP CHEEP. . . CHEER CHEER CHEER* , and a rising series of shrill reedy or wiry notes may end with a loud *chew-WHEER!* or *chew-WHIP!* **Range**: Lake Victoria basin and highlands from Mt Elgon south to Serengeti NP, and from se. Mt Kenya to Nairobi NP, Taita Hills, Usambara Mts and Arusha NP. (Old records from coast near Tanga and Malindi.)

ROCK or ROCK-LOVING CISTICOLA *Cisticola aberrans* Plate 97

Length 5″. A scarce, *plain-backed rufous-crowned* bird of *barren rock outcrops and sparsely vegetated boulder-strewn slopes*. Seasonal plumage differences within each race poorly known. **Breeding** *C. a. emini* of sw. Kenya and adjacent Tanzania has *grey-brown back and wings contrasting with rufous crown and nape, long superciliary stripes* and at close range shows a narrow buff eye-ring; underparts buff, tawnier on sides and flanks; tail indistinctly pale-tipped and with poorly defined subterminal dark band. Undescribed **non-breeding plumage** may resemble that of eastern *teitensis*. This is brighter brown above than breeding *emini*, and rufous of nape extends onto back; throat and lower belly whitish; tail spots larger, pale grey with no rufous tinge. (Similar Rattling and Lynes's Cisticolas often among rocks, and the former's back streaks can be inconspicuous, but those species prefer well vegetated sites.) **Calls** (*emini*) a mournful piping *pee-u,* a squeaky *squee-a or squee-e-a,* and an insistent nasal *tchaa* or *zheea,* frequently repeated and sometimes followed by a rapid *tsip-tsip-tsip-tsip* or a louder song-like churring or buzzing *tsirrrrrrrrrrr.* **Range**: *C. a. teitensis* known from a few specimens and sight records in Taita and Sagala hills near Voi, Tsavo West NP, Mkomazi GR and the West Usambaras; *emini* from 3 early specimens collected near s. Lake Victoria; recent records from nw. Mara GR and Serengeti NP probably of this race.

TRILLING CISTICOLA *Cisticola w. woosnami* Plate 97

Length 4.75–5.75″. A *bulky, large-billed, mostly western* cisticola of open woods and bushy grassy hillsides. The *dull chestnut crown and wing-edging contrast only slightly with the plain brown back*; tail spots noticeable only in flight when feathers are spread. Underparts white, washed with yellowish buff on breast, sooty grey on flanks; leg feathers rufous-brown; lores dull white. *Bill prominently curved*, black above, grey below (male) or whitish pink with dark culmen (female). Female much smaller, paler, more reddish-crowned than male. (Partially sympatric Rock C. has contrasting rufous crown, prominent superciliary stripes, smaller bill and occupies rocky sites.) **Song** a far-carrying trill, *trrrrrrrrrr-RRRRRRRRRRRRRR,* lasting several seconds and increasing in volume; often preceded by a loud metallic *quink . . . quink. . ..* Calls a single *tchaaa* and an emphatic nasal *cha-cha-cha.* Sings with quivering tail from tree, turning head and thus changing apparent volume and direction of song. Usually shy. **Range**: nw. Mara GR and Lolgorien to Ruma NP and Rapogi Dist., Mt Hanang, Arusha and Lake Manyara NPs and Moshi area.

WHISTLING CISTICOLA *Cisticola lateralis antinorii* Plate 97

Length 5–5.5″. A *plain, heavy-billed, west Kenyan* bird of damp brush and forest edge; a darker, duller, *dusky-crowned* version of Trilling Cisticola. Skulks in undergrowth, sometimes in family groups. Black tail spots well defined even on central feathers (most obvious in flight). Male much larger than female. (Rufous-backed birds unreported from our region.) **Juvenile** similar to young Trilling. Unique **song** a loud rich whistling of several patterns but usually involving repetition of a single

note, *keuw, keuw, keuw, keuw. . .*, or *whoi,* chu-chu-chu-chu-chu-chu-chu (reminds Americans of *Cardinalis*). Also a shorter *witilew t'wee tew* and a somewhat nuthatch-like *kree, kew-kew-kew-kew.* Calls include a scolding chatter and *tew* or *chew* notes, plus a *chea* of alarm. **Range:** North of Trilling Cisticola's range from n. shore of Lake Victoria north to Mumias and Kakamega districts; an old record from lower Mt Elgon.

HUNTER'S CISTICOLA *Cisticola hunteri* Plate 97

Length 5.75". A *slim, black-lored, fairly long-tailed* cisticola of herbage and shrubbery at *high elevations,* dark and sombre in plumage, but *animated and vocal.* At a distance or in dim light, adult dark brown above, except for chestnut-tinged crown, with broad diffuse streaks or mottling evident at close range. (Mt Elgon birds nearly plain.) Underparts light to dark grey or (Mt Elgon) dusky. Display involves exuberant **song**, a duet or chorus in which birds enthusiastically bob, flutter and pump their spread tails. One of a pair sings *weet-cheeeeer* or *see-wit-cheeeeer,* the other gives a long reeling trill, *tweeeeeeeeeeeeeerrrrrrrrrr;* performance repeated many times in quick succession, and with increasing excitement and activity. (Similar Chubb's Cisticola behaves and looks much like Hunter's, but its crown is lighter and brighter, contrasting with the back. Singing C. shows reddish wing edging and is much paler below. Both vocally distinct.) **Range:** From Mt Elgon (above 2500 m; Chubb's largely below that level), the Cheranganis and Mt Uraguess, south through the Mau, Aberdares and Mt Kenya to the Ngurumans, Crater Highlands, Mt Meru and Kilimanjaro.

CHUBB'S CISTICOLA *Cisticola c. chubbi* Plate 97

Length 5.5". A *plain, black-lored* western species resembling Hunter's Cisticola but shorter-tailed, brighter rufous on crown and nape, and with *no streaks* on the back. Whitish breast washed with grey at sides, buff on flanks and crissum. **Song** an energetic piping, chattering or babbling as a pair or group of birds bob and bow excitedly with tails spread and erect; the phrases *whi-cheery* and *see-whi-cheery* are distinctive, more shrill than Hunter's C. but with the same reeling quality. Like that species, noisy and conspicuous when courting; otherwise retiring. **Range:** Mt Elgon (usually below 2000 m) and Saiwa NP south to Kakamega, Eldama Ravine, Kericho, Sotik and Lolgorien.

FOXY CISTICOLA *Cisticola t. troglodytes* Plate 97

Length 3.75". A *small, richly coloured northwestern* species of *Erythrina–Combretum* savanna and open woodland with tall grass. Bright rufous above, warm buff below, with *no obvious tail spots* (central rectrices blackish toward tip); *eyes grey.* Forages in tall grass. **Call** a soft *tsit, tsit-tsit,* and a rapid series of similar wispy notes may serve as a song. **Range:** Ne. Mt Elgon (1993–97, but suitable habitat vanishing). Early specimens from the Cheranganis, Suk and w. Turkana districts.

TINY CISTICOLA *Cisticola nanus* Plate 97

Length 3.5". A *very small, short-tailed* bird of low *dry country,* mainly east of the Rift Valley. Clean-cut with *bright rufous crown, light loral lines* and clear white or buffy white underparts; *faintly streaked pale grey back* may appear plain. Forages from ground level into low trees; usually sings from high perch. Courtship flight involves short spurts of flight on whirring wings with occasional quick swerves or side-slips (Lynes). **Song** a loud, rapid, clear whistling: *TEW-teu-eet, t'TCHEW-tchew-eet, t'TCHEW-tchew-eet. . .,* or *tidiTUwe, tidiTUwi, tidiTUwe. . .* the phrases repeated with interspersed high-pitched *tsick* or *tseep* notes; some songs consist largely of these thinner notes. Also a simpler, monotonous *tseetsiup-tseetsiup-tseetsiup . . ..* Call note *churr-it-it* . **Range:** Ethiopian border areas south to Samburu GR, Meru and Tsavo NPs and Kajiado east to Mkomazi GR, South Pare foothills and Naberera. Rare west of Rift Valley.

*RED-PATE CISTICOLA *Cisticola ruficeps mongalla* Plates 97, 98

Length 4". A small, seasonally varying cisticola of *northwestern border* areas. Bill rather large for size of bird. **Breeding** bird plain or faintly mottled above with noticeable *white* supraloral stripes and dull rufous forehead, crown and nape. **Non-breeding** bird short white superciliary stripe, bright rufous head top and broad dark brown back streaks. Blackish subloral spot most evident in males. Throat whitish, breast buff with some grey at sides; tail narrowly white-tipped. **Juvenile** resembles non-breeding bird but yellowish below. (Allopatric Long-tailed Cisticola is much longer-tailed. Tiny C. is smaller, brighter and very short-tailed.) **Song** a rapid insect-like trill on one pitch (1–2 sec. duration), *tsee-seeseeseeseeseesee*; or a trill followed by forceful, terminally accented double notes: *teeeeeeeeeeeeeee tseWE tseWE tseWE tseWE* (or latter notes given alone). **Range**: Lokichokio area, nw. Kenya.

LONG-TAILED or TABORA CISTICOLA *Cisticola angusticaudus*   Plate 97

Length 4″. *Slender and prinia-like*, its long thin dark tail (shorter in non-breeding plumage) often cocked; *crown and nape bright rufous; back plain grey-brown.* **Juvenile** duller on crown with darker brown on back and yellow-tinged below. (Somewhat similar Red-fronted Warbler is more uniform above, shows conspicuous white in tail. See Tawny-flanked Prinia.) Usually in pairs or small active groups foraging in low trees or grass. Favours grassy stands of *Acacia gerrardii*. **Song** three-part-ed: *see-chew-chew* or *chew-see-see*. **Range**: Kendu Bay, Ruma NP, Rapogi and Lolgorien districts to the Mara GR and n. Serengeti NP. **Taxonomic Note**: Formerly considered conspecific with s. African *C. fulvicapillus*.

LEVAILLANT'S CISTICOLA *Cisticola tinniens oreophilus*   Plate 98

Length 5″. A slender montane *wetland* cisticola with *bright rufous tail, wing edgings, crown and nape; back and nape heavily streaked* (sometimes so densely as to appear black-backed). Upper tail-coverts mottled black and rufous. (Winding Cisticola in breeding plumage is striped black on *grey* above; its shorter tail lacks reddish tint, rump and upper tail-coverts are grey, not rufous. Non-breeding Winding, sandy buff overall, is streaked from forehead to nape.) **Song** a rapid warbling or partly trilled *tee-tiurrrrip* or *che-cheeureeeueep*. Calls *trrt-trrt* and a high *tee-tee-tee*. **Range**: Uasin Gishu and Elgeyu to Mau Summit, Molo, Nyahururu, the Aberdares, Kinangop Plateau and Mt Kenya (rare).

WINDING CISTICOLA *Cisticola galactotes*   Plate 98 ✔

Length 4.25–5″. A slender *boldly streaked* bird typical of wet places (or adjoining grass and thickets). Most adult *C. g. amphilectus* bright rufous on crown and wings. In **normal perennial plumage**, this inland race has rufous forehead and face, the *pale grey back heavily black-streaked*, and *grey tail shows extensive black subterminal band*; dark pectoral patches often present. *Some* individuals assume a **non-breeding plumage** with buff-edged back feathers, streaked crown, and *rufous*-and-black central rectrices. Coastal *haematocephalus* (perennial plumage only), is paler, less heavily streaked, much less reddish, more whitish-faced, shows little rufous on crown (none in worn plumage), and lacks marked pectoral patches (thus resembling inland Tanzanian *suahelicus* whose dorsal colour is intermediate between the two Kenyan races). **Juvenile** (all races) pale yellowish below; these and first-year birds have crown and back streaked buff and black as in non-br. adults. (See Levaillant's and Carruthers's Cisticolas. Stout C. is heavier, broader-tailed, with dull tawny wing edging, often on drier ground.) **Song** of *amphilectus* a dry creaking trill, likened to winding a clock; somewhat insect-like and quite prolonged, *krrrrrrRRRRRRRRRRRRRRrrrrrrrrrr*. Also gives a weak rasping *zhree-eeeeeee*, a ringing *chwee-chwee-chwee-chwee*, a loud *chew-chew-chew-chewip*, and a series of *trit-trit* notes by low-flying displaying male. *C. g. haematocephalus* bleats rather than trills, an upslurred *brrrrRRIP*; also gives excited twittering *tic-titic-tic-tic-titic* in dancing flight around bushes. **Range:** *C. g. amphilectus* widespread in Kenya (where sympatric with *C. carruthersi*, it is confined to *edges* of papyrus stands); *suahelicus* of interior Tanzania intergrades with *amphilectus* in s. Kenya and Lake Victoria basin. *C. g. haematocephalus* is the most conspicuous coastal cisticola.

CARRUTHERS'S CISTICOLA *Cisticola carruthersi* Plate 98

Length 5". A streak-backed, *galactotes*-like cisticola strictly confined to the *interior of western papyrus swamps*. Differs from Winding Cisticola in its *brown wing edgings*, plain *dusky or blackish tail, chestnut-brown crown*, and slimmer straighter bill. Paler **juvenile** has brown back lightly streaked with darker brown, quite unlike bold pattern of adult; underparts faintly yellowish. **Song**, a chatter followed by a rapid series of high scratchy or squeaky notes, these run-together and higher-pitched at the end, *chchchchchchchch tsik-tseeosisitseek*. Calls include a scolding nasal *cheeya!* or *nyaaa!*, and a protracted scolding. **Range:** Lake Victoria basin from n. shore of Winam (Kavirondo) Gulf south through Kisumu to Homa Bay.

STOUT CISTICOLA *Cisticola robustus nuchalis* Plate 98

Length 4.25–5.5". A *stocky* cisticola of moist shrubby grassland, with *unstreaked bright rufous nape* contrasting with buffy grey, black-streaked back; reddish brown crown also streaked with black. *Short blackish tail* has buff feather edges and dull whitish tips conspicuous in flight. Female much smaller than male. (Similar Aberdare Cisticola somewhat darker throughout, its rufous nape patch black-streaked and duller than in Stout, its outer rectrices grey-tipped and wings slightly brighter. See Croaking Cisticola.) **Song** types include (1) two or three introductory notes followed by a musical trill, *twi-twi-TWRRRRRRRRRRRR*; (2) a thinner lisping *tsee tsee tsiptsiptsiptsiptsip*; (3) a long, rapidly descending, almost tremulo series of identical notes, *tew-tew-tew-tew-tew-tew*. . .. Calls, a loud *chip-chip-chip* and a softer *tsi-tsi-tsi-tsi*. Less vocal than many cisticolas. **Range:** Mt Elgon, Trans-Nzoia and Uasin Gishu districts south to Ngong and Loita Hills, Nairobi NP, Mara GR and Serengeti NP; also from lower slopes of Mt Meru and Kilimanjaro east to Taveta, Maktau and Lake Jipe. Formerly on Laikipia Plateau.

ABERDARE CISTICOLA *Cisticola aberdare* Plate 98

Length 4.75–6". Only *above 2300 m*; a *dark, montane* version of Stout Cisticola, its *rufous nape streaked with black, hence not conspicuous and contrasting*; back streaks heavier, wing panels more rufous, and tail somewhat longer than in Stout C. **Songs**: *pieu pieu pieu pieu twirrrrrrr chip-chip-chip* and *pieu pieu pieu pieu tew-tew-tew-tew tschweep tchweep tchweep chew-chew-chew-chew-chew*; also a series of short trills. **Range:** Local around Molo, Mau Narok and on the Aberdares.

CROAKING CISTICOLA *Cisticola natalensis* Plate 98

Length 5.5". A streaky, *stout-bodied* cisticola with a *heavy decurved bill*, usually in *tall grass* on slopes and hillsides. Usual **perennial plumage** streaked or mottled dark sepia and pale brown above, but some birds in w. and se. Kenya (including Chyulu Hills) assume a **non-breeding dress** (Aug.–Oct.). This boldly striped black and tawny above, rich buff below, and with a considerably longer tail. Adults in perennial plumage show *some rufous on nape*, most pronounced in *C. n. kapitensis*; crown rusty buff, well mottled with dark brown; the race *matengorum* less prominently streaked than *kapitensis*; *argentea* paler and greyer. **Juvenile** similar to non-br. adult but yellowish below. (Stout C. has brighter nape and smaller bill, but some *C. n. kapitensis* approach that species in bill size.) **Song** often with unique 'klunking' notes, e.g. *k'lonk-i, chee-u-onk, chee-wunk, tweeonk*, etc. repeated several times then often changing into a rasping or croaking *kwerrrrrrrrrr*. Less metallic notes, *whut-CHI, klee klock, chiop-chiop* or an aspirate *wreeenh-YUK*, may be given in simple series. A single rolling *rrreek* may be repeated indefinitely. Aerial vocalizations composed either of klunking notes or of guttural, croaking or wheezing sounds as male circles high above ground. Alarm note an emphatic *chee-YRRR* or *chi-WUNK*. **Range**: *C. n. kapitensis* from Mathews Range and the Nyambeni Hills south to Thika, Nairobi, Machakos and Sultan Hamud; *strangei* from Mt Elgon south to Lake Victoria basin and Kericho; *matengorum* from n. Tanzania to Mara GR, Chyulu and Shimba hills and Mombasa; *argenteus* on Mt Marsabit and Huri Hills.

✓ RATTLING CISTICOLA *Cisticola chinianus* Plates 97, 98

Length 4.5–5.75". The common streak-backed brush-inhabiting cisticola in many areas, typically seen chattering from bushtop or low tree in thorn-bush or dry savanna (occupies other habitats along coast). Medium-sized, with whitish lores, *no well-defined superciliary stripes*, and *low-contrast, dull rufous wing edgings and crown* (brightest in *C. c. ukamba*). Western *C. c. victoria* and the duller (less reddish) *fischeri* heavily streaked on the back; most races also streaked on head, but highland *humilis* plain-crowned as is eastern *heterophrys* (which is so faintly streaked on the greyish back as to appear plain, its *crown, wing edgings and tail more rufous* than on inland birds). **Juveniles** typically rustier above than adults, pale yellowish below. (Similar Lynes's Cisticola is reddish-faced, prefers rocky hillsides or gorges. Winding C. has more rufous crown and wing panels, bolder streaking on a grey back, often a grey tail; Croaking C. larger, heavier, with stouter, more curved bill. In n. Kenya see Boran C.) **Songs** loud and distinctive despite much variation, typically of 2–4 rasping or grating introductory notes followed by harsh trill or rattle: *chr chr chititititititititititi* or *chi chi chi chrrrrrrrrr*, or *sk-sk-skiirrrrrrr*; the 'rattle' brief or prolonged, with or without additional short notes. Less common songs include *chuk-chuk-chuk tswi-tswi-tswi-tswi*, and *tseutseu seetsitisew*. **Range**: *C. c. heterophrys* in coastal lowlands inland to lower Tana River and East Usambaras; *humilis* from Mt Elgon, Maralal and Mt Kenya south to Nairobi, intergrading with *ukamba* which extends from Embu and Kitui south to Magadi, Tsavo area, Taita Hills, South Pare and West Usambara mts; *victoria* from Kakamega south to Serengeti NP; *fischeri* from Crater and Mbulu highlands east to Arusha and Moshi, meeting *keithi* near Lake Manyara and Tarangire NP and *victoria* in sw. Kenya. (Reports of Rattling C. from Moyale and Marsabit possibly refer to *C. bodessa*.)

LYNES'S or WAILING CISTICOLA *Cisticola (lais) distinctus* **Plate 98**

Length 5.5". A bird of ravines and rocky brushy slopes. Suggests Rattling Cisticola but *russet-tinged on face and underparts*. Wing edgings pale reddish brown; *back grey, dappled or streaked with black*, contrasting with streaked reddish crown; long tail tipped with dull reddish buff. **Juvenile** yellowish below. Shy; flits and scurries among shrubs and boulders, calling frequently; runs mouse-like on rocks and ground, recalling Rock Cisticola. (Sympatric race of Rattling C. and Boran C. are both browner, less grey on back, less reddish on face. Rattling is usually on flatter terrain. Rock C. is unstreaked above.) **Song** a reiterated loud thin whistle, *peeee*, at times preceding a dry trill, or the trill alone; also *t'pee t'pee t'pee t'pee chwer-chwer-chwer-chwer-chwer* and a variable series of repeated harsh notes, e.g. *squee squee squee, wich-wich-wich, squi WEE-WEE-WEE, skerk-cher wee-wee-wee chrk. . ..* Less often a rough wiry *spiiiiiii* or *swirrrrr* embellished with other notes in a discordant medley. Contact call a simple loud *SPEEEEE*. Alarm calls a loud shrill *SPEEK SPEEK . . .* and a squeaky *tskTWEEa*. **Range**: Lake Nakuru and Hell's Gate NPs south through Kedong Valley to Ngong and Loita hills, Lukenya Hill (se. of Nairobi) and Gol Mts (e. Serengeti NP). Early records from Laikipia Plateau, Mt Uraguess and Mt Kulal.

BORAN CISTICOLA *Cisticola b. bodessa* **Plate 98**

Length 5–5.5". A *northern* species of scrub- and grass-covered slopes. Closely resembles Rattling Cisticola but *crown browner* (*less rufous*) and usually so *faintly streaked* as to appear plain; back mottled, less boldly streaked; wing-coverts, light-margined when fresh, contrast more with deep buff flight-feather edges than in sympatric race of Rattling; underparts less buffy. Plumage differences subtle and affected by abrasion and earth-staining. Rely on distinctive **songs**—loud, emphatic and *hurriedly uttered*, usually with some less rapid initial notes: (1) *tchip-tchip-tchip-chipi CHU-uuuu-uuuuu* or *ti-ti-ti TliiiiiiiiiiiiiiiiiiiiiEW*. Initial part can also be rapid: *chuchuchu CHIchichichichichichi-chichichiCHEW*. A loud *chip* or *tsip*, repeated indefinitely as an agitation note, often accelerates abruptly and leads into a song. **Range**: Moyale, Marsabit, Mt Kulal, Maralal, the Kongelai, Iten and Tambach escarpments, ne. Mt Elgon, Kito Pass, Laikipia Plateau and n. Mt Kenya.

TANA RIVER CISTICOLA *Cisticola restrictus* **Plate 99**

Length 5". A very rare and enigmatic streak-backed cisticola of limited range in se. Kenya. Resembles a pale Lynes's Cisticola (but occupies different range and habitat). Also suggests both Ashy and Rattling Cisticolas; reported to sing like the latter, and perhaps a mere variant of that species or of hybrid origin. Underparts almost white, *pale grey on sides of breast and flanks*; *crown finely streaked and rufous-tinted*, distinct from duller back which, like rump, is narrowly streaked with dark brown. Differences between the few known specimens may reflect existence of distinct breeding and non-breeding plumages. Duller-crowned individuals resemble Ashy Cisticola which has uniform, more broadly streaked upperparts with (as seen in the hand) white bases to the nape feathers, and (in Kenya) a proportionately shorter, white-tipped tail; Ashy also lacks grey wash on sides. Those browner *restrictus* with stronger rufous tinge to crown recall Rattling Cisticola, but more like upland *C. c. ukamba* than the almost plain-backed sympatric *heterophrys*. (Coastal Winding Cisticola more streaked above, and wing edgings more rufous than back.) **Range**: The 7 specimens (1932–1972) all from dry bush on flat sandy or black 'cotton' soils at Mnazini, Garsen and Karawa in the lower Tana River basin, and at Ijara and Sangole, 50 km east of the river.

ASHY CISTICOLA *Cisticola cinereolus*   Plate 99

Length 5". A *greyish, dry-country* cisticola with a *pleasing song. Pale and uniformly streaked above*, the dark brown feather centres bordered with grey; crown slightly browner than back. Side of face plain, with very narrow white eye-ring. No rufous wing edgings. Tail feathers white-tipped. Underparts with buff or pale tawny wash. (See Siffling, Rattling, Boran, Lynes's, Croaking and Tana River Cisticolas.) **Song** quite musical and lark-like (regularly imitated by Red-winged Lark); a warbling, loud, rapid and accelerating *tiew-tiew, tawa-tiwi-twiwi* (rising) or *tee-tee-tee-titititititew* (falling); *chew chi-weeto* (last three syllables also used as an alarm call), or *twi-twi-twi-tweeo*, or *sri, sree-turee turEEileu*. Calls are a sharp *tsee tseet tseet tseet* and a monotonous *pee-pee-pee* . . .. **Range**: Lokichokio, Huri Hills, Mt Marsabit, Samburu GR south to Meru NP, lower Tana River, Tsavo and Amboseli NPs and Magadi, Lake Natron, Longido, Sanya Plains and Mkomazi GR.

SIFFLING or SHORT-WINGED CISTICOLA *Cisticola brachypterus*
Plates 97, 99

Length 4.25–4.75". Small and nondescript, with an undistinguished song, and in varied bushy, grassy habitats. Lacks useful field marks; upperparts either plain or streaked. Western *C. b. brachypterus* differs seasonally: **breeding plumage** nearly uniform and *unmarked* above, sometimes slightly dappled; light tail tip well defined and *grey* above. **Non-breeding** bird has mottled crown, *bold back streaks*; tail longer than in breeding plumage. Other races have a streaky perennial plumage. (Pectoral-patch, Wing-snapping, Zitting and Desert Cisticolas are more boldly patterned, shorter-tailed, and usually deliver aerial songs. Ashy C. larger, greyer, more obviously streaked. Boran and Rattling Cisticolas larger and longer-tailed. All have loud vocalizatiions.) **Song** a feeble, monotonous 'siffling' or lisping sound, like whistling softly through the teeth, delivered from bush or tree: *ssiwi-ssiwi-ssiwi.* . ., the typically three-parted phrases oft-repeated. A different *ssee-ssee-ssee-ssee*, drops slightly in pitch; more structured is a reit-erated scratchy *su-SEET su-SEET su-SEET*. Alarm note a squeaky *tsick*. Courting *reichenowi* has slow, spiralling flight up to 60 m, followed by circling with pumping tail, then a spectacular steep dive with audible wing sound. Displaying *katonae* (always?) less impressive with limited circling c.10 m above ground, followed by return to song perch. **Range**: *C. b. katonae* from cent. Kenya south to Crater Highlands, Arusha and Moshi; intergrades with nominate race in w. Kenya south of Mt Elgon, and presumably with *kericho* of West Mau–Kilgoris area; *reichenowi* along the coast, in the Shimba Hills and East Usambaras.

ZITTING CISTICOLA or FAN-TAILED WARBLER *Cisticola juncidis uropygialis*
Plates 99, 124

Length 4". A *short-tailed, heavily striped* little bird of moist grassy terrain. **Male** has *rusty buff rump and pale collar contrasting with black-striped crown and back*. **Female** less contrasting above, whiter below. Although most Kenyan birds have only one annual moult and wear a perennial plumage, adults from Tanzania north into cent. Kenya may moult into a **non-breeding plumage** in the dry season: brighter with longer tail, paler back-feather edges and buffier rump. Erythristic birds present on Pemba Island. **Juvenile** rustier above than adult, yellowish below. (Desert C. of dry plains, has nearly black upper tail surface with pale tip; juv. not yellow below. Pectoral-patch C. and Wing-snapping C. are much shorter-tailed.) Aerial **song** of sharp scratchy notes, *tseek . . . tseek . . . tseek . . .*, or *zit . . . zit . . .* at 1- or 2-sec. intervals, each note synchronized with low point of a dip in the courtship flight. Alarm call a rapid *zitzitzit.* Male displays to 30–40 m above ground, cruising back and forth with strongly undulating flight; never snaps wings. **Range:** Local in n. Kenya , Lake Victoria basin, around Rift Valley lakes, from Mara GR, Nairobi, Amboseli and Tsavo West NPs south to Serengeti NP, east to Tarangire and Arusha NPs; also along coast from Tana River delta south to Mombasa and locally on Pemba Island.

DESERT CISTICOLA *Cisticola aridulus tanganyika*   Plate 99

Length 4″. A small striped cisticola of *dry short-grass plains; resembles Pectoral-patch Cisticola but has longer tail and unstreaked light rufous-buff rump.* (Pectoral-patch C. and Wing-snapping C. are both shorter tailed and usually in more luxuriant grass; Zitting C. has black spots on paler brown tail, occupies taller grass, often near lakes, never open dry plains. Juveniles of these species are yellow below.) Aerial **song** a single, repetitive tinking *pinc . . pinc . . . pinc,* or *twing . . . twing . . .*, the note repeated several times at half-second intervals; sometimes almost bisyllabic: *tuink, tuink . . .*; audible wing-snaps with or between groups of notes. Also a dry sharp *tuk . . . tuk . . .*, accompanied by wing-snaps. **Range:** n. Kenyan deserts south to Marsabit and Shaba GR. Farther south, from Elmenteita, Hell's Gate and Nairobi NPs, the Athi and Kapiti plains, Kajiado, Amboseli and Tsavo area to n. Tanzanian Masailand where the commonest cisticola.

BLACK-BACKED CISTICOLA *Cisticola e. eximius*   Plate 99

Length 4″. A small species of *western grasslands.* Stub-tailed **breeding male** *brightly coloured, with reddish rump and upper tail-coverts, dark chestnut crown, black-streaked back and rusty buff flanks.* Longer-tailed **non-breeding male**'s *black crown* narrowly streaked with white and separated from black back by *red-brown nape;* rump and upper tail-coverts as in breeding plumage. Pectoral patches fainter than in *C. brunnescens;* tail black with white tip (as in *ayresii* and *brunnescens,* but their tails very short.) **Female** like non-br. male but shorter-tailed. **Juvenile** rusty above, yellow on throat and breast. (Desert C. has lighter buff-and-black back pattern. Pectoral-patch C. is uniformly buff-and-black-striped above or with buffy brown crown, and shows little or no collar or rump contrast. Zitting C. has more patterned brown tail, duller rump, and longer tail than breeding *eximius.*) Flight **song** varies, but most notes repeated several times, e.g. *tsi tsi tsi tsi, tsew tsew tsew, tsi tsi tsi. . .* Vocal in ascent (to 50–60 m), throughout the circular cruising (with wing-snapping) and during final near-vertical plunge (with audible whir of wings). **Range:** Rediscovered Ruma NP (July 2000). Formerly near Mumias and Yala in w. Kenya.

PECTORAL-PATCH CISTICOLA *C. brunnescens*   Plate 99

Length 3.75″. A *diminutive, stub-tailed, grassland* species, heavily *streaked buff and black above,* often showing a faint collar across nape, but the streaked *rump no brighter than the back.* **Breeding male** has *unstreaked rufous* (fading to rich buff) *crown with dark edges* just above the superciliaries, and *dark-streaked nape and back;* blackish breast patches and subloral spots faint or obsolete in **non-breeding plumage** which is *uniformly streaked above.* **Breeding female** resembles non-br. male but forehead and forecrown rufous. **Juvenile** rufous-tinted above, bright yellowish below. **Song** given in steady circling flight (with few or no undulations) a monotonous repetition of sharp *tsik* notes in groups often alternating with loud wing-snaps: *tsik tsik tsik* (SNAP) *tsik tsik tsik* (SNAP) *tsik tsik tsk tsk. . .* eventually accelerating into chatter as bird descends. Separate snap may be given with each vocal chip; at times a short volley of snaps. Sometimes calls and snaps from grass stem. (See Wing-snapping, Desert and Zitting Cisticolas.) **Range:** *C. b. nakuruensis* from Laikipia Plateau south to Loita Plains,

Mara GR, Serengeti NP and Crater Highlands. *C. b. hindii* east of Rift Valley from Thika and Nairobi south to Athi/ Kapiti plains and Arusha area. Huri Hills birds may be s. Ethiopian *C. b. brunnescens*; race on Mt Hanang is *C. b. cinnamomeus.*

WING-SNAPPING CISTICOLA *Cistiola ayresii mauensis* Plate 99

Length 3.5". A tiny grassland bird of *high elevations.* Recalls Pectoral-patch Cisticola but brighter and darker above, and still shorter-tailed in breeding plumage. *Rusty-tinged rump contrasts* with boldly streaked buff-and-black back; pale collar and faint pectoral patches evident. **Breeding male** *becomes black- or chestnut-crowned* as wear reduces the pale feather edges of non-br. plumage; *forehead dark rusty red*, usually mottled with black; underparts strongly tinged with reddish buff. **Non-breeding male** longer-tailed, brighter above with broad reddish buff feather edges and *bright rust-red rump*; head like back, with no rufous on forehead. **Female** resembles non-br. male. **Song** in high display flight, a high-pitched, wispy, squeaky *tsi-tsi-tsu TUwi-TUwi wi-wi* (last two notes higher) or *tsee, seese, seese-see*, or *seet sweeet twee turee seet twiulee . . .*, or *tsu-TSEW-wi chew werk.* Each dip in circular cruise accompanied by volleys of *loud*, rattle-like wing-snapping suggesting Flappet Lark's display sound; after 4–5 minutes, a rapid vocal *tsiktsiktsik . . .* as bird descends. Also snaps wings in erratic low flight when alarmed. (Pectoral-patch Cisticola's wing-snaps given singly and usually well spaced; its plumage most like female *ayresii* but rump and nape lack rufous. Longer-tailed Desert C. ranges entirely below Wing-snapping. Zitting C., also lower, has longer brown tail, does not snap wings.) **Range**: Kaptagat, Molo and the Mau, Aberdares, South Kinangop Plateau and Mt Kenya. Formerly Ngong Hills.

TAWNY-FLANKED PRINIA *Prinia subflava melanorhyncha* Plate 101

Length 4.25-5". A sprightly shrub-inhabiting warbler, tawny brown with *creamy white superciliary stripes, blackish lores*, and a long narrow tail with a dark subterminal band and pale feather tips; *flanks and under tail-coverts pale tawny*; tarsi flesh-pink; eyes light brown; bill colour varies seasonally. Tail often held high and wagged back and forth. Tail shorter in breeding season. See Pale Prinia. **Song** a monotonous, measured *cheeup cheeup cheeup . . .* or *chip chip. . .*, repeated 15–20 times; also a dry *brzzt* and a harsh scolding *sbeee.* **Range**: w., cent. and s. Kenya, n. Tanzania, and on coast north to Lamu. Where sympatric with Pale Prinia (Baringo and Tsavo areas), Tawny-flanked occupies the more verdant sites.

PALE PRINIA *Prinia somalica erlangeri* Plate 101

Length 4.5". Inhabits drier country than the similar Tawny-flanked Prinia from which it differs in its *plain creamy underparts* with no tawny on flanks, and *pale brownish grey back.* **Juvenile** tawny or sandy above, with *buff breast and flanks.* **Song** a buzzy note repeated without variation, *dzik, dzik, dzik, dzik . . .* or *zhree zhree zhree . . .*. **Range**: n. and ne. Kenya south to Pokot, Baringo, Isiolo and Garissa districts to Tsavo East NP, and (wanderers?) Tsavo West NP.

BANDED PRINIA *Prinia bairdii melanops* Plate 101

Length 4.5". A unique warbler of western forests. Heavily barred black and white below, dark brown above, black on head, with white tips to wing-coverts, secondaries and tail; eyes yellowish. **Juvenile** brown-eyed, grey or brownish grey on throat and breast, with faint barring. **Song** an emphatic ringing *plee plee plee . . .* or *pink pink pink . . .* in prolonged series; also a metallic *tu-tu-tu-tu-tu-tu* and *pipik-pipik-pipik. . ..* Call note, a hard *chip.* **Range**: Kakamega and Nandi districts south to Sotik, Kericho, Mau and Trans-Mara forests, east to Mau Narok and Molo. Formerly on Mt Elgon.

WHITE-CHINNED PRINIA *Prinia leucopogon reichenowi* Plate 101

Length 4.75–5.5". A long-tailed *western* warbler of moist bush and woodland undergowth. Bluish grey above with a *creamy white throat*; belly and under tail-coverts buff or pale tawny. Scaly-looking forehead and black lores noticeable at close range; eyes dark red. **Song** *tsu-tsu chipichew*, or *tswipi-chew chew-pi-chew tswe tsipi-tsew*. Call a loud chattering by two or more individuals. **Range**: Mt Elgon and Saiwa NP south to Lake Victoria basin, South Nyanza, and nw. Mara GR (Kichwa Tembo); locally in Kabarnet Forest.

RED-WINGED WARBLER *Heliolais erythroptera rhodoptera*   Plate 101

Length 4.75–5.5″. *Prinia-like* with *maroon-rufous wings*; mostly brownish grey (breeding) or dull rufous-brown (non-breeding) above, pale buffy or creamy white below. *Long, strongly graduated tail white-tipped and with black subterminal spots.* Bill long, thin, slightly decurved, brown above, pale pink or whitish below becoming black in breeding season. **Juvenile** resembles non-br. adult but has faint or obsolete tail markings. More arboreal than most prinias, but also forages in bushes, in shrub-grassland, open woods and abandoned cultivation. Smaller Long-tailed Cisticola somewhat similar but lacks rufous on wings. **Song** a loud monotonous *tseep tseep tseep tseep tseep*. Calls include a thin *sit-sit-sit. . .*, and a high-pitched churring. **Range**: E. Tanzania north to East Usambara foothills and Tarangire NP. Also rarely in w. Kenya at Fort Ternan, Muhoroni and Ng'iya.

GREY WREN-WARBLER *Calamonastes simplex*   Plate 100

Length 5″. A *dark brownish grey* bird of undergrowth in dry bush country. Forages low, *slowly moving its black tail up and down.* At close range, shows *faint whitish barring on sides and flanks* and pale tawny leg feathering above *blue-grey tarsi*; eyes red. **Juvenile** paler below with fainter barring. **Song** a distinctive sharp note repeated steadily, suggesting striking of two stones together, *tsuk, tsuk, tsuk, tsuk . . ..* See Pale Wren-Warbler. **Range**: Kenya, north, east and south of the highlands, and ne.Tanzania from Lake Natron east to Mkomazi GR and the Masai Steppe.

PALE WREN-WARBLER *Calamonastes undosus*   Plate 100

Length 5″. Paler and browner than Grey Wren-Warbler, with *pinkish-orange tarsi; tail uniform with rump and back*, not darker as in that species; *underparts greyish white with conspicuous barring* on throat, lower breast and upper belly. Tail motion less persistent than that of *simplex*. **Song** a rather sharp, measured *wheet* or *weeu* repeated several times, with an occasional more plaintive trisyllabic note: *weeu, weeu, weeu, weeu, weeu, teeueet*. **Range** primarily Tanzanian; in our area from Serengeti NP and Loliondo north to Mara GR and Loita Hills in sw. Kenya.

GREY-BACKED CAMAROPTERA or BLEATING WARBLER *Camaroptera brachyura*   Plate 103

Length 4″. A small *short-tailed* warbler, common and widespread in tangled vegetation and forest undergrowth. Varies subspecifically and seasonally; most are grey-backed (some non-breeders much browner) with *yellow-green wings; tail has indistinct dark subterminal band.* Northern races *tincta* and *abessinica* dark grey to brownish grey above, dull white or grey below and on face (*tincta* has no non-br. dress but *abessinica* becomes brownish above); *griseigula* always more brownish grey with brown flanks; *erlangeri* grey-backed but olive-green on scapulars, silky white below, though non-br. plumage greyer or buff on sides, and washed with brown above. These races all grey-tailed. Southeastern *pileata* has *yellow-green back, wings and tail*, grey head and underparts. **Juvenile** *erlangeri* and *pileata* yellowish below; young of interior races resemble adults but paler, with or without yellow ventral wash. In w. Kenya see Olive-green Camaroptera. Usual **song** of inland birds a repeated hard *CHITIP CHITIP CHITIP . . .* . Also a loud, continuous, petulant *pyaa pyaa . . .* or *tee-tee-tee-tee. . .*, a querulous bleating *squeeee* and a short *spee*. Produces a loud *trrip* sound with wings. **Range**: *C. b. pileata* on Tanzanian coast and East Usambaras; *erlangeri* in interior ne.

Tanzania (intergrading with *pileata* in Usambaras) and coastal Kenya inland to edge of cent. plateau; *griseigula* from n.-cent. Tanzania north to Kapenguria and Maralal; *abessinica* from Ethiopian border south to Marsabit and Baringo; *tincta* in w. Kenya south of Mt Elgon, east to Kakamega.

OLIVE-GREEN CAMAROPTERA *Camaroptera chloronota toroensis* Plate 103

Length 4″. A small, *short-tailed* warbler of *west Kenyan forests*. Dull brownish olive above, the wings brighter olive-green. *Sides of face, including short superciliaries, tawny*, and a tawny brown band across lower throat and breast. *Juvenile* *olive-green above, pale yellowish below with lower throat, breast and flanks olive*. Some birds have dark greenish throat and breast contrasting with yellowish chin and belly. (Young Grey-backed Camaroptera is yellowish below but greyer above than *chloronota*, with contrasting olive-green wings. Green Crombec is much shorter-tailed, longer-billed, dingier, lacks tawny face and is not a forest species.) **Song** loud, remarkably prolonged and ventriloquial, consisting of a single short penetrating note repeated *for several minutes without pause: pee-ee-ee-ee-ee-ee-ee-ee-ee-ee-ee-ee-ee.* . .. Less frequent is a prolonged *tewi-tewi-tewi-tewi* . . .. Usual contact call a plaintive *wheet-wheet*. Annoyance call a clear *pwee, pwee, pwee* . . .. **Range**: Kakamega and Nandi forests. Formerly on Mt Elgon.

YELLOW-BREASTED APALIS *Apalis flavida*   Plate 100

Length 4–5″. A common arboreal warbler with a broad *yellow breast band*, yellow-olive upperparts and *yellowish tail-feather tips*. *Central black spot* in breast band reduced or lacking in females and some males. Racially variable: southwestern *caniceps* has top of head grey, little or no black in breast band in any plumage, short tail, and small, pale rectrix tips; Tanzanian *golzi* is grey on crown, but long-tailed and has large black breast spot; long-tailed *pugnax* of Kenyan highlands has only forehead, forecrown and sides of face grey, broad yellow breast band with central black spot in male, and broad yellow rectrix tips; under tail-coverts yellow, not white as in southeastern *tenerrima* (or *neglecta*) which also has black breast spot. *These races are green-tailed*. Northern and eastern *A. f. flavocincta*, a dry-country bird, has *brown upper tail surface*, is *grey only on forehead*, has *no black breast spot in any plumage* and *pale yellow to whitish rectrix tips*. **Juveniles** paler dull olive above, yellow on breast, show a whitish eye-ring. **Song** (*A. f. pugnax* and *caniceps*): *chidiup chidiup chidiup* . . . or a camaroptera-like *chidip chidip* . . . (male) and *cheeea-cheea-cheea-cheea* (female). Other songs include *cheedo cheedo cheedle cheedle cheedle cheedle*, or *chier chier chier*, and a distinctive *sqieeu-kik-kik-kik-kik-kik*. Songs of *flavocincta* faster and higher-pitched. Call a single *cheerr*. **Range**: *caniceps* in Lake Victoria basin (Siaya and Kisumu districts); *pugnax* in the Kenyan highlands from Karissia Hills south to Chyulu Hills (possibly to Kilimanjaro and Mt Meru); *flavocincta* in n. Kenya, south in the east to Taita District (said to reach Lamu and Manda islands and Tanga by some authors) and the Usambaras where intergrading with *golzi* of dry interior Tanzania (Traylor), which ranges north to Taita Hills; *tenerrima*, of humid coastal lowlands in se. Kenya and ne. Tanzania where it apparently meets *golzi* without intergradation. **Taxonomic Notes:** *A. f. pugnax* is the race called *flavocincta* by most authors prior to 1986; current *flavocincta* is the former *malensis*. Some merge *tenerrima* with s. African *neglecta*.

CHESTNUT-THROATED APALIS *Apalis p. porphyrolaema*   Plate 100

Length 4.5″. A distinctive arboreal warbler of highland forest; *grey*, with *rufous chin and throat*; outer tail feathers with small pale tips and edges. **Juvenile** olive-tinged above, with *yellowish chin, throat and cheeks*; rest of underparts yellowish white. **Song** a high trill preceded by 1–2 chipping notes: *chi-chi trrrrrrrrrrrr*, or a simpler *chirrrreeeeeeeeeee* repeated several times. **Range**: Mt Elgon and Cherangani Hills to Aberdares and Mt Kenya, south to Mau Forest, Nguruman Hills and Crater Highlands.

BUFF-THROATED APALIS *Apalis rufogularis nigrescens*   Plate 100

Length 4″. A dimorphic arboreal bird of *west Kenyan forests. Tail appears white from below*; upperparts blackish brown in both sexes. **Male** white below, faintly buff on throat. **Female** *tawny buff from chin to upper breast*. **Juvenile** *greyish olive above, the female* faintly tinged buff on chin and throat; male evenly yellow below. (Chestnut-throated Apalis suggests female, but is grey below with a rufous throat. Black-headed Apalis resembles male, but longer tail is dark beneath with white only at tip. Tail of Grey Apalis appears all white below, but crown is brownish and underparts wholly white.) Two **song** types: *sureet sreet sreet sreet sreet sreet*, and a loud emphatic *chirrip* or *chidip* (recalling Yellow-breasted A.), often slightly trilled. **Range**: Mt Elgon, Kakamega and Nandi forests; formerly at Mumias.

GREY APALIS *Apalis c. cinerea*   Plate 100

Length 4.75". An active warbler of highland forest canopy. *Tail appears entirely white from beneath; crown brown* in male, grey-brown (contrasting little with the grey back in female); underparts white; eyes red-brown. **Juvenile** tinged yellow below, especially on throat. In w. Kenya see male Buff-throated Apalis; in Nguruman Hills and Tanzania see Brown-headed Apalis. **Song** a somewhat metallic *chip chip chip chip . . . or chip-it chip-it . . .* the note repeated up to 30 times, by both sexes; also a high trill ending with a few chips. **Range:** Marsabit, Mathews Range and Mt Elgon south to Mau and Trans-Mara forests, the Aberdares, Mt Kenya and Nairobi, and from the Nguruman Hills to Loliondo in n. Tanzania.

*BROWN-HEADED APALIS *Apalis alticola*   Plate 100

Length 4.75". A southern species closely resembling Grey Apalis; *crown and face dark chocolate-brown or rufous brown, and outer tail feathers grey with white outer webs and tips* (not entirely white); next three pairs of feathers have smaller white tips. Sexes alike. Eyes pale orange or orange-brown. **Juvenile** more olive-grey above, faintly yellowish below. Where sympatric with Grey Apalis (Nguruman Hills) apparently only at edges, not in forest interior. **Song** a loud *chip-it, chip it . . .* recalling Grey Apalis but sometimes accelerated as a rattle. **Range:** Mbulu and Crater highlands north to Loliondo and the Nguruman Hills.

BLACK-HEADED APALIS *Apalis melanocephala*   Plate 100

Length 4.75–6". A *dark-backed* arboreal forest warbler *with black face and whitish underparts*. **Male** *A. m. melanocephala* is dusky or brownish black above, darker on head, black on sides of face; breast sometimes buff-tinged; *tail dark grey with white feather tips*. (Similar Grey and male Buff-throated Apalises have the tail largely white below.) **Female** paler and faintly olive above, the face contrastingly blackish. Darker, very long-tailed race *nigrodorsalis* velvety brownish black above. *A. m. moschi*, also long-tailed, has paler dusky grey upperparts. **Juvenile** greyish olive above, black on lores and below eyes, pale yellow from chin to breast and along mid-ventral line to belly. **Song** loud and monotonous, *wheet wheet wheet wheet wee wee wee . . . or uwee uwee uwee . . .*. Birds may duet. **Range**: *A. m. melanocephala* in coastal forest, inland to East Usambaras, Shimba Hills and lower Tana River; *moschi* from West Usambara and Pare mts to Kilimanjaro, Mt Meru and on Mt Kasigau; *nigrodorsalis* in Kenyan highlands from Nairobi north to the Aberdares, Mt Kenya and Meru forests. Specimens from Mt Endau and Chyulu Hills intermediate between *nigrodorsalis* and nominate race.

BLACK-THROATED APALIS *Apalis j. jacksoni*   Plate 100

Length 4.5". A handsome yellow-bellied warbler of Kenyan highland forests. **Male** has *black face and black throat* separated by *long white malar stripes*; back and rump bright olive-green. **Female** duller with paler grey crown, face and throat. **Juvenile** still duller, greenish yellow on crown and throat in female, greyer in male. **Song** a loud monotonous *chu chu chu . . .* or *chip chip chip . . .*, or *kreek-kreek-reek-reek-reek . . .*; may be disyllabic *che-chip, che-chip . . .* or *tuTEE-ku, TEE-ku, TEE-ku . . .*; these typically duet performances by members of a pair, but notes are neither perfectly synchronised nor regularly antiphonal. Several birds may call together. **Range**: Mt Elgon and Cheranganis south through Nandi, Mau and Trans-Mara forests to Lolgorien

and Nguruman Hills; east of the Rift Valley from Meru, Mt Kenya and the Aberdares south to Limuru and Nairobi.

WHITE-WINGED APALIS *Apalis c. chariessa*   **Plate 100**

Length 5″. A rare arboreal bird of the lower Tana River gallery forests. **Male** glossy greenish black above with *white stripe on wing. Upper throat and cheeks white,* with lower throat and foreneck black. Underparts otherwise bright yellow, deepening to orange on breast; tail (except central feathers) tipped white. **Female** has head, sides of face, wings, tail and part of lower neck grey, the back and rump olive-green. (Highland Black-throated Apalis has entire throat black, lacks white wing-stripe.) **Juvenile** resembles female, but centre of lower neck yellow. **Song** (of *A. c. macphersoni* in Malawi) reportedly a rather slow, repeated *tweety tweety* . . . and a more rapid *teety-teetup* or *tweety-chy*. **Range:** Mitole and near Baomo (3 specimens, 1878 and 1961). Mitole forest now cleared, but possibly suitable habitat remains near Baomo in the Tana River Primate Reserve.)

BLACK-COLLARED APALIS *Apalis p. pulchra*   **Plate 100**

Length 4.5–5″. An attractive *tail-wagging* warbler of highland forest undergrowth and creepers. *Broad black breast band and rufous flanks and belly* distinctive. **Juvenile** has dark grey breast band. **Song** a series of loud complaining notes, *pweu PYEE PYEE PYEE PYEE* . . ., or *cher, CHEWI CHEWI CHEWI*. . . or *PEET-PEET-PEET, PEET*. . .; also *kwi-kwi, kwer kwer*. **Range:** Mt Elgon, Saiwa NP and the Cheranganis south to Mau and Trans-Mara forests, Nairobi, the Aberdares, Mt Kenya and Meru District.

BAR-THROATED APALIS *Apalis thoracica*   **Plate 100**

Length 4.5″. A rather stocky apalis represented in our region by 4 distinct races: *A. t. griseiceps* is brown- or grey-capped, bright yellow-olive on back, with *narrow black breast band* and yellow belly. **Juvenile** more greenish on head, with less distinct breast band. *A. t. murina* has *grey upperparts and little yellow* on belly. Similar *A. t. pareensis* has trace of yellow on lower belly and flanks. *A. t. fuscigularis* has brownish chin and *entire throat and breast black* and upperparts mostly dark grey. **Song** of *murina* involves fairly rapid repetition of one syllable, with short pause between sequences: *tjil tjil-tjil, tjil tjil-tjil tjil* . . .; alarm call a sharp, almost metallic ticking, one note uttered in rapid sequence without pause: *tik-tik-tik-tik* (Ripley and Heinrich). Usual call of *griseiceps* a frequently repeated *pii*, slightly disyllabic and recalling Grey-backed Camaroptera. *A. t. fuscigularis* has a loud penetrating *chwee-chwee-chwee* . . . or *chewik chewik chewik*, reminiscent of songs of more southern races; also some high thin notes. **Range:** *murina* in West Usambaras; *pareensis* in South Pare Mts, *griseiceps* in Mbulu Highlands, Oldeani, Longido, Monduli, Arusha NP, on Kilimanjaro and in Chyulu Hills; *fuscigularis* restricted to Taita Hills.

LONG-BILLED APALIS or MOREAU'S TAILORBIRD *Apalis* [*Artisornis*] *m. moreaui*   **Plate 123**

Length 4.25″ A *long-billed* grey warbler of dense vine tangles in the East Usambara Mts. Shy and elusive. Grey with tawny-tinged face. **Song** a whistled *tcheu-tcheu-tcheu-tcheu-tcheu*, sharp and mechanical. At times almost disyllabic: *tchwee-tchwee* . . . or *t'wee-t'wee* . . . . **Range:** Rare and extremely local between 900 and 1000 m around Amani and at 1200 m on Mt Nilo. Formerly recorded only in dense forest undergrowth, but the few recent records are mainly in cultivated valleys or adjacent to tea plantations.

RED-CAPPED FOREST WARBLER or AFRICAN TAILORBIRD *Orthotomus* [*Artisornis*] *m. metopias*   **Plate 123**

Length 4″. A long-billed, chestnut-headed warbler of forest undergrowth in the Usambara Mts. **Juvenile** duller and greyer than adult, with olive-yellow wash on underparts. **Song** of two short loud notes followed by a trill. Call, a soft *swee-swee-swee* or more wiry *siree-siree-siree* . . . also low humming notes. **Range:** 1200–2100 m in the West Usambaras; rare in the eastern range where formerly at Amani (900 m). **Taxonomic Note:** Many authors consider this and the previous species to be related to the Asian tailorbirds.

RED-FRONTED WARBLER *Spiloptila [Urorhipis] rufifrons*   **Plate 100**

Length 4.25". A *rufous-capped, apalis-like* warbler of low *dry bush; tail long and black, white-tipped* except for central feathers, often *held erect or bent forward and incessantly wagged sideways.* Rufous may be restricted to forehead or extend to nape or back. The race *rufifrons* grey-brown above; *rufidorsalis* brighter, with entire back washed rufous and underparts more tawny. Some (oldest?) adult males of this race have black band across upper breast. See Long-tailed Cisticola. **Songs** (*S. r. rufifrons*) include a high *tsee-it tsee-it tsee-it.* . ., suggesting a thin apalis song, and a louder *chee-ip chee-ip chee-ip.* . .. Alarm call, *seep-seep* or *speek, speek. S. r. rufidorsalis* gives a *spi-spi-hee-hee-hee* (Moreau). **Range**: *S. r. rufifrons* (= *smithi*) in n. Kenya south to Kerio Valley, Baringo, Isiolo, Wajir and Garissa districts, and along the Tana River to Bura and Ijara; also from Mosiro and Olorgesailie south to Lake Natron and across the Masai Steppe to Mkomazi GR, Pare foothills and around Lake Jipe; *rufidorsalis* in Tsavo area.

GREY-CAPPED WARBLER *Eminia lepida*   **Plate 101**

Length 6". A unique thickset warbler, yellowish green above, and the *grey crown bordered by a broad black line* through eyes and around occiput; *throat patch and bend of wing chestnut.* **Juvenile** duller with little chestnut on throat. Stays well hidden, but highly vocal, especially during rainy season. Pairs duet from rank cover in damp ravines, on riverbanks, etc. Male's **song** loud and variable with reeling, trilling and/or explosive notes, e.g. *churrrrrrrrr, WEE-WEE-WEE-WEE,* or *WHER-CHEEW-CHEEW-CHEEW-CHEEW,* or *TWEE TWEE CHU-CHU-CHU-CHU*; to these, female often adds a loud *WIRRRRRRR.* Call a short trilled *treeee.* **Range**: Lake Victoria basin and Kenyan highlands south to the Crater Highlands.

KRETSCHMER'S LONGBILL *Macrosphenus k. kretschmeri*   **Plate 101**

Length 5.75". A shy *greenbul-like* forest bird, olive with a greyish head, *white eyes* and *long straight bill;* tail olive-brown. Bill dark above, pale below; feet whitish flesh or lilac-pink. (Sympatric Little Greenbul is stockier and with a much shorter bill. Tiny Greenbul is more olive on head, greyer below, and has yellow eyes. Grey-olive Greenbul is browner above with more rufous tail.) **Song** also somewhat bulbul-like, of 3 or 4 notes, and uttered once every five or six seconds for long periods: *week, tyeuk-er-eek* or *tweet, euker-rik.* Also a clear *ker-ip* and a low *charr* . **Range**: In our region largely between 900 and 1550 m in the Usambara Mts, but recently (July 1996) rediscovered on Kilimanjaro (above Moshi). Formerly to Kenya's Kitovu Forest near Taveta (where no suitable habitat remains).

NORTHERN CROMBEC *Sylvietta brachyura*   **Plate 103**

Length 3". A 'nuthatch-warbler' with a *distinct facial pattern.* Typically pale grey above and rufous below, *whitish on throat and belly.* Side of face with whitish superciliary stripe (pale tawny in western *S. b. carnapi*) and *dusky eye-line.* **Juvenile** has tawny-tipped wing-coverts. (Larger Red-faced Crombec is plain-faced and uniformly rufous-buff below.) **Song** a short *chiorchi-chiririchi chiorchi-chiririchi.* Calls include a dry *trrr,* a sharp double *tick-tick* and an excited *chichichichi.* **Range**: *S. b. carnapi* local on north shore of Lake Victoria and in drier northern parts of Trans-Nzoia District. *S. b. leucopsis* is north, east and south of the highlands from northern border areas south to Amboseli and the Tsavo parks, and in northernmost Tanzania including Mkomazi GR (where common).

RED-FACED CROMBEC *Sylvietta whytii*   **Plate 103**

Length 3.5" A plain, stub-tailed warbler, typically with *uniformly rufous or rufous-buff face and underparts; no eye-lines or superciliary stripes* as in Northern Crombec. Pale northwestern *loringi* is more olive-brown above, whitish on belly, and coastal *minima* is also somewhat paler than the more richly coloured widespread race *jacksoni.* **Juvenile** has tawny-edged wing-coverts. **Song** a thin, decidedly patterned *WEE-see-see, WEE-wee-*

see or see-si-si SEEEEE, repeated; varied to a rhythmic chichirri-chichirri-chichirri. Less common is a louder chit-wit-weer-CHWEER-CHWEER-CHWEER. Contact note between members of a pair a dry chick. **Range**: loringi at Lokichokio, s. Turkana and Pokot districts; jacksoni from Mt Elgon and Baringo District south to Serengeti NP, the Masai Steppe and Mkomazi GR; minima in coastal areas, intergrading with jacksoni inland.

SOMALI LONG-BILLED CROMBEC Sylvietta isabellina   Plate 103

Length 3.75". A pale crombec of dry northern and eastern Kenya. Bill nearly as long as the head. Ash-grey above; underparts buffy white or cream, occasionally pale tawny on flanks. **Juvenile** duller than adult, with slightly mottled throat. (Somewhat similar dry-country birds are Yellow-vented Eremomela, which has shorter bill and some pale yellow on lower belly/vent region, and Mouse-coloured Penduline Tit with longer tail and shorter bill.) **Song** a repeated tichit-tichit-tiri-chirichirichirichiri. **Range**: Ethiopian border areas south to Tsavo East NP, occasionally to the Tsavo River and Maktau areas of Tsavo West NP.

WHITE-BROWED CROMBEC Sylvietta l. leucophrys   Plate 103

Length 3.5". An 'eye-browed' crombec of highland forest, usually in undergrowth and among vines. Chestnut-brown crown, bold white superciliary stripes and dark eye-lines create striking head pattern; yellow green wing edgings noticeable; back dark olive. **Juvenile** at fledging has brown crown with no trace of superciliary stripes, is pale yellow on lower breast and belly, brown from chin to chest and along sides. Older immature has pale greenish yellow superciliaries, and dark olive-brown of breast extends in a point onto centre of throat. **Song** short, clear and ending in a trill: tee-tee-tee-trrrrrrrrrrrrrrrr. **Range**: Mt Elgon south to Trans-Mara forest, and from the Aberdares to Limuru, Naro Moru and Mt Kenya. Formerly in Nairobi area.

*GREEN CROMBEC Sylvietta virens baraka   Plate 103

Length 3.5". A dull-coloured, slender-billed crombec of dense high bush near the Kenya/Uganda border. Dark olive or olive-brown above, with brighter olive-green on primaries visible on unworn birds. Crown and nape sepia-brown; sides of face, throat and chest cinnamon-brown; chin whitish; rest of underparts greyish, almost white in centre of belly. Indistinct short pale buff superciliary stripes noticeable at close range. (Short-tailed juv. Olive-green Camaroptera, sometimes mistaken for this species, is a forest bird, yellowish below with olive on lower throat, breast and flanks. Adult growing new tail is even more similar, but wings brighter olive and face tawny.) **Juvenile** paler with greenish yellow wash on underparts. **Song** variable, loud and rapid: stereeetisu, seet-seet-seet and sit-sit-stueetsisew CHEEsu CHEEsu. Call, chi-chi-chit. **Range**: Busia and Mumias districts. Reports from Kakamega Forest not substantiated. Documented in our region by tape recordings.

YELLOW-BELLIED EREMOMELA Eremomela icteropygialis   Plate 102

Length 3.75". A short-billed, short-tailed warbler of moist bush. Greyish above with bright yellow belly; chin to breast white. Some populations show dusky eye-lines and faint whitish superciliary stripes. Yellow paler and restricted to lower belly in western griseoflava, the colour only marginally more extensive than in Yellow-vented Eremomela. **Juvenile** (both races) paler yellow below than adult and often washed with olive on back. **Song** a repeated, short, cheerful cheri-chee-chit-chit CHWEER or a shorter chee-churi CHEEa. Call note a high chit. **Range**: E. i. abdominalis at Moyale and Mandera, and from Isiolo south through Magadi and Ambolesi to Tarangire NP, the Masai Steppe and Mkomazi GR; griseoflava from Lokichokio and Turkana south to Serengeti NP and Maswa GR.

YELLOW-VENTED EREMOMELA Eremomela flavicrissalis   Plate 102

Length 3.5". A tiny warbler of dry northern and eastern Kenya; suggests a pale Yellow-bellied Eremomela with the yellow paler and restricted to lower belly/vent region (often difficult to see); under tail-coverts largely white. Most Yellow-bellied Eremomelas have yellow brighter and more extensive. Even in race *griseoflava* the colour extends slightly higher on the belly, and the lower back has an olive tinge. In some ne. border areas sympatric with Yellow-bellied, but the two ecologically separated. Song a high *sureet-seet-seet-seet or seet-seet-seet-seet*. **Range**: Turkana district south to Samburu, Shaba and Kora reserves, lower Tana River and Tsavo East NP.

GREEN-CAPPED EREMOMELA *Eremomela scotops*   Plate 102

Length 4″. An active arboreal warbler of open wooded areas. Pale ashy grey above with greenish crown and sides of head, and bright yellow superciliaries. Eye colour and extent of yellow on underparts vary: coastal birds entirely pale yellow below, and (always?) with buffy yellow eyes; *kikuyuensis* of cent. Kenya bright yellow on throat and breast, otherwise yellowish white below and eyes usually hazel brown; southwestern *citriniceps* has greyish white belly. **Juvenile** paler than adult, more olive above. (Similar Yellow-throated Woodland Warbler has tawny brown crown and yellow under tail-coverts.) **Song** (*E. s. citriniceps*) a loud repeated chatter, *tsip-tsip, chip-chip-chip-chip*, a uniform *tew-tew-tew-tew-tew-tew*, and a short low musical trill, *tur-rrrrrrrr*. Also has a churring alarm call. Reportedly makes snapping sound with wings. **Range**: *E. s. citriniceps* from Mara GR and Loita Hills to n. Serengeti NP; *kikuyuensis* in Thika and Embu districts; nominate *scotops* (incl. 'occipitalis') in open *Brachystegia* stands of coastal Arabuko–Sokoke Forest (and old records from East Usambara foothills).

GREEN-BACKED EREMOMELA *Eremomela pusilla canescens*   Plate 102

Length 4.5″. A warbler of savanna and open woodland, typically foraging in small vocal groups among low trees and shrubs. Mostly yellowish, but grey from forehead to nape, with white throat and a *narrow black mask* through the buffy yellow to yellowish brown eyes. **Juvenile** more olive above and paler yellow below. **Song** rapid, somewhat guttural, of rising and falling phrases, *erreee-turtreeeureeee-tureeeutree*; also a more rolling *urrreet-urreet-rreet-rreet*, and a shorter *reelu reelu reelu*, commonly from several birds together. Call a thin *see-see*. **Range**: ne. Mt Elgon to Kongelai Escarpment and Kerio Valley. Old records from Muhoroni, Kericho and Sotik districts where now little suitable habitat. **Taxonomic Note**: This race sometimes considered specifically distinct from west African *pusilla*.

TURNER'S EREMOMELA *Eremomela turneri*   Plate 102

Length 3.25″. A *tiny*, grey-backed warbler of w. Kenyan forest treetops, often with mixed-species flocks. Shows *black band across the lower throat*, and a *chestnut forehead patch extending back over the eyes*; throat white. **Juvenile** olive-brown above with no chestnut on head or merely a faint rufous wash; pale yellow below with only a suggestion of breast band or unmarked; difficult to identify high in canopy. **Song** a high-pitched rapid series of 8–10 notes, fluctuating little in pitch, *titititititititi*, followed by a slightly louder *si-si-chick or weet-su-sweet*. **Range**: Kakamega Forest. Formerly along the Yala River.

BUFF-BELLIED WARBLER *Phyllolais pulchella*   Plate 100

Length 3.75″. A small plain warbler of acacia woodland and savanna. Dull grey-brown (with slight olive wash) above and pale *creamy yellow below* with a *featureless face*. Narrow blackish tail with white sides and tip. *Bill pinkish at base below*; eyes pale hazel-brown; *tarsi pale pinkish brown*. **Juvenile** darker above, more yellowish below than adults. **Song** a dry ascending trill, uneven, with a terminal buzzy chip or two: *chirrrrrrreerrrr-chk or zhrrrrreeeeeeerreet-chewk-chk*. Contact call, *cht-cht-cht-cht* or *cher cher chit*. **Range**: Lokichokio, Lodwar, the Turkwell and Kerio valleys and Mt Elgon east to Meru NP, south to Serengeti NP, Crater and Mbulu highlands, Tarangire and Arusha NPs. Formerly in Tsavo East NP.

BROWN PARISOMA *Parisoma lugens jacksoni*   **Plate 101**

Length 5.75". A *plain dull brown warbler* partial to acacia trees. *Outer tail feathers narrowly edged and tipped with white*; a little white on edge of wing alongside dark alula; dull whitish throat mottled with dusky at sides; centre of belly whitish. Short **song** begins with a husky slurred whistle, *zuree serichew wurEET*; or *wureet TWEEotew*; sometimes ends in a trill: *dzree suicherrrrrrr*. Alarm call a loud, tit-like, scolding *chee-chee-chee-chee* or *skwee-skwee-skwee*. **Range**: Mt Elgon to Kakamega and Laikipia Plateau, south to Nairobi area; also from Nguruman Hills to the Crater Highlands. Most numerous in and near Rift Valley among *Acacia abyssinica* and *A. xanthophloea*.

BANDED PARISOMA *Parisoma boehmi*   **Plate 101**

Length 4.75". A distinctly patterned arboreal warbler, and like the preceding two species partial to groves of acacia trees (especially *A. tortilis*) where it often feeds near the ground. Greyish brown above and white below with a *black band across upper breast, dusky-spotted throat, and tawny under tail-coverts* (duller in northern birds); much white in wings and at edges of tail. Eyes pale yellow. **Juvenile** has buffy wing-covert tips; lacks breast band and throat spots. **Song** of 'bouncing ball' pattern, sometimes ending in a rapid trill: *chip, chip, chip, chip-chip-chip-ipipipipipip*, or *prit-prit-prit-pruprupririririririri*. **Range**: *P. b. marsabit* from Marsabit and South Horr south to Nanyuki and Meru NP. *P. b. boehmi* is southern, from Mara GR and Serengeti NP east to the Tsavo parks, Mkomazi GR and the Masai Steppe.

SOUTHERN HYLIOTA *Hyliota australis*   **Plate 101**

Length 4.5". A gleaning and flycatching arboreal warbler of forest or forest-edge trees. Shows a *broad white band across the wing-coverts*, and the slightly forked tail has white-edged outer feathers. **Male** velvety brownish black above, including ear-coverts; **female** *grey-brown above*. Both sexes tawny yellow below. Slightly smaller Usambara birds, considered a separate species by some, have the underparts deeper in colour and are said not to be sexually dimorphic. (Similar Yellow-bellied H. has metallic blue gloss on upperparts, inhabits open savannas or shrubby hillsides.) **Song** reportedly of squeaky whistles ending in a trill. Call note a sharp *tsik*. **Range**: *H. a. slatini* in Kakamega and Nandi forests of w. Kenya. Rare Tanzanian *usambarae* between 350 and 1000 m in the Usambara Mts.

YELLOW-BELLIED HYLIOTA *Hyliota flavigaster*   **Plate 101**

Length 4.5". Patterned like the preceding species but **male** *iridescent blue-black above*; **female** *dark grey above, appearing almost blackish*, and with *faint blue-green lustre*. **Juvenile** buff-barred on upperparts, paler below than adult. A bird of savanna, bush and open woodland. **Call** *seek-seek* or *pit-seet* that may lead into a short sputtering song. **Range**: ne. slopes of Mt Elgon, Kongelai Escarpment, and Nambale District, and from Fort Ternan, Kericho and Sotik districts south to nw. Mara GR, occasionally to Sand River area on Kenya/Tanzanian border.

GREEN HYLIA *Hylia p. prasina*   **Plate 96**

Length 4.75". A stocky, dark olive bird of w. Kenyan forests. Note the long pale yellowish superciliaries and strong black bill. (Somewhat similar Uganda Woodland Warbler is smaller, more slender, much paler on belly.) Presumed **song** a loud penetrating double whistle, *tyee-tyee* or *tee-yew*, the first note higher. Alarm call, a rapid harsh chatter, *chreeeeee-che*. **Range**: Kakamega and Nandi forests; formerly Mt Elgon.

WHITE-EYES, FAMILY ZOSTEROPIDAE

Small, warbler-like birds of uncertain affinities. Typically yellow or olive, sometimes greyish below, with conspicuous white or silvery white eye-rings for which the group is named (the eyes are brown). Sexes are alike, and young differ little from adults. White-eyes move among trees and shrubs in restless, softly vocal flocks or in pairs, feeding on insects plus nectar and juices from soft fruits obtained with the brush-tipped tongue. Taxonomic treatments vary. The non-intergrading montane forms, here considered races of *Z. poliogaster*, are merged with *Z. senegalensis* or maintained as several separate species by others. Mt Kulal birds, originally described as a race of *Z. pallidus*, may well belong with that species. The pale *flavilateralis*, now treated as a race of Abyssinian White-eye, has been placed in *senegalensis* and called Yellow White-eye by some authors. Birds here considered *senegalensis* were included in *Z. virens* (Green White-eye) in earlier East African books.

ABYSSINIAN WHITE-EYE *Zosterops abyssinicus*   Plate 102

Length 4". The *pale yellow* white-eye below 1800 m in bush and open wooded areas *in and east of the Rift Valley*. Shows *no contrasting yellow forehead patch*, is black only at base of mandible and below the *narrow white eye-ring*; no black on lores. Greenish yellow above, light powdery yellow below with no trace of green, duller in northern *jubaensis*. (More western Yellow White-eye has greenish sides and flanks, is brighter yellow below, greener above, and eye-ring is broader. Yellow-bellied forms of Montane White-eye are larger with broader eye-rings and broad contrasting forehead patches.) **Call** a buzzing and twittering from foraging groups. Song unrecorded. **Range**: From northern border areas south through lower parts of the cent. Kenyan highlands to Tarangire NP, lowlands near Arusha and Mkomazi GR; also on coast from Sabaki Estuary northwards, and inland along lower Tana River to Baomo. Only known west of the Rift near the Cherangani Hills (specimens, July 1926) and on Kongelai Escarpment (sight records, Sept. 1988, July 1994). Sympatric with *Z. p. kikuyuensis* in n. Nairobi suburbs, with *Z. p. silvanus* in the Taita Hills. Northern birds, south to lowlands around Mt Kulal, are considered *jubaensis*, all others *flavilateralis*.

MONTANE WHITE-EYE *Zosterops poliogaster*   Plates 102, 124
(Includes Kikuyu, Taita, Kulal, South Pare and Broad-ringed White-eyes)

Length 4.5–4.75". A diverse group of *highland* forest forms, probably embracing more than one species, but still poorly known. Widespread central Kenyan *kikuyuensis* is large and bright, with *very broad eye-ring, well-defined golden-yellow forehead*, and black lores. On Kilimanjaro and Mt Meru, *eurycricotus* also has *broad eye-ring but no yellow on forehead*, and *underparts are mostly dark greenish*. Equally large *mbuluensis*, also largely Tanzanian, is golden-yellow below, but *yellow forehead is not sharply defined*, and eye-ring is narrower. Small, *grey-bellied silvanus* of the Taita Hills has a *broad eye-ring but no yellow on forehead*; *winifredae* of South Pares is also *grey-bellied but has yellow forehead and throat*, and narrower eye-ring; *grey-sided kulalensis* of Mt Kulal has relatively narrow eye-ring margined by black below and on lores, and a distinct yellow forehead. (Abyssinian White-eye is smaller, paler, has narrow eye-ring, and less yellow on forehead. Yellow White-eye is more greenish, with much narrower forehead band; eye-ring varies, but never as broad as in *kikuyuensis*.) **Call** a typical white-eye buzzing or twittering from flock. Distinctive calls of *silvanus* include a clear, slightly querulous but not buzzing *rree-tree, ter-ree-tee* or *kwerakwee-kwee-kwee*. Comparable call of *kikukyensis, whii-tu-tu-her-tu* or *whii-tew*. Song of *silvanus* a slow, slightly rising and falling warbling, *see tee tew chew, tew see te tew see-chew. . .*; that of *kikuyuensis* a similar *zhree zhree zhri zhree zhri zhree zhri zhew*. Songs of *kulalensis* and *winifredae* unrecorded. **Range**: Grey-bellied forms isolated on Mt Kulal (*kulalensis*), Mt Kasigau/Taita Hills (*silvanus*), and South Pare Mts (*winifredae*). *Z. p. kikuyuensis* in cent. Kenyan Highlands south to Nairobi; *mbuluensis* from the Mbulu and Crater highlands to the North Pares, Ol Doinyo Orok (Namanga) and the Chyulu Hills; *eurycricotus* in Arusha NP, on Kilimanjaro and nearby mountains.

YELLOW WHITE-EYE *Zosterops senegalensis*   Plate 102

Length 4.5". The common *northern and western forest* white-eye, darker, greener above and brighter yellow below than Abyssinian, and distinguished from yellow-bellied forms of Montane by the *much narrower eye-ring* and *limited forehead band* (obscure in some western birds). Black of loral area extends back under the eye-ring. *Sides, flanks and often a diffuse band across the breast are greenish*, contrasting with yellow throat and belly. Usambara *stierlingi* is darker green above and on flanks, and deeper yellow below than widespread *jacksoni*. Dawn **song** a rising and falling series of 12–30 burry notes of typical *Zosterops* quality, often introduced by 4–5 clear slurred notes: *tree-turri weeeu-teu, dzree-dzriri-dzree chrirri-tseeu-tseu zhree-zhree chew-chew-chew dzi-chew dzi-chew dzi-chew tzee-zizi-chew*, repeated. Calls a repeated rolling raspy *sreeeep*, and a faster *sreep-sreep-sreep*. **Range**: Mainly above 1100 m (and with absence of Montane White-eye on Mt Elgon, there extends to 3400 m in giant heath and moorland.) *Z. s. jacksoni* from mts Marsabit, Nyiru, Loima and Elgon, the Ndotos, Mathews Range and the Karissia Hills south through the w. Kenyan highlands to Mara GR, Loita and Nguruman hills and Loliondo. Ugandan *stuhlmanni* (specimens from Kapenguria) seems to intergrade with *jacksoni* near Busia and Kakamega. *Z. s. stierlingi* in Usambara Mts. Birds in Serengeti NP and near Lake Eyasi not racially assigned.

PEMBA WHITE-EYE *Zosterops vaughani*   **Plate 124**
Length 4″. The only white-eye on Pemba Island. Yellow, brightest on forehead, crown and underparts, with black loral spot and narrow white eye-ring. **Song** high and sweet, shorter than that of Yellow White-eye: *sreet, seweet-sureeteet-twerila-eeta-eet*, the first note distinct, others often run together in a brief warbling. **Range**: Pemba Island and adjacent coral islets. **Taxonomic Note**: Treated by some authors as a race of *Z. senegalensis*, a species absent from the adjacent mainland coastal region.

TITS, FAMILY PARIDAE

Small, rather plump arboreal birds, their tails longer and their short bills less conical than those of penduline tits (Remizidae). The sexes are alike or nearly so. Except when breeding, tits tend to be sociable, moving in noisy restless groups of their own kind or with mixed-species flocks. Busy, active and acrobatic birds, they may hang upside-down as they forage for insects and larvae on twigs. They occupy various wooded habitats, and all nest in tree cavities.

NORTHERN GREY TIT *Parus thruppi barakae*   **Plate 103**

Length 4.5″. Characteristic of dry country. Black crown and bib surround the *large white patch from bill to sides of neck*, and a black mid-ventral streak extends downward from the breast. Grey above with whitish wing edgings, and may show a white nape spot. **Juvenile** has adult's pattern, but black parts duller and wing edgings buff. **Song** a clear whistled *twee-tew-tew-tew* or *tui-tui-tui-tui*, usually of 4–6 notes, frequently repeated. Contact note a buzzy *chya chya*. Annoyance call, a harsh raspy nasal *chewy chewy chewy chewy*, or *tchwaa, tchwaa*. . . . **Range**: North and east of the Kenyan highlands, mainly below 1000 m, south to Baringo and Isiolo districts, the Tsavo NPs and Mkomazi GR .

NORTHERN BLACK TIT *Parus leucomelas guineensis*   **Plate 103**
Length 5.5″. A *black* tit with a *large white patch on wing-coverts*, white-edged flight feathers and *pale yellow eyes*. Rare in moist bush and other wooded habitats in western Kenya. Plumage glossed with violet; *eyes pale yellow*. **Juvenile** duller with no gloss, the white wing patch tinged yellowish. **Song** a clear repeated *cherwee* . Calls weak and rasping. **Range**: Wandered formerly from Uganda to Mt Elgon, Saiwa Swamp, Bungoma and in the Nyando Valley. Most recently at Kapenguria (April 1972), W. Pokot (Nov. 1985) and near Mumias (Dec. 1989).

DUSKY TIT *Parus funereus*   **Plate 103**
Length 5–5.5″. A dark, *red-eyed* tit of west Kenyan forests, often in mixed-species flocks. **Male** blackish slate with very slight green gloss. **Female** slightly duller and greyer. **Juvenile** similar to female, but browner and with narrow whitish wing-covert tips; eyes brown. **Song** a loud persistent *see-er, see-er, see-er*. **Range**: Kakamega and Nandi forests. Formerly on Mt Elgon.

WHITE-BELLIED TIT *Parus albiventris*   **Plate 103**

Length 5.5". Largely black with contrasting *white belly* and *large white patch on wing-coverts*. Secondaries and outer tail feathers conspicuously white-edged in fresh plumage. Female slightly duller than male. **Juvenile** much duller than adult, with yellowish tinged wing edgings. **Song** *chee-er-weeoo, chee-er-wheeoo*. Call a harsh *tss-tss-tcher-tcher-tcher*. **Range**: Generally above 1200 m in the Kenyan highlands, south to the Lake Victoria basin, Mara GR, Amboseli and Tsavo NPs, sparingly in Serengeti and Lake Manyara NPs and Mkomazi GR (where largely replaced by Red-throated Tit).

RED-THROATED TIT *Parus fringillinus*   **Plate 103**

Length 4.5". A small rufous-headed tit of acacia woodland and bush. *Blackish crown* contrasts with pale dull rufous-buff face, throat and breast; back greyish; prominent white wing-feather edges in fresh plumage. **Juvenile** browner on crown and back. **Song** a persistent *see-er, see-er, see-er*. Call a repeated rattling *tsi-chur-ur-ur-ur*, and a a chattering *ch-ch-ch-ch*, often with some squeaky notes. **Range**: Between 1000 and 1600 m in Masailand from Serengeti, Tarangire and Arusha NPs across the Masai steppe, and north (less commonly) through the Mara GR, Namanga, Kajiado and Selengai to s. boundary of Nairobi NP at Athi River. In places, sympatric with White-bellied Tit.

PENDULINE TITS, FAMILY REMIZIDAE

Tiny short-billed birds resembling parids in general habits, but differing in their short tails and sharp conical bills. Like true tits, they are agile and acrobatic in their search for insects. They frequently visit parasitic mistletoe flowers and blooming acacias. The unique nest (see figure overleaf) is a remarkable, tightly woven, felt-like bag of plant down with a tubular side entrance near the top, and suspended from a thin branch. That of *A. caroli* (and presumably *A. musculus*) has a false opening below the real entrance hole which is reportedly closed by the bird on leaving and sometimes after entering.

MOUSE-COLOURED PENDULINE TIT *Anthoscopus musculus*   **Plate 103**

Length 2.5–3.25". A tiny tit-like bird of *dry country*, plain, short-tailed and with a short sharp bill. Upperparts grey to brownish grey; *forehead same colour as crown*; underparts pale creamy or whitish, often faintly buffy on flanks and belly as well as on lores and ear-coverts; side of face marked only by a short dark eye-line; eyes brown. (African Penduline Tit, typically in moister areas, has the forehead paler than the crown. Faded individuals of *A. c. sylviella* suggest Mouse-coloureds, but are buff, not whitish below, on forehead and ear-coverts. Buff-bellied Warbler is long-tailed. Eremomelas and crombecs have longer bills.) **Song** high-pitched and sibilant, a rattling *di-di-di-di-di-di* and a *thin tsee-tsi tsee-tsi tsee-tsi. . ..* Call a short *tsrr* and a squeaky *tsi*. **Range**: Widespread north and east of the Kenyan highlands, south to Baringo and Isiolo districts, Meru and both Tsavo NPs, the North Pare foothills and Mkomazi GR; also (at least formerly) around lakes Magadi and Natron.

AFRICAN PENDULINE TIT *Anthoscopus caroli*   **Plate 103**

Length 3–3.5". Typically in moister regions than *A. musculus*, in open wooded areas and forest edge. Differs from *musculus* in its *brighter plumage and pale forehead*, but racially variable: *A. c. sylviella* is grey above, deep buff or pale rusty buff below and *forehead usually rusty buff*; similar **sharpei** of Lake Victoria basin is darker below with *whitish* forehead; eastern **robertsi** is grey or greyish olive above, buffy to yellowish or pale tawny below; western **roccattii** bright greenish olive above with *yellowish forehead and underparts*. (Mouse-coloured Penduline Tit is paler, lacks pale forehead and inhabits drier country.) **Song**: (*sylviella*) a somewhat metallic thin 2–3-sec. trill, *sreeeeeeeee-ee-ee-ee*. Other calls (subspecies?) include a rasping *chiZEE, chiZEEE, chiZEE* and a squeaky *skee-chi-skee-chi-zee*. **Range**: Local, mainly below 2000

African Penduline Tit at nest

m: *sylviella* in interior e. Kenya from Kitui and Athi River south to Voi, Taita Hills, Simba, and Longido; *robertsi* formerly in coastal Kenya, inland to Taru, Usambara Mts. and Naberera, but no recent records; *roccattii* from Mt Elgon to Kongelai Escarpment and Saiwa NP; *sharpei* from Kakamega south to Lake Victoria basin, Mara GR, Nguruman Hills and Serengeti NP. Also (subspecies?) Lake Baringo, Kerio Valley and Nakuru area.

CREEPERS, FAMILY CERTHIIDAE

Our single species differs from holarctic treecreepers in that the tail is not specialised for support, being soft and rounded, and held away from the bark during climbing. Like other creepers, it has a slender curved bill, strong feet, and sharply curved claws adapted to bark-clinging. The sexes are alike, and plumage is cryptically patterned. The nest is a compact lichen-covered cup in or near a horizontal tree fork.

SPOTTED CREEPER *Salpornis spilonotus salvadori*   **Plate 103**
Length 5.5". A boldly *white-spotted tree-climbing* bird with a thin, decurved bill and white superciliary stripes; tail barred black and white. Favours large, flat-topped acacias. Flight undulating and woodpecker-like. Joins foraging mixed species flocks. **Song** a shrill, thin, high-pitched *sweepy-swip-swip-swip*. Call a single *swee*. **Range**: Endangered. Extirpated from most areas owing to loss of habitat. Now localized around Kapenguria in nw. Kenya.

MONARCH FLYCATCHERS, FAMILY MONARCHIDAE

Active birds of tree canopy in forest, woodland, and gardens. Excepting *Erythrocercus*, they are crested, with long to very long graduated tails and rather broad flat bills. The sexes are alike or similar; juveniles differ from those of true flycatchers (Muscicapidae) in their unspotted plumage. Most are foliage-gleaners but they also pursue aerial prey.

LITTLE YELLOW FLYCATCHER *Erythrocercus holochlorus*   **Plate 102**

Length 3.75". A *warbler-like* bird of coastal forest, yellow-olive above and *bright yellow below;* face rather plain, but shows a narrow yellowish eye-ring at close range. **Song** of 3 or 4 notes, sweet, snappy and warbler-like, *wee-see-SEEu; si-SEEu-WEET;* or *sweechee-seeu; wichi-see-see,* any of these sometimes modified by addition of a chattering initial trill, *trrrrrrrrr.* Call an emphatic *cheu.* **Range**: Coastal areas, lower Tana River, Shimba Hills, and below 1000 m in the East Usambara Mts.

AFRICAN BLUE FLYCATCHER *Elminia longicauda teresita*   **Plate 88**

Length 5.5". A dainty crested monarch, *cerulean blue* above. Lively and conspicuous, fanning the long graduated tail (which shows no white), drooping the wings, twisting about and darting between perches. (Tanzanian White-tailed Blue Flycatcher has conspicuous white outer tail feathers.) **Juvenile** paler with buff-edged feathers above. **Song** a rapid featureless sputtering, *chiti-chi-chee-chee spitisti chitisi chi-chi-chi chi-tisee chit . . .* and a sharper *dzreet tsit stereeeu tsit-tsit-tsit tsereee tsit . .* . . Calls include a sharp high *chink* and a thin *chee*. **Range**: Below 2400 m in w. Kenya, from Mt Elgon, Kapenguria and Saiwa NP south to Kericho, Lolgorien and w. Mara GR.

WHITE-TAILED BLUE FLYCATCHER *Elminia albicauda*   **Plate 124**

Length 5.5". Tanzanian. Suggests a dull African Blue Flycatcher but shows *much white in the tail*, and is less blue than preceding species, especially on breast. **Call** a sharp *tip-tip*, alternating with whistled *teereet* notes. Song described as a short pretty warbling. **Range**: Mbulu Highlands north to Karatu and Marang forests in the Crater Highlands.

WHITE-TAILED CRESTED FLYCATCHER *Trochocercus albonotatus*   **Plate 88**

Length 5". The *broadly white-tipped tail* of this *montane forest* monarch is *frequently spread* as the bird flits about. Shows black head, throat and upperparts, whitish breast, flanks and belly. *T. a. subcaeruleus* is slightly paler above than nominate *albonotatus*. **Juvenile** dark grey on face and throat. (Blue-mantled Crested Flycatcher is more bluish grey above, with white wing markings, and lacks white in the tail.) **Song** of 4–5 thin sharp notes, *tseu, tseu-tseu-tseu*. Common call a high-pitched metallic *pink-pink*. **Range**: *T. a. albonotatus* in the w. and cent. Kenyan highlands, from Mt Elgon and Saiwa NP south to the North Nandi, Kericho, Mau and Trans-Mara forests, east to s. Aberdares, e. Mt Kenya and the Nyambenis. *T. a. subcaeruleus* in the Usambara Mts (mainly 900–2000 m, lower in cold seasons).

BLUE-MANTLED CRESTED FLYCATCHER *Trochocercus cyanomelas bivittatus*
Plate 88

Length 5". A small eastern forest monarch with a prominent floppy crest erected in display or excitement. Forages in undergrowth or lower canopy. Acrobatic and restless, frequently fanning tail, clinging first to one side of a branch, then the other. **Male** *glossy blue-black from head to breast*, slaty blue above with a *conspicuous white wing patch*. **Female** paler with grey head and upperparts, conspicuous white eye-ring and two *narrow white wing-bars*; underparts white except for *grey-mottled breast*. **Juvenile** resembles female but has buff-tipped wing-coverts. **Song** a loud mellow *kew-wu-wu-wu-wu and tew-witi-tew-ti-tee-tew*, at times ending with several chips. Calls include a rasping *zhi* or *zhi-wa* and a harsh *zwer-zwer-zwer-zwer*; also has a high twittering *tit-titititititi* and a repeated *skwi-yaa-yaa* followed by some high soft whistled notes. **Range:** Coastal lowlands, inland to Mt Kasigau, Taveta District (formerly?), Kitovu, Chyulu Hills and Mt Endau. Records from Meru Forest (1993) and w. Nairobi suburbs (1994) unique in recent decades. In n. Tanzania scarce and local up to 900 m in the East Usambara Mts, more numerous above 1500 m in Arusha and Moshi districts and North Pare Mts.

DUSKY CRESTED FLYCATCHER *Trochocercus nigromitratus*   **Plate 88**

Length 5". A small dark crested monarch of *west Kenyan forest undergrowth*. **Male** *dark bluish slate* with *top of head, wings and tail black*. **Female** and **juvenile** duller and less bluish. **Song** of clear, shrill, short notes, *sreet tseeu seet* (last note higher), *sreet tseu* (second note lower), or any of these notes given singly. Contact call a rather harsh *tick*. Annoyance call a harsh chattering. **Range**: Kakamega Forest, Chemoni Forest, Nandi Hills, and formerly Mt Elgon.

AFRICAN PARADISE FLYCATCHER *Terpsiphone viridis*   Plate

Length 7–7.5" excluding adult male's *long central tail feathers* which may extend 6–7" beyond other rectrices. An active dimorphic monarch with dark crested head and *grey belly*; bill and orbital ring bright blue. Some birds bright orange-rufous on back and tail, others (**white morph**) with white back and tail and much white in wings. **Female** and **young male** have only slightly elongated central rectrices. *T. v. ferreti* is glossy greenish black from head to breast with large white wing patch in male; eastern *ungujaensis* may lack white in the wings but has some whitish on belly; coastal *plumbeiceps* is dull bluish black from forehead to nape, and generally lacks white in wings. In w. Kenya see Red-bellied Paradise Flycatcher. **Song** of rapidly delivered, mellow ringing notes, *whee-wheeo-whit-whit* or *tu-whiddle tuWEE*; or *zwitty-weep-weepa-weep*. Has various rasping calls, e.g. *zwa-i-zer*; *zhweet-zhwait*; *wiZHEER* and *skwee-chi-chi-chwee*. **Range**: *T. v. ferreti* is widespread (most breeding records in or near the highlands); white morph common in eastern bush country but scarce at higher elevations; *ungujaensis* in ne. Tanzania from Usambara Mts southward, intergrading with *ferreti* in North Pare Mts and Moshi District; *plumbeiceps* along the coast north at least to Arabuko–Sokoke Forest, mainly as a non-breeding visitor from the southern tropics, but may breed on Pemba Island.

RED-BELLIED PARADISE FLYCATCHER *Terpsiphone rufiventer emini*   **Plate 88**
Length 6.25–8″. A western *forest-interior* bird with an entirely *orange-rufous* body. **Male** has *black head* sharply separated from colour of back and breast; crest short or lacking; central tail feathers only slightly elongated but sometimes extending well beyond rest of tail. **Female** may be greyer on throat. Hybridizes with preceding species producing intermediates with well-developed crests, elongated central tail feathers, grey or whitish breast feathers, a little white on the wings, or some combination of these characters. Most birds observed in recent years appear to be hybrids. **Call** a harsh *zhre-zhre* or *zree-zree*, much like that of African Paradise Flycatcher. **Range**: Kakamega Forest (where increasingly scarce, possibly genetically 'swamped' through interbreeding with African Paradise Flycatcher as remnant forest stands are thinned).

BATISES, WATTLE-EYES AND RELATIVES, FAMILY PLATYSTEIRIDAE

Small birds with somewhat flattened bills and pronounced rictal bristles; formerly considered muscicapids. The two *Bias* species are unique, sexually dimorphic, flycatcher-like birds. **Wattle-eyes** are forest birds sporting brightly coloured orbital wattles. Both *Platysteira* are relatively slender with ample tails, *Dyaphorophyia* are plump and stubtailed. As in *Batis*, their long fluffy rump feathers can be raised in a puff above the back. They also share with *Batis* various wing-flicking sounds and intriguing semi-musical songs. **Batises** (pronounced with a long 'a') are small foliage-gleaners that also indulge in flycatching. Some are quite vocal; true songs are supplemented by quaint piping contact notes often accompanied by audible wing sounds—*prrrt, prrrt* or *firrrrup*—as the bird flies from branch to branch. Bill-snapping is frequent. General behaviour is quite uniform throughout the genus. Most batises are confusingly similar in plumage. Males are grey, black and white with a black breast band; females have some chestnut or tawny below, often including a breast band. Both sexes show a white spot on the nape. Species recognition involves knowledge of *crown colour, relative tail length, throat pattern, eye colour and extent of the superciliary stripes*, although the last feature is affected by plumage wear and by degree of feather erection (a batis can show conspicuous superciliaries one minute and none the next). Grey crown feathers become blackish with wear, and a glossy black cap appears deceptively lighter in strong light. Our six species tend to segregate geographically and/or ecologically, although 2 or 3 may be sympatric in some areas.

CHIN-SPOT BATIS *Batis molitor*   **Plate 86**

Length 4″. The most widespread inland batis; typically at higher elevations. Does not reach the coastal lowlands which are occupied by other species. **Female** readily identified by *sharply defined dark chestnut throat spot*. **Male** has broad black breast band. The *slate-grey crown* can appear blackish when worn, but is *always lighter than the jet-black ear-coverts*; narrow white superciliary stripes extend back to the (sometimes hidden) white nape spot; eyes yellow. **Juvenile** resembles female but black feathers have buff tips. **Immature female** brown above with tawny median wing-coverts. (Male Black-headed Batis has black or blackish crown of same shade as ear-coverts. Pale Batis is shorter-tailed, paler grey above; female has paler, more diffuse patch on throat and a paler breast band. Forest Batis is still shorter-tailed, orange- or red-eyed, the female tawny/cinnamon below with no throat spot; also has conspicuous tawny wing band. Smaller Pygmy Batis inhabits drier country, has short white stripe leading from bill to eye only; female lacks throat spot. Rare far-northern Grey-headed Batis has shorter tail, larger nape spot.) **Song** of several penetrating, clear piping whistles in descending semi-tones, reminiscent of Common Wattle-eye: *hee-her, hee-her. . .* or *hee-her-her. . .*; the higher initial note may be repeated indefinitely, as can a metallic descending *weenh whenh wherr* or *tee quee queu*. Courting birds give a soft *querk querk querk*. Annoyance call a harsh scolding *chh-chh-chh*. **Range**: Widespread between 600 and 2600 m; absent from Lake Victoria basin, coastal lowlands and arid regions.

BLACK-HEADED BATIS *Batis minor* Plate 86

Length 4". **Male** much like Chin-spot Batis but *crown jet-black (same hue as auriculars) in western erlangeri, medium grey to dark charcoal-grey or blackish in nominate eastern race.* (Grey crown of worn male Chin-spot appears dark, but never as black as the ear-coverts.) *Long white superciliary stripes extend to or near nape* in fresh plumage. (Rare Grey-headed Batis also has long superciliary stripes but is grey or bluish grey on crown.) **Female** has *dark chestnut breast band and no throat spot*. Eyes yellow in both sexes. **Juvenile** blackish above with buff speckling, as in young Chin-spot. **Calls** of *B. m. erlangeri* tend to be more drawn out, less sharp, than those of Chin-spot. Most common is a penetrating, monotonous *eent eent eent . . .* or *reehn reehn. . .* repeated indefinitely. Pair members may call antiphonally, the notes well separated and unhurried. Male also has clearer whistled *ureet-eet*, oft-repeated, and another song with a high introductory *seent*, followed by *wree wree wree wree*. Female gives rough *skaow* of alarm. Eastern *B. m. minor* sings a thin, slightly ascending *ureet-weet-weet* or *yeeo-eet-eet* similar to that of western birds. **Range**: *B. m. minor* in coastal lowlands (including mangroves), inland along lower Tana River and to Mt Endau, the Tsavo parks, Kibwezi and Mkomazi GR. *B. m. erlangeri* in w. Kenya from Mt Elgon and the Kongelai Escarpment south to Lake Victoria basin, east to slopes above the Kerio Valley near Kabarnet where sympatric with *B. molitor* (as at Kapenguria).

FOREST BATIS *Batis mixta* Plates 86, 124

Length 3.75". A small batis of coastal evergreen forest and some ne. Tanzanian mountains. With its *broad breast band*, **male** suggests a *short-tailed* Chin-spot, but *eyes orange or red*, not yellow as in other coastal batises. **Female** *B. m. ultima* is distinctive, with *frosty cinnamon throat and upper breast, long black mask bordered above with white, and unique tawny wing-stripe.* Female *B. m. mixta* of Tanzanian highlands is darker, more chestnut below with reduced superciliary stripes and *brown eyes*. **Juvenile** resembles female but is buff-speckled above. **Immature** similar to female but crown olive-brown. **Song** a monotonous hollow piping, recalling that of Chestnut Wattle-eye, long-continued and at times ventriloquial. Call (*ultima*) a hollow, minor-key *yeu* or *ooo* repeated at 3- or 4-sec. intervals, often antiphonally by pair members; also a rough nasal *rrrannh* in series. A soft *nyemp* may be given with the piping. Annoyance call a mechanical *ch-ch-ch-ch . . .*. Piping of *B. m. mixta, eee . . . eee . . . eeeuk . . eee . . . eeeuk . . .*, the notes at 2- to 4-sec. intervals. **Range**: *B. m. ultima* is coastal from Arabuko–Sokoke Forest south to Shimba Hills, Shimoni and Mrima Hill; *mixta* between 1500 and 2300 m in Arusha NP, on Kilimanjaro, Mt Meru, Pare Mts and apparently intergrading with *ultima* in the Usambara Mts.

PALE BATIS or EAST COAST BATIS *Batis soror* Plate 86

Length 3.75". An *eastern woodland* species, similar to and replacing Chin-spot Batis in coastal areas. **Male** paler grey and *shorter tailed* than Chin-spot (but not stub-tailed like Forest Batis); best separated by range and accompanying **female** whose *throat patch is pale tawny and diffuse*, and whose *breast band is pale tawny or cinnamon*, not chestnut; eyes yellow in both sexes. **Call** of male a soft metallic piping, *yeenk-yeenk-yeenk-yeenk*

. . ., or an almost creaking *trree trree trree* . . ., the series often coinciding or alternating with female's louder and harder *pik-pik-pik-pik*. . .. These may alternate with soft *whit* notes and *prrrt* of wings. Harsh alarm calls like those of Chin-spot. **Range**: Arabuko–Sokoke Forest north to Marafa Forest (mainly in *Brachystegia*). In ne. Tanzania up to 1000 m in East Usambara Mts. Unconfirmed reports from the Tana River and forests south of Mombasa.

PYGMY BATIS *Batis perkeo*   Plate 86

Length 3.5–3.75". The *short-tailed*, grey-crowned batis of *arid and semi-arid country*. Prefers uniformly low acacia scrub-savanna. Suggests Chin-spot but *white superciliary stripes are reduced to short supraloral marks*. **Male**'s black breast band narrows noticeably in centre as does *orange-tawny* band of **female** whose white *throat is faintly washed with buff*. Eyes golden-yellow in female, almost orange-yellow in male. (Male of rare Grey-headed Batis on northern border has broader breast band and longer superciliaries; female's breast band is chestnut.) **Call** of penetrating piping notes suggests those of Black-headed Batis, but are typically sharper, more ringing, less drawn-out: *ting, ting, ting*. . ., in long measured series of 20 or more notes; sometimes each note slightly more extended, *een, een, een*. . .. **Range**: Widespread in n. and e. Kenya south to West Pokot and Baringo districts, Samburu and Shaba GRs, the Tsavo parks and Mkomazi GR.

GREY-HEADED BATIS *Batis o. orientalis*   Plate 86

Length 4". A northern batis known in our region only from the Ethiopian border at Moyale. **Male** similar to sympatric Pygmy Batis, but *long superciliary stripes extend back to nearly or actually merge with the broad white nape spot*; tail also somewhat longer, and *breast band typically broad*, not narrow as in eastern race of Black-headed Batis. Crown *blue-grey to medium grey*, as in Pygmy, but always lighter than the black ear-coverts (*contra* Black-headed). **Female** has *chestnut breast band* and *pure white throat*; eyes yellow in both sexes. **Call** of Ethiopian birds, described in the literature as *WEET, weet, weet, seerr* , would seem distinctive, but recent Ethiopian recordings are of clear piping whistles indistinguishable from those of Kenyan Chin-spot Batis. **Range**: Moyale area (2 specimens, Oct. 1910). Possibly elsewhere along northern boundary as specimens are known from se. Sudan and (one) from Mt Moroto, Uganda. **Taxonomic Note**: Relationship between this species and *B. minor* is as perplexing here as near Lake Chad in west-cent. Africa where an apparent cline exists between *B. o. chadensis* and *B. m. erlangeri*.

COMMON or BROWN-THROATED WATTLE-EYE *Platysteira cyanea nyansae*
Plate 86

Length 5". A western woodland and forest-edge species with prominent *scarlet eye-wattles*. **Male** glossy black above, white below, with a black breast band, *long white wing-stripe* and white-edged tail. **Female** has *throat and breast dark maroon-chestnut*. Eyes of both sexes blue-grey with narrow white inner ring around pupil. Buff-speckled **juvenile** has tawny wing-stripe and is pale buff on throat and breast. **Immature female** grey above with tawny-rufous wing-stripe and scattered chestnut feathers on face and throat; eye-wattles dull orange-red. (Black-throated Wattle-eye lacks white wing-stripe; female has black throat.) Pleasing **song** of somewhat mechanical-sounding notes, in variable groups of 3–5, often given by both members of a pair: *eee-tee-EENH-eu, ee-EENH-eu* or *sherrink rawnk rink, ee-ee-ree-eu* and variations. Has a buzzy alarm note and various churring calls. **Range**: Ugandan border areas south of Mt Elgon to Kakamega and Nandi forests and south to Lake Victoria basin, Mara GR and w. Serengeti NP.

BLACK-THROATED WATTLE-EYE *Platysteira peltata*   Plate 86
Length 5". Recalls Common Wattle-eye but *wings entirely dark*. **Male** has *narrow black breast band* and tail is very narrowly edged with white; eye wattles scarlet, eyes dark grey with narrow white ring around pupil. **Female** similar but *throat and upper breast black*.

490

Juvenile has tawny-edged wing-coverts and inner secondaries; lacks broad tawny stripe of Common Wattle-eye. **Song** a batis-like *er-er-fee-eu*. Calls include a harsh *zik-keek* and a sharp staccato *chit-chit-chit* or *keek keek keek*. **Range**: *P. p. mentalis* above 2000 m in and west of the Rift Valley, from Mt Elgon and the Cheranganis south to North Nandi, Mau, Trans-Mara and Nguruman/Loliondo forests, east to Nakuru; *P. p. peltata* on coast north to Witu and Lamu, along Tana River to Bura, in Shimba Hills and East Usambara Mts. Also Mt Endau, Meru and Nyeri districts, Laikipia Plateau and Ndaragwa (probably this race), n. Nairobi suburbs, near Taveta, Arusha and Moshi areas, North Pare Mts and Crater highlands.

CHESTNUT WATTLE-EYE *Dyaphorophyia c. castanea*   **Plate 86**
Length 4″. A plump and almost tailless bird of west Kenyan forests. **Male** black above with *white collar and lower back*; below, *broad black breast band* contrasts with white throat and belly. Feathers of hind crown form low crest in display or alarm. **Female** *pale chestnut above and on breast, rest of underparts white*; top of head dull purplish grey. Both sexes have *purple eye wattles*. **Juvenile** resembles female but with band of pale grey and chestnut across breast. Forages actively in tall shrubs and low trees, 3–7 m above ground, seldom lower; less often in canopy 30 m high where it sings. Shy and retiring except when several courting birds assemble in one spot. **Song** a rather loud tinkerbird-like *tonk-tonk-tonk-tonk. . .* may continue for 2 min. without a break (Yellow-rumped Tinkerbird pauses periodically in its singing). Displaying male gives penetrating hollow *p'qwonk* or *twonk* 6–10 times, mingled with nasal *chwaa* notes, a hiccough-like *p'kwup*, and sharper *pwick* and *kwink* notes, plus various popping and snapping sounds produced by wings and bill—all delivered in a soft, apparently patternless medley. **Range**: Kakamega and South Nandi forests.

JAMESON'S WATTLE-EYE *Dyaphorophyia jamesoni*   **Plate 86**
Length 3–3.5″. A tiny, stub-tailed bird of west Kenyan forest undergrowth. *Shows large turquoise-blue eye-wattles* and a bright chestnut patch on each side of neck; upperparts otherwise glossy greenish black as are throat and breast; posterior underparts silky white; eyes dark red-brown, feet light purple. Female greyer above than male. **Juvenile** dark grey above, white below with pale chestnut throat and upper breast. Forages at lower levels and in denser undergrowth than Chestnut Wattle-eye. Often produces loud wing-snapping noises. Song *chiddy SING* or *chun chiddy SING*, the terminal note far-carrying and of similar tonal quality to the whistle of Scaly-breasted Illadopsis. Usual call a subdued *chawuk-chawuk-chawuk. . .* and a very soft *wuk, wuk, wuk. . .*. Seemingly much less vocal than other wattle-eyes. **Range:** Kakamega and South Nandi forests.

YELLOW-BELLIED WATTLE-EYE *Dyaphorophyia concreta graueri*   **Plate 86**
Length 3.5″. The name describes this rarest of west Kenyan wattle-eyes. Its *bright apple-green eye-wattles* surround dark maroon eyes. **Male** is dark olive-green above. **Female** has duller upperparts and is chestnut from throat to upper breast. **Juvenile** dark grey above, pale yellow below. Inhabits undergrowth and lower mid-level of forest, particularly well-shaded sites with clumps of *Dracaena*. **Song** a distinctive emphatic *tchwik! tch-wik!* or *whick! whick! whick!* variously repeated and at times leading into a longer *whick! whick! tch'wee WHERNK!*, the last note strongly accented and frequently repeated by itself. All notes have a whistled nasal quality and possess considerable carrying power. **Range**: Kakamega, South and North Nandi forests.

AFRICAN SHRIKE-FLYCATCHER *Bias flammulatus aequatorialis*   **Plate 87**
Length 6″. A compact flycatcher-like bird of the forest canopy in w. Kenya. Sexes markedly different; **male** glossy black above with *white rump* and underparts, **female** brown above with *rufous rump, lower belly and crissum*, and rufous-edged wing and tail feathers; chin to belly white with *long brown streaks*. Black bill rather long and prominently hooked; *eyes of both sexes bright red to dark orange*. Perches quietly, alone or in pairs, typically high on large limbs near opening in forest. *Slowly wags tail from side to side*. (Female might be mistaken for African Broadbill which is smaller, short-billed and black-streaked below. Male somewhat resembles a puffback shrike.) **Call** a musical *chuik* plus whistling and churring notes. **Range**: Kakamega, North and South Nandi forests.

491

BLACK-AND-WHITE FLYCATCHER *Bias musicus changamwensis* **Plate 88**
Length 5". A compact, sexually dimorphic flycatching bird with a *pointed crest, short tail* and *bright yellow eyes*. **Male** glossy greenish black on upperparts, head and breast; rest of underparts white as is small patch near edge of wing. **Female** black on top and sides of head, otherwise tawny brown above, white below with pale chestnut tinge. **Juvenile** resembles adult female but top of head streaked with brown. **Song**, in flight, a sharp series of varied whistled notes, *wit-tu-wit-tu-tui-tu-tu. . . or twi-twi-trwirri-tuwoo. . .* with pronounced changes in pitch. A harsh *chuur* is also given on the wing. **Range/status**: Cent. Kenya's Meru and Ngaia forests and along northern boundary of Meru NP (Campi ya Nyati). Formerly common from Mombasa north to Takaungu, but now virtually gone from coastal lowlands (seen at Shimoni, Oct. 1997). At least formerly in the Usambara Mts.

HELMET-SHRIKES, FAMILY PRIONOPIDAE

The typical helmet-shrikes are noisy sociable birds, travelling restlessly through bush or woodland in parties of a few to 15 or 20 individuals. They feed mainly among branches and foliage. *Eurocephalus* is more sedentary and shrike-like than *Prionops* and takes most of its food from the ground. It is sometimes placed in the Laniidae, but it builds a neat, compact, well-camouflaged nest like *Prionops*, and its tarsal scutellation differs from that of true shrikes. Several *Prionops* possess circular, more or less pectinate eye-wattles. The firm plumage is black and white or of other contrasting pattern, and the sexes are alike. At least some species breed co-operatively and roost communally.

WHITE-CRESTED or WHITE HELMET-SHRIKE *Prionops plumatus* **Plate 85**

Length 6–10". The commonest and most widespread helmet-shrike, usually in small wandering flocks. *Black-and-white* with *bushy frontal crest* and *bare yellow wattles around bright yellow eyes*. Shows a prominent *white band across the primaries in flight*. Racially variable: curly-crested *cristatus* is large, with little or no white on the closed wing, much like smaller and shorter crested *vinaceigularis*; still smaller *poliocephalus* has long white wing-stripe and very short crest. **Juvenile** tinged brown above with white-tipped wing-coverts, brown eyes and no wattles. (Grey-crested Helmet-shrike lacks wattles, has part of crest dark grey and more or less erect; is much larger than mostly allopatric *P. p. poliocephalus* with similar wing pattern.) **Song** of *P. p. cristatus* a squeaky *tsirreek tsrick srech, chreek-chreek*, and a repeated nasal *KWEE-we-wiro* or *CHIri-ri-ro*. All races have various harsh scratchy calls and strident chattering or buzzy growling from a flock; *poliocephalus* gives a noisy rough *cherrow cherrow cherrow cree cree cerwow cerwow*. **Range**: *P. p. cristatus* is northwestern, east to the Turkwell River delta, Lake

White-crested Helmet-shrike

492

Turkana, south to Mt Elgon, Kerio Valley and Baringo District; *vinaceigularis* in e. and ne. Kenya south to the Tsavo parks and Mkomazi GR, inland along the lower Tana River to Garsen; *poliocephalus* is mainly a non-breeding visitor May–Sept. from south of our region to Serengeti, Lake Manyara and Tarangire NPs, Arusha Dist. and Mkomazi GR, north to Kibwezi, Machakos and Kitui districts, rarely Nairobi, overlapping *vinaceigularis* in several areas.

GREY-CRESTED HELMET-SHRIKE *Prionops poliolophus*　　　Plate 85

Length 9.5–10″. A large and conspicuously crested helmet-shrike, similar in plumage to the preceding species, but has *a partly erect, dark grey crest* and *no eye-wattles*; wings show a long white stripe and, in flight, a white band across the primaries. (The race *poliocephalus* of White-crested Helmet-shrike has similar wing pattern but is much smaller and short-crested.) Typically in whistling-thorn acacia or leleshwa (*Tarchonanthus*) woodland. **Calls** include a single *chwerr* and descending churrring phrases such as *chichi cherrrrro*. These elaborated upon with additional harsh scratchy, chattering in group vocalizations, *chikiki-chi-chirrrrow chi-chirrro che-chiwow-cherrow chk chk skrrk cherrk*. . ., often mixed with bill-snapping. **Range:** Local from Serengeti NP, Loliondo, Mara GR, the Loita and Nguruman hills north to Narok District, and in cent. Rift Valley from Kedong north to lakes Elmenteita and Nakuru (where scarce).

RETZ'S HELMET-SHRIKE *Prionops retzii graculina*　　　Plate 85

Length 7.5–8″. A highly gregarious bird of coastal forest and riverine woods. *Black and grey-brown above, with white belly and large white tail corners* (conspicuous as flock takes flight); *short shaggy frontal crest, largely red bill and serrated red wattles* around yellow eyes apparent in perched bird. Small white spots on inner webs of primaries are not always present. **Juvenile** has black replaced by barred dull brown, a dull horn-brown bill and dark eyes; whitish feather tips disappear, leaving a plainer immature stage. **Calls** include varied chattering, churring or grating sounds, often by several birds together. Individuals give a harsh *tsurrrEEoo-errrrEEo*, or a descending creaky trill, *crrreeeeeo*, alone or quickly repeated several times and often followed by a clearer *RRRREEO cho-wo cho-wo cho-wo*, or *choCAo, cho-CHO, cho-CHO*. **Range:** Coastal lowlands and (more locally) inland along the Tana River to Meru NP, Kamburu and Mwea NR, also the Tsavo parks and Kibwezi Forest, Arusha NP, Mkomazi GR and the Usambara Mts. Formerly near Nairobi.

CHESTNUT-FRONTED HELMET-SHRIKE *Prionops scopifrons*　　　Plate 85

Length 6.5–7″. Often in flocks with Red-billed Helmet-shrike. Smaller than that species, slate-grey with white belly and under tail-coverts, large white tail corners, a *chestnut frontal patch* of short bristly feathers, and pectinate *bluish* wattles around the yellow eyes. Rare inland race *keniensis* shows more white in the tail, and forehead patch is darker, with a narrow dark grey (not whitish) band between it and the dark crown. **Juvenile** has blackish forehead and white-tipped alular feathers on wings. **Call** a unique loud churring or chattering with a strange nasal whirring or humming quality; often accompanied by softer whistled notes, *char-rer wit-wit-chirro, trree trree trree trree*. Call a sharp *shuk*. **Range:** *P. s. scopifrons* in the East Usambara foothillls (has wandered to North Pare Mts); *kirki* on coast and in Shimba Hills; *keniensis* now confined to remnants of the Meru and Ngaia forests.

NORTHERN WHITE-CROWNED SHRIKE *Eurocephalus rueppelli*　　　Plate 85 ✔

Length 7.5–8″. A stocky, dark brown-and-white shrike-like bird, its large head distinctively patterned. Usually in pairs or groups of 3 or 4. *White crown conspicuous*, as are *white upper tail-coverts* when the bird glides from tree to tree on stiff wings. (Sustained flight distinctively quivering.) Most of face and underparts white except for *dull brown patch on sides*; bill black. **Juvenile** has *pale bill, brown forehead and crown*, and *black mask dipping below eyes*; brownish patches at sides connected by narrow band across breast. **Call** a harsh *kaak-kaak* or *weeyer WOK, weeyer WOKE*; similar

493

notes in song-like series: *chrrk, wirk-wirk, yerk-yerk, wuk-wuk, yerk. . ..* **Range:** Widespread except in Lake Victoria basin and coastal lowlands south of Malindi.

SHRIKES, FAMILY LANIIDAE

Bold and aggressive predatory birds of relatively open country. The head is large with a short hooked bill, and the narrow tail may be quite long. Sexes are alike or similar, although most female fiscals differ from males in their small chestnut flank patches. Adults are commonly black, grey, white and chestnut, but most juveniles are brownish with fine barring. Some shrikes are solitary, spending much time hunting from exposed perches. Others are gregarious, associating in noisy social groups. Harsh scolding vocalizations are the rule but some produce musical notes. The nest is a bulky cup of grasses and other plant material in bush or tree. Five of our species are regular palearctic migrants.

YELLOW-BILLED SHRIKE *Corvinella corvina affinis*   **Plate 84**

Length 12". Highly sociable; usually in small noisy parties in open woodland and savanna. *Long-tailed*, grey-brown above, and with pale buff underparts. Profusely *streaked with black above and below*; ear coverts dark brown. *Rufous primary bases are conspicuous in flight*, and most individuals show a small rufous patch on the flanks. *Bill and eyelids yellow*; eyes dark brown; feet dark grey-brown. **Juvenile** barred and mottled rather than streaked. **Call** a harsh rasping buzzing from a flock. Individuals also utter a repeated *scis-scis*. **Range:** Now largely restricted to ne. slopes of Mt Elgon around the Suam River from Kanyakwat to Kacheliba and base of Kongelai Escarpment. A few still survive around Soy and Awasi. Formerly more widespread.

✓ MAGPIE SHRIKE *Urolestes melanoleucus aequatorialis*   **Plate 84**

Length 14.5–17". Unmistakable with its *very long pointed tail* which it flirts as it calls. Mainly black with a long white patch on scapulars and some on secondaries, a smaller white spot on primary bases, and a greyish white rump; tail feathers white-tipped in fresh plumage. Female resembles male but has white patches on flanks. **Juvenile** browner than adult. Flight rapid and undulating. **Song** of various loud squeaky or squealing whistles, often from small groups in chorus, *KWEEKio KWEEKio . . ., kee-ur keeureek . . ., TWEO WHEEO WEEO. . .,* or *tlee-teeooo . . .,* the phrases repeated and variously combined. Also harsh sparrow-weaver-like *squee-er* notes and a grating scolding *skaaa.* **Range:** Serengeti, Lake Manyara and Tarangire NPs, and (a few) in e. Mara GR near Siana Springs.

RED-BACKED SHRIKE *Lanius collurio*   **Plate 85**

Length 6.5–7". A small, compact, short-billed shrike of open bush. **Male** *chestnut or red-brown on back* with *grey crown and rump*, black facial mask, white chin and throat; rest of underparts pinkish; flight feathers blackish, at times showing small white patch at base of primaries; tail black, edged with white, broadly so at base. *L. c. collurio* and the paler *pallidifrons* have bright rufous-chestnut back; *L. c. kobylini* is duller, and grey extends from nape onto back. **Female** brown above and on face, greyer on head and rump, white below with barring on breast and flanks; tail brown or rufous-brown above, greyish below. **First-winter** bird resembles female but crown and rump of same tone as back, varying from grey-brown to russet-brown, and barred with black. (First-winter Red-tailed Shrike is paler and greyer, and less heavily barred above than corresponding plumage of Red-backed. Slightly more rufous upper tail surface difficult to assess, but usually contrasts with sandy-brown back. Rufous-chestnut underside of tail often evident in the field.) **Call** a harsh repeated *chack.* A soft scratchy warbling song is heard after January. **Range/status:** Common palearctic migrant, Nov.–Dec. and April. A few (mainly *kobylini*) winter in greener parts of se. Kenya and ne. Tanzania.

RED-TAILED or ISABELLINE SHRIKE *Lanius isabellinus*   **Plate 85**

Length 6.5–7". Similar to Red-backed Shrike and in the same habitats. Usually *paler* and the tail slightly longer. **Male** *L. i. phoenicuroides* pale brown above, more rufous on crown, rufous on rump and tail; underparts whitish; black mask bordered above by narrow whitish superciliary stripes; blackish flight feathers show white patch at base of primaries. Some birds much paler on crown and back. *L. i. isabellinus* is more uniform sandy brown above and creamier below. **Female** and **first-winter** birds as in Red-backed Shrike but barring reduced; tail rufous-brown above contrasting with back, and appears pale rufous from below. Female usually shows cream patch at base of primaries. In the hand shows 9th primary to be much shorter than 6th (equal to or longer than 6th in Red-backed). **Call** and soft warbling song similar to those of Red-backed Shrike. **Range/status**: Common palearctic migrant (mostly *L. i. phoenicuroides*), Nov.–early April, mainly below 1700 m and east of the Rift Valley, especially in the Tsavo parks and Mkomazi GR.

LESSER GREY SHRIKE *Lanius minor*   Plate 84 ✓

Length 8–8.5″. Medium-sized, with rather long pointed wings and strong flight. **Spring adult** pale grey above with black wings and *black mask extending to forehead.* White tail edges and white patch on primary bases conspicuous in flight; white *underparts tinged pink.* **Autumn adult** has forehead mixed grey and black. **First winter** bird brown-tinged above, with no black on forehead. In w. Kenya see Mackinnon's Fiscal. **Call** a harsh *chek*. **Range/status**: Palearctic passage migrant, widespread in April from the coast to above 2200 m. Scarce in autumn.

*SOUTHERN GREY SHRIKE *Lanius meridionalis pallidirostris* Illus. opp. Plate 85

Length 9″. Accidental in our region. Longer-tailed and with more rounded wings than Lesser Grey Shrike. White superciliary stripes separate black mask from grey crown, and this subspecies is *pale*, with a *horn-coloured bill*, and *no black frontal band on forehead* (unlike Lesser Grey). White patch on primary bases larger than in Lesser Grey, and secondaries broadly tipped with white. **Call** a harsh *sheck-sheck* or *sheenk-sheenk*. **Status**: One record, Feb.1988, from Ilemi Triangle near Sudan border. **Taxonomic Note**: Formerly considered conspecific with *L. excubitor*.

MACKINNON'S FISCAL *Lanius mackinnoni*   Plate 84

Length 8″. A slender western shrike of forest edges and cultivation. Dull grey above with *wholly black wings* and white scapulars; tail narrow and graduated, black with white corners. *Black facial mask* is bordered by *white superciliary stripes.* Underparts all white in **male**; chestnut flank patch in **female**. **Juvenile** narrowly barred with dark grey above and on breast and flanks. (First-winter Lesser Grey Shrike, unlikely in same habitat, shows prominent white patch in primaries, and lacks white superciliaries.) **Call** a musical *chickerea*. Rich, varied and warbling song includes mimicry of other species. **Range**: Between 1500 and 2000 m in w. Kenya from Nandi and Kakamega districts south to Kericho, Sotik, and Kilgoris. Wanders to Mara GR and Saiwa NP. Formerly on Mt Elgon and at Elgeyu.

GREY-BACKED FISCAL *Lanius excubitoroides*   Plate 84 ✓

Length 10″. Pale grey back and *broad white side panels at base of the long broad black tail* mark this distinctive gregarous shrike; shows a wide black mask from forehead to sides of neck, black wings and scapulars and white underparts; **female** has small chestnut flank patch. The 3 races display only minor differences, although *boehmi* is more dusky grey above. **Juvenile** pale brownish above with narrow barring and with buffy white underparts. Pairs or groups chatter excitedly, wave their tails and flutter their wings. When dispersing they follow one another in slow flight. **Call** a chattering *teudleeoo-teudleeoo* and similar sounds often in chorus. **Range**: Low to medium elevations in areas of higher rainfall than those favoured by Long-tailed Fiscal. *L. e. intercedens* from Mt Elgon and Kapenguria south to Lake Victoria basin; nominate *excubitoroides* in the Kerio and Rift valleys from Baringo District south to Naivasha and Longonot, occasionally east to Laikipia Plateau; Tanzanian *boehmi* in Serengeti NP, Mara GR and Loita Hills.

✔ LONG-TAILED FISCAL *Lanius cabanisi*   Plate 84

Length 12–12.5″. The large size and *long rounded black tail* distinguish this rather sociable shrike of dry savannas. Small noisy groups often gather on bushtop, wire or low tree, excitedly waving their tails from side to side. Black from forehead to wings, dark grey on back, white on rump and upper tail-coverts; underparts and patch at base of primaries also white. **Female** shows some chestnut on flanks. **Juvenile** grey-brown above with narrow black barring; rump buff and underparts buffier than in adult. (Smaller Common Fiscal has much narrower white-sided tail, white scapulars and black back. Taita Fiscal has much shorter, white-sided tail and pale grey back.) Common **call** a chattering, harsh *chit-er-row* or other scolding sounds; also a mellow whistle. **Range**: From sea level to 1600 m, mainly east of the Rift Valley, from Isiolo District and Meru NP south to the Tsavo parks, Nairobi, Amboseli, Lake Manyara, Tarangire NP and the Masai Steppe. Also coastal lowlands north to the Tana River delta and Lamu District.

TAITA FISCAL *Lanius dorsalis*   Plate 84

Length 8″. A *short-tailed*, solitary *dry country* shrike. *Pale grey on back*, black from bill to hindneck, and *wings black except for white patch in primaries* (lacks white secondary tips of Somali Fiscal); graduated black tail has white sides and corners; underparts white, with some chestnut on flanks in female. **Juvenile** dark grey above finely barred with dusky, and wing feathers edged with buff; underparts white with sparse dark barring. *Flight direct* (not undulating as in Somali Fiscal). **Song** a quaint mixture of churrs, hollow sounds and ticking notes, *chwaaa pikereek chrrrrrrr yook pikerchik . . . skyaaa, week kiook-tiureek tik . . .*. **Range**: Widespread below 1500 m north and east of the Kenyan highlands; south of the highlands, ranges west to lakes Magadi, Natron and Eyasi. Absent from the coast south of Malindi.

SOMALI FISCAL *Lanius somalicus*   Plate 84

Length 8″. A medium-sized shrike of barren *northern Kenya*. Suggests Taita Fiscal, with glossy black top and sides of head and pale grey back, but *broad white tips to secondaries* show as bird swoops up to perch or flies off with *undulating flight*. **Female**, unlike other fiscals, lacks chestnut on flanks. **Juvenile** brownish above with buffy edges to wing-coverts and secondaries; some faint barring on scapulars, and buffy white underparts. **Song** composed of short variable phrases, *bur-ur-ur bit-it-it . . .*. Alarm call a low churring. **Range**: Lake Turkana area east to Turbi and Marsabit, south to Kapedo and Laisamis, infrequently wandering to Baringo, Wamba and Merti districts.

✔ COMMON FISCAL *Lanius collaris humeralis*   Plate 84

Length 8–9″. The common and conspicuous highland shrike, often seen on wires and other exposed perches, its *long narrow tail* identifying it even in silhouette. Black above from forehead to dark grey lower back, with contrasting *white scapulars that form a prominent V*. Black wings show small white area at base of primaries; tail black with white sides, and most feathers white-tipped. Dull chestnut flanks in female. **Juvenile** brown above, brownish white below, finely barred throughout; the well-defined scapular areas whitish or buff. **Song** consists of varied phrases including piping and rasping notes. Usual call a harsh grating *ghreeee* or *ghree ghree ghree*, sometimes accompanied by two soft piping notes from bird's mate. Also gives an extended plaintive *tweeeeeer*, soft and reedy. **Range**: Widespread above 1400 m in Kenyan highlands, including isolated northern mountains, the Chyulu Hills and Taita Hills (occasional), south to Lake Victoria basin, Serengeti NP, the Crater and Mbulu highlands, Arusha, and highland areas from Kilimanjaro and Mt Meru to the Pare and Usambara mts.

WOODCHAT SHRIKE *Lanius senator niloticus*   Plate 84

Length 7–7.5″. The *rufous or chestnut crown and nape* distinguish this rather thickset, large-headed shrike of acacia-grassland. *White scapulars prominent in any plumage; patch at primary bases, upper tail-coverts, base and sides of tail also white.* **Male** has black mask and blackish back. **Female** duller and browner above. **First-autumn** bird barred brown above with pale scapulars and rump, faintly barred breast and flanks, and with some rufous on nape. (Masked Shrike has different head pattern and in flight appears dark above except for white scapulars and wing patch.) **Call** a dry chattering *schrrrrret* or *kschaaa*. Song variable, with whistles, trills and mimicry. **Range/status**: Uncommon palearctic migrant, Nov.–March, in w. and nw. Kenya, south to Busia and Baringo districts and northern Mara GR, once to Nairobi NP.

MASKED SHRIKE *Lanius nubicus*   Plate 84
Length 6.75". A slim, narrow-tailed shrike with *orange-buff sides and flanks*; shows *white on scapulars, forehead, superciliaries*, at base of primaries and narrowly along sides of tail. **Male** *black above including rump and upper tail-coverts.* **Female** similarly patterned but brownish instead of black above and flank patches duller. **First-winter** bird barred brownish grey with paler forehead and superciliaries; scapular patches prominent, but no orange-buff on flanks; adult feathering appears by late Nov. or Dec. Typically winters in acacia groves near water, and often secretive, perching *within* thick shrubbery or *tree canopy*. **Call** a hard chattering *chek-chek* and a grating *krrrr* recalling Woodchat Shrike. **Range/status**: Palearctic migrant, annual at Lake Baringo, 1982–91. Also recorded at Lake Kanyaboli, south Kerio Valley and Lake Naivasha.

BUSH-SHRIKES, FAMILY MALACONOTIDAE
Typically retiring birds, mostly foliage-gleaners in undergrowth or canopy. Often shy and difficult to study as they skulk in dense vegetation, although their loud and unusual calls attract attention. Certain species become quite tame around safari lodges. Plumage is often contrastingly patterned, either brightly coloured or black and white, the sexes alike or different. The usually barred juvenile plumage is soon replaced by an immature dress similar to, but not always identical with, adult plumage. Some species feed on the ground, and all prey on insects and at times small vertebrates. Although often treated as a subfamily of the true shrikes (Laniidae), the two groups do not appear to be closely related.

BRUBRU *Nilaus afer*   Plate 82

Length 5". A small chestnut-sided bird of low savanna trees; unlike other bush-shrikes. **Male** black above with white superciliary stripes, *broad white streak down middle of back and a narrower one on the wings; sides and flanks chestnut.* **Female** has black replaced by blackish brown, and shows some dark streaks on throat. Eastern/northeastern birds have paler sides than those in the west. **Juvenile** heavily barred white, buff and blackish brown above, with irregular brown bars below. **Song** a distinctive prolonged trilling or purring sound, droning and slightly metallic in quality, *kuu-uurrrrrrrrrrr*, not loud but far-carrying; also a penetrating high whistled *wutitititititi*. **Range**: Widespread below 2500 m, but absent from the coast. *N. a. massaicus* in w. and cent. Kenya south to Lake Natron, Serengeti NP and Maswa GR; *minor* in n. and e. Kenya, south to n. Tanzania east of the Rift Valley.

BLACK-CROWNED TCHAGRA *Tchagra s. senegala*   Plate 82

Length 8". A brown-backed bush-shrike with *bright rufous wings and white-tipped black tail* prominent in flight. Shows solid *black crown margined by bold whitish or buff superciliary stripes.* Eyes dark blue. (Male Marsh Tchagra has black cap extending down below eyes; female has white superciliaries but is smaller than Black-crowned, with broken blackish 'V' on back and red eyes.) **Juvenile** duller, with brownish crown (but lacks narrow black lines above the superciliaries, thus differing from Brown-crowned Tchagra); eyes brownish grey, underparts buffier. **Song** a distinctive *slow* whistling, the clear lilting phrases run together in a pleasing sequence, often descending, *chweee, chew, chewee, cheee, chewi . . .*, or *teyo, weeo, queeo, tew*, or *queeo tew EEo-tew, tew, tew, tew.* Calls include a harsh *churr*, a low *tchuk*, and a desending soft rattle, *chrrrrrrrr.* Alarm call a clear liquid *chu-tu-woi.* Sings from concealed perch or on the wing. **Range**: Extreme nw. Kenya near Lokichokio (and old records from Moyale and Karo Lola); otherwise across much of s. Kenya and n. Tanzania, including coastal lowlands (where more common than Brown-crowned Tchagra).

BROWN-CROWNED TCHAGRA *Tchagra australis*   **Plate 82**

Length 7". Resembles larger Black-crowned Tchagra but *crown brown* and bordered by *narrow black lines above the buff superciliary stripes; eyes brown*. Eastern races slightly paler than western *emini*. **Juvenile** tawnier below, head stripes much less pronounced, bill horn-brown, not black. See juv. Black-crowned Tchagra. **Song** rapid and explosive, unlike that of Black-crowned, usually with some oriole-like whistles: WEEo, WEwo-wo, WEEwo kew kew kew tu-tut-tu-tu, or queeri, TWEEo, weeo weeo-kew-kew-kew. . ., or beginning with some soft notes and a short descending whinny, tok-tok-tok queero SKWIAAaaaa tyu-yeu-yeu-yeu. . .. Flight song a long, rapid series of *weeo* or *weewo* notes, beginning loudly and gradually diminishing, with increasingly prolonged syllables. Usual call note a low *cheerk*, but also gives a single oriole-like *quweeo*. Song, from bushtop, accompanied by much posturing and extreme tail movement. Fluttering vocal courtship flight given with loudly beating wings, erected rump feathers and broadly fanned tail. **Range**: Much as for Black-crowned Tchagra, between sea level and 2000 m, but absent from nw. Kenya. Western *T. a. emini* from Mt Elgon east to Laikipia Plateau and Nairobi, south to Mara GR and Serengeti NP; *minor* in e. and se. Kenya, along Tana River to Bura, at Lamu, and east of *emini* in n. Tanzania; *littoralis* on coast north to Malindi, Shimba Hills and East Usambara foothills.

THREE-STREAKED TCHAGRA *Tchagra jamesi*   **Plate 82**

Length 6.5". A small pale bush-shrike typical of dry thorn-bush. Differs from other tchagras in size, pallid appearance, and a *black streak of variable width down centre of crown and nape*, in addition to those through the eyes. The peculiar iris pattern, a ring of silvery dots surrounding the pupil, is rarely seen in the field. Eastern birds are sandier and less grey above than nominate *jamesi*, with broader crown stripe. Melodious flight **song** an emphatic series of down-slurred whistles, wi-weo-weo-weo-weo or chweeo-chweeo-chweeo, similar to song of Brown-crowned Tchagra. Call a scolding *chuwaa* or *cherraa-cherraa*. **Range**: *T. j. jamesi* local below 1000 m in n. and ne. Kenya, south to lakes Baringo and Bogoria, Samburu and Shaba GRs, Meru and Tsavo NPs, and the Mkomazi GR. *T. j. mandana* on Manda and Lamu islands, west to Witu and the Tana River delta.

MARSH TCHAGRA *Tchagra minuta*   **Plate 82**

Length 6–7.5". A small tchagra of *low wet grasslands*. Solid black cap to below eyes identifies **male** which also shows a *black 'V' on the back* (except in the scarce coastal *reichenowi*); eyes rose-pink or red. **Female** has *white superciliary stripes* and black streak through the eyes. **Juvenile** resembles female, but has a distinctive *whitish crown*. The short warbling **song**, *tewayo tuwaro*, given in low flight, suggests the words "today or tomorrow" (Chapin). Alarm note a hoarse *charr*; also a scolding *kiop*, *klock*, or *tchup*. **Range**: Western *T. m. minuta* from Kapenguria and Saiwa NP south to Lake Victoria basin and South Nyanza, wandering to Mara GR and w. Serengeti NP; formerly in cent. Kenyan highlands. Coastal *reichenowi* formerly known north to Lamu, but few recent records.

BOCAGE'S or GREY-GREEN BUSH-SHRIKE *Malaconotus bocagei jacksoni*
Plate 82

Length 6–6.5". This uncommon foliage-gleaning bird of western forest treetops usually appears *black above and white below*, with prominent *white lores, forehead and superciliary stripes*. Viewed nearer, the back is dark grey, and the breast and sides faintly buffy; there is *no white in wings*. **Juvenile** tinged yellow and faintly barred with grey below, barred yellowish and black on grey above; wings and tail with light greenish feather edgings and buff tips. **Song** a monotonous loud clear whistle, usually *peeeu-peeeeu* or *pureet-ureet*, sometimes *twee-teeeeu*, the second note lower, at times a rapid whistled *uwee-wee-wee-wee-wee*, all on the same pitch. Also harsh scolding notes. **Range**: Nandi and Kakamega forests. Formerly at Nyarondo and Kericho.

SULPHUR-BREASTED BUSH-SHRIKE *Malaconotus sulfureopectus similis*
Plate 83

Length 6.5–7". A colourful but shy bird of acacia woodland and savanna. Olive-green above and yellow below, with grey crown, *orange breast, narrow black mask and yellow superciliary stripes*; eyes dark brown. **Immature** lacks striking facial pattern and has whitish throat. **Juvenile** similar but finely barred with dusky above and below. See Grey-headed Bush-shrike. **Song** a characteristic sound of acacia woodland, a short ringing whistle of 4–8 notes, *twi-twu-twu-twurrr* or *whi-whi-whi-whi-her*, the last note lower and more emphatic (may recall opening notes of Beethoven's 5th symphony). A longer song has first note slightly lower-pitched, *kew-tee-tee-tee-tee-tee-tee*. Also frequent are a clear whistled *hooi hooi hooi* plus various rasping and clicking calls. **Range**: Widespread, mainly below 2000 m, except in arid n. and e. Kenya.

BLACK-FRONTED BUSH-SHRIKE *Malaconotus nigrifrons*　　Plate 83

Length 7". This shy arboreal bird of *montane or submontane forest canopy* exhibits considerable colour variation, but all are *olive-green above with grey head/upper back,* and a *black mask extending across the forehead.* Of the 4 colour morphs, golden-breasted birds are most numerous. A red-breasted form is known from the Cherangani Hills, Elgeyu-Maraquet, Meru, Nairobi and Mt Kilimanjaro. Some Kenyan birds are red only from chin to breast, with yellow abdomen; others are orange below. Buff-breasted individuals recorded on Mt Kenya, Taita Hills and Usambara Mts; rare black-breasted males known only in the East Usambaras. **Juvenile** yellowish-olive above with greyer crown to upper back, and narrow whiteish eye-ring; underparts olive-yellow with diffuse darker barring; wing-coverts and tail feathers tipped yellow. (Similar immature Sulphur-breasted Bush-shrike is in different habitat.) **Song** of various hollow bell-like phrases, e.g. *whoop-whoop . . .* or *WHEEo worik. . .* frequently repeated; or *kwo-kwo kwo, whoop-WEEup . . .* . Any of these, and a simple *oook,* commonly answered by mate's very loud nasal rasping *CHAAAAAAA , NYAAAA* or *SHNARR* (also given alone as an alarm). Pair duets with a soft mellow *woo woo woo woo . . .* or *uwoo-uwoo.* **Range**: Mt Elgon, Saiwa NP, the Cheranganis, Elgeyu-Maraquet and Tugen Hills, the Kericho, Mau, Trans-Mara, Lolgorien, Nguruman, Meru, Embu, s. Aberdare and Taita Hills forests; in n. Nairobi suburbs until 1980. In n. Tanzania, in Marang Forest above Lake Manyara, on Kilimanjaro and in Arusha NP, the Pare and Usambara mts.

DOHERTY'S BUSH-SHRIKE *Malaconotus dohertyi*　　Plate 83

Length 7". A colourful bush-shrike of *highland forest undergrowth. Bright red on forehead and throat, the latter separated from yellow belly by a broad black band* which extends up around throat and through the eyes. Under tail-coverts also red; back and wings green, tail black in **male. Female** has narrow olive-green edges and tips to the rectrices. Rare yellow morph lacks red. (Similar Four-coloured Bush-shrike of eastern lowlands has yellow or orange forehead and superciliary stripes.) **Juvenile** mainly yellow and olive-green, finely barred above and below; shows narrow yellow eye-ring and dull pink under tail-coverts. **Song** a whistled phrase of short notes, *we-week u-week-u-week,* and an almost liquid *wurk wurk wurwurwurwurk,* varied to *weeo-weeo-weeo-weeo-werk,* slightly accented terminally. Call-note, *quip* followed by a rising whistled *whee-u* (Chapin). **Range**: Typically above 2200 m on Mt Elgon, the Cheranganis, Mt Kenya, Aberdares and the Mau. Old records from Limuru, Kiambu, Kericho and Sotik.

FOUR-COLOURED BUSH-SHRIKE *Malaconotus quadricolor nigricauda*
Plate 83

Length 7". Inhabits *eastern lowland forest* and thickets. Skulks in the densest of undergrowth where hard to see, but responds to imitation or playback of song. Much like montane Doherty's Bush-shrike but *forehead and superciliary stripes orange or yellow*, sometimes red-tinged; *breast below the black band is red* . Tail of **male** black, that of **female** olive-green; her red throat shows some yellow feathers. **Immature** plain olive above and on flanks; throat orange-yellow tinged red posteriorly; lower breast and belly more lemon yellow; lores and eye-ring yellow. **Juvenile** similar with some barring below. **Song** a loud clear whistled *hooi-hooi-hooi-hooi*. . .; also has various harsh scolds. **Range**: Coastal areas north to Lamu, inland along lower Tana River to Baomo, Mt Endau and Mt Kasigau, Shimba Hills and North Pare Mts. Formerly in Chyulu and Sagala hills, Tsavo East NP (Voi River) and East Usambara foothills.

GREY-HEADED BUSH-SHRIKE *Malaconotus blanchoti* Plate 83

Length 9-10". A *large*, yellow-bellied bush-shrike, often in tree canopy. *Massive black bill and bright yellow eyes* impart distinctive facial expression to the *grey-head*; back and wings olive-green, the latter white-spotted. Variable chestnut patch on breast (and sometimes flanks) in *M. b. approximans* lacking in northwestern birds. **Juvenile** pale yellow below, mottled brown on head; bill brownish horn; eyes brown. **Song**, *wik-uraaanh-uraaanh-uraaanh* . . ., the main note repeated 5–12 times; may be given by one bird or in duet by members of a pair. Common call a far-carrying (yet often soft) hollow, whistled *whoonh*, mechanical-sounding, and repeated monotonously for an hour or more. Equally repetitive is a thinner *wheeu. . ., wheeu. . .*, sometimes preceded by soft notes audible only at close range; these may be accompanied by a variety of *click, tik* or *clink* notes. Also gives a single metallic bell-like note, and a harsh rasping alarm call. Highly vocal. **Range**: *M. b. approximans* north and east of the Kenyan highlands, usually below 1500 m, including coastal areas north of Mombasa, and south into n. Tanzania east of the Rift Valley; disjunct population from Lolgorien south to Nguruman Hills and cent. Serengeti NP. *M. b. catharoxanthus* from Karasuk Hills to near Mt Elgon. **Taxonomic Note:** The unique specimen (now lost) from the Kakamega Forest, considered to be *M. monteiri* (Monteiro's Bush-shrike) by some and *M. cruentus* (Fiery-breasted Bush-shrike) by others, was possibly an aberrant *M. b. catharoxanthus*.

ROSY-PATCHED BUSH-SHRIKE *Rhodophoneus cruentus* Plate 83

Length 8.75–9.25". A unique dry-country species, *slim, pinkish tan above with large white tail corners* and a *rosy red rump patch*, conspicuous as the bird flies just above ground in low open scrub. **Male** of the southern *R. c. cathemagmena* has the rose-coloured throat and breast patch bordered by black. Largely north of the Equator is *R. c. hilgerti*, less rosy tan above, and the male with no black. **Females** of both races have a black-bordered white throat. **Juvenile** shows buff feather edges on back and wings. Duet or antiphonal **song** by members of a pair is a loud, piercing, somewhat slurred *TWEE-u, TWEE-u* . . . or *TSWEE-UR, TSWEE-UR*. . . repeated indefinitely. **Range**: Mainly below 1300 m. *R. c. hilgerti* in n. and e. Kenya at Lokichokio and from Lake Turkana east to Mandera, south to Samburu GR, Meru NP and middle Tana River; *cathemagmena* from the Tsavo parks, Amboseli and Kiboko west to Olorgesailie and Mosiro, south to Lake Natron, Tarangire NP and the Masai Steppe.

✓ BLACK-HEADED GONOLEK *Laniarius erythrogaster* Plate 83

Length 8–8.5". An impressive *black-and-red* bush-shrike of woodland and thicket undergrowth in the west. Scarlet below except for black tibial feathers and *yellowish buff lower belly and crissum*; upperparts glossy black, sometimes with a few white spots on wing-coverts; eyes white or yellow. **Juvenile** blackish brown with faint buff barring above, closely barred yellowish buff and black below; eyes brown. Birds in post-juvenile moult boldly splotched red and black. See Papyrus Gonolek. **Song** a hollow whistled *chuyo-chuyo, chyochochocho* involving members of a pair. Male also gives a loud, resonant somewhat bell-like whistle, *Oiyo* or *WEEyo*, to which female immediately responds with a harsh grating *TURRRR* or *KSSRRRRR*, sounding like violent tearing of cloth. Alarm calls include a loud rapid *chk-chk-chk*. . ., the notes run together in a continuous rail-like chatter. **Range**: Lake Victoria Basin, Tanzania's Mara Region and

w. Serengeti NP, along Suam River around Kacheliba, Nasolot NR and parts of s. Kerio Valley, wandering to Lake Baringo. Birds in the north, at Lokichokio and Lake Turkana (Omo delta), represent southern limits of Sudanese and Ethiopian populations. **Taxonomic Note**: At times considered a race of *L. barbarus.*

PAPYRUS GONOLEK   *Laniarius mufumbiri*   **Plate 83**

Length 7.5″. Restricted to *western papyrus swamps.* Resembles preceding species but has *dull golden yellow crown* and shows variable white spotting on wing-coverts; posterior underparts dingy white, and throat somewhat orange-tinged, not pure red. **Immature** dull (not glossy) black above with some pale feather tips; crown dull greyish olive; underparts brick red to yellowish pink with yellowish buff throat. **Juvenile** undescribed. Occasionally overlaps Black-headed Gonolek at disturbed swamp edges, but *mufumbiri* rarely if ever leaves the papyrus except for short flights over open water. **Song** a double mellow whistle, *yong-yong* or *chyo-chyo,* varied to *yoo yong-yong.* **Range:** In and around Lake Victoria east to Kisumu and Kendu Bay.

LUHDER'S BUSH-SHRIKE   *Laniarius l. luehderi*   **Plate 83**

Length 7″. Restricted to forest undergrowth in western Kenya. *Orange-tawny on crown and from throat to breast, with a broad black mask. Upperparts mainly black with long white wing-stripe;* belly white. **Juvenile** largely olive above with rufous upper tail-coverts, and buffy yellow below, finely barred with blackish except on pale yellow belly and dark rufous tail. Wing-coverts and secondaries edged with yellowish or buff. **Song** a liquid whistling *weeo-k'wee* apparently given by males and females together. Common call a throaty, somewhat amphibian-like *whook* or *wurrk,* at times followed by a low *chk-chk-chk* from second bird. **Range:** Mt Elgon and Saiwa NP, the Nandi, Kakamega, Kericho, Mau and Trans-Mara forests south to Lolgorien, the Migori River and nw. Mara GR (Olololoo Escarpment).

RED-NAPED BUSH-SHRIKE   *Laniarius ruficeps*   **Plate 83**

Length 7″. An eastern species of dry bush thickets. Skulks in dense cover, but sings from bushtops just after dawn. The *orange-red crown and nape* are separated from *prominent black mask* by narrow white superciliary stripes; forecrown black in *L. r. rufinuchalis,* orange-red in *kismayensis; wings black with long white stripe;* tail also black with white-edged outer feathers; back grey or grey and black (male), or olive-grey (female); underparts pinkish or cream, white on belly and throat. **Juvenile** olive-grey above, dull white below. **Song** a continuously repeated *kwoi kwoi kwoi . . .,* and a low whistling *whooi-whooi. . ..* Harsh notes include a loud *K-K-K-K-K-K-K,* and a repeated scolding *KWERR, KWERR . . ..* Reportedly duets like other bush-shrikes. **Range:** Below 1000 m in e. and ne. Kenya. *L. r. rufinuchalis* from Garissa, Mwingi and Kitui districts south to the Tsavo NPs and Galana ranch. Status in Mandera and Wajir districts unclear. *L. r. kismayensis* around Kiunga on Somali border.

TROPICAL BOUBOU   *Laniarius aethiopicus*   **Plate 82** ✓

Length 8″. The common pied bush-shrike of dense undergrowth in woods and gardens. *Mainly black above and white below,* the 4 subspecies differing in amount of white in the wings: a bar on middle coverts only in *ambiguus,* extending as a stripe along secondaries in *major,* on middle coverts and edges of some secondaries in nominate *aethiopicus,* and lacking in *sublacteus* which also has an *all-black* coastal morph. **Juvenile** resembles adult but upperparts with tawny or ochre feather tips, and dull white underparts usually with limited dusky barring (lacking in *sublacteus*); nominate *aethiopicus* has pale brown breast and flanks. (Less robust and more arboreal Black-backed Puffback is smaller, with white rump in male; white of face extends above eyes in grey-rumped female. Fiscals differ in posture, proportions and habits. In coastal thickets, Slate-coloured Boubou can be mistaken for sympatric black morph of *L. a. sublacteus* but is dull bluish-slate, not glossy black.) **Song** of highland *ambiguus* a short, oft-repeated bell-like or metallic duet, *hooo-i-hoo* or *onk-hi-wong* or *ki-wahng,* as if a single bird were calling (as is sometimes the case). Calls include a quavering prolonged *hoooooooooo*, a *quu-wi* or *qui-u* and *kwi-u-eee* from male, accompanied by *heur* or *hoooo* from female. Also a repeated *hoo-anh* or *hoo-wanh* duet, the second note apparently from the female. Courting male gives a harsh jarring *SCHRANG! SCHRANG!* to which female responds *oo-yuu*. Common duet of *sublacteus* in the Usambaras, *hoongg-a-hoongg* (Moreau). **Range**: *L. a. ambiguus* in highlands east of the Rift Valley south to Arusha and Moshi districts (incl. Kilimanjaro and Mt Meru); western *major* from Mt Elgon and Kitale east into the Rift at Nakuru, Elmenteita and Naivasha, and south to Lake Victoria basin, Mara GR, Serengeti NP, Crater and Mbulu highlands; *aethiopicus* at Moyale on Ethiopian border; *sublacteus* on coast north to Lamu, inland along lower Tana River to Garissa, and to Taita hills, Mt Kasigau, East Usambara and North Pare mts.

SLATE-COLOURED BOUBOU *Laniarius funebris*   Plate 82

Length 7.25–8″. The dark slate-grey bush-shrike of scrub, thicket and bush. Vocal but shy and skulking; forages on or near ground in thick vegetation. *Slaty with a blackish head* (male dark bluish slate, female a little paler). **Juvenile** dull blackish brown barred with black below. (Black flycatchers, drongos and male cuckoo-shrikes differ in bill shape and behaviour. Coastal all-black morph of Tropical Boubou is glossy black. Fulleborn's Black Boubou differs vocally, and in our region only in West Usambara Mts.) **Song** loud and variable, e.g. a flute-like *cho-ko-WI*, given by male and often followed by female's harsh snarling *CHUERR*. Alarm note a harsh *CHERRK*. **Range**: Widespread below 2000 m except in northeast and much of w. Kenya and the coast south of Malindi.

SOOTY BOUBOU *Laniarius leucorhynchus*   Plate 82

Length 8.25″. A forest bird, in our region a vagrant to western Kenya. Sooty black or brownish black throughout, female slightly less glossy than male; eyes reddish brown or brown; bill and feet black. Bill of **juvenile/immature** *ivory white*. **Song** a fluty whistle, *oo-oo-ooi*, preceded or followed by female's grating *skaaaa*. **Status**: Ugandan. A specimen collected in Kaimosi Forest, April 1931.

FÜLLEBORN'S BLACK BOUBOU *Laniarius fuelleborni*   Plate 123

Length 7.5″. A *slaty black* bush-shrike of *Tanzanian mountain forests*. Uniformly dark, the female somewhat less black about the head and with a faint olivaceous wash on the breast; no white in rump feathers. Eyes brown; bill and feet black. **Juvenile** dark olive-grey above, olive-green or olive-grey below. (Allopatric Slate-coloured Boubou, not a forest species, is more bluish slate in colour.) **Song** a short liquid *wick-wick-WEE* or *hooi-hooi*, varied to *wu-wu-WEET* or *o-EEK*; may be preceded or followed by a melodious descending *turrrrrrrr* or rapid *u-u-u-u-u* from the female. Duet phrases include *weeuwee-tu-WEE*, *oogle-WEEK*, *ooi-ooi-ooWEE* and *wuk-WEEK k'WEEEE* and a harsh *nyaaa-skereeeee*. **Range**: West Usambara Mts where common between 1500 and 2200 m.

NORTHERN PUFFBACK *Dryoscopus gambensis*   Plate 82

Length 7–7.5″. Largely replaces the smaller Black-backed Puffback *north of the Equator*. Arboreal. **Male** distinguished from Black-backed (nowhere sympatric) by *larger size, stouter bill, duller white underparts* and *grey scapulars; rump is grey* (as in female Black-backed); *eyes bright orange-red*. Far northern *D. g. erythreae* is darker on back than the widespread *malzacii*. Distinctive **female** *tawny-buff below*, dusky brown above, the wing-coverts and secondaries edged with buff (not white). **Juvenile** resembles female but has buff wing-feather edges and grey feather tips on head and back. **Immature** has buffy white (male) or deep tawny (female) underparts. (Pringle's Puffback of dry bush country is much smaller, has conspicuously pale mandible base, white tail tip and edges; female much paler below and with distinctive facial pattern.) **Song** a whistled *keow* or *keewu*, repeated several times after a short pause. Varied call notes include a sharp *kek*, a *chuck-chack* of alarm; a harsh, slow *wrrich, wrrich, wrrich*; and a rasping *zhiuu* or *zhrraanh*. **Range**: *D. g. malzacii* from Bondo, Ng'iya and Nandi districts east to Elmenteita, Lake Nakuru NP and Laikipia Plateau, north to the Horr Valley, mts Loima, Nyiru and Marsabit. *D. g. erythreae* near Moyale.

BLACK-BACKED PUFFBACK *Dryoscopus cubla*   **Plate 82**

Length 6-7″. A clean-cut *red-eyed* bush-shrike of wooded areas, mainly south of the Equator. *Arboreal*, and often in mixed-species flocks. **Male** has *bright white* underparts and *black-and-white upperparts; black cap extends to below eyes*. **Female** *has white supraloral stripes and sides of* face; rump grey. Bill black. Inland *D. c. hamatus* has white-edged wing feathers, those of coastal *affinis* all-black. (Intergrades common where ranges overlap.) **Immature** tinged buff below and on wings. **Juvenile** resembles female but is buff below and greyer on flanks; upperparts dull black with grey feather tips; bill brownish. (Male Northern Puffback has dull white underparts and grey rump as does female Black-backed, buff-edged scapulars and more orange-red eyes. In dry e. and ne. Kenya see Pringle's Puffback. Tropical Boubou is larger, shows different wing pattern, and has dark brown eyes.) **Song** a loud repetitive hollow whistle, *WEEO* or *tu-WEEEO,* and a clear *TYEW . . . TYEW . . .,* that can change to an emphatic grating *TCHEW. . . TCHEW. . ..* Other notes include a repeated loud *TSUIK* and a prolonged harsh *ki-eeh.* Courting male calls *chak-chak-chak* on the wing (as rump feathers are puffed out to form a remarkable white ball). Coastal *affinis* incorporates *TYEW* note into an extended song with most notes repeated several times: *tsik-tsik-tsik-tsik skweea, chyaa chyaa chyaa chyaa kyah kyah kyah, TYEW TYEW TYEW TYEW.* **Range:** *D. c. hamatus* widespread inland south of the Equator. *D. c. affinis* in coastal lowlands, inland along lower Tana River to Bura, and in the Shimba Hills.

PRINGLE'S PUFFBACK *Dryoscopus pringlii*   **Plate 82**

Length 5.5″. A *small, dry-country puffback.* Note the *bicoloured bill* (black in other puffbacks) and *grey scapulars* (black in *D. cubla*). **Male** resembles a diminutive Northern Puffback but *basal half of mandible pale* and *tail edged and tipped with dull white* in fresh plumage; brownish grey wash on breast and flanks; *eyes crimson.* **Female** *entirely light grey-brown above with whitish wing edgings* and *narrow, inconspicuous white eye-ring surrounding crimson eye*; pale buff on breast and flanks; narrow white rectrix tips soon wear away. **Juvenile** resembles female but duller. **Call** a sharp repeated *keu* . **Range:** Below 1000 m in e. and ne. Kenya from Mandera, Moyale and Marsabit, and from Samburu GR south to the Tsavo parks and Mkomazi GR. Small disjunct populations in Turkwell River Valley and near Olorgesailie.

PINK-FOOTED PUFFBACK *Dryoscopus angolensis nandensis*   **Plate 82**

Length 6″. Inhabits canopy of west Kenyan forests. **Male** has *black crown, nape* and *upper back; pale grey lower back and rump;* white underparts and dark brown eyes. **Female** grey-headed, *rich tawny buff below except for white belly and under tail-coverts;* olive-brown above with brown eyes. **Juvenile** similar to female but duller. (Female Northern Puffback resembles female Pink-footed, but is larger, browner above with buff or tawny wing edgings and orange eyes. See Bocage's Bush-shrike.) **Song** an emphatic *TCHEW, TCHEW, TCHEW. . .,* the note repeated 10–30 times. Also a harsh churring sound. **Range:** Kakamega and Nandi forests. Formerly on Mt Elgon.

EASTERN NICATOR *Nicator gularis*   **Plate 75**

Length 8–9″. A long-tailed, pale-spotted *olive-and-brownish grey* bird of eastern forests and dense thickets. Shy and skulking but highly vocal. Flicks wings nervously when disturbed. *Large yellow spots on wing-coverts and secondaries unique; under tail-coverts and tips of tail feathers yellow.* Lores yellow in male, white in female. *Bill heavy and hooked.* **Juvenile** at first has unfeathered face. **Immature** has yellow-tipped remiges and wing-coverts. **Song** a loud, liquid whistling, *WEEo WEE, WEE-EE-OO-choWEE,* and a pleasing *chwik, cheerrk, chwick, wherrreek, cho-CHIDilee,* the softer notes audible only at close range. Commonly mimics other species. Alarm call a powerful *TSUCK!;* also a softer *tsuk-tsuk* and a whistled *WEE-oo.* **Range:** Coastal woods, inland to Mkomazi GR, North Pare Mts, s. Moshi District, Taveta, Kibwezi, Endau and along Tana River to Bura. In the north, on Mt Uraguess and the Karissia Hills. The similar (and possibly conspecific) *N. chloris* recorded on Ugandan side of Mt Elgon. **Taxonomic Note:** Formerly in Pycnonotidae.

CUCKOO-SHRIKES, FAMILY CAMPEPHAGIDAE

These birds have no affinities with either shrikes or cuckoos. Our species are starling-sized with rather long, pointed wings and ample, slightly rounded tails. The tarsi are short, the bill usually quite small with slight terminal hook. The dense matted feathers of lower back and rump may be partly erected, giving the bird a hump-backed, somewhat trogon-like outline. Sexual dimorphism pronounced in *Campephaga* species: males glossy blue-black, with the rictal skin often swollen into colourful 'gape flanges'; females yellow, olive and whitish, often extensively barred. Juveniles resemble females, but have pointed rectrices. All cuckoo-shrikes are quiet, unobtrusive arboreal birds, solitary or in pairs, often accompanying mixed-species flocks. They feed on insects (particularly larvae) gleaned from foliage, and on small fruits.

BLACK CUCKOO-SHRIKE *Campephaga flava*   Plate 81

Length 7–8". A sluggish arboreal bird of bush and woodland. The black **male** has blue or greenish blue sheen and vaguely resembles a drongo or glossy starling, but *gape noticeably yellow or orange-yellow*, and *tail tip rounded or square*. Some birds have a black-edged yellow 'shoulder' patch. **Female** greyish olive above, mostly whitish below, *heavily black-barred* and suggesting a small cuckoo; shows noticeable dark eye-lines and *bright yellow wing and tail edgings*. *Underside of tail appears mostly yellow*, and some yellow on sides of breast, leg feathers and rump. **Juvenile** resembles adult female but black-spotted above, and spotted rather than barred below. (Male Petit's Cuckoo-shrike, a forest species, has more obvious, bright orange-yellow gape. Male Purple-throated shows purple gloss on throat. Female Red-shouldered has different tail pattern.) **Song** a rather shrill, loud *tutututu chee-chee-chee-chee wureet-reet-seetiti* and a simpler *tu, chri-chri-chri-chri-chri-chri*. Also gives a high-pitched insect-like trill. Call notes high and sibilant. **Range/status**: Mainly a widespread non-breeding migrant from the southern tropics, May–Oct. Some present all year; has bred at several localities.

RED-SHOULDERED CUCKOO-SHRIKE *Campephaga phoenicea*   Plate 81

Length 7–8". Scarce and local in *western Kenya*. **Male** similar to Black Cuckoo-shrike but has *large scarlet or orange-red epaulettes* and *pale pink gape flanges*. **Female** much like female Black, but *underside of tail feathers black with broad yellow tips; crown and back grey-brown with olive tinge*; rump and upper tail-coverts black-barred. **Juvenile** resembles female but *spotted* (not barred) above and below. Where sympatric with other cuckoo-shrikes (e.g. near Kakamega), mainly a *savanna or open woodland* bird, with Black in second-growth woods or forest edge, slightly overlapping Petit's and Purple-throated in true forest. Often remains hidden in foliage, seldom perching on exposed branches. Rarely heard **call** a soft double whistle. **Range**: Ugandan border areas from Malaba and Alupe to Mumias and Kakamega districts.

PETIT'S CUCKOO-SHRIKE *Campephaga petiti*   Plate 81

Length 7.5". A *west Kenyan forest* species. **Male** closely resembles Black Cuckoo-shrike, but has more *conspicuous orange or orange-yellow gape flanges,* narrow bare orbital ring dull apple-green, and mouth-lining orange-yellow. **Female** *largely yellow, almost unmarked below*, but *heavily barred with black above*, with short yellowish superciliary stripe. **Immature male** resembles female but at least some birds *essentially unmarked above* except on wings; lower back, rump and upper tail-coverts plain rich yellow; tail as in female, largely yellow below; *underparts plain bright yellow with band of faint blackish bars across upper breast*; gape and inside of mouth bright yellow-orange. **Juvenile** resembles adult female or immature but *head and underparts spotted with black*. **Song** a high-pitched, scratchy warbling *sueet-sueet, siueet-seet-seet-sireet*. Infrequent call a short whistled *seep*. **Range**: Kakamega and Nandi forests.

PURPLE-THROATED CUCKOO-SHRIKE *Campephaga quisqualina martini*
Plate 81

Length 7–7.5". A *highland* bird of *forest and forest edge*. Slightly heavier-looking and broader-tailed than Black Cuckoo-shrike. Blue-black **male** has dull *purple gloss on throat and neck*, less prominent on rest of underparts which lack the bluish or greenish sheen of *C. flava*. Velvety black feathers at base of culmen and on lores somewhat better developed than in that species. Rictal skin yellow or orange but *inconspicuous and not swollen*; *mouth-lining red or orange-red* (obvious when the bird 'gapes'). **Female** *plain olive above with contrasting grey head, whitish or greyish throat*, streaked cheeks, dark-eye-lines and narrow white superciliaries; underparts yellow, with variable black barring (rarely lacking). Underside of tail olive-grey, yellow at tip and sides; mouth-lining orange. **Juvenile** resembles female but dark-barred above, faintly barred below, head browner and wing-coverts tipped white. (Petit's Cuckoo-shrike, also in forest, shows bright orange-yellow gape flanges and mouth-lining; female lacks contrasting grey head.) **Song** a monotonously repeated slurred whistled note, *sweep* or *tseeu*, loud and shrill. **Range**: W. and cent. Kenyan highlands. In n. Tanzania known from Loliondo, Mbulumbulu, Mt Hanang and Arusha NP.

GREY CUCKOO-SHRIKE *Coracina caesia pura*   Plate 81

Length 8.5". The *all-grey* cuckoo-shrike of *highland forest. Large whitish eye-ring conspicuous.* Sexes similar but **male** has blackish lores and dusky chin; **female** paler below, especially on chin. **Juvenile** finely barred above and below, with whitish flight-feather edging, and white tail-feather tips. **Immature** resembles adult, but may retain some spotted or barred juvenile feathers. **Calls** a descending nasal *meeeaa,* somewhat cat-like, and a feeble, high-pitched *tseeu* or *tsiu-tsiu.* **Range**: Widespread above 1600 m in the Kenyan highlands. In n. Tanzania at Loliondo, and from 900 to 1900 m in the Usambara Mts. Has wandered rarely to Mrima Hill and the Shimba Hills.

WHITE-BREASTED CUCKOO-SHRIKE *Coracina pectoralis*   Plate 81

Length 10". A rare, large *grey and white* cuckoo-shrike of west Kenyan savanna and woodland. Light grey above with primaries and outer rectrices black; *lower breast and belly white.* **Male** has *dark grey throat and upper breast.* **Female** has *whitish forehead, incomplete eye-ring and chin; throat and upper breast are pale grey.* **Juvenile** barred black, grey, and white above; black-spotted below. Flight flapping and gliding. Frequently joins mixed-species flocks. **Call** of male a soft whistled *duid-duid,* of female a drawn-out trilled *chrreeeeee. . ..* **Range**: Ne. Mt Elgon. Formerly in Busia and Kakamega districts. Vagrant to Tsavo River (July 1914), Arusha NP (Nov. 1969) and near Kondoa (Jan. 1982).

DRONGOS, FAMILY DICRURIDAE

Distinctive black-plumaged birds with rather long, more or less forked tails, the outer feathers of which are splayed out terminally in some species. The head is large and quite flat, the bill stout, somewhat hooked, and basally subtended by strong rictal bristles. The tarsi are short. Decidedly aggressive toward hawks and corvids, often pursuing them in the air. They feed by flycatching or pouncing on insect prey which is held down with the toes and dispatched in raptorial fashion.

COMMON DRONGO *Dicrurus adsimilis*   Plate 81 ✔

Length 9-10". A common and conspicuous 'fish-tailed' black bird. Inner webs of flight feathers greyish tan, producing a *pale silvery flash in flight.* Plumage mainly glossy blue-black except for velvety black forehead; *eyes red.* **Juvenile** blackish brown on head and crissum, dull grey-brown on rest of underparts, with extensive buff feather tips, less deeply forked tail than adult, and amber, grey-brown or light yellowish grey eyes. **Immature** uniformly blue-black but less glossy than adult, brown-eyed, with shallow tail fork, and with faint whitish barring on belly and crissum. (This plumage easily mistaken for Southern Black Flycatcher; note drongo's much larger bill with yellowish white gape.) **Song** of varied short phrases or single notes, often rasping or banjo-like in quality, unhurried and with frequent long pauses, e.g. *skerrik . . . tchwang, skiiing, seeeeek, tsurik-tssrng-cherrinka. . .,* sometimes including parrot-like squeals, other discordant sounds and mimicry. A simpler song consists of a repeated *wurchee-wurchee* with a few different notes. Prolonged pre-dawn song of well-separated phrases contains fewer metallic notes. Call a nasal *chwang.* **Range:** *D. a. adsimilis* widespread from the coast up to 2200 m (said to intergrade with *D. a. divaricatus* in n. Kenya).

VELVET-MANTLED DRONGO *Dicrurus modestus coracinus*   **Plate 81**
Length 9.5–11". A scarce *western forest* drongo. Differs from Common Drongo in having a *velvety black back and rump* and little gloss below. *Inner webs of flight feathers black-ish*, thus no silvery wing flash in flight. Eyes orange-red to deep scarlet. **Juvenile** brown-eyed. Dull **immature** has pale rictal skin and less deeply forked tail. **Song** prolonged, halting, semi-musical, many notes with a pronounced twang; much repetition of notes or phrases: *tsik, chk cher we wee-wee-weu, stik tser-eu, stick ter-eu, tsik-ter wee-tsik-twer-wee-wee, tser, suk, chk, ker-wee-quanh, chick cher-wi -squanh. . ..* Has various harsh scolding calls. **Range**: Kakamega Forest. Formerly on Mt Elgon.

SQUARE-TAILED DRONGO *Dicrurus ludwigii*   **Plate 81**

Length 7". A small forest drongo with a *slightly notched tail* (often twitched sideways) and bright *orange-red eyes*. **Male** glossy black (duller, more bluish/purplish in western *sharpei*, greener in eastern *ludwigii*). **Female** all black in *sharpei*, but with dark *slate-grey underparts* and (rarely?) whitish-tipped under tail-coverts in eastern birds. **Juvenile** resembles female but is speckled pale grey on mantle and breast; eyes brown. A rather secretive bird, usually in leafy cover, low or high. Persistently vocal. **Song** less jangling and more structured than that of Velvet-mantled Drongo, variable but often with repeated phrases; typically loud, strident or ringing: *SKI-tsi-chee si-chee-chee see-see*, or *cherk, chichi chwerk-chwerk*, or *cherk whuit whuit whuit*. Calls include a harsh rasping *chyaa*, a ringing *WEEK-yer* and *yerk-yerk*. **Range**: *D. l. ludwigii* in coastal lowlands from Tana delta northward, and inland along the Tana River to Garissa; also up to 2000 m in the Usambara Mts. *D. l. sharpei* in Kakamega and South Nandi forests (formerly on Mt Elgon).

ORIOLES, FAMILY ORIOLIDAE

Arboreal, starling-sized birds (not to be confused with New World orioles of family Icteridae). *Oriolus* species are stout-billed and long-winged with rather short tails. The sexes are alike or (in the migratory species) different, the plumage largely yellow and olive, often with black on head or wings. Most species are shy and remain hidden in high foliage, their presence revealed only by loud fluty whistles. Foraging movements are slow and deliberate, but flight tends to be swift and undulating.

✓ **BLACK-HEADED ORIOLE** *Oriolus larvatus rolleti*   **Plate 80**

Length 8–8.5". The commonly seen dark-headed oriole, typical of acacia woods and savanna. Central rectrices are *olive, not black*. Yellowish olive above and yellow below, with black head and throat; outer secondaries edged with greyish white, and primary coverts with a conspicuous white spot; closed tail olive above and yellow below, showing large yellow corners when spread. Bill deep pink or reddish; eyes red. (Montane Oriole of mountain forests has more contrasting pattern with black central rectrices. Western Black-headed Oriole of Kakamega Forest has duller wings with greyer feather edges.) **Juvenile** similar but head duller, with yellow-green feather edges, a yellow half-collar on sides of neck, obscurely streaked back, and *boldly streaked underparts* (streaks dense on throat); eyes grey-brown, bill dull black. **Song** a short liquid whistle, *ku-WEEo* or *weelka-WEEo* or *QU-o-wo*, and a shorter *keeWO* or *CLUeo*, repeated; alarm call a harsh *kwarr*. **Range**: Widespread below 2300 m (except in dry n. and ne. Kenya).

MONTANE ORIOLE *Oriolus percivali*   **Plate 80**

Length 7.75–8.5". A *highland forest* bird, closely resembling Black-headed Oriole but pattern more contrasting with deeper blacks and brighter, more extensive yellows above. *Central tail feathers black*, not olive, and in fresh plumage shows whitish stripe formed by edges of outer secondaries; *inner wing feathers mainly black but both inner and outer webs contrastingly margined with yellow-olive*, but colour of flight feathers often hard to see, and subject to wear and hybridization (see below). However, *greater coverts mainly dull yellowish* with less grey than in *larvatus*. **Juvenile**

much less heavily streaked on breast than young *larvatus*. **Song** similar to that of Black-headed Oriole and not always distinguishable. Typical are a short *e'YO* or *EE-yo*, a squealing *chaeWEE* or *CHWEE* which may flow into a liquid *qua-WEEo*. Common is a loud *weeka-ku-WEEU* to which female may reply with a higher *weekla-wee-er*. **Range**: Above 1850 m in w. and cent. Kenya from Mt Elgon and the Cheranganis south to the Mau, Trans-Mara, Aberdares and Mt Kenya. (Known to hybridize with *O. larvatus* in remnant forest patches north of Nairobi, reflecting incomplete reproductive isolation from that species. The two forms are increasingly in contact as forest habitat of *percivali* shrinks.)

WESTERN BLACK-HEADED ORIOLE *Oriolus brachyrhynchus laetior* Plate 80

Length 8–8.5". In our region restricted to *Kakamega Forest* where the only oriole. Resembles Black-headed Oriole, the differences difficult to see on birds high in forest trees. *Central tail feathers yellowish olive, not darkening terminally,* and *outer secondaries edged with slate-grey, not whitish; exposed webs of inner wing feathers olive, with no pale yellow edges,* and black inner webs also lack contrasting pale edges. **Juvenile** has dark olive head indistinctly streaked with black. **Song** a rapid *tututuWEEah* or *cucuWEEa*, more shrill than calls of Black-headed and Montane Orioles. Some shorter, more fluty calls resemble those of related species. **Range**: Kakamega Forest, w. Kenya.

GREEN-HEADED ORIOLE *Oriolus chlorocephalus amani* Plate 80

Length 8.5". A distinctive oriole of *coastal forest and the Usambara Mts.* Adult has dull *velvety green head,* throat and upper breast and dark olive-green back; most underparts and *collar on hindneck bright yellow; wings pale blue-grey with no white spot* on primary coverts; tail dark green with yellow corners and sides. Bill pink, eyes red. **Juvenile** *streaked with olive-green below;* yellowish on chin and throat; wing-coverts tipped yellow; bill dark. (Juv. Black-headed Oriole shows some dark greenish olive on head, but streaking on underparts is blackish.) **Song** slightly more liquid than that of Black-headed, the phrases often less abrupt: *ku-WEE-oo* or *kwee-WO* (each utterance accompanied by a quick fanning of the tail). A longer *onk-onk-co-WOyo* or simpler *coWOyo* characteristic as is a distinctive nasal mewing, *kweee-aaah*. **Range**: Local on Kenyan coast from Diani and Shimba Hills (uncommon) north to Arabuko–Sokoke Forest (rare). Common up to 1200 m in the Usambaras.

AFRICAN GOLDEN ORIOLE *Oriolus auratus* Plate 80

Length 8". In all plumages distinguished from Eurasian Golden Oriole by *broadly yellow-edged greater coverts and secondaries.* **Male** bright golden yellow with conspicuous *black streak through eyes;* black *wings have broad yellow feather edges;* tail mostly yellow with black central feathers; (yellow extends to base of outer rectrices in southern *notatus* but not in nominate *auratus*). Bill dull brownish red; eyes bright red. **Female** yellowish olive above with olive-grey eye-line and yellow upper tail-coverts; underparts yellow with some short olive streaks and an olive wash on sides of breast. **Juvenile** and **immature** similar to adult female above but underparts heavily black-streaked. Easily confused with streaky female or immature Eurasian Golden, but *bend of wing mainly yellow-olive,* not much darker than sides of neck and scapulars; bill black; eyes dull brown. **Song** a liquid *cuWEERo* and *turereeo-ki*, and a longer *weeka-la-weeoo*, more fluty and prolonged than those of Black-headed Oriole. Alarm note, a harsh mewing *mwaaa* or *mwaaarr*. **Range/status**: *O. a. notatus* is a non-breeding migrant from the southern tropics, mainly April–Aug., common in Tanzania and coastal Kenya north to the Tana River and Lamu; ranges north and west to Lake Victoria, and the w. and cent. Kenyan highlands. Nominate *auratus* from the northern tropics recorded on Mt Elgon and ne. base of the Cheranganis; sight records from Baringo and Kapedo districts may be of this form.

EURASIAN GOLDEN ORIOLE *Oriolus o. oriolus* Plate 80

Length 8.25–9". **Male** bright yellow with *black wings* (yellow spot on primary coverts), *black lores,* and black tail with yellow corners. Bill dark pink; eyes dark red. (African Golden Oriole shows much yellow on wings, has black streak *through* eye.) **Female/ immature male** yellow-olive above with brighter yellow upper tail-coverts; usually *grey-*

ish white below with dark brownish streaks and pale yellow sides and under tail-coverts; wings dark olive-brown with little pale feather edging; dark 'shoulder' contrasts with scapulars and sides of neck; tail blackish with yellow corners. **Older female** yellower below (more olive on throat and breast), with narrow olive streaks (suggests dull male but *loral spot olive-grey*); bill pinkish red. **First-winter** bird (both sexes) has brown bill and (usually) a yellow wing-bar; more whitish below than adult female, with darker streaks. **Song** a liquid fluty whistle, *weeka-laweela-weeoo*, or a shorter *weela-woo*. Call a harsh *kraa* or *kree-er*, and a *churr* of annoyance or alarm. **Range/status:** Palearctic passage migrant, Oct.–Dec. and late March–April, frequent in cent. and se. Kenya, less regular in n. Tanzania. On return, common along coast north to Malindi. A few winter in Tsavo area.

CROWS AND ALLIES, FAMILY CORVIDAE

Conspicuous and adaptable birds, some of them numerous around human habitation where their raucous nasal calls are a common sound. Our species are residents, one of them introduced. They are primarily black-plumaged, but some show white, grey or brown. The bill is strong, often heavy, the nostrils concealed by forward-directed bristles; feet are large and strong; tail varies greatly in length and shape; wings are broad and, in *Corvus*, often used for soaring. Gregarious for much of the year.

PIAPIAC *Ptilostomus afer*   Plate 80
Length 14″. A small sociable corvid of Ugandan border areas, where scarce. *Long grad- uated tail* distinctive as it feeds on the ground, often with domestic mammals. Walks and runs as well as hops. Flies with rapid wingbeats. Mainly black with faint purplish/bluish gloss; rump and upper tail-coverts dark brown; wings dusky brown, the *primaries almost silvery below, appearing noticeably pale in flight*; tail soon fades to light brown; eyes pur- ple or violet; bill and feet black. **Juvenile** has brown eyes and pink or light reddish bill with dark tip, the colour persisting for some months in immature birds. **Call** a shrill pip- ing *pee-ip* repeated in series; also a short rasping *kweer* and a scolding chatter. **Range:** Busia, Alupe, Mumias, Maseno and (formerly) Kisumu districts.

✓HOUSE CROW *Corvus s. splendens*   Plate 80

Length 13″. A slender *black and grey* crow with relatively large bill and fairly long tail extending well beyond wing tips in perched bird. Black on forecrown and from face to central breast. Nape, neck and lower breast dull buffy grey shading to sooty on belly; back, wings and tail black, well glossed with green, blue and purple. **Juvenile** duller, more brownish black and paler grey than adult. **Call**, *kwaa, kwaa,* more nasal and higher-pitched than call of Pied Crow. **Range:** Introduced and in- creasing on coast (displacing Pied Crow in many places). Abundant from Mombasa south to Diani, less common north to Malindi, and inland to Mackinnon Road. (Control mea- sures initiated in 1990s).

DWARF or BROWN-NECKED RAVEN *Corvus (ruficollis) edithae*   Plate 80

Length 18″. An all-dark corvid of *arid northern Kenya*, often in small groups around villages and camps. 'Desert Crow' would be a better name. Size, proportions and voice like those of Pied Crow. *At rest, wing tips extend to tip of moderately long wedge-shaped tail.* Bill rather long and slim (but less extreme than in Cape Rook). Sometimes dark brown on head; upper back bronze-glossed; rest of upperparts, wings and tail with faint bluish or purplish blue sheen. Concealed bases of pointed throat feathers and those of nape and breast *snow-white,* evident in display or when feathers disarranged by wind. **Juvenile** light brown (at times almost rufous) on head; underparts and upper back; bases of neck and breast feathers whitish, not pure white. **Call** a nasal croaking, *kwaar-kwaar-kwaar,* varied to *waaa or yaaa.* Also a short metallic *onk* or *kwonk,* a double *rrawnk-rrawnk,* a guttural rattle or purr, and a flat *yack, yack.* **Range:** N. Kenya south to Kapedo, Laisamis, Mado Gashi and Wajir. **Taxonomic Note:** Probably not conspecific with extralimital *C. ruficollis,* compared to which *edithae* is smaller, has more consistently white (not dusky) neck-feather bases, shorter primary extension, shorter and more slender bill, tree-nesting (instead of generally cliff-nesting) habits, and at least some different vocalizations.

PIED CROW *Corvus albus* — Plate 80 ✓

Length 18″. The familiar black-and-white crow in much of East Africa, present in all urban areas. Easily identified by *white breast and belly continuous with broad white collar across hindneck*; adult plumage otherwise glossy black. **Juvenile** duller black, the white feathers dusky-tipped. **Call** a harsh, nasal *kwah* or *kwar, kwar*, more rasping in alarm. Other sounds a snoring *khrrrr*, a hard hollow *clock, clock . . .*, a nasal *whawnk* or *aahnk*, a flat *ack-ack* and a throaty *glupp*, some of these given with raised head and exaggerated movements of wings and tail. Displaying bird gives a creaky growling *urrrrrkkk*, answered by mate's higher clicking *tkkk*. These accompany deep bowing with fluffed head feathers, partially spread wings and downward-pointing bill. **Range:** Widespread in open country up to 3000 m; in arid n. Kenya mainly in towns and villages where sympatric with Dwarf Raven.

WHITE-NAPED RAVEN *Corvus albicollis* — Plate 80 ✓

Length 22″. A large black corvid with *broad white collar on hindneck* and a *very deep, ivory-tipped black bill*; head and neck bronzy brown, the face black. Wings broad, tail quite short. **Juvenile** duller than adult with black streaks on the white nape, and in some birds scattered white-edged or all-white feathers on neck and breast. Often in mountains, but scavenges around villages in lower country. See Pied Crow. **Calls** include a high-pitched, almost falsetto croak, typically repeated: *krerk krerk krerk. . .*, a short guttural *wuk* or *raak*, and a soft husky *haa*. A short, somewhat metallic clattering *cluk-cluk-cluk* is given with head bowed in presence of presumed mate. **Range:** As low as 400 m in e. Kenya (Voi) to above 4000 m on high mountains. Sympatric with Fan-tailed Raven north of the Equator.

FAN-TAILED RAVEN *Corvus rhipidurus* — Plate 80

Length 18″. Stocky and all black. The *extremely short tail and broad wings* provide a unique flight silhouette; wing tips extend well beyond tail when perched. Adult plumage shows bronze or blue gloss but young birds duller and browner. Often near cliffs or rocky slopes. **Calls** include a guttural *waak*, a high, Pied Crow-like *kwaa-kwaa*, a longer growling *errrraak* or *errrrow* repeated numerous times, a high hollow *WOK* and a louder, more nasal *YAHNK* or *WHONK*, separate or in series. Some of these and other notes are combined in extended 'songs.' **Range:** Local in n. Kenya, mainly below 1500 m, south to Mt Elgon, the Kerio Valley, Marigat, Isiolo and Kitui districts.

CAPE ROOK or BLACK CROW *Corvus capensis* — Plate 80

Length 17″. A lightly built black corvid with a *slender bill*. Forages in groups on fields and plains, and (in n. Kenya) semi-deserts. Plumage glossed with purplish and steel-blue. Throat feathers lax, often raised to some degree; head blackish brown with slight gloss, purplish coppery on crown and nape. Bases of neck feathers dark grey. Juvenile and worn birds browner throughout. **Call** a loud harsh *RRRAK-raaah* or *Rrraak-aawah*, the second note higher. A liquid *kwer-kaplop* or *gur-lalop* given with head and throat feathers erected. Bowing call, a low gurgling *gwurrr* followed by a sharp *tik*. Also a guttural cackle. **Range:** Widespread between 1350 and 2500 m in cent. Rift Valley and adjacent highlands. Also in dry n. Kenya (where sympatric with Dwarf Raven) from Lake Turkana basin east to Turbi and Moyale. In n. Tanzania from e. Serengeti Plains, Ngorongoro Crater and around Monduli.

STARLINGS AND OXPECKERS, FAMILY STURNIDAE

Most starlings (Subfamily Sturninae) are medium-sized, sturdy birds with strong feet and bills. Many are dark or brightly plumaged. The glossy starlings (*Lamprotornis*) and some others display intense iridescence with satiny greens, blues and purples. The sexes may be alike or, less often, differently patterned. Long graduated tails characterize *Cosmopsarus* and most *Onychognathus*. Forest starlings (e.g. *Cinnyricinclus* and *Poeoptera*) are arboreal, whereas open-country species are equally at home on the ground. None has an accomplished song, but most utter a variety of whistled, chattering, twittering and squeaking notes. Many are gregarious when not breeding. A few species build cup-shaped or domed nests, but the majority breed in tree cavities. The two oxpeckers (Buphaginae) are aberrant starlings that accompany large game mammals and livestock in search of ticks.

KENRICK'S STARLING *Poeoptera kenricki*   **Plate 79**

Length 7.5". A slender gregarious starling of *montane forest canopy* in e. Kenya and ne. Tanzania. The glossy black **male** resembles western Stuhlmann's Starling, but has faint *bronzy* (not blue) gloss; wings and tail dull blackish; *eyes slate-grey in all Kenyan bensoni examined; grey or pale yellowish in smaller nominate kenricki* of Tanzania, the variation poorly understood. **Female** slate-grey, weakly glossed bronzy black on back, wings and tail; *inner webs of primaries rufous*, broadly edged and tipped black, obvious only in flight; eyes as in male. **Juvenile** sooty grey below; primaries black in male, largely chestnut in female; eyes duller. Sympatric Waller's Starling (which flocks with Kenrick's) is larger and broader-tailed. **Call** a loud monotonous and repetetive *pleep, pleep*. Flocks produce a musical babbling. **Range**: *P. k. bensoni* between 1500 and 2500 m on Mt Kenya, in nearby Meru Forest and the Nyambeni Hills; *kenricki* in Arusha NP, on Kilimanjaro, Mt Meru, the Pare and Usambara mts.

STUHLMANN'S STARLING *Poeoptera stuhlmanni*   **Plate 79**

Length 7". A *west Kenyan* forest species. High-flying and gregarious. *Eyes brown, the iris with a yellow peripheral ring*. **Male** *glossy blue-black* on head and underparts, dull brownish black on back, wings and tail; no chestnut in wings. **Female** *dark grey with faint bluish gloss; primaries rufous* with dark edges and tips. **Juvenile** sooty-black below; both sexes with rufous in wings, lost by male in post-juvenile moult. (Male of eastern Kenrick's Starling is bronzy black with grey or yellowish eyes; female has bronzy gloss. Waller's Starling is larger, stockier and broader-tailed.) **Song** of clear slurred whistles, *creep-creep turreep-chlerreep-tleeoo* and *TREEoup, turEEP twilieu, sureep-treep-creep-keew*; also a higher, thinner song and a loud squealing *werk-REEK* or *wee-YEW*. Trilling flight call suggests Eurasian Bee-eater. **Range**: Above 1500 m in Nandi, Kakamega, Kericho, Eldama Ravine and Kabarnet areas. One sight record from Mt Elgon.

WALLER'S STARLING *Onychognathus walleri*   **Plate 79**

Length 9". Another gregarious *highland forest* starling, stockier and *shorter-tailed* than the two *Poeoptera* species (with which Waller's is sympatric). Both sexes have *black-tipped rufous-chestnut primaries* and red eyes. **Male** glossy black with violet sheen (more greenish blue on head). **Female** *O. w. walleri* less glossy than male, the head and throat dark grey, nape and hindcrown densely streaked with shiny greenish blue-black; similar streaks on lower throat merge with faintly glossed breast. *O. w. elgonensis* is grey only on throat, and is less streaked. **Juvenile** dull black. (Kenrick's and Stuhlmann's Starlings are smaller, slimmer and longer tailed. Slender-billed Starling is larger with still longer, more steeply graduated tail.) **Song** a series of high slurred whistles, *weer-tew t'wee* or *wee-turr-tree-wureet*. Common calls are a repeated clear whistle, *cheer-whew* , or *TEE, pew-pew*, the first note higher. Call *errack, yak yak* and a low *werk*. **Range**: *O. w. elgonensis* is local west of Rift Valley from Mt Elgon and Saiwa NP south to the Mau, Trans-Mara and Nguruman forests, locally in the Crater Highlands and Nou Forest near Mbulu. *O. w. walleri* above 1600 m east of the Rift, from Marsabit and Maralal south to Aberdares, Mt Kenya and Meru Forest, Kilimanjaro, Mt Meru, Pare and Usambara mts. May move down to 300 m in the East Usambaras.

RED-WINGED STARLING *Onychognathus morio*   Plate 79

Length 11–12". Commonest of the rufous-winged starlings; a robust dark bird with a *long pointed tail.* Inhabits escarpments, gorges and cities. Black **male** has slight violet-blue gloss and dark-tipped *rufous primaries;* eyes brown. Similar **female** has *grey head and neck with narrow glossy violet streaks* broadening on upper breast. **Juvenile** dull sooty black; wings as in adult. Mt Elgon birds are more slender-billed. Flies rapidly, calling repeatedly. (Montane Slender-billed S. has longer, more graduated tail and slim bill; male glossed green on head; female with grey-tipped body feathers. Waller's Starling has short tail and smaller bill.) **Song** a series of whistles, *tuwhee tuwer teweedle tuwurtelee turdilee . . ..* Various whistling calls loud, drawn-out, and quite oriole-like: *tu-whee orpeeeo, sometimes pee-teeeo* or a simple soft *tew.* In flight utters a high-pitched twittering. **Range:** Widespread from 1000 to 2400 m (600 m near Voi, and to 3000 m on Mt Elgon). From the Ndotos and Mt Kulal south to the Crater and Mbulu highlands east to Arusha and Moshi districts, the Pare Mts and Mkomazi GR. Scarce in Usambara foothills. Common around kopjes in Serengeti NP.

SLENDER-BILLED STARLING *Onychognathus tenuirostris theresae*   Plate 79

Length 11.5–13". A *slender-billed* 'red-winged' starling of *high elevations,* typically around moorland waterfalls where often in noisy flocks. *Tail much longer* and more graduated than in *O. morio.* **Male** black with green-glossed head, back and rump tinged violet, throat glossy blue darkening to violet on belly; eyes brown. **Female** duller blue-black, many head and body feathers tipped with dull buff and grey. **Juvenile** uniformly dull black. (Stockier larger-billed Red-winged Starling is rarely above 2400 m except on Mt Elgon.) **Song** (often in chorus) a prolonged series of soft and semi-harsh notes mixed with short whistles and other sounds, many of the notes repeated: *quek-quek-quek-quek, tchuEK-tchuEK-tchuEK, seeWEEowee, cur-cur-cur-cur-cur-SWEEo-sqeeik. . ..* Call note a clear *teeo.* **Range:** Cent. Kenyan highlands, especially Aberdares and Mt Kenya; also at Nyahururu and on Mau, Elgeyu and Kongelai escarpments. One record from West Usambara Mts.

BRISTLE-CROWNED STARLING *Onychognathus salvadorii*   Plate 79

Length 15.5–16.5". A *very long-tailed* rufous-winged starling with prominent *'cushion' of erect velvety black feathers on forecrown.* Typically near cliffs and gorges in dry bush country. **Male** black, glossed with violet on head, bluish on body and greenish on tail. The rufous primaries have black tips. **Female** has greyer head with a smaller 'cushion.' **Juvenile** much duller. **Call** a sharp whistle, *suk-SWEEK* or *su-WEER,* and a high 2-syllabled whistling *chreep-rr,* often in flight. Annoyance call a harsh scolding *schwaah.* **Range:** Below 1300 m from Baringo and Isiolo districts north to Sudanese and Ethiopian borders.

BLACK-BELLIED STARLING *Lamprotornis corruscus*   Plate 77

Length 7.5". A small dark glossy starling of eastern and coastal forest (including mangroves). Arboreal, in pairs or noisy flocks. Shiny blue-green on head, upper breast, wings and back; ear-coverts, 'shoulders', rump and tail glossed with violet; *no black spots on wing-coverts;* lower breast bluish purple; *belly and crissum black* in male, sooty in female; eyes golden yellow. *L. c. vaughani* of Pemba Island has violet crown. **Juvenile** sooty black below with little iridescence. (Lesser Blue-eared Starling has violet belly and black spots on wing coverts. Imm. Greater Blue-eared is black-bellied but longer tailed, dark-eyed and is mainly a ground feeder.) **Song** (*L. c. mandanus*) includes squawks, trills, warbling and fluty whistles; a short phrase, *tcherk WHEEO* or *tchuk WEEO WEEO,* is repeated many times. Flocks produce a continuous babbling chorus, including imitations of other birds. **Range:** *L. c. mandanus* coastal, inland along Tana River to Kora NR, in Shimba Hills and to 1000 m in East Usambaras; *jombeni* above 1500 m in Meru and Nyambeni forests. Wanders (subspecies?) to Samburu GR, Meru NP, Kibwezi and s. slopes of Kilimanjaro; *vaughani* is restricted to Pemba Island.

SPLENDID GLOSSY STARLING *Lamprotornis s. splendidus* **Plate 77**
Length 9.5–11". Well named, this *large western* starling is highly coloured and magnificently iridescent. **Male** shining *golden green above*, blue on back, scapulars, and rump, with small bright coppery patch on side of neck, and a velvety black band across wing (below lower row of black covert spots); *throat and breast brilliant shining violet with brassy or coppery reflections* on breast; belly and crissum blue; *eyes pale creamy yellow.* **Female** noticeably smaller, *bluer below* with less brassy/coppery iridescence. **Juvenile** blackish brown (female) or blue-black (male) below; no brassy sheen. Arboreal and shy. Wings produce *loud 'swishing' sound in flight* when *broad tail* also apparent. (Purple Starling is smaller with large, bright yellow eyes and purple belly. Greater Blue-eared is blue and green with bright orange-yellow eyes.) *Distinctive* **call** of nasal, metallic and grating notes such as *nya-au*, *spi-yonk*, *kahn* and *kua-kuonk* mixed with whistles in various combinations. **Range**: Owing to extensive deforestation now only in Mt Elgon and Saiwa NPs, Oct.–May. Six birds in w. Mara GR (Aug. 1997) may have been wandering *L. s. bailundensis* (from Ukerewe Islands in s. Lake Victoria) which has reached n. Tanzania west of our area.

PURPLE STARLING *Lamprotornis purpureus amethystinus* **Plate 77**

Length 10.5". Local in western Kenya. A large starling with *rich metallic purple head and underparts*, and with *bright yellow eyes that appear unusually large*. Also appears *longer-billed, longer-necked and shorter-tailed than its relatives*. Glossy green on back and wings shading to blue on rump and tail. **Juvenile** less iridescent but head, rump and tail blue or violet, back golden green or blue, and underparts violet-black. (Greater Blue-eared Starling is more blue and green, less purple, and has longer tail. Splendid Glossy Starling is larger, broad-tailed and has pale creamy yellow eyes.) **Song** incorporates a variety of squeaky whistles and chattering calls, sometimes in chorus. **Range**: From Maseno, Akala and Ng'iya west to Ukwala and Busia; a few on Mt Elgon, in Saiwa NP and near Kapenguria.

✔ **GREATER BLUE-EARED STARLING** *Lamprotornis chalybaeus* **Plate 77**

Length, *L. c. cyaniventris*, 9–9.5"; *L. c. sycobius*, 8.5–9.25". The common blue or blue-green glossy starling with dark purplish blue ear-coverts (often appearing black). Brilliantly iridescent when feeding on the ground in full sunlight. The larger *L. c. cyaniventris* is dark green with blue sheen on head and back, bluer on rump and upper tail-coverts, greenish blue on tail; lower breast shining blue-green merging with blue-violet on belly; black spots on wing-coverts; *eyes orange-yellow*. Often in large noisy flocks. Smaller, less sociable race *sycobius* of Tanzania and se. Kenya is brighter, *much greener on head and neck*, with well-developed (but normally concealed) *violet patch near bend of wing*, dark purplish blue ear-coverts and *bright magenta-violet flanks and belly*; easily mistaken for Lesser Blue-eared Starling (but note tail length, narrower ear patch, different voice). **Juvenile** sooty brown heavily washed with bottle-green or greenish blue above; belly dull black; eyes grey-brown. In nw. Kenya see Bronze-tailed Starling. **Song** a succession of harsh chatterings whistles and nasal or guttural notes, *squeer-weer*, *tsuck-tsick*, *cherrrk-skwiiiiii*, *squirk* . . . .. Distinctive call a nasal, somewhat querulous *chweer* or *chweer-weer*; also a rough *yeeeah* or *wreeeak*. **Range**: *L. c. cyaniventris* widespread in the Kenyan highlands north to Mt Elgon and Mathews Range, and around Moyale, south to Mara GR and Crater Highlands. Wanders in non-breeding season to Lake Victoria, nw borders, Lake Turkana and elsewhere. *L. c. sycobius* in Tanzania north to Serengeti and Tarangire NPs, Arusha and Moshi districts, Mkomazi GR, and se. Kenya north to Malindi, west to Kibwezi.

LESSER BLUE-EARED STARLING *Lamprotornis chloropterus* **Plate 77**
Length 7–8". Relatively scarce. Distinguished from widespread Greater Blue-eared Starling by much *shorter tail, greener iridescence, narrower dark ear-covert patch, little or no blue or purple except on rump and belly*; eyes orange-yellow. (In se. and coastal Kenya *L. chalybeus sycobius* easily mistaken for *L. chloropterus*.) **Juvenile** has green gloss on back and wings, dark brownish head and dull brown or brownish grey underparts, these rufous-brown in Tanzanian race *elisabeth*. (Bronze-tailed Starling is bluer, less green,

above with purple lower breast and belly; tail purple or bronze.) **Song** a succession of short squeaks, squawks and throaty whistles, higher-pitched than those of Greater Blue-eared, and with fewer guttural sounds. In flight, a clear *wirri-wirri* or *wi-WIri*. When perched, a rising *cherwee* or *chirrriree-ree; also we-wuREET*. **Range**: In w. Kenya, *L. c. chloropterus* on Kongelai Escarpment, rarely near South Horr. *L. c. elisabeth* is a miombo woodland bird of interior Tanzania (formerly wandered north to Mombasa and Malindi).

BRONZE-TAILED STARLING *Lamprotornis chalcurus emini*   **Plate 77**

Length 8–9″. An uncommon *northwestern* starling resembling a *short-tailed* Greater Blue-eared, but bluer above and *rich purple on belly and tail*, the latter bluer at sides and tip and showing bronze or bronzy purple reflections at some angles; *upper tail-coverts and rump purplish blue to bronzy purple, contrasting with blue-green back*; eyes deep yellow or orange. **Juvenile** blackish, tinged blue above, dull sooty black below with greenish blue sheen on breast; tail greenish blue; eyes dark. Wings noisy in flight like those of Splendid Glossy Starling. (The two blue-eared starlings have greenish blue tails, that of *L. chalybeus* quite long; rump of *chalybeus* may appear purplish. Purple Starling has blue rump and tail, much purple on head and breast.) **Call** a loud nasal and throaty chattering like Greater Blue-eared Starling but harsher. **Range**: Lokichokio area, Kapenguria and parts of the Kerio Valley. Formerly at Kitale and Kakamega.

RÜPPELL'S LONG-TAILED STARLING *Lamprotornis purpuropterus*   **Plate 77**

Length 10.5–12.5″ The *long graduated purple or bronzy tail* and *creamy white eyes* set this dark glossy starling apart from others in our region. Largely *blue-black with violet/purple reflections*; belly and under tail-coverts black; *no spots on wing-coverts*. **Juvenile** dark-eyed and shorter-tailed; head sooty with violet gloss; underparts dull black with some blue on breast. **Song** contains a variety of rolling whistles, high squeaks, harsh grating sounds, nasal sounds and short warbling notes, each phrase distinct but part of a rather pleasing prolonged utterance, *chawaaa chwaa chuweeer-rrrrrrooo, wha-cheeer chiWEEEK, whaaaah, kwa-kwa QUEEEEEEEERRRR, tsuck-wiiiiiiiii-iiiiiii, tsickWEEEEEO. . .*. Common call, *kewo KWEERR KWEWEERR*. **Range**: In and west of the Rift Valley, south to Serengeti NP and Maswa GR. Uncommon east of the Rift, mainly around the Athi, Galana, Tiva and Tana rivers; locally on Laikipia Plateau and from Garsen northward.

HILDEBRANDT'S STARLING *Lamprotornis hildebrandti*   **Plate 77** ✔

Length 7.5–8″. A *rufous-bellied* starling with *no white breast band* (as in juvenile Superb Starling). Darker than Superb, iridescent *violet-blue on head and breast*, greenish on wings and hindneck, pale rufous on lower breast, darker from belly to under tail-coverts; *eyes red*. **Juvenile** duller, *bluish above*, with shiny *blue-green wings*; head brown with some rufous on face; underparts generally dull rufous, browner on upper breast, below which obscurely spotted; eyes brown. (Juv. Superb is dull black on breast and brown-eyed. Shelley's Starling is uniformly dark *chestnut* below, has orange eyes.) **Song** of harsh creaky notes and high clear whistles, slowly uttered with many distinct pauses: *cherrraaa-cherrraaa, turlewp. . ., queeleree. . ., cherrrah, eeeep . . ., the clearer notes higher-pitched. Also has a low guttural subsong, *kwa-aa kw-kweeo, kwer-kwee-er*. One call a repeated *chiweh-chiweh-chiweh*. **Range**: Between 700 and 1700 m in interior n. Tanzania and in s. Kenya north to Kibwezi, Sultan Hamud and Nairobi NP. Also from Maralal and Laikipia Plateau east to Isiolo, Meru NP and the upper Tana River.

SHELLEY'S STARLING *Lamprotornis shelleyi*   **Plate 77**

Length 7–7.5″. Suggests Hildebrandt's Starling but has *deep chestnut belly* and *orange eyes*. An uncommon bird of dry thorn-bush and scrub (especially *Commiphora*) in n. and e. Kenya. **Juvenile** differs from young Hildebrandt's in its greyer brown head and back, the latter without gloss; underside of flight feathers greyish, not blackish as in Hildebrandt's. Usually alone or in small groups, at times with Magpie Starlings. **Call** strident and harsh, recalling Superb Starling. **Range:** Mainly below 1300

m. Perhaps resident around Lokichokio, Mandera, El Wak and Wajir. In e. and se. Kenya, a non-breeding visitor Aug.–March, south to the Tsavo parks and Mkomazi GR.

✓ SUPERB STARLING *Lamprotornis superbus*　　　Plate 77

Length 7–7.5". Brightly iridescent, with *cream-coloured eyes*. The *narrow white band separating rufous-orange belly from blue upper breast* marks this familiar species. Head and spots on wings velvety black; *under tail-coverts and wing-linings white*. (Neither Hildebrandt's nor Shelley's Starlings have white on underparts.) **Juvenile** duller, the head and breast dull black with little or no suggestion of adult's white band; eyes brown at first, later greyish white. **Song** loud and sustained, of trilling and chattering notes, often in chorus. Mimics other birds. Midday subsong of slower softer phrases, *cheeeerit tsweee-eur, sweeshi-ee swee-eee, chwee-eu chwee-eu, whicher-which*, etc. in varying patterns. Alarm note an extended *chiiirrrr*. Also gives a rasping trilled *cherrah-cherrreet*, and a shrill screeching *skerrrreeee-cherrrrroo-tcherreeeeeet*. **Range**: Widespread below 2000 m, but largely absent from Lake Victoria basin (except around Ahero and Ruma NP), the coast south of Malindi, and Usambara Mts.

GOLDEN-BREASTED STARLING *Cosmopsarus regius*　　　Plate 77

Length 13.5–14". Unmistakable. A resplendent, multicoloured, long-tailed starling of eastern dry bush and bushed grassland. Brilliant iridescent blue above, purple on wings, rich coppery red-violet on flight feathers, *shining satiny green on head and throat*, and with a *patch of iridescent reddish violet on breast*; rest of *underparts rich golden yellow*; tail slender and strongly graduated, black with bronze or old-gold reflections; eyes white. **Juvenile** much duller; head to breast and upperparts brownish with traces of iridescence; lower breast/belly dull yellow; eyes greyish. **Call**, in flight, a whistling chattering *cherrrreeeeeeter-cherrrree*. **Range**: Northern border areas south (east of Rift Valley) to Samburu and Shaba GRs, Meru and the Tsavo NPs, Mkomazi GR and adjacent parts of the Masai Steppe; reaches the coast north of Malindi.

✓ ASHY STARLING *Cosmopsarus unicolor*　　　Plate 122

Length 11–12". A *plain brownish grey, long-tailed* starling of thorn-bush and woodland in dry *interior Tanzania*. Paler and greyer on crown, ear-coverts and breast; faintly glossed with greenish on wings and tail; eyes creamy yellow, contrasting with black lores. Darker-eyed **juvenile** dull ashy grey with pale horn-coloured bill and pale eye-ring. **Call** a plaintive *kuri-kiwera*, second note higher; song *kioorra-tcheeo chink- chink* with variations. **Range**: Local between 1000 and 1850 m north to Tarangire NP where common.

VIOLET-BACKED or PLUM-COLOURED STARLING *Cinnyricinclus leucogaster*　　　Plate 78

Length 6–7". **Male** *shining metallic violet or plum colour above* and on throat and breast (blue or bronze reflections in certain lights; more pinkish when worn); rest of underparts white. Outer tail feathers partly white on outer webs in *C. l. verreauxi*. **Female** and **juvenile** brown above (rufous-tinged on head) with dark streaks; *underparts white, heavily brown-streaked*. Eyes of both sexes dark brown, the iris with narrow yellow outer rim. Arboreal and highly gregarious. Flight fast and direct. **Call** a series of rapidly delivered metallic squawks and trills, often in chorus. **Range/status**: *C. l. leucogaster* is a vagrant from the northern tropics south to Lake Turkana; *verreauxi* largely a non-breeding migrant from the southern tropics, March–Sept., north to Mt Elgon, Maralal, Meru NP and along coast to Lamu. Some remain all year.

ABBOTT'S STARLING *Cinnyricinclus femoralis*　　　Plate 78

Length 6.5–7". A little-known *highland forest* species. Gregarious except when breeding. **Male** *glossy blue-black except for white belly and crissum; eyes pale yellow*. **Female** brown above and from head to breast; rest of underparts whitish, *uniformly streaked with brown*; eyes yellow. **Juvenile** similar to female but streaking limited to sides and flanks, and eyes brown. Presumed **immature** male streaked below, but grey above and dusky brown on breast, other underparts buffy white with broad dark streaks; eyes yellow. See Sharpe's Starling. **Song** short, high-pitched and squeaky, sometimes with banjo-like elements recalling those of Violet-backed Starling or the 'squeaking hinge' notes of Dark-backed Weaver: *skeek seeu wee-seek-useek*, or *sklieu sqew-iuwee, tsiueek seeuseet* or *skeek swuiu-weenk seekuweenk*. Widely spaced soft *tseet* or *tsuik* notes may separate the main song phrases. **Range**: Between 1800 and 2500 m on Mt Kenya, Aberdares, Mt Meru and Mt Kilimanjaro. Early records from the Chyulu Hills. Flocks (with Sharpe's Starlings) at 1600 m in the North Pare Mts, 1993–94.

SHARPE'S STARLING *Cinnyricinclus sharpii*   Plate 78

Length 6–7″. A short-billed bicoloured starling of highland forest. Pairs or small flocks often rest on bare branches above the canopy or on isolated trees in clearings. Shiny blue-black above, including sides of head; *underparts pale buff, tawnier on belly, flanks and crissum*; wing-linings black; eyes golden yellow; black bill rather broad at base. **Juvenile** duller with dusky arrowhead-shaped spots on underparts and orange-brown eyes. See female Violet-backed Starling. **Song** high-pitched, squeaky and metallic, reminiscent of Dark-backed Weaver's: *speenk spee-spee tsink-seresee-see cheenk seekserawn speek-speek. . .* and variations. Call a sharp *speek, spink* or *cheenk*. **Range**: Above 1400 m from the w. and cent. Kenyan highlands south to Arusha NP, Mt Meru, Kilimanjaro and North Pare Mts. Recorded twice in West Usambara Mts.

FISCHER'S STARLING *Spreo fischeri*   Plate 78

Length 7–7.5″. A *grey-and-white* starling of dry eastern/northeastern bush country. Pale brownish grey above with faint greenish blue gloss; *head pale grey, shading to dark brownish grey on breast*; belly white; dark grey patch on sides; *white eyes* contrast with black lores. **Juvenile** browner on back with tawny-rufous feather edges; *bill yellow below, eyes brown*. (Wattled Starling shows conspicuous whitish rump in flight.) **Song** a sequence of rather high strident trills and short notes, *prrrreeeo-prrrreee, squirrreee-squew sri-sri-sri-sri-shiaaa skew. . ..* Flocks indulge in prolonged chattering. **Range**: Below 1400 m, from far ne. Kenya south to Mkomazi GR, the Masai Steppe and Tarangire NP.

WHITE-CROWNED STARLING *Spreo albicapillus*   Plate 78

Length 10–11″. Unique. A *large white-capped, white-eyed* starling of dry bush in *northern border areas*. Gregarious. *Shiny olive-green above*, with *white-streaked brown underparts* and *a long buffy white patch in secondaries*; white wing-linings, belly and under tail-coverts are often earth-stained. Much variation in amount of white on throat and breast. Bill black. The more western race *horrensis* is much smaller than nominate *albicapillus*. Dark-eyed **juvenile** has tawny white crown, a brown-tipped yellow bill, and reduced streaking on underparts. **Call** a shrill rising *tschurreeeet* or *tchu-tchu tsureeeeet*. **Range**: *S. a. horrensis* along northern edge of the Dida Galgalu Desert from North Horr east to Maikona and Turbi, north to Ethiopian border. *S. a. albicapillus* of Ethiopia and Somalia reaches ne. Kenya near Mandera and Ramu.

MAGPIE STARLING *Speculipastor bicolor*   Plate 78

Length 6.5–7.5″. A nomadic pied starling of dry bush and thorn-scrub in n. and e. Kenya. Gregarious. *White patches at base of primaries obvious in flight.* **Male** *shiny blue-black on upperparts, head and upper breast; mostly white below; eyes blood-red.* **Female** dull blackish above with dark grey crown; *dark grey throat is separated from white belly by a glossy black breast band; eyes red or orange-red.* **Juvenile** brown with white belly; eyes brown, becoming orange-red in **immature**. Exceptional young birds are entirely whitish below, including chin and throat. **Song** a prolonged soft babbling *quereeeh quaaa kereek quak-quak, quereek suaaaa, cherak-chak-chak. . .* mixed

with higher harsh notes; lacks strident trills of Fischer's Starling song. Also has a shrill whistling flight call. **Range**: Below 1200 m in the north, breeding May–June, dispersing south to the Kerio Valley, Lake Baringo and Isiolo. Flocks regular Aug.–Nov. south to Garsen, the coast north of Malindi, and Tsavo East NP. Old records from Nairobi, Lake Magadi and from lowlands at base of the Pare Mts.

◀ **WATTLED STARLING** *Creatophora cinerea* **Plate 78**

Length 7.5–8″. A highly gregarious grey or grey-brown starling with a *pale rump*. **Non-breeding** bird *pale grey* or brownish grey, the *whitish rump contrasting with black flight feathers and tail*; head feathered except for yellow postocular patch and grey streak on each side of throat. **Breeding male** loses feathers on top of head, exposing bare skin: *bright yellow from eyes to hindcrown*, black on front part of head and throat; at same time develops pendent black wattles on forehead and chin, and small ones on crown; eyes brown, bill pinkish white, dark at base. **Breeding female** much like non-breeding bird but primary coverts blackish or brown; occasionally wings all brown. **Juvenile** resembles female but browner above, sometimes with suggestion of streaks below; bill dusky or yellowish *streak on each side of throat*. See Fischer's Starling. **Song** high and squeaky, *tsirrit-tsirrit tseep, seeet-seeereeet*. Has harsh 3-note flight call; alarm note a rasping nasal *graaaah*. Flocks maintain a varied babbling of squeaks, squawks and squeals. **Range**: Seasonally throughout, from sea level to over 2000 m. Breeds mainly in and east of the Rift Valley.

✓ **RED-BILLED OXPECKER** *Buphagus erythrorhynchus* **Plate 78**

Length 7.5–8″. A slender, *red-billed* brown bird invariably *associated with large mammals*. Uniformly brown above, the *rump little or no paler than the back*; eyes vermilion with *broad yellow orbital ring*; feet dark brown. **Juvenile** darker than adult; at fledging, bill yellow with dark culmen, darkening to dusky brown in 2 months; eyes and orbital skin then brown; 2 months later bill becomes red at base, all-red after 6–7 months. (Adult Yellow-billed Oxpecker has two-toned bill and rump is much paler than back.) **Call** when flying or in a hissing *krisss, krissss. . .*, or a buzzing *zhhhhhhhh*; also *tsee-tsee-tsee-tsee-tsee* and a harsh *tsik-tsik-tsik*. Usually silent when on animals. **Range**: Widespread up to 2500 m wherever large wild mammals and undipped livestock are present; local and scarce in coastal areas.

✓ **YELLOW-BILLED OXPECKER** *Buphagus a. africanus* **Plate 78**

Length 8-8.5″. Much less numerous than Red-billed Oxpecker. Resembles that species, but *basal half of bill bright yellow*, and *rump and upper tail-coverts pale creamy buff*, noticeably lighter than the brownish back; eyes scarlet, with no yellow orbital ring. At fledging, bill of **juvenile** yellow without dark culmen of preceding species, but soon entirely brown or blackish; eyes brown. Older **immature** has scarlet-tipped yellow bill blackish at base above; eyes brownish grey. **Call** a hissing churring alarm call similar to that of Red-billed. Also a reedy rattling. **Range**: Except on the Laikipia Plateau, now largely absent outside national parks and game reserves.

SUNBIRDS, FAMILY NECTARINIIDAE

Small, flower-probing passerines superficially resembling the unrelated New World hummingbirds (Trochilidae) in their highly developed iridescence, and occupying a similar ecological niche in Africa. Although extremely active and restless they lack the extraordinary specialized flight of hummers and normally feed from a perch. *Nectarinia* species have long curved bills with which they probe open blossoms or pierce the bases of deep tubular corollas to reach otherwise inaccessible nectaries. The more warbler-like *Anthreptes* have relatively short straight bills and glean foliage for insects, although they also visit flowers and eat small fruits. Some male sunbirds (and a few females) have coloured erectile pectoral tufts, more or less concealed at the sides of the breast except during display. After breeding, certain males moult into a duller 'eclipse' plumage which can vary among closely related forms. Seasonal movement occurs in response to flowering, and numbers of sunbirds concentrate at favoured food-plants such as *Aloe*, the orange-flowered mint *Leonotis* and *Erythrina* (coral-bean) trees. The typical nest is a domed pouch, often with a porch-like projection above the side entrance, and usually suspended from a branch.

Some female and young sunbirds are difficult to identify. Juvenile males may have a dusky or black throat patch; their plumage otherwise resembles that of adult females (a few of which are also black-throated). Moulting birds in mixed plumage are commonly seen. Immature males in moult may show a broad black mid-ventral line as incoming dark belly and breast feathers replace the paler juvenile plumage. Patchy adult males moulting in and out of breeding dress usually show sufficient iridescence to provide identification clues.

PLAIN-BACKED SUNBIRD *Anthreptes reichenowi yokanae*   Plate 106

Length 4–4.5". A small *coastal forest* sunbird often with mixed-species flocks. **Male** has *black forehead, face and throat* with some metallic blue reflections; otherwise pale olive, more yellow in centre of breast and belly, with yellow pectoral tufts. **Female** olive above with faint whitish superciliary stripes and eyelids; underparts yellowish white. **Juvenile** resembles female but upperparts olive-brown. **Song** *tee-tee-tee-tee* followed by a lower, often descending *tew-tew-tew-tew-tew. . .*; may end with some higher warbling notes. Also *tsee-tsee-tsee-tsee su-seeu seeu seeu seeu tsu*, the last 2 or 3 notes lower. Alarm call a prolonged *tew-tew-tew. . .*, or a complaining *eea-eeea-eeea* which may change to a chatter. **Range:** From Tanga north to the lower Tana River, inland to Shimba Hills and to 1000 m in the East Usambaras.

WESTERN VIOLET-BACKED SUNBIRD *Anthreptes l. longuemarei*   Plate 106

Length 5". A scarce *western* species of *high-rainfall areas*. **Male** *uniformly iridescent violet above* and on *throat*, otherwise white below with yellow pectoral tufts. **Female** grey-brown above with white superciliary stripes, dark violet tail/upper tail-coverts; white throat and breast contrast with *yellow belly, flanks and crissum*. **Juvenile** olive-brown above, *pale yellow below*. **Song** a rapid twittering. Call note a hard *tit*. **Range**: Kapenguria district, nw. Kenya. Old records from Bungoma and Muhoroni.

EASTERN VIOLET-BACKED SUNBIRD *Anthreptes orientalis*   Plate 106 ✓

Length 4.5–5". The common violet-backed sunbird of *dry bush and savanna*. **Male** shining violet above with greenish or blue-green rump and turquoise patch on bend of wing; tail violet-blue, narrowly edged with white; *snowy white* below except for violet chin and yellow pectoral tuft. **Female** mostly brown above with grey rump, *dark blue tail* and bold white superciliary stripes; *underparts white*. **Juvenile** similar to female but faintly yellow-tinged on belly. (Male Uluguru Violet-backed also has blue-green rump, is more bluish-violet above, but best separated by habitat. Females and young of both Western and Uluguru are yellow-bellied; Uluguru female is violet-backed.) **Call** a nasal *chwee* or *tswee-tswee*. **Range:** Below 1300 m in n. and e. Kenya and ne. Tanzania. Absent from Lake Victoria basin and adjacent highlands, and from coastal lowlands south of the Tana delta.

ULUGURU VIOLET-BACKED SUNBIRD *Anthreptes neglectus*   Plate 106

Length 4.75". An eastern *forest* sunbird, *violet-backed in both sexes*, and *greyish or grey and yellow below*. **Male** more bluish violet than the two preceding species, with yellowish olive flight-feather edges; dull underparts often washed with brown posteriorly; pectoral tufts yellow (rarely orange). **Female** iridescent violet on crown, upper back and upper tail-coverts; lower back dull brown with turquoise-green iridescence on rump; sides of face and ear-coverts grey-brown, extending as a broad dull collar around back of neck. *Underparts pale grey*, with *olive-yellow belly and crissum*. (Eastern Violet-backed S. has pure white underparts.) **Juvenile** duller above and yellower on belly. **Song** a loud persistent *sweep, sweep, sweep* or *seep-sureep, sureep* . . .. **Range**: Local along lower Tana River, in Shimba Hills, East Usambara Mts, and at Ambangulu (1200 m) in the West Usambaras.

AMANI SUNBIRD *Anthreptes pallidigaster* **Plate 106**
Length 3.25". A tiny, white-bellied sunbird of coastal *Brachystegia* woodland. Scarce and local. **Male** *dark iridescent bottle-green* above and from head to breast; tail glossy blue-black; underparts white with *orange pectoral tufts*. **Female** grey above with faint violet reflections, entirely white below; tail blue-black. **Juvenile** resembles female but paler grey. **Song** a colourless series of high notes, *su-su-suweet sususuweet-schweeeeet*. Call, *seeeet-seeeet*. **Range:** Arabuko–Sokoke and Marafa forests near Malindi, and up to 900 m in East Usambara Mts.

GREEN SUNBIRD *Anthreptes rectirostris tephrolaemus* **Plates 106, 107**
Length 3.5–4". A canopy species of west Kenyan forests. **Male** unique among Kenyan sunbirds with *broad green band across grey lower throat/upper breast, this bordered below by a narrow dull ochre band*; chin greyish; pectoral tufts bright yellow; upperparts bright golden green, the wings and short dusky tail edged with yellow-olive. **Female** mostly olive, more yellowish on belly, grey on chin; yellowish superciliary stripes contrast slightly with darker crown and lores; some dull green iridescence at bend of wing, but bird appears plain in the treetops. **Juvenile** olive above, paler below, darker on sides and flanks; throat and breast faintly mottled; centre of belly dull yellow. **Voice** not reliably described. **Range:** Kakamega, Nandi and Kericho forests. (Formerly on Mt Elgon and the Yala and Sio rivers.)

BANDED GREEN SUNBIRD *Anthreptes rubritorques* **Plate 123**
Length 3.5". A short-tailed *canopy* sunbird of the Usambara Mts. Somewhat gregarious. **Male** distinctive with *narrow scarlet band across grey breast*; belly and under tail-coverts pale yellow; pectoral tufts bright yellow (or yellow and orange); upperparts shining green. **Female** lacks breast band, is green above and pale greyish yellow below with indistinct yellowish streaks. **Juvenile** more olive above, yellowish olive below. (Eastern Double-collared Sunbird, of gardens and forest edge, has more curved bill; male has green throat and broad red breast band; female paler above with dark tail and more yellowish underparts.) **Call** a repeated chirp of remarkable carrying power, the note repeated several times, sometimes accelerating into a song. **Range:** Usambara Mts (where locally common).

✓ **COLLARED SUNBIRD** *Anthreptes collaris* **Plate 105**
Length 4–4.5". *Short-billed, glittering green and bright yellow.* **Male** iridescent green above and *from head to upper breast*, the latter separated from otherwise *yellow underparts* by a narrow violet band; flanks washed with olive. **Female** similar but entirely yellow below, tinged olive on throat (more so in western *A. c. garguensis*). **Juvenile** resembles female except for dusky yellowish chin and neck. (Yellow-bellied race of Variable Sunbird is longer-billed, has darker throat and breast with much blue and purple. See Green Sunbird.) **Song** of mostly distinct notes, not run together, e.g. *tsit-tsit-chuweet chuweet chueet chueet chueet chueeet eet*; also a more ringing *chwer-chwer-chwer-chwer. . ..* Calls include a thin nasal *tuwee, tuwee* or *tchee tchee*, and a hard *tik*. **Range:** Widespread (except in dry areas) from sea level to above 2200 m. *A. c. elachior* from the coast inland to the eastern plateau, Usambara and Pare mts and Kilimanjaro lowlands. *A. c. garguensis* in other Tanzanian highlands and north to the Mathews Range, Ndotos, Mt Marsabit and Mt Kulal. **Taxonomic Note:** This and the following species may be more closely allied to the genus *Nectarinia*.

PYGMY SUNBIRD *Anthreptes p. platurus* **Plates 105, 107**
Length, breeding male 7"; female 3.5". A tiny, short-billed, *yellow-bellied* sunbird of dry bush in *nw. Kenya*. **Breeding male** bright metallic green with rich yellow lower breast and belly, and greatly elongated narrow central tail feathers which may exceed bird's body length. **Non-breeding male** (Apr.–Oct.) and **female** *pale ash-brown above* with faint yellowish superciliary stripes and *blue-black, whitish-cornered tail*; underparts plain, whitish on throat shading to lemon yellow on breast and belly. (Female Beautiful S. has yellowish chin, and longer, moderately curved bill.) **Song** a soft trill. Call note *twee* or *twee-weet*. **Range/status:** Casual visitor to S. Turkana, Lodwar, Kerio Valley, Kapedo and Baringo districts. No recent records.

OLIVE SUNBIRD *Nectarinia olivacea*   **Plates 106, 107**

Length 4–5″. *Plain olive* with no iridescence. Favours cool damp forests and other wooded habitats. Both sexes resemble females of other sunbirds, but note the *long, well-curved bill* and *bright yellow pectoral tufts* (absent in female of *granti* and the large dark western *vincenti*). Coastal birds are noticeably small, both sexes with yellow tufts. **Juvenile** resembles female but more yellow below and without tufts. **Song** of coastal *N. o. changamwensis* a deliberate series of loud sharp clear notes, *tew-tew-twit-twit*; can be longer, accelerating and falling slightly in pitch toward end, *teu. . . teu . . . twit-twit-twit-twit-tit-tit-tit*; or *tsee-tseep tsee-tseep tsep-turp*. Western *vincenti* has a brief *weet-tur-weet* which can lead to a longer *tee tee-tew-tu-tur-TEE, TEE-tee-tee-tew-tew-tew tu-weet*. Usual call a staccato *tuc...tuc*, often in flight. Also gives a persistent high-pitched squeak and a scolding *dya-dya*. **Range**: *N. o.changamwensis* in coastal lowlands, inland along Tana River to Garissa, on Mt Kasigau, Taita Hills, Usambara and South Pare mts; *neglecta* from cent. Kenyan highlands south to Arusha NP, Kilimanjaro, Mt Meru and North Pare Mts; *vincenti* in w. Kenya from Mt Elgon south to the Migori River; *granti* on Pemba Island.

MOUSE-COLOURED SUNBIRD *Nectarinia veroxii fischeri*   **Plate 106**

Length 5″. A *grey sunbird of coastal areas*, both sexes with *scarlet pectoral tufts*. Slaty above, slightly darker on wings and tail; light glossy blue wash sometimes visible on crown, back and wing-coverts; underparts pale ash-grey. **Song** a fairly loud series of short, well-separated phrases, *ee-sew. . . tsu-ee-see. . . ee-see. . . tsu, ee-su ee-chew. . .*; occasional longer phrases such as *tchew-wee-tsi-see-chew* are repeated frequently. Sharp call-notes, *tsip* and *cheep-chew*. **Range**: Tanga north to the Somali border, and inland along lower Tana River to Baomo; most numerous south of Malindi.

GREEN-HEADED SUNBIRD *Nectarinia verticalis viridisplendens*   **Plate 105**

Length 5.5″. Often appears *blue*-headed (and sometimes misidentified as extralimital Blue-headed Sunbird, *N. alinae*). A sturdy bird, *golden-olive above* and *grey below*; head of **male** entirely iridescent green, bluer on chin and throat; rest of underparts ash-grey. **Female** green only on top and sides of head; entirely grey below. Pectoral tufts yellowish cream in male, smaller and whitish in female. **Juvenile** olive above with *black forehead, crown, chin and throat*, the latter separated from olive breast and belly by narrow yellow band. **Song** a prolonged twittering preceded by rapid *chip* notes. Calls include soft, high-pitched notes such as *chip, whew* or *tzit* in varied combinations, and a plaintive mewing *chiuwee* or *tseea-wee, cheea-weu*. Alarm call a harsh *chee*. **Range**: Widespread in cent. and w. Kenyan highlands between 1500 and 2400 m. In n. Tanzania known only from the Grumeti River in w. Serengeti NP.

GREEN-THROATED SUNBIRD *Nectarinia rubescens kakamegae*
Plates 105, 107

Length 5.5″. A dark sunbird of west Kenyan forests. **Male** *black* with *shining blue-green forecrown* (bordered posteriorly by violet), similar malar streaks, and paler *green throat and upper breast* (a thin line of violet bordering the breast patch is seldom visible). **Female** dusky brown above with olivaceous wash, yellowish underparts *broadly streaked with dusky brown*, and faint yellowish superciliary stripes. **Juvenile** less streaked, more mottled below; crown and face darker brown than back, contrasting with pale yellow malar streaks and narrow pale superciliaries. (Similar female Amethyst Sunbird, unlikely in forest interior, closely resembles Green-throated but is paler olive-brown or olive-grey above, less heavily streaked below.) **Songs** include *seet-seet-seet-seet* and *chereet, see-seet*; also a loud *sweeu-sweeu-sweeu*. Call a hard *tsick*. **Range**: Nandi and Kakamega forests. Formerly along the upper Yala River.

AMETHYST SUNBIRD *Nectarinia amethystina*   **Plates 105, 107**

Length 5.5″. A fairly common dark sunbird of woodlands and gardens. **Male** *velvety black*, more brownish on back, with *brilliant turquoise-green crown*; throat and 'shoulder' patch shining ruby or rose-purple. Coastal male may show purple on upper tail-coverts. **Female** pale brown or olive-grey above with dark lores, *whitish superciliary stripes,* and *pale yellowish underparts streaked with dusky brown.* Some coastal females are paler and more lightly streaked below than inland birds. **Juvenile** resembles female but throat dusky or blackish, upperparts with yellowish wash, and flight feathers edged yellow. **Immature male** similar but with some iridescence on throat and scattered black body feathers. (Female Scarlet-chested Sunbird lacks superciliary stripes, has barred throat and white-edged primary coverts. In w. Kenya see Greenthroated Sunbird.) **Song** a loud sustained twittering. Call a succession of clear, sharp penetrating notes, *chip chip-tew, chewit,* or *chewit-chewit,* or *tyi-tyi-tyi-tyi.* **Range**: Widespread below 2000 m; *N. a. kalckreuthi* in coastal lowlands, *kirkii* in the n. Kenyan mountains, w. and cent. Kenyan highlands, n. Tanzanian mountains, Crater Highlands, Arusha NP and Mkomazi GR.

✓ **SCARLET-CHESTED SUNBIRD** *Nectarinia senegalensis* **Plates 105, 107**

Length 6″. Stocky and dark, with a long, well-curved bill. Widespread except in dry areas occupied by Hunter's Sunbird. **Male** blackish brown with *iridescent green crown, chin and upper throat; lower throat and breast scarlet* with minute blue bars at close range. Small violet 'shoulder' patch present in coastal birds. **Female** greyish brown above with white-edged outer wing-coverts and *no superciliary stripes; underparts dull yellowish, heavily marked* with brown except on belly; *dark brown chin and throat narrowly barred* with lighter brown and with yellowish white tips producing a mottled effect; breast and belly dull yellowish white, streaked with dark brown. **Juvenile** resembles female but *throat uniform dusky or greyish black,* and *yellow breast and belly heavily mottled and barred with black.* **Immature male** has scarlet breast patch but otherwise resembles female or juvenile. (Male Hunter's has violet rump, black throat, brighter scarlet breast with few blue-banded feathers. Female Hunter's is paler than Scarlet-chested, more *mottled* on throat.) **Song** a loud, penetrating *cheet cheet chueet sweet-seechu-sweet sweet-seechu-seet seechu-sheechu-seechu. . .,* the notes distinct. Another song begins with a few *tchik* or *chewit* notes continuing with a weak *see tsee tsewit, tsick, tsetsee tsick chewik. . .,* this at times more warbling and long-continued. Call a loud clear *tew tew tew. . .* or *tee-tee tew-tew.* **Range**: *N. s. lamperti* in w. and cent. Kenya south to Serengeti NP and the Crater Highlands; *gutturalis* in Tanzania north to Lake Manyara, Tarangire and Arusha NPs, and coastal lowlands north to Malindi, inland to Usambara Mts and Shimba Hills.

HUNTER'S SUNBIRD *Nectarinia hunteri* **Plates 105, 107**

Length 5–5.75″. The *dry-country* counterpart of Scarlet-chested Sunbird. **Male** differs in being velvety black with *lower rump, upper tail-coverts and 'shoulder' patch iridescent violet* and the *black throat bordered laterally by thin metallic green streaks; breast pure vivid scarlet* (blue feather bars confined to edges of the red patch). **Female** greybrown above, paler than Scarlet-chested; underparts dull white, mottled with dark brown on throat and breast, less so on belly; flanks washed with brown. *Chin and throat become much darker as pale feather edges wear off;* worn female closely resembles Scarlet-chested as does **juvenile** which, however, is often pale-throated and does not have blackish appearance of that species; dark-throated young birds best distinguished by habitat and range. **Immature male** shows scarlet breast patch and black throat separated by a narrow violet border, but almost no blue bars within the red. **Call** a loud *TEW* repeated frequently, sometimes in a song-like series ending with *tee-tee-tee-tee;* also a harsher scolding *tchew-tchew-tchew* or *tchi-tchi-tchi-tchi.* **Range**: Below 1000 m in n., e. and se. Kenya, west to the Kerio Valley, south to Mkomazi GR.

✓ **VARIABLE SUNBIRD** *Nectarinia venusta* **Plates 105, 107**
Length 4–4.5″. A small and often familiar sunbird of gardens, bush and open woodland. **Breeding male** iridescent blue above, more violet on crown; chin to upper breast blue-violet; rest of underparts yellow to orange-yellow in *N. v. falkensteini,* white in northern *albiventris;* pectoral tufts orange or yellow; black tail shows a trace of blue. **Non-breed-**

ing **male** resembles female but some blue retained on wings and upper tail-coverts, occasionally on body. **Female** *falkensteini* brownish olive above with *blue-black tail* and upper coverts; buffy white to clear yellow on belly; breast clouded with olive; female *albiventris* grey-brown above, white below with grey wash on breast. **Juvenile male** similar to adult female of same race but with blackish or dusky throat patch. (Female Olive-bellied S. has pale superciliary stripes and is more streaked below. Females of both double-collared sunbirds have darker olive underparts with little or no clear yellow on the belly.) **Song** a fairly loud short *tsip-tsip-tsip chuchuchuchuchu.* Alarm call an insistent *tcheer-tcheer* or *chiu-chee-cheer.* Other calls include a scolding *tschew-TSEEP* or *chew-tsew-EEP.* **Range**: *N. v. falkensteini* in the cent. and w. Kenyan highlands and in n. Tanzania east to Kilimanjaro, Pare Mts and West Usambaras. *N. v. albiventris* in e. and ne. Kenya south along Tana River and along coast north from Lamu.

OLIVE-BELLIED SUNBIRD *Nectarinia chloropygia orphogaster*
Plates 106, 107

Length 4–4.5". Resembles both double-collared sunbirds, but lives at *lower elevations*, locally in *west* Kenyan edge habitats and cultivation; little or no overlap with those species. In **male**, *no blue or violet line separates green throat from scarlet breast band*; belly and crissum dark olive-brown; long pectoral tufts bright yellow. **Female** *dark olive above*, with narrow pale superciliary stripes; mostly pale olive-yellow below, with soft olive streaking on breast and flanks. **Juvenile** grey-brown above, dusky from head to upper breast; rest of underparts yellowish. Primary **song** an ascending, rapid, scratchy trill with 1–3 introductory notes and a terminal phrase, *ski ski-skir-rrrrrrrrrr su-skitsue-skitsu-sit*; a simpler slower song, *tsureep-seep-seep seep seep.* Call note a thin squeaky *chwee.* **Range**: Between 1150 and 1550 m from Kakamega, Mumias and Busia districts south to Ukwala, Yala, Ng'iya and Rapogi. Formerly at Sotik.

NORTHERN DOUBLE-COLLARED SUNBIRD *Nectarinia preussi kikuyuensis*
Plates 106, 107

Length 4–4.5". The two double-collared sunbird species can be difficult to separate. **Male** Northern is dark iridescent *blue-green* above with *violet or bluish purple upper tail-coverts* (not easily seen). *Scarlet breast band*, usually noticeably wider than in Eastern Double-collared, is separated from green throat by line of iridescent *violet*; pectoral tufts yellow; belly olive-brown, darker in Mt Kenya birds; *tail and bill relatively short.* **Female** and **juvenile** olive-brown above, greenish yellow below with olive wash on flanks; throat slightly greyer. (Eastern Double-collared S. is vocally distinct, and appears longer-tailed and longer-billed; male is more golden green above and in *N. m. mediocris* has contrasting *blue*, not violet, upper tail-coverts; scarlet breast band is narrower. At lower elevations in w. Kenya, see Olive-bellied Sunbird. Females best separated by bill and tail length, although Eastern has somewhat darker throat.) **Song** of 2 well-separated notes followed by a short fast sizzling twitter and ending with more distinct lower notes: *tsip. . . . . sweet. . . sususususrisrisri-tsew-tsutsu-tsu.* Call a hard *chick* or *chip-chip.* **Range**: Between 1700 and 2800 m in w. and cent. Kenyan highlands, most numerous around Mt Elgon, Kapenguria, Naro Moru, Limuru and n. Nairobi suburbs. In Kieni Forest (s. Aberdares) found alongside Eastern Double-collared.

EASTERN DOUBLE-COLLARED SUNBIRD *Nectarinia mediocris*
Plates 106, 107 ✔

Length 4.5". *Longer-billed, longer-tailed* and with *narrower scarlet breast band* than the preceding species, and generally at *higher elevations.* **Male** has brilliant *golden green* head and upperparts with (in Kenyan birds) contrasting steel-blue upper tail-coverts (violet in Tanzanian *usambarica*). Scarlet breast band (especially narrow in *usambarica*) separated from green throat by iridescent *blue* line; belly and crissum *pale* yellowish olive. **Female** and **juvenile** resemble those of Northern Double-collared but *bill and tail somewhat longer.* Female *usambarica* is greener above and has a more distinctly streaked throat than nominate *mediocris.* **Song** high and thin,

the introductory notes highest and not separated as in song of preceding species, *tsit-tsit-tsit, see-see-see-see-see* or *tsip tsip tsee-see-ch-tsitsitsi-su-see-see-tsip-su-sisisi*. Also gives isolated *tsip* notes. **Range**: *N. m. mediocris* between 1850 and 3700 m in the w. and cent. Kenyan highlands (recorded once on Mt Elgon); common on the Cheranganis, Mau, Aberdares and Mt Kenya (descends to lower elevations in cold seasons), Crater and Mbulu highlands, Arusha NP, Kilimanjaro and Mt Meru. Also attributed to North Pare Mts and the Taita and Chyulu hills, but replaced by *N. m. usambarica* in the South Pares and West Usambaras. (The latter race reportedly bred in Taitas, March 1993.)

MARICO SUNBIRD *Nectarinia mariquensis*   Plates 105, 107

Length 4.25–5". A dark sunbird of open bush and savanna. *Larger and longer-billed than the similar Purple-banded Sunbird*; not as restless as that species. **Male** glittering golden green on head and upperparts; a narrow blue band below the green throat, and below this a *broader band of deep maroon* (more violet in Purple-banded); underparts otherwise black (*osiris*) or greyish black (*suahelica*). **Female** ashy brown above with indistinct superciliary stripes; *pale yellow below with dark streaking* on breast and belly; tail edged and tipped with white. (Female Purple-banded is paler yellow below and often has a dusky throat.) **Juvenile** brown above, yellowish below with blackish chin/throat patch and much coarse dark diffuse mottling on breast; white on outer and inner webs of outer rectrices near tips. (Juv. male Red-chested S. is paler yellow below, and pale parts of outer tail feathers are grey, not white. Juv. Green-throated S. of forest canopy is much longer-billed.) **Song** distinctive, much louder than that of Purple-banded, usually a few high notes preceding a loud long squeaky chatter, *tse-tse-tseetsee chip-chip-chip tsitsitsitsee chick-che-chee-chu, tsee-che tseeu, tsik-tsik-tsik-cheeeeu tseu, chwee-chwee . . .*. Sharp *chic-chip* call notes often interspersed throughout the song. **Range**: *N. m. osiris* is scarce at Moyale, Mt Kulal, Mt Nyiru, the Ndoto foothills and from Kapenguria and Kerio Valley east to Maralal, Laikipia Plateau, Samburu GR and Meru NP. *N. m. suahelica* is common from the Lake Victoria basin east to Mara GR, Nairobi and Machakos districts, Serengeti NP and Maswa GR, Tarangire NP and (reportedly) Mkomazi GR.

PURPLE-BANDED SUNBIRD *Nectarinia bifasciata*   Plates 105, 107

Length 3.75–4". **Breeding male** mainly shining blue-green and black, the race microrhyncha almost identical in plumage to the larger Marico Sunbird, but with a *shorter* (14 mm), *less strongly decurved bill*; slightly more blue-green (less golden green) above than Marico, and breast band more violet, less maroon, but colour differences subtle and unreliable. Maroon band 7–10 mm wide in *microrhyncha*, and bordered with blue or violet; only 3–5 mm of maroon in *tsavoensis*, sometimes lacking or evident only at sides; lower breast and belly jet-black. (Male Violet-breasted S. is larger, longer-billed, with *broad* shining violet breast band extending almost to throat, which is bluer green, less brassy, than in Purple-banded.) **Non-breeding male** *microrhyncha* suggests a black-throated female, but has dark wings and iridescent green wing- and upper tail-coverts. *N. b. tsavoensis* apparently has no eclipse plumage. **Females** of both forms pale *yellowish below, dusky-streaked on breast* (but less heavily streaked than Marico); throat white, or dusky with contrasting long white malar stripes; grey-brown above, with faint superciliaries, black lores and some white on lower eyelids; tail blue-black with pale greyish feather tips and outer edges. (Female Black-bellied S. has fainter ventral streaking and may show a trace of red; otherwise nearly identical to Purple-banded.) **Juvenile male** resembles dark-throated female. **Immature male** has green feathers mixed with black on throat and wing-coverts, and often a broad black mid-ventral line. Typical **song** of *microrhyncha* high-pitched, softer, thinner, much less emphatic than that of Marico, typically with distinct short initial notes leading into high twittering, *tsi tsi tsi tsee-tsee-tsee-tsee-tsee seeseetsew seesueet tseet tseu cheet sitisitisitisreeee*. Simpler song, *chitisee-see-see-see-see-see*. Song of *tsavoensis* a rapid sputtering *tsusitiseesee, chuchiti-tsi-tsi-tsi-tsi sitisee-see-see-see chitisee . . .*, and *sitisee-see-see tseu-tseu-chiti-tisiti-see-swee*, or shortened to only the last few notes. Loud annoyance chatter, *chi-chi-chi-chi . . .*. Call a high *tsik-tsiki-tsik* or *brrrzi*. **Range**: *N. b. tsavoensis* in dry *Commiphora* and *Acacia* bush centred in Tsavo region and adjacent n. Tanzania. *N. b. microrhyncha* in moist coastal bush, mangroves and gardens north to Malindi, and disjunctly in Lake

Victoria basin east to Lolgorien, wandering seasonally to Mara GR and Serengeti NP. **Taxonomic Note:** The two forms have at times been treated as separate species.

VIOLET-BREASTED SUNBIRD *Nectarinia chalcomelas*   Plates 105, 107

Length 4.25″. Uncommon in *moist coastal scrub and thickets*. Suggests Purple-banded Sunbird but *larger, longer-billed* and somewhat *shorter tailed*. **Male** has *broad breast band of brilliant iridescent violet, not bordered below with maroon, and extending nearly to the blue-green throat*. **Female** quite *plain*: dull brownish grey above with faint whitish superciliary stripes and prominent whitish primary edges; *grey underparts immaculate or with suggestion of streaks/mottling on breast, yellowish or creamy on belly*. **Juvenile** like female, but male has black throat. **Immature male** has green or green and black throat, may show broad black mid-ventral line. **Song** a thin rapid *tsewtsi-tse-tseep-sisisisi-tsewtsi-tsi-tsi . . .* or *whichichee-see-tsiseesee*. Calls include *tsik* and *chiew-chiew-chiew*, and a fast loud monotonous chatter, *chee-chee-chee-chee-chee . . . .* **Range**: Local from Kiunga south to Tana delta and up that river to Ijara, and Bura. Status farther inland (within range of *N. bifasciata tsavoensis*) unclear, perhaps seasonal after rains.

PEMBA SUNBIRD *Nectarinia pembae*   Plate 124

Length 4″. Restricted to Pemba Island, where common in all habitats. **Male** resembles a small Violet-breasted Sunbird (not on Pemba), but has *iridescent violet and green lesser wing-coverts*. **Female** olive-brown above with narrow whitish superciliary stripes; darker and more blue-black on tail; whitish from chin to breast but pale yellow on belly, sometimes with suggestion of streaks at sides of breast. **Juvenile** similar but more yellowish; young male has blackish throat. **Call** *tslink* or a high-pitched *ssweek* sometimes repeated persistently. Song unrecorded. **Range**: Pemba and adjacent coral islets.

ORANGE-TUFTED SUNBIRD *Nectarinia bouvieri*   Plates 105, 107

Length 4.5″. A scarce western species resembling Marico Sunbird, but **male** has *purple and blue forecrown, blue chin* and often shows *conspicuous bright orange, yellow-tipped pectoral tufts* (lacking in Marico); *upperparts shiny brassy green*, much less blue-green (especially on lower back and rump) than in Marico. **Female** recalls female double-collared sunbirds, but more brownish (less olive) above, with *faint buff or whitish superciliary stripes*; underparts olive-yellowish (clearer yellow on belly) with *indistinct dusky streaks or mottling, these marks coalescing on throat and chin which appear dark*. (Female Marico S. is more heavily streaked below; Olive-bellied S. faintly streaked but has whitish chin and pale yellow throat, brighter yellow belly, sharper superciliaries; Copper S. diffusely streaked below, paler on throat. Variable S. lacks superciliaries, is bright yellow on belly and crissum.) **Juvenile** similar to female but young male has dark throat. **Immature male** grey-brown above, with faint pinkish coppery or brassy iridescence above and on the black throat; broad blackish mid-ventral line from throat to belly; may show blue-green/violet iridescence on breast. **Song** short, rapid, not very high, *tsit-sip-chip* or *ch-ch-sirrrip*, rising at end; sometimes a longer *sit-sit-sit-tsewtsewtsew*. Call a low *cheep* or *chip-ip*, and a loud *tchew*. **Range**: Glades and edges of Kakamega Forest; also margins of riverine woods in Busia District.

SUPERB SUNBIRD *Nectarinia superba buvuma*   Plate 106

Length 6.5–7″. A thickset, *large-billed* sunbird. Rare in Ugandan border areas. **Male** dark metallic golden green above, the *crown blue* with greenish and violet reflections; throat and upper breast shining ruby-red to violet-blue; *lower breast and belly deep non-iridescent maroon*. **Female** olive above with pale superciliary stripes; yellowish olive below, sometimes more orange on belly and crissum. **Juvenile** resembles female but posterior underparts olive-yellow; moults gradually to adult plumage, and in Uganda some birds breed in this patchy intermediate dress. **Call** a sharp *tsirp*, seldom heard. **Range**: Busia and Mumias districts in w. Kenya; possibly resident around Alupe.

COPPER SUNBIRD *Nectarinia cuprea*   Plates 106, 107

Length 5.25″. A dark western species of bush, thickets and forest borders. **Breeding male** shining *burnished copper* with ruby and pink reflections on head and breast, purple on rump and upper tail-coverts, blue-black on wings and tail; belly and crissum black. **Non-breeding** (and **immature?**) **male** similar to female but with iridescent wing- and tail-coverts; may show black mid-ventral line or blotching. **Female** brownish olive above with *dusky or blackish lores,* some dark postocular feathers and indistinct buff superciliary stripes; underparts dull olive-yellow, more yellow on belly; breast obscurely and diffusely streaked; tail blue-black with obscure pale tips and sides. (Female Variable Sunbird has clear yellow belly, no superciliary stripes; Olive-bellied is much darker above, somewhat streakier below, and with whitish, not yellowish, chin; Orange-tufted is darker, longer billed, with dusky or olive chin; Northern Double-collared is much darker above, more olive throughout, lacks superciliaries and is shorter-billed.) **Juvenile** resembles female but male has dusky throat. **Song** distinctive, of several thin notes followed by an accelerating 'bouncing ball' trill, *tsip, tsip, tsip, tsip, tsee-see-see-see-see-seeseesee.* Gives a repetitive *chip-chip-chip...* when feeding, and a hoarse *tsit-chit* in flight between flowers. **Range:** Lake Victoria basin north to Kakamega and Kitale, east to Muhoroni and south to Tanzanian border areas.

TACAZZE SUNBIRD *Nectarinia tacazze jacksoni*   Plates 104, 107

Length, male 9"; female 5.5–6". A large, dark, *highland* sunbird. Long-tailed **breeding male** blackish with head, throat and neck burnished bronzy green (inviting confusion with Bronze Sunbird); back purple (may be mixed with bronzy green); *wing-coverts, rump and upper tail-coverts shining purple; breast ruby-red and violet;* rest of underparts, flight-feathers and tail black. **Non-breeding male** brownish grey with black belly, wings and tail; black mask bordered below by whitish streaks; bend of wing, lower back, rump and upper tail-coverts shining purple; incoming iridescent body feathers producing mottled effect. **Female** duller and greyer than more yellowish Bronze and Malachite Sunbirds, with *whitish facial stripes outlining dark mask; underparts greyish olive, pale yellow in centre of belly;* pointed central tail feathers a little longer than the others, the outermost edged and tipped with white. **Juvenile** usually yellower than female, similar to young Malachite. **Song** a sibilant sputtering twitter, often extended, interspersed with occasional louder single notes, but with little fluctuation in pitch, *sweetsiuswitter TSEU seet-swirursittii, tsit-tsit-tsit-chitichitichit . . .* **Range:** Between 1800 and 4000 m on Mt Nyiru, Ndotos, Mt Elgon, Cheranganis, Mau, Aberdares, Mt Kenya, Kilimanjaro, Mt Meru, above 2150 in the Crater Highlands, and at 2900 m on Mt Hanang; descends during cold wet months.

BRONZE SUNBIRD *Nectarinia k. kilimensis*   Plates 104, 107

Length, male 8.5–9"; female 5". The familiar long-tailed sunbird of highland gardens. **Male** generally black with *gold, bronze and green reflections;* belly, wings and tail non-metallic black with slight purplish wash. Bill shorter but more *deeply curved* than in Tacazze Sunbird (otherwise easily mistaken for Bronze in dull light when both show bronzy green head reflections. Look for Tacazze's purple or red-violet on wing- and upper tail-coverts.) **Female** brownish olive above with *dusky facial mask outlined by whitish stripes* as in Tacazze, but *underparts yellow with diffuse greyish olive streaks,* the whitish throat finely streaked; most tail feathers white-tipped, the outermost also white edged and the central pair slightly elongated. (Female Malachite S. is browner above, less yellow below, unstreaked on throat and breast.) **Juvenile** more greenish olive above than female, with dusky forehead and short yellowish superciliary stripes; underparts more mottled than streaked; bill shorter and straighter than adult's; male has brown sides of face, dusky throat fading into olive breast and greenish yellow belly. **Song** an extended rapid sputtering with occasional louder harsher notes, *spitisew-spit-spit-spit-spit-chitisewsi-sweet-chirwee, chiwee, tsip-tsip-tsip. . .* etc. Territorial female has an insistent *psew-psew-seep* or *tsew-EEP.* Male calls *chee-wit-chee, chee-wit-wit* in pursuit of other sunbirds. **Range:** Between 1200 and 2800 m from cent. and w. Kenyan highlands south to the Crater and Mbulu highlands, Kilimanjaro and Mt Meru, Arusha and Moshi districts. Some post-breeding dispersal to lower drier areas.

GOLDEN-WINGED SUNBIRD *Nectarinia reichenowi* Plate 104

Length, male 9.5"; female 5". Unmistakable. A *long-tailed* highland sun-bird with *bright yellow wing and tail patches and strongly decurved bill in both sexes.* **Breeding male** iridescent bronzy gold on head, neck, back and lesser wing-coverts; most *wing and tail feathers black with broad yellow edges; central tail feathers elongated*; throat and upper breast coppery, grading to black on lower breast and belly. **Non-breeding male** velvety black on head, back and entire underparts; wings and tail as in breeding dress. **Female** olive above, black around eyes, yellowish below with olive mottling, entirely olive on belly and flanks. **Juvenile female** resembles adult; **juvenile male** dull blackish below with some olive; yellow plumage duller than in adult. **Song** a prolonged twittering warble interspersed with high *chi-chi-chi-chi* phrases. Calls are a rapid *chuk-chi-chi-chek*, an insistent *cher-cher-cher* and a single *tweep*. **Range:** *N. r. lathburyi* in Mathews Range, Mt Uraguess, Mt Nyiru and Mt Kulal. *N. r. reichenowi* between 1800 and 3000 m in cent. and w. Kenyan highlands and south to the Crater and Mbulu highlands, Arusha NP, Kilimanjaro and Mt Meru, uncommonly in South Pare and West Usambara mts. Moves lower, and into atypical localities in cold wet months.

MALACHITE SUNBIRD *Nectarinia famosa cupreonitens* Plates 104, 107

Length, male 9–9.5"; female 6". A long-tailed sunbird of grassy highland forest edges. **Breeding male** *brilliant emerald-green* with *bright yellow pectoral tufts* and *long central tail feathers.* **Non-breeding male** (Aug.–Oct.) female-like, but wings and tail as in breeding plumage. In moult, may have dark mid-ventral line. **Female** ashy olive-brown above, with dim yellowish superciliary and moustachial stripes; slightly pointed blackish tail narrowly edged with white, and *yellowish underparts mottled* with olive-brown on throat and breast. **Juvenile** greener above, yellower below than female, dusky olive on throat and breast; male may have blackish throat. (Female Scarlet-tufted Malachite is dusky below, with orange-red tufts and square-tipped tail. Female Tacazze is greyer, less yellow, and with more curved bill.) **Song** of several short notes, *chip. . . chi. . . chew-chew-chew. . .* accelerating into a sputtering warble. Call a sharp *chip-chip* or *chi-cheer*. **Range:** Between 1850 and 3000 m in w. and cent. Kenyan highlands (up to 3400 m on Mt Elgon). Also Mt Nyiru, Chyulu Hills, Crater Highlands, Mt Meru and Kilimanjaro; down to 1650 m in West Usambaras.

SCARLET-TUFTED MALACHITE SUNBIRD *Nectarinia j. johnstoni*
Plates 104, 107

Length, male 10.5"; female 5.5". The only sunbird on high *moorlands* where it feeds on insects in giant *Lobelia* and *Senecio* plants. Long-tailed **breeding male** mainly metallic green with *bright scarlet pectoral tufts*; blue reflections on rump and upper tail-coverts; wings and tail blue-black, the elongated central tail feathers green-edged. **Non-breeding male** brownish with wings and tail as in breeding plumage. **Female** *dark brown* above, somewhat paler below, with faint whitish moustachial stripes and *orange-red pectoral tufts*; tail black, square-tipped with no white. **Juvenile** resembles female but lacks pectoral tufts. (Juv. Tacazze S. has paler underparts and pointed, white-edged tail.) **Song** a rather mellow *sreep-sreep cheeureeeeep-reep*. Call a harsh rasping *chk-k* or *chaa-chaa*. **Range:** Between 3000 and 4500 m on Mt Kenya, Aberdares, Kilimanjaro, Mt Meru, and on Olosirwa in the Crater Highlands. Recorded once in the North Pare Mts.

RED-CHESTED SUNBIRD *Nectarinia erythrocerca* Plates 104, 107 ✔

Length, male 5.25–6"; female 4–4.5". A *western lakeshore* sunbird. **Male** shining blue-green above; green throat separated from broad non-irides-cent *crimson breast band* by narrow line of shining violet; posterior underparts black; *central rectrices extend an inch beyond rest of tail.* (Beautiful Sunbird is yellow on sides of breast; Black-bellied S. geographically distant.) **Female** brownish olive above, heavily streaked/mottled dusky on pale yellowish underparts, more or less solid dusky on throat, with *short-pointed, white-tipped, blue-black tail*; also has pale yellow eyelids, and yellowish edges of primaries form obvious wing panel in fresh plumage. **Juvenile male** like female above, yellowish below with dark mottling on breast and belly; *chin and throat black, bordered by pale yellowish moustachial stripes.* (Female Beautiful S. has narrow yellowish superciliaries and is brighter yellow and faintly streaked below. Female Marico has paler chin and throat. Juv. Amethyst shows no yellowish wing panel, is more streaked than mottled below. Juv. Marico is brighter yellow on belly.) **Song** a short thin twitter on the same pitch, *tsi-si-sip-see-see-swee* or *tsi-tsi-tsi-tsi-tsi-tsi-tsip.* Call a sharp *spink* or *spink-spink.* **Range**: Shores and islands of Lake Victoria.

BLACK-BELLIED SUNBIRD *Nectarinia nectarinioides*   Plates 104, 107

Length 4.75–5.5". Smallest of the long-tailed sunbirds. Prefers riverine acacias and adjacent dry bush with baobab trees. **Male** shining green above and on throat. (In bright light, green head shows faint brassy pink iridescence.) *N. n. nectarinioides* has a broad *orange-red breast band and yellow pectoral tufts,* rest of underparts black. Northern *erlangeri* has breast *pure red* and *no pectoral tufts.* In both races, central rectrices extend 2 in. beyond others, but worn, brown-bellied birds may lack these extensions. (Beautiful Sunbird has red breast patch bordered laterally by yellow, and head shows no pink sheen. Red-chested Sunbird of Lake Victoria is larger, more blue-green, with crimson breast band bordered below by violet.) **Female** ashy olive-brown above with faint superciliary stripes; underparts pale yellow, *faintly streaked with dusky brown on breast and sides;* throat greyish; *sometimes a trace of red or orange on the breast;* tail bluish, tipped with white. (Female Marico and Purple-banded Sunbirds are more heavily streaked.) **Juvenile** olive above with short pale superciliary stripes, yellowish malar streaks and blackish chin/throat patch extending into mottled streaking on olive-yellow breast and sides. **Song** a thin, two-parted *tsit-tsit-tsit-tsit-tsitsereetsereet* or *tsit-tsit, sit-sreet sit-sreet.* **Range**: Highly local *N. n. erlangeri* in ne. Kenya at Doua River and Wajir, intergrading on Northern Uaso Nyiro River with nominate *nectarinioides,* which extends along the Tana River and south through Tsavo region to Mkomazi GR.

BEAUTIFUL SUNBIRD *Nectarinia pulchella*   Plates 104, 107

Length male, 5.5-6"; female, 3.5". Another small, long-tailed sunbird of dry thorn-bush. **Breeding male** glittering green above and on throat, with coppery reflections on back; *longitudinal scarlet stripe down centre of yellow breast;* rest of underparts shining green in *N. p. pulchella,* black in *melanogastra.* Central tail feathers extend 2 in. beyond others. **Non-breeding male** resembles adult female but has black flight feathers, long central rectrices and, often, green wing-coverts. **Female** *N. p. pulchella* pale olive above with narrow yellowish superciliary stripes beginning over eyes; underparts *plain* creamy yellow, whitish toward chin; tail tipped white. *N. p. melanogastra* said to show some dusky streaking below. **Juvenile** male black on chin and throat. **Song** a high-pitched *shrrrr-tsit-tsit-sitisit-cheet-tsitsiseet-seet. . . .* Calls a weak *chip. . . chip,* and a loud *tseu-tseu-tseu-tseu . . . .* **Range**: The nominate race is widespread below 1300 m in nw. Kenya from Lokichokio and Turkana District south to the Kerio Valley and Lake Bogoria; *N. p. melanogastra* east and south of the cent. highlands, in low dry parts of Nyanza, south to Mara Region, Serengeti, Lake Manyara, Tarangire NP, Masai Steppe and Mkomazi GR. Moves higher (e. g. to Nairobi) during severe droughts.

SHINING SUNBIRD *Nectarinia habessinica turkanae*   Plates 106, 107

Length 5.25". An uncommon thorn-bush species in *northern Kenya.* **Male** the *only far northern sunbird with broad scarlet breast band* (sometimes bordered above and below by narrow blue lines) and yellow pectoral tufts. Iridescent green above, including head; coppery reflections on back, coppery and violet on crown, bluish on rump and upper tail-coverts; *posterior underparts black.* **Female** rather plain *pale brownish grey,* with faint *whitish superciliary stripes;* paler below, almost white on throat and obscurely streaked on breast and sides; *under tail-coverts whitish with bold dark feather centres;* tail black, the outer feathers narrowly tipped and edged with white. (Female Marico S. has faint yellow wash on lower breast and belly, and dusky streaks which coalesce on throat. Other similar species are allopatric.) **Juvenile** resembles female

526

but chin and throat blackish. **Call** a sharp *spik-spik* or *speek-speek*. Song (in Yemen) a low-pitched *skieu-ek-ek, skieu-tsek-tsek-tsek* . . .. **Range:** Below 1000 m from Lokichokio east to Mandera and south to Kongelai Escarpment, Lake Baringo, Isiolo and Meru NP.

SPARROWS AND PETRONIAS, FAMILY PASSERIDAE

Sometimes included with weavers in the family Ploceidae, the two groups being similar in palate structure, nesting habits, and social behaviour. The main external feature distinguishing them from weavers is their dorsally positioned and greatly reduced outer (10th) primary, its tip projecting only slightly from under the outermost upper primary covert. Sparrows differ from fringillids in their complete postjuvenile moult, and in building a bulky domed nest with a side entrance (in trees, cavities, under eaves of buildings or in thatched roofs). They are granivorous, ground-feeding, open-country birds, some adaptable species closely associating with humans. Vocally, they rank low, most having only simple chirps, sometimes run together to serve as a song.

GREY-HEADED SPARROW *Passer griseus*   **Plate 108**

Length 5–7".The most common and widespread East African sparrow, represented by 4 races in our region: **P. g. ugandae** with relatively small bill, *rich tawny rufous upperparts* and generally *pale greyish white underparts*; larger **P. g. gongonensis** ('Parrot-billed Sparrow') with more swollen bill, and uniform darker grey underparts (typically no white on throat); **P. g. suahelicus** ('Swahili Sparrow') like *ugandae* below, but duller above, the dusky brown back almost uniform with the crown; **P. g. swainsonii** ('Swainson's Sparrow') smaller than similar *gongonensis* with *smaller bill, darker and duskier head and face*, grey underparts, and *dull brownish back contrasting with tawny rufous rump/upper tail-coverts*. In all forms bill black when breeding, otherwise horn-brown. **Juvenile** has buffy horn bill and dusky-streaked back. Chirping, chattering **calls** suggest House Sparrow. *P. g. ugandae* gives a single *chirp* or *cheep*, a short rapid *chchchch* and *ch-ch-ch-chiwirp*; also a thin *tseup seep chirp tseep*, repeated. Another 'song' of *ugandae* and *gongonensis* is a long monotonous series of loud sharp notes, *TCHEW TCHEW TCHEW* . . .; *gongonensis* also monotonously alternates notes: *chew chur, chew chur, chew chur*. . ., or a more slurred *tcheew chirrup, tchewew tchewer, tchwe tchwer*. . . Comparable song of *ugandae*, *dzreep dzhirp dzreep dshirp dzhreep* . . .; *gongonensis* also has isolated churring notes, e.g. *chrrrrrrryek*, and a longer *tserkiseechirrrr*. Other races give similar calls. **Range:** *P. g. ugandae* in and west of Rift Valley, intergrading with *gongonensis* in several Rift localities, and apparently with *suahelicus* in Tanzania; may reach the coast at Tanga. *P. g. gongonensis* east of the Rift, north to Lake Turkana, south to n. and ne. Tanzania, and on Kenyan coast, intergrading with *ugandae* and possibly with *suahelicus*, whose range is centred in sw. Kenya/n. Tanzania (Narok to Mara GR, south to Serengeti NP and Crater Highlands); *suahelicus* also alongside *gongonensis* and *ugandae* at Lake Elmenteita. Ethiopian *swainsonii* reaches Moyale, and intergrades with *gongonensis* in Turkana and Marsabit districts. **Taxonomic Note:** In places, some of the forms seem to behave as separate species, occupying the same or adjacent areas and apparently remaining distinct. Elsewhere 2 or 3 forms mingle with one another and with intermediate birds. How they segregate for breeding is unknown; detailed study is needed.

SOUTHERN GREY-HEADED SPARROW *Passer diffusus mosambicus*
       Plate 124

Length 5–6.25". In our region, restricted to Pemba Island. Resembles a small, *pale* Grey-headed Sparrow with a *noticeably small bill*, black when breeding, otherwise pale brown. **Range:** Pemba Island, Tanzania.

RUFOUS SPARROW *Passer rufocinctus*   **Plate 108** ✓

Length 5–5.5". The brightly coloured *pale-eyed* sparrow of the highlands. **Male** has top and sides of head grey, bordered by *rufous streak from eyes and around ear-coverts* to sides of breast; *chin and throat black*; rufous above with black streaks on back. Northwestern *shelleyi* has black postocular lines and a smaller black bib than nominate birds. **Female** has dusky grey throat patch. **Juvenile** brown-eyed, dull tawny above;

male's throat black, female's grey. **Calls** include a sharp *tsui* or *tseuPEE*, a squeaky *tsweet*, a louder rolling *tchweep*, and a loud *CHEWP* recalling *P. griseus*. Song of thin sharp metallic notes, often alternating with lower chirps: *tseup CHREE, tseup CHREE, tsweet SHREEP. . ..* A repeated *chiREET* may serve as a song. **Range**: Nominate race in Rift Valley and adjacent highlands from Eldoret and Maralal south to the Crater Highlands and Arusha; *shelleyi* along Ugandan border, at base of Kongelai Escarpment and around Kunyao. **Taxonomic Note**: Treated as races of either *P. iagoensis* or *P. motitensis* by some authors.

SOMALI SPARROW *Passer castanopterus fulgens*   Plate 108

Length 4.5". A small brightly coloured sparrow of arid n. Kenya where it nests in villages and in tree cavities along dry watercourses. **Breeding male** *yellow below* and on cheeks, with black bib and bill. *Crown, nape and wing-coverts rich rufous-brown*; back streaked grey and black. **Non-breeding male** less yellow, greyer on crown, with less black on throat; bill yellowish brown. **Female** resembles female House Sparrow but *pale lemon yellow below*, buffier on breast, sides and flanks. **Juvenile** similar but dingier below. Chirping **call** much like House Sparrow's. **Range**: Lake Turkana and Ethiopian border areas south to Marsabit, Laisamis and Kapedo.

√ HOUSE SPARROW *Passer domesticus indicus*   Plate 108

Length 5.5". The familiar urban sparrow in much of the world. East African birds are smaller, paler and with brighter white cheeks than the European subspecies. Male black-bibbed and grey-crowned; bill black when breeding, otherwise horn-brown. **Female** and **juvenile** buffy brown with broad pale buff superciliary stripes, yellowish horn bill and white wing-bars. In n. Kenya see female Somali Sparrow. **Call**, chirping notes like those of European birds. **Range**: Introduced at Mombasa in early 1900s. Local in coastal towns north to Malindi, along highways and railways inland to Sultan Hamud and Nairobi (first, 1992), Thika and in some national park lodges. Recent records at Same, Kilimanjaro Int. Airport near Moshi and in Arusha.

CHESTNUT SPARROW *Passer eminibey*   Plates 108, 115

Length 4.25". **Male** *largely rich chestnut-rufous,* darker on head and face; wings and tail blackish with pale rufous feather edges; r*esembles a miniature Chestnut Weaver.* **Female** chestnut only on lower back and rump, with variable amounts on throat and above eyes; head greyish, back grey-brown with blackish streaks. **Juvenile** male resembles a dull female, becoming mottled as adult feathers appear. **Song** thin and high-pitched, *tchiweeza tchiweeza tchi-tchi-tchi-tchi see-see-see-see-serichi.* Flight call a ringing *chew chew.* **Range**: Mainly in cent. and s. Rift Valley and adjacent plateau country, south to Tsavo West, Serengeti and Tarangire NPs and the Masai Steppe.

YELLOW-SPOTTED PETRONIA *Petronia pyrgita*   Plate 108

Length 6". A drab, dry-country sparrow with heavy *pale bill*, narrow broken *white eye-ring* and pale wing-bars. The small yellow throat spot is seldom visible in the field, but can be conspicuous in calling birds. **Juvenile** browner, with buffier wing-bars, flight-feather edgings and superciliary stripes. **Song** a simple *chiew-chiew-chiew-chiew-chiew-tcheep.* Call a double *Passer*-like *cherp-cherp.* **Range**: Widespread, except in highland areas, coastal lowlands south of the Sabaki River and Lake Victoria basin.

WEAVERS AND RELATIVES, FAMILY PLOCEIDAE

A large family of typically thick-billed, strong-footed birds. Plumage is highly variable, and there are pronounced seasonal changes in some species. Sexes are alike in *Sporopipes*, the sparrow-weavers and some buffalo-weavers. Habitats and breeding habits are diverse; some species are solitary, others colonial, but all construct covered (and often distinctive) nests that are conspicuous features of many East African landscapes. The family as treated here excludes the sparrows (Passeridae), waxbills, whydahs and indigobirds (Estrildidae).

WHITE-HEADED BUFFALO-WEAVER *Dinemellia dinemelli*   Plate 109 ✔

Length 7". A striking bird with *white head, bright orange-red upper and under tail-coverts* and *white wing-patches*; back, wings, and tail are dusky brown in northern birds, black in southern *boehmi*. **Juvenile** resembles adult. Noisy and gregarious, often foraging with starlings. The large stick **nest** is somewhat flattened (not as high and rounded as those of *Bubalornis*). **Calls** include a shrill, strident, somewhat parrot-like *skwieeeer*, a more rasping metallic *errrrrrrh*, and a loud ringing *TEW*. **Range**: *D. d. dinemelli* widespread in Kenya below 1400 m except for Lake Victoria basin and southern coastal lowlands; scarce in the highlands. *D. d. boehmi* of interior Tanzania intergrades with the nominate race in se. Kenya.

RED-BILLED BUFFALO-WEAVER *Bubalornis niger intermedius*   Plate 109 ✔

Length 8.5–9". Starling-sized and sturdy. **Male** black with *stout reddish bill* and white-edged primaries; irregular white patches on sides of breast and flanks. **Female** dark brown above, white below with *heavy streaking and mottling; bill horn-brown, pinkish at base.* **Juvenile** pale brown above; *bill largely yellow-orange or pinkish*; underparts spotted and barred; some black-and-white blotches on sides. Noisy and gregarious. Builds massive thorny stick **nest** (1 m or more in length) usually in acacia or baobab. In nw. Kenya replaced by White-billed Buffalo-Weaver. **Call** of male a strident chattering *chi-chi-chi-skwi-chiree-chiree-skwiree-skirrow*, and a drier *chyerr chyerr cherk-cherk-cherk-cherk;* the loud rapid chatter may be followed by a skirling or squealing *skeekia-skeekia-skeekia;* female has a more musical *chwee*. **Range**: Mainly east of the Rift Valley, in low dry country. Widely sympatric with the preceding species.

WHITE-BILLED BUFFALO-WEAVER *Bubalornis albirostris*   Plate 109

Length 8.5–9". **Breeding male** similar to preceding species but *bill mostly ivory-white,* rough and somewhat swollen at base, becoming black in **non-breeding male; female** like male, but black bill lacks basal swelling. **Juvenile** dusky brown above, mottled or streaked with dusky and white below. **Nest** of dry sticks like that of preceding species which it replaces in nw. Kenya. **Call** a harsh dry rattle, *tshutchutchutchu*, preceding a rapid strident squealing *skwee-skwee-skwee-kerEEkerilli-kerilli-kerEE. . .; also a rollicking mechanical cue-cue-cue-cue-cue . . .,* rapidly delivered. **Range**: From nw. Kenyan border areas and Turkana District south to the Turkwell and Kerio valleys, lakes Baringo and Bogoria.

DONALDSON-SMITH'S SPARROW-WEAVER *Plocepasser donaldsoni*
Plate 109

Length 6.5". *Scaly crown, buff cheeks and dark malar lines* mark this weaver of northern acacia bush and savanna. Shows white lower rump and upper tail-coverts (as does White-browed Sparrow-weaver with which it is sympatric in Samburu, Buffalo Springs and Shaba GRs). **Juvenile** browner above than adult, with tawny-buff feather edges. **Nest** similar to that of White-browed. **Song** prolonged and varied, of harsh and soft notes interspersed with whistles and short warbling notes, somewhat starling-like: *tsick-tsurr-sweeet, chirrrrr, tsurr-suweep, chuWEE. . .*. **Range**: N. Kenya (east of Lake Turkana) south to Isiolo area.

WHITE-BROWED SPARROW-WEAVER *Plocepasser mahali melanorhynchus*
Plate 109

Length 6.5". A widespread dry-country bird, brown above with *white rump and upper tail-coverts, broad white superciliary stripes, and 2 broad white wing-bars.* **Juvenile** similar but has paler bill. **Nest** untidy, rounded or ovoid; with short entrance tube. Breeds in small noisy colonies in acacias. **Song** a chattering squealing performance, often pro-

Kenyan Weaver Nests (*Malimbus, Anaplectes, Amblyospiza, Plocepasser, Pseudonigrita, Bubalornis* and *Dinemellia*)

1 Red-headed Malimbe, *Malimbus rubricollis*. Solitary. Western forest trees only. Similar nests of *Anaplectes* not in forest.

2 Red-headed Weaver, *Anaplectes rubriceps*. Solitary or two or three nests in close proximity. Typically of firm materials; many projecting ends. Length of entrance tube varies. Conspicuous, often near buildings. Uncommon but widespread in savanna, riverine trees, gardens.

3 Black-capped Social Weaver, *Pseudonigrita cabanisi*. Colonial in isolated trees in dry areas of north and east. Often of inverted-cone shape, but may be more spherical. Typically with two entrance holes. Sometimes compound (3c). Often on thin dangling twig stripped of its leaves.

4 Grosbeak-Weaver, *Amblyospiza albifrons*. Solitary or in small groups in marshes. Compact and tightly woven between upright reed stems or *Typha* leaves. Roosting nest (4a) with larger entrance than those used for breeding (4b).

5 Grey-capped Social Weaver, *Pseudonigrita arnaudi*. Colonial in acacias (especially *A. drepanolobium*) or tall spindly saplings. Variable in shape; rather large for size of bird; may show two entrances after eggs hatch. Two nests sometimes attached to one another.

6 White-browed Sparrow-Weaver, *Plocepasser mahali*. Colonial. Locally common in acacias, often on safari-lodge grounds and in campsites. Bulky, untidy, rounded or ovoid, sometimes curved downwards. One entrance when containing eggs, two after hatching.

7 Chestnut-crowned Sparrow-Weaver, *Plocepasser superciliosus*. Northwestern. Solitary or a few nests in small leafy tree. Loosely constructed with long projecting grass stems.

8 Donaldson-Smith's Sparrow-Weaver, *Plocepasser donaldsoni*. Local south to Isiolo District. Colonial, usually in acacias, often low. Resembles nest of partly sympatric *P. mahali*, but sometimes more elongate.

9 White-headed Buffalo-Weaver, *Dinemellia dinemelli*. Northern and eastern. Solitary or a few together in a tree. Large, of twigs, stems or coarse grasses.

10 Red-billed Buffalo-Weaver, *Bubalornis niger*. Common, widespread. Bulky masses of dry, often thorny twigs, typically several in one large tree (10a). Old nests frequently used as supports for colonies of Chestnut Weaver nests.

11 White-billed Buffalo-Weaver, *Bubalornis albirostris*. Northwestern, south to Lake Bogoria. Resembles nest of *B. niger*. Variable. May have long tunnel of thorny twigs as shown.

longed and given in chorus, the shrill notes distinct or rapidly run together, e.g. *chiwerp skiweep tsweee skeeep skeweeerk, chirrup-chirru, squeek squew-weechiew. . ..* Has various squealing and chirping calls. **Range:** N, e. and se. Kenya, reaching Tanzania at Longido and Mkomazi GR. Largely absent from Lake Victoria basin and the coast. Scattered colonies in Kenyan highlands (including Nairobi area).

CHESTNUT-CROWNED SPARROW-WEAVER *Plocepasser superciliosus*
Plate 109

Length 6". Sparrow-like with a *striking head pattern*: long white superciliary stripes, subocular marks and submoustachial stripes, plus black malar lines; crown and ear-coverts chestnut. Upperparts rufous-brown with *two white wing-bars and conspicuous whitish flight-feather edges.* **Juvenile** paler than adult. Quiet and unobtrusive; pairs and small groups feed on ground. **Nest** globular, of dry grass and leaves in leafy tree. **Song** short and undistinguished: *wit SEEU witiseet-seet-seet,* often ending in a dry metallic trill. **Range:** Karasuk Hills south to Kongelai Escarpment and Marich Pass; also in Kerio Valley and the Tugen Hills.

✓ RUFOUS-TAILED WEAVER *Histurgops ruficaudus*
Plate 122

Length 8–8.5". Characteristic of n. Tanzanian acacia savannas is this large, *scaly-looking* weaver with *pale eyes* and much *tawny rufous in tail and wings.* **Juvenile** darker brown than adult, with extensive scaly mottling on underparts, yellowish horn bill and brown eyes. Gregarious and noisy. Feeds on the ground alone or with starlings and buffalo-weavers. **Nest** of grass, large and untidy, with short entrance tube, in loose scattered colonies in acacias. **Call** an emphatic strident *schweezzee* or *squeeeur,* sometimes in series. **Range:** Tarangire and Lake Manyara NPs west to Serengeti NP, Maswa GR and the Wembere Steppe.

✓ GREY-CAPPED SOCIAL WEAVER *Pseudonigrita arnaudi*
Plate 109

Length 4.5". The *short, pale-tipped tail and grey crown* distinguish this small weaver of thorn-bush and light woodland. Pale grey crown appears whitish in strong light; narrow white eye-ring is prominent; bill black. *P. a. arnaudi* is grey-brown with black primaries and tail. The race *dorsalis* has centre of back grey. **Juvenile** buffy brown, the grey-brown contrasting little with back; bill brownish. Breeds in small dense colonies. **Nest** of grass, compact, usually in tall spindly sapling or ant-gall acacia. **Calls** include a sharp, high-pitched *tew tew tew, tu-tew, tu-tew,* or *SPI-chew-SPI-chew, spik-spik, PI-tsew-PI-tsew;* also a shrill trilling and a loud, strident *sreet-sreet-sreet . . ..* (Juv. Black-capped Social Weaver resembles young Grey-capped but upper half of head is brown, bill larger and tail longer.) **Range:** *P. a. arnaudi* in and east of the Rift Valley south to Tarangire NP. *P. a. dorsalis* from Mara GR south to Serengeti NP, Lake Eyasi and beyond.

BLACK-CAPPED SOCIAL WEAVER *Pseudonigrita cabanisi*
Plate 109

Length 5". Sparrow-sized with *tail and top half of head black;* otherwise pale brown above; white underparts have black streak along each side of breast and another from lower breast to mid-belly. Eyes red; *bill ivory,* tinged yellow-green below. **Juvenile** similar but dark brown instead of black on head, bill horn-coloured. (Juv. Grey-capped Social Weaver has short, pale-tipped tail.) Breeds in colonies in isolated acacias, the **nest** somewhat cone-shaped and frequently on slender drooping branchlets. Non-breeding flocks partially nomadic. **Call** at nest a high-pitched squealing chatter, *sk'peee chwee-cher skiieer chir-chir squirrrrrr chirr-chrii-chirr. . .,* more wiry, less coarse than chattering of Donaldson-Smith's Sparrow Weaver often vocal in same areas. **Range:** From ne. Kenyan border areas south to the Tsavo region. Wanders to base of Pare Mts and lowlands south of Kilimanjaro at Naberera.

SPECKLE-FRONTED WEAVER *Sporopipes frontalis emini* Plate 108

Length 4.5". Small and *sparrow-like*, with *black-and-white-speckled forecrown and moustachial stripes, rufous nape and similar band behind ear-coverts* . **Juvenile** resembles adult but hindneck pale tawny. Breeds singly or in small groups; builds large untidy grass **nest** with porch-like extension over entrance, usually in a low acacia. **Song** thin, silvery and slightly accelerating, *tsitsitsi tee-tee-tee-teetee-teee*. Call, upon taking flight, *tsip-tsip-tsip-tsip*. **Range**: Nw. Kenya south to Meru and the Tsavo parks, Amboseli NP and Narok Dist. south across much of n. Tanzania.

GROSBEAK-WEAVER *Amblyospiza albifrons* Plate 109

Length 6-6.5". The heavy grosbeak-like bill identifies this thickset, sexually dimorphic weaver. **Male** blackish, with the head either black (*A. a. unicolor* and *montana*) or rusty brown (*melanota*). Forehead white when breeding or brownish or black at other times; *white patch at base of primaries conspicuous in flight*. **Female** brown above, *boldly streaked dark brown on white below*; bill yellowish horn. **Juvenile** resembles female but is more rufous above, buffy below. Flight undulating, often high. (Flying female might be mistaken for female Violet-backed Starling if bill not visible.) Small groups breed in marshes and reedbeds. **Nest** neat, ovoid, of leaf fibres and strips, with side entrance. **Song** a pleasing medley of chirps, high squeaky notes and buzzy sounds: *khhzz, sip-sip-sip, tip-tip seet. . .*, interspersed with a twangy musical *tur-treee* or *twaa-weee. . ..* Also a chattering or twittering flight call. **Range**: *A. a. melanota* in w. Kenya from Mt Elgon south to Lake Victoria basin; *montana* in cent. Kenyan highlands south to Mara GR and (locally) n. Tanzania; *unicolor* on coast from lower Tana River south to Pemba Island and Tanga, inland from Kibwezi to Lake Jipe, Taveta, Rombo, Moshi and Arusha districts.

PLOCEUS WEAVERS are widely distributed birds, some noisy and obtrusive, breeding colonially, whereas others are inconspicuous solitary breeders. The remarkable woven nests of numerous species are noticeable features of the landscape. They vary greatly and can be useful in identifying their builders. Male weavers are readily identified in breeding dress, but several assume a duller, female-like eclipse plumage after nesting. Some females also undergo a seasonal plumage change. Young birds are generally female-like, but tend to be browner above, buffier below and paler-billed. During much of the year these dull-plumaged birds wander through the countryside in great numbers and pose decided identification problems. Naming them requires attention to size, proportions, bare-part colours and plumage details.

COMPACT WEAVER *Ploceus superciliosus* Plates 114, 116

Length 4.5–5". An uncommon west Kenyan weaver with short tail and *thick conical bill*. **Breeding male** dusky olive with *yellow underparts and crown grading to chestnut on forehead; face and throat black*; bill black above, pale grey-blue below. **Breeding female** similar, but with dark brown crown and broad yellow superciliary stripes. **Non-breeding** bird brown above; paler, more tawny below, with buff superciliary stripes and cheeks, darker crown and eye-lines; bill slate. **Juvenile** resembles non-breeding bird but pale yellow below and on superciliaries, bill brown and buff. Typical of moist bush and wet grassland. Not colonial. **Nest** small, ovoid, attached to tall grass stems (resembles small Grosbeak Weaver's nest). **Song** a melodious *cheewery-cheewery-cheewery* (Marchant). Call a short, harsh *cheee*. **Range**: From Bungoma, Busia and Mumias districts south to Lake Victoria basin, Kisii and Lolgorien.

BAGLAFECHT or REICHENOW'S WEAVER *Ploceus baglafecht*
Plates 113, 114, 116

Length 5.5–6". Most birds are the familiar *P. b. reichenowi*, adults of which are black above and yellow below, the **male** with yellow forehead/forecrown, and a *black mask enclosing the yellow eyes*; **female** has entire *top and sides of head black*. Both sexes show yellow wing edgings. **Juvenile** olive-brown and heavily streaked above, *uniformly* *deep buffy yellow below* with *much yellow on the wings*. Distinctive northwestern **P. b. emini** is white on lower breast and belly, **breeding male** with yellow forehead/forecrown, throat, upper breast and wing edgings, black face, hindcrown and back, with grey rump and olive-green tail. **Breeding female** similar, but top and sides of head black. **Non-breeding** birds (both sexes) are grey above with black streaks. **Juvenile** is yellowish green on head, with buffy brown, dusky-streaked back and plain brown rump; yellow underparts fade to white on lower breast and belly. Around Mt Elgon, *reichenowi* X *emini* intergrades are white-bellied; intergrades between *reichenowi* and Ugandan *stuhlmanni* south of Elgon are yellow below, black-headed, olive and black on back. **Nest** solitary, coarse, with short entrance porch, the roof often attached to foliage of tree. **Calls** (*reichenowi*) include a dry *rink* or *errink*, a chirping *chweeeup*, a chattering *chwi, chi-chi-chichit*, and a sharp *spee spee spee*. Patternless unimpressive song infrequent. **Range:** *P. b. reichenowi* in Kenyan highlands, including most isolated northern mountains, south to the Crater and Mbulu highlands, Arusha NP, Mt Meru, Kilimanjaro, the Pare and Usambara mts; *emini* on Mt Loima and Kongelai Escarpment (*P. b. emini* and *reichenowi* intergrade in Kitale–Kapenguria area; black-and-green-backed birds in nw. Kenya may be intergrades between *reichenowi* and nominate *baglafecht* of w. Ethiopia/s. Sudan.)

SLENDER-BILLED WEAVER *Ploceus p. pelzelni*   Plates 113, 115
Length 4.5". A small western wetland species with very slender bill. **Male** olive above; the black of forehead and face extends to a point on upper breast; rest of underparts yellow; wings and tail dusky with yellow edgings. **Female** plain yellowish olive above, with yellow face and underparts. **Juvenile** olive above with dusky back streaks, pale yellow superciliaries and buffy yellow underparts; bill pale horn-brown. (Little Weaver has smaller bill, avoids lakeshore swamps, preferring acacia bush or woodland.) **Nest** small, spherical, loosely woven and with short entrance tube, usually over water. **Call**, a buzzing *bzzzzzt*, recalls Sedge Warbler. Song unrecorded. **Range:** Lake Victoria basin.

LITTLE WEAVER *Ploceus luteolus*   Plates 115, 116

Length 4.25". The diminutive small-billed weaver of dry western acacia bush and woodland. **Breeding male** has black forehead, face and throat; underparts mostly yellow. **Breeding female** yellow below and on face; olive above as in male. **Non-breeding male** has olive crown, is streaked black-and-buff on back; face, throat and breast buff, belly white, bill pale brown. **Non-breeding female** and **juvenile** greyish above, yellowish on face, buff on breast and flanks, whitish on belly; bill pale brown. (Similar Slender-billed Weaver of wetlands has a longer thinner bill. Northern Masked W. is larger, bigger-billed, and the male has rufous around the black mask. Lesser Masked W. is larger-billed and pale-eyed.) **Nest** tiny, spherical, neatly woven, with very short to fairly long entrance tube, typically on low acacia branch. **Song** varied, of typical harsh weaver quality but containing numerous clear notes. Call a soft *tsip*. **Range:** *P. l. luteolus* from nw. Kenya south to lakes Baringo and Bogoria. Scarce *kavirondensis* is local from s. Uganda to our region at Lake Kanyaboli, Muhoroni, Rapogi and parts of Mara GR.

✔ SPECTACLED WEAVER *Ploceus ocularis*   Plate 115

Length 5.5". Slender-billed and pale-eyed, with a narrow black mask. No seasonal plumage change. **Male** has black throat patch. **Female** yellow below, shading to saffron and washed with orange-rufous (less so in western *P. o. crocatus*) on face and throat. **Juvenile** resembles female, but bill pale buffy brown. (Slender-billed Weaver is smaller with still slimmer bill, and male has entire front of head black.) Usually in pairs, skulking in woodland tangles. Weaves compact **nest** of fine palm, banana, or grass leaf strips, with long spout 7–8 cm wide, usually conspicuous at end of drooping acacia branch or palm frond. **Song** a rapid trilling *pi-sir-see-sir-sit*. Calls include a resonant descending *chirr-r-r*, and a loud, even-pitched metallic rattling, *CHEE-CHEE-CHEE-CHEE-CHEE*. Foraging call *peeit*. **Range:** *P. o. suahelicus* in and east of the Rift Valley, on coast north to lower Tana River, inland to Usambara and Pare mts and Kilimanjaro; *cro-*

catus from Mt Elgon south to Lake Victoria basin, Mara GR, Serengeti NP and east to Arusha District.

BLACK-BILLED WEAVER *Ploceus melanogaster stephanophorus*   Plate 114

Length 5–5.5". A solitary *black forest weaver with a yellow face*. No seasonal plumage change. **Male** has black throat and narrow line through eyes. **Female** has entire head yellow apart from dark eye-lines. Eyes dark red. **Juvenile** dull sooty black above, greenish olive-yellow around face, blending with greenish brown on breast and belly. **Immature** dull sooty brown below (brighter on breast); yellow forehead, face and throat washed with chestnut; bill blackish. *Forages noisily in hanging creepers, vines and clumps of dry leaves.* **Nest** retort-shaped with short entrance tube, in tall shrub or tree. **Song** unrecorded. **Range**: Western Kenya from Mt Elgon and Saiwa NP south to the Nandi, Kakamega, Mau and Trans-Mara forests, east to the Karissia and Tugen hills; isolated records at East Mau, Subukia and Aberdare NP (The Ark).

BLACK-NECKED WEAVER *Ploceus nigricollis*   Plate 114

Length 5.5–6". *Dark above and bright yellow below.* **Male** has deep golden yellow head with *black eye-lines, throat patch and nape*. **Female** has *bold yellow superciliary stripes and no throat patch*. Eastern *melanoxanthus* is black above, western *nigricollis* dark sepia. **Subadult** tinged olive, and tail feathers yellow-edged. **Juvenile** resembles female, but dull olive-brown above and pale-billed. Shy and retiring. **Nest** neat and firm, of wiry grasses, with downward-projecting entrance tube *c.* 20 cm long and usually under 5 cm in diameter (narrower than Spectacled Weaver's), well concealed in shrub or low tree. **Calls** include a semi-metallic *trreeng-trreeng* with trilling or quavering quality, a dry *tswick-tswick-tswick-tswick* and a single *chwick*. **Range**: *P. n. nigricollis* in *moist* western woodland edges from Bungoma and Kakamega south to Lake Victoria basin, w. Serengeti and Mara Region; *melanoxanthus* in *dry* areas from the Ndotos south to Tarangire NP and the Masai Steppe; scarce on coast from Mombasa north.

BROWN-CAPPED WEAVER *Ploceus insignis*   Plate 114

Length 5". A montane forest weaver with yellow back and underparts contrasting with black scapulars, wings and tail. **Male** has black face and throat and chestnut crown. **Female** is entirely black-headed. **Juvenile male** has olive-green crown and face speckled with black; bill pale horn-brown; **juvenile female** has yellow flecks on black crown. Pairs work nuthatch-like along large tree branches and trunks. **Nest** has a long pendent entrance tube, and is woven to underside of branch. Usually silent, but **song** (West Africa) a nasal whistling *twit chirr, chirr, chirr, chitt, twit chirr*. **Range**: Marsabit, Mathews Range, Maralal, w. and cent. Kenyan highlands and Nguruman Hills to Loliondo.

HOLUB'S GOLDEN WEAVER *Ploceus xanthops*   Plate 113

Length 6.5". *Large, greenish yellow*, with *pale yellow eyes* and a large black bill. **Male** has orange wash on throat and upper breast, largely or entirely lacking in duller female. **Juvenile** resembles adult female but is greener and indistinctly streaked; bill brownish above, dull yellow below. (Other golden weavers are smaller, the males have brighter orange on head, and with red, pink or brown eyes.) Rather solitary, but a few pairs may nest close together. **Nest** rounded, loosely woven, near water in trees, reeds or cultivated bamboo. **Song** short and chattering, with a dry trill followed by various squeaky notes, *chichi-chichi-chi-squirrrrrrrrrr ski-wee*, and sometimes a final descending rail-like whinny, *qui-ee-ee-eh-er*. Call a loud sparrow-like *chirp*. **Range**: W. and cent. Kenyan highlands south to Serengeti NP, Crater and Mbulu Highlands.

AFRICAN GOLDEN WEAVER *Ploceus subaureus aureoflavus*   Plate 113

Length 4.5–5.5". Bright yellow with *pink or red eyes*. **Breeding male** has orange-rufous crown, face and throat, and *black bill*. **Non-breeding male** olive on crown and face, with a touch of rufous on the throat below the *pale brown bill*. **Breeding female** black-billed,

Kenyan Weaver Nests (*Ploceus* spp.)

(Nests may vary geographically, individually and even locally depending on available nest materials.)

1 African Golden Weaver, *P. subaureus aureoflavus*. Eastern. Spherical, neat and strong, of grass or palm-leaf strips; often near or over water in reeds, shrubs, palms or other trees; usually attached from a single support point. May be in mixed colony with Golden Palm Weaver.

2 Golden Palm Weaver, *P. bojeri*. Similar to No. 1, typically in palms or reeds, but may be in *Typha*, ornamental vines or shrubs. Nest of Taveta Golden Weaver, *P. castaneiceps* (not figured), similar but less neat and typically attached to several stems.

3 Vitelline Masked Weaver, *P. velatus uluensis*. Solitary or a few together. Suspended from branch tip, usually in acacia; very short entrance tube or none.

4 Northern Masked Weaver, *P. taeniopterus*. Colonial. In trees, shrubs or reeds near water, often with other weavers. More or less spherical, with no tube. In our area only in vicinity of lakes Baringo and Bogoria.

5 Holub's Golden Weaver, *P. xanthops*. Solitary or in small groups, in trees, shrubs, cultivated bamboo, low or high. Often in towns and gardens.

6 Baglafecht (Reichenow's) Weaver, *P. baglafecht reichenowi*. Solitary or a few together. Coarse, spherical to ovoid, with entrance tube short or vestigial; roof often well attached to leaf and twig support; among foliage of tree or shrub, low or high.

7 Lesser Masked Weaver, *P. intermedius*. Usually in colony in acacia. Untidy, often rough, with short but variable entrance tube. Two extremes shown.

8 Black-necked Weaver, *P. n. nigricollis*. Well woven, often concealed in foliage of tree or shrub; long tube narrower (to *c.* 6 cm wide) than in Spectacled Weaver's nest.

9 Dark-backed Weaver, *P. bicolor kersteni*. Woven of coarser materials (creeper tendrils, rootlets) than smoother nest of Black-necked Weaver. Often conspicuous.

10 Spectacled Weaver, *P. ocularis crocatus*. Woven of fine grasses, typically conspicuous on drooping branch tip or palm frond. Wide tube (7–8 cm) characteristic; length variable (two extremes shown).

11 Black-headed (Village) Weaver, *P. cucullatus paroptus*. Eastern. Large colonies, in low shrub or high in tree; often near or in villages. Entrance tube typically short, sometimes lacking, occasionally conspicuous (two extremes shown).

12 Black-headed (Village) Weaver, *P. c. bohndorfii*. Western. Large colonies in trees or shrubs. Spherical, with short tube.

13 Northern Brown-throated Weaver, *P. castanops*. Solitary or colonial. Small with short tube, often loosely woven; in papyrus, shrubs or trees near Lake Victoria.

14 Jackson's Golden-backed Weaver, *P. jacksoni*. Colonial in reeds, tall grass or on branch tips over water. (Nest of Yellow-backed Weaver, *P. melanocephalus*, is similar.)

15 Heuglin's Masked Weaver, *P. heuglini*. Western. Small colonies in trees. Globular, with short tube or none. Scarce.

16 Vieillot's Black Weaver, *P. nigerrimus*. Western. Large colonies, usually at forest edge. Spherical, with no tube or mere vestige of one.

17 Little Weaver, *P. l. luteolus*. Solitary in low acacia. Small size diagnostic for species. Compact and firm; tube may be shorter than shown.

18 Little Weaver, *P. l. kavirondensis*. Lake Victoria basin/Mara GR. Solitary. Small, well woven but rough if made of coarse grasses.

19 Compact Weaver, *P. superciliosus*. Solitary in tall grass or reeds. Resembles small nest of Grosbeak-Weaver (p. 531).

20 Chestnut Weaver, *P. rubiginosus*. Coarse, unkempt, typically few to several nests clustered together, usually in huge colonies in low trees, shrubs or tall grass.

21 Speke's Weaver, *P. spekei*. Coarse, bulky and untidy, generally rounded, with short entrance tunnel opening laterally or downwards, but bristly projecting grass stems may obscure basic structure. Close together or in clusters, commonly in acacia.

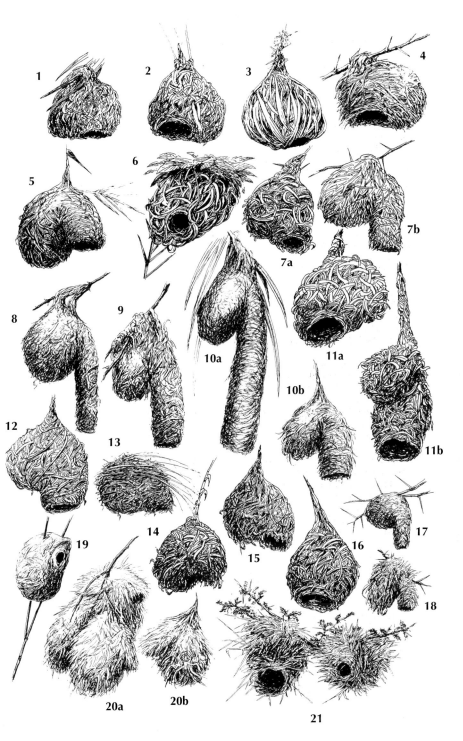

with *indistinctly streaked olive upperparts*, and yellow below except for *white in centre of belly*. **Non-breeding female** more greenish olive with distinct *blackish streaks on back; belly white or yellow and white; bill pale buffy brown*. **Juvenile** also heavily streaked above, pale yellow below with *white belly centre* (male) or pale yellow on throat/breast, and otherwise *mostly white below* (female). (Similar Golden Palm Weaver, with which it may share nesting colony, has almost black eyes, shows no white on underparts in any plumage; adult male's head bright orange with rufous on the throat.) Highly gregarious, often nesting near water. **Nest** spherical, of grass or palm-leaf strips with bottom entrance. **Call** a prolonged featureless chattering in colony. **Range:** Coastal lowlands south of the lower Tana River; local inland along Galana, Tsavo, Athi and Tana rivers, to Sultan Hamud, Kiboko, Kibwezi and Taveta, Usambara foothills and Mkomazi Valley.

ORANGE WEAVER *Ploceus aurantius rex* Plates 113, 116

Length 5.5". **Male** of this Lake Victoria endemic is *orange-yellow* except for the yellow-ish olive back and dusky wings with yellow feather edgings; *eyes pale grey*. **Female** and **juvenile** dull olive above with faint dark streaking, greenish yellow superciliary stripes, and whitish underparts (greyer on breast and flanks, or a trace of pale yellow on breast). In Uganda, breeds in colonies, often with other weavers, in trees or reeds over water. **Nest** compact, ovoid or globular, of grass or palm leaf strips; entrance opens downward under small portico. Largely silent except for noisy chattering in nesting colony. **Status:** Vagrant to Kisumu area (Aug. 1961, Nov. 1981, Nov. 1984).

GOLDEN PALM WEAVER *Ploceus bojeri* Plate 113

Length 5.5". *Brilliant yellow* with *dark brown eyes* (*appearing black* in the field). Often associated with palms. **Male** has bright orange head shading to orange-rufous on the lower throat; bill black when breeding, otherwise black above and yellow below. Yellow-headed **subadult male** developing orange on nape and with some orange-rufous on the lower throat, is easily mistaken for Taveta Golden Weaver, but lacks well defined rufous occipital crescent and rufous patch on upper breast of that species. **Female** mustard-yellow above with indistinct back streaking; *underparts entirely yellow*. (African Golden shows some white on belly. Taveta Golden is darker, more olive and prominently streaked above.) **Juvenile** resembles female but is paler. Gregarious, sometimes in colonies with *P. subaureus*. **Nest** spherical with no entrance tube, typically suspended under palm leaf. **Call** mainly a high-pitched chattering in breeding colony. **Range:** Coastal lowlands from Lamu south to Tanzanian border; inland locally along Tana River to Meru NP, and on Northern Uaso Nyiro River from Shaba and Samburu GRs east to the Lorian Swamp. Also along the Athi River, and (with African Golden Weaver) at Hunter's Lodge.

TAVETA GOLDEN WEAVER *Ploceus castaneiceps* Plates 113, 116

Length 5.75". A bright yellow, brown-eyed weaver in lowlands *around the base of Mt Kilimanjaro*. **Male** has *well-defined rufous crescent on back of head and rufous patch on breast*. (See subadult Golden Palm Weaver.) **Female** yellow below with yellow superciliary stripes and wing edgings. Back yellowish olive with dark stripes; eyes brown, bill dusky above, yellow below. **Juvenile** dull brownish olive above, heavily streaked with dusky; noticeable yellowish superciliary stripes and dark eye-lines; pale yellow on face and throat, more buff on breast and flanks and white on lower belly; bill as in female. Gregarious; flocks disperse into dry bush following breed-ing. **Nest** spherical or ovoid with no entrance tube, usually of green grass and suspend-ed over water. **Song** a twittering *creee-er-curee-twee-twee*. The chattering in a colony is lower-pitched than that of *P. bojeri*. **Range:** Local in Amboseli NP, Kimana and Taveta districts and at Lake Jipe; in Tanzania around Himo, Moshi, Usa River and in Arusha NP; at least formerly in the Mkomazi Valley.

NORTHERN BROWN-THROATED WEAVER *Ploceus castanops*
Plates 113, 115, 116

Length 5.5". A western lakeside weaver with *dark chestnut face, pale eyes and rather slender bill*. **Male** golden yellow with faintly streaked olive back, and deep chestnut face and throat that often appear black. **Female** olive-brown or olive-buff above with dusky streaking; underparts pale tawny buff; *lores and small patch around eyes blackish; eyes cream or creamy buff*. **Juvenile** streaked buff and brown above with yellow wing-feather edgings; underparts pinkish buff except for white belly; eyes brown. **Immature male** shows adult's pattern, but little or no chestnut on lores and forehead, and that on throat dull; yellow head feathers veiled with grey; dusky streaks on back; eyes variable, often pale tan. Nests alone or colonially. (Males of all 'masked' weavers are larger-billed and have *black* on the face. Female Spectacled Weaver, also pale-eyed, is plain olive-green above. Female Yellow-backed W. closely resembles female *castanops*, but is dark-eyed and heavier billed.) **Nest** rounded, of grass fibre, thickened on threshold of the side-bottom entrance). **Call** a soft chatter. **Range**: Local in papyrus and ambatch in Lake Victoria basin, from Port Victoria, Usengi and Lake Kanyaboli east to Kisumu and Kendu Bay.

RÜPPELL'S WEAVER *Ploceus galbula*
Plates 115, 116

Length 5–5.5". A rare golden weaver of ne. Kenyan border areas. **Breeding male** rich yellow with chestnut forehead, face and lower chin; lores and upper chin black; back olive-yellow mottled with dusky; eyes orange-red, bill black. **Non-breeding male** has yellowish olive crown, nape and back and brown bill. **Female** and **juvenile** nearly identical with female Vitelline Masked Weaver but eyes dark red-brown, not red or orange-red.) **Immature male** has pale brownish bill, paler and less extensive chestnut than in adult, none on chin. In Somalia, breeds in colonies near water. **Nest** spherical, with or without short entrance tube. **Song** a wheezy chatter ending in insect-like hissing sounds. Call a dry *cheee-cheee*. **Status**: One Kenyan record (near Mandera, May 1901). Possibly overlooked.

JUBA WEAVER *Ploceus dichrocephalus*
Plates 115, 116

Length 5". Restricted to riverine vegetation in extreme ne. Kenya. **Male** yellow above, often with *rich chestnut head, darker on crown and more dusky on throat; breast and sides paler rufous;* some have *black crown and cheeks and chestnut throat*. **Female** brownish above, with broad dusky streaks; face and superciliaries dull yellow; throat yellowish white, and pale buff band across breast; sides pinkish buff, belly whitish; eyes dark brown, bill blackish above, yellow below. **Juvenile** said to resemble young Yellow-backed Weaver, but upper tail-coverts olive, not buff. **Call** undescribed. **Range**: Daua River Valley west of Mandera.

YELLOW-BACKED WEAVER *Ploceus melanocephalus fischeri*
Plates 115, 116

Length 5.5". Confined to wetlands of the Nile watershed. *Culmen distinctly curved*. **Breeding male** has *black head separated from olive-yellow back by bright yellow nuchal collar;* underparts orange-chestnut, with yellow belly; *eyes brown*. **Breeding female** *buffy brown above* with *blackish streaks on back and scapulars,* and *upper tail-coverts brown or buff; yellow superciliary stripes* on olive-yellow head; *underparts whitish with tawny buff wash on breast and flanks; eyes brown;* bill blackish above, pale below. **Non-breeding** birds similar to breeding female, but with broader black streaks above. **Juvenile** resembles female but only faintly buff below. (Similar but largely allopatric *P. jacksoni* has almost straight culmen; male's back all yellow, black of head extends to nape, eyes crimson; female has eyes more reddish brown, upper tail-coverts bright olive, underparts pale yellow with buff flanks.) Gregarious; associated with water. **Nest** spherical, with or without small entrance tube, in reeds, grass or shrubs. **Call** a wheezy chatter and a nasal *chaa*. **Range**: Lake Victoria, Lake Kanyaboli, and along Nzoia River to Mumias.

JACKSON'S GOLDEN-BACKED WEAVER *Ploceus jacksoni*   Plates 113, 115

Length 5". Similar to the preceding species, but more widespread and often in acacia or ambatch woods near water. Culmen nearly straight. **Breeding male** *plain golden-yellow on back* with black head and nape; underparts bright chestnut except for yellow belly;

eyes crimson; bill black. **Breeding female** and **non-breeding** birds as in preceding species but *olivaceous above from head to upper tail-coverts,* the back dusky-streaked; superciliaries and *underparts pale yellow with some buff or orange-buff on breast,* and white in centre of belly; eyes red-brown (male) or dark brown (female). **Juvenile** resembles female, but is buffier below. Nests in small colonies beside or over water. **Nest** compact, ovoid or spherical, of fine grass or palm-leaf fibres. **Song** a sizzling wheezing chatter. **Range**: Nw. Kenya from Turkwell and Kerio rivers south to lakes Baringo and Bogoria; Lake Victoria basin and adjacent n. Tanzania; s. Kenya from Amboseli NP and Tsavo West NP to Arusha, Lake Manyara and Tarangire NPs and the Masai Steppe.

HEUGLIN'S MASKED WEAVER *Ploceus heuglini* Plates 115, 116

Length 4.5–5". A scarce northwestern 'masked' weaver with pale yellowish eyes. **Breeding male** *yellow from bill to nape with black face, ear-coverts and throat patch* narrowing to point on upper breast. Back olive-yellow, faintly streaked; rump and underparts pale lemon yellow; bill black. (Most male 'masked' weavers have black or chestnut forehead and are brighter yellow below.) **Non-breeding male** greener above and on face; entire underparts yellow; bill pale buffy brown. **Breeding female** olive above, streaked dusky; yellow breast and under tail-coverts separated by whitish belly; bill brown or blackish; *feet pinkish* (grey in female Lesser Masked Weaver; female VItelline Masked W. has dark eyes.). **Non-breeding female** and **juvenile** duller above and paler below than breeding female, with ochre wash on breast. Usually in pairs, but nests in small colonies in savanna or near habitation. **Nest** ovoid, rather coarse, with short entrance tube. **Song** a wheezy chattering *tsureet tsureet wichichichi tseet-tseet tzwee-tzwee-tzwee. . .* and a shorter *tsuree-tsee-tsee-tsee-tsee.* Breeding female sings *seet seet seet sueet sureet chree chree chree chroo.* **Range** Occasional in the Kerio Valley and near Kapenguria, Soy and Kitale.

√ VITELLINE MASKED WEAVER *Ploceus velatus uluensis* Plates 115, 116

Length 4.5–5.25". *Reddish eyes* (except juvenile) and *pale pinkish feet* distinguish this small *dry-country* weaver. **Breeding male** has black mask confined to face, chin and upper throat; little black at base of culmen; most of forehead/forecrown chestnut. (Breeding males of other 'masked' weavers are larger-billed, with more black on throat; male Heuglin's Masked and Speke's have yellow foreheads and yellowish eyes. Lesser Masked has whitish eyes.) **Non-breeding male/breeding female** yellowish olive above with dark streaks; pale yellow below with greyish olive flanks and white belly. **Non-breeding female** more whitish below, yellowish buff on upper breast and pinkish buff on flanks, streaked grey-brown and black on back; head more olive, *superciliary stripes not prominent.* (Heuglin's Masked has yellowish buff eyes; Northern Masked has yellowish superciliaries contrasting with dark crown and brown eyes; Lesser Masked is pale-eyed, grey-footed, mostly yellow below.) **Juvenile** browner and buffier than female, with *brown eyes*; probably not safely told from young Lesser Masked until adult bill shape develops. Less gregarious than other masked weavers; usually in pairs but nests in small colonies in trees. **Nest** *onion-shaped*, with no entrance tube. **Song** a dry sputtering leading into a squeaky trill, *tsuk, tsik- skikit-sker skeeeeerrrrrrrrr.* **Range**: Plateau country north, east and south of the Kenyan highlands and much of n. Tanzania.

√ LESSER MASKED WEAVER *Ploceus intermedius* Plates 115, 116

Length 5". Easily identified by *blue-grey tarsi/toes and cream or pale yellow eyes* in all adult plumages. **Breeding male** has black mask continuing to forehead and forecrown, and black of throat extends to the breast. Coastal birds are plain bright yellow below; those inland darker and more saffron; Tanzanian *cabanisii* has crown and breast clearer yellow. **Breeding female** and **non-breeding male** yellowish olive above with dark streaking; superciliary stripes and underparts pale yellow becoming white on belly. **Juvenile** similar but eyes dark brown; face and breast buffy yellow, flanks pale buffy grey; throat and breast may be almost white. Feet brownish pink, and until the tarsi turn grey, young birds distinguished from Vitelline Masked Weaver only by more slender bill. (Immature Northern Masked is whitish-eyed but has much heavier bill than Lesser Masked.) Breeds in large colonies or isolated pairs, often by water. **Nest** of dry grass, untidy, more or less spherical with short (6 cm) entrance tube. **Song** a rapid wheezy chattering or babbling, somewhat squeaky and metallic. **Range**: *P. i. intermedius* is widespread below 1500 m in humid and dry areas. Often sympatric with other 'masked' weavers. *P. i. cabanisii* only in Arusha–Moshi area.

NORTHERN MASKED WEAVER *Ploceus t. taeniopterus*   Plates 115, 116

Length 4.75–5.25". Likely to be seen only near Lake Baringo. Resembles Lesser Masked Weaver but *thicker-billed* and (except juvenile) *brown-eyed*. **Breeding male** *chestnut on forehead/forecrown*, with *black of face and throat extending to breast*; upperparts largely unstreaked yellow-olive, rump and underparts bright yellow; bill black, feet brown or pinkish. **Non-breeding male** streaked buff and black on back; head olive-tinged, with fine dark streaking and *bold yellow superciliary stripes*; black wings have 2 white bars and pale flight-feather edges; underparts buffy white (plain white on belly); bill dark brown. **Female** paler buff below, with grey-brown tail. (Vitelline Masked Weaver is olive on back, whitish below, buff only on breast and flanks, usually with red or deep orange eyes.) **Juvenile** resembles female, but buff from head to upper breast, and *eyes whitish*, inviting confusion with Lesser Masked W., but *bill much thicker and plumage buffier*. Breeds in loose colonies of 30–100 pairs, in lakeside sedges, shrubs and low tree branches over water. **Nest** spherical, with downward-opening entrance but no tube. **Song** a wheezy chatter recalling Lesser Masked; also a harsh grating alarm call. **Range**: Lake Baringo and swamps north of Lake Bogoria. (Also at n. end of Lake Turkana.)

SPEKE'S WEAVER *Ploceus spekei*   Plates 115, 116

Length 5.75". A *large-billed, pale-eyed* weaver of the highlands. **Male** bright yellow from nape to forehead, on rump and underparts; *back mottled black and yellow* (sometimes largely black); face and throat black, the latter edged rufous; *eyes whitish; bill black*. **Female** dull greyish olive above, heavily streaked with dusky brown; *superciliaries indistinct; lores and short postocular line dusky*; chin to breast pale yellow, almost white on belly, greyer on flanks; eyes pale buff. (Female Black-headed W. is red-eyed, with distinct yellow superciliary stripes and yellowish olive head contrasting with back; in breeding plumage bright yellow below.) **Juvenile** similar but duller brownish grey or greyish olive-brown above, duller yellowish below, with *brown eyes and pale bill*. Nests in large colonies, sometimes as isolated pairs. **Nest** bulky, untidy, with many projecting grass stems, spherical with short entrance tube, in acacia. **Song** *pew. . . pew . . .tew, chinkichi-chewchew-skerinkitsitew. . .*, with variations. Also harsh chattering at nests, and a single sharp *tseep!* **Range**: Cent. Kenyan highlands, cent. Rift Valley, the Crater and Mbulu highlands and Arusha District.

BLACK-HEADED or VILLAGE WEAVER *Ploceus cucullatus*   Plates 115, 116 ✔

Length 5.25–6". Large and sturdy, with *red or red-brown eyes*. Two distinct races. **Breeding male** of larger <u>*P. c. bohndorffi*</u> has *black of head and throat terminating in a point on the breast* bordered by chestnut. Bright yellow from hindcrown to rump except for *black scapulars*; underparts bright yellow. **Breeding female** *largely or entirely yellow below, on face and superciliaries. Yellowish olive head contrasts with browner dusky-striped back*; eyes pale orange-red. **Non-breeding birds** (both sexes) have *back and rump ashy grey or grey-brown, streaked with dusky*; **male** mostly pinkish buff below with yellow throat and upper breast; *bill pale buffy brown, lighter below*; **female** whiter below than male, with yellow throat. (See female Yellow-backed W.) **Juvenile** similar to non-br. adult but brownish above with brown eyes, becoming orange-red with age. **Breeding male** *P. c. paroptus* is smaller with smaller bill, *entirely black head* and *yellow back densely spotted with black*; in other plumages resembles *bohndorffi*. Traditional tree nesting sites (often in villages) used for years. **Nest** coarse and spherical, with short entrance tube added during incubation. **Song** a wheezy chattering interspersed with squeaking and various sibilant notes, usually by several males in unison. Large colonies produce a continuous roar. **Range**: Western *P. c. bohn-*

dorffi from Mt Elgon south to Lake Victoria basin and n. Tanzania; *paroptus* from Northern Uaso Nyiro River and Meru NP south through cent. and e. Kenya, including the coast, to Mkomazi GR, Usambara foothills and Tanga area.

VIEILLOT'S BLACK WEAVER *Ploceus n. nigerrimus*   Plate 114
Length 5.25–6". A dark, yellow-eyed western weaver. **Male** *all black with bright yellow eyes* and grey-brown feet. **Female** dusky olive above with darker head and heavily streaked back; *dark brownish olive below* with dull yellowish throat and centre of belly; *eyes tan or yellow*; bill horn-brown. **Juvenile** resembles adult female, but eyes at first dark grey. Yellow-eyed **immature male** similar, but central crown and underparts blackish. **Immature female** brown-eyed. Nests in large colonies, sometimes with *P. cucullatus*, near forest edge. **Nest** of long coarse leaf blades or strips; resembles that of Black-headed Weaver, but short entrance tube usually does not extend below bottom of nest. **Song** an insistent sputtering and chattering in colony. **Range**: Vicinity of the Nandi, Kakamega and Kaimosi forests. Has wandered to Nambale, Ng'iya and Kisumu districts.

CHESTNUT WEAVER *Ploceus r. rubiginosus*   Plate 115

Length 5.5". Seasonal 'rains migrant' in dry bush and savanna. **Breeding male** *bright chestnut with black head*; wings and tail black with buff edgings; eyes red or orange-red; bill black or slate; feet grey. **Non-breeding male** *buffy brown, broadly streaked with black above* except on rump; wing edgings buffy white; *superciliaries and sides of face buff; breast, sides, and flanks pale tawny or cinnamon buff, contrasting with white throat and belly*; eyes red. **Female** and **juvenile** similar to non-br. male but buffier below and eyes brown. See much smaller Chestnut Sparrow. Highly gregarious, breeding in hundreds or thousands among thorn-trees and shrubs. **Nest** rounded, rather bulky and untidy. **Call** *squip* or *tseup*, plus chattering. Flocks produce a quelea-like sizzling, the sound from a large colony far-carrying. **Range**: Widespread except in ne. Kenya, Lake Victoria basin, coastal lowlands and areas above 1700 m.

CLARKE'S WEAVER *Ploceus golandi*   Plate 114
Length 5". Confined to *Brachystegia* woods in coastal lowlands north of Kilifi. Gregarious, often with helmet-shrikes. Small and slender-billed. **Male** *black on head, back, throat, breast and wings*, but *'shoulders,' wing-bars and many wing-feather edges yellow*; lower belly white; bill mostly black, eyes brown, feet pink. **Female** olive above with dark back streaks and bold yellow wing edgings; underparts yellow except for yellow-streaked white belly; bill grey. **Juvenile** olive with indistinct dark streaking on back; underparts pale yellow, becoming white on belly; bill pale pink below. (Dark-backed Weaver, the only other forest *Ploceus* within known range of Clarke's, is more golden below, has no yellow wing edging, no white on belly.) **Nest** undescribed. **Call**, various loud chattering, chirping, and sizzling sounds from foraging flocks, audible for some distance. **Range**: Arabuko–Sokoke Forest to remnant *Brachystegia* patches on e. edge of Galana Ranch and at Marafa and Hadu. Most records Aug.–Nov. Flying but dependent juveniles seen near Sokoke, April 1982. Juveniles also near Dakacha north of the Sabaki River, July 1994.

YELLOW-MANTLED WEAVER *Ploceus tricolor interscapularis*   Plate 114
Length 5–6". A very rare weaver of the Kakamega Forest canopy. *Forages nuthatch- or tit-like* on branches and tree limbs, usually in pairs. **Male** *black with chestnut breast and belly, and bright yellow crescent between nape and back*. **Female** more brownish below, but *appears all black with a yellow band on upper back*. Eyes of both sexes dark red; bill black; feet brown or grey-brown. **Juvenile** paler dusky brown from cheeks to under tail-coverts; *face and throat tinged rufous; forehead to upper back dull orange-rufous*, and rest of upperparts black. **Call** reportedly a sharp *tsst* or *chirr-it*. **Status**: Possibly extirpated from Kenya. Last recorded in Kakamega Forest July 1972.

DARK-BACKED WEAVER *Ploceus bicolor*   Plate 114
Length 5–5.5". A *stocky, black-headed forest weaver* with *bright yellow underparts, red eyes,* and a *greenish white bill*. Sexes alike. Western *P. b. mentalis* has dark grey back, with black of face barely extending beyond chin; eastern *kersteni is* all black above and on throat, with rest of underparts bright golden- or saffron-yellow. **Juvenile** resembles

adult but chin and throat yellow flecked with black. See Black-necked Weaver. Usually in pairs or with mixed-species flocks. Feeds tit-like, often upside-down, and clings to tree trunks. Distinctive **nest** of hard vine tendrils is compact, smooth and with long entrance tube. **Song** (*kersteni*), a pleasing reedy arpeggio of 5 reedy notes, *ronh roonh raank rernh reenh*, punctuated by soft rapid clicks (audible only at close range), louder wheezy 'rusty hinge' squeaks and whistles. Call a loud *wheet-wheet*; also a soft *heeew*. **Range:** *P. b. mentalis* in Nandi and Kakamega forests; *kersteni* on coast, inland along lower Tana River to Garissa, in Shimba Hills NP and the Usambara Mts.

USAMBARA WEAVER *Ploceus n. nicolli* Plate 123
Length 5.5″. Rare. Confined to forest and forest edge in the Usambara Mts. Singles or pairs join mixed-species flocks. Actions tit-like; hangs upside down to probe among lichens and leaves. **Male** dull black above, largely brown-headed with *dull yellow forehead and brownish yellow wash on nape*; sides of face and entire throat dusky olive-brown; *breast rich rufous-chestnut; underparts otherwise yellow*; bill black, eyes yellow. **Female** similar but entire head brownish-black. **Juvenile** resembles adult except for slate-grey crown with some yellowish feathers in male. (Dark-backed Weaver, with which *nicolli* associates, lacks chestnut on breast and has all-black head and throat.) **Nest** undescribed. **Call** a soft *swi-swee-ee*. **Range:** East and West Usambaras (900–2000 m; recent records only above 1350 m). Total population probably fewer than 100 birds.

RED-HEADED MALIMBE *Malimbus r. rubricollis* Plate 114
Length 6.5″. *A jet-black western forest weaver with bright scarlet hood.* Usually in pairs high in canopy. *Climbs nuthatch-like on large limbs.* **Male** has the red extending from forehead to nape and down each side of the neck as a partial collar; eyes reddish; bill and feet black. **Female** similar but forehead and forecrown velvety black. **Juvenile** duller black, the coloured parts of head orange or red-orange; bill horn-brown. **Nest** suspended from high outer tree branch; retort-shaped, untidy; resembles that of Spectacled Weaver, but spout shorter and much broader. **Call** a wheezing, squeaking chatter reminiscent of calls of Dark-backed Weaver. Also a harsh *tsirp*. **Range:** Kakamega Forest (formerly at Nyarondo).

Ring stage of nest of Red-headed Weaver

543

✓ RED-HEADED WEAVER *Anaplectes rubriceps*   Plates 109, 114

Length 5–5.5″. Suggests a red-plumaged *Ploceus*. Note the bright orange-red bill in all plumages except juvenile. **Breeding male *A. r. leuconotus*** has *scarlet head, throat and breast and a black mask*; back blackish with some red feathers; flight feathers and tail edged with pale scarlet; belly white. **Non-breeding male** grey or brownish grey above. Striking **breeding male *A. r. jubaensis*** is *almost entirely bright scarlet* with some black on wings, tail and scapulars. Non-br. male undescribed. **Females** of both races grey above, white below with greyish wash on breast; *wings and tail edged with pale scarlet or yellow*; bill pinkish orange. **Juvenile** *leuconotus* olive or yellowish on head, throat and breast; *wings and tail edged with orange or scarlet*; bill pale brown. **Nest** coarse but well woven, the long spout with *numerous straggling ends projecting*, suspended by woven stalk from branch or wire; solitary or (*jubaensis*) in small colonies. **Song** (*leuconotus*) a high-pitched squeaky *sizzi-sizzi-sizzi-sizzi, tsrrrrrr, siss-siss-siss-siss tsik-tsiksizzi-sizzisizzisizzi . . ..* Call a sharp *spik* or *tswik*. **Range**: *A. r. leuconotus* generally below 2000 m in w, cent, and s. Kenya, Ethiopian border areas between Moyale and Lake Turkana, much of n. Tanzania except coastal lowlands. Local *A. r. jubaensis* in moist coastal bush from near the Somali border at Kiunga south to Kiwayu.

RED-BILLED QUELEA *Quelea quelea aethiopica*   Plates 110, 112

Length 4.5–5″. Highly gregarious; seasonally abundant in bushed grassland. A small weaver with a *large rosy red bill* in most plumages. **Breeding male** typically has black face and throat, and pale tawny breast; back is streaked buff and black. **Female** and **non-breeding male** have crown and nape grey-brown, *finely* streaked dusky; face and *superciliary stripes whitish, auriculars dusky grey; throat buffy white*; breast mottled. **Juvenile** resembles female, but bill greyish brown. **Immature** has pinkish brown bill. (Female-plumaged Cardinal and Red-headed Queleas have yellow superciliary stripes; Cardinal also has yellow throat. No female-plumaged *Euplectes* has red bill. Some female and eclipse whydahs have *small* red bills and bold black head stripes.) **Nest** of grasses, small and spherical with large side entrance. **Song** a nondescript wheezing and chattering. Alarm call, a sharp *chak-chak*. Flocks produce a noisy chatter. **Range**: Greatest concentrations south and east of the Kenyan highlands and in n. Tanzania. Breeds Nov.–Dec. near Ethiopian border, and in vast numbers in e. and se. Kenya and ne. Tanzania.

CARDINAL QUELEA *Quelea cardinalis*   Plates 110, 112

Length 4–4.5″. *Smaller billed* than preceding species. Gregarious and nomadic; common in tall grassland during or after heavy rain. **Breeding male** *black-billed, bright red on head and breast*; occiput and nape brownish, streaked buff and black, washed with crimson in nominate race but not in *Q. c. rhodesiae*. (Male Red-headed Q. has entire head scarlet, the red throat barred with blackish.) **Non-breeding male** similar to female but usually some red on head and throat. **Female** best distinguished from Red-headed Q. by *yellow throat*. **Juvenile** lacks yellow on throat, has dark-flecked brownish breast band. **Nest** semi-domed with large side entrance, suspended between stems. **Song** a sputtering buzzy *dzeee-dzeee-dzeeee-tsiki-dzee-dzee*, and a rapid sizzling *chhhz-chhhz-chhhz*; at times a simple thin chatter. **Range**: *Q. c. cardinalis* from Kerio Valley through w. and cent. Kenya to Lake Victoria, Rongai and Nairobi NP. Largely Tanzanian *rhodesiae* extends north to Amboseli and Tsavo NPs, s. Rift Valley, Mara GR and South Nyanza.

RED-HEADED QUELEA *Quelea erythrops*   Plates 110, 112

Length 4.5″. The least common quelea in our region. **Breeding male** has entire *head and throat scarlet*; usually densely to finely *barred blackish on throat*; bill large and black. **Female** has *yellow superciliary stripes and face*, especially in breeding season, *white or buffy white throat*, and orange-tawny wash on breast; bill brownish. Short dark moustachial marks more pronounced than in yellowish-throated Cardinal Quelea. **Non-breeding male** similar but may show red wash on face. **Juvenile**

resembles female but upperparts have broad, pale buff feather edges. **Song** a wheezy churring or chattering. **Range**: Small flocks regular around Kisumu, April–July. Sporadic in coastal lowlands north to Mombasa.

BISHOPS AND WIDOWBIRDS (*EUPLECTES*)

Breeding male widowbirds are black with coloured 'shoulders' and prominent tails. Bishops are short-tailed, the breeding males orange-red and black, or yellow and black. Most *Euplectes* are polygamous; a male defends a territory, but mates with several females and builds a nest for each. This is a spherical structure, with a side entrance, woven of grass strips and placed low in grass or shrubs. Breeding is correlated with rains and grass development. After nesting, males moult into a streaky female-like plumage before joining the post-breeding flocks, often of mixed species, which wander widely. Female and young *Euplectes* pose identification problems, as do non-breeding male bishops. Range considerations may assist in identification.

YELLOW-CROWNED BISHOP *Euplectes afer ladoensis*   Plates 111, 112

Length 4". Gregarious and nomadic. Breeds in marshes and wet grassland. **Breeding male** black with *bright yellow crown*, back, rump, upper and under tail-coverts and flanks. Face, breast to belly, wings, short tail and bill black. **Breeding female** streaked buff and black above, with broad whitish or pale yellow superciliary stripes; *blackish auriculars contrast with otherwise pale face*; underparts yellowish white with dark streaks on breast and sides; non-breeding plumage buff below, more distinctly streaked. (Other small female bishops have brown or tan postocular/auricular areas, lacking the contrast of Yellow-crowned.) **Non-breeding male** more heavily streaked above than female; **juvenile** browner above, with broad buff wing edgings. **Song** a high sizzling or buzzing. Call a sharp *tsip tsip*. **Range**: Regular in Baringo, Mwea, Thika and Nairobi districts; recorded in Turkwell delta, Kerio Valley, Lake Victoria basin and Southern Uaso Nyiro swamps. In n. Tanzania, irregular in Arusha District and Masailand.

FIRE-FRONTED BISHOP *Euplectes diadematus*   Plates 111, 112

Length 4". A gregarious and nomadic species of eastern bush country, often with weavers and queleas. **Breeding male** *small*, largely black, with *red-orange forehead patch and bright yellow rear parts*; upper back streaked yellow and black. **Non-breeding male, female** and **juvenile** *the only streaked 'sparrowy' bishop with yellow-edged flight feathers.* **Song** of sizzling quality. Call a sharp *zee-zee*. **Range**: Laisamis and Habaswein south to the Tsavo area and Mkomazi GR; on coast from Lamu south to the Sabaki River. Breeds regularly in and near Tsavo East NP. Occasional around Olorgesailie.

BLACK BISHOP *Euplectes gierowii*   Plates 111, 112

Length 5.5–6". A *large* bishop. Not gregarious when nesting. **Breeding male** black with *orange or orange-red hindcrown, nape and breast band; under tail-coverts pale buff with black streaks. Upper back yellow or orange-yellow in ansorgei, orange in friederichseni.* **Female** *dark*, with *dark sides of face*, boldly spotted under tail-coverts, and *dark spots on buff breast. Wing-linings black,* separating it from all but Black-winged Red Bishop. Female red bishops are smaller and unspotted below. **Non-breeding male** *black on back, wings and rump*, with yellowish superciliaries and chin; sides of face and breast band tawny buff. **Juvenile** resembles female but has smaller breast spots. **Song** of some clear notes followed by a sizzling *see-zee see-zee see-zhe see-zhe SEE-ZHEE*, accelerating as volume increases. Another aerial song a buzzing *zee-zee-zee-zee-zee*, combined with a wheezy *hishaah, hishaah, SHAAAAAH, tsee-tseet-tseet-tseet.* **Range**: *E. g. ansorgei* in Lake Victoria basin and Kakamega. Mainly Tanzanian *friederichseni* around Babati, and sporadically to Lake Manyara and Serengeti NP; possibly along Southern Uaso Nyiro River.

BLACK-WINGED RED BISHOP *Euplectes hordeaceus*   Plates 111, 112

Length 5". Larger than other red bishops. **Breeding male** has *black wings* and wing-linings, and *black tail projects well beyond the orange-red upper coverts.* (Other breeding male red bishops have paler wings.) Face, chin and broad belly band black. *Lower belly and crissum buff* (*hordeaceus*) *or white* (*craspedopterus*). **Non-breeding male, female** and **juvenile** have *rich tawny buff breast band* and necklace of short pale brown streaks; sides and flanks buffy brown, *dimly streaked;* superciliary stripes pale yellow. (Female/non-br. male Black Bishop larger, heavier and darker. Northern and Southern Red Bishops paler with little or no streaking below.) **Range**: *E. h. hordeaceus* coastal, north to Sabaki River, inland to Lake Jipe and Usambara lowlands. *E. h. craspedopterus* from Mt Elgon south to Lake Victoria basin and adjacent n Tanzania.

ZANZIBAR RED BISHOP *Euplectes nigroventris*   Plates 111, 112

Length 4" A *small* southeastern red bishop, often sympatric with *E. hordeaceus.* In pairs or loose groups during nesting season. **Breeding male** *black below except for orange-red under tail-coverts; orange-scarlet from forehead to nape.* Some inland birds have variable amounts of red on throat. In other plumages similar to larger Black-winged Red Bishop, but wing-linings pale buff. (Northern and Southern Red Bishops, unlikely in Zanzibar's range, are somewhat larger with paler ear-coverts.) **Song** not well described. **Range**: Coastal areas north to Lamu and Manda islands, inland to the Tsavo parks, Rombo, Taveta, Lake Jipe and Mkomazi GR.

✔ SOUTHERN RED BISHOP *Euplectes orix nigrifrons*   Plates 111, (112)

Length 4". The gregarious red bishop of Tanzania and the Lake Victoria basin. **Breeding male** *vivid orange-red or scarlet with black forehead, face and chin; lower breast to belly also black; wings and tail dusky, broadly edged with pale brown; orange or scarlet under tail-coverts shorter than tail.* (Northern Red Bishop has entire top of head black, longer tail-coverts covering the tail. Black-winged Red has black wings and longer black tail. Zanzibar Red is smaller with entire crown orange-red, underparts black except for orange-red crissum.) **Female** and **non-breeding male** much like other bishops (virtually identical to Northern Red); primaries edged pale brown (unlike Fire-fronted.) In w. Kenya see Black-winged Red Bishop. **Juvenile** resembles female but has broader and paler feather edges. **Song** a patternless sizzling or wheezy *tssssssss, zeeeeeeeee tsipitsiptsipi tsip-tsip-tsip-ts-ts-tsip.* Call a sharp *bzzz-bzzz.* **Range**: Interior Tanzania north to Serengeti NP, the Mbulu and Crater highlands, Lake Manyara NP, Southern Uaso Nyiro River and Lake Victoria basin. Has wandered to Lake Naivasha. Largely allopatric with other red bishops.

NORTHERN RED BISHOP *Euplectes franciscanus*   Plates 111, 112

Length 4". The red bishop of *Lake Baringo and northern Kenya.* **Breeding male** differs from Southern Red Bishop in having *entire top of head black* and both *upper and under tail-coverts longer, effectively concealing the tail.* **Female** indistinguishable from Southern Red Bishop. **Song** similar to that of Southern Red Bishop. **Range**: *E. f. franciscanus* in Rift Valley around lakes Baringo and Bogoria. Records in n. and ne. border areas may represent the Ethiopian race *pusillus.*

✔ YELLOW BISHOP *Euplectes capensis crassirostris*   Plates 111, 112

Length 6". A large dark bishop with diagnostic *yellow patch on rump/ lower back* and usually on 'shoulders.' Nests in scattered pairs. **Breeding male** black with bright yellow on bend of wing, lower back and rump; bill light blue-grey above, black below. Occasional males lack yellow. **Non-breeding male** mostly streaky brown but yellow on rump and wings conspicuous in flight. **Female** boldly streaked buff and black above except for *plain yellowish rump.* **Juvenile** less heavily streaked below; dorsal streaks dark brown, not black; *buffy brown rump streaked like back.* In w. Kenya see Yellow-mantled Widowbird. **Song** of weak nasal notes with occasional louder sizzling, *tzeemp tzeemp zziiiiiiiiiiiiiiiit zeemp-zeemp-zeemp.* Call a thin *tseep* or *tsip.*

Range: Widespread in w. and cent. Kenya, mainly above 1400 m. In n. Tanzania from n. Serengeti NP, the Crater and Mbulu highlands east to Arusha.

FAN-TAILED WIDOWBIRD *Euplectes axillaris* Plates 111, 112

Length 6". A *broad-winged*, rather *short-tailed* widowbird of *marshy sites*. Gregarious. **Breeding male** largely black with *buff-bordered, orange-red epaulettes* conspicuous in flight, largely concealed when perched. Bill (larger in coastal birds) pale blue-grey. **Non-breeding male** retains scarlet epaulettes; otherwise heavily streaked above and below, and with prominent pale buff superciliary stripes. Similar **Female** and **juvenile** have ochre, orange-yellow or russet 'shoulders.' (Male Hartlaub's Marsh Widowbird has much longer tail; other female-plumaged *Euplectes* lack orange or russet on wing-coverts.) **Song** weak, high-pitched and scratchy, *shreep skrik skrik wirra skreek skreek wirrily wirrily wirrily . . ..* **Range**: *E. a. phoeniceus* in w. Kenya from Mt Elgon south to the Lake Victoria basin, w. Mara GR/Serengeti region, Crater and Mbulu highlands. Wanders to cent. Rift Valley wetlands. *E. a. zanzibaricus* along the coast north to Lamu.

YELLOW-MANTLED WIDOWBIRD *Euplectes macrourus* Plates 111, 112

Length, male 7.5"; female 5–5.5". Solitary when breeding. Two discrete populations. **Beeding male** of nominate *macrourus* is black with *yellow back and 'shoulders'*; shorter-tailed *macrocercus* ('Yellow-shouldered Widowbird') has *yellow only on bend of wing*. In both forms, nuchal ruff is often evident; partly concealed white patch on centre of breast shows in display when ruff is expanded. **Female** and **juvenile** striped buff and black above; *lesser and median wing-coverts yellow margined;* whitish underparts often washed with yellow, and breast faintly streaked. **Non-breeding male** (both races) resembles female, but retains yellow wing-coverts of breeding plumage. **Calls** include a buzzing or sizzling *zeeeeeeee* and a thin *tseep*. **Range**: *E. m. macrourus* in moist lush grassland from Mara GR and Loita Plains/Hills south to n. Serengeti NP and Loliondo. Yellow-shouldered *macrocercus* in bushed grassland and cultivation in w. Kenya from Kapenguria south to Busia, Mumias, Ng'iya and Maseno districts. The two forms do not meet within our area.

WHITE-WINGED WIDOWBIRD *Euplectes albonotatus eques* Plates 111, 112

Length, male 6.5"; female, 5". Gregarious. **Breeding male** mostly black with ill-defined cinnamon-rufous 'shoulders' and *white wing patches* conspicuous in flight; wing-linings and primary bases also white. Bill pale blue-grey. **Non-breeding male** retains rufous and white wing-patches and has yellowish superciliary stripes; upperparts streaked yellowish buff and black; *breast faintly streaked with brown*. **Female** and **juvenile** similar but lack white in wings, and bend of wing (often concealed) is dark orange or rufous; edge of wing, supraloral and submalar areas yellow; throat and breast slightly yellowish. Young male may show pale buff patch on wing-coverts. (Female Yellow-mantled Widowbird is duller, less yellowish, with no rufous at bend of wing.) **Song** a rustling *shwrrrrr* followed by two throaty chirps. **Range**: Cent. Kenyan highlands and adjacent eastern plateau. Seasonal in dry areas, e.g. from Kibwezi and the Tsavo NPs south to Mkomazi GR, where it appears after heavy rains. In the west, with rains, around Saiwa NP and Kitale, w. Mara GR and n. Serengeti NP.

RED-COLLARED WIDOWBIRD *Euplectes ardens* Plates 111, 112

Length, male 10"; female 5". Gregarious. **Breeding male** black with a long flexible tail and, in *E. a. suahelica*, *scarlet crown, nape and collar*. Eastern race *tropicus* lacks red on the head, and has a red, orange or yellow band across throat only. (Some birds in interior Tanzania and Uganda are entirely black.) **Non-breeding male, female** and **juvenile** buff with black streaks above, have at least partly *yellow superciliary stripes*, are streaked on sides and flanks but not on breast. From Feb. to April males are in mottled intermediate plumage with some black body feathers and rectrices. (Female White-winged Widowbird also has yellowish superciliaries but breast is faintly streaked.) **Song** a rapid, insect-like *chisisisi chisisisi chisisisi*. **Range**: *E. a. suaheli-ca* in w. and cent. Kenyan highlands above 1500 m, south to the Crater Highlands, Arusha NP, Mt Meru and Mt Kilimanjaro. *E. a. tropicus* is known in our area only from old records in East Usambara Mts, Taita District and lower Tana River valley.

HARTLAUB'S MARSH WIDOWBIRD *Euplectes hartlaubi humeralis*
Plates 111, 112

Length, breeding male 8"; female 6". Only in marshes or tall moist grass-land in *western Kenya*. **Breeding male** has *moderately long tail* (unlike sympatric Fan-tailed W.) and *buffy orange epaulettes*; most wing feathers buff-edged; bill bluish white. **Female** and **juvenile** streaked pale brown and black above; underparts buff; shows short dark moustachial marks and dark streaks on breast, sides, and flanks. **Non-breeding male** female-like but larger, with buffy orange epaulettes. (Male Fan-tailed W. has *red* epaulettes; female is smaller, brighter, with russet or orange-brown on 'shoulders.') **Song** a short, abruptly rising metallic *turrrreeek* or a loud abbreviated *yecck*, immediately followed by a high-pitched faint *su-sitisit* or *see-seepeeu*; *yecck* or *yerk* note may also precede a rising buzzy trill with a prolonged ending: *chrrrrrrittter-weeeeeeeeeeee*. **Call** a short dry *drrrt*, like that produced by running fingernail along teeth of a comb. **Range**: Bungoma, Busia, Mumias and Kakamega districts.

LONG-TAILED WIDOWBIRD *Euplectes progne delamerei*   Plates 111, 112

Length, breeding male 24–28"; female 6". **Breeding male** unmistakable with *extraordinary long floppy tail*; plumage mainly black with *white-bordered scarlet epaulettes*. Bill pale blue-grey. Wings noticeably broad in flight. **Female** and **juvenile** much smaller, streaked buff and black, with buff patch formed by broad wing-covert margins but no red epaulettes. (Similar female Jackson's W. has larger bill and is more heavily streaked below.) **Non-breeding male** stocky, boldly streaked black and buff above, and with *orange-red shoulders bordered below by buff band; tail somewhat elongated and pointed*. Often solitary, but breeding males roost communally. Nests in marshy spots in high open grassland. **Song** a repeated *twi-twi-twi-twi-zizizizizi*, and a sharp *zik zik zik* in display flight. **Range**: Centred around the Aberdare Range and Mt Kenya; small disjunct population on the Uasin Gishu Plateau around Eldoret and Kaptagat.

Displaying Jackson's Widowbird

JACKSON'S WIDOWBIRD *Euplectes jacksoni* **Plates 111, 112**

Length, breeding male 11–12"; female 5.5". A high-elevation grassland species, always gregarious. **Breeding male** black with long *broad de-curved tail* and light brown, tawny or buffy tan 'shoulders'; bill pale. **Female** and **juvenile** streaked buff and black above; *underparts pale buff to bright orange-buff* with dark streaks on breast and sides. **Non-breeding male** darker and browner than female, breast almost unstreaked except at sides; wings as in breeding plumage but with broad tan feath-er edges. Wheezing, sizzling **song** combined with rattling sound (from vibrating wings?) given by displaying male. Flight call a soft *tu*. **Range**: W. and cent Kenyan highlands south to Nairobi NP, Mara GR, Loita and Nguruman hills, n. Serengeti NP, Loliondo and the Crater Highlands.

PARASITIC WEAVER or CUCKOO FINCH *Anomalospiza imberbis*
Plates 112, 113

Length 4.5". *Suggests a short-tailed canary with a dark, deep-based bill.* Solitary or in small flocks. Flight rapid, direct and weaver-like. **Breeding male** bright yellow with orange tinge to crown; upperparts olive with heavy black streaking; *bill black*. **Female** tawny buff, *broadly black-streaked above*; face yellowish buff with dusky eye-lines; throat buffy white, merging with buffy brown breast; flanks faintly streaked and washed with brown (worn birds paler, less tawny, with sharper streaks). **Non-breeding male** olive above, the head more yellowish and contrasting with *black-streaked back*; underparts yellow with pale feather tips; wings and tail dusky, edged olive-yellow; *bill dusky brown*. (Canaries are longer-tailed and have undulating flight.) **Song** of displaying male a nasal *chi-wee, chi-wee, chi-wee*. Usual calls a high, thin, sibi-lant *tissiwick* (rising) and *tissiway* (falling), often followed by *djzing-ji-ji*; also a separate *dzi-bee-chew*. Flight call a thin hard *jit jit*. **Range**: W. Kenyan border areas and Lake Victoria basin; Nairobi–Thika area (after heavy rains); Mara GR and Serengeti NP. Status on Pemba Island unclear.

WAXBILLS, FAMILY ESTRILDIDAE, SUBFAMILY ESTRILDINAE

Small finches of open savanna, bush, forest clearings, cultivation and suburban environ-ments. Most are granivorous, feeding mainly on grass seeds (but *Nigrita* species are insec-tivorous and frugivorous forest birds). Many are gregarious after breeding. Plumage and bills are often brightly coloured. Estrildine songs tend to be soft, high-pitched and unim-pressive. Numerous species are regularly parasitized by their relatives, the whydahs and indigobirds of the subfamily Viduinae (p. 557).

GREY-HEADED NEGROFINCH *Nigrita canicapilla* **Plate 119**

Length 5". A dark forest finch of canopy, mid-level and undergrowth. Grey above and black below, with *white-dotted wing-coverts; a whitish line separates grey crown from black face and forehead*; rump pale grey; eyes red. **Juvenile** uniform dark grey with suggestion of adult's head pat-tern and wing spots. **Song** a sweet, plaintive 3- or 4-note whistle, *eeee-teuWEEE-weu*. **Range**: *N. c. diabolica* in cent. Kenyan highlands, Crater and Mbulu highlands, on Mt Meru and Kilimanjaro; *schistacea* in w. highlands from Mt Elgon and the Cheranganis south to Nandi, Kakamega, Mau and Trans-Mara forests.

WHITE-BREASTED NEGROFINCH *Nigrita f. fusconota* **Plate 119**
Length 4.5". A *slender-billed, black-capped* finch of the *Kakamega Forest*. Mainly pale brown above and white below. **Juvenile** has dark brown cap, grey throat and flanks. **Song** a prolonged sizzling *tz-tz-tz-tz-tzeeeeeeee*; the high terminal trill may slow before end-ing with a few *tsip* notes. **Range**: Kakamega Forest. (Formerly on Mt Elgon.)

GREEN-WINGED PYTILIA or MELBA FINCH *Pytilia melba* **Plate 118**
Length 5.5". Golden olive wings and *red rump and tail* are conspicuous as this skulker flits into brushy cover; perched bird shows much dark barring on underparts. **Male** is

scarlet from forehead to breast, including bill; crown, sides of face grey. **Female** similar but *entire head grey,* and rump and tail duller. **Juvenile** plain grey- or olive-brown with dull red upper tail-coverts and tail edges. See rarer Orange-winged Pytilia. **Song** a variable plaintive trilled whistle mixed with *kwik* and *plink* notes. Call a loud sharp *tsip* and a soft, insect-like *kwik-kweek*. **Range:** Widespread; *P. m. soudanensis* north, east, and south of the Kenyan highlands, including the coast north of Malindi, south to Tarangire NP and the Masai Steppe; *belli* from Lake Victoria basin to Mara GR and Serengeti NP, east to lakes Eyasi and Manyara.

ORANGE-WINGED PYTILIA *Pytilia afra*   Plate 118

Length 4.5″. A rare waxbill with much *bright orange on the wings.* Smaller than Green-winged Pytilia and pattern similar, but in **male** red of face does not extend onto breast. **Female** barred below *from chin* to belly, and bill is brown with some orange-red below; wings as in male but duller. **Juvenile** resembles female but rump more orange. **Call** a sharp *tsip* and a higher-pitched *tseemp.* Song not recorded in our region; in s. Africa, said to begin with 2–3 rattling notes followed by a soft fluty series ending with a short crackling *kay.* **Range:** Formerly more widespread; largely extirpated by habitat change. Unknown in cent. Kenyan highlands for past 50–75 years. Recent records centred around Kongelai Escarpment and ne. Mt Elgon; small numbers may survive in the Shimba Hills.

GREEN-BACKED TWINSPOT *Mandingoa nitidula chubbi*   Plate 119

Length 4″. *A small, greenish-backed, forest-undergrowth bird with white-spotted underparts.* **Male** red-faced, golden green on throat and breast; rest of underparts black *with round white spots;* some red on bill. **Female** similar but *face and chin pale orange-tawny,* and breast dull olive. **Juvenile** dull greenish olive above, plain brownish grey below with some mottling on breast. Contact **call** a sharp *tik-tik;* alarm note a low *tirrrr.* Song, in s. Africa, described as a mixed series of *tick* notes and whistles; apparently not recorded in our region. **Range:** Coastal areas north to the lower Tana River. Occasional inland, perhaps in part displaced or wandering birds. Small populations may remain in s. Aberdares, Meru Forest, Arusha NP, Taveta District and the Taita Hills.

PETERS'S or RED-THROATED TWINSPOT *Hypargos niveoguttatus macrospilotus*   Plate 119

Length 5″. A 'polka-dotted' eastern waxbill of forest undergrowth. *Tawny russet above with dull red rump and tail.* **Male** has dark *red face, throat and breast;* rest of underparts black with *white spots on sides and flanks.* Orbital ring vivid electric blue; bill darker metallic blue. **Female** similar, but *face grey, throat tawny buff* and red areas duller. **Juvenile** plain russet-brown above and on breast, throat paler; lower breast and belly dull brown; bill dull bluish. See Green-backed Twinspot. **Song** a wispy insect-like trill, at times with 'bouncing-ball' rhythm: *tsit, tsit, tsit-tsit-tsit-tsisitsitsitsit;* or a single chip followed by a rattling trill, *spit cheeeeeeeeeeeeeee.* **Range:** Coastal, and local inland from Shimba Hills to Mkomazi GR and North Pare Mts; (regularly?) west to Kibwezi and Moshi areas. At least formerly in Lake Manyara NP and near Arusha.

ABYSSINIAN CRIMSONWING *Cryptospiza salvadorii kilimensis*   Plate 119

Length 4.25″. A reddish-backed, dull olive finch of montane forests. **Male** crimson on back, scapulars, rump, upper tail-coverts and flanks, with conspicuous *red or pink eyelids.* **Female** shows less red above, only a trace on flanks, none on eyelids. **Juvenile** crimson only from lower back to upper tail-coverts, and a trace on flanks. In n. Tanzania see male Red-faced Crimsonwing. **Call** a soft *tsip-tsip* when flushed. **Range:** N. Kenyan mountains south to Kilimanjaro and Mt Meru where sympatric with Red-faced Crimsonwing (perhaps also in parts of the Crater Highlands). Birds from the Ndotos northward show evidence of intergradation with the nominate Ethiopian race.

RED-FACED CRIMSONWING *Cryptospiza reichenovii*   Plate 124

Length 4.25". A Tanzanian species, darker than Ayssinian Crimsonwing. **Male** distinctive with *bright red on lores and around eyes.* **Female** has no red on face, reduced crimson on body, and eyes are more or less ringed by a diffuse pale area extending to lores. **Call** a high-pitched *tseet.* Song reportedly 4 descending notes followed by a chirp. **Range**: Kilimanjaro, Mt Meru, Pare and Usambara mts (as low as 300 m in East Usambara foothills). Possibly in the Crater Highlands.

RED-HEADED BLUEBILL *Spermophaga ruficapilla*   Plate 119

Length 5–5.5". A stocky *red-and-black* forest finch with a *heavy* iridescent *blue-and-red bill.* **Male**'s red head and upper tail-coverts obvious as bird flies away. When foraging, often assumes crouching posture, the red underparts then inconspicuous. Frequently flicks wings and tail. Upper back and belly are black in widespread nominate race, slate-grey in Tanzanian *cana.* **Female** slaty and dull red, the *blackish belly densely white-spotted.* **Juvenile** blackish above, sooty brown below; *head, throat and breast rich brown*, often scattered red feathers; upper tail-coverts tinged crimson; bill mostly bright blue. (Rare Black-bellied Seed-cracker shows red in tail, none on bill; female unspotted.) **Song** a thin squeaking *spit-spit-spit. . .* barely audible. Call a brief *skwee* or *speek.* **Range**: *S. r. ruficapilla* from Mt Elgon and Saiwa NP south to Kakamega, w. Mau and Mara River; in Meru and Embu forests; *cana* in East Usambara Mts.

*BLACK-BELLIED SEED-CRACKER *Pirenestes ostrinus*   Plate 119

Length 5.5". A rare, heavy-billed finch of thick riverine vegetation near Kenya-Ugandan border. **Male** recalls Red-headed Bluebill but *central rectrices and outer webs of others crimson, widened parts of eyelids above and below eye pale blue; bill darker blue, with no red.* **Female** has black replaced by brown; red of tail duller. **Juvenile** largely brown with duller red tail. **Call** a low metallic *peenk.* **Status**: Vagrant to extreme w. Kenya; two sight records from Busia District.

BROWN TWINSPOT *Clytospiza monteiri*   Plate 119

Length 4–4.5". A western bird of moist savanna undergrowth. Dark olive-brown above with grey head and *crimson upper tail-coverts at base of short dark tail; underparts cinnamon, densely spotted with white.* Male has triangular red spot in centre of lower throat, lacking in female. **Juvenile** grey-throated, with no white spots. **Song** a variable twittering. Call a sharp, frequently repeated *vay, vay, vay.* **Range**: Busia and Mumias districts south to Siaya, Ng'iya and Akala.

BAR-BREASTED FIREFINCH *Lagonosticta rufopicta*   Plate 118

Length 4". Largely replaces Red-billed Firefinch in extreme w. Kenya. Darker than that species and washed with *dark vinous red on forehead, face and throat. Some breast feathers tipped with tiny broken white bars;* belly and tail blackish, but *under tail-coverts buff,* not brown; bill rose-red with darker culmen. Brown **juvenile** has crimson wash on breast and upper tail-coverts. See Red-billed and African Firefinches. **Call** a soft *cheup.* **Range**: Busia and Mumias districts south to n. shore of Lake Victoria.

RED-BILLED FIREFINCH *Lagonosticta senegala ruberrima*   Plate 118 ✔

Length 3.5–3.75". The familiar firefinch of towns and villages. **Male** reddish brown washed with pinkish red above; face, upper tail-coverts, and underparts brighter red with *pale grey-brown belly and crissum;* tail black with crimson edges. Eyes red; *eyelids yellow or olive; bill rose-red below, dark grey above with some red at sides.* **Female** brown with *red lores and lower mandible;* red rump and upper tail-coverts; small white dots on sides; under tail-coverts spotted or barred. **Juvenile** resembles female but lacks white dots on sides, and has little or no red on face; bill dusky. In w. Kenya see Bar-breasted Firefinch. **Calls** a soft *sweet-fsseeet,* a sharp abrupt *chick,* and a

slurred, rising *peee,* the latter two sometimes combined as *chick-pee-pee.* **Range:** Widespread except in arid n. and e. Kenya; scarce on coast away from habitation.

AFRICAN FIREFINCH *Lagonosticta rubricata hildebrandti*　　**Plate 118**

Length 4". The *bluish-billed* firefinch of high-rainfall areas. Not a bird of towns and villages. *Darker* than Red-billed Firefinch, *both sexes with black belly and crissum; female has no red on face or bill.* **Juvenile** resembles female, but is pale buffy brown below except for black under tail-coverts. In dry bush country see Jameson's Firefinch. **Call** a sharp *pit* or *pit-pit,* or *chit-chit-chit-chit,* in irregular series, sometimes included in songs along with trills; also a slurred whistled *bzz-too,* and a repeated *too-too.* **Range:** W. and cent. Kenya, Chyulu Hills, Arusha NP, Kilimanjaro and Mt Meru, possibly East Usambara Mts. Birds on Mt Hanang may represent the race *haemato-cephala.*

JAMESON'S FIREFINCH *Lagonosticta rhodopareia*　　**Plate 118**

Length 4". A *paler, more rosy* version of *African Firefinch,* often in lower drier country (but northern birds are at higher elevations). Avoids towns and villages. *Bill bluish slate.* **Male** of southeastern *taruensis* more *rose-pink* above than the cinnamon-brown northern nominate birds, which lack pink wash on head and back; *upper tail-coverts bright red contrasting with jet-black tail.* Underparts rose-pink with black lower belly and under tail-coverts; some white dots on sides. **Female** *orangey brick-red below,* with *buff lower belly and dark-barred under tail-coverts* (as in Red-billed Firefinch, which is much darker below and with red mandible). Southern birds are pinker than female African, and often show a *red loral spot* (as does Red-billed but not African). Sides and flanks sparsely white-dotted in fresh plumage. **Juvenile** brown above, tawny russet-brown below. **Song** of southern birds a melodious trilled *teu-uuuuuuuuuu,* or a slower *tew-eu-eu-eu-eu-eu.* A musical *tew-twe-twe-twe,* and a thin *eet-eeeeet-eet* may serve as contact calls. Alarm call a rapid purring trill (in contrast to separate *pit* notes of African Firefinch). **Range:** *L. r. taruensis* below 1400 m in Tsavo area, Mkomazi GR and on coast. Western *L. r. rhodopareia* is around Kongelai Escarpment, Sigor and Kerio Valley; old records from near Wamba and Isiolo.

BLACK-BELLIED FIREFINCH *Lagonosticta r. rara*　　**Plate 118**

Length 4.5-5". A large *western* firefinch resembling Red-billed, but **male** is brighter, more scarlet, and *black of underparts extends up to breast; no white dots on sides; bill black with pink patch on mandible.* **Female** dark brown above, pinkish *red on lores and rump;* underparts rosy with *blackish lower belly and crissum.* **Juvenile** brown with red upper tail-coverts. (Red-billed and Bar-breasted Firefinches have no black on underparts.) **Song** usually 3-parted, ending with long trills. Alarm call a sharp nasal *chek.* **Range:** Bungoma, Busia, Mumias, Kakamega and Siaya districts of w. Kenya.

RED-CHEEKED CORDON-BLEU *Uraeginthus bengalus*　　**Plate 118**

Length 4.5". The common 'blue waxbill,' often around habitation. Brownish tan above with azure-blue face, underparts, rump and tail; bill dull red with dark tip; **male** has *red patch on ear-coverts. U. b. ugogoensis* is greyer brown above; **female** of nominate western race has *face and throat blue, uniform with breast and flanks;* in *brunneigularis* entire *head (including cheeks) pale brown; littoralis* similar but paler. (Blue-capped Cordon-bleu is paler, brighter and *longer-tailed;* bill bright pink.) **Juvenile** largely buffy brown below; throat blue in male, brown in female; bill dark slate. **Song** a thin *tse tse tseee,* frequently repeated. Call a thin *tseek.* **Range:** *U. b. bengalus* in w. Kenya; *littoralis* on coast and inland in se. Kenya/ne. Tanzania; *brunneigularis* in the cent. Kenyan highlands; *ugogoensis* in interior Tanzania.

BLUE-CAPPED CORDON-BLEU *Uraeginthus cyanocephalus*　　**Plate 118**

Length 5.25". A *pale, long-tailed* 'blue waxbill' of *dry country.* **Male** has *entire head azure-blue uniform with throat and breast;* belly pale tan, rump and tail blue; bill bright pink with black cutting edges and tip. **Female** paler and with less blue than Red-cheeked Cordon-bleu. **Juvenile** resembles female but breast is buffy tan. **Song** a high-pitched *see-pee-see-see-pee*. Call-note *seeee* or *see-see*. **Range**: North, east and south of the Kenyan highlands, near Lokichokio, from West Pokot to Lake Baringo, Isiolo, Meru NP, the Tsavo parks, Amboseli and Olorgesailie to se. Serengeti NP, Lake Eyasi, Tarangire NP and the Masai Steppe.

SOUTHERN CORDON-BLEU or BLUE WAXBILL *Uraeginthus angolensis niassensis* Plate 122 ✓

Length 5.25″. A southern African species barely reaching our area in n. Tanzania. Both sexes *pale brown from forehead to lower back;* cheeks and anterior underparts pale blue; belly to under tail-coverts pale buffy brown; bill pinkish grey with black cutting edges and tip. Female has less blue on sides and flanks. **Juvenile** paler, with no blue on sides, but *face and breast pale blue;* bill dark. (Female Red-cheeked C. has less blue on sides of head and neck. Female Blue-capped is paler; juvenile has tan breast.) **Song** a mixture of stuttering phrases; also a high-pitched sibilant *seet seet seet seet* and a semi-musical weaver-like series, *skwee-kwee q'wurr yur spee qyur-qyur.* Call note a thin *tseep.* **Range**: Reportedly sympatric with Blue-capped C. in lowlands south of Arusha, but no dated records.

PURPLE GRENADIER *Uraeginthus ianthinogaster* Plate 118

Length 5.25″. A *red-billed, cinnamon and violet-blue finch of bush and thicket.* **Male** cinnamon-rufous on head, neck, and throat, with *blue patch around eyes;* rump purplish blue; tail black; *underparts violet-blue,* often with rufous patches. **Female** has smaller, silvery blue eye patches, *cinnamon underparts barred with white.* **Juvenile** resembles female but head to breast uniformly tawny and bill red-brown. **Song** a high thin *chit-cheet tsereea-ee-ee tsit-tsit,* or *cheerer cheet tsee-tsee surchit.* **Range**: Widespread below 2200 m except in arid n. and e. Kenya, coastal lowlands and most of the Masai Steppe.

YELLOW-BELLIED WAXBILL *Estrilda quartinia kilimensis* Plate 117

Length 3.5–4″. A small highland waxbill with pale *olive-green back and wings.* Pale grey on head and breast, yellow from lower breast to under tail-coverts; rump and upper tail-coverts red; tail black; *bill black above, scarlet below.* **Juvenile** has orange rump and upper tail-coverts and black bill. (Fawn-breasted Waxbill has tawny brown back and all-red bill.) **Call** a weak *swee* or *sree.* Song *tsee-tsee-tsee-tsueeeee.* **Range**: Widespread in highlands above 1500 m.

FAWN-BREASTED WAXBILL *Estrilda p. paludicola* Plate 117

Length 3.5–4″. A *pale* western waxbill of moist grassy areas. *Bill entirely scarlet* in adults. Tawny brown above with indistinct narrow barring; *grey head blends to creamy throat and breast;* latter often with pale fawn wash merging to pink on lower belly (male only?); rump and upper tail-coverts red; tail black with narrow white feather edges. **Juvenile** resembles adult but has dark bill and no pink on belly. **Song** said to be a harsh *tek, tek, tek, teketree, teketree.* Call a nasal *tyeek* or *tsyee.* **Range**: Local in w. Kenya from Mt Elgon and Saiwa NP south to Mumias, Kakamega, Kisii, Kilgoris and wandering to nw. Mara GR.

CRIMSON-RUMPED WAXBILL *Estrilda rhodopyga centralis* Plate 117

Length 4.25″. A common *red-rumped* waxbill with red eye streaks and a *grey or black bill.* Warm brown above with indistinct fine barring; *rump and upper tail-coverts red;* tail dusky brown with central feathers tinged crimson as are the wing-coverts. **Juvenile** lacks red eye-streaks. Usual **call** a soft *tsip-tsip-tsip;* also a soft *tyeek* and a nasal *tchair* or *cheee,* sometimes double. (Common and Black-rumped Waxbills lack red on rump.) **Range**: Widespread. Scarce and local in arid n. and e. Kenya but influxes occur following heavy rains.

BLACK-RUMPED WAXBILL *Estrilda troglodytes* **Plate 117**

Length 4". A local west Kenyan species. Resembles a *pale* Common Waxbill with *black rump and tail* (*outer rectrices narrowly white-edged*) and *dark carmine bill.* **Juvenile** lacks red eye streaks and has black bill. (Darker Common W. has brown rump and tail. Crimson-rumped W. has red rump.) **Song** a loud *che-cheer, chee-eeer.* Call a loud repeated *cheu-cheu* or *chit-chit;* flocks in flight give a continuous *tiup-tiup-tiup* or a soft lisping twittering like that of Common Waxbill. **Range:** Ukwala, Siaya, Mumias and Kisumu areas including rice fields near Ahero.

COMMON WAXBILL *Estrilda astrild* **Plate 117**

Length 4". Distinguished from Crimson-rumped Waxbill by *brown rump* and *bright red bill.* **Male** warm brown with narrow blackish barring above; sides of face white, throat pinkish or pale tan; pinkish breast and sides are barred with dusky and white; centre of belly red, under tail-coverts black. **Female** is paler than male with less pink. Western *E. a. peasei* is much pinker than interior *massaica;* coastal *minor* is browner below with a white throat. **Juvenile** has *black bill, orange eye streaks* and more suffused barring. **Song** a variable hesitant sputtering mixed with a few semi-musical notes, *skwitchi tsitsi-chwee qyurr . . . tweep . . .qyurr . . . tsip-tsip . . .ckwee-chirree cheee skurrrrrree. . ..* Flock utters a soft buzzy twitter. **Range:** *E. a. minor* on coast, inland to the Usambara and Pare mts, Mkomazi GR, Taveta and Moshi, Tsavo West and Amboseli NPs; *peasei* from Mt Elgon and Cheranganis south to the Lake Victoria basin; *massaica* in interior Kenya/n. Tanzania between *minor* and *peasei.*

BLACK-CROWNED WAXBILL *Estrilda n. nonnula* **Plate 117**

Length 4". A black-capped western waxbill with *whitish belly,* and *black of head is confined to forehead and crown.* (Allopatric Black-headed Waxbill is black from crown to nape, on belly and under tail-coverts.) **Male** has grey back and wings with fine dusky barring, deep red rump/ upper tail-coverts and black tail; flanks washed with red; bill black with red patches on sides. **Female** is paler, less red on flanks. **Juvenile** has underparts tinged buffy brown. **Song** high-pitched and short: *speet-speet, p'seet-seet,* or *sureeeaseet seet-seet-seet.* Contact call a thin *pee-pee-pee.* **Range:** Between 1500 and 2000 m, from Saiwa NP south through Nandi, Kakamega, Mau and Trans-Mara forests to Lolgorien.

BLACK-HEADED WAXBILL *Estrilda atricapilla graueri* **Plate 117**

Length 4.25". A *dark-bellied* montane waxbill with *entire top of head and nape black.* Greyish white on sides of face and breast; remaining underparts blackish except for *bright crimson flanks;* rump and upper tail-coverts red; tail black; bill all black or with triangular crimson patch on side. See Black-crowned Waxbill. **Juvenile** dusky brown above, blackish below with no red on flanks. Chippering **song** louder and longer than that of Black-crowned Waxbill: *chureeecheet cher-wee-wee-wee chit-chit.* Flocks utter a lisping twittering. Contact call similar to that of Black-crowned. A bird of forest edges and clearings. **Range:** between 2500 and 3300 m on Mt Elgon, the Aberdares and Mt Kenya.

BLACK-FACED WAXBILL *Estrilda erythronotus delamerei* **Plate 117**

Length 4–4.5". A *red-rumped* waxbill with *black of face extending to chin and upper throat.* Crown and back pale vinaceous grey; wings with narrow black-and-white barring; rump and upper tail-coverts dark red; tail black; underparts pinkish grey shading to dull red on flanks; *belly and crissum black in male;* bill black. **Juvenile** resembles adult female but young male is blackish on belly and under tail-coverts. See Black-cheeked Waxbill. **Song/call** a repeated musical whistle, *tyur-ee* or *pee-tyee,* the second note rising, recalling Rufous-naped Lark. This usually combined with various *cht, tst-tst* and *seet* notes in an extended series. Inhabits dry woodland and acacia groves. **Range:** Lake Victoria basin and Thika–Nairobi area southward. In Tanzania,

widespread from Serengeti NP east to Mkomazi GR. **Taxonomic Note:** formerly considered conspecific with Black-cheeked Waxbill.

BLACK-CHEEKED WAXBILL *Estrilda charmosyna*   **Plate 117**

Length 4–4.5″. Closely resembles female Black-faced Waxbill, but *black of head confined to sides of face and a narrow strip on upper chin; lower chin and throat pinkish white,* shading to dull greyish pink on breast and sides; *rear underparts usually pale pink.* **Female** and **juvenile** duller, less vinaceous above and less pink below. Some individuals are darker, greyish-tinged, on belly. Black-faced W. has the chin and upper throat black; male also has black belly and crissum. **Song/call** apparently similar to those of Black-cheeked W., but past confusion between the two species may have concealed differences. Mainly in dry thorn-bush. **Range:** Widespread below 1000 m in dry n. and e. Kenya. Has wandered west to Thika district. A disjunct dark population in Olorgesailie–Magadi area.

ZEBRA WAXBILL *Amandava subflava*   **Plate 117**

Length 3.5″. A tiny waxbill of moist grassland; *yellow or orange underparts* unique. **Male** olive-brown above with *bright red upper tail-coverts* and black tail; superciliary stripes red; chin and *throat yellow, deepening to orange in western birds;* in east, orange only on breast and under tail-coverts; sides barred; bill scarlet, black on culmen. **Female** lacks red superciliaries, is pale yellow below, orange on under tail-coverts. **Juvenile** brown above with no red or orange, and no bars on flanks; bill black. **Calls** include a rapid *trip-trp-trp-trp* when taking wing, and a soft *chit-chit.* Song a series of high notes, not well described. **Range:** Nominate *subflava* in w. Kenya from Mt Elgon south to Lake Victoria basin (at times common in Ahero rice fields). *A. s. clarkei* in coastal lowlands inland locally to Lake Jipe, Arusha NP, Ngorongoro Crater, Nairobi NP, Thika and Murang'a .

QUAIL-FINCH *Ortygospiza atricollis muelleri*   **Plate 117**

Length 3.5″. A *tiny, short-tailed, heavily barred* ground bird of open moist grassland. Rises quickly with metallic ticking calls, flies a short distance and plummets back into cover. **Male** shows *distinctive pied face, white chin patch and black throat;* breast, sides and flanks are barred; rich buff patch in centre of lower breast; tail black with narrow white sides and corners. Bill reddish. **Female** is paler with grey throat. **Juvenile** still paler with unbarred breast and light feather edges. Usual flight **call** a sharp *djink* or *tink-tink.* Song a rising and falling series of creaky notes. **Range:** Above 1500 m, especially on black soils in w., cent. and s. Kenya south to Serengeti, Arusha, and Tarangire NPs.

*LOCUST-FINCH *Ortygospiza locustella uelensis*   **Plate 117**

Length 3.5–4″. A *tiny, short-tailed grassland bird, pale-eyed* and with *much red-orange in wings.* **Male** distinctive with *bright red face, throat and upper breast,* rest of underparts black with white bars on flanks; bill reddish. **Female** has black face, whitish underparts *heavily barred with black on sides and flanks.* **Call** a soft *pink-pink.* **Range:** Rare or vagrant in w. Kenya. Small numbers possibly established in parts of Busia and Mumias districts.

AFRICAN SILVERBILL *Lonchura cantans orientalis*   **Plate 117**

Length 4.5″. A *black-tailed, black-rumped* finch of dry country. Pale brown above with *prominent black primaries,* rump, upper tail-coverts and tail; throat and breast buff, otherwise white below; sometimes mottled on throat. Bill and bare orbital ring bluish. **Juvenile** similar but most feathers edged buff and rectrices edged brown. Prolonged **song** of twittering or sizzling notes. **Range:** Widespread in n. Kenya south to edge of highlands; in the south, from Olorgesailie to Arusha District and east to the Tsavo parks and Mkomazi GR. **Taxonomic Note:** Considered conspecific with Asian *L. malabarica* by some authors.

GREY-HEADED SILVERBILL *Lonchura griseicapilla* **Plate 117**

Length 4.5". The only finch-like bird showing a *prominent white rump in flight. Blue-grey head is speckled with white and black* on ear-coverts, cheeks and throat; back and underparts are rich pinkish cinnamon-brown, primaries and tail black, bill blue-grey. **Juvenile** duller, with no facial speckling. **Song** a weak high-pitched trill, starting with soft notes and becoming louder. **Range**: One population north of cent. Kenyan highlands, another to the south, and in interior Tanzania.

BRONZE MANNIKIN *Lonchura cucullata* **Plate 119**

Length 3.5". A tiny dark bird with a *blackish head, black tail* and a *large, two-toned bill.* Grey-brown above with *iridescent green shoulder patch,* barred rump and upper tail-coverts; *flanks barred brown and white.* Glossy green patch on sides in western *L. c. cucullata* lacking in *L. c. scutata.* **Juvenile** *plain dull brown* above; brown throat, breast, and sides contrast with paler belly; *under tail-coverts barred;* bill black. See Black-and-white Mannikin. Flock **call** a frequent soft buzzy or wheezy twittering, recalling white-eyes (*Zosterops*). **Range**: Western nominate race from Lake Victoria basin east to the Rift Valley where intergrading with *scutata*; the latter occupies other highland areas in cent. Kenya and n. Tanzania; also along coast and on Pemba Island.

✓ BLACK-AND-WHITE (incl. <u>RUFOUS-BACKED) MANNIKIN</u> *Lonchura bicolor*
Plate 119

Length 3.25". Two forms, both more sharply patterned than Bronze Mannikin: *L. b. poensis is glossy black on head, throat and breast,* dark brown on back, barred black and white on flight feathers, rump, upper tail-coverts and flanks; bill blue-grey. **Juvenile** sepia above, including crown and cheeks, greyish buff below, lightly barred on sides; *under tail-coverts plain*; bill black. (Juv. Bronze Mannikin is paler above, browner and buffier below, with less contrast between head and throat/breast. *L. b. nigriceps* ('Rufous-backed Mannikin') is like *poensis*, but back and innermost wing feathers are rufous. **Juvenile** rich brown with rufous wash on back. **Call** a soft *kip* or *tik.* Flock gives a low buzzy twittering. **Range**: *L. b. poensis* below 2000 m west of Rift Valley; *nigriceps* in cent. Kenyan highlands, on coast north to Lamu, inland to the Usambara and Pare mts, Taveta, Moshi and Arusha; locally at Oldeani, Loliondo and the Nguruman Hills. (Early specimens from Moyale and Marsabit.)

MAGPIE MANNIKIN *Lonchura fringilloides* **Plate 119**

Length 4.5". Rare. A *very large-billed, brown-backed* mannikin, glossy blue-black on head, sides of breast, tail and upper tail-coverts. Scapulars and wings mainly dark brown, and a few short white streaks on wing-coverts and back; *sides and flanks blotched with black* around a buffy tan patch; largely white underparts tinged buff on crissum; bill black above, grey-blue below. **Juvenile** dusky brown above, with blue-black rump and tail, pale buff underparts. (Smaller Black-and-white Mannikin has much smaller bill, glossy black or rufous back; lacks large blue-black pectoral patches.) **Call** a loud *pee-oo-pee-oo*; alarm call a thin *cheep.* **Range**: Recent records from East Usambara Mts. (1977–81), Taveta area (1989), and Busia District (1991). East African populations have declined greatly in the past 50 years.

CUT-THROAT FINCH *Amadina fasciata* **Plate 117**

Length 4". *Pale* and *scaly-feathered.* **Male** has *red band across the throat,* and a *dull cinnamon belly patch* on buffy white underparts marked with dark wavy bars and chevrons; upperparts pale greyish tan heavily barred and flecked with black. **Female** and **juvenile** lack red, the face is barred, and there is little or no cinnamon on belly. **Calls** are a sparrow-like chirp and a loud plaintive *kee-air.* Song reportedly a low buzzing broken by toneless warbling notes. **Range**: Widespread below 1300 m. Sporadic in Lake Victoria basin and coastal lowlands. Birds in nw. Kenya (Lokichokio to Lake Turkana) probably represent the nominate race; all others are *alexanderi.*

JAVA SPARROW *Padda oryzivora* **Plate 124**
Length 6–6.5". The *massive bright pink bill* and *large white patch on sides of the black head* distinguish this introduced Tanzanian finch. **Juvenile** is pale buffy grey above, buffy white below; bill dark brown with pink base; orbital ring pink. **Call** a liquid *t'lup*. **Range**: Mainly in and around Chake-Chake on Pemba Island.

WHYDAHS AND INDIGOBIRDS, SUBFAMILY VIDUINAE

Uniquely African birds that are host-specific brood-parasites on their estrildine relatives. Pattern and colour of palate and gape markings of the host species' nestlings are matched by those of the young viduine which (unlike some brood-parasites) does not evict the host's own offspring, and its close association with the foster family continues for some time after fledging. Male whydahs acquire a striking breeding plumage marked by exceptionally long central tail feathers. Females and non-breeding males have 'sparrowy' patterns dominated by buff-and-brown streaking. Although viduines have calls of their own, all except Pin-tailed and Steel-blue Whydahs regularly mimic songs of their host species. The short-tailed indigobirds parasitize firefinches, and each male generally mimics the voice of a single firefinch species. Females appear to select a male on the basis of his mimetic songs (probably learned when young from the foster parents). A male uses traditional singing stations year after year, and females visit these sites for mating. No pair bonds are formed. Indigobirds are difficult to identify. More important than morphology for delimiting their species are mating behaviour and song type. Different forms may share an area without interbreeding.

VILLAGE or COMMON INDIGOBIRD *Vidua chalybeata* **Plate 110**

Length 4". **Breeding male** bluish black, slightly more blue-green in the red-billed coastal race *amauropteryx*, more indigo-blue in white-billed *centralis*. In both races wings are brownish and the feet salmon-pink (whitish pink in some southern birds). See Purple Indigobird. **Non-breeding** birds (both sexes) closely resemble female Pin-tailed Whydah, with prominent pale buff and dark brown head stripes, but Pin-tailed is often red-billed and has warm buffy brown underparts. (Female Steel-blue Whydah is stubbier-billed, and largely white below with faint buff tinge to breast.) **Juvenile** resembles a small female House Sparrow with buff superciliaries (most noticeable behind eyes); bill colour varies. **Call** a clear *swee*. One song, a sputtering chatter, typically includes the *chick-pee-pee* phrase of Red-billed Firefinch, the host species. Complex non-mimetic songs differ from one population to another. **Range**: *V. c. centralis* is widespread, usually below 1800 m; *amauropteryx* is coastal, from Kwale north to Lamu.

PURPLE INDIGOBIRD *Vidua purpurascens* **Plate 110**

Length 4". A bird of dry areas occupied by its host, Jameson's Firefinch. **Breeding male** black with *dull purplish or purplish blue gloss*. Wings paler brown than in Village Indigobird; *bill and feet white or pinkish white*, thus identical in appearance with Variable Indigobird. **Female** and **non-breeding** male probably indistinguishable from other indigobirds in the field. **Song** harsh and chattering; differs from other indigobirds' songs only by the included mimetic 'purr' of Jameson's Firefinch. **Range**: Local; reported from Kongelai Escarpment, Sigor, Kerio Valley, probably Lake Baringo, Kibwezi, Tsavo West NP and Taita District.

VARIABLE INDIGOBIRD *Vidua funerea nigerrima* **(Not illustrated)**
Length 4". Identical in appearance to the preceding species, but male vocally mimics African Firefinch (the *bzz-tu* and *too-too* notes). **Song** includes a rapid trilled *pit-pitpit-pitpitpit. . .* (slower, but not always easily distinguished from faster purring trill of Jameson's Firefinch). **Range**: Known in Tanzania from Tanga, North Pare Mts and Moshi District. In Kenya, in the Kerio Valley (alongside *V. purpurascens* and *V. chalybeata*). Perhaps overlooked elsewhere.

STEEL-BLUE WHYDAH *Vidua hypocherina*   Plate 110

Length, breeding male, 11"; female, 4". **Breeding male** shiny blue-black with 4 long thin central tail feathers when breeding; has *white wing-linings*, unlike indigobirds (confusable with moulting male whydah without long rectrices). **Female** and **non-breeding male** distinguished from female indigobirds and Pin-tailed Whydah by smaller whitish or pale grey bill; from Paradise Whydah by bill colour and brighter pattern. **Juvenile** resembles young Straw-tailed Whydah but belly is whiter and bill whitish, not red-brown. Parasitises Black-cheeked and possibly Black-faced Waxbills. **Song** a series of simple *chiff, tik* or *wheez* notes, 1–4 per sec., repeated for several minutes. Probably mimics songs of other birds. **Range:** Local in dry bush; Kongelai Escarpment, Lake Victoria basin, Rift Valley north and south of the highlands, Samburu GR to Meru and Kitui districts and Tsavo East NP; sporadic in e. Serengeti; Lake Manyara and Tarangire NPs.

✓ PIN-TAILED WHYDAH *Vidua macroura*   Plate 110

Length, breeding male 12"; female 4". Most widespread and conspicuous of the whydahs. **Male** black and white with a red or orange bill; retains breeding plumage longer than other whydahs but tail length varies (in full plumage, 4 long central rectrices conspicuous). **Female** boldly streaked buff and black on head; *bill coral-red in non-br. season, blackish when breeding*. Female/non-br. male have *inner half of each rectrix white, obvious in flight*; male has black-and-white head stripes and red bill. **Juvenile** plain dull grey-brown, paler below; bill blackish at first, later dull reddish. (Most other female/young whydahs distinguished by bill colour. Female and young Straw-tailed also have rusty on head; pale-billed female Steel-blue has whiter underparts; juv. Paradise is larger, bigger-billed, has darker breast, at times with short streaks, and a darker face with superciliaries little paler than ear-coverts. Female indigobirds have duller, grey-brown or buffy brown underparts.) Parasitises various waxbills. **Song** a repetitive high-pitched *tseet tseet tsuweet* or *si-swirt-sweeu-see*. Call a low *peeee* and a thin double or triple *chip*. **Range:** Widespread below 2500 m except in the driest areas. Also at Lokichokio and Mandera. Occasional at Marsabit and Lake Turkana.

✓ STRAW-TAILED WHYDAH *Vidua fischeri*   Plate 110

Length, breeding male, 11"; female, 4". **Breeding male** mostly black above, with sandy buff forehead and crown, and 4 long, slender, straw-coloured central tail feathers. Bill and feet coral-red. **Female** and **non-breeding male** streaked buffy brown and sepia above, the head plain rufous-buff, darker on crown; whitish underparts tinged buff on breast and sides; bill pink, feet dusky pink. **Juvenile** dull rusty brown, paler below; feet and bill pinkish brown. **Immature male** resembles adult female, but may have short straw-like central rectrices; bill pink or coral-red. Parasitises Purple Grenadier. **Song** of 4–5 thin notes followed by a short trill, *p'tchewi-tchui-chitisee-tseeeeeeeeee*, or *tsu-tsu-tsewit cheeeeee*, frequently repeated. Call note a sharp *tseep*. **Range:** Extreme ne. Kenya, Lokichokio and from Kongelai to the Kerio and Rift valleys, Isiolo and Meru districts, south through Tsavo and Amboseli NPs; Olorgesailie–Lake Natron area and the Masai Steppe.

PARADISE WHYDAH *Vidua paradisaea*   Plate 110

Length, breeding male, 13"; female, 5". **Breeding male** unmistakable with black body, golden buff nape, chestnut breast, and remarkable tail with the 2 central feathers broad and short, their bare shafts projecting; adjacent pair narrower but greatly elongated and tapering. In flight has distinctive 'hunch-backed' appearance. **Female** and **non-breeding male** streaked tawny or cream and black; breast with black streaks. Female has *C-shaped mark on side of face* (lacking in Broad-tailed Paradise W.) **Juvenile** plain, similar to smaller-billed juv. Pin-tailed Whydah. (Female and imm. Pin-tailed are usually red-billed, have less patterned face, and no black streaks within the pale central crown stripe.) Long **song** includes mimicry of its host Green-winged Pytilia, *shree-shree sreeeeeeeeeee chrrrrr sreeeeee sreet sreet surreeet sreet skirrreet . . ..* Call a sharp *chip* or *chip-chip*; flight call a long thin whistle. **Range:** Parallels that of its pytilia host. Wanders to 2000 m or higher, and reaches coastal lowlands near Tana River delta and Kilifi.

BROAD-TAILED PARADISE WHYDAH *Vidua obtusa*   **Plate 110**

Length, breeding male, 12"; female, 5". **Breeding male** resembles widespread Paradise Whydah but has shorter and much wider elongated tail feathers which are equally broad throughout; hindneck coppery rufous, darker than in *paradisaea*, and breast deeper chestnut. Female lacks distinctive facial C-mark of *paradisaea*, and in breeding condition, the paler bill is at least partly pinkish or whitish grey, not all blackish. **Song** a mixture of whistling, chattering and churring notes, *skew chwew sreet skew chrrrrrrr chk-chk-chk-chk-tweeeeu chk-chk skweeeeu sweet-sweet sweeeeo.* **Status**: Probably now extirpated from our area (formerly in Meru District). Its host species, Orange-winged Pytlia, is itself extirpated from the cent. Kenyan highlands.

SEEDEATERS, CANARIES AND RELATIVES, FAMILY FRINGILLIDAE

Relatives of the holarctic siskins and goldfinches, these birds are characterized by a short, conical and often sharp-pointed bill designed for extracting and cracking seeds. The commissure is strongly angled, and the mandible edges fit closely together throughout their length (unlike buntings' bills). Most species feed on and near the ground, but usually sing from elevated perches. Many are gregarious except when breeding. Seedeaters are brown-backed, typically streaky birds, whereas most canaries, African Citril and Oriole-Finch are olive and yellow, often brightly plumaged.

STREAKY-HEADED SEEDEATER *Serinus (gularis) elgonensis*   **Plate 121**

Length 5". A rare, largely unstreaked finch with *bold white superciliary stripes and dark brown ear-coverts.* Shows *fine whitish lines on crown and nape* and an almost plain grey-brown back; underparts mostly pale brownish grey with a *contrasting white throat*; some birds have a few *short streaks on upper breast.* **Juvenile** perhaps indistinguishable from young Stripe-breasted Seedeater. **Song** a variable prolonged medley of twittering, whistles and buzzy notes, sometimes with long trills added. Also sings a prolonged, monotonous repetition of a single phrase, e.g. *we see-see SLIP* or *wee sieu TSIP.* **Range**: Mt Elgon–Kongelai area (one specimen, June 1900). **Taxonomic Note:** Possibly conspecific with the following form. See note below.

STRIPE-BREASTED SEEDEATER *Serinus (reichardi) striatipectus*   **Plate 121**

Length 5". A *heavily streaked*, brown-backed finch, local and uncommon on escarpments and shrub-covered hillsides. *Obscurely to boldly streaked above, the crown and nape more finely streaked with dark brown and white; broad white superciliary stripes contrast with dark brown sides of face and ear-coverts.* Buff-tinged *underparts broadly streaked with brown.* **Juvenile** warmer brown, the streaks somewhat bolder. See Streaky Seedeater. **Song** a series of buzzy trills, at times melodious, but joined with unmusical twittering and *multiple repetitions of single notes and phrases,* often mingled with imitations of other birds. **Range**: Kongelai, Tambach and Tugen escarpments east to Laikipia and Mt Kenya. **Taxonomic Note**: The form *striatipectus* has been linked to both *S. reichardi* and *S. gularis.*

STREAKY SEEDEATER *Serinus s. striolatus*   **Plate 121**

Length 5.25–5.5". A common terrestrial highland finch with *boldly streaked underparts*; broad pale superciliary stripes and dark jaw lines add to the overall streaky effect. Many individuals show yellowish green flight-feather edges. **Juvenile** duller than adult, with more diffuse streaking. (Other seedeaters lack the heavy malar/moustachial stripes.) One **song** is short, *chididi see-leep,* high and thin at end. A longer song, recalling canary or goldfinch, is composed of *see-leep* notes combined with thin, clear whistles and 'sizzling'; still longer warbling song consists of *distinctly separated phrases.* **Calls** include a high-pitched, long-drawn *seeeeeeit* and a trio of soft notes, the first highest. **Range**: Above 1300 m in w. and cent. Kenyan highlands and in most of n. Tanzania above 1500 m.

YELLOW-RUMPED SEEDEATER *Serinus reichenowi*   **Plate 121**

Length 4–4.5". Small, dull and streaky except for the *bright yellow rump, conspicuous in flight.* Sides of face below the whitish superciliaries dull brown, with prominent malar stripes; dull brown streaks on upper breast contrast with the white throat. Coastal birds are smaller, greyer above and whiter below. **Juvenile** more diffusely streaked, often tinged yellow on lower breast and belly. See female Northern Grosbeak-Canary, and in far west Kenya see Black-throated Seedeater. **Song** a *continuous* rapid warbling with rich trills and whistles, sweet and canary-like, *not divided into short phrases* like Streaky Seedeater's song. Call a clear rising *twee*. **Range**: Widespread below 2000 m, mainly in low dry brushy areas, but absent from more arid n. and e. Kenya.

BLACK-THROATED SEEDEATER *Serinus atrogularis somereni*   **Plate 121**

Length 4.5". A scarce and local yellow-rumped finch of *w. Kenya,* darker and darker-faced than Yellow-rumped Seedeater, and with *indistinct superciliary stripes; densely spotted throat appears black;* underparts otherwise light brown or dusky and less heavily streaked than *reichenowi.* **Range**: Kakamega, Siaya and Sioport areas.

THICK-BILLED SEEDEATER *Serinus burtoni*   **Plate 121**

Length 6–6.5". A *stocky, dull-plumaged* seedeater of the highlands, *heavy-billed* and *dark-faced,* with a narrow white forehead patch in the race *albifrons.* Throat variably mottled with dusky and white; faintly streaked buff below, darker and brighter in southern *tanganjikae; wing-coverts, primaries and tail feathers* all edged with olive-yellow. Usual **call** a thin, high-pitched *seeeeeeet* or *sweet-seeut,* sometimes followed (at dawn) by a short song of fairly loud sharp notes. Featureless sibilant songs later in the day vary from a shorter, barely audible *sss, sss, sss* or *tsee-tsee-tsew* to a longer *seee-sew, seweeee-see-see sewit-sit, tsee-tsee-tsew.* **Range**: *S. b. albifrons* above 1700 m in cent. Kenyan highlands; *tanganjicae* west of the Rift Valley from Mt Elgon and the Cheranganis south to Mau Narok; *kilimensis* in Mara River forests, Nguruman Hills and n. Tanzanian highlands.

YELLOW-CROWNED CANARY *Serinus canicollis flavivertex*   **Plate 120**

Length 4.5–5". A small *montane* canary. **Male** has *bright yellow crown,* yellowish olive rump, and *much yellow in the wings; yellow-edged tail is quite long and distinctly forked.* **Female** duller, more streaked, with whitish belly. **Juvenile** paler, streaked buffy brown and black above, the yellow wing- bars tinged buff or olive. Male performs a slow 'butterfly' courtship flight. **Song** a prolonged, bright, rapidly delivered and prolonged jumble of canary-like trills, twittering and warbling phrases, sometimes in chorus; quality suggests European Goldfinch. Call a rising, double or triple-noted *sweet pee* or *peet, swee-ee.* **Range**: From 2200 to over 4000 m in w. and cent. Kenyan highlands, and higher parts of the Crater and Mbulu highlands, Mt Meru and Kilimanjaro.

AFRICAN CITRIL *Serinus citrinelloides*   **Plate 120**

Length 4.5". Siskin-like, streaked olive and black above, more yellow on the rump. **Females** extensively streaked below. Variable **males** range from black-faced *kikuyuensis* with distinct yellow superciliaries (which may meet in *narrow* band above the black forehead) and plain yellow underparts, to female-like *brittoni* and *hypostictus,* with greyish faces and well-streaked underparts; narrow yellow forehead and superciliaries evident in *brittoni;* in *hypostictus* both sexes show grey cheeks and chin. (In race *frontalis,* which may reach our region, female has bright yellow forehead band and unstreaked yellow underparts; male resembles *kikuyuensis* but with broad yellow forehead band.) See Papyrus Canary. Usual **song** of *kikuyuensis* composed of sweet, unhurried short phrases separated by brief pauses, often with a longer complex series following or mixed in: *eee-turr-eeee tsurr. . . seeet tsew eeet. . . seeet tsew eeeet. . . sweet seeeet tsrrrr. . ..* A high, twittering dawn song is faster and more canary-like. Call a rising *t'tweee;* also a soft chittering in flight. Song of *brittoni* loud, musical and canary-like. Calls of *hypostictus* not well documented; its alarm note is a soft *t't'tee.* **Range**: *S. c.*

kikuyuensis in w. (Mau and Trans-Mara) and cent. Kenyan highlands, meeting *brittoni* (without intergradation) near Siaya and Kakamega; *brittoni* ranges north to Kitale and Mt Elgon. Southern *hypostictus* extends from Lolgorien, Mara GR, the Loita, Nguruman and Chyulu hills to the Crater and Mbulu highlands, and east to Arusha NP, Kilimanjaro, the Pare and Usambara mts. **Taxonomic Notes:** The grey-faced *brittoni* and *hypostictus* may constitute a species separate from *kikuyuensis*. Ugandan/nw Tanzanian *frontalis* now treated as specifically distinct by some authors.

PAPYRUS CANARY *Serinus koliensis*   Plate 120

Length 4.25". Confined to the Lake Victoria basin. Similar to some African Citrils (*brittoni* and female *kikuyuensis*), but the *bill stubbier and more curved*. Both sexes streaked on crown, back and breast. **Juvenile** buffier and browner, lacking olive tone of adult. **Songs** distinct from those of *citrinelloides*, usually a rapid series of short chippering notes ending with (or including) a rising slurred *surrreet*. Also gives a more broken song of highly varied, more or less separated notes, *sweet tsiew chip, TSUWEEE, chrrrr, chweet-chweet-chweet-chwee. . ..* **Range**: Port Victoria, Lake Kanyaboli and Usengi east to Kisumu and Kendu Bay.

YELLOW-FRONTED CANARY *Serinus mozambicus*   Plate 120

Length 4–4.5". A small, brightly coloured, short-tailed canary of moist bush, scrub and cultivation. Distinctive contrasting face pattern includes broad yellow forehead/superciliaries and black malar stripes. **Female** Underparts, rump and upper tail-coverts are bright yellow. **Female** slightly duller and paler. Western birds are larger, brighter, less heavily streaked than those at coast. **Juvenile** has white throat, obscure face pattern and dusky streaks on a pale yellow breast. (*Southern nominate race of White-bellied Canary is easily mistaken for this species.*) **Song** a series of sweet whistled twittering phrases, repetitive, but shorter than songs of most *Serinus*; suggests domestic canary. **Calls** *tseeu-tseeu* and *tseeup*. **Range**: *S. m. mozambicus* on coast north to Lamu and Manda islands, inland along Tana River to Baomo, in the Shimba Hills and East Usambara foothills; *barbatus* from Mt Elgon south to Lake Victoria basin, Mara GR and w. Serengeti NP.

WHITE-BELLIED CANARY *Serinus dorsostriatus*   Plate 120

Length 4.5–5". The dry-country counterpart of Yellow-fronted Canary; similarly patterned, but generally duller and longer tailed. White belly is most noticeable in northern *maculicollis*; southern nominate birds have only lower belly and flanks white. **Female** more heavily streaked on back than male, yellow frontal band less clear, paler below with some white on throat, and breast has *obvious short dusky streaks*. **Juvenile** more streaked below, with obscure malar stripes. **Song** of variable, short, often slurred phrases e.g. *sweet suer weet-sip, sweeur-tsee-tsip, chweeur wee-chip, swee tsur-eep*, at times with a short trill near end. Another song of several emphatic sharp notes ends with a loud rising trill. Call-note *zhuree* or *twee*. **Range**: Widespread below 1600 m in n. Kenya, south to edge of the highlands, Lake Victoria basin, and dry areas from Nairobi and the Tsavo parks south into interior Tanzania. Northern *maculicollis* intergrades with the nominate race in cent. and s. Kenya.

BRIMSTONE CANARY *Serinus sulphuratus sharpii*   Plate 120

Length 5.5". Sparrow-sized, with a *large yellow-brown bill and little contrast between rump and back*. Upperparts uniform greenish yellow with only faint dark streaking on the back. **Male** has bright yellow superciliary stripes, is plain yellow below. **Female** and **juvenile** are duller, with fainter facial marks, and may be obscurely streaked on breast. (Grosbeak-Canaries are duller, often brownish, and broadly streaked, with more rump/back contrast.) **Song** loud and prolonged, of sweet twittering phrases and trills, rising at end. **Range**: W. and cent. Kenyan highlands from Mt Elgon, the Cheranganis and Mt Kenya south to Mara GR and Serengeti NP; also in Kilimanjaro area.

SOUTHERN GROSBEAK-CANARY *Serinus buchanani* Plate 120

Length 6". The pale pinkish grosbeak-like bill separates this *large, dull-coloured* canary from all others *south of the equator*. The yellowish rump contrasts with a greener back; olive-yellow underparts have a few streaks on sides. **Juvenile** duller, rump less contrasting, lightly streaked on breast, and with whitish horn bill. (Brimstone Canary is much brighter, with no streaks on sides.) **Song** a series of low, almost guttural ticking or chipping notes with much higher and longer penetrating 'squeals': *chrk chrk chrk chrrrrr seeeeeee, tk-tk chrk chrk chrk chrk tsik tsur squeeeeeeeeeeeeee*. Calls include a whistled *tuweea*, a slurred *queeuleet*, and a prolonged *seeeek*. **Range**: Kajiado and Sultan Hamud areas to Olorgesailie, Ngong and Mua hills; also from Bura west to Maktau. Few n. Tanzanian records.

NORTHERN GROSBEAK-CANARY *Serinus donaldsoni* Plates 120, 121

Length 6". The northern counterpart of the preceding species, but *sexes markedly different*. Stocky, with a *heavy pale bill*. **Male** *dull olive with dark brown streaks on back, bright yellow superciliaries, rump and underparts; lower belly white*, sparse dark streaks on sides and flanks; bill salmon-pink. (Brimstone Canary is brighter, shows no side/flank streaking and little contrast between rump and back; bill yellow-tinged.) **Female** suggests a large Yellow-rumped Seedeater: *brown-streaked* above, a *golden yellow rump*, and buffy white *underparts with broad diffuse brown streaks*; bill pale horn-colour. **Songs** include a rapid *seu-seu-seu-seu. . .*, the note repeated 10–20 times, the series punctuated by *suWEEEER*; also *sreeeet . . . wriseet . . . sew . . . sreet . . . wreet . . .*, separate, sweet yet piercing notes, many upslurred; at times a ringing *tri-tri-tri-tri-tri-tri-tri*. Call a loud *tweea*, repeated at intervals, similar to one call of Southern Grosbeak-Canary. **Range**: Baringo and Rumuruti north to the Ndotos, Marsabit, e. side of Lake Turkana and Ethiopian border.

ORIOLE-FINCH *Linurgus olivaceus* Plate 121

Length 4.75". A shy forest finch with a *bright orange bill*. **Male** resembles a miniature Black-headed Oriole. **Female** olive, brighter on tail, more olive-yellow on belly; wing feathers edged olive-yellow; bill much duller than male's. May show obscure streaks below. Southern race *kilimensis* more greenish above and on flanks. **Juvenile** resembles female but has pale olive wing-covert tips and yellowish horn bill. **Song** of *L. o. elgonensis* varies from a rapid *tsew-tsew-tsew seeeeeeeeee* with variable thin notes added, to several high *seet* notes grading into a thin twittering or tinkling. *L. o. kilimensis* has a more canary-like song with marked fluctuation in pitch, and a terminal upslurred *chereeep*. Usual call a high *tseet-tseet*, barely audible to humans. **Range**: *L. o. elgonensis* from Mt Elgon and the Cherangani Hills to North Nandi, Kakamega, Mt Kenya and Meru forests (absent from Mau and Aberdares). *L. o. kilimensis* is Tanzanian, with a small disjunct population on Ol Donyo Orok at Namanga in s. Kenya.

OLD WORLD BUNTINGS, EMBERIZIDAE

Ground-feeding birds with short, deep, conical bills narrower than those of canaries and seedeaters; the mandibular cutting edges slightly separated centrally, not in contact throughout their length.

ORTOLAN BUNTING *Emberiza hortulana* Plate 121

Length 6.5". In **first-winter plumage** (the most likely in East Africa), a streaky brown bird with *short conical pinkish bill* and *prominent whitish eye-ring. White in tail conspicuous in flight.* May suggest lark or pipit, but bill distinctive. Note also the *dark malar stripes* and *ear-coverts bordered below by a dusky line*. Adult male greyish olive from head to breast, with yellow eye-ring, throat and cheeks. **Call** a whistled *tew* or a hard *twick*. **Range/status**: Palearctic vagrant; 3 Kenyan records, Oct.–March.

HOUSE BUNTING *Emberiza striolata saturatior*   **Plate 121**

Length 5.5″. A largely rufous-brown, stripe-headed bunting of *northern Kenyan deserts*, often around wells and water holes. In flight, shows much *rufous in wings and outer tail feathers*. **Male** has black-and-white-streaked forehead/crown bordered by bold whitish superciliary stripes. **Female** has streaked sandy brown head, with no black on ear-coverts or cheeks; wings dull cinnamon with rufous 'shoulders.' See Cinnamon-breasted Rock Bunting. **Calls** a hard *tsick* and a nasal *zwee*. Song a short wheezy twitter. **Range**: E. shore of Lake Turkana to base of Mt Marsabit; also near Sudan border.

CINNAMON-BREASTED ROCK BUNTING *Emberiza t. tahapisi*   **Plate 121**

Length 6″. A dark ground bird of rough or rocky terrain. Head prominently striped (black and white in male, dusky and tawny buff in female). Underparts cinnamon-chestnut, much duller in female; dark tail edged with tawny. **Juvenile** has head streaked tawny russet and black. In arid n. Kenya see House Bunting. **Song** a rapid *tserk tser sidisidisi-seet*, rising at end. **Range**: Lake Turkana basin south through the Rift Valley and adjacent highlands to most n. Tanzania parks and reserves.

GOLDEN-BREASTED BUNTING *Emberiza flaviventris kalaharica*   **Plate 121**

Length 6–6.5″. A *highland* bunting with *black-and-white-striped head*, *broad white wing-bars* and white tail edges. *Golden yellow below*, *deeper orange-tawny on breast*, *dark grey at sides;* back rufous with grey feather edges; *rump and upper tail-coverts grey.* **Juvenile** duller with dusky streaks across breast. (Somali Golden-breasted Bunting of low dry country is brighter, and appears more mottled above. In ne. Tanzania see Cabanis's Bunting.) **Song** a single repeated phrase, highly variable: a penetrating *sitsit EEU, sitsit EEU. . .*, a shrill whistled *cheRI cheRI cheRI. . .*, *seesher seesher seesher . . .*, or a husky, tit-like *seeDJEERit, seeDJEERit . . ..* **Range**: w. and cent. Kenyan highlands; Mara GR, Loita and Nguruman hills south to Serengeti NP. Also on Mts Meru and Kilimanjaro.

SOMALI GOLDEN-BREASTED BUNTING *Emberiza poliopleura*   **Plate 121**

Length 6″. A shy *dry-country* bunting, brighter than the preceding species, but *back appears mottled*, with pale feather edgings. *Sides and flanks largely whitish*; rump paler grey and *outer tail feathers with more white* than in Golden-breasted Bunting. **Juvenile** has fewer breast streaks than young Golden-breasted. **Song** high-pitched, *tsu weetsu weetsu weetsu* or *tseeper-tseepa-tseepa-tsee*. **Range**: n. and e. Kenya below 1200 m, south to the Tsavo parks and Mkomazi GR. Sporadic in the Rift Valley.

CABANIS'S BUNTING *Emberiza cabanisi orientalis*   **Plate 123**

Length 7″. The yellow-breasted bunting of Tanzania's Usambara Mts. Resembles preceding two species but *lacks white stripe below eye*. At least some females have duller crown stripe than males, and black areas of head replaced by brown; breast may be tawny buff. **Juvenile** has pale tawny brown upperparts and head stripes, pale yellowish underparts with dark streaks on upper breast and sides. **Song** loud and whistling with much individual variation. **Range**: In our region, only in the East Usambaras and at Ambangulu in W. Usambaras.

BROWN-RUMPED BUNTING *Emberiza affinis forbesi*   **Plate 121**

Length 5.5″. A rare bunting of *northwestern Kenya*. Similar to Golden-breasted Bunting but with *no wing-bars* and a *brown rump; yellow of underparts includes belly and sides.* Calls apparently unknown. **Range**: North Kerio River and base of the Kongelai Escarpment.

INDEX TO ENGLISH NAMES

Numbers in **bold** refer to plate numbers, and are followed by the page on which the species appears.

INDEX TO SCIENTIFIC NAMES